Fodor's

THE CAROLINAS & GEORGIA

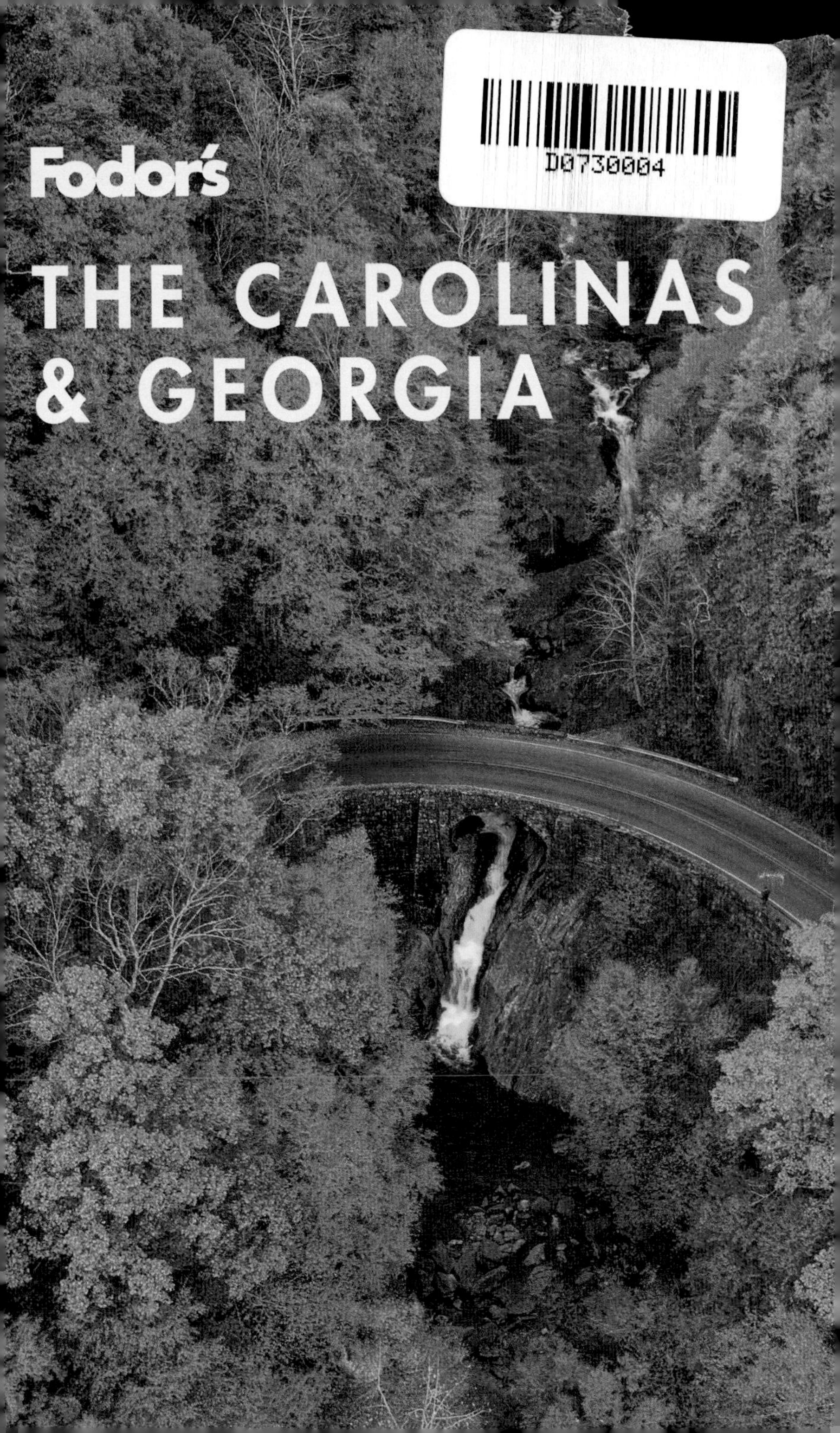

Welcome to the Carolinas and Georgia

In the Carolinas and Georgia, you can stroll beneath the Spanish moss–draped live oaks of Savannah, learn more about civil rights history in Atlanta, and discover secluded barrier islands. The Great Smoky Mountains provide plenty of outdoor recreation, while Hilton Head Island's resorts make the perfect retreat. This book was produced in the middle of the COVID-19 pandemic. As you plan your upcoming travels to the Carolinas and Georgia, please confirm that places are still open and let us know when we need to make updates by writing to us: editors@fodors.com.

TOP REASONS TO GO

★ **Southern Food:** Fried chicken, barbecue, shrimp and grits, plus fresh takes on tradition.

★ **Glorious Beaches:** From family-friendly Myrtle Beach to the serene Outer Banks.

★ **Hip Small Towns:** Asheville, Raleigh, Durham, Chapel Hill, Athens, and more.

★ **History:** From Gullah culture and Civil War battlefields to Dr. King's legacy.

★ **Outdoors:** Hiking, biking, fishing, scenic drives, and lovely gardens to explore.

★ **Southern Culture:** Slow down and sit a spell—Southern hospitality is infectious.

Contents

Fodor's Features

MAPS

Chapter 1

EXPERIENCE THE CAROLINAS AND GEORGIA

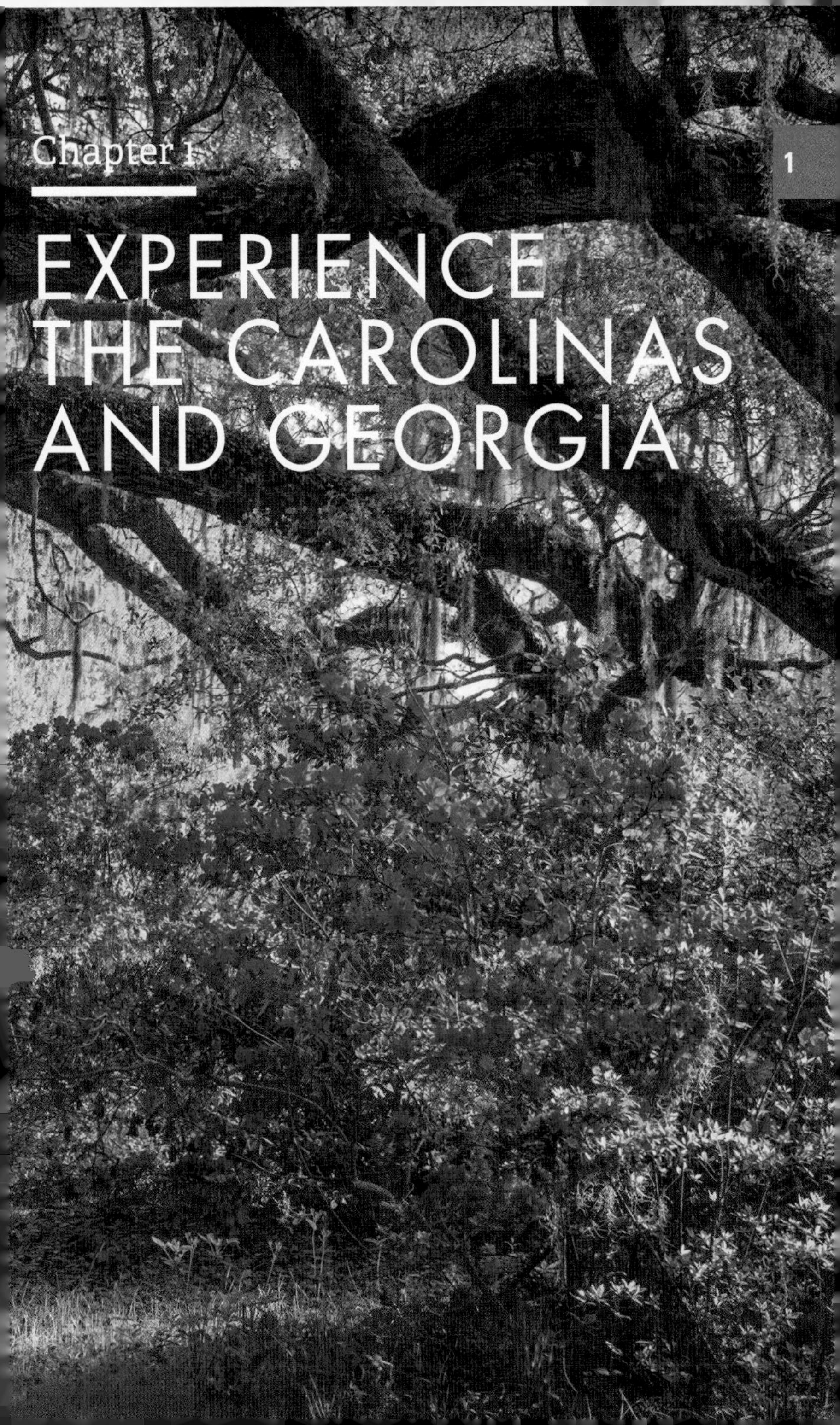

1 Hit the Trails of North Carolina

Roughly 100 miles of the nation's famous Appalachian Trail run through the western section of North Carolina, with another 200 or so following along the Tennessee border. *(Ch. 6)*

2 Get Hip in the Triangle

Chapel Hill, Raleigh, and Durham draw tourists to nationally renowned museums and some of the hottest restaurants and chefs in the American South. *(Ch. 4)*

3 Shop in Little Five Points

From vintage gear to crystals and sage, Atlanta's Little Five Points is home to a variety of stores perfect for the eclectic shopper. *(Ch. 14)*

4 Explore Natural Wonders

The Nantahala and Pisgah National Forests, Great Smoky and Blue Ridge Mountain ranges, and rivers and lakes fill North Carolina with gorgeous vistas. *(Ch. 5, 6)*

5 Embrace the History of the Outer Banks

See the feral horses that have roamed Ocracoke for over 500 years, or learn about the "Lost Colony," an entire British settlement that disappeared from the area in the 1500s. *(Ch. 3)*

6 Visit the Home of Dr. Martin Luther King Jr.

Dr. Martin Luther King Jr. grew up in a home off of Auburn Avenue, which is now a National Historic Site. *(Ch. 14)*

7 Walk or Bike the Atlanta BeltLine

The Atlanta BeltLine connects numerous neighborhoods. On any given day, catch a yoga class or a festival in one of the green spaces that run alongside. *(Ch. 14)*

8 Make a Splash at the Georgia Aquarium

Be prepared to stay awhile at the Georgia Aquarium, home to more than 100,000 animals, including whale sharks, beluga whales, and colorful angelfish. *(Ch. 14)*

9 Walk Savannah's Squares

There are 22 squares—small parks designed by Savannah founder General James Oglethorpe—in Savannah's Historic District. *(Ch. 11)*

10 Smell the Flowers

The State Botanical Garden of Georgia in Athens covers more than 300 acres with 5 miles of nature trails. *(Ch. 15)*

11 Visit the Biltmore Estate

In 1889, George Washington Vanderbilt began construction on a 250-room mansion on a vast estate that would become the largest private residence in the country. *(Ch. 5)*

12 Revisit the Civil Rights Movement

Visit the former Woolworth's in Greensboro, where in 1960 four African Americans sat down at a whites-only counter and sparked sit-ins and nonviolent protests. *(Ch. 4)*

13 Explore Civil War History

Between 1861 and 1865, 20 American Civil War battles were fought along the North Carolina coast and at Fort Sumter in Charleston. *(Ch. 3, 8)*

14 Climb Aboard the Historic Ships of Coastal Carolina

The USS *North Carolina* starred in the Pacific theater naval battles and was the most decorated U.S. battleship in World War II. Today it's a museum in Wilmington. *(Ch. 3)*

15 Nosh On Southern Cuisine

You can't visit the city of Atlanta without treating your taste buds. From Mary Mac's Tea Room to Old Lady Gang, there are plenty of options for classic Southern fare. *(Ch. 14)*

16 Visit a Brewery or Two (or Twenty)

Micro- and craft breweries have taken over North Carolina: there are more than 300 breweries and brewpubs, the most of any state in the South. *(Ch. 4, 5)*

17 Paddle to the Cockspur Lighthouse

See dolphins while kayaking to the Cockspur Island Lighthouse, then walk along North Beach to catch a glimpse of the Tybee Island Lighthouse. *(Ch. 11)*

18 Ride Horses on the Beach

On Seabrook Island, near Charleston, an equestrian center offers a unique experience—horseback riding on a pristine, sparsely populated stretch of Atlantic sand. *(Ch. 8)*

19 See the Boneyard Beach at Botany Bay Plantation

Spanish moss drapes from live oak limbs over the road as you pass centuries-old plantations on your way to sleepy Edisto Beach, South Carolina. *(Ch. 8)*

20 Stroll Through a Swamp at Congaree National Park

South Carolina's Congaree is the largest hardwood bottomland forest in the southeast; explore it via a trail network that allows for 10-plus-mile hikes. *(Ch. 10)*

21 Camp on Cumberland Island

On Georgia's Cumberland Island, you can either camp or stay at the famed Greyfield Inn. *(Ch. 12)*

22 Check Out a Live Show in Athens

From the Foundry to the 40 Watt Club, Athens venues are part of music history. Seminal bands that got their start here include R.E.M. and the B-52s. *(Ch. 15)*

23 Eat Until You Pop in Charleston

The jewel in South Carolina's crown, you'll never have a bad meal in Charleston. Upper King is a hot spot for new restaurant openings. *(Ch. 8)*

24 Visit the Telfair Family of Museums

With a Telfair Museums ticket, you'll have access to modern art, beautiful antiquities, and a traditional 19th-century Savannah mansion for a full week. *(Ch. 11)*

25 Ride the SkyWheel at the Myrtle Beach Boardwalk

The massive SkyWheel along Myrtle Beach's main strip forms a landmark you can see from a mile away—but the view is even better from 200 feet up. *(Ch. 7)*

WHAT'S WHERE

1 The North Carolina Coast. Nothing in the region compares with the Outer Banks. This band of barrier islands with wind-twisted oaks and pines has some of the East Coast's best beaches.

2 Central North Carolina. The New South comes alive in three major metropolitan centers: Charlotte; the Triangle, which consists of Raleigh, Durham, and Chapel Hill; and the Triad, which consists of Greensboro, Winston-Salem, and High Point. Shopping, dining, and nightlife abound.

3 Asheville and the North Carolina Mountains. Western North Carolina is home to more than 1 million acres of stupendous vertical scenery. In addition to opportunities for outdoor adventures, visitors find edgy art galleries and sophisticated eateries in Asheville.

4 Great Smoky Mountains National Park. Eleven million annual visitors can't be wrong; while the most visited of the national parks, there is more than enough beauty and deserted woodland in

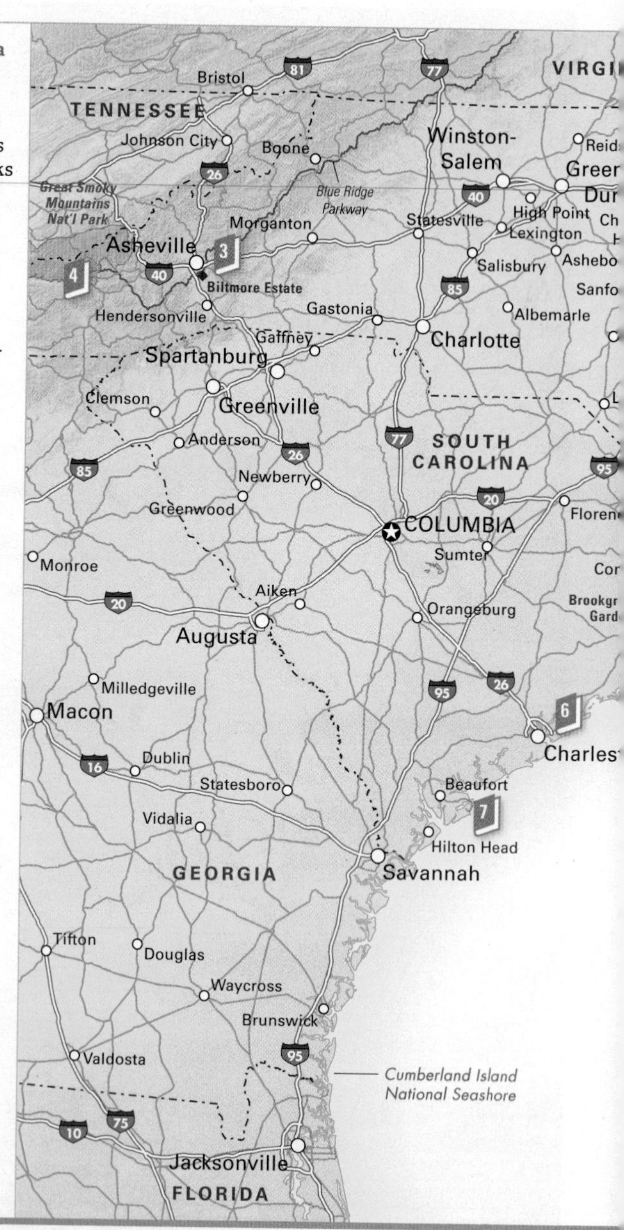

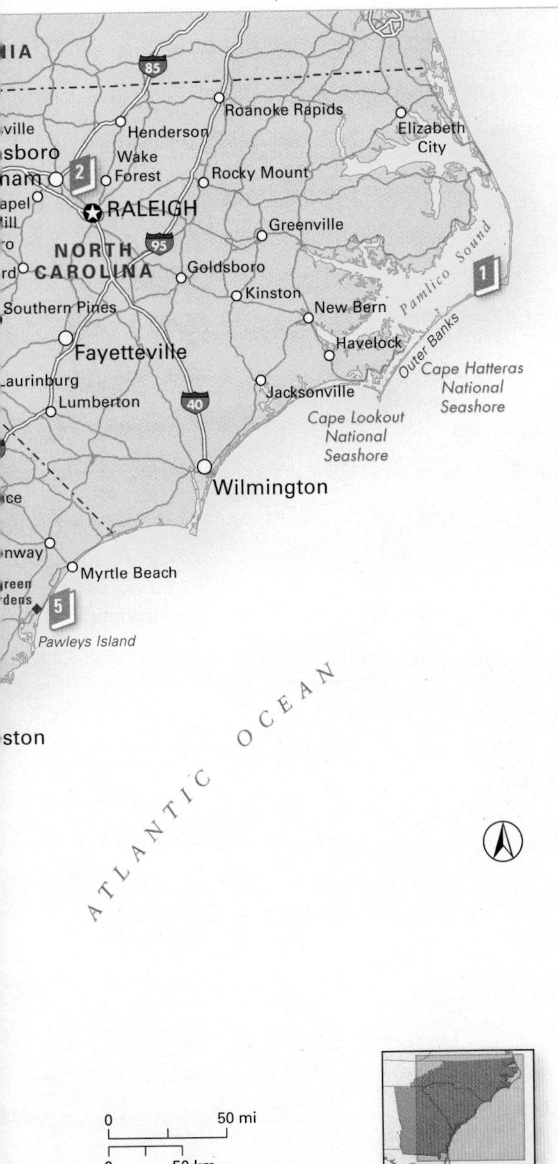

the Smokies for peaceful communion with nature.

5 Myrtle Beach, SC, and the Grand Strand. South Carolina's Grand Strand, a 60-mile expanse of beaches, offers varied pleasures: the quiet refuge of Pawleys Island; Brookgreen Gardens, with its magnificent sculptures and landscaped grounds; dozens of golf courses; and the bustle of Myrtle Beach.

6 Charleston, SC. Charleston anchors the Lowcountry in high style. The city's past, dating to 1670, is evident in cobblestone streets, antebellum mansions and plantations, and Gullah accents. Today, it hosts the renowned Spoleto performing arts festival and a celebrated food and wine festival. The city is home to numerous award-winning chefs and top-rated restaurants.

7 Hilton Head, SC, and the Lowcountry. The coastal lowlands feature picturesque landscapes of coastal forests and open marshes, undisturbed beaches, and quaint fishing villages. Hilton Head Island is home to more than 24 world-class golf courses and even more resorts, hotels, and top restaurants.

WHAT'S WHERE

8 The Midlands and the Upstate, SC. Radiating out from Columbia, South Carolina's engaging capital, the area's small towns have their claims to fame: Aiken is a national equestrian center; Camden is the place to go for well-priced antiques; Abbeville is steeped in Civil War history.

9 Savannah, GA. Georgia's oldest and grandest city is known for its elegant mansions, Spanish moss, and summer heat. It has more than 1,200 restored or reconstructed buildings dating from 1733 on.

10 Georgia's Coastal Isles and the Okefenokee. Stretching south from Savannah, Georgia's coastal isles are "almost Florida," but more appealing. Cumberland Island National Seashore—with more than 120 wild horses—and the wild and mysterious Okefenokee Swamp are must-sees. Upscale visitors favor Sea Island, while St. Simons Island and Jekyll Island have something for everyone.

11 Southwest Georgia. The serenity of this quiet corner of Georgia has been a refuge for two former U.S.

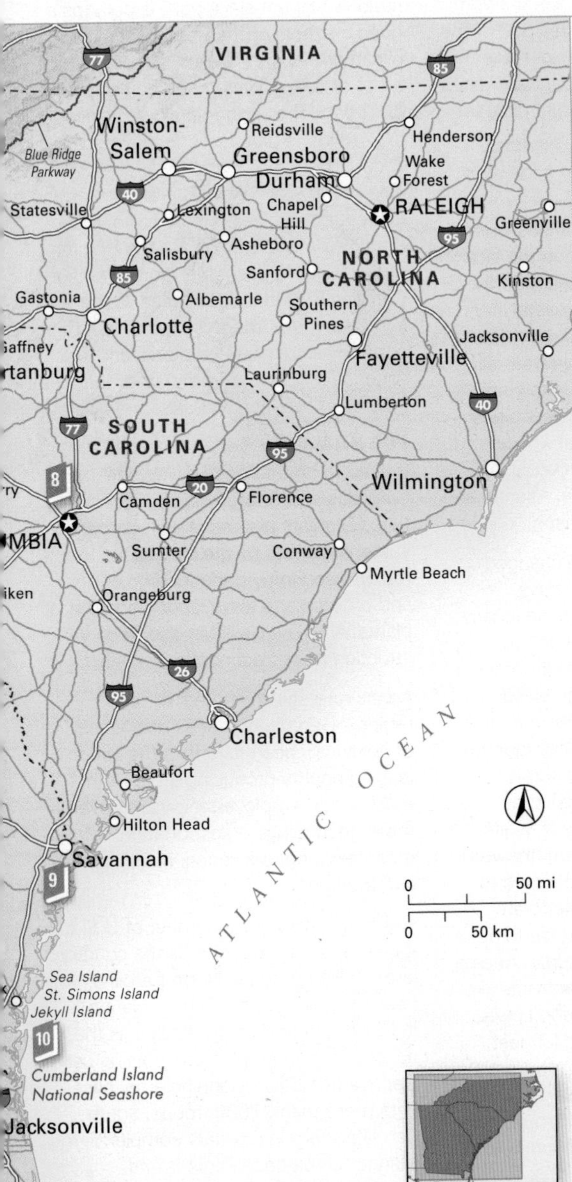

presidents. Franklin Delano Roosevelt had a summer home, the Little White House, in Warm Springs. Jimmy Carter, a Plains native, returned there to begin work as one of America's most active former presidents.

12 Atlanta, GA. The Georgia Aquarium, World of Coca-Cola, the High Museum and great shopping and restaurants keep visitors busy in the capital of the New South. The Martin Luther King Jr. National Historic Park and the National Center for Civil and Human Rights bring to life Atlanta's racially divided past and its ties to the civil rights movement, as well as human rights efforts worldwide.

13 Central and North Georgia. Stretching from Augusta to Macon, Central Georgia was the heart of the Old South. Azalea and cherry blossoms bloom along the Ocmulgee and Savannah Rivers. The pace picks up in Athens, home to the University of Georgia. Near Dahlonega, site of America's first gold rush, vineyards now produce new "gold" for the region. In the northwest, visit Chickamauga, the site of one of the Civil War's bloodiest battles.

The Carolinas and Georgia Today

THE PEOPLE

The Carolinas and Georgia are known for their friendliness. Folks in this part of the Southeast like to say hello—or rather hey and how y'all doin'. Such openness dates back to 18th- and 19th-century plantation days when scattered neighbors in remote, rural areas had only each other to depend on.

Among many factors, migrations from the Northeast and Midwest in the late 20th century dramatically changed the region's agrarian lifestyle. Coastal and metropolitan areas boomed. New job opportunities brought people from all over the country and world, allowing diversity to flourish. The region's cities host some of America's best-known colleges, including Duke University in Durham; Emory University in Atlanta; and Clemson University in Clemson.

But as much as things have changed since the region's plantation days, reckoning with the past, and the legacy of slavery, is a difficult reality in the Carolinas and Georgia. In the summer of 2020, the killing of George Floyd, the Black Lives Matter movement, and protests against police brutality (during a pandemic that disproportionately affected BIPOC communities) shed light on enduring remainders of white supremacy. All over the region, the work of black activists and organizers led to government removal of Confederate statues—what many considered to be long overdue, symbolic gestures. Atlanta, home of historic civil rights activists like Martin Luther King Jr. and John Lewis, held some of the largest and longest protests in the country. In North Carolina, three Confederate statues were toppled at the capitol in Raleigh, and around two dozen have been removed around the state since then.

Charleston, South Carolina, once the nation's biggest slave port, is perhaps a good example of the Southeast's complicated relationship with its past, where a city of beautifully preserved history can't deny the large role slavery played in forming its picture-perfect landscape. Today, efforts are made to tell the other side of the story, with Charleston and the Lowcountry's black history tours, museums, and monuments, and the forming of the Gullah Geechee Cultural Heritage Corridor. Still, in the Carolinas, Georgia, and elsewhere, there is much work to be done toward a more equitable and just America that learns from, rather than ignores or repeats, its past.

ECONOMY

It used to be that nearly everyone in the Carolinas and Georgia had agricultural ties. Colonists planted the first crops for sustenance, but by the mid-1800s the region's economy depended on cotton and tobacco and slave labor worked large plantations. The Civil War and Reconstruction forced economic diversity.

Agriculture still characterizes the region—Georgia produces nearly half of America's peanuts and is the nation's leading poultry-producing state—but much larger employers now are government, technology, transportation, retail, manufacturing, education, health care, and tourism.

The region also has a number of U.S. military bases. Among them is the country's largest: Fort Bragg in North Carolina, with nearly 54,000 troops. Camp Lejeune, in North Carolina's coastal plain, is the nation's largest amphibious training base. Georgia hosts Fort Benning army base, with more than 27,000 troops. South Carolina's famous military complex is the Marine recruit base Parris Island.

Other government employers, like the Centers for Disease Control and Prevention, are based in Atlanta. Georgia also ranks high in aerospace exports and is home to 15 Fortune 500 companies. Corporate headquarters include Coca-Cola, UPS, and Delta Airlines. North Carolina's Piedmont is a research and science hub, and Charlotte is a major U.S. banking center. South Carolina claims BMW's only American assembly plant; Michelin's American headquarters; and Boeing South Carolina's assembly plants, as well as research, design, and engineering facilities.

SPORTS

During one week each spring everyone is drawn to the college basketball craze. Schools in these three states make up nearly half of the 15-member Atlantic Coast Conference (ACC), and when the mighty league hosts its March college basketball tournament, fans here have much to cheer about. Top teams include the UNC Tar Heels, Duke Blue Devils, Clemson Tigers, and Georgia Tech Yellow Jackets.

On the pro side, tailgaters root for the NFL's Atlanta Falcons and Carolina Panthers. Mild winters don't deter hockey madness in Raleigh, home to the Carolina Hurricanes, while baseball fans have the Atlanta Braves and hoops lovers cheer for the Atlanta Hawks and the Charlotte Hornets.

NASCAR races were born on North Carolina's mountain roads, where drivers ran bootleg whiskey during Prohibition. The first NASCAR "strictly stock" car race took place in 1949 in Charlotte. Today, the region boasts major NASCAR tracks Charlotte Motor Speedway in Concord, North Carolina; Atlanta Motor Speedway in Atlanta, Georgia; and Darlington Raceway in Darlington, South Carolina.

Golf lovers relish the region's hundreds of courses, some of the world's most challenging. Pinehurst in North Carolina has staged more golf championships than any other American golf resort, and the Masters Golf Tournament is played annually in Augusta, Georgia.

CUISINE

Early explorers arriving in what would become the Carolinas and Georgia found Native Americans eating corn, beans, pecans, and seafood. These foods, combined with imported ingredients, shaped the region's cuisine and inspired cooks to create distinctive local fare.

Soul food and Southern cooking can be found throughout the area, but Georgia's rich African American culture may lay claim to fried chicken. Enslaved Africans brought deep-fat frying to the area, along with many favorites like candied yams and stewed collards with cornbread. African and Caribbean influences also season Lowcountry cuisine, associated mainly with South Carolina's shore, but stretching south to Savannah and north to Wilmington. Bountiful seafood and coastal rice plantations provided ingredients for famous dishes like shrimp and grits, she-crab soup, and the rice-and-black-eyed-pea dish named hoppin' John.

Barbecue debates rage in North Carolina. Westerners prefer tomato-based sauce, while easterners want vinegar-based. Everyone agrees on one thing: barbecue means pork butts, pork shoulders, or whole hogs roasted slowly over a wood or charcoal fire and then shredded or "pulled" after cooking.

Each state also claims popular foodstuffs. Coca-Cola was invented in Georgia, Pepsi in North Carolina, and Firefly Iced Tea Vodka in South Carolina.

What to Eat and Drink in Georgia

Pecan pie

MEXICAN TORTAS
This mouthwatering sandwich with Mexican origins can be stuffed with just about any meat imaginable but always inside a crusty, chewy sandwich roll complete with sliced avocado. Thanks to its hearty offering of international options, the strip of road known as Buford Highway is home to several Atlanta restaurants serving delicious tortas.

FRIED CHICKEN
Crispy, crunchy, and with just the right amount of savory flavor, fried chicken is a staple throughout Georgia. In fact, debates about who serves up the best fried chicken in the state have gone on for decades. Many soul food restaurants, including the historic Mary Mac's Tea Room, have been serving the dish for years.

BOURBON
From distilleries in Kennesaw to Atlanta's Old Fourth Ward neighborhood, bourbon has increasingly become a go-to spirit in Georgia, and local cocktails abound. For booze enthusiasts who prefer a more mature sip, Old Fourth Distillery recently released a straight bourbon whiskey that has been aged four years.

Crispy fried chicken

LEMON PEPPER WINGS
Although the hot wing does hold a tender (though spicy) spot in the hearts of those in Georgia, lemon pepper wings are the true wings of choice. Buttery with a subtle kick of tangy and tart, lemon pepper wings can be found in just about any sports bar in the city.

SHRIMP AND GRITS
Foodies would be hard-pressed to find a restaurant in Georgia that doesn't serve shrimp and grits. Thankfully, each restaurant does provide its own unique twist on this classic Southern dish, from creamy to spicy to decadent additions like lobster. In Savannah, The Olde Pink House is best for a traditional taste, with rich country ham gravy and cheddar grits cakes.

SWEETWATER BREWING COMPANY'S 420 EXTRA PALE ALE
In the past decade, the craft beer scene in Georgia has soared. Among the most popular and tried-and-true beers is SweetWater's 420 Extra Pale Ale. The herbal and floral year-round brew gets its name from the date it was born. The brewery also hosts its annual music festival in April.

VEGAN JUNK FOOD
Atlanta's Slutty Vegan, a vegan food truck and restaurant, swiftly garnered praise for satisfying burgers like the One Night Stand made using a plant-based patty; it also features a sizable helping of vegan bacon, vegan American cheese, grilled onions, lettuce, tomato, and special sauce.

PHO
Although pho is Vietnamese in origin, bowls of broth and noodles (topped with herbs) are slurped with enthusiasm throughout restaurants in Georgia. Located east of Atlanta, the city of Norcross serves as a one-stop shop for pho lovers.

ICE CREAM
For something unique, head to Decatur's Butter & Cream. Specializing in small-batch ice cream, they offer flavors like honeycomb forest and cashew crème brûlée.

PECAN PIE
Pecan pie might just be the official dessert of Georgia. With locations in Atlanta, Alpharetta, and Gainesville, Southern Baked Pie Company makes it easy to get your hands on one of its famed caramel pecan pies.

What to Eat and Drink in the Carolinas

Lowcountry boil

BARBECUE
Expect slow-cooked, pulled pork that is lightly sauced, seasoned, and served on a bun or plate with sides. Sauce varies from region to region. Enjoy vinegar-based sauce in eastern North Carolina, ketchup as the main ingredient in the western part of the state, and mustard-based barbecue sauce in most of South Carolina.

BOILED PEANUTS
Green peanuts are boiled, salted, and served warm in brown paper bags sold at small stores and stands throughout the Carolinas (advertised by a handwritten sign). The texture is quite different than regular roasted peanuts (think chewy, not crunchy), but it's an acquired taste that keeps you coming back for more.

CHEERWINE
The cherry-red "Drink Cheerwine" logo is a beacon of rural North Carolina, appearing on any worthwhile storefront. This cola has remained popular since the family-run company introduced it in 1917. North Carolina's state soda can be found everywhere, from fast food restaurants to grocery stores.

She-crab soup

SWEET TEA
You'd be hard-pressed to find a restaurant in the Carolinas that doesn't offer this beloved drink, iced tea sweetened with loads of sugar and usually served with a lemon wedge. South Carolina grew some of the first tea leaves in the states.

BRUNSWICK STEW
This stew—of slow-simmered meat, tomato, beans, and corn—was traditionally made with small game like rabbit or squirrel. At the many, many roadside restaurants where you'll find it today, it is often cooked with chicken or pork instead (and is always delicious).

LOWCOUNTRY BOIL
This casual, one-pot meal (also called Frogmore stew) abounds in the backyards and casual restaurants of Charleston and the South Carolina coast and coastal isles.

CHOW-CHOW
North Carolina's most popular pickle is said to have evolved in resourceful country kitchens, where vegetable scraps were thrown into a relish rather than wasted.

MORAVIAN COOKIES
The Moravians, an early Protestant sect originally from Germany, settled in the area around Winston-Salem, North Carolina, as early as the 18th century. Moravian cookies, paper-thin wafers spiced and sweetened with molasses, are especially popular around Christmastime.

OYSTERS
Charleston is full of year-round oyster restaurants and celebrates seasonal oyster roasts (mostly during the winter months). In North Carolina, small oyster farms have recently increased in number, and mollusks at restaurants in Wilmington and the Piedmont compete with Charleston's.

SHE-CRAB SOUP
This creamy seafood bisque, comprised of Atlantic blue crab, fish stock, heavy cream, and a small amount of crab roe has Scottish origins, when Scottish immigrants brought a similar recipe to Charleston in the 1700s.

FRIED SEAFOOD PLATTER
On the Carolina coast, sample this comforting staple: fried fish (flounder, catfish, shrimp, or anything fresh) served with a basket of hot hush puppies and sides of coleslaw and fries.

Best Beaches in the Carolinas and Georgia

CAPE HATTERAS NATIONAL SEASHORE, NORTH CAROLINA
Long stretches of unspoiled beaches hide behind tall dunes, interspersed with small villages along this 60-mile geographical treasure.

EAST BEACH, ST. SIMONS ISLAND, GEORGIA
Serving as one of the premier beaches on St. Simons Island, people flock to East Beach for sunbathing, water sports, horseback riding, and a wide selection of local seafood. The hard-packed sand makes it possible to bike along the beach.

GLORY BEACH, JEKYLL ISLAND, GEORGIA
Glory Beach, which was featured in the film *Glory*, is ideal for taking in some peace and quiet and observing nature from sand dunes to sea oats. A neighboring soccer complex is a short walk away.

NORTH BEACH, TYBEE ISLAND, GEORGIA
A short drive from downtown Savannah, Tybee Island's North Beach is a destination for its local boutiques, water sports, eclectic dining, and birding trails. If the surroundings look familiar, it's because it's become a hot spot for filming. Most recently, the big-screen version of *Baywatch* was filmed here.

DRIFTWOOD BEACH, JEKYLL ISLAND, GEORGIA
Easily one of the most scenic beaches in the state, Driftwood Beach is filled with driftwood and trees that add unique charm. Driftwood is one of several beaches that can be found on Jekyll Island, which is a part of Georgia's Golden Isles.

NORTH MYRTLE BEACH, MYRTLE BEACH, SOUTH CAROLINA
It's easy to think that Myrtle Beach is little more than pancake houses, seafood buffets, and trinket shops, but off the main drag, downtown North Myrtle Beach still feels like the hopping little town where shag dancing first took off in the '50s. Main Street dead-ends into the Atlantic at Ocean Park, a popular beach access with a kids' water-slide, showers, bathrooms, and concessions.

BULLS ISLAND, SOUTH CAROLINA
Surrounded by wilderness in the Cape Romain National Wildlife Refuge, remote Bulls Island is unlike any other beach in the state. Although

Driftwood Beach

the human population is zero, the alligators, deer, and birds number in the thousands. To visit, take the Bulls Island Ferry over in the morning and spend the day exploring and relaxing on the boneyard beach, an eerily beautiful feature where the ocean has eroded the forest, leaving the petrified skeletons of trees emerging from the surf.

ISLE OF PALMS, CHARLESTON, SOUTH CAROLINA
The northernmost of Charleston's beaches, "IOP" boasts some of the widest beaches in the Lowcountry and some of the best surfing waves. The island's north end is home to Wild Dunes, a family vacation and golfing paradise, while the strip along Ocean Boulevard features hot spots for food and live music.

NAGS HEAD, NORTH CAROLINA
Here, 11 miles of beaches include many with lifeguards. Plenty of accommodations line the shore. There are 42 public access points, many with wheelchair access, so you're always within a short driving distance of one.

SULLIVAN'S ISLAND, CHARLESTON, SOUTH CAROLINA
No beach in South Carolina is more steeped in history than Sullivan's, where at the island's southern terminus, Fort Moultrie has guarded Charleston Harbor for centuries. It's here that the state's iconic palmetto flag was born and where writer Edgar Allan Poe found inspiration for stories like "The Gold-Bug." It's also an excellent family swimming beach, thanks to broad swaths of sand and an offshore sandbar that limits the surf along much of the beachfront. Biking the quiet neighborhoods of this small island, and renting a stand-up paddleboard on the intracoastal waterway, are other favorite activities.

What to Watch and Read

THE SECRET LIFE OF BEES BY SUE MONK KIDD

This is the story of a young girl with a troubled past and the adoptive family (a group of beekeeping women) that takes her in. Rich, dark, and brimming with heart, the novel takes on South Carolina's complicated history of race relations, racism, and forced segregation.

THE LAST CASTLE: THE EPIC STORY OF LOVE, LOSS, AND AMERICAN ROYALTY IN THE NATION'S LARGEST HOME BY DENISE KIERNAN

This dense nonfiction account reads more like an epic novel, telling the story of George Vanderbilt and the greed, love, and logistics that went into building what is still the largest private home in the United States. *The Last Castle* helps makes sense of the Biltmore Estate's original purpose and existence, and the (sometimes bizarrely behaved) wealthy family at its founding. The author largely credits George's wife, Edith Dresser, for turning the estate—and the greater Asheville area—into a center of business and tourism after its original decline.

BASTARD OUT OF CAROLINA BY DOROTHY ALLISON

Dorothy Allison's semi-autobiographical bildungsroman stars Bone, a headstrong tomboy born under a bad sign and raised in Greenville, South Carolina, by tough women and often cruel, sometimes well-meaning men. Allison's burning prose is full of sympathetic characters and portrayals of life under poverty, abuse, and other socioeconomic circumstances prevalent in this 1950s northwest corner of South Carolina—but seldom represented as well as in Allison's work. Anjelica Huston directed the movie adaptation in 1996, starring Jennifer Jason Leigh and Jena Malone as Bone.

COLD MOUNTAIN BY CHARLES FRAZIER

Charles Frazier's debut novel and opus is an Odyssey-like love story about a Confederate deserter trying to get home to his wife. Running a farm alone near Cold Mountain, North Carolina (where the Pisgah National Forest is today), Ada, a city girl from Charleston, learns some tough lessons about adjusting to rural mountain life. If you can get past the very mediocre Southern accents, the movie adaptation (starring Nicole Kidman and Jude Law), full of sweeping views of this gorgeous region, is worth a watch.

WISTERIA: TWILIGHT POEMS FROM THE SWAMP COUNTRY BY KWAME DAWES

Kwame Dawes's lyrical, narrative-based poems tell the stories of African American women in rural central South Carolina. Dawes wrote his *Twilight* poems based on interviews he conducted with the elderly African American population of a small town in Sumter County, giving a beautiful and empathetic voice to these women's powerful stories and generations of life, love, and survival.

SOUTH OF BROAD BY PAT CONROY

Conroy, who was born and raised in Beaufort, South Carolina, often incorporates dark, complicated elements of the state's history into his narratives. *South of Broad* digs the deepest into Charleston and its history of racism, with a troubled but likeable narrator and a full spectrum of diverse Charlestonians at the novel's center.

MIDNIGHT IN THE GARDEN OF GOOD AND EVIL BY JOHN BERENDT

Novel-turned-movie *Midnight in the Garden of Good and Evil* is set in historic Savannah. The cover of the true-crime book quickly garnered fame thanks to the image of the *Bird Girl* sculpture, which has since moved from the Bonaventure Cemetery to a local museum. Released in 1997, the film adaptation was directed by Clint Eastwood and stars John Cusack.

AN AMERICAN MARRIAGE BY TAYARI JONES

An official Oprah Book Club selection from 2018 and a favorite of Barack Obama, Tayari Jones's *An American Marriage* puts words to both the triumph and the turmoil of the New South. The novel tells the story of Atlanta couple Celestial and Roy as they navigate marital and societal challenges after an unfortunate turn of events.

LOWCOUNTRY: A SOUTHERN MEMOIR BY J. NICOLE JONES

The child of a prominent South Carolina family responsible for developing much of Myrtle Beach, Jones tells her story of Southern secrets, money, and debt and conveys the region's great myths, ghosts, and beauty. This is a sweeping and heartfelt journey through the contemporary Southeast.

WHERE THE CRAWDADS SING BY DELIA OWENS

This *New York Times* best-selling novel is part bildungsroman, part murder mystery, set in the wild and isolated marshland of coastal North Carolina. The young narrator, Kya, is a talented naturalist from a young age; the coastal land and waterways, and the birds and marine life that call them home, play an important role in the novel. Reese Witherspoon is behind a movie adaptation of the best seller, currently in the works.

ATLANTA

Created and produced by Stone Mountain native Donald Glover (aka Childish Gambino), this television series provides an accurate portrayal of the city while also garnering praise from critics and viewers across the country. The show has racked up a number of awards, including Golden Globes for Best Television Series (musical or comedy) and Best Actor in a Television Series (musical or comedy).

ATL

ATL is a coming-of-age tale featuring a backdrop of Atlanta's famed roller rinks. It offers a candid glimpse into the life of Rashad, an Atlanta teen transitioning into adulthood. The film also stars several well-known Atlanta musicians, including Clifford "T.I." Harris, who plays Rashad. Outkast wordsmith Antwan "Big Boi" Patton also makes an appearance in the film.

THE HATE U GIVE BY ANGIE THOMAS

Both a highly successful young-adult novel and a hit movie, *The Hate U Give* is a poignant tale told from the perspective of an astute 16-year-old girl, centered around her experiences with racism, code-switching, police brutality, and the Black Lives Matter movement. The film adaptation, set throughout Atlanta, stars Amandla Stenberg, Regina Hall, Anthony Mackie, and Issa Rae, and is a moving, heartfelt watch for adults and teenagers alike.

OUTER BANKS

What may seem like a simple teen soap opera at first is full of action and satisfying humor, with plenty of mystery, buried treasure, and thrilling boat chases throughout. The two seasons of this Netflix series are a fun exploration of the North Carolina barrier islands and some of its main characters, from full-time fishermen to the wealthy seasonal crowd.

With Kids

Try these sights and events for guaranteed family fun.

WET AND WILD

NASCAR's slick **Charlotte Motor Speedway** in Concord holds up to 89,000 fans on race days. On non-race days, racetrack tours—including a drive around the track—are available for kids and adults.

Get a look at 18 stock cars spanning the history of NASCAR in the *Glory Road ICONS* exhibit, test your tire-changing skills at a pit stop, or get the driver's experience by sitting inside a racing simulator that provides virtual laps around a speedway at the **NASCAR Hall of Fame** in Charlotte.

Atlanta's **Georgia Aquarium** is the largest in the Western Hemisphere, with sea creatures in 10 million gallons of water. Special programs are aimed at toddlers, and families with kids can take a behind-the-scenes tour to learn about all the aquarium's animals and the care they receive.

Riverbanks Zoo and Garden in Columbia, South Carolina, supplies grounds for exotic animals like Siberian tigers, siamang apes, lemurs, and giraffes. More than 2,000 animals occupy natural habitats, while around 4,200 native and exotic plant species fill gardens. Civil War ruins dot the landscape, too.

EMBRACE HISTORY

Take a self-guided tour or follow guides in native costume at the **Oconaluftee Indian Village,** which tracks back more than 250 years, with demonstrations of weaving, hunting techniques, and canoe construction. The nearby **Museum of the Cherokee Indian** contains artifacts and displays that cover 11,000 years. Nature walks, dance programs, and traditional Cherokee dinners are available, in addition to museum tours. Both the village and the museum are near Cherokee, North Carolina, and the entrance to the Great Smoky Mountains National Park.

In Atlanta, the **National Center for Civil and Human Rights** has interactive exhibits geared toward a younger audience. Likewise, the *Children of Courage* exhibit at **The King Center** in the **Martin Luther King, Jr. National Historical Park** is a hands-on lesson about younger activists' role in the movement.

Kids can climb Big Kill Devil Hill, where Wilbur and Orville Wright tested their gliders, at the **Wright Brothers National Memorial,** south of Kitty Hawk, North Carolina. Stand right on the spot where the Ohio bicyclists first took flight on December 17, 1903. Kids can bring their kites for a flight here, but no motorized aircraft are allowed.

HANDS-ON ADVENTURES

Along the way to major attractions, take side trips to spots guaranteed to please. **EdVenture Children's Museum** in Columbia, South Carolina, is nothing but hands-on fun, from science experiments to climbing in a 24-foot fire truck and manning the siren.

Myrtle Beach is awash with activities guaranteed to bring smiles—and squeals—from the more than 35 rides at **Family Kingdom Amusement Park** to **Myrtle Waves,** South Carolina's largest water park, and the many colorful Putt-Putt golf courses.

Meet Big Bird, Kermit the Frog, and Miss Piggy at Atlanta's **Center for Puppetry Arts,** which houses the largest Jim Henson display in the world. The collection includes more than 500 puppets and artifacts donated by the Henson family. Another centerpiece at the attraction is a large global collection, with puppets dating back to the 1500s.

Chapter 2

TRAVEL SMART

Updated by
Rachel Roberts Quartarone

★ **CAPITAL**
Atlanta, GA; Raleigh, NC; Columbia, SC

POPULATION
Georgia: 10.6 million; North Carolina 10.5 million; South Carolina 5.2 million

LANGUAGE
English

$ **CURRENCY**
U.S. Dollar

AREA CODES
Atlanta, GA: 404, 470, 678, 770; Raleigh, NC: 919, 984; Columbia, SC: 803

⚠ **EMERGENCIES**
911

DRIVING
On the right

ELECTRICITY
120–220 v/60 cycles; plugs have two or three rectangular prongs

TIME
Same as New York

WEB RESOURCES
www.exploregeorgia.org
www.visitnc.com
discoversouthcarolina.com

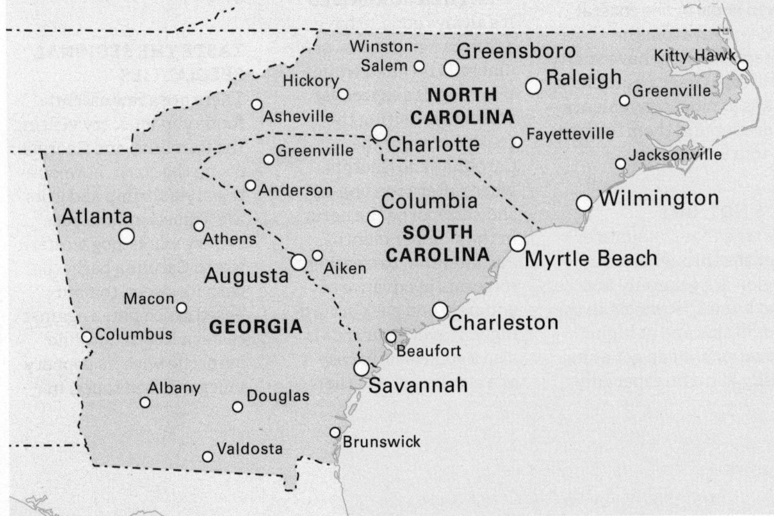

Know Before You Go

The Carolinas and Georgia cover a lot of ground—over 145,000 square miles combined! The somewhat unpredictable Southern climate and changing landscapes keep things interesting. There is a wealth of things to see and do—in fact, so much so that trip planning can often be overwhelming. Whether you are heading to the coastal areas, the mountains, or the modern metropolises, here are some tips to help you make the most of your visit.

GET OUT THE MAP

Yes, real-time GPS navigation is wonderful, but there are rural stretches throughout the Carolinas and Georgia where you can't necessarily depend on cell coverage. Be sure to have a map handy for those instances where you may find yourself lost on a country road or detoured due to roadwork. There are still largely undeveloped patches of farmland and/or mountain terrain where you won't find a cell tower. Even some of the coastal areas away from the interstates may have spotty coverage. You can purchase maps at most convenience stores or find them for free at tourism offices.

IT'S HOT, BUT ...

It's true that the summer months throughout this region are generally hot and humid. However, in the mountains and at higher elevations, it can get quite chilly at night, especially if you are camping. Also, even though it may be hot outside, you may be freezing inside. Air-conditioning is a pretty common and essential amenity throughout the region. Restaurants, shops, and other attractions in the Carolinas and Georgia aren't shy about cranking the ice-cold a/c. A light sweater or jacket may serve you well even in the heat of summer.

BE PREPARED FOR WEATHER SURPRISES

It's always good to have a rain jacket, poncho, or umbrella on hand while traveling. It's especially true when visiting the coastal areas of the Carolinas and Georgia, where afternoon pop-up showers can be the norm in the summer months. Pay attention to weather forecasts in advance of your trip and pack accordingly. Travel insurance is also a good idea, in case of a significant weather event like a hurricane or snowstorm. Believe it or not, snowstorms can still happen during the winter months in much of the region and can effectively shut a city down.

LOOK FOR "MOM AND POP"

The familiarity of national chains can be nice while traveling, but to really get a true sense of local culture, look for the "mom and pop" independently owned businesses where you can. Some of the best small inns, shops, and restaurants are owned and operated by people who have a vested interest in their communities. Even if it isn't a perfect meal or stay, odds are that you will remember it, and maybe even make new friends along the way. Especially in rural or less touristy areas where you aren't going to find many travel recommendations, it's fun to head off the beaten path, explore, and discover your own hidden gems.

TASTE THE REGIONAL SPECIALTIES

There are a few essential foods you must try visiting the Carolinas and Georgia. Along the coast, Lowcountry-style shrimp and grits are a must! Inland, you can try whole-hog western North Carolina barbecue with its sweet, tomato-based sauce pitted against eastern North Carolina barbecue with its peppery vinegar-based sauce. In

South Carolina, there's barbecue with a tangy mustard sauce. And, you can't get through Georgia without trying something with peaches, peanuts, pecans, or Vidalia onions. To round out the list, here are a few other essentials: Cheerwine in North Carolina, hoppin' John in South Carolina, and Brunswick stew in Georgia.

WALK WHERE YOU CAN

For the most part, a car is essential in this region. But, you will find most of the cities are extremely walkable and offer a variety of public transit options. Historic colonial cities like Charleston and Savannah are best seen on foot. If a walking tour is too much, book a hop-on/hop-off trolley tour for the most flexibility. In Atlanta, Charlotte, Raleigh, Columbia, and other large cities, look for walking tours that help you discover the neighborhoods and historic sites that define the character of local communities.

GET CULTURED

The Carolinas and Georgia offer some world-class museums and arts institutions, and some of them are even free to visit. Look ahead to see what exhibits and events are planned as some may require advanced tickets. In Atlanta, there's the High Museum of Art and the Woodruff Arts Center, while Charlotte is home to the Mint and the Blumenthal Performing Arts Center. In Raleigh, you can visit the North Carolina Museum of Art and the North Carolina Museum of History (both free), and in Columbia, check out the South Carolina State Museum and the Columbia Museum of Art.

HIT THE PARKS

From the Great Smoky Mountains National Park in western North Carolina to Cumberland Island National Seashore in Georgia, there are several national parks and federally managed recreation sites in this region. If you plan on visiting multiple parks, consider investing in a U.S. Park Pass, which is good for 12 months (🌐 *www.usparkpass.com*). They are free for U.S. residents over age 62. Also, if you plan on visiting multiple state parks within the Carolinas and Georgia, you may be able to save on parking by purchasing an annual park pass for each respective state.

BEWARE SUNDAYS AND MONDAYS

When you're planning your trip, watch out for these two tricky days of the week. In the smaller towns and rural areas of the region especially, you may find many shops and restaurants shuttered on Sundays, particularly in the off-season. Even in the cities you may find some restaurants open for Sunday brunch but closed for Sunday dinner. Monday is also a popular day for museums and cultural institutions to be closed and for higher-end restaurants to take the night off.

EMBRACE THE OFF-SEASON

Consider traveling in the off-season for a different perspective on the region. The coast can be just as gorgeous and relaxing in October as it is in June, for example. Plus, a mountain escape in January and February can sometimes offer even more wide-open scenery than the packed-out leaf season. Off-season rates are usually much lower, there are fewer people, and you can experience an area more like a local.

Getting Here and Around

 Air

Flying time to Atlanta is four hours from Los Angeles, two hours from New York, two hours from Chicago, two hours from Dallas, and nine hours from London. By plane, Charlotte is an hour northeast of Atlanta, Raleigh 75 minutes northeast, Wilmington 1½ hours east, Asheville an hour north, and Charleston, Hilton Head, and Savannah an hour east–southeast.

Travelers flying into the Carolinas or Georgia are likely to pass through Hartsfield-Jackson Atlanta International Airport. It's by far the most popular airport in the region and is the busiest in the world, at least in terms of number of passengers—more than 100 million annually.

AIRPORTS

Hartsfield-Jackson Atlanta International Airport (ATL) sees more than 2,700 arriving and departing flights daily. There are 263 concessionaires at the airport, and Wi-Fi is available throughout, as are laptop plug-in stations. Hartsfield-Jackson has three interfaith chapels; the chapel in the atrium is open from 9 to 5 daily, and the chapels on Concourses E and F are open 24 hours a day. A customer-service office and staffed customer-service desks answer questions. Waiting passengers can also check out museum exhibits throughout the airport, including a display of Martin Luther King Jr. memorabilia on Concourse E. The international terminal, Concourse F, has several art installations to explore. Smoking areas are located on Concourses B, C, E, F, and T. Overnight visitors can choose from over 70 hotels and motels near the airport, most with free shuttle service. Give yourself extra time, as you'll have to tackle crowds whether waiting to buy a burger, getting through security, or boarding the underground train to other concourses. The airport's website regularly updates estimates of waits at security areas and on-site parking areas. Arrive 90 minutes before a flight in the United States and allow two hours for international flights. Allow enough time to be at the gate 30 minutes before boarding. Those returning rental cars need to allow time for that process and a short ride on the ATL SkyTrain (to the domestic terminal) or a shuttle bus (to the international terminal) from the rental car center. Keep track of laptops and be ready to collect suitcases as soon as they arrive at the carousels for security's sake.

North Carolina's Charlotte Douglas International Airport (CLT), near the border of North Carolina and South Carolina, is an American Airlines hub. Tired travelers can plop down in one of the trademark, handcrafted white rocking chairs in the Atrium, a tree-lined indoor crossroads between airport concourses that also offers a food court with mostly fast-food outlets. Within a few miles are more than a dozen hotels, most with free airport shuttles. In the center of the state, right off Interstate 40, is Raleigh-Durham International Airport (RDU), a prime gateway into central and eastern North Carolina. Its two terminals serve 11 million passengers annually. GoTriangle provides bus transportation from the airport to the surrounding communities of Raleigh, Durham, and Chapel Hill. Those who live in the western reaches of the Triangle are just as likely to use the Piedmont Triad International Airport (GSO), at the convergence of four interstates in North Carolina. It primarily serves the Triad area—Greensboro, Winston-Salem, and High Point—as well as some cities in southwestern Virginia.

The portal to western North Carolina is Asheville Regional Airport (AVL). It provides nonstop flights to Atlanta; Charlotte; Chicago; Dallas; Denver; New

York; Newark; Philadelphia; Washington, DC; and, in Florida, Fort Lauderdale, Fort Myers, Punta Gorda, Sanford (Orlando), Tampa, and St. Petersburg.

For visits to the North Carolina coast, fly into Wilmington International Airport (ILM), a small facility with service by three carriers. Upstate South Carolina has the small but user-friendly Greenville–Spartanburg International Airport (GSP), which sometimes has lower fares than either the Charlotte or Asheville airport.

GROUND TRANSPORTATION

Of all the airports in the region, only Hartsfield-Jackson Atlanta International is well served by public transportation. The Metropolitan Atlanta Rapid Transit Authority, better known as MARTA, has frequent service to and from the airport. It's the quickest, cheapest, and most hassle-free way into the city. MARTA's north–south line will get you downtown in 15 to 20 minutes for just $2.50. MARTA riders can also travel to Midtown, Buckhead, Sandy Springs, and Doraville—reaching into north suburban Atlanta. MARTA's Airport Station is located inside the terminal and can be accessed from the north and south sides of the terminal near the baggage claim area. Trains run weekdays 4:45 am to 1:15 am, and weekends and holidays 6 am to 1:15 am. Most trains operate every 15 to 20 minutes; during weekday rush hours, trains run every 10 to 15 minutes. You can print out a copy of the rail map from the MARTA website or pick one up at any station.

Charlotte's Area Transit System (CATS) connects passengers to several city center locations with its "Sprinter" express bus service. The Sprinter operates every 20 minutes weekdays 5:05 am to 10:54 pm, and every 30 minutes weekends 5:05 am to 12:55 am.

GoTriangle provides public bus service from RDU to its Regional Transit Center, where riders can connect to bus routes throughout the region. There are designated pickup spots at both terminals.

Most of the airports in the region are served by rideshare, taxi, and shuttle services. Private limousine or van services also serve the major airports. In Atlanta, use only approved vehicles with the airport decal on the bumper, which ensure the drivers are charging legal fares and have knowledge of local destinations.

Bicycle

Throughout the coastal areas of Georgia and the Carolinas, hills are few and the scenery is remarkable. Many bike routes are marked on North Carolina's Outer Banks, around Savannah and Georgia's coastal islands, and in greater Charleston and South Carolina's Lowcountry. Mountain biking trails have popped up all over the Carolinas and North Georgia. The Pisgah National Forest and the Great Smoky Mountains are both national hotbeds for premier mountain biking. Cycling in larger cities in the region, especially Atlanta, can prove difficult. Although bike paths are available, riding on streets is often necessary and can prove daunting. However, biking is becoming more prevalent as public bike shares are available in Atlanta and the larger cities in the region. In Atlanta, dockless electric bikes and scooters are also widely available.

Printed state maps, available in bike shops and drugstores, contain useful topographic detail. Many tourist boards and local bike clubs also distribute bike maps. Google Maps can also be helpful in mapping out a bike route in real time.

Getting Here and Around

Southeastern Cycling (🌐 *www.sadlebred.com*) has information on road and trail riding throughout the Southeast and free ride maps. Mountain Biking in Western North Carolina (🌐 *www.mtbikewnc.com*) has information on mountain trails. AllTrails.com (🌐 *www.trails.com*) offers information on more than 30,000 bike trails, including many in Georgia and the Carolinas.

 Boat

Ferries are a common, and often necessary, way to get around coastal areas, and especially to visit North Carolina's Outer Banks and Georgia's Sea Islands.

The Ferry Division of the North Carolina Department of Transportation operates seven ferry routes over five separate bodies of water: the Currituck and Pamlico Sounds and the Cape Fear, Neuse, and Pamlico Rivers. Travelers use the three routes between Ocracoke and Hatteras Island, Swan Quarter, and Cedar Island; between Southport and Fort Fisher; and between Cherry Branch and Minnesott Beach. Ferries can accommodate any car, trailer, or recreational vehicle. Pets are permitted if they stay in the vehicle or are on a leash. Telephone and online reservations for vehicles are available for the Cedar Island–Ocracoke and Swan Quarter–Ocracoke routes; on other routes space is on a first-come, first-served basis. Schedules generally vary by season, with the largest number of departures May through October.

Ferries are the only form of public transportation to Sapelo and Cumberland Islands in Georgia. The Georgia Department of Natural Resources operates a ferry between Meridian and Sapelo. Advance reservations are required and can be made by phone or at the Sapelo Island Visitor Center in Meridian. A privately run passenger ferry, contracted by the National Park Service, runs daily between St. Marys and Cumberland Island from March to November. The rest of the year the ferry does not operate on Tuesday and Wednesday. Reservations are essential, especially in March and April.

In North Carolina, the Cedar Island–Ocracoke and Swan Quarter–Ocracoke ferries cost $1 for pedestrians, $3 for bicycles, $10 for motorcycles, $15 for cars, and up to $45 for other vehicles (trailers, boats, motor homes). The Southport–Fort Fisher ferry costs $1 for pedestrians, $2 for bicycles, $3 for motorcycles, and $7 to $28 for vehicles. Tickets can be purchased with cash or traveler's checks or online via credit card. Personal checks are not accepted. The other North Carolina ferries are free.

In Georgia, the pedestrian round-trip ferry to Sapelo Island costs $15 for adults and $10 for children. Advance reservations are required. The pedestrian ferry to Cumberland Island costs $30 round-trip, plus a $10 national park fee.

 Car

A car is the most practical and economical means of traveling around the Carolinas and Georgia. Atlanta, Savannah, Charleston, Myrtle Beach, and Asheville can also be explored fairly easily on foot or by using public transit and cabs, but a car is helpful to reach many of the most intriguing attractions, which are not always downtown. ■ **TIP→ When returning rental cars to airports, always allow extra time to check in vehicles.**

Although drivers make the best time traveling along the South's extensive network of interstate highways, keep in mind that U.S. and state highways offer some delightful scenery and the opportunity to stumble on funky roadside diners, leafy state parks, and historic town squares. Although the area is rural, it's still densely populated, so travelers rarely drive for more than 20 or 30 miles without passing roadside services, such as gas stations, restaurants, and ATMs.

Among the most scenic highways in the Carolinas and Georgia are **U.S. Route 78,** running east–west across Georgia; **U.S. Routes 25, 19, 74,** and **64,** traveling through the Great Smoky Mountains of western North Carolina; **U.S. Route 17** from Brunswick, Georgia, along the coast through South Carolina and North Carolina; and the **Blue Ridge Parkway** from the eastern fringes of the Great Smoky Mountains through western North Carolina into Virginia.

Unlike some other areas of the United States, the Carolinas and Georgia have very few toll roads. Currently, the Cross Island Parkway on Hilton Head, South Carolina, the Southern Connector in Greenville, South Carolina, and the Triangle Expressway in Wake and Durham Counties, North Carolina, are toll roads.

CAR RENTAL

It's important to reserve a car well in advance of your expected arrival. Rental rates vary from city to city but are generally lowest in larger cities where there's a lot of competition. Economy cars cost between $27 and $61 per day, and luxury cars go for $70 to $198. Weekend rates are generally much lower than those on weekdays, and weekly rates usually offer big discounts. Rates are also seasonal, with the highest rates coming during peak travel times, including Thanksgiving and Christmas holiday seasons. Local factors can also affect rates; for example, a big convention can absorb most of the rental-car inventory and boost rates for those remaining.

Travel Times Around the Carolinas and Georgia by Car

From	To	Time/ Distance
Atlanta, GA	Savannah, GA	4 hours / 248 miles
Asheville, NC	Great Smoky Mountains National Park, Cherokee entrance	1 hour / 50 miles
Charlotte, NC	Atlanta, GA	4 hours / 244 miles
Charleston, SC	Raleigh, NC	4 hours / 279 miles
Durham, NC	Asheville, NC	3½ hours / 224 miles
Hilton Head, SC	Columbia, SC	2½ hours / 152 miles
Winston-Salem, NC	Charlotte, NC	1½ hours / 84 miles

Don't forget to factor in the taxes and other add-ons when figuring up how much a car will cost. At Atlanta's Hartsfield-Jackson International Airport, add the 8% sales tax, 11.11% airport concession-recovery fee, 3% city rental car tax, $5 daily customer facility charge, and $0.80 to $1.30 vehicle license-recovery charge. These "miscellaneous charges" mean that a weekly rental can jump in price far higher than the rental agency cost.

Some off-airport locations offer lower rates, and their lots are only minutes from the terminal via complimentary shuttle. Also ask whether certain frequent-flyer, American Automobile Association (AAA), corporate, or other such promotions are accepted and whether the rates might be lower for other arrival and departure dates. National agencies include Alamo, Avis, Dollar, Enterprise, and National Car Rental.

Getting Here and Around

ROADSIDE EMERGENCIES

Travelers in Georgia and the Carolinas have help as close as their cell phones in case of emergencies on roadways. The Georgia Department of Transportation's Intelligent Transportation System works on three levels. First, drivers statewide can call 511 to report problems and get directions and information on traffic, MARTA, and Hartsfield airport. Next, on the 400 miles of metro Atlanta interstate highways, Highway Emergency Response Operators (HEROs) help motorists with everything from empty gas tanks to medical emergencies. Finally, the Georgia Navigator system provides statewide information on the Internet on roadway conditions and, in Atlanta, everything from drive times to incident locations and roadway conditions. Welcome centers statewide can also access that information.

In an emergency, drivers in North Carolina should call 911. In metro areas, such as Raleigh, Durham, Burlington, Greensboro, Winston-Salem, Charlotte, and Asheville, and in the Pigeon River Gorge area, drivers on major U.S. highways and interstates receive roadside assistance through the Department of Transportation's Incident Management Assistance Patrols (IMAPs). The IMAP staff remove road debris, change tires, clear stalled vehicles, and can call a private tow truck. Motorists should dial *HP to reach the highway patrol and have an IMAP truck dispatched. In North Carolina's congested metro and construction areas, use the NCDOT Traveler Information Management System (TIMS) on the Internet or via cell phone. Go to 🌐 *www.ncdot.org* and click the link for "Travel & Maps." Search for travel updates by region, roadway, or county. Both the Great Smoky Mountains National Park and the Blue Ridge Parkway lure travelers to North Carolina. The state's western area has many narrow, steep, and winding roads near such towns as Asheville, Boone, Sylva, and Waynesville. Use extra caution there, and pay extra attention to winter weather reports for snow and ice when roads may be closed. You can also access travel information by dialing 511.

South Carolina's Incident Response Program operates on interstate highways in urban areas including Charleston, Columbia, Florence, and the constantly busy Myrtle Beach area (specifically the U.S. Route 17 bypass and U.S. Route 501). Stranded motorists can call *HP for help and reach the local highway patrol dispatch system. The state operates hundreds of traffic cameras to monitor traffic flow and identify accident sites on all five interstates and in the Myrtle Beach area. They also have a camera at the intersection of Interstate 95 and Interstate 26, in case of hurricane evacuations. You can also get up-to-date travel information and traffic updates by calling 511.

RULES OF THE ROAD

Both of the Carolinas and Georgia prohibit all drivers from texting while driving. Georgia law goes further and prohibits drivers from using cell phones or other handheld electronic devices for any purposes while driving. North Carolina prohibits drivers under 18 from using handheld devices, but there are fewer restrictions for those over 18. Unless otherwise indicated, motorists may turn right at a red light after stopping if there's no oncoming traffic. When in doubt, wait for the green. In Atlanta, Asheville, Charleston, Columbia, Charlotte, Savannah, and the Triangle and Triad cities of North Carolina, be alert for one-way streets, "no left turn" intersections, and blocks closed to vehicle traffic.

In Georgia, always strap children under age eight or under 40 pounds (regardless of age) into approved child-safety seats or booster seats appropriate for their height and weight in the back seat. Children younger than age eight and weighing less than 80 pounds must be properly secured in child restraints or booster seats in North Carolina. Child-safety seats or booster seats are required for children younger than six and weighing less than 80 pounds in South Carolina.

Watch your speed, as police are more than happy to write tickets to speedy out-of-towners. In Georgia, a "Super Speeder Law" allows the state to issue an additional $200 fine to drivers exceeding 75 mph on a two-lane road or 85 mph on any roadway.

Cruise

Carnival has ships to Bermuda, the Bahamas, and the Caribbean that depart from Charleston primarily in spring and fall. Princess Cruises, Holland America, Regent Seven Seas Cruises, and Crystal Cruises occasionally call at Charleston. American Cruise Lines offers intracoastal tours that wind through historic Savannah, Charleston, and Beaufort.

Train

Several Amtrak routes pass through the Carolinas and Georgia; however, many areas are not served by train, and those cities that do have service usually only have one or two arrivals and departures each day. The *Crescent* runs daily through Greensboro, Charlotte, and Atlanta as it travels between New York and New Orleans. Three trains, the *Palmetto,* the *Silver Meteor,* and the *Silver Star,* make the daily run between New York and Miami via Raleigh, Charleston, Columbia, and Savannah. The *Carolinian* runs daily from New York to Charlotte, via Raleigh.

Amtrak offers rail passes that allow for travel within certain regions, which can save you a lot over the posted fare. Amtrak has several kinds of USA Rail Passes, offering unlimited travel for 15, 30, or 45 days, with rates of $459 to $899, depending on the area traveled, the time of year, and the number of days. Amtrak has discounts for students, seniors, military personnel, and people with disabilities.

Essentials

Dining

The increase of international flavors in the region reflects the tastes and backgrounds of the people who have flooded into the Carolinas and Georgia over the past couple of decades. Bagels are as common nowadays as biscuits, and, especially in urban areas, it can be harder to find country cooking than a plate of hummus. For the most part, though, plenty of traditional Southern staples—barbecue, fried chicken, greens, and the like—are available.

Atlanta now has a big-city mix of neighborhood bistros, ethnic eateries, and expense-account restaurants. A new wave of restaurants in Charleston and Savannah serves innovative versions of Lowcountry cooking, with lighter takes on traditional dishes. In North Carolina, you can find some nationally recognized restaurants in Charlotte, Asheville, Raleigh, and Durham. Outside the many resort areas along the coast and in the mountains, dining costs in the region are often lower than those in the North.

Vegetarians will have no trouble finding attractive places to eat in any of the larger metropolitan areas, although in small towns they may have to stick with pizza. Asheville is a haven for vegetarians; it has been named in many lists of the top vegetarian cities, including being named the most vegetarian-friendly city in the United States by People for the Ethical Treatment of Animals (PETA).

The food truck scene has made its way to most major cities in the Carolinas and Georgia, providing a quick way to grab decently priced cross-cultural eats at all hours. Websites like Roaming Hunger (🌐 *www.roaminghunger.com*) provide details on local food truck whereabouts.

MEALS AND MEALTIMES

The Southern tradition of Sunday dinner—usually a midday meal—has morphed to some degree, at least in urban areas, to Sunday brunch. For many people this meal follows midmorning church services, so be advised that restaurants will often be very busy through the middle of the day. In smaller towns many restaurants are closed Sunday. On weekdays in larger cities, restaurants will be packed with nearby workers from before noon until well after 1:30 pm. On Saturday, eateries in cities can be packed from morning through night. In small towns and big cities, weekday nights—when crowds are less likely and the staff can offer diners more time—can be the most pleasant for fine dining.

Southerners tend to eat on the early side, with lunch crowds beginning to appear before noon. The peak time for dinner is around 7. However, late-evening dining is not unusual in big cities, college towns, and tourist destinations.

RESERVATIONS AND DRESS

For the most part, restaurants in the Carolinas and Georgia tend to be informal. A coat and tie are rarely required, except in a few of the fanciest places. Business-casual clothes are safe almost anywhere.

WINE, BEER, AND SPIRITS

Blue laws—legislation forbidding sales on Sunday—have a history in this region dating to the 1600s. These bans are still observed in many rural areas, particularly with regard to alcohol sales. Liquor stores are closed Sunday in the Carolinas. Beer and wine can't be sold anywhere before noon in North Carolina and South Carolina on Sunday. There are entire counties in the Carolinas and Georgia that prohibit the sale of alcoholic beverages in restaurants. Some cities and towns allow the sale of beer and wine in restaurants but not mixed drinks. In North Carolina, bottled distilled spirits are sold only through "ABC" (Alcoholic Beverage Control) outlets; beer and wine are available in most grocery and convenience stores.

Although the Carolinas and Georgia will never be a Napa Valley, the last decade has seen a huge increase in the number of vineyards. North Carolina now has more than 200 wineries, and the Yadkin Valley is the state's first federally recognized American Viticultural Area, with more than 400 acres of vineyards in production. Asheville's Biltmore Estate Winery is the most popular in the United States, with about 1 million visitors each year. Georgia's Wine Highway, which guides visitors to a number of wineries, runs from just north of Atlanta up through the North Georgia mountains. Muscadine and scuppernong grapes are native to warmer parts of the region; the sweetish wine from these grapes is gaining more respect. Traditional wine grapes are also widely grown.

Microbreweries are common all over the region, with hot spots being Atlanta, Asheville, Wilmington, Charlotte, and Charleston, as well as the Triangle of Raleigh, Durham, and Chapel Hill. There are more than 300 microbreweries and brewpubs in North Carolina, close to 50 in South Carolina, and more than 100 in Georgia, despite state laws on alcohol distribution that have crimped their growth.

Lodging

With the exception of Atlanta, Savannah, Charleston, Asheville, and Charlotte, most lodging rates in the region fall at or below the national average. They do vary a great deal seasonally, however; coastal resorts and mountainous areas tend to have significantly higher rates in summer. Fall color creates demand for lodging in the mountains; expect high-season rates. All major chains are well represented in this part of the country, both in cities and suburbs, and interstates are lined with inexpensive to moderate chains.

In many places, consider forgoing a modern hotel in favor of a historic property. There are dozens of fine old hotels and mansions that have been converted into inns, many of them lovingly restored. Some may offer better rates than chain hotels. Bed-and-breakfasts are big in some cities, notably Charleston, Savannah, and Asheville. Each of these cities has two dozen or more B&Bs. There also are loads of B&Bs in many small towns along the coast and in the North Georgia and western North Carolina mountains.

In many coastal resort areas, vacation-home and condo rentals dominate the lodging scene. The North Carolina Outer Banks, Myrtle Beach, and Hilton Head are major rental areas, each with several thousand rental properties. Rental prices vary by season, with peak summer rental rates that can double or more over off-season rates.

In the North Carolina and Georgia mountains, cabins are popular. These are usually owner-operated businesses with only a few cabins. In Georgia many state parks rent cabins, and they're often excellent values. In the mountains a number of lodges are available. These vary from simple accommodations to deluxe properties with spas, golf courses, and tennis courts. Many attract families that come back year after year. Mountain lodges are closed for several months in winter.

Thousands of families camp in the Carolinas and Georgia. The North Carolina Outer Banks, the Sea Islands of Georgia, and the Great Smoky Mountains National Park and Pisgah and Nantahala National Forests in western North Carolina are especially popular with campers.

Essentials

APARTMENT AND HOUSE RENTALS

The far-flung resort areas of the Carolinas and Georgia are filled with rental properties—everything from cabins to luxury homes. Most often these properties, whether part of a huge corporation or individually owned, are professionally managed; such businesses have become an industry unto themselves.

Carolina Mornings and Carolina Mountain Vacations rent cabins in the high country of North Carolina. Georgia Mountain Rentals rents cabins and vacation homes in the northeast Georgia mountains around Helen. Intracoastal Vacation Rentals has long-term as well as off-season rentals on the coast of Cape Fear. Hatteras Realty, Midgett Realty, and Sun Realty handle properties on North Carolina's Outer Banks. Island Realty focuses on the Charleston and Isle of Palms area in South Carolina. Hilton Head Rentals and Resort Rentals of Hilton Head Island offer rentals on Hilton Head. StayTybee handles properties on Georgia's tiny Tybee Island.

BED-AND-BREAKFASTS

Historic B&Bs and inns are found in just about every region in the Carolinas and Georgia and include quite a few former plantation houses and lavish Southern estates. In many rural or less touristy areas, B&Bs offer an affordable and homey alternative to chain properties. In tourism-dependent destinations, expect to pay about the same as for a full-service hotel. Many of the South's finest restaurants are also found in country inns.

CAMPING

The Carolinas and Georgia are popular for trailer and tent camping, especially in state and national parks. Georgia offers camping sites at more than 40 state parks across the state. Popular private and/or national park supervised campgrounds along its Atlantic coastline include River's End on Tybee Island and those on Jekyll Island, Cumberland Island, and Sapelo Island. In South Carolina a similar number of state parks offer campsites. North Carolina's unique coastline offers primitive campsites on beachfronts and among southern swamp forests and sounds, including Hammocks Beach State Park on Bear Island. There are 29 other state parks that offer campsites across the state. For detailed information on the state parks and to reserve a site, visit the state parks' websites.

A variety of camping experiences are available at Great Smoky Mountains National Park, including backcountry and horse camping. Reservations for Elkmont, Smokemont, Cades Cove, and Cosby, the park's most popular developed campgrounds (with flush toilets and running water), can now be made online at 🌐 *www.recreation.gov*.

HOTELS

In summer, especially July and August, hotel rooms in coastal areas and the mountains can be hard to come by unless you book well in advance. In the mountains, the autumn leaf-peeping season, typically early October to early November, is the busiest time of the year, and on weekends nearly every room is booked. Lodging in North Carolina's Triad area is difficult during the twice-yearly international furniture shows: in April and October all rooms are booked within a 30-mile radius of the show's location in High Point. Lodging in downtown Atlanta, despite its density of hotels, can be problematic during trade shows at the Georgia World Congress Center and the AmericasMart complex.

Some of the most interesting hotels in the region are housed in historic buildings, particularly in well-preserved old cities like Charleston and Savannah. To find notable historic hotels, visit the National Trust for Historic Preservation's

Historic Hotels of America website (🌐 *www.historichotels.org*).

Health/Safety

HEALTH

With the exception of the mountains of North Georgia and western North Carolina, in the Carolinas and Georgia, it's hot and humid for at least six months of the year. Away from the coast, midsummer temperatures can reach the high 90s, making heat exhaustion and heatstroke real possibilities. Heat exhaustion is marked by muscle cramps, dizziness, nausea, and profuse sweating. To counter its effects, lie down in a cool place with your head slightly lower than the rest of your body. Sip cool, not cold, fluids. Life-threatening heatstroke is caused by a failure of the body to effectively regulate its temperature. In the early stages, heatstroke causes fatigue, dizziness, and headache. Later the skin becomes hot, red, and dry (due to lack of sweating), and body temperatures rise to as high as 106°F. Heatstroke requires immediate medical care.

At the beach or anywhere in the sun, slather on sunscreen. Reapply it every two hours, or more frequently after swimming or perspiring. Remember that many sunscreens block only the ultraviolet light called UVB but not UVA, which may be a big factor in skin cancer. Even with sunscreen it's important to wear a hat and protective clothing and to avoid prolonged exposure to the sun.

The coastal areas of the Carolinas and Georgia, especially the swamps and marshes of the Lowcountry, are home to a variety of noxious bugs: mosquitoes, sand flies, biting midges, black flies, chiggers, and no-see-ums. Most are not a problem when the wind is blowing, but when the breezes die down—watch out! Experts agree that DEET is the most effective mosquito repellent, but this chemical is so powerful that strong concentrations can melt plastic. Repellents with 100% DEET are available, but those containing 30% or less should work fine for adults; children should not use products with more than 10%. Products containing the chemical picaridin are effective against many insects and don't have the strong odor or skin-irritating qualities of those with DEET. The plant-based oil of lemon eucalyptus, used in some natural repellents, performed well in some studies. Mosquito coils and citronella candles also help ward off mosquitoes.

For sand flies or other tiny biting bugs, repellents with DEET alone are often not effective. What may help is dousing feet, ankles, and other exposed areas with an oily lotion, such as baby oil, which effectively drowns them.

The mountains of western North Carolina and North Georgia generally have few mosquitoes or other biting bugs, but in warm weather hikers may pick up chiggers or ticks. Use repellents with DEET on exposed skin. Wasps, bees, and small but ferocious yellow jackets are common throughout the region.

Feel free to drink tap water everywhere in the region, although in coastal areas it may have a sulfur smell. Many visitors to the beaches prefer to buy bottled water.

COVID-19

COVID-19 brought all travel to a virtual standstill in the first half of 2020, and interruptions to travel have continued into 2021. Although the illness is mild in most people, some experience severe and even life-threatening complications. Once travel started up again, albeit slowly and cautiously, travelers were asked to be particularly careful about hygiene and to avoid any unnecessary travel, especially if they are sick.

Essentials

Older adults, especially those over 65, have a greater chance of having severe complications from COVID-19. The same is true for people with weaker immune systems or those living with some types of medical conditions, including diabetes, asthma, heart disease, cancer, HIV/AIDS, kidney disease, and liver disease. Starting two weeks before a trip, anyone planning to travel should be on the lookout for some of the following symptoms: cough, fever, chills, trouble breathing, muscle pain, sore throat, new loss of smell or taste. If you experience any of these symptoms, you should not travel at all.

And to protect yourself during travel, do your best to avoid contact with people showing symptoms. Wash your hands often with soap and water. Limit your time in public places, and, when you are out and about, wear a face mask that covers your nose and mouth. Indeed, a mask may be required in some places, such as on an airplane or in a confined space like a theater, where you share the space with a lot of people. You may wish to bring extra supplies, such as disenfecting wipes, hand sanitizer (12-ounce bottles were allowed in carry-on luggage at this writing), and a first-aid kit with a thermometer.

Given how abruptly travel was curtailed in March 2020, it is wise to consider protecting yourself by purchasing a travel insurance policy that will reimburse you for any cancellation costs related to COVID-19. Not all travel insurance policies protect against pandemic-related cancellations, so always read the fine print.

SAFETY

In general, the Carolinas and Georgia are safe destinations for travelers. Most rural and suburban areas have low crime rates. However, some of the region's larger cities, such as Atlanta, have higher crime rates.

In urban areas, follow proven traveler's precautions: don't wander on to deserted streets after dark, avoid flashing large sums of money or fancy jewelry, and keep an eye on purses and backpacks. If walking, even around a historic district, ask about areas to avoid at a hotel or a tourist information center; if in doubt, take a taxi.

In the Smoky Mountains the greatest concerns are driving on some of the curving and narrow roads—sometimes in heavy traffic—and theft of property and credit cards from vehicles in parking lots. Sometimes thieves will watch for motorists locking valuables in their trunks before leaving their cars. Single-car collisions, with motorists hitting trees or rocky outcroppings, are the cause of most accidents. Stolen property is rare in campsites. Drivers should also keep in mind that cell phones don't often work in the park. If visitors encounter bears, they are advised not to move suddenly but to back away slowly.

$ Money

Although the cost of living remains fairly low in most parts of the South, travel-related costs (such as dining, lodging, and transportation) have become increasingly steep in Atlanta. Tourist attractions are pricey, too. For example, a tour of CNN Center is $15, admission to the High Museum of Art in Atlanta is $15, and getting into Georgia Aquarium is a steep $36. Costs can also be dear in resort communities throughout the Carolinas and Georgia.

If you plan on seeing multiple attractions in a city, look for money-saving passes sold at local visitor centers. Atlanta, for instance, participates in the national CityPASS program. The pass includes admission to six key attractions for $77, which is half of what you'd pay if buying individual admissions. Check out *www.citypass.com* for more information.

Prices throughout this guide are given for adults. Substantially reduced fees are almost always available for children, students, military personnel, and senior citizens.

Tipping

Tipping in the Carolinas and Georgia is essentially the same as tipping anywhere else in the United States. A bartender typically receives from $1 to $5 per round of drinks, depending on the number of drinks. Tipping at hotels varies with the level of the hotel, but here are some general guidelines: bellhops should be tipped $1 to $5 per bag; if doormen help to hail a cab, tip $1 to $2; maids should receive $1 to $3 in cash daily; room-service waiters get $1 to $2 even if a service charge has been added; and tip concierges $5 or more, depending on what service they perform.

Taxi drivers should be tipped 15% to 20% of the fare, rounded up to the next dollar amount. Tour guides receive 10% of the cost of the tour. Valet parking attendants receive $1 to $2 when you get your car back. Tipping at restaurants varies from 15% to 20% by level of service and level of restaurant, with 20% being the norm at higher-end restaurants.

Packing

Smart but casual attire works fine almost everywhere. A few chic restaurants in the cities prefer more elegant dress, and tradition-minded lodges in the mountains and resorts along the coast still require jackets and ties for men at dinner. For colder months pack a lightweight coat, slacks, and sweaters; bring along heavier clothing in some mountainous areas, where cold, damp weather prevails and snow is not unusual. Keeping summer's humidity in mind, pack absorbent natural fabrics that breathe; bring an umbrella, but leave the plastic raincoat at home. A jacket or sweater is useful for summer evenings and for too-cool air-conditioning. And don't forget insect repellent and sunscreen.

When to Go

Spring is the best time to see the Carolinas and Georgia in bloom. Fall can bring spectacular foliage in the mountains and stunning coastal sunsets. Spring and fall daytime temperatures are delightful; bring a jacket for cool nights. Summer is hot and humid, especially along the coast. In winter, mild weather is punctuated by brief bouts of cold. Short afternoon thunderstorms are common in spring and summer.

Contacts

Air

AIRPORT INFORMATION **Asheville Regional Airport.** *61 Terminal Dr., Fletcher* *828/684–2226* *www.flyavl.com*. **Charlotte Douglas International Airport.** *5501 Josh Birmingham Pkwy., Charlotte* *704/359–4013* *www.charlotteairport.com*. **Greenville–Spartanburg International Airport.** *2000 GSP Dr., Suite 1, Greer* *864/877–7426* *www.gspairport.com*. **Hartsfield-Jackson Atlanta International Airport.** *6000 N. Terminal Pkwy., Atlanta* *404/530–7300* *www.atl.com*. **Piedmont Triad International Airport.** *1000A Ted Johnson Pkwy., Greensboro* *336/665–5600* *www.flyfrompti.com*. **Raleigh-Durham International Airport.** *2400 John Brantley Blvd., Morrisville* *919/840–2123* *www.rdu.com*. **Wilmington International Airport.** *1740 Airport Blvd., Wilmington* *910/341–4125* *www.flyilm.com*.

AIRPORT TRANSFERS **Charlotte Area Transit System.** *704/336–7433* *www.ridetransit.org*. **GoTriangle Transit.** *919/485–7433* *www.gotriangle.org*. **Metropolitan Atlanta Rapid Transit Authority.** *404/848–5000* *www.itsmarta.com*.

Bicycle

CONTACTS **Georgia Bikes.** *706/740–2453* *www.georgiabikes.org*. **South Carolina Trails Program.** *1205 Pendleton St., Columbia* *803/734–1700* *www.sctrails.net*. **WalkBikeNC.** *Division of Bicycle and Pedestrian Transportation, 1552 Mail Service Center, Raleigh* *919/707–2600* *www.walkbikenc.com*.

Boat

BOAT INFORMATION **Cumberland Island National Seashore.** *113 St. Marys St. W, St. Marys* *912/882–4336, 877/860–6787 ferry reservations,* *www.nps.gov/cuis*. **North Carolina Department of Transportation Ferry Division.** *2300 Ferry Rd.* *800/293–3779* *www.ncdot.gov/divisions/ferry*. **Sapelo Island Visitor Center.** *1766 Landing Rd. SE, Darien* *912/437–3224* *www.sapelonerr.org*.

Car

ROADSIDE ASSISTANCE CONTACTS **Georgia Department of Transportation Travel Programs.** *511, 877/694–2511* *www.511ga.org*. **North Carolina Department of Transportation Travel Information.** **HP, 877/511–4662* *www.ncdot.gov/travel*. **South Carolina Department of Transportation Customer Service.** *877/511–4672, *HP* *www.511sc.org*.

Lodging

APARTMENT AND HOUSE CONTACTS **Carolina Mornings.** *855/398–0712* *www.carolinamornings.com*. **Carolina Mountain Vacations.** *877/488–8500,* *www.carolinamountainvacations.com*. **Georgia Mountain Rentals.** *844/328–8278* *www.georgiamtnrentals.com*. **Hatteras Realty.** *800/428–8372* *www.hatterasrealty.com*. **Hilton Head Rentals.** *843/342–4444* *www.hiltonheadrentals.com*. **Intracoastal Vacation Rentals.** *855/346–2463* *www.intracoastalrentals.com*. **Island Realty.** *800/707–6421* *www.islandrealty.com*. **Midgett**

Realty. ☎ *252/986–2841, 866/348–8819* 🌐 *www.midgettrealty.com.* **Resort Rentals of Hilton Head Island by Vacasa.** ☎ *800/845–7017, 843/686–6008* 🌐 *www.hhivacations.com.* **StayTybee.** ☎ *912/786–0531* 🌐 *www.staytybee.com.* **Sun Realty, Outer Banks.** ☎ *888/853–7770* 🌐 *www.sunrealtync.com.*

CAMPING CONTACTS Georgia State Parks. ☎ *800/864–7275* 🌐 *www.gastateparks.org.* **Great Smoky Mountains National Park.** ☎ *865/436–1200* 🌐 *www.nps.gov/grsm.* **North Carolina State Parks.** ☎ *877/722–6762* 🌐 *www.ncparks.gov.* **South Carolina State Parks.** ☎ *866/345–7275* 🌐 *www.southcarolinaparks.com.*

RESERVATION SERVICES Asheville Bed and Breakfast Association. ☎ *828/633–1110* 🌐 *www.ashevillebba.com.* **Association of Historic Inns of Savannah.** ☎ *912/232–5678* 🌐 *www.historicinnsofsavannah.com.* **South Carolina Bed and Breakfast Association.** 🌐 *www.southcarolinabedandbreakfast.com.*

Activities

GOLF Georgia State Park Golf Courses. 🌐 *gastateparks.org/golfing.* **Golf Link.** 🌐 *www.golflink.com.* **Golf North Carolina.** 🌐 *www.golfnorthcarolina.com.*

OUTDOORS Appalachian Trail Conservancy. 🌐 *www.appalachiantrail.org.* **Blue Ridge Parkway.** ☎ *828/670-1924* 🌐 *www.blueridgeparkway.org.* **Georgia State Parks.** 🌐 *www.gastateparks.org.* **National Forests in North Carolina.** ☎ *828/257–4200* 🌐 *www.fs.usda.gov/nfsnc.* **National Park Service.** ☎ *865/436-1200* 🌐 *www.nps.gov/grsm.* **North Carolina State Parks.** ☎ *919/707-9300* 🌐 *www.ncparks.gov.* **South Carolina State Parks.** ☎ *803/734-0156* 🌐 *www.southcarolinaparks.com.*

Tours

CONTACTS Georgia Travel and Tourism. ✉ *Technology Sq., 75 5th St. NW, Suite 1200, Midtown* ☎ *800/847–4842* 🌐 *www.exploregeorgia.org.* **North Carolina Travel and Tourism Division.** ✉ *301 N. Wilmington St., Raleigh* ☎ *800/847–4862* 🌐 *www.visitnc.com.* **South Carolina Department of Parks, Recreation, and Tourism.** ✉ *1205 Pendleton St., Columbia* ☎ *803/734–0124* 🌐 *discoversouthcarolina.com.*

Visitor Information

ARTS Penland School of Crafts. 🌐 *www.penland.org.* **Southern Highland Craft Guild.** 🌐 *www.southernhighlandguild.org.*

HISTORY AND CULTURE Doc South. 🌐 *docsouth.unc.edu.* **Garden & Gun.** 🌐 *www.gardenandgun.com.* **Southern Living.** 🌐 *www.southernliving.com.*

WINERIES NC Wine. 🌐 *www.ncwine.org.* **Winegrowers Association of Georgia.** 🌐 *www.georgiawine.com.*

Great Itineraries

Asheville and the Great Smoky Mountains

The soft mountain peaks, blue fog, and fall leaves of the Great Smoky Mountains have long inspired painters, writers, and musicians. Art-centric Asheville edges this great American landscape and makes the perfect launchpad for mountain touring. Pack your hiking boots to see the natural beauty up close.

DAY 1: DOWNTOWN ASHEVILLE

Drive into **Asheville** or land at pleasant **Asheville Regional Airport,** one of the South's best small airports, and rent a car. Stay downtown at **Haywood Park Hotel**—the expansive suites are close to the action. Hip Asheville is a center of North Carolina's craft beer and local food movements, so lunch at the lively **Wicked Weed Brewing Pub.** Pair a beer flight with small plates like fish-and-chips and lobster mac and cheese in the sprawling building with inviting outdoor dining spaces. Hit the sidewalks for a look at Asheville's art scene; watch glass artists work and patiently explain their craft at **Lexington Glassworks,** which also hosts a monthly concert series. Check out incredible architecture at the elaborate bricked and polychrome-tiled **Basilica of St. Lawrence** and the **Black Mountain College Museum + Arts Center.** The legendary college nurtured maverick 20th-century artists. Alternately, kick around the architectural wonder that is the **Grove Arcade,** built in 1929. Armies of stone gargoyles guard numerous locally owned stores and restaurants. Make advance reservations for a dinner of extraordinary tapas at **Cúrate,** one of the hottest restaurants in town, which is partially owned by chef Felix Meana, formerly of the famed elBulli restaurant on the Costa Brava of Spain. An early dinner allows time for a show at **Asheville Community Theatre,** which stages productions year-round.

DAY 2: GREAT SMOKY MOUNTAINS

(1½ hours by car)

Rise early to visit one of Asheville's more than 50 tailgate markets, including **Asheville City Market.** Stock up on locally made foods for the ride to **Great Smoky Mountains National Park.** Interstate 40 heading west is the quickest route out of Asheville. Take the highway to U.S. Route 19, which links to the spectacular **Blue Ridge Parkway** just west of Maggie Valley. The parkway leads into Great Smoky Mountains National Park. At the park entrance, stop by the **Oconaluftee Visitor Center** for maps and information. Spend the day exploring by vehicle and on foot. **Newfound Gap Road** (U.S. Route 441) is one of the park's most scenic drives and leads to **Clingmans Dome Trail.** This moderately difficult 1-mile trail ends at a 54-foot-tall observation tower affording amazing mountain views from the highest point in the Smoky Mountains. The round-trip hike takes about an hour, a nice warm-up before a picnic lunch and then another hike along **Trillium Gap Trail** to **Grotto Falls**. The 1.3-mile, moderately difficult hike ends at the 30-foot-high falls, the only falls in the park that you can walk behind. Stick around the park for sunset views at **Chimney Tops Overlook.** Camp at the park or depart for two luxurious nights at the nearby **Omni Grove Park Inn.** The grand hotel, built in 1913 with locally mined stone, is home to the world's largest collection of arts and crafts furniture. The 43,000-square-foot spa offers massages, skin-care treatments, indoor lap pools, outdoor whirlpools, and a subterranean sanctuary to ease tired hiking muscles.

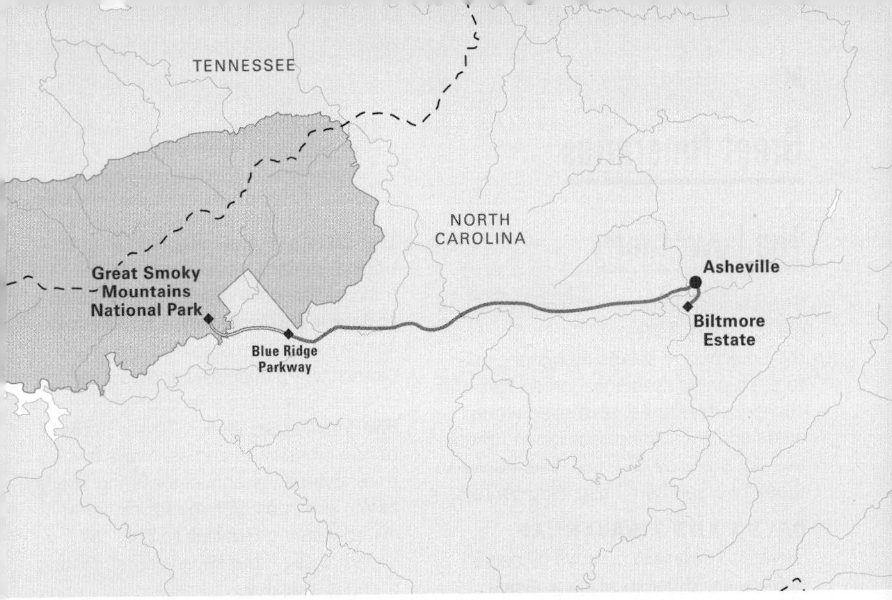

DAY 3: BILTMORE ESTATE

(15 minutes by car from Omni Grove Park Inn)

Stick around the Omni Grove Park Inn for a sunrise breakfast. If the weather is warm, book a day of kayaking, canoeing, or white-water rafting at the **Nantahala Outdoor Center,** the nation's largest outdoor recreation company. The center also offers mountain biking, hiking, climbing, fishing, and horseback riding adventures in the Blue Ridge and Great Smoky Mountains.

If the weather is chilly, set off instead for a morning tour of **Biltmore Estate,** America's largest privately owned home. Built in the 1890s as George Vanderbilt's private residence, this castle of sorts has 250 rooms, including its own bowling alley, and 75 acres of gardens and grounds. Be sure to visit the complex's state-of-the-art winery and tasting rooms.

Spend the late afternoon at the **North Carolina Arboretum,** created by Frederick Law Olmsted, designer of New York City's Central Park, and part of the original Biltmore Estate. See 65 acres of cultivated gardens and a bonsai exhibit of native trees. You can also explore a 10-mile network of trails.

Biltmore Village boasts many fine eateries, including **Corner Kitchen.** The renovated Victorian cottage has a fireplace in one dining room. The restaurant serves American classics with a twist like pecan-crusted mountain trout with bourbon sauce or Jamaican jerk smoked chicken breast over black beans.

DAY 4: HEAD HOME

If you're flying out of Asheville, enjoy breakfast at the Omni Grove Park Inn, where window-lined dining rooms provide fantastic views. Think house-cured pork belly, goat-cheese grits, and caramelized sweet-onion sauce. Don't forget a souvenir: a slice of Tupelo Honey Café brown-butter pecan pie to go.

Great Itineraries

The Lowcountry

Stretching from genteel Savannah, Georgia, to lively Charleston, South Carolina, the Lowcountry serves up history, culture, stunning coastlines, urban flair, and culinary adventures. Unspoiled natural areas and captivating seaside communities dot the easy 150-mile drive between these two Southern hospitality centers.

DAYS 1 AND 2: SAVANNAH

Drive into **Savannah** or arrive by plane at **Savannah/Hilton Head International Airport** and rent a car. Immerse yourself in the feel of old Savannah with a stay at the elegant but inviting **Foley House Inn,** where you'll be treated to complimentary breakfast, afternoon tea, and evening wine and hors d'oeuvres.

Once refreshed, spend a few leisurely hours strolling Bull Street. Enjoy beautifully landscaped squares and the **Green-Meldrim House,** a Gothic Revival mansion that was General Sherman's headquarters when the Union Army occupied Savannah, then head on to **Forsyth Park.** Massive, moss-draped oaks line wide park lanes leading to war memorials, an old fort, and a magnificent fountain.

For dinner, head to historic (and supposedly haunted) **The Olde Pink House** in Planters Inn, where you can enjoy cocktails and classic Southern cuisine like fried chicken, mac and cheese, and shrimp and grits.

Savannah's various tours offer fun and easy overviews of the city's rich history. On Day 2, step back in time on a morning horse-drawn history tour with **Carriage Tours of Savannah.** The 50-minute journey winds through the historic district as drivers narrate. Afterward, set out on foot for the **Owens-Thomas House & Slave Quarters,** one of America's finest examples of English Regency architecture, with an original carriage house that includes rare intact urban slave quarters. Grab lunch at **Back in the Day Bakery,** a favorite for sandwiches on fresh-baked bread and old-fashioned cupcakes and Southern sweets. Spend the afternoon shopping at **Riverfront/Factors Walk,** where a network of iron crosswalks and stairways leads to renovated warehouses hosting shops, cafés, and pubs. Splurge for dinner at award-winning **Elizabeth on 37th**; call ahead to see if the seven-course tasting menu is available.

DAY 3: HILTON HEAD ISLAND

(1 hour by car from Savannah)

Hilton Head Island beaches span 12 miles, offering respite after busy Savannah. **Burkes Beach,** mid-island, is a quiet place to stroll or sunbathe before being pampered at **Spa Montage at Palmetto Bluff,** a 13,000-square-foot full-service spa and hair salon. Tucked under an umbrella of old oaks hung with Spanish moss, the restaurant has near-panoramic views of stunning sunsets and sweeping marshlands, not to mention an impressive wine list and a tasting menu. Classic she-crab soup might share space with a prime pork chop with whipped potatoes, French beans, baby apples, onions, ginger, and hard-cider sauce. **The Jazz Corner** serves a musical nightcap.

DAY 4: ST. HELENA ISLAND

(1 hour by car from Hilton Head Island)

The Lowcountry is rooted in Gullah culture. The Gullah people, descendants of 18th-century slaves, maintain their dialect and heritage, much of it centered on **St. Helena Island,** where Gullahs still catch shrimp with hand-tied nets. **Penn Center,** the first school for freed slaves, is the official Gullah headquarters and part of the Penn School Historic District, which includes old burial grounds and

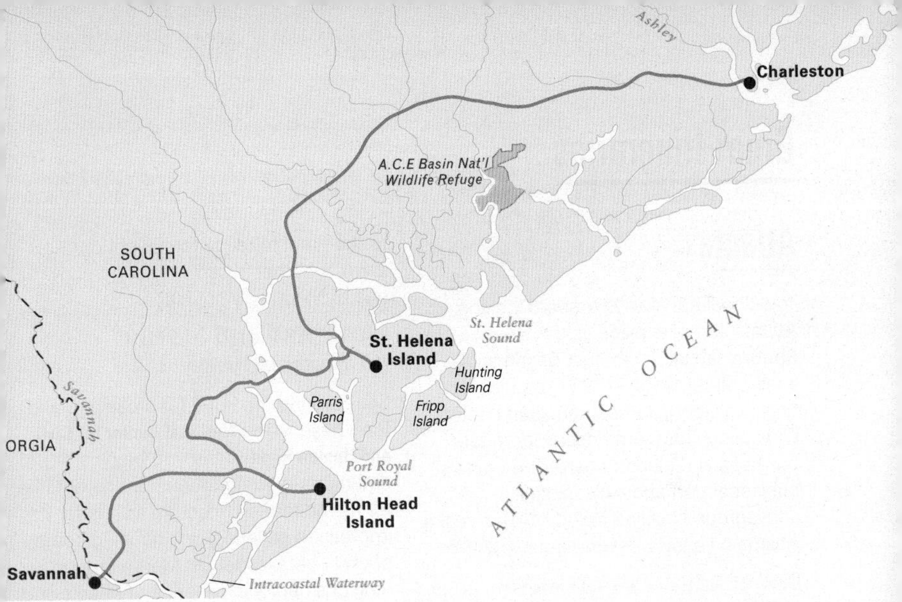

Gantt Cottage, where Dr. Martin Luther King Jr. stayed. At the **York W. Bailey Museum,** request to see Gullah indigo stamping, wood-burning art, and sweet-grass basketmaking demonstrations. **The Gullah Grub Restaurant** features authentic Lowcountry cooking.

DAYS 5 AND 6: CHARLESTON

(2½ hours by car from Hilton Head Island)

Charleston's status as the South's foodie capital gives the city a delicious layer of appeal atop all the art, architecture, history, and natural beauty there. Arrive in time for freshly made breakfast crepes and cold-pressed coffee at **Queen Street Grocery.** Walking **Charleston's Historic District** is a great way to see key landmarks, such as the 1752 **St. Michael's Church,** the city's oldest surviving church, and a National Historic Landmark. For lunch, take a seat at the **Slightly North of Broad** chef's table, which overlooks the kitchen, giving you a view of all that goes into your meal preparation at the lively Lowcountry bistro.

No culinary tour of Charleston is complete without visiting James Beard Award–winning chef Sean Brock's **McCrady's** and **Husk** restaurants. Book a tasting-menu dinner at McCrady's and lunch the next day at Husk or McCrady's Tavern (which is also open for dinner). All three spots highlight new Southern cooking and local ingredients. Husk also has a reputation for cool cocktails and an amazing weekend brunch. The historic Charleston Light Dragoon's Punch recipe blends California brandy, Jamaican rum, peach brandy, black tea, lemon juice, and raw sugar.

With a Husk lunch reservation secured, spend Day 6 working up an appetite by touring Charleston's magnificent plantations. **Magnolia Plantation and Gardens** has a huge array of blooming plants on more than 70 acres of gardens and a rebuilt 19th-century plantation house. **Drayton Hall,** where building began in 1738, is a National Trust for Historic Preservation site and the only plantation on the road that is a complete original (the rest were burned during the Civil War). Stunning **Middleton Place** has terraced lawns, butterfly-shaped lakes, and, for dinner, Lowcountry specialties at Middleton Place Restaurant.

After dinner, toast this grande dame of Southern cities at the swanky outdoor Pavilion Bar atop **Market Pavilion Hotel.** Terrific views and creative cocktails make this Charleston's best rooftop bar.

Great Itineraries

Atlanta

Traditional but always forward-looking Atlanta earns its place as the New South's capital. A city that began as a railroad terminus in 1837 grew to become Georgia's cosmopolitan center. Old-school Southern hospitality meets business and industry here. The world's busiest airport and a clean, safe, aboveground rail line called MARTA make Atlanta an easy weekend getaway.

DAY 1: ARRIVE IN ATLANTA

Landing early at **Hartsfield-Jackson Atlanta International Airport** means plenty of time to dive into Atlanta's thrilling urban scene. Sleek glass, steel, and stone towers and grand city views at **Omni Hotel at CNN Center** set the mood, and the hotel puts you close to public transportation. Start with a 50-minute, behind-the-scenes tour of **CNN Center,** but make sure to get reservations at least 24 hours in advance. Next stop: **Georgia Aquarium.** That this landlocked city is home to the largest aquarium in the Western Hemisphere (10 million gallons of water) is testimony to Atlanta's progressive attitude. Take the MARTA metro or grab a rideshare (Uber or Lyft) to West Midtown for a contemporary Southern lunch at **JCT Kitchen and Bar.** Billed as a "farmstead bistro" with Southern flair, JCT is the place for deviled eggs with country ham, pimento cheese with serrano chilies, shrimp and grits, and chicken and dumplings. In the same complex and nearby are lots of fun shops and art galleries to explore. Don't leave Midtown without checking the evening lineup at the **Fox Theatre.** The vintage movie palace built in 1929 is worth seeing for its Moorish-Egyptian style alone. The ceiling has moving clouds and twinkling stars. These days, it's a venue for dance, concerts, musicals, and film festivals. Head back to the hotel to ready for a night on the town, whether it's a Fox Theatre show or one of Midtown's hot clubs.

DAY 2: ART AND HISTORY

(15 minutes by subway)

Stick around the hotel for breakfast, and then head to the **National Center for Civil and Human Rights** nearby to begin a day of civil-rights-themed touring. It's as notable for its modern architecture as it is for its impressive galleries, one housing some of civil rights leader Dr. Martin Luther King Jr.'s personal papers and effects and others devoted to human rights campaigns worldwide. Next find your way to Atlanta's **Sweet Auburn** district to tour the area where King was born, raised, and later returned, making Atlanta a center for social change. Sign up early in the day for a guided tour of the **Birth Home** site at the **Martin Luther King, Jr. National Historical Park,** as a limited number of visitors are allowed to visit the home daily. Nearby **Ebenezer Baptist Church** is where King was baptized and later preached alongside his father. Pay tribute to King and his compatriots at **The King Center,** which houses the Eternal Flame and the Kings' final resting place. Note the inscription on King's white marble tomb: "Free at last, Free at last, Thank God Almighty I'm Free at last." Have a late lunch at the **Sweet Auburn Curb Market,** named for the days when whites were allowed to sell their goods inside while African Americans had to sell theirs along the curb. Cafés, meats, and fresh produce fill the market.

After lunch, make your way to fashionable **Buckhead.** With its history museums, cool shopping, and hot restaurants, the neighborhood is a perfect example of Atlanta's Old South/New South blend. While in Buckhead, visit **Atlanta History Center,** which focuses on Atlanta and the South. Its 9,200-square-foot Civil War

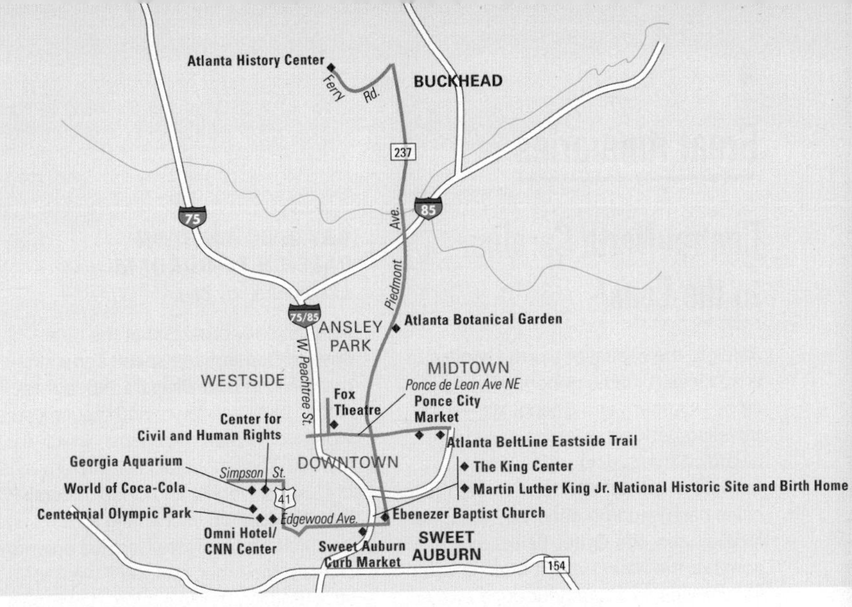

gallery displays 1,500 of the center's 7,500 war artifacts. Items are as large as a railroad engine and as small as a button. Speaking of large, the museum's newest permanent exhibit, *Cyclorama: The Big Picture,* features the fully restored cyclorama painting *The Battle of Atlanta.* The 132-year-old hand-painted masterpiece stands 49 feet tall, is longer than a football field, and weighs 10,000 pounds. It's one of only two cycloramas remaining in the United States. A period farm and a 1928 mansion, the Swan House, are on the 33-acre complex, too. Stick around Buckhead for shopping and dinner. Colorful **Eclipse di Luna** is a fun place for a glass of wine and shared tapas like duck empanadas, although you may want to hoard your own paella.

DAY 3: BRUNCH AND STROLL

(15 minutes by subway)

Rise early for a walk on the **Atlanta BeltLine Eastside Trail.** The BeltLine will eventually be a 33-mile loop around Atlanta's urban center—the Eastside Trail was the first to be developed. Parks, an urban farm, and public art are located on the portions of the trail that are already opened (the rest are expected to be complete by 2030). Breakfast is at **Flying Biscuit,** an easy mark for tall, pillowy biscuits with cranberry-apple butter or full-on grilled flatiron steak and eggs. Choosing the Midtown location will put you near **Ponce City Market,** a retail, entertainment, and residential complex inside the historic Sears & Roebuck Co. building. At 2.1 million square feet, it's the largest brick structure in the South. Some of the city's top chefs offer meals in the Central Food Hall. The complex continues to add high-end retailers and features Skyline Park, a rooftop arcade of vintage games and a spot for great city views. Nearby, the 30-acre **Atlanta Botanical Garden,** inside Piedmont Park, boasts the nation's largest orchid center, conservation gardens, a Japanese garden, a hardwood forest with a canopy walkway, and an interactive kids garden. Stroll-and-stop options are plenty at **Centennial Olympic Park,** where you'll find the College Football Hall of Fame and its massive wall holding the helmets of 700 teams. Before departing the Centennial Olympic Park area, stop by **World of Coca-Cola,** a shrine to the famous soda corporation based in Atlanta. Sample more than 100 Coke beverages sold around the world, see more than a century's worth of marketing, and, of course, buy a refrigerator magnet to take home.

Great Itineraries

Central North Carolina to the Coast

Raleigh, the capital of North Carolina, is so close to its neighboring Triangle cities—Durham and Chapel Hill—that traveling between them is easy. With award-winning restaurants, great farmers' markets, and food tours, these cities have become nationally recognized foodie hubs. The Outer Banks, home to some of the nation's best beaches and lighthouses, is a four-hour drive away.

DAY 1: DOWNTOWN RALEIGH

Fly into no-fuss **Raleigh-Durham International Airport,** not far from downtown Raleigh, and rent a car, or cruise in driving your own vehicle. Stay at centrally located **Raleigh Marriott City Center,** walking distance from sights, shopping, and the city's best restaurants. Before you head out, book a Durham Afternoon Tasting Tour with Taste Carolina for Day 2 of your trip. The company stages gourmet foodie tours throughout the Triangle, but this one blends local history and farm-to-table restaurants. After, take a walk to get your bearings, starting with a local beer and inventive dim sum fare at **Brewery Bhavana.** Fortified, stroll **City Market's** cluster of shops, galleries, and restaurants on cobblestone streets. If you love museums (and a bargain), check out North Carolina's free state museums of history and natural history in the heart of the city. For dinner, the options are plentiful. Stroll around the easily walkable downtown and see what strikes your fancy. After dinner, grab a classic cocktail at the underground speakeasy **Watts & Ward.**

DAY 2: DOWNTOWN RALEIGH TO DURHAM

(30 minutes by car)

After an early breakfast at the hotel, drive to Durham and spend some time marveling at **Duke Chapel's** 210-foot-tall Gothic-style bell tower and the intricate woodwork inside the chapel, which dates to 1930. The cathedral is on the grounds of Duke University and close to **Sarah P. Duke Gardens'** 55 enchanting acres. Lunch is your afternoon Taste Carolina downtown Durham food tour, and you'll want to stick around after to explore downtown shopping or the **North Carolina Museum of Life and Science's** three-story Magic Wings Butterfly House. For dinner, consider **The Durham,** a hip mid-century modern hotel with an equally hip restaurant and rooftop bar. James Beard Award–winning chef Andrea Reusing's menu changes daily but focuses on local ingredients and the freshest North Carolina seafood. Close the night strolling around the **American Tobacco Historic District** or taking in some live music at **Motorco Music Hall.**

DAY 3: DOWNTOWN RALEIGH TO CHAPEL HILL

(40 minutes by car)

Check out of your hotel and plan to spend the night at Chapel Hill's **Fearrington House Inn.** Accommodations and the Fearrington Village Center, totaling 100 acres, sit on a former dairy farm. The Fearrington House restaurant here is one of the country's best, and it was doing farm-to-table cooking years before it was cool. Challenge your foodie sensibilities with the likes of venison with quince and rutabaga. You could book spa services and relax the entire day here or take the 20-minute drive into Chapel Hill to visit **Morehead Planetarium and Science Center,** one of America's largest planetariums.

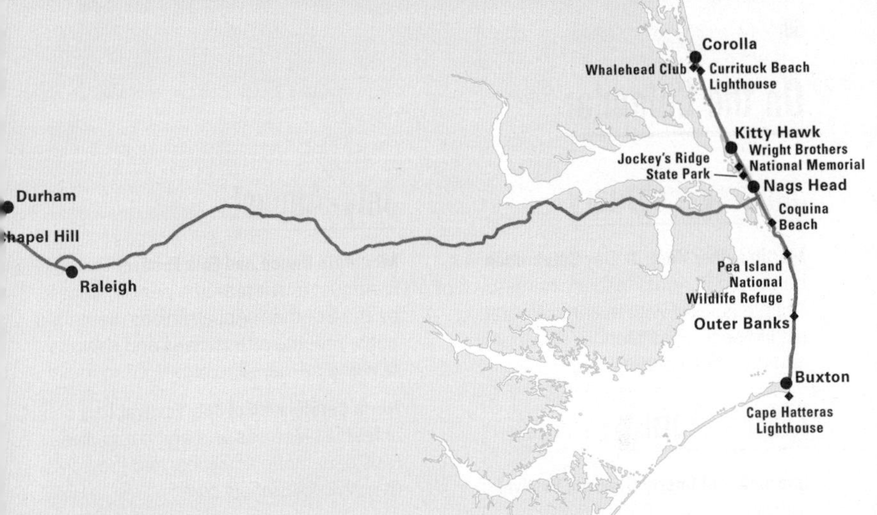

More than 60 NASA astronauts trained here in celestial navigation. It's also fun just to stroll down Franklin Street and take in the college-town scene.

DAY 4: CHAPEL HILL TO THE OUTER BANKS

(4 hours by car)

Get an early start for the drive to the **Outer Banks.** Book the centrally located **First Colony Inn** at Nags Head. Spend your first day chilling at **Coquina Beach,** which locals consider the OBX's nicest beach. Fish, take a long walk, and hunt for shells before dinner at **Basnight's Lone Cedar Café.** The huge, lively restaurant with waterfront views has its own herb garden and a specials menu that lists the names of the fishermen who supplied the day's catch.

DAY 5: NAGS HEAD TO BUXTON

(1 hour by car)

Grab a hearty breakfast at local favorite **Sam and Omie's,** open since 1937 and still serving salty country ham steaks with eggs. Today's mission is climbing the 210-foot-tall **Cape Hatteras Lighthouse,** the nation's tallest brick lighthouse. On the way, driving across the 5,800-acre **Pea Island National Wildlife Refuge,** watch for some of the more than 365 birds that have been spotted here.

DAY 6: NAGS HEAD TO KITTY HAWK

(40 minutes by car)

Book your last two nights at the oceanfront **Sanderling Resort.** On the way there, stop for a tour of **Wright Brothers National Memorial** in Kill Devil Hills, where America's first powered flight took place. Nearby, hike **Jockey's Ridge State Park,** home to the East Coast's tallest sand dunes, 80 to 100 feet high, depending on which way the wind blows the sand. Visitors can also stroll on a 384-foot boardwalk.

DAY 7: COROLLA

(20 minutes by car)

Corolla is home to the impressive redbrick **Currituck Beach Lighthouse,** which you may climb, and the historic **Whalehead Club,** a former luxury home and hunting lodge built between 1922 and 1925. Both spots are open for touring, and the pair stand on beautifully landscaped grounds perfect for a day of strolling. Stop at a grocery store on the way for lunchtime picnic provisions. Back at the resort, spend the late afternoon lazing on the beach or relaxing at the Spa at Sanderling. Then dine at **Kimball's Kitchen** for a perfect end to your vacation week before driving home or flying out of Norfolk International airport two hours north in Virginia.

On the Calendar

January-February

Martin Luther King, Jr. Day Celebration The beloved civil rights leader's hometown of Atlanta is filled with events celebrating his life each third Monday of January. 🌐 *www.thekingcenter.org*

March-April

International Cherry Blossom Festival In Macon, Georgia, 350,000 cherry trees glow pink and white. 🌐 *www.cherryblossom.com*

Newport Pig Cookin' Contest In April (sometimes late March) head to Newport, North Carolina, for eastern-style 'cue with vinegar-based sauce. 🌐 *www.newportpigcooking.com*

North Carolina Azalea Festival Since 1948, Wilmington has been celebrating all things azalea with live music, crafts, food, and more. The festival takes place each April. 🌐 *www.ncazaleafestival.org*

Savannah St. Patrick's Day The river runs green on March 17 in Savannah for the second-largest St. Patrick's Day celebration in the country (next to New York). 🌐 *www.savannahsaintpatricksday.com*

May-June

Atlanta Jazz Festival This long-running event takes place in Piedmont Park each Memorial Day Weekend. 🌐 *www.atlantafestivals.com*

Gullah Festival This Beaufort, South Carolina, festival highlights the fine arts, customs, and language of Lowcountry African Americans. 🌐 *www.originalgullahfestival.org*

Spoleto Festival USA This Charleston festival features classical and jazz music, dance, and theater. 🌐 *www.spoletousa.org*

July-August

Mountain Dance and Folk Festival The early-August event features performances by the Southern Appalachians' best traditional mountain musicians and dancers. 🌐 *www.folkheritage.org*

North Carolina 4th of July Festival This annual festival features arts and crafts, live music, patriotic activities, and fireworks. 🌐 *www.nc4thofjuly.com*

September-October

Helen Oktoberfest The festival features German music, food, a beer hall, and polka dancing. 🌐 *www.helenchamber.com*

Little River Shrimp Fest On the banks of the Little River near Myrtle Beach, South Carolina, this annual October festival features live music and lots of tasty shrimp. 🌐 *www.littlerivershrimpfest.org*

Lexington's Barbecue Festival One of the most popular events in North Carolina, this festival and cook-off is where barbecue legends are made. It takes place the last two weekends of October. 🌐 *www.barbecuefestival.com*

November-December

Dahlonega's Old Fashioned Christmas Dahlonega goes all out with a tree lighting and events filled with holiday spirit. 🌐 *www.dahlonegachristmas.com*

Nights of a Thousand Candles In coastal Murrells Inlet, South Carolina, Brookgreen Gardens celebrates with over 2,800 hand-lit candles. 🌐 *www.brookgreen.org*

Chapter 3

THE NORTH CAROLINA COAST

Updated by
Stratton Lawrence

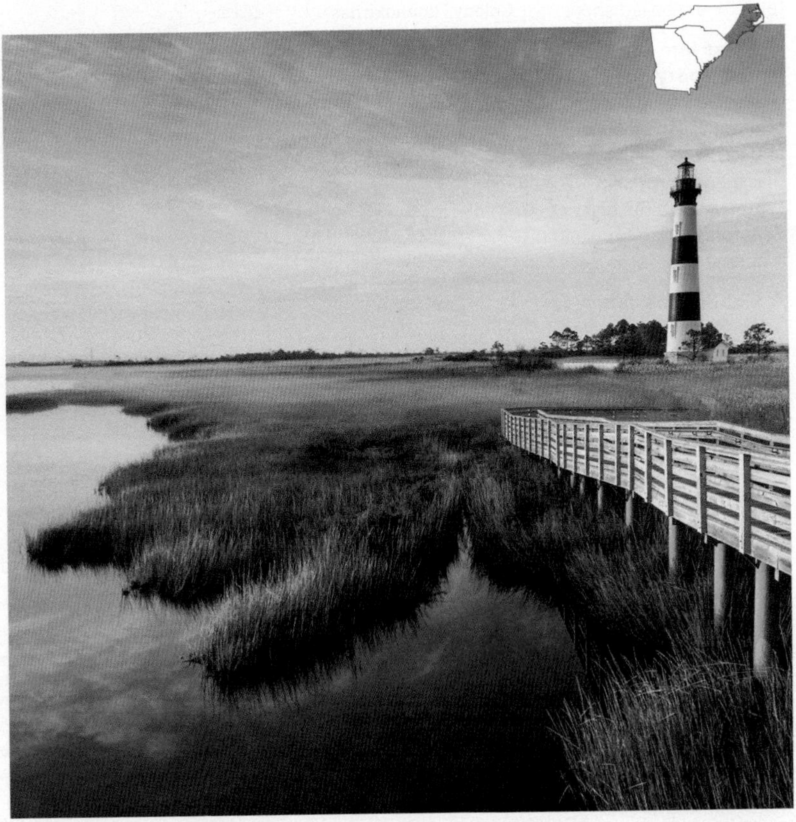

Sights	Restaurants	Hotels	Shopping	Nightlife
★★★★★	★★★★☆	★★★☆☆	★☆☆☆☆	★★☆☆☆

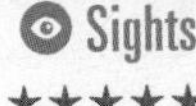

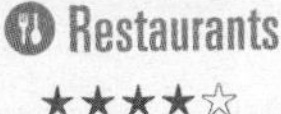

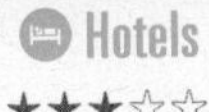

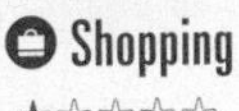

WELCOME TO THE NORTH CAROLINA COAST

TOP REASONS TO GO

★ **Water, water everywhere:** Surfers delight in Cape Hatteras's formidable waves. Kayakers and boaters prefer the Crystal Coast's sleepy estuaries. Beach strollers love Ocracoke's remote, unspoiled shore.

★ **Pirate lore and hidden booty:** The Graveyard of the Atlantic is littered with shipwrecks to dive. See artifacts from Blackbeard's flagship *Queen Anne's Revenge* at Beaufort's North Carolina Maritime Museum.

★ **Lighting the darkness:** North Carolina has seven lighthouses, each with its own personality; a few, you can climb to the top.

★ **The Lost Colony:** In a mystery for the ages, 117 settlers disappeared without a trace. Their story is presented both in historical context and dramatic entertainment in Manteo.

★ **Fresh seafood:** Prepared practically every way possible—fried, grilled, steamed, stuffed, blackened, or raw—the bounty of the ocean is available all along the coast.

1 **Northern Beaches.** Destinations include charming Corolla and vacation hot spot, Duck.

2 **Kitty Hawk and Nags Head.** Aviation history and gorgeous beaches along North Carolina Highway 12.

3 **Roanoke Island.** Home to the mysterious "Lost Colony," Roanoke has natural and historic appeal.

4 **Hatteras Island.** Beaches here are protected as part of the Cape Hatteras National Seashore.

5 **Ocracoke Island.** This island—once inhabited by pirates—is only reachable by ferry or boat.

6 **Beaufort.** History and maritime charm abound.

7 **New Bern.** Pepsi-Cola was invented here.

8 **Wilmington.** Abuzz with haute cuisine, music, and culture.

9 **Wrightsville Beach.** A surfer's paradise.

10 **Kure Beach.** Beaches, historic sites, and the North Carolina Aquarium.

11 **Southport.** Southport is the access point to Bald Head Island via ferry.

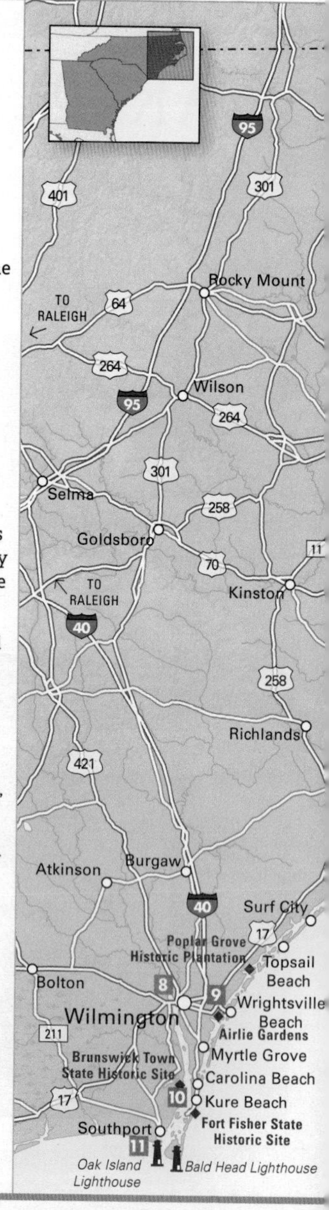

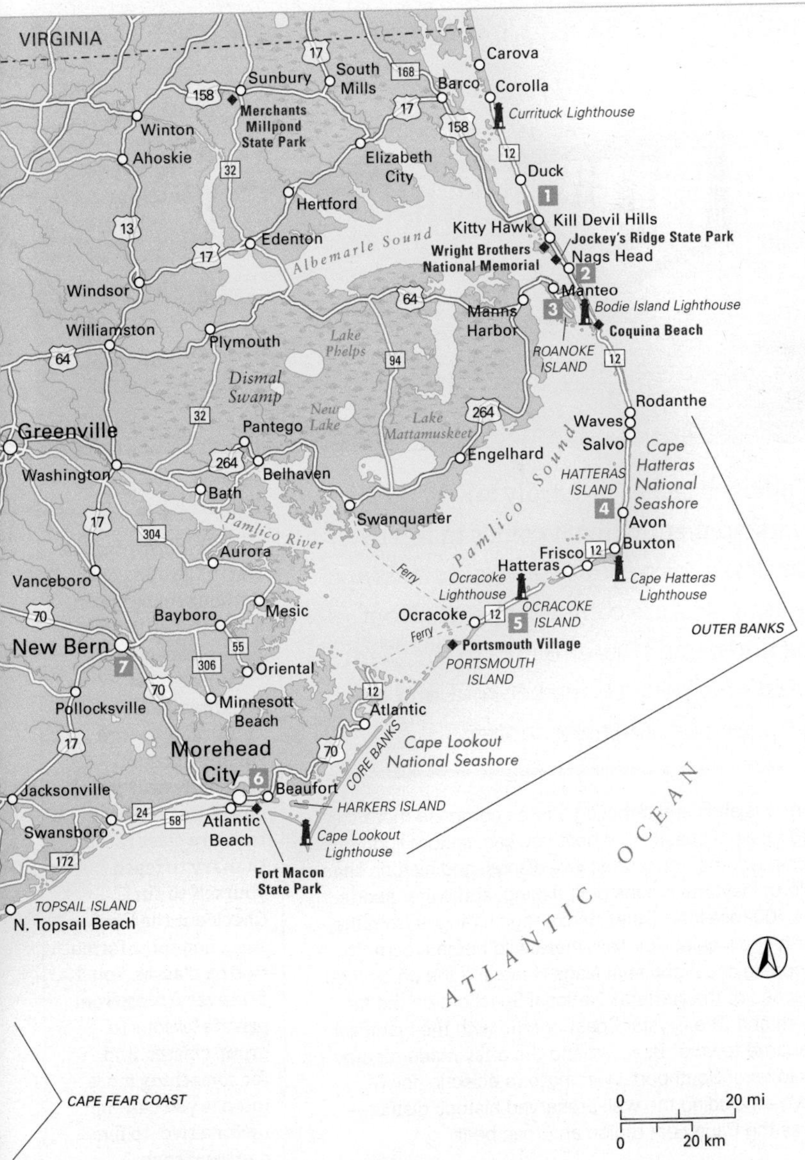
VIRGINIA
Carova
Sunbury
South Mills
Barco
Corolla
Merchants Millpond State Park
Currituck Lighthouse
Winton
Ahoskie
Elizabeth City
Duck
Hertford
1
Kill Devil Hills
Kitty Hawk
Jockey's Ridge State Park
Edenton
Wright Brothers National Memorial
Nags Head
Albemarle Sound
2
Windsor
Manteo
Bodie Island Lighthouse
Manns Harbor
3
Coquina Beach
Williamston
Plymouth
Lake Phelps
ROANOKE ISLAND
Dismal Swamp
Rodanthe
New Lake
Lake Mattamuskeet
Waves
Greenville
Pantego
Salvo
Cape Hatteras National Seashore
Engelhard
Washington
Belhaven
HATTERAS ISLAND
Bath
4
Swanquarter
Avon
Pamlico Sound
Pamlico River
Buxton
Aurora
Frisco
Hatteras
Ferry
Ocracoke Lighthouse
Cape Hatteras Lighthouse
Vanceboro
Mesic
Bayboro
Ocracoke
OCRACOKE ISLAND
5
OUTER BANKS
New Bern
Ferry
Portsmouth Village
7
Oriental
PORTSMOUTH ISLAND
Pollocksville
Minnesott Beach
Atlantic
Morehead City
Cape Lookout National Seashore
CORE BANKS
6
Jacksonville
Beaufort
HARKERS ISLAND
Atlantic Beach
Swansboro
Cape Lookout Lighthouse
Fort Macon State Park
TOPSAIL ISLAND
N. Topsail Beach
ATLANTIC OCEAN
CAPE FEAR COAST
0
20 mi
0
20 km
17
168
158
17
158
12
32
13
17
64
64
94
12
32
264
264
17
304
12
70
55
12
306
70
12
17
70
24
58
172

NORTH CAROLINA BEACHES

Wrightsville Beach is a family favorite.

"Endless beaches" is hardly an overstatement when it comes to North Carolina's coast. White or khaki sands and pristine seas are common themes from the north end's Outer Banks to the Central Coast's unspoiled Cape Lookout and the cottage-lined southern shores.

Barrier islands and rambling shores comprise more than 300 miles of coastline, where you can explore lighthouses, aquariums, museums, woodlands, and historic sites galore. Playtime means golf, fishing, and water sports. The 100-mile-long Outer Banks region ranges from the north end's quiet Corolla, where wild horses roam, to shopping and nightlife in Nags Head and the untouched beaches of the Hatteras National Seashore on the far south end. The Crystal Coast beams with the historical maritime town of Beaufort and the artsy made-for-movies town of Southport. Wilmington's eclectic downtown—including the well-preserved historic district—gives the Cape Fear region an urban beat.

HANG TEN

You can hardly walk a North Carolina beach without encountering a surfer. The Outer Banks (especially Cape Hatteras), Wrightsville Beach, and Ocean Isle are surfing hot spots, especially near piers and jetties. It's best to take a class rather than try to teach yourself to surf. Check out the local surf shop for information on classes. You'll find everything from private lessons to group classes, and for something more intense you can sign up for a two- to five-day "surf camp."

North Carolina's Best Beaches

NAGS HEAD

Couples, families, and friends all find options along **Nags Head,** where 11 miles of beaches include many with lifeguards. Plenty of accommodations—vacation homes, hotels, and cozy inns—line the shore, and getting onto the beach is no problem. There are 41 public access points, many with wheelchair access, so you're always within a short driving distance.

CAPE HATTERAS NATIONAL SEASHORE

Long stretches of unspoiled beaches hidden behind tall dunes, interspersed with small villages, along this 60-mile geographical treasure provide opportunities for shelling, surfing, birding, fishing, camping, lighthouse exploring, or simply getting lost in thought. The park's undeveloped **Coquina Beach** and **Ocracoke Island beaches** are considered by locals to be the Outer Banks' loveliest shorelines.

CAPE LOOKOUT NATIONAL SEASHORE

Exchange real-world stress for the magical wonderlands of this 56-mile stretch extending from the historic Portsmouth Island village to **Shackleford Banks,** where wild horses roam. The 28,400 acres of uninhabited land and marsh include remote, sandy islands linked to the mainland by nothing more than private ferries.

Sunsets on the North Carolina coast are stunning.

The coast has remote beaches where wild horses roam.

WRIGHTSVILLE BEACH

Quiet and moderately upscale, with longtime family homes and striking contemporary cottages jamming the lifeguard-protected shore, **Wrightsville Beach** is a perfect family or couple's retreat. The white-sand beaches are sports lovers' favorites. Surfers, kayakers, paddleboarders, and bodyboarders dig Wrightsville's tasty waves while anglers love its concrete fishing pier. Arrive early, as parking spaces fill up quickly.

KURE AND CAROLINA BEACHES

Aptly named, **Pleasure Island** offers all sorts of fun for families and singles. On the south end kids will love the **Kure Beach** aquarium, while history buffs can discover a Civil War fort. Beaches are wide, with plenty of room for fishing and surfing. Head north to **Carolina Beach** for charter-boat fishing excursions and the nostalgic charm of an old-fashioned, somewhat funky boardwalk.

Three hundred miles of breathtaking barrier islands and mainland beaches make North Carolina's coastline a beach lover's dream. White sands and pristine waters, lighthouses, and a plethora of vacation homes mark the shore. Athletes and anglers, history buffs and gallery hoppers, and singles, couples, and families of every configuration find plenty to do here, but snoozing along the quiet shore is just as appealing.

Distinctive port cities dot broad rivers that lead inland from the sounds. You'll find American Revolution and Civil War battle sites, elegant golf links and kitschy Putt-Putt courses, upscale boutiques and big-box beach shops. Aquariums, fishing charters, and museum outreach programs put you up close and personal with the seashore critters. North Carolina's small towns (mostly of 1,000 to 3,000 people) offer their own special brand of genuine warmth and hospitality.

The coast is divided into three broad sections that include islands, shoreline, and coastal plains: the Outer Banks, or OBX (Corolla south through Ocracoke, including Roanoke Island), the Crystal Coast (Core and Bogue Banks, Beaufort, Southport, Morehead City, and the inland river cities of New Bern and Edenton), and the greater Cape Fear region (Wrightsville Beach south through Wilmington to the Brunswick Isles). The Outer Banks are visible from space: the thin, delicate white tracings are barrier islands that form a buffer between the Atlantic Ocean and the mainland.

Although other states' coasts have wall-to-wall hotels and condominiums, much of North Carolina's coast belongs to the North Carolina Division of Parks and Recreation and the U.S. National Park Service. This arrangement keeps large chunks of the coast accessible to the public for exploration, athletic activities, picnicking, and camping. Still, property values have skyrocketed as summer residents' dream houses continually replace generations-old beach cottages.

Some of the coast either closes or operates on reduced hours during midwinter, which makes the colder season a special time to escape both crowds and peak prices but still enjoy seafood, beaches, and museums. Whether you're seeking peace or adventure, or a combination of both, you can find it on the coast.

The North Carolina coast has been no stranger to the occasional hurricane and tropical storm, especially in recent years.

Visitors to areas like New Bern and Wilmington, where 2018's Hurricane Florence had the most impact, will be impressed by the region's resilience and find that most things are back to business as usual. While spared in more recent years, ongoing projects in the Outer Banks, like bridge construction north of Hatteras Island and beach erosion renourishment in Nags Head, demonstrate the result of wear and tear caused by storms throughout the last decade. Though it's rare that a tropical storm or hurricane should occur during your trip, rest assured that these coastal communities and islands have the proper evacuation and safety plans in place. It's never a bad idea to purchase travel insurance, especially when visiting the coast during hurricane season.

MAJOR REGIONS

The Outer Banks. Long stretches of wild beach are intermingled with small, lively towns on this ribbon of sand. The north end is a tourist mecca of shops, resorts, restaurants, beach cottages, and historic sites. Quieter villages and open, undeveloped beaches mark the south end, where travelers often hear nothing but surf and shorebirds. With just one two-lane road stretching the length of the Outer Banks, locals refer to mile markers instead of street numbers when giving directions.

Cape Hatteras National Seashore. With challenging waves, myriad fish, and the impressive Cape Hatteras lighthouse anchoring the south end, this part of the Outer Banks is a surfer's playground, an angler's dream, and a history buff's treasure.

The Crystal Coast and New Bern. History here ranges from historical colonial sites to the birthplace of Pepsi, while extensive stretches of ocean, sound, and rivers please boaters, anglers, water-sports lovers, and those who just want to relax on a big Southern porch with a glass of sweet tea.

Wilmington and the Cape Fear Coast. Part cosmopolitan, part old-fashioned Southern charm, the Cape Fear region has attracted people from all over the world since the early 1500s, when explorers first arrived. You can still cast a line off an old wooden pier or spend the day roaming art galleries and wine bars.

Planning

When to Go

North Carolina's coast shines in spring (March to May) and fall (September and October), when the weather is most temperate and the water reasonably warm. Traveling during these times means you can avoid long lines and higher prices associated with the peak summer tourist season.

Planning Your Time

The North Carolina coast is a string of beach and inland towns, each with its own character. Pick one and plan day trips from there. Boisterous Nags Head and sophisticated Wilmington provide dining, shopping, and nightlife, but they are only short drives from lovely gardens, quiet beaches, dense woodlands, and historic landmarks. Front-porch-friendly Beaufort is a brief, private ferry ride away from barrier islands where wild horses roam. Southport is a living backdrop for movie filming. Just an hour inland are New Bern's charming downtown and historic Tryon Palace and gardens, and nearby Edenton's outstanding collection of colonial structures. In summer, secondary roads and some major highways are lined by fresh-seafood vendors and colorful produce stands.

Getting Here and Around

AIR TRAVEL

The closest large, commercial airports to the Outer Banks are Norfolk International Airport (ORF) in Virginia, a two-hour drive, and Raleigh-Durham International Airport (RDU), a four-hour drive. Norfolk International is served by American, Delta, Southwest, and United; Raleigh-Durham International has service by nine airlines, including Air Canada, Alaska, Allegiant, American, Delta, Frontier, JetBlue, Southwest, and United. Coastal Carolina Regional Airport in New Bern has connector flights, charter service, and car rentals available. Wilmington International Airport serves the Cape Fear Coast.

Barrier Island Aviation provides charter service between the Dare County Regional Airport and major cities along the East Coast. American and Delta fly into Coastal Carolina Regional Airport in New Bern as well as Wilmington International Airport.

AIR CONTACTS Barrier Island Aviation. ✉ *407 Airport Rd., Manteo* ☎ *252/473–4247* 🌐 *www.barrierislandaviation.com.* **Coastal Carolina Regional Airport.** ✉ *200 Terminal Dr., New Bern* 🌐 *www.flyewn.com.* **Dare County Regional Airport.** ✉ *410 Airport Rd., Manteo* ☎ *252/475–5570* 🌐 *www.darenc.com/departments/airport.* **Norfolk International Airport.** ✉ *2200 Norview Ave., Norfolk* ☎ *757/857–3351* 🌐 *www.norfolkairport.com.* **Raleigh-Durham International Airport.** ✉ *2400 John Brantley Blvd., Morrisville* ☎ *919/840–2123* 🌐 *www.rdu.com.* **Wilmington International Airport.** ✉ *1740 Airport Blvd., Wilmington* ☎ *910/341–4125* 🌐 *www.flyilm.com.*

CAR TRAVEL

Getting around the Outer Banks is a snap because there's only one road—North Carolina Highway 12. Sometimes, though, traffic can make that one road a route of pure frustration, especially on a rainy midsummer day when everyone is looking for something to do besides sunbathing. Low-lying areas of the highway are also prone to flooding.

Highways into the other areas along the coast—U.S. Route 158 into Kitty Hawk and Nags Head; U.S. Route 64 around Nags Head and Manteo; Interstate 40, which can take you from Wilmington all the way to Las Vegas or California if you desire, or Raleigh if you're catching a plane; and U.S. Route 17, which services Wilmington and New Bern—usually run smoothly during all but weekday rush hours and the busiest days of the high summer season.

Driving on the beaches is allowed in designated areas only, and permits are usually required. The most notable off-road vehicle (ORV) driving area is north of Corolla where the North Carolina Highway 12 pavement ends. Continuing on the beach where North Carolina Highway 12 ends, by four-wheel drive vehicle only, brings you to the village of Carova, where there are rental cottages and wild ponies and a few year-round residents. Other popular seasonal ORV areas include Hatteras and Ocracoke islands in the Cape Hatteras National Seashore; advance permits are required. A 10-day permit is $50. Visit 🌐 *www.outerbanks.com/driving-on-the-beach.html* for more information. The 15 mph on-the-beach speed limit is strictly enforced, and pedestrians always have the right-of-way. Driving on sand can be tricky, so be careful to lower the air pressure in your tires. Locals are happy to instruct.

FERRY TRAVEL

The state-run car ferry system operates 21 ferries on seven regular routes over five bodies of water: Currituck and Pamlico Sounds and the Cape Fear, Neuse, and Pamlico Rivers. Emergency routes are also provided when storms damage the main coastal highways. The North Carolina Department of Transportation's ferry information line and website have full details. ■ **TIP→ There's a charge for most ferries, but the Hatteras–Ocracoke ferry is free.**

FERRY CONTACTS Island Ferry Adventures. ✉ *610 Front St., Beaufort* ☎ *252/728–4129* 🌐 *www.islandferryadventures.com.* **North Carolina Department of Transportation Ferry Division.** ☎ *800/293–3779* 🌐 *www.ncdot.gov.*

TAXI TRAVEL

Island Limousine, headquartered in Nags Head, serves the entire area, including Norfolk International Airport, although its main service area is the Outer Banks. Getting to the airport in a van costs about $160 from Nags Head. Uber and Lyft also are options for getting around the Outer Banks and for transportation to and from airports and ferries.

TAXI CONTACTS Island Limousine. ✉ *6933 S. Croatan Hwy., Nags Head* ☎ *252/441–5466* 🌐 *www.islandlimo.com.*

Restaurants

Seafood houses and many restaurants sell each day's local catch: tuna, wahoo, mahimahi, mackerel, sand dabs, scallops, shrimp, or blue crabs. Raw bars serve oysters and clams on the half shell. For years, the coast has been a magnet for highly trained chefs, and emerging talents are constantly raising the bar with creative preparations and diversified menu options. Seafood dishes—broiled, fried, grilled, or steamed—are listed alongside globally inspired entrées fusing Asian, European, and Latin flavors with traditional Southern ingredients, such as black-eyed peas. On the negative side, restaurants in beach areas often close in winter and may have to hire new chefs and staff for the high season, leading to quality that can vary from year to year.

Expect up to hour-long waits, sometimes longer, at many restaurants during summer and festival periods. Many places don't accept reservations. Restaurant hours are frequently reduced in winter, and some restaurants in remote beach communities close for several months. Casual dress is acceptable in most restaurants. *Restaurant reviews have been shortened. For full information, visit Fodors.com.*

Hotels

Most visitors to the Outer Banks and other beach areas rent vacation homes instead of motels or hotels. Thousands of rental properties are available. Small beach cottages can be had, but, increasingly, so-called sand castles—large multistory homes with every imaginable amenity (private pools, movie theaters, elevators, etc.)—suit families and large groups. These can cost up to $15,000 a week or more in summer, but prices off-season often are slashed by 75% or more. Motels and hotels clustered along the coast are usually the more affordable way to go for couples or small families.

Throughout the North Carolina coast, you have a choice of cottages, condos, and waterfront resorts. Chain hotels have a presence here, but you can also stay at a surprising number of small, family-run lodgings. You might also consider selecting from a variety of bed-and-breakfasts, usually owned and managed by resident hosts. Always ask about special packages (price breaks on multiple-night stays) and off-season rates. Most hotels, inns, and B&Bs on the coast offer free parking on their property. A few have street parking only, but you can expect not to pay parking fees even at the priciest hotels. *Hotel reviews have been shortened. For full information, visit Fodors.com.*

What It Costs

	$	$$	$$$	$$$$
RESTAURANTS				
	under $15	$15–$19	$20–$24	over $24
HOTELS				
	under $150	$150–$200	$201–$250	over $250

Restaurant prices are the average cost of a main course at dinner or, if dinner is not served, at lunch. Hotel prices are the lowest cost of a standard double room in high season.

Visitor Information

CONTACTS National Park Service–Cape Hatteras National Seashore. ✉ *1401 National Park Dr., Manteo* ☎ *252/473–2111 park information for Hatteras National Seashore* 🌐 *www.nps.gov/caha.*

Northern Beaches

Corolla: 91 miles south of Norfolk, VA; 230 miles east of Raleigh. Duck: 16 miles south of Corolla.

The small northern beach settlements of Corolla and Duck are largely seasonal, residential enclaves full of summer rental homes and condominiums. The tony village of Duck, named for its waterfowl-hunting history, has expensive homes and is dotted with upscale restaurants and shops. A waterfront boardwalk connects the town, which lacks a true center. Drive slowly in charming Corolla, where freely wandering, federally protected wild horses always have the right-of-way. North of Corolla, the road disappears, giving way to miles of isolated, 4x4-accessible beach all the way to the Virginia border.

VISITOR INFORMATION

CONTACTS Aycock Brown Welcome Center. ✉ *5230 N. Croatan Hwy., MM 1, Kitty Hawk* ☎ *252/261–4644* 🌐 *www.outerbanks.com/aycock-brown-welcome-center.html.*

Sights

★ Currituck Beach Lighthouse

LIGHTHOUSE | FAMILY | The 1875 lighthouse was built from nearly 1 million bricks, which remain unpainted on the exterior. Except in high winds or thunderstorms, or during winter when the lighthouse is closed, you can climb 220 steps to the top of the northernmost lighthouse on the Outer Banks, taking in the view toward Virginia and south to Nags Head. ✉ *1101 Corolla Village Rd., Corolla* ✣ *Off NC 12* ☎ *252/453–4939* 🌐 *obcinc.org* 🎫 *Lighthouse $10, grounds free* 🕑 *Closed Dec.–early Mar.*

★ Historic Corolla Village

TOWN | FAMILY | What was once an aging, isolated beach town is now a vibrant year-round community where the tiny chapel schoolhouse again educates children and restored buildings house art galleries, a coffee shop, a bookstore, a barbecue restaurant, and a nonprofit dedicated to the wild horses that wander the beach and surrounding maritime forest. ⚠ **The road ends in Corolla—to access the beach north of here, you need a 4x4 vehicle.** ✉ *Corolla* ☎ *252/453–9612* 🌐 *visitcurrituck.com.*

Whalehead Club

HOUSE | This 21,000-square-foot monument to gracious living was built in the 1920s as the private residence of a northern couple attracted by the area's reputation for waterfowl hunting (the home was given its current name by the second owner). After having been abandoned, sold, and vandalized, it was renovated and opened for tours in 2002. Inside the ornamental art nouveau structure, a floral motif is evident in Tiffany lamps with flower detailing and mahogany woodwork carved with water lilies. The home is on 39 waterfront acres inside Currituck Heritage Park and is now listed on the National Register of Historic Places. ■ **TIP→ Even if you don't tour the mansion, it's worth a sunset visit to walk the waterfront yard and grounds.** ✉ *Currituck Heritage Park, 1100 Club Rd., Corolla* ⊕ *Off NC 12* ☎ *252/453–9040* 🌐 *visitcurrituck.com* 🎫 *$7, ghost tour $15* ⏲ *Closed weekends.*

Restaurants

AQUA Restaurant
$$$$ | **MODERN AMERICAN** | This beautifully located restaurant offers creative takes on locally sourced seafood and other dishes; there's seating on a waterside patio for great sunset views, at the bar (live music some nights), or in the main dining area. You can also get a massage at AQUA Spa upstairs or relax with a craft cocktail at the restaurant's popular afternoon happy hour. **Known for:** waterfront dining on Currituck Sound; fresh, locally caught seafood; sunset bar scene with live music. $ *Average main: $28* ✉ *1174 Duck Rd., Duck* ☎ *252/261–9700* 🌐 *aquarestaurantobx.com* ⏲ *Closed Mon. and Tues.*

★ The Blue Point
$$$$ | **SEAFOOD** | The Outer Banks' first farm-to-table restaurant, this upscale foodie haven marries Southern roots with contemporary flair and Currituck Sound views. During its three decades of existence, the Blue Point has maintained a commitment to a sustainable menu sourced as locally as possible, with seafood, beef, and other dishes prepared to highlight their texture and flavor. **Known for:** locally sourced seafood, done right; sunset views over Currituck Sound; back bar with outdoor seating in Adirondack chairs. $ *Average main: $32* ✉ *1240 Duck Rd., Duck* ☎ *252/261–8090* 🌐 *www.thebluepoint.com* ⏲ *Closed Mon.*

★ NC Coast Grill & Bar
$$$$ | **SEAFOOD** | The small plates and seafood that emerge from the open kitchen at this bold and bright waterfront eatery are a lot more creative than the name, although it is fitting—sunsets from the dining room or the outdoor tables along the deck are truly stunning. If there's a long wait or you'd like more of a great experience, the same chef owns Red Sky Cafe across the street. **Known for:** shareable plates like Korean fried cauliflower; local seafood fusing European and Asian flavors; quality local draft beer list. $ *Average main: $30* ✉ *1184 Duck Rd., Duck* ☎ *252/261–8666* 🌐 *nccoastobx.com.*

Urban Kitchen
$$$$ | **MODERN AMERICAN** | Don't be fooled by the strip-mall location—this tiny dining room is a haven for farm-fresh, creatively constructed dishes served in generous portions. The menu changes frequently, but you can always expect interesting versions of seafood, beef, pork, and other standards. **Known for:** seasonal menu that shows off what's fresh; whitewashed coastal chic decor; innovative dishes like smoked rockfish with trout roe. $ *Average main: $27* ✉ *603-B Currituck Clubhouse Dr., Corolla* ☎ *252/453–4453* 🌐 *www.urbankitchenobx.com.*

Coffee and Quick Bites

Duck Donuts
$ | **BAKERY** | **FAMILY** | Each doughnut at this Duck original starts with a coating—traditional favorites like vanilla and chocolate, or more daring varieties like lemon, peanut butter, and maple; then, you pile on toppings like shredded coconut, chopped peanuts, or even bacon. Duck Donuts has become so popular it has expanded to nearly 100 locations in several states, but the original is right here in Duck. **Known for:** maple-icing doughnut with chopped bacon and caramel; specialty espresso drinks; doughnut sundaes. $ *Average main: $3* ✉ *1190 Duck Rd., Duck* ☎ *252/480–3304* 🌐 *www.duckdonuts.com.*

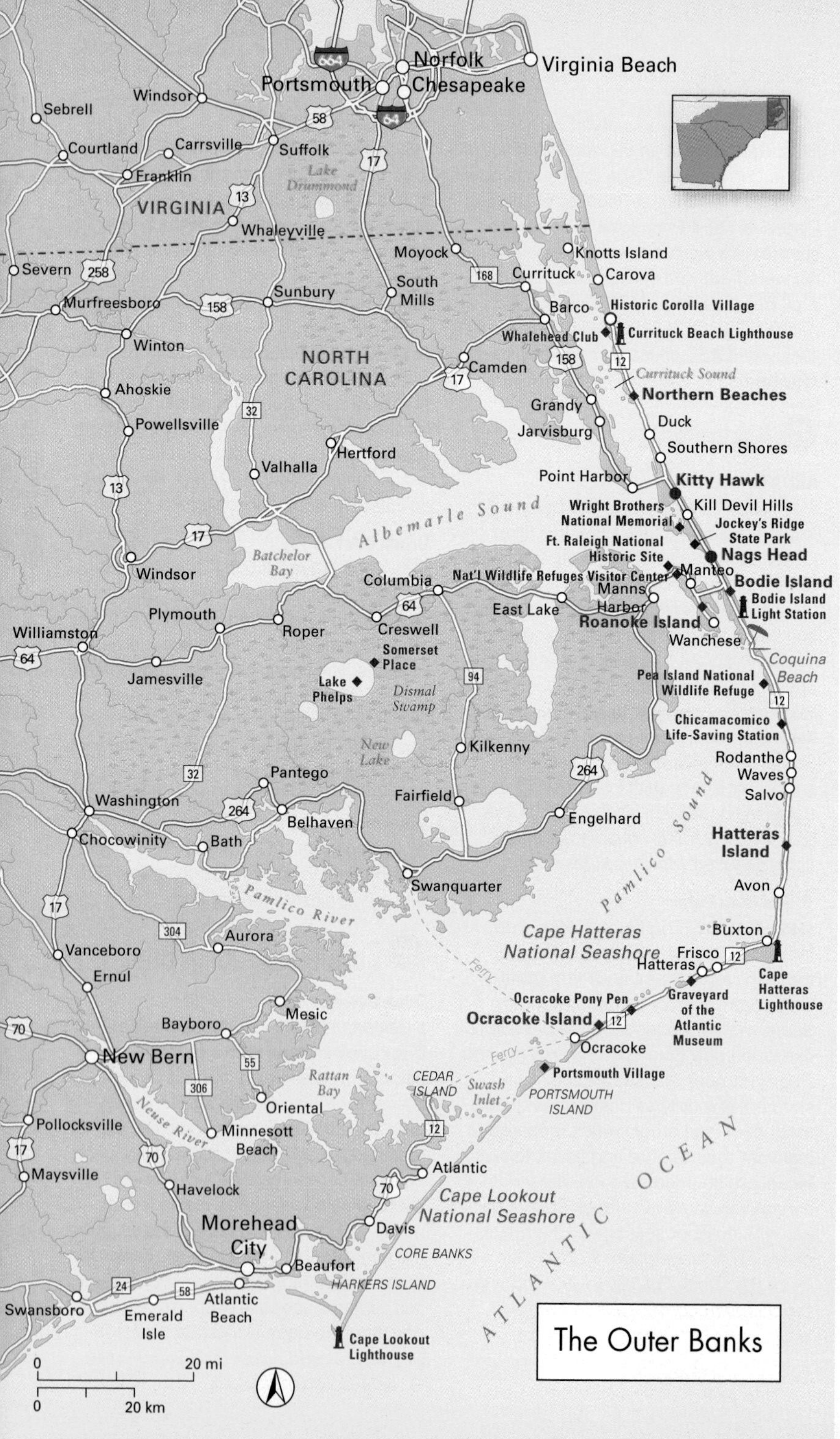

The Outer Banks
Norfolk
Virginia Beach
Portsmouth
Chesapeake
Windsor
Sebrell
Suffolk
Courtland
Carrsville
Franklin
Lake Drummond
VIRGINIA
Whaleyville
Moyock
Knotts Island
Severn
Currituck
Carova
South Mills
Sunbury
Murfreesboro
Barco
Historic Corolla Village
Whalehead Club
Currituck Beach Lighthouse
Winton
NORTH CAROLINA
Camden
Currituck Sound
Ahoskie
Northern Beaches
Grandy
Duck
Powellsville
Jarvisburg
Hertford
Southern Shores
Valhalla
Point Harbor
Kitty Hawk
Wright Brothers National Memorial
Kill Devil Hills
Albemarle Sound
Jockey's Ridge State Park
Ft. Raleigh National Historic Site
Nags Head
Batchelor Bay
Windsor
Manteo
Columbia
Nat'l Wildlife Refuges Visitor Center
Bodie Island
Manns Harbor
Bodie Island Light Station
East Lake
Plymouth
Roanoke Island
Williamston
Roper
Creswell
Wanchese
Somerset Place
Coquina Beach
Jamesville
Lake Phelps
Dismal Swamp
Pea Island National Wildlife Refuge
Chicamacomico Life-Saving Station
New Lake
Kilkenny
Rodanthe
Waves
Pantego
Salvo
Washington
Fairfield
Belhaven
Engelhard
Pamlico Sound
Chocowinity
Bath
Hatteras Island
Swanquarter
Avon
Pamlico River
Cape Hatteras National Seashore
Buxton
Aurora
Frisco
Vanceboro
Hatteras
Ernul
Ferry
Cape Hatteras Lighthouse
Ocracoke Pony Pen
Graveyard of the Atlantic Museum
Mesic
Ocracoke Island
Bayboro
Ocracoke
New Bern
Ferry
Portsmouth Village
Rattan Bay
CEDAR ISLAND
Swash Inlet
PORTSMOUTH ISLAND
Oriental
Pollocksville
Neuse River
Minnesott Beach
Atlantic
ATLANTIC OCEAN
Maysville
Havelock
Cape Lookout National Seashore
Morehead City
Davis
CORE BANKS
Beaufort
HARKERS ISLAND
Swansboro
Emerald Isle
Atlantic Beach
Cape Lookout Lighthouse
0
20 mi
0
20 km

Island Smoothie

$ | **VEGETARIAN** | Come early to beat the line at this strip-mall joint mixing acai bowls, avocado toast, nitro cold brew, and a full menu of sandwiches and wraps. **Known for:** elaborate fruit-filled acai bowls like the Blackbeard Treasure; power smoothies; turkey-avocado flatbread sandwich. *Average main: $10 ✉ 603 C Currituck Clubhouse Dr., Corolla ☎ 252/453–4545 🌐 islandsmoothiecafe.com ⏲ Closed Mon. and Tues.*

Hotels

Hampton Inn and Suites Outer Banks

$$$$ | **HOTEL** | **FAMILY** | If you need a family-friendly resort hotel with a range of amenities or simply want a no-surprises oceanfront property with plenty of extras, this hotel fits the bill. **Pros:** fewer crowds on the beach than at comparable hotels further south; free self-parking; fitness and business centers. **Cons:** pets not allowed; no restaurant for dinner; beachfront prices for standard hotel rooms. *Rooms from: $329 ✉ 333 Audubon Dr., Corolla ☎ 252/453–6565 🌐 hilton.com 123 rooms 🍽 Free breakfast.*

★ **Sanderling Resort**

$$$$ | **RESORT** | **FAMILY** | This luxury resort comprising three multistory buildings and five large rental homes spreads over 16 quiet acres of ocean-to-sound property that include two outdoor pools (one that's adults only), hot tubs, an indoor pool, firepits, and a boccie court. **Pros:** on-site spa with views across the sound; private balconies with hammock chairs; oversized bathrooms. **Cons:** no elevator in primary building; pricey rooms leave something to be desired; high-traffic areas like hallway carpets show their age. *Rooms from: $395 ✉ 1461 Duck Rd., Duck ☎ 855/412–7866 toll-free reservations 🌐 www.sanderling-resort.com 128 rooms 🍽 No meals.*

Activities

GOLF

The Currituck Club

GOLF | Rolling fairways with bent-grass greens and a sweeping view of Currituck Sound characterize this 18-hole semi-private championship course designed by Rees Jones. Anchoring the Currituck Club resort community, the course also serves as an Audubon Society Cooperative Sanctuary, which makes it an environmental host for a variety of wildlife. During summer, the club's PGA professionals schedule instructional clinics for adults and juniors of all skill levels. Additionally, Currituck's popular practice facility comprises an 8,000-square-foot putting green and bunker, plus a driving range. Family members of golfers who rent Currituck accommodations have access to beaches, lighted tennis courts, a fitness center, five swimming pools, biking and walking trails, and a valet trolley service. *✉ 619 Currituck Clubhouse Dr., Currituck ☎ 252/453–9400 🌐 clubcorp.com $69–$165 ($45–$85 for 9 holes), 18 holes, 6885 yds, par 72.*

Kitty Hawk and Nags Head

Kitty Hawk: 9 miles south of Duck. Nags Head: 9 miles south of Kitty Hawk.

Kitty Hawk and contiguous Kill Devil Hills, with a combined population of about 10,000 residents, have fewer rental accommodations but more chain retail. The towns' respective roles in the drama of the first powered flight occasionally create some confusion. When arriving at the Outer Banks, the Wright brothers first stayed in the then-remote fishing village of Kitty Hawk, but their flight took place some 4 miles south on Kill Devil Hills, a gargantuan sand dune where the Wright Brothers National Memorial now stands.

It's widely accepted that Nags Head got its name because pirates once tied lanterns around the necks of their horses to lure merchant ships onto the shoals, where they would be wrecked and pilfered for profit. Dubious citizenry aside, Nags Head was established in the 1830s and has become a classic North Carolina tourist haven.

The town—one of the largest on the Outer Banks even though it has fewer than 3,000 residents—lies between the Atlantic Ocean and Pamlico Sound, along and between U.S. Route 158 ("the bypass") and North Carolina Highway 12 ("the beach road," or Virginia Dare Trail). Both roads are congested in the high season, and the entire area is commercialized, but dip off Route 158 and on almost any street you'll find an endearing mix of weathered beach cottages sharing the roadway with shiny new mansions. Many lodgings, whether they're shingled older houses or sprawling estates with plenty of bells and whistles, are available through the area's plentiful vacation rentals. Numerous restaurants, motels, hotels, shops, and entertainment opportunities keep the town hopping day and night.

Nags Head has 11 miles of beach with 41 public access points from North Carolina Highway 12, some with paved parking, many with wheelchair access, and some with restrooms and showers. **■TIP➔ It's easy to overlook the flagpoles stationed along many area beaches, but if there's a red flag flying from one of them, it means the water is too rough even for wading. These are not suggestions—ignoring them is dangerous and carries hefty fines.**

GETTING HERE AND AROUND

From the west, arrive by car on U.S. Route 64, or arrive from the north, on U.S. Routes 17 and 158. Although many people cycle and walk on designated paths, most exploring requires a car.

VISITOR INFORMATION

CONTACTS Aycock Brown Welcome Center. ✉ *5230 N. Croatan Hwy., MM 1, Kitty Hawk* ☎ *252/261–4644* 🌐 *www.outerbanks.com/aycock-brown-welcome-center.html.* **Whalebone Welcome Center.** ✉ *2 NC Hwy. 12, MM 17* ☎ *877/629–4386* 🌐 *www.outerbanks.com/whalebone-junction.html.*

Sights

★ Jockey's Ridge State Park

NATIONAL/STATE PARK | FAMILY | The 427 acres of this park encompass the tallest sand dune system on the East Coast (about 80 to 100 feet). Walk along the 384-foot boardwalk from the visitor center to the edge of the dune. The climb to the top is a challenge; nevertheless, it's a popular spot for hang gliding (Kitty Hawk Kites has an outpost here for beginner lessons), kite flying, and sand boarding. You can also explore an estuary, a museum, and a self-guided trail through the park, which also has eight picnic shelters. In summer, join the free Sunset on the Ridge program: watch the sun disappear while you sit on the dunes and learn about their local legends and history. Covered footwear is a wise choice here, as the loose sand gets quite hot (25–30 degrees hotter than air temperature) in the summer months. ✉ *300 W. Carolista Dr., MM 12* ⊕ *Off U.S. 158 Bypass (S. Croatan Hwy.)* ☎ *252/441–7132* 🌐 *ncparks.gov* 🎫 *Free.*

★ Wright Brothers National Memorial

HISTORIC SITE | FAMILY | One of the most popular photo sites on the Outer Banks, 5 miles south of Kitty Hawk, is the 60-foot granite airplane's tail that stands as a tribute to Wilbur and Orville Wright, two bicycle mechanics from Ohio who took to the air here on December 17, 1903. A sculptured replica of their *Wright Flyer* and stone markers showing the exact points and distances soared help you experience the historic day humans first made powered flight—and the

At Jockey's Ridge State Park, you can hike to the top of the tallest natural sand dune in the eastern United States.

multiyear, trial-and-error process the perseverant brothers endured leading up to it. Informative talks by National Park Service rangers also help bring the event to life. The museum and visitor center, completely renovated in 2018, uses historical artifacts, reproductions, and displays to dive into the lives, legends, and flight process of the brothers. ✉ *1000 N. Croatan Hwy., Kill Devil Hills* ✣ *Off U.S. 158 at MM 7.5* ☎ *252/473–2111* 🌐 *www.nps.gov/wrbr* 🎫 *$10 (free for National Park pass holders).*

Beaches

Nags Head Beaches

BEACH—SIGHT | FAMILY | Forty-three public Atlantic beach access points and five sound-side access points make Nags Head the perfect place to hit the shore, no matter what your needs may be. Access points are marked with white signs clearly stating "Public beach access," and 15 of them are suitable for wheelchairs; beach wheelchairs are available at the Bonnett and Hargrove accesses, and the 8th Street access has a stability mat that makes getting a stroller or wheelchair onto the beach easy. Many other areas have lifeguards and bathhouses. The town website lists all the accesses and provides a map. No matter where you land, expect clean sand and water. Vehicles are allowed on Nags Head beaches October through April with a town-issued permit. Leashed pets (maximum 10-foot leash) are allowed on Nags Head beaches year-round. **Amenities:** food and drink; lifeguards (late May–early September); parking (fee and no fee); showers; toilets. **Best for:** sunrise; sunset; swimming. ✉ *S. Croatan Hwy.* ☎ *252/441–5508 town office* 🌐 *www.nagsheadnc.gov* 🎫 *Free.*

Restaurants

Basnight's Lone Cedar Café

$$$$ | SEAFOOD | FAMILY | Despite a modern rebuild after a fire, this classic seafood house directly on the water (there's an osprey nest mere feet from the dining-room window) feels old-school,

First in Flight

December 17, 1903, was a cold and windy day on the Outer Banks, but Wilbur and Orville Wright took little notice. The slightly built brothers from Ohio were undertaking an excellent adventure. With Orville at the controls, Wilbur running alongside, and the men of the nearby Lifesaving Service stations acting as ground crew, the fragile *Wright Flyer* lifted off from the Kill Devil Hills dune near Kitty Hawk and flew 120 feet in 12 seconds.

Outer Banker John Daniels photographed the instant the world forever changed: a heavier-than-air machine was used to achieve controlled, sustained flight with a pilot aboard. To prove they were not accidental aviators, the Wrights took two flights each that day, and in Wilbur's second attempt, he flew 852 feet in 59 seconds.

Others were attempting—and dying in the attempt of—powered flight as the Wright brothers opened their Dayton bicycle-repair shop in 1892. Using information on aerodynamics from the Smithsonian Institution and observation of birds in flight, they began experimenting with a box kite roughly shaped like a biplane and a makeshift wind tunnel. Strong, steady winds drew them to the then-remote Outer Banks, where they could test their next phase, manned glider flights, in privacy. In time, by adding power to the three-axis control they had developed, they eventually solved the problems of mechanical flight, lift, and propulsion that had vexed scientists for hundreds of years.

Their success is honored at the Wright Brothers National Memorial in Kill Devil Hills and by the North Carolina boast emblazoned on millions of license plates: "First in Flight."

thanks to nautical decor and the laid-back atmosphere. North Carolina produce and seafood star here, including OBX-style clear clam chowder and whole fried flounder. **Known for:** local seafood and produce; extra-friendly service; massive glass-walled wine rack. 💲 *Average main: $28* ✉ *Nags Head–Manteo Causeway, 7623 S. Virginia Dare Trail* ☎ *252/441–5405* 🌐 *www.lonecedarcafe.com* 🕑 *Closed Mon.*

The Black Pelican

$$$ | SEAFOOD | The views across the Atlantic are just part of the appeal at this casual, multiroom seafood spot built into a U.S. Lifesaving Station dating to 1874. **Known for:** smaller lunch portions of dinner entrées, priced right; thin-sliced rare tuna nagano; nautical decor and horizon views. 💲 *Average main: $24* ✉ *3848 N. Virginia Dare Trail, Kitty Hawk* ☎ *252/261–3171* 🌐 *blackpelican.com.*

★ Blue Moon Beach Grill

$$$ | SEAFOOD | "Once in a blue moon, you have to taste life on a sandbar," says the sign over the bar at this small, quirky, and locally popular restaurant set in a small strip center. The generously portioned fresh seafood and Southern comfort food, lively vibe, friendly bartenders, and an open kitchen make first-timers feel at home and keep regulars returning. **Known for:** chef-driven, moderately priced seafood; fun, local bar scene; authentic, not tourist-driven vibe. 💲 *Average main: $20* ✉ *Surfside Plaza, 4104 S. Virginia Dare Trail, MM 13, Shop 16* ☎ *252/261–2583* 🌐 *www.bluemoonbeachgrill.com.*

Outer Banks Brewing Station

$$$ | **AMERICAN** | **FAMILY** | Craft beer rules at this wind turbine–powered brewery and British Isles–style pub. Upscale pub fare complements the beer—opt for seared local tuna atop a garden salad or noodle bowl, or go for a bratwurst sausage plate. **Known for:** the bison, elk, pork, and Wagyu beef combo Beast Burger; full bands inside and singer-songwriters outside; big backyard with picnic tables. *Average main: $20* *600 S. Croatan Hwy. (U.S. 158, MM 8.5), Kill Devil Hills* *252/449–2739* *www.obbrewing.com* *Closed Tues.*

Owens' Restaurant

$$$$ | **SEAFOOD** | **FAMILY** | Family owned since 1946, this restaurant, housed in a replica of an early-19th-century Outer Banks Lifesaving Station, feels like dining in a nautical museum: classic clapboard construction, pine paneling, and walls of maritime artifacts. The traditional crab cakes are popular, and the 14-layer chocolate cake is a long-standing favorite. **Known for:** fresh-off-the-boat local seafood; filet mignon topped with lump crabmeat and asparagus with béarnaise sauce; history as a Nags Head institution. *Average main: $30* *7114 S. Virginia Dare Trail, MM 16.5* *252/441–7309* *www.owensrestaurant.com* *Closed Mon. and Tues.*

Sam and Omie's

$$$ | **SEAFOOD** | **FAMILY** | Named after two fishermen, father and son, this no-nonsense shack opened in 1937 and is one of the Outer Banks' oldest restaurants. Fishing photos hang between mounted catches on the walls, and classic country music twangs in the background. **Known for:** big breakfasts; local-style steamed and fried seafood; oysters lauded as the best on the beach. *Average main: $22* *7228 S. Virginia Dare Trail, MM 16.5* *Across from Jennette's Pier* *252/441–7366* *www.samandomies.net* *Closed Wed.*

Coffee and Quick Bites

★ Freshfit Cafe

$ | **VEGETARIAN** | When you need a break from seafood platters, head here for smoothies, local kombucha, and tasty wraps and BLTs. **Known for:** picnic-table seating directly on the water; fun bar with beer and wine; vegan breakfast and lunch options. *Average main: $11* *7531 S. Virginia Dare Trail* *252/715–6444* *obxfreshfitcafe.com* *Closed Thurs.*

★ John's Drive In

$ | **FAST FOOD** | **FAMILY** | When a large milk shake is the only thing that will do on a hot summer day, this is the place to head for—locals say they are the best on the Outer Banks, or even on the planet. And when you just can't take one more night out at a fancy restaurant, John's will come to the rescue with the best hand-held food on the Outer Banks: burgers, subs, sandwiches (including grouper), all-beef hot dogs, and sides. **Known for:** the Dolphin Boat mahi sandwich; laid-back beachfront drive-in vibes; 24-ounce milk shakes. *Average main: $12* *3716 N. Virginia Dare Trail* *252/261–6227* *www.johnsdrivein.com* *Closed Dec.–Feb.*

Hotels

★ First Colony Inn

$$$ | **B&B/INN** | Relax in a rocking chair on the verandas that encircle this classic, three-story, cedar-shingle inn (it's on the National Register of Historic Places) and admire the ocean views. **Pros:** lovely grounds and pool; free bicycles and beach chairs; microwaves and refrigerators in rooms. **Cons:** room access is from outside; hotel across the street blocks some of the view; it's an old building, so noise carries. *Rooms from: $229* *6715 S. Croatan Hwy., MM 16* *252/441–2343, 855/207–2262* *www.firstcolonyinn.com* *26 rooms* *Free breakfast.*

Hilton Garden Inn

$$$$ | **HOTEL** | **FAMILY** | This beachside resort is one of the largest of the chain properties on the Outer Banks; the U-shaped hotel has a patio and large pool on the ocean side, as well as easy access to the beach (a seasonal nesting ground for sea turtles) and the Kitty Hawk Pier for fishing (closed in winter) via a short walkway over the dunes. **Pros:** full-service beachfront resort with all amenities; spacious rooms; every room has a balcony. **Cons:** beach is fairly narrow in this area; breakfast is an additional charge if you're not a Hilton Gold or Diamond member; fills up for special concerts and events. *Rooms from: $325 ✉ 5353 N. Virginia Dare Trail, Kitty Hawk ☎ 252/261–1290 🌐 hilton.com 180 rooms No meals.*

Shutters on the Banks

$$$ | **HOTEL** | This oceanfront, family-owned hotel is a bargain hunter's dream (at least by Outer Banks standards), with spacious, spartan rooms equipped with microwaves, refrigerators, and full-size coffeepots. **Pros:** beachfront and near attractions; less expensive than some of the chain motels; some rooms have full kitchens. **Cons:** not all rooms face the ocean; outside entrances to rooms; pools are by parking lot and not beachfront. *Rooms from: $229 ✉ 405 S. Virginia Dare Trail, Kill Devil Hills ☎ 252/441–5581, 800/848–3728 🌐 www.shuttersonthebanks.com 94 rooms Free breakfast.*

Surf Side Hotel

$$$ | **HOTEL** | **FAMILY** | This midsize resort near Jennette's Pier is Nags Head's best independent beachfront hotel. **Pros:** attractive coastal in-room decor; great views of the beach and ocean; cooked-to-order breakfast. **Cons:** no elevator in the two-story building; some bathrooms are small; rooms closer to the road on the side of the building have less of an ocean view. *Rooms from: $249 ✉ 6701 S. Virginia Dare Trail ☎ 252/441–2105, 800/552–7873 🌐 www.surfsideobx.com 76 rooms Free breakfast.*

Shopping

Gallery Row

ART GALLERIES | A two-block side street off the beachfront S. Virginia Dare Trail road, now known officially as Gallery Row, is home to several local artist studios and retail displays, including the Glenn Eure Ghost Fleet Gallery and the Seagreen Gallery, where works are created from driftwood, buoys, and other reclaimed maritime items. There's plenty of parking on this quiet residential street, meaning you can easily walk from gallery to gallery. *✉ Nags Head ✣ North of Bonnett St., between S. Virginia Dare Trail and the Rte. 158 Bypass 🌐 obxgalleryrow.com.*

Activities

FISHING

★ Jennette's Pier

MARINA | **FAMILY** | Built in 1939, Jennette's Pier was North Carolina's oldest wooden ocean-fishing pier until 2003 when Hurricane Isabel knocked it down. In 2009, the state of North Carolina came to the rescue, breaking ground for not only a new, 1,000-foot-long concrete pier but also a public beach access point with 262 free parking spaces. Operated by North Carolina Aquariums, this is a great spot for fishing—depending on the time of year, you can catch black and red drum, flounder, king mackerel, mahimahi, gray trout, and others—and the website gives a daily fishing report along with details of notable catches. Non-anglers can walk on the pier, check out the aquarium fish tanks in the two-story, 16,000-square-foot pier house, or just laze on the wide, clean beach. *✉ 7223 S. Virginia Dare Trail ✣ Just north of the U.S. 64/NC 12 intersection 🌐 www.ncaquariums.com/jennettes-pier Walk-on $2, fishing $14.*

Golf courses along the Outer Banks often have beautiful water views.

GOLF

Nags Head Golf Links

GOLF | Opened in 1986, this Scottish-links-style course borders Roanoke Sound, which is visible from five holes. Sea grass and rolling dunes separate most tees and greens, and brambles growing in the rough make accurate shots a priority. Make sure you bring plenty of spare golf balls. Together with coastal winds and a rugged shoreline, this makes for one of the area's most challenging courses, best suited to long hitters. This is a membership golf club, but the public can play the course. ✉ *5615 S. Seachase Dr.* ✣ *Off NC 12, MM 15* ☎ *252/441–8073* 🌐 *www.clubcorp.com/Clubs/Nags-Head-Golf-Links* *$63–$133, 18 holes, 6126 yds, par 71.*

Sea Scape Golf Links

GOLF | Winds from the nearby ocean and sound make this short links course an unexpected challenge, while sand dunes and a maritime forest provide a serene setting. The course, which opened in 1965, was designed by Art Wall, a Masters champion. It's kept in good condition and features some tricky par 3s and dogleg par 4s. It offers a satisfying round to all levels of ability. ✉ *300 W. Eckner St., Kitty Hawk* ☎ *252/261–2158* 🌐 *www.seascapegolf.com* *$45–$115 ($28–$50 for 9 holes), 18 holes, 6231 yds, par 70.*

HANG GLIDING

Kitty Hawk Kites

HANG GLIDING/PARAGLIDING/PARASAILING | If you've ever wanted to hang glide, this is one of the top outfitters in the country, with 12 locations along the North Carolina coast. Kids as young as four and people with most types of physical challenges can be accommodated for beginner dune lessons. Jockey's Ridge is a favorite spot to learn, and instruction packages start at $109. A lesson and 2000-foot tandem flight starts at $264. Kitty Hawk Kites also sells wind toys and gives kayaking, kiteboarding, parasailing, surfing, and paddleboarding classes and leads guided walking, Segway, and horseback riding tours. You can pick up sports gear and sportswear, plus souvenirs. ■ **TIP→ History buffs can**

try flying a reproduction of the Wright Brothers' 1902 glider. ✉ *3933 S. Croatan Hwy.* ☎ *877/359–8447 reservations, 252/441–2426 Nags Head Hang-Gliding School* 🌐 *www.kittyhawk.com.*

SURFING

Outer Banks Boarding Company

WATER SPORTS | Rent or buy surfboards, skateboards, skimboards, bodyboards, and stand-up paddleboards—or trendy bathing suits and beach gear—at this shop that also offers private or group lessons. ✉ *103 E. Morning View Pl. (U.S. 158, MM 11)* ☎ *252/441–1939* 🌐 *www.obbconline.com.*

Roanoke Island

10 miles southwest of Nags Head.

On a hot July day in 1587, 117 men, women, and children left their boat and set foot on Roanoke Island to form the first permanent English settlement in the New World. Three years later, when a fleet with supplies from England landed, the settlers had disappeared without a trace, leaving a mystery that continues to baffle historians. Much of the 12-mile-long island, which lies between the Outer Banks and the mainland, remains wild. Of the island's two towns, Wanchese is the fishing village and Manteo is tourist oriented, with an aquarium and sights related to the island's history. Even with limited time, it's worth an hour to stroll around downtown Manteo, where a waterfront boardwalk frames the town and includes a dock out to the charming, rebuilt Roanoke Marshes Lighthouse.

GETTING HERE AND AROUND

From the west, drive to the island on U.S. Route 64; from the Outer Banks, follow U.S. Route 158 to U.S. Route 64. Although Manteo's main drag and historic waterfront have sidewalks, a car is useful for visiting the town's various sites. Charter flights are available at Dare County Regional Airport.

VISITOR INFORMATION

CONTACTS Outer Banks Welcome Center on Roanoke Island. ✉ *1 Visitors Center Circle, Manteo* ☎ *252/473–2138* 🌐 *www.outerbanks.org.*

Sights

Elizabethan Gardens

GARDEN | FAMILY | These lush gardens are a 10-acre re-creation of 16th-century English gardens, established as an elaborate memorial to the first English colonists. Walk through the brick and wrought-iron entrance to see antique statuary, wildflowers, rose gardens, a 400-year-old giant oak tree, and a sunken garden—something will be in bloom almost any time you visit. The gatehouse, designed in the style of a 16th-century orangery, serves as a reception center and gift and plant shop. There's also a butterfly garden and a kids' pirate-themed play area. Dogs (one per person) are permitted for an additional $3. ✉ *1411 National Park Dr.* ☎ *252/473–3234* 🌐 *www.elizabethangardens.org* 🎫 *$10* ⊗ *Closed Feb.*

★ Fort Raleigh National Historic Site

HISTORIC SITE | FAMILY | Fort Raleigh is a restoration of the original 1584–90 earthworks that mark the beginning of English-colonial history in America. The site has been identified as the original site of the doomed Lost Colonists, and the question that hangs in the air here is "What happened to the 117 men, women, and children of the 1587 expedition who disappeared without a trace?" ■ **TIP→ Be sure to see the orientation film before taking a guided tour of the fort.** A nature trail through the 513-acre grounds leads to an outlook over Croatan Sound. Native American and Civil War history is also preserved here. ✉ *1401 National Park Dr., Manteo* ☎ *252/473–2111 general information number for all Outer Banks NPS parks* 🌐 *www.nps.gov/fora* 🎫 *Free.*

Island Farm

FARM/RANCH | FAMILY | Outer Banks Conservationists operates this demonstration farm that lets visitors experience 19th-century life on the island. Reenactors in period dress spin wool, blacksmith, and cook over an open hearth. A wooden windmill and farmhouse set the scene, as do horses, cows, sheep, and chickens that guests can pet and feed. ✉ *1140 N. Hwy. 64, Manteo* ☎ *252/473–6500* 🎫 *$8* ⏲ *Closed Sat.–Mon.*

Lake Phelps

NATIONAL/STATE PARK | FAMILY | At 16,600 acres, 5 miles across, and about 4 feet deep, Lake Phelps is North Carolina's second-largest natural lake. It's also part of Pettigrew State Park and has long been considered a treasure by boaters and anglers. In 1985 researchers began to prize it for other reasons. Discovered underneath the sand in the beautifully clear water were ancient Native American artifacts, including 30 dugout canoes, one of which dates back some 4,400 years; Native Americans are believed to have settled here some 8,000 years ago. Two canoes are displayed in the Pettigrew Park information center. The park also includes a boat ramp, canoe launch, fishing pier, and camping sites. ✉ *2252 Lake Shore Rd., Creswell* ✢ *Take U.S. 64 west to Exit 558 and follow signs for 8 miles to the park office* ☎ *252/797–4475* 🌐 *www.ncparks.gov/pettigrew-state-park* 🎫 *Free, charge for camping.*

The Lost Colony

ARTS VENUE | FAMILY | Pulitzer Prize–winner Paul Green's drama was written in 1937 to mark the 350th birthday of Virginia Dare, the first English child born in the New World; in 2013 the show won a Tony Honor for Excellence in the Theatre. Except from 1942 to 1945 (when enemy German U-boats prowled the nearby Atlantic Ocean during World War II), it has played every summer since then in Fort Raleigh National Historic Site's Waterside Theatre, on the same grounds where the doomed English settlers tried to establish their new home. On a huge stage—larger than any on Broadway—and with a cast and crew of more than 130, the story of the first colonists, who settled here in 1587 and mysteriously vanished, is reenacted. Cast alumni include Andy Griffith and Lynn Redgrave. **■ TIP→ Try to buy tickets at least a week in advance. Preshow, hour-long backstage tours, dinner packages, and afternoon shows for children are available.** ✉ *1409 National Park Dr.* ✢ *Off U.S. 64, 3 miles north of downtown Manteo* ☎ *252/473–6000 box office* 🌐 *thelostcolony.org* 🎫 *Tickets start at $20* ⏲ *No performances mid-Aug.–mid-May; no performances Sun.*

National Wildlife Refuges Visitor Center

NATURE PRESERVE | FAMILY | In a new LEED-certified facility run by the U.S. Fish and Wildlife Service, you'll find lifelike dioramas and fun interactive exhibits, including a virtual "flyover" of 11 national wildlife refuges in a digital Cessna aircraft. Three crackerjack films are shown in a cushy 130-seat auditorium. If you're into native landscaping, you'll appreciate the plantings around the building, consisting entirely of vegetation exclusive to eastern North Carolina. The center's 35 acres include four hiking trails. ✉ *100 Conservation Way, Manteo* ☎ *252/473–1131* 🌐 *www.fws.gov/ncgatewayvc* 🎫 *Free.*

North Carolina Aquarium at Roanoke Island

ZOO | FAMILY | Occupying 68,000 square feet of space overlooking Croatan Sound, this modern aquarium includes exhibits on sea turtles, shipwreck marine life, and wild wetlands. *The Graveyard of the Atlantic*—a 285,000-gallon ocean tank containing sharks and the re-created remains of the USS *Monitor,* which sunk off Hatteras Island in 1862—remains the centerpiece exhibit. The aquarium hosts a slew of activities and field trips, from feeding fish to learning about medicinal aquatic plants and participating in a workshop on injured sea turtles. It also manages the 1,000-foot-long Jennette's Pier in Nags Head. ✉ *374 Airport Rd., Manteo* ☎ *252/475–2300* 🌐 *www.ncaquariums.com* 🎟 *$13.*

Roanoke Island Festival Park

MUSEUM VILLAGE | **FAMILY** | This multifunctional attraction sits on the waterfront in Manteo. Costumed interpreters conduct tours of the 69-foot ship *Elizabeth II*, a representation of a 16th-century vessel, but you can also help them set the sails, plot a course, and swab the decks. The 25-acre park is home to the interactive Roanoke Adventure Museum, representing 400 years of local history. There's also a re-created 16th-century settlement site, a Native American exhibit, a fossil pit, arts-and-crafts exhibitions, boardwalk trails along the marsh, and seasonal plays and concerts at the impressive outdoor stage fronting Shallowbag Bay. ✉ *1 Festival Park, Manteo* ✣ *Off Budleigh St.* ☎ *252/423–5200* 🌐 *www.roanokeisland.com* 🎟 *$11* ⏲ *Closed Sun., Mon., and Jan.–early Mar.*

Somerset Place

NATIONAL/STATE PARK | This former plantation—one of the country's largest—once claimed 100,000 acres along Lake Phelps, producing rice, corn, oats, peas, beans, and flax. Its sophisticated sawmills handled thousands of feet of lumber from 1785 to 1865. The 800 enslaved people who were forced to live and work here throughout the plantation's 80 years planted and harvested crops and worked as carpenters, brickmasons, cobblers, and weavers. The site, which originally consisted of more than 50 buildings, has nine original 19th-century buildings, and four others have been reconstructed, including slave quarters. ✉ *Pettigrew State Park, 2572 Lake Shore Rd., Creswell* ✣ *Take U.S. 64 west to Exit 558, then follow signs to Somerset Place* ☎ *252/797–4560* 🌐 *www.nchistoricsites.org* 🎟 *Free; tours $2* ⏲ *Closed Sun. and Mon.*

Restaurants

Avenue Waterfront Grille

$$$ | **SEAFOOD** | Expect local shrimp and fish at this relaxed but upscale seafood spot, where you can watch boats come and go along Manteo Harbor (or tie your own up at the dock while you dine). Avenue emphasizes its efforts to accommodate diners with food allergies. **Known for:** sushi-style tuna, when the fresh catch is in; indoor and patio seating, all with a view; blue crab dip. 💲 *Average main: $22* ✉ *207 Queen Elizabeth Ave., Manteo* ☎ *252/473–4800* ⏲ *Closed Tues. and Wed.*

Lost Colony Brewery and Cafe

$ | **SEAFOOD** | In a renovated gas station, this cheerful bistro has large front windows and lots of patio seating, plus an eclectic menu of seafood entrées, tacos, burgers, and hearty sandwiches. **Known for:** award-winning porter; fried oysters and shrimp; homemade root beer. 💲 *Average main: $14* ✉ *208 Queen Elizabeth Ave., Manteo* ☎ *252/473–6666* 🌐 *lostcolonybrewery.com* ⏲ *Closed Sun. and Mon.*

Coffee and Quick Bites

★ **Poor Richard's Sandwich Shop**

$ | **DELI** | **FAMILY** | Open since 1984, there is often a long line at the rear of this downtown Manteo institution serving gourmet classics like BLTs, Reubens, tuna melts, and pimento cheese sandwiches. Enjoy your snacks up front in the friendly, honey-blond wood bar or on the waterfront deck around back. **Known for:** hearty, inexpensive sandwiches; after-hours pub scene; battered rockfish wrap. 💲 *Average main: $10* ✉ *303 Queen Elizabeth Ave., Manteo* ☎ *252/473–3333* 🌐 *www.poorrichardsmanteo.com.*

At Roanoke Island Festival Park, you can help costumed 16th-century "sailors" set the sails and swab the decks of the *Elizabeth II*.

Hotels

Tranquil House Inn

$$$ | B&B/INN | This charming 19th-century-style waterfront inn would look perfectly in place on Martha's Vineyard and is just steps from shops, restaurants, and Roanoke Island Festival Park. **Pros:** rear porches overlook the water; complimentary evening wine reception; convenient location. **Cons:** no pool; some rooms need updating; not ideal for beach vacations. *Rooms from: $230 ✉ 405 Queen Elizabeth Ave., Manteo ☎ 252/473–1404, 800/458–7069 ⊕ www.tranquilhouseinn.com 25 rooms Free breakfast.*

White Doe Inn

$$$$ | B&B/INN | Just up the street from Manteo's romantic waterfront, this B&B is listed on the National Register of Historic Places and meets all the criteria for luxury wrapped in serenity. **Pros:** two levels of wraparound porches with rocking chairs; two-person whirlpools in some rooms; four-course breakfast. **Cons:** a popular wedding venue, so high-season availability can be scarce; rooms not individually climate-controlled; not directly on the water. *Rooms from: $275 ✉ 319 Sir Walter Raleigh St., Manteo ☎ 252/473–9851 ⊕ www.whitedoeinn.com 8 rooms, 1 cottage Free breakfast.*

Shopping

Downtown Books

BOOKS/STATIONERY | With strong local support, this enduring mainstay has survived hurricane flooding to stock an admirable collection of literature on the Outer Banks, cuisine, history, nature, lighthouses, shipwrecks, and folklore, as well as related fiction. Local author readings are frequent. *✉ 103 Sir Walter Raleigh St., Manteo ☎ 252/473–1056 ⊕ duckscottage.com.*

Outer Banks Distilling

WINE/SPIRITS | Tour the production room and take home a bottle of Kill Devil Rum from this small-batch distillery, where the Wheel House Lounge bar doubles as a popular hangout for locals sipping sweet rum cocktails. ✉ *510 Budleigh St., Manteo* ☎ *252/423–3011* 🌐 *outerbanks-distilling.com.*

Activities

SAILING

Pirate's Cove Marina

BOATING | A leaping full-size marlin sculpture leaps from the fountain to greet you at this 195-slip marina on the west side of Roanoke Sound. There's a deep-water charter dock as well as the Blue Water Grill seafood restaurant, a swimming pool, a kiddie pool and playground, a fitness center, tennis courts, and a 13,000-square-foot pavilion for private events. A fleet of 24 sport-fish boats offers offshore and nearshore excursions. ✉ *2000 Sailfish Dr., Manteo* ☎ *252/473–3906, 800/367–4728* 🌐 *www.fishpiratescove.com.*

SCUBA DIVING

Roanoke Island Outfitters and Dive Shop

SCUBA DIVING | Run by NAUI-, SDI-, and TDI-certified instructors, this outfit runs a 36-foot Bertram dive boat docked in Wanchese and a full-service dive shop in Manteo. The dive shop, which operates charters May to September, offers scuba, free-diving, and spearfishing classes, beach and night dives, bike rentals, and fishing charters. There are also guided diving trips to more than 20 wreck sites including the *Huron,* a gunship steamer that went down in 1877; the *U-85* U-boat; the *York,* a 253-foot freighter; and the *Benson,* a 465-foot tanker. Half-day dives start at $130 per person, and full-day at $165. ✉ *627 U.S. 64, Manteo* ☎ *252/473–1356* 🌐 *www.roanokeisland-outfittersanddivecenter.com.*

Hatteras Island

15 miles south of Nags Head.

The Herbert C. Bonner Bridge arches for 3 miles over Oregon Inlet and carries traffic to Hatteras Island, a 42-mile-long curved ribbon of sand and starkly beautiful dunes dividing the Atlantic Ocean and Pamlico Sound. At its most distant point (Cape Hatteras), the island is 25 miles from the mainland. About 88% of the island belongs to Cape Hatteras National Seashore and the state of North Carolina; the remainder is privately owned in seven quaint villages strung along the two-lane North Carolina Highway 12, the only main road on the island.

Hatteras Island is known as the blue marlin (or billfish) capital of the world. The continental shelf, 40 miles offshore, and its current, combined with the nearby Gulf Stream and Deep Western Boundary Current, create an unparalleled fish habitat.

The total population of the seven villages—from north to south, Rodanthe, Waves, Salvo, Avon, Buxton, Frisco, and Hatteras Village—is around 4,500, but in summer when the hundreds of vacation rental houses fill up, the island's population swells by several-fold. Each town has its own identity—Waves and Salvo are known for their windsurfing and kiteboarding, while Hatteras Village is dominated by fishing charters, with life centered around marinas. Buxton and Frisco feel trapped in time—you've left the busy highway of Nags Head far behind when you reach here, and you'll see few signs of corporate infiltration in the local businesses—even the grocery stores are independent.

Likewise, there are not many motels on Hatteras as most visitors stay in vacation houses. Avon is the village with the largest number of vacation rentals. Large waterfront houses with 6 to 10 bedrooms, private swimming pool, an elevator, and even a movie theater can go for $15,000 or more a week in summer, although many more-modest rentals are available.

GETTING HERE AND AROUND

From the north, reach Hatteras Island via U.S. Route 158. From the west, take U.S. Route 64 to U.S. Route 158. South of the Outer Banks on the mainland, U.S. Route 70 leads to an auto ferry at Cedar Island and U.S. Route 264 leads to one at Swan Quarter; both take you to Ocracoke village and North Carolina Highway 12. From the north end of Ocracoke Island, another auto ferry (free) gets you to Hatteras Village. Small planes can land at the National Park Service's Billy Mitchell Airfield in Frisco. Some charter flights are available from nearby airports.

VISITOR INFORMATION

CONTACTS Hatteras Welcome Center. ✉ *57190 Kohler Rd., Hatteras Village* ☎ *252/986–2203* 🌐 *www.outerbanks.com/hatteras-welcome-center-and-us-weather-bureau-station.html.*

Sights

★ Bodie Island Light Station

LIGHTHOUSE | FAMILY | The original Bodie (pronounced "body") lighthouse was constructed in 1847 but had to be abandoned in 1859 because of structural issues; the replacement lighthouse was destroyed by Confederate troops in 1861. The current black-and-white-banded, 156-foot-tall lighthouse was completed in 1872 and has been restored several times. The original lightkeepers' home, last remodeled in 1992, now serves as a ranger station and information center. From the third Friday in April to Columbus Day, you can climb the 214 steps to the top. (Children must be at least 42 inches tall, and climbers must weigh less than 260 pounds.) ✉ *Cape Hatteras National Seashore, 8210 Bodie Island Lighthouse Rd., Bodie Island* ☎ *252/473–2111* 🌐 *www.nps.gov/caha/planyourvisit/bils.htm* 🎫 *Grounds and visitor center free, lighthouse climb $10* 🕒 *Lighthouse tower closed mid-Oct.–late Apr.*

★ Cape Hatteras Lighthouse

LIGHTHOUSE | FAMILY | Authorized by Congress in 1794 to help prevent shipwrecks, this was the first lighthouse built in the region. The original structure was lost to erosion and Civil War damage; this 1870 replacement is, at 210 feet, the tallest brick lighthouse in the United States. Endangered by the sea, in 1999 the lighthouse, with its distinctive black-and-white spiral paint and red-and-tan base, was raised and rolled some 2,900 feet inland to its present location. A visitor center is located near the base of the lighthouse. In summer the Museum of the Sea in the former keeper's quarters is open, and you can climb the lighthouse's 257 narrow steps to the viewing balcony. Children under 42 inches tall aren't allowed to climb. Offshore lie the remains of the USS *Monitor,* a Confederate ironclad ship that sank in 1862. ✉ *46379 Lighthouse Rd., Buxton* ☎ *252/473–2111* 🌐 *nps.gov/caha/planyourvisit/chls.htm* 🎫 *Visitor center and keeper's quarters free, lighthouse climb $8* 🕒 *Lighthouse and museum closed mid-Oct.–late Apr.*

Chicamacomico Life-Saving Station

HISTORIC SITE | FAMILY | This restored lifesaving station is now a museum that tells the story of the brave people who manned 29 stations that once lined the Outer Banks. These were the precursors to today's Coast Guard, with staff who rescued people and animals from seacraft in distress. Eight incredibly well-preserved buildings (given the frequency of hurricanes here) on 7 acres include a cookhouse, bathhouse, stables, workshop, and the original 1874 lifesaving station. You'll see original equipment and tools, artifacts, and exhibits. A 1907 cottage moved to the site portrays 19th- and early-20th-century life along the Outer Banks. **■ TIP→ "Chicamacomico" is an Algonquin word meaning "land of shifting sands."** ✉ *23645 NC 12, MM 39.5, Rodanthe* ☎ *252/987–1552* 🌐 *www.chicamacomico.org* 🎫 *$8 (admission good for 1 wk)* 🕒 *Closed late Nov.–mid-Apr.*

Graveyard of the Atlantic Museum

MUSEUM | FAMILY | In a large building designed to emulate the spines of a ship, this fascinating museum tells the story of the hundreds of shipwrecks off the Outer Banks, including artifacts salvaged from dives to their wreckage. A scavenger hunt provides a fun way for kids to explore. *59200 Museum Dr., Hatteras Village* *252/986–0720* *graveyardoftheatlantic.com* *Closed Sun.*

Pea Island National Wildlife Refuge

NATURE PRESERVE | FAMILY | Heading south from Nags Head, Pea Island's miles of undeveloped coastline kick off one of the East Coast's most scenic drives. The refuge consists of 5,834 acres of marsh on the Atlantic Flyway, plus 25,700 acres of refuge waters. To the delight of birders, more than 365 species have been sighted from its observation platforms and spotting scopes and by visitors who venture into the refuge. Pea Island is home to threatened peregrine falcons, piping plovers, and tundra swans, which winter here, and to 25 species of mammals, 24 species of reptiles, and 5 species of amphibians. A visitor center on North Carolina Highway 12 has an information display and maps of the two trails, including one named for the late broadcaster Charles Kuralt, a Tar Heel native who wrote extensively about the North Carolina coast. On the west side of North Carolina Highway 12 are more than 12 miles of pristine beach. **■ TIP→ Remember to douse yourself in bug spray, especially in spring. Also, there's no tree coverage on trails, so plan peak-summer walks early and late in the day.** *15440 NC 12, Rodanthe* *252/473–1131* *www.fws.gov/refuge/pea_island* *Free.*

Beaches

Coquina Beach

BEACH—SIGHT | FAMILY | In the Cape Hatteras National Seashore, but just a few miles south of Nags Head, Coquina is considered by locals to be one of the loveliest beaches in the Outer Banks. The wide-beam ribs of the 1921 shipwreck *Laura Barnes* rest in the dunes here. Hurricanes have scattered the remains and covered them with sand, making them difficult, if not impossible, to discern. **Amenities:** lifeguards (late May–early September); parking (no fee); showers; toilets. **Best for:** sunrise; swimming. *Hatteras National Seashore, NC 12* *www.nps.gov/caha* *Free.*

Restaurants

Breakwater

$$$ | SEAFOOD | Perched atop Oden's Dock with views across the sound, this midpriced, seafood-oriented spot serves broiled and fried shrimp and fish, and plenty of specialty entrées like Cajun scallop tortellini and veggie options like coconut-curry stir-fry. The dining room is a bit small, but waiting for a table in comfortable chairs on the deck overlooking Pamlico Sound is not a chore. **Known for:** crab-stuffed flounder; live acoustic music; stunning sunset views. *Average main: $24* *57878 NC 12, Hatteras Village* *252/986–2733,* *dine.breakwaterhatteras.com* *Closed Mon. and Tues.*

★ Café Pamlico

$$$$ | SEAFOOD | Overlooking Pamlico Sound, this upscale bistro puts the focus squarely on locally sourced seafood, vegetables from the accompanying inn's own garden, and friendly service by local staff. Among the favorites are shrimp and grits, grilled catch of the day, tuna ceviche, and crab cakes. **Known for:** gorgeous sunsets; fine-dining atmosphere rare on Outer Banks; crab cakes that don't skimp on the crab. *Average main: $30* *The Inn on Pamlico Sound, 49684 NC 12, Buxton* *252/995–4500* *innonpamlicosound.com.*

Hatteras Sol Waterside Grill

$$$ | SEAFOOD | The Widespread Panic concert posters lining the walls are the first clue that this isn't the usual waterfront seafood spot; the next is the quality of the non-seafood options, like a strawberry and arugula salad, or the spicy margherita flatbread pizza. Of course, the ocean's bounty is well represented, from seafood corn chowder to a creamy shrimp carbonara. **Known for:** upscale food with a laid-back vibe; sunset views across the sound; creative approach to fresh seafood. *$ Average main: $23 ✉ 58646 NC 12, Hatteras Village ☎ 252/986–1414 ⊕ hatterassol.com ⊙ Closed Sun. and Mon.*

Oceanas Bistro

$$$ | **AMERICAN** | Open year-round for lunch and dinner (seasonally for breakfast), this long-established and popular roadside restaurant is a great spot to get local seafood and a variety of other dishes at moderate prices. Daily specials range from prime rib to tacos and grillers, a cross between a pizza and a quesadilla that's topped with tuna, crab, chicken, or veggies. **Known for:** well-prepared seafood and other dishes; moderate prices; tuna, crab, or chicken grillers. *$ Average main: $23 ✉ 40774 NC 12, Avon ☎ 252/995–4991 ⊕ www.oceanasbistro.com.*

Coffee and Quick Bites

Buxton Munch Company

$ | **CAFÉ** | **FAMILY** | This casual lunch spot, tucked away in a strip center, has been going strong for over 20 years, specializing in fish and shrimp tacos, wraps, burgers, salads, and sandwiches. There's nothing fancy here, but prices are reasonable, and there may be a line at peak times. **Known for:** crabby pattie crab cakes; inexpensive and fairly quick; local institution. *$ Average main: $10 ✉ Osprey Shopping Center, 47359 NC 12, Buxton ✣ Next to ABC store ☎ 252/995–5502 ⊕ www.buxtonmunch.com ⊙ Closed Sun.*

★ **Dancing Turtle Coffee Shop**

$ | **BAKERY** | The long list of mocha varieties at this early-morning hot spot tempt you to deviate from your usual latte, and the fluffy muffins and scones only add to the decadence. All-fruit smoothies offer a healthy balance. **Known for:** long specialty smoothie menu; coffee drinks with elaborate flavor options; grab-and-go pastries. *$ Average main: $6 ✉ 58079 NC 12, Hatteras Village ☎ 252/986–4004 ⊕ thedancingturtle.com ⊙ Closed Mon.–Wed.*

Orange Blossom Bakery & Cafe

$ | **BAKERY** | **FAMILY** | There's a line out the door during summer for this bakery's "Apple Uglies," fried amalgams of doughnut dough and apples. There's also a full menu of breakfast burritos and egg sandwiches. **Known for:** the Apple Ugly pastry—straight up or doused in chocolate; homemade biscuit sandwiches; birthday cake catering. *$ Average main: $6 ✉ 47206 NC 12, Buxton ☎ 252/995–4109 ⊕ orangeblossombakery.com ⊙ Closed Jan.–Mar.*

Hotels

Breakwater Inn

$$ | **HOTEL** | **FAMILY** | At this comfortable inn with spacious rooms with kitchenettes—suitable for a long weekend or short vacation—you can kick back on your wide, private balcony and watch the action as boats come and go from the Oden's Dock marina just below. **Pros:** oversized mini-refrigerators; sound views from your porch; walking distance to several restaurants. **Cons:** buildings across the marina block the sunset during some months; no elevator; no views from Fisherman's Quarters annex. *$ Rooms from: $189 ✉ 57896 NC 12, Hatteras Village ☎ 252/986–2565 ⊕ breakwaterhatteras.com ⇐ 35 rooms 🍽 No meals.*

Cape Pines Motel

$ | **HOTEL** | **FAMILY** | Though most visitors to Hatteras Island stay in a vacation rental house, this small, 1950s-era motel fits the bill for a night or two. **Pros:** large, very clean rooms in main building and new section; swimming pool; modest prices, even in season. **Cons:** old-looking brick style of the main building may be off-putting; no water views; basic amenities only. $ *Rooms from: $149* ✉ *47497 NC 12, Buxton* ☎ *252/995–5666* 🌐 *www.capepinesmotel.com* 🛏 *29 rooms* 🍽 *No meals.*

★ The Inn on Pamlico Sound

$$$ | **B&B/INN** | You'll feel like an honored houseguest in this casually elegant, full-service boutique hotel, with sweeping waterfront views, intuitive rather than intrusive service, and an indoor-outdoor fine-dining restaurant, Café Pamlico. **Pros:** rooms come in a variety of configurations and price ranges; complimentary fishing and beach gear; 14-seat private theater with film library. **Cons:** pool is small enough to only be comfortable for one party at a time; popular wedding and event venue may limit availability during high season; no elevators. $ *Rooms from: $230* ✉ *49684 NC 12, Buxton* ☎ *866/995–7030* 🌐 *www.innonpamlicosound.com* 🛏 *12 rooms* 🍽 *Free breakfast.*

Watermen's Retreat

$$$$ | **RENTAL** | This waterfront resort takes advantage of the perfect kiteboarding conditions just outside its door, offering an everything-you-need complex that includes modern, luxury suites with views of the action, an upscale restaurant and rum bar, and the REAL water-sports store, all on-site. **Pros:** suites feel like fresh, well-appointed condos; on-site lessons for kiteboarding beginners; excellent waterfront café. **Cons:** complex feels slightly sterile and removed from the rest of the community; kiteboarding launch site gets crowded; parking lot is cramped. $ *Rooms from: $350* ✉ *25706 NC 12, Rodanthe* ☎ *252/987–6060* 🌐 *watermens-retreat.com* 🛏 *14 rooms* 🍽 *No meals.*

Shopping

★ Buxton Village Books

BOOKS/STATIONERY | **FAMILY** | This independent bookstore in an old cottage on North Carolina Highway 12 has been a fixture for decades and hosts local book launches and readings. The knowledgeable owner stocks a large selection of regional books, as well as used and new books in all genres, plus greeting cards and gifts. The bookshop is open year-round but only three days a week in winter. ✉ *47918 NC 12, Buxton* ☎ *252/ 995–4240* 🌐 *www.buxtonvillagebooks.com.*

Activities

FISHING

Oregon Inlet Fishing Center

FISHING | This full-service marina at the north end of Oregon Inlet Bridge on Hatteras Island offers charter-boat sound and deep-sea fishing excursions and has supplies, such as bait, tackle, ice, and fuel, for the angler. The National Park Service maintains an adjacent boat launch. ✉ *98 NC 12, Nags Head* ☎ *252/441–6301, 800/272–5199 toll-free charter boat reservations* 🌐 *www.oregon-inlet.com.*

Ocracoke Island

Ocracoke Village: 15 miles southwest of Hatteras Village.

Around 950 people live on what is the farthest inhabited island in the Outer Banks, which can be reached only by water or air. The village, one of the most charming on the entire North Carolina coast, is in the widest part of the island, cradled around a harbor called Silver Lake. Inns, motels, and shops line the main street, while the Ocracoke Lighthouse is in a nearby residential area at the end of Lighthouse Road. Man-made canals form the landscape of a smaller residential area called Oyster Creek.

Centuries ago, Ocracoke was the stomping ground of Edward Teach, the pirate better known as Blackbeard, and a major treasure cache from 1718 is still rumored to be hidden somewhere on the island. Fort Ocracoke was a short-lived Confederate stronghold that was abandoned in August 1861 and blown up by Union forces a month later.

Although the island remains a destination for people seeking peace and quiet, silence can be hard to find in summer, when tourists and boaters swamp the place. About 90% of Ocracoke is within Cape Hatteras National Seashore, and the island is on the Atlantic Flyway for many migrating land and water birds. The 16 miles of Ocracoke Beach are wild, wide, and pristine, and many argue that it's the best beach in North Carolina.

GETTING HERE AND AROUND

The only way to reach Ocracoke Island is by ferry or private boat. A free auto ferry leaves hourly, and more frequently in peak summer season, from Hatteras Island and arrives 55 minutes later; toll ferries ($15 one way) connect with the mainland at Swan Quarter (2½ hours) and at Cedar Island (2¼ hours). Depending on the season, state ferries land at either end of the island and depart as late as 8 pm to Cedar Island and midnight to Hatteras Island. The ferry to and from Hatteras Island is first come, first served, but reservations should be made in advance for Cedar Island and Swan Quarter.

Only one road, North Carolina Highway 12, traverses the island. Quiet streets shoot off to the left and right at the south end. Lots of cyclists come to Ocracoke, and many inns have bikes or golf carts for their guests. Use caution when biking North Carolina Highway 12, especially in summer; traffic can be heavy, and the designated bike path doesn't extend the highway's entire 13-mile length.

VISITOR INFORMATION

CONTACTS Ocracoke Island Visitor Center. ✉ *NC 12 (38 Irvin Garrish Hwy.)* ✣ *At Ocracoke Village ferry landing* ☎ *252/473–2111* 🌐 *www.nps.gov/caha/planyourvisit/visitor-centers.htm.*

Sights

British Cemetery

CEMETERY | On May 11, 1942, the HMS *Bedfordshire*, an armed British trawler on loan to the United States, was torpedoed by a German U-boat and sank with all 37 hands lost off the coast of Ocracoke Island. The men were buried on Ocracoke in a corner of the community graveyard. The wreck was discovered in 1980 and some artifacts were recovered. It's still frequented by divers. ✉ *British Cemetery Rd., Ocracoke Village* 🌐 *www.outerbanks.com/british-cemeteries.html* 🎫 *Free.*

Ocracoke Light Station

LIGHTHOUSE | Built in 1823, Ocracoke's 77-foot tower is the second-oldest operating lighthouse in the United States. (Sandy Hook, New Jersey, has the oldest.) It was first fueled by whale oil, then kerosene, and finally electricity. The lighthouse is built entirely of brick, 5 feet thick at the base and 2 feet thick at the top, with a white finish once achieved with a blend of unslaked lime, glue, rice, salt, and powdered fish. Although it's not open to the public for climbing, the grounds are accessible year-round. ✉ *360 Lighthouse Rd., Ocracoke Village* ☎ *252/473–2111* 🌐 *www.nps.gov/caha/planyourvisit/ols.htm* 🎫 *Free.*

Ocracoke Pony Pen

NATURE PRESERVE | FAMILY | From a small observation platform, 6 miles southwest of the north Hatteras–Ocracoke ferry landing, you can look out at the descendants of the Banker ponies that roamed wild before the island came under the jurisdiction of Cape Hatteras National Seashore. The National Park Service manages the population of 25–30 animals; the wild herd once numbered nearly 500. All the animals you see today were born in captivity and are fed and kept on a 180-acre range. Legends abound about the arrival of the island's Banker ponies. Some believe they made their way to the island after the abandonment of Roanoke's Lost Colony. Others believe they were left by early Spanish explorers or swam to shore following the sinking of the *Black Squall,* a ship carrying circus performers. ✉ *NC 12* ☎ *252/473–2111 general park information* 🌐 *www.nps.gov/caha/historyculture/ocracokeponies.htm* 🎫 *Free.*

Ocracoke Preservation Society Museum
MUSEUM | FAMILY | This small museum and gift shop is located in a restored American Foursquare house built more than 100 years ago, containing photographs and artifacts illustrating the island's lifestyle and history. On display in the backyard is a round-stern fishing boat from 1934. ✉ *49 Water Plant Rd., Ocracoke Village* ☎ *252/928–7375* 🌐 *www.ocracokepreservation.org* 🎫 *Free* ⏲ *Closed Sun. and early Dec.–late Mar.*

★ **Portsmouth Village**
GHOST TOWN | FAMILY | This coastal "ghost town" is like nowhere else on the southeastern Atlantic coast, and the few thousand people that make it here each year are stunned to realize it exists.

Inhabited from 1753 until the early 1970s, Portsmouth had 685 permanent residents at its peak in 1860, making it one of the largest settlements on the Outer Banks. It was a "lightering" town, where ships heavy with cargo had to unload to smaller boats that could navigate the shallow Ocracoke Inlet. But the Civil War and the dredging of a deeper inlet at Hatteras were the beginning of the end for the town. By 1956 there were 17 inhabitants; the last two left in 1971. Today the public can tour the one-room schoolhouse, the Methodist church, the post office and general store, and the turn-of-the-20th-century lifesaving station (a multiroom Coast Guard station), each of which has been restored following the devestating flooding of Hurricane Dorian in 2019. Guided tours are available June 1 to September 1. Bring your own food, water, and bug spray (the mosquitoes could carry you away). Rudy Austin's Portsmouth Island Boat Tours runs a small passenger boat from Ocracoke. ✉ *Portsmouth Island* ✣ *Take private ferry from Ocracoke* ☎ *252/728–2250 park information line, 252/928–4361 Rudy Austin's Portsmouth Island Boat Tours (passenger ferry)* 🌐 *www.nps.gov/calo/planyourvisit/visit-portsmouth.htm* 🎫 *Passenger ferry $40 per person.*

Springer's Point Preserve
NATURE PRESERVE | FAMILY | This quarter-mile trail through a 124-acre preserve leads to Springer's Point, a sound-side beach where Edward Teach (aka Blackbeard) gathered with fellow pirates and ultimately met his demise in a battle with British naval lieutenant Robert Maynard. The enchanting trail traverses maritime forest and coastal marsh. ⚠ **There is no parking at the trailhead—walk or bike from the village.** ✉ *104 Loop Rd.* ☎ *910/790–4524* 🌐 *coastallandtrust.org.*

Beaches

★ **Ocracoke Island Beaches**
BEACH—SIGHT | FAMILY | The 16 miles of undeveloped shoreline here are often considered some of the best beaches in America. These beaches are among the least visited and most beautiful on the Cape Hatteras National Seashore. The shelling is amazing, the solitude unparalleled. Four public-access areas are close to the main beach road, North Carolina Highway 12, and easy to spot; just look for large brown-and-white wooden signs. ■ **TIP→ There are lifeguards only at the day-use beach ½ mile north of Ocracoke Village in late May through early September.** **Amenities:** lifeguards; parking (no fee); toilets. **Best for:** sunset; swimming. ✉ *Irvin Garrish Hwy. (NC 12)* 🌐 *www.nps.gov/caha/planyourvisit/wateractivities.htm* 🎫 *Free.*

Restaurants

Back Porch Restaurant and Wine Bar
$$$$ | **SEAFOOD** | This cozy little cottage under a stand of pines serves stellar seafood like crab cakes and fresh diver sea scallops. Other highlights include a pecan-crusted chicken breast in bourbon sauce and the seasonal veggie Dragon Bowl. **Known for:** fresh local seafood in creative preparations; charming dining space; respectable wine list. *Average main: $27* *110 Back Rd., Ocracoke Village* *252/928–6401* *www.backporchocracoke.com.*

★ **The Flying Melon Café**
$$$$ | **SEAFOOD** | This inviting neighborhood restaurant, with picnic tables and string lights setting an inviting scene in the yard, focuses on seafood with Louisiana Creole and Southern twists (the owners lived in New Orleans), creating dishes like seafood gumbo and fried green tomatoes with rémoulade. The atmosphere is lively, the service is friendly, and there's a full bar to quench your thirst. **Known for:** fresh seafood provided by local Ocracoke fishermen; some dishes done in a New Orleans Creole style; nice blend of modern and rustic. *Average main: $27* *181 Back Rd.* *252/928–2533* *Closed Sun. and Mon.*

Howard's Pub
$$ | **AMERICAN** | This long-established pub is a boisterous and friendly place to eat and drink, with a quick-footed staff who aim to please. Don't miss the fresh-cut pub fries, half-pound burgers, grilled fresh catch, oysters shucked to order, or appetizers like conch fritters or steamed shrimp. **Known for:** large selection of draft and bottled beer; good island bar food like fresh-shucked oysters and conch fritters; burgers and hand-cut pub fries. *Average main: $18* *1175 Irvin Garrish Hwy. (NC 12), Ocracoke Village* *252/928–4441* *www.howardspub.com* *Closed mid-Nov.–mid-Mar.*

★ **1718 Brewing**
$$ | **MODERN AMERICAN** | Coastal North Carolina's best beer is brewed at this outpost by the sea that doubles as a sunset hangout (the views from the rooftop deck are stunning) and a purveyor of next-level pub grub, courtesy of its partner business, Plum Pointe Kitchen. Order a hazy IPA or a coffee Kölsch, plus a slider platter or the catch of the day, and soak up the last rays of sunlight. **Known for:** Mexican chocolate stout; crab-stuffed pretzel with beer cheese; buzzy evening scene with stellar views. *Average main: $17* *1129 Irvin Garrish Hwy.* *252/928–2337.*

Coffee and Quick Bites

Ocracoke Coffee Co.
$ | **BAKERY** | The inviting front-yard seating at this neighborhood fixture fills most mornings with patrons enjoying healthy smoothies, tasty lattes, and fresh-baked pastries. **Known for:** relaxed vibe with indoor and outdoor seating; a chocolate, mint, and toffee Grasshopper latte; chocolate croissants. *Average main: $7* *226 Back Rd., Ocracoke Village* *252/928–7473* *ocracokecoffeeco.com.*

Hotels

Blackbeard's Lodge
$ | **HOTEL** | **FAMILY** | Step into Ocracoke history—and be greeted by a life-size statue of Blackbeard himself and a front desk shaped like the bow of the sloop *Adventure*—at this classic hotel that first opened as the Wahab Village Hotel in 1936. **Pros:** game room with billiards, foosball, and air hockey; fun pool scene; lots of porches and communal spaces. **Cons:** many guests come to party; fills up with families during summer months; the rustic exterior and old-school decor isn't at all fancy. *Rooms from: $109* *111 Back Rd.* *252/928–3421* *blackbeardslodge.com* *36 rooms* *No meals.*

★ **Captain's Landing Waterfront Inn**

$$$ | **B&B/INN** | This small, yellow inn is perched right on Silver Lake, within walking distance of most restaurants, bars, and the lighthouse. **Pros:** private balconies are directly over the water; large suites comfortable for week-long stays; very well managed. **Cons:** no elevator; breakfast not included; carpets and antique furniture aren't for everyone. *Rooms from: $220 ✉ 324 NC 12, Ocracoke Village ☎ 252/928–1999 🌐 www.thecaptainslanding.com 10 rooms No meals.*

★ **Ocracoke Harbor Inn**

$$ | **B&B/INN** | Comfort and convenience are yours in these water-facing rooms, stocked with plenty of amenities like fiber Wi-Fi, individual climate control, refrigerators, and coffeepots. **Pros:** most upscale inn on island; well-managed and meticulously maintained inn; away from busiest part of village but within walking distance. **Cons:** rooms are across the street from (not on) the harbor; some rooms may have noise from adjacent rooms; office not staffed overnight. *Rooms from: $170 ✉ 144 Silver Lake Rd. ☎ 252/928–5731, 888/456–1998 🌐 www.ocracokeharborinn.com Closed Dec.–mid-Mar. 29 suites Free breakfast.*

Shopping

Books to be Red

BOOKS/STATIONERY | In an 1898 cottage, this independent book store features a large children's selection, the latest novels and nonfiction, and everything ever published related to Ocracoke. A section of the building serves as a gift shop and local pottery gallery. *✉ 34 School Rd., Ocracoke Village ☎ 252/928–3936 🌐 ocracokebookstore.com.*

Moonraker Tea Shop

FOOD/CANDY | Hundreds of loose-tea varietals line the walls of this quaint shop devoted to wellness. Pick up a bag of the local yaupon holly tea, sample the day's tea special, and treat yourself to a magic color-changing lemonade (sparkles are 25 cents extra). *✉ 587 Irvin Garrish Hwy., Ocracoke Village ☎ 252/928–0443 🌐 moonrakerteashop.com.*

Beaufort

20 miles west of Harkers Island–Cape Lookout ferry; 150 miles southeast of Raleigh.

There's a feeling of having stepped back in time in this small, historic seaport with a charming boardwalk. Residents take great pride in the city's restored public buildings and homes—and in their homes' histories, which sometimes include tales of pirates and sea captains. **■ TIP→ Don't make the mistake of pronouncing the town's name as "BEW-furt"—that's how South Carolinians pronounce their state's city of Beaufort. North Carolina's Beaufort is pronounced "BOW-furt."** Established in 1713, the third-oldest town in North Carolina was named for Henry Somerset, Duke of Beaufort, and it's hard to miss the English influence here, particularly in the historic district's street names. Many are named after British royalty and colonial leaders.

GETTING HERE AND AROUND

Beaufort is near the far eastern end of U.S. Route 70, which intersects U.S. Route 17 to the northwest at New Bern. The town has a small airstrip but no commercial flights. For boaters, it's located along the intracoastal waterway, and downtown docks are available. The closest airport is in New Bern. The town is a perfect park-and-stroll location, with historic sites, museums, heritage B&Bs, and a retail center all within walking distance of each other.

The Crystal and Cape Fear Coasts

Sights

Beaufort Historic Site

HISTORIC SITE | **FAMILY** | In the center of town, the historic site consists of 10 buildings dating from 1732 to 1859, eight of which have been restored, including the 1796 **Carteret County Courthouse** and the 1859 **Apothecary Shop and Doctor's Office** . Don't miss the **Old Burying Grounds** (1709), where Otway Burns, a privateer in the War of 1812, is buried under his ship's cannon; a nine-year-old girl who died at sea is buried in a rum keg; and an English soldier saluting the king is buried upright in his grave. Tours of the entire 12-block historic site, which is now on the National Register of Historic Places, either on an English-style double-decker bus or by guided walk, depart from the visitor center. For a self-guided tour, download the free walking tour brochure from the website and put on your walking shoes—Beaufort has about 150 historic houses with plaques that list their date of construction and original owner. ✉ *100 Block Turner St.* ☎ *252/728–5225, 800/575–7483* 🌐 *www.beauforthistoricsite.org* 🎫 *Guided walking tour $12; bus tour $12; combined tickets: $18.*

★ **Cape Lookout Lighthouse**

LIGHTHOUSE | **FAMILY** | This distinctive 1859 lighthouse's double walls allow the tower to rise as tall as required—169 feet—without making the building unstable. This lighthouse on Core Banks island withstood retreating Confederate troops' attempts to blow it up to keep it out of Union hands (they stole the lens instead). With its white-and-black diamond markings, the beacon continues to function as a navigational aid. A small museum inside the visitor center over on Harkers Island tells the story of the lighthouse from its first incarnation in 1812. Anyone 44 inches or taller may climb the tower's 207 steps from mid-May to mid-September. The climb is worth it for an incomparable view of Cape Lookout's wild shores. A private ferry, Island Express Ferry Service, runs between both Beaufort and Harkers Island to the lighthouse. ✉ *Cape Lookout National Seashore Administration Office, 131 Charles St., Harkers Island* ☎ *252/728–7433 Island Express Ferry Service (private ferry), 252/728–2250 Cape Lookout park service information line* 🌐 *www.nps.gov/calo/planyourvisit/lighthouse-climbs.htm* 🎫 *Grounds free; lighthouse $8; round-trip for pedestrian ferry from Harkers Island $18, from Beaufort $40* 🕒 *Lighthouse closed mid-Sept.–late May; Harkers Island and Beaufort ferries closed Oct.–Feb.*

★ Fort Macon State Park

NATIONAL/STATE PARK | FAMILY | The centerpiece of this multiuse state park is the 1834 pentagon-shape fortress, built under the supervision of a young Robert E. Lee. From atop its walls, where six cannons still point out toward the harbor, take in the gorgeous 360-degree views of Beaufort and across the ocean. The fort was briefly used by the Confederacy against the Union during the Civil War, but was quickly surrendered under siege in 1862. The 365-acre park also offers picnic areas, hiking trails through the maritime forest, and a mile-long beachfront with a large bathhouse, showers, and refreshments. The beach has lifeguards on duty June through Labor Day and is known as one of the best surfing breaks in the Crystal Coast area. ✉ *2303 E. Fort Macon Rd., Atlantic Beach* ✣ *On east end of Rte. 58 about 3 miles south of Morehead City* ☎ *252/726–3775* 🌐 *www.ncparks.gov/fort-macon-state-park* 🎫 *Free.*

North Carolina Maritime Museum

MUSEUM | FAMILY | An exhibit about the infamous pirate Blackbeard includes artifacts recovered from the discovery of his flagship, *Queen Anne's Revenge,* near Beaufort Inlet. Other exhibits feature coastal culture and the state's rich marine-science history. You'll see seashells, fossils, duck decoys, and commercial fishing gear. The associated **Watercraft Center,** across the street, has lectures and classes on boatbuilding, and you can see various projects under construction. ✉ *315 Front St.* ☎ *252/504–7740* 🌐 *ncmaritimemuseumbeaufort.com* 🎫 *Free* 🕒 *Closed Sun.*

Shackleford Banks

BEACH—SIGHT | FAMILY | Wild, wooded, and undeveloped, this 7½-mile-long barrier island, the southernmost part of Cape Lookout National Seashore, is made even more magical by myriad seashells along the shore and about 100 free-roaming horses. Folklore offers two reasons for the Banker ponies' presence. One tale claims they swam ashore from a long-ago Spanish shipwreck, but some locals say early settlers first put these horses to pasture on the island. The horses may look friendly, but it's best to view them from a distance. The island hosted various settlements in the 1800s, but storms drove residents inland. Today, gravestones here and there are the only remaining evidence of the people who lived here. Island access is by ferry only, from Beaufort and Harkers Island, and although primitive camping is allowed (at no fee), there are no amenities aside from composting toilets. **Amenities:** toilets. **Best for:** swimming; walking. ✉ *Cape Lookout National Seashore* ☎ *252/728–7433 Island Express Ferry Service (private ferry)* 🌐 *www.nps.gov/calo* 🎫 *Island beaches free, Harkers Island or Beaufort ferry $18* 🕒 *Ferry times vary, closed Oct.–Mar.*

Beaches

Atlantic Beach
BEACH—SIGHT | FAMILY | Just across the harbor from Beaufort—but three bridges driving—this beach is a family-friendly spot known for its wide stretches of sand (even at high tide) and beautiful green water. Free outdoor movies, movie festivals, playgrounds, and a park are featured on the town's Circle. A boardwalk fronts part of the clean, wide beach, where buoys mark lifeguard-protected swimming areas. **Amenities:** food and drink; lifeguards; toilets. **Best for:** surfing; swimming; windsurfing. ✉ *W. Atlantic Blvd., Atlantic Beach* 🌐 *atlanticbeach-nc.com.*

Restaurants

Beaufort Grocery Company
$$$$ | MODERN AMERICAN | Well known for its lunchtime sandwiches, salads, and gumbo, this quaint neighborhood bistro's dinner menu expands and goes upscale, with an emphasis on duck, pork, and local seafood. Seating expands from the rustic, black-and-white-checkered-floor dining room out onto the sidewalk. **Known for:** big selection of soups, salads, and sandwiches for lunch; gougères (Parmesan pastries filled with shrimp or chicken salad); upmarket dinners like pan-seared duck with candied orange rind. $ *Average main: $30* ✉ *117 Queen St.* ☎ *252/728–3899* 🌐 *www.beaufortgrocery.com* ⏲ *Closed Tues.*

City Kitchen
$$$ | ECLECTIC | At an otherwise working marina, this small-plates restaurant and cocktail bar offers a touch of upscale class with its excellent water views. The rotating "Littles" menu is globally inspired and full of flavor, while the "Bigs" are heartier, meatier choices for dinner. **Known for:** small menu with a diverse selection; sticky-toffee pudding; sophisticated but local vibes. $ *Average main: $24* ✉ *114 A Town Creek Dr.* ☎ *252/648–8141* 🌐 *www.towncreekmarina.com.*

Clawson's 1905 Restaurant and Pub
$$ | AMERICAN | FAMILY | A combination of fresh seafood, local beers, and live music make this a Front Street staple, especially for lunch. Housed in a 1900s grocery building, Clawson's is stuffed with memorabilia dedicated to preserving the history and heritage of Beaufort. **Known for:** casual atmosphere for lunch or a hearty dinner; good selection of microbrews; historic memorabilia about Beaufort. $ *Average main: $18* ✉ *425 Front St.* ☎ *252/728–2133* 🌐 *www.clawsonsrestaurant.com* ⏲ *Closed Sun.*

★ Moonrakers
$$$$ | SEAFOOD | There's a lot to love at this gorgeous three-story destination restaurant, from the blackened grouper that emeges from the open kitchen's wood-fired grill, to the sunset views, enjoyed with a signature mai tai on the appropriately named Sky Deck. **Known for:** the best views in town; award-winning wine list; seafood cooked to perfection on a wood-fired grill. $ *Average main: $26* ✉ *326 Front St.* ☎ *252/838–0083* 🌐 *moonrakersbeaufort.com* ⏲ *Closed Tues. and Wed.*

The Ruddy Duck
$$ | SEAFOOD | Next door to the far more famous Sanitary Restaurant, this tavern churns out seafood that's a step above its competition along the Morehead City waterfront, and with views and open-air seating on the water to boot. **Known for:** the fried flounder Reuben; duck hunting and nautical decor, including a long rack of antique outboard engines; Cajun fish bites from the day's local catch. $ *Average main: $19* ✉ *509 Evans St., Morehead City* ☎ *252/726–7500* ⏲ *Closed Mon.*

Coffee and Quick Bites

CRU

$ | **DELI** | In the morning, pick up a bagel, a breakfast burrito, and a latte at this downtown coffee shop. Grab a sandwich or wrap to go for lunch, and come back in the evening for ice cream or to enjoy one of coastal North Carolina's best wine selections, by the glass or the bottle. **Known for:** house-made chocolate bars; gourmet coffee drinks; ice-cream cones and floats. *Average main: $6 ✉ 120 Turner St. ☎ 252/728–3066 🌐 beaufortcru.com.*

Hotels

Ann Street Inn

$$ | **B&B/INN** | Experience front-porch hospitality and mix with lively locals in this elegant 1830s home, complete with original details, such as the wood plank flooring. **Pros:** genuine historic Beaufort experience; gracious, generous host; delicious hot breakfast (plus complimentary wine and cocktails). **Cons:** no elevator; noise transfers within the house; no individual climate control. *Rooms from: $179 ✉ 707 Ann St. ☎ 252/723–8134 🌐 www.annstreetinn.com 3 rooms Free breakfast.*

★ Beaufort Hotel

$$$$ | **HOTEL** | **FAMILY** | Tasteful and modern decor adorns the rooms at this recent addition to downtown Beaufort, set directly on Taylor Creek, where the whinnies of wild horses at the Rachel Carson Reserve can be heard from your private balcony. **Pros:** state-of-the-art in-room luxuries; fine-dining restaurant with views; private dock and waterfront. **Cons:** some rooms have views of adjacent industrial buildings; too far to walk to other restaurants; wedding parties take over communal spaces on summer weekends. *Rooms from: $284 ✉ 2440 Lennoxville Rd. ☎ 252/728–3000 🌐 beaufforthotelnc.com 133 rooms No meals.*

Pecan Tree Inn

$$ | **B&B/INN** | This comfortable, well-kept B&B's seven rooms include pencil-post canopy beds and bay windows, offering a historic, authentic base for exploring. **Pros:** historic 1860s house with elegantly furnished rooms; maple-butter pecan cookies as an afternoon snack; gourmet breakfasts. **Cons:** books up far in advance; two-night minimum most weekends; some bathrooms are small. *Rooms from: $190 ✉ 116 Queen St. ✣ Across the street from Beaufort Grocery Co. ☎ 252/728–6733 🌐 www.pecantree.com 7 rooms Free breakfast.*

Activities

KAYAKING

★ Beaufort Paddle

KAYAKING | **FAMILY** | To fully appreciate a city that exists because of its maritime shipping and fishing history, you have to see it from the water. This full-service outfitter offers a range of beginner-friendly and advanced-level kayak and paddleboard tours to private beaches in the Rachel Carson Reserve, along the Beaufort waterfront, and through the marina that harbors the local fleet of shrimping boats. Rent kayaks for a self-guided adventure (including overnights to Shackleford Banks) or let one of their friendly, experienced guides lead a loop trip, pointing out birds, wild horses, and the best shelling beaches along the way. *✉ 424 Old Causeway Rd. ☎ 252/725–3065 🌐 beaufortpaddle.com.*

New Bern

41 miles northeast of Beaufort.

This city of nearly 30,000 was founded in 1710 by a Swiss nobleman who named it after his home, Bern, Switzerland. Since *bern* means "bear" in German, the black bear is New Bern's mascot—you'll see over 70 of them all over town, painted and named by local artists. New

Bern had the state's first printing press in 1749, the first newspaper in 1751, and the first publicly funded school in 1764. For nearly 30 years it was the state capital, until it moved to Raleigh in 1792. George Washington even slept in New Bern ... *twice.* In 1898, New Bern cemented its place in pop-culture history when pharmacist Caleb Bradham mixed up a digestive aid that eventually became known as Pepsi-Cola.

Today New Bern has a 20-block historic district that includes more than 150 significant buildings, about a third of which are on the National Register. The diverse architecture covers colonial, Georgian, Federal, Greek revival, and Victorian styles. Since 1979, more than $200 million has been spent preserving and revitalizing the downtown area, now a pleasant mix of shops, restaurants, and museums, with an authentic Small Town, U.S.A., feel to it. Sailors and sunseekers enjoy the area, too, as the Neuse and Trent Rivers provide the perfect environment for such activities as boating, waterskiing, and crabbing. The town has several marinas and seven public or semipublic golf courses that are open year-round.

GETTING HERE AND AROUND

The east–west U.S. Route 70 and north–south U.S. Route 17 intersect at New Bern, allowing highway access from all directions. The city also has the Coastal Carolina Regional Airport, a medium-size airport with commercial flights on Delta and American. You can walk around downtown, but you'll need a car to maneuver around the city.

TOURS

New Bern Trolley Tour

BUS TOURS | Hop on the trolley for an engaging 90-minute ride around town, including stops at the Cedar Grove Cemetery and the New Bern Academy. Dozens of historic homes and their roles in the nation's founding are highlighted along the way. ✉ *610 Pollock St.* ☎ *252/637–7316* 🌐 *newberntours.com* 🎟 *$18.*

VISITOR INFORMATION

CONTACTS Visit New Bern. ✉ *316 S. Front St.* ☎ *800/437–5767* 🌐 *www.visitnewbern.com.*

Sights

Birthplace of Pepsi-Cola

STORE/MALL | FAMILY | In honor of the soda's 100th anniversary in 1998, the local bottling company opened the Birthplace in the same corner store where teacher-turned-pharmacist Caleb Bradham brewed his first batch of "Brad's Drink." He later renamed it Pepsi-Cola, marketing the syrup to other soda fountains, and a conglomerate was born. This old-fashioned shop feels like a museum, with its reproduction of Bradham's fountain and exhibits of memorabilia, including the original recipe that included coriander, nutmeg, and a half gallon of alcohol. Enjoy an ice-cold bottle of Pepsi while roaming the gift shop, full of Pepsi history and souvenirs ranging from T-shirts to thimbles. ✉ *256 Middle St.* ☎ *252/636–5898* 🌐 *www.pepsistore.com* 🎟 *Free.*

★ Tryon Palace

CASTLE/PALACE | This elegant reconstructed 1770 Georgian building was the colonial capitol and originally the home of Royal Governor William Tryon. Tours are led by witty, engaging docents dressed in period attire and sometimes include cooking demonstrations in the freestanding kitchen. The palace burned to the ground in 1798, and it wasn't until 1959 that a rebuilt, scale replica of the home was completed. Today, only the stable and one basement wall are original, and the foundation has been restored to its original footprint. Everything else has been reconstructed from architectural plans, maps, and letters; and the palace is furnished with English and American antiques corresponding to Governor Tryon's inventory. Additionally, 85% of the books in the library are the same titles as those that were there 200 years ago. The stately **John Wright Stanly House** (circa 1783), the

George W. Dixon House (circa 1830), the **Robert Hay House** (circa 1805), and the **New Bern Academy** (circa 1809) are also part of the 13-acre Tryon Palace complex. You can also stroll through the 18th-century-style formal gardens, which bloom year-round but are especially popular during spring tulip and fall mum seasons. The complex's 60,000-square-foot **North Carolina History Center** contains two museums providing interactive displays that trace the history of New Bern and the central North Carolina coast. ✉ *529 S. Front St.* ☎ *800/767–1560* 🌐 *www.tryonpalace.org* 🎫 *Guided tours of Governor's Palace $20; galleries and gardens access only $6.*

Restaurants

Bay Leaf

$$ | **INDIAN** | The wonderful smells of freshly prepared curries and tandoori chicken beckon diners to enter this windowless but lovely restaurant in the restored Kress Mall. Known for its inexpensive lunch buffet, Bay Leaf offers the best Indian food in the region. **Known for:** lunch buffet; notable tandoori-style, seafood, and vegetarian dishes; exceptionally friendly staff. $ *Average main: $17* ✉ *309 Middle St.* ☎ *252/638–5323* 🌐 *www.bayleafnewbern.com* ⏲ *Closed Sun.*

The Chelsea

$$$ | **AMERICAN** | In the former drugstore of the pharmacist who invented Pepsi-Cola, this tile-floored, light-filled corner café is a magnet for visitors and local businesspeople wanting a quick sandwich or large salad for lunch. In the evening the Chelsea is more upscale, with entrées in the upstairs dining rooms (there's an elevator) including shrimp and grits and a candied-bacon rib eye. **Known for:** sandwiches, crab cakes, and lighter fare for lunch; fine dining for dinner; pleasant, historic dining room. $ *Average main: $23* ✉ *335 Middle St.* ☎ *252/637–5469* 🌐 *www.thechelsea.com* ⏲ *Closed Sun.*

★ Cypress Hall

$$$$ | **MODERN AMERICAN** | Chef Ashley Moser's open kitchen at this magnificent, brick-walled, fine-dining hall (it's arguably the best restaurant in a 100-mile radius) generates intensely pleasant flavors, from the charred octopus with pea and mint *romesco* to the kimchi pork belly and mushrooms, served as a wrap with Bibb lettuce. The wine list is excellent, but don't overlook cocktails like a margarita that's crowned with sea-salt foam. **Known for:** strawberry cake that's a local legend; excellent cocktails using house-made ginger beer; informed service and a relaxed dining experience. $ *Average main: $25* ✉ *219 Middle St.* ☎ *252/633–5909* 🌐 *cypresshallrestaurant.com* ⏲ *Closed Mon.*

MJ's Raw Bar and Grille

$$ | **SEAFOOD** | **FAMILY** | This little downtown seafood joint with sidewalk and indoor seating serves fresh coastal food in a setting full of local charm. You'll see plenty of fried seafood on the menu, but reasonably priced plates from the raw bar (combination platters of oysters, clams, steamed shrimp, and crab) do not disappoint. **Known for:** crab cakes; steamed seafood platters; Bloody Marys. $ *Average main: $18* ✉ *216 Middle St.* ☎ *252/635–6890* 🌐 *www.mjsrawbar.com* ⏲ *Closed Mon.*

Morgan's Tavern and Grill

$$ | **AMERICAN** | **FAMILY** | Skylights illuminate exposed redbrick walls and weathered wooden ceiling beams at this downtown, circa-1912 building, originally a garage and filling station. Today it's one of the town's most popular eateries, with steaks, fried seafood, big burgers, all types of salads and sandwiches, and its own craft beers. **Known for:** rustic, appealing, and lively atmosphere; burgers, steaks, and seafood at moderate prices; craft beers. $ *Average main: $18* ✉ *235 Craven St.* ☎ *252/636–2430* 🌐 *www.morganstavernnewbern.com* ⏲ *Closed Sun. and Mon.*

Stroll through 16 acres of 18th-century formal gardens at Tryon Palace.

Persimmons

$$$ | SEAFOOD | New Bern's only waterfront restaurant doesn't rely on geography to impress—the craft cocktails, seared scallops, and entrées like salmon and local littleneck clams over angel-hair pasta taste even better when you're seated directly over the water, but this inspired menu is a win even without the stunning views. **Known for:** rich tomato pie; live music on the waterfront deck; inspired takes on the local catch. *Average main: $22* *100 Pollock St.* *252/514–0033* *persimmonsrestaurant.net* *Closed Mon.*

Coffee and Quick Bites

Cow Café

$ | CAFÉ | FAMILY | This black-and-white-spotted café and ice cream parlor is popular with families. Sandwiches, "cow-lossal" all-beef hot dogs, "cowsadillas," house-made caramel corn, and apple pie "à la moo" are served, too. **Known for:** many varieties of ice cream; black-and-white cow toys, gifts, and memorabilia; kid-friendly fun. *Average main: $7* *319 Middle St.* *252/672–9269* *www.cowcafenewbern.com.*

Hotels

★ The Aerie

$ | B&B/INN | Rooms in this 1882 Italianate Victorian residence—priced very reasonably for the value—received a full update in 2021, balancing modern fixtures with well-curated antiques and reproductions, premium linens, and thoughtful amenities. **Pros:** lovely outdoor patio and firepit; gourmet breakfast included; convenient location within walking distance of Tryon Palace and historic district. **Cons:** no elevator; some noise transfer between rooms; two suites are in the building across the street. *Rooms from: $138* *509 Pollock St.* *252/636–5553* *aerienc.com* *8 rooms* *Free breakfast.*

Benjamin Ellis House
$ | **B&B/INN** | The new owners of this impressive 1850 Greek revival inn (it lodged Yankee soldiers during the Civil War), formerly known as Harmony House, have spruced things up with attractive paintings and a decor scheme heavy on antiques but light on clutter. **Pros:** excellent breakfast; easy walking distance to shops, restaurants, and the waterfront park; moderate rates. **Cons:** no pets allowed; no elevator; no pool. *Rooms from: $145* *215 Pollock St.* *252/259–2311* *www.harmony-houseinn.com* *8 rooms* *Free breakfast.*

DoubleTree by Hilton — New Bern Riverfront
$$ | **HOTEL** | **FAMILY** | At the confluence of the Neuse and Trent Rivers within the historic district, this comfortable hotel—with marina facilities—has rooms and suites with terrific views of the city and waterfront. **Pros:** free parking; on riverfront away from downtown bustle; recent upgrades and renovations. **Cons:** some maintenance is lacking; entire hotel has two luggage carts; gets busy with conference groups. *Rooms from: $169* *100 Middle St.* *252/658–9000* *hilton.com* *99 rooms* *Free breakfast.*

Hanna House Bed and Breakfast
$ | **B&B/INN** | Innkeepers Camille and Joe Klotz's renovation of the Rudolph Ulrich House (circa 1896) resulted in moderately priced accommodations in antiques-filled rooms that attract guests again and again. **Pros:** a short walk from downtown shops and a riverfront park; special breakfast requests taken; modest rates. **Cons:** no phones or televisions in rooms; no small children; floral wallpaper with Oriental rugs decor scheme feels dated. *Rooms from: $109* *218 Pollock St.* *252/635–3209, 866/830–4371* *www.hannahousenc.net* *5 rooms* *Free breakfast.*

Shopping

C. Foy Tonsorial Parlor
PERFUME/COSMETICS | Located in the historic Kress Mall, C. Foy Tonsorial Parlor and its third-generation owner are bringing back old-fashioned (but upscale) barbering, complete with hot-towel shaves, shoulder massages, and shoeshines. There's a shoeshine booth and a chess table to pass the time before your appointment. For the ne plus ultra, ask for the New York Mint Julep Cocktail Facial. *Kress Mall, 309 Middle St.* *252/636–2369* *www.cfoyparlor.com.*

Carolina Creations
ART GALLERIES | Fine American crafts and fine art represented by regional and national artists of every genre are the focus at this art gallery and gift shop. You can find blown glass, pottery, jewelry, wood carvings, and all manner of paintings and prints. *317 Pollock St.* *252/633–4369* *www.carolinacreations.com.*

★ **Surf, Wind and Fire**
CLOTHING | **FAMILY** | This fun outfitter sells clothing designed for the outdoors, from brands like Patagonia and Free Fly, plus outdoor gear and attractive New Bern souvenirs. The in-store Surfing Pig taproom includes sidewalk seating and stocks local craft beers. *230 Middle St.* *252/288–5823* *surfwindandfire.com.*

Wilmington

89 miles southwest of New Bern; 130 miles southeast of Raleigh.

The city's long history, including its part in the American Revolution, is revealed in sights downtown and in the surrounding area. The Cotton Exchange is a complex of old mills, warehouses, and cotton export buildings now used as shopping and entertainment centers. On 3rd Street are blocks of stately mansions, while historic Front Street now boasts one of

North Carolina's liveliest nightlife scenes, with clubs and restaurants packed with revelers on most weekends. The city also fills up for annual events, such as the Azalea Festival, North Carolina Jazz Festival, Christmas candlelight tours, fishing tournaments, and the Cucalorus Film Festival. EUE/Screen Gems Studios has turned out more than 400 film, television, and commercial productions, including *Iron Man 3* for Marvel; *Under the Dome* for CBS; TNT's *Good Behavior*, A&E's *Six*, about a Navy SEAL team; and the popular CW network shows *Dawson's Creek* and *One Tree Hill*. Wilmington's sprawling suburban areas are of less interest to visitors, but many of the chain motels and restaurants are located outside the downtown historic sections.

GETTING HERE AND AROUND

Wilmington is at the crossroads of U.S. Route 17 and the Interstate 40 terminus. Commercial flights land at Wilmington International Airport. The downtown historic district along the riverfront is easily walkable and also offers free trolley service. Downtown parking decks and lots are plentiful and reasonably priced. As you move away from this immediate area, however, a car becomes necessary for visits to places such as the Cameron Art Museum, Airlie Gardens, and the USS *North Carolina* Battleship Memorial. In summer and during rush hours year-round, the major thoroughfares are busy, and seemingly thousands of red lights create stop-and-go traffic, so allow more time than the distance would indicate. North Carolina Highway 132 (College Road), the main north–south road through the city, continues south where Interstate 40 leaves off. U.S. Route 76/17 (Market Street) runs from downtown east to the vicinity of Wrightsville Beach; U.S. Route 421 goes south to Carolina and Kure Beaches.

TOURS

Haunted Wilmington

WALKING TOURS | Give yourself chills even on a sultry night. Choose between the Ghost Walk of Old Wilmington, with its stories of privateers, murderers, and unmarked graves, or a Haunted Pub Crawl, where you wash down tales of madmen and saucy wenches with Dutch courage. ✉ *8 Market St., Downtown* ☎ *910/794–1866* 🌐 *www.hauntedwilmington.com* 🎫 *$17.*

Wilmington Ale Trail

SELF-GUIDED | Wilmington has nearly 20 craft breweries, and the Wilmington Ale Trail website helps you navigate the tasting rooms and taverns where you can try them all. A beer tour, **Port City Brew Bus** (🌐 *www.portcitybrewbus.com*), offers a three-stop brewery tour for $55. ✉ *Wilmington* ☎ *910/679–6023* 🌐 *www.wilmingtonaletrail.com.*

VISITOR INFORMATION

CONTACTS Downtown Wilmington Visitor Information Booth. ✉ *Riverwalk at the foot of Market St. and Water St., Downtown* ☎ *877/406–2356* 🌐 *www.wilmingtonandbeaches.com.*

Airlie Gardens

GARDEN | FAMILY | This garden's 67 lush acres feature azaleas, magnolias, and camellias that flourish near two freshwater lakes that attract waterfowl. This is not an ornate flower garden—it's more of a naturally beautiful place to take a stroll beside the river, enjoying native plants in bloom, trailside sculptures, and abundant birdlife. Take note of the greatest specimen in the gardens: a gargantuan five-century-old oak. ■ **TIP→ May through October you can flutter among 300 to 400 butterflies in the huge butterfly house.** The last tickets of the day are sold a half hour before closing. No pets (except service animals) are permitted. ✉ *300 Airlie Rd., Midtown* ✥ *8 miles east of downtown*

Downtown Wilmington
Isabel Holmes Bridge
Smith Creek
Corbett Street
King Street
Stanley Street
Mc Rae Street
Swann Street
Harnett Street
Bladen Street
Brunswick Street
North 11th Street
Oakdale Cemetery
Pine Forest Cemetery
Hanover Street
Campbell Street
Campbell Street
Red Cross Street
Rankin Street
North 3rd Street
North Front Street
North 2nd Street
North 4th Street
North 5th Street
North 6th Street
North 7th Street
Grace Street
Chestnut Street
Princess Street
N. 9th Street
N. 10th Street
N. 11th Street
N. 12th Street
N. 14th Street
N. 15th Street
N. 16th Street
N. 17th Street
Market Street
Dock Street
Orange Street
Ann Street
Cape Fear River
South Front Street
South 2nd Street
South 4th Street
South 5th Street
South 6th Street
South 7th Street
South 8th Street
South 10th Street
South 11th Street
South 13th Street
South 14th Street
South 15th Street
South 16th Street
Cape Fear Memorial Bridge
Dram Tree Park
Battleship Road NW
Castle Street
Queen Street
S. 9th Street
Wooster Street
Dawson Street
Wright Street
Mears Street
Marstellar Street
Kidder Street
Martin Street
Greenfield Street
South Front Street
South 3rd Street
Optimist Park

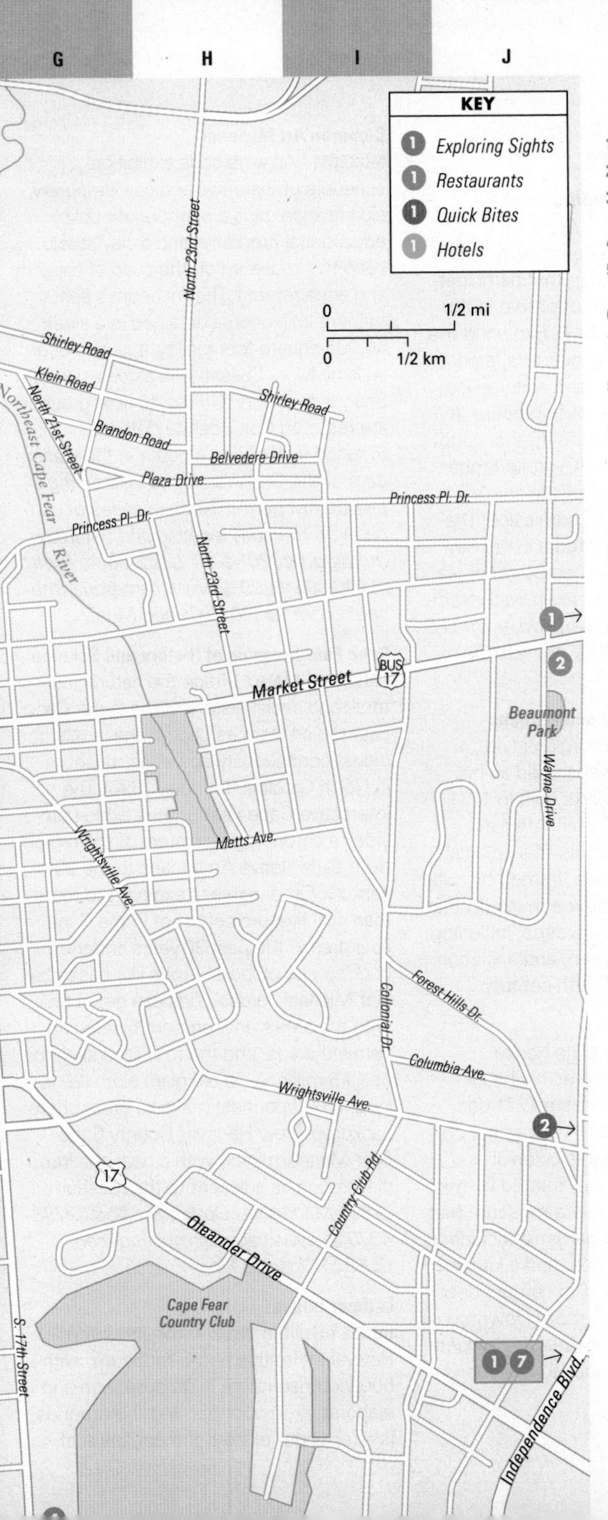

Sights

1 Airlie Gardens........................J8
2 Battleship *North Carolina*......... A4
3 Burgwin-Wright House and Gardens.........................C5
4 Cameron Art Museum G9
5 Cape Fear Museum of History and Science........................ D5
6 Latimer House........................C5
7 New Hanover County Arboretum...........................J8
8 Poplar Grove Historic Plantation................. D1
9 Wilmington Railroad Museum ... B3

Restaurants

1 Catch..................................J4
2 Indochine.............................J4
3 Manna C4
4 PinPoint Restaurant............... B5
5 Seabird.............................. B5

Quick Bites

1 Bespoke C4
2 Sealevel City Vegan Diner.........J7

Hotels

1 C.W. Worth House B&B............C6
2 Embassy Suites by Hilton Wilmington Riverfront............. B3
3 Graystone Inn........................C5
4 Hotel Ballast B4
5 The Verandas C6

via U.S. 76 ☎ *910/798–7700* 🌐 *www.airliegardens.org* 🎟 *$9.*

★ Battleship *North Carolina*

MILITARY SITE | FAMILY | Across the Cape Fear River from downtown, take a self-guided tour of a ship that participated in every major naval offensive in the Pacific during World War II. Exploring the floating city, with living quarters, a post office, chapel, laundry, and even an ice cream shop, takes about two hours. A climb down into the ship's interior is not for the claustrophobic. A ½-mile timber walkway lets visitors tour the ship's exterior with no cost of admission. The ship, which is open for tours every day of the year, can be reached by car or via river taxi from the downtown waterfront. ✉ *1 Battleship Rd., Downtown* ✣ *Off U.S. 74/76* ☎ *910/399–9100* 🌐 *www.battleshipnc.com* 🎟 *$14.*

Burgwin-Wright House and Gardens

HOUSE | The colonial Georgian-style house General Cornwallis used as his headquarters in 1781 was built in 1771 on the foundations of a jail. After a fine, furnished restoration, this colonial gentleman's town house, framed by two stately magnolias, is now a museum that includes seven period gardens, including an orchard, a rose garden, and a kitchen garden, along with an 18th-century debtors prison.

The colonial Georgian-style house General Cornwallis used as his headquarters in 1781 was built in 1771 on the foundations of a jail. After a fine, furnished restoration, this colonial gentleman's town house, framed by two stately magnolias, is now a museum that includes seven period gardens, including an orchard, a rose garden, and a kitchen garden, along with an 18th-century debtors prison. ✉ *224 Market St., Downtown* ☎ *910/762–0570* 🌐 *www.burgwinwright-house.com* 🎟 *House tour $14, gardens free* ⏲ *Closed Sun.*

Cameron Art Museum

MUSEUM | An ambitious exhibition schedule of historical and contemporary significance, plus a plethora of public educational programs and a clay studio, keep this museum on the cusp of capacity and engagement. The museum's permanent collection, contained in a sleek 40,000-square-foot facility, includes originals by Mary Cassatt and a collection of Seagrove pottery. On the 10-acre grounds are restored Confederate defense mounds built during a battle in the waning days of the Civil War. *Try to visit during a Live@CAM performance, a series of concerts on Thursday evening and Saturday morning.* ✉ *3201 S. 17th St., South Metro* ☎ *910/395–5999* 🌐 *www.cameronartmuseum.com* 🎟 *$10* ⏲ *Closed Mon.*

Cape Fear Museum of History and Science

MUSEUM | FAMILY | Trace the natural, cultural, and social history of the lower Cape Fear region from its beginnings in this, the oldest continuously operating museum in North Carolina (founded 1898). The interactive Cape Fear Stories exhibit provides a chronological history of the region from early Native Americans to the 20th century. Other exhibits explore the more than 400 film projects shot in the Cape Fear area in the past 30 years and the back stories of local heroes like basketball star Michael Jordan. Kids can get in touch with the area's environment by feeding Venus flytraps, and the fossilized skeleton of a 1.5-million-year-old giant sloth (20 feet long, 6,000 pounds) makes a great photo backdrop. New Hanover County Cape Fear Museum Park, with a neat children's playground, is adjacent to the museum. ✉ *814 Market St., Downtown* ☎ *910/798–4370* 🌐 *www.capefearmuseum.com* 🎟 *$8* ⏲ *Closed Mon.*

Latimer House

HOUSE | Built in 1852 in the Italianate Revival style, this home museum, with 600 Victorian items in its collection and elaborate ironwork framing the grounds, is a reminder of both the opulence of antebellum living and its tortuous underbelly. Guided tours of the home and the quarters that housed 11 enslaved people are available. Tours begin on the hour from 10 am to 2 pm. The Lower Cape Fear Historical Society is also based here. ✉ *126 S. 3rd St., Downtown* ☎ *910/762–0492* 🌐 *www.lcfhs.org* 🎫 *$14* ⏲ *Closed Sun. and Mon.*

New Hanover County Arboretum

GARDEN | FAMILY | Lose yourself along magnolia-lined natural trails that wind through rose beds and dozens of varieties of shade-loving camellias on this 7-acre site, just across the water from Airlie Gardens. Relax in the Japanese teahouse, spend a moment of reflection by the water garden, or admire the native carnivorous plants like the Venus flytrap. ✉ *6206 Oleander Dr., Midtown* ✥ *Off U.S. 76* ☎ *910/798–7660* 🌐 *arboretum.nhcgov.com* 🎫 *Free.*

Poplar Grove Historic Plantation

HOUSE | FAMILY | Take a tour of what was once a major peanut and sweet potato farm in North Carolina, with an 1850 Greek revival manor house and its outbuildings. Watch a blacksmith at work, admire the farm animals, see weaving and basket-making demonstrations, and learn about the difficult lives of the people who were enslaved here. On Wednesday from 8 to 1, mid-April through late September, local farmers, growers, and artisans sell their produce, plants, and crafts. The site adjoins the hiking trails of the 67-acre Abbey Nature Preserve. ✉ *10200 U.S. 17, North Metro* ✥ *9 miles northeast of downtown* ☎ *910/686–9518* 🌐 *www.poplargrove.org* 🎫 *Guided tours $12* ⏲ *Closed Sun.–Tues.*

Wilmington Railroad Museum

MUSEUM | FAMILY | Wilmington was once a major railroad hub on the East Coast, and that legacy lives on at this museum that includes a caboose, engine, and freight car (complete with hobos), a children's play area, and a huge model-train display. The museum holds the record for the longest model train ever assembled, a feat that's commemorated among the exhibits. ✉ *505 Nutt St., Downtown* ☎ *910/763–2634* 🌐 *wrrm.org* 🎫 *$10* ⏲ *Closed Sun.*

Restaurants

Catch

$$$$ | SEAFOOD | Native Wilmingtonian chef Keith Rhodes is a James Beard Award finalist who sources local seafood for inspired, beautifully plated Asian- and Southern-influenced dishes. Copper fish sculptures decorate the dining room's sky-blue walls and watch you enjoy lump crab cakes, blackened swordfish, pan-roasted grouper, and other seafood dishes. **Known for:** locally sourced seafood; artistic presentations; celebrity chef owner, of Top Chef fame. [$] *Average main: $29* ✉ *6623 Market St., Midtown* ☎ *910/799–3847* 🌐 *www.catchwilmington.com* ⏲ *Closed Sun. and Mon.*

Indochine

$$ | ASIAN FUSION | FAMILY | Walk through the doors of this colorful restaurant and you'll feel as if you're in another country, whether you're seated in an authentic Thai hut outdoors or under elaborate Asian artifacts indoors. Flavor-packed Vietnamese and Thai dishes can be ordered in your choice of meat, seafood, or vegetarian options, each prepared to order with customized levels of spiciness. **Known for:** huge, diverse menu of various Asian dishes; exotic decor; lunch specials. [$] *Average main: $18* ✉ *7 Wayne Dr., Midtown* ☎ *910/251–9229* 🌐 *www.indochinewilmington.com.*

★ Manna

$$$$ | MODERN AMERICAN | Sleek design, creative lighting, and carefully orchestrated music provide a mesmerizing backdrop to chef Carson Jewell's locally sourced ingredients and culinary artistry and the talented mixologists who create cocktails using seasonal ingredients and house-made bitters. Try the braised pork shank with sweet-potato puree, collards, and radish *pico de gallo,* or the pan-seared Virginia scallops with parsnip puree, braised leeks, and apple salsa. **Known for:** incredible desserts, like a deconstructed peanut butter cheesecake; creative, locally sourced dishes; impeccable service. *Average main: $30* *123 Princess St., Downtown* *910/763–5252* *mannaavenue.com* *Closed Mon.*

PinPoint Restaurant

$$$$ | **MODERN AMERICAN** | The sophisticated dining room delivers inventive new American dishes, crafted out of local ingredients and coastal catches. There are no wrong choices on the menu, from cornmeal-crusted North Carolina catfish to beef tartare, but the smoked trout with baked oysters is especially noteworthy. **Known for:** triggerfish with ramp bisque; polished farm-to-table experience; raw and baked oysters. *Average main: $30* *114 Market St., Downtown* *910/769–2972* *www.pinpointrestaurant.com.*

★ **Seabird**

$$$$ | **SEAFOOD** | On a prominent Market Street corner, chef Dean Neff's long-awaited seafood-and-cocktail lounge fully delivers, from the selection of local raw oysters to the impossibly buttery swordfish schnitzel, served with lemon jam and a mustard emulsion. The throwback style of the comfortable bar and small dining room invites leisurely meals, lubricated by addictive concoctions like the Hummingbird, made with local End of Days rum and honey-rhubarb simple syrup. **Known for:** a seafood tower, featuring seasonal catches like blue crab claws and littleneck clams; creative, delicious cocktails; wine and oyster pairings. *Average main: $28* *1 S. Front St., Downtown* *910/769–5996* *seabirdnc.com* *Closed Tues.*

Coffee and Quick Bites

Bespoke

$ | **BAKERY** | The drinks extend beyond coffee at this attractive, airy spot for a pick-me-up, from turmeric to matcha lattes, where the sign on the wall reads "Death Before Decaf." There's a small selection of scones and muffins and plenty of room—indoors and out—to kick back and work for a while. **Known for:** delicious iced drinks; quick service; creative skeleton-oriented branding and merchandise. *Average main: $5* *202 Princess St., Downtown* *910/769–4088* *bespokecoffeenc.com.*

Sealevel City Vegan Diner

$ | **VEGETARIAN** | The culinary creations here may be free of animal products, but they're certainly not lacking in flavor, from the addictive lentil burger patty melt to a kimchi tempeh Reuben that hits all the right notes. **Known for:** healthy, filling burgers and sandwiches; a towering plate of nachos; relaxed, courteous service. *Average main: $12* *1015 S. Kerr Ave., North Metro* *910/833–7196* *Closed Sun. and Mon.*

Hotels

C. W. Worth House B&B

$$ | **B&B/INN** | This 19th-century Queen Anne–style B&B, with fascinating turrets and period details, is a companionable sister to the family of architectural beauties in Wilmington's 230-block historic district, putting it within easy walking distance of the city's riverfront shopping and dining. **Pros:** enchanting courtyard and lawn; cozy bedrooms and suites with antique furnishings; innkeepers are welcoming and professional. **Cons:** no elevator; rooms do not have individual climate control; older carpets make some rooms feel dated. *Rooms from: $164* *412 S. 3rd St., Downtown* *910/762–8562* *www.worthhouse.com* *7 rooms* *Free breakfast.*

Embassy Suites by Hilton Wilmington Riverfront

$$$$ | **HOTEL** | Roomy suites at this riverfront chain by the Convention Center provide comfortable stays for business travelers and families alike. **Pros:** contemporary, roomy suites; free hot breakfast in the restaurant; convenient, central location. **Cons:** front desk and valet area gets congested, especially during conventions; self parking is $16; small indoor pool only. *Rooms from: $281 ✉ 9 Estell Lee Pl., Downtown ☎ 910/765–1131 🌐 www.embassysuiteswilmington.com 186 rooms 🍽 Free breakfast.*

Graystone Inn

$$ | **B&B/INN** | Even the name Graystone evokes an air of elegant sophistication, and entering this imposing 1905 mansion's stately formal areas and guest rooms feels like stepping back in time. **Pros:** luxurious lobby and elegant public spaces; hot breakfast served in the formal dining room; spacious, stately rooms. **Cons:** on a busy street with mostly street parking; TVs are old, and fireplaces are nonfunctional; no elevator. *Rooms from: $179 ✉ 100 S. 3rd St., Downtown ☎ 910/763–2000, 888/763–4773 🌐 www.graystoneinn.com 9 rooms 🍽 Free breakfast.*

★ Hotel Ballast

$$$ | **HOTEL** | The nine-story Hotel Ballast, part of Hilton's Tapestry Collection, aptly contains features of both a boutique hotel and a corporate chain. **Pros:** convenient to river, downtown restaurants, and shops; on-site Ruth's Chris Steak House; elegantly designed lobby, bar, and outdoor lounge. **Cons:** no complimentary breakfast; only some rooms have river views; crowded during events and weekends during wedding season. *Rooms from: $206 ✉ 301 N. Water St., Downtown ☎ 910/763–5900 🌐 www.hotelballast.com 272 rooms 🍽 No meals.*

★ The Verandas

$$ | **B&B/INN** | Built in 1853 in the Italianate style, the 8,500-square-foot Verandas underwent a full renovation in 2019 after damage from Hurricane Florence, bringing the beautiful mansion to its original glory with elegant and magnificent—but functional—furnishings. **Pros:** convenient location in historic district; lavishly furnished rooms; gourmet hot breakfasts. **Cons:** high percentage of returning guests can sometimes make availability scarce; no elevator; not appropriate for families with young children. *Rooms from: $179 ✉ 202 Nun St., Downtown ☎ 910/251–2212 🌐 www.verandasbedandbreakfast.com 8 rooms 🍽 Free breakfast.*

Performing Arts

North Carolina Jazz Festival

FESTIVALS | Since 1979, the North Carolina Jazz Festival has heated up a chilly early February weekend with nightly sets in the Hotel Ballast on the riverfront (special overnight rates for festival attendees). World-famous musicians perform in a variety of styles, including swing and Dixieland. *✉ Hotel Ballast, 301 N. Water St., Downtown ☎ 910/793–1111 🌐 www.ncjazzfestival.org.*

Thalian Hall Center for the Performing Arts

CONCERTS | A restored opera house in continuous use since 1858, Thalian Hall hosts dozens of theater, dance, stand-up comedy, cinema society, and musical performances each year. *✉ 310 Chestnut St., Downtown ☎ 910/632–2285 🌐 www.thalianhall.org.*

Shopping

Cotton Exchange

SHOPPING CENTERS/MALLS | **FAMILY** | Once the headquarters for the largest cotton exporter in the world, this historic warehouse complex now comprises a dense concentration of locally owned boutiques and restaurants—nearly 30 of them—in a rambling maze of courtyards and hallways. Clothing and footwear, arts and crafts, gourmet food supplies, books, and comics are all here. While you're here, check out the Wilmington Walk of Fame honoring local celebrities like David Brinkley, Michael Jordan, Charlie Daniels, Roman Gabriel, and nearly a dozen more. ✉ *321 N. Front St., Downtown* ☎ *910/343–9896* 🌐 *www.shopcottonexchange.com.*

Old Books on Front Street

BOOKS/STATIONERY | If you're intoxicated by the smell of well-worn books, you'll be addicted as soon as you step inside this store. Among its thousands of treasures are rare paperbacks, gently used cookbooks, and recent novels. Grab a coffee or a local beer from the small bar while you peruse the largest collection of African American literature in town and a huge selection of Judaica, plus theater books and movie and film scripts. The shop hosts events, such as a book club and literary walks. ✉ *249 N. Front St., Downtown* ☎ *910/762–6657* 🌐 *www.oldbooksonfrontstreet.com.*

Activities

BOATING

Cape Fear Riverboats

BOATING | **FAMILY** | This company runs a variety of cruises on three riverboats—*Captain J. N. Maffitt, Henrietta,* and *Jacob's Run*—from docks at Water and Dock Streets. There's a one-hour Wilmington riverfront tour and a four-hour Black River trip. Dinner tours are offered, as are private charters. ✉ *101 S. Water St., Downtown* ☎ *910/343–1611* 🌐 *www.cfrboats.com.*

GOLF

Beau Rivage Golf and Resort

GOLF | This public-access golf course includes its own resort, comprised of 900-square-foot villas overlooking the course. Against the backdrop of Cape Fear (visible from eight holes), the course changes elevation up to 75 feet, challenging players to dance with the wind for accurate placement. A well-equipped practice facility (driving range, chipping and putting area, sand bunkers, rough grass, and putting green) is among a nice group of amenities here. ✉ *649 Rivage Promenade, South Metro* ☎ *800/628–7080* 🌐 *www.beaurivagegolf.com* *$64–$69, 18 holes, 6709 yds, par 72.*

SCUBA DIVING

Aquatic Safaris

DIVING/SNORKELING | Wrecks, such as the World War II oil tanker *John D. Gill,* sunk by Germans in 1942, make for exciting scuba diving off the Cape Fear Coast. Aquatic Safaris has charter trips to about 30 wrecks and other dive sites on two dive boats. Charters cost $55 to $170 per person and take place between May and October when the water is warmer. ✉ *7220 Wrightsville Ave., Suite A, North Metro* ☎ *910/392–4386* 🌐 *www.aquaticsafaris.com.*

Wrightsville Beach

12 miles east of Wilmington.

A short drive from Wilmington, Wrightsville Beach is a good day-trip destination. This is a small (5-mile-long), partly upscale, and quiet island community.

GETTING HERE AND AROUND

U.S. Route 74/76 (Eastwood Drive) is the only road access to this small, friendly enclave. In town you can walk and bike or boat on the intracoastal waterway.

VISITOR INFORMATION

CONTACTS Wrightsville Beach Visitor Center. ✉ *305 Salisbury St.* ☎ *910/341–4030* 🌐 *www.wilmingtonandbeaches.com.*

Beaches

Wrightsville Beach

BEACH—SIGHT | FAMILY | Clean, wide beaches here provide the setting for all sorts of water sports. Surfers dominate the sunrise waves at Crystal Pier. Kayakers, parasailers, paddleboarders, bodyboarders, and windsurfers all share the waters here while shoreline runners and walkers hit the sand, which is also perfect for sandcastle building and people-watching. **Amenities:** food and drink; lifeguards (Memorial Day to Labor Day); parking (fee); toilets. **Best for:** surfing; swimming. *N. Lumina Ave.* *Take U.S. 76 (Causeway Dr.) to N. Lumina Ave. and turn left or right to find parking* *www.townofwrightsvillebeach.com* *Free (fee for most parking Mar.–Oct.).*

Restaurants

Ceviche's

$$ | LATIN AMERICAN | Panamanian-inspired food is the focus of this lively rum bar and restaurant just across the bridge from the beach. The eponymous ceviches—traditional Panamanian corvina, lobster, and tuna "cooked" in lime juice—are all wonderful, but *ropa vieja* (flank steak served over coconut rice) and blackened tuna are tasty, too. **Known for:** flavorful empanadas and tacos; four house ceviche blends; big selection of high-quality rum drinks. *Average main: $17* *7210 Wrightsville Ave., Wilmington* *910/256–3131* *www.wbceviche.com* *Closed Sun.*

Oceanic

$$$ | SEAFOOD | At Crystal Pier, this casual fine-dining destination lets you indulge in entrées like crab-stuffed salmon or a platter of Calabash seafood while sitting directly over the sand and surf. Sunday brunch—when specialties like crab and wild mushroom hash make their appearance—is particularly popular. **Known for:** Carolina crab dip; upscale but reasonably priced seafood; stunning location with outdoor seating directly on the ocean. *Average main: $24* *703 S. Lumina Ave.* *910/256–5551* *oceanicrestaurant.com.*

Coffee and Quick Bites

The Workshop

$ | BAKERY | The owner of this coffee, smoothie, and sandwich shop is a scuba diver and fossil hunter, and the bustling counter-service operation doubles as a gallery for her shark and megalodon jewelry and art. Most of the seating is outside at picnic tables. **Known for:** cold-brew coffee with coconut water; turmeric smoothies; toasted baguette sandwiches. *Average main: $8* *86 Waynick Blvd.* *910/679–8605* *theworkshopwb.com.*

Hotels

Blockade Runner

$$$$ | RESORT | FAMILY | The seven-story, 1960s-vintage Blockade Runner is pure class, from the large, modern rooms (upper floors have terrific ocean views) to the sparkling lobby, where cool blue drapes create the feel of waves all around you. **Pros:** prime beachfront location; remodeled, attractive rooms, many with balconies and beach views; gorgeous lawn and communal areas. **Cons:** unpretentious 1960s-era exterior; hotel can't run a/c and heat at the same time, so if you come during a winter hot spell, ask for a fan; parking is $10 and the lot is very tight for larger vehicles. *Rooms from: $335* *275 Waynick Blvd.* *877/684–8009* *www.blockade-runner.com* *165 rooms* *No meals.*

Holiday Inn Resort

$$$$ | RESORT | FAMILY | This reliable, seven-story mainstay sports a top beachfront location and a stellar and attentive staff, plus spacious rooms with fridges and microwaves. **Pros:** two pools, including a heated indoor pool; great views from higher-story rooms on ocean side; kids eat free at the on-site restaurant, OCEANS. **Cons:** a few rooms don't have balconies, and only half have ocean views; $7 charge for parking; breakfast not included in room rate. *Rooms from: $322 ✉ 1706 N. Lumina Ave. ☎ 910/256–2231 🌐 ihg.com 184 rooms No meals.*

Kure Beach

17 miles southwest of Wrightsville Beach; 21 miles southwest of Wilmington.

A resort community on a strip of sand locals know as Pleasure Island, Kure Beach is home to Fort Fisher State Historic Site, a 712-foot fishing pier, and one of North Carolina's three aquariums. At the southern end of the beach, twisted live oaks still grow behind the dunes. The community has miles of beaches; public access points are marked by orange-and-blue signs.

GETTING HERE AND AROUND

Drive to Kure Beach on U.S. Route 421 or take the ferry from North Carolina Highway 211 in Southport. Once at the beach, you'll want a car to get up and down the island, although some people walk and bike along the narrow, main highway.

VISITOR INFORMATION

CONTACTS Pleasure Island Visitor Center. *✉ 1121 N. Lake Park Blvd., Suite B, Carolina Beach ☎ 910/458–8434 🌐 www.pleasureislandnc.org.*

Sights

★ Fort Fisher State Historic Site

MILITARY SITE | FAMILY | This is one of the South's largest and most important earthworks fortifications from the Civil War, so tough and strategically placed along the Cape Fear River that it was known as the Southern Gibraltar. The fall of the fort in January 1865, closing the last supply lines for the South, helped seal the fate of the Confederacy. You can explore the restored battery with its reconstructed artillery and follow trails along the river. Inside, displays range from Civil War relics and a fiber-optic battle map to artifacts from sunken blockade runners. It's also known for its underwater archaeology sites. **■ TIP→ Fort Fisher also includes a beach access point with showers. It's one of the most attractive beaches in the area.** *✉ 1610 Fort Fisher Blvd., Kure Beach ☎ 910/251–7340 🌐 historicsites.nc.gov/all-sites/fort-fisher Free ⊙ Closed Sun. and Mon.*

North Carolina Aquarium at Fort Fisher

ZOO | FAMILY | This small but beautiful oceanfront aquarium features a 235,000-gallon saltwater tank that's home to sharks, stingrays, and a Goliath grouper and green moray eel. There's a touch tank with rays, a room of glowing jellyfish, an albino alligator, and turtle ponds. Kids love the life-size replica of a megalodon shark, complete with fossilized teeth found in North Carolina, and enjoy the daily feeding times and animal encounters. In the Butterfly Bungalow you can wander among hundreds of colorful free-flying butterflies. *✉ 900 Loggerhead Rd., Kure Beach ☎ 910/772–0500 🌐 www.ncaquariums.com $13.*

Southport/Fort Fisher Ferry

TRANSPORTATION SITE (AIRPORT/BUS/FERRY/TRAIN) | If you're approaching the town from Kure Beach and Fort Fisher via U.S. Route 421, the state-operated year-round car ferry provides a 35-minute Cape Fear River ride between Old Federal Point at the tip of the spit and the mainland. **Bald Head Lighthouse** on Bald Head Island is seen en route, as well as the **Oak Island Lighthouse** and the ruins of **Price's Creek Lighthouse**—in fact, this is the only point in the United States where you can see three lighthouses at the same time. It's best to arrive early (30 minutes before ferry departure), as it's first come, first served. During peak season, there are 16 scheduled ferries each day. *✉ 2422 S. Fort Fisher Blvd., Kure Beach*

☎ 800/368–8969 ferry information and reservations *$7 per car, one way.*

Beaches

Carolina Beach

BEACH—SIGHT | FAMILY | With ice cream cones, flashing arcade lights, seashell souvenirs, and paddleboats on the small inland lake, Carolina Beach's old-fashioned boardwalk is steeped in nostalgic charm, most evident at **Britts Donut Shop,** an institution since 1939 that still sells its glazed beauties for an even buck. **Amenities:** food and drink; lifeguards; parking (fee); toilets. **Best for:** sunrise; windsurfing. ✉ *U.S. 421, off U.S. 17, Carolina Beach* 🌐 *carolina-beach.wilmingtonandbeaches.com* *Free.*

★ Kure Beach

BEACH—SIGHT | FAMILY | Family memories are made here on tall ocean piers where kids reel in their first big catches. You can swim, beachcomb, kiteboard over the big blue sea, or scuba dive down to find some of the Cape Fear Coast's dozens of shipwrecks. Wildlife excursions set off from various nature trails, birding sites, and miles of undeveloped beach at the southern end. Shorebirds and loggerhead sea turtles inhabit the remote reserve of Zeke's Island. At Fort Fisher, the Confederacy's largest earthen fort, you can track Kure Beach's history. **Amenities:** food and drink; lifeguards (generally Memorial Day to Labor Day); parking (mostly no fee). **Best for:** sunrise; sunset; surfing; swimming; windsurfing. ✉ *U.S. 421, off U.S. 17, Kure Beach* 🌐 *kure-beach.wilmingtonandbeaches.com* *Free.*

Restaurants

COAST Craft Cocktails & Calabash

$$$ | SEAFOOD | In 2021, the popular Surf House rebranded into this laid-back spot for tasty cocktails, inviting seafood-leaning small plates, and the most upscale fried seafood platter in town. White shiplap, rustic wood accents, and surfboards keep the beach vibe rolling, even though it's in a small shopping center on the island's main drag. **Known for:** mini lobster rolls; Calabash-style fried seafood; thoughtful cocktails. *Average main: $22* ✉ *604 N. Lake Park Blvd., Carolina Beach* ☎ *910/707–0422* 🌐 *eatatcoast.com* *Closed Sun. and Mon.*

Freddie's Restaurant

$$ | ITALIAN | Dining at this family-run Italian joint—steps from the beach but in dark-wood-laden environs that feel like a haunt from *The Sopranos*—is an experience, but to enjoy the hearty pastas, lasagna, and pork chops without a wait, arrive early. **Known for:** massive center-cut pork chop; martinis; classic atmosphere, with a lively bar sharing space in the tiny dining room. *Average main: $18* ✉ *105 K Ave., Kure Beach* ☎ *910/458–5979* 🌐 *freddiesitalianrestaurant.com* *Closed Sun.*

Hotels

The Kure Lighthouse Inn

$$$$ | B&B/INN | The bright and spacious suites at this oceanfront inn feature wide private balconies, letting you idle close to home and soak in the view all day long. **Pros:** modern, luxurious rooms; walkable to restaurants; back porch patio and firepit. **Cons:** limited communal space; no pool; ground-floor room lacks the views of the others. *Rooms from: $359* ✉ *329 Atlantic Ave., Kure Beach* ☎ *910/444–4734* 🌐 *kurelighthouseinn.com* *9 suites* *No meals.*

Southport

10 miles southwest of Kure Beach; 30 miles south of Wilmington.

This small town, quietly positioned at the mouth of the Cape Fear River, is listed on the National Register of Historic Places. An increasingly desirable retirement spot, Southport retains its village charm and front-porch hospitality.

GETTING HERE AND AROUND

From U.S. Route 17, North Carolina Highways 211 and 133 both land in Southport. A state-operated car ferry arrives every 45 minutes from Kure Beach to the north. Once downtown, you can park your car and walk or bike throughout the waterfront area. Commercial airports are located at nearby Wilmington and Myrtle Beach, South Carolina.

VISITOR INFORMATION

CONTACTS Fort Johnston–Southport Museum and Visitor Center. ✉ *203 E. Bay St.* ✣ *Behind NC Maritime Museum* ☎ *910/457–7927* 🌐 *www.cityofsouthport.com.*

Brunswick Town/Fort Anderson State Historic Site

ARCHAEOLOGICAL SITE | FAMILY | About 10 miles north of Southport, you can explore the ruins and excavations of a colonial town and see the Civil War earthworks of Fort Anderson. The visitor center has a video presentation and a museum of historical items found at the site. Living-history events with costumed interpreters range from Civil War reenactments to colonial-era cooking demonstrations. It's also a great spot for a picnic. ✉ *8884 St. Phillip's Rd. SE, Winnabow* ✣ *Off NC 133* ☎ *910/371–6613* 🌐 *historicsites.nc.gov/all-sites/brunswick-town-fort-anderson* *Free* *Closed Sun. and Mon.*

Provision Company

$$ | SEAFOOD | FAMILY | This laid-back, colorful joint right on the water is the place to enjoy the day's catch with zero pretension, prepared to simple perfection, from steamed local shrimp and clams to a 10-ounce yellowfin tuna steak. **Known for:** grouper salad; peel-and-eat shrimp; waterfront dining. $ *Average main: $17* ✉ *130 Yacht Basin Dr.* ☎ *910/457–0654* 🌐 *provisioncompany.com.*

Trolly Stop

$ | FAST FOOD | FAMILY | An institution in the Cape Fear region (there are also locations in Wrightsville Beach and Wilmington, as well as inland in Chapel Hill), this hot dog joint is known for various wieners, all with individual names. You have a choice of five kinds of hot dogs, including vegetarian, with 13 choices of toppings. **Known for:** big variety of hot dogs and toppings; casual eating on picnic tables; local favorite since 1976. $ *Average main: $6* ✉ *111 S. Howe St.* ☎ *910/457–7017* 🌐 *www.trollystophotdogs.com* *No credit cards.*

★ Bald Head Island

$$$$ | RESORT | FAMILY | Reached by ferry from Southport, this beautiful 12,000-acre island resort is a self-contained, car-free community, complete with a grocery store, restaurants (Jules' Salty Grub, on the harbor, and AQUA, at the Shoals Club, are highlights), marina, a 50-room hotel, a 13-room B&B, two club complexes with restaurants and pools, and the gorgeous 18-hole George Cobb golf course. **Pros:** vast beaches all to yourself; resort amenities and restaurants when you need a touch of civilization; no cars allowed on island. **Cons:** island is accessible only by ferry; pricey; activities at the island's recreation clubs are not available to all accommodations. $ *Rooms from: $300* ✉ *Bald Head Island* ☎ *844/833–6320, 910/457–5003 for ferry reservations* 🌐 *www.baldheadisland.com* *$85–$195 for guest members with golf privileges, 18 holes, 6823 yds, par 72; guest club membership fees for those staying on island start at $125 per week* *63 rooms, 200 units* *No meals.*

Chapter 4

CENTRAL NORTH CAROLINA

4

Updated by
Stratton Lawrence

Sights
★★★★☆

Restaurants
★★★★★

Hotels
★★★★★

Shopping
★★☆☆☆

Nightlife
★★★☆☆

WELCOME TO CENTRAL NORTH CAROLINA

TOP REASONS TO GO

★ **Raleigh museums:** More than a dozen museums and historical sites—several within an easy walk of one another—cover every aspect of North Carolina life, from its prehistoric roots to its arts achievements and sports heroes.

★ **Old Salem:** Costumed guides fill this restored village in the heart of Winston-Salem, founded by the Moravian sect in the mid-18th century.

★ **Sports and recreation:** College basketball is serious business in these parts. You'll also find some of the best golf courses in the Southeast and abundant opportunities to get out and enjoy the Piedmont's lakes, rivers, and lovely landscapes.

★ **Wineries:** North Carolina has over 200 wineries, and many of the finest are in the Piedmont. Sample a few fine vintages in their tasting rooms.

North Carolina's dramatic mountains and beaches tend to overshadow the state's central regions. However, visitors who take the time to experience the woodlands and hills that grace the heart of the state will find themselves enchanted by the same sturdy beauty that has nurtured generations of intellectuals and artists, from early-20th-century wit O. Henry to the modern humorist David Sedaris.

1 **Raleigh.** Something new and hip is always on the horizon, yet the old-world charm of the capital city remains.

2 **Durham.** People know Durham as "Bull City" for the tobacco industry that once dominated here.

3 **Chapel Hill.** Centered around the University of North Carolina, the nation's first public university, Chapel Hill is a college town through and through. In spite of growing into a city of close to 60,000, it retains that small-town feel that truly makes it a special place.

4 **Greensboro.** The third-largest city in North Carolina, Greensboro has a long and rich history as a center of commerce.

5 **Winston-Salem.** Winston-Salem is literally a tale of two cities that merged in the early 20th century.

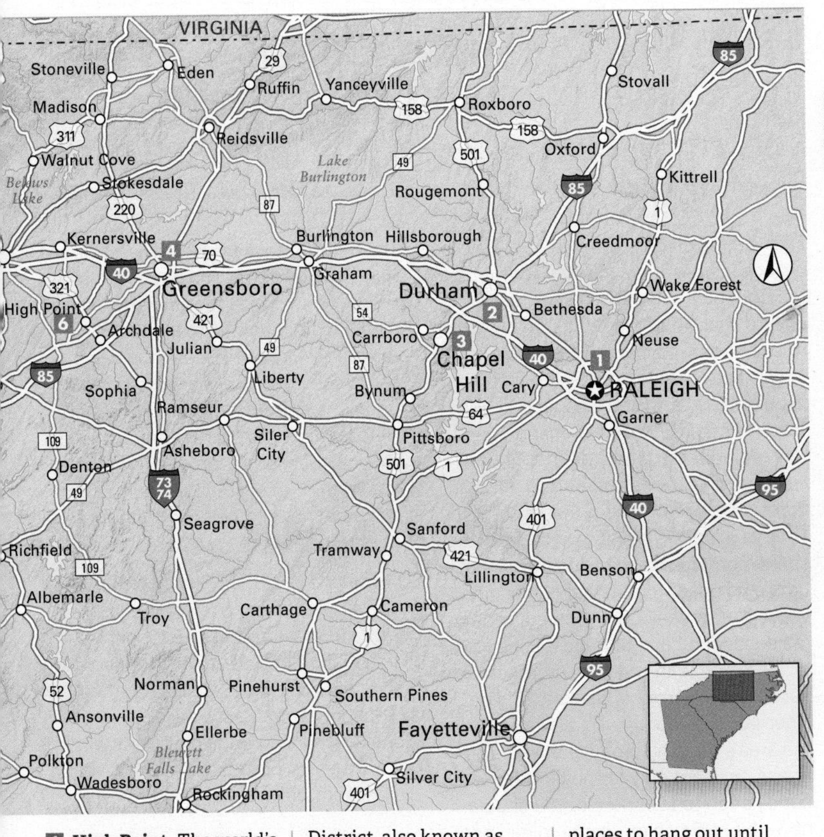

6 High Point. The world's largest furnishings industry trade show happens here each spring and fall.

7 Charlotte. There are many facets to the city of Charlotte. The business and cultural center, Uptown, is bustling during the week and a little quieter on the weekends, except for when there's a big show or game in town. The North Davidson Arts District, also known as NoDa, is Charlotte's artsy enclave. It's where you can explore art galleries or catch an acoustic live-music show. Another area to explore is Plaza Midwood. Once a streetcar suburb of Charlotte, Plaza Midwood is where you'll find vibrant street art, funky vintage shops, locally made artisan goods, comfort-food eateries, low-key dive bars, and places to hang out until the wee hours of the morning. And the area known as Greater Charlotte has numerous offerings in which to enjoy nature. The rolling hills outside the city are filled with golf courses, nature preserves, and outdoor recreation opportunities galore, including the U.S. National Whitewater Center.

While visiting the Piedmont, it's easy to forget what state you're in. Though it's in the geographic center of North Carolina, this collection of growing urban areas and college towns is like nothing else in the Tar Heel State—or the Southeast.

This is a region on the move, where change is constant and often for the better. Continual evolution keeps the local culture vital. The Piedmont's gently rolling hills are home to North Carolina's three major metropolitan areas—the Triangle (Raleigh, Durham, and Chapel Hill), the Triad (Winston-Salem, Greensboro, and High Point), and Charlotte. Though their histories differ, these sprawling population clusters now have much in common. They're full of big-city highlights like huge sports complexes, sparkling new museums, and upscale restaurants. Hip, innovative elements abound, fueled by new residents combining the best aspects of the South with modern, progressive sensibilities. Farmers' markets, indie cinemas, and monthly art walks show off the area's growing creative scene. The transition is not only fascinating to watch but also fun to take part in. You should never be at a loss for things to eat, see, or do.

MAJOR REGIONS

The Triangle: Raleigh, Durham, and Chapel Hill. The region is home to North Carolina State University, Duke University, and the University of North Carolina at Chapel Hill, so life in the Triangle revolves around basketball and higher education. Leafy campuses offer architectural delights, and the surrounding communities reflect the universities' progressive spirits with a vibrant farm-to-table food scene and a passion for learning and the arts.

The Triad: Greensboro, Winston-Salem, and High Point. The past and present fuse in fascinating ways in these vastly different cities. History comes to life in the restored Moravian village of Old Salem, and twice a year the furniture-making traditions of the Piedmont thrive at the High Point Market, a home furnishings show. Greensboro, famous for its role in the fight for desegregation half a century ago, continues to be one of the most diverse cities in the state.

Charlotte. The Queen City's contemporary facade dazzles, and its skyline gleams with the most impressive modern architecture in the region. Alongside fans cheering the NFL's Carolina Panthers and partiers hitting the city's sleek nightspots, you'll find traditional Southern hospitality and a lot of good eating inspired by regions around the world.

Planning

When to Go

North Carolina's central region shines particularly in spring (April and May) and fall (September and October), when the weather is most temperate and the trees and flowers burst with color.

Planning Your Time

Because the areas within the Piedmont are fairly compact, it makes sense to tackle them one at a time. Downtown Raleigh, with its expanding array of restaurants and hotels, makes a good base for exploring Durham and Chapel Hill on day trips. Take on Charlotte and the Triad separately. In Charlotte, Uptown is centrally located and provides plenty of entertainment, dining, and lodging within walking distance.

Getting Here and Around

AIR TRAVEL

The Raleigh-Durham International Airport (RDU), off Interstate 40 between the two cities, is served by most major airlines. Uber and Lyft each operate at RDU.

Charlotte-Douglas International Airport (CLT), served by most major airlines, is west of Charlotte off Interstate 85. From the airport, taxis charge a set fee of $25 to Uptown and surrounding neighborhoods (plus a $2.50 drop charge) and most destinations in Charlotte. Just west of Greensboro, the Piedmont Triad International Airport (GSO) is off North Carolina Highway 68 north from Interstate 40; it's served by Allegiant, American Airlines, Delta, Spirit, and United. Rideshare and taxi service to and from GSO are provided by Uber, Lyft, and Yellow United Taxi.

AIR CONTACTS Charlotte-Douglas International Airport. (*CLT*) ✉ *5501 Josh Birmingham Pkwy., Airport/Coliseum* ☎ *704/359–4013* 🌐 *www.cltairport.com.* **Piedmont Triad International Airport.** (*GSO*) ✉ *1000 Ted Johnson Pkwy., Greensboro* ☎ *336/665–5600* 🌐 *www.flyfrompti.com.* **Raleigh-Durham International Airport.** (*RDU*) ✉ *2400 John Brantley Blvd., Morrisville* ☎ *919/840–2123* 🌐 *www.rdu.com.*

BUS TRAVEL

GoRaleigh is Raleigh's public transport system, Chapel Hill Transit serves Chapel Hill and Carrboro, and GoDurham is Durham's intracity bus system. The fares are $1.25 for Raleigh and $1 for Durham. Chapel Hill Transit is free. Downtown Raleigh also has a free circulator bus route called the R-LINE.

GoTriangle, which links downtown Raleigh with Cary, Research Triangle Park, Durham, Chapel Hill, and the airport, runs weekdays except major holidays. Rates start at $2.25.

BUS CONTACTS Chapel Hill Transit. ☎ *919/969–4908* 🌐 *www.chtransit.org.* **GoDurham.** ☎ *919/485–7433* 🌐 *www.godurhamtransit.org.* **GoRaleigh.** ☎ *919/485–7433* 🌐 *www.goraleigh.org.* **GoTriangle.** ☎ *919/485–7433* 🌐 *www.gotriangle.org.*

CAR TRAVEL

Although it's possible to use buses and trains for travel within the Piedmont, they're usually not convenient or quick. Interstates 40, 85, and 77, as well as several state highways, offer easy access to most of the region's destinations. Traffic is an issue in the metropolitan areas during morning and evening rush hours, but this is hardly D.C. or L.A.

TAXI TRAVEL

Taxis and airport vans service all the area towns and airports and are an alternative to renting a car if you don't plan on doing a lot of sightseeing. Rideshare services, such as Uber and Lyft, also operate in the larger towns throughout the region.

TAXI CONTACTS Crown Cab. ✉ *1541 St. George St., Charlotte* ☎ *704/334–6666* 🌐 *www.crowncabinc.com.* **Durham's Best Cab.** ✉ *1005 W. Chapel Hill St., Durham* ☎ *919/680–3330* 🌐 *www.durhamtaxi.com.* **Yellow United Taxi.** ✉ *801 S. Elm St., Greensboro* ☎ *336/273–9421* 🌐 *yellowunitedtaxi.com.*

TRAIN TRAVEL

From Charlotte there's daily service to Washington, D.C., Atlanta, and points beyond, as well as daily service to the Triangle cities of Raleigh, Durham, and Cary. In Greensboro, Amtrak's *Crescent* stops in before continuing from New York to New Orleans (or vice versa). And the *Carolinian* also stops in Greensboro as it goes from Charlotte to Raleigh and then north to Baltimore, Washington, and New York. The in-state *Piedmont* connects nine cities—including Greensboro—between Raleigh and Charlotte each day.

TRAIN CONTACTS Amtrak. ☏ *800/872–7245* 🌐 *www.amtrak.com.*

Restaurants

In the Piedmont it's almost as easy to grab a bagel, empanada, or spanakopita as it is to grab a biscuit. That said, the region is still dominated by barbecue: wood-fired, pit-cooked, chopped, or sliced pork traditionally served with coleslaw and hush puppies. Southern specialties, such as catfish, fried green tomatoes, grits, collard greens, fried chicken, sweet potatoes, and pecan pie, are also favorites. *Dining reviews have been shortened. For full information, visit Fodors.com.*

Hotels

It's not usually a problem to find a place to stay in one of the Piedmont's resorts, bed-and-breakfasts, motels, or hotels. But during the High Point Market, a home-furnishings show held in spring and fall, tens of thousands of people descend on the area, making rooms almost impossible to find. May is graduation time for the region's colleges and universities. If you're planning on visiting central North Carolina during these peak times, book accommodations well in advance. **■ TIP→ Because many of the cities in the Piedmont are destinations for business travelers, hotel rates are often much higher during the week than over the weekend. You can also expect lots of up-charges in fancier business-oriented hotels for such things as breakfast, parking, and Internet fees.** *Hotel reviews have been shortened. For full information, visit Fodors.com.*

What It Costs

	$	$$	$$$	$$$$
RESTAURANTS				
	under $15	$15–$19	$20–$24	over $24
HOTELS				
	under $150	$150–$200	$201–$250	over $250

Restaurant prices are the average cost of a main course at dinner or, if dinner is not served, at lunch. Hotel prices are the lowest cost of a standard double room in high season.

Raleigh

85 miles east of Greensboro; 160 miles northeast of Charlotte.

For a state capital, Raleigh is surprisingly approachable. The hilly but very walkable downtown, smaller than you might think, is not only home to a multitude of government buildings but also to many friendly pubs and cafés. The shaded parks and the quiet Historic Oakwood District nearby add to the city's comfortable feel. Raleigh has both a sense of history and a cutting-edge coolness (that contributes to the constant hum of new apartment high-rise construction). Home to 11 universities and colleges, this bustling, modern city is a great place to get your fill of urban living (and some great food). Take in a play, visit a museum, and stroll along the wide city streets filled with tall and impressive buildings. When you finally feel the need to connect with nature once more, do as the locals do and grab your running shoes or bike and hit the Capital Area Greenway, Raleigh's well-loved series of trails, more than 68 miles in length and still growing.

GETTING HERE AND AROUND

Like Washington, D.C., Raleigh has a highway that loops around the city. Interstate 440, previously called the "Inner Beltline" and "Outer Beltline," circles Raleigh before meeting Interstate 40 to the south of the city.

If you come by train or bus, you'll step off in Raleigh's Warehouse District, a developing area of cool clubs and restaurants a few blocks west of downtown. RDU is a 25-minute cab ride, depending on rush-hour traffic, from downtown. Buses and taxis serve all parts of the city, including the suburbs. The city has its own private bike-share network, called Citrix, with bicycles and kiosks on corners all over downtown. **■ TIP→ This is the easiest city in the Triangle to get around without a car. Not having your own transportation will make exploration outside the city a pain, however.**

TOURS

Historic Raleigh Trolley Tours

GUIDED TOURS | Board one of this company's trolleys for a narrated hour-long tour of historic Raleigh. Tours depart from Moore Square on Thursdays and Fridays, and from Mordecai Historic Park on Saturdays. Sites include the State Capitol Bicentennial Plaza, the Joel Lane House, and City Market. ✉ *Downtown* ☎ *919/996–4364* 🌐 *raleighnc.gov* 🎫 *$10.*

VISITOR INFORMATION

CONTACTS Raleigh Visitor Information Center. ✉ *500 Fayetteville St., Downtown* ☎ *919/834–5900* 🌐 *www.visitraleigh.com.*

Sights

Artspace

ARTS VENUE | A nonprofit visual-arts center, Artspace offers open studios, where artists are happy to talk to you about their work. The gift shop showcases the work of the resident artists. **■ TIP→ The place bustles with visitors during the seasonal Stroll & Roll art walks, when galleries and museums throughout the city host public receptions to show off new work.** ✉ *201 E. Davie St., Downtown* ☎ *919/821–2787* 🌐 *www.artspacenc.org* 🎫 *$5 suggested donation* ⏲ *Closed Sun. and Mon.*

Executive Mansion

GARDEN | Since 1891, this 37,500-square-foot brick Queen Anne–style structure, made entirely from materials from the Tar Heel State, with elaborate gingerbread trim and manicured lawns, has been the home of the state's governors. Encompassing an entire city block, the brick-walled gardens explode with color during the spring. Reservations for tours must be made at least two weeks in advance. ✉ *200 N. Blount St., Downtown* ☎ *919/715–3962* 🌐 *nccapvisit.org* 🎫 *Free.*

JC Raulston Arboretum at North Carolina State University

GARDEN | The university's working, research, and teaching 10-acre garden holds the most diverse collection of hardy temperate-zone plants in the southeastern United States. There's also a garden featuring plants with white flowers and foliage and a 300-foot-long perennial border. ✉ *4415 Beryl Rd., University* ☎ *919/515–3132* 🌐 *jcra.ncsu.edu/* ⏲ *Closed weekends.*

Joel Lane Museum House

GARDEN | Dating to 1769, the oldest dwelling in Raleigh was the home of Joel Lane, known as the "Father of Raleigh" because he sold 1,000 acres of his property to the state of North Carolina on which the beginnings of the capital city were built. Costumed docents lead tours

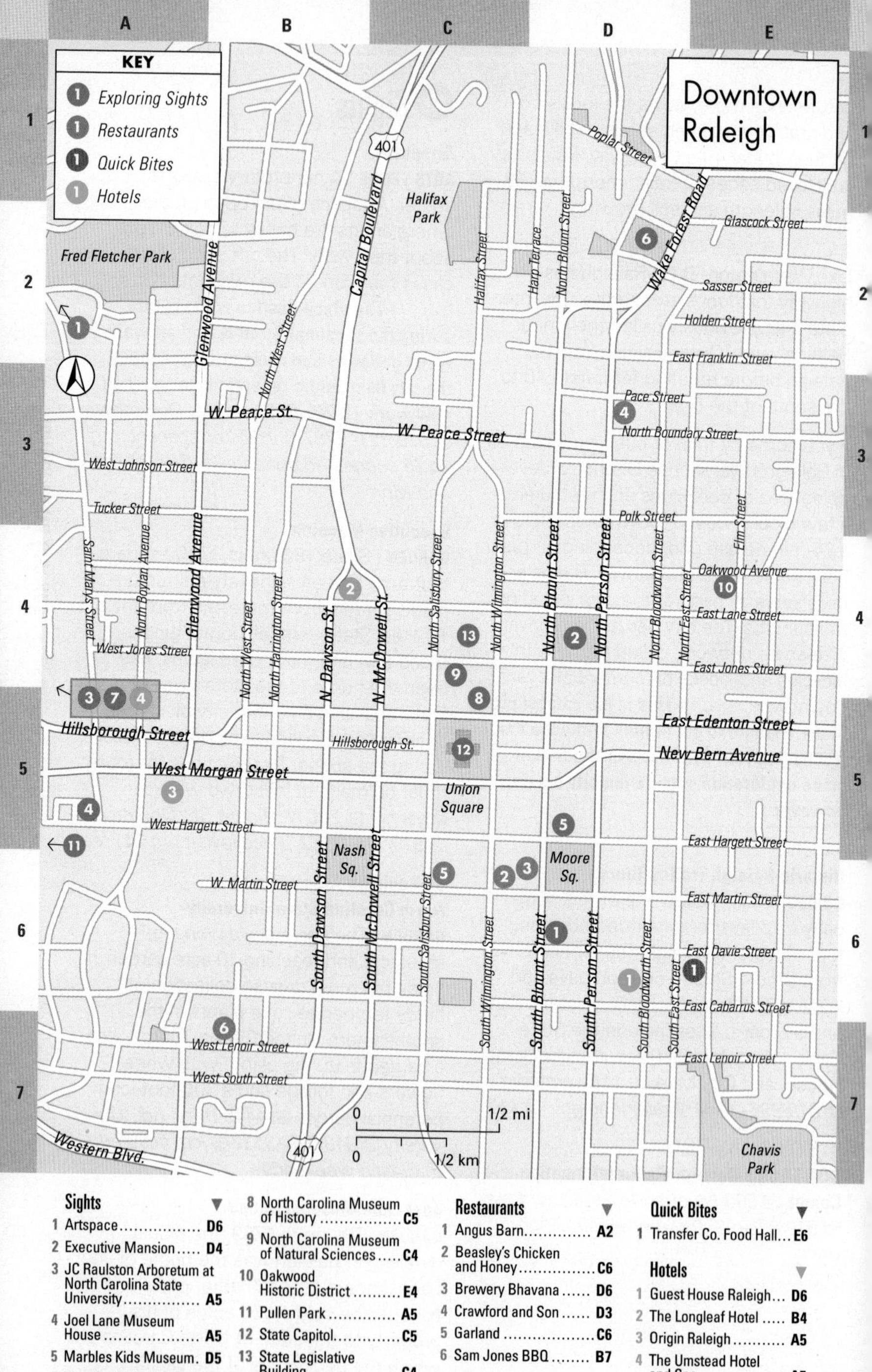

Sights

1 Artspace **D6**
2 Executive Mansion **D4**
3 JC Raulston Arboretum at North Carolina State University **A5**
4 Joel Lane Museum House **A5**
5 Marbles Kids Museum. **D5**
6 Mordecai Historic Park **D2**
7 North Carolina Museum of Art (NCMA) **A5**
8 North Carolina Museum of History **C5**
9 North Carolina Museum of Natural Sciences **C4**
10 Oakwood Historic District **E4**
11 Pullen Park **A5**
12 State Capitol **C5**
13 State Legislative Building **C4**

Restaurants

1 Angus Barn **A2**
2 Beasley's Chicken and Honey **C6**
3 Brewery Bhavana **D6**
4 Crawford and Son **D3**
5 Garland **C6**
6 Sam Jones BBQ **B7**

Quick Bites

1 Transfer Co. Food Hall... **E6**

Hotels

1 Guest House Raleigh... **D6**
2 The Longleaf Hotel **B4**
3 Origin Raleigh **A5**
4 The Umstead Hotel and Spa **A5**

of the restored house and beautiful period gardens. The last tour starts an hour before closing: 1 pm Wednesday through Friday, and 3 on Saturday. ✉ *160 S. St. Mary's St., Downtown* ☎ *919/833–3431* 🌐 *www.joellane.org* 🎫 *$8* ⏲ *Closed Sun.–Tues.*

Marbles Kids Museum

MUSEUM | FAMILY | This 84,000-square-foot cathedral of play and learning is aimed at children 10 and younger. Everything is hands-on, so your child is free to fill a shopping cart in the marketplace, don a fireman's hat, clamber through the cab of a city bus, scale the crow's nest of a three-story pirate ship, or splash in numerous water stations. Older children can play chess with 2-foot pawns, perform simple science experiments, or learn about the value of cash at the *Moneypalooza* exhibit. Toddler Hollow, designed with an enchanted forest in mind, is meant for kids under two. The space's wide-open design and its architectural details, including a suspension bridge and a courtyard with a 6-foot marble fountain, give adults something to look at as well. There's also an IMAX theater. ✉ *201 E. Hargett St., Downtown* ☎ *919/834–4040* 🌐 *www.marbleskidsmuseum.org* 🎫 *Museum $9, museum and IMAX $7–$12* ⏲ *Closed Mon. and Tues.*

Mordecai Historic Park

GARDEN | This 3-acre downtown historic site dating to 1785 includes President Andrew Johnson's birthplace and the Mordecai family's Greek revival plantation home. Moses Mordecai, a well-respected lawyer, married two granddaughters of Joel Lane, the "Father of Raleigh." Mordecai's descendants lived in the house until 1964. Exhibits acknowledge the struggle of the enslaved people who once toiled here. There are guided tours hourly from 10 to 3. ■ **TIP→ The historical figure's name is pronounced MOR-de-key. Using a long "i" will mark you as a newcomer immediately.** ✉ *1 Mimosa St., Downtown* ✣ *At Wake Forest Rd.* ☎ *919/996–4364* 🌐 *www.raleighnc.gov/mordecai* 🎫 *Free, guided tours $7* ⏲ *Visitor center closed Mon.*

★ North Carolina Museum of Art (NCMA)

GARDEN | On the west side of Raleigh, the NCMA houses more than 5,000 years of artistic heritage, including one of the nation's largest collections of Jewish ceremonial art. The museum hosts touring exhibitions of works by such artists as Caravaggio and Rodin. There are gallery tours offered daily, and on Saturdays at 10:30 you can catch a guided tour of the surrounding park. The 164-acre park features nine monumental works of art, which visitors can view on foot or by bike. ✉ *2110 Blue Ridge Rd., North Raleigh* ☎ *919/839–6262* 🌐 *ncartmuseum.org* 🎫 *Free* ⏲ *Closed Mon. and Tues.*

North Carolina Museum of History

MUSEUM | FAMILY | Founded in 1902, this Smithsonian-affiliated museum is now in a state-of-the-art facility on Bicentennial Plaza. Its signature exhibit, *The Story of North Carolina*, traces over 14,000 years of the state's history. The museum also houses the North Carolina Sports Hall of Fame, which displays memorabilia from hundreds of inductees, from college heroes to pro superstars and Olympic contenders. You can see Richard Petty's race car, Arnold Palmer's Ryder Cup golf bag, and Harlem Globetrotter Meadowlark Lemon's uniforms. Even if your time is short, it's worth popping in to admire the wall-sized oil paintings of the state's most beautiful natural vistas. ✉ *5 E. Edenton St., Downtown* ☎ *919/814–7000* 🌐 *www.ncmuseumofhistory.org* 🎫 *Free.*

★ North Carolina Museum of Natural Sciences

ARCHAEOLOGICAL SITE | FAMILY | With seven floors of immersive exhibits spread across two buildings connected via sky bridge, this museum is the largest of its kind in the Southeast. Exhibits and dioramas celebrate the incredible diversity of species in the state's various regions. There are enough live animals and insects—including butterflies, snakes, and a two-toed sloth—to qualify as a mid-size zoo. Massive and rare whale skeletons hang from the ceiling. The pièce de résistance, however, is the *Terror of the South* exhibit, featuring the dinosaur skeleton of "Acro," a giant carnivore that lived in the region 110 million years ago. The impressive bones are the world's most complete Acrocanthosaurus dinosaur skeleton. In the Nature Research Center, visitors can have live conversations with scientists. ✉ *11 W. Jones St., Downtown* ☎ *919/707–9800* 🌐 *www.naturalsciences.org* 🎫 *Free.*

Oakwood Historic District

HISTORIC SITE | Several architectural styles—including Victorian buildings—can be found in this tree-shaded 19th-century neighborhood. During spring, the well-manicured lawns and flower gardens make it an especially lovely place for a stroll. Brochures for self-guided walking tours of the area, which encompasses 20 blocks bordered by Person, Edenton, Franklin, and Watauga–Linden Streets, are available at the N.C. Museum of History. ✉ *Downtown.*

Pullen Park

AMUSEMENT PARK/WATER PARK | **FAMILY** | The state's first public park includes train rides, paddleboat rentals, and a 1911 Dentzel carousel. You can also swim in a large indoor aquatic center, play tennis, or, if the timing is right, see a summer play at the Theatre in the Park. ✉ *520 Ashe Ave., University* ☎ *919/996–6468* 🌐 *raleighnc.gov* 🎫 *Free; $1.50 per ride on the carousel and other amusements.*

State Capitol

GOVERNMENT BUILDING | This beautifully preserved example of Greek revival architecture from 1840 once housed all the functions of state government. Today it's part museum, part executive offices. Under its domed rotunda is a copy of Antonio Canova's statue of George Washington depicted as a Roman general. Guided tours are given Saturday starting at 11 and 2. Self-guided tours are available throughout the week. ✉ *Capitol Sq., 1 E. Edenton St., Downtown* ☎ *919/733–4994* 🌐 *www.historicsites.nc.gov/capitol* 🎫 *Free* ⏲ *Closed Sun.*

State Legislative Building

GOVERNMENT BUILDING | One block north of the State Capitol, this complex hums with lawmakers and lobbyists when the legislature is in session. It's fun to watch from the gallery. Free guided tours are available but must be scheduled in advance through Capitol Area Services. ✉ *16 W. Jones St., Downtown* ☎ *919/733–7929* 🌐 *www.ncleg.net* 🎫 *Free.*

Restaurants

Angus Barn

$$$$ | **STEAKHOUSE** | Dinner at this huge, rustic barn (a Raleigh legend) is a real event and certainly worth the sizable prices. With its big portions, kitschy surroundings, and 89-page wine and beer list, this steak house is both traditional and fun. **Known for:** classic steaks and baby back ribs; huge wine and beer list; special-occasion dining. 💲 *Average main: $42* ✉ *9401 Glenwood Ave., North Raleigh* ☎ *919/787–2444* 🌐 *www.angusbarn.com.*

Beasley's Chicken + Honey

$ | **SOUTHERN** | James Beard Award–winning chef Ashley Christensen (also behind Poole's Diner) opened this hip fried chicken spot, which serves the namesake dish as well as modern takes on Southern classics. Sit at the bar and wash down the restaurant's hearty cuisine with a craft cocktail or glass of champagne. **Known for:** elevated Southern classics; fried chicken and honey, duh; hip atmosphere. 💲 *Average main: $10* ✉ *237 S. Wilmington St., Downtown* ☎ *919/322–0127* 🌐 *www.ac-restaurants.com/beasleys* ⏲ *Closed Tues.*

★ Brewery Bhavana

$$ | ASIAN | A brewery, dim sum restaurant, flower shop, and bookstore, this open and airy dining spot downtown tries to do a lot, and succeeds wonderfully at all of them. The restaurant's light-filled atrium has become a culinary destination. **Known for:** unique concept in a room filled with books, trees, and natural light; delicious craft beers; flavorful and inventive dim sum cuisine. *Average main: $15 ✉ 218 S. Blount St., Downtown ☎ 919/829–9998 ⊕ www.brewerybhavana.com ⏲ Closed Sun. and Mon.*

Crawford and Son

$$$$ | MODERN AMERICAN | Five-time James Beard Award semifinalist Scott Crawford founded this comfy but sophisticated restaurant in the historic Oakwood neighborhood to showcase his unique approach to cooking and the seasonal bounty of his adopted hometown. The ever-changing menu is focused on seasonal, local produce that truly belongs to its community. **Known for:** award-winning chef and his take on seasonal, local ingredients; intimate, cozy dining experience (reservations a must); outstanding desserts and bar program. *Average main: $26 ✉ 618 N. Person St., Oakwood Historic District ☎ 919/307–4647 ⊕ www.crawfordandsonrestaurant.com ⏲ Closed Sun. and Mon.*

Garland

$$ | ASIAN FUSION | Chef Cheetie Kumar is a rock star in the Raleigh culinary scene, and her popular restaurant showcases the cuisine of her native India. Kumar, who really is a rock guitarist, is passionate about melding the flavors of India and Asia with the best seasonal and locally sourced ingredients. **Known for:** Indian and Asian flavors featuring local ingredients; fun and colorful dining space; inventive cocktails and adjacent nightlife venues. *Average main: $19 ✉ 14 W. Martin St., Downtown ☎ 919/833–6886 ⊕ garlandraleigh.com ⏲ Closed Sun. and Mon.*

Sam Jones BBQ

$ | BARBECUE | The Jones family have been smoking whole hogs in the Carolina Piedmont for three generations, so Raleigh urbanites greeted Sam's chopped pork and slow-cooked ribs with open arms. Order a platter and a craft cocktail and grab a seat in the light-filled dining room or at a picnic table in the yard. **Known for:** slow-smoked pulled pork, eastern North Carolina style; local fried catfish; laid-back bar scene. *Average main: $14 ✉ 502 W. Lenoir St., Downtown ☎ 984/206–2555 ⊕ samjonesbbq.com.*

Coffee and Quick Bites

★ Transfer Co. Food Hall

$ | INTERNATIONAL | The city's best food hall has a soaring ceiling with giant skylights, filling the room and its many stalls with natural light. Grab a hearty burrito, an empanada, or a sandwich from Benchwarmers Bagels, where heirloom grains and a wood-fired oven result in one of the Southeast's best. **Known for:** outpost for Asheville's Burial Beer Co.; an A-plus bagel shop; a fun raw oyster bar. *Average main: $12 ✉ 500 E. Davis St., Oakwood Historic District ☎ 984/232–8122 ⊕ transfercofoodhall.com.*

Hotels

Guest House Raleigh

$$ | B&B/INN | This architecturally inspiring inn in an 1880s home and adjacent Roger's Cottage blend perfectly into the neighborhood setting, offering eight rooms and suites that are calm, soft, and flooded with daylight, along with common spaces like a parlor, a porch with rocking chairs, and an open kitchen where daily continental breakfast is served. **Pros:** unique historic home with skyline views; bright, comfy rooms with modern architectural touches; quiet, restful environment with personalized service. **Cons:** no elevator to upstairs rooms; may be too small and intimate

Meet "Acro," the world's most complete Acrocanthosaurus dinosaur skeleton, at the North Carolina Museum of Natural Sciences.

for some; light breakfast of granola and yogurt may leave some hungry. *Rooms from: $199* *420 S. Bloodworth St., Downtown* *919/533–3052* *www.guesthouseraleigh.com* *8 rooms, 1 cottage* *Free breakfast.*

★ The Longleaf Hotel

$ | HOTEL | What was once a run-down mid-century motor lodge is now downtown's coolest place to stay, thanks to an overhaul with retro-chic furnishings, trellises with climbing vines, and a sage-and-neutrals color scheme that extends to the lobby coffee shop and lounge. **Pros:** fixtures, furnishings, and amenities from local artisans; hip, funky motif that's cool as can be; one of the best bars in town. **Cons:** no pool; no common spaces outside of the bar-lounge; it's a hike if you walk to the heart of downtown. *Rooms from: $145* *300 N. Dawson St., Downtown* *919/867–5770* *thelongleafhotel.com* *57 rooms* *No meals.*

Origin Raleigh

$$ | HOTEL | This sleek new-construction high-rise is mostly modern and professional, yet stays just funky enough with geometric designs and artwork like a giant white squirrel sculpture and a colorful mural of Sir Walter Raleigh in the lobby. **Pros:** walkable to most of downtown; spacious, modern fitness center; covered on-site parking ($14). **Cons:** no pool; very little communal lounge space outside of the restaurant; nothing historic about it. *Rooms from: $199* *603 W. Morgan St., Downtown* *984/275–2220* *wyndhamhotels.com* *126 rooms* *No meals.*

★ The Umstead Hotel and Spa

$$$$ | HOTEL | There's a sumptuous sense of escape at this modern, luxurious hotel where wall-sized portraits and sculpture (including a large-scale Chihuly) balance the gorgeous outdoor surroundings, including a 3-acre lake (with walking trail) and an infinity pool framed by comfy chairs and cabanas. **Pros:** luxurious hotel with a full-service spa; lovely natural setting; award-winning restaurant on-site. **Cons:** outside Raleigh and not in walking distance of any sights; I–40 traffic is audible from porches; can be difficult to get a spa appointment. *Rooms from: $369* ✉ *100 Woodland Pond Rd., Cary* ☎ *919/447–4000, 866/877–4141* 🌐 *www.theumstead.com* *150 rooms* *No meals.*

Nightlife

Raleigh Beer Garden

BREWPUBS/BEER GARDENS | This two-level pub claims to have the world's largest draft-beer selection. If that's not enough, it's just plain fun to drink here—there's a tree in the ground-level bar and junglelike patio seating amidst walls of green vines. ✉ *614 Glenwood Ave., Cameron Village* ☎ *919/324–3415* 🌐 *theraleighbeergarden.com.*

Raleigh Times Bar

BARS/PUBS | Faces of early-20th-century newsboys stare out from a 20-foot photo mural covering one wall at this 1906 newspaper office, artfully restored into a gastropub. The bar features a great selection of Belgian beers and thoughtful wine and cocktail lists. ✉ *14 E. Hargett St., Downtown* ☎ *919/833–0999* 🌐 *www.raleightimesbar.com.*

Watts & Ward

BARS/PUBS | There's definitely a speakeasy vibe going on at this subterranean club downstairs from Caffé Luna. In fact, Watts & Ward is named for the legislative acts that first sought prohibition in North Carolina. With several bars, a terrace, and nooks with sofas and cozy seating, it's the perfect setting for sipping a scotch or expertly mixed cocktail. There's often live music. ✉ *200 S. Blount St., Downtown* ☎ *919/896–8016* 🌐 *www.wattsandward.com.*

Performing Arts

Duke Energy Center for the Performing Arts

ARTS CENTERS | The Duke Energy Center for the Performing Arts has several different performance spaces. The 2,369-seat **Memorial Auditorium ,** the crown jewel of the complex, is home to the North Carolina Theatre and the nationally acclaimed Carolina Ballet. The 1,700-seat **Meymandi Concert Hall** hosts the North Carolina Symphony. The 600-seat **Fletcher Opera Theater** provides a showcase for the A. J. Fletcher Opera Institute, while the 170-seat **Kennedy Theater** stages shows by smaller theater groups. ✉ *2 E. South St., Downtown* ☎ *919/996–8700* 🌐 *www.dukeenergycenterraleigh.com.*

Walnut Creek Amphitheatre

CONCERTS | Accommodating up to 20,000 fans, the Coastal Credit Union Music Park at Walnut Creek amphitheater hosts big-name touring musicians like Widespread Panic and the Black Crowes. ✉ *3801 Rock Quarry Rd., Southeast Metro* ☎ *919/831–6400* 🌐 *www.livenation.com.*

Shopping

FOOD

Historic City Market

SPECIALTY STORES | Specialty shops, art galleries, restaurants, and a small farmers' market are found in this cluster of cobblestone streets. A beautifully lit and festive Night Market, featuring live music and local artisans, is held once a month from March to November. ✉ *215 Wolfe St., Downtown* 🌐 *citymarketraleigh.com.*

State Farmers Market

FOOD/CANDY | Open year-round, this 75-acre market is the place to go for locally grown fruits and vegetables, flowers and plants, and North Carolina crafts. There is also a host of restaurants serving down-home cooking. ✉ *1201 Agriculture St., Southwest Metro* ☎ *919/733–7417* 🌐 *www.ncagr.gov/markets/facilities/markets/raleigh.*

Videri Chocolate Factory

FOOD/CANDY | Prepare to be overwhelmed by the sweet aroma of chocolate when you step through the doors of this fully operational factory and retail space in the heart of Raleigh's Warehouse District. You can tour the self-guided factory floor and trace the chocolate-making process from bean to bar. The chocolate counter offers samples of Videri's high-quality chocolate bars and confections. There's also a coffee counter where you can grab fresh-roasted coffee and hot chocolate, of course. ✉ *327 W. Davie St., Downtown* ☎ *919/755–5053* 🌐 *www.videri-chocolatefactory.com.*

MALLS

Village District

SHOPPING CENTERS/MALLS | Raleigh's first shopping center continues to reinvent itself with new upscale boutiques and restaurants. Expect everything from home decor to yoga studios to locally roasted coffee. ✉ *2108 Clark Ave., Cameron Village* ☎ *919/821–1350* 🌐 *www.shopvillagedistrict.com.*

Activities

BASKETBALL

Wolfpack

BASKETBALL | Raleigh's Atlantic Coast Conference entry, North Carolina State University, plays basketball in the PNC Arena, which is also home to the NHL team, the Carolina Hurricanes. ✉ *1400 Edwards Mill Rd., University* ☎ *919/865–1510* 🌐 *www.gopack.com.*

GOLF

Hedingham Golf Club

GOLF | Designed by architect David Postlethwait, this semiprivate course has water hazards on eight holes. Watch out for Hole 1, where a large pond affects your play three times. ✉ *4801 Harbour Towne Dr.* ☎ *919/250–3030* 🌐 *hedinghamgolfnc.com* *$27–$52, 18 holes, 6529 yds, par 71.*

Lochmere Golf Club

GOLF | Designed by Carolina PGA Hall of Famer Gene Hamm, this semiprivate course meanders through the tree-lined links, challenging players with several different types of water hazards. A tiered green makes Hole 3 a difficult par 3. ✉ *2511 Kildaire Farm Rd., Cary* ☎ *919/851–0611* 🌐 *lochmeregolf.com* *$55–$65, 18 holes, 6627 yds, par 71.*

Lonnie Poole Golf Course

GOLF | With scenic views of the Raleigh skyline, this golf course is located on Centennial Campus, of North Carolina State University. It's the only collegiate course in the world designed by Arnold Palmer. ✉ *1509 Main Campus Dr., University* ☎ *919/515–6527* 🌐 *www.lonniepoolegolfcourse.com* *$52–$85, 18 holes, 7358 yds, par 71.*

HOCKEY

Carolina Hurricanes

HOCKEY | The NHL's Carolina Hurricanes play in the PNC Arena, which has a capacity of nearly 20,000. ✉ *1400 Edwards Mill Rd., North Raleigh* ☎ *919/467–7825* 🌐 *hurricanes.nhl.com.*

JOGGING

Capital Area Greenway

BICYCLING | Nearly 40 years in the making, this series of trails links the city's parks for runners and bikers. It currently consists of 28 trails making up over 100 miles, with new trails opening regularly. ✉ *Raleigh* ☎ *919/996–3285* 🌐 *www.raleighnc.gov/find-a-trail.*

Durham

23 miles northwest of Raleigh.

For many, Durham and Duke University are synonymous, and for good reason. Duke's well-manicured lawns, tree-lined streets, and stately buildings run right into town. With more than 37,000 employees, the university is also the city's biggest employer and famous for its renowned medical and research facilities. Having a university of such magnitude in their backyard means that Durhamites and visitors alike can attend all kinds of world-class lectures, exhibits, and sports events. This is not purely a college town, however, but a former tobacco hub that's grown into central North Carolina's most arts-minded, urbane city. This is a place where any exterior wall is a mural canvas, and bathrooms are more likely to be gender-neutral than defined as men's and women's—a rarity in the South. For years, old brick factory buildings have been slowly turned into shopping malls, theater spaces, and trendy restaurants. Although neighboring Chapel Hill often steals its thunder when it comes to attracting visitors, many locals prefer Durham's calmer and more mature vibe. Add Durham's long list of historic sites and museums to its ever-evolving sense of self, and you've got a city that's rooted in history but reinventing what it means to be a Southern city in the 2020s.

GETTING HERE AND AROUND

Durham's city center has grown rather haphazardly around its universities and commercial districts over the past 100 years. One-way streets and roads that change names can make navigation tricky. Using Durham Freeway, aka North Carolina Highway 147, as a guide helps. This thoroughfare bisects the city diagonally, connecting Interstates 85 and 40, and most places of interest can be reached via its exits.

TOURS

Taste Carolina

SPECIAL-INTEREST | This local outfit offers Saturday tasting tours of Durham's farm-to-table restaurants, artisanal foods, and craft beer scenes. ✉ *Durham* ☎ *919/237–2254* 🌐 *www.tastecarolina.net* 🎫 *From $65.*

VISITOR INFORMATION

CONTACTS Discover Durham Visitor Info Center. ✉ *212 W. Main St., Suite 101, Downtown* ☎ *919/687–0288* 🌐 *www.discoverdurham.com.*

Sights

American Tobacco Campus

COMMERCIAL CENTER | FAMILY | This complex, adjacent to the Durham Bulls Athletic Park, houses apartments, offices, a theater, bars, and restaurants in a series of beautifully refurbished warehouses left over from the city's cigarette-rolling past. Free summer concerts are staged on a central lawn, in the shadow of a Lucky Strike water tower, and the place comes alive with lights and decorations during the holidays. It's a great place to stroll around and take in the scenery. Despite the history, it's a nonsmoking development. Burt's Bees is also headquartered here, and you can tour Burt's intact original cabin, brought here from Maine. Don't miss the tucked-away bee mural behind the office building. ✉ *318 Blackwell St., Downtown* ☎ *919/433–1566* 🌐 *americantobacco.co.*

Bennett Place State Historic Site

HISTORIC SITE | In April 1865, Confederate general Joseph E. Johnston surrendered to U.S. general William T. Sherman in this humble Piedmont farmhouse, 17 days after Lee's surrender to Grant at Appomattox. The two generals then set forth the terms for a "permanent peace" between the South and the North. Live historical events, held throughout the year, demonstrate how Civil War soldiers drilled, lived in camps, got their mail, and received medical care. ✉ *4409 Bennett Memorial Rd., Duke University* ☎ *919/383–4345* 🌐 *bennettplacehistoricsite.com* 🎫 *Free* ⏲ *Closed Sun. and Mon.*

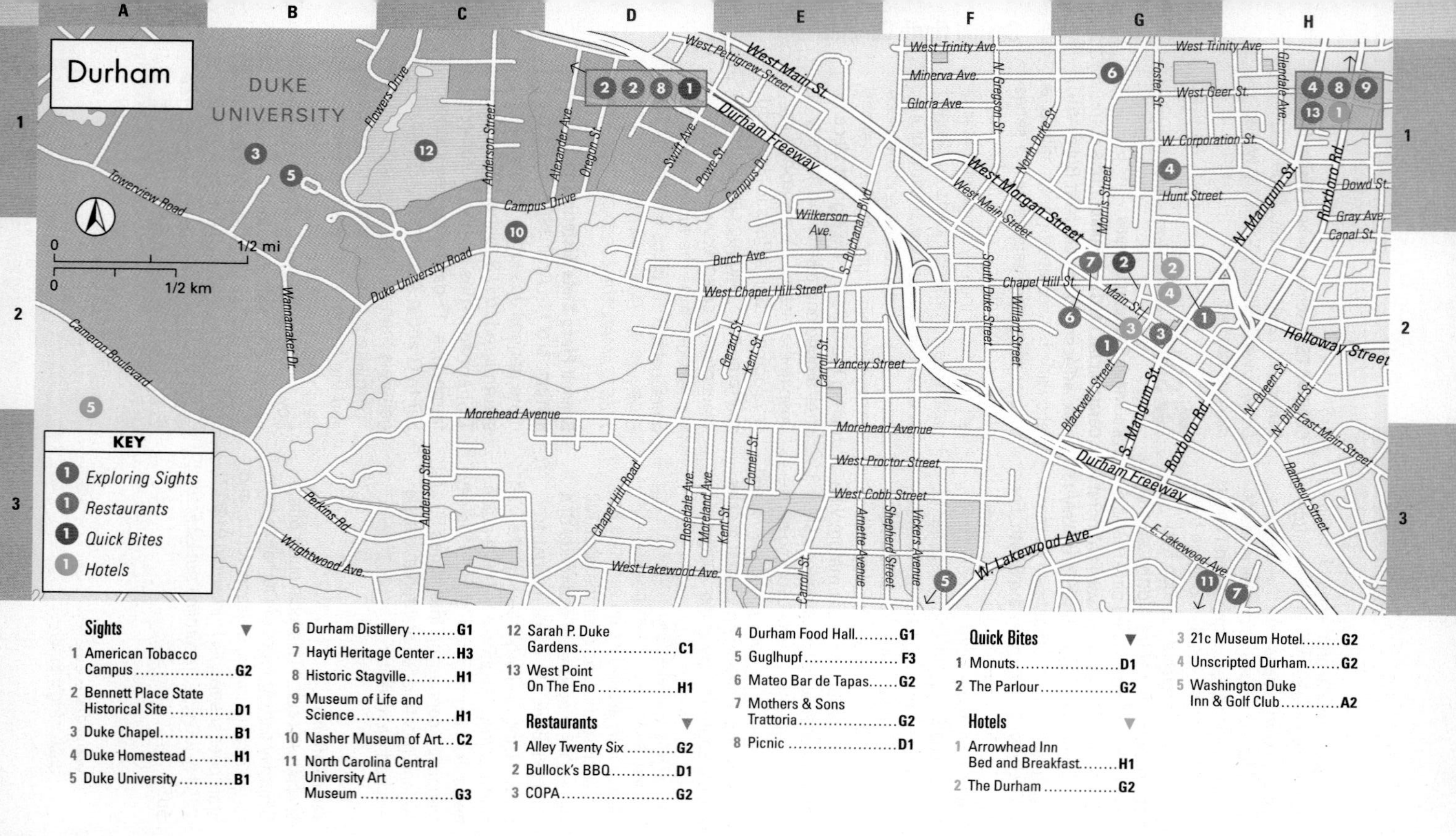

Sights ▼

1 American Tobacco Campus G2
2 Bennett Place State Historical Site D1
3 Duke Chapel B1
4 Duke Homestead H1
5 Duke University B1
6 Durham Distillery G1
7 Hayti Heritage Center H3
8 Historic Stagville H1
9 Museum of Life and Science H1
10 Nasher Museum of Art C2
11 North Carolina Central University Art Museum G3
12 Sarah P. Duke Gardens C1
13 West Point On The Eno H1

Restaurants ▼

1 Alley Twenty Six G2
2 Bullock's BBQ D1
3 COPA G2
4 Durham Food Hall G1
5 Guglhupf F3
6 Mateo Bar de Tapas G2
7 Mothers & Sons Trattoria G2
8 Picnic D1

Quick Bites ▼

1 Monuts D1
2 The Parlour G2

Hotels ▼

1 Arrowhead Inn Bed and Breakfast H1
2 The Durham G2
3 21c Museum Hotel G2
4 Unscripted Durham G2
5 Washington Duke Inn & Golf Club A2

★ Duke Chapel

RELIGIOUS SITE | A Gothic-style gem built in the early 1930s, this chapel is the centerpiece of Duke University. Modeled after England's Canterbury Cathedral, it has a 210-foot-tall bell tower. Weekly services are held here Sunday at 11 am. The chapel is a popular wedding spot, so check the website before trying to visit on Saturday. ✉ *West Campus, 401 Chapel Dr., Duke University* ☎ *919/681–9488* 🌐 *www.chapel.duke.edu.*

Duke Homestead

HISTORIC SITE | **FAMILY** | Washington Duke, patriarch of the now famous Duke family, moved into this house in 1852. It wasn't until he heard how the Union soldiers were enjoying smoking his tobacco that he decided to market his "golden weed." Explore the family's humble beginnings at this State Historic Site, which includes the first ramshackle "factory" as well as the world's largest spittoon collection. Guided tours demonstrate early manufacturing processes; the visitor center exhibits early tobacco advertising. ✉ *2828 Duke Homestead Rd., Downtown* ☎ *919/ 627–6990* 🌐 *www.dukehomestead.org* 🎫 *Free; guided tours $2* ⏲ *Closed Sun. and Mon.*

Duke University

COLLEGE | A stroll along the tree-lined streets of this campus, founded in 1924, is a lovely way to spend a few hours. Tours of the campus, known for its Georgian and Gothic revival architecture, are available during the academic year and can be arranged in advance. ✉ *Karsh Alumni and Visitors Center, 2080 Duke University Rd., Duke University* ☎ *919/684–5114* 🌐 *www.duke.edu.*

Durham Distillery

WINERY/DISTILLERY | This small craft distillery is racking up national and international awards for its Conniption American dry and navy-strength gins, as well as its cold-distilled cucumber vodka and Damn Fine Liqueurs made in collaboration with Raleigh's Videri Chocolate and Slingshot Coffee Company. The intimate tasting room is open on the weekends for quick tastes and for more involved behind-the-scenes tours that give you a look at the unique two-step distillation process. Downstairs, the Corpse Reviver bar, with its velvety blue lounge seating, is a new hot spot for craft cocktails showing off the best iterations of the products made upstairs. ✉ *711 Washington St., Downtown* ☎ *919/937–2121* 🌐 *www.durhamdistillery.com* 🎫 *$10 for tours* ⏲ *Closed Sun.–Thurs.*

Hayti Heritage Center

FESTIVAL | One of Durham's oldest houses of worship houses this center for African American art and culture. In addition to local theater productions and exhibitions of traditional and contemporary art by regional and national artists, the center hosts events like the Bull Durham Blues Festival and the Hayti Heritage Film Festival. ✉ *St. Joseph's AME Church, 804 Old Fayetteville St., Downtown* ☎ *919/683–1709* 🌐 *www.hayti.org* 🎫 *Free* ⏲ *Closed Sun.*

Historic Stagville

HISTORIC SITE | Owned by the Bennehan and Cameron families, Stagville was one of the largest plantations in antebellum North Carolina, at 30,000 acres. Over 900 people were enslaved here, and the story of their struggle for freedom and independence, even after Emancipation, is told through exhibits that include four original two-story slave cabins. The plantation today sits on 71 acres and has many original buildings, including the Bennehans' two-story wood-frame home, built in the late 1700s; the Great Barn, built by enslaved workers; and the family cemetery. Call for guided tour times. ✉ *5828 Old Oxford Hwy.* ☎ *919/620–0120* 🌐 *www.stagville.org* 🎫 *Free; $2 tours* ⏲ *Closed Sun. and Mon.*

★ Museum of Life and Science

COLLEGE | **FAMILY** | This interactive science park on 84 acres is packed full of attractions designed to spark wonder and curiosity. There's a two-story science center, one of the largest butterfly conservatories on the East Coast, and 60 species

Did You Know?

In addition to trying to inspire awe and reverence, the architects of Duke Chapel also added a touch of whimsy. Look for two wooden mice hidden within the intricate woodwork: one is in the choir stalls near the altar; the other is on top of a wooden pillar on the organ. If you still can't find them, take the tour.

of live animals in its outdoor exhibits. The *Hideaway Woods* exhibit features eight tree houses, a flowing stream, and fanciful nature sculptures. *Earth Moves* invites visitors to climb a large formation of Tennessee sandstone or explore a cave underneath it and control the flow of water from a 20-foot freestanding waterfall. ✉ *433 W. Murray Ave., Downtown* ✣ *Off I–85* ☎ *919/220–5429* 🌐 *www.lifeandscience.org* 🎫 *Museum $23* ⏲ *Closed Mon. and Tues.*

Nasher Museum of Art

MUSEUM | A highlight of any Duke visit, this museum displays African, American, European, and Latin American artwork. The collection includes works by Rodin, Picasso, and Matisse. The museum offers a steady stream of engaging events throughout the year. ✉ *2001 Campus Dr., Duke University* ☎ *919/684–5135* 🌐 *www.nasher.duke.edu* 🎫 *$7.*

North Carolina Central University Art Museum

MUSEUM | Located in the first publicly supported liberal arts college for African Americans, this gallery showcases work by black artists. The permanent collection includes 19th-century masterpieces and 20th-century works created during the Harlem Renaissance. ✉ *1801 Fayetteville St., South/NCCU* ☎ *919/530–6211* 🌐 *www.nccu.edu* 🎫 *Free* ⏲ *Closed Mon. and Sat.*

★ Sarah P. Duke Gardens

GARDEN | **FAMILY** | A wisteria-draped gazebo, the Carnivorous Plant Collection, and a Japanese garden with a lily pond teeming with fat goldfish are a few of the highlights of these 55 acres in Duke University's West Campus. More than 5 miles of pathways meander through formal plantings and woodlands. The Terrace Café serves lunch weekdays and brunch Saturday and Sunday seasonally. ✉ *West Campus, 420 Anderson St., Duke University* ☎ *919/684–3698* 🌐 *www.gardens.duke.edu* 🎫 *Free.*

West Point on the Eno

NATURE PRESERVE | **FAMILY** | This 388-acre city park on the banks of the Eno River boasts a restored mill dating from 1778—one of 32 that once dotted the area. Also on-site are a 19th-century Greek revival farmhouse that was occupied by John Cabe McCown, the onetime owner of the mill, and a museum that showcases early-20th-century photographer Hugh Mangum's pictures of the surrounding area. The Festival for the Eno, held around July 4, includes musicians, artists, and craftspeople from around the region. ✉ *5101 N. Roxboro Rd./U.S. 501 N, North Metro* ☎ *919/471–1623* 🌐 *www.enoriver.org* 🎫 *Free.*

Restaurants

★ Alley Twenty Six

$$$ | **MODERN AMERICAN** | Named for the alley it borders (the exposed brick walls and overhead string lighting make it absolutely charming), this celebrated bar and restaurant is known for its top-notch cocktail program. You'll find some of the city's most creative and locally sourced cocktails here, plus an impressive food menu. **Known for:** shared plates of upscale comfort food; late-night menu; craft cocktails with food pairings. 💲 *Average main: $20* ✉ *320 E. Chapel Hill St., Downtown* ☎ *984/439–2278* 🌐 *www.alleytwentysix.com* ⏲ *Closed Mon. and Tues.*

Bullock's BBQ

$ | **BARBECUE** | Durham's oldest restaurant sticks to the finely chopped vinegar barbecue that made it an institution. Pair a sandwich or platter with a bowl of beans or mac and cheese and you'll be in hog heaven. ⚠ **It's cash only, so head to an ATM before you arrive.** **Known for:** a tradition since 1952; hearty Brunswick stew; photos of former presidents and celebrities dining here line the walls. 💲 *Average main: $8* ✉ *3330 Quebec Dr., West Metro* ☎ *919/383–3211* 🌐 *bullocks-bbq.com* ⏲ *Closed Sun. and Mon.* 💳 *No credit cards.*

COPA

$$ | **CUBAN** | Cuban tapas and cocktails are paired with delicious sandwiches at this nod to Old Havana, where the tile floor and sidewalk dining add to the vibe. Everything is fresh and sourced from local farms and purveyors. **Known for:** focus on farm-fresh ingredients; Cuban dishes that pay tribute to the country's culinary history; fun and inventive cocktails with a lively bar. *Average main: $16* *107 W. Main St., Downtown* *919/973–0111* *Closed Sun. and Mon.*

Durham Food Hall

$ | **MODERN AMERICAN** | **FAMILY** | This repurposed warehouse includes 10 counter-serve restaurants, offering pizza, raw oysters, and gourmet coffee. The soaring ceilings and industrial-mod decor make it a pleasant place to explore and dine. **Known for:** Bowerbird Flowers & Apothecary brightens the room with scores of flowers; single-origin coffee from Liturgy; tempting desserts from Afters. *Average main: $12* *530 Foster St., Suite 1, Five Points* *919/908–9339* *durhamfoodhall.com.*

Guglhupf

$$ | **GERMAN** | **FAMILY** | Locals have flocked to this upscale German bakery, café, and biergarten for more than 20 years, drawn by the delicious pastries, lively brunch, and expansive dining patio. While the restaurant doesn't skimp on the classic sausage-and-schnitzel fare, the menu is enlivened by frequently rotating seasonal entrées that showcase central North Carolina's farm bounty; vegans and vegetarians will be pleasantly surprised by the range of elegant and inventive plant-based dishes. **Known for:** European pastries (especially the namesake guglhupf cake); vegetarian and vegan takes on German classics; hearty brunch. *Average main: $15* *2706 Durham-Chapel Hill Blvd., Duke University* *919/401–2600* *guglhupf.com* *Closed Mon.*

Mateo Bar de Tapas

$$ | **SPANISH** | When you mix the flavors and small-plate dining tradition of Spain with the beloved ingredients and dishes of the American South, the results are delicious. The ever-changing seasonal menu features *pintxos* (small bites) like Spanish deviled eggs and smoked barbecue marcona almonds with heartier tapas like charred octopus and pork ribs with pepper jelly. **Known for:** inventive Southern-inspired Spanish-style tapas; extensive wine, sherry, and cocktail offerings; fun, plate-sharing atmosphere. *Average main: $19* *109 W. Chapel Hill St., Downtown* *919/530–8700* *mateotapas.com* *Closed Sun. and Mon.*

★ Mothers & Sons Trattoria

$$$ | **ITALIAN** | Order a table of small plates to share, or dive into an entrée from the open kitchen's wood-fired grill at this Italian-themed café (no pizza though) that's known for making its own pasta. **Known for:** bruschetta menu; spaghetti with pork and beef meatballs, done right; laid-back but elegant dining scene. *Average main: $20* *107 W. Chapel Hill St., Downtown* *919/294–8247* *mothersandsonsnc.com* *Closed Sun. and Mon.*

Picnic

$ | **BARBECUE** | If you're craving Carolina-style whole-hog barbecue, head to this quaint little spot outside of town that's the partnership of a chef, heritage pig farmer, and seasoned pitmaster. You'll also find fried chicken, mac and cheese, smoky collard greens, and all the proper fixings. **Known for:** unique farm-to-plate concept; whole-hog barbecue with tangy vinegar-based sauce; deviled eggs, mac and cheese, and all the fixin's. *Average main: $14* *1647 Cole Mill Rd., North Metro* *919/908–9128* *www.picnicdurham.com.*

Coffee and Quick Bites

Monuts
$ | **BAKERY** | **FAMILY** | Whether you opt for a hearty avocado-stuffed breakfast burrito, go healthy with a granola bowl, or just stop in for a drip coffee, you'd be remiss to leave without one of the signature house doughnuts. Don't even try to fool yourself into just eating half. **Known for:** sea salt dark chocolate glazed doughnuts; seasonal coffee like iced mint lattes; build-your-own biscuit sandwiches. *Average main: $10 ✉ 1002 Ninth St., West Metro ☎ 919/286–2642 🌐 monuts-donuts.com.*

The Parlour
$ | **BAKERY** | **FAMILY** | It's worth the line down the sidewalk for the house-made ice cream with seasonal flavors at this boutique spot with a dozen daily flavors. **Known for:** fun flavors like guava cheesecake; the chocolate habanero float, with spicy cold brew over vanilla ice cream; vegan baked treats. *Average main: $6 ✉ 117 Market St., Downtown ☎ 919/564–7999 🌐 theparlour.co ⏲ Closed Mon. and Tues.*

Arrowhead Inn Bed and Breakfast
$$$ | **B&B/INN** | This sprawling 6-acre property dates to 1775, with rooms spread across the Manor House, a Garden Cottage, and a cabin, all amidst gardens and green space. **Pros:** comfortable inn offers suites and roomy cottages; beautiful country setting; upscale dinners can be arranged. **Cons:** it's a 15-minute drive to the city center; no entertainment or dining nearby; old-fashioned decor. *Rooms from: $219 ✉ 106 Mason Rd., North Metro ☎ 919/477–8430 🌐 www.arrowhead-inn.com 9 rooms No Free breakfast.*

The Durham
$$$ | **HOTEL** | This boutique hotel in the heart of downtown displays mid-century modern decor and emphasizes everything local, from its overall design to the in-room snacks. **Pros:** walking distance to restaurants and sights; friendly staff; great on-site dining and rooftop bar. **Cons:** no pool; rooftop bar is crowded on nice nights; only one elevator in the building makes for long waits. *Rooms from: $209 ✉ 315 E. Chapel Hill St., Downtown ☎ 919/768–8830 🌐 www.thedurham.com 53 rooms No meals.*

21c Museum Hotel
$$ | **HOTEL** | This innovative hotel, housed in a historic bank building, is the perfect fusion of art museum and boutique hotel. **Pros:** located in the heart of downtown; unique features, like an old bank vault to explore; cutting-edge art and fun decor throughout. **Cons:** the check-in desk can be hard to find for newcomers; frequently hosts events that can be noisy; ultramodern style and edgy sexualized art might be off-putting for some. *Rooms from: $199 ✉ 111 N. Corcoran St., Downtown ☎ 919/956–6700, 877/226–9957 🌐 www.21cmuseumhotels.com/durham 125 rooms No meals.*

★ Unscripted Durham
$$ | **HOTEL** | Once a 1960s motor lodge, this fun and quirky building downtown has been transformed into a boutique hotel with a rooftop pool and lots of retro touches. **Pros:** fun and hip environment; rooftop pool and bar; comfy retro-styled rooms with modern conveniences. **Cons:** exterior corridor rooms can be noisy; weekend events can fill the pool area with nonguests; hotel charges a facility fee plus $20 for parking. *Rooms from: $189 ✉ 202 N. Corcoran St., Downtown ☎ 984/329–9500 🌐 www.unscriptedhotels.com 74 rooms No meals.*

Washington Duke Inn & Golf Club
$$ | **HOTEL** | On the campus of Duke University, this luxurious hotel evokes the feeling of an English country inn. **Pros:** well-appointed and service-oriented; luxury travelers will feel right at home; allows all pets (for a fee). **Cons:** must be booked well in advance for any stays during graduation or other Duke events; many of

the rooms have views of the parking lot; dining options are pricey. $ *Rooms from: $189* ✉ *3001 Cameron Blvd., Duke University* ☎ *919/490–0999, 800/443–3853* 🌐 *www.washingtondukeinn.com* *271 rooms* *No meals.*

Nightlife

Fullsteam Brewery
BREWPUBS/BEER GARDENS | Local ingredients are used to make the traditional and experimental beers at this regionally celebrated brewery. Beer-friendly food is served at the tavern. ✉ *726 Rigsbee Ave., Downtown* ☎ *919/682–2337* 🌐 *www.fullsteam.ag.*

★ Kingfisher
WINE BARS—NIGHTLIFE | The subterranean digs at this choice cocktail bar make it feel like a speakeasy, but there's no secret password required to enjoy bespoke cocktails like the Celebrity Sour, an addictive amalgam of mezcal, cinnamon, pomegranate, and caramelized goat yogurt. ✉ *321 E. Chapel Hill St., Downtown* 🌐 *kingfisherdurham.com.*

Motorco Music Hall
MUSIC CLUBS | This former mid-century car dealership is now one of Durham's top places to hear live music and enjoy cocktails with friends. Motorco is made up of four parts: the eclectic Garage Bar, Parts and Labor restaurant, a spacious patio with outdoor seating, and the 450-seat Showroom, where you can catch both nationally touring acts and favorite local bands and performers. ✉ *723 Rigsbee Ave., Downtown* ☎ *919/901–0875* 🌐 *www.motorcomusic.com.*

Performing Arts

American Dance Festival
DANCE | This internationally known festival, held annually in June and July, brings dance performances to various locations throughout town. ✉ *715 Broad St., Downtown* ☎ *919/684–6402* 🌐 *www.americandancefestival.org.*

Carolina Theatre
CONCERTS | Dating from 1926, this Beaux Arts space hosts classical, jazz, and rock concerts, as well as film events and international film festivals. Check online for a full calendar of indie, retro, and all-around interesting films and live performances. ✉ *309 W. Morgan St., Downtown* ☎ *919/560–3030* 🌐 *www.carolinatheatre.org.*

Durham Performing Arts Center (DPAC)
ARTS CENTERS | With its impressive modernist glass structure and adjacent hotel and restaurants, DPAC offers panoramic views of the city and a world-class performing arts experience. The 2,700-person theater is the place to catch touring Broadway productions and big-name artists traveling through the region. ✉ *123 Vivian St., Downtown* ☎ *919/680–2787* 🌐 *www.dpacnc.com.*

Shopping

CRAFTS

Bull City Fair Trade
CRAFTS | Browse 2,000 square feet of unique, affordable home accessories, children's toys, and other arts and crafts collected from around the world. The market, a nonprofit, sells crafts from fair-trade vendors, which aim to provide artisans in developing countries (and poor areas of the United States) a living wage. ✉ *811 9th St., West Metro* ☎ *919/286–2457* 🌐 *bullcityfairtrade.com.*

FOOD

★ Parker and Otis
FOOD/CANDY | This shop and gourmet sandwich counter offers kitchenware, cookbooks, local produce, and specialty foods, as well as wines, chocolates, teas, coffees, and scads of candy. Breakfast is served until 11 and into the afternoon on weekends. Lunch lasts until 4 pm. Gift baskets can be shipped all over the country. ■ **TIP→ This shop is known for**

its pimento cheese. Take some to go, or have it spread on a shrimp BLT to enjoy at the tables just outside. ✉ *324 Blackwell St., Bay 4, Downtown* ☎ *919/683–3200* 🌐 *www.parkerandotis.com.*

SHOPPING AREAS AND MALLS

Brightleaf Square

SHOPPING CENTERS/MALLS | In the former Watts and Yuille warehouses, Brightleaf Square is named for the tobacco that once filled these buildings. The two long structures—now filled with shops, restaurants, and a brewery—sandwich an attractive brick courtyard. Shopping standouts include James Kennedy Antiques, Indio, Bull City Olive Oil, and Wentworth and Leggett Rare Books and Prints. ✉ *905 W. Main St., Downtown* 🌐 *www.historicbrightleaf.com.*

9th Street

SHOPPING CENTERS/MALLS | Durham's funky 9th Street is lined with shops and restaurants and has a distinct college-town feel. ✉ *9th St. at Markham Ave., West Metro* 🌐 *discover9thstreet.com.*

The Streets at Southpoint

SHOPPING CENTERS/MALLS | This village-like mall has restaurants, a movie theater, and nearly 150 stores, including Nordstrom and Crate & Barrel. ✉ *6910 Fayetteville Rd., Southeast Metro* ✣ *Off I–40* ☎ *919/572–8800* 🌐 *www.streetsat-southpoint.com.*

BASEBALL

Durham Bulls

BASEBALL/SOFTBALL | **FAMILY** | Immortalized in the hit 1988 movie *Bull Durham* and a tradition since 1902, this AAA affiliate of the Tampa Bay Rays plays in the 10,000-seat Durham Bulls Athletic Park. ✉ *Durham Bulls Athletic Park, 409 Blackwell St., Downtown* ☎ *919/687–6500* 🌐 *www.dbulls.com.*

BASKETBALL

Blue Devils

BASKETBALL | Duke's Atlantic Coast Conference team plays home games at the 9,291-seat Cameron Indoor Stadium. ✉ *115 Whitford Dr., Duke University* ☎ *919/681–2583* 🌐 *www.goduke.com.*

GOLF

Duke University Golf Club

GOLF | Twice host of the NCAA men's championship, this course was designed in 1957 by the legendary Robert Trent Jones; his son, Rees Jones, completed a renovation of the links in 1993. The whopping 455-yard par 4 on Hole 18 separates serious players from duffers. ✉ *3001 Cameron Blvd.* ✣ *At Science Dr.* ☎ *919/681–2288* 🌐 *www.golf.duke.edu* ⛳ *$80–$100, 18 holes, 7154 yds, par 72.*

Hillandale Golf Course

GOLF | The oldest course in the area, Hillandale was designed by the incomparable Donald Ross but then redesigned by George Cobb following the course's move in 1960. The course, with a couple of doglegs and a creek running through it, gives even experienced golfers a strategic workout. ✉ *1600 Hillandale Rd.* ☎ *919/286–4211* 🌐 *www.hillandalegolf.com* ⛳ *$21–$41, 18 holes, 6339 yds, par 71* ⚠ *Reservations essential.*

HIKING

Eno River State Park

HIKING/WALKING | **FAMILY** | This 4,231-acre park includes miles of hiking trails, a picnic area, and backcountry camping sites. Though only 15 minutes from downtown Durham, the Eno is a slice of secluded wilderness. ✉ *6101 Cole Mill Rd., North Metro* ☎ *919/383–1686* 🌐 *www.ncparks.gov.*

Basketball Rivalries

North Carolinians are famously split when it comes to the sport of basketball. Most locals will tell you that this long tradition of great collegiate basketball is ultimately the product of a larger state commitment to education. North Carolina stands out in the South and indeed the nation as a center for medicine, research, and education. Today "Tobacco Road" runs through a lengthy section of one of the largest medical, pharmaceutical, and tech regions in the nation. For basketball fans, Tobacco Road is all about the rivalry between the Duke Blue Devils and the Tar Heels of UNC-Chapel Hill. While this rivalry is legendary, North Carolina also boasts several other championship schools, such as Wake Forest University, North Carolina State University, and Davidson College, who have helped keep the tradition of great basketball strong for half a century.

Chapel Hill

28 miles northwest of Raleigh; 12 miles southwest of Durham.

Chapel Hill is the smallest city in the Triangle, but it probably has the biggest personality. Home to the nation's first state university, the University of North Carolina, this is a college town through and through. With its prestigious yet offbeat reputation, UNC draws all kinds of students, from West Coast hippies to fraternity-loving members of the Southern aristocracy. Part of the fun of the area is the push–pull between this motley crew of students and the wealthy retirees who call Chapel Hill home. Although there are fancy restaurants and hotels, there are also cheap pizza joints and dive bars. Franklin Street, located downtown, caters to both these communities with a mixture of boutiques, restaurants, and galleries.

GETTING HERE AND AROUND

Chapel Hill is a wonderful place to walk around but a difficult place to park a car. Find a parking space in one of the lots along Rosemary Street, one block off Franklin, and give yourself a chance to enjoy the Carolina blue skies. Start at the Old Well on Cameron Avenue and wander through campus, or eat, sip, and shop your way down Franklin Street, beginning at the Morehead Planetarium and heading west to Carrboro.

VISITOR INFORMATION

CONTACTS Chapel Hill/Orange County Visitors Bureau. ✉ *501 W. Franklin St., Downtown* ☎ *919/245–4320, 888/968–2060* 🌐 *www.visitchapelhill.org.*

Sights

Ackland Art Museum

MUSEUM | The permanent holdings at this impressive museum include 19,000 works, with one of the Southeast's strongest collections of Asian art. There's an outstanding selection of drawings, prints, and photographs as well as Old Master paintings and sculptures. The museum hosts regular lunch panels, film forums, and guest lectures. Be sure to say hello to the museum's namesake, William Hayes Ackland, whose modernist tomb is on-site. ✉ *101 S. Columbia St., University* ☎ *919/966–5736* 🌐 *www.ackland.org* *Free* *Closed Sun.–Tues.*

Carolina Basketball Museum

MUSEUM | You don't have to be a basketball fan to appreciate the passion and deep love for the game you'll encounter in Tar Heel country. This state-of-the-art museum features a film, artifacts, and interactive exhibits that celebrate some of the most famous Tar Heel coaches and players of all time, including Dean Smith, Roy Williams, and Michael Jordan. ✉ *450 Skipper Bowles Dr., University* ✣ *On the campus of UNC, next to the Dean E. Smith Center* ☎ *919/962–6000* 🌐 *www.goheels.com* 🎟 *Free* 🕑 *Closed Sun.*

Morehead Planetarium and Science Center
MUSEUM | FAMILY | The original Apollo astronauts trained here, at one of the largest planetariums in the country. A $9.2 million renovation, completed in 2020, expanded the exhibition areas. You can see planetarium shows, science demonstrations, and interactive STEM exhibits for children and adults. ✉ *250 E. Franklin St., University* ☎ *919/962–1236* 🌐 *www.moreheadplanetarium.org* 🎟 *$15* 🕑 *Closed Mon.*

★ **North Carolina Botanical Garden**
GARDEN | FAMILY | Part of the University of North Carolina, this tribute to native plants includes wildflowers, shrubs, trees, ferns, and grasses of the Southeast. Other highlights include nature trails that wind through a 300-acre Piedmont forest, a green education center, and an impressive collection of herbs and carnivorous plants. ✉ *100 Old Mason Farm Rd., South Metro* ☎ *919/962–0522* 🌐 *ncbg.unc.edu* 🎟 *Free* 🕑 *Garden closed Mon. Trails open daily.*

University of North Carolina
COLLEGE | Franklin Street runs along the northern edge of the campus, which is filled with oak-shaded courtyards, stately old buildings, and tucked-away gems like the mystical Forest Theatre and the gorgeous Coker Arboretum. Regarded as one of the top public institutions in the United States, UNC-Chapel Hill is also one of the country's oldest public universities and was the first to admit students (it opened its doors in 1795). To this day, it remains the very heart of Chapel Hill, which has grown up around it for more than two centuries. ✉ *Visitor Center, 134 E. Franklin St., University* ☎ *919/962–1630 Visitor Center* 🌐 *www.unc.edu/visitors.*

Restaurants

Il Palio
$$$$ | ITALIAN | A real find for food lovers willing to stray from Chapel Hill's lively downtown, this small, independently owned restaurant inside the Siena Hotel serves high-class Italian fare with an emphasis on local and seasonal ingredients (the menu lists the nearby farms and purveyors used). Although the dishes change frequently, previous offerings have included pappardelle Bolognese and pan-seared scallops served with corn succotash. **Known for:** house-made pasta dishes; intimate dining room; thoughtful, Italian-focused wine list. 💲 *Average main: $31* ✉ *Siena Hotel, 1505 E. Franklin St., North Metro* ☎ *919/918–2545* 🌐 *www.ilpalio.com.*

Lantern
$$$$ | ASIAN FUSION | James Beard Award–winning chef Andrea Reusing's flagship restaurant brings together Asian flavors and North Carolina ingredients sourced mostly from local farms and purveyors. The menu changes seasonally, but the legendary tea-smoked roast chicken and chive-and-pork dumplings are staples. **Known for:** award-winning chef and dishes; melding of Asian cuisine with local ingredients; intimate dining space and bar. 💲 *Average main: $26* ✉ *423 W. Franklin St., Downtown* ☎ *919/969–8846* 🌐 *www.lanternrestaurant.com* 🕑 *Closed Sun.*

Coffee and Quick Bites

Brandwein's Bagels
$ | BAKERY | North Carolina–grown and –milled flour, boiled and baked in the New York style, make these perfect bagels both local and authentic. Toasted and smothered with pimento cheese, bacon, and avocado, they're perfection. **Known for:** house-made sweet and savory bagel spreads, including vegan options; hefty

bagel lunch sandwiches like the Hot Honey Turkey; gluten-free bagel options. *Average main: $11 505 W. Rosemary St., Downtown 919/240–7071 brandweinsbagels.com.*

Neal's Deli

$ | **DELI** | Sweet-potato biscuits, muffulettas, and classics like grilled pimento cheese are among the staples at this breakfast and lunch nook with serious culinary street cred. **Known for:** the daily bag o' biscuits specials; local roasted coffee; soup and sandwich combos. *Average main: $10 100 E. Main St., Carrboro 919/967–2185 nealsdeli.com Closed Sun. and Mon.*

Hotels

★ Carolina Inn

$$ | **HOTEL** | The only hotel located on the campus of UNC-Chapel Hill, this century-old historic property features modern amenities in a charming setting. **Pros:** historic inn in easy walking distance to Franklin Street and UNC campus; easy, free on-site parking; lovely, historic gathering spaces and communal areas. **Cons:** frequently booked for meetings and university events; some rooms are on the small side; no pool. *Rooms from: $169 211 Pittsboro St., University 919/933–2001 www.carolinainn.com 185 rooms No meals.*

The Fearrington House Inn

$$$$ | **B&B/INN** | This luxury inn sits on a nearly 250-year-old farm that has been remade to resemble a country hamlet. **Pros:** a country inn with up-to-date luxuries; surrounded by plenty of shops and restaurants; fantastic breakfast. **Cons:** visitors may mind the 15-minute drive to the center of Chapel Hill; very expensive; might be too quiet for some. *Rooms from: $375 2000 Fearrington Village Center, Pittsboro 919/542–2121 www.fearrington.com 32 rooms Free breakfast.*

Graduate Chapel Hill

$$ | **HOTEL** | In the center of this hotel, three floors of rooms overlook a carpeted basketball court, where guests can shoot hoops with soft basketballs handed out at the front desk. **Pros:** great location, with on-site parking ($22); luxurious amenities and friendly staff make stays memorable; small touches everywhere to delight UNC fans. **Cons:** Franklin Street can get noisy when the campus is buzzing with students; no pool; reservations are scarce during busy times. *Rooms from: $179 311 W. Franklin St., University 919/442–9000 graduatehotels.com/chapel-hill 69 rooms No meals.*

The Siena Hotel

$$ | **HOTEL** | Experience a taste of Italy at this fanciful and friendly hotel, where the lobby and rooms are filled with imported carved-wood furniture, fabrics, and artwork that conjure up the Renaissance. **Pros:** the interior is impressively elegant; pet-friendly rooms available; free shuttle service to downtown. **Cons:** not within walking distance to downtown; property feels a little dated; setting by the highway doesn't feel so fancy until you go inside. *Rooms from: $199 1505 E. Franklin St., North Metro 919/929–4000 www.sienahotel.com 79 rooms No meals.*

Nightlife

The Chapel Hill area is a great place to hear live rock and alternative bands. Many of the best music venues are in adjacent Carrboro, while Chapel Hill's Franklin Street is the spot to create your own pub crawl. As a rule of thumb, the younger crowd heads east of Columbia Street, while the older, post-college set steers west of it.

Carolina Brewery

BREWPUBS/BEER GARDENS | Sip a Sky Blue Kölsch or an American IPA at this Franklin Street brewpub, where the production beer tanks are on full display. Plenty of TVs mean the crowd fills in on game days. ✉ *460 W. Franklin St., Downtown* ☎ *919/942–1800* 🌐 *carolinabrewery.com.*

Cat's Cradle

MUSIC CLUBS | The Triangle's premier live-music club since the late '70s, this legendary venue hosts local and regional bands as well as nationally known indie acts. ✉ *300 E. Main St., Carrboro* ☎ *919/967–9053* 🌐 *www.catscradle.com.*

The Crunkleton

BARS/PUBS | Setting the standard for craft cocktail bars in North Carolina, the Crunkleton has a knowledgeable staff of mixologists ready to stir and shake drinks. You can also select from a pages-long whiskey list—it includes antique spirits that seem to taste even better in the dark, parlorlike surroundings, with elk and deer busts lording it over the room. ✉ *320 W. Franklin St., Downtown* ☎ *919/969–1125* 🌐 *www.thecrunkleton.com.*

Top of the Hill (TOPO)

BARS/PUBS | A restaurant, brewery, and distillery all in one, TOPO has an impressive cocktail list featuring drinks made with homegrown spirits. As for beers, the refreshing Kenan lager and Old Well White wheat beer are always on tap. The top-floor space overlooks Franklin Street and is the place to be on UNC game days. ✉ *100 E. Franklin St., Downtown* ☎ *919/929–8676* 🌐 *thetopofthehill.com.*

Performing Arts

Memorial Hall

DANCE | Home to Carolina Performing Arts, you can catch music, dance, and other performances in this historic 1,400-seat auditorium on the campus of UNC. ✉ *114 E. Cameron Ave., University* ☎ *919/843–3333* 🌐 *www.carolinaperformingarts.org.*

PlayMakers Repertory Company

THEATER | The professional theater in residence at UNC, PlayMakers Repertory's productions range from old-time radio dramas to large-scale musicals, using a variety of ingenious sets. ✉ *Paul Green Theatre, 120 Country Club Rd., University* ☎ *919/962–7529* 🌐 *www.playmakersrep.org.*

Shopping

BOOKS

McIntyre's Books

BOOKS/STATIONERY | You can read by the fire in one of this little shop's cozy rooms. The independent bookstore has a big selection of mysteries, as well as gardening and cookbooks. It also hosts weekly readings. There are other interesting shops in Fearrington Village to explore as well. ✉ *Fearrington Village, 2000 Fearrington Village Center, Pittsboro* ☎ *919/542–3030* 🌐 *mcintyresbooks.com.*

CLOTHING

Julian's

CLOTHING | Franklin Street's premier clothier since 1942 is known for outfitting former UNC men's basketball coach Roy Williams when he takes the court. The traditional haberdashery creates unique and custom suits, shirts, ties, and women's clothing. ✉ *135 E. Franklin St., Downtown* ☎ *919/942–4563* 🌐 *julianstyle.com.*

LOCAL CRAFTS

WomanCraft Gifts

CRAFTS | This Carrboro institution is a co-op of about 70 artisans (and not just women) who sell the unique goods they create. All of the artists live within the surrounding counties. Handcrafted pottery, jewelry, textiles, blown glass, paintings, and photography are just a few of the items you'll find. Co-op members staff the store and love sharing their craft with guests. ✉ *360 E. Main St., Carrboro* ☎ *919/929–3300* 🌐 *www.womancraftgifts.com.*

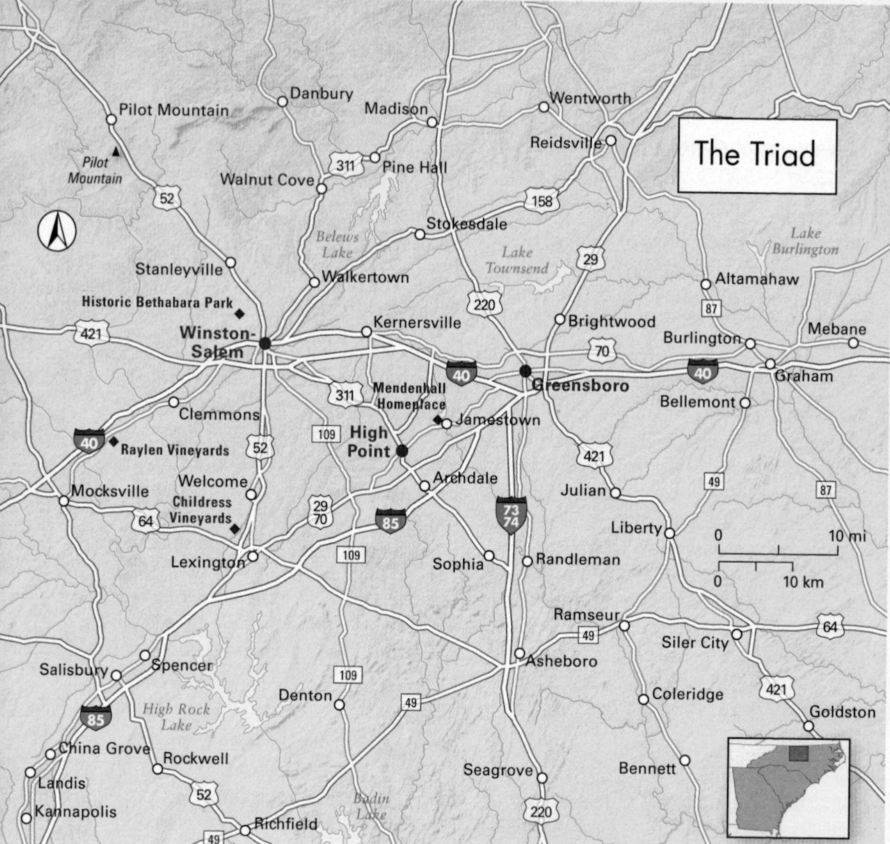

Activities

BASKETBALL

Tar Heels

BASKETBALL | The University of North Carolina Tar Heels are Chapel Hill's Atlantic Coast Conference team. They play in the Dean E. Smith Student Activities Center, aka the "Dean Dome," where the banners celebrating their seven NCAA national championships hang from the rafters. ✉ *Dean E. Smith Student Activities Center, 300 Skipper Bowles Dr., University* ☎ *919/962–2296, 800/722–4335* 🌐 *www.goheels.com.*

GOLF

UNC Finley Golf Course

GOLF | This public golf course was designed by golf legend Tom Fazio, who gave the links wide fairways and fast greens. ✉ *500 Finley Golf Course Rd., South Metro* ☎ *919/962–2349* 🌐 *www.uncfinley.com* *$58–$90, 18 holes, 7328 yds, par 72.*

Greensboro

96 miles northeast of Charlotte; 26 miles east of Winston-Salem; 58 miles west of Durham.

With its aging brick buildings and outer ring of small-city sprawl, Greensboro might not seem all that romantic at first, but let it grow on you. There's a feeling of possibility here created by a constant influx of new residents, which include college students and immigrants from around the world. This mixture of new folks and natives makes this unassuming city surprisingly diverse. Like Winston-Salem with tobacco and High Point with furniture, Greensboro's historical claim to relevance lies in textiles. In the early 20th century, it was the country's largest producer of denim, and Wrangler jeans is still headquartered here. Greensboro is also known for its role in the fight for civil rights (the most well-known lunch counter sit-in of the mid-'60s occurred here). Today, the multifaceted city is creating a brand-new identity.

For a night out, choose between an edgy play, live music, or a second-run movie at the inexpensive RED Cinemas theater outside town. A growing craft brewery presence is highlighted by slick spots like SouthEnd downtown and Oden Brewing near the UNC-Greensboro campus, where the back-porch scene overflows into the yard on sunny afternoons. There's also a vibrant LGBTQ scene, anchored by popular hangouts like the Bearded Goat, just off South Elm Street.

To watch the city's work in progress, take an early-evening stroll through Old Greensborough, which has been the city's eclectic epicenter for years. You'll find everything from vintage stores to bubble tea.

GETTING HERE AND AROUND

Interstates 40 and 85 diverge just to the northeast of Greensboro, which means getting here is easy. Navigating the city is easy, too, especially in the booming and walkable downtown.

VISITOR INFORMATION

CONTACTS Greensboro Convention and Visitors Bureau. ✉ *2411 W. Gate City Blvd.* ☎ *800/344–2282, 336/274–2282* 🌐 *www.visitgreensboronc.com.*

Sights

The Blandwood Mansion

HISTORIC SITE | The elegant home of former governor John Motley Morehead is considered the prototype of the Italian-villa architecture that swept the country during the mid-19th century. Noted architect Alexander Jackson Davis designed the house, which has a stucco exterior and towers and still contains many of its original furnishings. A kitchen garden and rose garden on the grounds are maintained by local volunteers. Guided tours highlight the architecture and history. The house also serves as the headquarters of Preservation Greensboro. Among the fascinating and well-preserved artifacts is a bracelet woven by Governor Moreland's daughter from her deceased husband's hair, featuring a posthumous portrait. ✉ *447 W. Washington St., Downtown* ☎ *336/272–5003* 🌐 *www.preservationgreensboro.org* 🎟 *$8* ⏲ *Closed Mon.*

Elsewhere

ARTS VENUE | This Greensboro original—a combination art museum, studio, theater, and school—brings complete sensory overload via an astounding explosion of art and artifacts collected over several decades by its former owner, Sylvia Gray, who ran it as a thrift store. Today, a colorful cast of resident artists creates new work from this treasure trove. Expect colorful plumes of fabric hanging from the walls and toys, books, jewelry, and so much more stuffed into every corner of this large space. You can't buy anything here, but you can touch it all. **■ TIP→ A great time to visit is during First Friday, when galleries and shops throughout downtown host an open house and art walk. Check out the scene every first Friday of the month, 6–9 pm.** ✉ *606 S. Elm St., Downtown* ☎ *336/907–3271* 🌐 *elsewheremuseum.org* 🎟 *$5 suggested donation* ⏲ *Closed Mon.–Thurs.*

Greensboro Children's Museum

MUSEUM | **FAMILY** | The exhibits at this fun museum are designed for children under 12, who can tour an airplane cockpit, explore a fire truck or police car, scale a climbing wall, create crafts out of recycled materials, or learn about buildings in the construction zone. **■ TIP→ Admission is reduced to $5 Friday 5–8.** ✉ *220 N.*

Church St., Downtown ☎ *336/574–2898* 🌐 *www.gcmuseum.com* 🎫 *$10* ⏲ *Closed Mon.–Wed.*

Greensboro History Museum

MUSEUM VILLAGE | Set in a Romanesque church dating from 1892, the museum has displays about the city's own O. Henry and Dolley Madison, plus a detailed timeline about the city's textile boom as the country's largest producer of denim. There's also an exploration of the Woolworth sit-in, which launched the civil rights movement's struggle to desegregate eating establishments. Permanent exhibits include a horse-drawn 1886 steam fire engine, an original Cadillac, and collections of Confederate weapons and Jugtown pottery. Behind the museum are an 18th-century homestead and the graves of several Revolutionary War soldiers. ✉ *130 Summit Ave., Downtown* ☎ *336/373–2043* 🌐 *www.greensborohistory.org* 🎫 *Free* ⏲ *Closed Mon.*

Greensboro Science Center

CAROUSEL | **FAMILY** | At this expansive park designed to fascinate children at every turn, you can roam through a room filled with dinosaurs, see tigers and red pandas in the 24-acre zoo, meet a penguin or shark in the aquarium, and soar through the treetops on the SKYWILD high ropes course. The grounds include a petting zoo, a reptile and amphibian house, a carousel, and a 3-D theater. ✉ *4301 Lawndale Dr., Northwest Metro* ☎ *336/288–3769* 🌐 *www.greensboroscience.org* 🎫 *$16.*

Guilford Courthouse National Military Park

ARCHAEOLOGICAL SITE | **FAMILY** | On March 15, 1781, the Battle of Guilford Courthouse so weakened British troops that they surrendered seven months later at Yorktown. This park was established in 1917 to memorialize that battle, one of the earliest events in the area's recorded history and a pivotal moment in the life of the colonies. There are more than 200 acres here, with wooded hiking trails. The visitor center features films and exhibits on the historic battle. ✉ *2332 New Garden Rd., Northwest Metro* ☎ *336/288–1776* 🌐 *www.nps.gov/guco* 🎫 *Free.*

★ The International Civil Rights Center and Museum

HISTORIC SITE | With an unflinching eye, this museum documents the beauty and horror of America's civil rights movement of the 1960s. The star attraction is the actual Woolworth's lunch counter where countless African Americans staged sit-ins to protest segregation for more than six months in 1960. A guided tour shows viewers how this act of defiance spread to more than 50 cities throughout the South and helped finally bring segregation to an end. Other exhibits uncover the brutality of America's racism throughout the South. ⚠ **Many of the museum's graphic images of historical violence may be too intense for young eyes.** ✉ *134 S. Elm St., Downtown* ☎ *336/274–9199* 🌐 *www.sitinmovement.org* 🎫 *$15* ⏲ *Closed Sun.*

★ Tanger Family Bicentennial Garden and Bog Garden

GARDEN | **FAMILY** | These two public gardens offer a relaxing retreat along a stream that runs between two busy roads. The Bicentennial Garden houses sculptures (including large-scale interactive wind chimes), a Sensory Garden, a pétanque court, and a reconstructed mill and waterwheel. The Bog Garden includes wooden walkways that meander over water and wetlands. ✉ *1105 Hobbs Rd.* ☎ *336/373–2199* 🌐 *www.greensborobeautiful.org* 🎫 *Free.*

Weatherspoon Art Museum

MUSEUM | Set on the campus of UNC Greensboro, the museum is known for its permanent collection, which includes lithographs and bronzes by Henri Matisse and over 400 Japanese woodblock prints. There's an outdoor sculpture garden, and ever-changing exhibitions of 20th-century and modern American art. ✉ *500 Tate St., University* ☎ *336/334–5770* 🌐 *weatherspoonart.org* 🎫 *Free* ⏲ *Closed Sun. and Mon.*

Restaurants

★ Crafted

$ | **MEXICAN FUSION** | This staple of Triad dining takes the gourmet taco to new levels. Try a Bowtie, stuffed with fried fish, cotija cheese, and honey mustard, or commit to the Big Truck's combo of mac and cheese, barbecue pork, and bacon sauce. **Known for:** stuffed avocado overflowing with queso, pico, and chorizo; a perfect house margarita; homemade flour tortilla chips and pico de gallo. *Average main: $12 ✉ 220 S. Elm St., Downtown ☎ 336/273–0030 🌐 www.eatatcrafted.com ⏲ Closed Mon.*

Hops Burger Bar

$ | **BURGER** | **FAMILY** | This Greensboro mainstay (now with two locations in town, plus a third in Winston-Salem) was early to the gourmet burger bandwagon. They keep up their sterling reputation with a commitment to well-sourced ingredients and inviting offerings like the North Carolinian (bacon, fried green tomato, pimento cheese, and a fried egg). **Known for:** the "wall of fries," including a hearty mound of poutine fries; fried goat cheese balls with fig jelly; packed house on weekends. *Average main: $14 ✉ 2138 Lawndale Dr., North Metro ☎ 336/663–0537 🌐 hopsburgerbar.com.*

Liberty Oak Restaurant and Bar

$$$$ | **AMERICAN** | Situated in a 19th-century building just off Elm Street, this inviting restaurant serves upscale food in relaxed surroundings. The constantly shifting menu always includes an array of seafood, steaks, pasta, and vegetarian dishes. **Known for:** top-notch seafood and steaks; historic building with patio dining; broad high-end menu. *Average main: $25 ✉ 100–D W. Washington St., Downtown ☎ 336/273–7057 ⏲ Closed Sun.*

★ Lucky 32 Southern Kitchen

$$$ | **SOUTHERN** | Gourmet meets fried catfish at this staple of Greensboro fine dining for three decades. A remodel in 2020 brought the chic dining room up to par with the elevated, Delta-inspired cuisine. **Known for:** silky sweet she-crab soup; short ribs braised in sweet tea; skilled, friendly service. *Average main: $23 ✉ 1421 Westover Terr., Friendly ☎ 336/370–0707 🌐 lucky32.com ⏲ Closed Sun. and Mon.*

★ Stamey's

$ | **BARBECUE** | **FAMILY** | This Greensboro staple (for nearly a century) is a pilgrimage spot for barbecue lovers from across the state. The chopped, Eastern-style pork is mostly shoulder meat already sauced in the kitchen, though there's also plenty of vinegary Stamey's Secret Sauce at your table. **Known for:** wood-smoked vinegar-based barbecue; traditional Brunswick stew; homemade peach cobbler. *Average main: $8 ✉ 2206 W. Gate City Blvd., Coliseum ☎ 336/299–9888 🌐 www.stameys.com ⏲ Closed Sun.*

Coffee and Quick Bites

Cheesecakes by Alex

$ | **BAKERY** | Swing by this local favorite for a café au lait and a chocolate croissant in the morning, and then visit again after dark for the decadent desserts. **Known for:** two dozen cheesecake flavors, from sweet potato to chocolate chip mint; coffee and pastries in the morning; rich cupcakes and muffins. *Average main: $6 ✉ 315 S. Elm St., Downtown ☎ 336/273–0970 🌐 cheesecakesbyalex.com.*

Hotels

The Biltmore Greensboro

$ | **HOTEL** | In the heart of the central business district, this historic spot (opened in 1903) has an old-world, slightly faded feel, with 16-foot ceilings, a cage elevator, and a lobby with walnut-panel walls and a fireplace. **Pros:** fans of old hotels will find the setting appealing; great downtown location; one of the best values in town. **Cons:** not very modern; small bathrooms; tiny fitness room.

$ Rooms from: $129 ✉ 111 W. Washington St., Downtown ☎ 336/272–3474, 800/332–0303 🌐 www.thebiltmoregreensboro.com 🛏 26 rooms 🍽 Free breakfast.

Grandover Resort

$$ | **RESORT** | Overlooking the Appalachian foothills and two world-class golf courses, this resort, spa, and conference center offers a luxurious escape. **Pros:** large, well-appointed rooms; luxurious amenities including a full-service spa; golf and tennis on-site. **Cons:** somewhat isolated from other attractions; service can be inconsistent; no shuttle service to downtown. *$ Rooms from: $199 ✉ 1000 Club Rd., Northwest Metro ☎ 336/294–1800 🌐 www.grandover.com 🛏 244 rooms 🍽 No meals.*

★ O. Henry Hotel

$$$$ | **HOTEL** | **FAMILY** | This boutique hotel (named for the renowned short-story writer, who grew up in Greensboro) was constructed in the late 1990s but evokes old-world European charm; expect lots of wood paneling, mohair club chairs, and an extremely friendly staff. **Pros:** nostalgic setting with modern comforts; daily afternoon high tea and live jazz in the evenings; free airport shuttle (often in a fun London-style taxi). **Cons:** some rooms have views of unattractive commercial properties; not in walking distance of Greensboro's city center; some furniture and wallpaper choices feel dated. *$ Rooms from: $269 ✉ 624 Green Valley Rd., Friendly ☎ 336/854–2000 🌐 www.ohenryhotel.com 🛏 130 rooms 🍽 Free breakfast.*

★ Proximity Hotel

$$$$ | **HOTEL** | With its high ceilings, big windows, and exposed beams, this modern hotel makes you feel like you're in the future—or perhaps just in a loft in a bigger city than Greensboro. **Pros:** striking blend of luxury and urban cool; large gym and an inviting outdoor pool; free bike rentals to explore the nearby greenway. **Cons:** the supersleek interior isn't for everyone; outside the city center; a bit too posh for most families with small children. *$ Rooms from: $279 ✉ 704 Green Valley Rd., Friendly ☎ 336/379–8200 🌐 www.proximityhotel.com 🛏 147 rooms 🍽 No meals.*

Nightlife

The Blind Tiger

MUSIC CLUBS | A Greensboro institution, this standing-room club is one of the best places in the Triad to hear live music. Previous headliners have included Ben Folds Five (their first show, no less) and members of the Neville Brothers. *✉ 1819 Spring Garden St., Coliseum ☎ 336/272–9888 🌐 www.theblindtiger.com.*

Natty Greene's Brewing Company

BREWPUBS/BEER GARDENS | Located on lively South Elm Street, this tavern keeps a dozen beers on tap, including several that it brews in-house. The bar food here's done right, including the potato chips and a generous tuna steak. Upstairs is a sports bar with pool tables. In nice weather, you can sit on the patio along the main drag. *✉ 345 S. Elm St., Downtown ☎ 336/274–1373 🌐 www.nattygreenes.com.*

Performing Arts

Carolina Theatre

CONCERTS | What opened in 1927 as a vaudeville theater has matured and diversified into a performing-arts center that showcases dance, music, films, and plays. The interior, with its gilded classical-style ornamentation and marble statues, is its own attraction. *✉ 310 S. Greene St., Downtown ☎ 336/333–2605 🌐 www.carolinatheatre.com.*

Community Theatre of Greensboro

THEATER | Founded in 1949, this playhouse stages professional shows and a host of children's programs in the Old Greensborough historic district. Little-known comedy gems are its specialty.

✉ 520 S. Elm St., Downtown ☎ 336/333–7470 🌐 www.ctgso.org.

Eastern Music Festival

FESTIVALS | The Eastern Music Festival, a classical music celebration whose guests have included Billy Joel, André Watts, and Wynton Marsalis, brings a month of more than four dozen concerts to Greensboro's Guilford College and music venues throughout the city. It starts in late June. ✉ *200 N. Davie St., Downtown* ☎ *336/333–7450* 🌐 *www.easternmusicfestival.org.*

Greensboro Coliseum Complex

ARTS CENTERS | The vast Greensboro Coliseum Complex hosts sporting, music, and entertainment events throughout the year, including the Central Carolina Fair. Jimi Hendrix, Phish, and Garth Brooks have all performed here. It's also home to the Greensboro Swarm, of the NBA's G League, and next door to the ACC Hall of Champions. ✉ *1921 W. Gate City Blvd.* ☎ *336/373–7400* 🌐 *www.greensborocoliseum.com.*

Greensboro Cultural Center

ART GALLERIES—ARTS | **FAMILY** | Home to the offices of more than a dozen art, dance, music, and theater organizations, like the Greensboro Ballet and Greensboro Opera, the cultural center also has several art galleries, a studio theater, an outdoor amphitheater, a sculpture garden, and a restaurant with outdoor seating. ✉ *200 N. Davie St., Downtown* ☎ *336/373–2712* 🌐 *visitgreensboronc.com.*

Triad Stage

READINGS/LECTURES | This nationally recognized professional theater company mixes classic and original plays. They perform in downtown Greensboro at the Pyrle Theater. ✉ *232 S. Elm St., Downtown* ☎ *336/272–0160* 🌐 *www.triadstage.org.*

Shopping

Replacements, Ltd.

CERAMICS/GLASSWARE | Located between Greensboro and Burlington, this is the world's largest seller of discontinued and active china, crystal, flatware, and collectibles. It stocks more than 12 million pieces in 425,000 patterns. Free tours of the massive warehouse are offered every hour until one hour before closing time. ✉ *1089 Knox. Rd., McLeansville* ✥ *I–85/I–40 at Mt. Hope Church Rd., Exit 132* ☎ *800/737–5223* 🌐 *www.replacements.com.*

Activities

GOLF

Bryan Park

GOLF | These two public courses, 6 miles north of Greensboro, have 36 holes of quality golf. The Players Course, designed by Rees Jones in 1988, features 79 bunkers and eight water hazards. Jones outdid himself on the lovely 1990 Champions Course, where seven holes hug Lake Townsend. ✉ *6275 Bryan Park Rd., Browns Summit* ☎ *336/375–2200* 🌐 *www.bryanpark.com* 🏌 *Players Course: $47–$55, 18 holes, 7057 yds, par 72; Champions Course: $50–$58, 18 holes, 7255 yds, par 72.*

Greensboro National Golf Club

GOLF | The clubhouse is known for its hot dogs, so you know this course lacks the pretense of others in the area. Called "a golf course for guys who like golf courses," the Don and Mark Charles–designed public links feature wide fairways, expansive greens, and layouts that are challenging without resorting to blind spots and other trickery. ✉ *330 Niblick Dr., Summerfield* ☎ *336/342–1113* 🌐 *www.greensboronationalgolfclub.com* 🏌 *$35–$57, 18 holes, 6261 yds, par 72.*

Winston-Salem

26 miles west of Greensboro; 81 miles north of Charlotte.

Even in the heart of downtown, there's something not entirely modern about Winston-Salem. And that's a good thing. The second-largest city in the Triad blends the past and the present nicely, creating a pleasant and low-key place for both history-minded tourists and people who work in the area. Historic skyscrapers like the R.J. Reynold's building (the architectural father of the Empire State Building) remind you that this small city once swung well above its weight, thanks to its history as the home of Camel cigarettes. And in the town that Big Tobacco built, it's now much easier to find an organic cold-pressed juice than a pack of smokes.

Two historical areas—Old Salem and Bethabara—celebrate the hardworking members of the Moravian Church, a Protestant sect that arose in what's now the Czech Republic in the 15th century. For nearly a hundred years, starting in the mid-18th century, the Winston-Salem region was almost entirely populated by Moravian settlers. With its Colonial Williamsburg–like period reconstruction (and delicious cookies), Old Salem in particular shouldn't be missed, even if you have only an afternoon to spend here.

For a taste of present-day Winston-Salem, check out the Downtown Arts District, centered on the intersection of 6th and Trade Streets. Once known for its bustling tobacco market, this area is now a sea of happening galleries and cafés.

With two impressive art museums, a symphony orchestra, a burgeoning brewery scene, and the internationally respected North Carolina School of the Arts, there's plenty to do within the city limits.

GETTING HERE AND AROUND

Easily accessed by Interstate 40, Winston-Salem is laid out in an orderly grid. Parts of the city are great for walking, especially Old Salem and the neighborhoods surrounding it. Parking anywhere except in the core five or six blocks of downtown is not a problem. On downtown street corners, pay-by-app electric scooters from Bird, Blue Duck, and Spin are abundant.

VISITOR INFORMATION

CONTACTS Visit Winston-Salem . ✉ *200 Brookstown Ave.* ☎ *336/728–4200* 🌐 *www.visitwinstonsalem.com.*

Childress Vineyards

WINERY/DISTILLERY | Modeled after an Italian villa, this stately winery provides both an atmosphere and a level of quality on par with vineyards in more lauded wine regions. Created by NASCAR driver and team owner Richard Childress, the winery offers more than 30 varieties, including its popular Reserve Chardonnay and Signature Meritage. Within its opulent 35,000-square-foot building, visitors can witness wine making firsthand or have lunch at the Bistro, which overlooks the vineyards. ✉ *1000 Childress Vineyards Rd., Lexington* ☎ *336/236–9463* 🌐 *www.childressvineyards.com.*

★ Historic Bethabara Park

MUSEUM VILLAGE | **FAMILY** | Set in a wooded 183-acre wildlife preserve, this was the site of the first Moravian settlement in North Carolina. The reconstructed village showcasing the mid-18th-century community includes the original 1788 Gemeinhaus congregation house, a colonial homestead, and well-maintained medicinal gardens. God's Acre, the first colony cemetery, is a short walk away. Children love the reconstructed fort from the French and Indian War, and hiking trails head off into the hills around the settlement. Brochures for self-guided walking tours are available year-round at the visitor center, where interpreters in period attire help bring this bygone era to life. ✉ *2147 Bethabara Rd., University* ☎ *336/924–8191* 🌐 *www.historicbethabara.org* 🎫 *Free, tours $4* ⏲ *Visitor center closed Mon.*

Kaleideum North

MUSEUM | FAMILY | This interactive science museum has 45,000 square feet of hands-on exhibits designed to engage kids of all ages, from a hurricane simulator to an indoor scooter racetrack. There's also a 120-seat planetarium and a 15-acre environmental park with a children's garden and paved walking trails. ✉ *400 W. Hanes Mill Rd., North Metro* ☎ *336/767–6730* 🌐 *north.kaleideum.org* 🎫 *$10* ⏲ *Closed Mon., Tues., and Thurs.*

Museum of Early Southern Decorative Arts

MUSEUM | This unique museum on the southern edge of Old Salem showcases the furniture, painting, ceramics, and metalware used in the area through 1820. The bookstore carries hard-to-find books on Southern culture and history. ✉ *924 S. Main St., Old Salem* ☎ *336/721–7360* 🌐 *www.mesda.org* 🎫 *Self-guided $10, guided tour $20, admission to both the museum and Old Salem Museums and Gardens $27* ⏲ *Closed Mon.*

★ Old Salem Museums and Gardens

HISTORIC SITE | FAMILY | Founded in 1766 as a backcountry trading center, Old Salem is one of the nation's most well-documented colonial sites. This living-history museum, a few blocks from downtown Winston-Salem, is filled with dozens of original and reconstructed buildings. Costumed guides demonstrate trades and household activities common in the late-18th- and early-19th-century Moravian communities, and an interactive audio tour tells the stories of the Native Americans, enslaved Africans, and European settlers that lived here. The preserved streets and buildings of the old town are still a functioning community that includes the campus of Salem College. Be sure to stop at Winkler Bakery, where you can buy bread, the pillowy, best-selling sugar cakes, and scrumptious Moravian ginger cookies, baked in traditional brick ovens. **■ TIP→ Don't miss "America's largest coffee pot," a 12-foot-tall vessel built by Julius Mickey in 1858 to advertise his tinsmith shop. After surviving two separate car collisions, it was moved to its present location at the edge of Old Salem in 1959.** ✉ *900 Old Salem Rd., Old Salem* ☎ *336/721–7300* 🌐 *www.oldsalem.org* 🎫 *$27, includes admission to Museum of Early Southern Decorative Arts* ⏲ *Museum closed Mon., although the town can be walked through any time of day.*

RayLen Vineyards and Winery

WINERY/DISTILLERY | This idyllic vineyard on rolling hills 20 miles west of Winston-Salem is an easy escape from city life. In its low-key country setting you can tour the vineyard and discover some of the state's most famous wines, including RayLen's Bordeaux-blend showstoppers Eagle's Select and Category 5. ✉ *3577 U.S. 158, Mocksville* ☎ *336/998–3100* 🌐 *www.raylenvineyards.com.*

Reynolda House Museum of American Art

GARDEN | The front yard of this home, built by Camel cigarette founder R. J. Reynolds and his wife, Katharine Smith Reynolds, seems to extend to the horizon. It's the first of many moments of grandeur at the 1917 dwelling that's now an art museum filled with paintings, prints, and sculptures by Thomas Eakins, Frederic Church, and Georgia O'Keeffe. There's also a costume collection, as well as clothing and toys used by the Reynolds children. The home is adjacent to the 134-acre Reynolda Gardens that include flower fields, wooded trails, and a nursery. Next door is **Reynolda Village**, a collection of shops and restaurants that fill the estate's original outer buildings. ✉ *2250 Reynolda Rd., University* ☎ *888/663–1149* 🌐 *www.reynoldahouse.org* 🎫 *$18* ⏲ *Closed Mon.*

Southeastern Center for Contemporary Art

MUSEUM | The always-changing exhibits at this expansive but tucked-away museum near the Wake Forest campus showcase artwork—including large-format sculpture displays—by nationally and internationally known artists. ✉ *750 Marguerite Dr., University* ☎ *336/725–1904* 🌐 *www.secca.org* 🎫 *Free* 🕒 *Closed Mon. and Tues.*

Tanglewood Park

BODY OF WATER | **FAMILY** | Once land claimed for Queen Elizabeth by Sir Walter Raleigh, this park's amenities include golfing, boating, hiking, fishing, horseback riding, and a large swimming pool with waterslides. There is also a dog park, campground, and an arboretum filled with plants native to the Carolina Piedmont. The Tanglewood Festival of Lights, one of the largest holiday-lights festivals in the Southeast, runs from mid-November to early January. ✉ *4061 Clemmons Rd., Clemmons* ☎ *336/703–6400* 🌐 *forsyth.cc/parks/tanglewood* 🎫 *$2 per car.*

Restaurants

Mozelle's

$$$ | **SOUTHERN** | Located in the historic West End neighborhood, this small, cheery café with shaded sidewalk seating offers Southern fare with a touch of elegance. The menu is based on seasonal local ingredients, with standouts that include the Southern spring rolls, bacon-wrapped meat loaf, and fried chicken with peach chutney. **Known for:** inspired Southern fare based on the freshest ingredients; legendary tomato pie; weekend brunch with both light and hearty options. 💲 *Average main: $22* ✉ *878 W. 4th St., Downtown* ☎ *336/703–5400* 🌐 *www.mozelles.com* 🕒 *Closed Mon.*

Sweet Potatoes

$$ | **SOUTHERN** | This restaurant's full name is Sweet Potatoes (Well Shut My Mouth!), and once you have a taste of these Southern classics, you'll know why. Expect friendly service and more food than you could possibly eat. **Known for:** fried chicken, biscuits, and other Southern staples; namesake-worthy sweet potatoes (including in fry and pie form); delicious Sunday brunch. 💲 *Average main: $16* ✉ *607 Trade St., Downtown* ☎ *336/727–4844* 🌐 *www.sweetpotatoes.ws* 🕒 *Closed Mon.*

Willow's Bistro

$$$$ | **FUSION** | This laid-back café in a former railroad building serves creative cocktails and Southern-fusion fare like salmon and grits and farro shiitake stir-fry. On warm evenings, grab a table along the lengthy side porch while you munch on appetizers like calamari with pickled peppers. **Known for:** a variety of Benedicts at Sunday brunch; thin cut, hearty flat iron steak; good food in a relaxed atmosphere. 💲 *Average main: $28* ✉ *300 S. Liberty St., Downtown* ☎ *336/293–4601* 🌐 *goodvibeshospitality.com/willowbistro.*

Coffee and Quick Bites

Grecian Corner

$ | **GREEK** | In an austere building underneath the highway, this out-of-the-way eatery has dished up gyros and souvlaki since 1970. Patrons, including workers at the nearby hospital and local families, enjoy the friendly service and ample portions of moussaka, spanakopita, and salads, plus more familiar fare like hamburgers and pizza. **Known for:** classic Greek dishes and wines; family-friendly service; the best gyro in the city. 💲 *Average main: $12* ✉ *101 Eden Terr., Downtown* ☎ *336/722–6937* 🌐 *www.greciancorner.com* 💳 *No credit cards* 🕒 *Closed Sun.*

★ Krankies Coffee

$ | **SOUTHERN** | Winston's hippest coffee joint is known for its biscuits and burgers as much as its espresso. A warehouse-like interior offers plenty of room to spread out, and ample outdoor tables fill with locals relaxing or working on sunny days. **Known for:** a chicken biscuit marinated in honey and Texas Pete; miel iced coffee lattes, flavored with spices and honey; full bar to get your midday drink on. $ *Average main: $8* ✉ *211 E. 3rd St., Downtown* ☎ *336/722–3016* 🌐 *krankiescoffee.com* ⏲ *Closed Mon.*

Hotels

★ Graylyn

$$ | **B&B/INN** | **FAMILY** | The former estate of R. J. Reynolds executive Bowman Gray and his wife, Nathalie, is now a luxurious inn 2 miles north of downtown, near the Wake Forest campus. **Pros:** 55 acres of gorgeous green space to roam; full breakfast buffet, including an omelet station; exceptional hospitality from butlers and front-desk staff. **Cons:** it's not directly in downtown Winston-Salem; conference groups sometimes fill the property; fitness center within the main inn has only two machines. $ *Rooms from: $159* ✉ *1900 Reynolda Rd., University* ☎ *800/472–9596* 🌐 *graylyn.com* *85 rooms* *Free breakfast.*

The Historic Brookstown Inn

$ | **HOTEL** | **FAMILY** | No two rooms are the same in this historic, affordable, and very pleasant lodging, built within two former cotton mills dating to 1837. **Pros:** historic setting is unique; walking distance to Old Salem; complimentary hot breakfast. **Cons:** dated carpets in hallways; some rooms have dim lighting; families might miss having a pool, especially in the sweltering summer. $ *Rooms from: $147* ✉ *200 Brookstown Ave., Old Salem* ☎ *336/701–3904* 🌐 *www.brookstowninn.com* *70 rooms* *Free breakfast.*

Hotel Indigo Winston-Salem Downtown

$$ | **HOTEL** | Built into the renovated art deco–era Pepper Building in the heart of downtown, this locally owned 2019 addition to the city's lodging doubles as a gathering place—the wide windows overlooking the street beckon passersby into the stunning lobby-level bar and restaurant, Sir Winston. **Pros:** colorful, fun aesthetic; pets are allowed, with no size restrictions, for a $25 fee; freshest, most modern option in town. **Cons:** parking is off-site and valet only ($23 per night); no pool; small gym. $ *Rooms from: $168* ✉ *104 W. 4th St., Downtown* ☎ *336/722–0720* 🌐 *ihg.com* *75 rooms* *No meals.*

★ The Kimpton Cardinal Hotel

$$$ | **HOTEL** | To understand Winston-Salem in the 2020s, consider that the former R. J. Reynolds headquarters is now a modern hotel where (of course) smoking is not allowed anywhere on the premises. **Pros:** architectural touches are stunning; dogs are welcome and even get their own bed upon request; fun amenities like bowling lanes. **Cons:** rooms fill up quickly during special events at nearby Wake Forest University; pet-friendly atmosphere doesn't work for everyone; no pool. $ *Rooms from: $246* ✉ *51 E. 4th St., Downtown* ☎ *855/546–7866* 🌐 *www.thecardinalhotel.com* *174 rooms* *No meals.*

Winston-Salem Marriott

$ | **HOTEL** | Soaring ceilings and elaborate, sculptural lighting set a striking, modern tone in the lobby of this central and reliable chain hotel. **Pros:** it's an easy walk to the arts district and jazz clubs; newly renovated rooms (as of 2019); on-site Butcher & Bull steak house is a solid dining option. **Cons:** sophisticated but dim lighting in communal areas brings down the vibe; lacks charm of nearby competitors; breakfast available but not included. $ *Rooms from: $128* ✉ *425 N. Cherry St., Downtown* ☎ *336/725–3500* 🌐 *www.marriott.com* *319 rooms* *No meals.*

The Zevely Inn

$$ | **B&B/INN** | This 1844 inn right on Old Salem's Main Street has a way of transporting guests back several centuries; it's also made a name for itself as a romantic getaway. **Pros:** only lodging in Old Salem; guests get a strong sense of history here; modern conveniences like televisions and free Wi-Fi. **Cons:** restaurants and nightlife are a drive away; bathrooms can be small; period furnishings aren't for everyone. $ *Rooms from: $169* ✉ *803*

S. Main St., Old Salem ☎ 336/748–9299 🌐 www.zevelyinn.com 🛏 12 rooms 🍽 Free breakfast.

★ **Foothills Brewpub**

BREWPUBS/BEER GARDENS | Winston-Salem's first craft brewery keeps a variety of year-round and seasonal brews on tap, including regional staples like their Hoppyum IPA and Torch Pilsner. The pub also serves up inspired bar food like dry-rubbed wings and daily flatbread and sandwich specials. It's a popular happy hour and weekend gathering spot. Try even more beers at the brewery and tasting room, just outside downtown. ✉ *638 W. 4th St., Downtown* ☎ *336/777–3348* 🌐 *www.foothillsbrewing.com.*

6th and Vine

CAFES—NIGHTLIFE | For a classy yet quirky evening out, try this wine bar–café. Outdoor patio seating (on the street and back patio), North Carolina wines, local brews, and frequent DJ dance parties make this a fun gathering place in the heart of the Arts District. ✉ *209 W. 6th St., Downtown* ☎ *336/725–5577* 🌐 *www.6thandvine.com.*

Wise Man Brewing

BREWPUBS/BEER GARDENS | Winston-Salem's downtown brewery scene is geographically compact yet expansive in variety, and Wise Man is arguably the best among a strong pack of contenders. Choose from over 20 rotating brews, like the punch-packing Body Electric double IPA or the Sufficient Wit Belgian witbier, and grab a seat at any of the shaded picnic tables lining the warehouselike brick taproom. ✉ *826 Angelo Bros. Ave., Downtown* ☎ *336/725–0008* 🌐 *wisemanbrewing.com.*

North Carolina Black Repertory Company

FESTIVALS | The first professional black theater company in North Carolina, this repertory offers performances throughout the year that educate and inspire. Every other August, it hosts the National Black Theatre Festival, a weeklong showcase of African American arts, which attracts tens of thousands of people to venues all over the city. ✉ *419 N. Spruce St., University* ☎ *336/723–2266* 🌐 *www.ncblackrep.org.*

The Ramkat

CONCERTS | There's a palpable energy in the room when national touring acts like Buddy Guy and Hiss Golden Messenger take the stage at this intimate 1,000-person venue. Seats and standing room are spread over two levels, and three bars ensure convenient access to libations and refreshments. ✉ *170 W. 9th St., Downtown* ☎ *336/754–9714* 🌐 *theramkat.com.*

Stevens Center

ARTS CENTERS | This restored 1929 movie palace hosts performances by the Winston-Salem Symphony and Piedmont Opera, as well as student productions by the University of North Carolina School of the Arts. ✉ *405 W. 4th St., Downtown* ☎ *336/721–1945* 🌐 *www.uncsa.edu/performances/stevens-center.*

CRAFTS

Moravian Book & Gift Shop

LOCAL SPECIALTIES | Discover Moravian crafts and heritage at this quaint gift shop in the heart of Old Salem. The collection of home goods includes local pottery, pillows, and gardening tools. ✉ *614 S. Main St., Old Salem* ☎ *336/723–6262.*

Piedmont Craftsmen's Shop and Gallery

CRAFTS | Contemporary and traditional works from nearly 400 craftspeople fill this gallery and shop in Winston-Salem's arty hub. The organization has held an annual fair in November since 1963. ✉ *601*

North Carolina Wineries

With over 200 wineries sprinkled throughout North Carolina's valleys, mountains, and coastal plain, the state's wine industry is huge yet intimate in its approach. When touring and tasting around these parts, don't be surprised if you end up sipping your vintage alongside the owner or head grower. Even the wildly successful folks at RayLen and Childress Vineyards, near Winston-Salem, remain approachable and focus on producing quality wine. This is especially true in the Yadkin Valley, the biggest wine-producing region in the state, located on and near the western edge of the Piedmont. Here, nearly 70 wineries have built their reputation by bucking North Carolina's centuries-old tradition of producing sweet muscadine and scuppernong wines and opting instead for the drier European varieties of the vinifera family. Though they were originally labeled rebels by the state's old-school wine producers, the Yadkin growers are now considered some of the finest in the Southeast. A few of the hot varietals to watch include the white Viognier and the red Cabernet Franc.

N. Trade St., Downtown ☎ 336/725–1516 🌐 www.piedmontcraftsmen.org.

BASKETBALL

Demon Deacons

BASKETBALL | Wake Forest University's Atlantic Coast Conference entry plays basketball in Lawrence Joel Veterans Memorial Coliseum. ✉ *2825 University Pkwy., University 🌐 www.godeacs.com.*

GOLF

Tanglewood Park Golf

GOLF | In addition to Tanglewood Park's Reynolds Course, there's the Championship Course, which once hosted the PGA Championship and was long home to the Vantage Championship. Both courses were designed by Robert Trent Jones in the mid-'50s, and both feature pine-lined fairways (narrower on the Reynolds course) and lakes that come into play several times. Golf cart fees are included in rates for both of these courses. ✉ *4201 Manor House Circle, Clemmons ✣ U.S. 158 off I–40 ☎ 336/703–6420 🌐 www.golf.tanglewoodpark.org 🏌 Reynolds Course: $29–$35, 18 holes, 6567 yds, par 72; Championship Course: $49–$59, 18 holes, 7101 yds, par 70; Par 3 Course: $10, 18 holes, 1445 yds, par 54.*

High Point

18 miles southeast of Winston-Salem; 76 miles northeast of Charlotte; 20 miles southwest of Greensboro.

High Point earned its name through simple geography: it was the highest point on the railroad line between Goldsboro and Charlotte. Nowadays the city's "high point" is hosting the semiannual High Point Market, the largest wholesale furniture trade show in the world. Each spring and fall for about a week, so many people flood "Furniture City" that its population of 112,000 nearly doubles. The rest of the year, the place can be pretty sleepy. Note that downtown High Point can feel like a ghost town on weekends, lorded over by massive buildings full of furniture but very few people. Thus, the town is lacking in memorable restaurants; for more varied eats, check out nearby Greensboro or Winston-Salem.

Don't miss the World's Largest Chest of Drawers in High Point, a city known for its superlative furniture.

GETTING HERE AND AROUND

High Point is one of the Piedmont's smaller cities, with very little traffic. Navigating it by car is fairly simple, and if you happen to get turned around, friendly folks are ready to offer help with directions.

VISITOR INFORMATION

CONTACTS High Point Visitor Center. *1634 N. Main St., Suite 102* *336/884–5255* *visithighpoint.com.*

Sights

★ High Point Museum and Historical Park
HISTORIC SITE | FAMILY | Wander through the 1786 John Haley House and the 1801 Hoggatt House, where rotating exhibits highlight Piedmont history and Quaker heritage with local artifacts. On Saturdays, costumed reenactors demonstrate trades like traditional blacksmithing. The museum is home to native son John Coltrane's childhood piano and a school bus cab with operational lights that's fun for kids. *1859 E. Lexington Ave.* *336/885–1859* *highpointnc.gov/2329/Museum* *Free* *Closed Sun. and Mon.*

Mendenhall Homeplace
GHOST TOWN | FAMILY | A well-preserved example of 19th-century domestic architecture, this homestead (including the main house and several outbuildings) sits in a cove along a peaceful creek. As Quakers, the Mendenhalls opposed slavery, and here you can find one of the few surviving false-bottom wagons used to help those enslaved escape to freedom on the Underground Railroad. **TIP→ Come in July, when kids can learn how to make a corn-husk doll or design a quilt square during the Village Fair.** *603 W. Main St., Jamestown* *336/454–3819* *www.mendenhallhomeplace.com* *$5* *Closed Sun. and Mon.*

World's Largest Chest of Drawers
BUILDING | In the 1920s, this building shaped like an 18th-century chest of drawers was constructed to call attention to the city's standing as the "furniture capital of the world." The 36-foot-high building, complete with a 6-foot-long pair

North Carolina Barbecue

Native Americans in what is today North Carolina are the first chapter in one of the longest continuous barbecue traditions anywhere. In fact, Native Americans, African slaves, and German and Scotch-Irish settlers have all had a hand in the evolution of two distinct styles of barbecue.

East vs. West

Vinegar and pepper sauces in the east highlight the flavor of the meat itself, while western barbecue mixes sweet sauces and smoky flavors in immense variety. Expect more of an eastern influence from Raleigh to the coast. From Charlotte to the mountains, the western style dominates. If you find yourself in between these two "barbecue boundaries," treat yourself to a blend of east and west in the form of North Carolina's third barbecue variety: Lexington Style, which adds ketchup to the vinegar-based sauce. However you slice, chop, or pull it, the barbecue debate has produced great meals and brought friends and family together for generations.

of socks dangling from one of its drawers, remains one of the strangest sights in North Carolina to this day. Nearby Furnitureland South has actually built a much larger chest of drawers as the facade to one of its showrooms, although it is not freestanding. ✉ *508 N. Hamilton St.*

Restaurants

Blue Water Grille

$$$$ | **SEAFOOD** | The menu at this intimate seafood spot includes Lowcountry favorites, often presented with an Asian flair and a bit of French influence. The standout ahi tuna varies by season in its preparation. **Known for:** creative seafood preparations; shared plates; classy night-on-the-town environment. *$ Average main: $25 ✉ 126 E. State Ave. ☎ 336/886–1010 🌐 www.bluewatergrillenc.com ⏲ Closed Sun. No lunch.*

Lexington Barbecue

$ | **BARBECUE** | **FAMILY** | The town of Lexington is the base for Carolina's sweet, red-sauce style of barbecue. At this mainstay where locals line up daily for takeout, meat is pulled from smoked pork shoulders and served up as a sandwich in a soft bun topped with red slaw. **Known for:** pulled pork smoked over hickory wood; fruit cobblers for dessert; old-school barbecue-joint atmosphere. *$ Average main: $11 ✉ 100 Smokehouse La., Lexington ✣ 20 miles southwest of High Point ☎ 336/249–9814 🌐 www.lexbbq.com ⏲ Closed Sun.*

Sweet Old Bill's

$ | **BARBECUE** | **FAMILY** | "SOB" dishes out a mean pulled-pork sandwich, but it's not your typical barbecue joint—the varied menu also includes grilled salmon with chimichurri and an array of gourmet burgers. Tables out front fill up on weekends—it doesn't hurt that it shares a wall with Brown Truck Brewery, whose fresh IPAs and lagers are a perfect accompaniment to the elevated pub grub. **Known for:** St. Louis–style racks of ribs on weekends; smoked meat loaf sandwich on Texas toast; weekend gathering place. *$ Average main: $13 ✉ 1232 N. Main St. ☎ 336/807–1476 🌐 sweetoldbills.com.*

Hotels

JH Adams Inn

$$ | **B&B/INN** | With its grand staircase, richly carved moldings, and marble fireplaces, the stately coral-colored 1918 Adams

Mansion is home to this boutique inn where each room is designed for comfort. **Pros:** historic inn with lots of charm; restaurant and wine bar on-site; nice outdoor spaces with balconies in some rooms. **Cons:** rooms facing street can be noisy; often booked for weddings and special events; no pool; small fitness room. *Rooms from: $154 1108 N. Main St. 336/882–3267 www.jhadamsinn.com 31 rooms Free breakfast.*

Performing Arts

Theatre Art Galleries

ART GALLERIES | Solo and group shows rotate through several exhibition spaces at this sculpture and painting gallery, in the same massive IHFC building as the High Point Theatre. The frequent art openings are always open to the public. Closed Saturday–Monday. *220 E. Commerce Ave. 336/887–2137 www.tagart.org.*

Shopping

Furnitureland South

HOUSEHOLD ITEMS/FURNITURE | With more than 1 million square feet of showroom space, this complex, the biggest furniture retailer in the world, makes an IKEA look like a corner store. This goes far beyond an average shopping experience—a visit here could easily take all day. Customers register with the front desk and are given tips by a Furnitureland consultant on how to maximize their time in the sprawling store, which includes innumerable galleries from leading manufacturers and a discount center. Meals and refreshments are available at a Starbucks and a Subway (the largest one in the United States, of course). *5635 Riverdale Dr., Jamestown 336/822–3000 www.furniturelandsouth.com.*

High Point Furniture Sales

HOUSEHOLD ITEMS/FURNITURE | Deep discounts are part of the draw to this furniture store. Don't be put off by the nondescript brick exterior beside the highway—inside, expect more than 150 well-known brands and some pieces offered at below manufacturer-direct prices. The **Discount Furniture Warehouse and Furniture Value and Clearance Center,** at 2035 Brentwood Street, is only one exit from the main store. *2000 Baker Rd. 336/841–5664 www.highpointfurnituresales.com.*

Activities

GOLF

Oak Hollow

GOLF | Designed by Pete Dye, this public course makes use of its lakeside position by including peninsula greens and an island tee on its par-5 fifth hole. *3400 N. Centennial St. 336/883–3260 www.oakhollowgc.com $18–$40, 18 holes, 6564 yds, par 72.*

HIKING

Piedmont Environmental Center

HIKING/WALKING | **FAMILY** | The 376-acre Piedmont Environmental Center has 11 miles of hiking trails—including several miles along High Point Lake—and a nearly 10-mile paved greenway adjacent to City Lake Park. A small visitor center includes live snake and turtle displays. *1220 Penny Rd. 336/883–8531 highpointnc.gov.*

Charlotte

Don't expect to hear many Southern accents in this melting pot, the biggest city in the state. Visiting this banking hub of the Southeast is much more of an urban experience than a down-home one, but that's all part of the fun of being in this bustling, forward-focused place. Here, local custom focuses less on preserving the old than building the new. Although controversial, this tradition is responsible for the ultramodern feel of Uptown Charlotte. With little doubt, it's also why the city is home to so many brand-new sports complexes, museums, and chic lofts. This lack of dwelling in the past brings

Golfing at Pinehurst

Pinehurst is a New England–style village with quiet, shaded streets and immaculately kept homes ranging from massive Victorians to tiny cottages. It was laid out in the late 1800s in a wagon-wheel pattern by Frederick Law Olmsted, who also designed Asheville's Biltmore Estate and New York City's Central Park. Annie Oakley lived here for a number of years and headed the local gun club. Today Pinehurst is renowned for its golf courses.

Although golfers will be in heaven, their nongolfing friends and family might be at a loss for entertainment around these sleepy parts. Don't expect to find much nightlife here or practically anything open late. Instead, this is a good place to stroll and sleep in. The town operates at a different pace than most of the world, and that's a big part of its charm.

TIP→ There are hardly any restaurants in Pinehurst that are not attached to hotels and lodges. When booking your trip, make sure to check out packages that include meals where you're staying.

Pinehurst Resort Pinehurst is famously known for its golf, and the courses—known by their numbers—can bring a tear to a golfer's eye with their beauty. The courses range from the first, designed in 1898 by legendary Donald Ross, to the most recent, designed in 1995 by Tom Fazio to mark the resort's centennial. No. 2 has hosted more single golf championships than any site in the country, and the U.S. Open will next return there in 2024. The hilly terrain of No. 7 makes it especially tough. ✉ *80 Carolina Vista Dr., Pinehurst* ☎ *855/235–8507 Ext. 4 reservations or tee times* 🌐 *www.pinehurst.com* *$95–$485, 9 18-hole courses, 5722–7588 yds, par 68–72.*

people from across the country to start new lives—and also to start restaurants, galleries, and high-concept bars.

Things are always in motion here, but history lovers shouldn't despair. Bits and pieces of Charlotte's past still linger. With their antique architecture and shaded streets, neighborhoods like Dilworth and the Fourth Ward offer lovely glimpses of what once was. Other areas, like hip Plaza Midwood and Montford, are a fusion of the new and old. There, historic houses have been converted into wine bars and late-night eateries.

Heavy development has created typical urban problems like traffic and restaurants that fill up quickly on weekends. But don't let that scare you away from the Queen City. When visiting the Piedmont, Charlotte is a must.

GETTING HERE AND AROUND

Charlotte is a driver's town, but its light-rail system makes going without a car possible if you stick to the central areas. Though its route is short and limited, the LYNX blue line is clean and fast. It runs from Uptown, through the convention center, to Interstate 485. Check for routes and schedules at 🌐 *charlottenc.gov*.

You'll be able to walk around Uptown and the historic Fourth Ward. Electric scooters from Bird, Spin, and Lime are also available for rent via phone app on nearly every corner in Uptown.

VISITOR INFORMATION

CONTACTS Visitor Info Center. ✉ *Convention Center, 501 S. College St., Uptown* ☎ *800/231–4636* 🌐 *www.charlottesgotalot.com.*

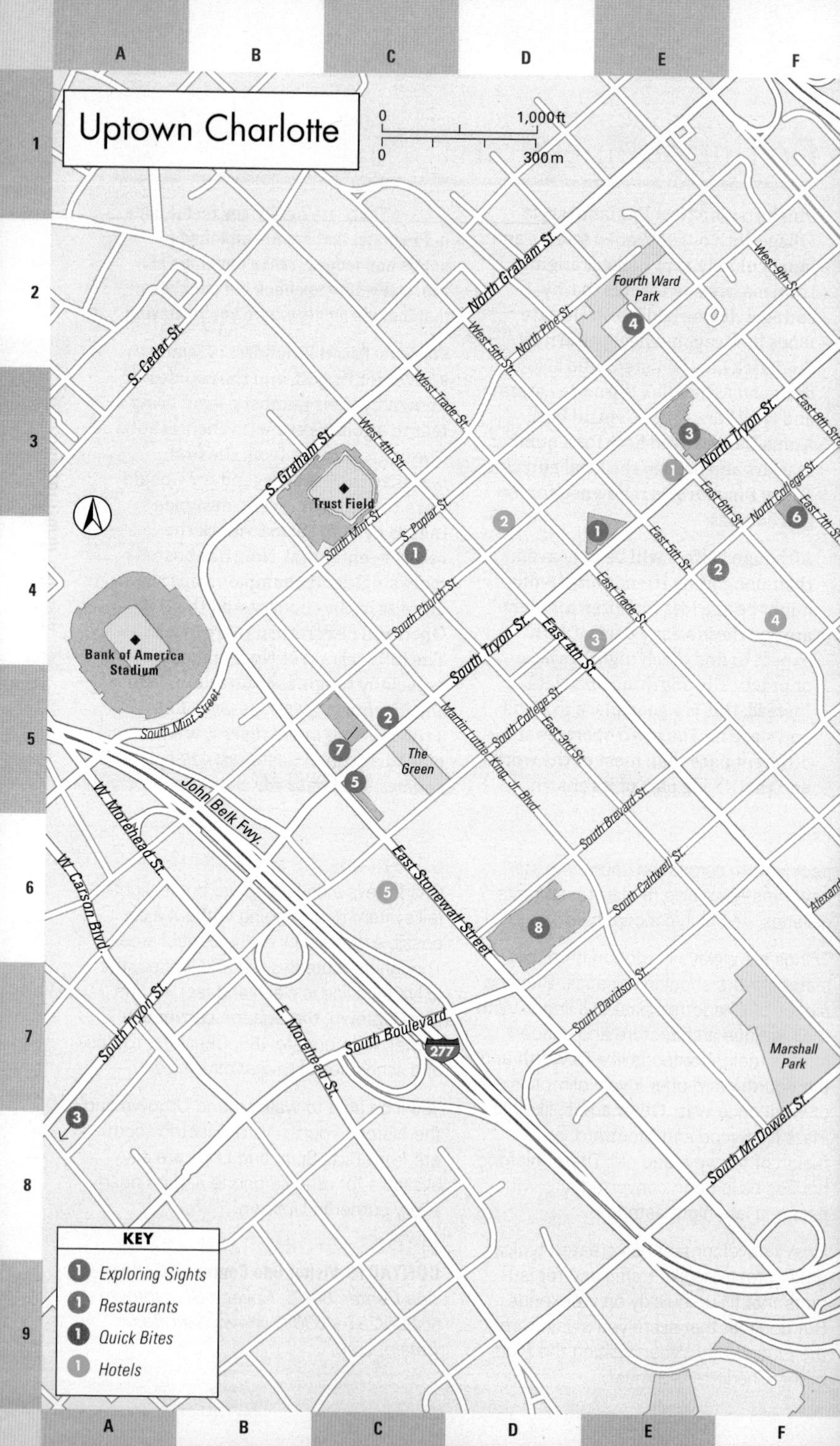
Uptown Charlotte
0
1,000ft
0
300m
A
B
C
D
E
F
1
2
3
4
5
6
7
8
9
North Graham St.
S. Graham St.
S. Cedar St.
West 5th St.
North Pine St.
West Trade St.
West 4th St.
Fourth Ward Park
West 9th St.
North Tryon St.
East 8th St.
East 6th St.
North College St.
East 7th St.
East 5th St.
East Trade St.
Trust Field
South Mint St.
S. Poplar St.
South Church St.
South Tryon St.
East 4th St.
Bank of America Stadium
South Mint Street
Martin Luther King, Jr. Blvd.
South College St.
East 3rd St.
The Green
John Belk Fwy.
W Morehead St.
W Carson Blvd.
East Stonewall Street
South Brevard St.
South Caldwell St.
Alexand
South Davidson St.
South Tryon St.
E Morehead St.
South Boulevard
277
Marshall Park
South McDowell St.
KEY
Exploring Sights
Restaurants
Quick Bites
Hotels

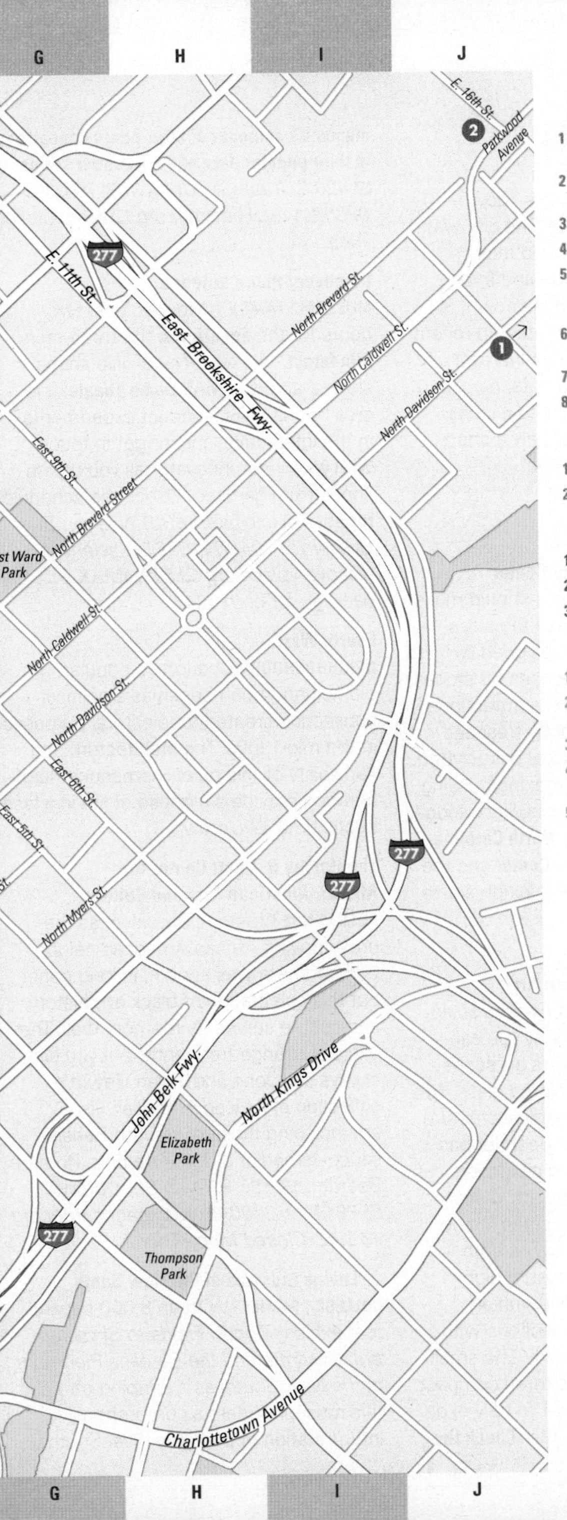

Sights

1 Bank of America Corporate Center E3
2 Bechtler Museum of Modern Art C5
3 Discovery Place Science E3
4 Fourth Ward E2
5 The Harvey B. Gantt Center for African-American Arts and Culture C5
6 Levine Museum of the New South F3
7 Mint Museum Uptown C5
8 NASCAR Hall of Fame D6

Restaurants

1 Haymaker C4
2 Mert's Heart and Soul E4

Quick Bites

1 Amélie's J2
2 Optimist Hall J1
3 Price's Chicken Coop A8

Hotels

1 The Dunhill Hotel E3
2 Grand Bohemian Hotel Charlotte D3
3 Omni Charlotte Hotel E4
4 SpringHill Suites Charlotte Uptown F4
5 Westin Charlotte C6

Uptown Charlotte

Uptown Charlotte, the city's "downtown," is ideal for walking. The city was laid out in four wards around Independence Square, at Trade and Tryon Streets. The Square, as it is known, is the center of the Uptown area. In recent years, Uptown has become increasingly user-friendly, with restaurants, bars, and museums tightly packed into a small area. If you're in town for only a short while, this is the place to be.

Sights

Bank of America Corporate Center
BUILDING | Architecture fans should make time for a trip to see one of the city's most striking buildings. Designed by César Pelli, this structure rises 60 stories to a crownlike top. The main attractions are three monumental lobby frescoes by the world-renowned local painter Ben Long—their themes are making/building, chaos/creativity, and planning/knowledge. Also in the tower are the **North Carolina Blumenthal Performing Arts Center** and the restaurants, shops, and exhibition space of **Founders Hall.** ⊠ *100 N. Tryon St., Uptown.*

Bechtler Museum of Modern Art
MUSEUM | With the famed *Firebird* sculpture out front, there's no way you can miss this staple of Uptown's art scene. Covered in mirrors and colored glass, Niki de Saint Phalle's 17-foot birdlike creature is just a taste of what the Bechtler has to offer inside. The rotating collection might include Warhol's pop art, Giacometti's dark sculptures, and ceramics by Picasso. Founded by the Swiss-born Andreas Bechtler, the museum highlights his family's love affair with art, as well as their deep connections with many of the artists on display. The small museum is spread across three compact floors—allow about an hour to fully experience the collections. **■ TIP→ Check the museum's calendar of after-hours concerts in their popular Jazz at the Bechtler series.** ⊠ *420 S. Tryon St., Uptown* ☎ *704/353–9200* 🌐 *www.bechtler.org* 🎟 *$9* ⏲ *Closed Tues.*

Discovery Place Science
MUSEUM | **FAMILY** | Allow at least two hours for the **aquariums,** the three-story **rain forest,** "Nose-to-Nose" live animal shows, and the **IMAX Dome Theater.** Lie on a bed of nails, conduct experiments in the interactive labs, or get in touch with your inner innovator as you create shoes from garbage. Check the schedule for special exhibits. ⊠ *301 N. Tryon St., Uptown* ☎ *704/372–6261* 🌐 *science.discoveryplace.org* 🎟 *$19, IMAX $10, package for both $24.*

Fourth Ward
NEIGHBORHOOD | Charlotte's popular old neighborhood began as a political subsection created for electoral purposes in the mid-1800s. The architecture and sensibility of this quiet, homespun neighborhood provide a glimpse of life in a less hectic time. ⊠ *Uptown.*

The Harvey B. Gantt Center for African-American Arts and Culture
ARTS VENUE | Historic Brooklyn, as the once-thriving African American neighborhood here was known, is long gone, but this celebration of black art, history, and culture serves its memory well. The exhibits change frequently, but you can always see John and Vivian Hewitt's collection of African American visual art, including those of Harlem Renaissance–famed and Charlotte-born Romare Bearden. ⊠ *551 S. Tryon St., Uptown* ☎ *704/547–3700* 🌐 *www.ganttcenter.org* 🎟 *$9* ⏲ *Closed Mon.–Thurs.*

★ Levine Museum of the New South
COLLEGE | **FAMILY** | With an 8,000-square-foot exhibit, *Cotton Fields to Skyscrapers: Charlotte and the Carolina Piedmont in the New South,* as a jumping-off point, this museum offers a comprehensive interpretation of post–Civil War Southern

history. Interactive exhibits and different "environments"—a tenant farmer's house, an African American hospital, a bustling street scene—bring to life the history of the region. Changing exhibits highlight current events and seek to engage the community in discussing historical events critical to Charlotte. Parking is free in the adjacent Seventh Street Station garage. Bring your parking ticket to the museum for validation. ✉ *200 E. 7th St., Uptown* ☎ *704/333–1887* 🌐 *www.museumofthenewsouth.org* 🎫 *$10* ⏲ *Closed Tues.–Thurs.*

★ Mint Museum Uptown

MUSEUM | With five stories and 145,000 square feet of space, this is a must-see for art lovers. Expect rotating special exhibits as well as permanent collections of American and contemporary work, plus craft and design. Be sure not to miss the museum's dramatic atrium, which houses a 60-foot-tall glass curtain that offers views of the surrounding cityscape. **■ TIP→ Use your ticket stub for free entrance to the Mint Museum Randolph (good for two days). Admission is free at both Mint Museums on Wednesday 5–9 pm.** ✉ *Levine Center for the Arts, 500 S. Tryon St., Uptown* ☎ *704/337–2000* 🌐 *www.mintmuseum.org* 🎫 *$15* ⏲ *Closed Mon.*

★ NASCAR Hall of Fame

MUSEUM | **FAMILY** | This 150,000-square-foot megamuseum has enough going on to intrigue even non-NASCAR fans. A complete visual overload, the racing palace features historic race cars, an enormous theater, and countless rotating exhibits highlighting the achievements of NASCAR's finest. Hands-on activities take visitors behind the scenes to see how the entire industry prepares for race day each week. Practice a pit stop, walk through a full-size NASCAR Sprint Cup hauler, and actually sit behind the wheel in one of eight iRacing simulators. ✉ *400 E. Martin Luther King Blvd., Uptown* ☎ *704/654–4400, 888/902–6463* 🌐 *www.nascarhall.com* 🎫 *$25; $9 upgrade for unlimited simulator rides* ⏲ *Closed Tues.*

Restaurants

Haymaker

$$$ | **SOUTHERN** | With a spacious bar and an open and inviting multilevel dining room overlooking Romare Bearden Park, Haymaker is focused on showcasing the bounty of the Piedmont and Appalachia regions with locally inspired, seasonal farm-to-table cuisine. The ever-changing menu features both small and large plates perfect for sharing. **Known for:** locally inspired, farm-fresh cuisine; weekend brunch; inviting dining room and outdoor patio overlooking a park. $ *Average main: $22* ✉ *225 S. Poplar St., Uptown* ☎ *704/626–6116* 🌐 *www.haymakerclt.com* ⏲ *Closed Mon. and Tues.*

★ Mert's Heart and Soul

$$ | **SOUTHERN** | Business executives and bohemians alike make their way to Mert's, an old-school gem that hides out under one of the city's many nondescript office buildings. Owners James and Reneé Bezzelle serve large portions of soul food and Lowcountry and Gullah staples, like fried chicken with greens, mac and cheese, and red beans and rice. **Known for:** classic soul food; pancakes for brunch; famous Soul Rolls: egg roll wraps filled with black-eyed peas, rice, chicken, and collard greens. $ *Average main: $16* ✉ *214 N. College St., Uptown* ☎ *704/342–4222* 🌐 *www.mertscharlotte.com.*

Coffee and Quick Bites

Amelie's

$ | **BAKERY** | Croissant breakfast sandwiches, gourmet coffee drinks, and tasty pastries make this a go-to for quality bites in the morning (or whenever the urge for a French treat arises, until 10 at night). There are four locations across Charlotte. **Known for:** all-day breakfast sandwiches; always changing quiche du jour; iced espresso with vanilla and cream.

The NASCAR Hall of Fame displays historic cars and racing memorabilia.

Average main: $8 2424 N. Davidson St., North Davidson 704/376–1781 ameliesfrenchbakery.com.

★ Optimist Hall

$ | **INTERNATIONAL** | **FAMILY** | Charlotte's most impressive food hall may be the state's biggest and best, with plenty of exposed brick painted in striking colors, multiple outdoor areas, and stall after stall of fresh-pressed juices, gourmet grilled cheese, ramen bowls, gelato, and craft cocktails. **Known for:** two dozen dining options in one location; gourmet coffee drinks; concerts in the courtyard. *Average main: $12 115 N. Brevard St., Uptown 980/701–0040 optimisthall.com.*

Price's Chicken Coop

$ | **SOUTHERN** | If you want to know where the locals eat, just follow the scent of oil to this counter-serve institution in the historic South End neighborhood, just across Interstate 277 from Uptown. The light, crispy coating—cooked to perfection in peanut oil—that covers the chicken is so juicy you'll begin to understand that there is indeed an art to running a deep fryer. **Known for:** some of the best fried chicken in the state; no dining room—take-out only; cash-only policy. *Average main: $9 1614 Camden Rd., South End 704/333–9866 www.priceschickencoop.com No credit cards Closed Sun. and Mon.*

Hotels

The Dunhill Hotel

$$ | **HOTEL** | You won't find many old buildings in Charlotte, and this 1929 structure in the center of downtown is Uptown's only historic hotel; the rooms have been updated with modern comforts without losing the period touches. **Pros:** in-house restaurant with inspired Southern cuisine at dinner and weekend brunch; one of few historic places in town; central location. **Cons:** rooms can be small; some bathrooms are a bit tight; gym and pool access are at the nearby YMCA. *Rooms from: $199 237 N. Tryon St., Uptown 704/332–4141 www.dunhillhotel.com 60 rooms Free breakfast.*

★ **Grand Bohemian Hotel - Charlotte**
$$$$ | HOTEL | Charlotte's take on this art-focused chain hotel is sleek and modern, like the Queen City, but with a subtle Argentinean undercurrent that's apparent in the paintings and sculptures, and in the food at Mico, the on-site restaurant. **Pros:** on-site Poseidon Spa is one of the city's best; lobby includes a Starbucks; feels like staying in a trendy art museum. **Cons:** the sixth-floor rooftop patio is great, but may not be available due to weddings; much of the art contains nudity, making it iffy for some families with small kids; off-site parking is valet-only. *Rooms from: $259 ✉ 201 W. Trade St., Uptown ☎ 704/372–1877 🌐 kesslercollection.com 254 rooms No meals.*

Omni Charlotte Hotel
$$ | HOTEL | This 16-story hotel is within walking distance of the convention center as well as many arts and sports venues. **Pros:** rooftop pool and bar; adjacent to a mall with tons of restaurant options; classic design and skyline views. **Cons:** busy setting can feel a bit hectic; valet parking only; newer luxury hotels now available. *Rooms from: $189 ✉ 132 E. Trade St., Uptown ☎ 704/377–0400 🌐 www.omnicharlotte.com 374 rooms No meals.*

SpringHill Suites Charlotte Uptown
$ | HOTEL | FAMILY | Located across the street from the Spectrum Center and a LYNX station, this clean and modern all-suites hotel is a great choice for families and those wishing to have a bit more space but still be in the heart of the action. **Pros:** affordable suites-style accommodations; central location close to public transit; generous breakfast included in rate. **Cons:** can be crowded during Spectrum Center events; valet parking only; rooms next to the light-rail line can be noisy. *Rooms from: $135 ✉ 311 E. 5th St., Uptown ☎ 704/439–8100 🌐 www.marriott.com 195 suites Free breakfast.*

Westin Charlotte
$ | HOTEL | For an upscale taste of Uptown, it's hard to get much better than this massive business hotel that's next to the convention center. **Pros:** helpful staff and beautiful surroundings; easy connection to mass transit; central location. **Cons:** they still charge for Internet ($13 per day); parking is $25 per day; indoor pool only. *Rooms from: $139 ✉ 601 S. College St., Uptown ☎ 704/375–2600 🌐 www.westincharlottehotel.com 700 rooms No meals.*

Nightlife

Duckworth's Grill and Taphouse
BARS/PUBS | Don't even try to count them—150 beer taps (and TVs galore) line the bar at this Uptown watering hole. It's the place to try a brew you've never seen before and a prime spot to watch basketball and other local sports. *✉ 330 N. Tryon St., Uptown ☎ 980/939–1166 🌐 www.uptown.duckworths.com.*

Merchant & Trade
GATHERING PLACES | Perched atop the stylish Kimpton Tryon Park Hotel, this rooftop bar and restaurant offers classic craft cocktails and sweeping 19th-floor views of the city. The outdoor terrace, complete with firepits, a "lawn," and comfy seating, is the place to be when weather is nice. *✉ 303 S. Church St., Uptown ☎ 704/445–2550 🌐 www.merchantandtrade.com.*

Performing Arts

AvidXchange Music Factory
CONCERTS | This massive entertainment center housed in a former mill complex includes popular venues the Fillmore, the Underground, and the Charlotte Metro Credit Union Amphitheatre. Here you'll find local, national, and international touring music acts and live entertainment. *✉ 1000 North Carolina Music Factory Blvd., Uptown ☎ 704/916–8970 🌐 www.avidxchangemusicfactory.com.*

Blumenthal Performing Arts Center

ARTS CENTERS | At its 2,100-seat Belk Theater and smaller Booth Playhouse and Stage Door Theater, this performing arts center houses several resident companies, including the Charlotte Symphony, Charlotte Ballet, and Opera Carolina. *130 N. Tryon St., Uptown 704/372–1000 www.blumenthalarts.org.*

Activities

FOOTBALL

Carolina Panthers

FOOTBALL | Charlotte's NFL team plays from August through December, and hopefully into the postseason playoffs, in the 75,000-seat Bank of America Stadium. *800 S. Mint St., Uptown 704/358–7800 www.panthers.com.*

North Davidson Arts District

Charlotte bills NoDa as "SoHo's little sister." Although this small, historic neighborhood 2 miles north of Uptown is quite a bit sleepier than its New York City namesake, it's still undeniably cool. Creative energy flows through the reclaimed textile mill and little houses, cottages, and commercial spaces. Here you'll find both the kooky and traditional—artists, musicians, dancers, restaurateurs, and even knitters—sharing space.

Nightlife

The Evening Muse

ARTS VENUE | Hear live music nightly at this popular venue situated in the center of the NoDa Arts District, or wait for "Find Your Muse," its frequent open-mic night. *3227 N. Davidson St., North Davidson 704/376–3737 www.eveningmuse.com.*

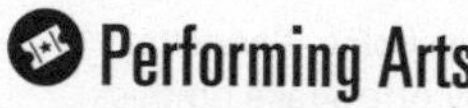

Performing Arts

Neighborhood Theatre

ARTS VENUE | Once called the Astor Theater, this circa-1945 former movie palace is now a venue that has hosted concerts by the likes of the Indigo Girls, Beach House, and Rooney. *511 E. 36th St., North Davidson 704/942–7997 www.neighborhoodtheatre.com.*

Plaza Midwood

Plaza Midwood, one of Charlotte's most diverse areas, is a fascinating place to spend an afternoon or evening. Located northeast of Uptown, on and near Central Avenue and the Plaza, it houses a hipster-approved collection of restaurants, shops, and galleries. After dark, it morphs into a colorful nightlife scene. This is a great spot to simply stroll and people-watch.

Restaurants

Midwood Smokehouse

$ | **BARBECUE** | **FAMILY** | Located in the funky Plaza Midwood neighborhood (and with satellite locations now in Ballantyne and Park Road Shopping Center), this barbecue joint carries a full range of sauces and meats and keeps its wood-fired smoker burning 24/7. This is no hole-in-the-wall joint but instead a fun and modern-looking place with something for just about every kind of barbecue lover. **Known for:** brisket, ribs, and pulled pork; banana pudding for dessert; pimento cheese fries. *Average main: $12 1401 Central Ave., Plaza Midwood 704/295–4227 www.midwoodsmokehouse.com.*

Soul Gastrolounge

$$ | **SUSHI** | Come for the elevated tapas and cocktails, stay for the dance party. This trendy hangout in a repurposed brick building dishes out quality sushi, skewers, and shareable plates, all served until midnight. **Known for:** tapas like tuna

nachos and veal short ribs; specialty sushi rolls; DJs in the evening. *Average main: $18 ✉ 1500B Central Ave., Plaza Midwood ☎ 704/348–1848 ⊕ soulgastrolounge.com.*

★ Supperland

$$$$ | STEAKHOUSE | Built into a former church, this grand, communal space books out far in advance, so reserve a table for their perfect steaks, veggie pot roast, and caviar service. The open kitchen and oversized wood-fired grill frame the high-ceilinged dining room. **Known for:** absinthe menu; a perfect 16-ounce rib eye; cool touches like church pew seating and a bar in an outbuilding. *Average main: $32 ✉ 1212 The Plaza, Plaza Midwood ☎ 704/817–7514 ⊕ supper.land ⊙ Closed Mon.*

Nightlife

Thomas Street Tavern

ARTS VENUE | In the heart of the "Thomas StrEATery" collection of restaurants and hangouts, this little bar is one of the best places in Plaza Midwood to grab a beer and play games like cornhole and ping-pong on the spacious patio. There's also live music. *✉ 1218 Thomas Ave., Plaza Midwood ☎ 704/376–1622.*

Greater Charlotte

Many of Charlotte's most interesting sights lie outside the city center. From gardens and museums to a racing speedway, there are plenty of reasons to leave Uptown if you have time—and wheels. While you can reach some of these spots by city bus, a car is essential for others.

Sights

Billy Graham Library

HOUSE | People from around the world come here to pay tribute to the life of beloved evangelist Billy Graham, a native of Charlotte. You can tour Graham's family homeplace and follow his 80-year-long ministry—including fascinating stories like his friendship with Johnny Cash—through films, memorabilia, and interactive exhibits. There's also a serene prayer garden and the grave sites of Graham and his wife, Ruth. *✉ 4330 Westmont Dr., Airport/Coliseum ☎ 704/401–3200 ⊕ www.billygrahamlibrary.org ⊙ Closed Sun.*

Carowinds

AMUSEMENT PARK/WATER PARK | FAMILY | Home of Fury 325, North America's fastest giga coaster (reaching 95 mph and 325 feet high), Carowinds is a place for thrill seekers. The 57 rides include multiple high-intensity roller coasters. Just across the South Carolina border on Interstate 77, Carowinds also boasts a water park, live concerts, and an interactive 3-D experience. ■ **TIP→ Check Carowinds's website for current hours and deals. It's usually cheaper to buy tickets online than at the gate.** *✉ 14523 Carowinds Blvd., South Charlotte ✣ Off I–77 at Carowinds Blvd. ☎ 704/588–2600 ⊕ www.carowinds.com 🎫 $40.*

Charlotte Museum of History

HISTORIC SITE | A 1774 stone building forms the centerpiece of this museum that traces central North Carolina's history over the last three centuries. Settler Hezekiah Alexander and his wife, Mary, reared 10 children in this house and farmed the land. Learn about the lives of early residents in the area through exhibits and displays. *✉ 3500 Shamrock Dr., East Charlotte ☎ 704/568–1774 ⊕ www.charlottemuseum.org 🎫 $10 ⊙ Closed Sun. and Mon.*

Daniel Stowe Botanical Garden

GARDEN | This bright garden is known for its painterly display of colors. There's a perennial garden, wildflower meadow, Canal Garden, an orchid conservatory, and other themed areas. *✉ 6500 S. New Hope Rd., Belmont ✣ 20 miles west of downtown Charlotte ☎ 704/825–4490 ⊕ www.dsbg.org 🎫 $15 ⊙ Closed Tues.*

Discovery Place Nature

COLLEGE | FAMILY | You'll find a butterfly pavilion, bugs galore, nature trails, a puppet theater, and hands-on exhibits just for children at this museum. Kids can experience up-close interaction with animals, and explore the Fort Wild outdoor play area. ✉ *1658 Sterling Rd., Freedom Park* ☎ *704/372–6261* 🌐 *nature.discoveryplace.org* 🎫 *$8* 🕓 *Closed Tues.–Thurs.*

Historic Latta Plantation

HOUSE | The last remaining Catawba River plantation open to the public, this living-history site interprets 19th-century farm life in North Carolina's backcountry. James Latta, a traveling merchant, built the plantation's Federal-style home in 1800 and soon became a cotton planter. According to family documents, the entire Latta family assisted with production on the 742-acre farm, but it would not have been possible to maintain the plantation without the back-breaking labor of more than 30 slaves. Today, visitors can tour the home as well as reconstructed slave quarters and a yeoman farmer's home. Historically appropriate farm animals and special weekend programs, such as folk craft demonstrations, round out the experience. ✉ *5225 Sample Rd., Huntersville* ☎ *704/875–2312* 🌐 *www.lattaplantation.org* 🎫 *$9* 🕓 *Closed Mon.*

Mint Museum Randolph

MUSEUM | Built in 1836 as the first U.S. Mint, this building has been a home for art since 1936. The holdings in its impressive permanent collections include fashion, ceramics, coins and currency, and art of the ancient Americas. **■ TIP→ Your ticket stub gets you free admission to the Mint Museum Uptown (good for two days).** ✉ *2730 Randolph Rd., East Charlotte* ☎ *704/337–2000* 🌐 *www.mintmuseum.org* 🎫 *$15* 🕓 *Closed Mon.*

President James K. Polk State Historic Site

HISTORIC SITE | FAMILY | This 22-acre state historic site 10 miles south of central Charlotte marks the humble birthplace and childhood home of the 11th U.S. president, nicknamed "Napoléon of the Stump" for his excellent speeches. Guided tours of the log cabins (replicas of the originals) show what life was like for settlers back in 1795. ✉ *12031 Lancaster Hwy., Pineville* ☎ *704/889–7145* 🌐 *www.jameskpolk.net* 🎫 *Free* 🕓 *Closed Sun. and Mon.*

Reed Gold Mine

HISTORIC SITE | FAMILY | This historic site, about 22 miles east of Charlotte, is where America's first documented gold rush began, after Conrad Reed discovered a 17-pound nugget in 1799. Guided underground tours of the gold mine are available, as well as gold panning (from roughly early April to late October), walking trails, and a stamp mill. ✉ *9621 Reed Mine Rd., Midland* ✥ *North of NC 24/27* ☎ *704/721–4653* 🌐 *www.nchistoricsites.org/reed* 🎫 *$2; gold panning $3* 🕓 *Closed Sun. and Mon.*

Wing Haven Garden and Bird Sanctuary

GARDEN | Set in Myers Park, one of the city's most exclusive neighborhoods, this 4-acre garden is a serene environment for feathered visitors and others. The grounds include a nursery and education building. ✉ *248 Ridgewood Ave., Myers Park* ☎ *704/331–0664* 🌐 *www.winghavengardens.org* 🎫 *$10* 🕓 *Closed Sun.–Tues.*

Restaurants

The Cowfish

$$ | ECLECTIC | This fusion spot is all about unexpected combinations: sushi packed with burger and beef components and burgers stuffed with rice, tempura, rare ahi tuna, and other traditional sushi elements. The out-of-the-way location on the ground floor of a modern apartment complex isn't too appealing, but the food makes up for the lack of charm, and it fills up fast on weekends. **Known for:** sushi rolls inspired by burgers; a "cowfish" sculpture out front that you can ride and pose with; huge bar menu, including sake. $ *Average main: $17* ✉ *4310 Sharon Rd., South Park* ☎ *704/365–1922* 🌐 *www.thecowfish.com.*

Good Food on Montford

$ | **AMERICAN** | This neighborhood café feels fancy without any pretension. Select from the brief menu highlighting seasonal seafood, meat, and veggie harvests, plus several daily pastas. **Known for:** an approachable and devourable charcuterie tray; high-end seafood at reasonable prices; laid-back dining on the glassed-in front porch. $ *Average main: $14* ✉ *1701 Montford Dr., Myers Park* ☎ *704/525–0881* 🌐 *goodfoodonmontford.com* ⏲ *Closed Sun.*

300 East

$$ | **AMERICAN** | Operated out of an old home in pleasant Dilworth, this comfortable little spot offers an always-changing menu blending Southern and Californian styles in its meat and fish dishes, pizza, salads, and pastas. Always available items include Chesapeake-style crab cakes and the Usual, a chicken salad sandwich that has been a local favorite for years. **Known for:** desserts by one of the best pastry chefs in North Carolina; historic building with inviting patio seating; creative cocktail list. $ *Average main: $19* ✉ *300 East Blvd., Dilworth* ☎ *704/332–6507* 🌐 *www.300east.net.*

The Ballantyne Hotel

$$$$ | **HOTEL** | This stately resort hotel offers a spa, indoor and outdoor pools, an expansive fitness center, and luxurious amenities, although the slightly gaudy nature of the Marriott property can feel more like the Bellagio than a classic Southern inn. **Pros:** luxurious amenities; spacious, lovely rooms, including many with large porches; relaxing on-site spa. **Cons:** not convenient for exploring city center; lacks the charm of more intimate options; on-site restaurant (The Gallery) is pricey. $ *Rooms from: $280* ✉ *10000 Ballantyne Commons Pkwy., South Charlotte* ☎ *704/248–4000* 🌐 *www.theballantynehotel.com* 🛏 *244 rooms* 🍽 *No meals.*

★ The Duke Mansion

$$$ | **B&B/INN** | Spending a night at this historic, luxurious inn seems more like borrowing a wealthy friend's estate than staying in a hotel. **Pros:** guests get a real sense of history and a neighborhood feel; the surrounding neighborhood is a great place to stroll; elegant full breakfast included in the rate. **Cons:** tiny fitness center; not in walking distance to nightlife spots; rooms have only one bed (king or queen). $ *Rooms from: $209* ✉ *400 Hermitage Rd., Myers Park* ☎ *704/714–4400* 🌐 *www.dukemansion.com* 🛏 *20 rooms* 🍽 *Free breakfast.*

The Morehead Inn

$$ | **B&B/INN** | Built in 1917, this grand Colonial Revival house has rooms filled with period antiques, including several with impressive four-poster beds. **Pros:** cozy and historic; known for its cooked-to-order breakfast; lovely grounds and residential setting. **Cons:** a popular spot for weddings and parties, so it can be noisy; not in walking distance to nightlife; it's been three decades since the last renovation. $ *Rooms from: $185* ✉ *1122 E. Morehead St., Dilworth* ☎ *704/376–3357* 🌐 *www.moreheadinn.com* 🛏 *12 rooms* 🍽 *Free breakfast.*

Shopping

ANTIQUES

Sleepy Poet Antique Mall

ANTIQUES/COLLECTIBLES | You may get lost among the rows at this antiques mall just outside Uptown. Vendors display their wide array of wares, ranging from books to furniture. ✉ *4450 South Blvd., South End* ☎ *704/529–6369* 🌐 *www.sleepypoetstuff.com.*

GIFTS

Paper Skyscraper

GIFTS/SOUVENIRS | As the name implies, you'll find books and paper goods here, but you'll also find an assortment of humorous and odd gifts. There is also a selection of Charlotte-themed items to remember the city. ✉ *330 East Blvd., Dilworth* ☎ *704/333–7130* 🌐 *www.paper-skyscraper.com.*

Activities

AUTO RACING

Charlotte Motor Speedway

AUTO RACING | **FAMILY** | This state-of-the-art facility, with a seating capacity of 89,000, is considered the heart of NASCAR. Hosting more than 300 events each year, this is one of the busiest sports venues in the United States. Racing season runs April to November, and tours are offered on non-race days. ✉ *5555 Concord Pkwy. S, Concord* ✣ *Northeast of Charlotte* ☎ *800/455–3267* 🌐 *www.charlottemotor-speedway.com.*

GOLF

Highland Creek Golf Club

GOLF | This semiprivate course is lovely to look at and challenging to play. You have to be careful with the water hazards; there are water features on 13 holes. It's consistently rated among Charlotte's toughest public golf courses. ✉ *7101 Highland Creek Pkwy.* ☎ *704/875–9000* 🌐 *www.highlandcreekgolfclub.com* *$35–$55, 18 holes, 7043 yds, par 72.*

Paradise Valley Golf Center

GOLF | This short course is perfect for players without much time: a round takes less than two hours. But don't let that fool you: the course can challenge the best of them. Unique elements include two island tees. ✉ *110 Barton Creek Dr.* ☎ *704/548–1808* 🌐 *www.charlottepub-licgolf.com* *$16–$20, 18 holes, 1264 yds, par 54; minigolf $5.*

WATER SPORTS

Catawba Queen

TOUR—SPORTS | **FAMILY** | On Lake Norman, the *Catawba Queen* paddle wheeler gives dinner cruises and tours. The *Lady of the Lake*, a 90-foot yacht, offers dinner cruises. ✉ *1459 River Hwy., Mooresville* ☎ *704/663–2628* 🌐 *www.queenslanding.com.*

Lake Norman State Park

BOATING | **FAMILY** | The largest man-made lake in North Carolina, Lake Norman is a recreational hot spot for the region. You can rent canoes, kayaks, paddleboards, and pedal boats here, and there's also a boat ramp, a beach for swimming, and a network of hiking and mountain biking trails. ✉ *759 State Park Rd., Troutman* ☎ *704/528–6350* 🌐 *www.ncparks.gov.*

★ U.S. National Whitewater Center

BICYCLING | **FAMILY** | At 1,300 acres, this renowned outdoor center on the Catawba River offers a wide variety of outdoor activities for all ages and skill levels. Guests can enjoy white-water rafting, kayaking, stand-up paddleboarding, rock climbing, ziplines, ropes courses, a canopy tour, and mountain biking. Recent additions include a free climbing wall over water and an ice-skating rink. ✉ *5000 Whitewater Center Pkwy.* ✣ *13 miles west of Uptown Charlotte* ☎ *704/391–3900* 🌐 *www.usnwc.org.*

Chapter 5

ASHEVILLE AND THE NORTH CAROLINA MOUNTAINS

Updated by
Cameron Roberts

Sights	Restaurants	Hotels	Shopping	Nightlife
★★★★★	★★★★★	★★★★☆	★★★☆☆	★★★☆☆

WELCOME TO ASHEVILLE AND THE NORTH CAROLINA MOUNTAINS

TOP REASONS TO GO

★ **Biltmore Estate:** The 250-room Biltmore House, modeled after the great Renaissance châteaux of the Loire Valley in France, is the largest private home in America.

★ **Blue Ridge Parkway:** This winding two-lane road, which ends at the edge of the Great Smokies and shows off the highest mountains in eastern America, is the most scenic drive in the South and the most visited national park site in the country.

★ **Asheville:** Hip and artsy with scores of restaurants and active nightlife, Asheville is one of America's coolest places to live and to visit.

★ **Engaging small towns:** It's easy to fall in love with the charm, style, and Southern hospitality of Black Mountain, Blowing Rock, Brevard, and Hendersonville, to name a few.

★ **Mountain art and crafts:** The mountains are a center of handmade art and crafts, with more than 4,000 working craftspeople.

1 Asheville. Asheville is a base for exploring the region, but it is also a destination unto itself for its arts, crafts, food, beer, and music scenes; just a short drive away are mile-high vistas that will take your breath away.

2 Blue Ridge Parkway. This two-lane mountaintop parkway, the most visited site of all national park units, is one of America's most scenic drives.

3 Black Mountain. Twenty minutes east of Asheville, Black Mountain, once home to a radical experimental college that helped birth the abstract impressionist art movement and the Beat poets, is now a charming and highly walkable small mountain town.

4 Hendersonville. Hendersonville has a classic Main Street filled with antiques shops, restaurants, and quaint boutiques.

5 Flat Rock. Flat Rock has poet Carl Sandburg's home and farm and the state theater of North Carolina.

6 Blowing Rock. Blowing Rock is Boone's more upscale sister town.

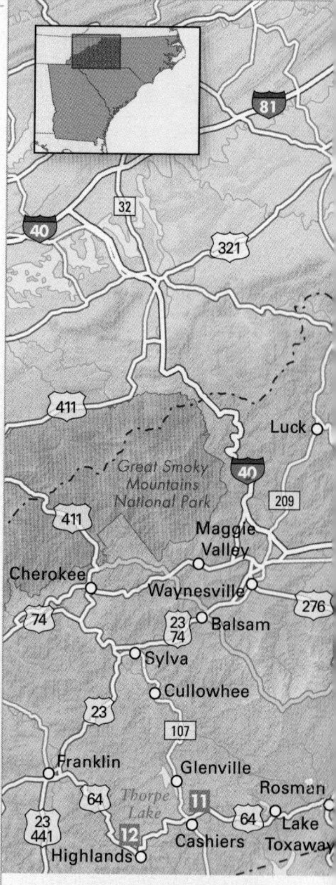

7 Boone. The heart of North Carolina's High Country is a college town near several snow ski resorts.

8 Valle Crucis. The state's first rural historic district is in a valley where you can shop at one of the oldest general stores in the South and enjoy a quiet, peaceful vacation in the mountains.

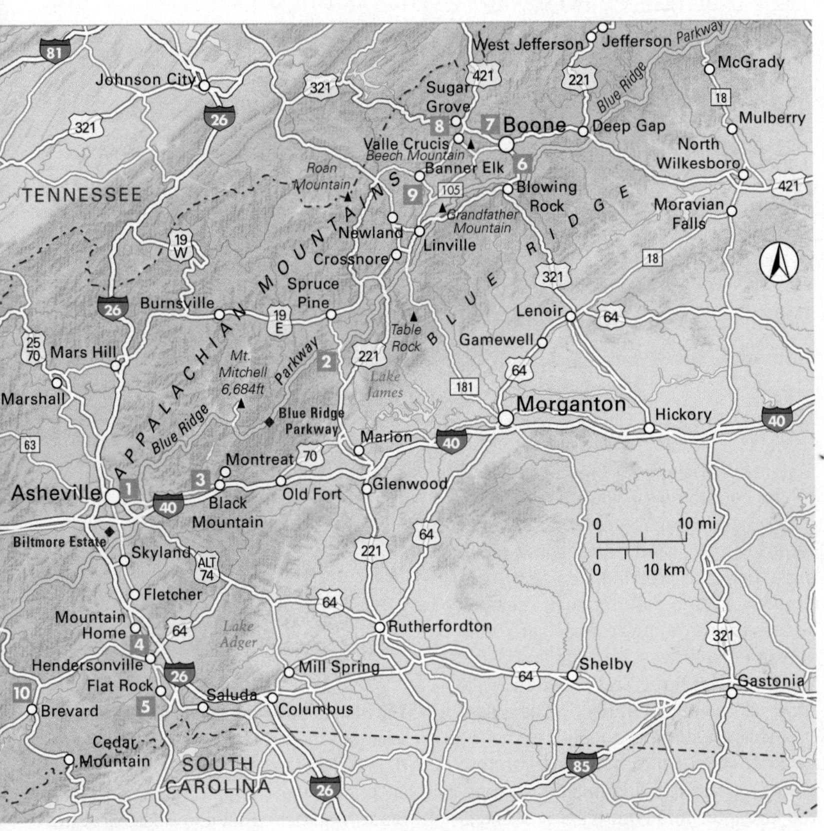

9 Banner Elk. Banner Elk, one of the highest elevation villages in the mountains, is home to ski resorts and the annual Woolly Worm Festival.

10 Brevard. This tiny, charming college town boasts a nationally known music center and festival and scurries of white squirrels.

11 Cashiers. Pronounced "CASH-ers," perhaps for its pricey gated developments, this town has a year-round population of about 2,000, which jumps to more than 25,000 in the summer and fall, as flatlanders flock to the high mountains and cool waterfalls.

12 Highlands. Sometimes called Buckhead North for its summer migrants from Atlanta, Highlands, on a high plateau at 4,118 feet, has tony shopping, one of the mountains' top resort spas, and stunning four-season views.

Majestic peaks, meadows, shrub-covered balds, and valleys of the Appalachian, Blue Ridge, and Great Smoky Mountains epitomize the western corner of North Carolina. The Great Smoky Mountains National Park, national forests, eclectic and sophisticated Asheville, the Biltmore Estate, and the Blue Ridge Parkway are the area's main draws.

Here you can shop, ski, hike, bike, camp, fish, canoe, or just take in the views. The city of Asheville is one of the stops on the counterculture trail, as well as a popular retirement area. Its restaurants regularly make the TV food show circuit, and it has craft breweries on nearly every block. Thanks to their moneyed seasonal residents and long histories as resorts, even smaller towns like Highlands, Cashiers, Flat Rock, and Hendersonville have restaurants with daring chefs and professional summer theater. In the High Country, where summer temperatures are as much as 15 degrees cooler than in the lowlands, and where snow skiing is a major draw in winter, affluent retirees and hip young entrepreneurs bring panache to even the most rural areas.

Some of the most important arts and culture movements of the 20th century, including abstract impressionist painting and the Beat movement, had roots just east of Asheville, at Black Mountain College, where in the 1930s to 1950s the notables included famed artists Josef and Anni Albers, Willem and Elaine de Kooning, Robert Rauschenberg, and Robert Motherwell, choreographer and dancer Merce Cunningham, musician John Cage, futurist Buckminster Fuller, architect Walter Gropius, and the writers Charles Olson and Paul Goodman.

MAJOR REGIONS

Asheville. This artsy and bohemian city is known for its excellent restaurants and numerous breweries. It's also home to the magnificent Biltmore Estate and is the launching off point for scenic drives in the Blue Ridge Mountains.

The High Country and the Southern Mountains. North Carolina's mountains–the Blue Ridge, Great Smoky, and Appalachian–brim with charming towns, such as Black Mountain, Blowing Rock, Brevard, and Hendersonville.

Planning

When to Go

Western North Carolina is a four-season destination. Dates for high season vary from hotel to hotel, but generally it's from Memorial Day through early November. It's most difficult to get a hotel reservation on weekends in October, which is peak leaf-peeping time. June to August draws a lot of families because kids are out of school. Around ski resorts at the higher elevations, winter, especially the Christmas season and the months of January and February, is prime time; elsewhere, these winter months are slow, and a few hotels and restaurants close. Spring, late March to late May, is a great time to visit, as the spring wildflowers bloom and the landscape turns green.

Planning Your Time

The Asheville area is a convenient base for day visits to Black Mountain and Hendersonville, and even to Brevard, Cashiers, and Highlands in the Southern Mountains. Of course, if you want to see these areas more completely, you're better off spending the night in one or several of these towns. You can also explore some of the most scenic parts of the Blue Ridge Parkway from Asheville, where it's headquartered. Likewise, it's easy to make day trips to Great Smoky Mountains National Park from Asheville. The Oconaluftee entrance to the Smokies is only an hour and 15 minutes drive from downtown Asheville. But if you want to spend several days or longer in the Smokies, you'll be better off staying in the park or at one of the small towns at the edge of it, such as Bryson City or Waynesville. The High Country is too far away to make a comfortable day trip from Asheville, especially considering the winding mountain roads and possible weather conditions (snow in winter and fog almost any time). To explore the High Country in detail, you'll want to make your headquarters in the appealing college town of Boone or one of the other towns nearby, such as Blowing Rock or Banner Elk.

Getting Here and Around

AIR TRAVEL

Asheville Regional Airport (AVL), one of the most pleasant and modern small airports in the South, is served by Allegiant, Delta, Spirit, United, and American. Most of the flights are on regional jets. A study by MIT found that Asheville had the best-connected non-hub airport in the country. There are nonstop flights (some are seasonal) to and from Atlanta, Baltimore, Charlotte, Chicago, Dallas–Fort Worth, Denver, Ft. Lauderdale, Ft. Myers, Orlando, Newark, New York's LaGuardia, Sarasota-Bradenton, St. Petersburg, Tampa, and Washington, D.C. A new airport garage added much-needed parking near the terminals. Charlotte Douglas International Airport (CLT), a major hub for American and with service by Air Canada, Delta, Frontier, Lufthansa, JetBlue, Southwest, and Via, is about a two-hour drive from Asheville or Boone.

AIRPORT INFORMATION Asheville Regional Airport. *(AVL) ✉ 61 Terminal Dr., Fletcher ☎ 828/209–3660 🌐 www.flyavl.com.* **Charlotte Douglas International Airport.** *(CLT) ✉ 5501 Josh Birmingham Pkwy., Charlotte ☎ 704/359–4013 🌐 www.cltairport.com.*

CAR TRAVEL

The coast-to-coast Interstate 40 runs west–east from the Pacific coast of California at Barstow through Asheville to the Atlantic shores of North Carolina at Wilmington. Interstate 26 runs from Charleston, South Carolina, to Asheville and, partly on a temporary route, continues northwest into Tennessee and the Ohio Valley. There are plans for a $1 billion upgrade and expansion of Interstate 26 in Asheville beginning in 2021. Interstate 240 forms a perimeter around Asheville. U.S. Route 19/23 is an important north and west route. The Blue Ridge Parkway runs northeast from Great Smoky Mountains National Park at Cherokee to Shenandoah National Park in Virginia, passing Asheville and the High Country. U.S. Route 221 runs north to the Virginia border through Blowing Rock and Boone and intersects Interstate 40 at Marion. U.S. Route 321 intersects Interstate 40 at Hickory and heads to Blowing Rock and Boone.

Restaurants

You can still get traditional mountain food, served family style, at inns and eateries around the region. Increasingly, though, mountain restaurants serve more elaborate dishes, often with a new Southern style. At many places the emphasis is on the farm-to-table dishes made with locally grown, often organic, ingredients. You can find nearly every U.S. and world cuisine somewhere in Asheville or the rest of the region. *Restaurant reviews have been shortened. For full information, visit Fodors.com.*

Hotels

Around the mountains, at least in the larger cities and towns, such as Asheville, Hendersonville, and Boone, you can find the usual chain motels and hotels. A building boom has brought more than a half dozen new hotels to downtown Asheville. For more of a local flavor, look at the many mountain lodges and country inns, some with just a few rooms with simple comforts, others with upmarket amenities like tennis courts, golf courses, and spas. Bed-and-breakfasts bloom in the mountains like wildflowers, and there are scores of them in the region; Asheville alone has more than 50. The mountains also have a few large resorts, including the Omni Grove Park Inn in Asheville. Visiting in the off-season can save you a third or more on hotel rates. Rates are highest during summer weekends and in October and early November, when the leaves change. *Hotel reviews have been shortened. For full information, visit Fodors.com.*

What It Costs

$	$$	$$$	$$$$
RESTAURANTS			
under $15	$15–$19	$20–$24	over $24
HOTELS			
under $150	$150–$200	$201–$250	over $250

Restaurant prices are the average cost of a main course at dinner or, if dinner is not served, at lunch. Hotel prices are the lowest cost of a standard double room in high season.

Visitor Information

CONTACTS Brevard/Transylvania County Chamber of Commerce. ✉ *175 E. Main St., Brevard* ☎ *800/648–4523, 828/883–3700* 🌐 *www.brevardnc.org.* **Cashiers Area Chamber of Commerce.** ✉ *202 U.S. 64 W, Cashiers* ☎ *828/743–5191* 🌐 *www.cashiersareachamber.com.* **Hendersonville Visitor Information Center.** ✉ *201 S. Main St., Hendersonville* ☎ *800/828–4244* 🌐 *www.visithendersonvillenc.org.* **High Country Host Regional Visitor Center.** ✉ *6370 U.S. 321 S, Blowing Rock* ☎ *800/438–7500* 🌐 *www.highcountryhost.com.* **Highlands Chamber of Commerce and Visitor Center.** ✉ *108 Main St., Highlands* ☎ *828/526–2112* 🌐 *www.highlandschamber.org.*

Asheville

Asheville is the hippest city in the South. At least that's the claim of its fans, who are legion. Visitors flock to Asheville for its arts and culture, which rival that of Charleston, South Carolina, or Santa Fe, New Mexico, and to experience its downtown, with myriad restaurants, coffeehouses, microbreweries, museums, galleries, bookstores, antiques shops, and boutiques.

Named "the best place to live" by many books and magazines, Asheville is also a destination for retirees escaping the cold North or for "halfbacks," those who moved to Florida but who are now coming half the way back North. Old downtown buildings have been converted to upmarket condos for these affluent retirees, and new residential developments seem to be constantly springing up around town.

As a result of this influx, Asheville has a much more cosmopolitan population than most cities of its size (over 90,000 people in the city, almost half a million in the metro area). Asheville has a diversity you won't find in many cities in the South. There's a thriving gay community, many self-described hippies and hipsters, young-at-heart retirees, and alternative-lifestyle seekers. *Rolling Stone* once called Asheville the "U.S. capital of weird" (sorry, Austin), but with more than 60 microbreweries and brewpubs in the area—and two large national craft breweries, New Belgium and Sierra Nevada, with their East Coast operations here—Asheville prefers the title of Beer City, USA. That said, you may be surprised to know that due to state law, bars are illegal in North Carolina. Public establishments that sell mostly alcohol and little food have to operate as private membership clubs. This just means you have to sign up and perhaps pay a nominal onetime membership fee (like a cover charge, often as low as $1, good for a year). You can do this at the door.

The city really comes alive at night, with restaurants, sidewalk cafés, and coffeehouses, so visit after dark to see the city at its best. Especially on summer and fall weekends, Pack Square, Biltmore Avenue, the "South Slope" area between Biltmore Avenue and Asheland Avenue south of Patton Avenue (fast becoming the craft brewery district), Broadway Street, Haywood Street, Wall Street, the Grove Arcade, Pritchard Park (site of a popular drum circle on Friday night), and Battery Park Avenue are busy until late.

GETTING HERE AND AROUND

From the east and west, the main route to Asheville is Interstate 40. Interstate 26 brings you from the Ohio Valley in the north or the coast of South Carolina in the south. The most scenic route to Asheville is via the Blue Ridge Parkway, which meanders between Shenandoah National Park in Virginia and Great Smoky Mountains National Park near Cherokee, North Carolina. Interstate 240 forms a freeway perimeter around Asheville, and Pack Square is the center of the city.

Although a car is virtually a necessity to explore Asheville thoroughly, the city does have a metropolitan bus system with nearly 20 routes radiating from the Asheville Redefines Transit (ART) Center downtown. Asheville also has a hop-on, hop-off, sightseeing trolley service and other tour services; tickets are available at the Asheville Visitor Center. The city is highly walkable, and the best way to see downtown is on foot.

FESTIVALS

★ Craft Fair of the Southern Highlands

ARTS FESTIVALS | FAMILY | One of the largest crafts events in the Southeast, the Craft Fair of the Southern Highlands is held for three days twice a year, in mid-July and mid-October. More than 200 of the 700 members of the Southern Highland Craft Guild, who qualify after a stringent jurying process, take over both the concourse and arena of the U.S. Cellular Center in downtown Asheville to display and sell their clay, wood, metal, glass, fiber, leather, jewelry, and other crafts. The fair, which has been in operation for more than 70 years, also features live mountain music. ✉ *U.S. Cellular Center, 87 Haywood St., Downtown* ☎ *828/298–7928 Southern Highland Craft Guild* 🌐 *www.southernhighlandguild.org* 🎫 *$8.*

★ Shindig on the Green

MUSIC FESTIVALS | FAMILY | Pack a picnic and bring a folding chair or blanket for this free mountain-music concert. Shindig on the Green has been held for more than 50 years most Saturdays from late June through August. The shows, held in Pack Square Park in the heart of Asheville, run from around 7 to 10 pm. The same sponsoring organization, the Folk Heritage Committee, also puts on the Mountain Dance and Folk Festival, the oldest music festival of its type in the United States, dating to 1928. It is held "along about sundown" on three nights the first weekend in August. ✉ *Pack Square Park, 121 College St., Roger McGuire Green, Downtown* ☎ *828/258–6101* 🌐 *www.folkheritage.org* 🎟 *Free.*

TOURS

Asheville Brewery Tours

GUIDED TOURS | Asheville Brewery Tours' guides are knowledgeable about beer and the booming Asheville craft brewery scene. After meeting at the Aloft Hotel downtown, you'll hop aboard a van and head out to three or four breweries and brewpubs, with flights of several beers served at each (there's a discounted rate for nondrinkers). You'll meet the brewmasters or owners. Dog-friendly walking tours of the South Slope brewery section of town are also offered. Tours, including small-group privates, are available daily year-round, except Monday, but there are more tours on weekends and from late spring through the fall. ✉ *Aloft Hotel Lobby, 51 Biltmore Ave., Downtown* ☎ *828/233–5006* 🌐 *www.ashevillebrewerytours.com* 🎟 *$49–$69.*

Asheville Food Tours

GUIDED TOURS | Asheville Food Tours was the first and still is one of the best of the city's half-dozen walking food tours. You visit six or seven of the better downtown restaurants, usually meeting the chef or owner, and sample the restaurants' food and drink specialties. Around 15 to 20 restaurants and bars participate, with different spots visited on different days. A brunch tour is also offered seasonally. Downtown tours last about three hours, and tickets must be purchased in advance. Tours operate year-round, and off-season may require a minimum number of participants. **■ TIP→ Tour hours and dates vary by month.** ✉ *Grove Arcade, 1 Page Ave., Downtown* ☎ *828/243–7401* 🌐 *www.ashevillefoodtours.com* 🎟 *$55–$65.*

★ Asheville Urban Trail

SELF-GUIDED | FAMILY | This 1.7-mile walk developed by the City of Asheville has 30 "stations" in five areas of downtown, each with a work of art and plaques marking places of historical or architectural interest. The free self-guided tour begins at Pack Square and takes about two hours to complete. Pick up free maps at the Asheville Visitor Center (36 Montford Avenue), the satellite visitor pavilion (121 College Street) in Pack Square Park, and at various shops in downtown Asheville. You can also download the map and brochure from the Asheville Visitor Center website. ✉ *Pack Square Park, 121 College St., Asheville Visitor Center Satellite Pavilion, Downtown* ☎ *828/258–6101 Asheville Visitor Center* 🌐 *www.exploreasheville.com* 🎟 *Free.*

★ Brew-Ed Asheville Brewery and History Walking Tours

WALKING TOURS | This tour company offers in-depth tours of two or three breweries and brewpubs on the South Slope of downtown Asheville. The owner and chief guide is a Certified Advanced Cicerone. Tours operate Thursday to Sunday and usually begin at Hi-Wire Brewing. ✉ *Hi-Wire Brewing, 197 Hilliard Ave., Downtown* ☎ *828/278–9255* 🌐 *www.brew-ed.com* 🎟 *$45–$60.*

★ Eating Asheville

GUIDED TOURS | Eating Asheville made its rep with its classic 2½-hour walking food tour of downtown Asheville, which visits about six restaurants and food shops to sample food and drinks and meet with chefs or owners. Now a High Roller Tour visits higher-end restaurants for food and beverage pairings. The restaurants and sections of town visited vary, but Eating Asheville has relationships with about 30 Asheville eateries. Tours operate year-round, although the number and frequency of tours increase in the summer and fall. Most tours start and finish at the Grove Arcade. ✉ *Grove Arcade, 1 Page Ave., Downtown* ☎ *828/489–3266* 🌐 *www.eatingasheville.com* 🎟 *$69–$79.*

The Flying Bike Electric Bike Tours
BICYCLE TOURS | FAMILY | The Flying Bike offers electric-assisted bike tours of Asheville. You have to pedal some, but the electric power helps you get up Asheville's hills. Two to seven riders go with a guide. Tours last about 2½ hours and cover 9 miles, usually visiting the downtown, Montford, South Slope, and Grove Park areas. Participants must be at least 16 years old and weigh less than 350 pounds. Tours are offered every two hours from 9 to 5 daily mid-February to mid-December but are weather dependent. The Flying Bike also rents electric bicycles. ✉ *225 Coxe Ave., Downtown* ☎ *828/450–8686* 🌐 *www.flyingbiketours.com* 🎟 *$65.*

Gray Line Historic Asheville Trolley Tours
BUS TOURS | FAMILY | Gray Line offers hop-on, hop-off tours in and around downtown Asheville in red motorized trolleys. Guided tours leave daily March through December, usually every 30 minutes from 10 to 3:30 from the Asheville Visitor Center, but you can get on or off and buy tickets at any of nine other stops, including the Omni Grove Park Inn, Biltmore Village, Pack Square, and the River Arts District. In January and February the tours operate with less frequency and on Monday, Thursday, Friday, and Saturday only. The entire tour takes less than two hours, and tickets are good for two consecutive days. ■ **TIP→ A tour without hop-on, hop-off privileges is cheaper.** A 75-minute ghost tour from April to mid-November leaves at 7 pm daily except Sunday, from Pack's Tavern at 20 Spruce Street. ✉ *Asheville Visitor Center, 36 Montford Ave., Downtown* ☎ *828/251–8687* 🌐 *www.graylineasheville.com* 🎟 *$27–$31.*

★ LaZoom Comedy Tours
BUS TOURS | On this popular and unusual tour, you ride in a big, open-air purple bus while you are entertained by actors who do comedy skits and over-the-top routines about the wacky side of Asheville. If you're over 21, you can purchase beer and wine at stops along the way and enjoy it on the bus. In peak periods such as summer and fall weekends, LaZoom has three or four tours a day, including 90-minute City Comedy Tours, 60-minute Haunted Comedy Tours, 60-minute Kids' Comedy Tours (family-friendly tours directed to kids 4–12), and three-hour Band and Beer Tours with live music and visits to three craft breweries. See their website for tour schedules. Due to the slightly risqué routines, riders must be at least 13 on the Comedy Tours, 17 on Haunted Tours, and 21 on Band and Beer tours. Many tours sell out, so it's best to reserve in advance; if seats are available you can buy when boarding. ✉ *LaZoom Room, 76 Biltmore Ave., Downtown* ☎ *828/225–6932* 🌐 *www.lazoomtours.com* 🎟 *$29–$49.*

VISITOR INFORMATION

CONTACTS Asheville Visitor Center. ✉ *36 Montford Ave., Downtown* ☎ *828/258–6129* 🌐 *www.exploreasheville.com.*

Downtown Asheville

A city of neighborhoods, Asheville rewards careful exploration, especially on foot. You can break up your sightseeing with stops at the more than 100 restaurants and bars in downtown alone, and at scores of unique shops (only a couple of downtown Asheville stores are national chains).

Asheville has the largest extant collection of art deco buildings in the Southeast outside Miami Beach, most notably the S&W Cafeteria (completed 1929), Asheville City Hall (1928), First Baptist Church (1927), and Asheville High School (1929). It's also known for its architecture in other styles: Battery Park Hotel (1924) is neo-Georgian; the Flatiron Building (1924) is neoclassical; the Basilica of St. Lawrence (1909) is Spanish baroque; the 15-story Jackson Building (1924), Asheville's first skyscraper, is neo-Gothic; and the old Pack Library (1926), now part of the Asheville Art Museum, is in the Italian Renaissance style.

Sights

★ Asheville Art Museum

MUSEUM | FAMILY | Established in 1948, the 68,000-square-foot museum kept the footprint of the old Pack Library, a 1926 Italian Renaissance–style building that houses the museum, but added a contemporary glass entrance, a sunny atrium, and a rooftop sculpture garden and café. Expanded galleries display more of the museum's permanent collection of American art since 1860, with an emphasis on Southeast regional artists, including those from Black Mountain College. ✉ *2 S. Pack Sq., Downtown* ☎ *828/253–3227* 🌐 *www.ashevilleart.org* 🎫 *$15* 🕒 *Closed Tues.*

Asheville Museum of Science

MUSEUM | FAMILY | The Colburn Earth Science Museum moved to a new space in the heart of downtown Asheville and has expanded into a full-fledged science museum. AMOS has interactive exhibits, special events, and educational programs. Among the exhibits are a large collection of North Carolina minerals, a small planetarium, and a Teratophoneus dinosaur skeleton. ✉ *43 Patton Ave., Downtown* ☎ *828/254–7162* 🌐 *www.ashevillescience.org* 🎫 *$8.*

Asheville Pinball Museum

MUSEUM | FAMILY | One of the more unusual attractions in town is the Asheville Pinball Museum, an arcade featuring dozens of vintage pinball machines and video games. Bring the kids, who'll probably ignore the modern machines in favor of those from the 1930s. There's also a bar serving snacks and craft beers and restrooms labeled Pac Man and Ms. Pac Man. ✉ *1 Battle Sq., Downtown* ⊕ *Just north of Grove Arcade* ☎ *828/776–5671* 🌐 *www.ashevillepinball.com* 🎫 *Museum free, unlimited play $15* 🕒 *Closed Tues.*

Basilica of St. Lawrence

RELIGIOUS SITE | A collaboration of Biltmore House head architect Richard Sharp Smith and the Spanish engineer-architect Rafael Guastavino, this elaborate Catholic basilica was completed in 1909. It follows a Spanish Renaissance design, rendered in brick and polychrome tile, and has a large, self-supporting dome with Catalan-style vaulting. Take a self-guided tour with one of the free brochures in the vestibule, or book a 25- to 45-minute guided tour at least a week in advance. ✉ *97 Haywood St., Downtown* ☎ *828/252–6042* 🌐 *www.saintlawrence-basilica.org* 🎫 *Free* 🕒 *Closed for tours during masses and other church events.*

Black Mountain College Museum and Arts Center

MUSEUM | Although it was around less than 25 years, the famed Black Mountain College was important in the development of several groundbreaking 20th-century art, dance, and literary movements. Some of the maverick spirits it attracted in its short lifetime were artists Willem and Elaine de Kooning, Robert Rauschenberg, Josef and Anni Albers, and M. C. Richards; dancer Merce Cunningham; musician John Cage; filmmaker Arthur Penn; futurist Buckminster Fuller; and writers Kenneth Noland, Charles Olson, and Robert Creeley. ✉ *120 College St., Downtown* ☎ *828/350–8484* 🌐 *www.*

blackmountaincollege.org 🎫 *Free, special exhibits from $5* ⏲ *Closed Sun. and between exhibitions.*

★ **Thomas Wolfe Memorial**

HOUSE | Asheville's most famous son, novelist Thomas Wolfe (1900–38), grew up in a 29-room Queen Anne–style home that his mother ran as a boardinghouse. In his prime in the 1930s, Wolfe was widely viewed as one of the best writers America had ever produced. The house—memorialized as "Dixieland" in Wolfe's novel *Look Homeward, Angel*—has been restored to its original 1916 condition, including the canary-color (Wolfe called it "dirty yellow") exterior. There are hourly guided tours of the house and heirloom gardens. ✉ *52 Market St., Downtown* ☎ *828/253–8304* 🌐 *www.wolfememorial.com* 🎫 *$5* ⏲ *Closed Sun. and Mon.*

Restaurants

Benne on Eagle

$$$$ | SOUTHERN | In the Foundry Hotel, James Beard Award finalist John Fleer's newest venture combines traditional Appalachian dishes with Lowcountry and Gullah flavors. The high-ceiling, industrial-style decor is softened by a collection of sketches of African American women who ran restaurants in the Block, a center of the black business community in Asheville. **Known for:** imaginative takes on soul food dishes; a taste of regional cuisines; updated historical setting. $ *Average main: $26* ✉ *The Foundry Hotel, 35 Eagle St., Downtown* ☎ *828/552–8833* 🌐 *www.benneoneagle.com* ⏲ *Closed Mon. and Tues. No dinner Sun. No lunch Wed.–Sat.*

Bouchon

$$$ | FRENCH | A French-style bistro, Bouchon ("cork" in French, and a type of Lyonnaise restaurant) serves simple Gallic comfort food, such as steak frites, bouillabaisse, and a version of chicken cordon bleu in a lemon juice, white wine, and butter reduction. The owner is from Lyon, and the casual spot fills up due to its prime location on Lexington Avenue. **Known for:** French fare like steak frites and escargots in garlic butter; steak tartare and ris de veau on Thursdays; all-you-can-eat mussels in savory sauces. $ *Average main: $22* ✉ *62 N. Lexington Ave., Downtown* ☎ *828/350–1140* 🌐 *www.ashevillebouchon.com* ⏲ *Closed Sun. and Mon. No lunch.*

Buxton Hall Barbecue

$$ | BARBECUE | FAMILY | In what was once a wood-floored skating rink in the now-hip South Slope section, this sprawling eatery serves traditional whole-hog, slow-pit barbecue in the eastern North Carolina style, infused with chef Elliott Moss's family vinegar mop sauce. The most popular dish is the pulled-pork plate with a side of Brussels sprouts cooked under the hog (available only at dinner). **Known for:** helmed by a James Beard Award nominee; Catawba Brewing in the same building; industrial-chic decor. $ *Average main: $16* ✉ *32 Banks Ave., Downtown* ☎ *828/232–7216* 🌐 *www.buxtonhall.com.*

★ **Chai Pani**

$ | INDIAN | Chef-owner Meherwan Irani, a James Beard Best Southeast Chef nominee, serves "Indian street food" from his hometown of Mumbai in this pleasant storefront eatery. Enjoy snacks like *bhel puri* (crispy puffed rice with a tamarind sauce) or chicken *pakoras* (savory fritters). **Known for:** perfect place to order a lot of dishes to share; vegetarian-friendly menu; very reasonable prices. $ *Average main: $11* ✉ *22 Battery Park Ave., Downtown* ☎ *828/254–4003* 🌐 *www.chaipani.net.*

Chestnut

$$$ | SOUTHERN | At this consistently good restaurant on Asheville's thriving "restaurant row," the food is local and seasonal, the prices are reasonable, the service is agreeable but not fawning, and there's a buzz without being overly loud. Chestnut is in a delightfully refurbished 1920s plumbing supply shop, updated

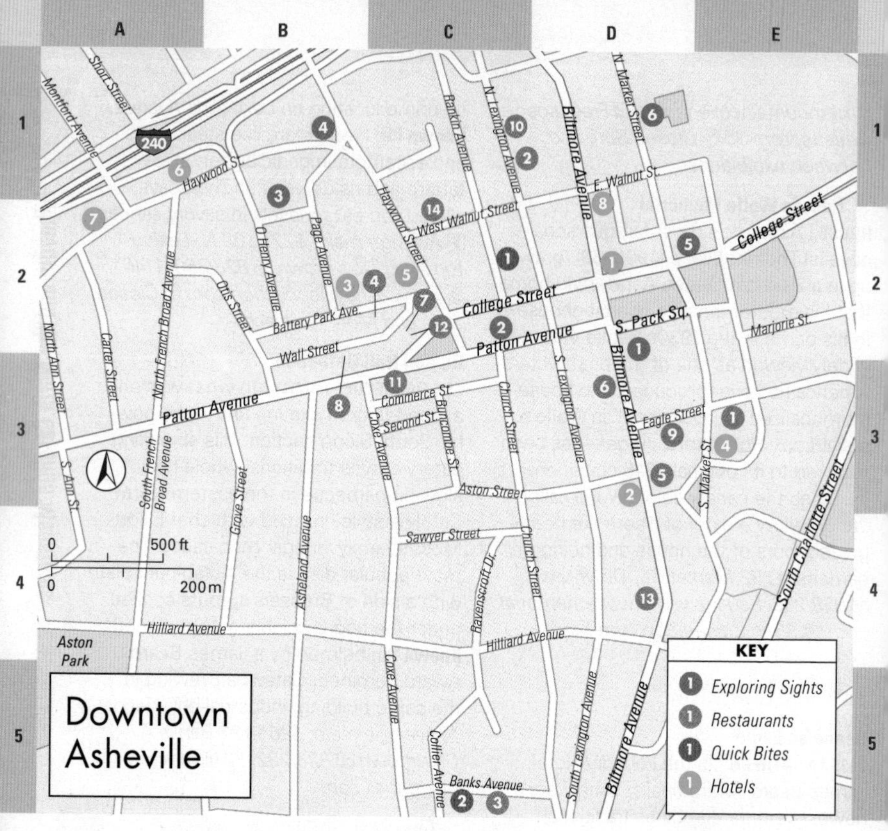

Sights

1 Asheville Art Museum.... **D2**
2 Asheville Museum of Science.................. **C2**
3 Asheville Pinball Museum................. **B1**
4 Basilica of St. Lawrence........... **B1**
5 Black Mountain College Museum and Arts Center.............. **E2**
6 Thomas Wolfe Memorial............... **D1**

Restaurants

1 Benne On Eagle.......... **E3**
2 Bouchon.................... **C1**
3 Buxton Hall Barbecue... **C5**
4 Chai Pani.................. **C2**
5 Chestnut................. **D3**
6 Cúrate..................... **D3**
7 Early Girl Eatery.......... **C2**
8 Laughing Seed Cafe.... **B3**
9 Limones................. **D3**
10 Mela....................... **C1**
11 Red Ginger **C3**
12 Tupelo Honey............ **C2**
13 Wicked Weed.......... **D4**
14 Zambra.................... **C2**

Quick Bites

1 High Five Coffee Bar **C2**
2 Vortex Doughnuts **C5**

Hotels

1 AC Hotel by Marriott ... **D2**
2 Aloft Asheville Downtown............... **D3**
3 Cambria Hotel Downtown Asheville **B2**
4 The Foundry Hotel Asheville **E3**
5 Haywood Park Hotel ... **C2**
6 Hotel Indigo Asheville Downtown.............. **A1**
7 Hyatt Place Asheville................. **A2**
8 The Windsor Boutique Hotel.......... **D1**

with art from a nearby gallery. **Known for:** delicious farm-to-table dishes; lively spot for a bite; moderate prices. $ *Average main: $22* ✉ *48 Biltmore Ave., Downtown* ☎ *828/575–2667* 🌐 *www.chestnutasheville.com.*

★ Cúrate

$$$ | SPANISH | If you have the blahs, Cúrate, with its extraordinary, authentic tapas and fun atmosphere, is the cure. The nationally known chef-owner, Katie Button, a James Beard Best Southeast Chef nominee, showcases the flavors of Spain in about four dozen small plates, with special attention to cured Iberian ham dishes and seafood items such as octopus and calamari. **Known for:** Spanish sherries and wines; convivial atmosphere; selection of hams. $ *Average main: $24* ✉ *13 Biltmore Ave., Downtown* ☎ *828/239–2946* 🌐 *heirloomhg.com/curate* ⏲ *Closed Mon.*

Early Girl Eatery

$ | SOUTHERN | FAMILY | Named after an early-maturing tomato variety, Early Girl Eatery is casually Southern, with a natural twist, as it partners with about two dozen local farms for its farm-to-table cuisine. Breakfast is served all day and includes stacks of multigrain pancakes with organic maple syrup, shrimp and grits, and sausage-and–sweet potato scramble. **Known for:** Southern comfort food; all-day breakfast; "meat and two" specials at lunch and dinner. $ *Average main: $13* ✉ *8 Wall St., Downtown* ☎ *828/259–9292* 🌐 *www.earlygirleatery.com.*

Laughing Seed Café

$ | VEGETARIAN | This vegetarian-vegan eatery is a longtime Asheville favorite on charming Wall Street. The extensive menu ranges from simple sandwiches and pizzas to dinner specialties influenced by the flavors of India, Cuba, Thailand, Mexico, and Morocco. **Known for:** fruits and vegetables from local organic farms; delicious juices and other beverages; breads baked in-house. $ *Average main: $14* ✉ *40 Wall St., Downtown* ☎ *828/252–3445* 🌐 *www.laughingseed.com* ⏲ *Closed Tues. and Wed.*

★ Limones

$$$$ | MODERN MEXICAN | Three components—a talented chef from Mexico City, locally sourced ingredients, and a San Francisco bistro atmosphere—combine to make this modern Mexican place a standout. Whet your appetite with the ceviche sampler and lobster nachos before going on to the regularly changing list of main dishes like carne asada with a *romesco* mole. **Known for:** the city's best margaritas; smart, unobtrusive service; airy and open space. $ *Average main: $27* ✉ *13 Eagle St., Downtown* ☎ *828/252–2327* 🌐 *www.limonesrestaurant.com.*

Mela

$$ | INDIAN | FAMILY | Rather than specialize in one type of Indian cuisine, Mela offers dishes from across the country. The traditionally prepared tandoori dishes (chicken, shrimp, and lamb) are especially delicious, and at lunch there's an extensive, inexpensive buffet. **Known for:** classic dishes nicely presented; bright and airy dining room; vegetarian and vegan options. $ *Average main: $16* ✉ *70 N. Lexington, Downtown* ☎ *828/225–8880* 🌐 *www.melaasheville.com.*

Red Ginger

$$$ | CHINESE FUSION | Although it's usually served earlier in the day, dim sum becomes an all-day affair at this upscale Chinese eatery. The resulting menu of farm-to-table small plates—don't miss the black truffle *shumai* (open-faced dumplings), crispy fish, or pork dumplings—is a feast for the eyes and the stomach. **Known for:** Asheville's best Chinese restaurant; farm-fresh ingredients; creative cocktails. $ *Average main: $23* ✉ *82 Patton Ave., Downtown* ☎ *828/505–8688* 🌐 *www.redgingerasheville.com.*

Tupelo Honey
$$ | **SOUTHERN** | **FAMILY** | This is the place for down-home Southern cooking with a frenetic twist. The mothership downtown Asheville location of this ever-expanding chain delivers a lot more than grits, with dishes like pan-roasted Gulf snapper, "Southernized" tacos, bottomless mac and cheese, and sassafras pork chops, plus good prices on craft brews and cocktails. **Known for:** Southernized takes on everything; loud, fun atmosphere; expanded downtown location. *Average main: $16 ✉ 12 College St., Downtown ☎ 828/255–4863 🌐 www.tupelohoneycafe.com.*

Wicked Weed
$ | **MODERN AMERICAN** | Pernicious IPA and another two dozen local brews are available at this popular restaurant, and they pair beautifully with steak tartare, bison meat loaf, and artisanal cheese plates. There's a bottle shop, a tasting room downstairs, and a patio with a firepit that's perfect on chilly evenings. **Known for:** award-winning beers and ales; lively atmosphere; popular patio. *Average main: $13 ✉ 91 Biltmore Ave., Downtown ☎ 828/575–9599 🌐 www.wickedweedbrewing.com.*

Zambra
$$$ | **SPANISH** | Zambra's sophisticated tapas—think grilled octopus in black ink sauce, pistachio-crusted veal sweetbreads with blackberries, and squash gnocchi—have made Zambra one of the most interesting restaurants in Asheville. Moorish colors, dim lighting, and an underground setting create a romantic atmosphere. **Known for:** Spanish and North African tapas; intimate, romantic atmosphere; 200 Spanish wines and sherries. *Average main: $23 ✉ 85 Walnut St., Downtown ☎ 828/232–1060 🌐 www.zambratapas.com ⊗ No lunch.*

Coffee and Quick Bites

High Five Coffee Bar
$ | **CAFÉ** | With exposed brick walls and antique wood floors, this is probably downtown Asheville's favorite spot to hang out, use free Wi-Fi, and sip fresh-brewed coffees and teas. There are also High Five locations in North Asheville and Woodfin. **Known for:** silky coffee and tea lattes; skilled baristas; laid-back atmosphere. *Average main: $4 ✉ 13 Rankin Ave., Downtown ☎ 828/713–5291 🌐 www.highfivecoffee.com.*

Vortex Doughnuts
$ | **BAKERY** | Doughnuts here are glazed, sugared, filled, served "old fashioned" or cake-style, and always fresh and handmade. The vegan choices are surprisingly decadent. **Known for:** vegan friendly; bacon-topped doughnuts; intriguing coffee drinks with ingredients like cardamom and turmeric. *Average main: $3 ✉ 32 Banks Ave., Suite 106, Downtown ☎ 828/552–3010 🌐 www.vortexdoughnuts.com.*

Hotels

★ AC Hotel by Marriott
$$$$ | **HOTEL** | With a distinctively modern facade, this gleaming hotel has a prime central location just north of Pack Square, within walking distance of most downtown restaurants, bars, galleries, and shops. **Pros:** unbeatable views from the rooftop terrace and bar; one of the city's sleekest lodgings; favorite of business travelers. **Cons:** priced like a premium brand; limited dining options in the hotel; more of a big-city vibe. *Rooms from: $340 ✉ 10 Broadway St., Downtown ☎ 828/258–2522 🌐 www.marriott.com 132 rooms No meals.*

Aloft Asheville Downtown
$$$$ | **HOTEL** | With a location just south of Pack Square, this hotel is very, very popular with travelers wanting to be in the heart of things. **Pros:** home of the trendy

WXYZ bar; easy parking under the hotel; nice extras like free Wi-Fi. **Cons:** perhaps a bit too trendy for some; not designed for families with kids; surprisingly pricey. *Rooms from: $350 51 Biltmore Ave., Downtown 828/232–2838 www.starwoodhotels.com/alofthotels 115 rooms No meals.*

Cambria Hotel Downtown Asheville
$$$ | **HOTEL** | Directly across from the Grove Arcade, the Cambria Hotel puts you near many restaurants and shops. **Pros:** complimentary glass of champagne at check-in; location couldn't be more central; one of the newest properties. **Cons:** rooms not as upscale as at some nearby hotels; lobby is at entrance to parking garage; pets not permitted. *Rooms from: $207 15 Page Ave., Downtown 828/348–4850 www.cambriadowntownasheville.com 136 rooms No meals.*

★ The Foundry Hotel Asheville
$$$$ | **HOTEL** | One of downtown Asheville's newest hotels, this boutique lodging occupies a former steel foundry and several other industrial buildings around a central courtyard. **Pros:** complimentary champagne on arrival; Tesla car service to nearby attractions; eager-to-help staff. **Cons:** not as central as other downtown hotels; near the top end in terms of prices; valet parking only. *Rooms from: $421 51 S. Market St., Downtown 828/552–8545 www.foundryasheville.com 87 rooms No meals.*

Haywood Park Hotel
$$$$ | **HOTEL** | Location is the biggest draw of this all-suites downtown hotel, which is within walking distance of many of Asheville's shops, restaurants, and galleries. **Pros:** small shopping mall and café in the atrium; Isa's Bistro has sidewalk seating; large and comfortable rooms. **Cons:** not as high-end as other nearby hotels; pricey in high season; no pool. *Rooms from: $299 1 Battery Park Ave., Downtown 828/252–2522 www.haywoodpark.com 33 suites No meals.*

Hotel Indigo Asheville Downtown
$$$$ | **HOTEL** | With views of the Blue Ridge Mountains from many of the rooms in this 12-story tower (especially the 16 upper-floor suites with floor-to-ceiling windows), Hotel Indigo is done up in striking colors like teal and aubergine and features furnishings and artworks by local craftspeople. **Pros:** short walk to Grove Arcade and many restaurants; nice extras like walk-in showers; better views the higher you go. **Cons:** some noise from nearby expressway; can be pricey in high season; no pool. *Rooms from: $375 151 Haywood St., Downtown 828/239–0239 www.ashevilleindigo.com 100 rooms No meals.*

Hyatt Place Asheville
$$$$ | **HOTEL** | **FAMILY** | Near Montford, the centrally located Hyatt Place is a short walk from the Grove Arcade and many restaurants; guest rooms are bright and airy, and higher-level corner rooms have floor-to-ceiling windows with city and mountain views. **Pros:** rooftop has great sunset views; walk to downtown destinations; spacious accommodations. **Cons:** fee for on-site parking; expensive in high season; not pet-friendly. *Rooms from: $379 199 Haywood St., Downtown 828/505–8500 www.hyatt.com 150 rooms Free breakfast.*

★ The Windsor Boutique Hotel
$$$$ | **B&B/INN** | Built in 1907, the Windsor Hotel shook off any signs of age with a top-to-bottom renovation. **Pros:** large, beautifully designed suites; perfect location in heart of downtown; decorated with local art. **Cons:** minimum stay in high season; no on-site parking; not pet-friendly. *Rooms from: $300 36 Broadway St., Downtown 844/494–6376 toll-free www.windsorasheville.com 14 suites No meals.*

Nightlife

Capella on 9

BARS/PUBS | Asheville's primo rooftop bar, Capella on 9 has expansive indoor and outdoor spaces tastefully designed and filled with local artworks. On the ninth floor of the centrally located AC Hotel, it offers dramatic views of downtown Asheville and the surrounding mountains. There's a first-rate selection of craft cocktails and a limited but locally sourced menu of small plates. ✉ *AC Hotel by Marriott, 10 Broadway St., 9th fl., Downtown* ☎ *828/258–2522* 🌐 *www.capellaon9.com.*

DSSOLVR

BREWPUBS/BEER GARDENS | This is one of the most exciting breweries to come out of the Asheville area in recent years, with a taproom open nightly (and all day weekends) right downtown. Branding is wacky and irreverent, and beers manage to be both inventive and traditional (there are also ciders and meads). The taproom has a small patio as well. There's plenty of merchandise to take home, including six-packs. ✉ *63 N. Lexington Ave., Downtown* 🌐 *www.dssolvr.com.*

★ The Orange Peel

DANCE CLUBS | Bob Dylan, Modest Mouse, and the Beastie Boys have played here. This midsize venue is far and away the best nightspot downtown. There's also a great dance floor, with springy wood slats, two bars serving wine and beer, and a private club for cocktail lovers on the lower level. ✉ *101 Biltmore Ave., Downtown* ☎ *828/225–5851* 🌐 *www.theorangepeel.net* 🎫 *Varies.*

★ Sovereign Remedies

BARS/PUBS | Offering creative craft cocktails and a classed-up-cool atmosphere (though it's still Asheville casual), Sovereign Remedies is one of the city's best spots for locally sourced farm-to-table and farm-to-glass delights. The light-filled space boasts high ceilings, large mirrors, locally built furnishings, and a huge array of spirits in the main bar, but there's also sidewalk seating and a space upstairs, so the place is even bigger than it first looks. Servers and bartenders are friendly and knowledgeable. ✉ *29 N. Market St., Downtown* ☎ *828/919–9518* 🌐 *www.sovereignremedies.com.*

Performing Arts

Asheville Community Theatre

THEATER | FAMILY | One of the oldest community theater groups in the country, Asheville Community Theatre stages amateur productions year-round in its own building. ✉ *35 E. Walnut St., Downtown* ☎ *828/254–1320* 🌐 *www.ashevilletheatre.org.*

Diana Wortham Theatre

ARTS CENTERS | The intimate 500-seat Diana Wortham Theatre is home to more than 200 musical, dance, and theatrical events each year. A planned $3 million expansion is expected to add two more smaller performance spaces and upgrade the main theater. There's parking next to the theater or nearby, under the Aloft Hotel. ✉ *2 S. Pack Sq., Downtown* ☎ *828/257–4530* 🌐 *www.dwtheatre.com.*

North Carolina Stage Company

THEATER | From an alley off Walnut Street, this professional company puts on edgy, contemporary plays, although it also does audience favorites, such as a series of Jeeves comedies. ✉ *15 Stage La., Downtown* ☎ *828/239–0263* 🌐 *www.ncstage.org.*

Thomas Wolfe Auditorium

ARTS CENTERS | FAMILY | The 2,400-seat Thomas Wolfe Auditorium, in the U.S. Cellular Center Asheville (formerly Asheville Civic Center), hosts larger events, including traveling Broadway shows and performances of the Asheville Symphony. In the U.S. Cellular Center is also the newly named ExploreAsheville.com Arena, which seats 7,200 and is used to stage concerts and other large events. ✉ *87 Haywood St., Downtown*

☎ *828/259–5736 box office* 🌐 *www.harrahscherokeecenterasheville.com.*

Shopping

BOOKS

★ Battery Park Book Exchange and Champagne Bar

STORE/MALL | At this unusual bookstore and bar, you can relax on an overstuffed chair or sofa while sipping one of 80 wines and champagnes by the glass. The inventory includes more than 20,000 secondhand books, with special strength in Civil War, American history, and North Carolina subjects. It's pet friendly, too, with an "espresso dog bar." ✉ *Grove Arcade, 1 Page Ave., southwest corner, Downtown* ☎ *828/252–0020* 🌐 *www.batteryparkbookexchange.com.*

★ Malaprop's Bookstore/Cafe

STORE/MALL | **FAMILY** | This is what an independent bookstore should be, with an intelligent selection of new books, many author appearances and other events, and a comfortable café. Staffers speak many foreign languages, including Hungarian, Russian, Italian, Spanish, French, and German. ✉ *55 Haywood St., Downtown* ☎ *828/254–6734* 🌐 *www.malaprops.com.*

CANDY AND CHOCOLATE

The Chocolate Fetish

FOOD/CANDY | **FAMILY** | Chocolate truffles and sea-salt caramels are favorites here, but you can also buy made-on-site items such as chocolate in the shapes of cowboy boots and high heels. Most items are sold for takeout, but there's limited in-store seating if you just can't wait to scarf down these delicious sweets with a cup of rich hot chocolate. ✉ *36 Haywood St., Downtown* ☎ *828/258–2353* 🌐 *www.chocolatefetish.com.*

★ French Broad Chocolate Lounge

FOOD/CANDY | **FAMILY** | French Broad Chocolate Lounge—so popular it had to move to this much-larger location on Pack Square (though the line is still sometimes out the door)—makes its own delicious chocolate candy, but that's just the start. As the name suggests, it's also a lounge, where you can sit in comfort and enjoy not only truffles and other premium chocolates but also ice cream, cookies, brownies, various kinds of hot and cold chocolate drinks, and specialty coffees and teas. Adjoining is the grab-and-go Chocolate Boutique. The owners also have a small chocolate factory and tasting room at 821 Riverside Drive, with guided tours daily, starting at $12. ✉ *10 S. Pack Sq., Downtown* ☎ *828/252–4181 lounge and boutique, 828/348–5187 factory* 🌐 *www.frenchbroadchocolates.com.*

FARMERS' MARKETS

The Asheville area has many tailgate markets, usually in parking lots where local growers set up temporary sales stalls on certain days, and farmers' markets, which are typically larger than tailgate markets and often have permanent booths. The website of Appalachian Sustainable Agriculture Project (ASAP) has up-to-date information on all the region's tailgate markets, U-pick farms, and farmers' markets.

ASAP

FARM/RANCH | More than 1,200 small family farms, tailgate markets, farm-to-table restaurants, and similar organizations in the region belong to the Asheville-based ASAP. ASAP lists more than 200 area restaurants and bakeries that buy direct from local farmers. A farm tour is held annually in September. ASAP also publishes a print and online guide to local food sources and tailgate markets. ✉ *306 W. Haywood St., Downtown* ☎ *828/236–1282* 🌐 *www.asapconnections.org.*

Asheville City Market

OUTDOOR/FLEA/GREEN MARKETS | **FAMILY** | Sponsored by ASAP, nearly everything at this downtown market is local. Offerings vary but usually include produce, free-range eggs, homemade breads, cheeses, and crafts from some 60 local farms, bakeries, and craftspeople. From early

April through December, every Saturday morning it covers an entire city block on North Market Street; January through March it moves indoors, to the Masonic Temple Building at 80 Broadway. ✉ *52 N. Market St., Downtown* ☎ *828/236–1282* 🌐 *www.asapconnections.org.*

GALLERIES

★ Blue Spiral 1

ART GALLERIES | The biggest and arguably the best art gallery in town has changing exhibits of regional sculpture, paintings, fine crafts, and photographs. ✉ *38 Biltmore Ave., Downtown* ☎ *828/251–0202* 🌐 *www.bluespiral1.com.*

Kress Emporium I and II

ART GALLERIES | **FAMILY** | In this 1928 landmark building decorated with polychrome terra-cotta tiles, about 100 artisans show and sell their crafts. A second location two doors away, Kress Emporium II, has about 25 art and crafts stalls. ✉ *19 and 27 Patton Ave., Downtown* ☎ *828/281–2252 Kress Emporium I, 828/232–7237 Kress Emporium II* 🌐 *www.thekressemporium.com.*

★ Woolworth Walk

ART GALLERIES | **FAMILY** | In a 1938 building that once housed a five-and-dime, Woolworth Walk features the curated work of more than 170 crafts artists, in 20,000 square feet of exhibit space on two levels. There's even a working soda fountain, built to resemble the original Woolworth luncheonette. ✉ *25 Haywood St., Downtown* ☎ *828/254–9234* 🌐 *www.woolworthwalk.com.*

SHOPPING CENTERS

★ Downtown Asheville

SHOPPING NEIGHBORHOODS | **FAMILY** | Shopping is excellent and local all over downtown Asheville, with around 200 boutiques, including more than 30 art and crafts galleries. Several streets, notably **Biltmore Avenue, Broadway Street, Lexington Avenue, Haywood Street,** and **Wall Street,** are lined with small, independently owned stores. In fact, there are only two chain retailers in all of downtown. ✉ *Downtown* 🌐 *www.ashevilledowntown.org.*

★ Grove Arcade

CLOTHING | **FAMILY** | Just before its opening in 1929, the Grove Arcade, which covers an entire city block, was trumpeted as "the most elegant building in America" by its builder, W. E. Grove, the man also responsible for the Grove Park Inn. He envisioned a new kind of retail, office, and residential complex. Grove died before completing the project, and a planned 14-story tower was never built. Still, the building is an architectural wonder, with gargoyles galore. Now it's a public market with about 40 locally owned shops and restaurants, along with apartments, office space, and an outdoor market. A self-guided architectural tour (download a map from the website) takes about 45 minutes. ✉ *1 Page Ave., Downtown* ☎ *828/252–7799* 🌐 *www.grovearcade.com.*

Activities

BASEBALL

Asheville Tourists

BASEBALL/SOFTBALL | **FAMILY** | A Class A farm team of the Colorado Rockies, the Asheville Tourists typically play April to early September at McCormick Field, the oldest minor league park in regular use. It appears briefly in the 1988 movie *Bull Durham.* ✉ *McCormick Field, 30 Buchanan Pl., Downtown* ☎ *828/258–0428* 🌐 *www.milb.com* 🎟 *$8.*

River Arts District

Asheville's former industrial and warehouse section, just southwest of downtown along the French Broad River, is the up-and-coming art-and-crafts center of the region, with many studios and galleries, plus cafés, breweries, and nightclubs. As industrial companies moved out, artists moved in, seeking cheaper rents for studios and loft apartments. Today the district is home to some 200 working artists—mainly pottery and ceramics artists, painters, fabric artists, and sculptors—and this doesn't include students taking courses. As many as 75 studios in around 20 late-19th- and early-20th-century industrial buildings are open free to the public (hours vary but many are open daily from 9 to 5). You can talk to artists and buy their work, often at lower prices than in galleries. On the second Saturday of each month, studios offer refreshments and demonstrations for visitors. Annually in early November, the district holds a Studio Stroll, when nearly all the studios and galleries are open to the public. Increasingly, restaurants, bars, and coffeehouses are setting up shop here as well, and a large national craft brewing company, New Belgium, opened its East Coast brewery and distribution center just across the French Broad River in West Asheville, overlooking the River Arts District (RAD). The City of Asheville's new $50 million access and infrastructure project, which got underway in 2018, means better access to the river, along with new roads, green spaces, and bike and pedestrian paths. For more information on what's going on in the neighborhood, see ⊕ *www.riverartsdistrict.com*.

Sights

Asheville Cotton Mill Studios

STORE/MALL | This 1887 brick building, one of the oldest industrial buildings in Asheville, is a former factory once owned by Moses H. Cone, whose family mansion is on the Blue Ridge Parkway. With an exterior covered by a colorful mural, it now has studios for artists and entrepreneurs. ✉ *122 Riverside Dr., River Arts District* ☎ *305/968–1300* ⊕ *www.cottonmillasheville.com* 🎫 *Free.*

Restaurants

★ The Bull and Beggar

$$$$ | **SEAFOOD** | The Bull and Beggar is decidedly warehouse hip, with brick walls, old wood floors, and high ceilings. Its most popular feature is Burger Monday, when fabulous double-patty burgers with fries go for $10, and oysters and clams on the half shell are half-price. **Known for:** kitchen turns out excellent surf, as well as turf; locals come out in droves for the burgers; best seats are on the sunny patio. $ *Average main: $32* ✉ *37 Paynes Way, No. 007, River Arts District* ✣ *Near original Wedge Brewery* ☎ *828/575–9443* ⊕ *www.thebullandbeggar.com* ⏲ *Closed Tues. and Wed.*

★ Smoky Park Supper Club

$$$ | **AMERICAN** | The restaurant itself is creatively constructed out of stacked shipping containers, but dining and drinking at this hip, young spot is best done outside, where you can choose a high-top on the deck, grab a picnic table on the lawn, or drink your cocktail in lounge chairs set up right along the river. This is one of those special places where the food is just as good as the atmosphere; affordable dishes highlight local ingredients like trout and ramps, and ordering the smoked burger is never a mistake. **Known for:** wood-smoked, farm-to-table ingredients; great atmosphere any time of day, from family fun to romantic; scenic views of the French Broad River. $ *Average main: $24* ✉ *350 Riverside Dr., No. 3141, River Arts District* ☎ *828/350–0315* ⊕ *www.smokypark.com* ⏲ *Closed Mon.–Wed.*

★ 12 Bones Smokehouse

$ | **BARBECUE** | **FAMILY** | Gentrification forced it out of its old digs, but 12 Bones now has a larger location with twice the seating and picnic tables for outdoor dining. The lively crowds still range from hippie potters to downtown suits—former president Barack Obama made 12 Bones his first stop on multiple trips to

Asheville—who come for the smoky baby back ribs, pulled pork, beef brisket, and corn pudding. **Known for:** smoky baby back ribs are worth the trip; waitresses who call you "sweetie"; collard greens and other Southern sides. *Average main: $10* ✉ *5 Foundy St., River Arts District* ☎ *828/253–4499* 🌐 *www.12bones.com* 🕒 *Closed weekends and most of Jan.*

Vivian

$$$$ | CONTEMPORARY | At this cozy eatery in the River Arts District, the emphasis is less on the atmosphere than on the cooking, which blends French techniques with some Southern ingredients, such as mountain trout and North Carolina shrimp. Expect the service to be top-notch. **Known for:** creative versions of contemporary dishes; interesting craft cocktails; unpretentious setting. *Average main: $28* ✉ *348 Depot St., Suite 190, River Arts District* ☎ *828/225–3497* 🌐 *vivianavl.com* 🕒 *Closed Mon.–Wed. No dinner Sun.*

Coffee and Quick Bites

Summit Coffee Co.

$ | CAFÉ | Serving third-wave coffee in a chic industrial space, this is a convenient stop for cold brew and more while visiting art studios. **Known for:** beans roasted in-house; great selections of beans and espresso drinks; bagels. *Average main: $3* ✉ *4 Foundy St., Suite 20, River Arts District* ☎ *828/705–8071* 🌐 *www.summitcoffee.com.*

Nightlife

Grey Eagle

BARS/PUBS | A RAD favorite, the Grey Eagle features popular local and regional bands four or five nights a week, with contra dancing and patio concerts on certain nights. During the day the space doubles as a restaurant serving tacos, burritos, and nachos. ✉ *185 Clingman Ave., River Arts District* ☎ *828/232–5800* 🌐 *www.thegreyeagle.com.*

Performing Arts

CURVE Studios and Garden

ART GALLERIES—ARTS | FAMILY | With working studios and exhibits by about a dozen artists, CURVE Studios displays ceramics, textiles, jewelry, sculpture, and furniture in three buildings. Many items are for sale direct from the artists. ✉ *6, 9, and 12 Riverside Dr., River Arts District* ☎ *828/388–3526* 🌐 *www.curvestudiosnc.com.*

Shopping

★ **Odyssey Center for the Ceramic Arts**

CERAMICS/GLASSWARE | FAMILY | Odyssey Center for the Ceramic Arts has the largest number of working clay artists in the region. It has two ceramics galleries, plus pottery studios and clay classes. The main gallery, **Odyssey Co-Op Gallery,** has a large and high-quality selection of ceramic works, both functional and decorative, as well as figurative and abstract sculpture, by 25 juried clay artists. **Odyssey Clayworks** offers classes and has a gallery of clay work by students and others. ✉ *238 Clingman Ave., River Arts District* ☎ *828/285–0210* 🌐 *www.odysseycoopgallery.com.*

Riverview Station

CRAFTS | FAMILY | More than 40 artists, craftspeople, and entrepreneurs in ceramics, painting, textiles, woodworking, and jewelry work in this complex of studios and galleries in the River Arts District. Several of the artists offer classes, and there's lots of free parking. ✉ *191 Lyman St., River Arts District* ☎ *828/231–7120* 🌐 *www.riverviewstation.com.*

Wedge Studios and Wedge Brewing Company

CRAFTS | Once the headquarters of Farmer's Federation, the region's leading agricultural co-op, this large brick building holds more than 30 independent art and crafts studios, along with the popular Wedge Brewery and other businesses. Grab a bite from one of the food trucks that appear in rotation in the Wedge parking lot and eat at a picnic table outside. Wedge Brewery has opened a second location in RAD behind Riverview Station next door to 12 Bones. *111–129 Roberts St., River Arts District 828/505–2782 www.wedgebrewing.com Free.*

West Asheville

West Asheville, across the French Broad River, has become a hot part of the city, with its main artery, Haywood Road, sporting new restaurants, edgy stores, and popular clubs. Despite the gentrification, some of the area still feels slightly scruffy.

Sights

★ New Belgium Brewing Company

WINERY/DISTILLERY | Opened on the former site of the Asheville Stockyards, New Belgium sits at the edge of the River Arts District, overlooking the French Broad River. Excellent 90-minute tours of this state-of-the-art brewery are free and can be booked online up to two months in advance. Tastings of several beers are included. *21 Craven St., West Asheville 828/333–6900 www.newbelgium.com.*

Restaurants

BimBeriBon

$ | ECLECTIC | Look past its location in a strip mall, because light-filled BimBeriBon brings fresh Asian, South American, and Middle Eastern flavors to the West Asheville restaurant scene. The café and bakery focuses on healthful, gluten-free, and mostly organic salads, sandwiches, bowls, and baked goods. **Known for:** flavors are like a trip around the world; great wines and craft cocktails; health-conscious dishes. *Average main: $12 697 Haywood Rd., West Asheville 828/505–0328 www.bimberibon.com.*

Ghan Shan West

$ | ASIAN FUSION | Inspired by the food of Southeast Asia, China, and Japan, Ghan Shan West has an eclectic and inventive menu of house-made dumplings, ramen, soups, and noodles. Choose between the colorful dining room and the breezy patio. **Known for:** pleasant outdoor dining; cool and casual vibe; exciting specials. *Average main: $14 285 Haywood St., West Asheville 828/417–7402 www.ganshangroup.com Closed Sun.*

★ Jargon

$$$ | ECLECTIC | As you enter this hipster haven in a historic building in a trendy part of West Asheville, you'll be taken by the charm of the intimate space, which features handmade shadowbox art from the 1950s, a collection of mirrors, and retro lava lamps above the bar. The menu is equally eclectic, with small and large plates, including deep-fried deviled eggs (far better than you'd think), calamari in a garlic marinara sauce, roasted octopus with fava beans, duck and andouille gumbo, elk meatballs, and trout with fennel. **Known for:** creative takes on traditional dishes; craft cocktails like the Ice Breaker; outdoor courtyard. *Average main: $22 715 Haywood Rd., West Asheville 828/785–1761 www.jargonrestaurant.com.*

Rocky's Hot Chicken Shack

$ | SOUTHERN | Serving Nashville-style fried chicken (at different levels of spiciness), this casual restaurant is a little ways from downtown, but a local's favorite and one of the best places for a cheap meal or takeout picnic. Large chicken platters, sandwiches, sides, and your pick of sauces are all loaded with flavor; order the fried pickles with zippy ranch as a snack. **Known for:** Nashville-style hot chicken; good Southern sides; food for the whole family. *Average main: $10 1455 Patton Ave., West Asheville 828/575–2260 www.rockyshotchickenshack.com.*

★ **Sunny Point Café**

$$ | SOUTHERN | FAMILY | The quintessential West Asheville eatery, Sunny Point serves food that is simple, well prepared, and not too expensive. Herbs and some veggies come from the restaurant's organic garden next door. **Known for:** your best intro to West Asheville; great breakfasts served all day; covered outdoor patio dining. *Average main: $16 ✉ 626 Haywood Rd., West Asheville ☎ 828/252–0055 🌐 www.sunnypointcafe.com ⏲ No dinner Sun. and Mon.*

Coffee and Quick Bites

BattleCat Coffee Bar and Tiger Bay Cafe

$ | CAFÉ | BattleCat Coffee Bar is one of the funkiest local coffeehouses in Asheville, in a boldly painted, old wood house with a porch and ample picnic tables that draws those who like the relaxed ambience, free Wi-Fi, and Counter Culture coffee. Tiger Bay Cafe shares the space and kitchen here, serving generous bagel sandwiches and breakfast burritos. **Known for:** plenty of outdoor seating; black-owned business; local art on the walls. *Average main: $4 ✉ 373 Haywood Rd., Metro West ☎ 828/713–3835 🌐 www.battlecatcoffeebar.com; www.tigerbaycafe.com.*

Nightlife

Fleetwood's

MUSIC CLUBS | This venue encompasses all that is good, holy, and hipster about West Asheville. Is Fleetwood's a dive bar? Vintage clothing store? Rock 'n' roll hall? Wedding chapel? The answer is, a resounding: all of the above. *✉ 496 Haywood Rd., West Asheville ☎ 828/505–5525 🌐 www.fleetwoodschapel.com.*

Isis Restaurant and Music Hall

MUSIC CLUBS | What was once a movie house—the marquee is a dead giveaway—is now an upscale music club. Early in the evening a full dinner menu is available. At night it's bar snacks and live music: bluegrass, blues, reggae, jazz, or rock. The venue also hosts lawn concerts. *✉ 743 Haywood Rd., West Asheville ☎ 828/575–2737 🌐 www.isisasheville.com.*

Montford, Grove Park, and North Asheville

The area north of downtown Asheville is largely residential and comprises several smaller neighborhoods. The historic Montford and Grove Park neighborhoods are the closest to downtown and home to fine Victorian-era houses, including many remarkable Queen Anne homes from the late 19th century. North of Montford is the campus of the University of North Carolina at Asheville, nationally known for its liberal arts focus.

Restaurants

Chiesa

$$ | ITALIAN | FAMILY | Named for its location in a former church, Chiesa feeds body and soul with heavenly Italian classics served under high vaulted ceilings. Pasta is certainly the focus here, be it house-made fettuccine, angel hair, or orecchiette, served with flavorful Sicilian red tomato gravy and paired with sweet Italian sausages or meatballs. **Known for:** friendly neighborhood feel; wonderful wines; patio seating. *Average main: $19 ✉ 152 Montford Ave., Montford ☎ 828/552–3110 🌐 www.chiesaavl.com ⏲ Closed Sun. No lunch.*

Nine Mile

$ | CARIBBEAN | FAMILY | This informal neighborhood spot in Montford serves what it bills as Jamaican food, although the not-too-spicy jerk dishes are served in bowls over linguine or basmati rice. Tofu can be substituted for any meat, and many of the ingredients are from local organic farms. (If you like more heat, ask for the Rasta Fyah hot sauce.)

Wine, beer, organic coffees and teas, and Cheerwine, a North Carolina soft drink with a cherry flavor, are among beverage offerings. **Known for:** Jamaican and Caribbean food; large servings at low-to-moderate prices; laid-back atmosphere. *$ Average main: $13 ✉ 233 Montford Ave., North Metro, Montford ☎ 828/505–3121 ⊕ www.ninemileasheville.com.*

★ Plant
$$ | **VEGETARIAN** | With a name that refers to the industrial vibe as much as the menu, Plant offers a sophisticated, frequently changing array of dishes from different cultures and cuisines, served in a minimalist setting. A typical menu might include seitan chili with cheese, lasagna with raw vegetables, smoked portobello mushrooms, and delicious "ice cream" made with coconut milk for dessert. **Known for:** wide range of vegan dishes; biodynamic cooking methods; organic wines and local beers. *$ Average main: $17 ✉ 165 Merrimon Ave., Chestnut Hill ☎ 828/258–7500 ⊕ www.plantisfood.com ⊙ Closed Mon. and Tues. No lunch.*

Hotels

Albemarle Inn
$$$$ | **B&B/INN** | This 1909 Greek Revival home in the upscale Grove Park residential area was home to Hungarian composer Béla Bartók when he wrote his famous Asheville Concerto. **Pros:** lovely residential neighborhood; lots of historic details; excellent breakfast. **Cons:** old-fashioned claw-foot tubs may not appeal to everyone; not within easy walking distance of downtown; some steps to climb. *$ Rooms from: $285 ✉ 86 Edgemont Rd., Grove Park ☎ 828/255–0027 ⊕ www.albemarleinn.com ⇨ 11 rooms ¶◎¶ Free breakfast.*

★ Chestnut Street Inn
$$$$ | **B&B/INN** | Even in a city with no shortage of excellent B&Bs, the Colonial Revival–style Chestnut Street Inn stands out for its location—easy walking distance of downtown, yet tucked away in the quiet, charming Chestnut Hill Historic District. **Pros:** award-winning restoration of a historic house; port is served in the afternoon; helpful, welcoming hosts. **Cons:** just-baked cookies will ruin your diet; a couple of rooms on the small side; breakfast is a fixed menu. *$ Rooms from: $255 ✉ 176 E. Chestnut St., Chestnut Hill ☎ 828/285–0705 ⊕ www.chestnutstreetinn.com ⇨ 8 rooms ¶◎¶ Free breakfast.*

1900 Inn on Montford
$$$$ | **B&B/INN** | Guests are pampered at this Arts and Crafts–style B&B, where all rooms have huge beds and most have whirlpool tubs and handsome fireplaces. **Pros:** filled with lovely antiques; lots of modern amenities; caring staff. **Cons:** not for families with small children; a bit of a hike from downtown; decor not for everyone. *$ Rooms from: $287 ✉ 296 Montford Ave., Montford ☎ 828/254–9569 ⊕ www.innonmontford.com ⇨ 8 rooms, 1 cabin ¶◎¶ Free breakfast.*

★ Omni Grove Park Inn
$$$$ | **RESORT** | This massive resort has hosted 10 U.S. presidents, from Woodrow Wilson to Barack Obama, and it's easy to see why: grand views of downtown and the Blue Ridge Mountains, a challenging golf course and top-rated spa, and a variety of dining options. **Pros:** imposing and historic property; magnificent mountain views; top-notch amenities. **Cons:** sometimes fills up with groups; expensive during high season; some small rooms. *$ Rooms from: $315 ✉ 290 Macon Ave., Grove Park ☎ 828/252–2711 ⊕ www.omnihotels.com/hotels/asheville-grove-park ⇨ 512 rooms ¶◎¶ No meals.*

The Reynolds Mansion
$$$$ | **B&B/INN** | In a beautifully restored Colonial Revival mansion, this inn dating from the 1840s has two levels of wraparound porches and a dozen fireplaces. **Pros:** handsome and historic building; gracious and friendly service; quiet setting.

Arts and Crafts Movement

The Arts and Crafts movement was an international movement of the late 19th and early 20th centuries that emphasized local and natural materials, craftsmanship, and a strong horizontal line in architecture and furniture. Inspired by the writings of British art critic John Ruskin, Arts and Crafts, along with the similar American Craftsman style, romanticized the role of the craftsperson and rebelled against the mass production of the Industrial Age. Prominent examples of Craftsman style include the furniture and other decorative arts of Gustav Stickley, first presented in his magazine, *The Craftsman*; the Roycroft community in Ohio, founded by Elbert Hubbard; the Prairie School of architect Frank Lloyd Wright; and the bungalow style of houses popularized in California. At its height between 1880 and 1910, the Arts and Crafts movement flourished in Asheville. The Grove Park Inn's construction was heavily influenced by Arts and Crafts principles, and today the resort hotel has one of the largest collections of Arts and Crafts furniture in the world. Several hundred Asheville bungalows were also built in the Arts and Crafts style. Today, the influence of the Arts and Crafts movement remains strong in the Asheville area, reflected in the large number of working craft studios in the region.

Cons: in a mixed-use neighborhood; not close to many restaurants; swimming pool has short season. *Rooms from: $283 ✉ 100 Reynolds Heights, North Asheville ☎ 828/258–1111 🌐 www.thereynoldsmansion.com 13 rooms Free breakfast.*

Nightlife

Asheville Pizza and Brewing Company

BARS/PUBS | FAMILY | More than a restaurant, more than a movie theater, Asheville Pizza and Brewing Company (also called the Brew 'n' View) is a popular spot to catch a second-run flick on a movie screen while lounging on a sofa, drinking a microbrew, and scarfing down a pizza. Kids and dogs are welcome for the food and movie, but movies are often sold out, so buy tickets before the show. There's a nice patio here, and an even bigger courtyard at the brewing company's second location in downtown's South Slope. *✉ 675 Merriman Ave., North Asheville ☎ 828/254–1281 🌐 www.ashevillebrewing.com.*

Shopping

ART GALLERIES

Grovewood Gallery

ART GALLERIES | The gallery's 9,000 square feet hold high-quality ceramic, glass, fiber, wood, and other crafts, along with furniture in what the gallery calls "the Asheville style." *✉ Grove Park, 111 Grovewood Rd., Grove Park ↔ On grounds of Omni Grove Park Inn ☎ 828/253–7651 🌐 www.grovewood.com.*

Activities

GOLF

★ Grove Park Golf Course

GOLF | Dating from 1899, this beautiful course has been played by several U.S. presidents, most recently Barack Obama. Flocks of wild turkeys regularly visit the fairway. The views of the Blue Ridge Mountains are well worth the trip. *✉ Omni Grove Park Inn, 290 Macon Ave., Grove Park ☎ 800/438–5800 🌐 www.omnihotels.com/hotels/asheville-grove-park/golf*

$70–$155, 18 holes, 6400 yds, par 70 *Reservations essential.*

Biltmore Village

Biltmore Village, across from the entrance to the Biltmore Estate, was constructed at the time that Biltmore House was being built in the 1890s and now holds boutiques, galleries, cigar bars, and restaurants.

Sights

★ Biltmore House and Estate
HOUSE | FAMILY | Built in the 1890s as the home of George Vanderbilt, the astonishing 250-room French Renaissance château is America's largest private house and the number one attraction of its kind in North Carolina. Richard Morris Hunt designed it, and Frederick Law Olmsted landscaped the original 125,000-acre estate (now 8,000 acres). It took 1,000 workers five years to complete the gargantuan project. On view are the antiques and art collected by the Vanderbilts, including notable paintings by Renoir and John Singer Sargent, along with 75 acres of gardens, formally landscaped grounds, and many hiking trails. You can also see the on-site Biltmore Winery, the most-visited one in America. Candlelight tours of the house are offered at Christmastime. Also on the grounds are a deluxe hotel, a more moderately priced hotel, many restaurants, and an equestrian center. Antler Hill Village includes a hotel, shops, restaurants, farm buildings, and crafts demonstrations. Most people tour the house on their own, but guided tours are available. Note that there are a lot of stairs to climb, but much of the house is accessible for guests in wheelchairs or with limited mobility. Pricing is complex, varying by month and day of the week, and not inexpensive, but a visit is well worth the cost for its access to the house, gardens, winery, and extensive grounds. **■ TIP→ Self-guided visits to the interior of the house typically require advance reservations.** *1 Lodge St., Biltmore Village* *828/225–1333* *www.biltmore.com* *From $64.*

Biltmore Village
HISTORIC SITE | FAMILY | Across from the main entrance to the Biltmore Estate, Biltmore Village is a highly walkable collection of restored English village–style houses dating from the turn of the 20th century, along with some newer buildings designed to blend in with the original architecture. Stroll the brick sidewalks and tree-lined streets and visit antiques stores, clothing and jewelry shops, art galleries, and restaurants. *Biltmore Village* *www.historicbiltmorevillage.com* *Free.*

Cathedral of All Souls
RELIGIOUS SITE | One of the most beautiful churches in America, the Episcopal Cathedral of All Souls was designed by Richard Morris Hunt following the traditional Greek Cross plan and inspired by abbey churches in northern England. It opened in 1896. *9 Swan St., Biltmore Village* *828/274–2681* *www.allsoulscathedral.org* *Free.*

Restaurants

★ Corner Kitchen
$$$$ | MODERN AMERICAN | FAMILY | Entrées such as pecan-crusted mountain trout with ginger sweet potatoes grace the frequently changing new American menu at Corner Kitchen. The charmingly renovated Victorian cottage in Biltmore Village has wood floors, plaster walls painted in serene colors, and a fireplace in one dining room. **Known for:** innovative versions of Southern and American favorites; charming Biltmore Village location; farm-to-table menu. *Average main: $27* *3 Boston Way, Biltmore Village* *828/274–2439* *www.thecornerkitchen.com.*

Biltmore, once the home of George Vanderbilt, is the largest private home in the United States; the estate grounds occupy some 8,000 acres.

★ Dining Room at the Inn on Biltmore Estate

$$$$ | **MODERN AMERICAN** | Romantic, impressive, delightful: that just begins to describe the field-to-white-linen-tablecloth dining experience at the Inn on Biltmore Estate, featuring lamb and beef from the estate's own farm and vegetables from its gardens. Afternoon tea is a favorite event. **Known for:** Asheville's most elegant dining; impeccable service; estate-grown ingredients. *Average main: $42 Inn on Biltmore Estate, 1 Antler Hill Rd., Biltmore Village 828/225–1699 www.biltmore.com.*

Hotels

Grand Bohemian Hotel

$$$$ | **HOTEL** | As close as you can get to the main gate of the Biltmore Estate and steps from all the best local shops and restaurants, this Tudor-style lodging is designed to blend in beautifully with the architecture of Biltmore Village. **Pros:** rooms are spacious and graciously appointed; a great location if you're touring the estate; very good on-site restaurant. **Cons:** in an area with many tourists; very pricey in high season; over-the-top decor. *Rooms from: $455 11 Boston Way, Biltmore Village 828/505–2949 www.bohemianhotelasheville.com 104 rooms No meals.*

★ The Inn on Biltmore Estate

$$$$ | **HOTEL** | Many visitors to the Biltmore Estate long to stay overnight; if you're one of them, your wish is granted at this posh property perched on a nearby hilltop. **Pros:** excellent, romantic restaurant; gorgeous vistas and outdoor terraces; shuttle to the Biltmore Estate. **Cons:** very expensive rates (though there are off-season discounts); can seem a bit formal to many travelers; some rooms are on the small side. *Rooms from: $495 1 Antler Hill Rd., Biltmore Village 828/225–1660 www.biltmore.com/inn 210 rooms No meals.*

Village Hotel on Biltmore Estate

$$$ | HOTEL | FAMILY | The Biltmore Estate's less pricey—though hardly inexpensive—lodging, the Village Hotel, in a prime location at Antler Hill, puts you near the winery, restaurants, and shops. **Pros:** in the middle of the Biltmore Estate; free shuttle around the property; walking distance to winery. **Cons:** atmosphere is more like a midpriced chain hotel; you'll still be spending a lot of cash; uninspired eatery. *Rooms from: $245 ✉ Biltmore Estate, 297 Dairy Rd., Biltmore Village ☎ 866/799–9228 🌐 www.biltmore.com 209 rooms No meals.*

Shopping

ART GALLERIES

New Morning Gallery

ART GALLERIES | FAMILY | Established by the late arts entrepreneur John Cram, New Morning Gallery has more than 13,000 square feet of exhibit space in a prime location in Biltmore Village. The gallery, which has a national reputation, focuses on more popular and moderately priced ceramics, garden art, jewelry, furniture, and art glass. *✉ 7 Boston Way, Biltmore Village ☎ 828/274–2831 🌐 www.newmorninggallerync.com.*

Activities

HORSEBACK RIDING

Biltmore Equestrian Center

HORSEBACK RIDING | FAMILY | The Biltmore Estate offers guided hour-long horseback rides on the estate trails as well as longer private rides, which usually must be reserved at least two days in advance. *✉ Biltmore Estate, Deer Park Rd., Biltmore Village ☎ 800/411–3812 🌐 www.biltmore.com From $65.*

Greater Asheville

The Greater Asheville area turns mountainous quite quickly. Several worthwhile attractions sit just outside downtown.

Sights

★ North Carolina Arboretum

GARDEN | FAMILY | Part of the original Biltmore Estate, these 434 acres completed Frederick Law Olmsted's dream of creating a world-class arboretum in the western part of North Carolina. The arboretum is now affiliated with the University of North Carolina and is part of Pisgah National Forest. Highlights include southern flora in stunning settings, such as the Blue Ridge Quilt Garden, with plants arranged in patterns reminiscent of Appalachian quilts. A 10-mile network of trails is great for hiking or mountain biking. The 16,000-square-foot Baker Exhibit Center hosts traveling shows on art, science, and history. Dogs are welcome on the grounds but must be leashed. *✉ 100 Frederick Law Olmsted Way, Greater Asheville ✣ 10 miles southwest of downtown Asheville ☎ 828/665–2492 🌐 www.ncarboretum.org Free.*

★ Sierra Nevada Brewery

WINERY/DISTILLERY | Sierra Nevada, one of the country's largest national craft breweries, situated its East Coast brewery and distribution center on a 190-acre site on the French Broad River. The beautifully landscaped complex includes a good restaurant, tasting room, gift shop, and hiking and biking trails. Sierra Nevada offers the best brewery tours in the region, ranging from a free 45-minute brewhouse tour to a three-hour Beer Geek tour. **■ TIP→ Tours book up quickly, so reserve as far in advance as possible.**

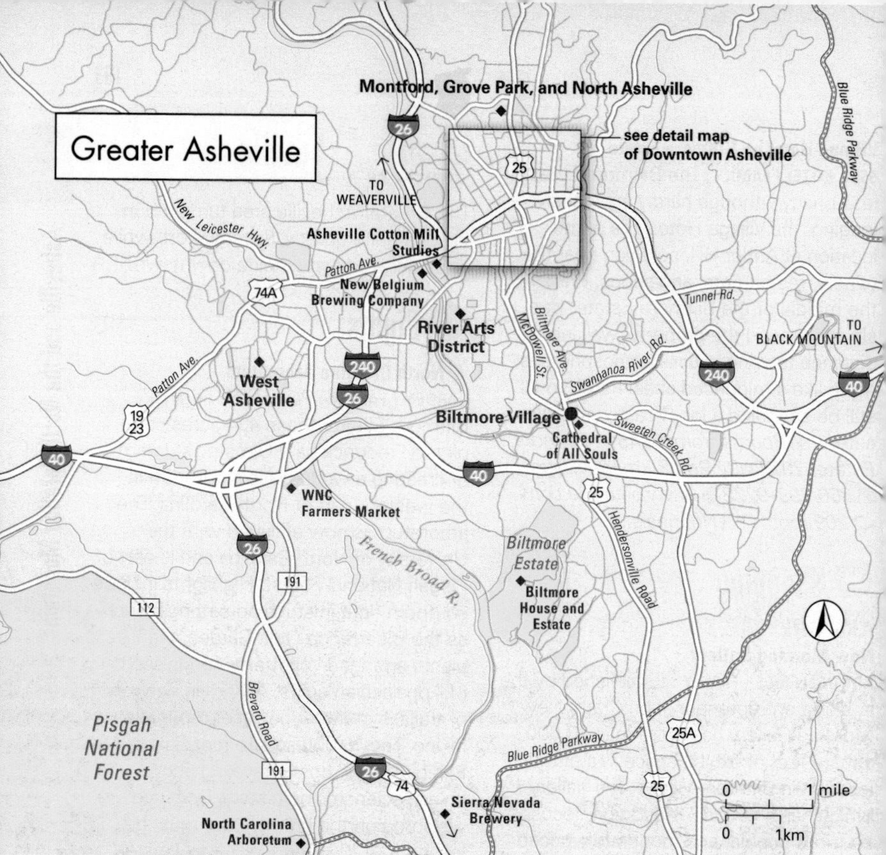

✉ *100 Sierra Nevada Way, Greater Asheville ✣ Near Asheville Regional Airport ☎ 828/681–5300 🌐 www.sierranevada.com 🎫 Tours free–$45.*

WNC Farmers Market

MARKET | FAMILY | The highest-volume farmers' market in North Carolina may not have the prettiest exterior, but it's a good place to buy local jams, jellies, honey, stone-ground grits and cornmeal, and, in season, local fruits and vegetables. An herb festival is held in the spring. On the grounds of the market is a Southern-style restaurant, Moose Café. ✉ *570 Brevard Rd., Greater Asheville ✣ 5 miles southwest of downtown Asheville ☎ 828/253–1691 🌐 www.ncagr.gov.*

Activities

GOLF

Asheville Municipal Golf Course

GOLF | FAMILY | This municipal course beside the Swannanoa River, owned by the city of Asheville but since 2012 under private management, is known for its firm and fast greens. Designed by famed golf architect Donald Ross, it opened in 1927 and is now in the National Register of Historic Places. ✉ *226 Fairway Dr., East Metro ☎ 828/298–1867 🌐 www.ashevillegc.com ⛳ $18–$36, 18 holes, 6420 yds, par 72 ✍ Reservations essential.*

SKIING

Wolf Ridge Ski Resort

SKIING/SNOWBOARDING | FAMILY | You can "Ski the Wolf" at Wolf Ridge Ski Resort, about 30 miles north of Asheville. There are 14 ski runs, four ski lifts, a rustic lodge, and cabin rentals. Snowboarding and tubing are also offered. Keep in mind that milder winters have impacted ski resorts in the South, including Wolf Ridge, which sometimes closes for a time even in January and February. ✉ *578 Valley View Circle, Mars Hill* ☎ *828/689–4111* 🌐 *www.skiwolfridgenc.com* 🎫 *Lift tickets from $26.*

ZIPLINING

Navitat Canopy Adventures

ZIP LINING | FAMILY | Zip through the treetops at Navitat, which has two different zipline complexes in Madison County, about 25 miles north of Asheville. One has ziplines up to 1,250 feet in length, with hiking trails. The other has three "racing style" ziplines as long as 3,600 feet. You need to be able to walk about a mile and be in generally good health. **■ TIP→ Make reservations two weeks in advance.** ✉ *242 Poverty Branch Rd., Barnardsville* ☎ *828/626–3700* 🌐 *www.navitat.com* 🎫 *Tours from $100.*

Blue Ridge Parkway

Entrance 2 miles east of Asheville.

The Blue Ridge Parkway's 252 miles within North Carolina wind down the High Country through Asheville, ending near the entrance of Great Smoky Mountains National Park. Highlights on and near the parkway include Mt. Mitchell (the highest mountain peak east of the Rockies), Grandfather Mountain, and Mt. Pisgah. Nearly all the towns and cities along the parkway route offer accommodations, dining, and sightseeing. In particular, Boone, Blowing Rock, Burnsville, Asheville, Waynesville, Brevard, and Cherokee are all near popular entrances to the parkway.

VISITOR INFORMATION

CONTACTS Blue Ridge Parkway Visitor Center. ✉ *195 Hemphill Knob Rd., Metro South* ☎ *828/348–3400* 🌐 *www.nps.gov/blri/index.htm.*

Sights

Craggy Gardens

TRAIL | At an elevation of 6,000 feet, Craggy Gardens has some of the Blue Ridge Parkway's most colorful displays of rhododendrons, usually blooming in June. You can also hike trails and picnic here. Craggy Pinnacle trail offers stunning 360-degree views. ✉ *Blue Ridge Parkway, MM 364* ☎ *828/298–0398* 🌐 *www.blueridgeparkway.org/poi/craggy-gardens* 🎫 *Free.*

Folk Art Center

ARTS VENUE | FAMILY | As the headquarters of the prestigious Southern Highland Craft Guild, the Folk Art Center regularly hosts exceptional quilt, woodworking, pottery, and other crafts shows and demonstrations. ✉ *382 Blue Ridge Parkway, East Metro* ☎ *828/298–7928* 🌐 *www.southernhighlandguild.org.*

★ Grandfather Mountain

MOUNTAIN—SIGHT | FAMILY | Soaring to almost 6,000 feet, Grandfather Mountain is famous for its Mile-High Swinging Bridge, a 228-foot-long footbridge that sways over a 1,000-foot drop into the Linville Valley. There are 12 miles of hiking trails and some 100 picnic tables. Part of the area is a state park, and part is private land with a small admission fee. ✉ *Blue Ridge Parkway and U.S. 221, Linville* ☎ *828/963–9522* 🌐 *www.ncparks.gov/grandfather-mountain-state-park/home* 🎫 *Free.*

Linville Falls

NATIONAL/STATE PARK | FAMILY | A half-mile hike from the visitor center leads to one of North Carolina's most photographed waterfalls. The easy trail winds through evergreens and rhododendrons to overlooks with views of the series of cascades tumbling into Linville Gorge. There's also a campground and a picnic area. ✉ *U.S. 221, Spruce Pine* ✣ *Off Blue Ridge Parkway* ☎ *828/298–0398* 🌐 *www.nps.gov/blri* 🎫 *Free.*

Moses H. Cone Memorial Park

NATIONAL/STATE PARK | **FAMILY** | On the grounds of this turn-of-the-20th-century manor house, and at the adjoining Julian Price Memorial Park near Grandfather Mountain, are about 100 picnic sites. The park is also known for its cross-country skiing trails. The Southern Highland Craft Guild often hosts traditional craft demonstrations and sales here. ✉ *Blue Ridge Parkway MM 292.7–295* ☎ *828/295–7938* 🌐 *www.nps.gov/blri/planyourvisit/moses-h-cone-memorial-park-mp-294.htm* 🎫 *Free.*

★ Mt. Mitchell State Park

NATIONAL/STATE PARK | **FAMILY** | This park—established in 1915 as North Carolina's first state park—includes the 6,684-foot Mt. Mitchell, the highest mountain peak east of the Rockies. The summit was named after Elisha Mitchell, a professor at the University of North Carolina at Chapel Hill, who died from a fall while trying to prove the mountain's true height. At the 1,946-acre park you can climb an observation tower and drive to a parking area where you can hike the short distance to the summit. Clouds obscure the views most days, but it's still worth the bragging rights. ✉ *2388 NC 128, Burnsville* ✣ *Off Blue Ridge Parkway* ☎ *828/675–4611* 🌐 *www.ncparks.gov/Visit/parks/momi/main.php* 🎫 *Free.*

★ Mt. Pisgah

MOUNTAIN—SIGHT | **FAMILY** | The 5,721-foot Mt. Pisgah is one of the most easily recognized peaks around Asheville due to the television tower installed here in the 1950s. It has walking trails, a picnic area, and an amphitheater where nature programs are offered most evenings from June through October. There is an inn, a restaurant, and a small grocery a short distance away. Nearby Graveyard Fields is popular for blueberry picking in midsummer. ✉ *Blue Ridge Parkway MM 408.6, Waynesville* ☎ *828/271–4779* 🌐 *www.nps.gov/blri/planyourvisit/mount-pisgah.htm* 🎫 *Free.*

Hotels

★ Pisgah Inn

$$ | **B&B/INN** | **FAMILY** | The spectacular setting is the main draw at the rustic Pisgah Inn, perched on a mountaintop at 5,000 feet. **Pros:** incredible views from its mile-high perch; rates are reasonable for the location; good on-site restaurant. **Cons:** motel-like rooms; remote setting; often fully booked. $ *Rooms from: $190* ✉ *Blue Ridge Parkway MM 408.6, Waynesville* ☎ *828/235–8228* 🌐 *www.pisgahinn.com* 🕒 *Closed Nov.–Mar.* *51 rooms* 🍽 *Free breakfast.*

Black Mountain

16 miles east of Asheville.

Black Mountain is a small town that has played a disproportionately large role in American cultural history because of the college located nearby. For more than 20 years in the middle of the 20th century, from its founding in 1933 to its closing in 1957, Black Mountain College was one of the world's leading centers for experimental art, literature, architecture, and dance, with a list of faculty and students that reads like a who's who of American arts and letters.

On a different front, Black Mountain was also the home of evangelist Billy Graham, who died in 2018. The Graham organization maintains a training center near Black Mountain, and there are several large church-related conference centers in the area, including Ridgecrest, Montreat, and Blue Ridge Assembly. Downtown Black Mountain is small and quaint, with a collection of little shops and several B&Bs.

Asheville Area Authors

They may not be able to go home again, but many famous writers have made their homes in the North Carolina mountains. The one most closely associated with the terrain is Thomas Wolfe (1900–38), author of *Look Homeward, Angel,* who was born and buried in Asheville. His contemporary, F. Scott Fitzgerald, visited Asheville and environs frequently in the 1930s, staying for long periods at the Grove Park Inn and at other hotels in the area. Author Zelda Fitzgerald died in a 1948 fire at Highland Hospital, then a psychiatric facility in North Asheville.

William Sydney Porter, who under the pen name O. Henry wrote "The Ransom of Red Chief," "The Gift of the Magi," and many other stories, married into an Asheville-area family and is buried in Asheville at Riverside Cemetery. Carl Sandburg, the Pulitzer Prize–winning poet and biographer of Lincoln, spent the last 22 years of his life on a farm in Flat Rock. A younger generation of poets, including Jonathan Williams, Robert Creeley, Robert Duncan, and Charles Olson, made names for themselves at Black Mountain College, an avant-garde hotbed for literature during the 1940s and early 1950s. Contemporary writers like award-winning poet Glenis Redmond, and journalist Denise Kiernan (author of *The Last Castle*) call Asheville home today.

Novelist Charles Frazier, born in Asheville in 1950, made Cold Mountain, in the Shining Rock Wilderness of the Pisgah National Forest, the setting (and the title) for his best-selling Civil War drama. The mountain can be viewed from the Blue Ridge Parkway at mile marker 412. (The 2003 movie, however, was filmed in Romania.) Enka-Candler native Wayne Caldwell writes eloquently of the people of the Cataloochee section of what is now the Great Smokies in 2007's *Cataloochee* and 2009's *Requiem by Fire.* In several books, Canton native and former North Carolina poet laureate Fred Chappell paints powerful images of his hometown and its odoriferous paper mill.

Sights

Black Mountain Cider + Mead

WINERY/DISTILLERY | **FAMILY** | Most of the apples for the cider at this mill come from Hendersonville, and it's the only type of alcohol in the area that can proudly say it's made from all local produce. Mead, a historic recipe for wine fermented from fruit and honey, is also interesting to try. Sample all flavors of both while here, an altogether pleasant and family-friendly stop in Black Mountain. ✉ *104 Eastside Dr., No. 307* ☎ *828/419–0089* 🌐 *www.blackmountainciderworks.com* ⏲ *Closed Mon.–Wed.*

★ **Black Mountain College**

COLLEGE | Originally housed in rented quarters at nearby Blue Ridge Assembly, southeast of the town of Black Mountain, Black Mountain College moved across the valley to its own campus at Lake Eden in 1941. Today the site is Camp Rockmont, a privately owned summer camp for boys. The school's buildings originally were designed by the Bauhaus architects Walter Gropius and Marcel Breuer, but the college turned to an American architect, Lawrence Kocher, and several intriguing buildings resulted, including one known as "The Ship," which still stands. BMC attracted maverick spirits in art, music, and literature, including Willem and Elaine de Kooning, Robert Rauschenberg, Josef and Anni Albers, Buckminster Fuller, M. C. Richards, Merce Cunningham, John Cage, Kenneth Noland, Ben Shahn, Arthur Penn, Charles Olson, Robert Creeley, and others. Black Mountain College Museum and Arts Center is in downtown Asheville at 120 College Street and holds occasional events at Lake Eden. ✉ *375 Lake Eden Rd.* ✣ *5 miles west of Black Mountain* ☎ *828/686–3885 Camp Rockmont, 828/350–8484 Black Mountain College Museum* 🌐 *www.blackmountaincollege.org.*

Restaurants

Veranda Café

$ | **AMERICAN** | **FAMILY** | With its gingham curtains and checkered tablecloths, this popular downtown lunch spot serves food that is both unpretentious and tasty. The soups are the best thing on the menu (the Hungarian mushroom soup is a longtime favorite), and the sandwiches are winners, too. **Known for:** home-style soups and sandwiches; friendly small-town ambience; spacious outdoor seating. 💲 *Average main: $9* ✉ *119 Cherry St.* ☎ *828/669–8864* 🌐 *www.verandacafeandgifts.com* ⏲ *Closed Sun. and Mon.*

Hendersonville

23 miles south of Asheville via I–26.

With about 14,000 residents, Hendersonville has one of the most engaging downtowns of any small city in the South. Historic Main Street, as it's called, extends over 10 winding blocks, lined with about 40 shops, including antiques stores, galleries, and restaurants. Each year from April through October, Main Street has displays of public art. Within walking distance of downtown are several B&Bs.

The Hendersonville area is North Carolina's main apple-growing area, and some 200 apple orchards dot the rolling hills around town. An apple festival, attracting some 200,000 people, is held each year in August. Whereas Asheville is liberal, progressive, and youthful in spirit and reputation, Hendersonville is predominantly a town of retirees and is considered conservative and as "American" as—yes—apple pie.

GETTING HERE AND AROUND

It is about 25 miles from Asheville to Hendersonville, via Interstate 26 East. From Interstate 26, take Four Seasons Boulevard through the typical suburban mix of motels, strip malls, and fast-food restaurants to downtown Hendersonville. Main Street, where there's free parking, runs through the center of town.

Restaurants

Daddy D's Suber Soulfood

$ | **SOUTHERN** | Family owned and friendly, this no-frills storefront is the place for soul food in the Asheville area. Fried chicken plates are the specialty; catfish or pork chops are a close second. **Known for:** generous portions; black-owned business; served with love. 💲 *Average main: $10* ✉ *411 7th Ave.* ☎ *828/698–7408* ⏲ *Closed Mon.*

Dandelion Eatery

$ | **SOUTHERN** | **FAMILY** | This downtown destination is more than a restaurant; it's a nonprofit organization that provides job training and other resources to those at risk of domestic abuse. Open for breakfast and lunch only, the ingredients are local, fresh, and delicious, with the emphasis on comfort food like chicken potpie and, in season, tomato pie. **Known for:** freshly made local dishes; very friendly service; sidewalk tables. 💲 *Average main: $8* ✉ *127 5th Ave. W* ☎ *828/595–9365* 🌐 *www.safelightfamily.org* ⏲ *Closed weekends. No dinner.*

★ **West First**

$ | **PIZZA** | **FAMILY** | Wood-fired, thin-crust pizzas made from organic flour are the specialty at this lively eatery. Besides the standard toppings are more unusual ones like roasted salmon and barbecued chicken. **Known for:** sit in the dining room, the loft, or on the patio; industrial-chic decor; eye-catching oven. *Average main: $12* ✉ *101B 1st Ave. W* ☎ *828/693–1080* *www.flatrockwood-fired.com* *Closed Sun.*

Hotels

1898 Waverly Inn

$$ | **B&B/INN** | On a warm afternoon you'll love to "sit a spell" in a rocking chair on the front porch of Hendersonville's oldest inn. **Pros:** historic home with lots of gingerbread; walking distance to downtown; cooked-to-order breakfast. **Cons:** in a fairly busy area with lots of traffic; some rooms are on the small side; some steps to climb. *Rooms from: $180* ✉ *783 N. Main St.* ☎ *828/693–9193* *www.waverlyinn.com* *15 rooms* *Free breakfast.*

Pinebrook Manor

$$ | **B&B/INN** | The four "bedchambers" in this B&B are named after British poets—Wordsworth, Lord Byron, Alfred Lord Tennyson, and Elizabeth Barrett Browning—which should give you an idea of what to expect: cozy rooms filled with antiques and creature comforts. **Pros:** on 5 acres of landscaped grounds; hospitable hosts go the extra mile; full breakfasts and afternoon treats. **Cons:** not within walking distance of town; not close to most restaurants; books up quickly. *Rooms from: $165* ✉ *2701 Kanuga Rd.* ☎ *828/698–2707* *www.pinebrookmanor.com* *4 rooms* *Free breakfast.*

Flat Rock

3 miles south of Hendersonville; 26 miles south of Asheville via I–26.

Flat Rock has been a summer resort since the early 19th century. It was a favorite of wealthy planters from Charleston eager to escape the Low-country heat. The trip from Charleston to Flat Rock by horse and carriage took as long as two weeks, so you know there must be something here that made the long trek worthwhile. Today, you can tour the home and farm where poet Carl Sandburg spent the last years of his life, take in some summer stock at the official state theater of North Carolina, or play a round of golf.

GETTING HERE AND AROUND

From Asheville, take Interstate 26 East 22 miles to Exit 53. Follow Upward Road about 2½ miles to Flat Rock.

Sights

★ **Carl Sandburg Home National Historic Site**

FARM/RANCH | **FAMILY** | Connemara Farm is where the famed poet and biographer Carl Sandburg moved with his wife, Lillian, in 1945; he lived there until his death in 1967. Guided tours of their 1830s house—beautifully reconstructed in 2017—are given by National Park Service rangers. Sandburg's papers still are scattered on his desk as if he had just stepped away for a moment, and there are 11,000 of his books on shelves. Kids enjoy cavorting around the 264-acre farm, which still maintains descendants of the Sandburg family goats. There are also miles of trails. ✉ *81 Carl Sandburg La.* ☎ *828/693–4178* *www.nps.gov/carl* *Free, tours $5.*

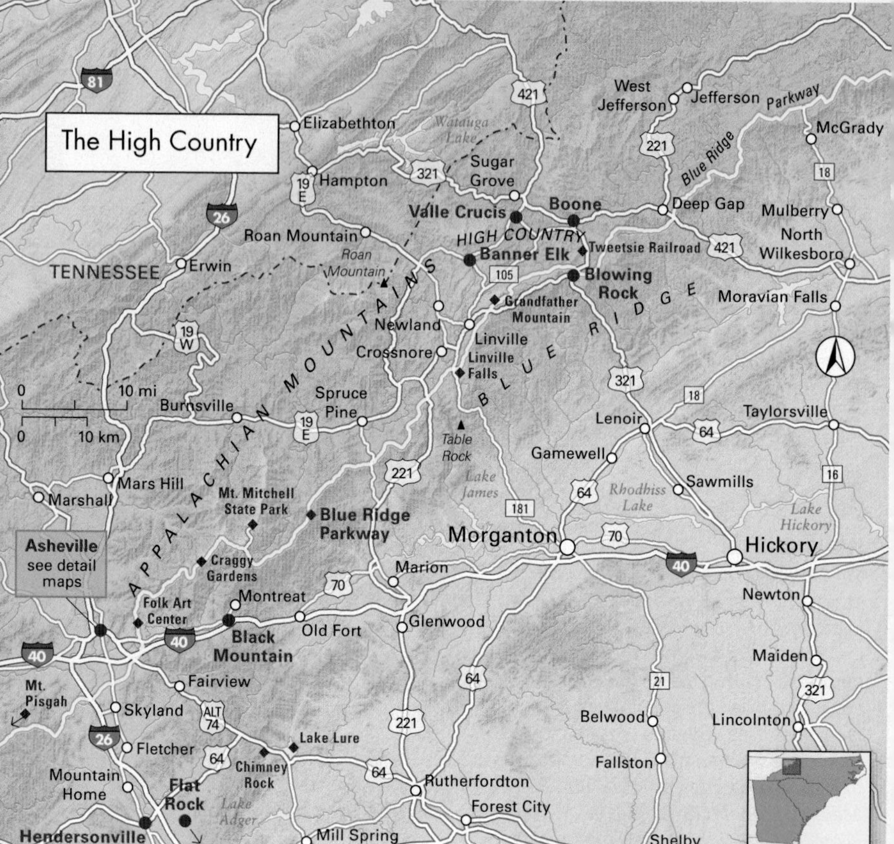

★ Flat Rock Playhouse

ARTS VENUE | FAMILY | This theater, the official state theater of North Carolina, is known for its high-quality productions, with sophisticated sets and professional actors. The productions are mostly well-known musicals and other classics. In a converted barn, Flat Rock holds summer and fall programs and classes for aspiring actors. The drama season, with about a dozen productions, typically runs from March to December. The theater ran an impressive fundraising campaign for its shows and arts education programs after having to postpone the 2020–21 season. ✉ *2661 Greenville Hwy.* ☎ *828/693–0731* 🌐 *www.flatrockplayhouse.org* ⏲ *Closed Jan.–mid-Feb.*

Blowing Rock

86 miles northeast of Asheville; 93 miles west of Winston-Salem.

Blowing Rock, a draw for mountain visitors since the 1880s, has retained the flavor of a quiet New England village, with stone walls and buildings with wood shakes or bark siding. About 1,200 people are permanent residents of this town at a 4,000-foot elevation, but the population swells each summer. On summer afternoons it seems as if most of the town's population is sitting on benches in the town park. To ensure that the town would remain rural, large hotels and motels are prohibited. Blowing Rock is the inspiration for Mitford, the small town in resident writer Jan Karon's novels about country life.

GETTING HERE AND AROUND

To get here from the Blue Ridge Parkway, take U.S. Route 221/321 at mile marker 292 near Moses H. Cone Park. U.S. Route 321 makes a loop around the village of Blowing Rock.

Sights

The Blowing Rock

NATURE SITE | **FAMILY** | The Blowing Rock, after which the mountain town is named, is a cliff, which at 4,000 feet looms over the Johns River Gorge about 3,000 feet below. If you throw your hat over the sheer precipice, it may blow back to you, should the wind gods be playful. The story goes that a Cherokee man and a Chickasaw maiden fell in love. Torn between his tribe and his love, he jumped from the cliff, but she prayed to the Great Spirit, and he was blown safely back to her. ✉ *432 Rock Rd.* ✣ *Off U.S. 321* ☎ *828/295–7111* 🌐 *www.theblowingrock.com* 🎫 *$7* ⏲ *Inclement weather may cause closures.*

Tweetsie Railroad

AMUSEMENT PARK/WATER PARK | **FAMILY** | A Wild West theme park built into the side of a mountain between Boone and Blowing Rock, Tweetsie Railroad is centered on coal-powered steam locomotives beset by robbers. A petting zoo, carnival amusements, gem panning, shows, food, and concessions are also here. Several of the attractions are at the top of the mountain and can be reached from the parking lot on foot, by bus, or by ski lift. ✉ *300 Tweetsie Railroad La.* ✣ *Near U.S. 321/221, off BRP at MM 291* ☎ *828/264–9061, 800/526–5740* 🌐 *www.tweetsie.com* 🎫 *$50* ⏲ *Park closed Jan.–Mar. and most of Nov. Closed weekdays Apr., May, Sept., Oct., and Dec.*

Restaurants

★ The Restaurant at Gideon Ridge

$$$$ | **MODERN AMERICAN** | Attached to the Gideon Ridge Inn, this intimate 10-table restaurant is your top choice in Blowing Rock. It sticks with dishes it carries off perfectly, such as lamb sirloin, pork loin chop, or duck breast, and most items are sourced from local suppliers. **Known for:** reputation as the best restaurant in Blowing Rock and a top spot in the region; locally sourced meats and vegetables; often being fully booked well in advance. 💲 *Average main: $34* ✉ *202 Gideon Ridge Rd.* ☎ *828/295–3644* 🌐 *www.gideonridge.com* ⏲ *Closed Sun. and Mon.*

Hotels

Gideon Ridge Inn

$$$$ | **B&B/INN** | At Gideon Ridge Inn, 2 miles from downtown Blowing Rock, you can take in long-range views of the mountains from the gardens and stone terraces or relax with a book by the fire in the library or in your own room. **Pros:** scenic mountaintop views; fireplace and grand piano in book-lined library; beautiful gardens. **Cons:** a few items could stand refurbishing; no pool; no room service. 💲 *Rooms from: $280* ✉ *202 Gideon Ridge Rd.* ☎ *828/295–3644* 🌐 *www.gideonridge.com* 🛏 *10 rooms* 🍴 *Free breakfast.*

Inn at Ragged Gardens

$$ | **B&B/INN** | With a stone staircase in the entry hall, colorful gardens, Arts and Crafts furnishings, and chestnut paneling and bark siding, it's no wonder that this 1900 manor-style house in the heart of Blowing Rock gets many return guests. **Pros:** historic old inn at moderate prices; within walking distance of Blowing Rock shops and restaurants; good restaurant on-site. **Cons:** if you're on the first floor, you may hear guests on the floor above; lots of steps to some rooms; no pool. 💲 *Rooms from: $175* ✉ *203 Sunset Dr.* ☎ *828/295–9703* 🌐 *www.ragged-gardens.com* 🛏 *11 rooms* 🍴 *Free breakfast.*

Activities

SKIING

Appalachian Ski Mountain

SKIING/SNOWBOARDING | **FAMILY** | There's downhill skiing, snowboarding, and ice-skating at this resort at around 4,000 feet, which has a dozen slopes, a half-dozen lifts, and a lodge. There are also cabin rentals and an RV park. Skiing and other snow sports are usually available mid-November to mid-March. ✉ *940 Ski Mountain Rd.* ☎ *828/295–7828, 800/322–2373* 🌐 *www.appskimtn.com* 🎫 *8-hr lift tickets $42 weekdays, $67 weekends.*

Boone

8 miles north of Blowing Rock.

This college town is home to Appalachian State University (ASU) and its 18,000 students. Suburban sprawl has arrived, especially along U.S. Route 321, with its clusters of fast-food restaurants, motels, and a small mall. Closer to ASU, however, you get more of the college-town vibe, with organic-food stores and boutiques. The town was named for frontiersman Daniel Boone, whose family moved to the area when Daniel was 15.

GETTING HERE AND AROUND

Boone, about 100 miles northeast of Asheville, is at the convergence of three major highways—U.S. Route 321, U.S. Route 421, and North Carolina Highway 105. From Asheville, take Interstate 40 East to U.S. Route 64. Follow U.S. Route 64 to U.S. Route 321, which leads into Boone.

Restaurants

Dan'l Boone Inn

$$$ | **SOUTHERN** | **FAMILY** | Near Appalachian State University, in a former hospital surrounded by a picket fence and flowers, Dan'l Boone serves old-fashioned Southern food family style. You can have any or all of the items on the menu, and seconds and thirds if you want them, for the same price—and the portions of fried chicken, country-style steak, ham biscuits, mashed potatoes, and green beans (to name a few) are generous. **Known for:** large portions; simple Southern dishes; friendly staff. $ *Average main: $20* ✉ *130 Hardin St.* ☎ *828/264–8657* 🌐 *www.danlbooneinn.com* 💳 *No credit cards* ⏲ *No breakfast weekdays. No lunch weekdays Jan.–late May* ☞ *No reservations except for large groups; cash or check only.*

Gamekeeper

$$$$ | **AMERICAN** | This stone cottage in the woods, off a winding country road between Boone and Blowing Rock, surprises newcomers with a rotating menu of unusual, sophisticated dishes like grilled elk, antelope Bolognese, bison steak, and other game. In cool weather, there's a roaring fire in the fireplace; when weather permits, eat on the deck with woodsy views. **Known for:** wild game on the menu; rustic setting; views from deck. $ *Average main: $38* ✉ *3005 Shull's Mill Rd.* ✣ *6 miles southwest of Boone* ☎ *828/963–7400* 🌐 *www.gamekeeper-nc.com* ⏲ *Closed Sun.–Wed.*

★ Vidalia

$$ | **SOUTHERN** | **FAMILY** | Named for Georgia's famous sweet onion, this small bistro in the middle of town brings creative regional American cooking to the High Country. The food, much of it from local organic farms, is standout good—for dinner, try the shrimp and grits, chicken with potato dumplings, or meat loaf with, of course, Vidalia onion rings. **Known for:** locally sourced Southern dishes for dinner; creative brunch on weekends; interesting wine list and array of craft beers. $ *Average main: $18* ✉ *831-35 W. King St.* ✣ *Across from Watauga Courthouse* ☎ *828/263–9176* 🌐 *www.vidaliaofboonenc.com* ⏲ *Closed Mon. No brunch Tues.–Fri.*

Hotels

The Horton Hotel

$$$$ | **HOTEL** | Billed as Boone's only boutique hotel (for now), the Horton's sophisticated accommodations right downtown—plus a lively lobby and rooftop bar and lounge—have a surprisingly cosmopolitan feel. **Pros:** in the heart of downtown; rooftop bar with 360-degree views; contemporary but charming. **Cons:** lower-level rooms can be noisy; not your typical remote mountain getaway; lively lounge and bar not for everyone. *Rooms from: $259* ✉ *611 W. King St.* ☎ *828/832–8060* 🌐 *www.thehorton.com* *15 rooms* *Free breakfast.*

Horn in the West

THEATER | **FAMILY** | A project of the Southern Appalachian Historical Association (SAHA), *Horn in the West* is an outdoor drama by Kermit Hunter that traces the story of Daniel Boone and other pioneers, as well as the Cherokee, during the American Revolution. The drama has been presented since 1952. Performances are held nightly, Tuesday through Sunday from late June to mid-August. SAHA also operates the **Hickory Ridge Living History Museum**, adjacent to the *Horn in the West* amphitheater. The museum can be visited before the show. ✉ *Amphitheater, 591 Horn in the West Dr.* ⊕ *Off U.S. 321* ☎ *828/264–2120* 🌐 *www.horninthewest.com* *Play $35, museum $5.*

Activities

CANOEING AND RAFTING

Near Boone and Blowing Rock, the New River, a federally designated Wild and Scenic River (Class I and II rapids) provides excitement for canoeists and rafters, as do the Watauga and Toe Rivers and Wilson Creek.

High Mountain Expeditions

WATER SPORTS | **FAMILY** | This 30-year-old outdoors company organizes white-water rafting on the Nolichucky River, Watauga River, and Wilson Creek, plus tubing on the New River. The company also does caving and hiking trips. It has outposts in Banner Elk and Asheville, as well as in east Tennessee. ✉ *1380 NC 105 S* ☎ *828/202–1556* 🌐 *www.highmountainexpeditions.com* *Half-day rafting $65, full day $85.*

Wahoo's Adventures

CANOEING/ROWING/SKULLING | **FAMILY** | This long-established outfitter offers rafting, kayaking, canoeing, paddleboarding, and tubing on several rivers in western North Carolina (including the Nolichucky, Watauga, and New Rivers) and Class V "extreme rafting" trips on Wilson Creek. Tubing on the New River is the most popular activity, and the most popular rafting is on the Nolichucky. Most activities are available April through October. ✉ *3385 S. U.S. 321* ☎ *828/262–5774, 800/444–7238* 🌐 *www.wahoosadventures.com* *Rafting $41–$75, tubing $20–$65.*

Valle Crucis

5 miles west of Boone.

This tiny mountain town has the state's first rural historic district; vintage stores line the downtown streets.

Restaurants

Over Yonder

$$ | **SOUTHERN** | **FAMILY** | Founded by the former chef of Simplicity restaurant at Mast Farm Inn—the two businesses still have a friendly, reciprocal relationship—Over Yonder serves an updated style of Appalachian food, with dishes such as tomato cobbler, grilled meat loaf with grits, and panfried rainbow trout with almonds. Over Yonder is in a charming 1861 farmhouse near the Mast Farm Inn.

Known for: updated, delicious versions of Southern mountain food; 1861 farmhouse with a fireplace in one dining room; reasonably priced cocktails, some made with moonshine. *Average main: $18* *3608 NC 194* *828/963–6301* *www.overyondernc.com* *Closed Mon. and Tues. Closed Mon.–Wed. Dec.–Mar.*

Hotels

★ Mast Farm Inn

$$$ | B&B/INN | FAMILY | You can turn back the clock and still enjoy modern amenities at this charming and pastoral inn, with parts built in the 1790s and now on the National Register of Historic Places. **Pros:** delightful and historic country inn; personalized service; discounts for teachers. **Cons:** a little off the beaten path; restaurant now only serves breakfast; a few creaks and squeaks (expected in historic old buildings). *Rooms from: $209* *2543 Broadstone Rd., Banner Elk* *828/963–5857* *www.themastfarminn.com* *15 rooms (7 rooms, 8 cottages)* *Free breakfast.*

Shopping

Mast General Store

CONVENIENCE/GENERAL STORES | FAMILY | This is the original Mast General Store, originally called Taylor General Store. Built in 1882–83, the store has plank floors worn to a soft sheen and an active, old-timey post office. Everything from ribbons and overalls to yard art and cookware is sold here. You can take a shopping break by sipping bottled "dope" (mountain talk for a soda pop) or a cup of coffee for 5¢ while sitting in a rocking chair on the store's back porch. For more shopping, an annex, which dates to 1909, is just down the road. Mast General Store has expanded to nine locations, but as the first, this one still has the most authentic atmosphere. *3567 NC 194, Sugar Grove* *828/963–6511, 866/367–6278* *www.mastgeneralstore.com.*

Banner Elk

6 miles southwest of Valle Crucis; 11 miles southwest of Boone.

Surrounded by the lofty peaks of Grandfather, Hanging Rock, Beech, and Sugar Mountains, this ski resort bills itself as the "highest town in the East." The massively ugly condo tower you'll see on top of Little Sugar Mountain (not a part of the Sugar Mountain ski resort) is the only scar on the scenic beauty of the area. At least something good came of the monstrosity—it so outraged local residents that it prompted the passing of a ridgeline law preventing future mountaintop development. A must-do in Banner Elk is the annual Woolly Worm Festival, held annually in mid- to late October. Woolly worms race to see which one gets to predict the winter weather forecast for North Carolina's High Country.

Restaurants

★ Artisanal Restaurant

$$$$ | MODERN AMERICAN | Artisanal is in a barn by a country stream, but don't let that fool you: this restaurant is elegantly designed, modern, and serious about first-rate food and service. The menu, which changes frequently, features only a few entrées, such as lamb tenderloin with charred eggplant and North Carolina flounder with morels, but they are prepared perfectly. **Known for:** sophisticated food and service in an upscale barnlike setting; craft cocktails and good wine list; chef's tasting menu. *Average main: $38* *1200 Dobbins Rd.* *828/898–5395* *www.artisanalnc.com* *Closed Nov.–Mar. Closed Sun. and Mon.*

Hotels

Banner Elk Inn

$ | **B&B/INN** | Here you have the choice of either traditional B&B rooms in a restored 1912 farmhouse or spacious, modern cottages with kitchens. **Pros:** variety of accommodations; delicious breakfasts; good value, especially for B&B rooms. **Cons:** away from center of town; rooms in main house aren't fancy; no kids allowed in the inn. *Rooms from: $125 407 Main St. E 828/898–6223 www.bannerelkinn.com 10 rooms (6 rooms, 4 cottages) Free breakfast.*

Shopping

Fred's General Mercantile

CONVENIENCE/GENERAL STORES | **FAMILY** | For hardware, firewood, a quart of milk, locally grown vegetables, deli sandwiches, pumpkins for Halloween, snowboard and ski rentals, gourmet birdseed, and just about anything else you need, Fred's General Mercantile, half general store and half boutique, is the place to go. At 5,049 feet, it's billed as the highest-elevation general store in America. *501 Beech Mountain Pkwy. 828/387–4838 www.fredsgeneral.com.*

Activities

GOLF

Sugar Mountain Golf Course

GOLF | **FAMILY** | Designed by Francis Duane, this short par-64 "people's course" sits at a 4,000-foot elevation. Tennis and cottage rentals are available. Sugar Mountain also has snow skiing in winter. *1054 Sugar Mountain Dr., Sugar Mountain 828/898–6464 www.seesugar.com $40–$50, 18 holes, 4560 yds, par 64 Golf and tennis closed Nov.–Mar.*

SKIING

Beech Mountain Resort

SKIING/SNOWBOARDING | **FAMILY** | At about 5,500 feet above sea level, Beech Mountain Resort is the highest ski area in the eastern United States. Beech also offers snowboarding, tubing, and ice-skating. There are a total of 15 ski trails and eight lifts. In warm weather (Memorial Day to Labor Day), the resort switches to mountain biking, hiking, and yoga. Beech Mountain Resort even has a craft brewery. Chalet and condo rentals are available year-round. *1007 Beech Mountain Pkwy., Beech Mountain 828/387–2011, 800/438–2093 www.beechmountainresort.com Full-day lift/slopes tickets $43 weekdays, $72 weekends.*

Sugar Mountain Resort

SKIING/SNOWBOARDING | **FAMILY** | One of the larger ski resorts in the High Country, with 21 ski slopes and nine lifts, Sugar Mountain has an equipment shop and lessons, along with snowboarding, tubing, and ice-skating. In warm weather, Sugar also offers rides on the ski lifts, tennis on six clay courts, and an 18-hole, par-64 golf course designed by Frank Duane, open April through October. Vacation rentals are offered year-round. *1009 Sugar Mountain Dr. Off NC 184 828/898–4521, 800/784–2768 www.skisugar.com Full-day lift/slopes tickets $46 weekdays, $77 weekends; lower rates in Mar.*

SNOW TUBING

Hawksnest Snow Tubing

SKIING/SNOWBOARDING | **FAMILY** | You can no longer ski here, but you can try snow tubing on any of 30 tubing lanes at what is claimed to be the largest snow-tubing resort in the East. In either snow or summer heat, Hawksnest also offers ziplining, with 20 ziplines that total 4 miles in length. *2058 Skyland Dr., Seven Devils 828/963–6561 www.hawksnesttubing.com 1 hr, 45 min snow-tubing session $33 weekdays, $42 weekends; ziplining $40–$90.*

Did You Know?

The Blue Ridge Parkway has more than 200 overlooks with breathtaking vistas of the Blue Ridge Mountains, old farmsteads, meadows, and valleys. Be sure to stop and smell the wildflowers as you make your way along America's favorite drive.

Brevard

40 miles southwest of Asheville on NC 280.

This small town in the Pisgah National Forest has a friendly, highly walkable downtown. In summer, more than 400 talented music students from around the country attend the music school at the Brevard Music Center, and the Brevard Music Festival features some 80 classical music concerts, some with such noted visiting artists as cellist Yo-Yo Ma, violinists Joshua Bell and Midori, and pianists André Watts and Emanuel Ax.

Brevard residents go nuts over the white squirrels, which dart around the town's parks and the campus of Brevard College. These aren't albinos but a variation of the eastern gray squirrel. About a quarter of the squirrels in town are white. The white squirrels are thought to have come originally from Hawaii by way of Florida; they possibly were released in Brevard by a visitor in the 1950s. Whatever the case, today Brevard capitalizes on it by holding a White Squirrel Festival in late May.

GETTING HERE AND AROUND

You can reach Brevard via U.S. Route 64 from Hendersonville, or from the U.S. Route 276 exit of the Blue Ridge Parkway. North Broad Street and Main Street are the two primary thoroughfares through Brevard. Brevard Music Center is less than a mile west of town—look for directional signs.

Sights

Cradle of Forestry in America

HISTORIC SITE | FAMILY | The home of the first forestry school in the United States is on 6,500 acres in the Pisgah National Forest. Started in 1898 by Carl Schenck, who came here to work for the Biltmore Estate, the school trained some 300 foresters. Today you can visit the school's original log buildings, a restored 1915 steam locomotive, 3 miles of interpretive trails, and a visitor center with many hands-on exhibits. It sits on a scenic byway that connects with the Blue Ridge Parkway near Mt. Pisgah. ✉ *11250 Pisgah Hwy., Pisgah Forest* ✣ *Off U.S. 276* ☎ *828/877–3130* 🌐 *www.cradleofforestry.com* 🎫 *$6* ⏲ *Closed mid-Nov.–early Apr.*

DuPont State Forest

NATIONAL/STATE PARK | FAMILY | Between Hendersonville and Brevard you'll find this 10,400-acre state forest with four waterfalls, five lakes, and 80 miles of dirt roads to explore. It's ideal for biking, hiking, or horseback riding. Fishing and hunting are permitted in season. ✉ *U.S. 64 and Little River Rd., Cedar Mountain* ☎ *828/877–6527* 🌐 *www.dupontstaterecreationalforest.com* 🎫 *Free.*

Looking Glass Falls

BODY OF WATER | FAMILY | Getting to this waterfall is easy, as it's right beside the road in Pisgah National Forest. Water cascades 60 feet into a clear pool, where you can wade or take a swim. There's a parking area and a sometimes slippery walkway down to the falls. ✉ *U.S. 276* ☎ *828/877–3265* 🌐 *www.fs.usda.gov* 🎫 *Free.*

Mountain Biking

The North Carolina mountains offer some of the best mountain biking in the East. Among the favorite places for mountain biking are **Tsali**, a peninsula sticking out into Lake Fontana near Bryson City, in the Nantahala National Forest; **DuPont State Forest**, just south of Brevard; and the **Bent Creek**, **Davidson River**, and **Mills River** sections of the Pisgah Ranger District of the national forest.

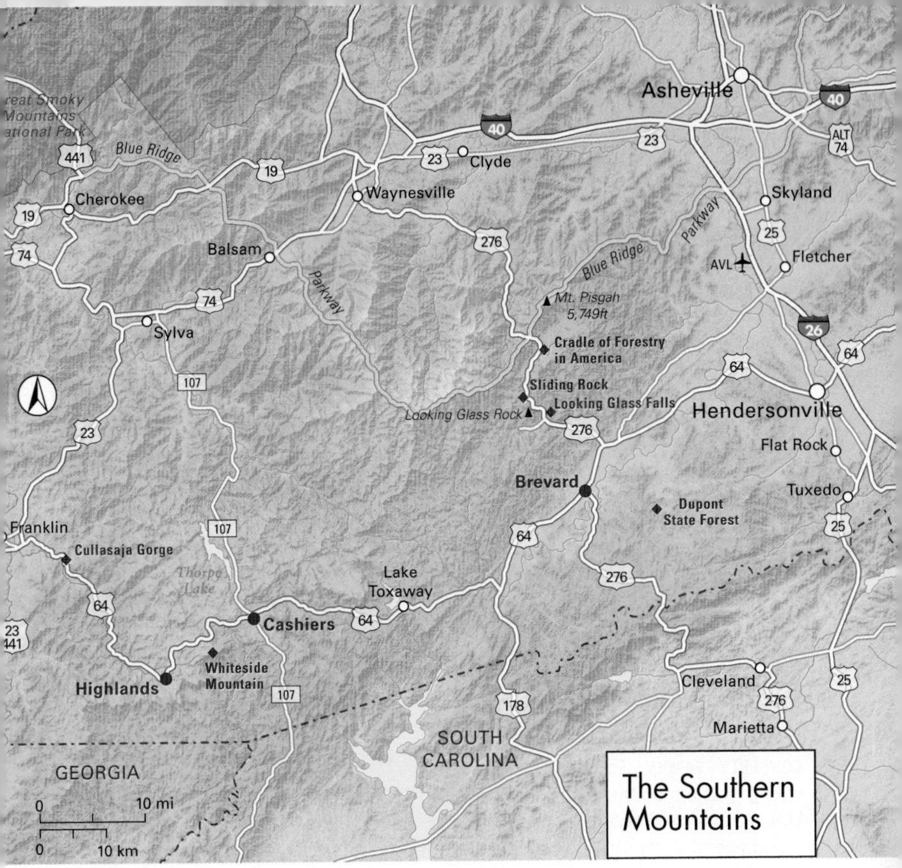

The Southern Mountains

★ **Sliding Rock**

BODY OF WATER | FAMILY | This natural rock waterslide, fueled by 11,000 gallons of mountain water every minute, deposits you into a clear, cold pool. Wear old jeans and tennis shoes and bring a towel. Lifeguards are on duty daily 10 to 6 from Memorial Day to Labor Day (and usually on the weekends in September and October). On warm summer days the parking area is often very crowded. No picnicking is allowed, but there are grounds nearby. ✉ *U.S. 276* ☎ *828/885–7625* 🌐 *www.fs.usda.gov* 🎟 *$4.*

 Restaurants

The Falls Landing Eatery

$$$ | SEAFOOD | FAMILY | The hands-on owner has made this storefront eatery in downtown Brevard probably the most recommended dining spot in town. The menu skews to seafood (the owner moved here from the U.S. Virgin Islands), with standouts including fish-and-chips, clam chowder, mountain trout, and blackened mahimahi, but lamb chops and filet mignon are good, too. **Known for:** dog-friendly sidewalk dining; locals love the place; friendly service. *$ Average main: $21* ✉ *18 E. Main St.* ☎ *828/884–2835* 🌐 *www.thefallslanding.com* ⏲ *Closed Sun. and Mon.*

Rocky's Grill and Soda Shop

$ | HOT DOG | FAMILY | This kitschy but fun version of an old-fashioned soda shop—an institution in Brevard since the early 1940s—has a wide range of ice cream creations. The burgers, hot dogs, and sandwiches are all tasty. **Known for:** the Elvis sandwich—grilled peanut butter and banana; delicious milkshakes, floats, and sundaes; perfect place to take the kids.

Average main: $8 50 S. Broad St. 828/877–5375 No dinner.

Hotels

Red House Inn

$$ | **B&B/INN** | **FAMILY** | One of the oldest houses in Brevard, the Red House Inn was built in 1851 as a trading post and later served as a courthouse, tavern, post office, and school. **Pros:** beautifully renovated historic house; relax on two wraparound porches; friendly, knowledgeable hosts. **Cons:** advance reservations a must; a few rooms are snug; not for swinging singles. *Rooms from: $165* *266 W. Probart St.* *828/884–9349* *www.brevardbedandbreakfast.com* *6 rooms* *Free breakfast.*

Performing Arts

★ **Brevard Music Festival**

CONCERTS | **FAMILY** | Some 400 talented young music students from nearly every U.S. state and 60 faculty from around the world spend summers at the 180-acre Brevard Music Center. Each year, from mid-June to early August, the center hosts about 80 public orchestral and chamber music concerts and operas featuring guest performers such as violinist Itzhak Perlman and pianist Garrick Ohlsson. Boston Pops conductor Keith Lockhart is the festival's artistic director. *349 Andante La.* *828/862–2100* *www.brevardmusic.org* *Concert prices vary; some are free.*

Activities

Davidson River Outfitters

FISHING | **FAMILY** | Catch rainbow, brown, or brook trout on the Davidson River, named one of the top 100 trout streams in the United States by Trout Unlimited. Davidson River Outfitters and its 15 guides arrange trips in the Pisgah and Nantahala National Forests and elsewhere, including private trout streams. It also has a fly-fishing school and a fly shop. *49 Pisgah Hwy., Pisgah Forest* *828/877–4181* *www.davidsonflyfishing.com* *One-person trout-fishing trips from $250.*

Cashiers

63 miles southwest of Asheville via U.S. 74 and NC 107.

Cashiers (pronounced CASH-ers) is not quite a town. Until recently, it was just a crossroads with a store or two, a summer getaway for wealthy South Carolinians escaping the heat. But after the building of many exclusive gated developments, the Cashiers area, at a cool 3,500-foot elevation, now has several new restaurants and stores. Most hotels and other accommodations are in nearby Highlands, about 20 minutes away by car via U.S. Route 64, the Waterfall Byway.

GETTING HERE AND AROUND

From Asheville, take NC 280 to U.S. Route 64 to get to Cashiers. Everything in Cashiers is within a mile or two of the intersection of NC 107 and U.S. Route 64.

Sights

Whiteside Mountain

NATURE SITE | Near Highlands and Cashiers, Whiteside Mountain is one of the highest continuous cliffs in the East. The sheer cliffs of white granite rise up to 750 feet, overlooking the Chattooga River in the Nantahala National Forest. A 2-mile loop (moderate) takes you to the top of the cliffs. The cliffs are also popular with rock climbers. Peregrine falcons nest here, and the cliffs are closed to climbers during falcon mating season. *Whiteside Mountain Rd.* *4.6 miles from Cashiers on U.S. 64. From Asheville, take I–26 East to Exit 40 (Asheville Airport). Turn right on NC 280 W. NC 280 W becomes U.S. 64 W in Pisgah Forest. Stay on U.S. 64 W through Cashiers, and*

For a thrilling ride through Class III and IV rapids, take a guided rafting trip on the Nantahala River.

go another 5 miles. Turn left on NC 1600 and turn left into Whiteside Mountain entrance and parking area ☎ 828/524–6441 Nantahala Ranger District, U.S. Forest Service 🎫 Day-use fee $3, annual pass $15 ⏲ Cliff closed to climbers Jan.–July.

Restaurants

★ The Orchard

$$$$ | SOUTHERN | Located in a century-old farmhouse in an old apple orchard, the Orchard is the best restaurant in Cashiers, putting a Southern twist on traditional American dishes. The decor is comfortable rather than fancy, with a few kitschy Southern touches. **Known for:** catering to upscale visitors and second-home owners; location in an old house, with outdoor seating in warm weather;, mountain trout prepared four different ways. $ *Average main: $28 ✉ 905 NC 107 S ☎ 828/743–7614 🌐 www.theorchardcashiers.com.*

Highlands

85 miles southwest of Asheville; 11 miles southwest of Cashiers on U.S. 64.

Highlands is a tiny town of only 900 people, but the surrounding area swells to 20,000 or more in summer and fall, when those with summer homes here flock back, like wealthy swallows of Capistrano. At 4,118 feet it is usually cool and pleasant when even Asheville gets warm. The five-block downtown is lined with upscale shops, antiques stores, restaurants, and coffeehouses, and there's a sniff of West Palm Beach in the air.

GETTING HERE AND AROUND

From Asheville, you can get to Highlands by two routes. One is via Interstate 40 West, U.S. Routes 23/74 and 441 to Franklin, then North Carolina Highway 28 and U.S. Route 64 to Highlands. Alternatively, you can drive North Carolina Highway 280 to Cashiers, and then U.S. Route 64, the Waterfall Byway, to Highlands.

Cullasaja Gorge
SCENIC DRIVE | West of Highlands via U.S. Route 64 toward Franklin, the Cullasaja Gorge (cul-lah-SAY-jah) is a 7½-mile gorge passing the Cullasaja River, Lake Sequoyah, and several waterfalls, including **Bridal Veil Falls, Dry Falls, Quarry Falls,** and the 200-foot **Cullasaja Falls.** The gorge and falls are in the Nantahala National Forest. **■ TIP→ Rocks around waterfalls are slippery, and it is dangerous to try to cross the top of the falls.** ✉ *U.S. 64* ✣ *From Highlands follow U.S. 64 W/NC 28 N to Franklin* ☎ *828/524–6441 Nantahala Ranger Station, Nantahala National Forest* 🌐 *www.fs.usda.gov/recarea/nfsnc* 🎫 *Free.*

Madison's
$$$$ | MODERN AMERICAN | In the Old Edwards Inn, Madison's is Highlands' most upscale restaurant. The dining room is gorgeous, light, and sunny, with stone floors and windows overlooking Highlands' Main Street. **Known for:** beautiful upscale setting; extensive dinner menu and wine list; impeccable tableside service. $ *Average main: $29* ✉ *445 Main St.* ☎ *828/787–2525* 🌐 *www.oldedwardsinn.com.*

★ Ristorante Paoletti
$$$$ | ITALIAN | A fixture on Main Street for more than three decades, Ristorante Paoletti serves sophisticated Italian cuisine with first-rate service, although this comes at a price. The menu includes a lengthy section of freshly made pastas, along with many excellent seafood dishes. **Known for:** extensive wine list; upscale Italian food; reputation as a long-time favorite with many repeat guests. $ *Average main: $35* ✉ *440 Main St.* ☎ *828/526–4906* 🌐 *www.paolettis.com* ⏲ *Closed Jan.–Mar.*

Wolfgang's Restaurant and Wine Bistro
$$$$ | ECLECTIC | Cheerful and unpretentious, though not inexpensive, Wolfgang's has an eclectic menu ranging from a Wiener schnitzel to venison au poivre to Cajun shrimp and grits (the founder was a chef in New Orleans). Several of the rooms have fireplaces, and in good weather there's outdoor seating. **Known for:** quaint bistro atmosphere; eclectic menu; extensive wine list. $ *Average main: $30* ✉ *474 Main St.* ☎ *828/526–3807* 🌐 *www.wolfgangs.net* ⏲ *Closed Tues. and most of Dec.–Feb.; closed dates vary annually.*

★ Old Edwards Inn and Spa
$$$$ | B&B/INN | Service at this posh inn is first-rate, starting with the complimentary champagne in the lobby and extending to elegantly furnished guest rooms in the main building, with period antiques and European linens, and more rustic but still luxurious accommodations in the lodge. **Pros:** deluxe inn with lots of amenities including golf course; central location in middle of town; top-notch spa. **Cons:** very pricey; often booked months in advance; complicated choice of accommodations in inn, lodge, cottages, and sister properties. $ *Rooms from: $395* ✉ *445 Main St.* ☎ *828/526–8008, 866/526–8008* 🌐 *www.oldedwardsinn.com* *93 rooms* 🍴 *No meals.*

Performing Arts

Highlands Playhouse
THEATER | The well-respected Highlands Playhouse, an Equity theater, puts on three or four productions each summer. It also doubles as a movie theater, with new and classic films screened year-round. ✉ *362 Oak St.* ☎ *828/526–2695* 🌐 *www.highlandsplayhouse.org* 🎫 *Theater $40, movies $10.*

Chapter 6

GREAT SMOKY MOUNTAINS NATIONAL PARK

Updated by
Cameron Roberts

Camping
★★★★★

Hotels
★☆☆☆☆

Activities
★★★★☆

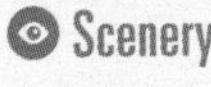
Scenery
★★★★★

Crowds
★★★★☆

WELCOME TO GREAT SMOKY MOUNTAINS NATIONAL PARK

TOP REASONS TO GO

★ **Witness the wilderness:** This is one of the last remaining big chunks of wilderness in the East. Get away from civilization in more than 800 square miles of tranquillity, with old-growth forests, clear streams, 900 miles of hiking trails, wildflowers, and panoramic vistas from mile-high mountains.

★ **Get your endorphins going:** Outdoor junkies can bike, boat, camp, fish, hike, ride horses, white-water raft, watch birds and wildlife, and even cross-country ski.

★ **Experience mountain culture:** Visit restored mountain cabins and tour "ghost towns" in the park, with old frame and log buildings preserved much as they were 100 years ago.

★ **Spot wildlife:** Biologists estimate there are more than 1,600 bears, 6,000 deer, and 150 elk now in the park.

★ **It's free!:** It's one of the few major national parks in the country with no admission fee (though charges apply for campgrounds and a few activities).

The Great Smoky Mountains National Park straddles parts of two states, North Carolina and Tennessee. The park headquarters is in Gatlinburg, Tennessee, and many people think of the Smokies as being a Tennessee national park. In fact, slightly more of the park is on the eastern, or North Carolina, side than on the Tennessee side—276,000 acres to 245,000 acres. The dividing line is at Newfound Gap. Once inside the park, you may not be aware of which state you're in except for practical considerations of geography and the time it takes to get from point to point.

1 North Carolina Side. A little quieter than the Tennessee side, the North Carolina side is home to the observation tower atop Clingmans Dome, the highest point east of the Rockies. Historical sites like Cataloochee are a ghostly reminder of the past. The park's main gateway, and location of the Oconaluftee Visitor Center, is at the bustling town of Cherokee, where numerous attractions tell the story of the Cherokee Nation.

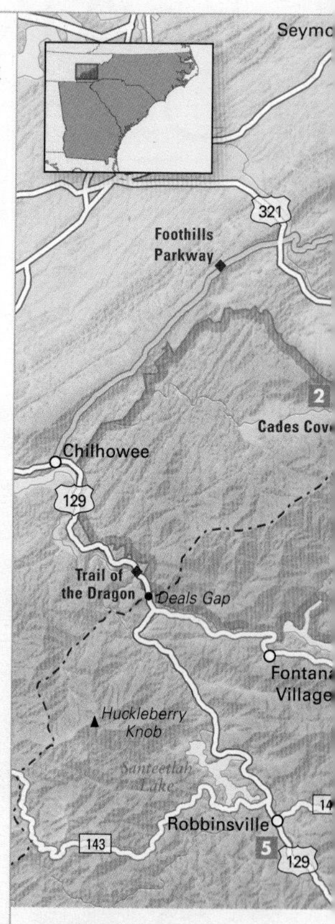

2 Tennessee Side. If you're looking for a family-friendly vacation, the Tennessee side is your best bet. Just inside the main entrances at Gatlinburg and Townsend are easy-to-reach attractions like Cades Cove, with its scenic wide valley, pioneer buildings, and extensive wildlife—you might catch a glimpse of black bears.

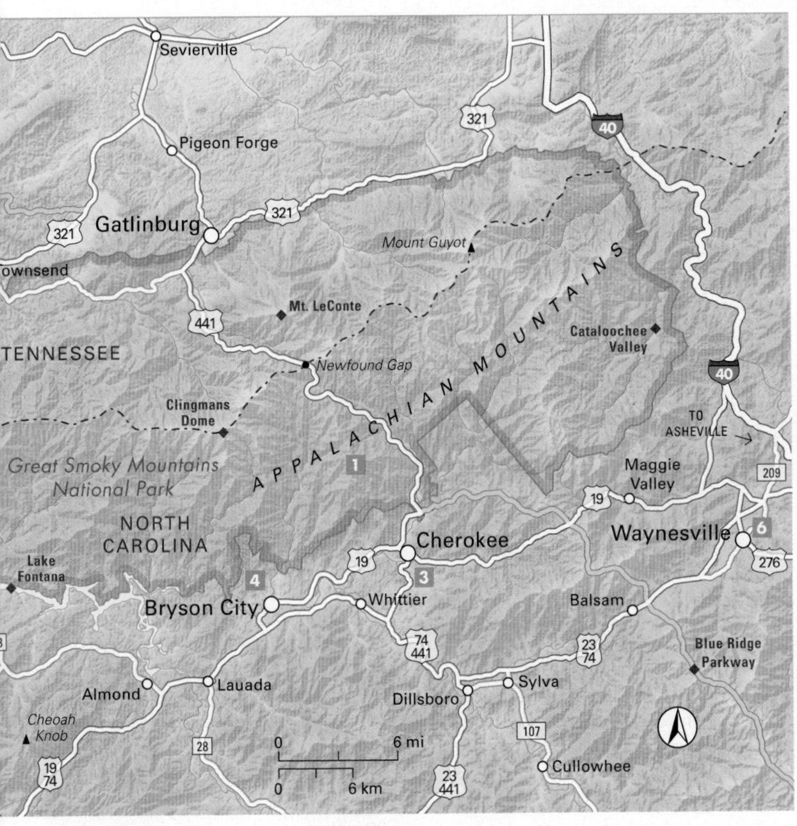

3 Cherokee. The Cherokee Indian Reservation and its principal community, the town of Cherokee, are at the border of the national park.

4 Bryson City. The headquarters of the Great Smoky Mountains Railroad is home to craft breweries, coffee shops, small inns, and good places to eat.

5 Robbinsville. Visit this remote area for the Joyce Kilmer Memorial Forest.

6 Waynesville. 30 minutes from the Oconaluftee entrance to the park, Waynesville has boutique shopping, a craft beer scene, good restaurants, and cozy inns.

Great Smoky Mountains National Park is one of the great wild areas of the eastern United States and the most visited national park in the entire country. From a roadside lookout or a clearing along a trail, in every visible direction you can see the mountains march toward a vast horizon of wilderness.

Some of the tallest mountains in the East are here, including 16 peaks over 6,000 feet. The highest in the park, Clingmans Dome, was reputedly the original inspiration for the folk song "On Top of Old Smoky." It rises 6,643 feet above sea level and 4,503 feet above the valley floor. These are also some of the oldest mountains in the world, far older than the Rockies, Alps, or Andes. Geologists say the Great Smokies began being built about 480 million years ago.

Today, the park hosts around 12 million visitors each year, over twice as many as the next most popular parks, the Grand Canyon and Yellowstone. Even so, with more than 814 square miles of protected land, if you get out of your car you can soon be in a remote cove where your closest neighbors are deer, bobcats, and black bears.

The Qualla Boundary, at the southeastern entrance to the park, belongs to the Eastern Band of Cherokees and represents a small part of their ancestral home. When you're in the Cherokee area, and the Smokies in general, respect the fact that this is sacred land. Take the time to learn about its fascinating history from places like the Cherokee Museum, and consider buying your souvenirs at shops like the Qualla Arts and Crafts Mutual. Some things are also a little different on Cherokee land: you'll see that signs posted in the Qualla Boundary include translations in the Cherokee language, and you need a special permit to fish here.

Due to a fortuitous combination of moderate climate and diverse geography, Great Smoky Mountains National Park is one of the most biologically rich spots on Earth. Bears are the most famous animal in the park, but elk are also making the Smokies their home for the first time in 150 years. It's not just large mammals that make the park special, however; the Smokies have been called the "salamander capital of the world," with at least 30 different salamander species. It is also one of the few places on the planet where, for a few evenings in June, you can see synchronous fireflies flashing in perfect unison.

The park offers extraordinary opportunities for other outdoor activities: it has world-class hiking, on nearly 900 miles of trails, ranging from easy half-hour nature walks to weeklong backpacking treks. Although backcountry hiking has its wonders, some of the most interesting sights in the park can be seen from the comfort of your car or motorcycle.

AVERAGE HIGH/LOW TEMPERATURES

JAN.	FEB.	MAR.	APR.	MAY	JUNE
41/18	45/21	54/27	63/34	69/43	75/51
JULY	**AUG.**	**SEPT.**	**OCT.**	**NOV.**	**DEC.**
78/55	77/54	72/48	63/36	53/27	44/21

MAJOR REGIONS

North Carolina Side. Bisecting the park, Newfound Gap Road offers amazing scenery. The Ocanaluftee Valley has many of the park's most historic sites and Clingmans Dome is its highest point. The Cataloochee Valley has early 20th-century settlements, and Fontana Lake is great for boating and fishing.

Tennessee Side. Close to Gatlinburg, the Sugarlands Visitor Center is the place to get oriented. Enjoy gorgeous views while on the 11-mile loop road at Cades Cove. Discover historic cottages at Elkmont, take a walking tour of a mountain farmstead at Roaring Forks, and explore the backcountry at Cosby.

Nearby North Carolina Towns. Sometimes called "the quiet side of the park," the North Carolina side of the Smokies is edged with a collection of small, low-key towns. The most appealing of these are Bryson City and Waynesville. Except for these towns, and the city of Asheville about 50 miles east , most of the area around the east side of the park consists of national forest lands and rural areas. On the southwestern boundary of the park is Lake Fontana, the largest lake in western North Carolina.

Planning

When to Go

High Season: There's no bad time to visit the Smokies. The biggest crowds in the park arrive mid-June to mid-August, and throughout the month of October for peak fall foliage viewing. Beat the crowds by coming on weekdays and also early in the day, before 10 am. By mid-June, haze, heat, and high humidity have arrived. In July, highs at the lower elevations average 88°F, but at Clingmans Dome (elevation 6,643 feet) the average high is just 65°F. In September a pattern of warm, sunny days and cool nights sets in.

Low Season: Winter in the park can be beautiful, especially when there's snow on the ground or frost on the tree limbs. The air is usually clearer in the winter, with less haze, and with leaves off the trees the visibility is excellent. Winters in the park see some snow, especially at the higher elevations. Many visitor centers, roads, campgrounds, and other services in and around the park close for the winter season. But on the other hand, January has just a sixth of the visitors you'd encounter in July.

Value Season: Late spring is a wonderful time to visit the park, as wildflowers are in bloom and it's before the heat, humidity, and crowds of summer. The weather in the park is highly changeable, especially in the spring. On one day it may be a balmy 70°F, and the next bitterly cold and snowy.

FESTIVALS AND EVENTS

Fall Heritage Festival and Old Timers' Day at Cades Cove. Visitors are invited to bring lawn chairs and a picnic along to Old Timers' Day at Cades Cove. Held in late September at the Cable Mill area of Cades Cove, Old Timers' Day allows former residents of Cades Cove and their descendants, along with the general public, to reminisce about the old days in the valley. The Cades Cove event is now part of a two-day Fall Heritage Festival at the Great Smoky Mountains Heritage Center in Townsend, just outside the park. In Townsend you can enjoy bluegrass music, clogging and square dancing, arts and crafts demonstrations, and mountain food. Both events are free, though there's a park fee for Townsend. 🌐 *www.smokymountains.org*

Spring Wildflower Pilgrimage. Each year in mid-to-late April, the Great Smoky Mountains National Park and the Great Smoky Mountains Association host the Spring Wildflower Pilgrimage. It attracts wildflower enthusiasts from all over the country for five days of wildflower and natural-history walks, seminars, classes, photography tours, and other events. Instructors include National Park Service staff, along with outside experts. Most of the activities are at various locations in the park, on both the North Carolina and Tennessee sides. Begun in 1951, the pilgrimage has grown to more than 150 different walks, classes, and events. Advance registration online begins in February of the year of the conference, and some events quickly sell out. Check the website for current details and dates. 🌐 *www.wildflowerpilgrimage.org*

Getting Here and Around

Although there are numerous entrances to the North Carolina side of the park, the main entrance is via U.S. Route 441 near Cherokee and the Oconaluftee Visitor Center.

Another, much more pleasant (but slower), route to the Smokies is the Blue Ridge Parkway, which has its southern terminus in Cherokee.

You can enter the park by car at nine different places on the Tennessee side. Most of these entrances take you just a short distance into the park to a developed campground or picnic area. The two major entrances to the park on the western side are from Gatlinburg and Townsend.

AIR

The closest airport on the North Carolina side with national air service is Asheville Regional Airport (AVL), about 60 miles east of the Cherokee entrance. On the Tennessee side, the closest major airport is Knoxville's McGhee Tyson Airport (TYS), about 45 miles west of the Sugarlands entrance.

AIRPORT INFORMATION Asheville Regional Airport. (*AVL*) ✉ *61 Terminal Dr., Fletcher* ✈ *Off I–26* 🌐 *www.flyavl.com.* **McGhee Tyson Airport.** (*TYS*) ✉ *2025 Alcoa Hwy., Alcoa* ☎ *828/684–2226* 🌐 *www.flyknoxville.com.*

CAR

The nearest sizable city to the park in North Carolina is Asheville. This hip, liberal-minded city is about 50 miles east of Cherokee and the Oconaluftee Visitor Center. It takes a little more than an hour to get from Asheville to the Cherokee entrance of the park, via Interstate 40 and U.S. Routes 19 and 441. If you aren't pressed for time, however, we advise traveling via the Blue Ridge Parkway—it takes longer, but the scenery is worth it.

The closest sizable city to the park in Tennessee is Knoxville, about 40 miles west of the Sugarlands entrance, via U.S. Route 441.

Coming either from the east or west, Interstate 40 is the main interstate access route to the Great Smokies; from the north and south, Interstates 75, 81, and 26 are primary arteries.

U.S. Route 441, also called Newfound Gap Road, is the main road through the park, and the only paved road that goes all the way through. It travels 31 miles between Cherokee and Gatlinburg, crossing Newfound Gap at nearly a mile high. Once out of the park on the Tennessee side, avoid driving through Gatlinburg (take the bypass option instead), as even in the off-season, intense traffic means you can spend an hour crawling through this small and very touristy town.

Restaurants

Besides the park's numerous picnic areas, the only food service in the park is a camp store deli in Cades Cove on the Tennessee side.

Outside the park you'll find many more dining options, from fast food to fine dining, the latter especially in Asheville, North Carolina, which is known for its farm-to-table, locavore food culture. On the Tennessee side, both Gatlinburg and Pigeon Forge, which might just rank among the most touristy towns in the country, have myriad fast-food and family dining choices. Knoxville also has many good dining options. *Dining reviews have been shortened. For full information, visit Fodors.com.*

Hotels and Campgrounds

The only accommodations actually in the park aside from the abundant and reasonably priced campgrounds are at LeConte Lodge. There are 939 tent and RV camping spaces at 10 developed campgrounds, two (Cades Cove and Smokemont) open year-round, in addition to more than 100 backcountry campsites, shelters, and horse camps. The cost for camping ranges from $4 per person per site (backcountry sites and shelters, up to a maximum of $20 per person) to $18–$27 per night for front-country sites. All but one of the campgrounds accept RVs and trailers, though most have size limits. Immediately outside the park are many commercial campgrounds and RV parks. Permits are required for all backcountry camping. Sites at all developed campgrounds can be reserved up to 6 months in advance by calling ☎ *877/444–6777* or visiting 🌐 *www.recreation.gov*; reservations are *required* at all campgrounds.

Outside the park, you have a gargantuan selection of hotels of every ilk. On the Tennessee side, in Gatlinburg you'll see a street sign that says "2,000 Hotel Rooms" and points up the hill, and that's just in one section of town. On the North Carolina side, lodging is mostly more low-key, but you can choose from old mountain inns, bed-and-breakfasts, and motels in the small towns of Bryson City, Waynesville, and Robbinsville. A seemingly ever-expanding number of hotel towers are connected to the giant Harrah's casino in Cherokee. About 50 miles away, in and around Asheville, you can choose from among one of the largest collections of B&Bs in the Southeast, along with hip urban hotels and classic mountain resorts. *Hotel reviews have been shortened. For full information, visit Fodors.com. Restaurant prices are the average cost of a main course at dinner or, if dinner is not served, at lunch. Hotel prices are the lowest cost of a standard double room in high season.*

What it Costs

$	$$	$$$	$$$$
RESTAURANTS			
under $15	$15–$19	$20–$24	over $24
HOTELS			
under $150	$150–$200	$201–$250	over $250

Inspiration

Asheville native Wayne Caldwell's 2007 novel, *Cataloochee* , tells the story of three generations of mountain families in Cataloochee Cove. As the government takes steps to relocate the settlers out of Cataloochee to make room for the Great Smoky Mountains National Park, a tragic act of violence touches the families.

Park Essentials

ACCESSIBILITY

The three main visitor centers are wheelchair-accessible and have accessible parking spaces; the Cades Cove ampitheater is level and easily accessible. Three campgrounds (Cades Cove, Elkmount, and Smokemont) have wheelchair-accessible campsites. Only the Sugarland Valley Nature Trail is paved and wheelchair-accessible; most historic buildings throughout the park are not, but the walkways surrounding them are mostly hard-packed gravel that can be navigated by wheelchair users with some assistance.

PARK FEES AND PERMITS

Unlike at most other national parks, admission to the Great Smokies is free. Admission to all historical and natural sites within the park is also free. Picnicking is free. Front-country campgrounds charge a nightly fee.

Camping and overnight hiking in the backcountry require a permit. General backcountry permits are $4 per night. To camp in the backcountry, you must complete a permit at one of the 14 self-registration stations in and near the park, which are available 24 hours a day, or by telephone or online. Your permit must designate the campsite or shelter at which you will stay for each night of your trip. Keep the permit with you and drop the top copy in the registration box. Download a park trail map to get the locations of all reserved and nonreserved backcountry campsites and shelters. Day hikes do not require a permit.

PARK HOURS

The park is open 24 hours a day, 365 days a year. Primary roads are always open (weather-permitting), but some secondary roads, campgrounds, and other visitor facilities close in winter.

CELL PHONE RECEPTION

Reception varies widely, but is generally not good. There are no towers within the park boundaries, so typically good reception is only available near park borders and around the three main visitor centers and in some areas of high elevation. Deeper within the park, you'll find almost no service, including at LeConte Lodge. The park service offers no public Wi-Fi service.

PETS

Pets are permitted in some areas of the park but are strictly prohibited in others. Dogs and other pets are allowed in most campgrounds and picnic areas and along roads, but at all times they must be kept on a leash measuring no more than 6 feet. Pets are not allowed on park trails, except the Gatlinburg and the Oconaluftee River trails, and they are not permitted anywhere in the backcountry. Pet excrement must be immediately collected and disposed of in a trash can.

Visitor Information

There are three main visitor centers in the park: Oconaluftee Visitor Center near Cherokee (looking great after a $3 million renovation and expansion), Sugarlands Visitor Center near Gatlinburg (featuring extensive exhibits in a nature museum about the park's incredibly varied flora and fauna), and Cades Cove Visitor Center on the 11-mile Cades Cove Loop. Some of the best hiking trails fan out

Flora and Fauna of the Smokies

The park is about 95% forested, home to almost 6,000 known species of wildflowers, plants, and trees. Many call the Smokies the "wildflower national park," as it has more flowering plants than any other U.S. national park. In October, hundreds of thousands of visitors jam the roads of the park to view the autumn leaf colors.

You can see wildflowers in bloom virtually year-round: ephemerals such as trillium and columbine in late winter and early spring; bright red cardinal flowers, orange butterfly weed, and black-eyed Susans in summer; and joe-pye weed, asters, and mountain gentian in the fall. However, the best time to see wildflowers in the park is the spring, especially April and early May. From early to mid-June to mid-July, the hillsides and heath balds blaze with the orange of flame azaleas, the white and pink of mountain laurel, and the purple and white of rhododendron.

Living in Great Smoky Mountains National Park are some 66 species of mammals, more than 200 varieties of birds, 67 native fish species, and more than 80 types of reptiles and amphibians.

The North American black bear is the symbol of the Smokies. Bear populations vary year to year, but biologists think that about 1,600 bears are in the park, a density of about two per square mile. Some experts put the number at 2,000 or higher. Many visitors to the park see bears, although sightings are never guaranteed.

The National Park Service has helped reintroduce elk, river otters, and peregrine falcons to the Smokies.

Because of the high elevation of much of the park, you'll see birds here usually seen in more northern areas, including the common raven and the ruffed grouse.

For a few short weeks, usually from late May to mid-June, synchronous fireflies put on an amazing light show. In this illuminated mating dance, the male *Photinus* fireflies blink four to eight times in the air, then wait about six seconds for the females on the ground to return a double-blink response. Inside the park, the Elkmont camping area on the Tennessee side is a popular place to see the fireflies.

Altogether, some 17,000 species of plants, animals, and invertebrates have been documented in the park, and scientists believe that up to 85,000 additional species of life, as yet unidentified, may exist here.

from these facilities, making them hard to pass up despite the crowds. In addition, there is a compact visitor contact station at Clingmans Dome.

There are five information centers in communities just outside the park (there's one in Bryson City on the North Carolina side, and on the Tennessee side one in Sevierville, one in Townsend, and two in Gatlinburg). All the gateway towns around the park entrances have their own visitor information centers with plenty of information about the park.

CONTACTS Great Smoky Mountains National Park. ☎ *865/436–1200* 🌐 *www.nps.gov/grsm/planyourvisit/index.htm.*

North Carolina Side

The Great Smoky Mountains National Park may be headquartered in Tennessee, but more of the park is on the North Carolina side. The North Carolina Side boasts the highest mountain in the park—Clingmans Dome, elevation 6,643 feet—and four more of the 10 highest peaks: Mount Guyot, Mount Chapman, Old Black, and Luftee Knob. It's also home to Fontana Lake, which forms much of the park's southwestern boundary. The small towns along the edge of the park—including Robbinsville, Bryson City, Dillsboro, and Sylva—sometimes bill themselves as "the quiet side of the park," and with good reason.

But there's no reason for Carolinians and Tennesseans to get into a bragging match. Within the park itself, both sides are actually quite similar in terms of scenery, activities, flora and fauna, and historical sites. Indeed, you probably won't even know when you go from one side of the park to the other. ■ **TIP→ There are numerous picnic areas and campgrounds but no food service or lodging options on the North Carolina side of the park.**

Sights

GEOLOGICAL FORMATIONS

★ Clingmans Dome

MOUNTAIN—SIGHT | FAMILY | At an elevation of more than 6,600 feet, this is the third-highest peak east of the Rockies, only a few feet shorter than the tallest, Mt. Mitchell. From the parking lot (where there are restrooms) at the end of Clingmans Dome Road, walk up a paved, but steep, half-mile trail to the observation tower offering 360-degree views from the "top of Old Smoky." There's also a small visitor center and bookshop (open April to November). Temperatures here are usually 10 to 15 degrees lower than at the entrance to the park. Clingmans Dome Road is closed to vehicular traffic in winter, but if there's snow on the ground you can put on your snowshoes and hike up to the peak. ✉ *Clingmans Dome Rd., Great Smoky Mountains National Park* ✣ *7 miles from U.S. 441* ☎ *865/436–1200* 🌐 *www.nps.gov/grsm/planyourvisit/clingmansdome.htm* 🎫 *Free* ⏲ *Closed Dec.–Mar.*

HISTORIC SIGHTS

★ Cataloochee Valley

HISTORIC SITE | FAMILY | This is one of the most memorable and eeriest sites in all of the Smokies. At one time Cataloochee was a community of more than 1,200 people. After the land was annexed for the national park in 1934, the community dispersed. Although many of the original buildings are gone, more than a dozen houses, cabins, barns, and churches still stand. You can visit the Palmer Methodist Chapel, the Beech Grove School, and the Woody, Caldwell, and Messer homesteads. You have a good chance of spotting elk here, especially in the evening and early morning. You'll also likely see wild turkeys, deer, and perhaps bears. Cataloochee is one of the most remote parts of the Smokies reachable by car via a narrow, winding, gravel road. The novels of Asheville-area native Wayne Caldwell, *Cataloochee* and *Requiem by Fire,* depict Cataloochee before the coming of the park. ✉ *Cove Creek Rd., off Rte. 276, Great Smoky Mountains National Park* ☎ *865/436–1200* 🌐 *www.nps.gov/grsm* 🎫 *Free* ⏲ *Often closed in winter due to snow and ice.*

Mingus Mill

FACTORY | FAMILY | In the late 19th century this was a state-of-the-art gristmill, with two large grist stones powered by a store-bought turbine rather than a hand-built wheel. From mid-March to just after Thanksgiving, you can watch the miller make cornmeal and even buy a pound of it. ✉ *U.S. 441, Great Smoky Mountains National Park* ✣ *2 miles north of Cherokee* ☎ *865/436–1200* 🌐 *www.nps.gov/grsm/planyourvisit/mfm.htm* 🎫 *Free* ⏲ *Closed late Nov.–mid-Mar.*

The North Carolina Side in One Day

Start early, pack a picnic lunch, and drive to the **Oconaluftee Visitor Center** to pick up orientation maps and brochures. While you're there, spend an hour or so exploring the **Mountain Farm Museum.** Drive the half mile to **Mingus Mill** and see corn being ground into meal in an authentic working gristmill. Head up Newfound Gap Road and Clingmans Dome Road to **Clingmans Dome.** The 25-mile drive takes you through a dizzying array of plants and trees. Stretch your legs and walk the half-mile paved, but fairly steep, trail to the observation tower on Clingmans Dome, the highest point in the Smokies. On a clear day you can see as far as 100 miles, though on most days air pollution limits views to about 20 miles. If you've worked up an appetite, head back down the mountain and stop for a leisurely picnic at **Collins Creek Picnic Area.** If you want a moderate afternoon hike, the 4-mile round-trip **Kephart Prong Trail** is nearby and wanders along a stream to the remains of a Depression-era Civilian Conservation Corps camp. Alternatively, drive via the Blue Ridge Parkway and Heintooga Ridge Road to the **Heintooga Picnic Area** at Balsam Springs. At a mile high, this part of the Smokies is usually cool even in mid-July. If you're up for it, you can hike all or part of the **Flat Creek Trail,** which begins near the Heintooga Picnic Area and is one of the hidden jewels of the park.

★ Mountain Farm Museum

MUSEUM VILLAGE | FAMILY | This is perhaps the best re-creation anywhere of an Appalachian mountain farmstead. The nine farm buildings, all dating from the late 19th century, were moved in the 1950s to this site next to the Oconaluftee Visitor Center from various locations within the park. Besides a furnished two-story chestnut log cabin, there is a barn, apple house, corncrib, smokehouse, bee gums, springhouse, chicken coop, and other outbuildings. In season, corn, tomatoes, pole beans, squash, and other mountain crops are grown in the garden, and the park staff sometimes puts on demonstrations of pioneer activities, such as making apple butter and molasses. Two easy 1½-mile walking trails begin near the museum. Dogs on leashes are allowed on the trail but not within the farm grounds. Elk are sometimes seen grazing in the pastures adjoining the farm, and occasionally you may see white-tailed deer and wild turkeys. ✉ *Oconaluftee Visitor Center, U.S. 441, Great Smoky Mountains National Park* ✣ *1½ miles from Cherokee* ☎ *865/436–1200* 🌐 *www.nps.gov/grsm/planyourvisit/mfm.htm* 🎫 *Free.*

Proctor

HISTORIC SITE | Once a thriving lumber and copper mining town on Hazel Creek, Proctor has mostly been taken over by nature. Among the structures remaining are the white-frame Calhoun House, probably built in the early 1900s; the foundations of a church and of several other buildings; and bridges over Hazel Creek. About half a mile away is the Proctor cemetery. Proctor is best reached by boat across Fontana Lake. After arriving on the north shore of the lake, it's a short walk to the site of the old town. Fontana Marina offers daily boat transport across the lake. ✉ *Great Smoky Mountains National Park* ☎ *828/498–2129* 🌐 *www.nps.gov/grsm/learn/historyculture/people.htm.*

Road to Nowhere

HISTORIC SITE | FAMILY | Lakeview Drive was originally proposed as a way for local communities to reach their family cemeteries, after being displaced from their homes for the Fontana Dam project in the 1940s. An environmental issue halted the construction of Lakeview Drive, earning it its nickname as the "Road to Nowhere." Today, the road begins at the park's entrance from Fontana Road in Bryson City, and ends at a tunnel 6 miles into the park. The drive is quite scenic, with an overlook of Fontana Lake and a few trailheads along the way. A network of hiking trails (including a 3.2-mile loop) begin at the tunnel. ✉ *Lakeview Dr., Great Smoky Mountains National Park* ☎ *865/436–1200* 🌐 *www.nps.gov/grsm* 🎫 *Free.*

Smokemont Baptist Church

RELIGIOUS SITE | Also known as the Oconaluftee Baptist Church, Smokemont Baptist Church is all that remains of the once-thriving lumbering community of Smokemont. Founded in 1832, and rebuilt in 1916, the church was added to the National Register of Historic Places in 1976. To get to the graceful, white-frame church, turn off Newfound Gap Road at the Smokemont Campground, cross the Oconaluftee, and park in the area just past the bridge. The church is across the road and up the hill. An old cemetery, the Bradley Cemetery, is nearby. ✉ *Newfound Gap Rd., MM 17.2, Great Smoky Mountains National Park* ☎ *865/426–1200* 🌐 *www.nps.gov/grsm.*

PICNIC AREAS

Picnic areas provide amenities such as restrooms—some with pit toilets and some with flush toilets—but not all have running water (bring hand sanitizer) or potable drinking water. Most of the 11 developed picnic areas in the park have raised grills for cooking. Picnic grounds in the park are free, except for group pavilions at several grounds, which can be reserved in advance and charge from $12.50 to $80 per group. To avoid future problems with bears, clean your grill and picnic area thoroughly before leaving.

Big Creek Picnic Area

LOCAL INTEREST | FAMILY | This is the smallest picnic area in the park, with only 10 picnic tables. It's accessible via Exit 451 of Interstate 40, or the unpaved Cove Creek Road from Cataloochee. There's a small campground here and restrooms but no pavilion. Several good hiking trails can be reached from the picnic area. Big Creek has some Class IV rapids nearby. ✉ *Off I–40 at Exit 451, Waynesville* ☎ *865/436–1200* 🌐 *www.nps.gov/grsm.*

Collins Creek Picnic Area

LOCAL INTEREST | FAMILY | The largest developed picnic area in the park, Collins Creek has 182 picnic tables. Collins Creek, which runs near the picnic area, is a small stream with above-average trout fishing (license required). The site has restrooms with flush toilets, potable water, and a 70-seat pavilion for groups that can be reserved in advance for $25. ✉ *Newfound Gap Rd., MM 25.4, Great Smoky Mountains National Park* ⊕ *About 8 miles from Cherokee* ☎ *865/436–1200* 🌐 *www.nps.gov/grsm* 🕒 *Closed late Oct.–late Mar.*

★ Deep Creek Picnic Area

LOCAL INTEREST | FAMILY | Deep Creek offers more than picnicking. You can go tubing (rent a tube for the day for around $5 or $6 at nearby commercial tubing centers), hike about 2 miles to three pretty waterfalls, or go trout fishing. You can even go mountain biking here, as this is one of the few park trails where bikes are allowed. The picnic area, open year-round (but no running water in winter), has 58 picnic tables, plus a pavilion that seats up to 70 (reserve in advance, $25 fee). There's also a campground here. ✉ *1912 E. Deep Creek Rd., Bryson City* ☎ *865/436–1200* 🌐 *www.nps.gov/grsm.*

★ Heintooga Picnic Area

LOCAL INTEREST | FAMILY | This is our favorite developed picnic area in the park. Located at more than a mile high and set in a stand of spruce and fir, the picnic area has 41 tables. Nearby is Mile High Overlook, which offers one of the most scenic views of the Smokies and is a great place to enjoy the sunset. For birders, this is a good spot to see golden-crowned kinglets, red-breasted nuthatches, and other species that prefer higher elevations. You're almost certain to see the common raven here. Nearby are a campground and trailheads for several good hiking trails, including Flat Creek. The disadvantage is that due to the high elevation (and the risk of snow and ice) the picnic area is open only from late May to mid-October. ✉ *Heintooga Ridge Rd., Great Smoky Mountains National Park* ☎ *865/436–1200* 🌐 *www.nps.gov/grsm* ⏱ *Closed mid-Oct.–late May.*

SCENIC DRIVES

Cove Creek Road

SCENIC DRIVE | FAMILY | This drive takes you to one of the most beautiful valleys in the Smokies and to one of its most interesting (and least visited) destinations. The first 7 miles of Cove Creek Road are on a mostly paved, winding, two-lane road through a scenic rural valley. As you enter the park, the road becomes gravel. Although in the park this is a two-way road, in places it is wide enough only for one vehicle, so you may have to pull over and let an oncoming vehicle pass. At points the curvy road hugs the mountainside, with steep drop-offs, making it unsuitable for larger vehicles. As you near the Cataloochee Valley, suddenly you're on a paved road again. Follow the paved road, as it is a shortcut to the historic buildings of Cataloochee. Keep a lookout for elk, wild turkey, deer, and other wildlife. Try to visit off-season, as you'll face less traffic on Cove Creek Road and the valley is so peaceful and relaxing. However, the road may close at times in winter. ✉ *Cove Creek Rd., Great Smoky Mountains National Park* ☎ *865/436–1200* 🌐 *www.nps.gov/grsm* 🎟 *Free.*

Heintooga Ridge Road–Balsam Mountain Road

SCENIC DRIVE | Begin this drive near mile marker 458 of the Blue Ridge Parkway, about 11 miles from Cherokee. Travel about 8 miles along the paved Heintooga Ridge Road, a mile-high drive that is lined with evergreens. At this elevation, you're often literally in the clouds. Near the Heintooga Picnic Area, take the narrow, unpaved 18-mile Balsam Mountain Road, sometimes called Roundbottom Road. Although it's only one lane wide and with many sharp curves, Balsam Mountain Road is well maintained and does not require a four-wheel-drive vehicle. Travel trailers and other large vehicles are prohibited. The roadside scenery changes as you descend from the higher elevations, with firs and hemlocks, of Balsam Mountain to the lowlands toward Cherokee. There is a profusion of flowers along Balsam Mountain Road especially in the spring. If you tire of driving, there are plenty of nearby trails, including the 11-mile Balsam Mountain Trail and 3.3-mile Palmer Creek Trail. Another 12 miles on Big Cove Road, mostly through rural areas outside the park, gets you back to Cherokee. ✉ *Heintooga Ridge Rd., off Blue Ridge Pkwy., Great Smoky Mountains National Park.*

★ Newfound Gap Road

SCENIC DRIVE | FAMILY | Newfound Gap Road is by far the busiest road on the national park's North Carolina side, with more than a million vehicles making the 16-mile climb from an elevation of 2,000 feet near Cherokee to almost a mile at Newfound Gap (and then down to Gatlinburg on the Tennessee side). It's the only paved road that goes all the way through the center of the park, so you definitely won't escape from the crowds. The scenery is memorable, however. If you don't have time to explore the back roads, Newfound Gap Road will give

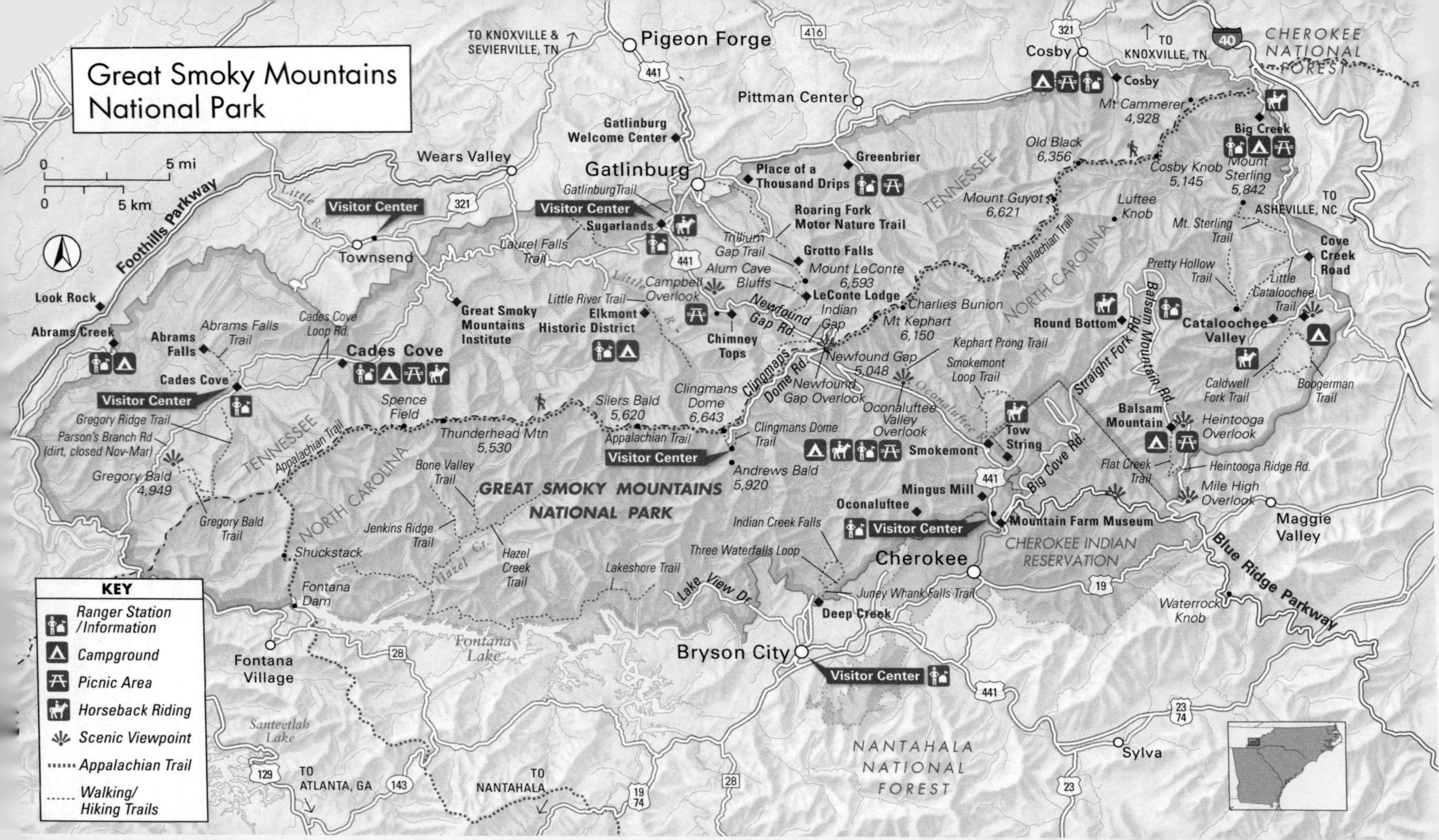
Great Smoky Mountains National Park
0 5 mi
0 5 km
KEY
Ranger Station /Information
Campground
Picnic Area
Horseback Riding
Scenic Viewpoint
Appalachian Trail
Walking/ Hiking Trails
TO KNOXVILLE & SEVIERVILLE, TN
Pigeon Forge
Pittman Center
Cosby
TO KNOXVILLE, TN
CHEROKEE NATIONAL FOREST
Gatlinburg Welcome Center
Wears Valley
Gatlinburg
Greenbrier
Place of a Thousand Drips
Roaring Fork Motor Nature Trail
Gatlinburg Trail
Visitor Center
Sugarlands
Townsend
Little R.
Foothills Parkway
Laurel Falls Trail
Trillium Gap Trail
Grotto Falls
Alum Cave Bluffs
Mount LeConte 6,593
LeConte Lodge
Campbell Overlook
Little River Trail
Elkmont Historic District
Chimney Tops
Great Smoky Mountains Institute
Look Rock
Abrams Creek
Abrams Falls
Abrams Falls Trail
Cades Cove Loop Rd.
Cades Cove
Spence Field
Gregory Ridge Trail
Parson's Branch Rd (dirt, closed Nov-Mar)
Gregory Bald 4,949
Gregory Bald Trail
TENNESSEE
NORTH CAROLINA
Appalachian Trail
Thunderhead Mtn 5,530
Silers Bald 5,620
Clingmans Dome 6,643
Clingmans Dome Trail
Andrews Bald 5,920
Newfound Gap Rd.
Indian Gap
Clingmans Dome Rd.
Newfound Gap 5,048
Newfound Gap Overlook
Mt Kephart 6,150
Charlies Bunion
Kephart Prong Trail
Smokemont Loop Trail
Oconaluftee Valley Overlook
Oconaluftee R.
Tow String
Smokemont
Mingus Mill
Oconaluftee
Mountain Farm Museum
Bone Valley Trail
Jenkins Ridge Trail
Hazel Creek Trail
Hazel Cr.
GREAT SMOKY MOUNTAINS NATIONAL PARK
Shuckstack
Fontana Dam
Lakeshore Trail
Lake View Dr.
Indian Creek Falls
Three Waterfalls Loop
Juney Whank Falls Trail
Deep Creek
Cherokee
CHEROKEE INDIAN RESERVATION
Mt Cammerer 4,928
Old Black 6,356
Mount Guyot 6,621
Cosby Knob 5,145
Big Creek
Mount Sterling 5,842
TO ASHEVILLE, NC
Luftee Knob
Mt. Sterling Trail
Cove Creek Road
Pretty Hollow Trail
Little Cataloochee Trail
Cataloochee Valley
Round Bottom
Balsam Mountain Rd.
Straight Fork Rd.
Caldwell Fork Trail
Boogerman Trail
Balsam Mountain
Heintooga Overlook
Flat Creek Trail
Heintooga Ridge Rd.
Big Cove Rd.
Mile High Overlook
Maggie Valley
Blue Ridge Parkway
Waterrock Knob
Fontana Village
Fontana Lake
Bryson City
Santeetlah Lake
TO ATLANTA, GA
TO NANTAHALA
NANTAHALA NATIONAL FOREST
Sylva
321
441
416
40
28
129
143
19 74
23 74
23
19

you a flavor of the richness and variety of the Smokies. Unlike most other roads in the park, Newfound Gap Road has mile markers; however, the markers run backward (as far as North Carolinians are concerned), starting at 31.1 where it intersects with the Blue Ridge Parkway near Cherokee. Among the sites on the road are the Oconaluftee Visitor Center and Mountain Farm Museum (mile marker 30.3); Mingus Mill (mile marker 29.9); Smokemont Campground and Nature Trail (mile marker 27.2); Web Overlook (mile marker 17.7), from which there's a good view almost due west of Clingmans Dome; and Newfound Gap (mile marker 14.7), the start of the 7-mile road to Clingmans Dome. The speed limit on Newfound Gap Road tops out at 45 mph. ✉ *Newfound Gap Rd., off Blue Ridge Pkwy., Great Smoky Mountains National Park* ☎ *865/436–1200* 🌐 *www.nps.gov/grsm/planyourvisit/nfg.htm* 🎫 *Free.*

SCENIC STOPS

Big Witch Overlook

VIEWPOINT | FAMILY | This overlook offers fine views into the eastern side of the Smokies, and in May and June the roadsides bloom with rosebay rhododendron. ✉ *Blue Ridge Pkwy. MM 461.9, Cherokee* ☎ *828/298–0398* 🌐 *www.nps.gov/blri* 🎫 *Free.*

Cataloochee Valley Overlook

VIEWPOINT | FAMILY | This is a great spot to take in the broad expanse of Cataloochee Valley. Cataloochee comes from a Cherokee word meaning "row upon row" or "standing in rows," and indeed you'll see rows of mountain ridges here. The overlook is well marked and has a split-rail fence. ✉ *Cataloochee Entrance Rd., Great Smoky Mountains National Park* ☎ *865/436–1200* 🌐 *www.nps.gov/grsm* 🎫 *Free.*

Heintooga Overlook

VIEWPOINT | FAMILY | One of the best spots to watch the sunset, Heintooga Overlook has sweeping views westward of the crest of the Great Smokies. ✉ *Heintooga Ridge Rd., Great Smoky Mountains National Park* ☎ *865/436–1200* 🌐 *www.nps.gov/grsm* 🎫 *Free* ⏲ *Closed Nov.–late May.*

★ Newfound Gap Overlook

VIEWPOINT | FAMILY | At 5,048 feet, Newfound Gap is a drivable pass through the top of the park and provides excellent views of a broad swath of the Smokies. The ridge at Newfound Gap marks the North Carolina–Tennessee state line. If you want to say you've been on the Appalachian Trail, it's a short and easy walk away here. Franklin Delano Roosevelt officially dedicated the park at this site in 1940. ✉ *Newfound Gap Rd., MM 14.7* ☎ *865/436–1200* 🌐 *www.nps.gov/grsm.*

Oconaluftee Valley Overlook

VIEWPOINT | FAMILY | From atop the Thomas Divide, just a little below the crest of the Smokies, you can look down at winding Newfound Gap Road. This is also a good spot to view the sunrise in the Smokies. ✉ *Newfound Gap Rd., MM 15.4, Great Smoky Mountains National Park* ☎ *865/436–1200* 🌐 *www.nps.gov/grsm* 🎫 *Free.*

TRAILS

Clingmans Dome Trail

TRAIL | FAMILY | If you've been driving too long and want a place to stretch your legs, unbeatable views of the Smokies, and an ecological lesson, take the ½-mile (1-mile round-trip) trail from the Clingmans Dome Visitor Center parking lot to the observation tower at the top of Clingmans Dome, the highest peak in the Smokies. While paved, the trail is fairly steep, and at well over 6,000 feet elevation you'll probably be gasping for air. Many of the fir trees here are dead, killed by an alien invader, the balsam woolly adelgid. There's a small visitor information station on the trail. In the parking lot, often full in season, there are restrooms. *Easy.* ✉ *Clingmans Dome Rd., Great Smoky Mountains National Park* ☎ *865/436–1200* 🌐 *www.nps.gov/grsm/planyourvisit/clingmansdome.htm* ⏲ *Clingmans Dome Rd. closed Dec.–Mar.*

Flat Creek Trail

TRAIL | FAMILY | This is one of the hidden gems in the park. It's little known, but it's a delightful hike, especially in summer when this higher elevation means respite from stifling temperatures. The 2.6-mile path stretches through pretty woodlands with evergreens, birch, rhododendron, and wildflowers. The elevation gain is about 570 feet. *Moderate.* ✉ *Heintooga Ridge Rd., MM 5.4, Great Smoky Mountains National Park* ☎ *865/436–1200* 🌐 *www.nps.gov/grsm* ☞ *Heintooga Ridge Rd. closed Nov.–late May.*

Forney Ridge Trail

TRAIL | Getting to Andrews Bald isn't easy. From Clingmans Dome you have to walk the 1.8-mile Forney Ridge Trail, a rocky path with an elevation gain of almost 600 feet, the equivalent of a 60-story skyscraper. The payoff is several acres of grassy bald at more than 5,800 feet, with stunning views of Lake Fontana and the southeastern Smokies. This is one of only two balds in the Smokies that the park service keeps clear (the other is Gregory Bald on the Tennessee side). *Difficult.* ✉ *Clingmans Dome Visitor Center, Clingmans Dome Rd., Great Smoky Mountains National Park* ☎ *865/436–1200* 🌐 *www.nps.gov/grsm/planyourvisit/forney-ridge-project-overview.htm* 🎫 *Free.*

Hazel Creek Trail

TRAIL | This hike begins with a boat ride across the lake from Fontana Resort Marina. Your captain will give you directions on how to get from the docking point to the trailhead. A half-mile on the Hazel Creek Trail (known on some park maps as Lakeshore Trail) will take you to the old lumber and mining town of Proctor. After about 5.1 miles, bear right onto the Jenkins Ridge Trail, which will take you to Bone Valley Trail. Bone Valley gets its name from the herd of cattle, moved here for summer pasture in 1888, that died in a spring snowstorm. This is an easy hike (as hikes go in the Smokies), mostly following an old road and railroad bed. However, it is also a long hike, but you could always do a shorter section. *Easy.* ✉ *Great Smoky Mountains National Park* ✣ *Trailhead near Backcountry Campsite 86* ☎ *828/498–2129 boat reservations* 🌐 *www.nps.gov/grsm.*

Kephart Prong Trail

TRAIL | A 4.2-mile round-trip woodland trail, named for one of the early promoters of the park, wanders beside a stream to the remains of a Civilian Conservation Corps camp. Close by, the trail takes a moderate slope to Mt. Kephart, gaining over 900 feet in elevation. *Moderate.* ✉ *Newfound Gap Rd., 5 miles north of Smokemont Campground, Great Smoky Mountains National Park* ☎ *865/436–1200* 🌐 *www.nps.gov/grsm.*

Little Cataloochee Trail

TRAIL | No other hike in the Smokies offers a cultural and historic experience quite like this one. In the early 20th century, Cataloochee Cove had the largest population of any place in the Smokies, around 1,200 people. Most of the original structures have been torn down or have succumbed to the elements, but a few historic frame buildings remain along this remote trail. Some have been restored by the park staff, such as the Cook Log Cabin near Davidson Gap, an apple house, and a church. You'll see several of these, along with rock walls and other artifacts, on the Little Cataloochee Trail. The trail is 6 miles each way, including a mile-long section of Pretty Hollow Gap Trail. Allow at least six hours for this hike. *Moderate.* ✉ *Little Cataloochee Trailhead, Old Cataloochee Tpk., Great Smoky Mountains National Park* ☎ *865/436–1200* 🌐 *www.nps.gov/grsm/planyourvisit/cataloochee.htm.*

Mt. Sterling Trail

TRAIL | A 5.4-mile round-trip hike takes you to an old fire watchtower, which you can climb, rewarding yourself with amazing views. The route is steep, with an elevation gain of almost 2,000 feet, so you should consider this a strenuous, challenging hike. *Difficult .* ✉ *Mt. Sterling Gap, Old Cataloochee Turnpike, Great Smoky Mountains National Park* ☎ *865/436–1200* 🌐 *www.nps.gov/grsm.*

Smokemont Loop Trail

TRAIL | A 6.1-mile round-trip loop takes you by streams and, in spring and summer, lots of wildflowers, including trailing arbutus. At Smokemont Campground near Cherokee, this is an easy trail to access. The only downside is that there are no long-range views. *Moderate.* ✉ *Smokemont Campground, Newfound Gap Rd., Great Smoky Mountains National Park* ☎ *865/436–1200* 🌐 *www.nps.gov/grsm.*

★ Three Waterfalls Loop

TRAIL | FAMILY | For the effort of a 2.4-mile hike at the Deep Creek entrance to the park near Bryson City, this trail will reward you with three pretty waterfalls: Tom Branch, Indian Creek, and Juney Whank, which you can see close-up from a 90-foot-long wooden bridge. *Moderate.* ✉ *Deep Creek Rd., Great Smoky Mountains National Park* ✣ *Near Bryson City entrance* ☎ *865/436–1200* 🌐 *www.nps.gov/grsm* ⏲ *Campground closed Nov.–mid-Apr.*

VISITOR CENTERS

Clingmans Dome Visitor Contact Station

INFO CENTER | FAMILY | While not a full-fledged visitor information center, Clingmans Dome has a staffed information kiosk, along with a small park store and bookshop. There are restrooms in the Clingsmans Dome parking lot. ✉ *Clingmans Dome, Great Smoky Mountains National Park* ☎ *865/436–1200* 🌐 *www.nps.gov/grsm/planyourvisit/visitorcenters.htm* ⏲ *Closed Dec.–Mar.*

★ Oconaluftee Visitor Center

INFO CENTER | FAMILY | The park's main information center on the North Carolina side is looking great after a $3 million renovation and expansion. It is 1½ miles from Cherokee and offers interactive displays, a 20-minute film, a large book and gift shop, ranger-led programs, and assistance from helpful volunteers. There are restrooms and vending machines. Adjoining the visitor center, in a large level field next to the Oconaluftee River, is the Mountain Farm Museum, a reconstruction of an early 1900s mountain farmstead. Herds of elk are sometimes seen here. ✉ *Newfound Gap Rd., MM 30.3, Great Smoky Mountains National Park* ☎ *865/436–1200* 🌐 *www.nps.gov/grsm/planyourvisit/visitorcenters.htm.*

Activities

BIKING

The North Carolina side of the Smokies offers excellent cycling, and bicycles are permitted on most roads. Avoid Newfound Gap Road, which can be clogged with vehicular traffic. Instead, head to the (mostly) paved roads of Lakeview Drive—the so-called Road to Nowhere near Bryson City—and the Cataloochee Valley. Balsam Mountain Road and Cove Creek Road also offer pleasant biking with very little auto traffic. Since these roads are unpaved, with mostly gravel surfaces, you should use a mountain bike or an all-terrain hybrid. Helmets are not required in the park, but are strongly recommended.

BIKE RENTALS

Nantahala Outdoor Center Bike Shop

BICYCLING | FAMILY | Watch river rafters swoosh by on the Nantahala River as you get your bike tuned up or rent a bike at this friendly outfitter. Avid bikers on staff will give you tips on the best biking spots. All rentals include a helmet and a bike rack to transport the bike on your car. During busy periods you should reserve well in advance. This is the closest bike rental to the Tsali Recreation Area, famous for its mountain biking. ✉ *13077 U.S. 19 W, Bryson City* ☎ *828/785–4846* 🌐 *www.noc.com* ☞ *$40 a day.*

BOATING

★ Fontana Lake

BOATING | FAMILY | Covering around 12,000 acres, Fontana Lake borders the southern edge of the Great Smokies. Unlike most other nearby lakes, Fontana's shoreline is almost completely undeveloped, since about 90% of it is owned by the federal government. Fishing here is excellent, especially for smallmouth bass, muskie, and walleye. On the downside, the Tennessee Valley Authority generates power at Fontana Dam, sometimes lowering the water level. The dam, completed in 1944, at 480 feet is the highest concrete dam east of the Rockies. The dam's visitor center gets about 50,000 visitors a year. The Appalachian Trail crosses the top of the dam. ✉ *Fontana Dam Visitor Center, 71 Fontana Dam Rd., Great Smoky Mountains National Park* ✣ *3 miles from Fontana Village off NC 28* ☎ *865/498–2234* 🌐 *www.visitnc.com/listing/UHdY/fontana-dam-visitors-center* 🎫 *Free* ☞ *Visitor center closed Nov.–Mar.*

BOAT RENTALS

Fontana Marina

BOATING | FAMILY | Boat rentals—including kayaks, canoes, pontoon boats, and paddleboards—are available at Fontana Marina. The marina runs a shuttle service across the lake twice daily, and can drop hikers, anglers, and campers at Hazel Creek, Eagle Creek, Pilkey Creek, Kirkland Branch, and other north shore locations. ✉ *300 Woods Rd., Fontana Dam* ✣ *Off NC 28 N* ☎ *828/498–2129* 🌐 *www.fontanavillage.com/marina* 🕒 *Closed Nov.–Apr.* ☞ *Shuttles to Hazel Creek $50 per person.*

CAMPING

Four developed campgrounds—Balsam Mountain, Big Creek, Cataloochee, and Deep Creek—require reservations, and reservations are strongly recommended at Smokemont during high season. Only Smokemont is open year-round, and from November to April sites are first-come, first-served.

Balsam Mountain Campground. If you like camping among the evergreens, tent-only Balsam Mountain is for you. It's the highest campground in the park, at more than 5,300 feet. You may want to warm up in the evening with a campfire, even in summer. Due to its remote location off the Blue Ridge Parkway, the 64-site campground is rarely full, even on peak weekends. It's closed mid-October though late May. The camping fee is $17.50. ✉ *Near end of Heintooga Ridge Rd., Cherokee* ☎ *65/436–1200* 🌐 *www.nps.gov/grsm/planyourvisit/balsam-mountain.htm.*

Big Creek Campground. With just a dozen campsites, Big Creek is the smallest campground in the park. This is a walk-in, not hike-in, campground. Five of the 12 sites sit beside Big Creek, which offers good swimming and fishing. Carefully observe bear protection rules, as a number have been spotted nearby. It's closed November through March. The camping fee is $17.50. ✉ *Cove Creek Rd., Newport* ☎ *865/436–1200* 🌐 *www.nps.gov/grsm/planyourvisit/camping-at-big-creek.htm.*

Cataloochee Campground. The appeal of this small campground is its location in the beautiful and historical Cataloochee Valley. Reservations are required for all 27 tent sites. Take care driving into the valley; the unpaved Cove Creek Road is narrow with sharp curves, and in some places you hug the mountainside. It's closed late October through late March. The camping fee is $25. ✉ *Cataloochee Valley, Cove Creek Rd., Waynesville* ☎ *877/444- 6777* 🌐 *www.nps.gov/grsm/planyourvisit/cataloochee-campground.htm.*

Deep Creek Campground. This campground at the Bryson City entrance to the park is near the most popular tubing spot on the North Carolina side of the Smokies. There are also several swimming holes. Of the 92 sites here, 42 are for tents only. It's closed late October through late March. The camping fee is $25. ✉ *1912 E. Deep Creek Rd., Bryson City* ☎ *865/436–1200*

🌐 *www.nps. gov/grsm/planyourvisit/deep-creek-campground.htm.*

Smokemont Campground. With 142 sites (98 for tents and 44 for RVs), Smokemont is the largest campground on the North Carolina side of the park and is open year-round. Some of the campsites are a little too close together, but the sites themselves are spacious. The camping fee is $25. ✉ *Off Newfound Gap Rd., 6 miles north of Cherokee* ☎ *877/444–6777* 🌐 *www.nps.gov/grsm/planyourvisit/smokemont-campground.htm.*

EDUCATIONAL OFFERINGS

Discover the flora, fauna, and mountain culture of the Smokies with scheduled ranger programs and nature walks.

Interpretive Ranger Programs

TOUR—SPORTS | **FAMILY** | The National Park Service organizes all sorts of activities, such as daily guided hikes and talks, from spring to fall. The programs vary widely, from talks on mountain culture, blacksmithing, and old-time fiddle and banjo music to tours through historical areas of the park. Many of the programs are suitable for older children as well as adults. The Oconaluftee Visitor Center is a good place to learn about park events. ☎ *865/436–1200* 🌐 *www.nps.gov/grca/planyourvisit/ranger-program.htm.*

Junior Ranger Program

TOUR—SPORTS | **FAMILY** | Children ages 5 to 12 can take part in these hands-on educational programs. Kids can pick up a Junior Ranger booklet at the Oconaluftee Visitor Center. Spring through fall the park offers many age-appropriate demonstrations, classes, and programs, such as Stream Splashin', Critters and Crawlies, and—our favorite—Whose Poop's on My Boots? For kids 13 and older (including adults), look for events in the park's Not-So-Junior-Ranger Program. ☎ *865/436–1200* 🌐 *www.nps.gov/grsm/learn/kidsyouth/beajuniorranger.htm.*

FISHING

The North Carolina side of the Smokies has one of the best wild trout fisheries in the East. It has more than 1,000 miles of streams, and all are open to fishing year-round except Bear Creek where it meets Forney Creek. Native brook trout thrive in colder high-elevation streams, while brown and rainbow trout (not native but now widely present in the region) can live in somewhat warmer waters. Among the best trout streams on this side of the park are Deep Creek, Big Creek, Cataloochee Creek, Palmer Creek, Twentymile Creek, Raven Fork, Hazel Creek, and Noland Creek. Fishing licenses are available online at 🌐 *www.ncwildlife.org.*

To fish in the Cherokee Reservation (Qualla Boundary), everyone over 12 needs a separate tribal permit, available at shops on the reservation.

North Carolina Wildlife Resources Commission

FISHING | You can order a North Carolina inland fishing license, valid throughout the park, by telephone or online or buy one from fishing shops or guides. The North Carolina license is good throughout the Great Smoky Mountains National Park, even on the Tennessee side (likewise, a Tennessee license is valid throughout the park). A 10-day nonresident inland fishing license is $23, while an annual license is $45. North Carolina residents pay $9 for a 10-day license and $25 for an annual license. To fish for trout outside the park, you'll also need a trout stamp, which costs an extra $18 for both North Carolina residents and nonresidents. To fish in the Cherokee Reservation (Qualla Boundary), those over 12 need a separate tribal permit, available at shops on the reservation for $10 per day, $17 for two days, $27 for three days, and $47 for five days. A tribal three-day catch-and-release permit allowing fishing in a special area of Raven Creek is an extra $25. ✉ *1751 Varsity Dr., Raleigh* ☎ *919/707–0391* 🌐 *www.ncwildlife.org.*

HIKING

Great Smoky Mountains National Park has almost 900 miles of hiking trails, about equally divided between the North Carolina and Tennessee sides. The trails range from short nature walks to long, strenuous hikes that gain several thousand feet in elevation. The Little Cataloochee Trail is a favorite, but Flat Creek and Smokemont Loop are also extraordinary hikes.

Although permits are not required for day hikes, you must have a backcountry permit for overnight trips.

HORSEBACK RIDING

Get back to nature and away from the crowds with a horseback ride through the forest. Guided horseback rides are offered by one park concessionaire at Smokemont near Cherokee. Rides are at a walking pace, so they are suitable for even inexperienced riders.

Smokemont Riding Stable

HORSEBACK RIDING | FAMILY | The emphasis here is on a family-friendly horseback-riding experience, suitable even for novice riders. Choose either the one-hour trail ride or a 2½-hour waterfall ride. If you don't feel like saddling up, Smokemont also offers wagon rides. ✉ *135 Smokemont Riding Stable Rd., Cherokee* ✢ *Off U.S. 441* ☎ *828/497–2373* 🌐 *www.smokemontridingstable.com* ⏲ *Closed mid-Nov.–early Mar.* ☞ *1-hr rides $35.*

TUBING

On a hot summer's day there's nothing like hitting the water. On the North Carolina side, you can swim or go tubing on Deep Creek near Bryson City. The upper section is a little wild and woolly, with white water flowing from cold mountain springs. The lower section of Deep Creek is more suitable for kids. There are several tubing outfitters near the entrance to the park at Deep Creek. Some have changing rooms and showers. Wear a swimsuit and bring towels and dry clothes to change into. Most outfitters are open April through October.

Smoky Mountain Campground

WATER SPORTS | FAMILY | Just outside the Bryson City Entrance to the national park, look for a rustic structure with "TUBES" in huge red letters across the roof. This highly commercial operation rents tubes and sells camping supplies. It also has a campground and rental cabins. ✉ *1840 W. Deep Creek Rd., Bryson City* ☎ *828/488–9665* 🌐 *www.smokymtn-campground.com* ⏲ *Closed Nov.–Mar.*

Tennessee Side

The Tennessee side of the Great Smokies gets heavy action. Some 2 million people a year tour Cades Cove, and on a busy fall weekend the traffic on the Cades Cove Loop may remind you of midtown Manhattan. The Tennessee side also has the largest and busiest campgrounds and picnic areas.

If you prefer peace and quiet and natural beauty, all is not lost. With just a little bit of effort, you can find your way to lovely and little-visited parts of the Tennessee side of the park. Greenbrier, for example, is a picnicking paradise that's often virtually deserted. The Roaring Fork Motor Trail, a 5-mile winding road that passes historic buildings, old-growth forests, and waterfalls, is a delight, and the Foothills Parkway, a scenic, unfinished road along the western and southern edges of the park, is an undiscovered gem. Several of the best hiking trails in the park are also in Tennessee.

The Tennessee side is also the family-fun side, particularly in the towns of Gatlinburg and Pigeon Forge. You can tour historical sites, treat the family to minigolf or go-karts, tire the kids out at nearby theme parks, try a different restaurant at every meal, or enjoy some grown-up time at a bar or music theater.

One Day on the Tennessee Side

If you have one day and are entering the park from the Tennessee side, start early, pack a picnic lunch, and drive to the **Sugarlands Visitor Center** to orient yourself to the park. Beat the crowds to the **Cades Cove Loop Road** and drive the 11-mile loop, stopping to explore the preserved farmsteads and churches. Spend some time in the **Cable Mill** area, visiting the gristmill, **Gregg-Cable House**, and other historic buildings. Depending on your timing, you can picnic at one of the stops in Cades Cove or Metcalf Bottoms. Take **Newfound Gap Road** up to **Newfound Gap.** Just over the state line is **Clingmans Dome Road**, but if you've come this far you'll want to drive up. Stretch your legs and walk to the observation tower at **Clingmans Dome.** Return down Newfound Gap Road and then proceed to **Roaring Fork Motor Nature Trail.** Stop to explore the preserved cabins and other sites along the trail. Park in the lot at the Trillium Gap trailhead and—if you have the time and are up to a moderate 2.6-mile hike—walk to **Grotto Falls.**

Sights

HISTORIC SIGHTS

★ Cades Cove

HISTORIC SITE | FAMILY | A 6,800-acre valley surrounded by high mountains, Cades Cove has more historic buildings than any other area in the park. Driving, hiking, or biking the 11-mile Cades Cove Loop Road gives you access to three old churches (Methodist, Primitive Baptist, and Missionary Baptist), a working gristmill (Cable Mill), a number of log cabins and houses in a variety of styles, and many outbuildings, including cantilevered barns, which used balanced beams to support large overhangs. The Cherokee name for this valley is *Tsiyahi*, "place of otters," but today you're more likely to see bears, deer, coyotes, and wild turkeys. For hundreds of years the Cherokee people hunted in Cades Cove, but there is no evidence of major settlements. Under the terms of the Calhoun Treaty of 1819, the Cherokee lost their rights to Cades Cove, and the first white settlers came in the early 1820s. By the middle of the 19th century, well over 100 settler families were growing corn, wheat, oats, and vegetables. For a while, when government-licensed distilleries were allowed in Tennessee, corn whiskey was the major product of the valley. After the establishment of the park in the 1930s, many of the nearly 200 buildings were torn down to allow the land to revert to its natural state. More recently, the remaining farmsteads and other structures have been restored to depict life in Cades Cove as it was from around 1825 to 1900. Keep in mind that this route gets 2 million visitors per year; at peak times traffic in and out of here can be extremely slow. ✉ *Cades Cove Loop Rd., Great Smoky Mountains National Park* ☎ *865/436–1200* 🌐 *www.nps.gov/grsm/planyourvisit/cadescove.htm.*

Dan Lawson Cabin

HISTORIC SITE | FAMILY | From many points along the 11-mile Cades Cove Loop Road, you'll enjoy impressive views of the broad Cades Cove Valley. The Park Service keeps hayfields and pastures cleared, so you can see how the valley may have looked in the late 19th century when it was farmed by more than 100

Continued on page 241

GREAT SMOKY MOUNTAINS THROUGH THE SEASONS

SPRING, SUMMER, AND FALL

by Lan Sluder

The changing seasons bring new experiences to the Great Smoky Mountains National Park. In spring you can tiptoe through the wildflowers; in fall a curtain of fiery red and gold leaves sets the trees ablaze; in summer shady paths and cool mountain streams beckon. Throughout the seasons, miles of hiking trails and wilderness await exploration beyond the car window.

Above: Newfound Gap, Great Smoky Mountains

Spring arrives at the lower elevations in March and April. With it, the wildflowers—buttercups, columbine, arbutus, and hundreds more—bloom, carpeting meadows and popping up near forest streams. Wildflower walks are a popular activity and the Spring Wildflower Pilgrimage in late April is a must for budding botanists.

The warm, hazy days of **summer** begin in June as do many of the park's best activities. You can hike to a cool, high peak in the clouds, walk part of the Appalachian Trail, splash or tube in a stream, or fish for native brook trout.

In **autumn**, the flaming golds of sugar maples, the rich reds of sumac and sourwoods, and the mellow yellows of birch and poplar make for memorable leaf peeping. Because elevations in the park range from 1,000 to over 6,000 feet, autumn color lasts for up to two months. Fall foliage generally peaks in mid- to late-October.

TOP SPRING WILDFLOWERS

❶ Trillium

The large flowered trillium, with blooms three to four inches across, is the most common of ten trillium varieties in the park. To identify this impressive flower, look for sets of three: three large pointed green leaves, three sepals, and three white petals. Trilliums bloom on woody slopes and along roadsides and trails at elevations up to 3,500 feet from April to May. **See it:** Middle Prong Trail (TN), Oconaluftee River Trail (NC).

❷ Lady Slippers

These delicate orchids come in pink, yellow, and white. The slender stalk rises from a pair of green leaves, and then bends a graceful neck to suspend the paper-thin flower, which resembles a woman's slipper. They favor wooded areas in dappled sunlight, often under oaks. **See it:** Cove Hardwood Nature Trail (TN).

❸ Fire pink

These brilliant red flowers have five notched petals and bloom in dry rocky areas in April and May. Look for the ruby-throated hummingbirds that pollinate the flowers. **See it:** Chestnut Top Trail (TN).

❹ Rhododendron

The park is famous for its displays of rhododendron. The rosebay's big clumps of white flowers appear in June around streams at the lower and middle elevations and as late as July at higher elevations. The Catawba, with stunning purple flowers, blooms at higher elevations in June. **See it:** rosebay, trails below 5,000 feet; Catawba, Newfound Gap Road (NC and TN).

❺ Flame azalea

Blooms can be found in white, peach, yellow, and red, but the most striking color is the namesake flame orange. They bloom in April and May at low to mid-elevation, and June to early July on the mountaintops. **See it:** Gregory Bald (TN), Andrews Bald (NC), Balsam Mountain Road (NC).

TOP TREES FOR FALL COLOR

❶ Tulip poplar
With its tall, straight trunk and light yellow leaves in the fall, the tulip poplar is hard to miss. Poplars are among the first to turn and often grow in stands of hundreds of trees, at elevations under 4,500 feet. **See it:** Cove Hardwood Nature Trail (TN), Fontana Lake (NC), Ramsey Cascades Trail (TN).

❷ Sugar maple
Sugar maples are the kings of the fall forest with brilliant orange-to-yellow leaves that appear like fire against the blue autumn sky. Each leaf has five multi-pointed lobes. Maples turn early in the season and are found at elevations up to 4,500 feet. **See it:** Sugarlands Valley (TN), Cataloochee (NC), Newfound Gap Road (NC and TN).

❸ Sumac
Sumac are small shrubs, but inch for inch they pack more fall color than almost any other tree in the mountains. You'll recognize them for their bright scarlet leaves and oblong clusters of red fruit. Staghorn sumac grows along roadsides at up to 5,500 feet. **See it:** Newfound Gap Road (NC and TN).

❹ Sourwood
In the fall, the sourwood leaves are among the first to turn, glowing deep red and orange. At this time the sourwood also bears sprays of small green fruit. The leaves have a slight sour taste. **See it:** low to middle elevations off Parson Branch Road (TN).

❺ Sweetgum
The spiny ball-shaped fruits of the American sweetgum can be annoying to step on, but the trees' showy fall colors make up for it. Orange-yellow and red leaves mix with dark purple and smoky brown. Sweetgums turn around the middle of the season. These medium-size hardwoods, grow at the lower elevations, especially near creeks and streams. **See it:** Cades Cove (TN), Lower Little Pigeon River (TN).

● =Common ● =Somewhat Common ● =Rare

CHOOSE YOUR DAY HIKE

Whether you just want to stretch your legs or you have a yen to climb a mountain, the Smokies has a hike for you. Here are a few of our favorite hikes to waterfalls, scenic overlooks, and historic sites.

Tom Branch waterfall, Deep Creek

BEST HIKES TO WATERFALLS

ABRAMS FALLS, TN

Moderate, 5 miles round-trip, 3 hours

From the trailhead off Cades Cove Loop Road, follow Abrams Creek to Abrams Falls, where you can take a dip in a lovely natural pool below the falls framed by laurel and rhododendron.

LAUREL FALLS, TN

Easy, 2.6 miles round-trip, 1.5 hours

Off Little River Road, this popular trail to 75-foot, multi-level Laurel Falls is paved and offers a mostly gentle walk in the woods. It's suitable for kids and strollers, though the trail is narrow in places with steep drop-offs.

THREE WATER-FALLS LOOP, NC

Easy, 2.4 miles round-trip, 1.5 hours

About 3 miles by car from Bryson City, Deep Creek offers something for the entire family, with river tubing, mountain biking, fishing, and several loop trails including this easy loop, which takes you by three small falls.

TRILLIUM GAP TRAIL TO GROTTO FALLS, TN

Moderate, 2.6 miles round-trip, 2 hours

From the trailhead off Roaring Fork Motor Trail, Trillium Gap Trail gains over 400 feet in elevation, crossing several small streams and passing old-growth hemlocks before reaching 30-foot Grotto Falls, the only falls in the park that you can walk behind.

BEST HIKES TO OVERLOOKS

CLINGMANS DOME TRAIL, NC

Moderate, 1 mile round-trip, 1 hour

Paved but steep, this trail leads you to the 6,643-foot Clingmans Dome, crosses the Appalachian Trail, and ends at a 54-foot tall observation tower with stunning views of the Smokies.

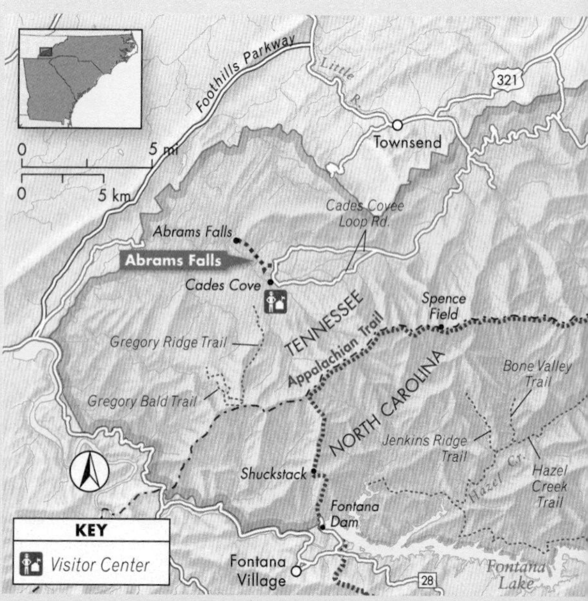

BEST HIKES TO HISTORIC SITES

KEPHART PRONG, NC

Moderate, 4 miles round-trip, 3 hours

Named for Horace Kephart, who was an advocate for the establishment of the park, the trail crosses the Oconaluftee River six times over footbridges, passing remains of a 1930s Civilian Conservation Corps camp that was later used to house conscientious objectors during World War II.

Clingmans Dome

Hikers in Great Smoky Mountains National Park

LITTLE CATALOOCHEE TRAIL, NC

Moderate, 5.9 miles one way, 6 hours

The Little Cataloochee Trail is one of the Smokies' most historically rich hikes, passing several old cabins and houses, cemeteries, a church, school, and other relics of early 20th-century life in the Cataloochee Valley before the coming of the national park. We recommend using a two-car shuttle for this hike.

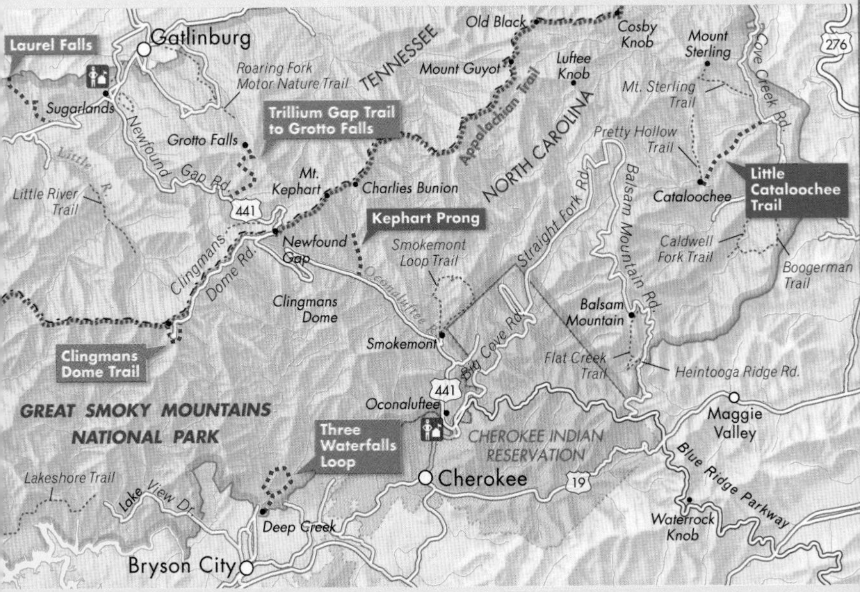

FUN SUMMER ACTIVITIES

Rafting on the Nantahala River

Summer is prime time for outdoor fun in the park and nearby.

BIKING

Main roads have a lot of traffic and lack bike lanes. For safer biking, choose back roads such as Balsam Mountain Road (NC) and Cove Creek Road (NC). A hybrid or mountain bike is best on these unpaved roads. For mountain biking, try the Tsali Recreation Area.

Best places to bike: Cades Cove Loop (TN), an 11-mile paved road, is closed to motor vehicles Wednesday and Saturday mornings until 10. Cataloochee Valley (NC) is another good place to bike.

BOATING

Rent a powerboat or pontoon boat and enjoy a lazy day on the water.

Best place for boating: Fontana Lake, bordering the southern edge of the park in North Carolina, has power and pontoon boats for rent.

FISHING

There's top-notch trout fishing in the 2,100 miles of trout streams in the park. You can catch rainbow, brown, and the native brook trout. Only artificial lures and flies can be used, not live bait.

Best places to fish: In North Carolina, Deep Creek, Little Cataloochee, and Hazel Creek are good trout streams. Little River, Abrams Creek, and Little Pigeon River are good choices on the Tennessee side.

RAFTING

Ride the white water! You can take a guided rafting trip, or rent your own raft on several rivers in and near the Smokies.

Best places to raft: The Nantahala just outside the park on the North Carolina side is the most popular river for rafting. On the Tennessee side, the Big Pigeon River offers rafting in mild white water.

TUBING

Few things are more pleasant than floating down a refreshing stream on a hot day. You can rent a large inner tube for less than $10 a day.

Best places to tube: Deep Creek (NC) and Little River (TN).

Cades Cove has a number of historical houses, log cabins, and barns.

families. Typical is the view across the valley from the front porch of the Dan Lawson Cabin, the original portion of which was built in 1856. ✉ *Cades Cove Loop Rd., Townsend* ☎ *865/436–1200* 🌐 *www.nps.gov/grsm.*

★ Elkmont Historic District

HISTORIC SITE | FAMILY | What began as a logging town in the early years of the 20th century evolved into a summer colony for wealthy families from Knoxville, Chattanooga, and elsewhere in Tennessee. Many prominent east Tennessee families bought land here and built vacation homes and the Wonderland Hotel. After the national park was established, parts of Elkmont were placed on the National Registry of Historic Places. Today, Elkmont is primarily a campground, although many of the original 74 cottages remain along Jakes Creek and Little River. Most of the cottages are at the far end of the campground—follow the Elkmont Nature Trail or drive along a separate paved road off Little River Road. In recent years, the Park Service has been stabilizing and restoring several homes along Jakes Creek. Four cabins were restored in 2017 and are open to the public. The Appalachian Clubhouse, built for a hunting and fishing club, has been restored to its 1930s appearance, complete with rocking chairs on the porch. ✉ *Little River Rd., Great Smoky Mountains National Park* ✣ *4½ miles west of Sugarlands Entrance* ☎ *865/436–1200* 🌐 *www.nps.gov/grsm/planyourvisit/elkmont.htm.*

Roaring Fork

NATIONAL/STATE PARK | FAMILY | Roaring Fork was settled by Europeans beginning in the 1830s. At its height around the turn of the 20th century, there were about two dozen families in the area. Most lived a simple, hardscrabble existence, trying to scrape out a living from the rough mountain land. The Noah "Bud" Ogle Self-Guided Nature Trail, on Orchard Road just before entering the one-way Roaring Fork Motor Nature Trail, offers a walking tour of an authentic mountain farmstead and surrounding hardwood forest. Highlights include a log cabin, barn, streamside mill, and a wooden flume system to bring water to the farm. Among the historic structures on the Motor Nature Trail, all open for you to explore, are the Jim Bales Cabin, the Ephraim Bales Cabin, and the Alfred Reagan House, one of the more "upscale" residences at Roaring Fork. ✉ *Orchard Rd., Great Smoky Mountains National Park* ☎ *865/436–1200* 🌐 *www.nps.gov/grsm/planyourvisit/roaringfork.htm* ⏲ *Closed late Nov.–Mar.*

PICNIC AREAS

Cades Cove Picnic Area

NATIONAL/STATE PARK | **FAMILY** | This picnic area, near the beginning of the Cades Cove Loop, has 81 picnic tables open all year. Its big advantage is that it's near the beautiful Cades Cove valley; the disadvantage is that as many as 2 million people come through this area each year. Also, at only 1,800 feet high, it can be hot and humid in summer. Potable water and flush toilets are available. Bears are fairly common, so closely observe food storage precautions. Several trailheads are at the picnic area. There is a campground store here that sells hot dogs, burgers, ice cream, basic grocery supplies, and firewood; it also rents bikes. ✉ *Great Smoky Mountains National Park* ✣ *9 miles east of Townsend, near the entrance to Cades Cove Loop and near the Cades Cove campground* 🌐 *www.nps.gov/grsm.*

★ Chimneys Picnic Area

NATIONAL/STATE PARK | **FAMILY** | Chimneys, just off Newfound Gap Road and a little more than 6 miles from the Sugarlands Visitor Center, may be the most loved picnic area in the park. Along both sides of a well-shaded loop road through the area are 68 picnic tables with grills. Some are wheelchair accessible. The prime spots along the wadeable stream that runs through the site fill up first. Huge boulders in the stream make for a striking view from your table. Potable water and flush toilets are available, but there is no group pavilion. ✉ *Newfound Gap Rd. (U.S. 441), MM 6.2, Gatlinburg* 🌐 *www.nps.gov/grsm* ⏲ *Closed late Nov.–mid-Mar.*

Cosby Picnic Area

NATIONAL/STATE PARK | **FAMILY** | On the northeast edge of the park, this picnic area has 35 tables in well-tended grassy areas under large poplar trees. Cosby Creek runs through the grounds. A wheelchair-accessible pavilion seats 55 and can be reserved for $25. There's a ranger station, restrooms, trailheads, and horse trails. Cosby has easy access from Interstate 40 via the Foothills Parkway and Tennessee State Route 32. ✉ *Cosby* ✣ *Off Exit 443 of I–40 via the eastern section of the Foothills Pkwy. and TN 32* 🌐 *www.nps.gov/grsm* ⏲ *Closed late Oct.–late Mar.*

Greenbrier Picnic Area

NATIONAL/STATE PARK | **FAMILY** | Greenbrier is one of the two smallest picnic areas in the park, with only 12 tables near a shady, boulder-strewn creek, plus a pavilion that seats 70 and can be reserved for $12.50. This picnic area off U.S. Route 321 is rarely busy, and it's one of only four in the park that's open year-round. There is a ranger station here and restrooms with pit toilets but no running water. The Ramsey Cascades Trail is nearby, leading to the Ramsey waterfalls about 4 miles away. ✉ *Great Smoky Mountains National Park* ✣ *Off U.S. 321 northeast of Sugarlands Visitor Center* 🌐 *www.nps.gov/grsm.*

Look Rock Picnic Area

LOCAL INTEREST | **FAMILY** | Accessed via the western section of the beautiful Foothills Parkway, Look Rock Picnic Area is almost never crowded. A ½-mile hike takes you to the observation tower, which offers panoramic views into the Smokies. There are 51 picnic tables, restrooms, and a ranger station. ✉ *Look Rock Picnic Area Rd., Off Foothills Pkwy., Great Smoky Mountains National*

Park ☎ 865/436–1200 ⊕ www.nps.gov/grsm/planyourvisit/picnic.htm ⊙ Closed Nov.–mid-May.

Metcalf Bottoms Picnic Area

LOCAL INTEREST | FAMILY | Midway between the Sugarlands Visitor Center and Cades Cove, Metcalf Bottoms Picnic Area is a great place to stop along the way. The Little River is nearby, where you can fish or take a cooling dip. There are restrooms with flush toilets, potable water, and a 70-seat pavilion (open early April to late October) that can be reserved in advance. Two easy hiking trails, Metcalf Bottoms and Little Brier, begin at the picnic area. ✉ *Metcalf Bottoms Picnic Area Rd., off Little River Rd., Gatlinburg* ☎ *865/436–1200* ⊕ *www.nps.gov/grsm/planyourvisit/picnic.htm.*

SCENIC DRIVES

★ Cades Cove Loop Road

SCENIC DRIVE | FAMILY | This 11-mile loop through Cades Cove is the most popular route in the park and arguably the most scenic part of the Smoky Mountains. The one-way, one-lane paved road starts 7.3 miles from the national park's Townsend Entrance. Stop at the orientation shelter and pick up a tour booklet. The drive begins with views over wide pastures to the mountains at the crest of the Smokies. Few other places in the Appalachians offer such vistas across wide valleys with hayfields and wildflower meadows framed by split-rail fences and surrounded by tall mountains. Along the way, you'll pass three 19th-century churches and many restored houses and barns that are open for exploration. A highlight is the Cable Mill area, with a visitor center, working water-powered gristmill, and a restored farmstead. The Cades Cove Loop Road is also an excellent place to see wildlife, including black bears, white-tailed deer, and wild turkeys. Whenever you visit, even in winter, you can expect traffic delays, as passing points on the one-way road are few and far between. Allow at least two to three hours to drive the loop, longer if you want to stop and explore the historic buildings. If you get frustrated with delays, there are two points at which you can cut across the loop on improved gravel roads, exiting sooner. A campground and picnic area are open year-round. The road is closed from sunset to sunrise. ✉ *Cades Loop Rd. , off Laurel Creek Rd., Townsend* ☎ *865/436–1200* ⊕ *www.nps.gov/grsm/planyourvisit/cadescove.htm.*

Foothills Parkway

SCENIC DRIVE | FAMILY | A 72-mile scenic roadway, Foothills Parkway has long been planned to parallel the northern, western, and southwestern edges of the Great Smoky Mountains National Park, providing dramatic views of the Smokies. Construction began in the 1960s, but due to funding problems it still hasn't been completed. About 17 miles from U.S. Route 129 at Chilhowee Lake to U.S. Route 321 at Walland were completed in 1966. In late 2018, another 16-mile section of the parkway was opened, connecting with this original section and running to Wears Valley. A 5.6-mile section runs from Interstate 40 south to U.S. Route 321. In between these sections are more than 33 miles where construction has not even begun. Rights-of-way have been purchased, but there is no state or federal money to build it. Known as the "Tail of the Dragon," a serpentine section of U.S. Route 129 is popular with motorcycle and sports car enthusiasts; it connects with the end of the Foothills Parkway at Chilhowee. ✉ *Gatlinburg* ☎ *865/436–1200* ⊕ *www.nps.gov/places/foothills-parkway.htm.*

★ Newfound Gap Road

SCENIC DRIVE | FAMILY | In a little more than 14 miles, Newfound Gap Road climbs more than 3,500 feet, from Gatlinburg to the gap through the crest of the Smokies at 5,046 feet. It takes you through Southern cove hardwood, pine-oak, and Northern hardwood forests to the spruce-fir forest at Newfound Gap. Unlike other roads in the park, Newfound Gap Road has mile markers, starting at the park entrance near Gatlinburg. The Sugarlands Visitor Center is at mile marker 1.7. At Newfound Gap (mile marker 14.7), you can straddle the Tennessee–North Carolina state line and also hike some of the Appalachian Trail. ✉ *U.S. Rte. 441 MM 14.7, Great Smoky Mountains National Park* ☎ *865/436–1200* 🌐 *www.nps.gov/grsm/planyourvisit/nfg.htm.*

Parson Branch Road

SCENIC DRIVE | **FAMILY** | Following a wagon track, this 8-mile unpaved road has been used for more than 150 years. Some believe that Parson Branch Road was named for ministers who held religious retreats nearby, but others believe they were named for Joshua Parson, an early settler in the area. The road begins at the southwestern edge of Cades Cove Loop Road just beyond the visitor center at the Cable Mill. Although unpaved, it doesn't require four-wheel drive except after heavy rains, when a few sections may become flooded or muddy. It offers no scenic vistas, but it runs through old-growth forests, with huge poplars and hemlocks along the roadway. RVs are prohibited on this road. ✉ *Parson Branch Rd., off Cades Cove Loop Rd., Townsend* ☎ *865/436–1200* 🌐 *www.nps.gov/grsm/planyourvisit/seasonalroads.htm* ⏲ *Closed mid-Nov.–mid-Mar.*

★ Roaring Fork Motor Nature Trail

SCENIC DRIVE | **FAMILY** | The 6-mile Roaring Fork offers a dramatic counterpoint to Cades Cove Loop Road, which meanders through a wide-open valley. Roaring Fork closes in, with the forest sometimes literally just inches from your fender. The one-way, paved road is so narrow in places that RVs, trailers, and buses are not permitted. The trail starts just beyond the Noah "Bud" Ogle Farmstead and the Rainbow Falls trailhead. Stop and pick up a Roaring Fork Auto Tour booklet at the information shelter. Numbered markers along the route are keyed to 16 stops highlighted in the booklet. Along the road are many opportunities to get closer to nature. A favorite sight is the old Alfred Reagan House, which is painted in the original blue, yellow, and cream, "all three colors that Sears and Roebuck had," according to a story attributed to Mr. Reagan. There are several good hiking trails starting along the road, including the Trillium Gap Trail to Mt. LeConte. The road follows Roaring Fork Creek a good part of the way, and the finale is a small waterfall called "The Place of a Thousand Drips," right beside the road. ✉ *Roaring Fork Motor Nature Tr., Gatlinburg* ✥ *To get to Roaring Fork from Gatlinburg from the parkway (U.S. 441), turn onto Historic Nature Trail at stoplight No. 8 in Gatlinburg and follow it to the Cherokee Orchard Entrance to the park* ☎ *865/436–1200* 🌐 *www.nps.gov/grsm/planyourvisit/roaringfork.htm* ⏲ *Closed Dec.–Mar.*

SCENIC STOPS

Campbell Overlook

VIEWPOINT | **FAMILY** | Named for Carlos Campbell, a conservationist who was instrumental in helping to establish the park, Campbell Overlook provides a good view up a valley to Bull Head peak and, farther up, to Balsam Point. An exhibit at the overlook explains the different types of forests within the park. ✉ *Newfound Gap Rd., MM 3.9, Great Smoky Mountains National Park* 🌐 *www.nps.gov/grsm.*

Chimney Tops Overlook

VIEWPOINT | **FAMILY** | From any of the three overlooks grouped together on Newfound Gap Road, you'll have a good view of the Chimney Tops—twin peaks that cap 2,000-foot-high cliffs. Sadly, you'll also see dozens of dead fir and spruce trees, victims of the invasive woolly adelgids. ✉ *Newfound Gap Rd., MM 7.1, Gatlinburg* ☎ *865/436–1200* 🌐 *www.nps.gov/grsm.*

Gatlinburg Bypass Overlook

VIEWPOINT | This 4-mile roadway runs just north of Gatlinburg toward Pigeon Forge. It tracks around the side of Mt. Harrison. Take this route to avoid the stop-and-go traffic of downtown Gatlinburg when leaving or entering the park. The second overlook when headed out of the park toward Pigeon Forge has the best views of Gatlinburg and Mt. LeConte. ✉ *Gatlinburg Bypass* ☎ *865/436–1200* 🌐 *www.nps.gov/grsm.*

Gregory Bald

VIEWPOINT | From almost 5,000 feet on Gregory Bald, you have a breathtaking view of Cades Cove and Rich Mountain to the north and the Nantahala and Yellow Creek mountains to the south. You can also see Fontana Lake to the southeast. Many colorful rhododendrons grow on and around the bald, blooming in late June. Gregory Bald is one of only two balds in the Smokies that are being kept cleared of tree growth by the Park Service. This is a view that just a few thousand people a year will see, as it's reachable only by a strenuous hike via the Gregory Ridge Trail of more than 11 miles round-trip. The trailhead is at the end of Forge Creek Road in Cades Cove. ✉ *Gregory Ridge Trail, off Forge Creek Rd., Townsend* ☎ *865/436–1200* 🌐 *www.nps.gov/grsm.*

Look Rock

VIEWPOINT | **FAMILY** | The viewpoints looking east on the western section of the Foothills Parkway around Look Rock have remarkable vistas. This is also a great spot to enjoy the sunrise over the Smokies. Stargazers gather at the five overlooks south of the Look Rock exit because light pollution is especially low. ✉ *Foothills Pkwy., Great Smoky Mountains National Park* ☎ *865/436–1200* 🌐 *www.nps.gov/grsm.*

Roaring Fork Motor Nature Trail Site Number 3

VIEWPOINT | **FAMILY** | While most of the Roaring Fork Motor Nature Trail takes you on a narrow and winding one-way road through forested areas where the views are limited, at the beginning of the drive the first and second overlooks present good views of the distant mountain ridges. The best scenery is from the second overlook, marked as the number 3 site on the Roaring Fork auto tour. ✉ *Roaring Fork Motor Tr.* ☎ *865/436–1200* 🌐 *www.nps.gov/grsm* ⏲ *Closed late Nov.–Mar.*

TRAILS

★ Abrams Falls Trail

TRAIL | This 5-mile round-trip trail is one of the most popular in the Smokies, thanks to its trailhead location on Cades Cove Loop Road. Beginning at the wooden bridge over Abrams Creek, the trail first follows a pleasant course through rhododendron, then becomes steeper at a couple of points, especially near Arbutus Ridge. The path then leads above Abrams Falls and down to Wilson Creek. Though only about 20 feet high, the falls are beautiful, with a large volume of water and a broad pool below. ⚠ **It is dangerous to climb, jump from, or swim near the falls.** *Moderate.* ✉ *Cades Cove Loop Rd., between signposts 10 and 11, Townsend* ☎ *865/436–1200* 🌐 *www.nps.gov/grsm/planyourvisit/abrams-falls.htm.*

★ Alum Cave Trail

TRAIL | One of the best and most popular hikes in the national park, the fairly short 2.3-mile one-way hike to Alum Cave Bluffs contains some of the most interesting geological formations in the Smokies. Arch Rock, a natural arch created by millions of years of freezing and thawing, and Alum Bluffs, a large overhanging rock ledge, are the highlights. This very well-known trail does not offer much solitude, especially on weekends. From the bluffs you can continue on another 2.8 miles to

Deer are a common sight throughout the Great Smoky Mountains, especially in the early morning and at dusk.

reach Mt. LeConte, passing awe-inspiring mountain vistas. Alum Cave Bluffs is the shortest of five trail routes to LeConte Lodge, but it is also the steepest, with an elevation gain of over 2,700 feet. *Moderate.* ✉ *Newfound Gap Rd. MM 10.4., Great Smoky Mountains National Park* ☎ *865/436–1200* 🌐 *www.nps.gov/grsm/planyourvisit/chimneys-alternative-alum-cave-bluffs.htm.*

Appalachian Trail at Newfound Gap

TRAIL | For those who want to say they hiked part of the Appalachian Trail, this 72-mile section through the Great Smokies is a great place to start. Park in the Newfound Gap Overlook parking lot and cross the road to the trail. From Newfound Gap to Indian Gap, the trail travels 1.7 miles through high-elevation spruce and fir forests, and in late spring and summer there are quite a few wildflowers. The total round-trip distance is 3.4 miles. *Easy.* ✉ *Newfound Gap Overlook, Newfound Gap Rd., Great Smoky Mountains National Park* ☎ *865/436–1200* 🌐 *www.nps.gov/grsm/planyourvisit/nfg.htm.*

Chimney Tops Trail

TRAIL | Pant, wheeze, and gasp. This is a fairly short yet steep trail that will take a lot out of you, but it gives back a lot, too. The payoff for the difficult climb is one of the best views in the Smokies. In places the trail has loose rock (hiking poles are recommended), and the elevation gain is 1,350 feet. Some sections have steep stairs. A new observation deck was built roughly ¼ mile from the summit, with views of Mt. LeConte and the pinnacles. The total distance round-trip is 3.6 miles. *Difficult.* ✉ *Newfound Gap Rd., 6.9 miles from Sugarlands Visitor Center, Gatlinburg* ☎ *865/436–1200* 🌐 *www.nps.gov/grsm/planyourvisit/chimney-tops.htm* 🎫 *Free.*

Elkmont Nature Trail

TRAIL | **FAMILY** | This 1-mile loop is good for families, especially if you're camping at Elkmont. It passes by many of the remaining buildings in the Elkmont Historic District. Pick up a self-guided brochure at the start of the trail. *Easy.* ✉ *Little River Rd., Great Smoky Mountains National Park* ✥ *Near Elkmont*

Campground ☎ *865/436–1200* 🌐 *www.nps.gov/grsm/planyourvisit/elkmont.htm.*

Gatlinburg Trail

TRAIL | FAMILY | This is one of only two trails in the park where dogs and bicycles are permitted (the other one is Oconaluftee River Trail on the North Carolina side). Dogs must be on leashes. The 1.9-mile trail starts at Sugarlands Visitor Center and follows the Little Pigeon River. *Easy.* ✉ *Sugarlands Visitor Center, Newfound Gap Rd., Gatlinburg* ☎ *865/436–1200* 🌐 *www.nps.gov/grsm/planyourvisit/gatlinburg-trail.htm.*

★ Gregory Ridge Trail

TRAIL | In early summer, this difficult hike through old-growth forests to Gregory Bald offers an astounding display of hybrid flame azaleas. When there are three or more varieties of rhododendrons in an area, crossbreeding creates dozens of hybrid varieties with different colored blossoms. Even if you miss the rhododendron in bloom, Gregory Bald has great views of Cades Cove, Fontana Lake, and the surrounding mountains. Gregory Bald is named for Russell Gregory, a pre–Civil War settler who at one time had a cabin on the bald. Parts of the hike are strenuous because of the elevation gain, about 2,700 feet. The total distance round-trip is 11.2 miles, so get an early start if you're doing this as a day hike. *Difficult.* ✉ *Forge Creek Rd.* ☎ *865/436–1200* 🌐 *www.nps.gov/grsm.*

Laurel Falls Trail

TRAIL | FAMILY | This paved trail is fairly easy. It takes you past a series of cascades to a 60-foot waterfall and a stand of old-growth forest. The trail is extremely popular in summer and on weekends almost anytime (trolleys from Gatlinburg stop here), so don't expect solitude. The 1.3-mile paved trail to the falls is wheelchair accessible. The total round-trip hike is 2.6 miles. *Easy.* ✉ *Little River Rd., between Sugarlands Visitor Center and Elkmont Campground, Gatlinburg* ☎ *865/436–1200* 🌐 *www.nps.gov/grsm.*

The Appalachian Trail

Each spring nearly 3,000 hikers set out to conquer the 2,190-mile Appalachian Trail. Most hike north from Springer Mountain, Georgia, toward Mt. Katahdin, Maine. By the time they get to the Great Smokies, 160 miles from the trailhead in Georgia, about half the hikers will already have dropped out. Typically, fewer than 800 hikers per year complete the entire AT, which takes an average of 165 days. At Newfound Gap Overlook, you can get on it for a short hike on the North Carolina–Tennessee line.

Little River Trail

TRAIL | This 5.1-mile loop (if Cucumber Gap and Jakes Creek trails are included) offers a little of everything—historical buildings, a waterfall, and wildflowers. The first part of the trail wanders past remnants of old logging operations and cottages that were once the summer homes of wealthy Tennesseans. Huskey Branch Falls appears at about 2 miles. The Little River Trail passes a junction with three other trails, offering the possibility for even longer hikes—Cucumber Gap at 2.3 miles, Huskey Gap at 2.7 miles, and Goshen Prong Trail at 3.7 miles. The trail is normally open even in winter. This is the habitat of the synchronous fireflies, which put on their light show on late May and June evenings. *Moderate.* ✉ *Little River Rd. , near Elkmont Campground, Gatlinburg* ☎ *865/436–1200* 🌐 *www.nps.gov/grsm.*

Sugarlands Valley Trail

TRAIL | FAMILY | The easiest trail in the park, it's only a quarter mile, virtually level, and paved, so it's suitable for young children, strollers, and wheelchairs. A brochure available at the start explains the numbered exhibits and features of the trail. *Easy.* ✉ *Newfound Gap Rd., south of Sugarlands Visitor Center, Gatlinburg* ☎ *865/436–1200* 🌐 *www.nps.gov/grsm.*

Trillium Gap Trail

TRAIL | FAMILY | Grotto Falls is the only waterfall in the park that you can walk behind. The Trillium Gap Trail, off the Roaring Fork Motor Nature Trail, takes you there through a hemlock forest. Only 1.3 miles long, with an easy slope, this trail is suitable for novice hikers and is one of the most popular in the park. The total round-trip distance to Grotto Falls is 2.6 miles. Trillium Gap Trail continues on to LeConte Lodge. It is a horse trail, and llamas resupplying the lodge also use it. *Easy.* ✉ *Roaring Fork Motor Nature Tr., Gatlinburg* ☎ *865/436–1200* 🌐 *www.nps.gov/grsm.*

VISITOR CENTERS

Cades Cove Visitor Center

INFO CENTER | FAMILY | Located near the midway point on the highly popular 11-mile Cades Cove Loop, the Cades Cove Visitor Center is especially worth visiting to see the Cable Mill, which operates spring through fall, and the Becky Cable House, a pioneer home with farm outbuildings. ✉ *Cades Cove Loop Rd., Great Smoky Mountains National Park* ☎ *865/436–1200* 🌐 *www.nps.gov/grsm/planyourvisit/visitorcenters.htm.*

Sugarlands Visitor Center

INFO CENTER | FAMILY | The main visitor center on the Tennessee side, Sugarlands features extensive exhibits in a nature museum about park flora and fauna, as well as a 20-minute film about the park. Ranger-led programs are held from spring to fall. There are hiking trails nearby. ✉ *1420 Fighting Creek Gap Rd.* ☎ *865/436–1200* 🌐 *www.nps.gov/grsm/planyourvisit/visitorcenters.htm.*

Hotels

★ LeConte Lodge

$$$$ | B&B/INN | FAMILY | Set at 6,360 feet near the summit of Mt. LeConte, this hike-in lodge is remote, rustic, and remarkable. **Pros:** unique setting high on Mt. LeConte; a true escape from civilization; breakfast and dinner included in rates. **Cons:** books up many months in advance; few modern conveniences; hike-in access only. $ *Rooms from: $303* ✉ *End of Trillium Gap Trail, Great Smoky Mountains National Park* ☎ *865/429–5704* 🌐 *www.lecontelodge.com* ⏲ *Closed mid-Nov.– late Mar.* *10 rooms* *Some meals.*

Shopping

The Sugarlands, Townsend, and Cades Cove Visitor Centers have attractive gift shops and bookstores, with first-rate selections of books and maps on the Smokies and nearby mountain areas, as well as some souvenirs. There is a small convenience store with some picnic and camping items, along with a snack bar at the Cades Cove Campground. Firewood is available at the Cades Cove and Elkmont Campgrounds. For groceries, camping supplies, and other shopping items outside the national park, your best bet is Sevierville. Pigeon Forge, Townsend, and Gatlinburg also have grocery stores and other places to stock up.

Activities

BIKING

Tennessee requires that youth age 16 and under wear a helmet, though it's strongly recommended that all riders do so, regardless of age.

Cades Cove Loop Road. Arguably the best place to bike in the national park, this 11-mile loop is mostly level and takes you through some lovely scenery. Vehicle traffic can be heavy, especially on weekends in summer and fall. Serious cyclists come here from early May to late September, when the loop is closed to motor vehicles on Wednesday and Saturday morning until 10. Bicycles and helmets can be rented in summer and fall at the Cades Cove Campground.

Foothills Parkway West. Parts of this scenic 72-mile road have light vehicular traffic, making it a fairly safe place for bicycling.

Gatlinburg Trail. This is the only hiking trail on the Tennessee side where bikes are permitted. The trail takes you 1.9 miles from the Sugarlands Visitor Center to the outskirts of Gatlinburg. Pets on leashes are also allowed on this trail.

Parsons Branch Road. This narrow, unpaved back road twists and dips from near the Cable Mill on the Cades Cove Loop Road to U.S. Route 129.

CAMPING

No matter your style of camping, there are plenty of campgrounds in the national park. Reservations for campgrounds on the Tennessee side can be made online or by phone up to six months in advance.

Backcountry permits are required for overnight camping, hiking, or backpacking, and generally cost $4 per night. Advance reservations are required for all backcountry campsites.

Abrams Creek Campground. Beside a meandering creek, this 16-site campground sits on the extreme western edge of the park, way off the beaten path. Although it sits at an elevation of 1,125 feet, summers can be hot and humid. Several excellent hiking trails, including Gold Mine, Cane Creek, Rabbit Creek, and Little Bottoms, begin at or near the campground. It's closed late October through late April. The daily fee is $17.50. ✉ *Abrams Creek Campground Rd., off Happy Valley Rd.* ☎ *865/436–1200* 🌐 *www.nps.gov/grsm.*

Cades Cove Campground. One of the largest campgrounds in the Smokies, the 159-site Cades Cove Campground also has the most on-site services. It has a small general store with a snack bar, bike rentals, horse stables, and an amphitheater. In spring it's covered with wildflowers, while in the fall the maples turn vivid reds and yellows. It's one of just two campgrounds in the national park that are open year-round (the other is Smokemont on the North Carolina side). This is a popular campground and often fills up in summer and fall, and reservations can be made up to six months in advance. The fee is $25. ✉ *10042 Campground Dr., at entrance to Cades Cove Loop Rd.* ☎ *865/448–2472* 🌐 *www.recreation.gov.*

Cosby Campground. Set among poplars, hemlocks, and rhododendrons, Cosby Campground sits near Cosby and Rock Creeks. Most of the campsites are reserved for tents, and RVs and trailers are limited to 25 feet. Bears are fairly common in the area, and several campsites may be temporarily closed due to bear activity. Nearby are the trailheads for the Snake Den Ridge and Gabes Mountain Trails. This rarely busy campground nearly always has sites available. It's closed November through early April. The daily fee is $17.50. ✉ *127 Cosby Park Rd., off TN 32* ☎ *423/487–2683* 🌐 *www.recreation.gov.*

Elkmont Campground. Easy access to hiking trails and swimming in the Little River make Elkmont ideal for families with kids. Nearby is the Elkmont Historic District, which has old vacation cabins to explore. Even though Elkmont is the largest campground in the park, with 200 tent and RV sites available, it is often fully booked. Rates are $25 to $27. Spots can be reserved up to six months in advance. It's closed early November through late March. ✉ *434 Elkmont Rd.* ☎ *877/444–6777* 🌐 *www.recreation.gov.*

EDUCATIONAL OFFERINGS

Great Smoky Mountains Institute at Tremont

TOUR—SPORTS | **FAMILY** | Located within the national park at Tremont, this residential environmental education center offers a variety of programs year-round for student groups, teachers, and families. Programs include photography, crafts, and backpacking trips. Accommodations are in Caylor Lodge, a climate-controlled dormitory that sleeps up to 125 people, as well as in tents on platforms. Meals are served family style in a large dining hall. Some 5,000 students and adults attend programs each year. ✉ *9275 Tremont Rd., Townsend* ☎ *865/448–6709* 🌐 *www.gsmit.org.*

Smoky Mountain Field School

TOUR—SPORTS | **FAMILY** | The University of Tennessee's Smoky Mountain Field School offers noncredit workshops, hikes, and outdoor adventures for adults and families. Participants choose from among more than 30 weekend programs held at various locations within the park. Fees vary, ranging from around $69 for courses such as wildflower identification and wild food foraging to $249 for a hike and overnight stay at LeConte Lodge. ✉ *Knoxville* ☎ *865/974–0150* 🌐 *smfs.utk.edu* ⏲ *No classes mid-Nov.–Feb.*

FISHING

There are more than 200 miles of wild trout streams on the Tennessee side of the park. Trout streams are open to fishing year-round. Among the best trout streams on the Tennessee side are Little River, Abrams Creek, and Little Pigeon River.

Everyone over 15 must possess a valid fishing license or permit from Tennessee or North Carolina. Either state license is valid throughout the park, and no trout stamp is required. Fishing licenses are not available in the park but may be purchased in nearby towns and online from the Tennessee Wildlife Resource Agency (🌐 *www.* tn.gov/twra.html).

For backcountry trips, you may want to hire a guide. Full-day fishing trips cost about $250–$300 for one angler, $250–$350 for two. Only guides approved by the National Park Service are permitted to take anglers into the backcountry.

Little River Outfitters

FISHING | This large fly-fishing shop and school has been in business since 1994. It specializes in fly tying and other skills. Although it does not offer guide services, it can hook you up with guides for fishing in the Smokies or elsewhere. ✉ *106 Town Square Dr., Townsend* ☎ *865/448–9459* 🌐 *www.littleriveroutfitters.com.*

Smoky Mountain Angler

FISHING | This well-equipped fly-fishing shop offers equipment rentals, fishing licenses, and half-day and full-day fly- and spin-fishing trips with one of its half dozen guides. Full-day guided trout fishing trips in the park are around $275 for one person and $325 for two. ✉ *469 Brookside Village Way, Gatlinburg* ☎ *865/436–8746* 🌐 *www.smokymountainangler.com.*

HIKING

The national park has more than 800 miles of hiking trails, about half of which are on the Tennessee side. The trails range from short nature walks to long, strenuous hikes that gain several thousand feet in elevation. Park trails are well maintained most of the year, but be prepared for erosion and washouts December through May.

Weather in the park is subject to rapid change. A day in spring or fall might start out warm and sunny, but by the time you reach a mile-high elevation the temperature may be near freezing. The higher elevations of the park can get up to 85 inches of rain and snow annually.

Although permits are not required for day hikes, you must have a backcountry permit for overnight trips.

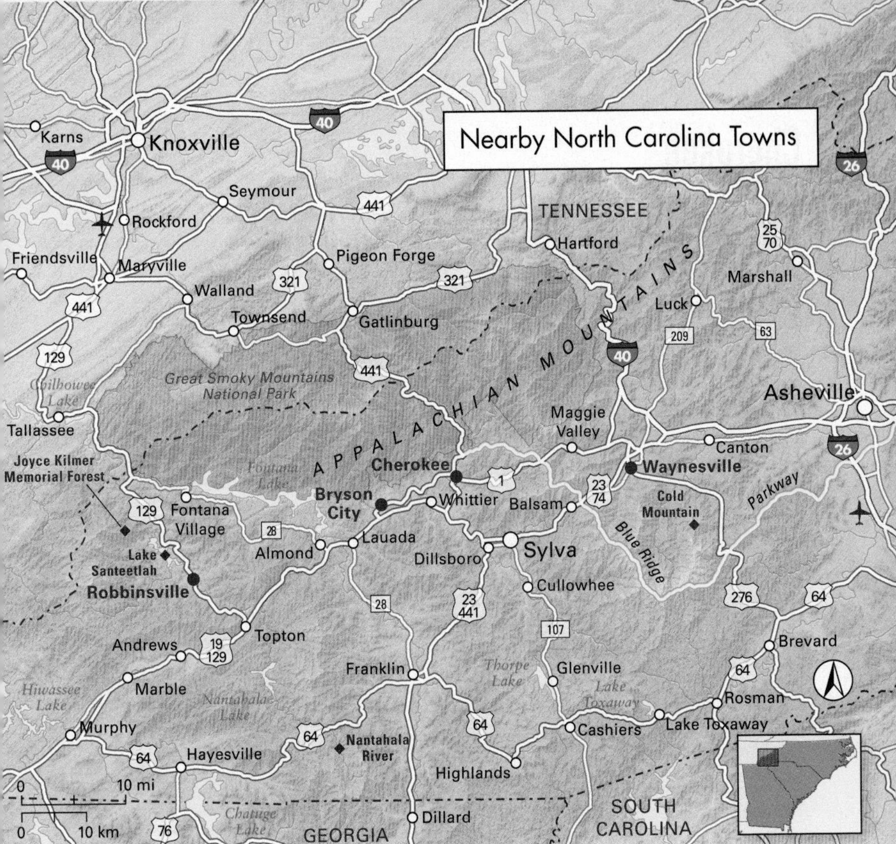

HORSEBACK RIDING

Several hundred miles of backcountry trails on the Tennessee side are open to horseback riders.

Cades Cove Riding Stables

HORSEBACK RIDING | FAMILY | Along with horseback riding this park concessionaire offers hayrides, carriage rides, and guided trail rides. It's first-come, first-served, with no reservations except for large groups. Call the stables to find out times and dates for ranger-led hayrides. Horseback riders must be at least six years old and weigh no more than 250 pounds. ✉ *Cades Cove Campground, 10042 Campground Dr., at entrance to Cades Cove Loop Rd., Townsend* ☎ *865/448–9009* 🌐 *www.cadescovestables.com* ⏲ *Closed Dec.–early Mar.* ☞ *From $15.*

TUBING

Little River is the most popular tubing river on the west side of the Smokies. It's mostly flat water, with a few mild rapids. Several outfitters in Townsend rent tubes and life jackets and provide shuttle buses or vans that drop you off upstream. Expect to pay from $10 to $18 per person. Outfitters are generally open May through September or October.

Smoky Mountain River Rat

WATER SPORTS | FAMILY | This outfitter, the best of the bunch in the Townsend area, offers tubing on the Little River during warmer months. Tube rental, life jacket, and a shuttle service is $18. ✉ *205 Wears Valley Rd., Townsend* ☎ *865/448-8888* 🌐 *www.smokymtnriverrat.com* ⏲ *Closed Nov.–Apr.*

Cherokee

178 miles east of Charlotte; 51 miles west of Asheville; 2 miles from entrance to Great Smoky Mountains National Park.

The Cherokee Qualla Boundary consists of almost 57,000 acres, and the town of Cherokee is its capital. Truth be told, there are two Cherokees. There's the Cherokee with the often-tacky pop culture, with junky gift shops full of cheap plastic "Indian crafts." These are designed to appeal to the lowest common denominator of the tourist masses. But there's another Cherokee that's a window into the rich heritage of the tribe's Eastern Band. Although now relatively small in number—Eastern Band tribal enrollment is about 14,000—these Cherokee and their ancestors have been responsible for keeping alive the Cherokee culture. They are the descendants of those who hid in the Great Smoky Mountains to avoid the Trail of Tears, the forced removal of the Cherokee Nation to Oklahoma in the 19th century. They are survivors, extremely attached to the hiking, swimming, trout fishing, and natural beauty of their ancestral homeland. You'll note that due to tribal efforts, all official signs in the Qualla Boundary, and many private commercial ones, are in the Cherokee language as well as in English. The reservation is dry, with no alcohol sales, except at the huge Harrah's casino complex. This means that there are few upscale restaurants in the area (because they depend on wine and cocktail sales for much of their profits), just fast-food and mom-and-pop places.

GETTING HERE AND AROUND

The Blue Ridge Parkway's southern terminus is at Cherokee, and the parkway is by far the most beautiful route to Cherokee and to Great Smoky Mountains National Park. A faster option is U.S. Route 23 and U.S. Route 74/441, connecting Cherokee with Interstate 40 from Asheville or from Franklin in the south. The least pleasant route is U.S. Route 19 from Interstate 40, a mostly two-lane road packed with touristy roadside shops.

VISITOR INFORMATION

CONTACTS Cherokee Welcome Center. ✉ *498 Tsali Blvd.* ☎ *800/438–1601* 🌐 *www.visitcherokeenc.com.*

Sights

★ Museum of the Cherokee Indian
MUSEUM | FAMILY | Covering 12,000 years of history, the Museum of the Cherokee Indian is one of the country's best Native American museums. Computer-generated images, video projections, and sound effects help bring to life events in the history of the Cherokee. For example, you'll see children stop to play a butter-bean game while adults shiver along the snowy Trail of Tears. The museum has an art gallery, a gift shop, and an outdoor living exhibit of Cherokee life in the 15th century. ✉ *589 Tsali Blvd.* ☎ *828/497–3481* 🌐 *www.cherokeemuseum.org* *$12.*

Oconaluftee Indian Village
NATIVE SITE | FAMILY | At the historically accurate Oconaluftee Indian Village, guides in traditional dress lead you through a 1760-era Cherokee village, while others demonstrate traditional skills, such as weaving, pottery, canoe construction, and hunting techniques. ✉ *564 Tsali Blvd.* ☎ *828/497–2111* 🌐 *www.visitcherokeenc.com/play/attractions/oconaluftee-indian-village* *$16* *Closed mid-Nov.–mid-Apr.*

Restaurants

Peter's Pancakes and Waffles
$ | AMERICAN | FAMILY | Pancake houses are big in Cherokee, and Peter's is at the top of the stack. Many locals are regulars here, and you'll see why when you try the blueberry pancakes with country ham in the dining room with wide windows overlooking the Oconaluftee River. **Known for:** breakfast served until the afternoon;

old-fashioned diner feel; perky service. *Average main: $8* *1384 Tsali Blvd.* *828/497–5116* *No dinner.*

Hotels

★ Harrah's Cherokee Casino Resort
$$$$ | HOTEL | The 21-story towers of North Carolina's largest lodging loom large over the mom-and-pop motels below. **Pros:** spa, fitness center, and indoor and outdoor pools; only place within the reservation selling alcohol; no need to ever leave the property. **Cons:** heavily booked year-round with high-rollers; state's no-smoking laws don't apply here; huge casino environment not for everyone. *Rooms from: $376* *777 Casino Dr.* *U.S. 19* *828/497–7777* *www.harrahscherokee.com* *1220 rooms* *No meals.*

Nightlife

Harrah's Casino
CASINOS | Owned by the Eastern Band of the Cherokee, Harrah's Casino has live blackjack, roulette, craps, and poker games along with some 5,000 electronic gaming machines in a huge casino larger than three football fields. Alcohol is available in the casino (the rest of the Cherokee Qualla Boundary is dry). Big-name stars like Chris Rock, Willie Nelson, and Reba McEntire provide entertainment at the casino's 3,000-seat theater. *777 Casino Dr.* *828/497–7777* *www.harrahscherokee.com.*

Performing Arts

Unto These Hills
THEATER | FAMILY | More than 6 million people have seen this colorful historical drama, which tells the story of the Cherokee people from about 1780 to the present day. First presented in 1950, the outdoor summertime spectacle has been updated over the years with new scripts and costumes. The show runs from early June to mid-August. Contemporary plays are also presented in the renovated 2,100-seat Mountainside Theater. *564 Tsali Blvd.* *828/497–2111* *www.cherokeesmokies.com/unto_these_hills.html* *From $28.*

Shopping

★ Qualla Arts and Crafts Mutual
CRAFTS | FAMILY | Across the street from the Museum of the Cherokee Indian, Qualla Arts and Crafts Mutual is the nation's oldest Native American co-op. It displays and sells items created by more than 250 Cherokee craftspeople. The store has a large selection of museum-quality baskets, masks, and wood carvings, some of which can cost hundreds of dollars. *645 Tsali Blvd.* *828/497–3103* *www.quallaartsandcrafts.com.*

Activities

FISHING

Cherokee Qualla Boundary
FISHING | FAMILY | There are 30 miles of regularly stocked trout streams on the Cherokee Indian Reservation, called the Qualla Boundary. The public can fish on most of the Raven Fork, Oconaluftee River, and Soco watersheds. To fish in these tribal waters you need a catch-and-keep fishing permit, available at many reservation businesses or online for $10. Fishing is permitted year-round, from dawn to one hour before dusk. Only artificial lures are permitted. A North Carolina fishing license is not required. *828/359–6110* *www.fishcherokee.com.*

GOLF

Sequoyah National Golf Club
GOLF | Owned by the Eastern Band of the Cherokee Nation, Sequoyah National Golf Club is open to the public. The challenging course, in a valley surrounded by green mountains, was designed by Robert Trent Jones II. It has groomed bent grass greens with bluegrass fairways.

Pricing varies significantly by day, time, and season. ✉ *79 Cahons Rd., Whittier* ☎ *828/538–4246* 🌐 *www.sequoyahnational.com* *$45, 18 holes, 6600 yds, par 72* *Reservations essential.*

HIKING

Oconaluftee Islands Park and Trail

HIKING/WALKING | **FAMILY** | In the downtown area of Cherokee you can cross the Oconaluftee River via a footbridge to the well-kept Oconaluftee Islands Park and Trail. The park has nice picnic facilities and walking trails. In warm weather, you can wade, tube, and swim in the river. On Thursday, Friday, and Saturday evenings in summer, there is often a bonfire and a Cherokee storyteller. ✉ *Tsali Blvd.* ☎ *800/438–1601* 🌐 *visitcherokeenc.com/play/outdoor-adventure/oconaluftee-islands-park.*

Bryson City

65 miles east of Asheville; 11 miles southwest of Cherokee.

Bryson City is a little mountain town on the Nantahala River, one of the lesser-known gateways to the Great Smokies. The town's most striking feature is the former city hall with a four-sided clock. Since becoming the depot and headquarters of the Great Smoky Mountains Railroad, the downtown area has been rejuvenated, mostly with gift shops, restaurants, craft breweries, and ice cream stands.

GETTING HERE AND AROUND

Bryson City is a 15-minute drive from Cherokee on U.S. Route 19. Near Bryson City are two entrances to the Great Smokies.

Sights

Great Smoky Mountains Railroad

TRANSPORTATION SITE (AIRPORT/BUS/FERRY/TRAIN) | **FAMILY** | Bryson City's historic train station is the departure point for the Great Smoky Mountains Railroad. Diesel or steam locomotives take you on a 32-mile journey along the Tuckasegee River or a 44-mile trip passing through the Nantahala Gorge. Trips are offered year-round, but with very limited schedules January to March. Open-sided cars or standard coaches are ideal for picture taking as the mountain scenery glides by. Your ticket gives you free admission to the nearby Smoky Mountain Trains Museum. ✉ *45 Mitchell St.* ☎ *800/872–4681 toll-free reservations line* 🌐 *www.gsmr.com* *From $56.*

★ Nantahala River

BODY OF WATER | **FAMILY** | The most popular river in western North Carolina for rafting and kayaking is the Nantahala, which races through the scenic Nantahala Gorge, a 1,600-foot-deep gorge that begins about 13 miles west of Bryson City on U.S. Route 19. Class III and Class IV rapids make for a thrilling ride. A number of outfitters run river trips or rent equipment. At several points along the river you can park your car and watch rafters run the rapids—on a summer day you'll see hundreds of rafts and kayaks going by. ✉ *Bryson City* ✣ *U.S. 19* ☎ *828/524–6441* 🌐 *www.fs.usda.gov.*

Swain County Heritage Museum

MUSEUM | Located in the gold-domed Swain County Courthouse dating from 1908, this charming museum has displays on the history of settlers of this mountain area, including a one-room schoolhouse and a log cabin. It also serves as a visitor information center for both Bryson City and Swain County and for the Great Smoky Mountains National Park. ✉ *255 Main St.* ☎ *828/488–7857* 🌐 *www.swainheritagemuseum.com.*

Restaurants

★ The Bistro at the Everett Hotel

$$$$ | **MODERN AMERICAN** | The best place to eat in Bryson City, this wood-paneled bistro serves hearty dinner entrées like mountain trout with quinoa and brown rice or meat loaf made from four different locally sourced specialty meats. It's in a rustic yet elegant space in a 1908 building that formerly housed Bryson City Bank. **Known for:** a favorite for any type of celebration; local twists on classic dishes; craft cocktails and craft beers. *Average main: $25 16 Everett St. 828/488–1934 www.theeveretthotel.com Closed Sun.-Tues.*

The High Test Deli and Sweet Shop

$ | **FAST FOOD** | **FAMILY** | This little sandwich shop is a popular place to grab a foot-long kosher hot dog, a roast beef hoagie, or a corned beef on rye, or you can opt for a bowl of chili. While you're waiting, look at the old service-station memorabilia. **Known for:** the Cuban sandwich is a local favorite; ice-cream sandwich cookies for dessert; friendly, upbeat owners. *Average main: $7 145 Everett St. 828/488–1919 www.thefillingstation-deli.com Closed Sun. and Mon.*

River's End

$ | **AMERICAN** | **FAMILY** | At Nantahala Outdoor Center, this eatery's riverside setting and high-energy atmosphere draw lots of hungry people returning from an invigorating whitewater rafting trip. Every seat has a view of the Nantahala River, and the menu is mostly salads, soups, and sandwiches. **Known for:** hearty, casual fare for adventurers; views of the Nantahala River; open year-round. *Average main: $12 Nantahala Outdoor Center, 13077 U.S. 19 W 828/488–7172 www.noc.com.*

Hotels

★ The Everett Hotel

$$$$ | **B&B/INN** | A handsome bank building in downtown Bryson City has been converted into this charming boutique hotel. **Pros:** surprisingly sophisticated rooms; good bistro on first floor; rooftop terrace with a firepit. **Cons:** priced a little higher than nearby lodgings; steps to climb; books up fast. *Rooms from: $279 16 Everett St. 828/488–1976 www.theeveretthotel.com 10 rooms Free breakfast.*

Hemlock Inn

$$ | **B&B/INN** | **FAMILY** | This folksy, friendly mountain inn on 55 acres on a hilltop near Bryson City, operated by the same family since 1969, is the kind of place where you can relax in a rocking chair, catch up on reading, or play a game of Scrabble. **Pros:** unpretentious vibe; delicious Southern-style food; peaceful surroundings. **Cons:** no Wi-Fi, TVs, or in-room phones; small a/c units may not do the job; no alcohol is served. *Rooms from: $195 911 Galbraith Creek Rd. 828/488–2885 www.hemlockinn.com 23 rooms Some meals.*

Nightlife

Mountain Layers Brewing Company

BARS/PUBS | Mountain Layers has a cozy bar adjoining the brewhouse on the first floor and another, larger space on the second floor with a rooftop deck with nice views of the mountains. It serves its own ales, porters, and stouts, but no food (but there's often a food truck parked out back). *90 Everett St. 828/538–0115 mountainlayersbrewingcompany.com.*

Activities

RIVER RAFTING AND KAYAKING

Alarka Boat Dock

BOATING | **FAMILY** | To rent a small powerboat on Fontana Lake, check with Alarka Boat Dock. A 16-foot boat with 20 horsepower outboard motor is $10 an hour or $50 a day, and a 24-foot pontoon boat is $250 a day or $150 for a half-day (each plus fuel). *7230 Grassy Branch Rd., off Lower Alarka Rd. 828/488–3841 www.alarkaboatdock.com.*

★ Nantahala Outdoor Center

WATER SPORTS | **FAMILY** | This center claims to be America's largest outdoor recreation company, with more than

1 million visitors a year arriving to raft on the mighty Nantahala, along with the Chattooga, Cheoah, French Broad, Nolichucky, Ocoee, and Pigeon Rivers. It also rents kayaks, mountain bikes, and other equipment. The bustling 500-acre complex is a tourist magnet, with three restaurants, a hotel, an outdoors store, a bike shop, a fly-fishing shop, and a stop for the Great Smoky Mountains Railroad. ✉ *13077 U.S. 19 W* ☎ *828/785–4834 local reservations* 🌐 *www.noc.com.*

Wildwater, Ltd.
WHITE-WATER RAFTING | FAMILY | This company offers whitewater rafting and kayaking on the Nantahala River, as well as ziplining for kids and adults. The operator also offers four-wheel-drive tours and glamping in yurts. ✉ *10345 U.S. 19 S/U.S. 74 W* ☎ *866/319–8870 toll-free reservations, 828/488–2384 Nantahala rafting* 🌐 *www.wildwaterrafting.com* 🎟 *Rafting on Nantahala River $50, kayaking from $25* 🕓 *Nov.–early Apr.*

Robbinsville

98 miles southwest of Asheville; 35 miles southwest of Bryson City.

If you truly want to get away from everything, head to the area around Robbinsville in the far southwest corner of North Carolina, a little south of the southern edge of the Great Smokies. The town of Robbinsville offers little, but the Snowbird Mountains, Lake Santeetlah, Fontana Lake, the rugged Joyce Kilmer–Slickrock Wilderness, and the Joyce Kilmer Memorial Forest, with its giant virgin poplars and sycamores, are definitely highlights of this part of North Carolina.

Sights

Joyce Kilmer Memorial Forest
FOREST | FAMILY | One of the last remaining sections of old-growth forests in Appalachia, Joyce Kilmer Memorial Forest, part of the 17,000-acre Joyce Kilmer–Slickrock Wilderness, has incredible 400-year-old yellow poplars that measure as large as 20 feet in circumference, along with huge hemlocks, oaks, and sycamores. If you haven't seen a true virgin forest, you can only imagine what America must have looked like in the early days of settlement. A 2-mile trail, moderately strenuous, takes you through wildflower- and moss-carpeted areas. During June, the parking lot is an excellent spot to see the light shows of the synchronous fireflies (*Photinus carolinus*), which blink off and on in unison. ✉ *5410 Joyce Kilmer Rd.* ☎ *828/479–6431* 🌐 *www.fs.usda.gov* 🎟 *Free.*

Lake Santeetlah
BODY OF WATER | FAMILY | Formed in 1928 with the construction of the Santeetlah Dam, Lake Santeetlah, meaning "blue waters" in the Cherokee language, has 76 miles of shoreline, with good fishing for crappie, bream, and lake trout. The lake is part of the Nantahala National Forest. ✉ *Cheoah Point Recreation Area , NC 1145* ☎ *828/479–6431* 🌐 *www.fs.usda.gov* 🎟 *Free.*

Hotels

Snowbird Mountain Lodge
$$$$ | B&B/INN | FAMILY | In the National Register of Historic Places, Snowbird Mountain Lodge is everything you expect in a rustic inn, with two massive stone fireplaces, solid chestnut beams across the ceiling, and beautiful views across the valley. **Pros:** 10,000 books in the impressive library; 100 acres of grounds to explore; historic flavor. **Cons:** remote location; books up fast; no kids under 12. $ *Rooms from: $325* ✉ *4633 Santeetlah Rd.* ☎ *828/479–3433* 🌐 *www.snowbirdlodge.com* 🛏 *23 rooms* 🍽 *All meals.*

Waynesville

17 miles east of Cherokee on U.S. 19.

This is where the Blue Ridge Parkway meets the Great Smokies. Waynesville is the seat of Haywood County. About 40% of the county is occupied by Great Smoky Mountains National Park, the Pisgah National Forest, and the Harmon Den Wildlife Management Area. The town of Waynesville is a rival of Blowing Rock and Highlands as a summer and vacation-home retreat for the well-to-do, though the atmosphere here is a bit more countrified. The compact downtown area is charming and walkable, and there are many small shops and restaurants.

Folkmoot USA, a two-week international festival that began in Waynesville in 1984 and is held annually in July, brings music and dancing groups from around the world to various venues in Waynesville and elsewhere in western North Carolina.

GETTING HERE AND AROUND

Waynesville is about 30 miles southwest of Asheville. From Asheville, take Interstate 40 West. At Exit 27, take U.S. Route 74 West to U.S. Route 23/74 West. At Exit 102, take U.S. Route 276 to Waynesville. If coming from Cherokee, about 19 miles west of Waynesville, you can take U.S. Route 74 East to U.S. Route 23 to Waynesville; the longer but much more scenic route is via the Blue Ridge Parkway. South Main Street is the main commercial street in Waynesville, lined for several blocks with small shops, craft breweries, and art galleries.

Sights

Cold Mountain

VIEWPOINT | FAMILY | The vivid best-selling novel by Charles Frazier, *Cold Mountain,* and its movie adaptation have made a destination out of the real Cold Mountain. About 15 miles from Waynesville in the Shining Rock Wilderness Area of the Pisgah National Forest, the 6,030-foot rise had long stood in relative anonymity. But with the success of Frazier's book, people want to see the region that Inman and Ada, the book's Civil War–era protagonists, called home. For a view of the splendid mass, stop at any of a number of overlooks off the Blue Ridge Parkway. Try the Cold Mountain Overlook, just past mile marker 411.9, or the Wagon Road Gap parking area, at mile marker 412.2. You can climb the mountain, but be prepared—the hike to the summit is strenuous. ✉ *Cold Mountain Overlook, Blue Ridge Parkway MM 411.9* ☎ *828/298–0398 parkway information line* 🌐 *www.nps.gov/blri.*

Museum of North Carolina Handicrafts

MUSEUM | Exhibits of 19th-century heritage crafts are on display at the Museum of North Carolina Handicrafts, located in the 1875 Shelton House. ✉ *49 Shelton St.* ☎ *828/452–1551* 🌐 *www.sheltonhouse.org* 🎟 *$7* ⏲ *Closed Sun. and Mon. and Nov.–Apr.*

Restaurants

Chef's Table

$$$$ | MODERN AMERICAN | At the region's most sought-after restaurant, chef-owner Josh Monroe uses ingredients from his own farm or other local farms to prepare dishes in an open kitchen. The award-winning menu includes dishes like lamb shank, trout, and deconstructed lasagna that are created with wine pairings in mind. **Known for:** hands-on chef who uses local ingredients; the best wine selection in town; alfresco dining on the patio. 💲 *Average main: $27* ✉ *30 Church St.* ☎ *828/452–6210* 🌐 *www.thechefstableofwaynesville.com.*

Frogs Leap Public House

$$$$ | SOUTHERN | This popular eatery partners with more than a dozen natural and organic producers to find the ingredients needed to create its rigorous "farm-to-fork" modern Southern menu, which changes frequently depending on what's in season. Several signature dishes, such as Sunburst trout and wood-grilled beef tenderloin, never leave the menu, and those are always dependable. **Known for:** charmingly rustic atmosphere; sophisticated meals; this place is a splurge. *$ Average main: $29 ✉ 44 Church St. ☎ 828/456–1930 🌐 www.frogsleappublichouse.com ⏲ Closed Sun. and Mon. and most of Jan. No lunch.*

The Sweet Onion

$$ | **SOUTHERN** | **FAMILY** | This casual downtown restaurant serves delicious Southern comfort food like country fried steak, meat loaf, shrimp and grits, and blackberry barbecue short ribs. Entrées come with two sides, so take your pick of mashed potatoes, collards, or fried okra. **Known for:** Southern comfort food; cheerful, friendly staff; beer and wine only. *$ Average main: $18 ✉ 39 Miller St. ☎ 828/456–5559 🌐 www.sweetonionrestaurant.com ⏲ Closed Sun. and Mon.*

Hotels

★ Andon-Reid Bed and Breakfast Inn

$$ | **B&B/INN** | The interior of this 1902 Victorian showplace is spacious and flooded with sunlight. **Pros:** hospitable owners know the area; cozy rooms and suites with fireplaces; delicious breakfasts served on the patio. **Cons:** a bit of a walk to downtown; steps to climb; often booked up. *$ Rooms from: $195 ✉ 92 Daisy Ave. ☎ 828/452–3089 🌐 www.andonreidinn.com 7 rooms Free breakfast.*

★ The Swag Country Inn

$$$$ | **B&B/INN** | Sitting high atop the Cataloochee Divide on 250 wooded acres bordering Great Smoky Mountains National Park, the Swag Country Inn has an away-from-it-all feel. **Pros:** nice touches like a sauna, hot tub, and racquetball court; fabulous location on a mile-high mountaintop; delicious meals included. **Cons:** two-night minimum stay; very expensive rates; books up fast. *$ Rooms from: $520 ✉ 2300 Swag Rd. ☎ 828/926–0430 🌐 www.theswag.com ⏲ Closed late Nov.–mid-Apr. 14 rooms All meals.*

The Yellow House on Plott Creek Road

$$ | **B&B/INN** | Just outside town, this lovely two-story Victorian, painted a cheerful sunflower yellow, sits on 5 acres with gorgeous gardens and hammocks under shady trees. **Pros:** warm and welcoming staff; great place to get away from it all; romantic atmosphere. **Cons:** very couples-oriented; not walking distance to restaurants and shops; no TVs in rooms. *$ Rooms from: $199 ✉ 89 Oak View Dr. ✥ At Plott Creek Rd., 1 mile west of Waynesville ☎ 828/452–0991 🌐 www.theyellowhouse.com 10 rooms Free breakfast.*

Nightlife

Frog Level Brewing Company

BREWPUBS/BEER GARDENS | Waynesville has several good craft brewers, but the original is still the best. Frog Level Brewing has a large, comfortable tasting room with lots of exposed brick and natural wood accents. In warm weather you can sit outside by the creek and enjoy beer and bar snacks. There's live music some nights. *✉ 56 Commerce St. ☎ 828/454–5664 🌐 www.froglevelbrewing.com.*

Chapter 7

MYRTLE BEACH, SC, AND THE GRAND STRAND

7

Updated by
Stratton Lawrence

Sights ★★★★★
Restaurants ★★★☆☆
Hotels ★★★★☆
Shopping ★★★☆☆
Nightlife ★★★★☆

WELCOME TO MYRTLE BEACH, SC, AND THE GRAND STRAND

TOP REASONS TO GO

★ **Sixty miles of beach:** From North Myrtle Beach south to Pawleys Island, Grand Strand sand is silky smooth—perfect for sunbathing and biking.

★ **Golf, golf, and more golf:** More than 100 golf courses for all skill levels meander through pine forests, dunes, and marshes.

★ **Southern culture:** Explore Southern culture and its troubled history on a plantation tour; taste it in the form of barbecue and other local foods; bring home a functional memento with a hammock woven right on Pawleys Island.

★ **Brookgreen Gardens:** More than 500 works from American artists are set among 250-year-old oaks, palms, and flowers in America's oldest sculpture garden.

★ **Water world:** Thanks to the area's rivers, waterways, inlets, and Atlantic coastline, you'll find yourself surrounded by water while you're here. Explore it any way you like: drop a hook, dip a toe or an oar, or dive right in and make your own waves.

Although most resort communities have beaches and water activities, the Grand Strand—the 60-mile stretch of beaches from Little River to Georgetown—is known for much more. Lush botanical gardens, quirky art galleries, theatrical shows, high-end and kitschy shopping, and fresh seafood are just some of the Strand's assets. Although other coastal communities, such as Charleston or Hilton Head Island, may cater to a wealthier lifestyle, the Grand Strand can accommodate a range of budgets.

1 **Myrtle Beach.** Walk the boardwalk, ride the SkyWheel, and enjoy family fun galore, from minigolf to go-karts to all-you-can-eat buffets.

2 **North Myrtle Beach.** Main Street is home to a row of clubs that hark back to the mid-20th century. Grab a partner and dance the shag in the place it originated.

3 **Murrells Inlet.** Stroll the Marsh Walk at sunset, and then dive into a plate of seafood (or catch your own) in this waterman's paradise.

4 **Pawleys Island.** Breathe deep, take a long walk on an uncrowded beach, and enjoy the slow pace of life on this quiet, family island.

5 **Georgetown.** Walk the historic waterfront and centuries-old downtown neighborhood before enjoying fine dining in this classic coastal town.

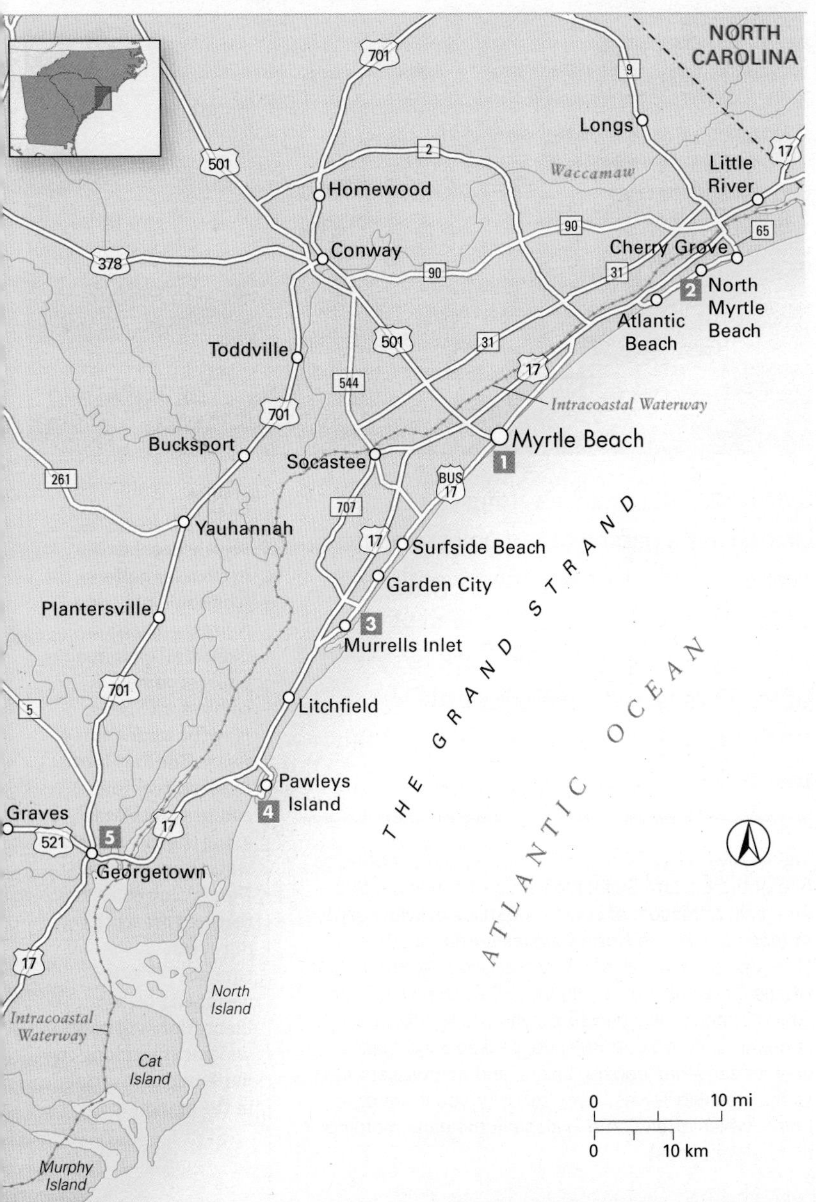
NORTH CAROLINA
Longs
Little River
Waccamaw
Homewood
Conway
Cherry Grove
North Myrtle Beach
Atlantic Beach
Toddville
Intracoastal Waterway
Myrtle Beach
Bucksport
Socastee
Yauhannah
Surfside Beach
Garden City
Plantersville
Murrells Inlet
Litchfield
Pawleys Island
Graves
Georgetown
THE GRAND STRAND
ATLANTIC OCEAN
North Island
Intracoastal Waterway
Cat Island
Murphy Island
0
10 mi
0
10 km

MYRTLE BEACH AND THE GRAND STRAND BEACHES

Myrtle Beach has a gorgeous strand—and so much more.

The broad, flat beaches along the Grand Strand are a patchwork of colorful coastal scenes—from the high-energy section of Myrtle Beach backed by a wall of hotel high-rises to the laid-back leisure of Pawleys Island, accessible only by two causeway bridges that cross the salt marsh.

The family-oriented Grand Strand is world-renowned as one of the Eastern Seaboard's megavacation centers. The main attraction, of course: 60 miles of white sand, stretching from the North Carolina border south to Georgetown, with Myrtle Beach as the hub. From North Myrtle Beach all the way down to Pawleys Island, the Grand Strand's silky beaches invite you to take your shoes off and relax. At low tide, packed sand makes way for early-bird joggers, bikers, and dog walkers next to the crashing waves. If you're lucky, you'll see dolphins, which often come in close in the early morning or just before sunset.

GOLF

Myrtle Beach is heaven for golfers, who could play two rounds a day for a month, all on immaculately groomed courses, and never play the same course twice. The Barefoot Resort offers four courses and vistas along the intracoastal waterway. The private Dunes Club course features breathtaking ocean views, and the Jack Nicklaus–designed Pawleys Plantation will have you putting among the pluff mud at low tide in the marshes.

MYRTLE BEACH

It's no secret **Myrtle Beach** is a big hit with families. The international praise it has received as a family destination put it on the summer vacation map, so if you're seeking peace and quiet, this isn't the place for you. What you will find here is a buzz of activity, from music spilling out of beachfront tiki bars to an overflow of excitement from the stretch of boardwalk shops and cafés between the piers at 14th and 2nd Avenues North. For sunseekers who prefer more peace, Myrtle Beach's residential section between 38th and 48th Avenues North, which is short on beach access parking (and thus people), is the best bet. **Myrtle Beach State Park,** just south of Springmaid Pier, is another peaceful spot with picnic areas, wooded nature trails, playgrounds, and a fishing pier.

NORTH MYRTLE BEACH

North Myrtle Beach is less crowded and steeped in history. You'll find a hodgepodge of smaller hotels, high-rises, and beach cottages along the coastline. North Myrtle's population increases in spring and fall when two national shag dance gatherings and two major motorcycle rallies take over the streets. The old shag dance clubs, as well as oodles of cute restaurants, still thrive along North Myrtle's Main Street. You may even see a few shaggers shuffling the dance steps on the sand, like they first did more than 50 years ago.

Family beach days are easy with so many amenities nearby.

You can rent sailboats along the beach.

SURFSIDE BEACH AND GARDEN CITY BEACH

Surfside Beach is a small, southern suburb of Myrtle Beach, touted as a family beach, that has a tight community of locals, parks, and a pier flanked by a block of seafood restaurants for visitors. **Garden City Beach** is south of Surfside off the Atlantic Avenue causeway, which ends at the Garden City Pier, boasting a fun arcade, fishing, and a one-of-a-kind bar that hosts live bands on summer nights. Garden City not only features beaches ocean-side but also has a beach inlet-side, called the Point, accessible by boat.

LITCHFIELD BEACH AND PAWLEYS ISLAND

When you go to the South Strand's **Litchfield Beach** and **Pawleys Island,** it's time to relax, slow down, and breathe in the fragrance of the saltwater marshes. Pawleys Island was once a summer retreat for wealthy rice plantation owners who lived inland and remains perfect for quiet relaxation. Kissing the northern cusp of Litchfield is **Huntington Beach State Park,** a coastal haven for hikers, bird-watchers, or history buffs.

The coastal beauty of the Myrtle Beach area is priceless, but its affordability for families helps rank this resort area as one of the most accessible beach destinations in the world. As Myrtle Beach's reputation as a family-friendly destination has grown, so have the size, sophistication, and number of activities available.

The main attraction is the broad, beckoning beach known as the Grand Strand—60 miles of white sand, stretching nearly from the North Carolina border to Pawleys Island, with Myrtle Beach centered at the hub. People come to "the Strand" for all of the traditional beach-going pleasures: swimming, sunbathing, sailing, surfing, shell hunting, fishing, jogging, and strolling. Away from the water, golfers have more than 100 courses to choose from, designed by the likes of Arnold Palmer, Robert Trent Jones, and Jack Nicklaus.

Golfing and beaching are far from "it" in Myrtle Beach, however. When it comes to diversions, you could hardly be better served, with acclaimed seafood restaurants, giant shopping complexes, trendy markets, factory outlets, Vegas-style live performance and concert venues, nightlife hot spots, amusement and water parks, arcades, a dozen shipwrecks for divers to explore, beachfront campgrounds, antique-car and wax museums, an award-winning aquarium, the world's largest outdoor sculpture garden, and a museum dedicated entirely to rice. There is a renewed interest in the oceanfront shops, ice cream parlors, restaurants, and arcades, and the beautiful new boardwalk is recapturing a pedestrian- and family-friendly Myrtle Beach that was alive with the Pavilion amusement park (demolished in 2006) in its 1960s heyday. The Myrtle Beach Boardwalk is constantly expanding with amusements and attractions, including the SkyWheel, one of the largest Ferris wheels on the East Coast by day and a sky-high spectacle at night.

You won't find centuries of history here—until 1901, Myrtle Beach didn't have an official name—but you'll find plenty of kitsch and nostalgia. More than 15 million people a year visit the region to stroll the boardwalk and see attractions like Family Kingdom amusement park, Broadway at the Beach, and Myrtle Waves Water Park. If a quiet vacation is more your speed, opt for dining in sophisticated restaurants following days lolling on relatively uncrowded beaches adjacent to the residential areas of Myrtle Beach at either end of the Strip.

⚠ **Be sure to take note of whether an establishment is on U.S. Route 17 Business or U.S. Route 17 Bypass—confusing the two could lead to hours of frustration. U.S. Route 17 Business is also referred to as Kings Highway.**

MAJOR REGIONS

The Myrtle Beach Area. Myrtle Beach has a colorful case of multiple personalities in its makeup, from exclusive resorts to gritty nostalgia. Try local muscadine wine, fill up at restaurants by renowned chefs, touch heaven in the SkyWheel Ferris wheel, play Skee-Ball at an oceanfront arcade, take in shops and variety shows, and of course, enjoy the miles of sandy beaches. North Myrtle Beach, including the small, waterfront fishing towns of Little River and Cherry Grove, has a diverse assortment of entertainment options, from casino riverboats to scuba diving in artificial reefs and shipwrecks to fishing off the Cherry Grove Pier. At the clubs along Main Street in North Myrtle Beach, learn about South Carolina's state dance, the shag, born on Ocean Drive.

The Southern Grand Strand. Where the busy highways and hotel high-rises of Myrtle Beach end at the border of Horry and Georgetown Counties, the South Strand begins. The coastal communities of Georgetown County—seafood-centric Murrells Inlet, arrogantly shabby Pawleys Island, and historic Georgetown—boast a slow-paced, rustic elegance. Poke around small shops surrounded by live oaks or sample the fresh catch of the day, with no pretense in sight.

Planning

When to Go

The Grand Strand was developed as a summer resort, and with its gorgeous beaches, flowering tropical plants, palmetto trees, and warm weather, it continues to shine during the height of the summer season. That said, the fall and spring shoulder seasons may be even better. Warm temperatures allow for beach activities, but the humidity drops, the crowds thin, and the heat of summer passes.

Winter—November through February—isn't usually considered a time to visit the beach, but the region can be quite pleasant. There are certainly cold days, but for the most part, golfers, tennis players, and other outdoors enthusiasts can enjoy their pursuits during these months—at rock-bottom prices.

■ TIP→ **From mid- to late May, much of the Grand Strand is inhabited by bikers in town for Myrtle Beach Bike Week and the Atlantic Beach BikeFest. Traffic and noise problems are common, and hotel space is scarce.**

Planning Your Time

Many visitors do Myrtle Beach in a long weekend: beach or golf by day, and nightlife, dining, and shows by night. But with the area's bounty of beaches, amusement parks, minigolf courses, and waterslides, you could easily fill a week, especially if you've got kids in tow. Enjoy the great outdoors by water or land (boardwalk, minigolf, and Market Common festivals year-round), or pass rainy days in indoor playgrounds with aquariums, museums, and arcades galore. If history is your passion, spend at least a day exploring Georgetown on foot, by boat, or with a guided tour. With all this to explore, we recommend you rent a car, as these treasures are spread out.

Getting Here and Around

AIR TRAVEL

Myrtle Beach International Airport (MYR) is served by Allegiant, American, Delta, Frontier, Porter, Spirit, Sun Country, United, and WestJet, flying nonstop to more than 30 cities. The terminal's 12 gates over two concourses include an array of shops and restaurants.

AIR CONTACTS Myrtle Beach International Airport. *(MYR) ✉ 1100 Jetport Rd., Myrtle Beach ☎ 843/448–1580 🌐 www.flymyrtlebeach.com.*

CAR TRAVEL

Midway between New York and Miami, the Grand Strand isn't connected directly to any interstate highways but is within an hour's drive of Interstates 95, 20, 26, and 40 via South Carolina Highway 22 (Veterans Highway), U.S. Route 501, and the newer South Carolina Highway 31 (Carolina Bays Parkway). U.S. Route 17 Bypass and U.S. Route 17 Business are the major north–south coastal routes through the Strand.

■ TIP→ **In summer, to bypass incoming southbound traffic jams on U.S. Route 501, take Interstate 95 to Interstate 40 to U.S. Route 17 (at Wilmington) to South Carolina Highway 31, which connects to Myrtle Beach via South Carolina Highway 544 or the tail end of U.S. Route 501.**

MOPED TRAVEL

Rent a moped for a fun way to travel with the slower traffic along Ocean Boulevard (state law maximum speed for mopeds is 30 mph), anywhere along the Grand Strand. Helmets are strongly advised within Myrtle Beach city limits and are required for riders under 21.

CONTACTS Go Fast Golf Cart and Moped Rentals. ✉ *609 S. Kings Hwy., Myrtle Beach* ☎ *843/712–2225.* **Scooter Rental of Myrtle Beach.** ✉ *300 S. Ocean Blvd., Myrtle Beach* ☎ *843/626–6900.* **Seaside Scooters and Bikes.** ✉ *14 S. Ocean Blvd., Surfside Beach* ☎ *843/315–8611* 🌐 *scooterseaside.com.*

TAXI TRAVEL

Taxi services are available at several locations along the Grand Strand. Uber and Lyft are both available in Myrtle Beach and are permitted at the airport for pickups and drop-offs—Uber is more popular and generally faster to get a car. Diamond Taxi Transportation serves the North Myrtle Beach area, Creekside Cab serves the South Strand, and Absolute Taxi serves the central Myrtle Beach area.

TAXI CONTACTS Absolute Taxi. ☎ *843/333–3333* 🌐 *www.absolutetaxi.com.* **Creekside Cab.** ☎ *843/357–8444* 🌐 *www.creeksidecab.com.* **Diamond Cab.** ☎ *843/448–8888* 🌐 *www.diamondcabmb.com.*

Restaurants

With the sand at your feet, seafood will most likely be on your mind. The nearly 2,000 restaurants on the Grand Strand boast all types of seafood, whether you're seeking a buffet or a more intimate dining spot. The summer months see an influx of visitors, so waits at popular restaurants can reach up to an hour or more. ■ TIP→ **To avoid long waits, take advantage of early-bird dinner specials, make a reservation, or opt for takeout.** Many spots oblige with free delivery to hotels. *Restaurant reviews have been shortened. For full information, visit Fodors.com.*

Hotels

High-rise hotels line the Grand Strand, but kitschy beach motels, beachside camping, luxury resorts, and weekly beach house or cottage rentals are popular choices, too. Most accommodations have pools, and many high-rises up the ante with lazy rivers or water-play areas. Advance reservations are recommended for the majority of beach properties. Ask about special packages that include golf, shows, and shopping. *Hotel reviews have been shortened. For full information, visit Fodors.com.*

What It Costs

$	$$	$$$	$$$$
RESTAURANTS			
Under $15	$15–$19	$20–$24	over $24
HOTELS			
Under $150	$150–$200	$201–$250	over $250

Restaurant prices are the average cost of a main course at dinner or, if dinner is not served, at lunch. Hotel prices are the lowest cost of a standard double room in high season.

Discounts and Deals

Visitor centers and grocery stores throughout the Grand Strand have free coupon books with discounts for minigolf, 18-hole golf courses, personal watercraft rentals, and parasailing, to name a few. Kiosks on the boardwalk and in area malls also have special offers.

Tours

The Big Red Bus and Gray Line offer tour packages and guide services.

TOUR CONTACTS The Big Red Bus. ☎ *843/286–5152* 🌐 *bigredbussc.com.* **Gray Line Tours Myrtle Beach.** ☎ *843/448–9483* 🌐 *www.graylinemyrtlebeach.com.*

Myrtle Beach

94 miles northeast of Charleston; 138 miles east of Columbia.

Myrtle Beach, with its high-rises and hyperdevelopment, is the nerve center of the Grand Strand and one of the major seaside destinations on the East Coast. Visitors are drawn here for the swirl of classic vacation activity, from beaches and golf to nightlife, live music, and theater shows.

To capture the flavor of the place, take a stroll along the sidewalks or boardwalk of Ocean Boulevard. Here you'll find an eclectic assortment of restaurants and gift and novelty shops. When you've had your fill, turn east and make your way back onto the beach amid the sunbathers, parasailers, kite fliers, and kids building sandcastles.

GETTING HERE AND AROUND

Most routes to Myrtle Beach run via Interstates 95 and 40, and connect to either U.S. Route 501, South Carolina Highway 31, South Carolina Highway 22, or U.S. Route 17. The main thoroughfares through the Grand Strand are U.S. Route 17 Bypass and U.S. Route 17 Business (aka Kings Highway); both run parallel to the beach. Most of the city's main streets are numbered and are designated north or south.

VISITOR INFORMATION

CONTACTS Visit Myrtle Beach. ✉ *1200 N. Oak St.* ☎ *843/626–7444, 800/356–3016* 🌐 *www.visitmyrtlebeach.com.*

Sights

Broadway Grand Prix Family Race Park
AMUSEMENT PARK/WATER PARK | FAMILY | This go-kart race park features seven different tracks, including one indoor slick track. The 26-acre facility also has bumper cars, kids' rides, an arcade, and miniature golf. ✉ *1820 21st Ave. N, Central Myrtle Beach* ✥ *At U.S. 17 Bypass* ☎ *843/839–4080* 🌐 *www.broadwaygrandprix.com* 🎟 *$45 all-you-can-ride.*

Conway
TOWN | For a break from the beach, or as a pleasant way to spend a cool or cloudy day, take a 15-mile day trip inland to the historic town of Conway. A huge source for lumber in the 1870s, the town is now an eclectic hub for art studios and the arts (take a glassblowing class at Conway Glass!), antiques stores, and a growing number of foodie hot spots, including the celebrated Rivertown

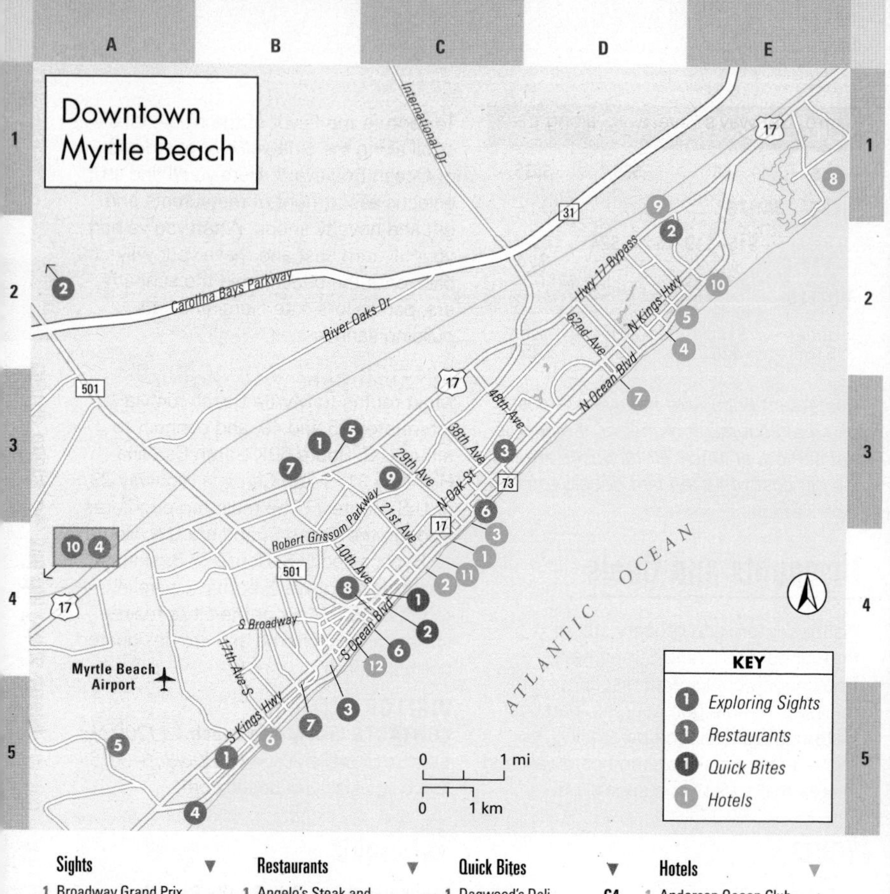

Sights

1 Broadway Grand Prix Family Race Park B3
2 Conway A2
3 Family Kingdom B4
4 Franklin G. Burroughs-Simeon B. Chapin Art Museum B5
5 Hollywood Wax Museum B3
6 Myrtle Beach Boardwalk and Promenade.......... C4
7 Myrtle Waves Water Park B3
8 Pavilion Park C4
9 Ripley's Aquarium C3
10 Wild Water and Wheels.............. A4

Restaurants

1 Angelo's Steak and Pasta B5
2 Drift.................... D2
3 44 & King.................. C3
4 Indo Asian Bistro and Sushi Bar A4
5 Nacho Hippo A5
6 Sea Captain's House C3
7 Villa Romana B5

Quick Bites

1 Dagwood's Deli C4
2 Hi-Fi Coffee Bar.......... C4

Hotels

1 Anderson Ocean Club and Spa.................. C4
2 The Breakers Resort.... C4
3 Caribbean Resort and Villas......... C3
4 Grand Cayman Resort .. D2
5 Grande Shores Ocean Resort E2
6 Hampton Inn and Suites Myrtle Beach–Oceanfront B5
7 Island Vista Resort...... D3
8 Kingston Resorts E1
9 Marina Inn at Grande Dunes D1
10 Myrtle Beach Marriott Resort and Spa at Grande Dunes E2
11 Ocean 22 .... C4
12 South Bay Inn and Suites............ C4

Bistro. Conway's Riverwalk, along the Waccamaw River, offers a peaceful respite for walkers, joggers, and bikers. If you're charmed and want to stay the night, the elegant Cypress Inn is a luxurious respite worlds away from the busy attractions of the Grand Strand. ✉ *Conway* 🌐 *cityofconway.com.*

Family Kingdom

AMUSEMENT PARK/WATER PARK | FAMILY | Dominated by a giant white wooden roller coaster called the Swamp Fox, **Family Kingdom amusement park** is quite an experience, and it's right on the ocean. There are thrill rides, children's rides, a log flume, a go-kart track, an old-fashioned carousel, and the Slingshot Drop Zone, which rockets riders straight down a 110-foot tower. It's a bit like going to a state fair that runs all summer long. Bring your bathing suit and cross the street for more fun at **Splashes Oceanfront Water Park .** Operating hours can vary, so check online before visiting, especially on Saturday when the parks are sometimes rented by groups. Money-saving bundled tickets and multiday passes are readily available. ✉ *300 S. Ocean Blvd., The Strip* ☎ *843/626–3447* 🌐 *www.familykingdomfun.com* 🎫 *$29 all-you-can-ride.*

★ Franklin G. Burroughs-Simeon B. Chapin Art Museum

MUSEUM | You're greeted by a giant octopus constructed of recovered plastic trash at this hidden gem in a 1920s beach cottage on the southern cusp of Ocean Boulevard. The museum has a permanent collection of surf-, coastal-, and wildlife-themed works, plus an ever-changing eclectic array of sculptures and paintings that will open your eyes to the art community that thrives on the Grand Strand. ✉ *3100 S. Ocean Blvd., South Myrtle Beach* ☎ *843/238–2510* 🌐 *www.myrtlebeachartmuseum.org* 🎫 *Donations accepted* ⏲ *Closed Sun. and Mon.*

Hollywood Wax Museum

MUSEUM | Grab props off the wall and pose with your favorite stars—from Harrison Ford to Rhianna, Audrey Hepburn to Snoop Dogg—at this expansive exhibit that's all about the photo op. Downstairs, there's the surprisingly difficult Hannah's Maze of Mirrors and a scream-inducing zombie haunted house, Outbreak. ✉ *1808 21st Ave. N, Central Myrtle Beach* ☎ *843/444–0091* 🌐 *hollywoodwaxentertainment.com* 🎫 *Wax museum $27; $37 three-attraction pass.*

Myrtle Beach Boardwalk and Promenade

PROMENADE | FAMILY | The heart of Myrtle Beach is this mile-long oceanfront destination that stretches from the 14th Avenue Pier, where seafood restaurant-café Pier 14 roosts, to the newly renovated 2nd Avenue Pier and its Wicked Tuna restaurant and open-air rooftop lounge. Take a sky-high seat on the SkyWheel, one of the largest Ferris wheels on the East Coast at 175 feet tall, with enclosed gondolas for a smooth ride (don't miss the light show at night), then stop in for a bite to eat at Jimmy Buffett's LandShark restaurant located right at the entrance. You can also take the kids to play in the old-time arcade, zip across the Myrtle Beach Zipline Adventures aerial course, break for a soft-serve ice cream cone, shop for a souvenir at the world-famous Gay Dolphin, shuck oysters at Dirty Don's, pull up a stool at the Bowery (the legendary bar that gave country band Alabama its start), or just stroll or sit, taking in the beach scene. A schedule of free live concerts, performances, fireworks, and children's carnivals abounds in summer at the boardwalk's Plyler Park. Don't miss the holiday, family-friendly block parties year-round. ⚠ **Bikes, pets, and skateboards are prohibited on the boards May–September.** ✉ *14th Ave. N to 2nd Ave. N and Ocean Blvd.* 🌐 *www.myrtlebeachdowntown.com* 🎫 *Free.*

Myrtle Beach's mile-long boardwalk is lined with restaurants to grab a bite.

Myrtle Waves Water Park

AMUSEMENT PARK/WATER PARK | FAMILY | At South Carolina's largest water park you can shoot through twisty chutes, swim in the Ocean in Motion Wave Pool, race your friends down the Turbo Twisters, or ride a boogie board on the Racin' River. Even the toddlers will enjoy splashing in Bubble Bay and Saturation Station playground. There's beach volleyball, too, for when you've had enough water. Shaded areas with lounge chairs offer respite from the sun, and private cabanas, complete with waitstaff, are available to rent for the day. ✉ *3000 Mr. Joe White Ave., Central Myrtle Beach* ☎ *843/913–9250* 🌐 *www.myrtlewaves.com* 🎫 *$32* ⏲ *Closed Oct.–Apr.*

Pavilion Park

AMUSEMENT PARK/WATER PARK | FAMILY | The historic oceanfront Pavilion (razed in 2006) lives on through its amusement rides that are now split between three sections at Broadway at the Beach. East Park features original Pavilion rides like the famous Herschell-Spillman Carousel, dating back to 1912. West Park is home to kiddie rides and the Myrtle Turtle coaster, while Central Park includes an array of modern thrill rides. In between, hit the snack stands vending funnel cakes and snow cones. ✉ *Broadway at the Beach, 1171 Celebrity Circle, Central Myrtle Beach* ☎ *843/839–0303* 🌐 *www.pavilion-park.com* 🎫 *Ride tickets $1.75, unlimited ride pass $38.50.*

Ripley's Aquarium

ZOO | FAMILY | Glide underwater (no need for a wet suit) through a winding tunnel exhibit that's longer than a football field, where sharks of all kinds and exotic marine creatures, including poisonous lionfish, moray eels, and an octopus, swim over and around you (or below you, if you spring for the glass-bottom boat tour). Children can examine horseshoe crabs and stingrays in touch tanks, and mermaid shows are offered regularly. There are also add-ons, like the up-close 30-minute, $70 Penguin Encounter. Admission discounts are available when combined with the price of Ripley's Ocean

Boulevard attractions. ✉ *Broadway at the Beach, 1110 Celebrity Circle, Central Myrtle Beach* ☎ *843/916–0888* 🌐 *www.ripleyaquariums.com/myrtlebeach* 🎫 *$35.*

Wild Water & Wheels

AMUSEMENT PARK/WATER PARK | **FAMILY** | This water park has 24 water-oriented rides and activities, along with go-carts and minigolf. If your children are old enough to navigate the park on their own, spend a few minutes at the adults-only lounge pool, where you can sit immersed in Jacuzzi-like bubbles, or rest in your own private cabana. ■ **TIP→ Admission is lower after 2 pm and on Sunday and Monday.** ✉ *910 U.S. 17 S, Surfside Beach* ☎ *843/238–3787* 🌐 *www.wild-water.com* 🎫 *$27* ⏲ *Closed Oct.–Apr.*

Beaches

There are nearly 150 public beach access points in the city, all marked with signs. Most are located off Ocean Boulevard and have parking and "shower towers" for cleaning up; few have restroom facilities. Parking can be scarce, but during summer the city allows metered parallel parking on Ocean Boulevard.

Because much of Myrtle Beach's coastline is dominated by high-rise hotels, there are plenty of places to get lunch or a cool drink without having to get back in your car. Many of these hotels also rent beach chairs, umbrellas, and boogie boards. Some have nets set up for beach volleyball. ■ **TIP→ For a quieter beach experience, look for beach access away from the high-rise hotels. The Strand's residential section between 30th and 48th Avenues North is a good bet.**

Dogs, kayaks, and surfboards are limited on many beaches from May through September. Be sure to read the ordinances posted at each access point for details. ■ **TIP→ Summer heat can be brutal, and the sand can scorch: don't step out of the hotel barefoot.**

Garden City Beach

BEACH—SIGHT | **FAMILY** | Horry County's southernmost beachfront is backed by a causeway that crosses creeks and tributaries feeding into Murrells Inlet. The coastline is a curious collection of a few high-rise hotels, older condo buildings, and cute, stilted beach houses. Beachfront disappears at high tide farther south—so much so that it slaps up against the pilings and sea wall. The Garden City Pier is a must for fishing (free), strolling, playing arcade games, or dancing to live music at the partially covered bar perched at the very end. Other beach activities include kayaking, Jet Skiing, kiteboarding, parasailing, banana-boat rides, and boogie boarding. **Best for:** sunrise; surfing; swimming; walking. **Amenities:** food and drink; lifeguards (sometimes); parking (no fee); showers; toilets; water sports. ✉ *Atlantic Ave. and S. Waccamaw Dr., Garden City Beach.*

Myrtle Beach

BEACH—SIGHT | **FAMILY** | The beachfront of the city of Myrtle Beach stretches from the Springmaid Pier at the south end up to 82nd Avenue North. Expect the entire length of this popular family beach to be busy from May to October with people fishing, boogie boarding, parasailing, surfing (only allowed before 10 am and after 5 pm), and sunbathing. In the off-season (November–February) you can take horseback rides on the beach. Restaurants and shops line the boardwalk section of 2nd to 14th Avenues. A beachfront trail of workout stations lines the north end. Note that an ordinance bans tents over 7½ feet in diameter from Memorial Day to Labor Day. **Best for:** partiers; sunrise; swimming; walking. **Amenities:** lifeguards (May–September; no lifeguards in residential section of 38th–48th Avenues North); parking (free at north-end beach access areas; metered on street along Ocean Boulevard; pay by day or hour at Pavilion Parking Garage at 8th Avenue North); showers; toilets; water sports. ✉ *32nd Ave. S to 82nd Ave. N, Central Myrtle Beach.*

★ Myrtle Beach State Park

NATIONAL/STATE PARK | FAMILY | Take a short hike through a forest canopy of pine, magnolia, and live oak, and escape the traffic of Highway 17 while discovering what Myrtle Beach looked like before all the neon. This state-protected parcel of land has a mile-long beach, 350 campsites, picnic pavilions, hiking trails, a fishing pier, an ice cream shop, and playgrounds. There are year-round family or children's activities offered through the park, like crabbing and nature programs, and lifeguards at the north section of the beach. **Best for:** sunrise; swimming; walking. **Amenities:** food and drink; parking (free with $8 admission to park); showers; toilets. ✉ *4401 S. Kings Hwy., South Myrtle Beach* 🌐 *www.southcarolinaparks.com/myrtle-beach* 🎫 *$8.*

Surfside Beach

BEACH—SIGHT | FAMILY | Dubbed "the Family Beach," this small strand just south of Myrtle Beach offers up about 2 miles of white sand. Here, the hotel high-rises, bright lights, and big city of Myrtle Beach disappear, replaced by beach houses, cottages, and peaceful views. The centerpiece Surfside Pier is the site of most of the town's festivals, burger and fried-fish joints, and Scotty's, a kickin' karaoke bar. **Best for:** solitude; sunrise; surfing; swimming; walking. **Amenities:** food and drink; lifeguards (May–September); parking (lots with meters at 12 out of 36 beach access areas); showers; toilets. ✉ *17th Ave. N to Melody La., Surfside Beach.*

Restaurants

Angelo's Steak and Pasta

$$$ | ITALIAN | Cut, trimmed, and seasoned to order, steaks sizzle on their way to the tables and then melt in your mouth at this Italian-style steak house. Pasta is served up on the daily Italian buffet, featuring standard favorites such as spaghetti, meatballs, lasagna, and tortellini Alfredo. **Known for:** tableside magic shows; longevity—Angelo's has been a fixture for four decades; Italian buffet. 💲 *Average main: $20* ✉ *2311 S. Kings Hwy., South Myrtle Beach* ☎ *843/626–2800* 🌐 *www.angelosteakandpasta.com.*

Drift

$ | CAFÉ | This bright, centrally located spot bills itself as a "coastal eatery," but it's breakfast entrées like the quinoa huevos rancheros and salmon avocado toast that make it an early morning staple. Lunch keeps the casual, upscale vibe going with chargrilled octopus and duck leg confit. **Known for:** inspired breakfast and lunch menu; strong value for lunch entrées; modern coastal decor that's heavy on wood accents. 💲 *Average main: $14* ✉ *980 Cipriana Dr., Unit A-6, Central Myrtle Beach* ☎ *843/879–4758* 🌐 *drifteatery.com.*

44 & King

$$ | SOUTHERN | FAMILY | Dining extends seamlessly from indoors to the game-filled outside at this laid-back pub known for fresh takes on Southern fare, from chicken pie to shrimp with sweet potato grits. The lawn includes a boccie court and cornhole boards. **Known for:** daily specials like chicken bog Thursday; shareable pub grub plates; fun outdoor atmosphere. 💲 *Average main: $16* ✉ *515 44th Ave. N, Central Myrtle Beach* ☎ *843/626–5464* 🌐 *44andking.com.*

Indo Asian Bistro and Sushi Bar

$$ | ASIAN | Owner Laura Smith is legendary in Myrtle Beach for her sushi artistry. In addition to sushi masterpieces, she creates a slew of authentic Thai noodle dishes and signature seafood creations like Coco Shrimp and jumbo soft-shell crabs. **Known for:** elaborate sushi rolls; Indonesian-style seafood specialties; an outpost of inspired eats. 💲 *Average main: $19* ✉ *4620 Dick Pond Rd., North End* ☎ *843/691–9557* 🌐 *www.indothairestaurant.com.*

Nacho Hippo

$ | MODERN MEXICAN | If you're a hungry hippo, then slide a stool over to a *maximo* plate of nachos at this hip corner cantina in three locations: the Market

Grand Strand Vacation Rentals

If a hotel just won't suit the size of your crew, the Grand Strand can accommodate with beach-house or cottage rentals aplenty.

Here are a few agencies to check out before you check in:

Dunes Realty ✉ *Surfside Beach* ☎ *888/889–0312, 843/651–2116* 🌐 *www.dunes.com.*

Elliott Realty ✉ *North Myrtle Beach* ☎ *888/669–7853* 🌐 *www.elliottrealty.com.*

Garden City Realty ✉ *Garden City Beach* ☎ *877/767–7737* 🌐 *www.gardencityrealty.com.*

Grand Strand Vacations ✉ *North Myrtle Beach* ☎ *800/722–6278* 🌐 *www.grandstrandvacations.com.*

North Beach Vacations ✉ *North Myrtle Beach* ☎ *800/274–1105* 🌐 *northbeachvacations.com.*

Surfside Realty Company ✉ *Surfside Beach* ☎ *800/833–8231* 🌐 *www.surfside-realty.com.*

Common, North Myrtle Beach, and inside the airport. It's bold, fresh, and fun—from the funky wall and ceiling decor to the creative Mexican dishes. **Known for:** budget-priced margaritas; massive, creative nachos piled high in seafood, vegan, and kamikaze versions; colorful, festive decor. 💲 *Average main: $10* ✉ *The Market Common, 1160 Farrow Pkwy., South Myrtle Beach* ☎ *843/839–9770* 🌐 *www.nachohippo.com.*

★ Sea Captain's House

$$$$ | **SEAFOOD** | The windowed porch overlooking the ocean houses the best seats at this nautical-themed restaurant in a 1930s beach cottage (unless it's a perfect spring or fall day to sit outside in the ocean breeze). Menu highlights include sautéed crab cakes and jambalaya; it's the rare Myrtle Beach seafood restaurant that offers vegetarian and gluten-free menus. **Known for:** historic oceanfront locale—an island of history amid high-rises; hearty breakfasts a step above the Strip's pancake-house fare; broiled and fried seafood. 💲 *Average main: $28* ✉ *3002 N. Ocean Blvd., The Strip* ☎ *843/448–8082* 🌐 *www.seacaptains.com.*

Villa Romana

$$$ | **ITALIAN** | It's all about family at Villa Romana, where owners Rinaldo and Franca come in early to make the gnocchi and stick around to greet customers. It's hard to resist filling up on the *stracciatella* (Italian egg-drop) soup, bruschetta, salad, and rolls (perhaps the best on the Strand) that accompany every meal, but try. **Known for:** homemade sauces, pastas, and gnocchi; live Italian accordion music during service; veal specialty dishes. 💲 *Average main: $23* ✉ *707 S. Kings Hwy., Central Myrtle Beach* ☎ *843/448–4990* 🌐 *www.villaromanamyrtlebeach.com* ⏲ *No lunch.*

Coffee and Quick Bites

Dagwood's Deli

$ | **DELI** | Comic-strip characters Dagwood and Blondie could split one of the masterful meat-packed sandwiches at Dagwood's Deli, where locals line up on their lunch break. There are the usual suspects—ham, turkey, and homemade chicken salad—but you won't regret trying one of the more distinctive creations like the Hogpound, pork tenderloin doused in melted Swiss and provolone. **Known for:** delivery to most of the Myrtle Beach area; catering for family and business groups; sandwiches piled high. 💲 *Average main: $10* ✉ *400 Mr. Joe White Ave., Central Myrtle Beach* ☎ *843/448–0100* 🌐 *www.dagwoodsdeli.com* ⏲ *Closed Sun.*

Hi-Fi Coffee Bar

$ | **BAKERY** | If you need a jolt to keep up with the kids while cruising the boardwalk—or want a late-night soft-serve cone—this newcomer is a rare island of independent creativity along the Strip. There are breakfast sandwiches and smoothies in addition to the regular coffee concoctions and pastries. **Known for:** frappés with flavors like cotton candy and orange cream; caramel macchiato; sweet and savory grab-and-go breakfast options. 💲 *Average main: $5* ✉ *918-B N. Ocean Blvd., The Strip* ☎ *843/626–0022* 🌐 *hificoffeebar.com.*

Hotels

Anderson Ocean Club and Spa

$$$ | **RENTAL** | Small touches of heavenly luxury greet you upon arrival, from the fountain in the front plaza to the stately double-door entrance flanked by large lanterns. **Pros:** generally upscale furnishings; central location; one of the most well-appointed resort complexes in the area. **Cons:** many units are individually owned so decor can vary; lots of resorts in this area can make for a crowded beach; no true lobby or indoor communal space. 💲 *Rooms from: $249* ✉ *2600 N. Ocean Blvd., The Strip* ☎ *844/887–9452* 🌐 *www.andersonoceanclub.com* *289 units* *No meals.*

The Breakers Resort

$$$$ | **RESORT** | **FAMILY** | This sprawling multitower oceanfront hotel, in the middle of the Myrtle Beach Strip, has airy and spacious rooms complete with contemporary furnishings. **Pros:** excellent views from the tower rooms; big water park for kids; multiple on-site dining options. **Cons:** pool areas can be crowded in high season; multiple buildings means it's a hike from some rooms to pools or dining; it's located in a high-traffic area of the beach. 💲 *Rooms from: $312* ✉ *2006 N. Ocean Blvd., The Strip* ☎ *855/861–9550* 🌐 *www.breakers.com* *343 units* *No meals.*

Caribbean Resort and Villas

$$$$ | **RESORT** | **FAMILY** | Four different properties make up the polished Caribbean, each offering access to the other's amenities. **Pros:** floor-to-ceiling windows for ocean views in the two towers; great family-geared water facilities; next door to Sea Captain's House restaurant. **Cons:** parking is across the street from the towers; pools and water-activity areas are designed for families more than couples; quality varies between buildings. 💲 *Rooms from: $292* ✉ *3000 N. Ocean Blvd., The Strip* ☎ *855/421–6947* 🌐 *www.caribbeanresort.com* *465 rooms* *No meals.*

Grande Cayman Resort

$$$$ | **RESORT** | **FAMILY** | This remodel of an older resort reopened in 2020, with suites featuring shiplap walls, light-colored wood floors, coastal decor, and Murphy beds for extra room. **Pros:** terrific on-site dining options; in-room decor feels bright and fresh; watch the sun rise over the ocean from bed in some rooms. **Cons:** gets very crowded with families; wear and tear adds up during high season; party scene means some noise into the evening. 💲 *Rooms from: $350* ✉ *7200 N. Ocean Blvd., North End* ☎ *855/820–4751* 🌐 *grandecaymanresort.com* *260 rooms* *No meals.*

Grande Shores Ocean Resort

$$ | **RESORT** | **FAMILY** | This classic spot, north of the Strip's crowds, is a combination of rentable condos with full kitchens and standard hotel rooms outfitted with refrigerators, coffeemakers, and, in a few cases, kitchenettes. **Pros:** water features for all age groups; spacious rooms with full kitchens are great for families; attractive rooftop pool and garden. **Cons:** only a select group of rooms actually face

the ocean; less flashy and fancy than newer competitors; exterior and entrance could use a little upkeep. *Rooms from: $159 ✉ 201 77th Ave. N, North End ☎ 888/974–1337 🌐 www.grandeshores.com ⇨ 233 rooms 🍽 No meals.*

Hampton Inn and Suites Myrtle Beach–Oceanfront

$$$ | **RESORT** | This property combines the reliability of an established hotel chain with the joys of a beach resort. **Pros:** tropical, beachy feel to rooms; free airport shuttle; free breakfast buffet. **Cons:** it's a drive or over a mile walk to the boardwalk and attractions along the Strip; older building than some competitors; more about the view than the luxuries. *Rooms from: $205 ✉ 1801 S. Ocean Blvd., South Myrtle Beach ☎ 843/946–6400 🌐 www.hamptoninnoceanfront.com ⇨ 228 rooms 🍽 Free breakfast.*

★ Island Vista Resort

$$$ | **RESORT** | **FAMILY** | Nestled along the residential north end of the Strand, this resort has room to breathe, instead of being smack up against the clutter of hotels clogging the coastline farther south. **Pros:** every room has an ocean view; room furnishings are tastefully tropical, not tacky; less crowded beach area than its peers. **Cons:** small lobby (communal space is mostly outside and around the pool); there's less to do within walking distance than at other resorts; low 6 foot, 9 inch clearance in parking garage. *Rooms from: $239 ✉ 6000 N. Ocean Blvd., North End ☎ 855/732–6250 🌐 www.islandvista.com ⇨ 172 rooms 🍽 No meals.*

Kingston Resorts

$$$$ | **RESORT** | **FAMILY** | This 145-acre ocean-side complex includes two hotels and two rental condo towers, as well as restaurants, shops, and a spa. **Pros:** lushly landscaped property; award-winning beachfront restaurant, Café Amalfi, on-site; expansive on-site water park with whirlpools, lazy river, and waterslides. **Cons:** some condos may include a sleeper sofa in the bed count; it's a drive to popular attractions along the Strip; resort feels densely developed. *Rooms from: $289 ✉ 10000 Beach Club Dr., North End ☎ 800/876–0010 🌐 www.kingstonplantation.com ⇨ 1458 units 🍽 No meals.*

Marina Inn at Grande Dunes

$$$ | **RESORT** | From the rich wood and sumptuous carpet in the lobby to the manicured lawns and amenities, this inn along the intracoastal waterway is a little slice of paradise. **Pros:** exemplary service; views of the waterway and Grand Dunes golf greens; daily schedule of activities for families and children. **Cons:** U.S. Route 17 runs adjacent to the complex; it's a drive to get to the beach; some rooms could use updating. *Rooms from: $229 ✉ 8121 Amalfi Pl., North End ☎ 843/913–1333 🌐 www.marinainnatgrandedunes.com ⇨ 210 rooms 🍽 No meals.*

★ Myrtle Beach Marriott Resort and Spa at Grande Dunes

$$$$ | **RESORT** | Entering this chic high-rise resort, with its airy wicker furniture, giant palms, and mahogany details, will take you away from the hubbub of Myrtle Beach and straight to a tropical locale. **Pros:** rope hammocks swing near the dunes with views of the ocean; large, adult-oriented pool complex; lifeguard stand on the beach directly in front of the resort. **Cons:** it's a drive to the hub of Myrtle Beach shopping; the pool area can be crowded in season; fills up with conference groups. *Rooms from: $313 ✉ 8400 Costa Verde Dr. ☎ 843/449–8880 🌐 www.myrtlebeachmarriott.com ⇨ 405 rooms 🍽 No meals.*

Ocean 22

$$$ | **RESORT** | At 24 floors, Hilton's Ocean 22 was briefly the tallest resort in the city, until Hilton built the 330-room Ocean Enclave just down the street. **Pros:** close proximity to the boardwalk and attractions along the Strip; free entry to Wild Water & Wheels water park; modern fitness center. **Cons:** pool complex doesn't feature the kid-oriented aspects of other resorts; close proximity of other resorts

can make for a crowded beach; the lobby's Sky Bar feels sterile. $ *Rooms from: $229 ✉ 2200 N. Ocean Blvd., The Strip ☎ 843/848–0022 🌐 www.hilton.com ⇝ 220 suites 🍽 No meals.*

South Bay Inn and Suites

$$$ | RESORT | FAMILY | Combining the appeal of a family-friendly resort with immediate proximity to the boardwalk, this newcomer features modern rooms and suites, most of which have an ocean view. **Pros:** big indoor water park; modern fitness center with new machines; if you're here for the beach and the boardwalk, you can park the car for your entire vacation. **Cons:** not the spot for a quiet romantic getaway; pool and water park get very crowded; parking is across the street. $ *Rooms from: $229 ✉ 520 N. Ocean Blvd., The Strip ☎ 833/585–5251 🌐 www.southbayinnandsuites.com ⇝ 242 rooms 🍽 No meals.*

Nightlife

★ The Carolina Opry Theater

MUSIC CLUBS | FAMILY | A Myrtle Beach show staple since 1986, the Carolina Opry is a polished, action-packed variety show featuring live country, light rock, show tunes, and gospel music, plus comedy skits. There's also a "Time Warp" show that pays tribute to the '60s, '70s, and '80s, and a celebrated Christmas Special. ✉ *8901 N. Kings Hwy., North End ☎ 800/843–6779 🌐 www.thecarolinaopry.com.*

Comedy Cabana

COMEDY CLUBS | Touring comedians—some of whom have made cable TV appearances—make their way to this little comedy club that's inspired belly laughs for over 20 years on the north side of town. There's an on-site restaurant serving pizza and burgers. ✉ *9588 N. Kings Hwy., North End ☎ 843/449–4242 🌐 www.comedycabana.com.*

★ Landing at the Boathouse

MUSIC CLUBS | If you're up for a rowdy evening of entertainment (and a worthy basket of grub for dinner), grab a spot in the backyard April–September for the annual free Sunday summer concert series featuring national touring acts; on Friday check out free local acts. It's quite a sight, as fleets of boats anchor for a waterway view of the stage and the landlocked crowd packs the bank to relax and sip on pales and lagers from the on-site brewery, Independent Republic. ✉ *201 Fantasy Harbour Blvd., Fantasy Harbor ☎ 843/903–2628 🌐 landingmb.com.*

Legends in Concert

THEMED ENTERTAINMENT | This venue features high-energy shows by impersonators of pop stars like Bruno Mars, Dolly Parton, Elvis, Garth Brooks, and the Blues Brothers. ✉ *Broadway at the Beach, 2925 Hollywood Dr., Central Myrtle Beach ☎ 843/238–7827 🌐 www.legendsinconcert.com.*

Pirates Voyage

THEMED ENTERTAINMENT | FAMILY | This Dolly Parton–owned production features a 15-foot-deep water lagoon staged with pirate ships *Crimson* and *Sapphire*. Ye families will enjoy a four-course feast while watching swashbuckling fights, pyrotechnics, acrobats, high dives, and mermaids in flight. ✉ *8907 N. Kings Hwy., North End ☎ 843/497–9700 🌐 www.piratesvoyage.com 🎟 $55.*

3001 Nightlife

DANCE CLUBS | This 21-and-older complex features three clubs, including a 6K DJ video system in the main nightclub, Envy. There's also Bourbon Cowboy, with live bands, and Club Rewind, which features songs from the '80s–'00s. ✉ *920 Lake Arrowhead Rd., North End ☎ 843/232–7941 🌐 3001nightlifemb.com.*

Shopping

★ Broadway at the Beach

SHOPPING CENTERS/MALLS | FAMILY | South Carolina's only Hard Rock Cafe and Jimmy Buffett's Margaritaville restaurant are among the many themed restaurants at this shopping complex set around Lake Broadway, where you can soar through the sky on a zipline or take a dizzying speedboat ride. It's the area's biggest mall, with shops ranging from the Man Cave Store and a Harley-Davidson outfitter to the Southern Living store, featuring home items curated by the magazine. Among the many attractions in the complex are Pavilion Park's kids' and thrill rides, a Topgolf, and the WonderWorks interactive museum, where kids can spend hours exploring and adults can strap into one of several simulators that send you twirling at dizzying speeds. ✉ *U.S. 17 Bypass, between 21st and 29th Aves. N, Central Myrtle Beach* ☎ *843/444–3200* 🌐 *www.broadwayatthebeach.com.*

The Market Common

SHOPPING CENTERS/MALLS | Combining high-end shopping with upscale living and dining spaces, the 114-acre Market Common features stores like Anthropologie, Barnes & Noble, Orvis, Pottery Barn, and a Southern Living store. A movie theater, playgrounds, bountiful year-round outdoor festivals, and a park with a man-made lake and bike path make it a day-trip destination. ✉ *4017 Deville St., South Myrtle Beach* ✥ *Off Farrow Pkwy., between U.S. 17 Business and U.S. 17 Bypass* ☎ *843/839–3500* 🌐 *www.marketcommonmb.com.*

THEBlvd

SHOPPING CENTERS/MALLS | Set right on the beachfront and framed in glass, this shopping and dining complex features a large arcade, a rooftop music venue, the Tin Roof, and three restaurant anchor tenants: Banditos (upscale Mexican), Burger Fi, and a Starbucks. ✉ *1410 Ocean Blvd., The Strip* 🌐 *www.theblvdmyrtle.com.*

Activities

BASEBALL

Myrtle Beach Pelicans Baseball

BASEBALL/SOFTBALL | FAMILY | Catch a minor-league baseball game April–September with this proud Chicago Cubs–affiliated team. Look for specials and promos, like $2 tacos on Tuesdays and Thirsty Thursdays. Distractions include a super-size playground and inflatable rides for kids, and contests and entertainment between innings. A sandy beach section, picnic area, and luxury suites can be reserved for groups. ✉ *1251 21st Ave. N, Central Myrtle Beach* ☎ *843/918–6000* 🌐 *www.myrtlebeachpelicans.com.*

FISHING

Fishing along the Grand Strand is best during the warm waters of late spring through December. Anglers can fish from 10 piers and jetties for amberjack, sea trout, and king mackerel. Surf casters may snare bluefish, whiting, flounder, pompano, and channel bass. In the South Strand, the tidal creeks weaving through the salt marsh yield flounder, blues, croakers, spots, shrimp, clams, oysters, and blue crabs.

■ TIP→ Swimmers, steer clear of the piers. Fishermen's bait is known to lure unwelcome sharks to the water as well.

Grand Strand Fishing Rodeo

FISHING | For more than 50 years, from April through October, the Grand Strand Fishing Rodeo has held a fish-of-the-month contest on participating area piers, with prizes for the largest catch of a designated species. There's no registration fee; entrants must take their catch to designated weigh stations for consideration. ✉ *Myrtle Beach* 🌐 *www.Facebook.com/GrandStrandFishingRodeo.*

GOLF

Known as the Golf Capital of the World, the Grand Strand is home to more than 100 courses. Many are championship layouts and most are public.

Arrowhead Country Club

GOLF | Known for its top-notch condition, regardless of the season, Arrowhead is the only Raymond Floyd–designed course in the region. Many of the scenic 27 holes, uniquely grouped into 9-hole themes, run along the intracoastal waterway. All greens are MiniVerde Bermuda grass, a grass species developed to tolerate high temperatures. Chomping at the bit? Arrowhead offers showers, towels, and amenities so you can sneak in one last round before heading to the airport, which is five minutes away. ✉ *1201 Burcale Rd., West Myrtle Beach* ☎ *843/236–3243* 🌐 *www.arrowheadcc.com* *$81, 27 holes, 6180 yds, par 72* *Reservations essential.*

Grande Dunes

GOLF | This course has some of the widest and purportedly fairest fairways in Myrtle Beach, a veritable kingdom of golf, with majestic, nationally award-winning views of the tranquil waterway. ✉ *8700 Golf Village La., North End* ☎ *877/283–2122* 🌐 *www.grandedunesgolf.com* *$128, 18 holes, 7618 yds, par 72* *Reservations essential.*

Pine Lakes

GOLF | Built in 1927 and listed on the National Register of Historic Places, Pine Lakes is reputed as the Grand Strand's "granddaddy" of courses. The patriarch, however, is kept in immaculate shape. A conversation here led to the creation of *Sports Illustrated* magazine, a piece of trivia proudly displayed on the walls of the clubhouse. ✉ *5603 Granddaddy Dr., Central Myrtle Beach* ☎ *877/283–2122* 🌐 *www.pinelakes.com* *$95, 18 holes, 6675 yds, par 70* *Reservations essential.*

The Witch

GOLF | Dan Maples–designed, this course is set amidst a pine forest, off the beaten path. True to its name, it can be quite bewitching throughout its 500-acre rolling layout over higher elevations and the lower wetlands connected by a mile of bridges. ✉ *1900 SC 544, Conway* ☎ *843/347–2706* 🌐 *www.witchgolf.com* *$79, 18 holes, 6796 yds, par 71* *Reservations essential.*

HELICOPTER RIDES

For a bird's-eye view of the beach, take to the sky in a helicopter to scoot along the coastline or explore more customized tours inland. The tours are great for aerial photo ops.

Helicopter Adventures

FLYING/SKYDIVING/SOARING | ✉ *1860 21st Ave. North, Central Myrtle Beach* ☎ *800/359–4386* 🌐 *www.helicopteradventures.com* *Flights start at $20.*

OceanFront Helicopters

FLYING/SKYDIVING/SOARING | ✉ *3000 S. Kings Hwy., South Myrtle Beach* ☎ *843/946–0022* 🌐 *www.huffmanhelicopters.com* *Flights start at $20.*

MINIGOLF

Nearly 50 minigolf courses, also known as "Putt-Putt" around here, are in full swing along the Grand Strand. It's practically a subculture of Myrtle Beach that will have you climbing through caverns, scaling volcanic mountains, crossing rapids, and dodging fire-breathing dragons to master the 18-hole minigreens. Beat the crowds by Putt-Putting in the morning or before the after-dinner rush.

Cancun Lagoon

MINIATURE GOLF | FAMILY | Putt over 27 holes inside or out of a massive 50-foot Mayan pyramid. The same owners also run the Molten Mountain and Mutiny Bay courses in North Myrtle Beach and offer a $20 three-course deal. ✉ *2101 S. Kings Hwy., South Myrtle Beach* ☎ *843/444–1098* 🌐 *www.paradiseadventuregolf.com* *$11.*

Captain Hook's Adventure Golf

MINIATURE GOLF | FAMILY | Putt your way through two 18-hole courses in Neverland at this Peter Pan–themed attraction that winds over and through a waterfall-covered mountain, complete with pirate ships and an animatronic alligator.

⊠ *2205 N. Kings Hwy., Central Myrtle Beach* ☎ *843/913–7851* 🌐 *myrtlebeachfamilygolf.com.*

Mt. Atlanticus

MINIATURE GOLF | FAMILY | Indoor and outdoor greens race around a giant mountain, past waterfalls, and into lagoons of this elaborate, impressive, tiki-themed 36-hole course. ⊠ *707 N. Kings Hwy., Central Myrtle Beach* ⊕ *Off 7th Ave. N, near U.S. 501* ☎ *843/444–1008* 🎟 *$10.*

TENNIS

There are more than 200 courts on the Grand Strand. Facilities include hotel and resort courts, as well as free municipal courts in Myrtle Beach, North Myrtle Beach, and Surfside Beach. ■ **TIP→ Many tennis clubs offer weekly round-robin tournaments that are open to players of all levels.**

Grande Dunes Tennis Club

TENNIS | A full fitness facility with 10 Har-Tru courts (eight lit), the club also offers lessons, clinics, camps, and match opportunities. ⊠ *8821 Marina Pkwy., North End* ☎ *843/449–4486* 🌐 *www.grandedunestennis.com.*

Prestwick Tennis Club

TENNIS | This club offers court time, instruction, and tournament opportunities on adult and junior levels; 11 clay and two hard courts are lighted for nighttime play. ⊠ *1375 McMaster Dr., South Myrtle Beach* ☎ *843/831–0117* 🌐 *www.prestwicktennisclub.com.*

WATER SPORTS

Don't forget to bring your own towels and sunscreen when you head out.

★ Downwind Sails Watersports

WATER SPORTS | Hobie Cats, personal watercraft, Jet Skis, and ocean kayaks are available for rent at this trusted company operating at the beach since 1981; it also has banana-boat rides (where you're towed in a long, yellow inflatable raft) and parasailing. There's a second location behind Family Kingdom at 410 S. Ocean Boulevard. ⊠ *2985 S. Ocean Blvd., South Myrtle Beach* ☎ *843/448–7245* 🌐 *www.downwindsailsmyrtlebeach.com.*

Island Adventure Watersports

WATER SPORTS | For water fun along the waterway, this rental spot at the Socastee Swing Bridge offers the standard water-sport vessels, plus wakeboards, paddleboards, and Jet Ski tours. ⊠ *5843 Dick Pond Rd., West Myrtle Beach* ☎ *843/650–7003* 🌐 *www.islandadventurewatersports.com.*

Ocean Watersports

WATER SPORTS | This outfit specializes in parasailing and also rents Jet Skis and gives banana-boat rides. ⊠ *404 3rd Ave. South, The Strip* ⊕ *On the beach at 3rd Ave. S* ☎ *843/445–7777* 🌐 *www.parasailmyrtlebeach.com.*

★ Village Surf Shoppe

WATER SPORTS | Learn how to ride the waves with a rental board or a surfing lesson from the crew led by local surfing legend Kelly Richards (father of pro surfer Cam Richards). Richards shapes his own Perfection Surfboards at the shop, while his national surf champion sons and staff (including USA Team members) take aspiring surfers out for camps and some hands-on action near the Garden City Pier, a tradition since 1969. ⊠ *500 Atlantic Ave., Garden City Beach* ☎ *843/651–6396* 🌐 *villagesurfshoppe.com.*

North Myrtle Beach

5 miles north of Myrtle Beach via U.S. 17.

North Myrtle Beach, best known as the site where the shag, South Carolina's state dance, originated, is made up of the beach communities Cherry Grove, Crescent Beach, Windy Hill, and Ocean Drive. Entering North Myrtle Beach from the south on U.S. Route 17, you'll see Barefoot Landing, a huge shopping and entertainment complex that sits on the intracoastal waterway. As you make your way east toward the ocean, then north on Ocean Boulevard South, high-rises give way to small motels, then to single beach houses, many of which are available for rent. This relaxed end of the Strand marks the tip of a large peninsula, and the view from the north end across to Hog Island makes it perhaps the most beautiful beach in the Grand Strand area. Along the entire North Myrtle Beach area, there are lots of little islands, creeks, and marshes between the ocean and the waterway to explore by kayak or canoe. **■ TIP→ Mosquitoes can be a problem on the marsh, especially in the early evening. Be sure to pack repellent.**

GETTING HERE AND AROUND

North Myrtle Beach is an easy jaunt up U.S. Route 17 or South Carolina Highway 31 from Myrtle Beach (South Carolina Highway 22 or Main Street exits) or just south of Little River. Once inside the city limits, the numbered cross streets connect to Ocean Drive, the beachfront road.

Sights

Alligator Adventure

ZOO | FAMILY | Interactive reptile shows, including an alligator-feeding demonstration, are the main attractions at this wildlife park. Boardwalks lead through marshes and swamps on the 15-acre property, where you'll see wildlife of the wetlands, including a pair of rare white albino alligators, the largest known crocodile in captivity, giant Galápagos tortoises, river otters, and all manner of reptiles, including boas, pythons, and anacondas. Unusual plants and exotic birds, as well as mountain lions and spotted hyenas, are also in residence. ✉ *U.S. 17 at Barefoot Landing* ☎ *843/361–0789* 🌐 *www.alligatoradventure.com* 🎫 *$28.*

Heritage Shores Nature Preserve

NATURE PRESERVE | This 7-acre park offers an easy escape into nature, via a series of raised wooden walkways through the marsh that runs a few streets behind the beach cottages and high-rise hotels lining the ocean. A small parking lot allows visitors to park and explore the preserve on foot. Common sights include ibis, herons, and kingfishers. The park is free to the public and open daily 7 am to 8:30 pm. ✉ *5611 Heritage Dr.* ✣ *At 53rd Ave. N and Ocean Blvd.* ☎ *843/280–5584* 🌐 *parks.nmb.us.*

La Belle Amie Vineyard

WINERY/DISTILLERY | This shaded vineyard makes its Twisted Sisters wines from the sweet muscadine grapes grown on the property. Tastings and tours are available during operating hours. Saturdays are typically festival days and usually feature live music, food, and free tours of the grounds. The gift shop offers everything from wine to savory dips and fun grape-themed items. ✉ *1120 St. Joseph Rd., at SC 90, Little River* ☎ *843/399–9463* 🌐 *www.labelleamie.com* ⏲ *Closed Sun. and Mon.*

Beaches

Cherry Grove Oceanfront Park

BEACH—SIGHT | FAMILY | Between two high-rises in the relatively quiet community of Cherry Grove, this small oceanfront park with pretty, budding landscaping has amenities for families, like a shaded gazebo, bench swings, and a ramp to the sand for strollers. **Best for:** solitude; sunrise; swimming; walking. **Amenities:** lifeguards; showers; toilets. ✉ *2108 N. Ocean Blvd.* ✣ *Near 21st Ave. N* 🌐 *nmb.us.*

North Myrtle Beach

BEACH—SIGHT | FAMILY | Choose from more than 240 access points to this beach, which is populated with fewer sunbathers than Myrtle Beach—especially farther south and north of Main Street's stretch of beachfront. Ocean Park, at 101 South Ocean Boulevard, offers a nice setting, with a beachfront picnic shelter and a giant, 40-foot-tall inflatable triple waterslide, dubbed the Trippo, open in summer (rides are $3). **Best for:** sunrise; surfing; swimming; walking; windsurfing. **Amenities:** food and drink; lifeguards; parking (metered); showers; toilets; water sports. ✉ *Ocean Blvd. from 63rd Ave. N to 47th Ave. S.*

Restaurants

Greg Norman's Australian Grille

$$$$ | **AUSTRALIAN** | Overlooking the intracoastal waterway, this large restaurant in Barefoot Landing has leather booths, Australian Aboriginal art on the walls, an extensive wine list, and an outdoor patio with a firepit. The menu features grilled meats and seafood, and many of the selections have an Asian flair. **Known for:** holiday and seasonal wine dinners; hearty surf-and-turf entrées; the classy Shark Club bar. *Average main: $38* ✉ *4930 U.S. 17 S* ☎ *843/361–0000* 🌐 *www.gregnormansaustraliangrille.com.*

Lucy Buffett's LuLu's

$$ | **SEAFOOD** | **FAMILY** | If the Jimmy Buffett tie-in (Lucy, or "LuLu," is his sister) doesn't get people in the door of this festive landmark at Barefoot Landing, the on-site aerial ropes course and arcade certainly will. The open-air environment and view of the intracoastal waterway make this a place where parents can while away the afternoon with a platter of fresh seafood and a margarita while the kids harness up and swing around up in the air. **Known for:** live music most evenings; Lucy's Key West Bowl, featuring turnip greens, Cuban rice, black beans, and your fish or meat of choice; key lime pie. *Average main: $17* ✉ *4954 U.S. 17 S* ☎ *843/491–5011* 🌐 *www.lulubuffett.com.*

★ The Parson's Table

$$$$ | **ECLECTIC** | It's a heavenly experience at this Little River staple housed in an old country church that dates back to 1885. Renowned chef-owner Ed Murray Jr. brings the finest steaks and local seafood and produce to the table. **Known for:** local fine dining (hard to find in Myrtle Beach); thoughtful wine and craft cocktail lists; long list of seafood entrées. *Average main: $30* ✉ *4305 McCorsley Ave., Little River* ☎ *843/249–3702* 🌐 *www.parsonstable.com* ⏲ *Closed Sun.*

Rockefellers Raw Bar

$$$ | **SEAFOOD** | Yes it's a raw bar—and a good one, with a bounty of fresh seafood—but don't sell the cooked items short at this small, casual locals' joint. The seasoned boiled shrimp are the real deal, and the mussels, clams, scallops, and other goodies steamed with spices in an iron pot is a terrific version of a Lowcountry staple. **Known for:** comfy boat-captain's chairs lining the wraparound bar; authentic, local hospitality (and attitude); affordable seafood, done right. *Average main: $20* ✉ *3613 U.S. 17 S* ☎ *843/361–9677* 🌐 *www.rockefellersrawbar.com.*

SeaBlue

$$$$ | **CONTEMPORARY** | Don't let the strip-mall location put you off; this restaurant's seafood and locally sourced entrées stand out. Blue mood lighting, a glowing aquarium, and abstract art combine to give this restaurant more of a Miami Beach than Myrtle Beach feel. **Known for:** contemporary, inspired cuisine from quality ingredients; chic, trendy vibe; hopping atmosphere on weekends. *Average main: $36* ✉ *501 U.S. 17 N* ☎ *843/249–8800* 🌐 *www.seabluerestaurant.com* ⏲ *Closed Sun. and Mon.*

Coffee and Quick Bites

Melt

$ | **FAST FOOD** | **FAMILY** | It's hard to walk past this inviting, family-owned nook on Main Street without ducking in for a cone of one of their homemade ice cream flavors like salted Bananas Foster or Midnight Caramel River. **Known for:** over 20 house-made flavors; vegan ice cream options; grab-and-go cones by the beach. *Average main: $5* ✉ *204 Main St.* ☎ *843/273–0284* 🌐 *cravemelt.com.*

Hotels

Best Western Ocean Sands Beach Resort

$$ | **HOTEL** | **FAMILY** | One of the few family-owned resort properties left in North Myrtle Beach, the Ocean Sands has a beachfront tiki bar and updated one- and two-bedroom suites with full kitchens. **Pros:** friendly, available staff; continental breakfast included; reasonably priced oceanfront digs. **Cons:** an annex building down the street does not have ocean views; shows some wear around the edges; lazy river is very short. *Rooms from: $190* *1525 S. Ocean Blvd.* *843/272–6101, 800/588–3570* *www.oceansands.com* *95 suites* *Free breakfast.*

Myrtle Beach Barefoot Resort

$$ | **RENTAL** | **FAMILY** | This luxury golf resort includes more than 160 one- to four-bedroom condominium units and Barefoot Yacht Club Villas. **Pros:** pretty views of the waterway surround the resort; Barefoot Landing shopping and entertainment center is just across the inlet; ideal for golfers. **Cons:** going to the Strip or boardwalk requires driving across a busy highway; condos are spread throughout golf course complex; not on the beach. *Rooms from: $160* *Barefoot Resort Bridge Rd.* *800/548–9904* *www.myrtlebeachbarefootresort.com* *322 condos* *No meals.*

North Beach Resort & Villas

$$$$ | **RESORT** | **FAMILY** | Two massive towers connect at the top of this massive resort, creating an arching, striking building design that's unlike anything else along the coast—think the Bellagio, or Atlantis in Nassau. **Pros:** sky-high surroundings make you feel like royalty; Cinzia Spa and fitness center are incomparable on the Grand Strand; the water park and pool complex is the area's largest. **Cons:** spa and fitness center are not in the towers; location is somewhat isolated from other attractions; feels more like Vegas than the Carolinas. *Rooms from: $429* *719 N. Beach Blvd.* *855/904–4858* *www.northbeachrentals.com* *300 condos* *No meals.*

Nightlife

Alabama Theatre

MUSIC CLUBS | The 2,250-seat Alabama Theatre has a regular variety show of singing and dancing with a wonderful patriotic closing; the theater also hosts guest music and comedy artists during the year and a holiday-themed show. *Barefoot Landing, 4750 U.S. 17 S* *843/272–1111* *www.alabama-theatre.com.*

Duck's Night Life

DANCE CLUBS | You can dance the shag and take lessons from the pros at this classic club that hosts shag events throughout the year for dedicated and novice dancers. There's also an on-site café. *229 Main St.* *843/663–3858* *www.ducksatoceandrive.com.*

★ **Fat Harold's Beach Club**

DANCE CLUBS | Step back to a bygone era when you enter the jukebox front door of this hip-movin' shag spot that's constantly hosting shag contests. Two different dance floors guarantee you can find a melody that gets you dancing, or just hang along the edges and take in the action. The Shag City Grill sells burgers and sandwiches. *212 Main St.* *843/249–5779* *www.fatharolds.com.*

House of Blues

MUSIC CLUBS | This giant shed (quite literally—its exterior facade is rusty corrugated steel) showcases up-and-coming talent and national names in blues, rock, jazz, country, and R&B in its 2,000-seat concert hall and on stages in its Southern-style restaurant with patio. The Sunday gospel brunch is a great deal, and there's free live music on the deck every evening. *Barefoot Landing, 4640 U.S. 17 S* *843/272–3000 for tickets* *www.houseofblues.com.*

OD Arcade and Lounge

MUSIC CLUBS | This place might be small, but it's big on the shag moves, cold drinks, and fish baskets. It has four pool tables and karaoke every Thursday and Sunday. ✉ *100 S. Ocean Blvd.* ☎ *843/249–6460* 🌐 *www.odarcade.com.*

Pirate's Cove Lounge

MUSIC CLUBS | The dance floor and rooftop bar at Pirate's Cove are packed every weekend for rock and R&B bands. The corner location and a bar that opens up to the sidewalk make this a hub of activity. ✉ *205 Main St.* ☎ *843/249–8942.*

Spanish Galleon Night Club

DANCE CLUBS | A '50s-era neon sign welcomes revelers into this classic dance hall inside the Ocean Drive Resort, where DJs and a regular rotation of rock and beach music bands perform every weekend. The Shaggers Hall of Fame is also located here, in the OD Beach Club. ✉ *Ocean Drive Beach and Golf Resort, 100 N. Ocean Blvd.* ☎ *800/438–9590* 🌐 *www.spanishgalleonbeachclub.com.*

Shopping

HOME DECOR

White Pine Artisan Market

HOUSEHOLD ITEMS/FURNITURE | This big red barn is set up like an antiques market but is full of newly built furniture and home decor items, most of which have a farmhouse or beach motif. Offerings range from colorful, funky wall hangings to elaborate, ornate dressers and hutches. ✉ *4340 Big Barn Dr., Little River* ☎ *843/734–1551* 🌐 *whitepine-artisanmarket.com.*

MALLS

Barefoot Landing

SHOPPING CENTERS/MALLS | **FAMILY** | This complex features more than 100 specialty shops, bars, and restaurants, plus amusement rides and the Crooked Hammock Brewery. Restaurants fronting the intracoastal waterway include Greg Norman's Australian Grille and LuLu's. In summer, check out the fireworks displays every Monday night. ✉ *4898 U.S. 17 S* ☎ *843/272–8349* 🌐 *www.bflanding.com.*

Myrtle Beach Mall

SHOPPING CENTERS/MALLS | This indoor mall sits in the Briarcliffe section just north of Tanger Outlets and just south of Barefoot Landing, offering department store and boutique standards, as well as a monstrous Bass Pro Shop, a movie theater, and a model train exhibit. ✉ *10177 N. Kings Hwy.* ☎ *843/272–4040* 🌐 *www.mymallmyrtlebeach.com.*

Activities

FISHING

Cherry Grove Fishing Pier

FISHING | **FAMILY** | This narrow, wooden pier has a two-story observation deck and reaches 985 feet into the ocean, making it the place to catch pompano, bluefish, and mackerel. You can rent tackle and buy bait at the pier. Early morning and late afternoon are the best time to catch fish. ✉ *3500 N. Ocean Blvd.* ☎ *843/249–1625* 🌐 *www.cherrygrovepier.com* 🎟 *$3 for walkers; $7.50 per rod to fish.*

Little River Fishing Fleet

FISHING | This outfitter offers half- and full-day excursions, as well as night fishing and dolphin cruises. ✉ *1901 U.S. 17 S* ☎ *843/361–3323* 🌐 *www.littleriver-fleet.com.*

GOLF AND MINIGOLF

★ Barefoot Resort and Golf

GOLF | The four 18-hole championship courses at Barefoot were designed by Tom Fazio, Davis Love III, Pete Dye, and Greg Norman with all skill levels in mind. Notable details include a replica of plantation ruins on the Love course and only 60 acres of mowable grass among the natural vegetation on the Norman course. The Dye course is the chosen site of the annual Monday After the Masters celebrity tournament, hosted by Hootie and the Blowfish. ✉ *4980 Barefoot Resort Bridge* ☎ *866/638–4818* 🌐 *www.barefootgolf.com* ⛳ *$65–$194, 72 holes; Dye course:*

7343 yds, par 71; Fazio course: 6834 yds, par 71; Love course: 7000 yds, par 72; Norman course: 7200 yds, par 72 *Reservations essential.*

★ Hawaiian Rumble Minigolf

MINIATURE GOLF | Host of the U.S. ProMiniGolf Association's Masters Championship, this course takes minigolf to a whole new level, especially with its centerpiece: a 40-foot-tall, fire-erupting volcano mountain that "rumbles" the ground every 20 minutes. *3210 U.S. 17 S* *843/272–7812* *www.hawaiianrumbleminigolf.com* *$10.*

Tidewater Golf Club

GOLF | Designed by Ken Tomlinson, the magnificent Tidewater peninsula is one of only two courses in the area with an ocean view; the marshes and waterway border other well-crafted parts of the course. Some say the challenging fairways and high bluffs are reminiscent of Pebble Beach. *1400 Tidewater Dr.* *843/913–2424* *www.tidewatergolf.com* *$99–$170, 18 holes, 7044 yds, par 72* *Reservations essential.*

WATER SPORTS

Coastal Scuba

WATER SPORTS | You don't have to go far off the coast of the Grand Strand to explore the underwater world. Man-made reefs boast an array of fish, including sea fans, sponges, reef fish, anemones, urchins, and crabs. A number of shipwrecks are also worth exploring under the waves. Paddle wheelers, freighters, and cargo ships lie in ruins off the coast and are popular scuba spots. Learn to scuba dive, take a dive trip, or just rent equipment at Coastal Scuba, which is PADI certified. *1903 U.S. 17 S* *843/361–3323* *www.coastalscuba.com.*

Myrtle Beach Watersports

WATER SPORTS | You can rent your own pontoon boats or Jet Skis, try parasailing, or book a dolphin cruise aboard the *Sea Screamer* or *Sea Thunder,* 72-foot speedboats that accommodate 141 passengers.

You can rent your own pontoon boats or Jet Skis, try parasailing, or book a dolphin cruise aboard the *Sea Screamer* or *Sea Thunder,* 72-foot speedboats that accommodate 141 passengers. *2111 Little River Neck Rd.* *843/280–7777* *www.myrtlebeachwatersports.com.*

Murrells Inlet

15 miles south of Myrtle Beach via U.S. 17.

Murrells Inlet, a fishing village that bills itself as the seafood capital of South Carolina, is a perfect place to rent a fishing boat or join an excursion. A notable sculpture garden and state park provide other diversions from the beach. Though there are a few chain hotels, they aren't anywhere near the water.

GETTING HERE AND AROUND

Driving south on U.S. Route 17 takes you through Murrells Inlet. If you stay on U.S. Route 17 Bypass, though, you'll miss some of the town's character. Try taking U.S. Route 17 Business to get a taste of the real Murrells Inlet. Most cross streets connect to the bypass if you get turned around.

Sights

★ Brookgreen Gardens

GARDEN | FAMILY | One of the Grand Strand's most magnificent hidden treasures, the 9,100-acre Brookgreen Gardens is the oldest and largest sculpture garden in the United States, with more than 550 examples of figurative American sculpture by such artists as Frederic Remington and Daniel Chester French. Each sculpture is carefully set within garden rooms and outdoor galleries graced by sprawling live oak trees, colorful flowers, and peaceful ponds. The gardens are lush and full in spring and summer, and in winter splashes of color from winter-blooming shrubs are set off against the stark surroundings.

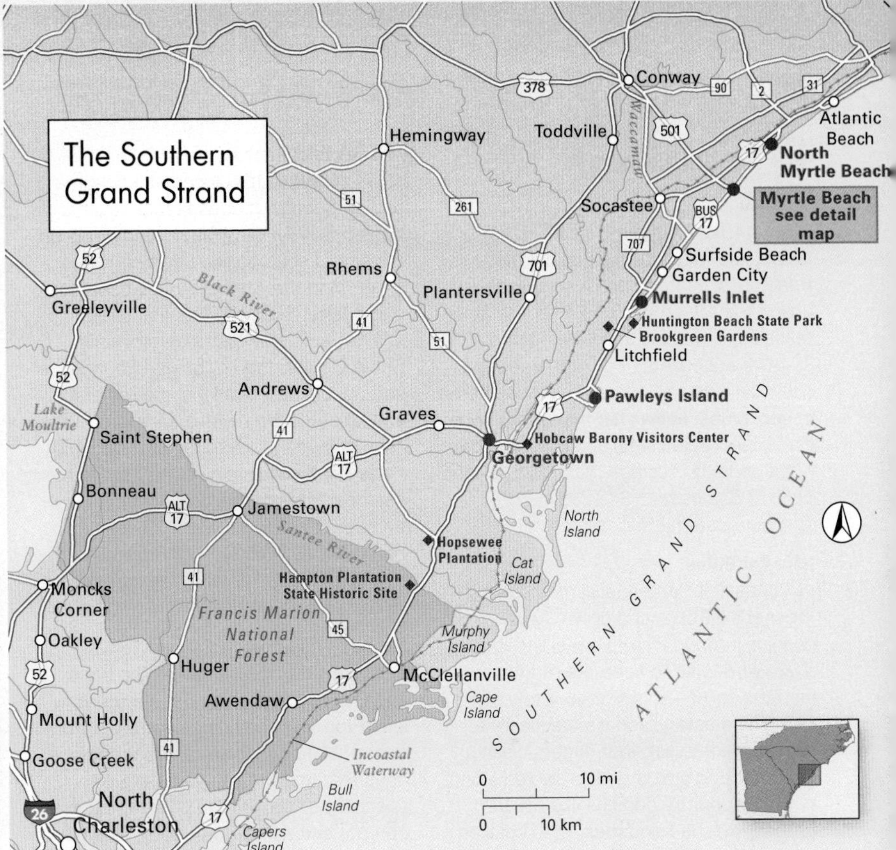

The property was purchased as a winter home for industrialist Archer Huntington and his wife, Anna Hyatt Huntington, in 1929, but they quickly decided to open it to the public as a sculpture garden and wildlife sanctuary. You'll find a Lowcountry zoo (including native red wolves, introduced in 2021), an aviary, a cypress swamp, nature trails, an education center, and a butterfly house. Summer concerts under the stars and the garden's breathtaking Night of a Thousand Candles during the Christmas season are Brookgreen traditions. The gardens are just beyond *The Fighting Stallions,* the Anna Hyatt Huntington sculpture alongside U.S. Route 17. ✉ *1931 Brookgreen Garden Dr.* ✣ *3 miles south of Murrells Inlet on U.S. 17* ☎ *843/235–6000* 🌐 *www.brookgreen.org* 🎫 *$18.*

★ Huntington Beach State Park

NATIONAL/STATE PARK | FAMILY | This 2,500-acre former estate of Archer and Anna Huntington lies east of U.S. Route 17, across from Brookgreen Gardens. The park's focal point is **Atalaya** (circa 1933), their Moorish-style 30-room home. New in 2021 is a $1.2 million nature center, with live native animals, including an aquarium with rays and horseshoe crabs. There are nature trails, ample areas for biking (including a bicycle path from Huntington Beach to Litchfield Beach), fishing, picnic areas, bird-watching expeditions, a playground, concessions, and a campground. ✉ *16148 Ocean Hwy.* ☎ *843/237–4440* 🌐 *southcarolinaparks.com* 🎫 *$8.*

 Restaurants

★ Costa

$$$$ | **ITALIAN** | Although it's billed as Italian, the focus at this popular bistro is fresh, local seafood, from savory local clams to juicy shrimp and diver scallops, tossed with pastas and worked into creative appetizers. The interior features open ceilings and a classy nautical theme in cool blues. **Known for:** thoughtful wine list; impeccable clams and mussels; date night go-to. *Average main: $25 4606 U.S. 17 Business 843/299–1970 www.costamyrtlebeach.com.*

Inlet Bar B Que

$$ | **BARBECUE** | When local mainstay Prosser's BBQ closed down, new owners jumped in with a rebrand, but they were wise to keep the menu and vibe the same—this ain't your four-star fine-dining eatery, and it's practically a requirement to lick your fingers clean. Lip-smacking pulled pork is served along with Lowcountry goodies like collard greens, mashed potatoes, fried chicken, macaroni and cheese, banana pudding, and peach cobbler. **Known for:** all-you-can-eat Southern barbecue buffet; bang-for-your-buck value; chicken bog. *Average main: $15 3750 U.S. 17 Business 843/357–1133 Closed Mon. and Tues.*

Inlet Provision Company

$$$ | **SEAFOOD** | Like most spots in Murrells Inlet, this newcomer focuses on seafood, but its approach adds much-needed flair, from a trio of lobster, crab, and shrimp cakes to peanuts boiled in local beer. Enjoy it all with a horizon view across the salt marsh, washed down with a local pale ale. **Known for:** quality local beer list; steam-pot entrées; key lime pie and banana pudding dessert jars. *Average main: $22 4891 U.S. 17 Business 843/299–2444 inletprovisioncompany.com Closed Sun.*

★ Lee's Inlet Kitchen

$$$$ | **SEAFOOD** | It's closed at lunchtime and on Sunday; it doesn't take reservations or have a view, but nobody fries up a mess of seafood like Lee's, which is something the restaurant has been doing since 1948. Even the biggest eaters will get their fill when they order the Shore Dinner: fried or broiled flounder, shrimp, oysters, scallops, deviled crab, and lobster, along with a shrimp cocktail, clam chowder, hush puppies, fries, and coleslaw. **Known for:** huge platters of fried seafood; Lowcountry authenticity; family owned for nearly 75 years. *Average main: $30 4460 U.S. 17 Business 843/651–2881 leesinletkitchen.com Closed Sun. No lunch.*

Nance's Creekfront Restaurant

$$$ | **SEAFOOD** | You can smell the brine and Old Bay seasoning the minute you leave your car and head toward the front door of Nance's. Oysters, the small local ones that taste of saltwater, are the specialty, available fried or steamed in an iron pot and served with butter. **Known for:** steamed local oysters; 10-layer chocolate cake for dessert; views across the marsh. *Average main: $24 4883 U.S. 17 Business 843/651–2696 nancescreekfront.com No lunch.*

Wahoo's Fish House

$$$$ | **SEAFOOD** | Whether you choose to sit inside the contemporary confines of this classy waterfront restaurant or outside at the tropical-tiki Raw Bar, you can't go wrong with atmosphere or cuisine. The menu features seafood and sushi, as well as Lowcountry-inspired dishes. **Known for:** an amalgam of sushi and fried seafood platters; live music in the evenings; beautiful views. *Average main: $27 3993 U.S. 17 Business 843/651–5800 www.wahoosfishhouse.com.*

The drive from the Grand Strand to peaceful Pawleys Island makes for an excellent road trip.

Nightlife

Hot Fish Club

MUSIC CLUBS | This happening waterfront joint is set up for a backyard party, featuring live music on the gazebo stage every Friday and Saturday night. There's also an excellent menu of steamed, fried, and broiled seafood. ✉ *4911 U.S. 17 Business* ☎ *843/357–9175* 🌐 *www.hotfishclub.com.*

Murrells Inlet Marsh Walk

GATHERING PLACES | **FAMILY** | You can have a drink, watch boats come back from a day of fishing, hear live music, and enjoy the evening breeze with a stroll along the Murrells Inlet Marsh Walk, a picturesque boardwalk that connects eight waterfront bars and restaurants, from Drunken Jack's on the north end to Wicked Tuna at the Crazy Sister Marina on the south end. On the Fourth of July, the Marsh Walk serves as your front-row seat to the wildly popular Boat Parade. Also included along the way are colorful waterfront stops with fanciful names like Dead Dog Saloon, Creek Ratz, Bubba's Love Shak, and Wahoo's. ✉ *4025 U.S. 17 Business* 🌐 *www.marshwalk.com.*

Activities

GOLF

Indigo Creek Golf Club

GOLF | Beauty and bargains await at Indigo Creek, a course cut through forests of huge oaks and pines that once surrounded an indigo plantation. The Willard Byrd design boasts tall oaks, meandering creeks, and stellar maintenance of the Tifdwarf Bermuda greens and tees. ✉ *9480 Indigo Club Dr.* ☎ *843/650–1809* 🌐 *www.indigocreekgolfclub.com* *$45–$75, 18 holes, 6747 yds, par 72* *Reservations essential.*

TPC Myrtle Beach

GOLF | Designed by the legendary Tom Fazio, this former home to the Senior PGA Tour Championship was also the training grounds for PGA Tour star and Myrtle Beach local Dustin Johnson, who founded the Dustin Johnson Golf School here. The scenery is both beautiful and challenging, with plenty of towering pines, wetlands, and water hazards. ✉ *1199 TPC Blvd.* ☎ *877/283–2122* 🌐 *www.tpcmyrtlebeach.com* *$112–$138, 18 holes, 6950 yds, par 72* *Reservations essential.*

Pawleys Island

10 miles south of Murrells Inlet via U.S. 17.

About 4 miles long and a half-mile wide, Pawleys, sometimes referred to as "arrogantly shabby," began as a resort before the Civil War, when wealthy planters and their families summered here. Today, it's mostly made up of weathered old summer cottages nestled in groves of oleander and oak trees. Headed south, this is the place where you've officially left behind the bustle of the Grand Strand and entered the slower pace of the Lowcountry. You can watch the famous Pawleys Island hammocks being made and bicycle around admiring the beach houses, many dating to the early 1800s. Golf and tennis are nearby. **TIP→ Parking is limited on Pawleys and facilities are nil, so arrive early and bring what you need.**

GETTING HERE AND AROUND

Pawleys Island is south of Murrells Inlet on U.S. Route 17. Take North Causeway Drive off the main highway to experience the natural beauty of the island. A 2-mile-long historic district is home to rustic beach cottages and historic buildings, including a church.

★ Pawleys Island

BEACH—SIGHT | FAMILY | Over 3 miles of tranquil and natural beach run along the shoreline of Pawleys Island. The surrounding architecture consists only of beach cottages and low-lying resorts, so it's a peaceful retreat. Lack of crowds allows for bicycling on packed sand, shelling, or napping on a hammock. Note that there aren't any lifeguards. **Best for:** surfing; swimming; walking. **Amenities:** parking (limited; on side streets). ✉ *Pawleys Island* 🌐 *www.townofpawleysisland.com.*

Frank's

$$$$ | ECLECTIC | This local favorite serves dishes that give traditional cooking methods and ingredients a new twist. The former 1930s grocery store now offers a fine dining experience with wood floors, framed French posters, and cozy fireside seating. **Known for:** local seafood dishes like grouper and shrimp with Dijon cream sauce and grits; informal vibe with sophisticated food; long by-the-glass wine list. $ *Average main: $28* ✉ *10434 Ocean Hwy.* ☎ *843/237–3030* 🌐 *www.franksandoutback.com* *Closed Sun.*

Habaneros

$ | MEXICAN | The fish tacos here are to die for, but the full menu of Mexican favorites at this colorful cantina proves that Pawleys Island is not just about seafood. Take a seat inside or on the festive deck and order a burrito with secret sauce and a margarita. **Known for:** the sunny outdoor bar and deck; margaritas priced right; party scene on weekend evenings. $ *Average main: $10* ✉ *11151 Ocean Hwy.* ☎ *843/235–9595* 🌐 *www.habanerosrestaurant.com.*

Hog Heaven

$ | BARBECUE | Part barbecue joint, part seafood shack (after 5), Hog Heaven has a wonderful smoky aroma that perfumes U.S. Route 17 as you approach. **Known for:** a generous all-you-can-eat buffet; the curious wedding of pork barbecue and fried seafood; laid-back country atmosphere. $ *Average main: $10* ✉ *7147 Ocean Hwy.* ☎ *843/237–7444* 🌐 *www.hogheaveninc.com.*

Did You Know?

The centuries-old community of Pawleys Island has a complex and fascinating history, including slave rebellions, shipwrecks, and rumors of supernatural occurrences.

Landolfi's

$ | **ITALIAN** | This fourth-generation-owned Italian pastry shop, deli, and restaurant has excellent coffee, hearty hoagies, pizzas, homemade sorbet, and delicious and authentic pastries, including cannoli and *pasticciotti* (rich cookielike pastries filled with jam). Both counter and table service are available. **Known for:** wood-fired pizza and panini; laid-back atmosphere; rich cakes and desserts. *Average main: $10* *9305 Ocean Hwy.* *843/237–7900* *Closed Sun. and Mon.*

Coffee and Quick Bites

Kudzu Bakery & Market

$ | **BAKERY** | Come here for the justifiably famous key lime pie and red velvet cake, both of which are available whole or by the slice. Kudzu is also a great source for ready-to-cook specialties, such as cheese biscuits, macaroni and cheese, and quiche. **Known for:** fresh bread and deli items; great wine selection; decadent desserts. *Average main: $12* *221 Willbrook Blvd.* *843/235–8560* *www.kudzubakery.com* *Closed Sun.*

Litchfield Beach and Golf Resort

$$$ | **RESORT** | **FAMILY** | This beautifully landscaped 4,500-acre resort features a nearly 2-mile stretch of oceanfront, marshfront, and golf course accommodations that range from high-rise condos to sprawling mansions. **Pros:** geared to all kinds of travelers; beautiful natural surroundings; modern amenities. **Cons:** some properties are at least a 15-minute walk to the beach; minimum stays during high season; it's a drive to non-resort restaurants. *Rooms from: $240* *14276 Ocean Hwy.* *888/734–8228* *www.litchfieldbeach.com* *560 units* *No meals.*

The Oceanfront Litchfield Inn

$$$ | **RESORT** | Head across the creek to this beachfront inn just minutes from U.S. Route 17, and you'll immediately feel the world slow down. **Pros:** on-site dining at the Cabana beach bar and Austin's Ocean One fine-dining restaurant; grab-and-go breakfast; beach chairs to borrow. **Cons:** views vary significantly; concrete building exteriors, although attractively painted, feel more utilitarian than cozy; it's a drive to other dining options. *Rooms from: $229* *1 Norris Dr.* *843/237–4211* *litchfieldinn.com* *160 rooms* *Free breakfast.*

Sea View Inn

$$$ | **B&B/INN** | A self-described "barefoot paradise," Sea View is a no-frills beachside boardinghouse (there are no TVs or in-room phones) with long porches. **Pros:** quaint, quiet oceanfront experience is completely unlike the megaresorts on the Grand Strand; all meals are included; on a quiet stretch of beach. **Cons:** not wheelchair accessible; credit cards not accepted; introverts may not love the close interaction with other guests. *Rooms from: $245* *414 Myrtle Ave.* *843/237–4253* *www.seaviewinn.net* *No credit cards* *Closed Nov.–Mar.* *16 rooms* *All meals.*

Pawleys Island Festival of Music and Art

ARTS FESTIVALS | Pawleys Island comes alive each October during this festival that brings national and local artists together for a month of concerts, exhibitions, and readings. Past performers have included David Sanborn and Delbert McClinton. *Pawleys Island* *843/626–8911* *www.pawleysmusic.com.*

Shopping

Hammock Shops Village

SHOPPING CENTERS/MALLS | Two dozen boutiques, gift shops, and restaurants, set in cottages built with old beams, timber, and ballast brick, under a canopy of live oaks, make up this charming shopping district. Outside the Original Hammock Shop, in the Hammock Weavers' Pavilion, craftspeople demonstrate the 19th-century art of weaving the famous cotton-rope Pawleys Island hammocks. Also look for jewelry, toys, antiques, and designer fashions. ✉ *10880 Ocean Hwy.* ☎ *843/350–2220* 🌐 *hammockshopsvillage.com.*

Litchfield Books

BOOKS/STATIONERY | This independent bookstore is the place to pick up a beach read or regional-interest book. It's also the home base for authors who want to return home after making it on the bestseller list, via Pawleys Island's Moveable Feast series of lectures and classes. ✉ *Fresh Market Commons, 11421 Ocean Hwy.* ☎ *843/237–8138* 🌐 *litchfieldbooks.com.*

Activities

GOLF

Caledonia Golf and Fish Club

GOLF | Designed by Mike Strantz, this course on a former Southern rice plantation is a stunning Lowcountry beauty, from its entrance avenue of live oaks, continuing around pretty streams, to its ending, with an 18th hole that borders an old rice field. ✉ *369 Caledonia Dr.* ☎ *843/237–3675, 800/483–6800* 🌐 *www.caledoniagolfandfishclub.com* 🏌 *$99–$189, 18 holes, 6526 yds, par 70* ✍ *Reservations essential.*

Pawleys Plantation Golf and Country Club

GOLF | This Jack Nicklaus–designed course demands respect from golfers for its several tricky holes surrounded by saltwater marshes. Off the course, many reserve the posh clubhouse and patio for four-course wedding receptions, with the 18th hole as a backdrop. ✉ *70 Tanglewood Dr.* ☎ *877/283–2122* 🌐 *www.pawleysplantation.com* 🏌 *$89, 18 holes, 7026 yds, par 72* ✍ *Reservations essential.*

Tradition Golf Club

GOLF | Rated as one of the best-maintained courses on the Grand Strand, this Ron Garl–designed beauty is known for its wide greens and fairways, and is also affordable. ✉ *1027 Willbrook Blvd.* ☎ *877/283–2122* 🌐 *www.traditionclub-myrtlebeach.com* 🏌 *$74, 18 holes, 6313 yds, par 72* ✍ *Reservations essential.*

Willbrook Plantation

GOLF | Dan Maples designed this course with nature in mind, on two former rice plantations that now wind past historical markers, a cemetery for the enslaved people that once toiled here, and a tobacco shack. Polls have ranked Willbrook high on the list with women, in particular, for its Southern hospitality and leafy surrounds. ✉ *379 Country Club Dr.* ☎ *877/283–2122* 🌐 *www.willbrookgolf.com* 🏌 *$89, 18 holes, 6704 yds, par 72* ✍ *Reservations essential.*

Georgetown

13 miles south of Pawleys Island via U.S. 17.

Founded on Winyah Bay in 1729, Georgetown was once the center of America's colonial rice empire. It had a prosperous plantation culture (built on the backs of enslaved people) developed on a scale comparable to Charleston's, and the historic district is among the prettiest in the state. Today, oceangoing vessels still come to Georgetown's busy port, and the **Harborwalk,** the restored waterfront, hums with activity. **■ TIP→ Many of the restaurants along the river side of Front Street have back decks overlooking the water that come alive in the early evening for happy hour.**

GETTING HERE AND AROUND

Georgetown is accessible from U.S. Route 17, as well as U.S. Route 701. The heart of the town is near the waterfront—an easy trip off the highway down any side street is worth it. Take Cannon Street to Front Street to see the harbor.

VISITOR INFORMATION

CONTACTS Georgetown Visitors Center. ✉ *531 Front St.* ☎ *843/546–8436* 🌐 *www.visitgeorge.com.*

Sights

★ Hampton Plantation State Historic Site
HOUSE | The true star of Archibald Rutledge's home (he was the poet laureate of South Carolina for 39 years until his death in 1973) may not be his 18th-century plantation house but the centuries-old Washington Oak in the yard, a now-massive tree saved by the first president. The mansion's exterior has been restored; cutaway sections in the finely crafted interior show the changes made through the centuries. There are walking trails and picnic areas on the grounds. You can also learn more about the slaves that toiled on the plantation, as well as freed people who made their homes in the area after empancipation. ✉ *1950 Rutledge Rd., McClellanville* ☎ *843/546–9361* 🌐 *www.southcarolinaparks.com/hampton* *Mansion $10; grounds free.*

Hobcaw Barony Visitors Center
NATURE PRESERVE | This historic landmark was once the vast estate of the late Wall Street financier Bernard M. Baruch. Franklin D. Roosevelt and Winston Churchill came here to confer with him. A small interpretive center has exhibits on coastal ecology and history, with special emphasis on the Baruch family. There are aquariums, touch tanks, video presentations, and guided two-hour tours of the 16,000-acre wildlife refuge. ✉ *22 Hobcaw Rd.* ✣ *Off U.S. 17, 2 miles north of Georgetown* ☎ *843/546–4623* 🌐 *www.hobcawbarony.org* *Visitor center free; tours $30* *Closed Sun.*

Hopsewee Plantation
HOUSE | Built in 1735, this National Historic Landmark overlooks the North Santee River and is surrounded by moss-draped live oaks, magnolias, and tree-size camellias. The mansion has a fine Georgian staircase and hand-carved lighted-candle moldings. Tours focused on the lives of the enslaved people who worked here and the Gullah culture of their descendents occur Tuesday through Thursday and sweetgrass basket-weaving workshops are held on Thursday. The River Oak Cottage Tea Room on-site serves a full menu of Southern treats. ✉ *494 Hopsewee Rd.* ✣ *Off U.S. 17, 12 miles south of Georgetown* ☎ *843/546–7891* 🌐 *www.hopsewee.com* *$20* *Closed Sun. and Mon.*

Kaminski House Museum
HOUSE | Overlooking the Sampit River from a bluff is this sprawling historic home (circa 1769) that's notable for its collections of regional antiques and furnishings and its Chippendale and Duncan Phyfe furniture, Royal Doulton vases, and silver. Events at the Kaminski House include summer outdoor concerts on the lawn. ✉ *1003 Front St.* ☎ *843/546–7706* 🌐 *www.kaminskimuseum.org* *Closed Sun.*

Prince George Winyah Church
RELIGIOUS SITE | Named after King George II, this church still serves the Anglican parish established in 1721. It was built in 1737 with bricks brought from England. ✉ *300 Broad St.* ☎ *843/546–4358* 🌐 *www.pgwinyah.com* *Donations accepted.*

Rice Museum
MUSEUM | A graceful market and meeting building in the heart of Georgetown, topped by an 1842 clock and tower, has been converted into a unique museum, with maps, tools, and dioramas that outline the history of rice in Georgetown. At the museum's Prevost Gallery next door

is the Brown's Ferry river freighter, the oldest American-built water-going vessel in existence. The museum gift shop has local pine needle baskets, African dolls, and art (including baskets made from whole cloves), as well as South Carolina rice and honey. *633 Front St. 843/546–7423 www.ricemuseum.org $7 Closed Sun.*

Wooden Boat Show

FESTIVAL | FAMILY | Each October, Front Street is transformed into a popular event where craftsmen showcase their works in the wooden boat exhibits. There's an intense boatbuilding competition (finished off by a rowing race on the river), kids' model-building contest, live music, and arts and crafts. All proceeds from the show are donated to the Harbor Historical Association's maritime museum. *Georgetown 843/520–0111 www.woodenboatshow.com.*

Restaurants

River Room

$$$$ | SEAFOOD | Enjoy Sampit River views from most tables at this upscale spot that's especially romantic at night, when the oil lamps and brass fixtures cast a warm glow on the dark wood and brick interior of the early-20th-century building. Menu highlights include chargrilled fish (especially the Carolina grouper), Cajun fried oysters, seafood pastas, and steaks. **Known for:** fresh fish entrées; lively waterfront atmosphere; boat slips to arrive by water. *Average main: $26 801 Front St. 843/527–4110 www.riverroomgeorgetown.com Closed Sun.*

★ Root

$$$ | MODERN AMERICAN | The menu at this farm-to-table kitchen along Front Street is helping to transform dining in the whole town, raising consciousness about ingredient sourcing and seasonality, not to mention creative presentations like blueberry jalapeño bacon scallops and crab cakes packed into eggrolls. **Known for:** outside-the-box menu; lots of veggie options; modern, relaxed dining room. *Average main: $24 919 Front St. 843/461–9344 rootgeorgetown.com.*

Coffee and Quick Bites

Thomas Café

$ | SOUTHERN | Though it might look the part, this isn't a greasy spoon: the luncheonette dishes up great fried chicken, homemade biscuits, and pie, plus grits, eggs, country ham, and other breakfast favorites. Join the regulars at the counter, or sit in one of the booths or café tables in the 1920s storefront building. **Known for:** classic Southern lunch fare; famous fried chicken; local hangout. *Average main: $10 703 Front St. 843/546–7776 thomascafe.net Closed weekends.*

Hotels

Hampton Inn Georgetown Marina

$$ | HOTEL | Watch boats cruise up and down the river at this riverside resort with spectacular views of the intracoastal waterway. **Pros:** there is a marina outside the hotel if you'd like to arrive by boat; walkable to Georgetown's old village; free breakfast. **Cons:** lacks the unique aspects of some other hotels; small pool; not near the beach. *Rooms from: $169 420 Marina Dr. 843/545–5000 hilton.com 98 rooms Free breakfast.*

★ 620 Prince

$$ | B&B/INN | A Pawleys Island local renovated this 19th-century home in 2017, transforming it into a luxury six-bedroom retreat with ample porches for relaxing. **Pros:** full continental breakfast, plus afternoon hors d'oeuvres; outdoor swimming pool; complimentary bikes to use. **Cons:** it's a 20-minute drive to the beach; two rooms are in a separate cottage, not the historic home; dining room lacks the modern flair of other spaces. *Rooms from: $200 620 Prince St. 843/485–4899 www.620prince.com 6 rooms Free breakfast.*

BOATING

Cap'n Rod's Lowcountry Tours

BOATING | FAMILY | Cruise up the river with Captain Rod, past abandoned rice plantations, and hear stories about the belles who lived there; another tour visits a lighthouse and an unspoiled barrier island beach. ✉ *701 Front St.* ☎ *843/477–0287* 🌐 *www.lowcountrytours.com* 🎫 *$38.*

Rover Boat Tours

BOATING | FAMILY | Book a three-hour tour to sail the high seas to an untouched barrier island past the Winyah Bay Lighthouse for an exclusive afternoon of shelling. Pack snacks for the nearly hour-long trip to and from the island. ✉ *735 Front St., on the harbor* ☎ *843/546–8822* 🌐 *roverboattours.com* 🎫 *$38.*

Wallace Sailing Charters

BOATING | Feel the spray on your face as you explore Winyah Bay aboard a 40-foot yacht with Captain Dave of Wallace Sailing Charters. Each trip is limited to six passengers, so it feels like you're touring on a private yacht. ✉ *525 Front St.* ☎ *843/902–6999* 🌐 *www.wallacesailingcharters.com* 🎫 *$369 for 6 guests* ☞ *All cruises are by appointment only.*

CANOEING AND KAYAKING

★ Black River Outdoors

CANOEING/ROWING/SKULLING | This outfitter offers naturalist-guided canoe and kayak tours of the tidelands and swamps of Georgetown County. Guides are well versed not just in the wildlife but also in local lore. Tours take kayakers past settings such as Drunken Jack's (the island that supposedly holds Blackbeard's booty), and Chicora Wood plantation, where dikes and trunk gates mark canals dug by the enslaved to facilitate rice growing in the area. It's said that digging the canals required as much manual labor as Egypt's pyramids. Wildlife tends to be more active during the early morning or late afternoon; there's a good chance you'll hear owls hooting on the evening tours, especially in fall. ✉ *Georgetown* ☎ *843/546–4840* 🌐 *www.blackriveroutdoors.com.*

GOLF

Wedgefield Country Club

GOLF | This premier Georgetown course on a former rice plantation has a ghost story: people have reported sightings of the ghost of a Revolutionary War–era British soldier, who lost his head to Francis Marion while guarding valuable prisoners in the plantation house. The spirit's appearance near the house is accompanied by the sound of horses' hooves. The 18th hole is surrounded by remnants from the original home. Most of the course is flat, a result of the rice fields' terrain. The on-site Manor House serves a menu of Southern-leaning surf and turf. ✉ *129 Clubhouse La., off U.S. 701* ☎ *843/546–8587* 🌐 *www.wedgefieldcountryclub.com* ⛳ *$35, 18 holes, 7072 yds, Par 71* ✍ *Reservations essential.*

Chapter 8

CHARLESTON, SC

Updated by
Stratton Lawrence
and Hanna Raskin

Sights ★★★★★ | Restaurants ★★★★★ | Hotels ★★★★★ | Shopping ★★★★☆ | Nightlife ★★★★☆

WELCOME TO CHARLESTON, SC

TOP REASONS TO GO

★ **Dining out:** Charleston is one of the country's biggest culinary destinations, with talented chefs who offer innovative twists on the city's traditional Lowcountry cuisine.

★ **Seeing art:** The city abounds with galleries, so you'll never run out of places to see remarkable art.

★ **Spoleto Festival USA:** If you're lucky enough to visit in late May and early June, you'll find a city under a cultural siege: Spoleto's flood of indoor and outdoor performances (opera, music, dance, and theater) is impossible to miss.

★ **The Battery:** The views from the terminus of Charleston's peninsula—of the elegant waterfront mansions that line White Point Garden and across the harbor to Fort Sumter—are the loveliest in the city.

★ **History lessons:** A wealth of markets, historic homes, and churches take you back in time.

1 South of Broad and the French Quarter. The southern tip of the peninsula is home to the Battery and many historic mansions.

2 Lower King and the Market. The majority of downtown Charleston's shops and hotels are clustered around these two perpendicular thoroughfares. King Street is the primary shopping artery that bisects the lower peninsula, while Market Street stays abuzz all day thanks to the City Market.

3 Upper King. The city's hottest new restaurants—and many of its new hotels—have emerged along upper King Street. On weekend nights, this is where the action is.

4 Mount Pleasant. East of Charleston, across the Cooper River, is Mount Pleasant, an affluent suburb with historic sites like the USS *Yorktown*.

5 Greater Charleston. Across the Ashley River lies the West Ashley suburb, with its three major historic plantations that offer visitors lessons about the city's integral role in the slave trade. Just south are low-key beaches and islands, including James Island and Folly Beach.

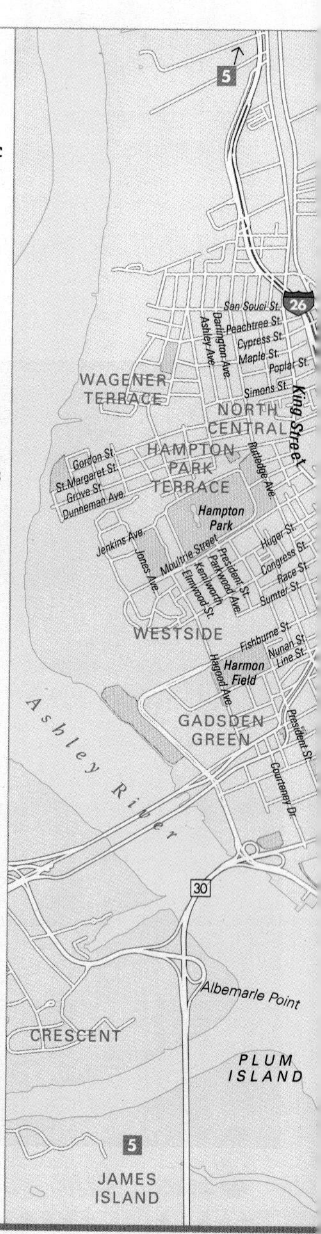

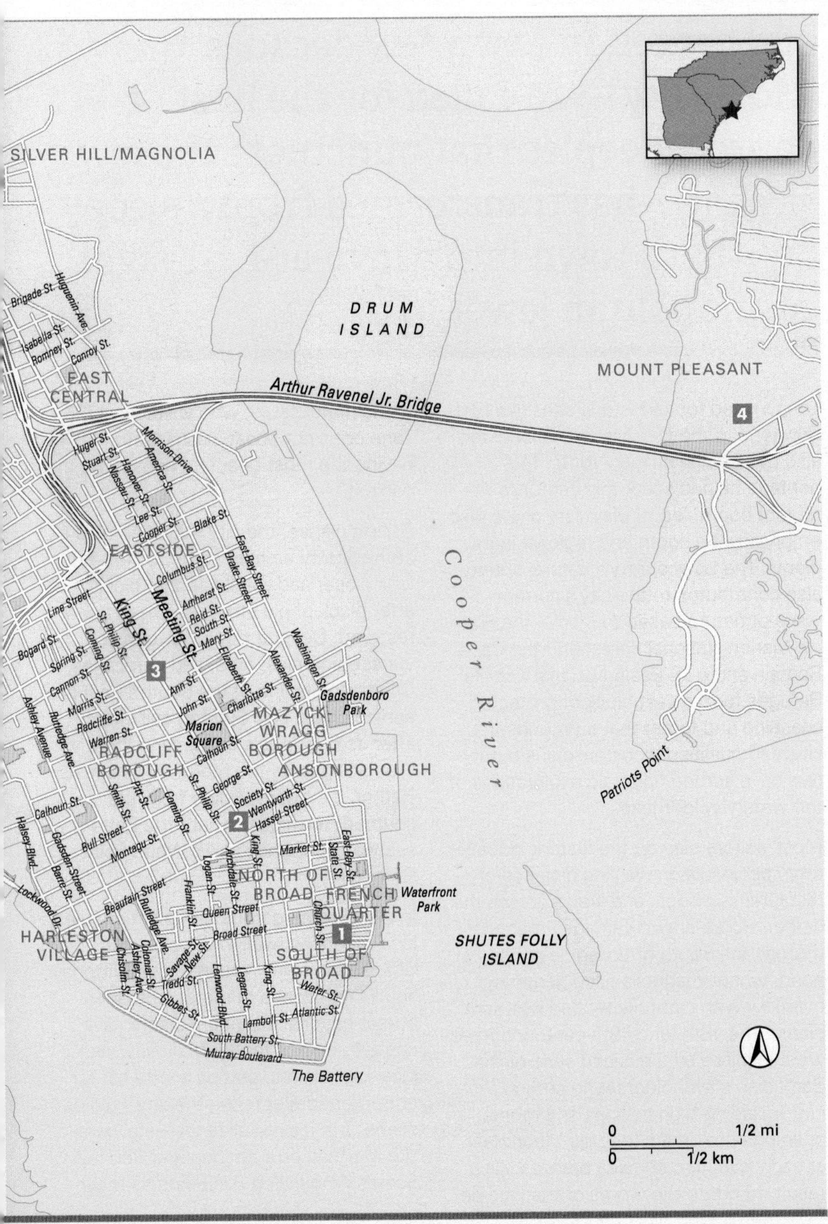
SILVER HILL/MAGNOLIA
DRUM ISLAND
MOUNT PLEASANT
EAST CENTRAL
Arthur Ravenel Jr. Bridge
EASTSIDE
Cooper River
King St.
Meeting St.
MAZYCK-WRAGG BOROUGH
RADCLIFF BOROUGH
ANSONBOROUGH
Gadsdenboro Park
Marion Square
Patriots Point
NORTH OF BROAD
FRENCH QUARTER
Waterfront Park
HARLESTON VILLAGE
SOUTH OF BROAD
SHUTES FOLLY ISLAND
The Battery
Brigade St.
Huguenin Ave.
Isabella St.
Romney St.
Conroy St.
Huger St.
Stuart St.
Morrison Drive
America St.
Hanover St.
Nassau St.
Lee St.
Cooper St.
Blake St.
East Bay Street
Drake Street
Columbus St.
Line Street
Amherst St.
Reid St.
South St.
Mary St.
Bogard St.
Spring St.
Coming St.
St. Philip St.
Washington St.
Cannon St.
Ann St.
Elizabeth St.
Alexander St.
John St.
Charlotte St.
Morris St.
Radcliffe St.
Ashley Avenue
Rutledge Ave.
Warren St.
Calhoun St.
George St.
Smith St.
Pitt St.
Society St.
Wentworth St.
Hassel Street
Bull Street
Montagu St.
Halsey Blvd.
Gadsden Street
Barre St.
Market St.
State St.
Logan St.
Archdale St.
Lockwood Dr.
Beaufain Street
Franklin St.
Queen Street
Church St.
Broad Street
Colonial St.
Ashley Ave.
Chisolm St.
Savage St.
New St.
Tradd St.
Lenwood Blvd.
Legare St.
Water St.
Gibbes St.
Lamboll St.
Atlantic St.
South Battery St.
Murray Boulevard
1
2
3
4
0
1/2 mi
0
1/2 km

From stately pastel-hued mansions to sweeping Lowcountry marsh vistas, Charleston shows off its charm, front and center. In just a few decades, the "Holy City"—so called for the host of church steeples that punctuate the low skyline—has transformed from a sleepy Southern town into a love-at-first-sight cosmopolitan jewel.

Long visited for its historic sites like Fort Sumter and the City Market, Charleston also boasts rich culinary roots. That heritage helped spark this century's restaurant boom, led by visionary chefs who emphasize heirloom and regional ingredients. The Lowcountry's natural bounty also contributes to the city's current wave of nature-based tourism—the Francis Marion National Forest and the Cape Romain and ACE Basin National Wildlife Refuges form a vast block of protected coastline and forest that surrounds the city, and qualified, eco-conscious outfitters have sprung up to aid explorations of the watery wilderness.

Most visitors stay on the historic downtown peninsula, in walking distance of restaurants, shops, and views across the harbor. Horse-drawn carriages meander through the South of Broad neighborhood, where magnolia-filled gardens overflow with carefully tended heirloom plants. The 18th- and 19th-century homes were inspired by the island style of the Barbadian slaveholders who settled the city, including high ceilings and rooms opening onto broad "piazzas" (porches) at each level to catch sea breezes. As a result, to quote the words of the Duc de La Rochefoucauld, who visited in 1796, "one does not boast in Charleston of having the most beautiful house, but the coolest."

At first glance, the city may resemble a 19th-century etching come to life—but look closer and you'll see that block after block of old structures have been restored. Despite three centuries of wars, epidemics, fires, and hurricanes, Charleston is one of the South's best-preserved cities. Fort Sumter, still intact after its critical role in sparking the Civil War, still guards the mouth of Charleston Harbor. It's clearly visible from the city's southern terminus, where the Battery sea wall surrounds idyllic White Point Garden.

In a city with rigorous preservation rules, locals literally dwell in the past, but Charleston is very much a town of today. You'll find dozens of restaurants that attract national attention; diners have come to expect thoughtfully sourced local ingredients, setting a lofty bar for entrepreneurs entering the city's dining scene. But it's not all fancy—stalwarts like Martha Lou's Kitchen and Rodney Scott's Whole Hog BBQ earn as much buzz as the detail-oriented white-tablecloth spots. The culinary scene culminates in March with the annual Wine + Food Festival, when the nation's celebrated chefs and food personalities flock to Charleston for a long weekend of noshing and imbibing. That influx is dwarfed in May and June during the internationally heralded Spoleto Festival USA, when arts patrons from around the world come to enjoy 17 days of international concerts, dance performances, operas, and plays at various venues citywide. During the day, attendees can shop for museum-quality paintings and antiques along King Street or just relax in the sand on Folly Beach or Sullivan's Island, just 20 minutes from downtown.

Planning

When to Go

Spring and fall are the most popular times to visit Charleston. The former sees courtyard gardens blooming and warm temperatures coaxing sundresses and seersucker suits out of local closets. The latter finds residents and tourists alike returning to the sidewalks to stroll, once summer's most intense heat (and hair-curling humidity) mellows out. There are truly only two slightly slower times for tourism in Charleston (July to mid-September and January to mid-February), so those loathe to brave crowds or vie for dinner reservations are best advised to visit during those months.

Planning Your Time

The best way to get acquainted with Charleston is to take a carriage ride or walking tour, especially one that takes you through the South of Broad neighborhood. You can get acquainted with Charleston's Historic District at your leisure, especially if you can devote at least three days to the city, which will allow time to explore the sights west of the Ashley River. With another day, you can explore Mount Pleasant, and if you have even more time, head out to the coastal islands, where golf and beach activities are the order of the day.

Getting Here and Around

AIR TRAVEL

Charleston International Airport (CHS) is about 12 miles west of downtown. Charleston Executive Airport on Johns Island is used by noncommercial aircraft, as is Mount Pleasant Regional Airport.

Charleston International Airport Ground Transportation arranges shuttles for $14 per person to downtown. You can arrange to be picked up by the same service when returning to the airport by making a reservation with the driver.

AIRPORT INFORMATION Charleston International Airport (CHS). ✉ *5500 International Blvd., North Charleston* ☎ *843/767–7000* 🌐 *www.iflychs.com.*

BOAT AND FERRY TRAVEL

Boaters—many traveling the intracoastal waterway—dock at Ashley Marina and City Marina, in Charleston Harbor. The Charleston Water Taxi is a delightful way to travel between Charleston and Mount Pleasant. Some people take the $12 round-trip journey just for fun. It departs from the Charleston Maritime Center. Do not confuse its address at 10 Wharfside as being near the area of Adger's Wharf, which is on the lower peninsula. The water taxi departs daily every hour from 9 am to 8 pm from mid-March to mid-November; 10 am to 6 pm Saturday only from mid-November to December 26; 10 am to 6 pm December 26–31; and 10 am to 6 pm Saturday only from January 1 to mid-March. It also offers dolphin cruises and harbor boat rides.

CONTACTS Ashley Marina. ✉ *33 Lockwood Dr., Medical University of South Carolina* ☎ *843/722–1996* 🌐 *www.theharborageatashleymarina.com.* **Charleston City Marina.** ✉ *17 Lockwood Dr., Medical University of South Carolina* ☎ *843/723–5098* 🌐 *www.charlestoncitymarina.com.* **Charleston Water Taxi.** ✉ *Charleston Maritime Center, 10 Wharfside St., Ansonborough* ☎ *843/330–2989* 🌐 *www.charlestonwatertaxi.com.*

CAR TRAVEL

You'll probably need a car in Charleston if you plan on visiting destinations outside the city's Historic District or have your heart set on trips to Walterboro, Edisto Island, Beaufort, Bluffton, or Hilton Head.

Although you'll make the best time traveling along the interstates, keep in mind that smaller highways offer some delightful scenery and the opportunity to stumble upon funky roadside seafood stands, marshy state parks, and historic town halls and churches. The area is rural, but it's still populated, so you'll rarely drive for more than 20 or 30 miles without passing roadside services, such as gas stations, restaurants, and ATMs.

PUBLIC TRANSPORTATION

The Charleston Area Regional Transportation Authority, the city's public bus system, takes passengers around the city and to the suburbs. The XP4 bus, which goes to the airport, is convenient for travelers. CARTA buses go to James Island, West Ashley, and Mount Pleasant.

CARTA operates DASH, which runs free buses that look like vintage trolleys along three downtown routes that crisscross at Marion Square.

PUBLIC TRANSPORTATION CONTACTS Charleston Area Regional Transportation Authority. (*CARTA*) ✉ *Downtown Historic District* ☎ *843/724–7420* 🌐 *www.ridecarta.com.*

TAXI TRAVEL

Taxis are easily accessible in Charleston. Circling the Historic District, pedicabs are a fun way to get around in the evening, especially if you are barhopping. Three can squeeze into one pedicab; the average cost is $5 per person for a 10-minute ride. Additionally, all of the major rideshare services are represented in the Charleston area, including Uber and Lyft.

TAXI CONTACTS Bike Taxi. ☎ *843/532–8663* 🌐 *www.biketaxi.net.* **Charleston Green Taxi.** ☎ *843/819–0846* 🌐 *www.charlestongreentaxi.com.* **Yellow Cab of Charleston.** ☎ *843/577–6565* 🌐 *www.yellowcabcharleston.com.*

Discounts and Deals

The $49.99 Charleston Heritage Passport, a digital ticket available exclusively for online purchase on the Explore Charleston website, is good for one-time admission to eight cultural and historic sites around the city, including the Charleston Museum, Gibbes Museum of Art, and SC Historical Society Museum, for three consecutive days. For an additional fee, passport buyers can add Drayton Hall and Middleton Place to the mix.

Restaurants

Charleston is blessed with a bevy of Southern-inflected selections, from barbecue parlors to fish shacks to casual places serving tourist favorites such as shrimp and grits. If you'd like to try something new, there are plenty of places serving updated, inspired versions of classic dishes. Before you leave, you'll definitely see why Charleston is considered one of the greatest food cities in the world.

As for attire, Charleston invites a crisp yet casual atmosphere. Don't forget, it was recognized as the Most Mannerly City in the country by Marjabelle Young Stewart, which means that residents are slow to judge (or, at the least, that they're doing so very quietly). On the whole, the city encourages comfort and unhurried, easy pacing. The result is an idyllic setting in which to enjoy oysters on the half shell and other homegrown delicacies from the land and sea that jointly grant the city its impressive culinary standing.

Restaurant reviews have been shortned. For full information, visit Fodors.com. Restaurant prices are for a main course at dinner, or if dinner is not served, at lunch.

What It Costs

	$	$$	$$$	$$$$
RESTAURANTS	under $15	$15–$22	$23–$30	over $30

Hotels

Charleston has a well-earned reputation as one of the most historic and beautiful cities in the country. Among travelers, it's also increasingly known for superior accommodations, ranging from lovingly restored mansions converted into atmospheric bed-and-breakfasts to boutique inns to world-class hotels, all found in the residential blocks of the historic downtown peninsula. Most are within walking distance of the shops, restaurants, and museums spread throughout the nearly 800-acre district.

Hotel reviews have been shortened. For full reviews, visit Fodors.com. Prices in the reviews are the lowest cost of a standard double room in high season.

What It Costs

	$	$$	$$$	$$$$
HOTELS	under $125	$125–$200	$201–$300	over $300

VACATION HOME RENTALS

Dunes Properties

For a wide selection of house and condo rentals on Folly Beach, Kiawah and Seabrook Islands, and Isle of Palms (including Wild Dunes Resort), call the Isle of Palms branch of locally owned Dunes Properties. ✉ *1400 Palm Blvd., Isle of Palms* ☎ *843/886–5600* 🌐 *www.dunesproperties.com.*

Wyndham Vacation Rentals

For condo and house rentals on Kiawah and Seabrook Islands and Isle of Palms (including Wild Dunes Resort), contact Wyndham Vacation Rentals. ✉ *354 Freshfields Dr., Johns Island* ☎ *843/768–5000* 🌐 *www.wyndhamvacationrentals.com.*

Tours

AQUATIC TOURS

AquaSafaris

BOAT TOURS | If you want a sailboat or yacht charter, a cruise to a private beach barbecue, or just a day of offshore fishing, AquaSafaris offers it all. Captain John Borden takes veteran and would-be sailors out daily on *Serena,* a 50-foot sloop, leaving from Shem Creek and Isle of Palms. A sunset cruise on the *Palmetto Breeze* catamaran offers panoramic views of Charleston Harbor set to a soundtrack of Jimmy Buffett tunes. Enjoy beer and cocktails as you cruise on one of the smoothest sails in the Lowcountry. ✉ *A-Dock, 24 Patriots Point Rd., Mount Pleasant* ☎ *843/886–8133* 🌐 *www.aqua-safaris.com.*

Charleston Harbor Tours

BOAT TOURS | FAMILY | This company's 90-minute sightseeing circuit through Charleston Harbor provides a great orientation to the city and its history, but those looking to spend more time on the water are bound to enjoy sailboat outings aboard the *Schooner Pride.* ✉ *Charleston Maritime Center, 10 Wharfside St., Ansonborough* ☎ *843/722–1112* 🌐 *www.charlestonharbortours.com* 🎟 *From $25.*

Charleston Kayak Company

GUIDED TOURS | FAMILY | Guided kayak tours with Charleston Kayak Company depart from the grounds of the Inn at Middleton Place. You'll glide down the Ashley River and through brackish creeks in a designated State Scenic River Corridor. Naturalists tell you about the wetlands and the river's cultural history. It's not uncommon to spot an alligator, but thankfully they take no interest in kayakers. Tours last two hours (reservations essential) and start at $55 per adult. There are private tours available, as well as trips through an adjacent swamp and to the marshes behind Folly Beach. For self-guided trips, both single and tandem kayak rentals are available starting at $25, including all safety gear. ✉ *Middleton Place Plantation, 4290 Ashley River Rd., West Ashley* ☎ *843/628–2879* 🌐 *www.charlestonkayakcompany.com.*

★ Coastal Expeditions

GUIDED TOURS | FAMILY | Coastal Expeditions owner Chris Crolley is the Lowcountry's preeminent naturalist, and his guides reflect that reputation. A kayak or stand-up paddleboard (SUP) tour with a naturalist guide starts at $65 per adult, and kayak rentals start at $45 for a half day. The company provides exclusive access to the Cape Romain Wilderness Area on Bulls Island via the Bulls Island Ferry. The ferry departs from Garris Landing in Awendaw and runs Tuesday, and Thursday to Saturday, from April through November. It costs $40 round-trip. Bulls Island has rare natural beauty, a "boneyard beach," shells galore, and nearly 300 species of migrating and native birds. Coastal Expeditions has additional outlets at Crosby's Seafood on Folly Beach, at Isle of Palms Marina, on Kiawah Island, and in Beaufort at St. Phillips Island. ✉ *Shem Creek Maritime Center, 514B Mill St., Mount Pleasant* ☎ *843/884–7684* 🌐 *www.coastalexpeditions.com.*

Ocean Sailing Academy

SPECIAL-INTEREST | Learn how to command your own 26-foot sailboat on Charleston's beautiful harbor with the guidance of an instructor. This academy can teach you and your family how to sail comfortably on any size sailboat and can take you from coastal navigation to ocean proficiency. Instructors are fun and experienced U.S. Sailing–certified professionals. Skippered charters and laid-back sunset cruises are also available. ✉ *24 Patriots Point Rd., Mount Pleasant* ☎ *843/971–0700* 🌐 *www.osasail.com.*

Sandlapper Water Tours

BOAT TOURS | FAMILY | These tours focus on regional history, coastal wildlife, and nocturnal ghostly lore. ✉ *Charleston Maritime Center, 10 Wharfside St., Ansonborough* ☎ *843/849–8687* 🌐 *www.sandlappertours.com* 🎟 *From $25.*

SpiritLine Cruises

BOAT TOURS | FAMILY | The local leader in dinner cruises, SpiritLine serves standout versions of Lowcountry classics, including shrimp and grits. The dishes are only enhanced by the scenery, including an uncommon view of the commanding Ravenel Bridge from below. ✉ *Aquarium Wharf, 360 Concord St., Ansonborough* ☎ *843/722–2628* 🌐 *www.spiritlinecruises.com* 🎟 *From $23.*

BIKE RENTALS AND TOURS

Cycling at your own pace is one of the best ways to see Charleston. Those staying at the nearby island resorts, particularly families with children, almost always rent bikes, especially if they are there for a week.

The Bicycle Shoppe

BICYCLING | Open seven days a week, this shop rents simple beach cruisers for $7 per hour, $28 per day, or $50 per week, and that includes a helmet, basket, and lock. For those wanting to tackle the Ravenel Bridge, the store offers geared bikes for slightly more. There's a second branch at 1539 Johnnie Dodds Boulevard in Mount Pleasant, and it offers free delivery to local beaches. ✉ *280 Meeting St., Market* ☎ *843/722–8168* 🌐 *www.thebicycleshoppe.com.*

Bilda Bike

BICYCLING | Bike rentals at this shop start at $25 for 24 hours (or $55 a week), and that includes a helmet, lock, and basket. Conveniently located in the Upper King area, it's open on Sunday—the best day for riding around downtown Charleston or across the Ravenel Bridge. ✉ *573 King St., Upper King* ☎ *843/789–3281* 🌐 *www.bildabike.com.*

Island Bike and Surf Shop

BICYCLING | FAMILY | At this shop, you can rent beach bikes for a very moderate weekly rate (starting at $40 per week), or check out hybrids, mountain bikes, bicycles built for two, and a wide range of equipment for everyone in the family. The shop will even deliver to Kiawah and Seabrook Islands. ✉ *3665 Bohicket Rd., Johns Island* ☎ *843/768–1158* 🌐 *www.islandbikeandsurf.com.*

CARRIAGE TOURS

Carriage tours are a great way to see Charleston. Each follows one of four routes (determined by a city-operated bingo lottery at the start of each tour) and lasts about one hour. Most carriages queue up at North Market and Anson Streets. In addition to public tours, each carriage company offers private tours and wedding rentals.

Carolina Polo & Carriage Company

CARRIAGE TOURS | FAMILY | Known for its blue carriages, Carolina Polo & Carriage Company boasts that its owners trace their Charleston roots back to the 17th century. ✉ *45 Pinckney St., Market* ☎ *843/577–6767* 🌐 *www.cpcc.com* 🎫 *From $35.*

Old South Carriage Company

CARRIAGE TOURS | FAMILY | This is the only carriage outfitter in town that consistently offers haunted carriage rides at night. ✉ *14 Anson St., Market* ☎ *843/723–9712* 🌐 *www.oldsouthcarriage.com* 🎫 *From $35.*

Palmetto Carriage Works

CARRIAGE TOURS | FAMILY | Palmetto started rolling through town in 1972, making it the oldest carriage tour company in Charleston. ✉ *8 Guignard St., Market* ☎ *843/723–8145* 🌐 *www.palmettocarriage.com* 🎫 *Evening tours $18, daytime tours $28.*

ECOTOURS

Barrier Island Eco Tours

BOAT TOURS | FAMILY | Located at the Isle of Palms Marina, Barrier Island Eco Tours runs three-hour pontoon-boat tours to the uninhabited Capers Island, with an optional Lowcountry boil on the beach add-on. ✉ *Isle of Palms Marina, 50 41st Ave., Isle of Palms* ☎ *843/886–5000* 🌐 *www.nature-tours.com* 🎫 *From $40.*

WALKING TOURS

Walking tours on various topics—horticulture, African American history, or women's history—are available from several city-certified tour companies, mostly located around the Market area.

Bulldog Tours

SPECIAL-INTEREST | The selection of strolls from Bulldog includes a walk through the stunning Magnolia Cemetery, the Victorian burial grounds that are the final resting place of 2,000 Confederate soldiers, including the men who went down with the *Hunley*. ✉ *18 Anson St., Market* ☎ *843/701–1419* 🌐 *www.bulldogtours.com* 🎫 *From $29.*

Charleston Culinary Tours

SPECIAL-INTEREST | A wide variety of "foodie" tours are offered in historic downtown Charleston, including culinary, mixology, and chefs' kitchens tours. And rather than miss out on the haunted fun that's a staple of non-food tours in the city, owner Guilds Hollowell has added a seated five-course dessert tasting to his repertoire of walking tours, and the evening includes plenty of ghost stories. ✉ *46B State St., Charleston* ☎ *843/806–0130* 🌐 *charlestonculinarytours.com* 🎫 *From $65.*

Tour Charleston

GUIDED TOURS | It's little wonder that Tour Charleston's tours are acclaimed for being so informative, since the company's owners also own the city's top bookshop. Tour Charleston stresses low-impact tourism and cultural sensitivity. ✉ *160 King St., Market* ☎ *843/723–1670* 🌐 *www.tourcharleston.com* 🎫 *From $28.*

Nightlife

Charleston loves a good party, and the city boasts an ever-growing array of choices for a night on the town. The more mature crowd goes to the sophisticated spots, and there are many wine bars, clubs featuring jazz groups, and trendy lounges with craft cocktail menus. Rooftop bars are a particular Charleston tradition, and the city has several good ones. Many restaurants offer live entertainment on at least one weekend night, catering to crowds of all ages. The Upper King area has grown exponentially in recent years, overtaking the Market area in terms of popularity and variety of bars and lounges. **■ TIP→ A city ordinance mandates that bars must close by 2 am, so last call is usually 1:30.**

Performing Arts

For a midsize metropolis, Charleston has a surprisingly varied and sophisticated arts scene, though the city really shines during its major annual arts festival, Spoleto Festival USA. Still, throughout the year, there are ample opportunities to explore higher culture, from productions by the Footlight Players and PURE Theatre to concerts at the historic Charleston Music Hall.

Festivals and Events

★ Charleston RiverDogs

BASEBALL/SOFTBALL | **FAMILY** | The local minor league baseball team—co-owned by actor Bill Murray, who is often in attendance—plays at "The Joe," on the banks of the Ashley River near the Citadel. Kids love the mascot, Charlie T. RiverDog, and adults love the beer deals and the creative, surprisingly tasty food concessions. After Friday night games, fireworks illuminate the summer sky in honor of this all-American pastime. The season runs from April through September. ✉ *Joseph P. Riley Jr. Stadium, 360 Fishburne St., Hampton Park Terrace* ☎ *843/577–3647* 🌐 *www.riverdogs.com* 🎫 *From $8.*

★ Charleston Wine + Food

FESTIVALS | Since 2005, this annual fete has served as the city's marquee event for foodies. Spread over five days, it brings together the nation's leading chefs (including local James Beard Award winners), food writers, and, of course, regular diners who love to eat and drink. Held the first full weekend of March, it emphasizes the Lowcountry's culinary heritage. Marion Square serves as the hub with its Culinary Village, but savvy attendees grab up tickets quickly for the numerous dinners and special events held around the city. ✉ *Charleston* ☎ *843/727–9998* 🌐 *www.charlestonwineandfood.com.*

MOJA Arts Festival

ARTS FESTIVALS | FAMILY | Held each year in late September and early October, this festival celebrates the region's African heritage and Caribbean influences on local culture. It includes theater, dance, and music performances, lectures, art shows, and films. The free Sunday afternoon finale, featuring concerts, dancing, and plenty of food, is a marquee city event each year. ✉ *Charleston* ☎ *843/724–7305* 🌐 *www.mojafestival.com.*

Piccolo Spoleto Festival

ARTS FESTIVALS | FAMILY | The spirited companion to Spoleto Festival USA showcases the best in local and regional talent from every artistic discipline. There are as many as 700 events—from jazz performances to puppet shows, chamber music concerts, and expansive art shows in Marion Square—from mid-May through early June. Many of the performances are free or inexpensive, and hundreds of these cultural experiences are kid-friendly. ✉ *Charleston* ☎ *843/724–7305* 🌐 *www.piccolospoleto.com.*

Southeastern Wildlife Exposition

CULTURAL FESTIVALS | FAMILY | One of Charleston's biggest annual events, this celebration of the region's flora and fauna takes place in mid-February, offering fine art by renowned wildlife artists, bird of prey demonstrations, dog competitions, an oyster roast, and a gala. Spread across three days, the expo generally attracts more than 500 artists and 40,000 participants to various venues around the city. ✉ *Charleston* ☎ *843/723–1748* 🌐 *www.sewe.com.*

★ Spoleto Festival USA

ARTS FESTIVALS | FAMILY | For 17 glorious days in late May and early June, Charleston gets a dose of culture from Spoleto Festival USA. This internationally acclaimed performing-arts festival features a mix of distinguished artists and emerging talent from around the world. Performances take place in magical settings, such as the College of Charleston's Cistern beneath a canopy of ancient oaks or inside a centuries-old cathedral.

A mix of formal concerts and casual performances is what Pulitzer Prize–winning composer Gian Carlo Menotti had in mind when, in 1977, he initiated the festival as a complement to his opera-heavy Italian festival. He chose Charleston because of its European look and because its residents love the arts—not to mention any cause for celebration. He wanted the festival to be a "fertile ground for the young" as well as a "dignified home for the masters."

Some 45 events—with most tickets averaging between $25 and $50—include everything from improv to Shakespeare, from rap to chamber music, from ballet to salsa. Because events sell out quickly, buy tickets several weeks in advance (book hotel rooms and make restaurant reservations early, too). Tickets to midweek performances are a bit easier to secure. ✉ *Charleston* ☎ *843/579–3100* 🌐 *www.spoletousa.org.*

Visitor Information

The Charleston Area Convention & Visitors Bureau runs the Charleston Visitor Center, which has information about the city as well as Kiawah Island, Seabrook Island, Mount Pleasant, North Charleston, Edisto Island, Summerville, and the Isle of Palms. The Preservation Society of Charleston has information on house tours.

VISITOR INFORMATION Charleston Visitor Center. ✉ *375 Meeting St., Upper King* ☎ *800/774–0006* 🌐 *www.charlestoncvb.com.* **Preservation Society of Charleston.** ✉ *147 King St., Lower King* ☎ *843/722–4630* 🌐 *www.preservationsociety.org.*

South of Broad and the French Quarter

Locals jokingly claim that just off the Battery (at Battery Street and Murray Boulevard), the Ashley and Cooper Rivers join to form the Atlantic Ocean. Such a lofty proclamation speaks volumes about the South of Broad area's rakish flair. To observe their pride and joy, head to White Point Garden at the point of the downtown peninsula. Here, handsome mansions and a large oak-shaded park greet incoming boats and charm passersby.

This heavily residential area south of Broad Street brims with beautiful private homes, many of which have plaques bearing brief descriptions of the property's history. Be respectful, but feel free to peek through iron gates and fences at the verdant displays in elaborate gardens. Although an open gate once signified that guests were welcome to venture inside, that time has mostly passed—residents tell stories of how they came home to find tourists sitting in their front-porch rockers. But you never know when an invitation to have a look-see might come from a friendly owner-gardener. Several of the city's lavish house museums call this famously affluent neighborhood home.

Just across Broad Street to the north, on the Cooper River side of Meeting Street, the mansions morph into centuries-old town houses in the charming French Quarter. This small borough is home to landmark churches, like St. Philip's, that help give the Holy City its moniker as well as most of the city's most impressive art galleries. Ducking into the Quarter off bustling East Bay or Broad Streets feels like slipping into a well-preserved—but still very vibrant—bygone era.

Sights

★ The Battery

HISTORIC SITE | FAMILY | During the Civil War, the Confederate army mounted cannons in the Battery, at the southernmost point of Charleston's peninsula, to fortify the city against Union attack. Cannons and piles of cannonballs still line the oak-shaded park known as White Point Garden—kids can't resist climbing them. Where pirates once hung from the gallows, walkers now take in the serene setting from Charleston benches (small wood-slat benches with cast-iron sides). Stroll the waterside promenades along East Battery and Murray Boulevard to enjoy views of Charleston Harbor, the Ravenel Bridge, and Fort Sumter on one side, with some of the city's most photographed mansions on the other. You'll find locals dangling their fishing lines, waiting for a bite. ■ **TIP→ There are no public bathrooms within a 10-minute walk of the Battery, so plan accordingly. A bicycle is a great way to tour South of Broad, and it allows for a quick exit to the commercial part of town.** ✉ *E. Battery St. at Murray Blvd., South of Broad* 🎫 *Free.*

Circular Congregational Church

RELIGIOUS SITE | The first church building erected on this site in the 1680s gave bustling Meeting Street its name. The present-day Romanesque structure, dating from 1890, is configured on a Greek-cross plan and has a breathtaking vaulted ceiling. While the sanctuary is not open to visitors except during Sunday morning service, you are welcome to explore the graveyard, which is the oldest English burial ground in the city, with records dating back to 1695. ✉ *150 Meeting St., Middle King* ☎ *843/577–6400* 🌐 *www.circularchurch.org* 🕐 *Graveyard closed Sat.*

Dock Street Theatre

ARTS VENUE | FAMILY | The original Dock Street, built in 1736, was the first theater building in America. The current structure, reopened in 1935, incorporates the

Did You Know?

The Battery, along the shores of the Charleston peninsula, is named after a Civil War coastal defense artillery battery.

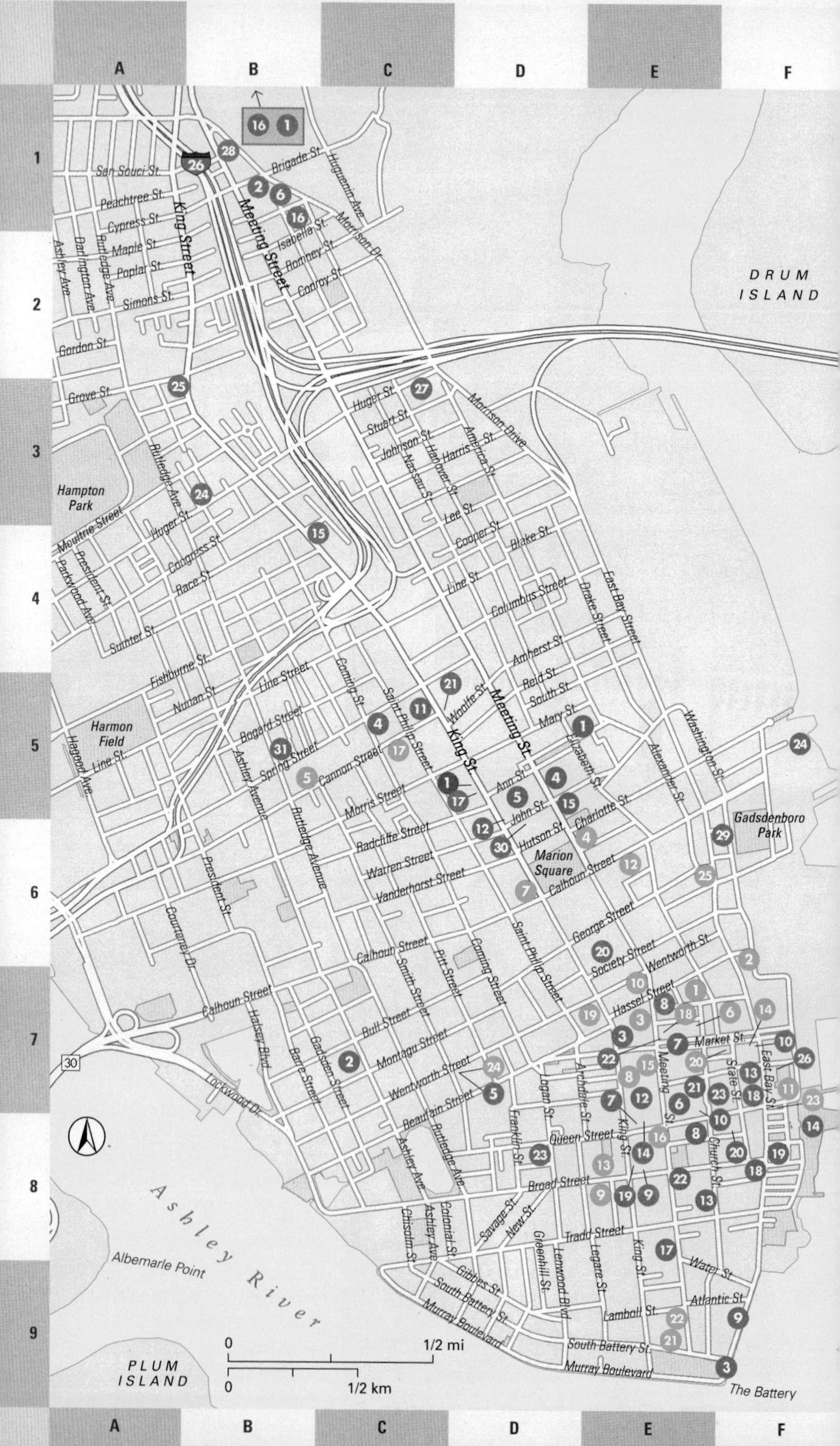
A
B
C
D
E
F
1
2
3
4
5
6
7
8
9
DRUM ISLAND
PLUM ISLAND
Ashley River
Albemarle Point
Hampton Park
Harmon Field
Marion Square
Gadsdenboro Park
The Battery
King Street
Meeting Street
San Souci St.
Peachtree St.
Cypress St.
Maple St.
Poplar St.
Simons St.
Gordon St.
Grove St.
Brigade St.
Huguenin Ave.
Isabella St.
Romney St.
Morrison Dr.
Conroy St.
Ashley Ave.
Darlington Ave.
Rutledge Ave.
Huger St.
Stuart St.
Johnson St.
Hanover St.
Harris St.
America St.
Nassau St.
Morrison Drive
Lee St.
Cooper St.
Blake St.
Line St.
Columbus Street
Moultrie Street
President St.
Parkwood Ave.
Congress St.
Race St.
Sumter St.
Fishburne St.
Line Street
Nunan St.
Bogard Street
Spring Street
Cannon Street
Coming St.
Saint Philip Street
Woolfe St.
King St.
Meeting St.
Amherst St.
Reid St.
South St.
Mary St.
Drake Street
East Bay Street
Elizabeth St.
Ann St.
Washington St.
Alexander St.
Hagood Ave.
Line St.
Ashley Avenue
Rutledge Avenue
Morris Street
Radcliffe Street
John St.
Hutson St.
Charlotte St.
Warren Street
Vanderhorst Street
Calhoun Street
President St.
Courtenay Dr.
Saint Philip Street
George Street
Calhoun Street
Smith Street
Pitt Street
Coming Street
Society Street
Wentworth St.
Hassel Street
Calhoun Street
Halsey Blvd.
Bull Street
Montagu Street
Barre Street
Gadsden Street
Wentworth Street
Beaufain Street
Market St.
Meeting St.
State St.
East Bay St.
Archdale St.
Logan St.
King St.
Franklin St.
Rutledge Ave.
Ashley Ave.
Lockwood Dr.
Queen Street
Church St.
Broad Street
Savage St.
New St.
Chisolm St.
Colonial St.
Tradd Street
Greenhill St.
Lenwood Blvd.
Legare St.
King St.
Water St.
Gibbes St.
South Battery St.
Murray Boulevard
Atlantic St.
Lamboll St.
South Battery St.
Murray Boulevard
26
30
0
1/2 mi
0
1/2 km

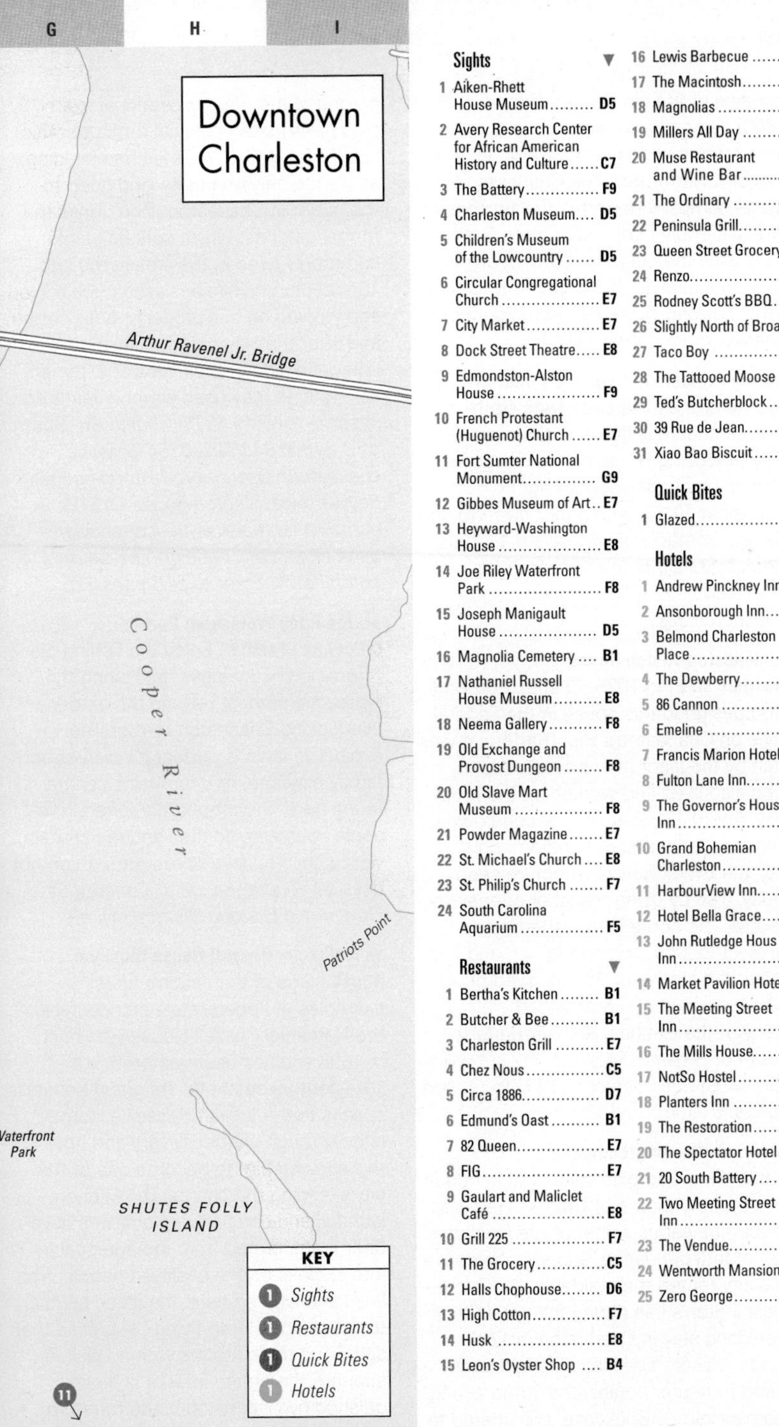

Sights

1 Aiken-Rhett House Museum D5
2 Avery Research Center for African American History and Culture C7
3 The Battery F9
4 Charleston Museum.... D5
5 Children's Museum of the Lowcountry D5
6 Circular Congregational Church E7
7 City Market E7
8 Dock Street Theatre..... E8
9 Edmondston-Alston House F9
10 French Protestant (Huguenot) Church E7
11 Fort Sumter National Monument.............. G9
12 Gibbes Museum of Art .. E7
13 Heyward-Washington House E8
14 Joe Riley Waterfront Park F8
15 Joseph Manigault House D5
16 Magnolia Cemetery B1
17 Nathaniel Russell House Museum E8
18 Neema Gallery F8
19 Old Exchange and Provost Dungeon F8
20 Old Slave Mart Museum F8
21 Powder Magazine E7
22 St. Michael's Church E8
23 St. Philip's Church F7
24 South Carolina Aquarium F5

Restaurants

1 Bertha's Kitchen B1
2 Butcher & Bee B1
3 Charleston Grill E7
4 Chez Nous C5
5 Circa 1886................ D7
6 Edmund's Oast B1
7 82 Queen.................. E7
8 FIG E7
9 Gaulart and Maliclet Café E8
10 Grill 225 .... F7
11 The Grocery C5
12 Halls Chophouse........ D6
13 High Cotton F7
14 Husk E8
15 Leon's Oyster Shop B4
16 Lewis Barbecue B1
17 The Macintosh.......... D5
18 Magnolias F7
19 Millers All Day E8
20 Muse Restaurant and Wine Bar E6
21 The Ordinary C5
22 Peninsula Grill............ E7
23 Queen Street Grocery.. D8
24 Renzo.................... B3
25 Rodney Scott's BBQ.... A3
26 Slightly North of Broad.. F7
27 Taco Boy C3
28 The Tattooed Moose ... B1
29 Ted's Butcherblock...... F6
30 39 Rue de Jean.......... D6
31 Xiao Bao Biscuit........ B5

Quick Bites

1 Glazed.................... D5

Hotels

1 Andrew Pinckney Inn ... E7
2 Ansonborough Inn....... F6
3 Belmond Charleston Place E7
4 The Dewberry............ E6
5 86 Cannon B5
6 Emeline E7
7 Francis Marion Hotel... D6
8 Fulton Lane Inn........... E7
9 The Governor's House Inn E8
10 Grand Bohemian Charleston................ E7
11 HarbourView Inn......... F7
12 Hotel Bella Grace........ E6
13 John Rutledge Hous Inn E8
14 Market Pavilion Hotel ... F7
15 The Meeting Street Inn E7
16 The Mills House.......... E8
17 NotSo Hostel C5
18 Planters Inn E7
19 The Restoration.......... E7
20 The Spectator Hotel..... F7
21 20 South Battery E9
22 Two Meeting Street Inn E9
23 The Vendue............... F7
24 Wentworth Mansion ... D7
25 Zero George.............. E6

remains of the old Planter's Hotel (circa 1809). Green velvet curtains and wonderful woodwork give it a New Orleans French Quarter feel. The Charleston Stage company performs full seasons of family-friendly fare, and Spoleto Festival USA uses the stage for productions in May and June. ✉ *135 Church St., Downtown Historic District* ☎ *843/720–3968* 🌐 *www.charlestonstage.com.*

French Protestant (Huguenot) Church
RELIGIOUS SITE | The circa-1845 Gothic-style church is home to the nation's only practicing Huguenot congregation. English-language services are held Sunday at 10:30, with a tour given to any visitors immediately afterward. ✉ *136 Church St., Downtown Historic District* ☎ *843/722–4385* 🌐 *www.huguenot-church.org.*

Edmondston-Alston House
HISTORIC SITE | In 1825, Charles Edmondston designed this house in the Federal style on Charleston's High Battery; it was built by the labor of enslaved people, who also lived and worked on the property. About 13 years later, second owner Charles Alston began transforming it into the Greek Revival structure seen today, also by using the labor of enslaved people. The home is furnished with family antiques, portraits, silver, and fine china; the stories of the enslaved people who lived here are intertwined with many of the exhibits. ✉ *21 E. Battery, South of Broad* ☎ *843/722–7171* 🌐 *www.edmondstonalston.com* 🎫 *$12* ⏲ *Closed Sun. and Mon.*

Heyward-Washington House
HOUSE | This Georgian-style double house was the townhome of Thomas Heyward Jr., patriot leader, signer of the Declaration of Independence, and slaveholder. The city rented the residence for George Washington's use during the president's weeklong stay in Charleston in 1791. Inside, visitors find historic Charleston-made furniture, notably the withdrawing room's Holmes Bookcase, considered to be one of the most exceptional examples of American colonial furniture. Also significant is the 1740s kitchen building, as it's the only one of its kind open to the public in Charleston. Don't miss the formal gardens, which contain plants commonly used in the area in the late 18th century. While enslaved people lived and worked on this property, both before and after the Heyward family, there's little reflection of their lives or experiences; artifacts they used are only featured in some exhibits. ✉ *87 Church St., South of Broad* ☎ *843/722–0354* 🌐 *www.charlestonmuseum.org/historic-houses/heyward-washington-house* 🎫 *$12, combination ticket with Joseph Manigault House or Charleston Museum $18, combination ticket to all 3 sites $25.*

★ **Joe Riley Waterfront Park**
CITY PARK | **FAMILY** | Enjoy the fishing pier's "front-porch" swings, stroll along the waterside path, or relax in the gardens overlooking Charleston Harbor. The expansive lawn is perfect for picnics and family playtime. Two fountains can be found here: the oft-photographed Pineapple Fountain and the Vendue Fountain, which children love to run through on hot days. ✉ *Vendue Range at Concord St., Downtown Historic District* 🎫 *Free.*

★ **Nathaniel Russell House Museum**
HOUSE | One of the nation's finest examples of Federal-style architecture, the Nathaniel Russell House was built in 1808 and has been restored to a 19th-century aesthetic. Its grand beauty speaks to the wealth Russell accumulated through chattel slavery and how this allowed him to become one of the city's leading merchants. The kitchen, laundry, and certain living quarters have been transformed from storage space into exhibits on the enslaved people who lived and labored here. Inside, in addition to the famous "free-flying" staircase that spirals up three stories with no visible support, the ornate interior is distinguished by Charleston-made furniture

as well as paintings and works on paper by well-known American and European artists, including Henry Benbridge, Samuel F. B. Morse, and George Romney. The extensive formal garden is worth a leisurely stroll. ✉ *51 Meeting St., South of Broad* ☎ *843/722–3405* 🌐 *www.historiccharleston.org/house-museums* 🎫 *$12, combination ticket with Aiken-Rhett House Museum $18.*

★ Neema Gallery

MUSEUM | Housed in a building that once printed Confederate money, Neema Gallery is the city's only gallery space dedicated exclusively to black artists from the South. The rotating collection of artwork features large-scale prints, jewelry, and ceramics from a range of local and award-winning artists. Classes and workshops are regularly offered. ✉ *3 Broad St., Suite 100, Broad Street* ☎ *843/353–8079* 🌐 *www.neemagallery.com* ⏲ *Closed Sun. and Mon.*

Old Exchange and Provost Dungeon

HISTORIC SITE | **FAMILY** | Built as a customs house in 1771, this building once served as the commercial and social center of Charleston and was the primary site of the city's public auctions of enslaved people. It was also the site of many historic events, including the state's ratification of the Constitution in 1788 and two grand celebrations hosted for George Washington. In addition to its role in the transatlantic slave trade, it was also used by the British to house prisoners during the Revolutionary War, experiences that are both detailed in exhibits. Costumed interpreters bring history to life on guided tours. ✉ *122 E. Bay St., South of Broad* ☎ *843/727–2165* 🌐 *www.oldexchange.org* 🎫 *$10.*

★ Old Slave Mart Museum

MUSEUM | Used as a site for the auctioning of enslaved people (as well as a jail and morgue) until 1863, this building is now a museum that educates visitors on Charleston's role in the transatlantic slave trade. Charleston was a commercial center for the South's plantation economy, and enslaved people were forced to perform most labor within and beyond the city, on the surrounding plantations. Galleries are outfitted with interactive exhibits, including push buttons that allow you to hear the historical accounts of enslaved people. The museum sits on one of the few remaining cobblestone streets in town. ✉ *6 Chalmers St., Downtown Historic District* ☎ *843/958–6467* 🌐 *www.oldslavemartmuseum.com* 🎫 *$8* ⏲ *Closed Sun.*

Powder Magazine

BUILDING | Completed in 1713, the oldest public building in South Carolina is one of the few that remain from the time of the Lords Proprietors. The city's volatile—and precious—gunpowder was kept here during the Revolutionary War, and the building's thick walls were designed to contain an explosion if its stores were detonated. Today, it's a small museum with a permanent exhibit on colonial and Revolutionary warfare. ✉ *79 Cumberland St., Downtown Historic District* ☎ *843/722–9350* 🌐 *www.powdermagazine.org* 🎫 *$6.*

St. Michael's Church

RELIGIOUS SITE | Topped by a 186-foot steeple, St. Michael's is the city's oldest surviving church building. The first cornerstone was set in place in 1752, and through the years, other elements were added: the steeple clock and bells (1764); the organ (1768); the font (1771); and the altar (1892). A claim to fame: George Washington worshipped in pew number 43 in 1791. Listen for the bell ringers on Sunday morning before worship services. ✉ *78 Meeting St., South of Broad* ✣ *Corner of Meeting and Broad Sts.* ☎ *843/723–0603* 🌐 *www.stmichaelschurch.net.*

★ St. Philip's Church

RELIGIOUS SITE | Founded around 1680, St. Philip's didn't move to its current site until the 1720s, becoming one of the three churches that gave Church Street its name. The first building in this location burned down in 1835 and was replaced with the Corinthian-style structure seen today. A shell that exploded in the churchyard while services were being held during the Civil War didn't deter the minister from finishing his sermon (the congregation gathered elsewhere for the remainder of the war). Amble through the churchyards, where notable South Carolinians are buried. If you want to tour the church, call ahead, as hours depend upon volunteer availability. ✉ *142 Church St., Market* ☎ *843/722–7734* 🌐 *www.stphilipschurchsc.org.*

Restaurants

Gaulart & Maliclet Café

$$ | FRENCH | This local favorite, also known as Fast & French, has been a fixture in the neighborhood for more than 35 years, thanks to the consistent food, the esprit de corps of the staff, and the family-style tables for sharing breakfast, lunch, or dinner. Its popular fondue grew from a once-a-week special to a daily affair, and you can also get your cheese fix with the wonderful Bucheron cheese salad. **Known for:** gourmet bites in an area of town short of restaurants; charming ambience; nightly specials, including fondue night. 💲 *Average main: $18* ✉ *98 Broad St., South of Broad* ☎ *843/577–9797* 🌐 *www.fastandfrenchcharleston.com* ⏲ *Closed Sun.*

High Cotton

$$$$ | SOUTHERN | This Charleston classic remains unchanged by time: lazily spinning paddle fans, lush palm trees, and exposed brick walls. The kitchen serves up regional classics like a Lowcountry boil and bacon-wrapped stuffed rabbit loin. **Known for:** live jazz and bluegrass music at the bar; one of the city's finest Sunday brunches; high-rising peanut butter pie for dessert. 💲 *Average main: $34* ✉ *199 E. Bay St., Downtown Historic District* ☎ *843/724–3815* 🌐 *www.highcottoncharleston.com* ⏲ *No lunch.*

Magnolias

$$$$ | SOUTHERN | The theme at this extremely popular—and worthy—tourist destination is evident in the vivid paintings of white magnolia blossoms that adorn the walls. The menu pays homage to classic dishes like fried green tomatoes with white cheddar grits, caramelized onions, and country ham. **Known for:** collard-green-and-tasso-ham egg rolls that spawned a Southern-fusion revolution; daily vegetarian entrée showcasing local produce; affordable Sunday brunch. 💲 *Average main: $33* ✉ *185 E. Bay St., Downtown Historic District* ☎ *843/577–7771* 🌐 *www.magnoliascharleston.com.*

★ Millers All Day

$$ | SOUTHERN | The owner of Marsh Hen Mill co-owns this breakfast joint that caters to the white-collar Broad Street crowd, balancing blue plate breakfasts with fancy morning entrées like lobster toast on house-baked brioche. It's hard to choose between the biscuits loaded with pimento cheese, fried chicken, or country ham with fig jam. **Known for:** grits prepared to perfection—there's even a grit mill in the storefront window; possibly the best Bloody Mary in town; to-go doughnuts and muffins. 💲 *Average main: $15* ✉ *120 King St., South of Broad* ☎ *843/501–7342* 🌐 *www.millersallday.com.*

★ Slightly North of Broad

$$$ | SOUTHERN | Affectionately known as S.N.O.B., this former warehouse with atmospheric brick-and-stucco walls has a chef's table that looks directly into the open kitchen. Many of the specialties, including wild game and other less common meats, are served as small plates that are perfect for sharing. **Known for:** bustling lunchtime service; history as the forefather of the farm-to-table movement in Charleston; upscale, authentic Southern fare. 💲 *Average main: $30* ✉ *192 E. Bay St., Downtown Historic District* ☎ *843/723–3424* 🌐 *www.snobcharleston.com.*

Hotels

The Governor's House Inn

$$$ | **B&B/INN** | The stately architecture of this quintessential Charleston lodging radiates the grandeur, romance, and civility of the city's bountiful colonial era. **Pros:** a true taste of the Charleston high life; chairs and beach towels provided for day trips; free off-street parking in an elegant courtyard. **Cons:** sophisticated vibe isn't ideal for families; period decor isn't as trendy as newer options; no elevator, so don't book an upstairs room if you need one. *Rooms from: $265 ✉ 117 Broad St., South of Broad ☎ 843/720–2070, 800/720–9812 ⊕ www.governorshouse.com ↩ 11 rooms 🍴 Free breakfast.*

HarbourView Inn

$$$ | **HOTEL** | If you ask for a room with a view or even a private balcony here, you can gaze out over Charleston Harbor and on to the fountain at the center of Waterfront Park. **Pros:** continental breakfast can be delivered to your room or the rooftop; attractive rooftop terrace with soaring views; lovely Lowcountry design. **Cons:** chain hotel feel in some parts; not as new and exciting as similarly priced options; no pool. *Rooms from: $279 ✉ 2 Vendue Range, Downtown Historic District ☎ 843/853–8439 ⊕ www.harbourviewcharleston.com ↩ 52 rooms 🍴 Free breakfast.*

John Rutledge House Inn

$$$ | **B&B/INN** | The New Orleans–esque exterior of this National Historic Landmark (the former residence of politician and slaveholder John Rutledge) has wrought-iron architectural details, and inside, parquet floors sit beneath 14-foot ceilings adorned with plaster moldings. **Pros:** incredibly comfortable Tempur-Pedic mattresses; afternoon tea in the former ballroom; carriage house rooms have privacy and quiet. **Cons:** you can hear some street and kitchen noise in the first-floor rooms; the two carriage houses are not as grand as the main house; limited restaurants within a five-minute walk. *Rooms from: $289 ✉ 116 Broad St., South of Broad ☎ 843/723–7999 ⊕ www.johnrutledgehouseinn.com ↩ 19 rooms 🍴 Free breakfast.*

The Spectator Hotel

$$$$ | **HOTEL** | The corner rooms at this elegant luxury hotel, with balconies overlooking the city's church steeples, are among the best accommodations in the city. **Pros:** central location; complimentary in-room snacks and drinks; free bike rentals. **Cons:** weekend prices nearly double; no on-site gym or pool; in the most heavily touristed part of town. *Rooms from: $329 ✉ 67 State St., Market ☎ 843/724–4326 ⊕ thespectatorhotel.com ↩ 41 rooms 🍴 Free breakfast.*

★ 20 South Battery

$$$ | **B&B/INN** | Facing White Point Garden, this 11-room inn within a five-story 1843 mansion makes you feel like you've stepped back in time. **Pros:** fully furnished by David Skinner Antiques, including four-poster beds in every room; excellent butler and concierge service; stunning restoration details, from original Italian tile to 175-year-old parquet flooring. **Cons:** some rooms are small; no pool or gym; it's a long walk to restaurants. *Rooms from: $299 ✉ 20 S. Battery, South of Broad ☎ 843/727–3100 ⊕ www.batterycarriagehouse.com ↩ 11 rooms 🍴 Free breakfast.*

Two Meeting Street Inn

$$$ | **B&B/INN** | As pretty as a wedding cake, this 1892 Queen Anne–style mansion wears overhanging bays, colonnades, balustrades, and a turret; two original Tiffany stained-glass windows (worth as much as the house itself), carved-oak paneling, and a crystal chandelier dress up the public spaces. **Pros:** free on-street parking; community refrigerator on each floor; ringside seat for a Battery view and horse-drawn carriages clipping by. **Cons:** decor might be too opulent for some; not equipped for handicapped guests; no restaurants

in easy walking distance. $ *Rooms from: $279* ✉ *2 Meeting St., South of Broad* ☎ *843/723–7322* 🌐 *www.twomeeting-street.com* 🛏 *9 rooms* 🍽 *Free breakfast* ☞ *No children under 12.*

★ The Vendue

$$$$ | HOTEL | Thanks to its gorgeous art-filled space, the Vendue feels as much like a contemporary art museum as it does a boutique hotel. **Pros:** free bike rentals; soundproofing masks street noise; terrific on-site restaurant. **Cons:** no complimentary breakfast; some halls and spaces are small as in centuries past; communal spaces are shared with nonguests. $ *Rooms from: $319* ✉ *19 Vendue Range, Downtown Historic District* ☎ *843/577–7970* 🌐 *www.thevendue.com* 🛏 *84 rooms* 🍽 *No meals.*

Nightlife

★ The Gin Joint

BARS/PUBS | The cocktails here—frothy fizzes, slings, smashes, and juleps—are retro, some dating back to before Prohibition. The bartenders don bow ties and suspenders, but the atmosphere is utterly contemporary, with slick gray walls, butcher-block tabletops, and subtle lighting. The kitchen serves up small plates like oysters, arugula salad, and Coca-Cola–braised ham. ✉ *182 E. Bay St., Downtown Historic District* ☎ *843/577–6111* 🌐 *www.theginjoint.com.*

The Griffon

BARS/PUBS | Dollar bills cover just about every square inch of the Griffon, helping the bar achieve nearly legendary status around the city. Its wood interior is dark, dusty, and well worn, yet charming. A rotating selection of draft beers comes from local breweries like Westbrook, Coast, and Holy City. It's a popular lunchtime and happy hour watering hole and hosts live music on weekend nights. ✉ *18 Vendue Range, Downtown Historic District* ☎ *843/723–1700* 🌐 *www.griffon-charleston.com.*

The Rooftop Bar at the Vendue

BARS/PUBS | Have a cocktail and appetizer as you watch the colorful sunset behind the church steeples. There are actually two bars at this venue atop the Vendue hotel; the lower Deck Bar has tables and chairs shaded by umbrellas, but the view of the water is partially obscured by condo towers. Keep going to the upper-level bar, which offers a 360-degree panorama and an open-air atmosphere. You'll find live music by local and regional bands on weekends. Get here early—it closes at 10 pm on weekdays and at midnight on weekends. ✉ *The Vendue, 19 Vendue Range, Downtown Historic District* ☎ *843/577–7970* 🌐 *www.thevendue.com.*

Shopping

Berlin's

CLOTHING | Family-owned since 1883, this Charleston institution has a reputation as a destination for special-occasion clothing. Expect preppy styles, suits, and stylish threads from European designers. There's a women's store next door to the men's shop and a complimentary parking lot across the street. ✉ *114–116 King St., Lower King* ☎ *843/722–1665* 🌐 *www.berlinsclothing.com.*

ellington

CLOTHING | Chic and classy, this shop is known for its washable, packable women's clothing made of feel-good fabrics like silk, linen, and cashmere. Its fashions have classic lines but always feel up-to-date. ✉ *24 State St., Downtown Historic District* ☎ *843/722–7999* 🌐 *ellington.business.site.*

★ Historic Charleston Foundation Shop

HOUSEHOLD ITEMS/FURNITURE | Bring home products inspired by Charleston furniture, china, and decorative accessories. These authentic Charleston mementos, including bags of Carolina Rice, avoid the kitsch of the City Market and make treasured gifts. ✉ *108 Meeting St., Downtown*

Historic District ☎ *843/724–8484* 🌐 *www.historiccharleston.org/store.*

Lower King and the Market

Wandering through the neighborhoods surrounding the City Market and Lower King Street, it's obvious why filmmakers look to Charleston as a backdrop for historic movies.

Dozens of church steeples punctuate the low skyline, and horse-drawn carriages pass centuries-old mansions, their stately salons offering a crystal-laden and parquet-floored version of Southern comfort. Outside, magnolia-filled gardens overflow with carefully tended heirloom plants. At first glance, the city may resemble a 19th-century etching come to life—but look closer and you'll see that block after block of old structures have been restored. Happily, after three centuries of wars, epidemics, fires, and hurricanes, Charleston has prevailed and is now one of the South's best-preserved cities.

During the early 1800s, large tracts of land were available North of Broad—as it was outside the bounds of the original walled city—making it ideal for suburban plantations. A century later, these Lower King and Market districts are the heart of the city, a vibrant mix of residential neighborhoods and commercial clusters, with verdant parks scattered throughout. The College of Charleston's idyllic campus anchors much of lower King Street, ensuring the thoroughfare remains alive with young people and hip shops and restaurants. Though there are a number of majestic homes and pre-Revolutionary buildings in this area, the main draw is the rich variety of stores, museums, restaurants, and historic churches.

Sights

★ Avery Research Center for African American History and Culture

MUSEUM | Part of the College of Charleston, this museum and archive was once a school for African Americans, training students for professional careers from approximately 1865 to 1954. The collections here focus on the civil rights movement, but also include artifacts from the era of chattel slavery, such as badges, manacles, and bills of sale, as well as other materials from throughout African American history. The free guided tours begin with a brief film. ✉ *125 Bull St., College of Charleston Campus* ☎ *843/953–7609* 🌐 *avery.cofc.edu* 🎫 *Free* ⏲ *Closed weekends.*

★ The Charleston City Market

MARKET | **FAMILY** | Most of the buildings that make up this popular attraction were constructed between 1804 and the 1830s to serve as the city's meat, fish, and produce market. These days you'll find the open-air portion packed with stalls selling handmade jewelry, crafts, clothing, jams and jellies, and regional souvenirs. The market's indoor section is a beautiful backdrop for 20 stores and eateries. Local craftspeople are on hand, weaving sweetgrass baskets—a skill passed down through generations from their African ancestors. From April through December, a night market on Friday and Saturday hosts local artists and food vendors. This shopping mecca's perimeters (North and South Market Streets) are lined with restaurants and shops, too. ✉ *N. and S. Market Sts. between Meeting and E. Bay Sts., Market* 🌐 *www.thecharlestoncitymarket.com.*

★ Fort Sumter National Monument

MILITARY SITE | **FAMILY** | Set on a manmade island in Charleston's harbor, this is the hallowed spot where the Civil War began. On April 12, 1861, the first shot of the war was fired at the fort from

Take the ferry to Fort Sumter National Monument to see where the first shots of the Civil War were fired.

Fort Johnson across the way. After a 34-hour battle, Union forces surrendered and Confederate troops occupied Fort Sumter, which became a symbol of Southern resistance. The Confederacy managed to hold it, despite almost continual bombardment, from August 1863 to February 1865. When it was finally evacuated, the fort was a heap of rubble. Today, the National Park Service oversees it, and rangers give interpretive talks. To reach the fort, take a private boat or one of the ferries that depart from Patriots Point in Mount Pleasant and downtown's Fort Sumter Visitor Education Center, which includes exhibitions on the period before, during, and after the Civil War. There are as many as seven trips daily to the fort between mid-March and mid-August, fewer the rest of the year. ✉ *Charleston* ☎ *843/883–3123* 🌐 *www.nps.gov/fosu* 🎫 *Fort free, ferry $24.*

★ Gibbes Museum of Art

MUSEUM | Housed in a beautiful Beaux Arts building with a soaring stained-glass cupola, this museum boasts a collection of 10,000 works, principally American with a local connection. A recent $11.5 million renovation expanded on-site studios, rotating exhibit spaces, and visiting artist programs. Permanent displays include a massive stick sculpture by Patrick Dougherty that visitors can step inside and life-size oil paintings from the 18th century. Different objects from the museum's permanent collection are on view in "The Charleston Story," offering a nice summary of the region's history. Leave time to sit for a spell in the tranquil Lenhardt Garden behind the building. ✉ *135 Meeting St., Downtown Historic District* ☎ *843/722–2706* 🌐 *www.gibbesmuseum.org* 🎫 *$12.*

South Carolina Aquarium

ZOO | **FAMILY** | Get up close and personal with more than 5,000 creatures at this waterfront attraction, where exhibits invite you to journey through distinctive habitats. Step into the Mountain Forest and find water splashing over a rocky gorge as river otters play. Enter the open-air Saltmarsh Aviary to feed stingrays and view herons, diamondback terrapins, and puffer fish; gaze in awe at the two-story, 385,000-gallon Great Ocean Tank, home to sharks, jellyfish, and a loggerhead sea turtle. Kids love the touch tank, and the Sea Turtle Recovery exhibition makes the celebrated sea turtle rehabilitation hospital accessible to all visitors. *100 Aquarium Wharf, Ansonborough 800/722–6455, 843/577–3474 www.scaquarium.org $30.*

Restaurants

★ Charleston Grill

$$$$ | SOUTHERN | This perennial favorite inside Belmond's Charleston Place hotel provides what many regard as the city's highest gastronomic experience, with a menu divided into three parts: Roots & Stems, Waves & Marsh, and Field & Pasture. Chef Michelle Weaver creates the groundbreaking New South cuisine, while sommelier Rick Rubel stocks 1,300 wines in his cellar, with many served by the glass. **Known for:** impeccable service; a wine selection that rivals the world's best; nightly tasting menu that spans genres. *Average main: $37 Belmond Charleston Place, 224 King St., Market 843/577–4522 www.charlestongrill.com Closed Mon. and Tues. No lunch.*

Circa 1886

$$$$ | MODERN AMERICAN | Located on-site at the Wentworth Mansion, this former residential home is full of hand-carved marble fireplaces and stained-glass windows. The locally sourced menu is designed as a journey through South Carolina history, with dishes like heart of palm soup and venison loin that highlight ingredients used by presettlement Native Americans along with ones that celebrate the Lowcountry's Gullah-Geechee culture, like shrimp and rice grits. **Known for:** outdoor dining in the courtyard; city views from the cupola atop the mansion; local crab and clam pie. *Average main: $40 149 Wentworth St., College of Charleston Campus 843/853–7828 www.circa1886.com Closed Sun. No lunch.*

82 Queen

$$$ | SOUTHERN | This landmark mainstay continues to thrive as an atmospheric, fine-dining establishment. As always, the food has strong Southern leanings, with seafood highlights, including Charleston bouillabaisse; don't miss the creamy grits (perfection) or authentic fried green tomatoes. **Known for:** one of the city's quintessential she-crab soups; romantic dining; extensive and unique wine list. *Average main: $29 82 Queen St., Lower King 843/723–7591 www.82queen.com.*

★ FIG

$$$$ | CONTEMPORARY | Spend an evening at this trendsetter for fresh-off-the-farm ingredients cooked with unfussy, flavorful finesse—the Food Is Good kitchen has produced two James Beard Best Chef: Southeast winners. The menu changes frequently, but the family-style vegetables might be as simple as young beets in sherry vinegar served in a plain white bowl. **Known for:** local, seasonal fare, prepared with intense care and creativity; nationally recognized wine program; lively bar scene. *Average main: $35 232 Meeting St., Market 843/805–5900 www.eatatfig.com Closed Sun. No lunch.*

★ Grill 225

$$$$ | STEAKHOUSE | The cuisine at this atmospheric establishment—combined with a staggering array of excellent wines and professional, caring service—makes Grill 225 a popular special-occasion spot. Take the opportunity to dress up; the elegant wood floors, white linens, and red-velvet upholstery call for it. **Known for:** glitz and glamour; one of the best steaks in town; signature Nitrotini cocktail. *Average main: $40 Market Pavilion Hotel, 225 E. Bay St., Market 843/723–0500 www.marketpavilion.com/grill225.cfm.*

★ Husk

$$$$ | SOUTHERN | With an abundance of accolades, Husk serves an ambitious menu steeped in the South, and the South alone—everything is sourced regionally, barring exceptions like chocolate and coffee. A large chalkboard lists the ever-changing artisanal dishes available, as the menu sometimes varies twice daily. **Known for:** the Husk burger, modeled after In-N-Out's famous offering; the throwback stand-alone bar with its great bourbon menu; smoky bacon cornbread for a side. *Average main: $30 ✉ 76 Queen St., Market ☎ 843/577–2500 🌐 www.huskrestaurant.com.*

Muse Restaurant and Wine Bar

$$$ | MEDITERRANEAN | Set in a pale yellow building on Society Street, Muse lays bare Mediterranean stylings in sophisticated, relaxed quarters. The menu offers standout versions of classic fine-dining fare like veal scaloppini and a grilled pork chop, as well as the signature dish: a delicious, scarcely fried sea bass, served with head and tail intact, over a ragù of butter beans and pancetta. **Known for:** 75 wines by the glass; late-night weekend menu; ricotta cheesecake with blueberry coulis. *Average main: $26 ✉ 82 Society St., Lower King ☎ 843/577–1102 🌐 www.charlestonmuse.com ⏲ No lunch.*

Peninsula Grill

$$$$ | SEAFOOD | This fine-dining stalwart melds Lowcountry produce and seafood into traditional but inspired dishes, at once eyeing the past and the future. The dining room fixtures (walls covered in olive-green velvet and 18th-century-style portraits, with wrought-iron chandeliers on the ceiling) serve as an excellent backdrop for Angus steaks, jumbo sea scallops, and Berkshire pork chops. **Known for:** sought-after coconut cake dessert; special-occasion splurging; knowledgeable and friendly sommelier. *Average main: $35 ✉ Planters Inn, 112 N. Market St., Market ☎ 843/723–0700 🌐 www.peninsulagrill.com ⏲ No lunch.*

Queen Street Grocery

$ | CAFÉ | Don't pass up the sweet and savory crepes, named for the islands surrounding Charleston, at this venerable neighborhood institution that also serves pressed breakfast and lunch sandwiches, smoothies, cold brew, and craft beer. The art-filled space doubles as a wineshop—pick up a bottle on the way to a picnic at nearby Colonial Lake. **Known for:** charming sidewalk and patio seating; grab-and-go picnic items; local gourmet grocery products. *Average main: $10 ✉ 133 Queen St., Broad Street ☎ 843/723–4121 🌐 www.queenstreetgrocerycafe.com.*

★ Ted's Butcherblock

$ | CAFÉ | Operating as a one-stop butcher shop and deli counter, Ted's sells beef, game, seafood, and homemade sausages to complement its selection of artisanal cheeses, wine, and other specialty foods. Among the lunchtime favorites are the house-roasted Wagyu beef panini and the ever-changing bacon-of-the-month BLT. **Known for:** Ultimate Burger Saturday, cooked on the Big Green Egg; Friday night dinners with wine pairings; daily sandwiches with memorable flavors. *Average main: $12 ✉ 334 E. Bay St., Ansonborough ☎ 843/577–0094 🌐 www.tedsbutcherblock.com ⏲ Closed Sun. and Mon.*

Hotels

Andrew Pinckney Inn

$$ | B&B/INN | Nestled in the heart of Charleston, this West Indies–inspired inn offers a range of accommodations, from charming rooms perfect for couples to two-level suites big enough for the whole family. **Pros:** the town houses are ideal for longer stays; afternoon wine and cheese with fresh-baked cookies; central location. **Cons:** elevator access in only one of the two buildings; nearby horse stables and restaurant deliveries can be noisy; no pool. *Rooms from: $199 ✉ 40 Pinckney St., Market ☎ 843/937–8800,*

800/505–8983 🌐 *www.andrewpinckney-inn.com* 41 *rooms* *Free breakfast.*

★ Ansonborough Inn

$$$ | **B&B/INN** | At this boutique hotel you can relax in your comfortable suite or indulge in evening wine and cheese on the expansive rooftop terrace while enjoying views of the city and Cooper River. **Pros:** lots of period details; 24-hour upscale supermarket across the street; easy walking distance to the Market. **Cons:** gym only has treadmill and weight machine; some rooms open to a central atrium directly over the lobby; no pool. *Rooms from: $219* ✉ *21 Hasell St., Market* ☎ *800/723–1655* 🌐 *www.ansonboroughinn.com* *45 suites* *Free breakfast.*

★ Belmond Charleston Place

$$$$ | **HOTEL** | Guests and casual passers-by alike enjoy gazing up at the immense handblown Murano glass chandelier in this hotel's open lobby, clicking across the Italian marble floors, and browsing the gallery of upscale shops that completes the ground-floor offerings of this landmark hotel with bright, modern rooms. **Pros:** at the heart of the city's best shopping district; excellent amenities, including salt-and-mineral-water pool; great on-site restaurants and bars. **Cons:** hosts lots of conference groups in shoulder seasons; lacks the charm of more historic properties; many common spaces are shared with nonguests. *Rooms from: $359* ✉ *205 Meeting St., Market* ☎ *843/722–4900, 888/635–2350* 🌐 *www.belmond.com/charleston-place* *435 rooms* *Some meals.*

★ Emeline

$$$ | **HOTEL** | The Market area's newest upscale lodging feels like a boutique hotel despite its size, thanks to an endless array of thoughtful touches, from welcome cocktails and staff who remember your name to in-room record players with classic albums like *Piano Man* and *Pet Sounds*. **Pros:** free bike rentals; excellent on-site dining options, including Clerks coffee shop; luxurious decor. **Cons:** some rooms are small; the gym is well equipped but cramped for a hotel this size; no pool. *Rooms from: $299* ✉ *181 Church St., Market* ☎ *843/577–2644* 🌐 *www.hotelemeline.com* *212 rooms* *No meals.*

Fulton Lane Inn

$$$ | **HOTEL** | This inn is both lovely and quirky: its Victorian-dressed rooms (some with four-poster beds, handsome fireplaces, and jetted tubs) are laid out in a bit of a floor-creaking maze, but it adds to its individuality. **Pros:** great central location; charming choice of rooms; evening wine, cheese, and sherry. **Cons:** nonsuite rooms are a bit cramped; street noise; the only communal spaces are next door at Kings Courtyard Inn. *Rooms from: $219* ✉ *202 King St., Lower King* ☎ *843/720–2600* 🌐 *www.fultonlaneinn.com* *47 rooms* *Free breakfast.*

Grand Bohemian Charleston

$$$$ | **HOTEL** | One of the entrances to this luxurious Marriott-affiliated hotel steers guests directly into an art gallery, an indication of the modern, creative flair that awaits inside the Instagram-worthy lobby. **Pros:** in-house wine-blending program offered for guests; one of the best rooftop bars in town; central location for walking the Historic District. **Cons:** priced higher than some competitors; the unique emphasis on art won't appeal to everyone; no pool. *Rooms from: $425* ✉ *55 Wentworth St., Market* ☎ *843/722–5711* 🌐 *www.grandbohemiancharleston.com* *50 rooms* *No meals.*

Hotel Bella Grace

$$$$ | **HOTEL** | Marriott's answer to the city's boutique hotel boom is quite charming, thanks in part to the adjacent Delaney Oyster House restaurant in an 1830 Charleston single house. **Pros:** nice fitness center with a Peloton; modern decor with a historic element; boutique hotel that's in the Marriott Rewards program. **Cons:** not as over-the-top charming as some boutique competitors; breakfast

not included; no pool. *Rooms from: $349 115 Calhoun St., Ansonborough 843/990–7500 hotelbellagrace.com 50 rooms No meals.*

★ Market Pavilion Hotel

$$$ | HOTEL | The hustle and bustle of one of the city's busiest corners vanishes as soon as the uniformed bellman opens the lobby door of the Market Pavilion Hotel to reveal wood-paneled walls, antique furnishings, and chandeliers hung from high ceilings; it resembles a European grand hotel from the 19th century, and you'll feel like you're visiting royalty. **Pros:** opulent furnishings; architecturally impressive, especially the tray ceilings; excellent on-site restaurant. **Cons:** gym is small; some may find the interior over the top; pool terrace is open to nonguests. *Rooms from: $279 225 E. Bay St., Market 843/723–0500 www.marketpavilion.com 70 rooms Free breakfast.*

The Meeting Street Inn

$$ | HOTEL | Guest rooms in this 1874 stucco mansion, with porches on the second, third, and fourth floors, overlook a lovely courtyard with fountains and a hot tub. **Pros:** some rooms have desks and other extras; bathrooms sport nice marble fixtures; fun wine-and-cheese nights. **Cons:** lacy canopy beds and exquisite wallpaper aren't for everyone; some rooms overlook a parking lot; parking is off-site and on the pricey side. *Rooms from: $159 173 Meeting St., Market 843/723–1882 www.meetingstreetinn.com 56 rooms Free breakfast.*

The Mills House

$$$ | HOTEL | The Wyndham-managed Mills House is the modern iteration of the original 1853 hotel by the same name. **Pros:** convenient to South of Broad and to Market and King Street shopping; a concierge desk so well regarded that locals call for neighborly assistance and advice; lovely rooftop pool. **Cons:** rooms are rather small, which is typical of hotels of this time period; on a busy street; pool can be crowded during summer. *Rooms from: $209 115 Meeting St., Market 843/577–2400 www.millshouse.com 216 rooms No meals.*

Planters Inn

$$$ | B&B/INN | Part of the Relais & Châteaux group, this boutique property with well-appointed, expansive, and beautifully maintained rooms is a stately sanctuary amid the bustle of Charleston's City Market. **Pros:** double-pane windows render the rooms soundproof; front desk staff knows your name upon arrival; complimentary evening cocktails and bedtime macarons. **Cons:** no pool; gym access is off-site; parking is valet only, at $34 a day. *Rooms from: $279 112 N. Market St., Market 843/722–2345 www.plantersinn.com 64 rooms No meals.*

★ The Restoration

$$$$ | B&B/INN | FAMILY | Charleston architect Neil Stevenson designed this boutique hotel to be swank and suave to the hilt, featuring several rooftop terraces with sleek sofas and prime views. **Pros:** many suites are larger than Manhattan luxury apartments, with full kitchens and complimentary snacks and drinks; great location without the street noise; excellent amenities like a rooftop pool and free bike rentals. **Cons:** no gym on the premises, but there are some within easy walking distance; views vary from room to room; very expensive. *Rooms from: $359 75 Wentworth St., Lower King 877/221–7202 www.therestorationhotel.com 54 suites Free breakfast.*

Wentworth Mansion

$$$$ | B&B/INN | The grandest inn in town features Second Empire antiques and reproductions, elaborate woodwork, and original stained-glass windows, as well as sweeping views from the rooftop cupola. **Pros:** fantastic on-site restaurant and spa; opulent guest rooms; free parking. **Cons:** style can strike some people as forbidding; outside the tourist areas; no on-site gym. $ *Rooms from: $349* ✉ *149 Wentworth St., College of Charleston Campus* ☎ *843/853–1886* 🌐 *www.wentworthmansion.com* *21 rooms* 🍴 *Free breakfast.*

★ Zero George

$$$$ | HOTEL | Five restored 19th-century residences have been joined together to create this hideaway in the heart of Charleston's leafy Ansonborough neighborhood that's surrounded by well-heeled homes and just a short walk from East Bay restaurants, the City Market, and Marion Square. **Pros:** convenient and quiet location; local charm; excellent on-site bar and restaurant. **Cons:** it's a bit of a walk to the Market and to King Street; gym access is at nearby Pivotal Fitness; no pool. $ *Rooms from: $339* ✉ *0 George St., Ansonborough* ☎ *843/817–7900* 🌐 *www.zerogeorge.com* *16 rooms* 🍴 *Free breakfast.*

Nightlife

Bin 152

WINE BARS—NIGHTLIFE | Husband and wife Patrick and Fanny Panella ply their guests with selections from more than 130 bottles of wine and 40 varieties of cheeses and charcuterie, freshly baked breads, contemporary art, and tasteful antique furniture. All of it is imminently available, too, from the Sauvignon Blanc and Shiraz to the tables and chairs. Cast in low lighting, the wine bar serves as a comfortable backdrop for a pre- or postdinner drink or for an entire evening. ✉ *152 King St., Lower King* ☎ *843/577–7359* 🌐 *www.bin152.com.*

★ Charleston Grill

MUSIC CLUBS | The elegant Charleston Grill hosts live jazz seven nights a week, drawing from the city's most renowned musicians. Performers range from the internationally acclaimed Brazilian guitarist Duda Lucena to the Bob Williams Duo, a father and son who play classical guitar and violin. The place draws an urbane crowd that spans generations. Down the hall, the neighboring Thoroughbred Club offers nightly live music and an impressive selection of bourbons. ✉ *Charleston Place Hotel, 224 King St., Market* ☎ *843/577–4522* 🌐 *www.charlestongrill.com.*

Henry's Restaurant, Bar & Music Hall

BARS/PUBS | The longest continuously operating restaurant and bar in South Carolina, Henry's has evolved since the opening of Henry's house in 1932. On the first floor is a large horseshoe bar and dining room with floor-to-ceiling windows looking out to the Market. The second floor is a classic jazz bar with exposed brick and rafters, and dim chandelier lighting. A few steps up is a rooftop deck and an enclosed dance lounge that attracts a younger crowd on weekends. ✉ *54 N. Market, Market* ☎ *843/723–4363* 🌐 *www.henrysonthemarket.com.*

★ Pavilion Bar

BARS/PUBS | Atop the Market Pavilion Hotel, the swanky outdoor Pavilion Bar offers panoramic views of the city and harbor, set around the hotel's posh swimming pool. Enjoy appetizers like lobster ceviche and duck nachos with a specialty mojito or martini. The dress code dictates no flip-flops, baseball caps, visors, or tank tops. ✉ *Market Pavilion Hotel, 225 E. Bay St., Market* ☎ *843/723–0500* 🌐 *www.marketpavilion.com.*

Shopping

ANTIQUES

★ George C. Birlant and Co.

ANTIQUES/COLLECTIBLES | You'll find mostly 18th- and 19th-century English antiques here, but keep your eye out for a Charleston Battery bench (seen at White Point Garden), for which the store is famous. Founded in 1922, Birlant's is fourth-generation family-owned and home to the oldest working freight elevator in the country. ✉ *191 King St., Lower*

King ☎ 843/722–3842 🌐 www.birlantantiquescharleston.com.

Jacques' Antiques

ANTIQUES/COLLECTIBLES | French imports make up much of the selection here, and the rest are either European or English from the 17th to the 20th centuries. Decorative arts include ceramics, porcelains, and crystal. From the candlesticks to the armoires, all are in exquisite taste. ✉ *160 King St., Lower King* ☎ *843/577–0104.*

CLOTHING

Ben Silver

CLOTHING | Charleston's own Ben Silver, premier purveyor of blazer buttons, has more than 800 designs, including college and British regimental motifs. The shop, founded in the 1960s, also sells British neckties, embroidered polo shirts, and blazers. ✉ *149 King St., Lower King* ☎ *843/577–4556* 🌐 *www.bensilver.com.*

Christian Michi

CLOTHING | Tony clothing and accessories by designers from Italy, such as Piazza Sempione, are represented here, as is the European line Intropia. Known for its evening wear, the shop has pricey but gorgeous gowns and a fine selection of cocktail dresses. High-end fragrances add to the luxurious air. ✉ *220 King St., Lower King* ☎ *843/723–0575.*

Copper Penny

CLOTHING | This longtime local clothier sells trendy dresses and apparel from designers like Trina Turk and BB Dakota. There's also an accompanying shoe store next door and two satellite locations in Mount Pleasant. ✉ *311 King St., Lower King* ☎ *843/723–2999* 🌐 *www.shopcopperpenny.com.*

Finicky Filly

CLOTHING | This mother/daughter-owned boutique carries exceptional apparel, jewelry, and handbags by such designers as Joie, Tory Burch, and Etro. ✉ *303 King St., Lower King* ☎ *843/534–0203* 🌐 *www.thefinickyfilly.com.*

★ **Hampden Clothing**

CLOTHING | One of the city's trendiest boutiques attracts the young and well-heeled, who come here for an edgier, New York–influenced style. Hot designers like Alexandre Birman and Mara Hoffman help make it a premier destination for the latest in fashion. ✉ *314 King St., Lower King* ☎ *843/724–6373* 🌐 *www.hampdenclothing.com.*

★ **Ibu Movement**

CLOTHING | Artisans from 38 countries contribute the elaborate and intricate textiles used to make the clothing for sale here. The brightly colored shop is nestled in an upstairs nook on Lower King. Purchases support the communities where the clothing and supplies originate. ✉ *183B King St., Lower King* ☎ *843/327–8304* 🌐 *www.ibumovement.com.*

Kids on King

CLOTHING | **FAMILY** | This shop's world-traveling owners offer the finest in children's apparel, accessories, and toys from just about everywhere. You'll be transported to other lands with the handcrafted designs. ✉ *310 King St., Lower King* ☎ *843/720–8647* 🌐 *www.kidsonking.com.*

FOOD AND WINE

Caviar and Bananas

FOOD/CANDY | This upscale specialty market and café features classic paninis, salads, and every type of fancy, fizzy drink imaginable. It's an ideal spot to prep for a picnic. Note the locally produced items, such as Callie's Pimiento Cheese and Jack Rudy Cocktail Co. Small Batch Tonic Syrup. There's even an airport location, which is your best bet for a quick before-flight bite. ✉ *51 George St., College of Charleston Campus* ☎ *843/577–7757* 🌐 *www.caviarandbananas.com.*

★ **Market Street Sweets**

FOOD/CANDY | **FAMILY** | Stop here for melt-in-your-mouth pralines, bear claws, fudge, and the famous glazed pecans—cinnamon and sugar is the favorite. It's a sister location of Savannah's River Street

Sweets. ✉ *100 N. Market St., Market* ☎ *843/722–1397* 🌐 *www.riverstreets-weets.com.*

Upper King

Spanning northward from Calhoun Street on Charleston's main peninsula, Upper King and the surrounding areas are home to the city's newest and hippest restaurants and bars (and its highest-end hotels). On weekends, college students and young professionals line up outside the thumping clubs and tony cocktail bars.

Formerly the heart of the city's black business district, the area between the Lower Peninsula and The Neck was dramatically changed with the opening of the Crosstown Expressway in 1968. Then in the 1990s, white restaurateurs started looking northward to open dining rooms in the vicinity of Upper King Street, due to its cheaper rents. This raised prices in the area and forced former residents to move farther afield in the city, and as is often the case with gentrification, it then paved the way for a tourism boom with food and drink at its center. While the neighborhood is still residential in spots, it's now dominated by short-term rentals, high-end restaurants, bars, coffee shops, breweries, and boutiques.

Sights

★ Aiken-Rhett House Museum

HISTORIC SITE | A prime example of the wealth derived from chattel slavery, the Aiken-Rhett House is considered one of the best preserved town-house complexes in the country. Built in 1820 and virtually unaltered since 1858, it boasts original wallpaper, paint, and some furnishings. Two of the former owners, Governor Aiken and his wife Harriet, bought many of the chandeliers, sculptures, and paintings in Europe. The carriage house remains out back, along with a building that contained the kitchen, laundry, and housing for enslaved laborers, making this the most intact property to showcase urban life in pre–Civil War Charleston. Be sure to take the audio tour, as it vividly describes the surroundings, giving historical and family details throughout. ✉ *48 Elizabeth St., Upper King* ☎ *843/723–1159* 🌐 *www.historiccharleston.org/house-museums* 🎫 *$12, with admission to Nathaniel Russell House Museum $18.*

Charleston Museum

MUSEUM | **FAMILY** | Although housed in a modern-day brick complex, this institution was founded in 1773 and is the country's oldest museum. The collection is especially strong in South Carolina decorative arts, from silver to snuffboxes. There's also a large gallery devoted to natural history (don't miss the giant polar bear). Children love the permanent Civil War exhibition and the interactive "Kidstory" area, where they can try on reproduction clothing in a miniature historic house. The Historic Textiles Gallery features rotating displays that showcase everything from uniforms and flags to couture gowns, antique quilts, and needlework. Combination tickets that include the Joseph Manigault House and the Heyward-Washington House are a bargain at $25. ✉ *360 Meeting St., Upper King* ☎ *843/722–2996* 🌐 *www.charlestonmuseum.org* 🎫 *$12; combination ticket with Heyward-Washington House or Joseph Manigault House $18, combination ticket for all 3 sites $25.*

Children's Museum of the Lowcountry

MUSEUM | **FAMILY** | Hands-on interactive exhibits at this top-notch museum will keep kids—from infants to 10-year-old children—occupied for hours. They can climb aboard a Lowcountry pirate ship, drive an antique fire truck, race golf balls down a roller coaster, and create masterpieces in the art center. ✉ *25 Ann St., Upper King* ☎ *843/853–8962* 🌐 *www.*

explorecml.org 🎫 *SC residents $10, non-SC residents $12* 🕓 *Closed Mon.*

Joseph Manigault House

HISTORIC SITE | An extraordinary example of Federal architecture, this 1803 residence and National Historic Landmark reflects the urban lifestyle of a well-to-do rice-planting family and the Africans they enslaved. Engaging guided tours reveal a stunning spiral staircase, rooms that have been preserved in period style, and American, English, and French furniture from the early 19th century. Outside, stroll through the artfully maintained period garden; unfortunately, most of the historic out buildings were torn down long ago, now replaced with interpretive signs that note their former locations. ✉ *350 Meeting St., Upper King* ☎ *843/723–2926* 🌐 *www.charlestonmuseum.org* 🎫 *$12; combination ticket with Heyward-Washington House or Charleston Museum $18; combination ticket for all 3 sites $25.*

Magnolia Cemetery

CEMETERY | Ancient oak trees drip Spanish moss over funerary sculptures and magnificent mausoleums in this cemetery on the Cooper River. It opened in 1850, beautifully landscaped (thanks to the rural cemetery movement of the era) with paths, ponds, and lush lawns. The people of Charleston came not only to pay respects to the deceased, but also for picnicking and family outings. Similarly, visitors still find joy in the natural surroundings—and intrigue in the elaborate structures marking the graves of many prominent South Carolinians. All three crews of mariners who died aboard the Civil War sub the *H. L. Hunley* are buried here, and more than 850 Confederate servicemen rest in the Soldiers' Ground. Walking maps are available in the front office. ✉ *70 Cunnington Ave., North Morrison* ☎ *843/722–8638* 🌐 *www.magnoliacemetery.net* 🎫 *Free.*

Restaurants

★ Bertha's Kitchen

$ | SOUTHERN | FAMILY | One of the Charleston area's great soul food institutions, Bertha's is owned and run by sisters Julie Grant, Linda Pinckney, and Sharon Grant Coakley, who have been awarded the America's Classic prize from the James Beard Foundation for being an essential component of the community (the restaurant was opened in their mother's honor). There's almost always a line at the counter-service restaurant, but it's worth waiting for exceptional okra soup, fried pork chops, and lima beans. **Known for:** home-cooking that most eaters can't get at home; strong family values and connection to the community ; serving everyone from construction workers to the mayor. $ *Average main: $6* ✉ *2332 Meeting St. Rd., North Charleston* ☎ *843/554–6519* 🕓 *Closed Sun. No dinner.*

★ Butcher & Bee

$ | MODERN AMERICAN | Healthy and light but always satisfying, this local favorite has grown into new digs and expanded its lunch and dinner menus. The seasonal menu features creative salads, craft sandwiches, and rice bowls. **Known for:** locally sourced ingredients filtered through a Middle Eastern lens; plant-forward sandwiches; big patio for outside dining. $ *Average main: $12* ✉ *1085 Morrison Dr., North Morrison* ☎ *843/619–0202* 🌐 *www.butcherandbee.com.*

★ Chez Nous

$$$ | FRENCH | The menu may be nearly illegible, the space minuscule, and locating the tucked-away location like finding Waldo, but the food is almost always sublime. Each night only two appetizers, two entrées (like snapper with a *vin jaune* [type of white wine] sauce or gnocchi with chanterelles), and two desserts are offered. **Known for:** romantic hideaway dining; unique French, Spanish, and Italian fare; constantly changing menu. [$] *Average main: $26 ⊠ 6 Payne Ct., Upper King ✥ Off Coming St. ☎ 843/579–3060 🌐 cheznouschs.com ⏲ Closed Mon.*

★ Edmund's Oast

$$$ | **SOUTHERN** | It's not just what's in the pint glasses at this upscale brewpub that has locals raving. The kitchen's mac-and-peas and pickled shrimp toast, featuring the region's hallmark ingredients, are almost universally adored. **Known for:** the best of the best for beer nerds; upscale Sunday brunch; sunshine-filled patio. [$] *Average main: $25 ⊠ 1081 Morrison Dr., North Morrison ☎ 843/727–1145 🌐 www.edmundsoast.com ⏲ No lunch.*

★ The Grocery

$$$ | **MODERN AMERICAN** | Executive chef and owner Kevin Johnson's outstanding restaurant sits in impressive quarters near the corner of Cannon and King Streets. The menu suggests a humble, considerate approach, as the dishes represent local flavors: the wood-roasted carrots come with feta, raisins, and pistachio crumble, while the wood-roasted whole fish is delivered with salsa *verde*. **Known for:** down-to-earth dishes designed for sharing; a monstrous wood-fired oven; decadent cassoulet. [$] *Average main: $28 ⊠ 4 Cannon St., Market ☎ 843/302–8825 🌐 www.thegrocery-charleston.com ⏲ No lunch.*

Halls Chophouse

$$$$ | **STEAKHOUSE** | Thanks to its impressive 28-day-aged USDA steaks, Halls Chophouse is regarded as one of the top steak houses in town. The 28-ounce Tomahawk rib eye, the New York strip, and the slow-roasted prime rib are especially recommended. **Known for:** hopping upscale bar scene; Sunday brunch featuring live gospel singers; amazing variety of steaks. [$] *Average main: $45 ⊠ 434 King St., Upper King ☎ 843/727–0090 🌐 www.hallschophouse.com ⏲ No lunch.*

★ Leon's Oyster Shop

$$ | **SOUTHERN** | Casual, quirky, and a tad Wes Anderson-y, this oysters-and-fried-chicken joint sports a kitschy ambience and blues-heavy soundtrack. Fried catfish, oyster, and chicken sammies come towering, dressed in fresh slaw or "comeback sauce" and nestled on perfectly prepared rolls. **Known for:** lively stand-up bar scene; extensive champagne list; old-school soft-serve ice cream. [$] *Average main: $15 ⊠ 698 King St., Upper King ☎ 843/531–6500 🌐 www.leonsoystershop.com.*

★ Lewis Barbecue

$ | **BARBECUE** | Austin pitmaster John Lewis transformed Charleston's smoked meat scene when he opened this Texas-style joint that serves prime rib, pulled pork, and "hot guts" by the pound. The meat is served on brown paper and the margaritas are tart; the Juan Luis trailer parked on Lewis's patio, uncannily evocative of Texas, serves breakfast tacos and other El Paso specialties. **Known for:** smoked prime rib Wednesday; monster El Sancho Loco sandwich; hatch green chile barbecue sauce. [$] *Average main: $12 ⊠ 464 N. Nassau St., North Morrison ☎ 843/805–9500 🌐 www.lewisbarbecue.com ⏲ Closed Mon.*

★ The Macintosh

$$$$ | **MODERN AMERICAN** | Once the local darling among the Indigo Road properties, which also includes Oak Steakhouse and O-Ku, the Macintosh lost some of its luster over the years, but a string of new executive chefs put the one-time trendsetter on a path back to relevance. The menu is still rife with house classics, including *gnudi*, strip steak, and the Mac's ever-popular truffle fries. **Known for:** creative seasonal starters; bone marrow bread pudding for dessert; sophistication without pretense. [$] *Average main: $30 ⊠ 478 King St., Upper King ☎ 843/789–4299 🌐 www.themacintoshcharleston.com ⏲ No lunch except for Sun. brunch.*

★ The Ordinary

$$$ | **SEAFOOD** | Award-winning chef Mike Lata delivers every possible type of underwater delight here, from local littleneck clams to wahoo carpaccio. The two-story dining room of this former bank building fills up fast, but you can always belly up to the stunning bar while you wait and enjoy a variety of clever cocktails. **Known for:** heady wine pairings; daily plat du jour; excellent oyster bar. *Average main: $28 544 King St., Upper King 843/414–7060 www.eattheordinary.com Closed Mon. No lunch.*

★ Renzo

$$ | **PIZZA** | Although it's billed as a pizza parlor, this neighborhood trattoria stuns taste buds with its entire menu, including anchovies in pepper and grapefruit and entrées like swordfish with horseradish mustard. The thin-crust pizzas are complemented by an impressive selection of natural wines and a daily cocktail special. **Known for:** collaborations with outside chefs; occasional bagel Sunday; after-dinner drinks at the Faculty Lounge across the street, a watering hole from the same owners. *Average main: $17 384 Huger St., Hampton Park Terrace 843/952–7864 www.renzochs.com Closed Sun. and Mon. No lunch.*

★ Rodney Scott's Whole Hog BBQ

$ | **BARBECUE** | Rodney Scott became a darling of the region's barbecue scene in the early 2010s, when with the help of the Southern Foodways Alliance, he branched out from his family's pit-cooked joint in Hemingway, South Carolina, to create this temple to whole hogs in downtown Charleston. Apart from the requisite sandwiches and platters, he also offers pit-cooked chicken, racks of ribs, and fried catfish. **Known for:** city's best steak sandwich; sealed plastic bags of pork rinds that should be added to every order; exceptional banana pudding. *Average main: $14 1011 King St., Hampton Park Terrace 843/990–9535 www.rodneyscottsbbq.com.*

Taco Boy

$ | **MEXICAN** | **FAMILY** | Accommodating locals and out-of-towners alike, Taco Boy delivers tasty Mexican American treats to a bustling patio crowd. The ambience is half the allure of this eclectic outpost featuring rehabbed or reclaimed materials—right down to the bar counter, carved from a fallen North Carolina walnut tree, and the funky Mexican folk art adorning every inch of wall space. **Known for:** funky, eclectic decor; creative, gourmet tacos; mean margaritas and micheladas. *Average main: $12 217 Huger St., North Morrison 843/789–3333 www.tacoboy.net.*

The Tattooed Moose

$ | **AMERICAN** | If it looks like a cross between a veterans' hall and a dive bar, that's because the Tattooed Moose is going for a decidedly unpretentious vibe. With 90-plus beers on the menu and a large moose head behind the counter, the place cuts a distinctive figure; homey eats like house-smoked barbecue brisket, chicken salad, jumbo chicken wings, and fried turkey breast are just some of the offerings. **Known for:** decadent duck club sandwich with apple-smoked bacon, garlic aioli, and ripened tomatoes bounded by sweet Hawaiian bread; weekend brunch that's a great value; chill and eclectic vibe. *Average main: $12 1137 Morrison Dr., North Morrison 843/277–2990 www.tattooedmoose.com.*

39 Rue de Jean

$$$ | **FRENCH** | Against a backdrop of classic French-bistro style—think gleaming wood, cozy booths, and white-papered tables—Charleston's night owls feast on such favorites here as steamed mussels in a half dozen preparations. Order them with *pommes frites,* as the French do. **Known for:** lively social scene; weekly specials, including Sunday bouillabaisse; amazing burgers. *Average main: $26 39 John St., Upper King 843/722–8881 www.39ruedejean.com.*

★ **Xiao Bao Biscuit**

$$ | **ASIAN FUSION** | Amid the boom in Charleston's dining scene in the early 2010s, one thing was distinctly lacking: Asian-influenced flavors, but then Xiao Bao came along and changed the city's trajectory. With curries, fried fish, and Sichuan pork dishes that draw on one of the three owners' Chinese heritage without directly replicating it, the casual eatery in a former gas station has gained national acclaim. **Known for:** okonomiyaki cabbage pancake topped with a farm egg and pork candy; seasonally updated menu full of surprises; dishes meant for family-style sharing. *Average main: $18* *224 Rutledge Ave., Cannonborough* *www.xiaobaobiscuit.com* *Closed Sun.*

Coffee and Quick Bites

Glazed

$ | **BAKERY** | **FAMILY** | Three words: maple bacon doughnuts. If that's not enough to get you in the door, any number of other creative options—think raspberry nutella or berries and mascarpone—should do the trick. **Known for:** unconventional doughnut flavors, made from scratch; constantly rotating daily specials; homemade jam fillings. *Average main: $3* *481 King St., Upper King* *843/577–5557* *www.glazedgourmet.com.*

Hotels

★ **The Dewberry**

$$$$ | **HOTEL** | Built in the renovated Federal Building overlooking Marion Square, the Dewberry exudes style and sophistication from the travertine marble to the mahogany and walnut that adorn the lobby and in-house bar and restaurant. **Pros:** one of the city's best cocktail bars on-site; perfectly central location; world-class spa. **Cons:** sheer indulgence doesn't come cheap; Hotel Bennett a block away may out-luxury its competitor; no rollaway beds or sleeper sofas. *Rooms from: $499* *334 Meeting St., Middle King* *888/550–1450* *www.thedewberrycharleston.com* *155 rooms* *No meals.*

86 Cannon

$$$$ | **B&B/INN** | Awash in style and modern luxury yet firmly rooted in historic authenticity, this boutique hotel caters to the well-to-do with a taste for understated class. **Pros:** posh amenities; thoughtful architectural and design details; wide porches are perfect for an afternoon spent reading. **Cons:** long walk to the heart of town; historic house converted into an inn means fellow guests are always nearby; quite expensive. *Rooms from: $429* *86 Cannon St., Cannonborough* *843/779–7700* *www.86cannon.com* *7 rooms* *Free breakfast.*

Francis Marion Hotel

$$ | **HOTEL** | Wrought-iron railings, crown moldings, and decorative plasterwork speak of the elegance of 1924, when the Francis Marion was the largest hotel in the Carolinas. **Pros:** in the midst of the peninsula's best shopping; on-site Spa Adagio; some of the best city views. **Cons:** rooms are small, as is closet space; on a busy intersection; often hosts conferences that fill the hotel. *Rooms from: $219* *387 King St., Upper King* *843/722–0600* *www.francismarionhotel.com* *235 rooms* *No meals.*

★ **NotSo Hostel**

$ | **B&B/INN** | A small enclave of 1840s-era buildings make up this homey, idyllic hostel. **Pros:** great price and sense of camaraderie; historic rooms have character; insider tips from fellow guests and staff. **Cons:** not for travelers who wish to keep to themselves; communal bathrooms; no extra amenities like pool or gym. *Rooms from: $68* *156 Spring St., Cannonborough* *843/722–8383* *www.notsohostel.com* *24 dorm beds, 1 room with private bath, 7 rooms with communal baths* *No meals.*

Nightlife

★ Babas on Cannon

WINE BARS—NIGHTLIFE | Order a pomegranate, juiced on the spot and spiked with the liquor of your choice, at this casual but stylish hangout for wine, cocktails, and tapas (try the pickled shrimp with fennel). It's a coffee shop by day and bar at night, but both iterations are distinguished by excellent service and impressive extras to go with your drinks. ✉ *11 Cannon St., Upper King* 🌐 *www.babasoncannon.com.*

★ The Belmont

BARS/PUBS | This place doesn't seek attention—heck, it won't even list its phone number. But with a soaring tin ceiling, exposed-brick walls, and a penchant for projecting black-and-white films onto the wall, the charisma comes naturally. An inventive cocktail menu served up by sharply dressed mixologists helps, too. Try their take on the spicy-sweet Brown Derby, a bourbon drink made with jalapeño-infused honey, or the Bells of Jalisco, featuring *reposado* tequila, more jalapeño honey, and lime juice. There's also a light menu of panini, charcuterie, and homemade pop tarts. ✉ *511 King St., Upper King* 🌐 *www.thebelmontcharleston.com.*

★ The Cocktail Club

BARS/PUBS | This establishment characterizes the craft cocktail movement with its "farm-to-shaker" seasonal selection of creative concoctions. The bar showcases exposed brick walls and wooden beams inside its lounge areas, though warm evenings are best spent outside on the rooftop patio. Inside, some of Charleston's best bartenders muddle and shake clever mixtures like the Dad Bod (Demerara rum, rye whiskey, Falernum, grenadine, and lime) and the Double Standard (a blend of serrano pepper–infused gin and cucumber vodka). ✉ *479 King St., Suite 200, Upper King* ☎ *843/724–9411* 🌐 *www.thecocktailclubcharleston.com.*

Dudley's on Ann

BARS/PUBS | A local landmark, the city's oldest gay bar hosts lively karaoke parties, DJs and dancing on weekends, and boisterous drag shows. ✉ *42 Ann St., Upper King* ☎ *843/577–6779* 🌐 *www.dudleysonann.com.*

★ Graft

WINE BARS—NIGHTLIFE | Two of Charleston's most respected sommeliers co-own this wineshop and oenophile haven that spins classic records and hosts live bands on weekends. The walls are lined with carefully curated bottles that can be taken to go or popped and enjoyed on the spot. ✉ *700B King St., Upper King* ☎ *843/718–3359* 🌐 *www.graftchs.com.*

Trio

DANCE CLUBS | Funky sounds from the '70s and '80s mix with the latest club anthems at this perennially popular dance club. Listen to the cover bands at the downstairs bar, mingle on the outdoor patio, or head upstairs for the DJ-led dance party. It's open only Friday and Saturday night. ✉ *139 Calhoun St., Upper King* 🌐 *www.triocharleston.com.*

Performing Arts

★ Charleston Music Hall

CONCERTS | Regularly hosting big-name bluegrass, blues, and country acts, the beautiful 900-seat Charleston Music Hall shines. Home to the Charleston Jazz Orchestra, it's in the heart of Upper King and within easy walking distance of numerous popular bars and restaurants for pre- and postshow refreshments. ✉ *37 John St., Upper King* ☎ *843/853–2252* 🌐 *www.charlestonmusichall.com.*

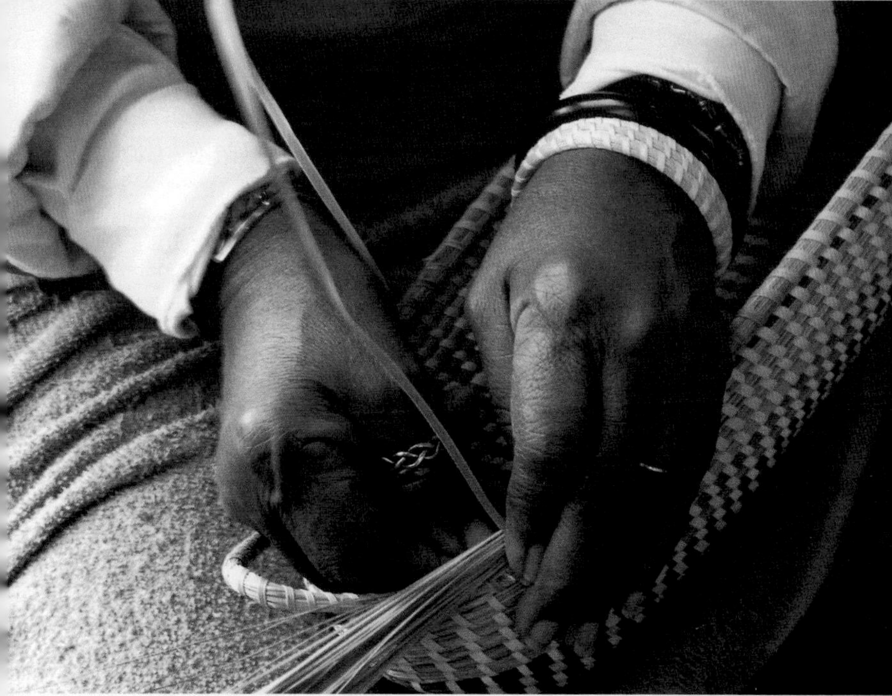

Women in Charleston keep alive the art of sweetgrass basket weaving brought over by enslaved people from Africa.

Shopping

SHOPPING DISTRICTS

King Street

SHOPPING NEIGHBORHOODS | The city's main shopping strip is divided into informal districts: Lower King (from Broad Street to Market Street) is the Antiques District, lined with high-end dealers; Middle King (from Market to Calhoun Street) is the Fashion District, with a mix of national chains like Anthropologie and Pottery Barn and locally owned boutiques; and Upper King (from Calhoun to Spring Street) has been dubbed the Design District, known for both its restaurant scene and its clothing and interior-design stores. Check out Second Sundays on King, when the street closes to cars all afternoon from Calhoun Street to Queen Street. Make sure to visit the Saturday farmers' market in Marion Square throughout the spring and summer months. ✉ *Charleston.*

BOOKS

★ Blue Bicycle Books

BOOKS/STATIONERY | Look for out-of-print and rare books, including hardcover classics and a large selection of Lowcountry fiction and nonfiction, at this locally adored bookstore offering everything from military history to cookbooks. It hosts frequent signings by local authors like Matt and Ted Lee. ✉ *420 King St., Upper King* ☎ *843/722–2666* 🌐 *www.bluebicyclebooks.com.*

CLOTHING

Indigo and Cotton

CLOTHING | This store is the go-to boutique for the latest in gentlemen's tailoring featuring brands such as Gitman Vintage, Filson Red Label bags, and Raleigh Denim. The Cannonborough shop is also brimming with bow ties, handkerchiefs, and other accessories. ✉ *79 Cannon St., Cannonborough* ☎ *843/718–2980* 🌐 *www.indigoandcotton.com.*

Did You Know?

One of the most popular places for a stroll is Waterfront Park but this patch of land was once a center of the city's maritime trade with numerous wharves and shipping terminals lining the water's edge.

Mount Pleasant

East of Charleston, across the beautiful Arthur Ravenel Jr. Bridge, is the town of Mount Pleasant, named not for a mountain but for a plantation that existed there in the early 18th century. In its Old Village neighborhood are historic homes and a sleepy, old-time town center with a drugstore where patrons still amble up to the soda fountain and lunch counter for egg-salad sandwiches and floats.

A lively African American community for decades following the Civil War, Mount Pleasant has emerged since the 2005 construction of the Ravenel Bridge as one of the state's most popular destinations for Northeasterners relocating to South Carolina; the result being that this fast-growing suburb is now 92% white, according to United States Census data. The town is home to an array of upscale shops and services, but is best known among fun-seekers for Shem Creek, a former working waterfront that's now dominated by outdoor bars specializing in day drinking.

Sights

Boone Hall Plantation and Gardens
FARM/RANCH | **FAMILY** | Celebrities Ryan Reynolds and Blake Lively have publicly distanced themselves from their 2012 wedding here at Boone Hall Plantation and Gardens, apologizing for mistaking the longtime site of human enslavement for a pastoral setting. Still, Boone Hall remains one of the former Lowcountry plantations that continues to actively market itself as a wedding backdrop, complete with a moss-draped live oak allée and an heirloom rose garden. Nonwedding guests can also visit the plantation; most significant from a historic standpoint is a set of brick cabins, built at the turn of the 19th century, which housed enslaved people. While Boone Hall's interpretative strategy generally doesn't stress African American contributions or culture beyond the cabins, each one is devoted to a topic in black history, such as civil rights and sweetgrass baskets. The venue occasionally hosts Gullah storytelling and song performances. ✉ *1235 Long Point Rd., Mount Pleasant* ⊕ *Off U.S. 17 N* ☎ *843/884–4371* 🌐 *www.boonehallplantation.com* 🎫 *$26.*

★ **Cape Romain National Wildlife Refuge**
NATURE PRESERVE | **FAMILY** | Maritime forests, barrier islands, salt marshes, beaches, and coastal waterways make up this 66,287-acre refuge established in 1932 as a migratory bird haven. The **Sewee Visitor and Environmental Education Center** has information and exhibits on the property and its trails, as well as an outdoor enclosure housing endangered red wolves. The refuge is aiding the recovery of the threatened loggerhead sea turtle, and a video details the work. **■ TIP→ From the mainland refuge, you can take a $40 ferry ride to remote and wild Bulls Island to explore its boneyard beach and freshwater ponds teeming with alligators.** ✉ *Sewee Center, 5821 U.S. 17 N, Awendaw* ☎ *843/928–3368* 🌐 *www.fws.gov/caperomain* 🎫 *Free* ⏲ *Closed Sun.–Tues.*

Charles Pinckney National Historic Site
HISTORIC SITE | This remnant of Charles Pinckney's 715-acre birthplace was winnowed down by development, but today the National Park Service uses archaeological findings to tell the story of the man who signed the U.S. Constitution and the people his family enslaved. While most structures linked to the site's history as a rice and indigo plantation no longer stand, an 1820s cabin erected after Pinckney's death is open to visitors, along with three buildings where enslaved people lived. ✉ *1254 Long Point Rd., Mount Pleasant* ⊕ *Off U.S. 17 N* ☎ *843/881–5516* 🌐 *www.nps.gov/chpi* 🎫 *Free* ⏲ *Closed Mon. and Tues.*

★ Mount Pleasant Memorial Waterfront Park

CITY PARK | FAMILY | Sprawling beneath the Ravenel Bridge, this beautifully landscaped green space invites lounging on the grass with views of Charleston Harbor. You can also take a path up to the bridge for a stroll. Find helpful info in the visitor center, chat with Gullah artists selling traditional baskets in the Sweetgrass Cultural Arts Pavilion, and spend a quiet moment listening to the waterfall fountain in the Mount Pleasant War Memorial. Kids love the playground modeled after the Ravenel Bridge, and parents appreciate that it's fenced, with benches galore. A 1,250-foot-long pier stretches into the water—grab a milkshake from the River Watch Cafe and a seat on one of the double-sided swings to watch folks fishing for their supper. Better yet, rent a rod and bait for $10 from the pier's tackle shop and cast for your own. ✉ *71 Harry Hallman Blvd., Mount Pleasant* ☎ *843/762–9946* 🌐 *www.ccprc.com.*

Old Village

HISTORIC SITE | FAMILY | The historic center of Mount Pleasant, this neighborhood is distinguished by white picket fences, storybook cottages, traditional homes with wide porches, tiny churches, and lavish waterfront homes. It's a lovely area for a stroll or bike ride, and Pitt Street offers a couple of locally loved eateries and boutiques. Head south along Pitt Street to the Otis M. Pickett Bridge and Park, popular for picnicking, fishing, and sunset views. ✉ *Pitt St. and Venning St., Mount Pleasant.*

★ Patriots Point Naval and Maritime Museum

MILITARY SITE | FAMILY | Climb aboard the USS *Yorktown* aircraft carrier—which contains the Congressional Medal of Honor Museum—as well as the destroyer USS *Laffey*. The carrier's flight deck features stunning views of the harbor and city skyline and up-close views of 25 airplanes and helicopters from throughout the last century of American warfare. A life-size replica of a Vietnam support base camp showcases naval air and watercraft used in that military action. ✉ *40 Patriots Point Rd., Mount Pleasant* ☎ *843/884–2727* 🌐 *www.patriotspoint.org* 🎟 *$24.*

Shem Creek Boardwalk

MARINA | FAMILY | Follow this quarter-mile-long boardwalk that stretches from Coleman Boulevard to the marshy mouth of Shem Creek for an up-close look at the recent past and vibrant present of Mount Pleasant's most important waterway. Decades ago, shrimping boats docked three or four abreast in the channel; now fewer than a dozen trawlers ply the creek, but visitors can buy crab and shrimp right off the working boats. ✉ *Shrimp Boat La., off Coleman Blvd., Mount Pleasant* ☎ *843/884–4440* 🌐 *www.experiencemountpleasant.com/explore/shem-creek-park.*

Restaurants

Jack's Cosmic Dogs

$ | AMERICAN | FAMILY | The Galactic, Krypto, Orbit City, and Blue Galactic hot dog varieties at Jack's Cosmic are otherworldly excellent, with blue-cheese slaw, spicy mustard, sauerkraut, zippy onion relish, and Jack's own sweet-potato mustard, all swaddled in Pepperidge Farms split-top buns. Akin to a diner, Jack's serves milkshakes and sundaes, real custard soft-serve ice cream, draft root beer, and hand-cut fries. **Known for:** eclectic, one-of-a-kind decor; creative topping combinations; an array of shakes and sundaes. $ *Average main: $5* ✉ *2805 N. Hwy. 17, Mount Pleasant* ☎ *843/884–7677* 🌐 *www.jackscosmicdogs.com.*

★ The Shellmore

$$ | WINE BAR | Mount Pleasant's culinary ambitions perhaps reached their apex at the Shellmore, an unassuming wine bar with a chalkboard menu and some of the most romantic nooks in town. Chef-owner Eric Milley always has cheese and cold shucked oysters at the ready, but devotees know he's prone to work wonders with hulking cuts of beef, including prime rib and veal chops. **Known for:** savvy wine selection; serene atmosphere; attentive cooking. *Average main: $18* *357 Shelmore Blvd., Mount Pleasant* *843/654–9278* *www.theshellmore.com* *Closed Sun. and Mon. No lunch.*

★ The Wreck of the *Richard and Charlene*

$$$ | SEAFOOD | FAMILY | At first glance, the odd name appears to refer to this waterfront restaurant's exterior, topped off with a shabby screened-in porch (in actuality, the *Richard and Charlene* was a trawler that slammed into the building during a hurricane in 1989). Located in the Old Village of Mount Pleasant, the kitchen serves up Southern tradition on a plate: boiled peanuts, fried shrimp, and stone-crab claws. **Known for:** generous platters of fried seafood; old-school ambience right on the shrimp docks; boiled peanuts served at every table. *Average main: $25* *106 Haddrell St., Mount Pleasant* *843/884–0052* *www.wreckrc.com* *No credit cards* *Closed Mon. No lunch.*

Hotels

★ The Beach Club at Charleston Harbor Resort and Marina

$$ | RESORT | FAMILY | Mount Pleasant's finest hotel sits on Charleston Harbor, so you can gaze at the city's skyline with your feet on this resort's sandy beach or from the waterfront pool. **Pros:** easy access to downtown but offers an away-from-it-all vibe; large pool and extensive grounds are perfect for enjoying a sunset glass of wine; on-site gym. **Cons:** a bit removed from the action; no complimentary breakfast; can be hard to navigate your way around. *Rooms from: $197* *20 Patriots Point Rd., Mount Pleasant* *843/856–0028* *www.charlestonharborresort.com* *92 rooms* *No meals.*

Shem Creek Inn

$ | HOTEL | FAMILY | Shem Creek is the heart of Mount Pleasant, and this long-standing inn makes the charming waterway an attractive place to call home for the night. **Pros:** daily continental breakfast; free on-site parking; easy access to Shem Creek's restaurants and kayak tours. **Cons:** the bars across the creek host live music and can get noisy on weekends; it's a drive or a cab ride to get downtown; the inn's location and affordability guarantee that some guests come here to party. *Rooms from: $109* *1401 Shrimp Boat La., Mount Pleasant* *843/881–1000* *www.shemcreekinn.com* *51 rooms* *Free breakfast.*

Activities

GOLF

Charleston National Golf Club

GOLF | The best nonresort golf course in Charleston tends to be quiet on weekdays, which translates into lower prices. The setting is captivating, carved along the intracoastal waterway and traversing wetlands, lagoons, and pine and oak forests. Finishing holes are set along golden marshland. Diminutive wooden bridges and a handsome clubhouse add to the natural beauty of this well-maintained course. *1360 National Dr., Mount Pleasant* *843/203–9994* *www.charlestonnationalgolf.com* *From $66* *18 holes, 7064 yds, par 72.*

Greater Charleston

Visitors to Charleston need never leave the peninsula to fill a week's itinerary, but those who do are treated to a taste of the real Lowcountry, from winding two-lane roads past massive live oaks on Johns Island to long stretches of sand within the series of barrier islands that stretch north and south of the city.

Along the Ashley River north of town, those who are interested in history may

Check out the shrimp boats and spot bottlenose dolphins on a kayak tour of Shem Creek.

need several days to explore former plantations like Drayton Hall, Middleton Place, and McLeod Plantation. Spring is a peak time for the flowers, although many of them are in bloom throughout the year. Folly Beach, Sullivan's Island, and Isle of Palms fill up during summer, but are perfect for a long beach stroll when the temperatures begin to drop in the fall. Golfers may visit Charleston just for the links—it's possible to play a different nationally ranked course every day of the week here.

Sights

★ Angel Oak Tree

LOCAL INTEREST | **FAMILY** | Live oak trees do as much to define the Lowcountry landscape as the salt marsh, and this gorgeous specimen is likely the oldest—and biggest—in the country. One branch reaches 187 feet. A 17-acre fenced park surrounds the tree, which is free to visit. Bring a picnic and bask in its magnificent shade. ✉ *3688 Angel Oak Rd., Johns Island* 🌐 *www.angeloaktree.com.*

★ Charles Towne Landing

MUSEUM VILLAGE | **FAMILY** | This off-the-radar gem of a park (and zoo) marks the site of the original 1670 settlement of Charles Towne, the first permanent European settlement in South Carolina. Begin with the visitor center's 12-room, interactive museum and exhibit hall that tells the history of the early settlers and their relationship with the Kiawah people who were here when they arrived. Be sure to visit the exhibits about the enslaved people and indentured servants who also arrived with the English. Kids will make a beeline for the *Adventure,* a full-size replica of the colonists' 17th-century tall ship that's docked on the creek running through the park. The grounds are threaded with 6 miles of paths through forest and marsh, including an Animal Forest zoo where you can see black bears, bobcats, pumas, and bison. All in all, there are 664 acres of gardens and forest, including an elegant live oak alley. Leashed dogs are allowed (although not in the Animal Forest), and rental bikes are available for $5 an hour. ✉ *1500*

Old Towne Rd., West Ashley ☎ *843/852–4200* 🌐 *southcarolinaparks.com/charles-towne-landing* 🎫 *$12.*

Drayton Hall

HISTORIC SITE | The only plantation house on the Ashley River to have survived the Civil War intact, Drayton Hall is considered the nation's finest example of Palladian-inspired architecture. A National Trust Historic Site built between 1738 and 1742, it's an invaluable lesson in history as well as in architecture. Visitors can pay their respects at the African American cemetery—one of the oldest in the nation still in use—and experience the 30-minute "Port to Plantation" program that uses maps and historic documents to examine the lives of the enslaved Africans who built Charleston's economy. Inside the main home, rooms are unfurnished to highlight the original plaster moldings, opulent hand-carved woodwork, and other ornamental details. Regular tours, with guides known for their in-depth knowledge, depart on the half hour. ✉ *3380 Ashley River Rd., West Ashley* ☎ *843/769–2600* 🌐 *www.draytonhall.org* 🎫 *$32* 🕒 *Closed Mon. and Tues.*

★ Fort Moultrie

MILITARY SITE | **FAMILY** | A part of the Fort Sumter National Monument, this is the site where Colonel William Moultrie's South Carolinians repelled a British assault in one of the first patriot victories of the Revolutionary War. Completed in 1809, the fort is the third fortress on this site on Sullivan's Island, 10 miles southeast of Charleston. Set across the street, the companion museum is an unsung hero. Although much is made of Fort Sumter, this smaller historical site is creatively designed, with figurines in various uniforms that make military history come alive. A 20-minute educational film that spans several major wars tells the colorful history of the fort. There's also an essential exhibit on Sullivan Island's role in the transatlantic slave trade. ■ **TIP→ Plan to spend the day bicycling through Sullivan's Island, where you'll find a cluster of century-old beach houses.** ✉ *1214 Middle St., Sullivan's Island* ☎ *843/883–3123* 🌐 *www.nps.gov/fosu* 🎫 *$10.*

The *Hunley*

MILITARY SITE | **FAMILY** | In 1864, the Confederacy's *H. L. Hunley* sank the Union warship USS *Housatonic,* becoming the world's first successful combat submarine. But moments after the attack, it disappeared mysteriously into the depths of the sea. Lost for more than a century, it was found in 1995 off the coast of Sullivan's Island and raised in 2000. The *Hunley* is now preserved in a 90,000-gallon tank, which you can see during an informative guided tour. An exhibit area includes artifacts excavated from the sub and interactive displays, including a model that kids will enjoy crawling inside. In downtown Charleston, there's also a full-size replica of the *Hunley* outside the Charleston Museum. ✉ *Old Charleston Naval Base, 1250 Supply St., North Charleston* ☎ *843/743–4865* 🌐 *www.hunley.org* 🎫 *$18* 🕒 *Closed weekdays.*

Magnolia Plantation and Gardens

HISTORIC SITE | **FAMILY** | Beautiful Magnolia Plantation is home to the oldest public garden in the country, a sprawling estate created entirely by the labor of enslaved people. Established in the 1670s by Thomas Drayton after he moved from Barbados (where he also enslaved people), the extensive garden was started in the late 17th century and has evolved into a Romantic-style green space overflowing with plants, including a vast array of azaleas and camellias and a topiary maze. Exhibits surrounding the plantation's five former slave dwellings give insight into the enslaved people who lived here, with tours curated by prominent African American historian Joseph McGill. Outside of the gardens and historic buildings, take a train or boat to tour the grounds, or traverse more than 500 acres of trails by foot or bike (bring your own). The adjacent Audubon Swamp Garden invites a long stroll on its network of boardwalks and bridges. There's also a petting zoo, a nature center, and a reptile house. ✉ *3550 Ashley River Rd., West Ashley* ☎ *843/571–1266* 🌐 *www.magnoliaplantation.com* 🎫 *Grounds $20, house tour $8, train $8, boat $8, From Slavery to Freedom exhibit $8, Audubon Swamp $8.*

★ McLeod Plantation Historic Site

HISTORIC SITE | FAMILY | Directly across the Ashley River from downtown Charleston, on James Island, this 37-acre site is the only former plantation in the area where the visitor experience is focused on the lives of the enslaved people who toiled here, encouraging visitors to compare the row of well-preserved slave quarters with the large plantation house. Guided and self-led tours are organized around a Transition to Freedom program that imagines what life was like for the people working on the cotton plantation and the ramifications these injustices still have on society today. ✉ *325 Country Club Dr., James Island* ☎ *843/762–9514* 🌐 *www.ccprc.com/1447/mcleod-plantation-historic-site* 🎫 *$15* ⏲ *Closed Mon.*

★ Middleton Place

HISTORIC SITE | FAMILY | Established in the 1730s, Middleton Place was at the center of the Middleton family's empire of rice plantations, where they enslaved 3,500 people on 63,000 acres of properties throughout the South Carolina Low-country. With its massive three-story brick manor home and prized gardens, Middleton Place continues to be a grand statement of wealth and the bitter injustice and cruely behind it.

To get the complete picture of life on the plantation, take the Beyond the Fields tour and film, focused on the lives of the Africans and African Americans who lived and worked at Middleton. The tour begins at Eliza's House, a restored 1870s sharecropper's home.

Middleton's original manor home was destroyed in the Civil War, but one of its flanking buildings, which served as the gentlemen's guest quarters, was salvaged and transformed into the family's post-war residence. It now serves as a house museum, displaying impressive English silver, furniture, original paintings, and historic documents, including an early silk copy of the Declaration of Independence. In the stable yards, historic interpreters use authentic tools to demonstrate spinning, weaving, blacksmithing, and other skills from the era. Heritage-breed farm animals, such as water buffalo and cashmere goats, are housed here, along with peacocks.

Restored in the 1920s, the breathtakingly beautiful gardens include camellias, roses, and blooms of all seasons that form floral allées (alleys) along terraced lawns and around a pair of ornamental lakes, which are shaped like butterfly wings. Wear comfortable walking shoes to explore Middleton's gardens, and dress to be outside. ✉ *4300 Ashley River Rd., West Ashley* ☎ *843/556–6020* 🌐 *www.middletonplace.org* 🎫 *$26, house tour $12.*

Beaches

★ Folly Beach

BEACH—SIGHT | FAMILY | Charleston's most laid-back beach community fills up on weekends, so head out early to avoid traffic if you're visiting on a Saturday. A rebuild of the beloved Folly Beach Fishing Pier is still in development and set to debut in 2022, but the familiar Morris Island Lighthouse yet rises from the water at the northeast end of the island. Surfers flock to the Washout, a renowned and consistent surf break, and the southwest end of the island has lifeguards and amenities at the county park. Street parking is free, but to avoid a ticket, all four wheels have to be off the pavement. Stock up on snacks and sandwiches at Bert's Market on East Ashley Avenue or grab a taco with the locals at Chico Feo across the street.

Amenities: food and drink; lifeguards; parking (fee); showers and toilets (at Washout, the pier, and the county park). **Best for:** surfing; swimming. ✉ *Folly Beach* 🌐 *www.cityoffollybeach.com.*

Isle of Palms County Park

BEACH—SIGHT | FAMILY | Play beach volleyball or soak up the sun in a lounge chair on this wide stretch of sand. This beach is as good as the island's idyllic name. The sands are golden, the waves are gentle, and there's a playground, so it's great for families with small children. Those seeking to avoid the crowds can venture a few blocks north down the beach. The county park is the only lifeguard-protected area on the Isle of Palms. **Amenities:** food and drink; lifeguards; parking (fee); showers; toilets. **Best for:** sunrise; swimming; walking. ✉ *Ocean Blvd., 1st to 14th Ave., Isle of Palms* ☎ *843/762–9957* 🌐 *www.ccprc.com* 🎫 *May–Labor Day $10 per car weekdays, $15 on weekends; Sept.–Apr. from $5.*

★ Sullivan's Island

BEACH—SIGHT | FAMILY | The pristine Sullivan's Island beachfront is owned by the town, including 200 acres of walkable maritime forest overseen by the Lowcountry Open Land Trust. The downside to this is that there are no amenities like public toilets and showers. There are, however, a number of good small restaurants on nearby Middle Street, the island's main drag. Approximately 30 public-access paths (four are wheelchair accessible) lead to the beach. "Sully's" is a delightful island with plenty to see, including Fort Moultrie National Monument. When parking or getting directions, note that the blocks are referred to as "Stations" on Sullivan's. Station 28.5 is the primary kitesurfing destination in Charleston and can be busy on windy days; lessons are available from Sealand Adventure Sports. **Amenities:** none. **Best for:** sunrise; sunset; walking; windsurfing. ✉ *Atlantic Ave., Sullivan's Island* 🌐 *www.sullivansisland.sc.gov.*

Restaurants

★ Bowens Island

$$ | SEAFOOD | FAMILY | This family-owned seafood shack has survived hurricanes, fires, and the onslaught of trendy restaurants hitting downtown. The menu at this funky spot littered with oyster shells and graffiti is reliable: big ol' shrimp, fried or boiled; shrimp and grits; hush puppies; and the biggie—trays of piping hot steamed oysters. **Known for:** one of the last old-school seafood shacks left; traditional Frogmore stew (aka Lowcountry boil); long lines on weekends. 💲 *Average main: $20* ✉ *1871 Bowens Island Rd., James Island* ☎ *843/795–2757* 🌐 *www.bowensisland.com* 🕒 *Closed Sun. and Mon. No lunch.*

★ Extra Virgin Oven

$$ | PIZZA | Known to locals as EVO, this Park Circle pizzeria is considered by many to be the area's best, doling out Neapolitan-style pies with super-thin and crunchy crusts. The Food Network chose EVO's pistachio pesto pie—containing goat, mozzarella, and Parmesan cheese on a pesto base whipped up with olive oil, salt, and pistachios—as the state's best slice. **Known for:** the standard bearer for craft pizza in town; hard-to-find local beers on tap; on-site bakery for breads to-go. 💲 *Average main: $18* ✉ *1075 E. Montague Ave., North Charleston* ☎ *843/225–1796* 🌐 *www.evopizza.com.*

The Glass Onion

$$ | SOUTHERN | The Alabama roots of this eatery's chef-owner show in the classic Southern eats like deviled eggs, meat loaf, fried catfish po'boys, and overstuffed pimento-cheese sandwiches, along with sweets like bread pudding with whiskey sauce. The Saturday brunch is a must, with fluffy buttermilk biscuits and gravy and savory pork tamales. **Known for:** addictive deviled eggs; consistent, seasonal Southern fare; delectable Saturday brunch that often sells out. 💲 *Average main: $22* ✉ *1219 Savannah Hwy., West*

Ashley ☎ *843/225–1717* 🌐 *www.ilovetheglassonion.com* ⏲ *Closed Sun.*

Home Team BBQ

$ | **BARBECUE** | **FAMILY** | This bar and restaurant swiftly earned the endorsement of even the old-school barbecue set (the restaurant's newfangled pork tacos notwithstanding), and Home Team has done so with time-honored adherence to the oft-preferred technique of low-and-slow grilling, producing St. Louis–style ribs and traditional smoked pork and chicken. Side offerings are a good measuring stick for any barbecue joint, and they deliver with mashed potatoes, collard greens, red rice, baked beans, poppy-seed slaw, and potato salad. **Known for:** delicious pulled pork and rich mac and cheese; live blues and rock music at all three locations; unique tableside sauces. 💲 *Average main: $12* ✉ *1205 Ashley River Rd., West Ashley* ☎ *843/225–7427* 🌐 *www.hometeambbq.com.*

★ **The Obstinate Daughter**

$$ | **ITALIAN** | Known for his fine Italian cuisine at Wild Olive on Johns Island, chef Jacques Larson expands his creative touch with this elegant seafood, pasta, and pizza outpost on Sullivan's Island. In the charming blue-and-white space—nautically styled, of course—choose from the excellent gnocchi, inventive pizzas, or fat strands of spicy bucatini pasta—or dive into grilled octopus with white beans, collard flower kimchi, and scallops and squid fra diavolo. **Known for:** bustling weekend brunch; local clam pizza, among other creative toppings; buzz-worthy dining at the beach. 💲 *Average main: $22* ✉ *2063 Middle St., Sullivan's Island* ☎ *843/416–5020* 🌐 *www.theobstinatedaughter.com.*

★ **Stono Market and Tomato Shed Cafe**

$$ | **SOUTHERN** | This Johns Island roadside joint presents a banquet of locally raised delicacies. Owners and farmers Pete and Babs Ambrose maintain a 135-acre farm on Wadmalaw Island, sourcing the grounds for the menu, which emphasizes seasonal choices, allowing for fresh butter beans, cabbage, collards, cucumber salad, and rutabaga casserole. **Known for:** tomato pie when it's in season; take-and-bake meals; true farm-to-table cuisine. 💲 *Average main: $16* ✉ *842 Main Rd., Johns Island* ☎ *843/559–9999* 🌐 *www.stonomarket.com* ⏲ *Closed Sun. and Mon.*

 Hotels

Kiawah Island Golf Resort

$$$$ | **RESORT** | **FAMILY** | Choose from one- to four-bedroom villas, three- to eight-bedroom private homes, or one of the fabulous 255 rooms at the Sanctuary at Kiawah Island at this luxury waterfront hotel and spa that is one of the most prestigious resorts in the country and yet still kid-friendly. **Pros:** smaller villas are more affordable; top-rated restaurant is an ideal venue for an anniversary or a proposal; the golf courses and tennis programs are ranked among the country's best. **Cons:** not all rooms have ocean views; a long drive from town; luxury comes at a price. 💲 *Rooms from: $350* ✉ *1 Sanctuary Beach Dr., Kiawah Island* ☎ *843/768–2121, 800/654–2924* 🌐 *www.kiawahresort.com* *750 rooms and villas* 🍽 *No meals.*

★ **Wild Dunes Resort**

$$$ | **RESORT** | **FAMILY** | Guests at this 1,600-acre island beachfront resort can choose from two Tom Fazio–designed golf courses, a nationally ranked tennis program, and miles of paved trails to walk and jog. **Pros:** first-rate Lowcountry cuisine and scenery in one location; family-friendly bike paths parallel every thoroughfare; rarely crowded beach. **Cons:** kid-friendly pools can get crowded during summer; beach traffic can make day trips a headache; views and porch sizes vary, so inquire when booking. 💲 *Rooms from: $285* ✉ *1 Sundial Circle, Isle of Palms* ☎ *866/359–5593* 🌐 *www.destinationhotels.com/wild-dunes* *646 rooms* 🍽 *No meals.*

Chapter 9

HILTON HEAD, SC, AND THE LOWCOUNTRY

Updated by
Stratton Lawrence

Sights ★★★★★ | Restaurants ★★★★★ | Hotels ★★★★★ | Shopping ★★★★★ | Nightlife ★★☆☆☆

WELCOME TO HILTON HEAD, SC, AND THE LOWCOUNTRY

TOP REASONS TO GO

★ **Beautiful beaches:** Swim, soak up the sun, take a walk and collect shells, or ride your bike along the 12 miles of beaches on Hilton Head Island.

★ **Golfing paradise:** With more than 24 challenging courses, Hilton Head has earned an international reputation as a top destination for golfers.

★ **Outdoor activities:** Visitors to Hilton Head can stay busy by enjoying land activities, such as tennis, cycling, and horseback-riding, or water activities, such as kayaking, fishing, and boating.

★ **Family fun:** This semi-tropical island has been a family-friendly resort destination for decades, thanks to its vast array of lodgings, a variety of amazing restaurants, and a laid-back vibe—all making for an ideal vacation.

★ **Beaufort:** This small coastal town offers large doses of heritage and culture; it's worth the day trip to experience the unique beauty and history of the area.

Hilton Head is just north of South Carolina's border with Georgia. The 42-square-mile island is shaped like a foot, hence the reason locals often describe places as being at the "toe" or "heel" of Hilton Head. This part of South Carolina is best explored by car, as its points of interest are spread across a flat coastal plain that is a mix of wooded areas, marshes, and sea islands. The more remote areas are accessible only by boat or ferry.

1 Hilton Head Island. One of the Southeast coast's most popular tourist destinations, Hilton Head is famous for activities like golf and tennis. The island's natural beauty attracts flocks of retirees and families alike, all looking to spend time outdoors and take in the sights that make the Lowcountry so unique. Bluffton is located on the mainland, just before you cross the bridge onto the island.

2 Beaufort. This charming town is a destination in its own right, with a lively dining scene, cute bed-and-breakfasts, and many historic and picturesque places to enjoy.

3 Daufuskie Island. A scenic ferry ride from Hilton Head, Daufuskie Island is a beautiful place to explore; visitors can delight in the nearly deserted beaches and strong Gullah culture.

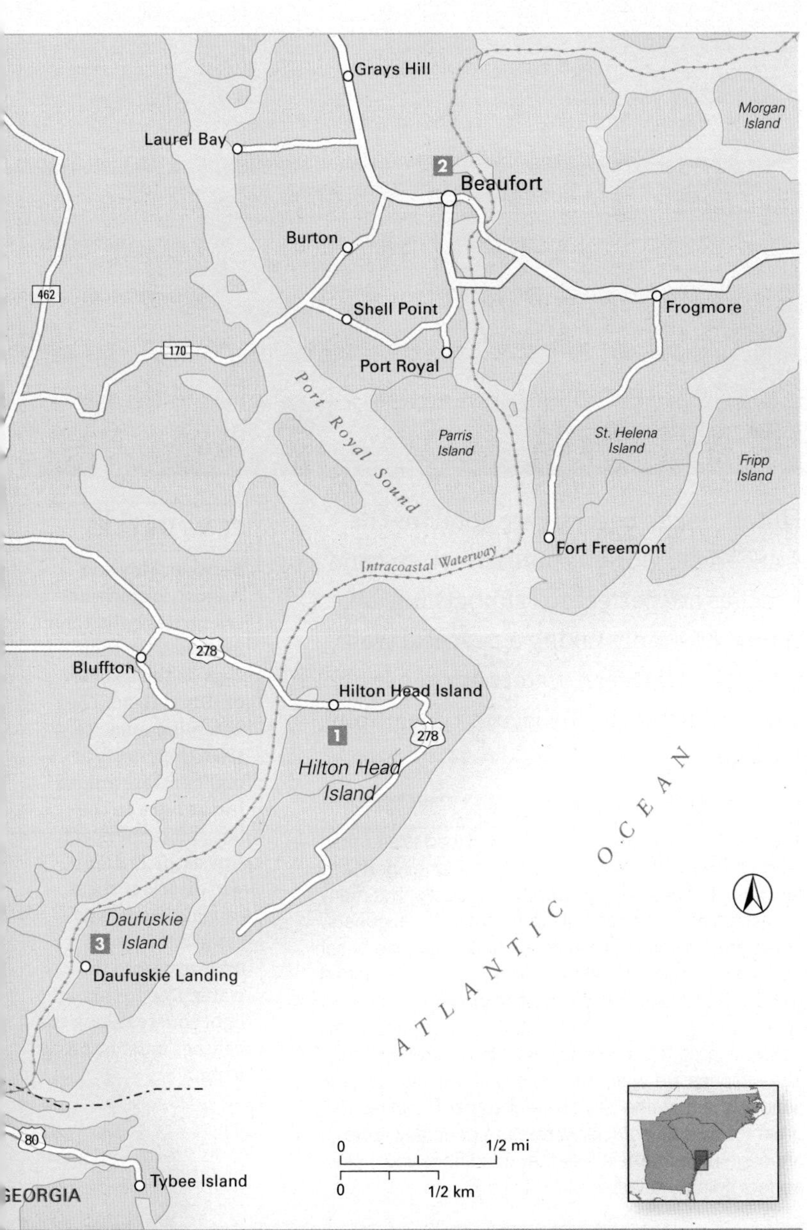
Grays Hill
Morgan Island
Laurel Bay
2
Beaufort
Burton
462
Shell Point
Frogmore
170
Port Royal
Port Royal Sound
Parris Island
St. Helena Island
Fripp Island
Fort Freemont
Intracoastal Waterway
Bluffton
278
Hilton Head Island
1
278
Hilton Head Island
ATLANTIC OCEAN
Daufuskie Island
3
Daufuskie Landing
80
Tybee Island
GEORGIA
0
1/2 mi
0
1/2 km

BEST BEACHES IN HILTON HEAD AND THE LOWCOUNTRY

Hilton Head Island has 12 miles of beaches.

Hilton Head's beaches are good for the soul. The 12 glorious miles of white-sand beaches are perfect for sunbathing, bike riding, or simply taking a peaceful walk. The Atlantic Ocean waters are generally smooth thanks to the island's geographic location.

There are several beaches on Hilton Head Island that range from the bucolic and peaceful to ones perfect for families. All beaches are open to the public, but many access points are open only to resort or hotel guests. There are several public access points that take beach-goers over small walkways or boardwalks surrounded by sand dunes and sea oats. Beachgoers might see a variety of critters, including crabs, sand dollars, starfish, pelicans, great blue herons, and many other species. The beaches are wide, particularly at low tide, and the sand at the mid-tide point is packed hard, making it great for bike riding. The waters are generally tame, although under certain weather conditions you'll see surfers riding the waves.

SEA TURTLES

Between May and August, loggerhead sea turtles build their nests and lay their eggs on the beaches of Hilton Head. The hatchlings emerge from their nests at night and are guided by the light on the horizon to the ocean. Any artificial light will disorient them, causing them to go toward the dunes instead of into the water. Due to this, all light sources along the beaches must be off by 10 pm.

ALDER LANE BEACH PARK

Alder Lane Beach Park is a nice spot for a swim or a romantic walk. This beach, which has lifeguards on patrol during the summer months, is less crowded than some of the more popular areas, like Coligny Beach. There are restrooms, outdoor showers, and vending machines. The beach, like almost all public beaches on Hilton Head, is wheelchair accessible. Alder Lane Beach Park is on the south end (near the toe) of Hilton Head Island, next to the Marriott Vacation Club Grande Ocean off South Forest Beach Drive.

BURKES BEACH

If you're looking to get away from the crowds, **Burkes Beach** is a great choice. It's located midisland, adjacent to the Chaplin Community Park at the end of Burkes Beach Road off William Hilton Parkway (U.S. 278). There are no lifeguards, so it's quieter than many of the other Hilton Head beaches. It's a great place for a quiet walk along the shore. If you get up early it's also a perfect spot to catch an amazing sunrise.

COLIGNY BEACH PARK

This south-end beach, located off Coligny Circle, is by far the most popular beach on Hilton Head Island. The entrance has choreographed fountains for children to play under, showers and changing rooms, large restroom facilities, swinging benches, and a boardwalk to the beach. Throughout the summer months there is children's entertainment starting at 6:30 pm weekdays at Coligny Plaza. There are chairs and umbrellas for rent, volleyball nets, and even Wi-Fi. For the grown-ups, the outdoor Tiki Hut bar at the Beach House, a Holiday Inn Resort, is a local favorite spot to drink a cool beverage while enjoying the ocean view. Parking is free at **Coligny Beach Park.**

Conservation efforts assure critters large and small a home.

A lighthouse keeps watch on Hilton Head.

DRIESSEN BEACH AND FOLLY FIELD BEACH

These beaches near the heel of Hilton Head Island are great spots for families. In fact, on many summer days you'll see bicyclists enjoying the day, beach-goers flying colorful kites, and children building sandcastles. **Driessen Beach** is accessible at Bradley Beach Road off William Hilton Parkway. Follow a wooden boardwalk to get to the beach. It's a hike, but it's worth the walk. There are barbecue grills, a playground, outdoor showers, restrooms, and a picnic pavilion. **Folly Field Beach** is next to Driessen Beach, off Folly Field Road, and also boasts outdoor showers, restrooms, and lifeguards in summer.

LOWCOUNTRY CUISINE

Shrimp po'boys are menu staples in the Lowcountry.

To understand Lowcountry cuisine, you have to dig in to the "what" and the "where" of its historic culinary conglomeration.

Although you can find Lowcountry cuisine along most of coastal South Carolina all the way down to Savannah, Georgia, the food's foundation feeds off the pulse of the Lowcountry, the Holy City of Charleston, where, centuries ago, European aristocrats would share kitchens with their African slaves. The result was a colonial European fusion with Caribbean and West African, otherwise known as Gullah, influences.

Seafood—shrimp, crabs, fish, and oysters—from the marshlands, combined with rice pulled from the countless coastal rice plantations' paddies, are the core ingredients of this specific cuisine. Add to that a twist of exotic African spices and citrus zest, as well as locally grown okra, corn, and benne seeds and you have Lowcountry staples like shrimp and grits, she-crab soup, hoppin' John, and perlau.

First-time visitors to the area will quickly realize that Lowcountry cuisine is pure Southern comfort.

A SWEET SIDE

While, it's true, you can't eat this Lowcountry must with a fork, sweet tea is an undoubtedly essential sidekick to South Carolina cuisine. Sugar is added to the brew before it cools, which makes this supersaturated beverage all the more sweet. Lowcountry visitors beware: when ordering at a restaurant, iced tea will most likely arrive as sweet tea.

Here are some Lowcountry staples:

SHRIMP AND GRITS

If you're not convinced that South Carolina is serious about grits, consider this: in 1976, it declared grits the official state food. In the South, grits are most commonly paired with their coastal-waters counterpart, making shrimp and grits a standard dish for breakfast, lunch, and dinner. Today, foodies will delight in discovering the dish dressed up with everything from sausage, bacon, and Cajun seasoning to cheese, gravy, and tomato-based sauces.

SHE-CRAB SOUP

Rich and creamy, with lumps of crabmeat and a splash of dry sherry, she-crab soup is to the Lowcountry as chowder is to New England. The "she" of this signature dish actually comes from the main ingredient, a female crab's orange crab roe. It is delicious as an appetizer and quite filling as an entrée.

STEAMED OYSTERS

Oyster beds are plentiful in the creeks and inlet waters along the Lowcountry coast. Also plentiful are those who can't get enough of shucking the fresh meat out of clasped shells and dipping it into warm, drawn butter or cocktail sauce. Oysters are usually served by the half dozen, with a side of Saltine crackers.

Once you taste shrimp and grits you may crave it morning, noon, and night.

Hoppin' John is often topped with salsa.

HOPPIN' JOHN

This rice-and-bean concoction is not only a favorite Lowcountry dish, but a lucky one at that. Families throughout the Lowcountry prepare hoppin' John on New Year's Day for lunch or dinner in hopes that it will provide them with a year's worth of good luck. It's all in the classic Lowcountry ingredients: black-eyed peas symbolize pennies (a side of collard greens adds to the wealth in the new year). Rice, chopped onions, bacon (or ham), and peppers are added to the peas. Add garnishes like a spoonful of salsa or a dollop of sour cream for an interesting Southwest spin.

PERLAU

South Carolina takes great pride in its perlau, more lovingly known at the table as "chicken bog." This rice-based dish is cooked with chunks of tender chicken and sausage slices, simmered in the chef's choice of Southern seasonings. For more than 30 years, in fact, the tiny town of Loris has been hosting its annual Loris Bog-off Festival, where hundreds of chefs compete to be awarded for the best bowl of bog.

Hilton Head Island is a unique and incredibly beautiful resort town that anchors the southern tip of South Carolina's coastline. What makes this semitropical island so unique? At the top of the list is the fact that visitors won't see large, splashy billboards or neon signs. What they will see is an island where the environment takes center stage, a place where development is strictly regulated.

There are 12 miles of sparkling white-sand beaches, amazing world-class restaurants, top-rated golf courses—Harbour Town Golf Links annually hosts the Heritage Golf Tournament, a PGA Tour event—and a thriving tennis community. Wildlife abounds, including loggerhead sea turtles, alligators, snowy egrets, wood storks, great blue heron, and, in the waters, dolphins, manatees, and various species of fish. There are lots of activities offered on the island, including parasailing, charter fishing, kayaking, and many other water sports.

The island is home to several private gated communities, including Sea Pines, Hilton Head Plantation, Shipyard, Wexford, Long Cove, Port Royal, Indigo Run, Palmetto Hall, and Palmetto Dunes. Within these you'll find upscale housing (some of it doubling as vacation rentals), golf courses, shopping, and restaurants. Sea Pines is one of the most famous of these communities, as it is known for the candy-cane-striped Hilton Head Lighthouse. There are also many areas on the island that are not behind security gates.

Planning

When to Go

The high season follows typical beach-town cycles, with June through August and holidays year-round being the busiest and most costly. Mid-April, during the annual RBC Heritage Golf Tournament, is when rates tend to be highest. Thanks to the Lowcountry's mostly moderate year-round temperatures, tourists are ever-present. Spring is the best time to visit, when the weather is ideal for tennis and golf. Autumn is almost as active for the same reason.

To get a good deal, it's imperative that you plan ahead. The choicest locations can be booked six months to a year in advance, but booking agencies can help you make room reservations and get good deals during the colder months, when the crowds fall off. Villa-rental companies often offer snowbird rates for monthly stays during the winter season. Parking is always free at the major hotels, but valet parking can cost from $20 to $32; the smaller properties have free parking, too, but no valet service.

Planning Your Time

No matter where you stay, spend your first day relaxing on the beach or hitting the links. After that, you'll have time to visit some of the area's attractions, including the Coastal Discovery Museum or the Sea Pines Resort. You can also visit the Tanger outlet malls on U.S. 278 in Bluffton. Old-town Bluffton is a quaint area with many locally owned shops and art galleries. If you have a few more days, visit Beaufort on a day trip or even spend the night there. This historic antebellum town is rich with history. Savannah is also a short drive away.

Getting Here and Around

AIR TRAVEL

Most travelers use the Savannah/Hilton Head International Airport (SAV), less than an hour from Hilton Head, which is served by Air Canada, Allegiant, American Eagle, Delta, JetBlue, United, and Suncountry. Hilton Head Island Airport (HHH) is served by American Airlines.

AIR CONTACTS Hilton Head Island Airport. *(HHH)* ✉ *120 Beach City Rd., North End* ☎ *843/255–2950* 🌐 *hiltonheadairport.com.* **Savannah/Hilton Head International Airport.** *(SAV)* ✉ *400 Airways Ave., Northwest* ☎ *912/964–0514* 🌐 *savannahairport.com.*

BOAT AND FERRY TRAVEL

Hilton Head is accessible via boat, with docking available at Harbour Town Yacht Basin, Skull Creek Marina, and Shelter Cove Harbour.

BOAT DOCKING INFORMATION Harbour Town Yacht Basin. ✉ *Sea Pines, 149 Lighthouse Rd., South End* ☎ *843/363–8335* 🌐 *seapines.com.* **Safe Harbor Skull Creek Marina.** ✉ *1 Waterway La., North End* ☎ *843/681–8436* 🌐 *www.shmarinas.com/locations/safe-harbor-skull-creek.* **Shelter Cove Harbour & Marina.** ✉ *Shelter Cove, 1 Shelter Cove La., Mid-Island* ☎ *866/661–3822* 🌐 *www.sheltercovehiltonhead.com.*

BUS TRAVEL

The Lowcountry Regional Transportation Authority, known as the Palmetto Breeze, has buses that leave Bluffton in the morning for Hilton Head, Beaufort, and some of the islands. The fare is $2.50, and exact change is required.

CAR TRAVEL

Driving is the best way to get onto Hilton Head Island. Off Interstate 95, take Exit 8 onto U.S. 278 East, which leads you through Bluffton (where it's known as Fording Island Road) and then to Hilton Head. Once on Hilton Head, U.S. 278 forks: on the right is William Hilton Parkway, and on the left is the Cross Island Parkway (a toll road that costs $1.25 each way). If you take the Cross Island (as the locals call it) to the south side where Sea Pines and many other resorts are located, the trip will take about 10 to 15 minutes. If you take William Hilton Parkway the trip will take about 30 minutes. Be aware that at check-in and checkout times on Friday, Saturday, and Sunday, traffic on U.S. 278 can slow to a crawl. **■ TIP→ Be careful of putting the pedal to the metal, particularly on the Cross Island Parkway. It's patrolled regularly.**

Once on Hilton Head Island, signs are small and blend in with the trees and landscaping, and nighttime lighting is kept to a minimum. The lack of streetlights makes it difficult to find your way at night, so be sure to get good directions.

TAXI TRAVEL

There are several taxi services available on Hilton Head, including Hilton Head Taxi and Limousine and Diamond Transportation, which has SUVs and passenger vans available for pickup at Savannah/Hilton Head International Airport and Hilton Head Airport. Prices range from $20 to $120, depending on where you're headed. Rideshare services Uber and Lyft also operate on the island.

TAXI CONTACTS Diamond Transportation. ☎ *843/247–2156* 🌐 *hiltonheadrides.com.* **Yellow Transportation HHI.** ☎ *843/686–6666* 🌐 *www.yellowtransportationhhi.com.*

TRAIN TRAVEL

Amtrak gets you as close as Savannah or Yemassee.

TRAIN CONTACTS Savannah Amtrak Station. ✉ *2611 Seaboard Coastline Dr., Savannah* ☎ *800/872–7245* 🌐 *www.amtrak.com/stations/sav.*

Restaurants

The number of fine-dining restaurants on Hilton Head is extraordinary, given the size of the island. Because of the proximity to the ocean and the small farms on the mainland, most locally owned restaurants are still heavily influenced by the catch of the day and seasonal harvests. Most upscale restaurants open at 11 and don't close until 9 or 10, but some take a break between 2 and 4. Many advertise early-bird menus, and sometimes getting a table before 6 can be a challenge. During the height of the summer season, reservations are a good idea, though in the off-season you may need them only on weekends. There are several locally owned breakfast joints and plenty of great delis where you can pick up lunch or the fixings for a picnic. Smoking is prohibited in Bluffton, Beaufort, and Hilton Head restaurants and bars. Beaufort's restaurant scene has certainly evolved, with more trendy restaurants serving contemporary cuisine moving into the downtown area. *Dining reviews have been shortened. For full information, visit Fodors.com.*

Hotels

Hilton Head is known as one of the best vacation spots on the East Coast, and its hotels are a testimony to its reputation. The island is awash in regular hotels and resorts, not to mention beachfront or golf-course-view villas, cottages, and luxury private homes. You can expect the most modern conveniences and world-class service at the priciest places. Clean, updated rooms and friendly staff are everywhere, even at lower-cost hotels—this is the South, after all. Staying in cooler months, for extended periods of time, or commuting from nearby Bluffton can save money. *Hotel reviews have been shortened. For full information, visit Fodors.com.*

What it Costs

$	$$	$$$	$$$$
RESTAURANTS			
under $15	$15–$22	$23–$30	over $30
HOTELS			
under $125	$125–$200	$201–$300	over $300

Nightlife and Performing Arts

Bars, like everything else on Hilton Head, are often in gated communities or shopping centers. Some are hangouts frequented by locals, and others get a good mix of both locals and visitors. There are a fair number of clubs, many of them restaurants that crank up the music after diners depart.

Tours

TOUR CONTACTS Bluewater Adventure. ✉ *Shelter Cove Marina, 1 Shelter Cove La., Mid-Island* ☏ *843/422–9119* 🌐 *www.bluewateradventurehiltonhead.com.* **Captain Mark's Dolphin Cruises.** ✉ *Shelter Cove Marina, 9 Harbourside La., Mid-Island* ☏ *843/785–4558* 🌐 *www.cruisehiltonhead.com.* **Gullah Heritage Trail Tours.** ✉ *Coastal Discovery Museum, 70 Honey Horn Dr., North End* ☏ *843/681–7066* 🌐 *www.gullaheritage.com.* **Live Oac Outdoor Adventure Co..** ✉ *Hilton Head Harbor, 43A Jenkins Rd., North End* ☏ *843/384–1414* 🌐 *www.liveoac.com.* **Low Country Nature Tours.** ✉ *Shelter Cove Marina, 1 Shelter Cove La., Mid-Island* ☏ *843/683–0187* 🌐 *www.lowcountrynaturetours.com.*

Visitor Information

As you're driving into town, you can pick up brochures and maps at the Hilton Head Island–Bluffton Chamber of Commerce and Visitor and Convention Bureau.

CONTACTS Hilton Head Island-Bluffton Chamber of Commerce and Visitor and Convention Bureau. ✉ *1 Chamber of Commerce Dr., Mid-Island* ☏ *843/785–3673* 🌐 *www.hiltonheadchamber.org.*

Hilton Head Island

Hilton Head Island is known far and wide as a vacation destination that prides itself on its top-notch golf courses and tennis programs, world-class resorts, and beautiful beaches. But the island is also part of the storied American South, steeped in a rich, colorful history. It has seen Native Americans and explorers, battles from the Revolutionary War to the Civil War, plantations and slaves, and development and environmentally focused growth.

More than 10,000 years ago, the island was inhabited by Paleo-Indians. From 8000 to 2000 BC, Woodland Indians lived here. A shell ring made from their discarded oyster shells and animal bones from that period can be found in the Sea Pines Nature Preserve.

The recorded history of the island goes back to the early 1500s, when Spanish explorers sailing coastal waters came upon the island and found Native American settlements. Over the next 200 years, the island was claimed at various times by the Spanish, the French, and the British. In 1663, Captain William Hilton claimed the island for the British crown (and named it for himself), and the island became home to indigo, rice, and cotton plantations.

During the Revolutionary War and the War of 1812, the British harassed islanders and burned plantations, but the island recovered from both wars. During the Civil War, Union troops took Hilton Head in 1861 and freed the more than 1,000 slaves on the island. Mitchelville, one of the first settlements for freed blacks, was created. There was no bridge to the island, so its freed slaves, called "Gullah," subsisted on agriculture and the seafood-laden waters.

Over the years, much of the plantation land was sold at auction. Then, in 1949, General Joseph Fraser purchased 17,000 acres, much of which would eventually become various communities, including Hilton Head Plantation, Palmetto Dunes, and Spanish Wells. The general bought another 1,200 acres, which his son, Charles, used to develop Sea Pines. The first bridge to the island was built in 1956, and modern-day Hilton Head was born.

What makes Hilton Head so special now? Charles Fraser and his business associates focused on development while preserving the environment. And that is what tourists will see today: an island that values its history and its natural beauty.

GETTING HERE AND AROUND

Hilton Head Island is 19 miles east of Interstate 95. Take Exit 8 off Interstate 95 and then U.S. 278 east, directly to the bridges. If you're heading to the southern end of the island, your best bet to save time and avoid traffic is the Cross Island Parkway toll road. The cost is $1.25 each way.

Sights

Your impression of Hilton Head depends on which of the island's developments you make your temporary home. The oldest and best known of Hilton Head's developments, Sea Pines occupies 4,500 thickly wooded acres. It's not wilderness, however; among the trees are three golf courses, tennis clubs, riding stables, and shopping plazas. A free trolley shuttles visitors around the resort. Other well-known communities are Palmetto Dunes and Port Royal Plantation.

Rain in Hilton Head

Don't be discouraged when you see a weather forecast during the summer months saying there's a 30% chance of rain for Hilton Head. It can be an absolutely gorgeous day, and suddenly a storm will pop up late in the afternoon. That's because on hot sunny days, the hot air rises up into the atmosphere and mixes with the cool air, causing the atmosphere to become unstable, thereby creating thunderstorms. These storms move in and out fairly quickly, and they can bring welcome respite from the summer heat. Pack a light jacket or a portable poncho.

Audubon Newhall Preserve

NATURE PRESERVE | FAMILY | There are walking trails, a self-guided tour, a pond, and eight distinct areas to explore on this 50-acre preserve located off Palmetto Bay Road. Native plant life is tagged and identified in the pristine forest, and many species of birds can also be found here. ✉ *Palmetto Bay Rd., off Cross Island Pkwy., South End* 🌐 *www.hiltonheadaudubon.org* 🎫 *Free.*

Ben Ham Images

MUSEUM | The extraordinary black-and-white large format photography of Ben Ham includes many stirring Lowcountry landscapes. ✉ *210 Bluffton Rd., Bluffton* ☎ *843/815–6200* 🌐 *www.benhamimages.com.*

★ Coastal Discovery Museum

MUSEUM | FAMILY | Located on the grounds of the former Honey Horn Plantation, this interactive museum features a butterfly enclosure, programs for children, and guided walks of the 68-acre property that includes historic buildings and barns, marsh front boardwalks, and a wide variety of magnificent trees, such as live oaks, magnolias, and one of the state's largest Southern red cedars. As a Smithsonian Affiliate, the museum hosts a variety of temporary exhibits that focus on a range of interesting historic topics and artistic mediums. Animal tours, history tours, and kayak tours are also available and should be booked in advance. Informative and inspiring, the Coastal Discovery Museum lets visitors experience the Lowcountry up close. ✉ *70 Honey Horn Dr., off Hwy. 278, North End* ☎ *843/689–6767* 🌐 *www.coastaldiscovery.org* 🎫 *Free; donation suggested; most tours and programs are individually priced.*

★ Harbour Town

MARINA | FAMILY | Located within the Sea Pines Resort, Harbour Town is a charming area centered on a circular marina that's filled with interesting shops and restaurants. Distinctive paths covered with white gravel and rows of red rocking chairs add to the small-town feel, while families are attracted to the large playground and live entertainment underneath the Liberty Oak during the summer. Stroll down the pier for excellent views of Daufuskie Island or catch one of the many vessels docked there and ready to set sail for adventure. Rising above it all is the landmark candy-cane-stripe Harbour Town Lighthouse, which visitors can climb to enjoy a view of Calibogue Sound. Summer nights are particularly lovely here, with a breeze coming off the water and music in the air; soak in the atmosphere with a drink at one of the welcoming outdoor bars and seating areas. ✉ *Lighthouse Rd., South End* ☎ *866/561–8802* 🌐 *www.seapines.com.*

★ Old Town Bluffton

HISTORIC SITE | Charming Old Town Bluffton has historic homes and churches on oak-lined streets dripping with Spanish moss, intermingled with newer businesses like the Salt Marsh Brewing Company. The Promenade Street area is newer and features trendy bars and restaurants. At the end of Wharf Street is the Bluffton Oyster Company (*63 Wharf St.*), a place to buy fresh local seafood. Grab a sandwich from the Downtown Deli (*1223 May River Rd.*) and head to the Calhoun Street Public Dock for a picnic with a view of the May River. Another incredibly beautiful spot to visit is the grounds of the historic Church of the Cross (*110 Calhoun St.*). Originally inhabited by Yemassee people who were driven out by the first English settlers, the town's later population of slaveholders played a key role in South Carolina's secession. ✉ *May River Rd. and Calhoun St., Bluffton* 🌐 *www.oldtownbluffton.com.*

★ Red Piano Gallery

MUSEUM | Sculptures, Lowcountry landscapes, and eccentric works by contemporary artists can be found at this upscale gallery in Bluffton. ✉ *Old Town Bluffton, 40 Calhoun St., Suite 201, Bluffton* ☎ *843/842–4433* 🌐 *redpianoartgallery.com.*

★ Sea Pines Forest Preserve

NATURE PRESERVE | **FAMILY** | Located within the gates of the Sea Pines Resort, the Sea Pines Forest Preserve is made up of 605 acres of protected wilderness. There are two entrances: one off Greenwood Drive, about a mile past the main gate, has a parking area; the other is located off Lawton Drive. Walking and biking trails take you past a stocked fishing pond, a waterfowl pond, a 3,400-year-old Native American shell ring, a wildflower field, wetland boardwalks, picnic areas, boat docks, and an outdoor chapel with five wooden pews and a wooden lectern engraved with the Prayer of St. Francis. Nature tours, boat tours, fishing expeditions, and wagon tours are available through Sea Pines and can be booked in advance. Nearby Lawton Stables offers a unique experience to explore the forest on a guided horseback tour. ✉ *The Sea Pines Resort, Greenwood Dr., South End* ☎ *843/671–1343 CSA office to call for permits for fishing or group outings, 843/671–2586 Lawton Stables, contact for tours on horseback* 🌐 *seapines.com* 🎫 *$9 per car; free for those staying at Sea Pines.*

SOBA Gallery

MUSEUM | Located in Old Town Bluffton, this small gallery for the Society of Bluffton Artists (SOBA) showcases the work of local painters, sculptors, and photographers. ✉ *8 Church St., Bluffton* ☎ *843/757–6586* 🌐 *www.sobagallery.com.*

Stoney-Baynard Ruins

HISTORIC SITE | **FAMILY** | This historic site contains the remains of four structures once part of Braddock's Point Plantation. Captain John "Saucy Jack" Stoney forced enslaved people to build the plantation in the 1790s; it was eventually bought by William Baynard in 1840. Union troops occupied the plantation home during the Civil War, and the home was burned in 1869. The 6-acre site, with the ruins of the main house, a plantation overseer's house, and housing for enslaved people, was listed on the National Register of

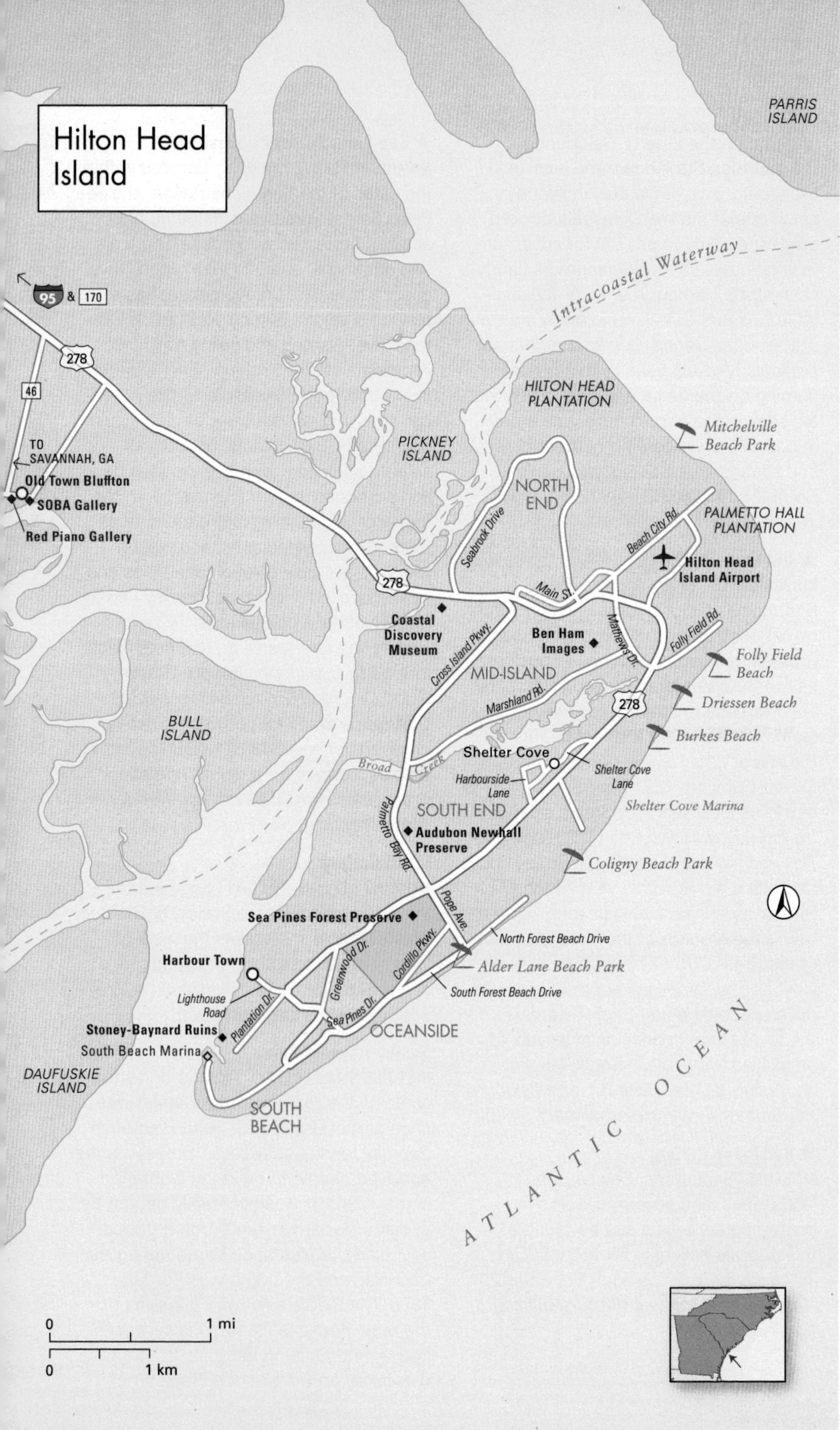

Hilton Head Island
PARRIS ISLAND
Intracoastal Waterway
95 & 170
278
46
TO SAVANNAH, GA
Old Town Bluffton
SOBA Gallery
Red Piano Gallery
PICKNEY ISLAND
HILTON HEAD PLANTATION
Mitchelville Beach Park
NORTH END
Seabrook Drive
Beach City Rd.
PALMETTO HALL PLANTATION
Hilton Head Island Airport
Main St.
Coastal Discovery Museum
Cross Island Pkwy.
Ben Ham Images
Mathews Dr.
Folly Field Rd.
Folly Field Beach
MID-ISLAND
Driessen Beach
Marshland Rd.
Burkes Beach
BULL ISLAND
Shelter Cove
Broad Creek
Harbourside Lane
Shelter Cove Lane
Shelter Cove Marina
SOUTH END
Palmetto Bay Rd.
Audubon Newhall Preserve
Coligny Beach Park
Pope Ave.
Sea Pines Forest Preserve
North Forest Beach Drive
Harbour Town
Greenwood Dr.
Cordillo Pkwy.
Alder Lane Beach Park
Lighthouse Road
Plantation Dr.
Sea Pines Dr.
South Forest Beach Drive
Stoney-Baynard Ruins
OCEANSIDE
South Beach Marina
DAUFUSKIE ISLAND
SOUTH BEACH
ATLANTIC OCEAN
0
1 mi
0
1 km

Island Gators

The most famous photo of Hilton Head's original developer, Charles Fraser, ran in the *Saturday Evening Post* in the late 1950s. It shows him outfitted with a cane and straw hat, with an alligator on a leash.

What you will learn if you visit the Coastal Discovery Museum, where the old photograph is blown up for an interpretive board on the island's early history, is that someone else had the gator by the tail (not shown) so that it would not harm Fraser or the photographer.

These prehistoric creatures are indeed indigenous to this subtropical island. Alligators can be found among the many ponds and lagoons in Sea Pines and islandwide. Spotting a live gator on the banks of a lagoon is a possibility while riding your bike or playing golf. But no matter where you happen to see these intriguing reptiles, do not feed them or attempt to get near them as they are fast and can be aggressive. Having respect for the gators in their natural habitat means keeping a safe distance, especially when children or small pets are involved.

Historic Places in 1994. Now located within the Sea Pines Resort, Baynard Ruins Park has a small parking area as well as trails and interpretative signs that describe the historical and archaeological significance of the area. If you are staying in Sea Pines, you can ride your bike to the site and explore at your leisure. Guided tours are also available through Sea Pines. ✉ *Plantation Dr., near Baynard Cove Rd., South End* 🌐 *seapines.com.*

Beaches

A delightful stroll on the beach can end with an unpleasant surprise if you don't put your towels, shoes, and other earthly possessions way up on the sand. Tides here can fluctuate by as much as 7 feet. Check the tide chart at your hotel.

Alder Lane Beach

BEACH—SIGHT | FAMILY | A great place for solitude during the winter—and popular with families during the summer season—this beach has hard-packed sand at low tide, making it ideal for walking. It's accessible from the Marriott Grande Ocean Resort. **Amenities:** lifeguards; parking; showers; toilets. **Best for:** swimming; walking. ✉ *2 Woodward Ave., off South Forest Beach Dr., South End.*

Burkes Beach

BEACH—SIGHT | This beach is usually not crowded, mostly because it is a bit hard to find and there are no lifeguards on duty. At sunrise, birds and deer bring the adjacent marsh to life. Visitors must park at the Chaplin Community Park at 11 Cast Net Drive, since there is no longer parking on Burkes Beach Road. **■ TIP→ Time a visit around low tide—the marsh flooding during high tide can cut off access.** **Amenities:** parking; showers. **Best for:** solitude; sunrise; swimming; windsurfing. ✉ *60 Burkes Beach Rd., off William Hilton Pkwy., Mid-Island.*

★ Coligny Beach Park

BEACH—SIGHT | FAMILY | The island's most popular public beach is a lot of fun, but during high season it can get very crowded. It has choreographed fountains that delight little children, bench swings, and beach umbrellas and chaise lounges for rent. If you have to go online, there's also Wi-Fi access. **Amenities:** food and drink; lifeguards; parking; showers; toilets. **Best for:** partiers; swimming; windsurfing. ✉ *1*

Coligny Circle, at Pope Ave. and South Forest Beach Dr., South End.

Driessen Beach
BEACH—SIGHT | **FAMILY** | A good destination for families, Driessen Beach Park has a playground and an attractive boardwalk and sandy path through the dunes. It's often peppered with people flying kites, making it colorful and fun. **Amenities:** lifeguards; parking; showers; toilets. **Best for:** sunrise; surfing; swimming; walking. ✉ *64 Bradley Beach Rd., off William Hilton Pkwy., Mid-Island.*

Fish Haul Beach Park
BEACH—SIGHT | Not ideal for swimming because of the many sharp shells on the sand and in the water, this public beach is a terrific spot for a walk or shell and shark tooth hunting. It is not on the Atlantic Ocean, but rather on Port Royal Sound. **Amenities:** parking; showers; toilets. **Best for:** sunrise; solitude; walking. ✉ *124 Mitchelville Rd., North End.*

Folly Field Beach Park
BEACH—SIGHT | **FAMILY** | Next to Driessen Beach, Folly Field is a treat for families. It can get crowded in high season, but even so it's a wonderful spot for a day of sunbathing and swimming. The best waves for surfing break here. **Amenities:** lifeguards; parking; showers; toilets. **Best for:** sunrise; surfing; swimming; walking. ✉ *55 Starfish Dr., off Folly Field Rd., Mid-Island.*

Islanders Beach Park
BEACHES | **FAMILY** | Featuring a boardwalk, a playground, a picnic pavilion, parking, and outdoor showers and restrooms, Islander Beach Park is a great spot for families looking to spend the day at the beach. **Amenties**: parking; showers; lifeguards (seasonal). **Best for:** swimming. ✉ *94 Folly Field Rd., off William Hilton Pkwy., North End.*

Sand Dollars

Hilton Head Island's beaches hold many treasures, including starfish, sea sponges, and sand dollars. Note that it is strictly forbidden to pick up any live creatures on the beach, especially live sand dollars. How can you tell if they are alive? Live sand dollars are brown and fuzzy and will turn your fingers yellow and brown. You can take sand dollars home only if they're white. Soak them in a mixture of bleach and water to remove the scent once you get home.

Restaurants

A Lowcountry Backyard Restaurant
$$ | **SOUTHERN** | **FAMILY** | This unassuming little restaurant located off Palmetto Bay Road serves excellent seafood dishes with Southern flavor in a laid-back setting with indoor and outdoor seating. Don't ignore the full bar that serves South Carolina moonshine. **Known for:** funky atmosphere; excellent shrimp and grits; fun for kids and families. *$ Average main: $20* ✉ *The Village Exchange Shopping Center, 32 Palmetto Bay Rd., South End* ☎ *843/785–9273* 🌐 *www.hhbackyard.com.*

Black Marlin Bayside Grill
$$$ | **SEAFOOD** | This busy restaurant specializing in seafood dishes such as chowder and fish tacos is open for lunch and dinner every day, and brunch on the weekend. Located in Palmetto Bay Marina, the Black Marlin has indoor and outdoor seating, as well as family-style meals available for takeout. **Known for:** a hopping happy hour; an outdoor Hurricane Bar; weekend oyster roasts during winter. *$ Average main: $23* ✉ *86 Helmsman Way, South End* ☎ *843/785–4950* 🌐 *www.blackmarlinhhi.com.*

The Shrimp Boat Tradition

Watching shrimp trawlers coming into the home port at sunset, with mighty nets raised and followed by an entourage of hungry seagulls, is a cherished Lowcountry tradition. The shrimping industry has been an integral part of the South Carolina economy for nearly a century, but farm-raised imported shrimp has had a big impact on the market and has caused the number of shrimpers to dwindle across the state.

The season for fresh-caught shrimp is May to December. People can support local fishermen by buying only certified, local wild shrimp from stores or from the shrimpers directly.

In restaurants, look for the "Certified Wild American Shrimp" logo or ask your server if they use local seafood.

On Hilton Head, Benny Hudson Seafood sells local shrimp straight from the dock at 175 Squire Pope Road, or visit South End Seafood at 18 Executive Park Road. In Bluffton, the Bluffton Oyster Company has been selling fresh oysters, clams, crabs, and shrimp since 1899 at 63 Wharf Street. Gay Fish Company on Saint Helena Island or Sea Eagle Market in Beaufort are other local businesses that are keeping the tradition alive in South Carolina.

★ Captain Woody's

$$ | SEAFOOD | FAMILY | If you're looking for a fun, casual, kid-friendly seafood restaurant, this vibrant joint offers creamy crab bisque, oysters on the half shell, and a sampler platter that includes crab legs, shrimp, and oysters. Open daily for lunch and dinner, plus a Sunday brunch, Captain Woody's has indoor and outdoor seating. **Known for:** grouper sandwiches, including the buffalo grouper, grouper melt, and grouper Reuben; a lively atmosphere; good happy hour. *Ⓢ Average main: $22 ✉ 6 Target Rd., South End ☎ 843/785–2400 ⊕ www.captainwoodys.com.*

Charlie's L'Etoile Verte

$$$ | FRENCH | This family-owned culinary landmark has been serving French cuisine with a Lowcountry flair since 1982. While the handwritten menu changes daily, classic dishes like escargot, pate, and rack of lamb remain the same. **Known for:** extensive wine list (more than 500 bottles); 14 varying seafood entrées offered nightly; fine dining in a relaxed atmosphere. *Ⓢ Average main: $27 ✉ 8 New Orleans Rd., Mid-Island ☎ 843/785–9277 ⊕ www.charliesgreenstar.com ⏲ Closed Sun. No lunch Sat.*

The Crazy Crab

$$ | SEAFOOD | FAMILY | With two distinct locations on Hilton Head, the Crazy Crab has been a long-time institution thanks to its quality seafood and friendly environment. Don't miss the she-crab soup and crab cakes. **Known for:** picturesque marsh views; spacious seating; she-crab soup and fried seafood platters. *Ⓢ Average main: $18 ✉ 104 William Hilton Head Pkwy., North End ☎ 843/681–5021 Jarvis Creek location, 843/363–2722 Harbour Town location ⊕ www.thecrazycrab.com.*

Frankie Bones

$$$ | ITALIAN | The early '60s theme here appeals to an older crowd that likes the traditional Italian dishes on the early dining menu, but younger patrons who order flatbread pizzas and small plates can be found at the bar area. Some dishes have innovative twists, including the 16-ounce rib eye with a sweetened coffee rub. **Known for:** cool twists on traditional dishes; drinks for dessert, like a key lime colada martini and house-made limoncello; the 24-ounce "Godfather Cut" prime rib. *Average main: $26* ✉ *1301 Main St., North End* ☎ *843/682–4455* 🌐 *www.frankieboneshhi.com.*

Harold's Country Club Bar & Grill

$ | **AMERICAN** | Not the "country club" you might expect, Harold's is a remodeled gas station in the little town of Yemassee, just east of Interstate 95 in northern Beaufort County. There's a buffet every Thursday and steak night on Saturday that requires ordering in advance. **Known for:** great live entertainment; kitschy dining rooms; a worthy stop on your way in or out of town. *Average main: $13* ✉ *97 U.S. 17A, Yemassee* ✣ *30 mins north of Beaufort* ☎ *843/589–4360* 🌐 *www.haroldscountryclub.com* ⊗ *Closed Sun.–Wed.*

Hinoki

$$ | **JAPANESE** | Slip into a peaceful oasis through a tunnel of bamboo at Hinoki, which has arguably the best sushi on the island. Try the Hilton Head roll, which is whitefish tempura and avocado; the Hinoki roll with asparagus, spicy fish roe, tuna and avocado; or the amazing tuna sashimi salad with spicy mayo, cucumbers, onions, salmon roe, and crabmeat. **Known for:** super-fresh sushi with more than 50 menu items; extensive sake menu; udon noodle dishes and bento boxes. *Average main: $20* ✉ *Orleans Plaza, 37 New Orleans Rd., South End* ☎ *843/785–9800* 🌐 *hinokihhi.com* ⊗ *Closed Sun. No lunch Mon. and Sat.*

Kenny B's French Quarter Cafe

$ | **CAJUN** | **FAMILY** | Surrounded by Mardi Gras memorabilia, owner Kenny himself cooks up jambalaya, gumbo, and muffaletta sandwiches at this family-run, Cajun-inspired restaurant that has been serving locals and tourists since 1999. The extensive menu also features Southern staples such as crab cakes and shrimp and grits. **Known for:** colorful mural and decor; no reservations, so be prepared to wait; beignets like they're made in New Orleans. *Average main: $14* ✉ *Circle Center, 70 Pope Ave., South End* ☎ *843/785–3315* 🌐 *www.eatatkennybs.com* ⊗ *Closed Mon. and Tues.*

★ Michael Anthony's Cucina Italiana

$$$$ | **ITALIAN** | This restaurant has a convivial spirit, and its innovative pairings and plate presentations are au courant. Expect fresh, top-quality ingredients, simple yet elegant sauces, and waiters who know and care about the food and wine they serve. **Known for:** cooking demonstrations; on-site market with fresh pasta; wine tastings. *Average main: $31* ✉ *Orleans Plaza, 37 New Orleans Rd., Suite L, South End* ☎ *843/785–6272* 🌐 *www.michael-anthonys.com* ⊗ *Closed Sun. and Mon. No lunch.*

Mi Tierra

$$ | **MEXICAN** | This traditional Mexican restaurant has tile floors, colorful sombreros, and paintings of chili peppers hanging on the walls. Don't forget to order the guacamole and bean dip with your margarita and try the *enchiladas suizas*, tortillas filled with chicken and topped with green tomatillo sauce, sour cream, and avocado. **Known for:** authentic Mexican comfort food; signature dish arroz con camarones—butterfly shrimp sautéed with garlic butter and vegetables; daily specials and affordable kids' menu. *Average main: $15* ✉ *130 Arrow Rd., South End* ☎ *843/342–3409* 🌐 *www.mitierrahiltonhead.com.*

One Hot Mama's

$$ | **BARBECUE** | **FAMILY** | This barbecue joint has an upbeat atmosphere, colorful walls, multiple flat-screen TVs, and an outdoor patio with a big brick fireplace. With baby back ribs, award-winning pulled pork sandwiches, great burgers, and a fun kids' menu, you should expect to bring your appetite to One Hot Mama's. **Known for:** lots of fun in the "Barmuda Triangle" (other bars are just steps away); award-winning wings with sauces like strawberry-jalapeño; a delectable rib sampler that includes "Hot Asian" and chocolate barbecue.

$ Average main: $19 ✉ 7A Greenwood Dr., South End ☎ 843/682–6262 ⊕ onehotmamas.com.

★ Red Fish

$$$$ | CONTEMPORARY | Appealing to locals and tourists alike, the menu at upscale Red Fish features classic seafood dishes, mouthwatering apps, and delicious desserts. The contemporary restaurant's wine cellar is filled with some 1,000 bottles, and there's also a retail wineshop as well as indoor and outdoor seating. **Known for:** award-winning burger; fabulous service; produce grown on the restaurant's own farm. *$ Average main: $32 ✉ 8 Archer Rd., South End ☎ 843/686–3388 ⊕ www.redfishofhiltonhead.com ⏲ No lunch.*

Santa Fe Cafe

$$$ | SOUTHWESTERN | The sights, sounds, and aromas of New Mexico greet you here: Native American rugs, Mexican ballads, steer skulls and horns, and the smell of chilies and mesquite on the grill. Listen to *guitarra* music in the rooftop cantina, enjoy the adobe fireplaces on chilly nights, or dine under the stars. **Known for:** rooftop cantina with a cozy fireplace and live music; signature grouper served with chipotle Parmesan au gratin; one of the island's best margaritas. *$ Average main: $28 ✉ 807 William Hilton Pkwy., Mid-Island ☎ 843/785–3838 ⊕ santafehhi.com ⏲ Closed Sun. and Mon.*

★ Signe's Heaven Bound Bakery & Café

$ | AMERICAN | Since 1972, Signe's has been serving freshly made baked goods as well as delicious breakfast and lunch options on Hilton Head. Signature dishes range from deep-dish French toast and crispy polenta to curried chicken salad and specialty quiches. **Known for:** homemade breads, cookies, cakes, and pies; the "beach bag" (a lunch packed with goodies to take to the beach); cozy, friendly atmosphere. *$ Average main: $12 ✉ 93 Arrow Rd., South End ☎ 843/785–9118 ⊕ www.signesbakery.com ⏲ Closed Sun.*

Skull Creek Boathouse

$$ | SEAFOOD | FAMILY | Soak up the salty atmosphere in this complex of dining areas where almost every table has a view of the water. Outside is a third dining area and a bar called the Marker 13 Buoy Bar, where Adirondack chairs invite you to sit back, listen to live music, and catch the sunset. **Known for:** an adjacent outdoor Sunset Landing beer garden; tasty sandwiches and po'boys with a Southern twist; sushi, ceviche, and carpaccio from the Dive Bar. *$ Average main: $17 ✉ 397 Squire Pope Rd., North End ☎ 843/681–3663 ⊕ www.skullcreekboathouse.com.*

Truffles Cafe

$$$ | MODERN AMERICAN | FAMILY | When a restaurant keeps its customers happy for decades, there's a reason, and in the case of Truffles, it's the consistently good service and excellent food. Popular entrées include grilled salmon with a mango-barbecue glaze and the chicken pot pie. **Known for:** wide-ranging, crowd-pleasing menu with plenty of seafood; very popular with locals; on-site market with thoughtful gifts. *$ Average main: $26 ✉ Sea Pines Center, 71 Lighthouse Rd., South End ☎ 843/671–6136 ⊕ www.trufflescafe.com.*

WiseGuys

$$$$ | STEAKHOUSE | The red-and-black decor is modern and sophisticated at this lively restaurant on the north end of the island. The food is a spin on the classics, from seafood to steak, and the shared plate menu is on point. **Known for:** a delightful crème brûlée flight and deep-fried bread pudding; extensive wine list and cocktail menu; charred rib-eye steak entrée. *$ Average main: $32 ✉ 1513 Main St., North End ☎ 843/842–8866 ⊕ wiseguyshhi.com ⏲ No lunch.*

Hotels

Beach House Hilton Head Island

$$$ | **RESORT** | **FAMILY** | Located along one of the island's busiest stretches of sand, this Holiday Inn–branded resort is within walking distance of Coligny Plaza's shops and restaurants. **Pros:** central location cannot be beat; spacious rooms; popular beach bar. **Cons:** in summer the number of kids raises the noise volume; small front desk can get backed up; not a spot for a quiet getaway. *Rooms from: $229 1 S. Forest Beach Dr., South End 843/785–5126 hotel staff, 855/474–2882 reservations www.beachousehhi.com 202 rooms No meals.*

Disney's Hilton Head Island Resort

$$$$ | **RESORT** | **FAMILY** | The cheery colors and whimsical designs at Disney's popular resort create a look that's part Southern beach resort, part Adirondack hideaway. **Pros:** family-friendly vibe; huge heated pool with a waterslide; charming porches with each villa. **Cons:** books up far in advance; expensive rates; it's a drive to the beach. *Rooms from: $414 22 Harbourside La., Mid-Island 843/341–4100 hiltonhead.disney.go.com 123 units No meals.*

Hampton Inn Hilton Head

$$$ | **HOTEL** | **FAMILY** | Although it's not on the beach, this attractive hotel is a good choice for budget travelers, with nice amenities and a lovely outdoor pool area. **Pros:** good customer service; moderate prices; close to the airport. **Cons:** not on a beach; parking lot views; lacks the charm of the island's resort hotels. *Rooms from: $219 1 Dillon Rd., Mid-Island 843/681–7900 www.hamptoninn.com 122 rooms Free breakfast.*

★ **Hilton Head Marriott Resort & Spa**

$$$$ | **HOTEL** | **FAMILY** | Private balconies with views of the palm-shaded grounds are the best reason to stay at this resort facing the Atlantic Ocean. **Pros:** steps from the beach; lots of amenities; accommodating staff. **Cons:** rooms could be larger; in summer, kids are everywhere; one of the older beachfront resorts on the island. *Rooms from: $359 1 Hotel Circle, Mid-Island 843/686–8400 www.marriott.com/hotels/travel/hhhgr-hilton-head-marriott-resort-and-spa 513 rooms No meals.*

★ **The Inn & Club at Harbour Town**

$$$$ | **HOTEL** | This European-style boutique hotel located within the Sea Pines Resort pampers guests with British service and a dose of Southern charm—butlers are on hand any time and the kitchen delivers around the clock. **Pros:** the staff spoils you from arrival to checkout; ideal location, walking distance to golf and tennis; complimentary valet parking. **Cons:** it's a drive to the beach; two-day minimum on most weekends; less appealing for families. *Rooms from: $309 The Sea Pines Resort, 7 Lighthouse La., South End 843/363–8100 seapines.com 60 rooms No meals.*

★ **Montage Palmetto Bluff**

$$$$ | **B&B/INN** | A 30-minute drive from Hilton Head, the Lowcountry's most luxurious resort sits on 20,000 acres that have been transformed into a perfect replica of a small Southern town, complete with its own clapboard church. **Pros:** 18-hole May River Golf Club on-site; tennis/boccie/croquet complex has an impressive retail shop; the river adds both ambience and boat excursions. **Cons:** the mock Southern town is not the real thing; isolated from the amenities of Hilton Head; escaping in luxury is priced accordingly. *Rooms from: $580 477 Mount Pelia Rd., Bluffton 843/706–6500 resort, 855/264–8705 reservations www.montagehotels.com/palmettobluff 50 cottages, 75 inn rooms No meals.*

Omni Hilton Head Oceanfront Resort

$$$$ | **RESORT** | **FAMILY** | At this beachfront hotel with a Caribbean sensibility, the spacious accommodations range from studios to two-bedroom suites. **Pros:** lots of outdoor dining options; well suited

for both families and couples; packages are often good deals, and many include breakfast, bottles of wine, or outdoor cabana massages. **Cons:** wedding parties can be noisy; pricey; noise travels through room walls. *Rooms from: $349 23 Ocean La., Palmetto Dunes, Mid-Island 843/842–8000 www.omnihiltonhead.com 323 rooms No meals.*

Palmera Inn and Suites

$$ | **HOTEL** | **FAMILY** | This property located just off William Hilton Parkway has private balconies and full kitchens in each suite. **Pros:** one of the island's most reasonably priced lodgings; parking and Wi-Fi are free; good place for an extended stay. **Cons:** doesn't have an upscale feel; more kids means more noise, especially around the pool area; going to the beach or to dinner requires a drive. *Rooms from: $176 12 Park La., South End 843/686–5700 www.palmerainnandsuites.com 156 suites No meals.*

Sonesta Resort Hilton Head Island

$$$ | **RESORT** | **FAMILY** | Set in a luxuriant garden that always seems to be in full bloom, the Sonesta Resort is the centerpiece of the Shipyard private community, which means guests have access to its amenities, such as golf and tennis. **Pros:** wonderful on-site spa; spacious rooms; beach access. **Cons:** crowded during summer; service is sometimes impersonal; doesn't have the views of competing resorts. *Rooms from: $299 Shipyard Plantation, 130 Shipyard Dr., South End 843/842–2400 www.sonesta.com/hiltonheadisland 340 rooms No meals.*

The Westin Hilton Head Island Resort and Spa

$$$$ | **RESORT** | **FAMILY** | A circular drive winds around a sculpture of long-legged marsh birds as you approach this beachfront resort inside Port Royal. **Pros:** the beach here is absolutely gorgeous; pampering spa; access to the Port Royal Golf & Racquet Club. **Cons:** lots of groups in the off-season; crowds during summer can back up the check-in process; on-site Carolina Room restaurant gets mixed reviews. *Rooms from: $314 Port Royal Plantation, 2 Grass Lawn Ave., North End 800/933–3102, 843/681–4000 www.marriott.com/hotels/hotel-information/restaurant/hhhwi-the-westin-hilton-head-island-resort-and-spa/ 416 rooms No meals.*

PRIVATE VILLA RENTALS

Hilton Head has some 6,000 villas, condos, and private homes for rent, almost double the number of the island's hotel rooms. Villas and condos seem to work particularly well for families with children, especially if they want to avoid the extra costs of staying in a resort. Often these vacation homes cost less per diem than hotels of the same quality. Guests on a budget can further economize by cooking some of their own meals.

Villas and condos are primarily rented by the week, Saturday to Saturday. It pays to make sure you understand exactly what you're getting before making a deposit or signing a contract. For example, a property owner in the Hilton Head Beach & Tennis Club advertised that his villa sleeps six. That villa had one small bedroom, a foldout couch, and a hall closet with two very narrow bunk beds. That's a far cry from the three-bedroom villa you might have expected. **■ TIP→ Before calling a vacation rental company, make a list of the amenities you want.** Ask for pictures of each room and ask when the photos were taken. If you're looking for a beachfront property, ask exactly how far it is to the beach. Make sure to request a list of all fees, including those for parking, cleaning, pets, security deposits, and utility costs. Finally, get a written contract and a copy of the refund policy.

RENTAL AGENTS

Hilton Head Rentals

Representing more than 150 vacation rentals ranging in size from one to seven bedrooms, this agency has villas, condos, and homes with oceanfront views. It offers various packages that include golf and other activities. Rentals are generally for three to seven days. ✉ *578 William Hilton Pkwy., Hilton Head Island* ☎ *888/599–5326* 🌐 *www.hiltonheadvacation.com.*

Resort Rentals of Hilton Head Island by Vacasa

This company represents some 500 homes and villas, including many located inside the gated communities of Sea Pines, Palmetto Dunes, and Shipyard. Others are in North and South Forest Beach and the Folly Field area. Most of the properties are privately owned, so decor and amenities can vary. ✉ *32 Palmetto Bay Rd., Suite 1B, Mid-Island* ☎ *800/845–7017* 🌐 *www.vacasa.com/usa/South-Carolina/Hilton-Head-Island.*

★ The Sea Pines Resort

The vast majority of the overnight guests at the Sea Pines Resort rent one of the more than 400 villas, condos, and beach houses through the resort itself. Staying within this gated community allows guests access to all the amenities Sea Pines has to offer—golf, tennis, a beach club, fitness center, restaurants, marinas, shopping, and 15 miles of biking trails. There's a wide selection of properties to meet your needs, whether it's a two-bedroom villa in Harbour Town or a five-bedroom oceanfront home. Prices depend on location and the length of your stay. ✉ *32 Greenwood Dr., South End* ☎ *843/785–3333, 866/561–8802* 🌐 *seapines.com/vacation-rentals.*

Nightlife

Big Bamboo Cafe

BARS/PUBS | This South Pacific–theme bar and restaurant features live music, a great selection of craft beers and cocktails, and a lunch and dinner menu serving up tasty tacos and burgers. Located on the second story in Coligny, there's indoor and outdoor seating. ✉ *Coligny Plaza, 1 N. Forest Beach Dr., South End* ☎ *843/686–3443* 🌐 *www.bigbamboocafe.com.*

Comedy Magic Cabaret

COMEDY CLUBS | Several nights a week this lounge brings top-flight comedic talent to Hilton Head. There's a light menu of appetizers and sandwiches, and a full bar. General admission tickets are $39.50 per person. **■ TIP→ Book ahead online because the shows sell out fairly quickly.** ✉ *South Island Square, 843 William Hilton Pkwy., South End* ☎ *843/681–7757* 🌐 *www.comedymagiccabaret.com.*

★ The Jazz Corner

BARS/PUBS | The elegant supper-club atmosphere at this popular spot makes it a wonderful setting in which to enjoy an evening of jazz, swing, or blues. There's a special martini menu, an extensive wine list, and a late-night menu. **■ TIP→ The club fills up quickly, so make reservations.** ✉ *The Village at Wexford, 1000 William Hilton Pkwy., Suite C-1, South End* ☎ *843/842–8620* 🌐 *www.thejazzcorner.com.*

★ Reilley's Plaza

BARS/PUBS | Dubbed the "Barmuda Triangle" by locals, the little cluster of bars and restaurants located just off Sea Pines Circle is a fun spot to grab a drink, eat wings and burgers, watch a game, or meet up with friends in the various outdoor areas. Reilley's Grill & Bar is the area's cornerstone, with a big outdoor bar, seating area, and delicious food. Elsewhere, the Lodge has great beer and games like pool and shuffleboard;

the Boardroom is open late with live music; One Hot Mama's has tasty wings and burgers; MidiCi Italian Kitchen has wooden tables and open-air seating; and Brother Shucker's Bar & Grill serves up fun with raw oysters, vodka specials, and trivia nights. ✉ *Reilley's Plaza, 7D Greenwood Dr., South End* 🌐 *www.reilleyshiltonhead.com.*

★ The Salty Dog Cafe

CAFES—NIGHTLIFE | **FAMILY** | The popular Salty Dog Cafe has been drawing crowds for more than 30 years with its lively atmosphere and outdoor bar and seating area overlooking scenic Braddock Cove at South Beach Marina. Serving breakfast, lunch, and dinner, guests can sit inside or outside and enjoy items such as crab dip, fish sandwiches, fried shrimp, and Jake's hush puppies. Adults can relax with a cocktail from the extensive drink menu and kids can hop over to the Salty Dog Ice Cream Shop located next door. Don't forget to bring home a T-shirt with the trendy Salty Dog Cafe logo at the nearby store. ✉ *South Beach Marina, 232 S. Sea Pines Dr., South End* ☎ *843/671–2233* 🌐 *www.saltydog.com.*

Performing Arts

Arts Center of Coastal Carolina

ART GALLERIES—ARTS | Locals love the theater productions at this arts hub that strives to enrich the community through performing and visual arts. The nonprofit supports youth education programs and showcases the works of more than 150 local artists in its Walter Greer Gallery. ✉ *14 Shelter Cove La., Mid-Island* ☎ *843/686–3945* 🌐 *www.artshhi.com.*

Hilton Head Island Gullah Celebration

ART GALLERIES—ARTS | **FAMILY** | This annual showcase of Gullah life through arts, music, and theater is held at a variety of locations throughout Hilton Head and the Lowcountry in February. ✉ *Hilton Head Island* ☎ *843/255–7303* 🌐 *www.gullahcelebration.com.*

Hilton Head Symphony Orchestra

CONCERTS | With nearly 100 musicians, the Hilton Head Symphony Orchestra is a fully professional ensemble devoted to bringing world-class music to the Lowcountry. In addition to year-round performances, the orchestra supports a host of youth programs, including an international piano competition. ✉ *First Presbyterian Church, 540 William Hilton Pkwy., Mid-Island* ☎ *843/842–2055* 🌐 *www.hhso.org.*

Shopping

Hilton Head is a great destination for those who love shopping, starting with the Tanger outlet malls. Although they're officially in Bluffton, visitors drive by the outlets on U.S. 278 to get to Hilton Head Island. Tanger Outlet I has been completely renovated and reopened with many high-end stores, including Saks OFF 5th, DKNY, Michael Kors, and more.

GIFTS

Harbour Town Lighthouse Gift Shop

GIFTS/SOUVENIRS | **FAMILY** | Located at the top of the striking red-and-white Harbour Town Lighthouse, this shop sells tasteful South Carolina–themed gifts and nautical souvenirs. ✉ *The Sea Pines Resort, 149 Lighthouse Rd., South End* ☎ *866/305–9814* 🌐 *www.harbourtownlighthouse.com/shop.*

Markel's Card & Gift Shop

GIFTS/SOUVENIRS | The helpful and friendly staff at Markel's is known for wrapping gifts with giant bows. You'll find unique Lowcountry gifts, including hand-painted wineglasses and beer mugs, lawn ornaments, baby gifts, greeting cards, and more. ✉ *1008 Fording Island Rd., Bluffton* ☎ *843/815–9500.*

Pretty Papers & Gifts

BOOKS/STATIONERY | This is the go-to local spot for wedding invitations, fine stationery, and gifts since 1983. ✉ *The Village at Wexford, 1000 William Hilton Pkwy.,*

Suite E7, Mid-Island ☎ *843/341–5116* 🌐 *www.prettypapershhi.com.*

★ Salty Dog T-Shirt Factory

GIFTS/SOUVENIRS | FAMILY | You can't leave Hilton Head without a Salty Dog T-shirt, so hit this factory store for the best deals. The trendy T-shirts are hard to resist, and there are lots of options for kids and adults in various colors and styles. ✉ *67 Arrow Rd., South End* ☎ *843/842–6331* 🌐 *www.saltydog.com.*

The Storybook Shoppe

BOOKS/STATIONERY | FAMILY | This charming, whimsical children's bookstore has a darling reading area for little ones as well as educational toys for infants to teens. ✉ *Old Town Bluffton, 41 Calhoun St., Bluffton* ☎ *843/321–8256* 🌐 *www.thestorybookshoppe.com.*

JEWELRY

Forsythe Jewelers

JEWELRY/ACCESSORIES | This is the island's leading jewelry store, offering pieces by famous designers. ✉ *The Shops at Sea Pines Center, 71 Lighthouse Rd., South End* ☎ *843/671–7070* 🌐 *www.forsythe-jewelers.biz.*

MALLS AND SHOPPING CENTERS

Coligny Plaza

SHOPPING CENTERS/MALLS | FAMILY | Things are always humming at this shopping center, which is within walking distance of the most popular public beach on Hilton Head. Coligny Plaza has more than 50 shops and restaurants, including unique clothing boutiques, souvenir shops, and a Piggly Wiggly grocery store. Don't miss Skillets for breakfast, Frozen Moo for ice cream, Frosty Frog for outdoor drinks, and Island Fudge Shoppe for homemade sweet treats. ✉ *Coligny Circle, 1 N. Forest Beach Dr., South End* ☎ *843/842–6050* 🌐 *colignyplaza.com.*

★ Harbour Town

CLOTHING | FAMILY | Located within the Sea Pines Resort, Harbour Town is a picture-perfect little area with plenty of shops that appeal to visitors young and old. S. M. Bradford Co., Currents, and Fashion Court specialize in upscale clothing, while Knickers and Harbour Town Surf Shop carry outdoor wear. Kids and families will enjoy the Cinnamon Bear Country Store and Hilton Head Toys. ✉ *The Sea Pines Resort, 149 Lighthouse Rd., South End* ☎ *866/561–8802* 🌐 *seapines.com/recreation/harbour-town.*

★ Old Town Bluffton

SHOPPING CENTERS/MALLS | FAMILY | Charming Old Town Bluffton features local artist galleries, antiques, shops, and restaurants. ✉ *Downtown Bluffton, May River Rd. and Calhoun St., Bluffton* ☎ *843/706–4500* 🌐 *www.oldtownbluffton.com.*

Shelter Cove Towne Centre

SHOPPING CENTERS/MALLS | FAMILY | This sprawling, bikeable complex is anchored by chains like Belk and Talbots, but is also home to charming local spots like Spartina 449 and the Palmetto Running Company. There's also a Kroger grocery store, several restaurants and bars, and a barre studio. An extra bonus is its location next to Shelter Cove Community Park, a spacious outdoor area that offers beautiful marsh views. ✉ *40 Shelter Cove La., Mid-Island* ☎ *843/686–3090* 🌐 *www.sheltercovetownecentre.com.*

Shops at Sea Pines Center

SHOPPING CENTERS/MALLS | Clothing, fine gifts and jewelry, and a selection of local crafts and antiques can be found at this quaint open-air shopping center located in the Sea Pines Resort. ✉ *71 Lighthouse Rd., South End* ☎ *843/363–6800* 🌐 *www.theshopsatseapinescenter.com.*

South Beach Marina Village

SHOPPING CENTERS/MALLS | FAMILY | Built to resemble a New England fishing village, this quaint area in the Sea Pines Resort is home to the Salty Dog Cafe and two stores selling signature Salty Dog T-shirts and a selection of other souvenirs and logo-ed items. There are several other little shops in South Beach, in addition to an ice cream spot and seafood restaurants. ✉ *South Beach Marina Village, 232 S. Sea Pines Dr., South End.*

Tanger Outlets

OUTLET/DISCOUNT STORES | FAMILY | There are two separate sections to this popular shopping center: Tanger Outlet I has more than 40 upscale stores, as well as eateries like Olive Garden, Panera Bread, and Longhorn Steakhouse. Tanger Outlet II has Banana Republic, the Gap, and Nike, along with 60 other stores that offer great discounts for shoppers. ✉ *1414 Fording Island Rd., Bluffton* ☎ *843/837–5410, 866/665–8679* 🌐 *www.tangeroutlet.com/hiltonhead.*

The Village at Wexford

SHOPPING CENTERS/MALLS | FAMILY | Upscale shops, including Lilly Pulitzer and Le Cookery, as well as several fine-dining restaurants can be found in this established shopping area. There are also some unique gift shops and luxe clothing stores, such as Currents, Evelyn & Arthur, Island Child, and Teagues Men's Clothing. ✉ *1000 William Hilton Pkwy., Hilton Head Island* 🌐 *www.villageatwexford.com.*

Activities

Hilton Head Island is a mecca for the sports enthusiast and for those who just want a relaxing walk or bike ride on the beach. There are 12 miles of beaches, 24 public golf courses, more than 50 miles of public bike paths, and more than 300 tennis courts. There's also tons of water sports, including kayaking and canoeing, parasailing, fishing, sailing, and much more.

BIKING

More than 50 miles of public paths crisscross Hilton Head Island, and pedaling is popular along the firmly packed beach. The island keeps adding more to the boardwalk network as visitors are using it and because it's such a safe alternative for kids. Bikes with wide tires are a must if you want to ride on the beach. They can save you a spill should you hit loose sand on the trails. Keep in mind when crossing streets that, in South Carolina, vehicles have the right-of-way. **■ TIP→ For a map of trails, visit www.hiltonheadislandsc.gov.**

Bicycles from beach cruisers to mountain bikes to tandem bikes can be rented either at bike stores or at most hotels and resorts. Many can be delivered to your hotel, along with helmets, baskets, locks, child carriers, and whatever else you might need.

Hilton Head Bicycle Company

BICYCLING | FAMILY | This local outfit rents bicycles, helmets, bike trailers, and adult tricycles. ✉ *112 Arrow Rd., South End* ☎ *843/686–6888, 800/995–4319* 🌐 *www.hiltonheadbicycle.com.*

Pedals Bicycles

BICYCLING | FAMILY | Rent beach bikes for adults and children, kiddy karts, jogging strollers, and mountain bikes at this local operation in business since 1981. ✉ *71 Pope Ave. A, South End* ☎ *888/699–1039* 🌐 *www.pedalsbicycles.com.*

South Beach Bike Rentals

BICYCLING | FAMILY | Rent bikes, helmets, tandems, and adult tricycles at this spot in the Sea Pines Resort. ✉ *South Beach Marina, 230 S. Sea Pines Dr., Sea Pines, South End* ☎ *843/671–2453* 🌐 *www.south-beach-cycles.com.*

CANOEING AND KAYAKING

This is one of the most delightful ways to commune with nature on this commercial but physically beautiful island. Paddle through the creeks and estuaries and try to keep up with the dolphins.

★ Outside Hilton Head

BOATING | FAMILY | Boats, canoes, kayaks, and paddleboards are available for rent from this local outfitter that has set the standard for outdoor adventures in the Lowcountry for decades. Outside Hilton Head also offers nature tours, surf camps, tubing, and dolphin-watching excursions as well as private charters

Biking is popular on the hard-packed sand at low tide.

and activities for kids and families. ✉ *Shelter Cove Marina, 50 Shelter Cove La., Mid-Island* ☎ *843/686–6996* 🌐 *www.outsidehiltonhead.com.*

FISHING

Although anglers can fish in these waters year-round, in April things start to crank up and in May most boats are heavily booked. May is the season for cobia, especially in Port Royal Sound. In the Gulf Stream you can hook king mackerel, tuna, wahoo, and mahimahi. ■ **TIP→ A fishing license is necessary if you are fishing from a beach, dock, or pier. They are $11 for 14 days. Licenses aren't necessary on charter fishing boats because they already have their licenses.**

Bay Runner Fishing Charters

FISHING | **FAMILY** | With more than four decades of experience fishing these waters, Captain Miles Altman takes anglers out for deep-sea fishing trips lasting three to eight hours. Evening shark trips are offered May to August. ✉ *Shelter Cove Marina, 1 Shelter Cove La., Mid-Island* ☎ *843/290–6955* 🌐 *www.bayrunnerfishinghiltonhead.com.*

Bulldog Fishing Charters

FISHING | **FAMILY** | Captain Christiaan offers his guests 4-, 6-, 8-, and 10-hour fishing tours on his 32-foot boat, the *Bulldog.* ✉ *1 Hudson Rd., departs from docks at Hudson's Seafood House on the Docks, North End* ☎ *843/422–0887* 🌐 *bulldog-fishingcharters.com.*

Capt. Hook Party Fishing Boat

FISHING | **FAMILY** | For those looking for a fun time out on the water with friends and family, deep-sea fishing tours are available on this large party boat. Public and private offshore fishing charters are also available. The friendly crew can teach kids how to bait hooks and reel in fish. ✉ *Shelter Cove Marina, 1 Shelter Cove La., Mid-Island* ☎ *843/785–1700* 🌐 *www.captainhookhiltonhead.com.*

Fishin' Coach Charters

FISHING | **FAMILY** | Captain Dan Utley offers a variety of inshore fishing tours on his 22-foot boat to catch redfish and other species year-round. ✉ *C.C. Haigh Jr. Boat Landing, 2 William Hilton Pkwy., North End* ☎ *843/368–2126* 🌐 *www.fishincoach.com.*

Hilton Head Charter Fishing
FISHING | FAMILY | Captain Jeff Kline offers offshore, sport-fishing adventure trips and four-hour family trips on a trio of 30-plus-foot boats, the *Gullah Gal, True Grits,* and *Honey B.* ✉ *Shelter Cove Marina, 1 Shelter Cove La., Mid-Island* ☎ *843/422–3430* 🌐 *www.hiltonheadislandcharterfishing.com.*

***Integrity* Charters**
FISHING | FAMILY | The 38-foot Hatteras Sportfisher charter boat *Integrity* offers offshore and near-shore fishing expeditions with U.S. Coast Guard licensed Master Captain Mike Russo. ✉ *Broad Creek Marina, 18 Simmons Rd., South End* ☎ *843/422–1221* 🌐 *www.integritycharterfishing.com.*

Palmetto Lagoon Charters
FISHING | FAMILY | Captain Trent Malphrus takes groups for half- or full-day excursions to the region's placid saltwater lagoons. Redfish, bluefish, flounder, and black drum are some of the most common trophy fish. ✉ *Shelter Cove Marina, 1 Shelter Cove La., Mid-Island* ☎ *843/301–4634* 🌐 *www.palmettolagooncharters.com.*

Stray Cat Charters
FISHING | FAMILY | Whether you want to fish inshore or go offshore into the deep blue to catch fish such as cobia and snapper, Captain Jim Clark offers options for charters on his 27-foot catamaran, *The Stray Cat.* ✉ *2 Hudson Rd., North End* ☎ *843/683–5427* 🌐 *www.straycatcharter.com.*

GOLF

Hilton Head is nicknamed "Golf Island" for good reason: the island itself has 24 championship courses (public, semiprivate, and private), and the outlying area has 16 more. Each offers its own packages, some of which are great deals. Almost all charge the highest greens fees in the morning and lower fees as the day goes on. Lower rates can also be found in the hot summer months. It's essential to book tee times in advance, especially in the busy spring and fall months; resort guests and club members get first choices. Most courses can be described as casual-classy, so you will have to adhere to certain rules of the greens. **■ TIP→ The dress code on island golf courses does not permit blue jeans, gym shorts, or jogging shorts. Men's shirts must have collars.**

★ The RBC Heritage PGA Tour Golf Tournament
GOLF | The most internationally famed golf event on Hilton Head Island is the RBC Heritage presented by Boeing, held mid-April at Harbour Town Golf Links. For more than 50 years, this PGA tournament has drawn flocks of fans and spectators to the island for a weeklong celebration of golf and tradition. ✉ *The Sea Pines Resort, 2 Lighthouse La., South End* 🌐 *www.rbcheritage.com.*

GOLF COURSES

Arthur Hills and Robert Cupp Courses at Palmetto Hall
GOLF | There are two prestigious courses at the Palmetto Hall Country Club: Arthur Hills and Robert Cupp. Arthur Hills is a player favorite, with its trademark undulating fairways punctuated with lagoons and lined with moss-draped oaks and towering pines. Robert Cupp is a very challenging course, but is great for the higher handicappers as well. ✉ *Palmetto Hall, 108 Fort Howell Dr., North End* ☎ *843/342–2582* 🌐 *www.palmettohallcc.com* 💳 *$99* 🏌 *Arthur Hills: 18 holes, 6257 yards, par 72. Robert Cupp: 18 holes, 6025 yards, par 72* ✍ *Reservations essential.*

Country Club of Hilton Head
GOLF | Although it's part of a country club, the semiprivate course is open for public play. A well-kept secret, it's rarely too crowded. This 18-hole Rees

Golden Bear Golf Club at upscale Indigo Run was designed by Jack Nicklaus.

Jones–designed course is a more casual environment than many of the other golf courses on Hilton Head. ✉ *Hilton Head Plantation, 70 Skull Creek Dr., North End* ☎ *843/681–2582* 🌐 *www.clubcorp.com/Clubs/Country-Club-of-Hilton-Head* 🎫 *$105* 🏌 *18 holes, 6543 yards, par 72.*

Golden Bear Golf Club at Indigo Run

GOLF | Located in the upscale Indigo Run community, Golden Bear Golf Club was designed by golf legend Jack Nicklaus. The course's natural woodlands setting offers easygoing rounds. It requires more thought than muscle, yet you will have to earn every par you make. Though fairways are generous, you may end up with a lagoon looming smack ahead of the green on the approach shot. ✉ *Indigo Run, 72 Golden Bear Way, North End* ☎ *843/689–2200* 🌐 *www.clubcorp.com/Clubs/Golden-Bear-Golf-Club-at-Indigo-Run* 🎫 *$99* 🏌 *18 holes, 6643 yards, par 72.*

★ Harbour Town Golf Links

GOLF | Considered by many golfers to be one of those must-play-before-you-die courses, Harbour Town Golf Links is extremely well-known because it has hosted the RBC Heritage PGA Golf Tournament every spring for more than 50 years. Designed by Pete Dye, the layout is reminiscent of Scottish courses of old. The 18th hole lies along the marsh and waterway, driving toward the Harbour Town Lighthouse. The Sea Pines Resort also has two other incredible courses—Heron Point by Pete Dye and Atlantic Dunes by Davis Love III—that make this a great destination for any golfer. ✉ *The Sea Pines Resort, 11 Lighthouse La., South End* ☎ *843/842–8484, 800/732–7463 to book tee times* 🌐 *seapines.com/golf* 🎫 *$350* 🏌 *18 holes, 7099 yards, par 71* ✍ *Reservations essential.*

★ Robert Trent Jones at Palmetto Dunes

GOLF | One of the island's most popular layouts, this course's beauty and character are accentuated by the 10th hole, a par 5 that offers a panoramic view of the ocean (one of only two on the entire island). There are two other golf courses located within the Palmetto Dunes Oceanfront Resort (George Fazio course and Arthur Hills course) and packages are available to play all three. ✉ *Palmetto Dunes Oceanfront Resort, 7 Robert Trent Jones La., North End* ☎ *888/909–9566* 🌐 *www.palmettodunes.com* 🎫 *$105* 🏌 *18 holes, 6570 yards, par 72* ✍ *Reservations essential.*

GOLF SCHOOLS

The Golf Learning Center at The Sea Pines Resort

GOLF | The well-regarded golf academy offers hourly private lessons by PGA-trained professionals and one- to three-day clinics to help you perfect your game. ✉ *The Sea Pines Resort, 100 N. Sea Pines Dr., South End* ☎ *843/785–4540* 🌐 *www.golfacademy.net.*

Palmetto Dunes Golf Academy

GOLF | There's something for golfers of all ages at this academy: instructional videos, daily clinics, and multiday schools. Lessons are offered for ages three and up, and there are special programs for women. Free demonstrations are held with Doug Weaver, former PGA Tour pro and director of instruction for the academy. Take advantage of the free swing evaluation and club-fitting. ✉ *Palmetto Dunes Oceanfront Resort, 7 Trent Jones La., Mid-Island* ☎ *888/909–9566 general info, 866/455-6890 private lessons* 🌐 *www.palmettodunes.com.*

BLUFFTON GOLF COURSES

There are several beautiful golf courses in Bluffton, which is just on the other side of the bridges to Hilton Head Island. These courses are very popular with locals and can often be cheaper to play than the courses on Hilton Head.

Crescent Pointe

GOLF | An Arnold Palmer Signature Course, Crescent Pointe is fairly tough, with somewhat narrow fairways and rolling terrain. There are numerous sand traps, ponds, and lagoons that make for demanding yet fun holes. Some of the par 3s are particularly challenging. The scenery is magnificent, with large live oaks, pine-tree stands, and rolling fairways. Additionally, several holes have spectacular marsh views. ✉ *Crescent Pointe, 1 Crescent Pointe, Bluffton* ☎ *843/706–2600* 🌐 *www.hallmarkgolf.com* 🎫 *From $55* 🏌 *18 holes, 6773 yards, par 71.*

Eagle's Pointe Golf Club

GOLF | This Davis Love III–designed course is one of the area's most playable, thanks to its spacious fairways and large greens. There are quite a few bunkers and lagoons throughout the course, which winds through a natural woodlands setting that attracts an abundance of wildlife. ✉ *Eagle's Pointe, 1 Eagle's Pointe Dr., Bluffton* ☎ *843/757–5900* 🌐 *www.hallmarkgolf.com/eagles-pointe* 🎫 *$59* 🏌 *18 holes, 6780 yards, par 71.*

The May River Golf Club

GOLF | This 18-hole Jack Nicklaus signature course at the Montage Palmetto Bluff resort has several holes along the banks of the scenic May River and will challenge all skill levels. The greens are Champion Bermuda grass and the fairways are covered by Paspalum, the latest eco-friendly turf. Caddy service is always required. No carts are allowed earlier than 9 am to encourage walking. ✉ *Palmetto Bluff, 477 Mount Pelia Rd., Bluffton* ☎ *855/377–3198* 🌐 *www.montagehotels.com/palmettobluff/experiences/golf* 🎫 *$315* 🏌 *18 holes, 7171 yards, par 72* ✍ *Reservations essential.*

Old South Golf Links

GOLF | There are many scenic holes overlooking marshes and the intracoastal waterway at this Clyde Johnson–designed course. It's a public course, but that hasn't stopped it from winning awards. It's reasonably priced, just over the bridge from Hilton Head, and reservations are recommended. ✉ *50*

Buckingham Plantation Dr., Bluffton ☎ *843/785–5353* 🌐 *www.oldsouthgolf.com* 💵 *$70* ⛳ *18 holes, 6772 yards, par 72.*

PARASAILING

For those looking for a bird's-eye view of Hilton Head, it doesn't get better than parasailing. Newcomers will get a lesson in safety before taking off. Parasailers are then strapped into a harness, and as the boat takes off, the parasailer is lifted about 500 feet into the sky.

★ H20 Sports

HANG GLIDING/PARAGLIDING/PARASAILING | **FAMILY** | Check out views up to 25 miles in all directions while parasailing with this popular outdoor adventure company located out of the Harbour Town Marina in the Sea Pines Resort. They also offer sailing, kayak, and SUP (stand-up paddleboard) tours, Jet Ski and boat rentals, and a private water taxi to Daufuskie Island. Nature lovers will enjoy dolphin or alligator tours with experienced local guides. ✉ *Harbour Town Marina, 149 Lighthouse Rd., South End* ☎ *843/671–4386* 🌐 *www.h2osports.com.*

Sky Pirate Parasail

HANG GLIDING/PARAGLIDING/PARASAILING | **FAMILY** | Glide 500 feet in the air over the water and get an aerial view of the Lowcountry on an adventure out of Broad Creek Marina. The outfitter also offers boat rentals, tubing trips, water skiing, and paddleboard rentals as well as dolphin eco-cruises. ✉ *Broad Creek Marina, 18 Simmons Rd., Mid-Island* ☎ *843/842–2566* 🌐 *www.skypirateparasail.com.*

SPAS

Spa visits have become a recognized activity on the island, and for some people they are as popular as golf and tennis. In fact, spas have become one of the top leisure-time destinations, particularly for "golf widows." And this popularity extends to the men as well; previously spa-shy guys have come around, enticed by couples massage, deep-tissue sports massage, and even the pleasures of the manicure and pedicure.

There are East Indian–influenced therapies, hot-stone massage, Hungarian organic facials—the treatments span the globe. Do your research, go online, and call or stop by the various spas and ask the locals their favorites. The therapists island-wide are noteworthy for their training, certifications, and expertise.

FACES DaySpa

FITNESS/HEALTH CLUBS | This local institution has been pampering loyal clients for more than three decades, thanks to body therapists, stylists, and cosmetologists who really know their stuff. Choose from fabulous facials, enjoy a manicure and pedicure, or have a relaxing massage treatment in a facility that is committed to providing a safe and clean environment for all guests and staff. ✉ *The Village at Wexford, 1000 William Hilton Pkwy., D1, South End* ☎ *843/785–3075* 🌐 *www.facesdayspa.com.*

Heavenly Spa by Westin

FITNESS/HEALTH CLUBS | As part of the oceanfront Westin Resort, this luxury spa provides a range of unique treatments designed to rejuvenate the body and renew your spirit. From massages to facials to salon services, the Heavenly Spa lives up to its name by offering guests a chance to relax and unwind. A variety of specials and seasonal packages are available. ✉ *The Westin Hilton Head Island Resort & Spa, 2 Grasslawn Ave., Port Royal Plantation, North End* ☎ *843/681–1019* 🌐 *www.westinhiltonheadspa.com.*

Spa Montage Palmetto Bluff

FITNESS/HEALTH CLUBS | Dubbed the "celebrity spa" by locals, this two-story facility is the ultimate pampering palace with treatments such as body wraps, facials, sensual soaks, and couples massages. Located at Montage Palmetto Bluff in Bluffton, the spa also offers a variety of other services, including pedicures, manicures, facials and other skin treatments, and a hair salon. Be sure to book appointments in advance. ✉ *Montage Palmetto Bluff, 477 Mount Pelia Rd., Bluffton* ☎ *855/264–8705* 🌐 *www.montagehotels.com/palmettobluff/spa.*

TENNIS

Tennis comes in at a close second as the island's premier sport after golf. The island has more than 300 courts so you'll be spoiled for choice. ■**TIP→ Spring and fall are the peak seasons for cooler play, with numerous tennis packages available at the resorts and through the schools.**

★ Palmetto Dunes Tennis and Pickleball Center

TENNIS | **FAMILY** | Ranked among the best in the world, this facility at the Palmetto Dunes Oceanfront Resort has 19 clay tennis courts (four of which are lighted for night play) and 24 dedicated pickleball courts. There are lessons geared to players of every skill level given by enthusiastic staffers. ✉ *Palmetto Dunes Oceanfront Resort, 6 Trent Jones La., Mid-Island* ☎ *888/879–2053* 🌐 *www.palmettodunes.com.*

Port Royal Racquet Club

TENNIS | **FAMILY** | Magnolia trees dot the grounds of the Port Royal Racquet Club, which has eight clay courts and two pickleball courts. Located in the Port Royal private community, this award-winning tennis complex attracts guests with its professional staff, stadium seating, and tournament play. ✉ *Port Royal Plantation, 15 Wimbledon Court, Mid-Island* ☎ *843/686–8803* 🌐 *www.hiltonheadgolf.net/port-royal/.*

Sea Pines Racquet Club

TENNIS | **FAMILY** | This award-winning club has 21 clay courts, as well as a pro shop and instructional programs, including weekend clinics with Wimbledon champ, Stan Smith. Guests of Sea Pines receive two hours of complimentary court time each day. ✉ *The Sea Pines Resort, 5 Lighthouse La., South End* ☎ *843/363–4495* 🌐 *seapines.com/tennis.*

Van Der Meer Tennis Center

TENNIS | Recognized for its tennis instruction for players of all ages and skill levels, this highly rated facility has 17 hard courts, 4 of which are covered and lighted for night play. The center is the main training location for students attending the Van Der Meer Tennis Academy. In a separate location within Shipyard, the Van Der Meer Shipyard Racquet Club has 13 Har-Tru courts, 7 hard courts, 3 indoor courts, and a pro shop with a certified racquet stringer. ✉ *19 DeAllyon Ave., South End* ☎ *843/785–8388* 🌐 *www.vandermeertennis.com.*

ZIPLINE TOURS

ZipLine Hilton Head

ZIP LINING | **FAMILY** | Take a thrilling tour on a zipline over ponds and marshes and past towering oaks and pines. This company offers eight ziplines, two suspended sky bridges, and a dual-cable racing zipline. ✉ *33 Broad Creek Marina Way, Mid-Island* ☎ *843/682–6000* 🌐 *ziplinehiltonhead.com.*

Beaufort

38 miles north of Hilton Head via U.S. 278 and Rte. 170; 70 miles southwest of Charleston via U.S. 17 and U.S. 21.

Charming homes and churches grace this old town on Port Royal Island. Come here on a day trip from Hilton Head, Savannah, or Charleston, or to spend a quiet weekend at a B&B while you shop and stroll through the historic district. Beaufort continues to gain recognition as an art town and supports a large number of galleries for its diminutive size. Visitors are drawn equally to the town's artsy scene and to the area's water-sports possibilities. The annual Beaufort Water Festival, which takes place over 10 days in July, is the premier event. For a calendar

Pat Conroy's Beaufort Legacy

Many fans of the late author Pat Conroy consider Beaufort his town because of his autobiographical novel *The Great Santini*, which was set here. He, too, considered it home base: "We moved to Beaufort when I was 15. We had moved 23 times. (My father was in the Marines.) I told my mother, 'I need a home.' Her wise reply was: 'Well, maybe it will be Beaufort.' And so it has been. I have stuck to this poor town like an old barnacle. I moved away, but I came running back in 1993."

Conroy lived on Fripp Island with his wife, author Cassandra King, for many years before he passed away in 2016. In order to honor his memory and the important role he played in introducing the Lowcountry to so many readers, the Pat Conroy Literary Center was founded in Beaufort. The nonprofit organization holds an annual literary festival with writing workshops and events, and also offers in-person tours at its downtown location. Call ☎ *843/379–7025* or visit 🌐 *www.patconroyliterarycenter.org* for more information about the center.

of Beaufort's annual events, check out 🌐 *www.beaufortsc.org*.

More and more transplants have decided to spend the rest of their lives here, drawn to Beaufort's small-town charms, and the area is burgeoning. A truly Southern town, its picturesque backdrops have lured filmmakers here to shoot *The Big Chill, The Prince of Tides,* and *The Great Santini,* the last two being Hollywood adaptations of best-selling books by the late author Pat Conroy. Conroy waxed poetic about the Lowcountry and called the Beaufort area home.

To support Beaufort's growing status as a tourist destination, it has doubled the number of hotels in recent years. Military events like the frequent graduations (traditionally Wednesday and Thursday) at the marine base on Parris Island tie up rooms.

GETTING HERE AND AROUND

Beaufort is 25 miles east of Interstate 95, on U.S. 21. The only way to get here is by private car or Greyhound bus.

TOURS

SouthurnRose Buggy Tours

CARRIAGE TOURS | FAMILY | These 50-minute horse-drawn carriage tours leave from Waterfront Park and offer a historical perspective of downtown Beaufort that's a great orientation to the charming town. Van and walking tours are also available. ✉ *1002 Bay St., Downtown Historic District* ☎ *843/524–2900* 🌐 *www.southurnrose.com.*

ESSENTIALS

Well-maintained public restrooms are available at the Beaufort Visitors Center. You can't miss this former arsenal; a crenellated, fortlike structure, it is now beautifully restored and painted ocher.

The Beaufort County Black Chamber of Commerce (🌐 *www.bcbcc.org*) puts out an African American visitor's guide, which takes in the surrounding Lowcountry. The Beaufort Visitors Center gives out copies.

VISITOR INFORMATION Beaufort Visitors Center. ✉ *713 Craven St., Beaufort* ☎ *843/525–8500* 🌐 *www.beaufortsc.org.*

Sights

Barefoot Farms

FARM/RANCH | Pull over for boiled peanuts, a jar of gumbo or strawberry jam, or perfect watermelons at this roadside stand and working farm on St. Helena Island. ✉ *939 Sea Island Pkwy., St. Helena Island* ☎ *843/838–7421.*

Beaufort National Cemetery

CEMETERY | Listed on the National Register of Historic Places in 1997, Beaufort National Cemetery is the final resting spot of both Union and Confederate soldiers from the Civil War. The peaceful, well-maintained grounds make this a nice spot to commemorate the dead. ✉ *1601 Boundary St., Beaufort* ☎ *843/524–3925* 🌐 *www.cem.va.gov/cems/nchp/beaufort.asp.*

★ Henry C. Chambers Waterfront Park

CITY PARK | **FAMILY** | Located off Bay Street in downtown Beaufort, Waterfront Park represents the heart of this charming coastal town. It's a great place to stroll along the river walk and enjoy the hanging bench swings. Parents enjoy the spacious park where kids can run in the grass or play on the enclosed playground with views of the Richard V. Woods swing bridge that crosses the Beaufort River. Trendy restaurants and bars overlook these seven beautifully landscaped acres that also feature a pavilion, stage, and historical markers and lead into the marina. ✉ *1006 Bay St., Beaufort* ☎ *843/525–7070* 🌐 *www.cityofbeaufort.org.*

Highway 21 Drive In

ARTS VENUE | **FAMILY** | An authentic drive-in experience, Highway 21 Drive In is a charming throwback that's fun for the whole family. Showing a variety of classic movies and recent hits, the family-owned facility has been attracting crowds for nearly 25 years. The old-school concessions stand has everything from popcorn and candy to burgers and corn dogs as well as funnel cakes and root beer floats. Even the ticket prices are a nod to another time, and include double features on two screens. It's totally worth the trip for this slice of nostalgia to see "where the stars come out at night." ✉ *55 Parker Rd., Beaufort* ☎ *843/846–4500* 🌐 *www.hwy21drivein.com* 🎫 *$7.*

John Mark Verdier House

HOUSE | Built and maintained by the forced labor of enslaved people, this 1804 Federal-style mansion has been restored and furnished as it would have been prior to a visit by Marquis de Lafayette in 1825. It was the headquarters for Union forces during the Civil War. The house museum also features historical photographs, a diorama of Bay Street in 1863, and an exhibit about Robert Smalls, the first African American U.S. congressman. Run by Historic Beaufort Foundation, the museum offers docent-guided tours. ✉ *801 Bay St., Downtown Historic District* ☎ *843/379–6335* 🌐 *historicbeaufort.org* ⏲ *Closed Sun.*

Kazoobie Kazoo Factory

LOCAL INTEREST | **FAMILY** | Taking a tour of this unique kazoo factory is a fun and informative experience; you even get to make your own kazoo at the end. ✉ *12 John Galt Rd., Beaufort* ☎ *843/982–6387* 🌐 *www.thekazoofactory.com* 🎫 *$9* ⏲ *Closed weekends.*

Parish Church of St. Helena

RELIGIOUS SITE | This 1724 church (founded in 1712) was turned into a hospital during the Civil War, and gravestones were brought inside to serve as operating tables. While on church grounds, stroll the peaceful cemetery and read the fascinating inscriptions. ✉ *505 Church St., Beaufort* ☎ *843/522–1712* 🌐 *www.sthelenas1712.org.*

★ St. Helena Island

ISLAND | Between Beaufort and Fripp Island lies St. Helena Island, a sizeable sea island that is less commercial than the other islands in the area and home to a tight-knit Gullah community. The highlight here is Penn Center, a historic school and museum that was the first

The World of Gullah

In the Lowcountry, Gullah refers to several things: a language, a people, and a culture. Gullah (the word itself is believed to be derived from *Angola*), an English-based dialect rooted in African languages, is the unique language, more than 300 years old, of the African Americans of the Sea Islands of South Carolina and Georgia. Most locally born African Americans of the area can understand, if not speak, Gullah.

Gullah History

Descended from thousands of enslaved people who were brought here by planters in the Carolinas during the 18th century, the Gullah have maintained not only their dialect but also their heritage. Much of Gullah culture traces back to the African rice-coast culture and survives today in the art forms and skills, including sweetgrass basketmaking, of Sea Islanders. During the colonial period, when rice was king, Africans from the West African rice kingdoms drew high premiums as slaves. Those with basketmaking skills were extremely valuable because baskets were needed for agricultural and household use. Made by hand, sweetgrass baskets are intricate coils of marsh grass with a sweet, haylike aroma.

Gullah Food

Nowhere is Gullah culture more evident than in the foods of the region. Rice appears at nearly every meal—Africans taught planters how to grow rice and how to cook and serve it as well. Lowcountry dishes use okra, peanuts, benne (a word of African origin for sesame seeds), field peas, and hot peppers. Gullah food reflects the bounty of the islands: shrimp, crabs, oysters, fish, and such vegetables as greens, tomatoes, and corn. Many dishes are prepared in one pot, a method similar to the stewpot cooking of West Africa.

Gullah Today

On St. Helena Island, near Beaufort, Penn Center is the unofficial Gullah headquarters, preserving the culture and developing opportunities for Gullahs. In 1852 the first school for freed slaves was established at Penn Center. You can delve into the culture further at the York W. Bailey Museum.

On St. Helena, many Gullahs still go shrimping with hand-tied nets, harvest oysters, and grow their own vegetables. Nearby on Daufuskie Island, as well as on Edisto, Wadmalaw, and John's Islands near Charleston, you can find Gullah communities. A famous Gullah proverb says, "*If oonuh ent kno weh oonuh dah gwine, oonuh should kno weh oonuh come f'um.*" Translation: "If you don't know where you're going, you should know where you've come from."

school for formerly enslaved people in 1862. Visitors can also see the Chapel of Ease ruins, go to Lands End and discover Fort Fremont Historical Park, or stop by roadside farms and local restaurants. ✉ *Rte. 21, St. Helena Island* 🌐 *www.beaufortsc.org/area/st.-helena-island.*

Beaches

★ Hunting Island State Park

BEACH—SIGHT | FAMILY | This state park located on a barrier island 18 miles southeast of Beaufort has 5,000 acres of rare maritime forest and 5 miles of public beaches—some which are dramatically eroding. The light sand beach decorated with driftwood and the subtropical vegetation is breathtaking; it almost feels like you're in Jurassic Park. You can kayak in the tranquil saltwater lagoon, stroll the 1,120-foot-long fishing pier, and go fishing or crabbing. For sweeping views, climb the 167 steps of the historic 1859 **Hunting Island Lighthouse .** Bikers and hikers can enjoy eight miles of trails. The nature center has exhibits, an aquarium, and tourist information. There is also a campground on the northern end that has 100 sites, but be sure to book in advance as these nearly oceanfront campsites fill up fast. **Amenities:** parking; toilets; grills. **Best for:** sunrise; swimming; walking. *2555 Sea Island Pkwy., St. Helena Island* *843/838–2011* *www.southcarolinaparks.com/hunting-island* *$8.*

Restaurants

Breakwater Restaurant & Bar

$$$ | **ECLECTIC** | This classy downtown restaurant offers small tasting plates such as tuna crudo and fried shrimp, as well as main dishes like lamb meat loaf and filet mignon with a truffle demi-glace. The presentation is as contemporary as the decor. **Known for:** contemporary approach to Lowcountry cuisine; elegant atmosphere; local loyalty. *Average main: $25* *203 Carteret St., Downtown Historic District* *843/379–0052* *www.breakwatersc.com* *Closed Sun.*

Johnson Creek Tavern

$$ | **AMERICAN** | There are times when you just want a cold one accompanied by some raw oysters. If that's the case, head out to Harbor Island to this relaxed hangout with outside seating and lovely marsh views. **Known for:** friendly atmosphere; fresh seafood; cheap happy hour specials. *Average main: $19* *2141 Sea Island Pkwy., Harbor Island* *843/838–4166* *www.johnsoncreektavern.com.*

★ Plums

$ | **AMERICAN** | This popular local eatery still uses family recipes for its soups, crab-cake sandwiches, and curried chicken salad. Open daily for breakfast and lunch, Plums is the perfect spot to enjoy a meal outside and to take in the beautiful views of downtown Beaufort. **Known for:** tasty raw bar; inventive burgers and sandwiches for lunch; great location on Waterfront Park. *Average main: $10* *904 Bay St., Downtown Historic District* *843/525–1946* *www.plumsrestaurant.com.*

Saltus River Grill

$$$$ | **SEAFOOD** | This upscale restaurant wins over diners with its sailing motifs, great cocktails, and modern Southern menu. Take in the sunset and a plate of seared sea scallops from the gorgeous outdoor seating area overlooking the waterfront park. **Known for:** signature crab bisque; raw bar with a tempting array of oysters and sushi; thoughtful wine list. *Average main: $32* *802 Bay St., Downtown Historic District* *843/379–3474* *www.saltusrivergrill.com* *No lunch.*

Hotels

★ Beaufort Inn

$$$ | **B&B/INN** | This 1890s Victorian inn charms with its handsome gables and wraparound verandas. **Pros:** in the heart of the historic district; beautifully landscaped space; breakfast is complimentary at three nearby restaurants. **Cons:** atmosphere in the main building may feel too dated for those seeking a more contemporary hotel; no water views; can fill up with wedding parties during spring. *Rooms from: $209* *809 Port Republic St., Downtown Historic District* *843/379–4667* *www.beaufortinn.com* *48 rooms* *Free breakfast.*

Beaulieu House

$$$ | **B&B/INN** | From the French for "beautiful place," this waterfront B&B on nearby Cat Island is a quiet, relaxing inn with airy rooms decorated in Caribbean colors. **Pros:** great views; lots of privacy; short drive to Beaufort's historic district. **Cons:** thin walls; hot water can be a problem; a bit off-the-beaten path. *Rooms from: $205 ✉ 3 Sheffield Ct., Beaufort ☎ 843/770–0303 ⊕ beaulieuhouse.com 5 rooms No meals.*

Best Western Sea Island Inn

$$ | **HOTEL** | **FAMILY** | This well-maintained hotel in the heart of the historic district puts you within walking distance of many shops and restaurants. **Pros:** only swimming pool in downtown Beaufort; directly across from marina and an easy walk to art galleries and restaurants; breakfast included. **Cons:** air-conditioning is loud in some rooms; breakfast room can be noisy; lacks the charm of nearby B&B alternatives. *Rooms from: $179 ✉ 1015 Bay St., Beaufort ☎ 843/522–2090 ⊕ www.sea-island-inn.com 43 rooms Free breakfast.*

City Loft Hotel

$$ | **HOTEL** | This 1960s-era motel was cleverly transformed by its hip owners to reflect their minimalist style. **Pros:** stylish decor; use of the adjacent gym; central location. **Cons:** the sliding Asian screen that separates the bathroom doesn't offer full privacy; no lobby or public spaces; not as charming as a B&B. *Rooms from: $189 ✉ 301 Carteret St., Downtown Historic District ☎ 843/379–5638 ⊕ www.cityloftthotel.com 22 rooms No meals.*

Cuthbert House Inn

$$$ | **B&B/INN** | This 1790 home is filled with 18th- and 19th-century heirlooms and retains the original Federal fireplaces and crown and rope molding. **Pros:** owners are accommodating; complimentary wine and hors d'oeuvres service; great walk-about location. **Cons:** history as a home to slaveholders; stairs creak; some furnishings are a bit busy. *Rooms from: $225 ✉ 1203 Bay St., Downtown Historic District ☎ 843/521–1315 ⊕ www.cuthberthouseinn.com 10 rooms Free breakfast.*

Fripp Island Golf & Beach Resort

$$$$ | **RESORT** | **FAMILY** | On the island made famous in Pat Conroy's *Prince of Tides,* with 3½ miles of broad, white beach and unspoiled scenery, this private resort has long been known as a safe haven where kids are allowed to roam free, go crabbing at low tide, bike the trails, and swim. **Pros:** fun for all ages; the beachfront Sandbar has great frozen drinks and live music; two golf courses: Ocean Creek and Ocean Point. **Cons:** far from Beaufort; some dated decor; could use another restaurant with contemporary cuisine. *Rooms from: $374 ✉ 1 Tarpon Blvd., Fripp Island ✣ 19 miles south of Beaufort ☎ 843/838–1558 ⊕ www.frippislandresort.com 180 rentals No meals.*

Two Suns Inn

$$ | **B&B/INN** | With its unobstructed bay views and wraparound veranda complete with porch swing, this historic home—built in 1917 by an immigrant Lithuanian merchant—offers a distinctive Beaufort experience. **Pros:** most appealing is the Charleston room, with its own screened porch and water views; truly peaceful ambience; breakfast prepared by the French owners. **Cons:** decor is dated; a bike ride or short drive downtown; third-floor skylight room is cheapest but least desirable. *Rooms from: $169 ✉ 1705 Bay St., Downtown Historic District ☎ 843/522–1122, 800/532–4244 ⊕ www.twosunsinn.com 6 rooms Free breakfast.*

Nightlife

Luther's Rare & Well Done

BARS/PUBS | A late-night waterfront hangout, Luther's is casual and fun, with a young crowd watching the big-screen TVs or listening to live music. There's also an appealing lunch and dinner menu with favorites such as Brewsky's burger and teriyaki wings. The decor features exposed brick, pine paneling, old-fashioned posters on the walls, a great bar area, and plenty of outdoor seating. ✉ *910 Bay St., Downtown Historic District* ☎ *843/521–1888.*

Shopping

Lulu Burgess

JEWELRY/ACCESSORIES | This amazing little shop in downtown Beaufort is overflowing with colorful, quality items from funny cards and locally made jewelry to kitchen accessories and novelty goodies. Owner Nan Sutton's outgoing personality and eye for adorable gifts make shopping at Lulu Burgess a real treat. ✉ *917 Bay St., Beaufort* ☎ *843/524–5858* 🌐 *www.luluburgess.com.*

Rhett Gallery

ANTIQUES/COLLECTIBLES | This family-owned gallery sells Lowcountry art by four generations of the Rhetts, including remarkable wood carvings and watercolor paintings. The historic, two-story building also houses antique maps, books, and Audubon prints. ✉ *901 Bay St., Downtown Historic District* ☎ *843/524–3339* 🌐 *rhettgallery.com.*

Activities

BIKING

Beaufort looks different from two wheels. In town, traffic is moderate, and you can cruise along the waterfront and through the historic district. However, if you ride on the sidewalks or after dark without a headlight and a rear red reflector, you run the risk of a city fine of nearly $150. If you stopped for happy hour and come out as the light is fading, walk your bike back "home." Some inns lend or rent out bikes to guests, but alas, they may not be in great shape and usually were not the best even when new. ■ **TIP→ The Spanish Moss Trail is the perfect place to ride bikes.**

Lowcountry Bicycles

BICYCLING | FAMILY | If you want a decent set of wheels—or need yours fixed—this affordable shop is the hub of all things bike-related in Beaufort. ✉ *102 Sea Island Pkwy., Beaufort* ☎ *843/524–9585.*

Spanish Moss Trail

BICYCLING | FAMILY | Built along former railroad tracks, this trail is the Lowcountry's answer to the Rails to Trail movement. The nearly 10-mile trail (16 miles once it's eventually complete) currently connects Beaufort, Port Royal, and Burton. It's open to walkers, runners, bikers, fishers, skaters, and scooters, offering great water and marsh views and providing ample opportunities to view coastal wildlife and historic landmarks. The train depot trailhead offers parking and restrooms and is located not too far from downtown Beaufort. ■ **TIP→ The website offers a downloadable trail guide.** ✉ *Spanish Moss Trail Train Depot, Depot Rd., Beaufort* 🌐 *spanishmosstrail.com.*

BOATING

Beaufort is where the Ashepoo, Combahee, and Edisto Rivers form the A.C.E. Basin, a vast wilderness of marshes and tidal estuaries loaded with history. For sea kayaking, tourists meet at the designated launching areas for fully guided, two-hour tours.

Barefoot Bubba's

KAYAKING | FAMILY | This eclectic surf shop on the way to Hunting Island rents bikes, kayaks, paddleboards, and surfboards for kids and adults and will deliver them to vacationers on the surrounding islands. They also serve ice cream. A second location on Bay Street in downtown

Beaufort sells clothing and souvenirs. ✉ *2135 Sea Island Pkwy., Harbor Island* ☎ *843/541–3400* 🌐 *barefootbubbasurfshop.com.*

★ Beaufort Kayak Tours

TOUR—SPORTS | FAMILY | Tours are run by professional naturalists and certified historical guides, and are designed to go with the tides, not against them, so paddling isn't strenuous. The large cockpits in the kayaks make for easy accessibility and offer an up-close observation of the Lowcountry wilds. Tours depart from various landings in the area. ✉ *Beaufort* ☎ *843/525–0810* 🌐 *www.beaufortkayaktours.com* 💵 *$50.*

GOLF

Most golf courses are about a 10- to 20-minute scenic drive from Beaufort.

Dataw Island

GOLF | This upscale gated island community is home to two top-rated championship golf courses. Tom Fazio's Cotton Dike golf course features spectacular marsh views, while Arthur Hills's Morgan River course has ponds, marshes, wide-open fairways, and a lovely view of the river from the 14th hole. To play these private courses, contact Dataw Island ahead of time with your request. ✉ *100 Dataw Club Rd., Dataw Island* ✢ *6 miles east of Beaufort* ☎ *843/838–8216* 🌐 *www.dataw.com* 💵 *From $75* ⛳ *Cotton Dike: 18 holes, 6787 yards, par 72. Morgan River: 18 holes, 6657 yards, par 73.*

Fripp Island Golf & Beach Resort

GOLF | This resort has a pair of championship courses. Ocean Creek was designed by Davis Love III and has sweeping views of saltwater marshes, while Ocean Point Golf Links was designed by George Cobb and runs alongside the ocean for 10 of its 18 holes. Fripp Island has been designated a national wildlife refuge, so you'll see plenty of animals, particularly marsh deer and a host of migratory birds. Be sure to book your tee times in advance since Fripp is a private island. ✉ *300 Tarpon Blvd, Fripp Island* ☎ *843/838–1576* 🌐 *www.frippislandresort.com/golf* ⛳ *Ocean Creek: 18 holes, 6613 yards, par 71. Ocean Point: 18 holes, 6556 yards, par 72.*

Daufuskie Island

13 miles (approximately 45 minutes) from Hilton Head via ferry.

From Hilton Head you can take a 45-minute ferry ride to nearby Daufuskie Island, the setting for Pat Conroy's novel *The Water Is Wide,* which was made into the movie *Conrack.* The boat ride may very well be one of the highlights of your vacation. The Lowcountry beauty unfolds before you, as pristine and unspoiled as you can imagine. The island is in the Atlantic, nestled between Hilton Head and Savannah. Many visitors come just for the day to have lunch or dinner; kids might enjoy biking or horseback riding. On weekends, the tiki hut at Freeport Marina whirrs out frozen concoctions as a vocalist sings or a band plays reggae and rock and roll. The island also has acres of unspoiled beauty. On a bike, in a golf cart, or on horseback, you can easily explore the island. You will find remnants of churches, homes, and schools—some reminders of antebellum times. Guided tours include such sights as an 18th-century cemetery, former slave quarters, a "praise house," an 1886 African Baptist church, the schoolhouse where Pat Conroy taught, and the Haig Point Lighthouse. There are a number of small, artsy shops like the Iron Fish Gallery.

GETTING HERE AND AROUND

The only way to get to Daufuskie is by boat, as it is a bridgeless island. The public ferry departs from Broad Creek Marina on Hilton Head Island several times a day. On arrival, you can rent a golf cart (not a car) or bicycle or take a tour. Golf carts are the best way to get around on the island. Enjoy Daufuskie (🌐 *www.*

Did You Know?

Daufuskie Island can only be reached by boat or ferry. Once on the island, golf carts are the main mode of transportation.

enjoydaufuskie.com) offers golf cart rentals to tourists when they come to visit. If you are coming to Daufuskie Island for a multiday stay with luggage and/or groceries, and perhaps a dog, be absolutely certain that you allow a full hour to park and check in for the ferry, particularly on a busy summer weekend. Whether you are staying on island or just day-tripping, the ferry costs $25 round-trip. Usually the first two pieces of luggage are free, and then it is $10 apiece.

Freeport Marina, where the public ferry disembarks on Daufuskie Island, includes the Freeport General Store, a restaurant, overnight cabins, and more. A two-hour bus tour of the island by local historians will become a true travel memory. The ferry returns to Hilton Head Island on Tuesday night in time to watch the fireworks at Shelter Cove at sundown.

Live Oac, based on Hilton Head, is an owner-operated company that offers Lowcountry water adventures such as nature tours, fishing excursions, and dolphin cruises. On its first-class hurricane-deck boats you are sheltered from sun and rain; tours, usually private charters, are limited to six people. Captains are interpretive naturalist educators and U.S. Coast Guard–licensed.

TOUR CONTACTS SouthurnRose Buggy Tours. ✉ *1002 Bay St., Downtown Historic District* ☎ *843/524–2900* 🌐 *www.southurnrose.com.* **Tour Daufuskie.** ✉ *50 Melrose Landing Rd., Daufuskie Landing, Daufuskie Island* ☎ *843/842–9449* 🌐 *www.tourdaufuskie.com.*

Restaurants

Old Daufuskie Crab Company Restaurant

$$ | **SEAFOOD** | **FAMILY** | This outpost, with its rough-hewn tables facing the water, serves up Gullah-inspired fare with specialties such as Daufuskie deviled crab and chicken salad on buttery grilled rolls. Entrées include shrimp and local seafood, while the Lowcountry buffet features pulled pork, fried chicken, and sides like butter beans and potato salad. **Known for:** incredible sunsets; colorful bar; reggae and rock music. $ *Average main: $17* ✉ *Freeport Marina, 1 Cooper River Landing Rd., Daufuskie Island* ☎ *843/785–6652* 🌐 *www.daufuskiedifference.com/pages/restaurant.*

Hotels

Bloody Point Resort

$$$$ | **RENTAL** | This resort offers guests open beaches, tennis, golf carts, and a pool. **Pros:** spacious and private rooms; range of lodgings available; complimentary golf carts. **Cons:** very few restaurant options for a weeklong vacation; no direct public ferry service; 20-minute golf cart ride from Freeport Marina. $ *Rooms from: $475* ✉ *2302 Sandy La., Daufuskie Island* ☎ *843/341–3030* 🌐 *www.bloodypointresort.com* *7 rooms, 34 villas* *No meals.*

Chapter 10

THE MIDLANDS AND THE UPSTATE, SC

Updated by
Stratton Lawrence

Sights	Restaurants	Hotels	Shopping	Nightlife
★★★★☆	★★★★☆	★★★★☆	★★★☆☆	★★☆☆☆

WELCOME TO THE MIDLANDS AND THE UPSTATE, SC

TOP REASONS TO GO

★ **Small-town charm:** Small towns—most of them with shady town squares, small shops, and a café—dot this region. Abbeville and Aiken are a couple of the nicest.

★ **Downtown Greenville:** This charming small city has reinvented itself with a revitalized Main Street area that features a walking bridge over a waterfall.

★ **Antiquing in Camden:** Camden's antiques and arts district is a trove of well-priced furniture, ironwork, and high-quality paintings.

★ **Congaree National Park:** Wander through 22 miles of trails or follow the 2½-mile boardwalk that meanders over lazy creeks and under massive hardwoods.

★ **Waterfalls:** There are more than 25 waterfalls in the Upstate; some, like 75-foot Twin Falls, are an easy walk from the road. Others, such as Raven Cliff Falls, are a 2-mile hike away.

South Carolina's gleaming coasts and rolling mountains are linked by its lush Midlands. Swells of sandy hills mark where the state's coastline once sat. As you drive farther inland you're greeted by the beauty of the Blue Ridge foothills. What lies between is a mixture of Southern living—with cities and rural farms—that is truly remarkable.

1 Columbia. The state capital is a hip college town with a growing restaurant scene.

2 Camden. Revolutionary War history and antiques shopping make Camden an attractive Midlands destination.

3 Aiken. Northerners used to winter in this idyllic Piedmont retreat that's surrounded by horse pastures.

4 Abbeville. Boasting an opera house and a Gothic revival church, this quaint town takes travelers back in time.

5 Greenville. The Upstate's hub is a budding urban metropolis, surrounded by nature.

6 Blacksburg. This colonial town just off Interstate 85 is a great place to take a hike or explore battlefields.

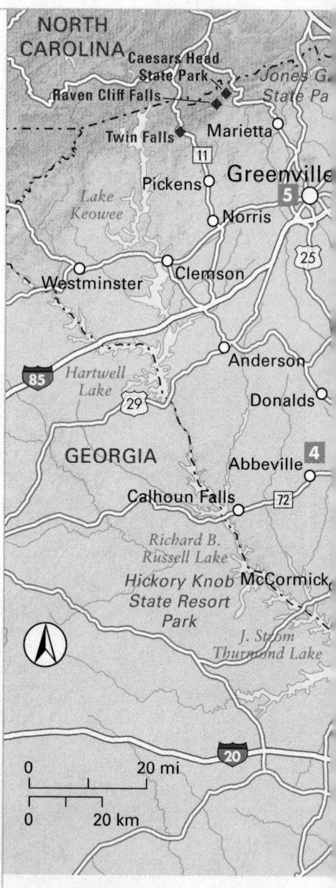

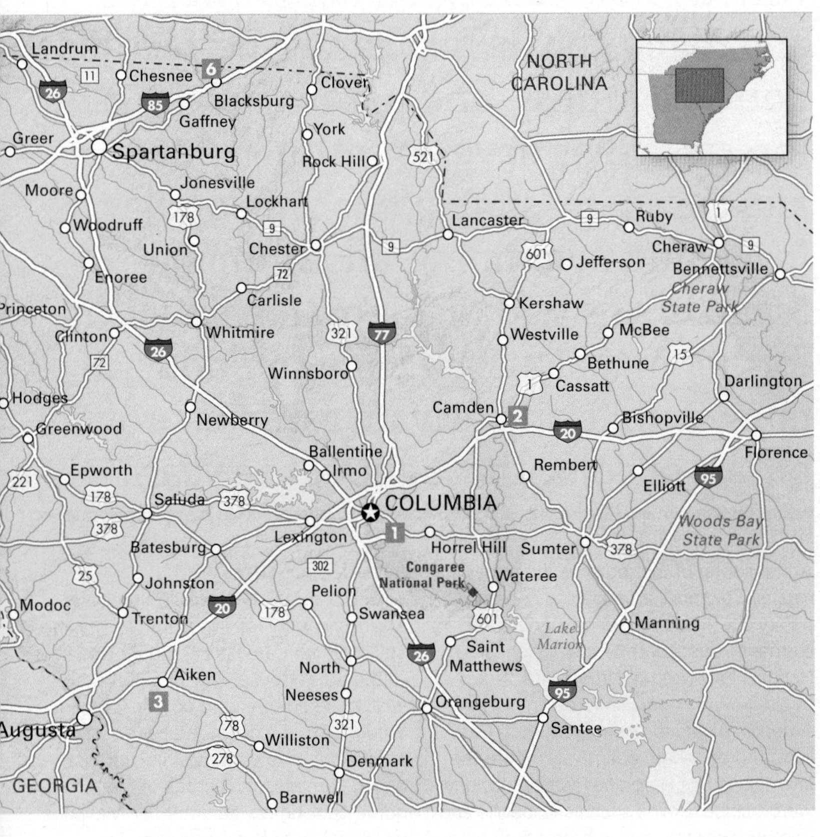
NORTH CAROLINA
GEORGIA
Landrum
Chesnee
Clover
Blacksburg
Gaffney
York
Greer
Spartanburg
Rock Hill
Moore
Jonesville
Lockhart
Woodruff
Union
Chester
Lancaster
Ruby
Cheraw
Jefferson
Bennettsville
Enoree
Carlisle
Kershaw
Cheraw State Park
Princeton
Clinton
Whitmire
Westville
McBee
Winnsboro
Bethune
Cassatt
Darlington
Hodges
Newberry
Camden
Bishopville
Greenwood
Ballentine
Irmo
Rembert
Florence
Epworth
Elliott
Saluda
COLUMBIA
Woods Bay State Park
Lexington
Horrel Hill
Sumter
Batesburg
Congaree National Park
Wateree
Johnston
Pelion
Modoc
Trenton
Swansea
Lake Marion
Manning
Saint Matthews
North
Aiken
Neeses
Orangeburg
Augusta
Williston
Santee
Denmark
Barnwell
1
2
3
6
11
26
85
521
178
9
601
72
321
77
15
20
221
378
95
302
25
78
278

Lying between the coastal Lowcountry and the mountains, South Carolina's varied Midlands region holds swamps and rivers, fertile farmland—perfect for horse pastures—and hardwood and pine forests. Lakes have bountiful fishing, and the many state parks are popular for hiking, swimming, and camping. Small towns with bed-and-breakfasts in former mansions are common, and the many public and private gardens provide bursts of color throughout the year.

At the center of the region is the state capital, Columbia, an engaging contemporary city enveloping cherished historic elements. Just south of town, Congaree National Park has the largest intact tract of old-growth floodplain forest in North America. Aiken, the center of South Carolina's Thoroughbred country, is where the champions Sea Hero and Pleasant Colony were trained. Towns such as Abbeville and Camden preserve and interpret the past, with historic house museums, colonial-era re-creations, and museum exhibits.

The Upstate of South Carolina is a land of waterfalls and wide vistas, cool pine forests, and fast rapids. Camping, hiking, white-water rafting, and kayaking are less than an hour from downtown Greenville and a paddle's throw from the small hamlets that are scattered about. Greenville itself, artsy and refined, is a modern Southern city with a thriving downtown full of trendy restaurants, boutiques, and galleries.

MAJOR REGIONS

Columbia and the Midlands. Columbia is swarming with activity, from the University of South Carolina campus to the halls of the State House. Day or night, there is always something to do. It's worth it, though, to slow down the pace and take a drive out of town. With thick forests, quaint hamlets, and scores of local home-cooking restaurants, the Midlands will take you back to a simpler time.

The Upstate. South Carolina's Upstate is a treasure trove of natural and historic sites. Hiking trails and waterfalls abound for visitors of all fitness levels. Even the most robust will enjoy the river and trails in Falls Park, right in the heart of downtown Greenville. History buffs will love following the South Carolina National Heritage Corridor through the area. The drive stretches through lush landscapes, making stops at historic sites and homes along the way.

Planning

When to Go

Central South Carolina comes alive in spring (beginning in early March), when the azaleas, dogwoods, wisteria, and jasmine turn normal landscapes into fairylands of pink, white, and purple shaded by a canopy of pines. The heat of late May through September can be oppressive, particularly in the Midlands. Festivals celebrating everything from peaches to okra are held in summer. Fall brings the state fair in Columbia, SEC and ACC football to the University of South Carolina and Clemson University, rich yellows and reds of the changing trees in the mountains, and a number of art and music festivals.

FESTIVALS

Summer kicks off the festival season in the Midlands, and there's plenty to celebrate. Check out *www.scbarbeque.com* for information on South Carolina barbecue festivals.

euphoria Greenville

FESTIVALS | Each September, downtown Greenville comes alive with this four-day event showcasing the Upstate's best farms and chefs, featuring ticketed dinners and live music. *Greenville* *864/617–0231* *www.euphoriagreenville.com.*

Irmo Okra Strut

FESTIVALS | **FAMILY** | September's Okra Strut in Irmo is slimy fun and includes live music, a craft market, and carnival rides. *Irmo* *803/781–7050* *okrastrut.com* *Free.*

Lexington County Peach Festival

FESTIVALS | **FAMILY** | Every Fourth of July in downtown Gilbert, indulge in fresh peach ice cream and take in live country music, or just bite into a sun-warmed peach while enjoying the peach parade and the evening fireworks. *Gilbert* *www.lexingtoncountypeachfestival.com* *Free.*

South Carolina Peanut Party

FESTIVALS | **FAMILY** | Boiled peanuts are royalty at this annual fest held in Pelion each fall, featuring rides, a parade, a pageant, and a fireworks show. *951 Pine St., Pelion* *discoversouthcarolina.com/products/2116* *Free.*

Planning Your Time

The Midlands and the Upstate have a good mix of larger cities and small towns. Columbia and Greenville are destinations on their own, with plenty of sights, stores, and high-end restaurants. The surrounding towns offer great day trips and shopping excursions, especially if you're looking to go antiquing. In Aiken you can spend the day with horses at events like Sunday polo matches and the Triple Crown each spring.

Miles of forested land and winding rivers offer plenty of reasons to stay outdoors. With your options covering everything from hiking and mountain biking to motorcycle paths and bridle trails, it's easy to find an excuse to head into the woods. The Palmetto Trail stretches across the entire state and can be walked in segments. The South Carolina National Heritage Corridor allows visitors to take a driving tour of some of South Carolina's major historic sites from the foothills of the Smokies to the coast of Charleston. The Ninety Six National Historic Site offers a mile-long loop through the woods, past Revolutionary War battlegrounds.

Getting Here and Around

AIR TRAVEL

Columbia Metropolitan Airport (CAE), 10 miles west of downtown Columbia, is served by American Airlines, Delta, and United. Greenville–Spartanburg International Airport (GSP), off Interstate 85 and between the two cities, is served by

Allegiant, American Airlines, Delta, Silver Airways, Southwest, and United.

AIR CONTACTS Columbia Metropolitan Airport. (*CAE*) ✉ *3250 Airport Blvd., West Columbia* ☎ *803/822–5000* 🌐 *www.flycae.com.* **Greenville Spartanburg International Airport.** (*GSP*) ✉ *2000 GSP Dr., Greer* ☎ *864/877–7426* 🌐 *www.gspairport.com.*

CAR TRAVEL

Interstate 77 leads into Columbia from the north, Interstate 26 runs through northwest–southeast, and Interstate 20 east–west. Interstate 85 provides access to Greenville, Spartanburg, Pendleton, and Anderson. Interstate 26 runs from Charleston through Columbia to the Upstate, connecting with Interstate 385 into Greenville. Car rental by all the national chains is available at the airports in Columbia and Greenville.

TAXI TRAVEL

Rideshare services Uber and Lyft are widely available in Columbia and Greenville. Other companies providing service in Columbia include Blue Ribbon and Checker Yellow Cab. American VIP Limo provides citywide service as well as service to other cities statewide. It's about $20 to $25 from the airport to downtown Columbia. Greenville is served by Yellow Cab Greenville. Fares from the Greenville airport to downtown Greenville run around $25.

TAXI CONTACTS American VIP Limo. ☎ *803/238–6669* 🌐 *www.theviplimo.com.* **Blue Ribbon Taxi Service.** ☎ *803/754–8163* 🌐 *www.originalblueribbontaxi.com.* **Checker Yellow Cab.** ☎ *803/799–3311* 🌐 *www.checkeryellowcab.com.* **Yellow Cab Greenville.** ☎ *864/233–6666* 🌐 *www.yellowcabgreenville.com.*

TRAIN TRAVEL

Amtrak's *Silver Service* makes stops at Camden, Charleston, Columbia, Denmark, Dillon, Florence, Kingstree, and Yemassee. The *Crescent* stops in Clemson, Greenville, and Spartanburg.

TRAIN CONTACTS Amtrak. ☎ *800/872–7245* 🌐 *www.amtrak.com.*

Restaurants

Most of the smaller towns have at least one dining choice that may surprise you with its take on sophisticated fare. Larger cities, such as Columbia and Greenville, have both upscale foodie haunts and ultra-casual grits-and-greens joints. Plan ahead: many places close on Sunday. *Restaurant reviews have been shortened. For full information, visit Fodors.com.*

Hotels

For an authentic taste of South Carolina's heartland, your best bet is to stay at an inn or B&B. Count on a handful of rooms, hearty breakfasts, and perhaps a garden for wandering and a restored town square nearby. What you gain in charm, however, you may have to give up in convenience. Our local writers vet every hotel to recommend the best lodging in each price category. Unless otherwise specified, you can expect a private bath, phone, and TV in your room. For expanded reviews, facilities, and current deals, visit Fodors.com. *Hotel reviews have been shortened. For full information, visit Fodors.com.*

What It Costs

$	$$	$$$	$$$$
RESTAURANTS			
under $15	$15–$19	$20–$24	over $24
HOTELS			
under $150	$150–$200	$201–$250	over $250

Columbia

112 miles northwest of Charleston via I–26; 101 miles southeast of Greenville via I–385 and I–26.

Old as Columbia may be, trendy and collegiate neighborhoods give the city an edge. The symphony, two professional ballet companies, several theaters that stage live, often locally written productions, and a number of engaging museums keep the arts thriving. The city is a sprawling blend of modern office blocks, suburban neighborhoods, and the occasional antebellum home. Here, too, is the expansive main campus of the University of South Carolina. Out of town, 550-acre Lake Murray is full of pontoon boats and Jet Skis, and Congaree National Park's swamps, creeks, and hiking trails are waiting to be explored.

In 1786, South Carolina's capital was moved from Charleston to Columbia, along the banks of the Congaree River. One of the nation's first planned cities, Columbia has streets that are among the widest in America, because it was then thought that stagnant air in narrow streets fostered the spread of malaria. The city soon grew into a center of political, commercial, and cultural activity, but in early 1865, General William Tecumseh Sherman invaded South Carolina and incinerated two-thirds of Columbia. Only a few homes, public buildings, and historic sights survived. The First Baptist Church, where secession was declared, still stands because a janitor directed Sherman's troops to a Presbyterian church instead.

GETTING HERE AND AROUND

Columbia lies in the heart of the state. It's two hours from the coast and just a little more than that from the mountains. Major interstates, along with airport, train, and bus terminals, make the city very accessible. Most of the action happens in the downtown neighborhoods of the Vista and Five Points. Devine Street, in the Shandon neighborhood, also offers plenty of boutique shopping and fine dining, and the university's football stadium, fairground, zoo, and gardens are all a short drive away. Historic Columbia runs guided house, garden, and walking tours and rents storied properties and gardens for events.

ESSENTIALS

TOUR CONTACTS Historic Columbia Foundation. ✉ *1601 Richland St.* ☎ *803/252–7742* 🌐 *www.historiccolumbia.org.*

VISITOR INFORMATION Columbia Metropolitan Convention Center and Visitors Bureau. ✉ *1120 Lincoln St.* ☎ *803/545–0000* 🌐 *www.experiencecolumbiasc.com.*

Sights

★ Columbia Museum of Art

MUSEUM | This attractive, expansive gallery contains art from the Kress Foundation collection of Renaissance and baroque treasures, sculpture, and decorative arts. There are prominent paintings by European and American masters, including a Monet and a Botticelli, as well as temporary exhibitions featuring world-famous works by artists like Salvador Dalí and M. C. Escher. ✉ *1515 Main St., Main Street Area* ☎ *803/799–2810* 🌐 *www.columbiamuseum.org* 🎫 *$10, free every first Thurs.* ⏲ *Closed Mon. and Tues.*

★ Congaree National Park

NATIONAL/STATE PARK | **FAMILY** | South Carolina's only national park is unlike any other—the park is the floodplain of the Congaree River, meaning that throughout the year, the majority of this bottomland forest is a true swamp. The wettest, hardest-to-reach areas survived centuries of logging, leaving towering cypress trees—some of the oldest and largest trees east of the Mississippi River—in the heart of the 27,000-acre park. Access varies by your ambition and tolerance for mud. A 2.6-mile loop via elevated boardwalk is handicap accessible and

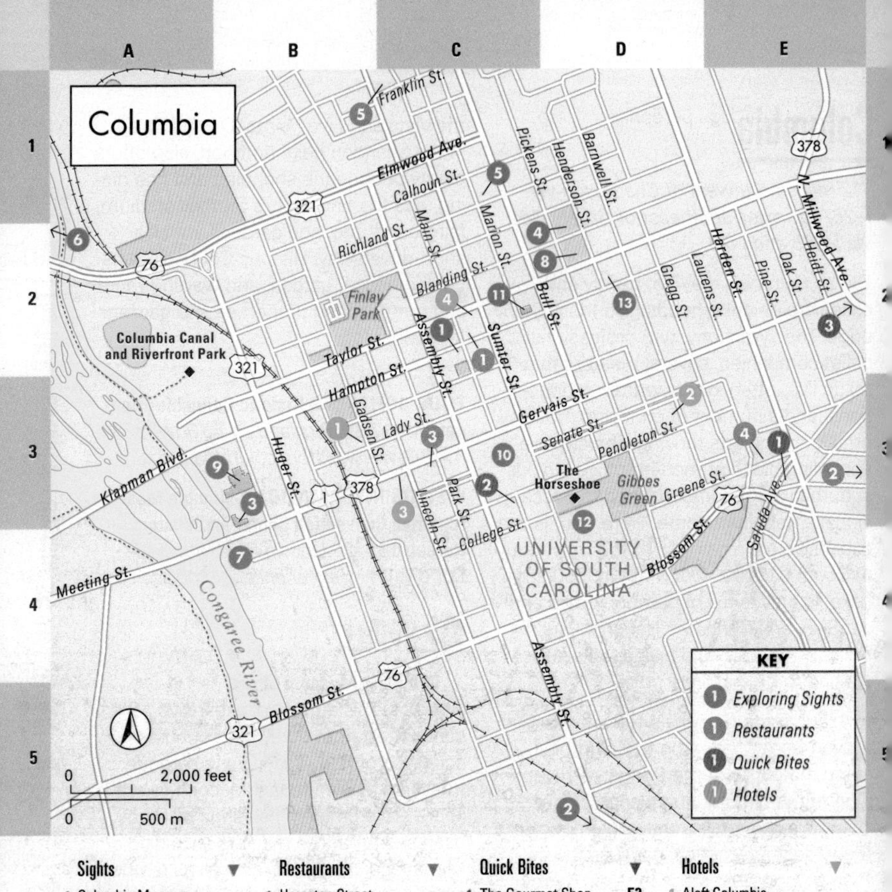

Sights

1 Columbia Museum of Art **C2**

2 Congaree National Park **D5**

3 EdVenture Children's Museum **B3**

4 Hampton-Preston Mansion and Gardens . **D2**

5 Mann-Simons Site **C1**

6 Riverbanks Zoo and Garden **A2**

7 Riverfront Park and Historic Columbia Canal **B4**

8 Robert Mills House and Gardens **D2**

9 South Carolina State Museum **B3**

10 State House **C3**

11 Tunnelvision Mural **C2**

12 University of South Carolina **D3**

13 Woodrow Wilson Family Home **D2**

Restaurants

1 Hampton Street Vineyard **C2**

2 Mediterranean Tea Room **E3**

3 Motor Supply Co. Bistro **C3**

4 Mr. Friendly's New Southern Cafe **E3**

5 The War Mouth **C1**

Quick Bites

1 The Gourmet Shop **E3**

2 Immaculate Consumption **C3**

3 Little Pigs Barbecue **E2**

Hotels

1 Aloft Columbia Downtown **B3**

2 Graduate Columbia **D3**

3 Hampton Inn Downtown Historic District **C3**

4 Hotel Trundle **C2**

meanders through perennial swamp, higher pine uplands, and past Weston Lake. Longer trails total 22 miles, allowing for loops and overnight treks into the park, but bring extra socks and boots suitable for wading, especially on the fantastic but especially soggy Oakridge Trail. A potentially drier method of exploring the interior is by kayak or canoe. Local outfitters, including River Runner Outdoor Center and Carolina Outdoor Adventures, run three-hour kayak tours from the Cedar Creek Canoe Access. Or, coordinate a shuttle and canoe rental and paddle Cedar Creek one way, putting in at Bannister Bridge Canoe Access. **■ TIP→ Bring binoculars and sharp ears—Congaree hosts a cacophony of birds and wildlife, including otters, wild boar, deer, and woodpeckers. The park also has two primitive campgrounds. Book in advance, especially during the two-week synchronized firefly season in May and June.** **⚠ Apart from packaged snacks at the visitor center, there are no concessions in the park, and nearby restaurants are limited.** ✉ *100 National Park Rd., Hopkins* ✣ *20 miles southeast of Columbia* ☎ *803/776–4396* 🌐 *www.nps.gov/cong* 🎟 *Free.*

EdVenture Children's Museum
MUSEUM | FAMILY | With more than 90,000 square feet for climbing, exploring, painting, playing, building—oh, and learning, too—this museum is a full day of hands-on fun. Eddie, a 40-foot-tall statue of a boy that can be climbed on (and in) by children and adults, is the centerpiece. Each of nine galleries has a theme, such as My Backyard, Wags & Whiskers, and Maker Works. Kids can shop in their own grocery store, act as firefighters in a full-size fire truck, and pretend to be newscasters. ✉ *211 Gervais St., Vista* ☎ *803/779–3100* 🌐 *www.edventure.org* 🎟 *$12* ⏲ *Closed Mon.*

Hampton-Preston Mansion and Gardens
HOUSE | Dating from 1818, this grand home is filled with lavish furnishings collected by three generations of two influential families. The mansion was rehabilitated and outfitted with new interactive exhibits and expanded gardens to celebrate its 200th anniversary in 2018. Buy tickets at the Robert Mills House. ✉ *1615 Blanding St., Main Street Area* ☎ *803/252–7742* 🌐 *www.historiccolumbia.org* 🎟 *$10* ⏲ *Closed Mon.*

Mann-Simons Site
HISTORIC SITE | This cottage and outdoor museum was the home of Celia Mann, one of only 200 free African Americans in Columbia in the mid-1800s. Buy tickets at the Robert Mills House. ✉ *1403 Richland St., Main Street Area* ☎ *803/252–7742* 🌐 *www.historiccolumbia.org* 🎟 *$10* ⏲ *Closed Mon.*

★ Riverbanks Zoo and Garden
ZOO | FAMILY | This top-notch zoo contains more than 2,000 animals and birds in natural habitats, including a sea lion exhibit and western lowland gorillas. Walk through landscaped gardens to see elephants, Siberian tigers, koalas, and penguins. The South American primate collection has won international acclaim, and the park is noted for its success in breeding endangered species. The Aquarium Reptile Complex has regional, desert, tropical, and marine specimens. Ride the carousel, and take a tram over the Saluda River to the 70-acre botanical gardens. A forested section with walking trails has spectacular views of the river and passes Civil War ruins. Stop by the Saluda Factory Interpretive Center for more information about the site's history and its connection to the Civil War. ✉ *500 Wildlife Pkwy., West Columbia* ✣ *At I–126 and U.S. 76* ☎ *803/779–8717* 🌐 *www.riverbanks.org* 🎟 *$22.*

Riverfront Park and Historic Columbia Canal
NATIONAL/STATE PARK | FAMILY | Where the Broad and Saluda Rivers form the Congaree River is the site of the city's original waterworks and hydroelectric plant. Interpretive markers describe the area's plant and animal life and tell the history of the buildings. A 2½-mile paved trail

weaves between the river and the canal and is filled with runners and walkers. ✉ *312 Laurel St., Vista* ☎ *803/917–5522* 🌐 *discoversouthcarolina.com* 🎫 *Free.*

Robert Mills House and Gardens

HOUSE | The classic, columned 1823 house was named for its architect, who later designed the Washington Monument. It has opulent Regency furniture, marble mantels, and spacious grounds. This is the home of the Historic Columbia Foundation, where you can get walking and driving tour maps of historic districts and buy tickets to other historic homes. ✉ *1616 Blanding St., Main Street Area* ☎ *803/252–7742* 🌐 *www.historiccolumbia.org* 🎫 *$10* 🕒 *Closed Mon.*

South Carolina State Museum

MUSEUM | **FAMILY** | Exhibits in this refurbished textile mill explore the state's natural history, archaeology, and historical development. An iron gate made for the museum by Philip Simmons, the "dean of Charleston blacksmiths," is on display, as is an exhibit on South Carolina's astronauts and artifacts associated with the state's cotton industry and slavery. Newer exhibits are geared toward the younger set, including a 4-D theater and nature-oriented rotating films shown in the planetarium. **■ TIP→ When skies are clear, the observatory stays open until 8 on Tuesday.** ✉ *301 Gervais St., Vista* ☎ *803/898–4921* 🌐 *www.scmuseum.org* 🎫 *$9* 🕒 *Closed Mon.*

State House

GOVERNMENT BUILDING | Six bronze stars on the western wall of South Carolina's grandest building mark where direct hits were made by General Sherman's cannons. Begun in 1851 and completed in 1907, the capitol is made of native blue granite in the Italian Renaissance style. The interior is richly appointed with brass, marble, mahogany, and artwork. Guided tours are available throughout the day. ✉ *1100 Gervais St., Main Street Area* ☎ *803/734–2430* 🌐 *southcarolinaparks.com/education-and-history/state-house* 🎫 *Free* 🕒 *Closed Sun.*

Tunnelvision Mural

PUBLIC ART | **FAMILY** | This glowing optical illusion painted on the wall of the Federal Land Bank Building in 1976 by local artist Blue Sky gives the appearance of a tunnel leading to the mountains. To celebrate the mural's 25th anniversary in 2001, the city hired Blue Sky to create another work in the same parking lot: the world's largest fire hydrant towers 40 feet here. ✉ *Taylor and Marion Sts., Main Street Area.*

University of South Carolina

COLLEGE | A highlight of this sprawling university is its original campus, founded in 1801. Stroll the historic buildings and gardens of the Horseshoe, or dive into the special collections at the South Caroliniana Library, built in 1840 as the first stand-alone college library in the nation. The McKissick Museum on campus features exhibits on geology, gemstones, and local folklife. ✉ *Sumter St., USC Campus* ☎ *803/777–7251 McKissick Museum* 🌐 *www.sc.edu/visit* 🕒 *Museum closed Sun. Library closed weekends.*

Woodrow Wilson Family Home

HOUSE | This boyhood home of President Woodrow Wilson displays the gaslights, arched doorways, and ornate furnishings of the Victorian period. Museum exhibits explore the life of the president and the South in the 1870s. **■ TIP→ Buy tickets at the Robert Mills House, where you get a discount if you plan to visit more than one historic home.** ✉ *1705 Hampton St., Main Street Area* ☎ *803/252–7742* 🌐 *www.historiccolumbia.org* 🎫 *$10* 🕒 *Closed Mon.*

Restaurants

Hampton Street Vineyard

$$$$ | **FRENCH** | This cozy bistro with upscale French fare is set inside one of the first buildings constructed in the city after Sherman's infamous march. It has exposed brick walls, arched windows,

A tour of the South Carolina State House reveals the location of six cannon hits made by General Sherman's army during the Civil War.

and original wide-plank floors. **Known for:** 650-bottle wine list that won Wine Spectator's Award of Excellence; locally inspired, seasonally changing menu; attractively presented entrées. $ *Average main: $28* ✉ *1207 Hampton St., Downtown* ☎ *803/252–0850* 🌐 *www.hamptonstreetvineyard.com.*

Mediterranean Tea Room

$ | **MIDDLE EASTERN** | This friendly little restaurant serves Middle Eastern and Greek food, such as a marinated chicken breast, that keeps people coming back. The *kofta* (spiced meatball), hummus, and vegetarian dishes offer patrons a break from the rich Southern cooking elsewhere. **Known for:** gyros and falafel; colorful, cheery atmosphere; a generous Greek salad. $ *Average main: $10* ✉ *2601 Devine St., Shandon* ☎ *803/799–3118* ⏲ *Closed Sun. No lunch Sat.*

★ Motor Supply Co. Bistro

$$$$ | **ECLECTIC** | The daily-changing menu at this stalwart of the Columbia dining scene highlights the best of what local farmers and purveyors have to offer, worked into eclectic dishes that span European to Asian influences. The artsy interior (a former engine parts building, on the National Register of Historic Places) and thoughtful service make it a standout. **Known for:** curated beer and wine selection; farm-to-table menu that changes daily; gorgeous setting in a renovated 19th-century building. $ *Average main: $26* ✉ *920 Gervais St., Vista* ☎ *803/256–6687* 🌐 *www.motorsupplycobistro.com* ⏲ *Closed Mon.*

Mr. Friendly's New Southern Cafe

$$$ | **SOUTHERN** | Who knew that barbecue sauce could be the base for such tasty salad dressing or that pimento cheese could elevate a fillet to near perfection? Appetizers of fried pickles and country ham–spinach dip only add to the creative thinking that makes Mr. Friendly's such a local treasure. **Known for:** seafood specials; impressive wine and beer list; attractive outdoor seating. $ *Average main: $22* ✉ *2001A Greene St., Five Points* ☎ *803/254–7828* 🌐 *www.mrfriendlys.com* ⏲ *No lunch Sat. Closed Sun. and Mon.*

★ The War Mouth

$$ | **SOUTHERN** | Named after a freshwater sunfish and set in a former auto repair garage, this casual-cool joint serves up whole-hog barbecue from its wood-fired outdoor pit as well as hearty Southern specialties like chicken bog, quail legs, and catfish stew. Stick around for nightcap craft cocktails at the popular bar. **Known for:** wood-fired meats; lively happy hour; craft cocktails. *Average main: $18 1209 Franklin St., Main Street Area 803/569–6144 www.thewarmouth.com Closed Mon. and Tues.*

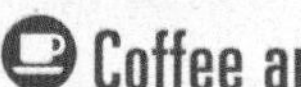

Coffee and Quick Bites

The Gourmet Shop

$ | **CAFÉ** | Mirrors and art adorn the walls at this French-inspired bakery and café serving coffee, sandwiches, soups, and cheese plates. Next door, the retail shop sells wine, kitchen gadgets, French table linens, and fancy food items. **Known for:** fresh baguettes and cookies; chicken salad sandwiches; more than 1,500 different wine labels. *Average main: $10 724 Saluda Ave., Five Points 803/799–3705 www.thegourmet-shop.net.*

Immaculate Consumption

$ | **DELI** | This coffee shop roasts its own beans, and from its location immediately next to the State House, it's helped to fuel many a legislative session for over two decades. **Known for:** generously portioned sandwiches and salads; "concentration coffee" with coconut oil and grass-fed butter; comfortable interior suitable for working. *Average main: $8 933 Main St., Main Street Area 803/799–9053 immaculate-consumption.com Closed weekends.*

Little Pigs Barbecue

$ | **BARBECUE** | **FAMILY** | Enjoy the laid-back Southern atmosphere at this Carolina barbecue joint. Grab a plate, get in the buffet line, and load up on brisket, pulled pork barbecue, fried chicken, ribs, and fried fish, along with fixings such as collards, coleslaw, and macaroni and cheese. **Known for:** all-you-can-eat buffet; real country cooking, priced right; mustard-, tomato-, and vinegar-base barbecue sauces—choose your favorite. *Average main: $10 4927 Alpine Rd., Northeast 803/788–8238 www.littlepigs.biz Closed Mon. and Tues. No dinner Sun. and Wed.*

Hotels

Aloft Columbia Downtown

$$ | **HOTEL** | A short walk from the convention center and hot spot restaurants and nightlife, and housing a lively bar of its own, this hotel is modern and customer focused. **Pros:** contemporary decor and gym; lively bar; Mexican restaurant COA is on the ground floor. **Cons:** no pool; no dining room or room service; lacks Southern charm. *Rooms from: $159 823 Lady St., Downtown 803/445–1900 www.marriott.com 107 rooms No meals.*

★ Graduate Columbia

$$ | **HOTEL** | **FAMILY** | This extremely colorful (think: plaids over pastels) yet tastefully decorated boutique inn expands upon a century-old historic home, whose original parlors and living rooms serve as a bar, library, and communal areas. **Pros:** on the attractive and walkable USC campus; Presidential Suites in the original home are luxurious; free bike rentals. **Cons:** no pool; no breakfast; small fitness center. *Rooms from: $170 1619 Pendleton St., USC Campus 803/779–7779 graduatehotels.com 119 rooms No meals.*

Hampton Inn Downtown Historic District

$ | **HOTEL** | This classy outpost is within walking distance of restaurants and nightlife in the Vista neighborhood. **Pros:** outdoor saltwater pool; walking distance to USC and the State House; free hot breakfast. **Cons:** rooms along Gervais Street can be noisy; parking lot can fill up on busy weekends; corporate feel lacks charm of a boutique hotel. *Rooms from: $119 822 Gervais St., Vista 803/231–2000 hilton.com 122 rooms Free Breakfast.*

Hotel Trundle

$$ | HOTEL | Built into a historic former furniture store building in the heart of downtown Columbia, Trundle stands out for its focus on service and eclectic decor highlighted by paintings and sculpture throughout the communal areas. **Pros:** complimentary draft beer or wine upon arrival; locally roasted coffee always available; welcoming aesthetic. **Cons:** $18 self-parking; no pets; no pool. *Rooms from: $159 1224 Taylor St., Downtown 803/722–5000 hoteltrundle.com 41 rooms Free Breakfast.*

Nightlife

Art Bar

MUSIC CLUBS | In the hopping Vista neighborhood, this funky spot has neon-painted walls, colorful string lights, and a lively crowd, making it the perfect setting for karaoke and dancing to live bands. *1211 Park St., Vista 803/929–0198 www.artbarsc.com.*

★ The Grand on Main

BREWPUBS/BEER GARDENS | This palace of fun combines a bowling alley, a restaurant, a taproom, an outdoor patio, and a game area into one establishment. Eat an upscale Southern entrée like shrimp and grits or espresso-rubbed rib eye before rolling for a turkey. *1621 Main St., Main Street Area 803/726–2323 www.thegrandonmain.com.*

★ Hunter-Gatherer Brewery and Alehouse

BREWPUBS/BEER GARDENS | This venerable local beer hall opened in 1995 as the city's first microbrewery and serves an excellent selection of beer and a menu of elevated pub fare and pizza. It also hosts occasional live bands. There's a second, larger location 3 miles south of town in a restored airplane hangar. *900 Main St., USC Campus 803/748–0540 hunter-gathererbrewery.com.*

The Whig

BARS/PUBS | Directly across from the State House, the subterranean Whig attracts an eclectic mix of patrons who are drawn to its dive bar vibe by the great drink specials, classic pub fare, and the wildly popular Taco Tuesday. *1200 Main St., basement, Main Street Area 803/931–8852 www.thewhig.org.*

Shopping

Many of Columbia's antiques outlets, boutique shops, and restaurants are in the Vista neighborhood around Huger and Gervais Streets, between the State House and the river. A number of intriguing shops and cafés are in Five Points, around Blossom and Harden Streets, as well as along Devine Street in the Shandon neighborhood to the east. There are also antiques shops across the river on Meeting and State Streets in West Columbia.

Old Mill Antique Mall

ANTIQUES/COLLECTIBLES | This sprawling complex with more than 75 dealers has a wide array of furniture, glassware, jewelry, and books. *310 State St., West Columbia 803/796–4229 oldmillantiquemall.com.*

★ Soda City Market

SHOPPING NEIGHBORHOODS | FAMILY | Every Saturday morning from 9 to 1, Soda City Market comes to life with 150 vendors along Main Street. Artists and artisans join the farm stands and food trucks, while shoppers browse to the sounds of local musicians. *1500 Block Main St., Main Street Area www.sodacitysc.com.*

State Farmers' Market

OUTDOOR/FLEA/GREEN MARKETS | South Carolina's state market, one of the 10 largest in the country, is open daily and features fresh vegetables, along with flowers, plants, seafood, and more.

✉ *3483 Charleston Hwy., West Columbia* ☎ *803/737–4664* 🌐 *www.scstatefarmers-market.com.*

Activities

CANOEING AND KAYAKING

The Saluda River near Columbia has challenging, seasonal Class III and IV rapids. Saluda access is out of town in Gardendale and Saluda Shoals Park, as well as at the Riverbanks Zoo. The Broad and the Saluda Rivers meet in the center of town to become the calmer Congaree River. There's public access for the Congaree behind EdVenture on Senate Street at the Senate Street Landing.

Carolina Outdoor Adventures

CANOEING/ROWING/SKULLING | FAMILY | This outfitter offers guided trips on the Saluda and Broad Rivers (including some rapids) and into the swampy wonderland of Congaree National Park. ✉ *Irmo* ☎ *803/381–2293* 🌐 *carolinaoutdooradventures.com.*

River Runner Outdoor Center

CANOEING/ROWING/SKULLING | FAMILY | This local outfitter rents and sells canoes, kayaks, and gear and can point you in the right direction for river or swamp expeditions. During spring and fall, they lead day trips through Congaree National Park, and they also coordinate shuttles for self-guided excursions. ✉ *905 Gervais St., Vista* ☎ *803/771–0353* 🌐 *www.shop-riverrunner.com.*

PARKS AND LAKES

Lake Murray

PARK—SPORTS-OUTDOORS | FAMILY | This 41-mile-long lake, 15 miles west of Columbia, has swimming, boating, picnicking, and superb fishing. There are many marinas and campgrounds in the area. A 1.7-mile pedestrian walkway stretches across the Dreher Shoals Dam offering panoramic views. In summer a massive flock of purple martins fills the sky at sunset, when the birds return to their roost on Bomb Island. ✉ *2184 N. Lake Dr.* ☎ *803/781–5940* 🌐 *www.lakemurraycountry.com.*

Saluda Shoals Park

CANOEING/ROWING/SKULLING | FAMILY | This 400-acre park has picnic shelters, an observation deck, an environmental education center, trails, and a splash zone for kids. You can explore the park by canoe and kayak (rentals available) on the Saluda River. ✉ *5605 Bush River Rd.* ✣ *12 miles northwest of downtown Columbia* ☎ *803/772–1228* 🌐 *www.icrc.net* 🎟 *$5 per car.*

Sesquicentennial State Park

HIKING/WALKING | FAMILY | The 1,419-acre Sesquicentennial State Park is not far from downtown but feels as if it's deep in the country. A 30-acre lake sits at the heart of the park, allowing for fishing and nonmotorized boating. Enjoy picnicking areas, playgrounds, a splash pad, campgrounds, and miles of nature, hiking, and mountain-biking trails. ✉ *9564 Two Notch Rd., Northeast* ☎ *803/788–2706* 🌐 *southcarolinaparks.com/sesqui* 🎟 *$6.*

Camden

35 miles northeast of Columbia via I–20.

A town with horse history and grand colonial homes, charming Camden has never paved some of its roads for the sake of the hooves that regularly trot over them. The steeplechase season-opening Carolina Cup is run here each spring.

Camden is South Carolina's oldest inland town, dating from 1732. British general Lord Cornwallis established a garrison here during the Revolutionary War and burned most of the town before evacuating it. A center of textile trade from the late 19th century through the 1940s, Camden blossomed when it became a refuge for Northerners escaping the cold winters. Because General Sherman spared the town during the Civil War, most of its antebellum homes still stand.

GETTING HERE AND AROUND

A roughly 40-minute day-trip drive northeast of Columbia takes you to Camden, whose distinct downtown holds many stores carrying antiques, collectibles, and one-of-a-kind art. Outside the downtown area are historic homes, museums, and horse-race courses. Camden Carriage Company can take you on a tour on a horse-drawn carriage through Camden's loveliest neighborhood and down unpaved roads.

ESSENTIALS

VISITOR INFORMATION Revolutionary War Visitor Center at Camden. ✉ *212 Broad St.* ☎ *803/272–0076* 🌐 *simplyrevolutionary.com.*

Sights

Camden Archives and Museum

MUSEUM | Inside a commanding, columned brick building just north of town, this museum includes an impressive antique gun collection, Native American artifacts, and horse-racing memorabilia. ✉ *1314 Broad St.* ☎ *803/425–6050* 🌐 *cityofcamden.org* ⏲ *Closed Sun.*

★ Historic Camden

HISTORIC SITE | **FAMILY** | This 107-acre outdoor museum complex and Revolutionary War historic site emphasizes the period surrounding the British occupation of 1780. Several structures dot the site, including the 1789 **Craven House** , the **Blacksmith Shed** , and the **Kershaw House,** a reconstruction of the circa-1770 home of Camden's founder, Joseph Kershaw, which also served as Cornwallis's headquarters; it's furnished with period pieces. A nature trail, fortifications, powder magazine, picnic area, and crafts shop are also here. Guided tours are available. ✉ *222 Broad St.* ✣ *1½ miles north of I–20* ☎ *803/432–9841* 🌐 *historiccamden.org* 🎫 *$5.*

National Steeplechase Museum

MUSEUM | This museum at the historic Springdale Race Course contains the largest collection of racing memorabilia in the United States. The Equicizer, a training machine used by jockeys for practice, lets you experience the race from the jockey's perspective; don't stay on too long, unless you want to feel the race all day. ✉ *200 Knights Hill Rd.* ☎ *803/432–6513* 🌐 *www.steeplechasemuseum.org* 🎫 *Free* ⏲ *Closed Sun.–Tues.*

Restaurants

Mill Pond Steakhouse

$$$$ | **STEAKHOUSE** | It's all about steak here, and what steaks they are: aged for at least 35 days before they're cut, the fillets, rib eyes, and strips are juicy, tender, and packed with flavor. You can dine alfresco overlooking the sprawling pond or enjoy the vintage saloon-style bar. **Known for:** homemade mixed-berry cobbler; high-end Southern cuisine; locally sourced produce. 💲 *Average main: $40* ✉ *84 Boykin Mill Rd., Rembert* ✣ *10 miles south of Camden* ☎ *803/425–8825* 🌐 *www.millpondsteakhouse.com* ⏲ *Closed Sun. and Mon.*

Salud Mexican Kitchen and Tequila Lounge

$$ | **MEXICAN** | Authentic street tacos (small and four to a plate), generous burritos, and what may be the state's best tequila collection come together in this modern Mexican-themed lounge with comfy seating and a *tranquilo* vibe. **Known for:** 100 tequila varieties; albondigas, a turkey meatball soup; fun, celebratory vibe on weekends. 💲 *Average main: $15* ✉ *1011 Broad St.* ☎ *803/425–4850* 🌐 *saludmexicankitchen.com* ⏲ *Closed Sun. and Mon.*

Sam Kendall's

$$$$ | **STEAKHOUSE** | The exposed brick wall and high-back booths offer the perfect upscale backdrop for steak or seafood, including tuna sashimi and shrimp in garlic chili sauce. The menu also features an

Did You Know?

Rangers provide free, guided canoe trips on weekends along Cedar Creek in Congaree National Park. The trips are an excellent way to experience the floodplain forest, which contains some of the tallest trees in eastern North America. You might also spot river otters, turtles, snakes, and wild pigs.

extensive list of more than 100 wines. **Known for:** fine dining in historic digs; signature cocktails; extensive wine list. *Average main: $28 ✉ 1043 Broad St. ☎ 803/424–2005 🌐 www.samkendalls.com ⏲ Closed Sun.*

Hotels

Bloomsbury Inn

$$$ | B&B/INN | Noted Civil War diarist Mary Boykin Chesnut wrote much of her famous account in this romantic, award-winning 1849 house built by her husband's family. **Pros:** impressive breakfast; richly decorated rooms; electric car charging stations on-site. **Cons:** no elevator; the four rooms can book far in advance; it's a bit too far to walk to dinner downtown. *Rooms from: $245 ✉ 1707 Lyttleton St. ☎ 803/432–5858 🌐 www.bloomsburyinn.com 4 rooms Free breakfast.*

Shopping

Camden is known for its antiques shopping, with the heart of the antiques and arts district along Broad Street, as well as on neighboring Rutledge, DeKalb, and Market Streets.

Camden Antiques Market

ANTIQUES/COLLECTIBLES | Among the finds here are well-priced furniture and decorative art dating back to the 18th century. The shop is open daily. *✉ 830 S. Broad St. ☎ 803/432–0818 🌐 www.camdenantiquesmarket.com.*

Rutledge Street Gallery

ART GALLERIES | The paintings, textiles, and sculptures of two dozen local and regional artists are on display at this light-filled studio. *✉ 508 Rutledge St. ☎ 803/425–0071 🌐 www.rutledgestreetgallery.com.*

Aiken

89 miles southwest of Camden via I–20; 56 miles southwest of Columbia via I–20 and U.S. 1.

This is Thoroughbred country. Aiken first earned its fame in the 1890s, when wealthy Northerners wintering here built stately mansions and entertained one another with horse shows, hunts, and lavish parties. Many up-to-60-room houses stand as a testament to this era of opulence. The town is still a center for all kinds of outdoor activity, including the equestrian events of the Triple Crown, as well as tennis and golf.

GETTING HERE AND AROUND

An hour's drive southwest of Columbia will take you to the rolling green horse country of Aiken. Though not a concise town square, Laurens Street and the surrounding streets offer plenty of shopping, dining, and entertainment. If you're headed to the polo matches or races, the horse district is only a five-minute drive outside the downtown area.

VISITOR INFORMATION

CONTACTS Aiken Chamber of Commerce. *✉ 121 Richland Ave. E ☎ 803/641–1111 🌐 www.aikenchamber.net.* **Aiken Visitors Center and Train Museum.** *✉ 406 Park Ave. SE ☎ 803/293–7846 🌐 www.visitaiken-sc.com.*

Sights

Aiken County Historical Museum

MUSEUM VILLAGE | FAMILY | One wing of this 1860 estate is devoted to early regional culture, including Native American artifacts, firearms, an authentically furnished 1808 log cabin, a schoolhouse, and a miniature circus display. *✉ 433 Newberry St. SW ☎ 803/642–2015 🌐 aikencountymuseum.org Donations suggested ⏲ Closed Mon. and Tues.*

Aiken Thoroughbred Racing Hall of Fame and Museum

MUSEUM | The area's horse farms have produced many national champions. Exhibits include horse-related decorations, paintings, and sculptures, plus racing silks and trophies. The Hall of Fame is on the grounds of the 14-acre **Hopelands Gardens,** where you can wind along paths past quiet terraces and reflecting pools. There's also a Touch and Scent Trail with Braille plaques. ✉ *135 Dupree Pl.* ✣ *Off Whiskey Rd.* ☎ *803/642–7631* 🌐 *www.aikenracinghalloffame.com* 🎟 *Free* ⏱ *Closed Mon.*

Hitchcock Woods

FOREST | **FAMILY** | At 2,100 acres and three times the size of New York's Central Park, this is one of the largest urban forests in the country and is listed on the National Register of Historic Places. It's a popular horseback-riding destination, but the double-track trails are also pleasant for hiking and jogging. Make use of the maps available at the entrances because it's easy to get lost. Note that there are seven entrances to the woods; the ones with the best parking are at 2180 Dibble Road Southwest and 430 South Boundary Road. ✉ *2180 Dibble Rd. SW* ☎ *803/642–0528* 🌐 *www.hitchcockwoods.org.*

Old Edgefield Pottery

MUSEUM | Peruse the extensive collection of Edgefield stoneware pottery on display at this shop and museum that's dedicated to a craft that began here and spread across the nation. **■ TIP→ Ask to see original pieces crafted by the famed and prolific African American potter known only as Dave. While enslaved, he created some of the first "face jugs."** ✉ *230 Simpkins St., Edgefield* ✣ *15 miles northwest of Aiken* ☎ *803/634–1634* 🌐 *www.oldedgefield-pottery.com* ⏱ *Closed Sun.–Wed.*

Redcliffe Plantation State Historic Site

HISTORIC SITE | **FAMILY** | Home to James Hammond, who is credited with being first to declare that "cotton is king," this wood-frame house remained in the family until 1975. The 13,000-square-foot mansion (which now sits on 369 acres) remains just as it was, down to the 19th-century books on the carved shelves. Exhibits in and around the former slave quarters contain photograph and textile exhibits that help visitors to understand the lives of the enslaved families that lived here and the atrocities they suffered. Once you've toured the house, be sure to explore the grounds on the 1-mile trail. ✉ *181 Redcliffe Rd., Beech Island* ✣ *15 miles southwest of Aiken* ☎ *803/827–1473* 🌐 *www.southcarolinaparks.com/redcliffe* 🎟 *Park entrance free, house tours $10* ⏱ *No tours Mon.–Wed.*

Restaurants

Malia's

$$$$ | **ECLECTIC** | Locals love this busy contemporary restaurant, with dim lighting and dark decor that conveys a cool class. The menu changes monthly and may include American, Caribbean, French, and Italian entrées. **Known for:** white-tablecloth dining on weekend evenings; small-town farm-to-table cuisine; casual lunch scene. $ *Average main: $28* ✉ *120 Laurens St. SW* ☎ *803/643–3086* 🌐 *www.maliasrestaurant.com* ⏱ *Closed Sun.–Tues.*

The Whitney

$$$$ | **STEAKHOUSE** | Exposed brick, plenty of wood, and a well-stocked bar set the tone at this downtown fine-dining spot known for its steak and Southern-style entrées like shrimp and grits. **Known for:** an 8-oz filet mignon; shrimp tempura appetizer or entrée; small-town fine-dining experience. $ *Average main: $28* ✉ *148 Laurens St. SW* ☎ *803/226–0911* 🌐 *thewhitneyaiken.com* ⏱ *Closed Sun.*

Coffee and Quick Bites

New Moon Café

$ | **CAFÉ** | This funky café pairs Aiken's best coffee (the coffee beans are roasted right next door) with freshly baked muffins and sweet rolls, panini sandwiches and salads, and homemade soups. The crab bisque is particularly good. **Known for:** healthy food made with heart; smoothies and milkshakes; quick, friendly service. *Average main: $9 116 Laurens St. NW 803/643–7088 www.newmoon-downtown.com No dinner.*

Hotels

★ Carriage House Inn

$$ | **B&B/INN** | This charming inn within walking distance of local boutiques and restaurants includes a historic mansion in front, with a modern hotel annex behind the courtyard, each offering well-appointed rooms with a mix of antique furnishings. **Pros:** full hot breakfast; special "pet suites" available; pleasant grounds and patios. **Cons:** only the Pendleton Guest House annex has an elevator; not the best for kids; sounds carry here. *Rooms from: $169 139 Laurens St. NW 803/644–5888 www.aikencarriagehouse.com 37 rooms Free breakfast.*

★ The Willcox

$$$ | **B&B/INN** | Winston Churchill, Franklin D. Roosevelt, and the Astors have slept at this 19th-century inn, where luxurious facilities—including a spa, restaurant, and a lovely outdoor pool—and authentic Southern hospitality come together to make an outstanding getaway. **Pros:** breakfast is a huge step above normal fare; terrific restaurant, including pizza service in the courtyard; on-site spa. **Cons:** slight walk to downtown shops and restaurants; large wedding parties can dominate communal spaces; some furniture looks more dated than vintage. *Rooms from: $218 100 Colleton Ave. SW 803/648–1898 www.thewillcox.com 22 rooms Free breakfast.*

Activities

Aiken Polo Club

POLO | Polo matches are played at Whitney Field on Sunday at 3, September through November and April through June. *420 Mead Ave. 803/643–3611 www.aikenpolo.org $5.*

Aiken Triple Crown

HORSE RACING/SHOW | Three weekends in late March and early April are set aside for Aiken's version of the Triple Crown—three races occuring over consecutive weekends. Events include Thoroughbred trials of promising yearlings, a steeplechase, and harness races by young horses making their debut. *538 Two Notch Rd. SE 803/648–9641 www.aikensteeplechase.com.*

Abbeville

63 miles northwest of Aiken via SC 19-N; 102 miles west of Columbia.

Abbeville is one of inland South Carolina's most satisfying lesser-known towns. An appealing historic district includes the old business areas, early churches, and residential areas. What was called the "Southern cause" by supporters of the Confederacy was born and died here: it's where the first organized secession meeting was held and where, on May 2, 1865, Confederate president Jefferson Davis officially disbanded the defeated armies of the South in the last meeting of his war council.

GETTING HERE AND AROUND

Abbeville is a little more than an hour west of Columbia. Most of the sites, including the opera house, are around its quaint town square, with shopping and restaurants all within walking distance. A short drive—or a long walk—past the square is the historic Burt-Stark Mansion.

VISITOR INFORMATION

CONTACTS Abbeville Welcome Center. ✉ *107 Court Sq.* ☎ *864/366–4600* 🌐 *www.abbevillechamber.org.*

Sights

Abbeville Opera House

ARTS VENUE | Built in 1908 along the old town square, this auditorium has been renovated to reflect the grandeur of the days when lavish road shows and stellar entertainers took center stage. Current productions range from contemporary light comedies to local renderings of Broadway musicals. Self-guided tours are available. ✉ *100 Court Sq.* ☎ *864/366–5017* 🌐 *abbevillecitysc.com.*

Burt-Stark Mansion

HOUSE | It was in this 1820 home that Jefferson Davis disbanded the Confederate armies, effectively ending the Civil War. Now a popular wedding venue, the house was a private residence until 1971, when Mary Stark Davis died. She willed the house to the Abbeville County Historic Preservation Commission, with a provision that nothing be added or removed from it; thus it's filled with lovely antiques, carved-wood surfaces, and old family photos. ✉ *400 N. Main St.* ☎ *864/366–0166* 🌐 *www.burtstark.com* *$10* *Closed Sun.–Thurs.*

★ Trinity Episcopal Church

RELIGIOUS SITE | Built in 1860, this is the town's oldest standing church and an architectural landmark that anchors the town. Complete with a 125-foot spire, the Gothic Revival structure has an original chancery window imported from England and a rare working 1860 John Baker tracker organ. ✉ *200 Church St.* ☎ *864/366–5186* 🌐 *www.trinityabbeville.org* *Free.*

Restaurants

Village Grill

$$ | **AMERICAN** | This popular restaurant with pomegranate-color walls and high ceilings has the fillets and pastas, but the reason many locals come is for the herb rotisserie chicken. The beef for the burgers is ground on the spot, and salads consist of locally grown organic vegetables. **Known for:** integrity in local ingredient sourcing; chicken and ribs; relaxed Southern atmosphere. *Average main: $17* ✉ *110 Trinity St.* ☎ *864/366–2500* 🌐 *www.abbevillevillagegrill.com* *Closed Sun.–Tues.*

Hotels

The Belmont Inn

$ | **B&B/INN** | This Spanish-style redbrick building with a colonnade, built in the 1900s, holds spacious rooms with high ceilings, pine floors, and period furniture. **Pros:** ideal location near opera house and town square; veranda has great views of town; period furnishings and building. **Cons:** the inn hosts weddings, so rooms book fast; some rooms feel dated; walls are thin. *Rooms from: $129* ✉ *104 E. Pickens St.* ☎ *864/459–9625* 🌐 *www.belmontinn.net* *26 rooms* *Free breakfast.*

Greenville

100 miles northwest of Columbia via I–26 and I–385.

Once known for its textile and other manufacturing plants, Greenville has reinvented itself as a trendy and sophisticated city that supports a growing number of restaurants, galleries, and boutiques along a tree-lined Main Street that passes a stunning natural waterfall. Anchored by two performance centers, the business district is alive well into most evenings with couples and families enjoying the energy of this revitalized

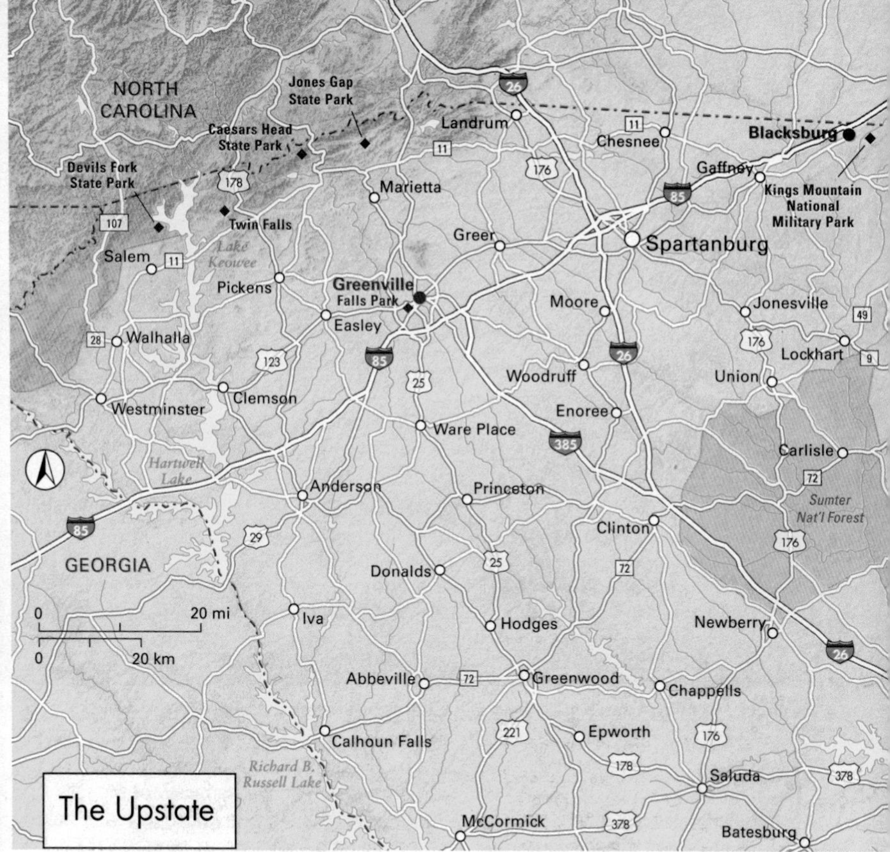

Southern city. Downtown development has been so successful that many young professionals have moved here to create interesting living spaces, food halls, breweries, and mixed-use developments from the old brick warehouses surrounding town. From May through October, Main Street comes to life with the Greenville State Farmers Market on Saturday morning.

GETTING HERE AND AROUND

Greenville is a little more than two hours northwest of Columbia. The area lies in the foothills of the Appalachian Mountains, so there is plenty of hiking and numerous waterfalls just outside town. The revitalized Main Street area, a long tree-lined stretch of shops, restaurants, and hotels, is a great base camp for your stay. To the south, the road runs through Falls Park and passes Fluor Field, home of the Greenville Drive baseball team. The northern end is home to Heritage Green, a block of museums, theaters, and a library. Be prepared with cash in hand when driving around the outskirts of Greenville—Interstate 185, a connector loop of Interstate 85 and Interstate 385, is a toll road.

VISITOR INFORMATION

CONTACTS Discover Upcountry Carolina Association. ☎ *864/233–2690* 🌐 *www.upcountrysc.com.* **VisitGreenvilleSC Visitor Center.** ✉ *206 S. Main St.* ☎ *864/233–0461, 800/717–0023* 🌐 *www.visitgreenvillesc.com.*

The unique Twin Falls, 24 miles outside Greenville, is also one of the easiest local waterfalls to get to.

Sights

★ BMW Performance Center

SCENIC DRIVE | If you missed your true calling as a race-car driver, BMW lets you live out your dreams at this two-hour experience. A pro driver radios in instructions while you put the pedal to the metal and slide around curves in each of the automaker's fastest cars, including the M8 Coupe. Afterward, cool down on the off-road course, where you'll drive an X5 through an artificial river and onto two wheels as you navigate rocky outcroppings. ✉ *1155 SC 101, Greer* ☎ *888/345–4269* 🌐 *bmwperformancecenter.com.*

Caesars Head State Park

NATIONAL/STATE PARK | **FAMILY** | Part of the Mountain Bridge Wilderness Area and best known for the Raven Cliff Falls here, Caesars Head State Park is about 30 miles north of Greenville. The trail leading to the 420-foot-tall falls can be reached a mile north of the park's main entrance; along the way there are spectacular views of river gorges and pine-covered mountains. Cross Matthews Creek on a suspension bridge; the view of the falls is worth the terror of knowing you're held in the air by nothing but wire. ✉ *8155 Geer Hwy., Cleveland* ☎ *864/836–6115* 🌐 *www.southcarolinaparks.com/caesars-head* 🎫 *Overlook free, hiking trails $3.*

Children's Museum of the Upstate

MUSEUM | **FAMILY** | This 80,000-square-foot facility is packed with hands-on exhibits that cover everything from science and music to construction and race cars. There are also special areas for kids five and younger. ✉ *300 College St., Heritage Green* ☎ *864/233–7755* 🌐 *www.tcmupstate.org* 🎫 *$10* ⏲ *Closed Mon.*

Devils Fork State Park

NATIONAL/STATE PARK | **FAMILY** | At this park on Lake Jocassee, known for its hiking, boating, and fishing, Lower Whitewater Falls plunges more than 200 feet over huge boulders to splash into the lake waters. You can view the falls from an overlook or from a boat on the lake. The park has accommodations, including both luxurious villas and camping facilities.

✉ *161 Holcombe Cr., Salem* ✣ *Off SC 11, north of Salem, 45 miles northwest of Greenville* ☎ *864/944–2639* 🌐 *www.southcarolinaparks.com/devils-fork* 🎫 *$8.*

★ Falls Park on the Reedy

NATIONAL/STATE PARK | FAMILY | In this urban outdoor oasis, sloping green hills, giant boulders, and winding walkways offer great views of the Reedy River, but the best views of the waterfalls are along the architecturally ingenious Liberty Bridge. The Peace Center amphitheater hosts moonlight movies, Shakespeare plays, and open-air concerts during the year. ✉ *601 S. Main St.* ☎ *864/467–4355* 🌐 *www.fallspark.com* 🎫 *Free.*

★ Greenville County Museum of Art

MUSEUM | This Southern-focused gallery is home to American paintings dating from the colonial era, along with more-modern works by Andy Warhol, Georgia O'Keeffe, and Jasper Johns. It hosts the world's largest public collection of Andrew Wyeth watercolors. ✉ *420 College St., Heritage Green* ☎ *864/271–7570* 🌐 *www.gcma.org* 🎫 *Free* 🕒 *Closed Mon. and Tues.*

Jones Gap State Park

NATIONAL/STATE PARK | FAMILY | Famous for its trout fishing and the Rim of the Gap Trail, which has views of Rainbow Falls, Jones Gap is 6 miles east of U.S. Route 276 and is part of the Mountain Bridge Wilderness Area. Pick up a trail map and register before venturing into the wilderness; some of the trails are long and strenuous. ✉ *303 Jones Gap Rd., Marietta* ✣ *6 miles east off U.S. 276* ☎ *864/836–3647* 🌐 *www.southcarolinaparks.com/jones-gap* 🎫 *$6.*

Shoeless Joe Jackson Museum and Baseball Library

HOUSE | This collection is housed in the former home of baseball great Joe Jackson, who along with seven other White Sox players, was accused of throwing the 1919 World Series. Though he was found not guilty, Jackson was banned from playing baseball. The museum, which is open only on Saturday from 10 to 2, has records, artifacts, photographs, and a film, along with a library of baseball books donated from fans around the country. At the end of each summer, staffers challenge their peers at Georgia's Ty Cobb Museum to a vintage baseball game. ✉ *356 Field St., Historic West End* ✣ *Across from Fluor Field* ☎ *864/346–4867* 🌐 *www.shoelessjoejackson.org* 🎫 *Free* 🕒 *Closed Sun.–Fri.*

★ Swamp Rabbit Trail

TRAIL | FAMILY | This rails-to-trails masterpiece runs 22 miles from downtown Greenville to Travelers Rest, with ample waypoints and scenic views along the way. **Reedy Rides** rents modern cruisers for $30 per day. Three miles out of town, the backyard seating at **Swamp Rabbit Cafe & Grocery** fills up on weekends with bikers grabbing gourmet sandwiches after a morning workout. If you push all the way to Travelers Rest, walk the charming downtown strip and fuel up for the return trip with an upscale burger or the lobster quesadilla at **Hare & Field**. ✉ *Greenville* ☎ *864/232–2273* 🌐 *greenvillerec.com/swamprabbit.*

Twin Falls

BODY OF WATER | It's a scenic drive and then an easy hike to these picturesque double falls, where the left and larger of the falls pitches from a height of 75 feet and white water swooshes over wide gray boulders on the right. Don't give in to the temptation to climb the rocks leading to the top of the falls; not only is the view not much better, but also the stones are very slippery. The trail is on public property, a ¼-mile hike one way. ✉ *Water Falls Rd., Pickens* ✣ *Take Cleo Chapman Rd. to Eastatoe Community Rd. to Water Falls Rd. (gravel).*

Upcountry History Museum

MUSEUM | FAMILY | This Furman University exhibit gives a visual portrait of the history of the 15 counties of the South Carolina Upstate, including lifesize diaromas. There are two floors of interactive displays and a small theater where special programs are regularly presented. ✉ *540 Buncombe St., Heritage Green* ☎ *864/467–3100* 🌐 *www.upcountryhistory.org* 🎟 *$10* ⏲ *Closed Sun. and Mon.*

Restaurants

Augusta Grill

$$$$ | AMERICAN | Wood paneling and modern art set the tone at this fine-dining stalwart, where the daily-changing menu (posted online) includes seafood like tempura soft-shell crabs, hearty steaks, and braised duck. Order ahead to be sure the kitchen hasn't run out of its signature blackberry cobbler. **Known for:** small plate options designed for sharing; varied, seasonal menu; quality service with Southern hospitality. $ *Average main: $28* ✉ *1818 Augusta St.* ☎ *864/242–0316* 🌐 *www.augustagrill.com* ⏲ *Closed Sun. and Mon.*

Husk Barbeque

$$ | BARBECUE | This spinoff of the famous Charleston restaurant rebranded in 2021, shifting toward a casual barbecue model, with long-time Husk butcher Dave Jensen at the helm. In addition to smoked meats, the outpost also offers the Husk empire's lauded fried chicken and cheeseburger. **Known for:** gorgeous exposed-brick interior balanced with industrial lighting; combo plates featuring prime beef brisket or pulled pork; top-shelf bourbon selection. $ *Average main: $16* ✉ *722 S Main St., Downtown* ☎ *864/627–0404* 🌐 *huskbbq.com* ⏲ *Closed Mon.*

Jianna

$$$$ | ITALIAN | Combining the best of Italy and coastal South Carolina, this downtown osteria serves house-made pastas and gnocchi, plus a selection of raw oysters from around the country, served with a house hot sauce and prosecco mignonette. The bright, modern interior features an open kitchen and a massive central bar that includes outdoor balcony seating when weather permits. **Known for:** raw oysters and negronis; hearty, authentic pasta entrées; light, lively atmosphere. $ *Average main: $26* ✉ *600 S. Main St., No. 2, Downtown* ☎ *864/720–2200* 🌐 *jiannagreenville.com* ⏲ *Closed Mon.*

★ Oak Hill Cafe

$$$$ | MODERN AMERICAN | In a simple home nestled just off a highway, this restaurant houses one of the most innovative kitchens in the Southeast. Owners David Porras and Lori Nelsen combine their chef and lab science histories to extract maximum flavors from the produce grown on their on-site farm. **Known for:** a deconstructed deviled egg featuring emulsified crème fraîche, honey Dijon, and roe; 2020 James Beard Best New Restaurant semifinalist; relaxed atmosphere indoors or at picnic tables outside. $ *Average main: $25* ✉ *2510 Poinsett Hwy.* ☎ *864/631–1397* 🌐 *oakhillcafe.com.*

Soby's

$$$$ | MODERN AMERICAN | The palette of plums and golds is a stunning contrast to the original brick and wood that was uncovered during the renovation of this 19th-century cotton exchange building. Although the menu changes seasonally, perennial favorites—a layered appetizer of fried green tomatoes and jalapeño pimento cheese, shrimp, and locally ground grits, and the wonderful white-chocolate banana-cream pie—are always available. **Known for:** popular Sunday brunch; one of the city's best wine lists; patio seating on Court Square. $ *Average main: $25* ✉ *207 S. Main St., Downtown* ☎ *864/232–7007* 🌐 *www.sobys.com.*

Stax Omega Diner

$ | DINER | FAMILY | This contemporary diner's menu features a little of everything, from bacon and eggs, burgers, and souvlaki to Greek-style chicken and shrimp and grits. Sit in the booths or at the half-circle counter with stools to enjoy your meal; when you're done, check out the sweets menu from the Stax Bakery next door. **Known for:** Greek and Italian desserts; popular local catering service; classic diner fare. $ *Average main: $12* ✉ *72 Orchard Park Dr.* ☎ *864/297–6639* 🌐 *www.staxs.net.*

Coffee and Quick Bites

Gather GVL

$ | **ECLECTIC** | The most unique of Greenville's growing food hall scene is Gather, where stacks of colorful shipping containers housing mini-kitchens circle a central courtyard. Grab an acai bowl, a signature sushi roll, or a basket of fried chicken, and find a spot to kick back and enjoy the live bands on weekends. **Known for:** on-site craft beer shop; pet-friendly atmosphere (leashed, and not on weekends); a hefty lobster roll from the Lob Father. $ *Average main: $10* ✉ *126 Augusta St., Downtown* ☎ *864/501–5008* 🌐 *gathergreenville.com* ⊙ *Closed Mon.*

Southern Pressed Juicery

$ | **VEGETARIAN** | Cold-pressed juices, energy bowls, and salads in a high-ceilinged, bright room make this an obvious spot for a pick-me-up when you're hoofing it around town. **Known for:** superfood coffee drinks; bottled fruit and veggie juices; creative, delicious smoothies. $ *Average main: $12* ✉ *2 W. Washington St., Downtown* ☎ *864/729–8626* 🌐 *southernpressedjuicery.com.*

Two Chefs Cafe and Market

$ | **DELI** | Adjacent to a grab-and-go market, this café has a selection of homemade sandwiches and healthy entrée options like roasted-potato salad and dried-cranberry-and-grilled-chicken salad. Tempting desserts include apple-brandy cake, flourless chocolate cake, and fruit tarts. **Known for:** salad-sandwich combos; daily entrée specials; second grab-and-go location on Pelham Road. $ *Average main: $8* ✉ *644 N. Main St., Suite 107* ☎ *864/370–9336* 🌐 *www.twochefscafeandmarket.com* ⊙ *Closed weekends.*

Hotels

Aloft Greenville Downtown

$$$ | **HOTEL** | This colorful, modern hotel offers rooms adorned with local art, including spacious suites. **Pros:** central location downtown; outdoor swimming pool is open late; pet friendly. **Cons:** not directly on Main Street; some rooms don't have a great view; no free parking. $ *Rooms from: $220* ✉ *5 N. Laurens St., Downtown* ☎ *864/297–6100* 🌐 *www.aloftgreenvilledowntown.com* *144 rooms* *No meals.*

Hyatt Regency Greenville

$$ | **HOTEL** | Ask for a room overlooking the pool or the palm-filled atrium at this conveniently located spot on the north end of Main Street. **Pros:** easy access to Main Street and Falls Park; popular on-site restaurant, Roost; light-filled, attractive communal spaces. **Cons:** the breakfast buffet served at the restaurant is not included; rooms see out into the atrium unless curtains are closed; noise carries through room walls. $ *Rooms from: $199* ✉ *220 N. Main St., Downtown* ☎ *864/235–1234* 🌐 *www.hyatt.com* *327 rooms* *No meals.*

The Westin Poinsett

$$$ | **HOTEL** | This 11-story downtown hotel built in 1925 combines old-fashioned appeal with Westin's modern upgrades. **Pros:** central location on Court Square; on-site coffee shop; fitness studio and spa. **Cons:** daily parking fee; small elevators; very busy during holidays. $ *Rooms from: $219* ✉ *120 S. Main St.* ☎ *864/421–9700* 🌐 *www.westinpoinsettgreenville.com* *223 rooms* *No meals.*

Performing Arts

Bon Secours Wellness Arena

CONCERTS | This 15,000-seat arena hosts major concerts and sporting events, including the minor league hockey Greenville Swamp Rabbits. ✉ *650 N.*

Academy St. ☏ *864/241–3800* 🌐 *www.bonsecoursarena.com.*

★ The Peace Center

ARTS CENTERS | Situated along the Reedy River, the Peace Center's theater, concert hall, and amphitheater present star performers, touring Broadway shows, dance companies, chamber music, and local groups. ✉ *300 S. Main St.* ☏ *864/467–3000* 🌐 *www.peacecenter.org.*

Shopping

Augusta Twenty

CLOTHING | This friendly women's clothing shop is filled with racks of designer threads and has frequent sales. ✉ *20 Augusta St., Downtown* ✣ *At S. Main St.* ☏ *864/233–2600* 🌐 *www.augustatwenty.com.*

MacGregor Orchard

FOOD/CANDY | **FAMILY** | The rustic stand offers a selection of fruits grown on their farm, such as peaches, blackberries, pears, apples, and raspberries. Owners Julia and Stephens Gregory make the jams and ciders that fill the shelves. ✉ *2400 SC 11, Travelers Rest* ☏ *864/320-2778.*

O.P. Taylor's

TOYS | **FAMILY** | Even adults love this supercool toy emporium, where many of the toys are on display for on-the-spot playtime. ✉ *117 N. Main St.* ☏ *864/467–1984* 🌐 *www.optaylors.com.*

Activities

GOLF

Links O'Tryon

GOLF | This 18-hole course with stunning views of the Blue Ridge Mountains and fieldstone bridges and walls was designed by Tom Jackson. ✉ *11250 New Cut Rd., Campobello* ☏ *864/468–5099* 🌐 *www.linksotryon.com* 🏌 *$26–$42, 18 holes, 6877 yds, par 72.*

The Rock Golf Club

GOLF | This mountain course features plenty of water hazards; its signature hole has a waterfall view. ✉ *171 Sliding Rock Rd., Pickens* ☏ *864/878–2030* 🌐 *www.therockgolfclub.com* 🏌 *$36–$42, 18 holes, 6710 yds, par 72.*

Blacksburg

70 miles northeast of Greenville via I–85.

Once a booming center during the "iron rush" of the late 1800s, Blacksburg is a quiet little town with a lot of history.

Sights

Kings Mountain National Military Park

NATIONAL/STATE PARK | A Revolutionary War battle considered an important turning point was fought here on October 7, 1780. Colonial Tories were soundly defeated by ragtag patriot forces from the Southern Appalachians. Visitor center exhibits, dioramas, and an orientation film describe the action. ✉ *Blacksburg* ✣ *Off I–85 Exit 2* ☏ *864/936–7921* 🌐 *www.nps.gov/kimo* 🎟 *Free.*

Kings Mountain State Park

NATIONAL/STATE PARK | **FAMILY** | This 6,000-acre park, adjacent to the National Military Park, has camping, fishing, boating, and nature and hiking trails. ✉ *1277 Park Rd.* ✣ *Off I–85 Exit 2* ☏ *803/222–3209* 🌐 *www.southcarolinaparks.com/kings-mountain* 🎟 *$3.*

Chapter 11

SAVANNAH, GA

Updated by
Summer Bozeman and
Jessica Leigh Lebos

Sights ★★★★★ Restaurants ★★★★★ Hotels ★★★★★ Shopping ★★★★★ Nightlife ★★★★★

WELCOME TO SAVANNAH, GA

TOP REASONS TO GO

★ **Winsome architecture:** Savannah has no shortage of architectural or historical marvels. The many building styles make strolling the tree-lined neighborhoods a delight.

★ ***Midnight in the Garden of Good and Evil:*** John Berendt's famous 1994 book about a local murder and the city's eccentric characters still draws travelers to the places described in the novel.

★ **Excellent restaurants:** Savannah's best restaurants, notably The Grey and The Olde Pink House, have exquisite Southern cuisine.

★ **Historic inns and bed-and-breakfasts:** One of Savannah's unique pleasures is the opportunity to stay in a historic home fronting a prominent square.

★ **Savannah by night:** Ubiquitous "to-go" cups make barhopping a popular pastime. Ghost tours are another fun nocturnal activity.

Although it's commonly referred to as "downtown," the Historic District lies on the northern edge of Savannah, just across the river from Hutchinson Island and South Carolina. The borders of the district are River Street to the north, Gaston Street to the south, and East Broad Street and Martin Luther King Jr. Boulevard to the east and west.

Tybee Island is 18 miles east of Savannah via Victory Drive (U.S. 80).

1 The Historic District. This area is home to the city's historic squares as well as many of its finest hotels, restaurants, and shopping. The borders of the district are River Street to the north, Gaston Street to the south, and East Broad Street and Martin Luther King Jr. Boulevard to the east and west.

2 The Victorian District and the Eastside. One of Savannah's oldest neighborhoods, the Victorian District is where you'll find gorgeous homes that date to the 1800s.

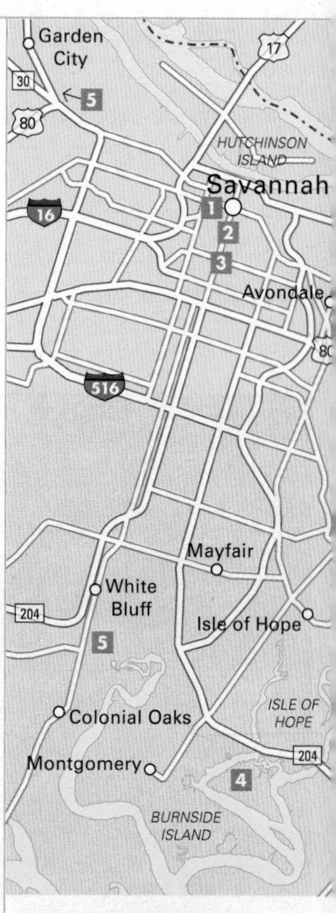

3 The Starland District, Thomas Square, and Midtown. Midtown Savannah includes neighborhoods south of Forsyth Park to Derenne Avenue, including the Starland District, the Thomas Square Streetcar Historic District, Baldwin Park, and Ardsley Park.

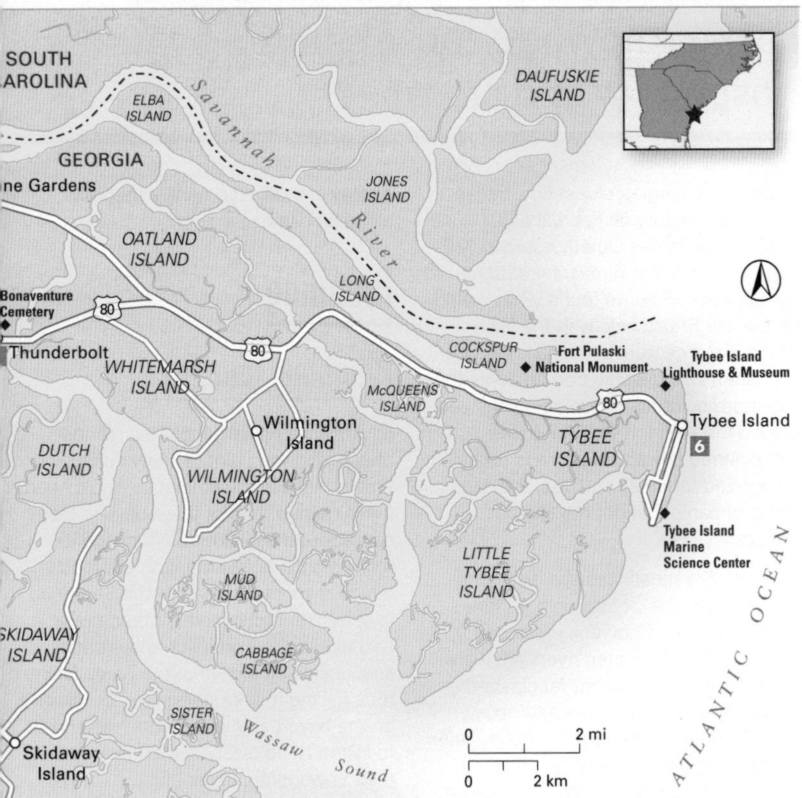

4 The Moon River District, Thunderbolt, and the Islands. Named after the song by Savannah native Johnny Mercer, this district includes the Sandfly, Isle of Hope, and Skidaway Island neighborhoods. Thunderbolt, bordering on Savannah's east side and the Wilmington River, is home to historic Bonaventure Cemetery and seafood restaurants. East on U.S. 80 leads to Wilmington Island. Historic Fort Pulaski and Oatland Island Wildlife Center are nearby.

5 The Southside, the Gateway, and Greater Savannah. Close to the airport, here's where you'll find big-box stores and affordable lodging.

6 Tybee Island. Tybee Island is home to North Beach, the Pier and Pavilion, and the South End. Souvenir shops and restaurants from the 1950s abound.

Savannah is such a warm, welcoming city that you may find it especially easy to get acquainted with the "Hostess City," as it is known to those smitten by its hospitality and charm.

Savannah, Georgia's oldest city, began its modern history on February 12, 1733, when James Oglethorpe and 120 colonists arrived at Yamacraw Bluff on the Savannah River to found what would be the last British colony in the New World. For a century and a half, the city flourished as a bustling port and was the departure point for cotton being shipped around the world. It was America's first planned city and is perhaps most recognized for its 22 squares, the diverse group of parks that dot the Historic District.

Although Savannah was spared during the Civil War, the city fell on hard times soon afterward. Cobwebs replaced cotton in the dilapidated riverfront warehouses. Historic buildings languished; many were razed or allowed to decay. The tide finally turned in the 1950s, when residents began a concerted effort—which continues to this day—to restore and preserve the city's unique architectural heritage.

The past plays an important role in Savannah. Standing in a tranquil square surrounded by historic homes, it's easy to feel as if you have stumbled through a portal into the past. Don't be fooled though, as the city offers much more than antebellum nostalgia for moonlight and magnolias. Savannah is home to several colleges and universities, including the prestigious Savannah College of Art and Design (SCAD), and since 2000 in particular has seen a surge of creative energy and development, especially along its namesake river.

Planning

Planning Your Time

Savannah is not large, but it is atmospheric, and you want to allow sufficient time to soak in the ambience. You'll need a minimum of two or three days to fully appreciate the Historic District and its many sights, not to mention the food, which is an integral part of the Savannah experience. You'll need another day or two to see the sights in the surrounding area, including a jaunt out to Tybee Island for a fishing trip, kayaking tour, or relaxing on the beach. Some travelers head north to Hilton Head or Charleston to round out their Lowcountry experience.

Getting Here and Around

You can fly into Savannah and catch a cab downtown, which is largely walkable. But you'll probably need a car if you want to explore beyond the Historic District.

AIR

Savannah and Hilton Head share an airport. Savannah/Hilton Head International Airport (SAV) is 11 miles west of downtown. The airport is only 20 minutes by car from the Historic District and around 40 minutes from Hilton Head Island.

There are plenty of taxis waiting outside the baggage claim area, and some of the larger hotels offer shuttles. **■TIP→If the flights into Savannah/Hilton Head International Airport aren't convenient, consider Jacksonville International Airport. The drive time to Savannah is just shy of 2½ hours.**

AIRPORT INFORMATION Savannah/Hilton Head International Airport. *(SAV)* ✉ *400 Airways Ave., Northwest* ☎ *912/964–0514* 🌐 *savannahairport.com.*

CAR

Interstate 95 slices north–south along the Eastern Seaboard, intersecting 10 miles west of town with east–west Interstate 16, which dead-ends in downtown Savannah. U.S. 17, the Coastal Highway, also runs north–south through town. U.S. 80 is another east–west route through Savannah.

Downtown parking can be a challenge; there are often more options in nearby residential neighborhoods. Tourists may purchase one- and two-day parking passes for $8 and $14 from the Savannah Visitors Center, the Parking Services Department, and some hotels and inns (several properties give you this pass for free if you're staying with them). Rates vary at local parking garages, but in a City of Savannah–owned lot you should expect to pay at least $1 to $2 per hour during business hours on weekdays, a $2 flat rate in the evenings, and a flat rate of $3 on weekends.

PUBLIC TRANSPORTATION

Chatham Area Transit (CAT) operates buses in Savannah and Chatham County Monday through Saturday from just before 6 am to just shy of midnight, Sunday from 7 am to 9 pm; download the app to see the full schedule. Visitors can also take advantage of "the Dot," Savannah's fare-free downtown transportation system. The express shuttle serves 24 stops through the Historic District and runs from 7 am to midnight weekdays, 10 am to midnight on Saturday, and 10 am to 9 pm on Sunday; it does not run on most holidays.

PUBLIC TRANSIT CONTACTS Chatham Area Transit. *(CAT)* ☎ *912/233–5767* 🌐 *catchacat.org.*

TAXI TRAVEL

You can hail cabs on the street if they don't have riders or assignments, though with the advent of Uber and Lyft these are few and far between. Most cab services offer flat rates to and from the airport, usually in the range of $28–$30, plus $5 for each additional person. Yellow Cab Company charges $2.70 per mile.

Pedicabs proliferate in the Historic District, operating from 10 am to midnight (until 2 am on weekends); expect to pay $5 to $10 for a short ride, or $45 per hour of touring.

CONTACTS Savannah Pedicab. ☎ *912/232–7900* 🌐 *savannahpedicab.com.* **Yellow Cab.** ☎ *912/236–1133, 912/236-1133* 🌐 *yellowcabsavannah.com.*

Tours

CARRIAGE TOURS

Carriage Tours of Savannah

CARRIAGE TOURS | Operating 50-minute tours out of City Market, Carriage Tours of Savannah travels the Historic District at a 19th-century clip-clop pace, with coachmen spinning tales and telling ghost stories along the way. During the winter months, the tours are not offered from Monday to Wednesday. ✉ *19 Jefferson St., Savannah* ☎ *912/236–6756* 🌐 *carriagetoursofsavannah.com* 🎟 *From $25.*

TROLLEY TOURS

Old Savannah Tours

DRIVING TOURS | This is the city's award-winning company, with years of experience, the widest variety of tours, and live historical reenactors. Popular options include the historic hop-on, hop-off trolley tour, the

90-minute Historic Overview, and the ghost tour that includes dinner at the Pirates' House. Leashed pets under 25 pounds are welcome to ride along. ✉ *215 W. Boundary St., Historic District* ☎ *912/234–8128* 🌐 *oldsavannahtours.com* 🎫 *From $28.*

Old Town Trolley Tours

BUS TOURS | Old Town Trolley Tours has narrated 90-minute tours traversing the Historic District. Trolleys stop at 15 designated stops every 30 minutes daily from 9 to 5 (August to March) or 9 to 6 (April to July). You can hop on and off as you please, and free parking is available. ✉ *Savannah* ☎ *855/245–8992 toll-free* 🌐 *www.trolleytours.com/savannah* 🎫 *From $33 (online purchases are discounted).*

WALKING TOURS

Creepy Crawl Haunted Pub Tour

GUIDED TOURS | This tour is a great option for anyone who loves a good ghost story while imbibing adult beverages. Believers say there are so many ghosts in Savannah they're actually divided into subcategories. These charismatic guides specialize in tavern ghosts, and they'll regale you with tales of secret subbasements, possessed gumball machines, and animated water faucets. Tours traditionally depart from the Six Pence Pub at 8 pm and last for 2½ hours. Because this is a cocktail tour, children are not permitted. Routes can vary, so call for departure times and locations. ✉ *Savannah* ☎ *912/238–3843* 🌐 *savannahtours.com* 🎫 *From $30.*

Ghost Talk Ghost Walk Tour

WALKING TOURS | FAMILY | Savannah's original, affordable ghost tour sends chills down your spine during an easygoing 1-mile jaunt through the downtown, the city's oldest area, but it's still appropriate for children. Tours last 1½ hours and leave from the middle of Reynolds Square at the John Wesley Memorial at 7:30 pm and 9:30 pm, weather permitting. Reservations are required. ✉ *Savannah* ☎ *912/233–3896* 🌐 *www.ghosttalkghostwalk.com* 🎫 *From $10.*

Festivals

Savannah Jazz Festival. Sponsored by the City of Savannah, this weeklong September extraganza of hot licks, big band sounds, and classic standards brings together different generations and multiple genres in a series of free concerts in Forsyth Park. 🌐 *savannahjazz.org*

Savannah Music Festival. Beginning in late March and running through April, this world-class showcase features more than 80 performances in classical, blues, and global genres for music lovers who travel from far-flung destinations to attend. Concerts take place around the city, from formal theaters to exquisite, intimate private rooms. 🌐 *www.savannahmusicfestival.org*

Savannah Rock 'n' Roll Marathon. Runners from all over come to pound 13 or 26 miles of pavement every November and compete for their best times, but you don't even have to own a pair of sneakers to enjoy the free music stationed all along the route, convening at the finish line with a big-name headliner in the park bandshell. 🌐 *www.runrocknroll.com/savannah*

St. Patrick's Day Festival. More than a million folks descend upon the city to carouse and take part in this annual parade and party dedicated to Irish heritage. Enjoy traditional Irish food, song, dance, and, if you're over 21, plenty of whiskey. Make sure to wear your green! 🌐 *savannahsaintpatricksday.com*

Restaurants

Southern cuisine is rich in tradition, but the dining scene in Savannah is more than just fried chicken and barbecue. Many of the city's restaurants have been exploring locally sourced ingredients as a way to tweak their usual homespun offerings, a change that is now attracting chefs and foodies alike. The mix of options includes newer, much-lauded restaurants like The Grey or Local 11ten as well as older, more established favorites like The Olde Pink House, Paula Deen's The Lady & Sons, and Mrs. Wilkes Dining Room.

That's just a few ideas to get you started. While exploring Savannah, you're sure to find any number of other exciting options as well, whether you're craving noodle bowls or a simple sandwich.

HOURS, PRICES, AND DRESS

Most popular restaurants serve both lunch and dinner, usually until around 9 pm, later on Friday and Saturday nights. Sunday brunch is a beloved institution, but be prepared to wait for a table at most of the popular spots.

Always make a reservation at an upscale restaurant when you can. Some are booked weeks in advance, but some popular restaurants don't accept reservations. Although some locals and restaurant owners have a laid-back attitude about dressing for a night out, the way you look can influence how you're treated—and where you're seated. People dress up at the city's high-end restaurants.

Restaurant listings have been shortened. For full information, visit Fodors.com.

What It Costs

$	$$	$$$	$$$$
RESTAURANTS			
under $15	$15–$19	$20–$24	over $24

Hotels

The Hostess City opens its doors every year to millions of visitors who are drawn to its historic and vibrant downtown. Because the majority of attractions are located within the Historic District, most of the city's best hotels are located there, too. In terms of accommodations, Savannah is best known for its many inns and B&Bs, which have moved into the stately antebellum mansions, renovated cotton warehouses, and myriad other historic buildings stretching from the river out to the Victorian neighborhoods in the vicinity of Forsyth Park. Most are beautifully restored with the requisite high ceilings, ornate carved millwork, claw-foot tubs, and other quaint touches. Sophisticated properties that might be at home in a much larger city have figured out how to introduce a sleek, cosmopolitan edge without bulldozing Savannah's charm. Airbnb and VRBO have made massive inroads in recent years, and these short-term vacation rentals can be condos, rooms in someone's home, or an entire private house.

HOTEL PRICES

The central location and relatively high standards of quality in Savannah's Historic District hotels do drive up room rates, especially during peak seasons, holidays, and special events like St. Patrick's Day. The number of hotel rooms continues to increase, and occupancy rates have grown accordingly, even in the former slow season from September through January. October is another relatively busy time thanks to the pleasant temperatures and packed events calendar.

Hotel reviews have been shortened. For full information, visit Fodors.com.

What It Costs

$	$$	$$$	$$$$
HOTELS			
under $150	$150–$200	$201–$250	over $250

Nightlife

As the old saying goes, "In Atlanta, they ask you what you do. In Macon, they ask you what church you go to. And in Savannah, they ask you what you drink." Congress Street and River Street have the highest concentrations of bars with live music, especially if you're looking for rock, heavy metal, or the blues. Many of the most popular dance clubs are scattered across the same area. If you're in the mood for something more sedate, there are plenty of chic enclaves known for their creative cocktails and cozy nooks that encourage intimate conversation.

Shopping

You would have to make a concerted effort to leave Savannah empty-handed. Whether you're on a quest for designer clothing or handmade candy, Savannah offers up a potent dose of shopping therapy on a silver platter.

Visitor Information

CONTACTS Savannah Visitor Information Center. ✉ *301 Martin Luther King Jr. Blvd., Historic District* ☎ *912/944–0455* 🌐 *visitsavannah.com.* **Tybee Island Visitor Information Center.** ✉ *802 1st St., Tybee Island* ☎ *877/344–3361* 🌐 *visittybee.com.*

The Historic District

Georgia's sage founder, General James Oglethorpe, laid out the city on a grid as logical as a geometry solution.

The Historic District is neatly hemmed in by the Savannah River, Gaston Street, East Broad Street, and Martin Luther King Jr. Boulevard. Streets are arrow-straight, and public squares are tucked into the grid at precise intervals. Bull Street, anchored on the north by City Hall and the south by Forsyth Park, charges down the center of the grid and maneuvers around the five public squares that stand in its way. The squares all have some historical significance; many have elaborate fountains, monuments to war heroes, and shaded resting areas with park benches. Beautiful homes and mansions speak lovingly of another era.

Sights

American Prohibition Museum

MUSEUM | FAMILY | In the heart of City Market, America's only museum dedicated to the Prohibition era shares history from 1907 to 1933. In the 6,000-square-foot space, guests wander 13 galleries, a theater, and a real speakeasy. From stories of Southern rumrunners to the history of moonshine, the museum offers a fun and informative look at the past—there are even four antique cars on the premises. Make sure to enjoy a specially crafted cocktail at the museum speakeasy bar, Congress Street Up, which stays open long after the museum closes and uses period-authentic recipes and ingredients. ✉ *209 W. Julian St., Downtown* ✣ *In City Market* ☎ *912/220–1249* 🌐 *www.americanprohibitionmuseum.com* 🎫 *$15.*

Andrew Low House

HOUSE | Built on the site of the city jail, this residence was constructed in 1848 for Andrew Low, a native of Scotland and one of Savannah's merchant princes. Designed by architect John S. Norris, the residence later belonged to Low's son, William, who inherited his father's wealth and married his longtime sweetheart, Juliette Gordon. The couple moved to England and several years after her husband's death, Juliette returned to this house and founded the Girl Scouts here on March 12, 1912. The house has 19th-century antiques, stunning silver, and some of the finest ornamental ironwork in Savannah, but it is the story and history of the family—even a bedroom named after family friend and visitor General Robert E. Lee—that is fascinating and well told by the tour guides. ✉ *329 Abercorn St., Historic District* ☎ *912/233–6854* 🌐 *www.andrewlowhouse.com* 🎫 *$12* ⏱ *Closed early Jan.*

Cathedral Basilica of St. John the Baptist
RELIGIOUS SITE | Soaring over the city, this French Gothic–style cathedral, with pointed arches and free-flowing traceries, is the seat of the Catholic diocese of Savannah. It was founded in 1799 by the first French colonists to arrive in Savannah. Fire destroyed the early structures; the present cathedral dates from 1876. Its architecture, gold-leaf adornments, and the entire edifice give testimony to the importance of the Catholic parishioners of the day. The interior spaces are grand and dramatic, including incredible stained glass and an intricately designed altar. ✉ *222 E. Harris St., at Lafayette Sq., Historic District* ☎ *912/233–4709* 🌐 *www.savannahcathedral.org* ⏱ *No tours Sun.*

Chippewa Square
PLAZA | Anchoring this square is Daniel Chester French's imposing bronze statue of General James Edward Oglethorpe, founder of both the city of Savannah and the state of Georgia. The bus-stop scenes of *Forrest Gump* were filmed on the northern end of the square. The historic Savannah Theatre, on the corner of Bull and McDonough Streets, claims to be the oldest continuously operated theater site in North America and offers a variety of family-friendly shows. ✉ *Bull St., between Hull and Perry Sts., Historic District.*

City Market
COMMERCIAL CENTER | Although the 1870s City Market was razed years ago, its atmosphere and character are still evident. Adjacent to Ellis Square, the area is a lively destination because of its galleries, boutiques, street performers, and open-air cafés. Local favorites include Byrd Cookie Company, a popular Savannah-based bakery with great edible souvenirs, and Pie Society, offering specialty British meat pies. City Market is also a good spot to purchase trolley tickets, take a ride in a horse-drawn carriage, or dive into history at the American Prohibition Museum. ✉ *W. St. Julian St., between Barnard and Montgomery Sts., Historic District* ☎ *912/232–4903* 🌐 *www.savannahcitymarket.com.*

Colonial Park Cemetery
CEMETERY | Stroll the shaded pathways and read some of the old tombstone inscriptions in this park, the final resting place for Savannahians who died between 1750 and 1853. Many of those interred here succumbed during the yellow fever epidemic in 1820. Notice the dramatic entrance gate on the corner of Abercorn and Oglethorpe Streets. Local legend tells that when Sherman's troops set up camp here, they moved some headstones around and altered inscriptions for their own amusement, which partially explains the headstones mounted against the far wall. This spooky spot is a regular stop for ghost tours. ✉ *Oglethorpe and Abercorn Sts., Historic District.*

Davenport House Museum
HOUSE | Semicircular stairs with wrought-iron railings lead to the recessed doorway of the redbrick Federal home constructed by master builder Isaiah Davenport for his family between 1815 and 1820. Three dormered windows poke through the sloping roof of the stately house, and the interior has polished hardwood floors and fine woodwork and plasterwork, showcasing Davenport's talents to potential clients. The proposed demolition of this historic Savannah structure galvanized the city's residents into action to save their treasured buildings. The home endured a history of dilapidation that had lingered since the 1920s, when it was divided into tenements. When someone proposed razing it to build a parking lot in 1955, a small group of neighbors

The Mercer Williams House is famous for being featured in the book and film *Midnight in the Garden of Good and Evil.*

raised $22,000 to buy and restore the property. This action was the inception of the Historic Savannah Foundation and the first of many successful efforts to preserve the architectural treasure that is the city today. ✉ *324 E. State St., Historic District* ☎ *912/236–8097* 🌐 *www.davenporthousemuseum.org* 🎟 *$10* ⏲ *Closed mid-Jan.*

★ Ellis Square

PLAZA | FAMILY | Converted from a public square to a parking garage in the 1970s, Ellis Square has been restored in recent years and is once again one of Savannah's most popular spots. Near the western end stands a statue of legendary songwriter Johnny Mercer, a Savannah native. Nearby is a visitor center with a touch-screen city guide, maps and brochures, and public restrooms. To the east is a life-size chess board; the pieces can be requested at the visitor center. A treat for youngsters (and the young at heart) is the square's interactive fountain, which is entertaining and refreshing in the warmer months. ✉ *Barnard St., between W. Congress and W. Bryan Sts., Historic District.*

Factors Walk

HISTORIC SITE | A network of iron crosswalks and steep stone stairways connects Bay Street to Factors Walk below. The congested area of multistory buildings was originally the center of commerce for cotton brokers (also called factors), who walked between and above the lower cotton warehouses. Ramps lead down to River Street. ■ **TIP→ This area is paved in cobblestones and features steep, historic stone staircases, so wear comfortable shoes.** ✉ *Bay St. to Factors Walk, Historic District.*

First African Baptist Church

RELIGIOUS SITE | Enslaved people constructed this church at night by lamplight after having worked the plantations during the day, finishing it in 1859. It is one of the first organized black Baptist churches on the continent, constituted in 1777. The basement floor still shows signs of its time as a stop on the Underground Railroad. Designs drilled in the floor are rumored to actually have been air holes for slaves hiding underneath, waiting to be transported to the Savannah River for their trip to freedom. It was also an important meeting place during the civil rights era. ✉ *23 Montgomery St., Historic District* ☎ *912/233–6597* 🌐 *www.firstafricanbc.com* 🎫 *$10* ⏲ *Closed Mon.*

★ Jepson Center for the Arts

MUSEUM | FAMILY | This contemporary building is one of a kind among the characteristic 18th- and 19th-century architecture of historic Savannah. The modern art extension of the adjacent Telfair Academy museum, the Jepson was designed by renowned architect Moshe Safdie. Within the marble-and-glass edifice are rotating exhibits, on loan and from the permanent collection, ranging from European masters to contemporary locals. There's also an outdoor sculpture terrace and an interactive, kid-friendly area on the third level called the ArtZeum. ✉ *207 W. York St., Historic District* ☎ *912/790–8800* 🌐 *www.telfair.org/visit/jepson-center* 🎫 *$20, includes admission to the Owens-Thomas House & Slave Quarters and the Telfair Academy.*

Johnson Square

PLAZA | The oldest of James Oglethorpe's original squares was laid out in 1733 and named for South Carolina governor Robert Johnson. A monument marks the grave of Nathanael Greene, a hero of the Revolutionary War and close friend of George Washington. The square has always been a popular gathering place: Savannahians came here to welcome President Monroe in 1819, to greet the Marquis de Lafayette in 1825, and to cheer for Georgia's secession in 1861. ■ **TIP→ Locals call this Bank Square because of the plethora of nearby banks—perfect if you need an ATM.** ✉ *Bull St., between Bryan and Congress Sts., Historic District.*

Juliette Gordon Low Birthplace

HOUSE | FAMILY | This early-19th-century town house, attributed to William Jay, was designated in 1965 as Savannah's first National Historic Landmark. "Daisy" Low, founder of the Girl Scouts, was born here in 1860, and the house is now owned and operated by the Girl Scouts of America. Mrs. Low's paintings and other artwork are on display in the house, restored to the style of 1886, the year of Mrs. Low's marriage. Droves of Girl Scout troops make the regular pilgrimage to Savannah to see their founder's birthplace and earn merit badges. In addition to its value as a pilgrimage site for Girl Scouts, the home is a beautiful look into the lives of Savannahians during the Victorian era. ■ **TIP→ Tickets sell fast, so book in advance if you want to tour the house on a specific day.** ✉ *10 E. Oglethorpe St., Historic District* ☎ *912/233–4501* 🌐 *www.juliettegordonlowbirthplace.org* 🎫 *$15* ⏲ *Closed Sun. and early Jan.*

Lafayette Square

PLAZA | Named for the Marquis de Lafayette, who aided the Americans during the Revolutionary War, the square contains a graceful three-tier fountain donated by the Georgia chapter of the Colonial Dames of America. The Cathedral Basilica of St. John the Baptist is located on this square, as are the Andrew Low House and the impressive and elegant Hamilton-Turner Inn. The childhood home of celebrated Southern author Flannery O'Connor also sits on this square. ✉ *Abercorn St., between E. Harris and E. Charlton Sts., Historic District.*

Madison Square

PLAZA | Laid out in 1839 and named for President James Madison, this square is home to a statue depicting Sergeant William Jasper hoisting a flag, a tribute to his bravery during the Siege of Savannah. Though mortally wounded, Jasper rescued the colors of his regiment in the assault on the British lines, and his valor

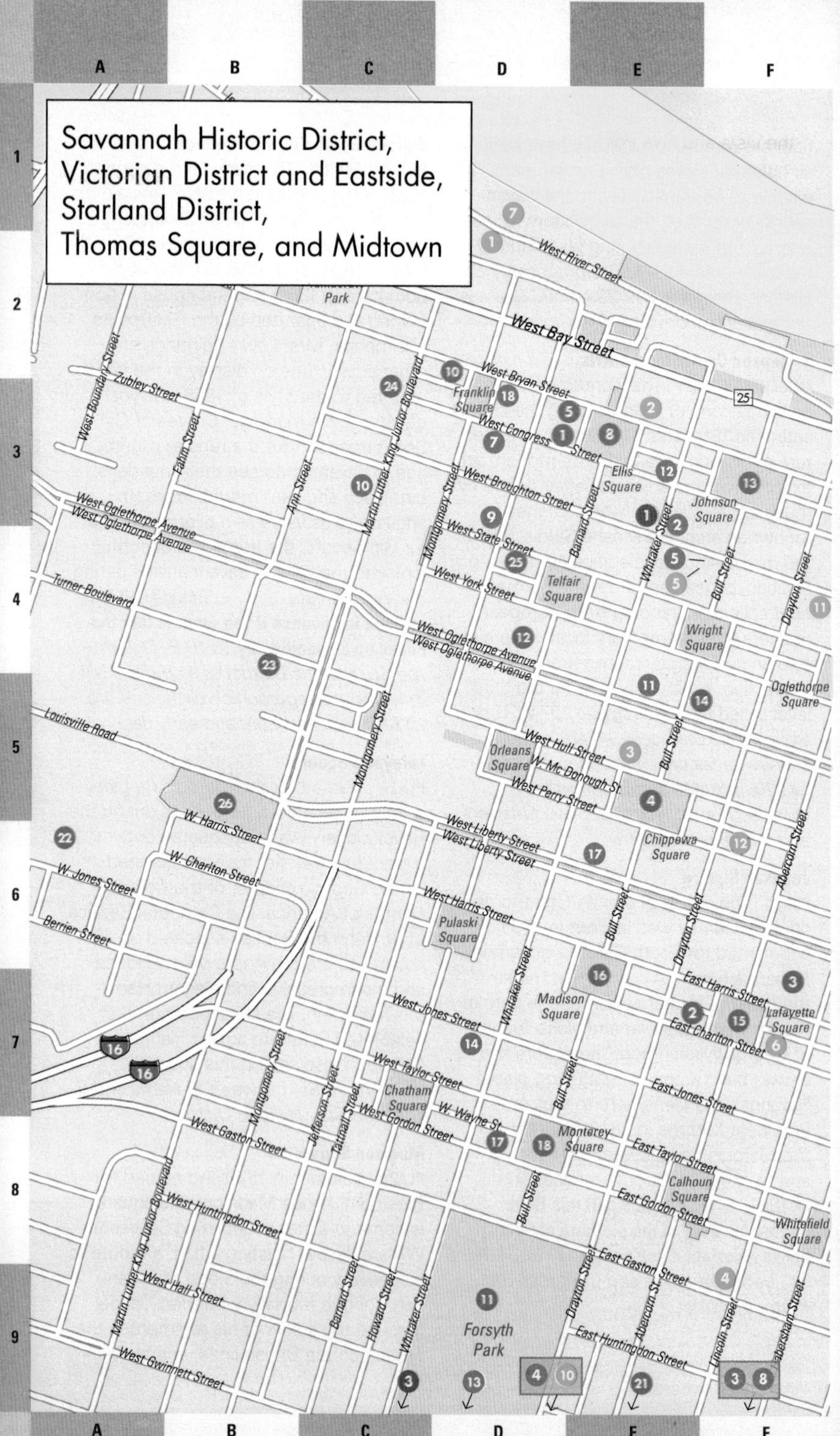

Savannah Historic District, Victorian District and Eastside, Starland District, Thomas Square, and Midtown
A
B
C
D
E
F
1
2
3
4
5
6
7
8
9
West River Street
West Bay Street
Park
West Boundary Street
Zubley Street
Fahm Street
West Bryan Street
Franklin Square
West Congress Street
Ellis Square
Martin Luther King Junior Boulevard
Ann Street
Montgomery Street
West Broughton Street
Barnard Street
Whitaker Street
Johnson Square
West Oglethorpe Avenue
West State Street
West York Street
Telfair Square
Bull Street
Drayton Street
Turner Boulevard
Wright Square
Oglethorpe Square
Louisville Road
West Hull Street
Orleans Square
W. Mc Donough St.
West Perry Street
W. Harris Street
West Liberty Street
Chippewa Square
Abercorn Street
W. Charlton Street
W. Jones Street
West Harris Street
Pulaski Square
Berrien Street
Madison Square
East Harris Street
Lafayette Square
East Charlton Street
West Jones Street
West Taylor Street
East Jones Street
Chatham Square
Jefferson Street
Tattnall Street
West Gordon Street
W. Wayne St.
Monterey Square
West Gaston Street
East Taylor Street
Calhoun Square
East Gordon Street
West Huntingdon Street
Whitefield Square
East Gaston Street
West Hall Street
Barnard Street
Howard Street
Forsyth Park
Abercorn St.
Lincoln Street
Habersham Street
East Huntingdon Street
West Gwinnett Street
16
25

G H I

HUTCHINSON ISLAND
Savannah River
John Rousakis Riverfront Plaza
East River Street
Morrell Park
Emmet Park
East Bay Street
East Bryan Street
Reynolds Square
East Congress Street
Warren Square
E. Saint Julian St.
Washington Square
Abercorn Street
East Broughton Street
Habersham Street
East State Street
Price Street
Houston Street
East Broad Street
East York Street
Columbia Square
E. President St.
Greene Square
Lincoln St.
East Oglethorpe Avenue
East Oglethorpe Avenue
East Hull Street
East McDonough St.
Crawford Square
East Perry Street
East Perry Lane
East Liberty Street
East Liberty Street
East Harris Street
Troup Square
East Macon Street
East Charlton Street
East Jones Street
East Taylor Street
Price Street
East Gordon Street
East Broad Street
East Gaston Street
Hartridge Street

KEY
Exploring Sights
Restaurants
Quick Bites
Hotels

G H I

Sights

1 American Prohibition Museum ... D3
2 Andrew Low House ... E7
3 Cathedral Basilica of St. John the Baptist ... F7
4 Chippewa Square ... E5
5 City Market ... D3
6 Colonial Park Cemetery ... G6
7 Davenport House Museum ... H5
8 Ellis Square ... E3
9 Factors Walk ... G3
10 First African Baptist Church ... D2
11 Forsyth Park ... D9
12 Jepson Center for the Arts ... D4
13 Johnson Square ... F3
14 Juliette Gordon Low Birthplace ... E5
15 Lafayette Square ... F7
16 Madison Square ... E7
17 Mercer Williams House ... D8
18 Monterey Square ... D8
19 Owens-Thomas House & Slave Quarters ... G5
20 Reynolds Square ... G3
21 Savannah African Art Museum ... E9
22 Savannah Children's Museum ... A6
23 SCAD Museum of Art ... B4
24 Ships of the Sea Maritime Museum ... C3
25 Telfair Academy ... D4
26 Tricentennial Park and Battlefield ... B5

Restaurants

1 Cha Bella ... I5
2 Circa 1875 ... E3
3 Cotton & Rye ... F9
4 Elizabeth on 37th ... D9
5 The Flying Monk Noodle Bar ... E4
6 Fox & Fig Cafe ... G7
7 Garibaldi ... D3
8 Green Truck Neighborhood Pub ... F9
9 The Grey Market ... D3
10 The Grey ... C3
11 Husk Savannah ... E5
12 The Lady & Sons ... E3
13 Local 11ten ... D9
14 Mrs. Wilkes' Dining Room ... D7
15 The Olde Pink House ... G3
16 Sisters of the New South ... I7
17 Soho South Cafe ... E6
18 Vinnie Van Go-Go's ... D3

Quick Bites

1 The Coffee Fox ... E3
2 Leopold's Ice Cream ... G4
3 Starland Yard Food Truck Park ... C9

Hotels

1 The Alida, Savannah, a Tribute Portfolio Hotel ... D2
2 Andaz Savannah ... E3
3 Foley House Inn ... E5
4 The Gastonian ... F9
5 The Grant ... E4
6 Hamilton-Turner Inn ... F7
7 JW Marriott Savannah Plant Riverside District ... D1
8 Kehoe House ... G5
9 The Kimpton Brice Hotel ... I4
10 Mansion on Forsyth Park ... D9
11 The Marshall House ... F4
12 Perry Lane Hotel ... F6
13 Westin Savannah Harbor Golf Resort & Spa ... I2

is celebrated each year with an annual memorial ceremony. A granite marker denotes the southern line of the British defense during the 1779 battle. The Green-Meldrim House, General Sherman's headquarters after capturing the city in 1864, is here. ✉ *Bull St., between W. Harris and W. Charlton Sts., Historic District.*

Mercer Williams House

MUSEUM | A staple on the tourist circuit, this house museum has been the stuff of legend since the release of the longtime best-selling novel *Midnight in the Garden of Good and Evil,* which was based on the murder trial of local antiques dealer Jim Williams. Williams, who purportedly killed his lover in the front den while sitting at the desk where he later died, purchased the house in 1969. Scandal aside, Williams was an aficionado of historic preservation, and the Mercer House was one of some 50 Savannah properties that he purchased and restored. Designed by New York architect John S. Norris for General Hugh Mercer, great-grandfather of Johnny Mercer, the home was constructed in 1860 and completed after the end of the Civil War in 1868. Inside are fine examples of 18th- and 19th-century furniture and art from Jim Williams's private collection. **■TIP→ Don't miss a look around the charming gift shop.** ✉ *429 Bull St., Historic District* ☎ *912/236–6352* 🌐 *mercerhouse.com* 🎫 *$12.50* ⏲ *Closed Tues. and Wed.*

Monterey Square

PLAZA | Commemorating the victory of General Zachary Taylor's forces in Monterrey, Mexico, in 1846, this is the southernmost of Bull Street's squares. A monument honors General Casimir Pulaski, the Polish nobleman who lost his life in the Siege of Savannah during the Revolutionary War. On the square sits Temple Mickve Israel (one of the country's oldest Jewish congregations) and some of the city's most beautiful mansions, including the infamous Mercer Williams House. ✉ *Bull St., between Taylor and Gordon Sts., Historic District.*

★ Owens-Thomas House & Slave Quarters

HOUSE | Designed by William Jay, the Owens-Thomas House is widely considered to be one of the finest examples of English Regency architecture in America. Built in 1816–19, the house was constructed with local materials. Of particular note are the curving walls, Greek-inspired ornamental molding, half-moon arches, stained-glass panels, original Duncan Phyfe furniture, the hardwood "bridge" on the second floor, and the indoor toilets, which it had before the White House or Versailles. In 2018, the site renamed itself the Owens-Thomas House & Slave Quarters and revealed a new interpretive exhibition that includes the restored dwellings of those enslaved here. Owned and administered by Telfair Museums, this home gives an inside perspective on Savannah's history. ✉ *124 Abercorn St., Historic District* ☎ *912/790–8889* 🌐 *www.telfair.org/visit/owens-thomas* 🎫 *$20, includes admission to the Jepson Center and the Telfair Academy* ⏲ *Closed Tues. and Wed.*

Reynolds Square

PLAZA | Anglican cleric and theologian John Wesley is remembered here. He arrived in Savannah in 1736 at the behest of General James Oglethorpe to minister to the newly established colony. During his short stay, the future founder of the Methodist Church preached and wrote the first English hymnal in the city. His monument in Reynolds Square is shaded by greenery and surrounded by park benches. The landmark Planters Inn, formerly the John Wesley Hotel, is also located on the square. Ironically, though it was named after a man of the cloth, it was considered the best brothel in town at the turn of the 20th century. ✉ *Abercorn St., between E. Congress and E. Bryan Sts., Historic District.*

Savannah Children's Museum

MUSEUM | FAMILY | Adhering to the principle of learning through doing, the Savannah Children's Museum has open green spaces with several stations geared toward sensory play, including a water–sand play excavation station, sound station of percussion instruments, and an organic garden. The storybook nook is a partnership with the public library and encourages visiting youngsters to balance physical and mental recreation. One station includes costumes for stage performances. ✉ *Tricentennial Park, 655 Louisville Rd., Historic District* ☎ *912/651–4292* 🌐 *www.chsgeorgia.org/scm* 🎫 *$8* 🕒 *Closed Sun. in June–Aug., and Mon. and Tues. in Sept.–May.*

★ SCAD Museum of Art

MUSEUM | This architectural marvel rose from the ruins of the oldest surviving railroad building in the United States. Appropriately, the architect chosen for the lofty design and remodel project was Christian Sottile, the valedictorian of Savannah College of Art and Design's 1997 graduating class and the current dean of the School of Building Arts. Sottile rose to the hearty challenge of merging the past with the present, preserving key architectural details of the original structure while introducing contemporary design elements. SCAD Museum of Art houses two main galleries with rotating exhibits by some of the most acclaimed figures in contemporary art: the Evans Gallery features works of African American arts and culture, while the André Leon Talley Gallery is devoted to fashion and high style. ✉ *601 Turner Blvd., Historic District* ☎ *912/525–7191* 🌐 *www.scadmoa.org* 🎫 *$10* 🕒 *Closed Mon.–Wed.*

★ Ships of the Sea Maritime Museum

HOUSE | FAMILY | This exuberant Greek Revival mansion was the home of William Scarborough, a wealthy early-19th-century merchant and one of the principal owners of the *Savannah,* the first steamship to cross the Atlantic. The structure, with its portico capped by half-moon windows, is another of architect William Jay's notable contributions to the Historic District. These days, it houses the Ships of the Sea Maritime Museum, with displays of model ships and exhibits detailing maritime history. The ambitious North Garden nearly doubled the original walled courtyard's size and provides ample space for naturalist-led walks and outdoor concerts. ✉ *41 Martin Luther King Jr. Blvd., Historic District* ☎ *912/232–1511* 🌐 *www.shipsofthesea.org* 🎫 *$9* 🕒 *Closed Mon.*

★ Telfair Academy

MUSEUM | The oldest public art museum in the South was designed by William Jay in 1819 as a residence for Alexander Telfair. Within its marble rooms are a variety of paintings from American and European masters, plaster casts of the Elgin Marbles and other classical sculptures, and some of the Telfair family furnishings, including a Duncan Phyfe sideboard and Savannah-made silver. ✉ *121 Barnard St., Historic District* ☎ *912/790–8800* 🌐 *www.telfair.org* 🎫 *$20, includes admission to the Jepson Center and the Owens-Thomas House & Slave Quarters.*

Tricentennial Park and Battlefield

NATIONAL/STATE PARK | FAMILY | This 25-acre complex is home to the Savannah History Museum, the Georgia State Railroad Museum, and the Savannah Children's Museum, as well as Battlefield Memorial Park. This site offers an unbeatable introduction to the city and a full day of fun for the whole family. The battlefield was the site of the second bloodiest battle of the Revolutionary War where, on October 9, 1779, 800 of the 8,000 troops who fought lost their lives. ✉ *303 Martin Luther King Jr. Blvd., Historic District* ☎ *912/651–6840* 🌐 *www.savannah.com/tricentennial-park.*

Restaurants

★ Cha Bella

$$$$ | **AMERICAN** | The first farm-to-table restaurant in Savannah, Cha Bella continues to serve only dishes made with the finest local ingredients, so even if you've been here recently, there may be some surprises. With no walk-in refrigerator, all ingredients must be used within three days of delivery, so the menu is guaranteed to be fresh. **Known for:** Savannah's first farm-to-table restaurant; a delightful array of cocktails; menu changes regularly based on what's fresh and available. *Average main: $27* *102 E. Broad St., Historic District* *912/790–7888* *www.cha-bella.com* *No lunch.*

Circa 1875

$$$$ | **FRENCH** | The closest thing you'll find to a Parisian bistro in Savannah, this intimate gastropub offers a menu of rich traditional French dishes; trust the well-trained staff to suggest a wine pairing for your meal. The escargot and pâté make excellent starters before you move on to main dishes like steak frites or cassoulet. **Known for:** Parisian atmosphere and authentic French cuisine; intimate, romantic space; fantastic mussels steeped in fennel, shallots, and white wine. *Average main: $31* *48 Whitaker St., Historic District* *912/443–1875* *www.circa1875.com* *No lunch. Closed Sun.*

The Flying Monk Noodle Bar

$ | **ASIAN FUSION** | Noodle, rice, and soup dishes from across Asia come together on the eclectic, flavorful menu at the Flying Monk. The well-appointed space and laid-back atmosphere complement the savory dishes. **Known for:** authentic Asian fare; quick service; vegetarian-friendly menu. *Average main: $9* *5 W. Broughton St., Historic District* *912/232–8888* *www.flywiththemonk.com.*

★ Fox & Fig Cafe

$ | **VEGETARIAN** | After gaining a cult following at Foxy Loxy Cafe, proprietor Jen Jenkins has created a haven for vegans, vegetarians, and omnivores with her plant-based menu that features all-day brunch, lunch, and dinner options. Popular items include the Fox Burger (a Beyond Burger with arugula, caramelized onions, and agave-dijon on pretzel bun), milky shakes that use Leopold's coconut cream ice cream, soaked chia porridge, and eggless quiche. **Known for:** vegan eats; house-made ingredients; all-day brunch. *Average main: $11* *321 Habersham St., Historic District* *912/297–6759* *www.foxandfigcafe.com.*

Garibaldi

$$$$ | **MODERN ITALIAN** | This well-appointed restaurant is known to locals and travelers alike for its contemporary cuisine and Italian classics at reasonable prices. Ask your knowledgeable and professional server to offer wine pairings. **Known for:** elegant and intimate setting; crispy flounder with apricot and shallot sauce; Italian classics. *Average main: $27* *315 W. Congress, Historic District* *912/232–7118* *www.garibaldisavannah.com* *No lunch.*

★ The Grey

$$$$ | **AMERICAN** | In a restored Greyhound bus depot, James Beard Award–winner Chef Mashama Bailey and her talented team create gorgeous dishes that fuse Southern cuisine with European inspiration. Whether you're tucked in the more casual diner car or perched in the luster of the art deco–inspired dining room, service is impeccable, and the ever-changing menu offers sumptuously made mains from water, earth, and sky. **Known for:** impressive collection of accolades; port city Southern cuisine; reservations recommended. *Average main: $31* *109 Martin Luther King Jr. Blvd., Downtown* *912/662–5999* *www.thegreyrestaurant.com* *Closed Mon.*

★ The Grey Market

$ | **DINER** | After the success of The Grey, a mecca of port city Southern cuisine, restaurateurs Johno Morisano and Chef Mashama Bailey created this hip bodega-inspired take on a Southern lunch counter. Whether you're looking for a breakfast sandwich, an egg cream, a bottle of wine, or a Band-Aid, the Market has you covered. **Known for:** NYC meets Southern lunch counter vibe; grab-and-go options; breakfast, like the Sizzlin' Smoky Pig (pulled pork, egg, and pepper relish on a roll). *Average main: $12 109 Jefferson St., Downtown 912/201–3924 www.thegreymkt.com.*

Husk Savannah

$$$ | **SOUTHERN** | After transforming the Charleston restaurant scene with internationally recognized, elevated Southern cuisine crafted from heirloom ingredients, James Beard Award–winning chef Sean Brock has brought his unique flavor to Savannah. Housed in a restored (and rumored to be haunted) Historic District home, Husk Savannah features an ever-changing menu of coastal Georgia and Deep South delights. **Known for:** award-winning chef Sean Brock as its creator; Sunday brunch; classic Southern building with modern decor. *Average main: $22 12 W. Oglethorpe Ave., Historic District 912/349–2600 www.husksavannah.com Closed daily 2–5:30.*

The Lady & Sons

$$$ | **SOUTHERN** | Y'all, this is the place that made Paula Deen famous. There are plenty of crowds these days, but everyone patiently waits to attack the buffet, which is stocked for both lunch and dinner with crispy fried chicken, mashed potatoes, collard greens, lima beans, and other favorites. **Known for:** celebrity chef Paula Deen; gut-busting Southern eats; homemade dessert classics like banana pudding. *Average main: $24 102 W. Congress St., Historic District 912/233–2600 www.ladyandsons.com.*

★ Mrs. Wilkes' Dining Room

$$$$ | **SOUTHERN** | **FAMILY** | The gold standard for authentic Southern fare in Savannah has kept folks lined up to enjoy family-style offerings at big tables for decades. Mrs. Wilkes's granddaughter and great-grandson are keeping it a family affair in more ways than one (kids under 10 eat for half-price). **Known for:** Southern cooking served family-style; former president Barack Obama and his entourage had lunch here when he visited Savannah; cash-only policy. *Average main: $25 107 W. Jones St., Historic District 912/232–5997 www.mrswilkes.com No credit cards Closed weekends and Jan. No dinner.*

★ The Olde Pink House

$$$$ | **SOUTHERN** | This Georgian mansion was built in 1771 for James Habersham, one of the wealthiest Americans of his time, and the historic atmosphere comes through in the original Georgia pine floors of the tavern, the Venetian chandeliers, and the 18th-century English antiques. The menu is just as classic and Southern, with chicken pot pie, shrimp and grits, and sweet potato biscuits gracing the menu. **Known for:** exceptional Southern dining; historical ambience; remarkable wine menu. *Average main: $27 23 Abercorn St., Historic District 912/232–4286 www.plantersinnsavannah.com/the-olde-pink-house-menu No lunch Sun. and Mon.*

★ Soho South

$ | **ECLECTIC** | This garage turned art gallery turned restaurant features a playful, Southern-inspired menu with a variety of fresh and beautiful salads and soups, plus a handful of entrées, like the chicken and waffles sandwich or the fried goat cheese salad—both best bets for lunchtime patrons. **Known for:** unique take on Southern lunch, informed by fresh, local ingredients; located in a renovated garage space; signature tomato-basil bisque accompanying the grilled cheese on sourdough with pimento aioli.

[$] *Average main: $12* ✉ *12 W. Liberty St., Historic District* ☎ *912/233–1633* 🌐 *www.sohosouthcafe.com* ⏲ *No dinner.*

Vinnie Van Go-Go's

$ | **PIZZA** | **FAMILY** | With a secret dough recipe and a homemade sauce, Vinnie's is critically acclaimed by pizza and calzone enthusiasts from around the Southeast. Lots of visitors get a kick out of watching the cooks throw the dough in the air in the big open kitchen, but there are only a few tables inside, along with a long stretch of stools at the bar; the heart of the restaurant is its plentiful outdoor seating, great for people-watching. **Known for:** outdoor seating; bustling, casual dining; long waits. [$] *Average main: $14* ✉ *317 W. Bryan St., City Market* ☎ *912/233–6394* 🌐 *www.vinnievangogo.com* 💳 *No credit cards* ⏲ *No lunch Mon.–Thurs.*

Coffee and Quick Bites

★ The Coffee Fox

$ | **CAFÉ** | Specializing in locally roasted PERC coffee, house-made baked goods, and craft beers, the Coffee Fox is a great stop whether you're on the run or looking to perch. The cold brew will win the hearts of coffee aficionados in the hot summer months. **Known for:** Cubano-style coffee and Latin-American-inspired drinks with horchata; vegan baked goods made by Auspicious Bakery; beer to go. [$] *Average main: $4* ✉ *102 W. Broughton St., Downtown* ☎ *912/401–0399* 🌐 *thecoffeefox.com.*

★ Leopold's Ice Cream

$ | **CAFÉ** | One of the best ice-cream parlors in the area is Leopold's, a Savannah institution since 1919. It's currently owned by Stratton Leopold, grandson of the original owner and the producer of films like *Mission: Impossible III*. Posters and paraphernalia from his films make for an entertaining sideline to the selection of ice cream made with the old family recipe, methods, and ingredients. **Known for:** lemon custard or honey almond and cream flavors; seasonal flavors like rose petal cream, Guinness, or mint-lime sorbet; floats and shakes. [$] *Average main: $5* ✉ *212 E. Broughton St., Historic District* ☎ *912/234–4442* 🌐 *www.leopoldsicecream.com.*

Hotels

The Alida, Savannah, a Tribute Portfolio Hotel

$$$$ | **HOTEL** | A newer addition to Savannah's Riverfront, the Alida collaborated with the Savannah College of Art and Design to create the industrial-meets-mid-century-modern vibe that's peppered with vibrant original, local artwork. **Pros:** local/artisanal details feel special; attentive staff; can be booked through Marriott with points. **Cons:** views from several floors are blocked by the new JW Marriott at Plant Riverside District; Williamson Street gets very busy and rowdy with partiers at night; no in-room coffee (though available on request). [$] *Rooms from: $288* ✉ *412 Williamson St., Historic District* ☎ *912/715–7000* 🌐 *www.thealidahotel.com* *194 rooms* *No meals.*

Andaz Savannah

$$$$ | **HOTEL** | The interiors at the Andaz make quite a statement: the exposed-brick walls in the spacious lobby are offset by cozy, nested seating areas. **Pros:** concierge with extensive insider knowledge; excellent location overlooking Ellis Square, two blocks from the river; cosmopolitan rooftop pool. **Cons:** sounds of revelers on Congress Street can sometimes be heard in rooms; no free parking; conference spaces don't match the designer appeal of the rest of the hotel. [$] *Rooms from: $279* ✉ *Ellis Sq., 14 Barnard St., Historic District* ✢ *At Barnard and Bryan Sts. on Ellis Sq.* ☎ *912/233–2116* 🌐 *savannah.andaz.hyatt.com* *151 rooms* *No meals.*

Foley House Inn

$$$$ | **B&B/INN** | In the center of the Historic District, this elegant inn is made up of two town houses built 50 years apart. **Pros:** gorgeous architecture and decor; luxury bath products; complimentary wine and hors d'oeuvres served in the evening. **Cons:** old pipes can make for slow drainage; fee for parking pass; no elevator. *Rooms from: $259* *14 W. Hull St., Historic District* *912/232–6622, 800/647–3708* *www.foleyinn.com* *19 rooms* *Free breakfast.*

★ The Gastonian

$$$$ | **B&B/INN** | Guest rooms—many of which are exceptionally spacious—in this atmospheric Italianate inn dating from 1868 all have fireplaces and are decorated with a mix of funky finds and antiques from the Georgian and Regency periods. **Pros:** cordial and caring staff; hot breakfast is hard to beat; afternoon tea and wine and cheese at night. **Cons:** accommodations on the third floor are a climb; some of the furnishings are less than regal; plumbing is old and sometimes problematic. *Rooms from: $279* *220 E. Gaston St., Historic District* *912/232–2869, 800/322–6603* *www.gastonian.com* *17 rooms* *Free breakfast.*

★ The Grant

$$ | **RENTAL** | Offering the best of both worlds, the Grant provides a boutique-hotel environment with the freedom of vacation-rental accommodations, the first establishment in Savannah to embrace the so-called urban suite trend. **Pros:** quality plus affordability; multiple-room suites great for large parties; overlooks Broughton Street. **Cons:** Broughton Street can be noisy at night; no hotel amenities; parking can be a challenge. *Rooms from: $174* *5 W. Broughton St., Downtown* *912/257–4050* *www.thegrantsavannah.com* *17 suites* *No meals.*

★ Hamilton-Turner Inn

$$$$ | **B&B/INN** | With bathrooms the size of New York City apartments, this French Empire mansion is celebrated, if not in song, certainly in story, and definitely has a "wow" effect, especially the rooms that front Lafayette Square. **Pros:** wonderfully furnished rooms; breakfast is a treat, with baked items such as scones and hot entrées like perfect eggs Benedict; long and interesting history. **Cons:** sedate atmosphere won't appeal to everyone; no guest elevator (except for accessible Room 201); street parking only. *Rooms from: $259* *330 Abercorn St., Historic District* *912/233–1833* *www.hamilton-turnerinn.com* *18 rooms* *Free breakfast.*

JW Marriott Savannah Plant Riverside District

$$$$ | **RESORT** | The name is a mouthful, and that's appropriate for this massive, entertainment-packed property with an enviable location on the Savannah riverfront. **Pros:** activity-packed area of town; plenty of dining options; Electric Moon Skytop Lounge is one of the city's best. **Cons:** this trendy area of River Street is noisy in the evenings; as Savannah's newest lodging property, prices are high; the decor can be gauche and overstimulating. *Rooms from: $429* *400 W. River St., Historic District* *912/373–9100* *www.marriott.com* *419 rooms* *No meals.*

★ Kehoe House

$$$$ | **B&B/INN** | Known for its remarkably friendly and attentive staff, this 1890s-era house, handsomely appointed in Victorian splendor, was originally the family manse of William Kehoe, a prominent Savannah businessman whose Kehoe Iron Works are now an event venue near the Eastern Wharf. **Pros:** romantic, photo-worthy setting; the two elevators are a rarity in a B&B; great, filling Southern breakfasts. **Cons:** a few rooms have the sink and shower in the room; soundproofing in guest rooms could be better; in-room

fireplaces don't work. $ *Rooms from: $251* ✉ *123 Habersham St., Historic District* ☎ *912/232–1020, 800/820–1020* 🌐 *www.kehoehouse.com* 🛏 *13 rooms* 🍴 *Free breakfast.*

★ The Kimpton Brice Hotel
$$$ | HOTEL | No detail was spared when they made a boutique hotel out of this 1860s warehouse, which later served as a Coca-Cola bottling plant and then a livery stable. **Pros:** staff is genuinely warm and helpful; artistic design mixed with old Southern touches; great view of the secret garden from many of the second-floor rooms. **Cons:** neighboring Bay Street can be loud; no free parking; given it's in a historic building, the rooms are smaller than one might expect for the price. $ *Rooms from: $224* ✉ *601 E. Bay St., Historic District* ☎ *912/238–1200* 🌐 *www.bricehotel.com* 🛏 *145 rooms* 🍴 *No meals.*

★ The Marshall House
$$$$ | B&B/INN | With original pine floors, handsome woodwork, and exposed brick, this hotel provides the charm and intimacy of a B&B. **Pros:** great location near stores and restaurants; exceptional restaurant; balconies offer great bird's-eye views of Broughton Street. **Cons:** no free parking; floors show their age in places; the sounds of bustling Broughton Street can be noisy. $ *Rooms from: $259* ✉ *123 E. Broughton St., Historic District* ☎ *912/644–7896* 🌐 *www.marshallhouse.com* 🛏 *68 rooms* 🍴 *No meals.*

★ Perry Lane Hotel
$$$ | HOTEL | Luxurious and artful with an edge, Perry Lane Hotel raises the bar for upscale accommodations in Savannah. **Pros:** beautiful and chic; staff goes above and beyond; a favorite spot for locals and tourists alike. **Cons:** in a high-traffic area that can be noisy; no coffee makers in rooms; expensive daily Destination Amenity Fee. $ *Rooms from: $226* ✉ *256 E. Perry St., Historic District* ☎ *912/244–9140* 🌐 *perrylanehotel.com* 🛏 *179 rooms* 🍴 *No meals.*

★ Westin Savannah Harbor Golf Resort & Spa
$$$ | RESORT | FAMILY | Within its own fiefdom, this high-rise property with more resort amenities than any other property in the area—including tennis courts, a full-service spa, and a golf course—presides over Hutchinson Island, five minutes by water taxi from River Street and just a short drive over the Talmadge Bridge. **Pros:** heated outdoor pool boasts a great view of River Street; dreamy bedding; great children's program. **Cons:** you are close, but still removed, from downtown; lacks atmosphere; an expensive and annoying resort fee. $ *Rooms from: $249* ✉ *1 Resort Dr., Hutchinson Island* ☎ *912/201–2000* 🌐 *www.westinsavannah.com* 🛏 *403 rooms* 🍴 *No meals.*

Nightlife

BARS AND CLUBS

Alley Cat Lounge
BARS/PUBS | A trendy spot in downtown Savannah, the Alley Cat Lounge is a backdoor bar with a refined cocktailer attitude. The well-designed subterranean space can only be accessed via the lane south of Broughton Street. The menu is a triumph of content marketing, resembling a newsprint, with entertaining articles, sketches, and quotes, and features impressive craft liquors and conceptual beverages. Space is limited, so come early to guarantee your spot. ✉ *207 W. Broughton St., Historic District* ☎ *912/677–0548* 🌐 *www.alleycatsavannah.com.*

★ Artillery
WINE BARS—NIGHTLIFE | A restored landmark, the award-winning Daniel Reed group renovated this unique, intimate space that was once home to the Georgia Hussars pre-Revolutionary cavalry regiment. The end result is one of Savannah's classiest cocktail bars and a resplendent example of contemporary design mixed with historical accuracy. Intricate cocktails feature inspired

Live oak allées draped with Spanish moss are a symbol of Savannah.

ingredients like muddled corn, shishito peppers, and smoked pipe tobacco. The wine list is as formidable as the cocktail menu. ■ **TIP→ There is an enforced code of conduct in a classy joint like this; usage of cell phones is highly frowned upon and the dress code is on the border of business-casual and semiformal.** ✉ *307 Bull St., Historic District* ☎ *912/335–5200* 🌐 *www.artillerybar.com.*

★ Lulu's Chocolate Bar

BARS/PUBS | This laid-back spot invites you to indulge your sweet tooth. Walking through the door, you're immediately greeted by a dessert case full of freshly baked specialties—try some of the homemade truffles. The menu also includes a spectacular list of specialty drinks, including champagne cocktails, chocolate martinis, and a modest selection of beer and wines. Warm up with an Irish coffee or the truly divine "drinkable chocolate," an especially fulfilling twist on hot chocolate. ✉ *42 Martin Luther King Jr. Blvd., Historic District* ☎ *912/480–4564* 🌐 *www.luluschocolatebar.com.*

The Original Pinkie Masters

BARS/PUBS | This dive bar's biggest claim to fame was that Georgia's own Jimmy Carter stood up on the bar to announce his bid for the presidency. The people are friendly, the drinks are cheap, the analog jukebox is loaded with an unexpected mix of soul, R&B, and punk, and the vibe is laid-back with zero frills. ✉ *318 Drayton St., Historic District* ☎ *912/999–7106* 🌐 *www.theoriginalsavannah.com* 🕙 *Closed Sun.*

★ Peregrin

BARS/PUBS | Perched on top of Perry Lane Hotel, Peregrin offers the best view of the city's church steeples and architectural details on a lush, colorful patio. Revelers can play cornhole while sipping frosé (frozen rosé) or the planter's punch. Wine lovers will revel in the curated menu, and there's a small array of bites, like dill pickle dip and crab-and-shrimp lettuce wraps, if you're feeling peckish. ✉ *Perry Lane Hotel, 256 E. Perry St., Historic District* ✥ *Between Parker's Urban Gourmet and Green Fire Pizza* ☎ *912/559–8365* 🌐 *www.peregrinsavannah.com.*

★ Planters Tavern

BARS/PUBS | Lighted by flickering candles, this tavern in the basement of The Olde Pink House is one of Savannah's most romantic late-night spots. There's a talented piano player setting the mood, two stone fireplaces, and an array of fox-hunt memorabilia. The upstairs menu is available, with the same quality of service but a slightly less formal approach. **■ TIP→ The handful of tables fill up fast, but the staff will serve you wherever you find a spot.** ✉ *The Olde Pink House, 23 Abercorn St., garden level, Historic District* ☎ *912/232–4286.*

Top Deck Rooftop Bar

BARS/PUBS | Enjoy the best views of the Savannah River and the cargo ships coming to port from this bar on the rooftop of the Cotton Sail Hotel. During the daytime Top Deck is quite low-key, but it gets lively and packed during the evening hours. Enjoy tasty, eclectic light bites with classic mixed drinks or more inspired signature cocktails. **■ TIP→ It's the best place in town to catch the sunset while enjoying a drink.** ✉ *125 W. River St., rooftop, Downtown* ☎ *912/436–6828* 🌐 *www.topdeckbar.com.*

GAY AND LESBIAN

Club One

DANCE CLUBS | Savannah's mainstay gay bar offers three levels of fun: drag shows and occasional burlesque and theater productions upstairs; dance parties on the main floor; and a relaxing spot for conversation or karaoke in the basement bar. Although the decor is a little tacky, the scene is wildly fun when the lights go down and the music starts. ✉ *1 Jefferson St., Historic District* ☎ *912/232–0200* 🌐 *www.clubone-online.com.*

LIVE MUSIC CLUBS

Casimir's Lounge

BARS/PUBS | This sleek nightspot regularly features live jazz, blues, and acoustic stylings. The decor is luxe, perhaps even a bit over-the-top. There's a great balcony on the side where you can have a drink while enjoying a view of lovely Forsyth Park. ✉ *Mansion on Forsyth Park, 700 Drayton St., Historic District* ☎ *912/721–5002* 🌐 *www.mansiononforsythpark.com* ⏲ *Closed Sun.–Tues.*

Shopping

SHOPPING DISTRICTS

Broughton Street

SHOPPING NEIGHBORHOODS | Savannah's "main street" has long served as an indicator of the city's changing economic and demographic trends. The first of Savannah's department stores, Adler's and Levy's, emerged on Broughton, followed by the post-WWII introduction of national chains Sears & Roebuck, JCPenney, and Kress. During the 1950s, ladies donning white gloves and heels did their shopping, while kids gathered at the soda counter or caught the matinee. Downtown's decline began in the late 1950s and continued through the '70s, when boarded-up storefronts were the norm rather than the exception. Today, Broughton is again thriving, not only with local boutiques and world-class shops, but with theaters, restaurants, and coffeehouses. ✉ *Broughton St., between Congress and State Sts., Historic District* 🌐 *www.broughtonstreetcollection.com.*

Downtown Design District

SHOPPING NEIGHBORHOODS | Known for its array of fine antiques shops, galleries, lighting showrooms, and interior design boutiques, the Downtown Design District is worth a visit. Stop in some of Savannah's trendier fashion stores, many of them housed in charming historic storefronts. Nearby are the famed Mercer Williams House and the landmark Mrs. Wilkes' Dining Room, known for some of the area's best family-style Southern food. The picturesque surrounding neighborhoods are also enjoyable for a nice afternoon stroll. ✉ *Whitaker St., between Charlton and Gaston Sts., Historic District.*

★ Liberty Street Corridor

SHOPPING NEIGHBORHOODS | With the redevelopment of Broughton Street came an influx of national and high-end retailers that left local shops in search of lower rent. Many set up shop a half-mile south along the oak-lined Liberty Street Corridor. The crossroads of Liberty and Bull is a particularly thriving shopping neighborhood, with outdoor cafés, pubs, clothing boutiques, art galleries, bookshops, and more. ✉ *Liberty St. at Bull St., Historic District.*

ANTIQUES

★ Alex Raskin Antiques

ANTIQUES/COLLECTIBLES | This shop is inside the four-story Noble Hardee Mansion, a gilded Italianate home. You can wander through almost all 12,000 square feet of the former grand residence and see how the landed gentry once lived. The building is a bit musty, with peeling wallpaper and patches of leaky ceiling, showcasing the fading grandeur of pre-restoration Savannah mansions, but the antiques within are in great condition and represent a colorful scrapbook of Savannah's past. They specialize in furniture, rugs, and paintings, but take note of more rare artifacts like tramp-art frames and antique doll furniture. Take in the view of Forsyth Park from one of the upper-level porches. **■ TIP→ The building lacks air-conditioning, so avoid the heat of midday or bring along a fan.** ✉ *441 Bull St., Historic District* ☎ *912/232–8205* 🌐 *www.alexraskinantiques.com.*

ART GALLERIES

Kobo Gallery

ART GALLERIES | Between the bustling hubs of Broughton Street and City Market sits the city's foremost cooperative art gallery. Near Ellis Square, the tasteful space is teeming with fine art across countless mediums. Noteworthy are industrial-style jewelry by Danielle Hughes Rose, the colorful landscapes of Dana Richardson, and Dicky Stone's intricate woodworking. ✉ *33 Barnard St., Historic District* ☎ *912/201–0304* 🌐 *kobogallery.com.*

★ Roots Up Gallery

ART GALLERIES | Opened in 2014 by longtime Savannah residents Leslie Lovell and Francis Allen, Roots Up is a testament to the charm and mystique of Southern folk art. Located in the heart of the Downtown Design District, Roots Up is home to such artists as Howard Finster, Willie Tarver, Jimmy Lee Sudduth, Antonio Esteves, Mr. Imagination, and local folk art notable Panhandle Slim. The collection includes everything from handmade dolls to vintage pieces. ✉ *412–C Whitaker St., Historic District* ☎ *912/677–2845* 🌐 *www.rootsupgallery.com.*

BOOKS

★ E. Shaver, Bookseller

BOOKS/STATIONERY | Among the city's most beloved bookshops, E. Shaver is the source for 17th- and 18th-century maps and new books on local history, recipes, artists, and authors. This shop occupies multiple rooms of a historic building, which alone is something to see. The whole family can explore the children's book sections. Enjoy a cozy cup of tea in the adjoining tearoom after you're finished perusing the many shelves. ✉ *326 Bull St., Historic District* ☎ *912/234–7257* 🌐 *eshaverbooks.com.*

CLOTHING

James Hogan

CLOTHING | Tucked in a storefront in the Historic District, this shop has brought a touch of glamour to the city. Featured here is apparel designed by James Hogan himself, as well as upscale women's fashions from well-regarded American and European designers. ✉ *412B Whitaker St., Historic District* ☎ *912/234–0374* 🌐 *www.jameshogan.com.*

Red Clover

CLOTHING | This is the place to be if you want fashionable and affordable apparel, shoes, and handbags. It features sharp looks from up-and-coming designers, all at under $100. It's also a great place to search for unique jewelry. ✉ *244 Bull*

St., Historic District ☎ 912/236–4053 🌐 shopredclover.com.

FOOD

★ Savannah Bee Company

FOOD/CANDY | FAMILY | Ted Dennard's Savannah Bee Company has been featured in such national magazines as *O, Vogue, InStyle*, and *Newsweek*, and with good reason—the whimsical shop features locally cultivated honey and bath products that are simply wonderful. You can sample and buy multiple varieties of honey and even raw honeycombs, and there's an entire bar dedicated to mead, a delicate honey wine; enjoy a tasting for a sweet experience. Children enjoy the life-size beehive. ✉ *104 W. Broughton St., Historic District* ☎ *912/233–7873* 🌐 *www.savannahbee.com.*

HOME DECOR

★ The Paris Market and Brocante

GIFTS/SOUVENIRS | A Francophile's dream from the time you open the antique front door and take in the intoxicating aroma of lavender, this two-story emporium is a classy reproduction of a Paris flea market. It sells furniture, vintage art, garden planters and accessories, and home fashions like boudoir items and bedding. Although the store will ship to your hometown, there are numerous treasures that can be easily packed away, like soaps, candles, vintage jewelry, kitchen and barware, and dried lavender. ✉ *36 W. Broughton St., Historic District* ☎ *912/232–1500* 🌐 *www.theparismarket.com.*

★ 24e

HOUSEHOLD ITEMS/FURNITURE | Owner Ruel Joyner has a keen eye for design. His eclectically sophisticated downtown shop is stocked floor to ceiling with luxurious housewares, like velvet sofas, stunning chandeliers, and conversation-starting accessories, from an array of revered design houses. 24e has also made a name for itself with custom-built furniture. Simply perusing the two stories of spectacular specimens is an inspiring way to spend some time—even if the store's big-ticket items are a little out of your price range. ✉ *24 E. Broughton St., Historic District* ☎ *912/233–2274* 🌐 *www.24estyle.com.*

SHOES, HANDBAGS, AND LEATHER GOODS

★ Satchel

JEWELRY/ACCESSORIES | This artisanal-leather studio and shop is owned by Elizabeth Seeger Jolly, a New Orleans native and graduate of SCAD. The store specializes in custom leather clutches, handbags, travel bags, and accessories and offers a wide selection of leathers to choose from, including python and alligator. At lower price points are the sharp and handy beverage cozies, cuff bracelets, and wallets. ✉ *4 E. Liberty St., Historic District* ☎ *912/233–1008* 🌐 *shopsatchel.com.*

SOUVENIRS

★ ShopSCAD

ART GALLERIES | Inside historic Poetter Hall, the Savannah College of Art and Design's shop is filled with handcrafted items guaranteed to be one of a kind. Handmade and hand-dyed silk accessories are cutting-edge, as are original fashion pieces and experimental purses by design students. Just remember that these originals are often one of a kind and do not come cheap. ✉ *340 Bull St., Historic District* ☎ *912/525–5180* 🌐 *www.shopscad.com.*

Activities

BIKING

Perry Rubber Bike Shop

BICYCLING | At the pulsing corner of Bull and Liberty Streets, Perry Rubber is the go-to shop for repairs and your best bet for rentals. It offers trendy hybrid or city bikes at $20 for a half-day or $35 for the full day—helmet, lock, and basket included. ✉ *240 Bull St., Historic District* ☎ *912/236–9929* 🌐 *www.perryrubberbikeshop.com.*

GOLF

★ The Club at Savannah Harbor

GOLF | The area's only PGA course, this resort property on Hutchinson Island is a free ferry ride from Savannah's riverfront. The lush championship course winds through pristine wetlands and has unparalleled views of the river and downtown. It is also home to the annual Liberty Mutual Legends of Golf tournament, which attracts golfing's finest each spring. A bit pricier than most local clubs, prices vary according to the season, but the course is packed with beauty and amenities. ✉ *Westin Savannah Harbor, 2 Resort Dr., Hutchinson Island* ☎ *912/201–2240* 🌐 *www.theclubatsavannahharbor.com* *Dynamic pricing $85–$145* *18 holes, 7300 yds, par 72* *Reservations essential.*

SPAS

★ Spa Bleu

FITNESS/HEALTH CLUBS | Consistently ranked as one of Savannah's top ways to pamper yourself, Spa Bleu offers a more contemporary feel. In keeping with trends of the "New South," Spa Bleu offers true Southern comfort in a modern space. The signature Organic Thermal Body Treatments are not to be missed, and neither are spa nights where you can stay late and indulge in hors d'oeuvres and champagne. ✉ *101 Bull St., Historic District* ☎ *912/236–1490* 🌐 *www.spa-bleu-sav.com.*

The Victorian District and the Eastside

Bordered by Gwinnett, Abercorn, and 31st Streets, the Victorian District is Savannah's first neighborhood, with the picturesque Forsyth Park at its heart. You'll find many historic bed-and-breakfasts here, including the Catherine Ward House Inn and Azalea Inn & Villas. The Mansion on Forsyth Park is nestled alongside the park.

Sights

★ Forsyth Park

FOUNTAIN | FAMILY | The heart of the city's outdoor life, Forsyth Park hosts a number of popular cultural events, including film screenings, sports matches, and the annual Savannah Jazz Festival. Built in 1840 and expanded in 1851, the park was part of General Oglethorpe's original city plan and made possible by the donation of land from Georgia governor John Forsyth. A glorious white fountain dating to 1858, Confederate and Spanish-American War memorials, a fragrant garden, multiple playgrounds, tennis and basketball courts, and an old fort (which houses the gorgeous new Collins Quarter Forsyth Café, with indoor/outdoor seating) are spread across this grand, green space. Be sure to stop by the south end on Saturday mornings for the bustling farmers' market. The park's 1-mile perimeter is among the prettiest walks in the city and takes you past many beautifully restored historic homes. ✉ *Gaston St., between Drayton and Whitaker Sts., Historic District* *If you're walking up Bull Street from downtown, you'll walk right into the park.*

Restaurants

★ Local 11ten

$$$$ | MODERN AMERICAN | This farm-to-table staple features an upbeat and contemporary menu that draws young chefs on their nights off. Seasonally driven, the menu is continually changing depending on the local harvest and the chef's vision, but dishes tend to be perfectly prepared and presented. **Known for:** seasonal menu with farm-sourced ingredients; sea scallops over black rice; open-air rooftop bar. *Average main: $33* ✉ *1110 Bull St., Victorian District* ☎ *912/790–9000* 🌐 *local11ten.com* *Closed Mon. and Tues. No lunch.*

Sisters of the New South

$ | **SOUTHERN** | Traditional Southern home cookin' comes with a smile at Sisters of the New South, where you'll be greeted as "honey" or "baby" (or both) as you place your order. Try the smothered pork chops or the fried whiting, though you can't go wrong with the generous "Meat & Three"—a choose-your-own foodie adventure. **Known for:** smothered pork chops; traditional Southern cooking; collard greens. *Average main: $12 2605 Skidaway Rd., Eastside 912/335-2761 thesistersofthenewsouth.com.*

Hotels

★ **Mansion on Forsyth Park**

$$$$ | **HOTEL** | Presiding over the eastern edge of Forsyth Park, this Marriott Autograph Collection property has dramatic design, opulent interiors with a contemporary edge, and a magnificently diverse collection of some 400 pieces of American and European art, all of which create a one-of-a-kind experience—sophisticated, chic, and artsy only begin to describe it. **Pros:** stimulating environment transports you from the workaday world; full-service spa; complimentary shuttle to River Street. **Cons:** very pricey; some of the art from the early 1970s is not appealing; location is a good walk from central downtown of Broughton Street, Bay Street, and so on. *Rooms from: $279 700 Drayton St., Historic District 912/238–5158 www.kesslercollection.com/mansion 125 rooms No meals.*

The Starland District, Thomas Square, and Midtown

Midtown Savannah includes neighborhoods south of Forsyth Park to Derenne Avenue, including the Starland District, the Thomas Square Streetcar Historic District, Baldwin Park, and Ardsley Park. The area is home to numerous B&Bs, fabulous dining (try an award-winning burger at Green Truck Neighborhood Pub or beautiful seasonal fare at Atlantic) and a vibrant arts and culture scene.

Sights

Savannah African Art Museum

MUSEUM | Once the private collection of Savannah businessman Don Cole, this assemblage of over a thousand sculptures, artifacts, tribal costumes, carved masks, pottery, and other sacred objects from West and Central Africa is now on display for the general public in a beautifully restored yellow mansion.The museum has works and artifacts from over 180 cultures and also hosts workshops and lectures relating to African history. *201 E. 37th St., Thomas Square 912/721–7745 savannahafricanartmuseum.org Free Closed Sun.–Tues.*

Restaurants

Cotton & Rye

$$$ | **SOUTHERN** | Embodying the new Southern cuisine, Cotton & Rye offers a menu that is creative and artistic with a strong sense of tradition. You'll see classic, recognizable comfort dishes like fried chicken and beef Stroganoff, but careful intention goes into the preparation and presentation that results in delightful sensory surprises. **Known for:** upscale take on gastropub fare; inventive, homemade desserts; patio dining. *Average main: $28 1801 Habersham St., Thomas Square 912/777–6286 www.cottonandrye.com Closed Sun. and Mon. No lunch.*

★ **Elizabeth on 37th**

$$$$ | **SOUTHERN** | This elegant turn-of-the-20th-century mansion has been feeding regional specialties to Savannah's upper crust for decades. Chef Kelly Yambor has helmed the kitchen since 1996, and she

masters dishes like Georgia shrimp and Savannah red rice, a double-cut Berkshire pork chop with apple-cabbage slaw, and local grouper Celeste (with a sesame-almond crust). **Known for:** impressive wine list; top fine-dining experience in town; seven-course tasting menu option. *Average main: $35 105 E. 37th St., Thomas Square 912/236–5547 elizabethon37th.net Dinner only.*

Green Truck Neighborhood Pub

$ | **BURGER** | **FAMILY** | Serving one of the best burgers in the state, this casual haunt draws diners from far and wide for its grass-fed beef; vegetarians find satisfaction with the hearty meatless patties. Everything from the coffee to the produce is locally sourced, and even the ketchup is made in-house. **Known for:** great beer selection; homemade ketchup and pimento cheese; big crowds and long waits. *Average main: $12 2430 Habersham St., Thomas Square 912/234–5885 greentruckpub.com Closed Sun. and Mon.*

Coffee and Quick Bites

Starland Yard Food Truck Park

$ | **AMERICAN** | Rotating food trucks means that menus revolve weekly at this literal playground constructed out of old shipping containers. Two permanent fixtures are a well-stocked central bar and Vittoria Pizzeria, whose piping hot oven is manned by award-winning chef Kyle Jacovino. **Known for:** amazing pizza; fun atmosphere; lots of variety. *Average main: $11 2411 De Soto Ave., Starland District 912/417-3001 starlandyard.com Closed Mon. No lunch.*

Lone Wolf Lounge

BARS/PUBS | Offering the warm vibe of a down-home, 1970s-era watering hole with an expertly crafted cocktail menu, Lone Wolf has quickly become the anti-hipster hangout, far from the madding crowd. Choose from a refreshing mix of high and low beverages, from a cold Schiltz for a couple bucks to a house cocktail made by some of Savannah's best bartenders for under $10. Toss back a Fernet or sip a Zippah, an invigorating crisp mix of gin, absinthe, and lemon with a touch of earthiness. A mix of townies, students, and neighborhood folks gather around the wood-paneled bar and booths and nosh on dinner from the food trucks frequently parked outside. The pandemic year 2020 brought an expansion, allowing for more seating and an extra bar when things get busy—which they do on weekend nights. *2429 Lincoln St., Thomas Square lone-wolf-lounge.business.site.*

Shopping

ANTIQUES

★ Picker Joe's Antique Mall & Vintage Market

ANTIQUES/COLLECTIBLES | A haven for lovers of architectural salvage, vintage treasures, mid-century furniture, and antique decor, Picker Joe's offers 10,000 square feet of discovery. A consistent receiver of local awards, the shop's many booths are carefully tended and offer a true variety of quality finds for pickers of all walks of life. *217 E. 41st St., Thomas Square 912/239–4657 pickerjoes.com.*

The Moon River District, Thunderbolt, and the Islands

Experience marshside tranquility in the Moon River District, named after the tune that made Savannah native Johnny Mercer famous. The area includes the Sandfly, Isle of Hope, and Skidaway Island neighborhoods and is a necessary stop for outdoor adventurers and history buffs. Learn about Gullah Geechee culture at Pin

Point Heritage Museum, see the area by water with Moon River Kayak Tours, and sip a handcrafted cocktail on the dock at The Wyld. See beautiful coastal homes on Isle of Hope, a historic community flanked by Herb River and Skidaway River. Wormsloe Historic Site, on Skidaway Road, is a beautiful visit. Carry on to Skidaway Island and enjoy a nature walk at Skidaway Island State Park.

Drive out of Savannah's downtown and you'll find one-of-a-kind marsh views and stunning sunset vistas. Thunderbolt, bordering on Savannah's east side and the Wilmington River, is a lush residential community that's home to historic Bonaventure Cemetery and delicious seafood spots like Tubby's Tank House. Head east on U.S. 80 and discover Wilmington Island, a cozy neighborhood on the Wilmington River. Historic Fort Pulaski and Oatland Island Wildlife Center are nearby.

Sights

★ Bonaventure Cemetery

CEMETERY | The largest and most famous of Savannah's municipal cemeteries, Bonaventure spreads over 160 acres and sits on a bluff above the Wilmington River. Once a sprawling plantation, the land became a private cemetery in 1846 and was established as a public cemetery in 1907. An emblematic destination for visitors, the evocative landscape is one of lush natural beauty transposed against an elegant, eerie backdrop of lavish marble headstones, monuments, and mausoleums as well as sweeping oaks and blooming camellia trees. John Muir reportedly camped at Bonaventure in 1867 on his legendary "thousand-mile walk," and local photographer Jack Leigh, novelist and poet Conrad Aiken, and singer-songwriter Johnny Mercer are among those interred here. Great tours of the cemetery are offered by "Bonaventure Don." ✉ *330 Greenwich Rd., Thunderbolt* ☎ *912/651–6843* 🌐 *bonaventurehistorical.org.*

★ Fort Pulaski National Monument

MILITARY SITE | FAMILY | Named for Casimir Pulaski, the Polish count and Revolutionary War hero, this must-see sight for history buffs was designed by Napoléon's military engineer and built on Cockspur Island between 1829 and 1847. Robert E. Lee's first assignment after graduating from West Point was as an engineer here. The fort was thought to be impervious to attack, but as weapons advanced, it proved penetrable. During the Civil War, the fort fell after bombardment by newfangled rifled cannons. The restored fortification, operated by the National Park Service, has moats, drawbridges, massive ramparts, towering walls, and an informative visitors center. Trails, picnic areas, and a protected bird refuge surround the park. ✉ *U.S. Hwy. 80, Thunderbolt* ☎ *912/786–5787* 🌐 *nps.gov/fopu* 🎟 *$10.*

Pin Point Heritage Museum

MUSEUM | The culturally rich community surrounding this museum lived in relative isolation for nearly 100 years before modern development reached Skidaway Island. Residents of Pin Point are Gullah/Geechee descendants of first-generation freed slaves from Ossabaw Island. Founded in 1890 on the banks of Moon River, this fishing community has a deep connection to the water. Many residents once worked at the A. S. Varn & Son oyster and crab factory, which has been transformed into this interactive museum to honor the life, work, and history of the community. ✉ *9924 Pin Point Ave., Moon River District* ☎ *912/355–0064* 🌐 *chsgeorgia.org/phm* ⏲ *Closed Sun.–Wed.*

Restaurants

★ Wiley's Championship BBQ

$ | BARBECUE | Tucked away in a strip mall on the way out to Tybee Island, this highlight of the local barbecue scene began with legendary pit master Wiley McCrary, who passed away in 2018. His recipes live on in the small space that's intimate and friendly; the staff is like long-lost family. **Known for:** slow-cooked barbecue staples; BBQ sampler feeds two people and lets you sample just about everything they make; Extra-Tingly Better Than Sex BBQ sauce. *Average main: $14 4700 U.S. 80 E, Moon River District 912/201–3259 wileyschampionshipbbq.com.*

★ The Wyld Dock Bar

$ | **SEAFOOD** | Enjoy elevated fish-shack food with yacht-rock vibes at this former marina where many of the patrons arrive by water. Order at the counter for a fresh catch of the day prepared perfectly; pair it with flavorful sides like Mexican corn and skillet okra. **Known for:** unparalleled marsh views; outdoor seating; local seafood. *Average main: $12 2740 Livingston Ave., Moon River District 912/692–1219 thewylddockbar.com Closed Mon.*

Activities

BOATING AND FISHING

Miss Judy Charters

FISHING | The legendary Captain Judy Helmey has headed up her charter fishing company for decades, and nobody knows the hidden honey holes better (locals swear by her weekly fishing report). Her 10-boat fleet offers packages ranging from 3-hour sightseeing tours to 14-hour deep-sea fishing expeditions, with plenty of delightful tales included. Expect to catch redfish, trout, and flounder in close waters and mackerel and barracuda on the open sea. *124 Palmetto Dr., Wilmington Island 912/897–4921 missjudycharters.com From $425 for 3 hours of inshore fishing; from $600 for 4 hours of offshore fishing.*

★ Savannah Canoe and Kayak

BOATING | Leading you through inlets and tidal creeks, Savannah Canoe and Kayak employs highly skilled guides that provide expert instruction for newbies and challenges for seasoned paddlers. You'll also learn about the history of these historic waterways and visit lesser-known spots, including hidden creeks and Little Tybee. Half-day tours start at $85 for three hours. *414 Bonaventure Rd., Thunderbolt 912/341–9502 savannahcanoeandkayak.com From $85.*

The Southside, the Gateway, and Greater Savannah

For bigger chains and shopping malls, head to the Southside; it's also where you'll find the majority of Savannah's movie theaters and cheaper rates on chain hotels. Gateway is conveniently located close to the Savannah/Hilton Head Airport off of Interstate 95 about 20 minutes from downtown. While it doesn't offer the Historic District's charm, the hotel and motel rates can't be beat.

Sights

National Museum of the Mighty Eighth Air Force

MILITARY SITE | Members of the "Greatest Generation" formed the famous World War II squadron called the Mighty Eighth in Savannah in 1942. Within a month, they answered the call to arms and shipped out to the United Kingdom as part of the Allied Forces. Flying in Royal Air Force planes, the Mighty Eighth was the largest Army Air Force during World War II and played a major role in defeating the Nazis. Exhibits at this museum begin with the prelude to World War II and the rise of Adolf Hitler, and continue through Desert Storm. You can see vintage aircraft, fly a simulated bombing mission with a B-17 crew, test your skills as a waist gunner, and view interviews with courageous World War II vets. The museum also has three theaters, a chapel, an art gallery, and a

7,000-volume library. ✉ *175 Bourne Ave., Pooler* ☎ *912/748–8888* 🌐 *mightyeighth.org* 🎫 *$12* ⏱ *Closed Mon.*

★ **Byrd Cookie Company**
FOOD/CANDY | Founded in 1924, this internationally renowned family-owned and -operated gourmet food company specializes in benne (sesame seed) wafers, trademark Savannah cookies (notably key lime), and other house-made sweets and crackers, all sold in decorative tins. Although you'll find locations around the city, the Waters Avenue flagship Byrd's Famous Cookies store sells picture tins of Savannah and the entire line of Byrd's gourmet foodstuffs, including condiments and dressings. Free cookie and cracker samples come with every visit. ✉ *6710 Waters Ave., Southside* ☎ *912/355-1716* 🌐 *byrdcookiecompany.com.*

Tybee Island

The native Yamacraw people originally came to this island in the Atlantic Ocean to hunt and fish, but these days, it's chock-full of seafood restaurants, chain motels, and souvenir shops—most of which sprang up during the 1950s and haven't changed much since. Fun-loving locals still host big annual parties like fall's Pirate Festival and spring's Beach Bum Parade. Tybee Island's entire expanse of taupe sand is divided into three public beach stretches: North Beach, the Pier and Pavilion, and the South End. Beach activities abound, including swimming, boating, fishing, sea kayaking, and parasailing. Newer water sports have gained popularity, including kiteboarding and stand-up paddleboarding.

Tybee Island Light Station and Museum
LIGHTHOUSE | FAMILY | Considered one of North America's most beautifully renovated lighthouses, the Tybee Light Station has been guiding Savannah River mariners since 1736. It's not the first lighthouse built on this site; the original was constructed on orders of General James Oglethorpe in 1732. You can walk up 178 steps for amazing views at the top. The lightkeeper's cottage houses a small theater showing a video about the lighthouse. The nearby museum is in a gun battery constructed for the Spanish-American War. ✉ *30 Meddin Dr., Tybee Island* ☎ *912/786–5801* 🌐 *www.tybeelighthouse.org* 🎫 *$10* ⏱ *Closed Tues.*

Tybee Island Marine Science Center
ZOO | FAMILY | Don't miss the Tybee Island Marine Science Center's interesting exhibit on Coastal Georgia, which houses local wildlife ranging from Ogeechee corn snakes to American alligators. Schedule one of two guided walks along the beach and marshes if you're interested in the flora and fauna of the Lowcountry. There is also a "Turtle Talk," which consists of a classroom discussion and hands-on workshop. ■ **TIP→ Arrive early, as parking near the center can be competitive in the busier months.** ✉ *37 Meddin Dr., Tybee Island* ☎ *912/786–5917* 🌐 *www.tybeemarinescience.org* 🎫 *$10* ⏱ *Closed Mon.–Wed.*

Tybee Island Pier and Pavilion
MARINA | This is Tybee's "grand strand," the center of the summer beach action. Anchored by a 700-foot pier that is sometimes host to summer concerts, this stretch of shoreline is your best bet for people-watching and beach activities. Just off the sand at the bustling intersection of Tybrisa Street and Butler Avenue, a cluster of watering holes,

Did You Know?

Tybee Island, a popular vacation spot since the 1800s, is home to three miles of beaches.

souvenir shops, bike shacks, and oyster bars makes up Tybee's main business district. ■ **TIP→ There's metered street parking as well as two good-size lots. Both fill up fast during the high season, so arrive early.** There are public restrooms at the Pier and at 15th and Tybrisa Streets. The pier is popular for fishing and is also the gathering place for fireworks displays. ✉ *Tybrisa St. at Butler Ave., Tybee Island* ☎ *912/652–6780.*

Restaurants

★ Huc-A-Poo's Bites & Booze

$$ | **AMERICAN** | **FAMILY** | Drink and eat like the locals do at this charming, laid-back spot. With walls covered in vintage signs, records, and various trash and treasure, guests enjoy a great breeze on a large porch or in the screened-in restaurant as they tuck into slices or 18-inch stone-baked pies loaded with tantalizing ingredients and unique combinations; the beer is ice-cold and best enjoyed in pitchers, and the prices can't be beat. **Known for:** authentic island relaxation; live music on the weekends; lively game nights during college football season. $ *Average main: $15* ✉ *1213 E. Hwy. 80, Tybee Island* ☎ *912/786–5900* 🌐 *www.hucapoos.com.*

★ Sundae Cafe

$$ | **AMERICAN** | Tucked into an unassuming strip mall off the main drag on Tybee Island, this gourmet restaurant is a diamond in the rough. Locals and tourists alike enjoy the diverse menu, fresh seafood, and brilliant food combinations—don't miss the unique seafood "cheesecake" starter, consisting of shrimp and crabmeat over greens with a hint of Gouda. **Known for:** generous portions at reasonable prices; tucked-away location; reservations recommended. $ *Average main: $19* ✉ *304 1st St., Tybee Island* ☎ *912/786–7694* 🌐 *www.sundaecafe.com* ⏲ *Closed Sun.*

Activities

BOATING AND FISHING

★ Captain Mike's Dolphin Tours

WILDLIFE-WATCHING | **FAMILY** | If boat-bound adventure is what you seek, look no further than Captain Mike. Widely popular with tourists and locals alike, Captain Mike's tours have been featured on the Discovery Channel and *Good Morning America* and in the pages of *Southern Living* . Choose from a 90-minute dolphin tour or a sunset tour (available May to September). Captain Mike has a 32-foot cabin cruiser in his fleet and offers inshore and offshore fishing charters. This business is family-owned and-operated, and kids are welcome. ✉ *Lazaretto Creek Marina, 1 Old U.S. Hwy. 80, Tybee Island* ☎ *912/786–5848* 🌐 *tybeedolphins.com* 🎟 *Tours from $15.*

Chapter 12

GEORGIA'S COASTAL ISLES AND THE OKEFENOKEE

Updated by
Rachel Roberts Quartarone

Sights ★★★★★ | Restaurants ★★★☆☆ | Hotels ★★★☆☆ | Shopping ☆☆☆☆☆ | Nightlife ★☆☆☆☆

WELCOME TO GEORGIA'S COASTAL ISLES AND THE OKEFENOKEE

TOP REASONS TO GO

★ **Saltwater marshes:** Fringing the coastline, waist-high grasses transform both sunlight and shadow with their lyrical textures and shapes.

★ **Geechee culture:** Vestiges of Georgia's Black Republic, an independent state of freed slaves established on the barrier islands in the mid-19th century, remain at the Sapelo Island settlement of Hog Hammock.

★ **Horses of Cumberland:** Some 200 feral horses, descendants of horses abandoned by the Spanish in the 1500s, roam the wilderness of Cumberland Island.

★ **Luxurious escapes:** Jekyll Island was originally the exclusive winter retreat of America's exceptionally rich, but today it's open to all.

★ **Go for a ride:** Jekyll Island has 25 miles of paved bike paths that traverse salt marshes, maritime forests, beaches, and the island's ever-charming National Historic Landmark District.

1 Sapelo Island. The historic home of the Geechee people, this island is a haven of salt marshes and pristine beaches.

2 St. Simons Island. Get active on this vacation island 4 miles from Brunswick and accessible via a causeway.

3 Sea Island. Relax in the lap of luxury at a historic, exclusive resort.

4 Jekyll Island. Explore the relics of an island resort once restricted to the rich and famous.

5 Cumberland Island. This small island is reachable only by ferry from St. Marys (115 miles south of Savannah).

6 Okefenokee National Wildlife Refuge. This 402,000-acre refuge is home to Okefenokee Swamp Park and Stephen C. Foster State Park.

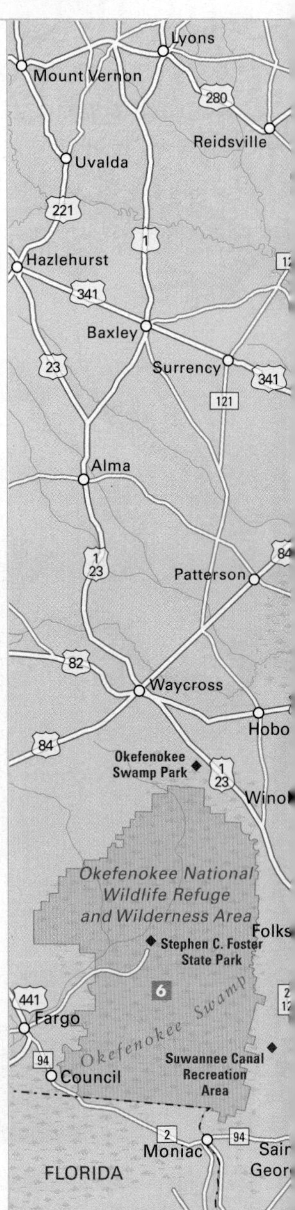

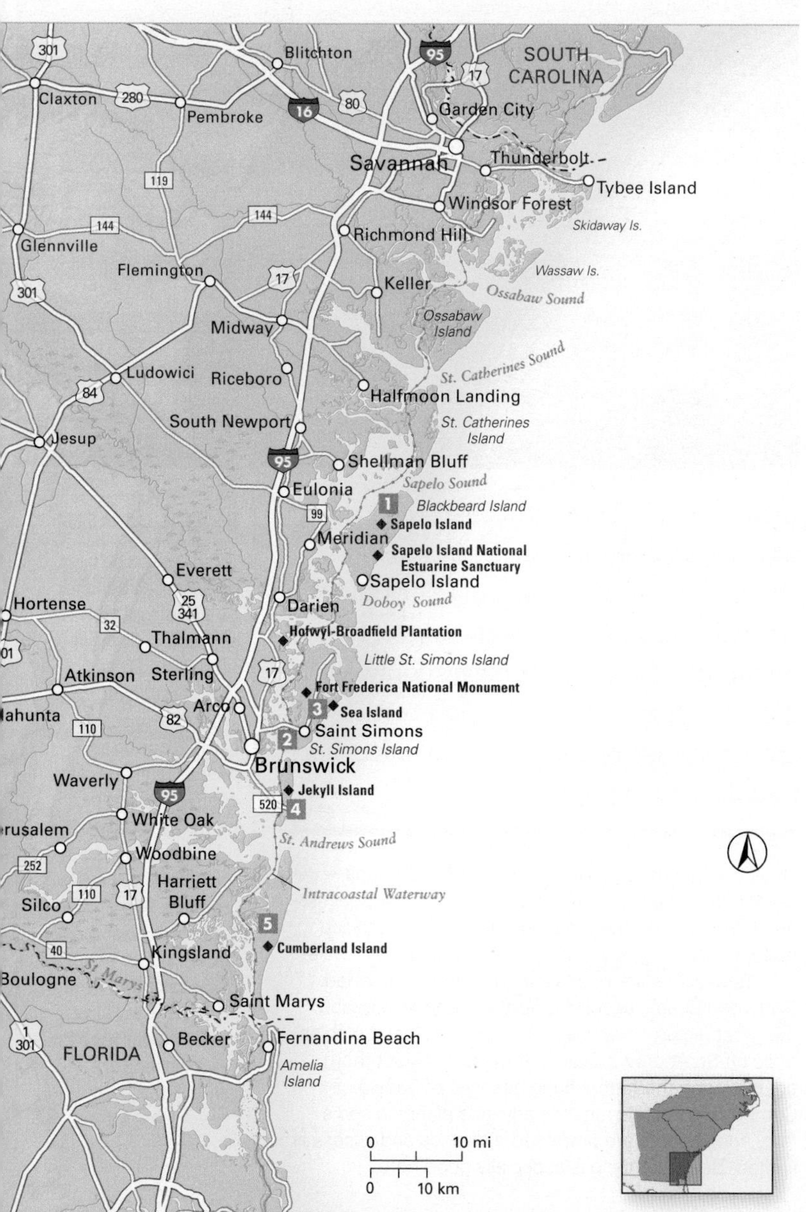

SOUTH CAROLINA
Blitchton
Claxton
Pembroke
Garden City
Savannah
Thunderbolt
Tybee Island
Windsor Forest
Skidaway Is.
Richmond Hill
Glennville
Flemington
Wassaw Is.
Keller
Ossabaw Sound
Ossabaw Island
Midway
St. Catherines Sound
Ludowici
Riceboro
Halfmoon Landing
South Newport
St. Catherines Island
Jesup
Shellman Bluff
Sapelo Sound
Eulonia
1
Blackbeard Island
Sapelo Island
Meridian
Sapelo Island National Estuarine Sanctuary
Everett
Sapelo Island
Hortense
Darien
Doboy Sound
Hofwyl-Broadfield Plantation
Thalmann
Little St. Simons Island
Atkinson
Sterling
Fort Frederica National Monument
Arco
3
Sea Island
Saint Simons
2
St. Simons Island
Brunswick
Waverly
Jekyll Island
4
White Oak
St. Andrews Sound
Woodbine
Harriett Bluff
Silco
Intracoastal Waterway
5
Cumberland Island
Kingsland
Boulogne
St Marys
Saint Marys
Becker
Fernandina Beach
FLORIDA
Amelia Island
0
10 mi
0
10 km

GEORGIA'S COASTAL ISLES BEACHES

Enjoy a sunset stroll on one of Georgia's remote beaches.

Remote and largely untouched, the beaches on Georgia's barrier islands sit at the confluence of rich salt marshes and the Atlantic Ocean. Nature-watching on foot or by canoe or kayak is the biggest draw, with dolphins, manatees, nesting sea turtles, more than 300 bird species, and much more found along these shores.

Of all the islands, only two—Jekyll and St. Simons—have undergone significant development. East Beach on St. Simons has the most facilities and is the place to go for sunbathing, swimming, and water sports, while Jekyll's beaches are both accessible and uncrowded. Driftwood Beach, at Jekyll's northern end, is arguably the most picturesque beach on the coast, and dolphins frolic off St. Andrews Beach, at the island's southern tip. Exploring the farther-flung beaches of Sapelo or Cumberland Islands requires advance planning and a ferry ride, as both are protected parklands and access is limited. Beachcombing is especially good here.

BEACH CAMPING

Experience the best of Georgia's beaches by pitching a tent shoreside. Cumberland Island has wonderful camping, with standard campgrounds as well as backcountry campsites that can be reached only by hiking trails taking you 5½ to 10½ miles from the ferry dock. There are no stores on the island, so bring all necessary food and supplies. Camping costs $22 per night; reservations are required.

Georgia's Coastal Isles Best Beaches

NANNY GOAT BEACH (SAPELO ISLAND)

Used as an outdoor classroom by the Sapelo Island National Estuarine Research Reserve, this remote beach, accessible only by boat, offers ample beachcombing and wildlife-watching opportunities. Look for conch shells on its 2 miles of sandy shore while pelicans and osprey fish among the shallows, or bring a seine (a large, weighted net) to dip for shrimp and crabs. Dunes give way to protected maritime forest, and a ¾-mile trail leads to the historic Reynolds Mansion.

EAST BEACH (ST. SIMONS ISLAND)

The Golden Isles' liveliest stretch of sand occupies the southeastern edge of St. Simons Island, from the Coast Guard station at the end of 1st Street to Massengale Park, both of which offer facilities and access to the hard-packed-sand beach. Here you can swim and sun, boogie board in the mild shore break, or kitesurf past the offshore sandbars. This is one of the few beaches in the area with lifeguards, making it a good family destination.

Bring your camera to Driftwood Beach—the downed trees make for great photo ops.

Wild horses roam Cumberland Island.

DRIFTWOOD BEACH (JEKYLL ISLAND)

The northern end of Jekyll Island offers beautiful views of St. Simons against a stark and dramatic backdrop. Accessible by trail from the Clam Creek Picnic Area or from North Beachview Drive, near the campground the beach has a graveyard of coastal trees slowly succumbing to the sea, reeling at odd angles as the encroaching tide loosens their roots. Drained of color by the sun and saltwater, they create a maze of craggy limbs. Come here for the view and the unique scenery, but use caution swimming among the branches.

DUNGENESS BEACH (CUMBERLAND ISLAND)

Nearly 18 miles of unspoiled beach fringe the eastern edge of this national-park island, off the coast of St. Marys. At the southern end, Dungeness Beach is accessible via the *Cumberland Queen II*, a reservations-only, 146-passenger ferry that stops here and at Sea Camp Beach to the north. Beachcombers can find shells and shark teeth here, and Pelican Flats, off the island's southern tip, offers good shore fishing. From the beach it's an easy hike to the ruins of Thomas Carnegie's great estate, Dungeness. Keep an eye out for the wild horses that roam the area.

Georgia's lush barrier islands meander down the Atlantic coast from Savannah to the Florida border. Notable for their subtropical beauty and abundant wildlife, the isles strike a unique balance between some of the country's wealthiest communities and some of its most jealously protected nature preserves. Until recently, large segments of the coast were in private hands, and as a result much of the region remains as it was when the first Europeans set eyes on it 450 years ago. Though the islands have long been a favorite getaway of the rich and famous, they no longer cater only to the well-heeled.

St. Simons, Jekyll, Little St. Simons, and Sea Island constitute Georgia's Golden Isles. And while even today Little St. Simons Island and Sea Island remain privately owned, each with its own exclusive resort catering to the very wealthy, St. Simons and Jekyll Islands have morphed into relaxed beach communities. These more developed islands—although by Georgia law, only 35% of Jekyll's land can be developed—have become diverse havens with something for everyone, from beach bums to family vacationers and the suit-and-tie crowd.

Sapelo Island and the Cumberland Island National Seashore are the least developed and, as protected nature preserves, the most ecologically intact of all the islands. With their miles of untouched beaches, forests of gnarly live-oak trees draped with Spanish moss, and rich swamps and marshlands, both islands are ideal camping destinations, with sites ranging from primitive to modern. Noncamping accommodations are available, but limited, and require booking well in advance. Many visitors opt to stay on the mainland and make day trips by ferry, private boat, or kayak.

The Okefenokee National Wildlife Refuge, 60 miles inland from St. Marys, near Folkston, is one of the largest freshwater wetlands in the United States. Spread over 700 square miles of southeastern Georgia and northeastern Florida, the swamp is a trove of flora and fauna that naturalist William Bartram called a "terrestrial paradise" when he visited in the 1770s. From towering cypress swamps to alligator- and snake-infested waters and prairie-like wetlands, the Okefenokee is a mosaic of ecosystems, much of which has never been visited by humans.

MAJOR REGIONS

Sapelo Island. Reachable only by ferry from Meridian, less-developed Sapelo is a protected state wildlife preserve and home to the Geechee, direct descendants of freed African slaves. You must have a reservation for a day tour or to camp or stay at one of the island's small hotels in order to take the ferry over.

St. Simons Island. The most developed of the Golden Isles is a well-rounded vacation destination with a variety of hotels and restaurants in varying price ranges.

Sea Island. Only 5 miles long, this small barrier island is attached to St. Simons by a causeway and is home to Sea Island Resort, where world leaders once met.

Jekyll Island. Once a playground for the rich and famous, Jekyll is now more widely accessible. Its pristine beaches are not commercialized and are open to all, and the range of resorts and restaurants appeals to a wide range of travelers.

Cumberland Island. Reachable only by ferry, this virtually pristine island is a National Seashore and has only one accommodation (a former Carnegie family mansion) and a few campgrounds.

Okefenokee National Wildlife Refuge. The Okefenokee is a mysterious world where, as a glance at a map will indicate, all roads disappear. A large, interior wetland navigable only by boat, it can be confusing and intimidating to the uninitiated. None of the individual parks within the area give a sense of the total Okefenokee experience—each has its own distinct natural features. Choose the park that best aligns with your interests and begin there.

Planning

When to Go

Early spring and late fall are ideal for visiting the coastal isles and the Okefenokee. By February, temperatures can reach into the 70s, while nights remain cool and even chilly, which keeps the bugs at bay. The high demand to visit these areas before the bugs arrive and after they depart necessitates ferry reservations to Sapelo Island and Cumberland Island National Seashore months in advance for spring and fall; without a reservation, you risk having to wait days at best for a cancellation. If you plan to stay in the immediate vicinity of St. Marys or Meridian, the respective docking points for the Cumberland and Sapelo ferries, or Folkston, the gateway to the Okefenokee, it's advisable to book rooms for these areas well in advance for spring or fall, as accommodations are scarce and the demand is high. The Cumberland Island ferry accepts reservations six months in advance. If you go during the warmer months, always bring water because these areas generally offer minimal services.

By May, sand gnats, deer flies, and mosquitoes swarm the coast and islands in abundance. Don't underestimate their impact: during peak times in some areas they are so thick they sound like hail hitting your car. And though many localities spray, it's imperative to have a good repellent handy, especially when traveling to outlying areas. Despite the subtropical heat and humidity, summer is busy with crowds flocking to the beaches, so you'll want to make reservations at least a couple of months in advance. The season lasts until Labor Day, but you can still expect travelers making weekend getaways until October or late November, when temperatures cool. Hurricane season officially runs from June through the end of November, but August and September are the peak months for them.

Planning Your Time

Although Georgia's coastal islands are along a strip of coastline that is less than 60 miles long, each has a different feel, and a visit to any of them requires at least a day. The complications of ferries to Sapelo or Cumberland make it difficult to visit either of those in less than a day, and these visits must generally be planned far in advance. It's possible to base yourself on busy St. Simons Island (or any of the Golden Isles for that matter) and visit much of the region on a series of day trips. The Okefenokee is a bit farther out of the way but can be visited on a day trip from almost any of the islands; if you have more time, it can be an overnight trip.

Getting Here and Around

Visiting the region is easiest by car, because many of the outer reaches of Georgia are remote places with little in the way of alternate transportation. Touring by bicycle is an option for most of the region; note that personal bicycles are allowed on the Cumberland ferry for an additional fee but prohibited on the ferry to Sapelo. Except for Little St. Simons, the Golden Isles are connected to the mainland by bridges around Brunswick and are the only coastal isles accessible by car. Sapelo Island and the Cumberland Island National Seashore can be reached only by ferry from Meridian and St. Marys, respectively.

AIR TRAVEL

The coastal isles are served by the Brunswick Golden Isles Airport (BQK), 6 miles north of Brunswick, and the Malcolm McKinnon St. Simons Airport (SSI) on St. Simons Island. McKinnon accommodates light aircraft and private planes. The closest major airports are in Savannah, Georgia, and Jacksonville, Florida.

AIR CONTACTS Brunswick Golden Isles Airport (BQK). ✉ *295 Aviation Pkwy., Brunswick* ⊕ *Off I–95* ☎ *912/265–2070* 🌐 *flygcairports.com/brunswick-airport.html.* **St. Simons Island Airport at McKinnon Field (SSI).** ✉ *115 Terminal Way, St. Simons Island* ☎ *912/638–8617* 🌐 *flygcairports.com/st-simons-airport.html.*

BOAT AND FERRY TRAVEL

Cumberland Island and Sapelo Island are accessible only by ferry or private launch. The *Cumberland Queen II* serves Cumberland Island (the National Park Service has a Cumberland Island ferry schedule at 🌐 *www.nps.gov/cuis/reservations.htm*), and the *Katie Underwood* serves Sapelo Island. Advance reservations are advised for Cumberland, but they are required for passage to Sapelo.

BOAT AND FERRY CONTACTS *Cumberland Queen II* ✉ *113 St. Marys St. W, St. Marys* ☎ *877/860–6787* 🌐 *www.cumberlandislandferry.com.* ***Katie Underwood*** ✉ *Sapelo Island Visitors Center, U.S. 1, 1766 Landing Rd. SE, Darien* ☎ *912/437–3224* 🌐 *www.sapelonerr.org/visitor-center.*

CAR TRAVEL

From Brunswick take the Jekyll Island Causeway ($8 per car per day) to Jekyll Island and the Torras Causeway to St. Simons and Sea Island. You can get by without a car on Jekyll Island, but you'll need one on St. Simons. You cannot bring a car to Cumberland Island or Sapelo.

TAXI TRAVEL

Island Transport and Taxi Service, as well as rideshare services like Uber and Lyft, can shuttle you around St. Simons for fares that range between $7 and $15 depending on your destination.

TAXI CONTACTS Island Transport and Taxi Service. ✉ *708 E. Islands Sq., St. Simons Island* ☎ *912/634–0113* 🌐 *www.islandtransportandtaxi.com.*

Restaurants

Restaurants range from fish camps—normally rustic dockside affairs—to the more upscale eateries that tend to spawn around the larger towns and resorts. And though there's still room for growth, the area now has several menus gaining not only local but nationwide attention. The rising tide of quality has begun to lift all boats. Some restaurants still serve food family style. *Restaurant reviews have been shortened. For full information, visit Fodors.com.*

Hotels

Hotels run the gamut from Victorian mansions to Spanish-style bed-and-breakfasts to some of the most luxurious hotel-spa accommodations found anywhere. Since options are somewhat limited, make your reservations as far in advance as possible. Most hotels offer the full range of guest services, but as a matter of philosophy some B&Bs do not provide televisions or telephones in the rooms. Lodging prices quoted here may be much lower during nonpeak seasons, and specials are often available on weekdays even in high season. *Hotel reviews have been shortened. For full information, visit Fodors.com.*

What It Costs

	$	$$	$$$	$$$$
RESTAURANTS	under $15	$15–$20	$21–$24	over $24
HOTELS	under $150	$150–$200	$201–$250	over $250

Restaurant reviews are the average cost of a main course at dinner or, if dinner is not served, at lunch. Hotel reviews are the lowest cost of a standard double room in high season.

Tours

Lighthouse Trolleys Land and Sea Tours offers year-round trolley and boat tours from St. Simons Island and Jekyll Island that explore the surrounding marshes and rivers and get you up close and personal with dolphins, manatees, and other marine life. Kayaks and canoes are also a great way to explore the creeks; SouthEast Adventure Outfitters is located on St. Simons Island and offers trips in Brunswick and Darien as well.

CONTACTS Lighthouse Trolleys Land and Sea Tours. ☎ *912/638–3333* 🌐 *lighthousetrolleys.com.* **SouthEast Adventure Outfitters.** ✉ *313 Mallory St., St. Simons Island* ☎ *912/638–6732* 🌐 *www.southeastadventure.com.*

Sapelo Island

8 miles northeast of Darien.

The fourth-largest of Georgia's coastal isles—and bigger than Bermuda—Sapelo Island is a unique community in North America. It still bears evidence of the Paleo-Indians who lived here some 4,500 years ago and is home to the Geechee, direct descendants of African slaves who speak a blend of English and various

The Geechee, a Culture Apart

Georgia's Geechee, like the Gullah people of South Carolina, are descendants of African slaves who have preserved a distinct culture and language, in large part due to the isolation of the remote coastal areas, such as Sapelo Island, where they live.

The Geechee take their name from the Ogeechee River in north coastal Georgia. Geechee ancestry includes a variety of African tribes but is particularly marked by the language and traditions of slaves from Sierra Leone, who were brought to work the vast coastal plantations because of their expertise in rice cultivation. Their native tongue, Krio (sometimes called Sierra Leone Creole), is still evident in the Geechee language of the region today: *tief/tif* (steal), *ooman/uman* (woman), and *enty/enti* (isn't it so?) are just a few of the easily recognizable words that are similar in Geechee and Krio, respectively. The two languages share similar sentence structures and grammatical elements as well. Interesting fact: Geechee, not English, was the first language of Supreme Court Justice Clarence Thomas, who was born and raised in Savannah.

African languages. This rapidly dwindling community maintains many traditional African practices, including the making of sweetgrass baskets and the use of herbal medicines made from recipes passed down for generations. It's also a nearly pristine barrier island with miles of undeveloped beaches and abundant wildlife. To take the 40-minute ferry ride from Meridian on the mainland through the expanse of salt marshes to Sapelo Island is to enter a world seemingly forgotten by time.

GETTING HERE AND AROUND

You can explore many historical periods and natural environments here, but facilities on the island are limited. Note that you can't simply walk up to the dock and catch the ferry—you need to have a reservation for a tour, a campsite, or one of the island's lodgings (or have prearranged plans to stay with island residents). The on-island vendors will typically book ferry reservations on your behalf to be included in the price of your tour or stay. Bring insect repellent, especially in summer, and leave your pets at home. You can rent a bicycle on the island, but you cannot bring a bicycle on the ferry. As there are no hotels on the island, many people choose to visit Sapelo Island for the day and stay overnight in nearby Darien. Founded by Scottish Highlanders in 1736, it's one of Georgia's oldest towns and has a quaint riverfront village with a few shops and restaurants.

TOURS

Sapelo Sights Tour

GUIDED TOURS | FAMILY | These private, guided tours are led by island native and slave descendant J. R. Grovner. He highlights island life, culture, and history with visits to Nanny Goat Beach, tabby (a building material made from oyster shells, sand, and water) ruins of estates and slave quarters, Native American shell mounds, the Sapelo Lighthouse, and the historic Hog Hammock community. ✉ *Hog Hammock* ☎ *912/506–6463* 🌐 *www.toursapelo.com.*

Sights

Hofwyl-Broadfield Plantation

HOUSE | Rice, not cotton, dominated Georgia's coast in the antebellum years, and the Hofwyl-Broadfield Plantation is the last remaining example of a way of

A ferry leads to Sapelo Island, one of Georgia's most pristine barrier islands.

life that fueled an agricultural empire. The main farmhouse, in use since the 1850s when the original house burned, is now a museum with family heirlooms accumulated over five generations, including extensive collections of silver and Canton china. A guide gives an insightful talk on rural plantation life. Though grown over, some of the original dike works and rice fields remain, as do some of the slave quarters. A brief film at the visitor center complements exhibits on rice technology and cultivation, linking them to Sierra Leone, the country from which many slaves were taken because of their expertise in growing rice. ✉ *5556 U.S. 17 N, Brunswick* ✣ *5 miles south of Darien* ☎ *912/264–7333* 🌐 *gastateparks.org/HofwylBroadfieldPlantation* 🎫 *$8* ⏲ *Closed Mon. and Tues.*

Hog Hammock Community

HISTORIC SITE | This small settlement near the southern end of Sapelo Island is one of the few remaining Gullah/Geechee communities on the south Atlantic Coast. The Saltwater Geechee people, Georgia's sea-island equivalent to the Gullah of South Carolina, are descendants of slaves who worked the island's plantations during the 19th century. Hog Hammock's roughly 50 residents still maintain their distinct language and customs, which share many characteristics with their West African origins. ✉ *Hog Hammock.*

Sapelo Island Visitors Center

INFO CENTER | Start your visit here, on the mainland near the Sapelo Island ferry docks, where you can view exhibits on the island's history, culture, and ecology, and get helpful trip planning tips from knowledgeable staff. Check in advance to see if they are offering a bus tour of the island on the day of your visit. The sights that make up the bus tour vary, but generally include the old sugar mill, the airfield, the cemetery, Nanny Goat Beach, and the 80-foot-tall **Sapelo Lighthouse .** Built in 1820, it's a symbol of the thriving cotton and lumber industry once based out of Darien. You may also book a tour with one of the residents on

Sapelo Island—staff can assist. To get to the visitor center and Meridian ferry dock from downtown Darien, go north on Georgia State Route 99 for 8 miles, following signs for the Sapelo Island National Estuarine Research Reserve. Turn right on to Landing Road at the Elm Grove Baptist Church in Meridian. The visitor center is about ½ mile down the road. ✉ *1766 Landing Rd. SE, Darien* ☎ *912/437–3224* 🌐 *www.sapelonerr.org* ⏲ *Closed Sun. and Mon.*

Beaches

Cabretta Beach

BEACH—SIGHT | Just north of Nanny Goat Beach, Cabretta Beach stretches along Sapelo's eastern shore, with its northern terminus at the outflow of Blackbeard Creek. This remote expanse of hard-packed sand is sometimes visited by fishermen or kayakers on their way to Blackbeard Island, and it's also the site of the Cabretta Campground, a group wilderness campsite that can be reserved via Georgia's Department of Natural Resources. **Amenities:** none. **Best for:** solitude; sunrise; walking. ✉ *End of Cabretta Rd.*

Nanny Goat Beach

BEACH—SIGHT | On the southeastern edge of the island, this beach sits at the heart of the rich ecological zones for which the island is known and protected. Naturalists with the Sapelo Island National Estuarine Research Reserve use this beach as an outdoor classroom, sometimes bringing groups here for beach walks. Visitors can hunt for sand dollars and whelk shells along nearly 2 miles of sandy shore; bird sightings include blue herons, egrets, ospreys, bald eagles, and the occasional plain chachalaca. A 1-mile trail connects this beach with the historic R. J. Reynolds House, crossing five ecological zones along the way. **Amenities:** toilets. **Best for:** solitude; walking. ✉ *Sapelo Island* ✣ *End of Beach Rd.*

Restaurants

B & J's Steak and Seafood

$$ | **AMERICAN** | **FAMILY** | While it's nothing fancy, this small and simple joint is beloved by locals for its fried shrimp, generous portions, and down-home country fare. The weekend seafood buffet is especially popular and is loaded with the freshest of local fish, shrimp, and other seafood staples. **Known for:** homestyle country fare; fried seafood and steaks; buffet-style dining. 💲 *Average main: $19* ✉ *901 North Way, Darien* ☎ *912/437–2122* 🌐 *www.bandjssteaksandseafood.com* ⏲ *Closed Sun.*

The Fish Dock Bar & Grill

$$$ | **SEAFOOD** | A local staple, this quintessential coastal restaurant, which overlooks the Sapelo River as it runs to the Sapelo Sound, offers fresh-from-the docks seafood dishes and surf-and-turf specialties. Menu favorites include the seafood linguine with Sapelo Sea Farms clams and whole fried Altamaha River catfish with hush puppies, local shrimp, and deviled crab. **Known for:** classic steak and seafood dishes; waterfront dining with deck seating; fresh Georgia oysters, shrimp, and clams. 💲 *Average main: $23* ✉ *1398 Sapelo Ave., Crescent* ☎ *912/832–4295* 🌐 *www.fishdockrestaurant.com* ⏲ *Closed Mon.*

Skipper's Fish Camp

$$$ | **SEAFOOD** | This upscale take on the fish camp theme lies at the foot of a public dock on the Darien River, where working shrimp boats moor. It has a beautiful courtyard pond and an open-air oyster bar. **Known for:** the views; catching the game; seafood and barbecue. 💲 *Average main: $22* ✉ *85 Screven St., Darien* ✣ *At the southern end of Darien, turn right at Broad just before the river bridge, then take the first left down to the waterfront* ☎ *912/437–3474* 🌐 *www.skippersfishcamp.com.*

Hotels

Open Gates Bed and Breakfast
$$ | **B&B/INN** | Built by a timber baron in 1876, this two-story, Italianate house on Darien's Vernon Square is filled with antiques that beautifully decorate each room and offers a relaxing library filled with books of local historical interest. **Pros:** beautiful setting; easy walking distance to Darien's restaurants and waterfront; outstanding gourmet breakfast. **Cons:** may be a bit too small and intimate for some; two rooms share a bath; upstairs rooms require a steep flight of stairs. *$ Rooms from: $157 ✉ 301 Franklin St., Darien ☎ 912/437–6985 🌐 www.opengatesbnb.com 5 rooms 🍽 Free breakfast.*

R. J. Reynolds Mansion
$$ | **ALL-INCLUSIVE** | A stay at this 10-bed, 10-bath historic Sapelo Island mansion is a rare treat reserved only for groups of 8–25, or a smaller group willing to pay the minimum nightly fee per person. **Pros:** surrounded by nature; all-inclusive with many program opportunities; a chance to have a historic mansion all to yourself. **Cons:** can stay booked years in advance during peak season; can be pricey if fewer than eight people; may be too remote for some. *$ Rooms from: $175 ✉ Sapelo Island ☎ 912/485–2299 🌐 www.gastateparks.org/ReynoldsMansion 10 rooms 🍽 All-inclusive ☞ Rate is per person with minimum of $1,400 (8 people).*

Sapelo Island Birdhouses
$$$ | **RENTAL** | **FAMILY** | Any one of these well-equipped stilt cottages offers a comfortable (yet rustic) lodging experience right along the shore of Sapelo Island. **Pros:** unprecedented views; central access to island's historical sites and remote beaches; friendly staff and nearby community. **Cons:** on-island stay can feel too remote for some guests; minimum two-night stay to book; a pricey choice for just two people. *$ Rooms from: $250 ✉ Hog Hammock ✥ About a mile south of the First African Baptist Church ☎ 912/223–6515 🌐 www.sapeloislandbirdhouses.com 4 cottages 🍽 No meals.*

Camping on Sapelo Island

Comyam's Campground. The name of Hog Hammock's only campground comes from the Geechee word meaning "come here." The campground has marsh views and is great for backpackers looking for a more rustic taste of the island life. Campsite reservations are essential and start at $10 per day. *✉ Hog Hammock, Sapelo Island* ☎ 912/602–4717 🌐 *www.gacoast.com/geecheetours.*

Activities

CANOEING AND KAYAKING

Altamaha Coastal Tours
CANOEING/ROWING/SKULLING | The Altamaha River, the largest undammed river on the East Coast, runs inland from near Darien. You can take expeditions along it with Altamaha Coastal Tours, which rents equipment and conducts guided trips from the waterfront in Darien. With them you can explore tidal swamps, marshlands, and Queens and Sapelo Islands. Kayak or canoe rentals start at $35 per day. *✉ 229 Fort King George Dr., Darien ☎ 912/437–6010 🌐 www.altamaha.com.*

Amble through the live oak allées on St. Simons Island.

St. Simons Island

22 miles south of Darien, 4 miles east of Brunswick.

St. Simons may be the Golden Isles' most developed vacation destination: here you can swim and sun, golf, hike, fish, ride horseback, tour historic sites, and feast on local seafood at more than 70 restaurants. (It's also a great place to bike and jog, particularly on the southern end, where there's an extensive network of trails.) Despite the development, the island has managed to maintain some of the slow-paced Southern atmosphere that made it such a draw in the first place. Upscale resorts and restaurants are here for the asking, but this island the size of Manhattan has only 15,000 year-round residents, so you can still get away from it all without a struggle. Even down in the village, the center of much of St. Simons's activity, there are unpaved roads and quiet back alleys of chalky white sand that seem like something out of the past.

GETTING HERE AND AROUND

Reach the island by car via the causeway from Brunswick.

TOURS

St. Simons Colonial Island Trolley Tours

TRAIN TOURS | For more than a decade, this locally owned and operated tour company has been introducing visitors to the history and culture of St. Simons Island. Reaching back 500 years, guides chronicle stories from the days of the island's early Native American inhabitants to modern history. No tour is the same, but the air-conditioned trolley passes by landmark sites of pre–Civil War African American churches, Christ Church, and the Battle of Bloody Marsh. The tour runs for 1½ hours and costs $20. The trolley departs from near the fishing pier at Pier Village up to three times daily depending on the season. ✉ *St. Simons Pier* ☎ *912/268–0363* 🌐 *www.colonialtrolley.com.*

VISITOR INFORMATION

CONTACTS The Golden Isles Convention and Visitors Bureau. *I–95 S, between Exits 42 and 38* *912/264–0202* *www.goldenisles.com.* **St. Simons Island Welcome Center.** *529 Beachview Dr.* *912/638–9014* *www.goldenisles.com.*

Sights

Christ Church, Frederica

RELIGIOUS SITE | Surrounded by moss-draped live oaks, dogwoods, and azaleas, this picturesque white-frame, Gothic-style church was built by shipwrights and consecrated in 1884 following an earlier structure's desecration by Union troops. The interior has beautiful stained-glass windows and several handmade pews. The congregation itself dates back to 1808 and is the second oldest Episcopal Church in the diocese of Georgia. In the adjacent cemetery grounds, you'll find the final resting place for Golden Isles historical fiction writer Eugenia Price. *6329 Frederica Rd.* *912/638–8683* *ccfssi.org* *Donations suggested* *Closed Mon.*

Fort Frederica National Monument

MILITARY SITE | Built by English troops in the mid-1730s, Fort Frederica was constructed to protect the southern flank of the new Georgia colony against a Spanish invasion from Florida. At its peak in the 1740s, it was the most elaborate British fortification in North America. Around the fort today are the foundations of homes and shops and the partial ruins of the tabby barracks and magazine. Start your visit at the National Park Service Visitors Center, which has a film and displays. *6515 Frederica Rd.* *912/638–3639* *www.nps.gov/fofr.*

Neptune Park

AMUSEMENT PARK/WATER PARK | FAMILY | Named after Neptune Small, a former slave who owned property where the park is now located, this lovely waterfront park is located near Pier Village on the island's south end. The expansive park boasts a picturesque oak canopy and picnic tables amid a sprawling lawn, beach access, and a large recreation area perfect for families. The Neptune Park Fun Zone has a free playground, a swimming pool ($8 per person) that opens in the warmer months, and a year-round miniature golf course ($8 per round). Also newly renovated, the adjacent pier is good for fishing or watching ships roll in. Public restrooms are outside the library. *550 Beachview Dr.* *912/279–2836* *www.glynncounty.org* *No golf Mon.–Thurs. fall–winter; pools closed Labor Day–May.*

St. Simons Lighthouse

LIGHTHOUSE | One of only five surviving lighthouses in Georgia, the St. Simons Lighthouse has become a symbol of the island. It's been in use since 1872; a predecessor was blown up to prevent its capture by Union troops in the Civil War. The **St. Simons Lighthouse Museum ,** occupying two stories of the lightkeeper's dwelling, tells of the history of the island, the lighthouse, and James Gould, the first lightkeeper of the original lighthouse. The keeper's second-floor quarters contain a parlor, kitchen, and two bedrooms furnished with period pieces, including beds with rope mattress suspension. The last climb of the lighthouse is at 4:30. *101 12th St.* *912/638–4666* *www.coastalgeorgiahistory.org* *$12, with combined access to WWII Museum $20.*

World War II Home Front Museum

MUSEUM | FAMILY | Set in a restored 1936 Coast Guard station and renovated in 2017, this museum—geared as much to kids as adults—features the life of a "Coastie" in the early 1940s, told through personal accounts of the WWII history of St. Simons Island. Exhibits explore how small communities like St. Simons came close to conflict due to the threat of German U-boats just offshore, and how the military shipbuilding industry sprung up in nearby Brunswick. The museum demonstrates how Georgia's Golden Isles were transformed during and after the Second World War and the important role civilians played on the home front. ✉ *4201 1st St.* ☎ *912/638–4666* 🌐 *www.coastalgeorgiahistory.org* 🎟 *$12, with combined access to lighthouse $20.*

Beaches

East Beach

BEACH—SIGHT | FAMILY | The most expansive stretch of public beach on St. Simons is also one of the most popular in all of the Golden Isles. Entrances sit on either end of the beach: at the Coast Guard Station on 1st Street to the north and Massengale Park on Oak Street to the south. Between the two entrances, this ½-mile stretch of hard-packed white sand is vacation central, with calm, shallow water perfect for swimming, boogie boarding, or windsurfing. Plenty of parking is available, lifeguards watch the waves all summer, and drinking is allowed in plastic containers (no glass bottles). **Amenities:** food and drink; lifeguards; parking (no fee); showers; toilets. **Best for:** swimming; windsurfing. ✉ *Ocean Blvd. from 1st St. to Oak St.* 🌐 *www.explorestsimonsisland.com.*

Restaurants

Coastal Kitchen and Raw Bar

$$$ | SEAFOOD | The fresh, locally sourced seafood at this spot overlooking the Morningstar Marina on the Frederica River, just inside the St. Simons Sound, is among the best on the island and perfectly complements the sunset views from the outdoor dining patio. The banks scallops and shrimp are a crowd-pleaser, perfectly paired with a butternut squash puree with hints of ginger and pistachio. **Known for:** waterfront views; Sunday brunch; fresh from the docks seafood. 💲 *Average main: $20* ✉ *102 Marina Dr.* ✣ *Just off the F.J. Torras Causeway on the way to St. Simons* ☎ *912/638–7790* 🌐 *www.coastalkitchenssi.com.*

The Half Shell at the Pier

$$ | SEAFOOD | FAMILY | On an island chock-full of seafood establishments, the Half Shell rises above the competition. It's beloved by locals and visitors alike for the combination of laid-back atmosphere, fresh seafood, and quality preparation and presentation—this is not the stereotypical fried-shrimp shack. **Known for:** fresh oysters—raw, shucked, or steamed; local Georgia shrimp and grits; crab cakes. 💲 *Average main: $18* ✉ *504 Beachview Dr.* ☎ *912/268–4241* 🌐 *thehalfshellssi.com* ⏲ *No lunch Mon.–Thurs.*

★ Halyards

$$$$ | AMERICAN | Chef-owner Dave Snyder's devotion to quality and homemade dishes (everything but the ketchup is made on the premises) has earned this elegant but relaxed restaurant a faithful following of discerning locals. Halyards, his flagship, is focused on the finest seasonal and local ingredients. **Known for:** signature coffee; vanilla bean crème brûlée with fresh strawberries; superb wine list. 💲 *Average main: $28* ✉ *55 Cinema La.* ☎ *912/638–9100* 🌐 *www.halyardsrestaurant.com* ⏲ *Closed Sun. No lunch.*

Porch

$ | AMERICAN | Located in a coastal-style shack on the edge of the Village, the porch is always packed at this casual order-at-the-counter eatery specializing in Nashville hot chicken, fried catfish, and fried local shrimp. Wash it all down with some Southern sweet tea or a chilly "frosé." There's tons of outdoor seating on the screened-in porch and at picnic tables on the lawn, making it popular with families and those with pups in tow. **Known for:** Nashville hot chicken; frosé and craft beer; large lawn and outdoor seating. 💲 *Average main: $10* ✉ *549 Ocean Blvd.* ☎ *912/634–5168* 🌐 *www.porchssi.com.*

Southern Soul Barbeque

$ | **BARBECUE** | This retro-inspired indoor-outdoor establishment with a more-than-12-hour hardwood-fired barbecue occupies a former gas station at a five-points crossroads in the heart of St. Simons Island. Locals claim this as the area's best barbecue, and diners flock here for the brisket, pulled pork, Brunswick stew, and homemade sauces and side dishes. **Known for:** retro atmosphere; sizable portions; Southern-style sides. *Average main: $10 ✉ 2020 Demere Rd. ☎ 912/638–7685 🌐 www.southernsoulbbq.com.*

Tramici

$$ | **ITALIAN** | **FAMILY** | Although it's in a shopping center, this Italian eatery with the same owner as the more refined Halyards bills itself as a neighborhood restaurant. It has spaghetti and meatballs and pizzas piled with favorite toppings, as well as a remarkable antipasto with prosciutto and various cheeses and a superb take on braised short ribs over goat cheese ravioli, with sun-dried tomatoes as the mystery ingredient. **Known for:** kid-friendly dining; authentic flatbreads; hearty Italian entrées. *Average main: $18 ✉ 75 Cinema La. ☎ 912/634–2202 🌐 www.tramicirestaurant.com ⏲ No lunch weekends.*

Coffee and Quick Bites

Palm Coast Coffee

$ | **AMERICAN** | The coffee is always on at this café in the Village where you'll also find delicious soups, salads, sandwiches, and desserts. Breakfast and lunch are served daily, and there's ample outdoor seating for relaxing and watching the world go by. **Known for:** great coffee; tasty breakfast and lunch entrées; pet-friendly outdoor seating. *Average main: $9 ✉ 318 Mallery St. ☎ 912/634–7515 🌐 www.palmcoastssi.com.*

Hotels

Holiday Inn Express

$$ | **HOTEL** | With clean, simple, brightly decorated rooms at great prices, this chain hotel is an attractive option in this price category. **Pros:** good value; no-smoking; swimming pool. **Cons:** guests have complained that walls are too thin; the breakfast is basic; a few miles away from the beach. *Rooms from: $156 ✉ Plantation Village, 299 Main St. ☎ 912/634–2175, 866/238–4218 🌐 www.ihg.com 60 rooms Free breakfast.*

King and Prince Beach and Golf Resort

$$$ | **RESORT** | Situated at the southern end of East Beach, this lovely historic inn and resort has some of the only true beachfront accommodations on the island. **Pros:** sprawling suites; golf-course access; on-site restaurant with pool and oceanfront dining. **Cons:** amenities are fairly basic; some rooms are small; tide levels can make it difficult to access the beach. *Rooms from: $235 ✉ 201 Arnold Rd. ☎ 912/638–3631 🌐 www.kingandprince.com 195 rooms No meals.*

★ The Lodge

$$$$ | **B&B/INN** | Although technically on St. Simons Island, this award-winning Sea Island resort has the charm and feel of an English country manor, with exposed ceiling beams, hardwood floors softened by Oriental rugs, and your own private butler, on call 24 hours a day. **Pros:** fantastic golfing; elegant, cozy interiors; stately, full marble baths. **Cons:** luxury comes at a high price; meals aren't included; hefty daily resort fee. *Rooms from: $679 ✉ 100 Retreat Ave. ☎ 855/572–4975 🌐 www.seaisland.com 61 rooms and cottages No meals.*

Saint Simons Inn

$$ | **B&B/INN** | In a prime spot by the lighthouse, and only minutes on foot from the Village and the beaches, this European-style inn is made up of privately owned guest rooms—nothing fancy, but they're clean, comfortable, and individually

decorated, many with furnishings and art that give off a beachy vibe. **Pros:** excellent location; affordable rates; some pet-friendly rooms. **Cons:** two-night minimum stay on weekends; some rooms are small; individually decorated rooms means some are not as nice as others. *Rooms from: $150 ✉ 609 Beachview Dr. ☎ 912/638–1101 ⊕ www.stsimonsinn.com 34 rooms Free breakfast.*

Sea Palms Resort and Conference Center

$$ | RESORT | Fully renovated in 2020, this full-service resort offers accommodations overlooking the beautiful "Marshes of Glynn" immortalized by poet Sidney Lanier, as well as condo-style suites near the ocean. **Pros:** guests have beach-club privileges; two lodging locations to choose from; some rooms have fantastic marsh views. **Cons:** no beach-club access for guests of Sea Gate Inn; complex often booked with events; no free breakfast. *Rooms from: $189 ✉ 515 N Windward Dr. ☎ 912/638–3351 ⊕ www.seapalms.com 64 rooms No meals.*

The Village Inn and Pub

$$ | B&B/INN | What was once a cinder-block beach house has since won awards for its environmentally friendly design that incorporated the original structure and preserved the surrounding live oaks. **Pros:** great location; courtyard pool and lively on-site pub; owners have taken care to preserve the mossy live oaks. **Cons:** basic rooms; the lively crowd at the pub can be noisy on weekends; on-site parking can be difficult. *Rooms from: $180 ✉ 500 Mallery St. ☎ 912/634–6056 ⊕ www.villageinnandpub.com 28 rooms Free breakfast.*

Activities

BIKING

Ocean Motion Surf Co.

BICYCLING | St. Simons has an extensive network of bicycle trails, and you can ride on the beach as well. Ocean Motion rents bikes for the entire family, from trail bikes and beach bikes to seats for infants. Rates start at $19 per day. *✉ 1300 Ocean Blvd. ☎ 912/638–5225 ⊕ www.stsimonskayaking.com.*

CRABBING AND FISHING

Shrimpin' Excursions

BOATING | FAMILY | If you've ever wondered what the life of a shrimper is like, then this is the cruise for you. This family-friendly excursion travels along the intercoastal waterway through the Marshes of Glynn on a retired shrimp trawler, *The Lady Jane.* On the two-hour cruise, you'll witness up to three net trawls bringing up a whole host of shrimp, crabs, and other wildlife to observe. An onboard tour guide and naturalist will help you identify the catch and provide hands-on opportunities to return the wildlife to nature. There's no actual shrimping involved—the purpose is wholly educational (and fun)! *✉ 1200 Glynn Ave., Brunswick ✥ Across the Torras Causeway from St. Simons Island, off Hwy. 17S ☎ 912/602–1677 ⊕ www.shrimpcruise.com.*

St. Simons Island Bait and Tackle

FISHING | FAMILY | There's no simpler fun for the kids than to grab a crab basket or fishing pole and head to the St. Simons Island Pier next to Neptune Park. This bait shop is near the foot of the pier and is open 364½ days a year. Owners Mike and Trish Wooten have everything from crabbing and fishing gear to snacks and cold drinks. They also sell locally made crab drop nets and fishing rigs. *✉ 121 Mallory St. ☎ 912/634–1888.*

GOLF

The top-flight golf facilities at the Lodge at Sea Island are available only to members and guests, but St. Simons has two other high-quality courses open to the general public.

The King and Prince Golf Course

GOLF | At the north end of St. Simons, on the site of the Hampton Plantation—an 18th-century cotton, rice, and indigo plantation—is a *Golf Digest* "Places to

Play" four-star winner. The course, originally designed by Joe Lee, lies amid towering oaks, salt marshes, and lagoons. ✉ *100 Tabbystone* ☎ *912/634–0255* 🌐 *www.kingandprince.com* *$79 resort guests, $115 nonguests, 18 holes, 6462 yds, par 72.*

Sea Palms Resort and Conference Center

GOLF | On a former cotton and indigo plantation, this resort offers a recently renovated 18-hole course plus a driving range. Discounts are available through online reservations. ✉ *5445 Frederica Rd.* ☎ *912/434–5336* 🌐 *www.seapalms.com* *$95, 6628 yds, par 71.*

KAYAKING AND SAILING

Barry's Beach Service

KAYAKING | If sailing is your thing, check out this shop in front of the King and Prince Beach and Golf Resort on Arnold Road for its Hobie Cat rentals and sailing lessons. Barry's also rents kayaks, boogie boards, stand-up paddleboards, beach chairs and umbrellas, and beach funcycles (low, reclining bikes) and conducts guided kayak tours. Locally owned and operated, Barry's has served the Golden Isles since 1977. ✉ *420 Arnold Rd.* ☎ *912/638–8053* 🌐 *www.stsimonskayaking.com* *Sailboat rentals from $120 an hour.*

Turtle Tides Outfitters

KAYAKING | This local outfitter offers kayak and paddleboard rentals, lessons, and guided eco tours. The three-hour guided tour takes you from the mouth of the Atlantic Ocean through the wetlands and to a preserve on Sea Island for shelling and bird-watching. ✉ *St. Simons Island* ☎ *912/ 222–2190* 🌐 *www.turtle-tides.com.*

SCUBA DIVING

Island Dive Center

DIVING/SNORKELING | Island Dive Center, a five-star PADI center, is the place to go for scuba and snorkeling instruction, equipment rental, and charter trips. Open by appointment only. ✉ *St. Simons Island* ☎ *912/638–6590.*

Sea Island

East of St. Simons Island, connected by a 1-mile causeway.

Tiny Sea Island—with a full-time population of less than 400—is one of the nation's wealthiest communities. Established by Howard Coffin, the wealthy Detroit auto pioneer who also owned Sapelo Island in the early 20th century, Sea Island has been a getaway for the well-heeled since 1928, when Coffin opened The Cloister hotel, which sits at the heart of this posh island retreat. Today Sea Island is a gated community accessible only to registered guests of the hotel and Sea Island Club members.

GETTING HERE AND AROUND

Though accessible by causeway, the island is restricted to owners and guests of Sea Island Club hotels.

Hotels

★ The Cloister

$$$$ | **RESORT** | This Mediterranean-style, waterside resort—tucked behind a secure gate and impeccably appointed with tropical landscaping, rich rococo fabrics, and stained glass—is fit for dignitaries (and hosted them during the 2004 G8 Summit). **Pros:** elegant getaway; horseback riding and a plethora of activities; pristine beach. **Cons:** the winding paths and property layout may be a bit confusing for first-time visitors; hefty daily resort fee; restaurants and amenities fill quickly. *Rooms from: $749* ✉ *100 Cloister Dr.* ☎ *855/572–4975 reservations, 800/732–4732 general information* 🌐 *www.seaisland.com* *265 rooms* *No meals.*

The Inn at Sea Island

$$ | **HOTEL** | Located just outside the gates of the Sea Island Resort, this self-service hotel offers comfortable accommodations with a much more affordable price tag. **Pros:** more affordable way to experience Sea Island; access to BMW courtesy cars, bikes, and a resort shuttle; free continental breakfast. **Cons:** resort access isn't always available (blackout dates); can be confusing what amenities are included in stay; less expensive options in the area. *$ Rooms from: $177 ✉ 100 Salt Marsh Dr., St. Simons Island ☎ 855/572–4975 🌐 www.seaisland.com 85 rooms 🍽 Free breakfast.*

Jekyll Island

18 miles south of St. Simons Island; 90 miles south of Savannah.

For 56 winters, between 1886 and 1942, America's rich and famous faithfully came south to Jekyll Island. Through the Gilded Age, World War I, the Roaring '20s, and the Great Depression, Vanderbilts and Rockefellers, Morgans and Astors, Macys, Pulitzers, and Goodyears shuttered their 5th Avenue castles and retreated to elegant "cottages" on their wild coastal island. It's been said that when the island's distinguished winter residents were all "in," a sixth of the world's wealth was represented. Early in World War II the millionaires departed for the last time. In 1947 the state of Georgia purchased the entire island for the bargain price of $675,000.

Jekyll Island is still a 7½-mile playground, but it's no longer restricted to the rich and famous. A water park, picnic grounds, and facilities for golf, tennis, fishing, biking, and jogging are all open to the public. One side of the island is lined by nearly 10 miles of hard-packed Atlantic beaches; the other by the intracoastal waterway and picturesque salt marshes. Deer and wild turkey inhabit interior forests of pine, magnolia, and moss-veiled live oaks. Egrets, pelicans, herons, and sandpipers skim the gentle surf. Jekyll Island's clean, mostly uncommercialized public beaches are free and open year-round. Bathhouses with restrooms, changing areas, and showers are open at regular intervals along the beach.

GETTING HERE AND AROUND

Jekyll Island is connected to the mainland by the Sidney Lanier Bridge. Visitors coming to the island by car must stop at the greeting station to pay a parking fee of $8 per vehicle per day. Once on the island, you'll need a car or a bicycle to get around.

VISITOR INFORMATION

CONTACTS Jekyll Island Welcome Center. *✉ 901 Downing Musgrove Causeway ☎ 912/635–3636 🌐 www.jekyllisland.com.*

Sights

★ Georgia Sea Turtle Center

INFO CENTER | FAMILY | A must-see on Jekyll Island, this is one of the few sea turtle centers in the country. This center aims to increase awareness of habitat and wildlife conservation challenges for endangered coastal turtles—loggerheads, green, Kemp's ridley, and diamondback terrapin—through turtle rehabilitation, research, and education programs. The center includes educational exhibits and a "hospital," where visitors can view rescued turtles and read their stories. Sea turtles lay their eggs along Jekyll Island beaches from May through August. Several hundred rehabilitated turtles have been released into the wild since the center opened. *✉ 214 Stable Rd. ☎ 912/635–4444 🌐 gstc.jekyllisland.com $10.*

★ Jekyll Island National Historic Landmark District

HISTORIC SITE | This 240-acre historic district encapsulates the village that once comprised the winter retreat and seasonal residences for America's wealthiest—Morgan, Pulitzer, Goodyear, Rockefeller, and Vanderbilt among them. Today, the original cottages still stand amid the historic grounds, with the Jekyll Island Club Hotel, founded in 1886, as the crown jewel. Nearby is **Faith Chapel** , built in 1904, which is illuminated by stained-glass windows, including one Tiffany original. The chapel is open daily 10 am to 12 pm for prayer and meditation. Free admission is included outside those hours with the purchase of any Historic Landmark District Tour. ✉ *Jekyll Island* 🌐 *www.jekyllisland.com.*

★ **Mosaic, Jekyll Island Museum**

MUSEUM | Reopened in spring 2019 after a massive renovation, the museum is housed in the island's former stables and offers guests a glimpse into Jekyll's rich history. A wide array of exhibits, interactive tools, and audio and visual effects tell the stories of the barrier island—from the life of original natives and the landing of one of the last slave ships at the south end to the golden age of the island, when America's rich and famous wintered here. Tram tours ($20) depart daily at 11, 1, and 3, weather permitting. The 60-minute tour covers the National Historic Landmark District and includes entry into a restored cottage and Faith Chapel. ✉ *100 Stable Rd.* ☎ *912/635–4036* 🌐 *www.jekyllisland.com/history/museum* 🎫 *$9.*

Summer Waves Water Park

AMUSEMENT PARK/WATER PARK | FAMILY | At this 11-acre park more than a million gallons of water are used in the 18,000-square-foot wave pool, waterslides, children's activity pool with two slides, splash zone, and circular river for tubing and rafting. Inner tubes and life vests are provided at no extra charge. ✉ *210 S. Riverview Dr.* ☎ *912/635–2074* 🌐 *www.summerwaves.com* 🎫 *$18* ⏲ *Closed Oct.–Apr.*

Beaches

Driftwood Beach

BEACH—SIGHT | For a firsthand look at the stunning effects of erosion on barrier islands, head at low tide to this oceanfront boneyard on North Beach, where live oaks and pines are being consumed by the sea at an alarming rate. The snarl of trunks and limbs and the dramatic, massive root systems of upturned trees are an eerie and intriguing tableau of nature's slow and steady power. It's been estimated that nearly 1,000 feet of Jekyll's beach have been lost since the early 1900s. ■ **TIP→ Bring your camera; the photo opportunities are terrific, and this is the best place to shoot the St. Simons Lighthouse. The snarling branches of submerged trees can make this a dangerous place to swim, however, so use caution in the water.** Restrooms and other facilities are at the Clam Creek Picnic Area. **Amenities:** parking (no fee); showers; toilets. **Best for:** solitude; sunrise. ✉ *Jekyll Island* ✣ *Walk from the trailhead at the east side of the Clam Creek Picnic Area or from the roadside parking area on N. Beachview Dr.*

Great Dunes Beach Park

BEACH—SIGHT | FAMILY | Starting just north of the entrance road on South Beachview Drive, this 20-acre stretch of beach runs alongside Main Street and the convention center to South Dunes Beach at Glory Boardwalk (built when the final battle scene of the film *Glory* was shot here), next to the soccer complex. This is one of the most accessible beaches on the island, with parking at both ends and good shower-restroom facilities. The white-sand beach is backed by dunes, which are protected wildlife areas, while calm, shallow water, and a mild shore break make this a good spot to swim and play in the surf. It's the most popular beach for families on the island. **Amenities:** parking (no fee); showers; toilets. **Best for:** swimming. ✉ *Jekyll Island* ✣ *S. Beachview Dr., from the beach deck to Glory Boardwalk* 🌐 *www.jekyllisland.com/activities/great-dunes-beach.*

St. Andrews Beach

BEACH—SIGHT | FAMILY | Stretching south of Glory Boardwalk to the St. Andrews Picnic Area at the very southern end of the island, this narrow beach backs up to dense maritime forest, making it a quiet, secluded bit of coast and a great spot for wildlife viewing or beachcombing. At the picnic area, a short trail leads to a viewing platform overlooking the outflow of Jekyll Creek—keep an eye out for dolphins cruising near the shoreline. A memorial and memory trail honors the landing of one of the last American slave ships, *The Wanderer*. **Amenities:** parking (no fee); toilets. **Best for:** solitude. ✉ *Jekyll Island ✣ Take S. Beachview Dr. or S. Riverview Dr. to the southernmost end of the island 🌐 www.jekyllisland.com/activities/st-andrews-beach.*

Restaurants

Driftwood Bistro

$$ | **SEAFOOD** | On-site at Villas by the Sea, Driftwood Bistro is an island favorite for its Lowcountry Southern cuisine and friendly, laid-back environment. Try the shrimp and grits, pork tenderloin, and crab bisque. **Known for:** Lowcountry cuisine; vegetarian options; outstanding seafood dishes. *$ Average main: $19 ✉ 1175 N. Beachview Dr. ☎ 912/635–2521 🌐 www.driftwoodbistro.com ⏲ No lunch. Closed Sun.*

★ Grand Dining Room

$$$$ | **SOUTHERN** | This colonnaded restaurant inside the Jekyll Island Club maintains a tradition of fine dining first established in the 19th century. Signature dishes are the rack of lamb, duck breast, and the filet mignon, all seasoned differently depending on the season. **Known for:** grand historical architecture; super Sunday brunch spread; Victorian tea service. *$ Average main: $35 ✉ Jekyll Island Club, 371 Riverview Dr. ☎ 912/635–5155 🌐 www.jekyllclub.com 👔 Jacket required.*

The Wharf

$$$ | **AMERICAN** | **FAMILY** | This casual waterfront spot, operated by the Jekyll Island Club, is a popular destination for fresh seafood, live music, and an alfresco lunch or cocktail hour. Bar snacks, raw oysters, and Lowcountry boils dominate a menu that also offers landlubber's choices like burgers and grilled steak. **Known for:** gumbo; live music; waterfront location. *$ Average main: $20 ✉ 370 Riverview Dr. ☎ 912/635–3612 🌐 www.jekyllwharf.com.*

Coffee and Quick Bites

Island Sweets Shoppe

$ | **FAST FOOD** | **FAMILY** | Head to this cute little cottage in Jekyll's historic district when the sweet tooth hits for handmade fudge, pralines, truffles, and other goodies made on-site. There's also ice cream and slushies. **Known for:** chocolate confections; ice cream; take-home treats. *$ Average main: $6 ✉ In the Jekyll Island Historic District, 150 Old Plantation Rd. ☎ 912/635–3135.*

Hotels

Beachview Club Hotel

$$ | **HOTEL** | Grand old oak trees shade the grounds of this quaint boutique hotel, where rooms are either on the oceanfront or have a partial ocean view. **Pros:** heated pool; relaxing location with beautiful grounds; property on the beach. **Cons:** not much for kids to do here; exterior corridors; breakfast not included in rate. *$ Rooms from: $200 ✉ 721 N. Beachview Dr. ☎ 912/635–2256 🌐 www.beachviewclubjekyll.com ⇆ 38 rooms 🍴 No meals.*

Holiday Inn Resort

$$$ | **HOTEL** | **FAMILY** | Decorated in coastal blue hues, the rooms here offer the standard comforts of a Holiday Inn but with sweeping views of the beach on the ocean side. **Pros:** lovely views; large oceanfront pool with whirlpool; multiple dining options on-site. **Cons:** good views only on ocean side; rooms near the restaurant are loud on the weekends; exterior corridors. *$ Rooms from: $205 ✉ 711 N. Beachview Dr. ☎ 912/635–2211 🌐 www.ihg.com ⇆ 157 rooms 🍴 No meals.*

★ Jekyll Island Club Hotel
$$$ | **RESORT** | This sprawling 1887 resort was once described as "the richest, the most exclusive, the most inaccessible club in the world," and its old-world charm persists. **Pros:** on the water; gorgeous grounds and common areas; close proximity to restaurants, shopping, and sea-turtle center. **Cons:** service can be varied; some rooms are small; can be noisy due to thin walls and older construction. *Rooms from: $229 371 Riverview Dr. 912/635–2600 www.jekyllclub.com 200 rooms No meals.*

Westin Jekyll Island
$$$ | **RESORT** | With expansive ocean views, this resort is well situated near Jekyll's beachfront and bike path and the shopping amenities of the beach village. **Pros:** ocean views and beach access; eco-friendly and pet friendly; close to convention center and shopping district. **Cons:** rooms are on the small side; resort fee added; restaurant service inconsistent. *Rooms from: $264 110 Ocean Way 912/635–4545 www.westinjekyllisland.com 200 rooms No meals.*

Activities

BIKING

The best way to see Jekyll is by bicycle: a long, paved trail runs right along the beach, and there's an extensive network of paths throughout the island.

Beachside Bike Rentals
BICYCLING | Located near the Days Inn, this one-stop rental shop offers everything from multispeed bikes to double surreys with Bimini tops that look like antique cars and carry up to six adults and two children. The shop also has beach chairs, umbrellas, stand-up paddleboards, and kayaks. *60 S. Beachview Dr. 912/635–9801 www.beachsidebikerentals.com.*

Camping on Jekyll Island

Jekyll Island Campground. At the northern end of Jekyll across from the entrance to the fishing pier, this campground lies on 18 wooded acres with more than 175 sites that can accommodate everything from backpackers looking for primitive sites to RVs needing full hookups. Pets are welcome. It's within walking distance of Driftwood Beach but far from the main activity of the island. *1197 Riverview Dr., Jekyll Island 912/635–3021 www.jekyllisland.com/lodging/jekyll-island-campground.*

Jekyll Island Mini Golf and Bike Rentals
BICYCLING | FAMILY | Play miniature golf or choose from a wide selection of rental bikes (including surrey pedal cars that can hold four people, recumbent bikes, and traditional bikes) at this shop located next to the Red Bug. Rates start at $15 daily for bike rentals and $7 for a round of minigolf. *N. Beachview Dr. at Shell Rd. 912/635–2648 www.jekyllisland.com/activities/miniature-golf.*

FISHING

Coastal Expeditions
FISHING | With 40 years of experience in local waters, Captain Eric Moody provides half-day and full-day trips inshore and offshore for fishing, dolphin-watching, and sightseeing. There's a six-person maximum. *Jekyll Harbor Marina 912/270–3526 www.coastalcharterfishing.com.*

Jekyll Fishing Center
FISHING | Get all your fishing gear right at the pier at this shop selling bait, tackle, and other supplies. They also rent rods and reels, pier carts, coolers, and more. *Jekyll Island Fishing Pier, 10 Clam Creek Rd. 912/635–3556.*

GOLF

Jekyll Island Golf Club

GOLF | A golf destination for nearly 90 years, this club today has four courses: the original 9-hole course called Oceanside Nine (now known as Great Dunes), built in 1926, and three beautifully designed 18-hole courses, plus a clubhouse. ✉ *322 Capt. Wylly Rd.* ☎ *912/635–2368* 🌐 *www.jekyllisland.com/activities-category/golf-club* ⛳ *$59 (9 holes $20), 18 holes, 6469–6701 yds, par 72.*

HORSEBACK RIDING

Golden Isles Carriage and Trail

HORSEBACK RIDING | **FAMILY** | See Jekyll by horseback with this well-regarded livery company, in business for more than 30 years. Trail rides include visits to the salt marsh and Driftwood Beach, a boneyard of live oaks and pine trees being reclaimed by the sea; narrated carriage tours explore the sights of the historic district. Rides leave from the Clam Creek Picnic Area across from the Jekyll Island Campground, and the carriages leave from the Riverview Drive location. Perks for families include a petting zoo, horse camp for children, and riding lessons for all ages. ✉ *364 Riverview Dr.* ☎ *912/635–9500* 🌐 *www.threeoaksfarm.org* 🎫 *Horseback rides from $65 an hour; historic carriage tours from $20 per person.*

Cumberland Island

47 miles south of Jekyll Island; 115 miles south of Savannah to St. Marys via I–95; 45 mins by ferry from St. Marys.

Cumberland, the largest of Georgia's coastal isles, is a national treasure. The 18-mile spit of land off the coast of St. Marys is a nearly unspoiled sanctuary of marshes, dunes, beaches, forests, lakes, and ponds. And although it has a long history of human habitation, it remains much as nature created it: a dense, lacework canopy of live oak shades, sand roads, and foot trails through thick undergrowth of palmetto. Wild horses roam freely on pristine beaches. Waterways are homes for gators, sea turtles, otters, snowy egrets, great blue herons, ibises, wood storks, and more than 300 other species of birds. And in its forests are armadillos, wild horses, deer, raccoons, and an assortment of reptiles.

In the 16th century the Spanish established a mission and a garrison, San Pedro de Mocama, on the southern end of the island. But development didn't begin in earnest until the wake of the American Revolution, with timbering operations for shipbuilding, particularly construction of warships for the early U.S. naval fleet. Cotton, rice, and indigo plantations were also established. In 1818 Revolutionary War hero General "Lighthorse" Harry Lee, father of Robert E. Lee, died and was buried near the Dungeness estate of General Nathanael Greene. Though his body was later moved to Virginia to be interred beside his son, the gravestone remains. During the 1880s, the family of Thomas Carnegie (brother of industrialist Andrew) built several lavish homes here. In the 1950s the National Park Service named Cumberland Island and Cape Cod as the most significant natural areas on the Atlantic and Gulf Coasts. And in 1972, in response to attempts to develop the island by Hilton Head developer Charles Fraser, Congress passed a bill establishing the island as a National Seashore. Today most of the island is part of the National Park system.

GETTING HERE AND AROUND

The only access to the island is via the *Cumberland Queen II*, a reservations-only, 146-passenger ferry based near the National Park Service Information Center at St. Marys. The round-trip ticket price is $30. The $10 entry fee to the Cumberland Island National Seashore applies to all island visitors. There are two Park Service docks at the island's south end: the main

Wild horses roam freely on Cumberland Island.

ferry dock is the Sea Camp Dock, with a secondary stop at Dungeness Dock farther south.

Ferry bookings are heavy in spring and early summer and then again in early fall. Cancellations and no-shows often make last-minute space available, but don't rely on it. You can make reservations up to six months in advance. The ferry operates twice a day in both directions between St. Marys and Cumberland Island. ■ **TIP→ Note that the ferry does not transport pets, kayaks, or cars.**

Getting around the island is solely by foot or bicycle, which can be rented at the Sea Camp Dock or brought aboard the ferry for a $10 fee.

ESSENTIALS

FERRY CONTACTS ***Cumberland Queen II*** ✉ *113 St. Marys St. W, St. Marys* ☎ *877/860–6787* 🌐 *www.cumberlandislandferry.com.*

Sights

★ Cumberland Island National Seashore

NATURE PRESERVE | Encompassing the vast majority of Cumberland Island, this 36,347-acre preserve has pristine forests and marshes marbled with wooded nature trails, 18 miles of undeveloped beaches, and opportunities for fishing, bird-watching, and viewing the ruins of Thomas Carnegie's great estate, **Dungeness.** You can also join history and nature walks led by Park Service rangers. Bear in mind that summers are hot and humid and that you must bring everything you need, including your own food, drinks, sunscreen, and insect repellent. The only public access to the island is via the *Cumberland Queen II* ferry. ✉ *Visitor Center, 113 St. Marys St. W, St. Marys* ☎ *912/882–4336* 🌐 *www.nps.gov/cuis* 🎫 *Preserve $10, ferry $30.*

The First African Baptist Church

RELIGIOUS SITE | This small, one-room church on the north end of Cumberland Island was rebuilt in 1937 to replace a

Georgia's Black Republic

After capturing Savannah in December 1864, General William Tecumseh Sherman read the Emancipation Proclamation at the Second African Baptist Church and issued his now famous Field Order No. 15, giving freed slaves 40 acres and a mule. The field order set aside a swath of land reaching 30 miles inland from Charleston to northern Florida (roughly the area east of Interstate 95), including the coastal islands, for an independent state of freed slaves.

Under the administration of General Rufus Saxton and his assistant, Tunis G. Campbell, a black New Jersey native who represented McIntosh County as a state senator, a black republic was established with St. Catherines Island as its capital. Hundreds of former slaves were relocated to St. Catherines and Sapelo Islands, where they set about cultivating the land. In 1865 Campbell established himself as virtual king, controlling a legislature, a court, and a 275-man army.

Congress repealed Sherman's directive and replaced General Saxton with General Davis Tillson, who was sympathetic to the interests of former plantation owners, and in 1867 federal troops drove Campbell off St. Catherines and into McIntosh County, where he continued to exert his power. In 1876 he was convicted of falsely imprisoning a white citizen and sentenced, at the age of 63, to work on a chain gang. After being freed, he left Georgia for good and settled in Boston, where he died in 1891.

cruder 1893 structure used by former slaves from the High Point–Half Moon Bluff community. Constructed of whitewashed logs, it's simply adorned with a cross made of sticks tied together with string and 11 handmade pews seating 40 people. John F. Kennedy Jr. and Carolyn Bessette were married here on September 21, 1996. The Kennedy–Bessette wedding party stayed at the Greyfield Inn, built on the south end of the island in 1900 by the Carnegie family. ✉ *Cumberland Island* ✣ *North end of Cumberland, near Half Moon Bluff, about 12 miles from Sea Camp Dock.*

St. Marys Aquatic Center

AMUSEMENT PARK/WATER PARK | FAMILY | If the heat has you, and the kids are itching to get wet, head to this full-service water park on the mainland, where you can get an inner tube and relax floating down the Oasis lazy river, hurtle down Splash Mountain, or corkscrew yourself silly sliding down the Orange Crush. ✉ *301 Herb Bauer Dr., St. Marys* ☎ *912/673–8118* 🌐 *www.stmarysga.gov/department/aquatic_center* 🎫 *$11* ⏲ *Closed Oct.–Apr.*

Beaches

Dungeness Beach

BEACH—SIGHT | From the Dungeness ferry dock to the southern tip of the island, Dungeness Beach covers nearly 2 miles of pristine, remote coast. This wild stretch of sand attracts beachcombers (shark teeth are a sought-after find) and fishermen, who cast for redfish and flounder at the southernmost point, called Pelican Flats. Trails lead to Thomas Carnegie's historic estate, Dungeness, and this is also a good area to spot Cumberland's famed wild horses that roam the beach and inland areas here. **Amenities:** none. **Best for:** solitude; sunrise. ✉ *Cumberland Island* ✣ *Dungeness ferry dock to Pelican Flats.*

Sea Camp Beach

BEACH—SIGHT | Proximity to the ferry makes this beach fronting the Sea Camp campground the most popular beach among day-trippers, though with only 300 visitors allowed on the island daily, it's never very crowded. Hard-pack trails and a boardwalk allow short nature walks, and the beach has good beach-combing. **Amenities:** showers; toilets. **Best for:** solitude; sunrise. ✉ *Cumberland Island* ✣ *½ mile north of Sea Camp Dock.*

Restaurants

There are no restaurants on Cumberland Island; it's a pack-in, pack-out destination. But St. Marys has several great dining options offering waterfront views in its quaint downtown area.

401 West

$$$ | **AMERICAN** | With spectacular views overlooking the marsh, this St. Marys eatery specializes in local farm-to-table cuisine including a relaxing weekend brunch. The menu ranges from burgers to house-made pastas to the quintessential shrimp and grits. **Known for:** sunset views; inventive cocktails; weekend brunch. $ *Average main: $20* ✉ *401 W. St. Marys St., St. Marys* ☎ *912/333–9515* 🌐 *www.eat401west.com* ⏲ *Closed Mon.*

Riverside Cafe

$$ | **AMERICAN** | **FAMILY** | Go for the authentic Greek food at this cozy café right across from the Cumberland Island Ferry. There's indoor and outdoor dining with great waterfront views. **Known for:** Greek-American specialties; fried seafood; family-friendly dining. $ *Average main: $17* ✉ *106 St. Marys St., St. Marys* ☎ *912/882–3466* 🌐 *www.riversidecafe-saintmarys.com* ⏲ *Closed Sun.*

Camping Near Okefenokee

Laura S. Walker State Park. One of the few state parks named for a woman, this 626-acre park honors a Waycross teacher who championed conservation. The park, 9 miles northeast of the Okefenokee Swamp Park, has campsites with electrical and water hookups. Be sure to pick up food and supplies on the way. Boating, skiing, and fishing are permitted on the 120-acre lake. ✉ *5653 Laura Walker Rd., Waycross* ☎ *912/287–4900* 🌐 *www.gastateparks.org/lauraswalker.*

Hotels

ON THE ISLAND

Greyfield Inn

$$$$ | **B&B/INN** | Once described as a "Tara by the sea," this turn-of-the-last-century Carnegie family home is Cumberland Island's only accommodation. **Pros:** unique lodging experience in historic home; lack of telephone service means complete solitude; social hour with hors d'oeuvres. **Cons:** pricey; no stores on Cumberland; communications to the mainland are limited. $ *Rooms from: $725* ✉ *Cumberland Island* ✣ *Southern end of the island, accessible by private boat from Fernandina Beach, FL* ☎ *904/261–6408* 🌐 *www.greyfieldinn.com* *16 rooms* *All meals.*

ON THE MAINLAND

Cumberland Island Inn and Suites

$ | **HOTEL** | **FAMILY** | Children under 18 stay free at this modern, moderately priced hotel 3½ miles from the St. Marys waterfront and near a shopping center. **Pros:** clean, large rooms; affordable rates; kids stay free. **Cons:** not in historic area; not in walking distance of the beach; location not special. $ *Rooms from: $79* ✉ *2710 Osborne Rd., St. Marys* ☎ *800/768–6250* 🌐 *www.cumberlandislandinn.com* 🛏 *79 rooms* 🍴 *Free breakfast.*

Goodbread House Inn
$ | **B&B/INN** | This 1870 Victorian home, named after the Goodbread family who once owned it, is a comfy bed-and-breakfast with six uniquely decorated rooms named for famous lovers like Scarlett and Rhett and Bogie and Bacall. **Pros:** friendly and accommodating innkeeper; golf cart available for exploring the town; excellent breakfast and afternoon reception. **Cons:** the inn's eclectic decor isn't for everyone; some rooms feel a bit dated; may be too small and intimate for some. $ *Rooms from: $139* ✉ *209 Osborne St., St. Marys* ☎ *912/882–7490* 🛏 *6 rooms* 🍴 *Free breakfast.*

Riverview Hotel
$ | **B&B/INN** | The front door to the Riverview could be a time machine transporting you straight to the Old West, circa 1916, the year the hotel was built. **Pros:** some rooms with river views; excellent location across from ferry; affordable rates. **Cons:** can be noisy due to old construction; some rooms are small; no elevator. $ *Rooms from: $135* ✉ *105 Osborne St., St. Marys* ☎ *912/882–3242* 🌐 *www.riverviewhotelstmarys.com* 🛏 *20 rooms* 🍴 *Free breakfast.*

Spencer House Inn
$$ | **B&B/INN** | At the heart of the St. Marys historic district, this pink, three-story Victorian inn, built in 1872, is a perfect base for touring the town and Cumberland Island. **Pros:** short walk to the ferry; big balconies with rocking chairs; elevator. **Cons:** some complain of hard beds; a/c units are near rooms and can be loud; historic house quirks aren't for everyone. $ *Rooms from: $175* ✉ *200 Osborne St., St. Marys* ☎ *912/882–1872, 888/840–1872* 🌐 *www.spencerhouseinn.com* 🛏 *14 rooms* 🍴 *Free breakfast.*

KAYAKING

Up the Creek Xpeditions
KAYAKING | Whether you're a novice or skilled paddler, Up the Creek can guide you on kayak tours through some of Georgia and Florida's most scenic waters. Classes include navigation, tides and currents, and kayak surfing and racing. Trips include the St. Marys River, Cumberland Sound, and Amelia Island. ✉ *St. Marys* ☎ *912/882–0911* 🌐 *jacksonvillekayakcompany.com.*

Okefenokee National Wildlife Refuge

Larger than all of Georgia's barrier islands combined, the Okefenokee National Wildlife Refuge covers 700 square miles of southeastern Georgia and northeastern Florida. From the air, all roads and almost all traces of human development almost disappear into this vast, seemingly impenetrable landscape, the largest intact freshwater wetlands in the contiguous United States. The rivers, lakes, forests, prairies, and swamps all teem with seen and unseen life: alligators, otters, bobcats, raccoons, opossums, white-tailed deer, turtles, bald eagles, red-tailed hawks, egrets, muskrats, herons, cranes, red-cockaded woodpeckers, and black bears all make their home here. The term "swamp" hardly does the Okefenokee justice. It's the largest peat-producing bog in the United States, with varied landscapes, including towering virgin cypress, sandy pine islands, and lush subtropical hammocks.

None of the parks encompass everything the refuge has to offer; you need to determine what your highest priorities are and choose your gateway on that basis. Day trips and boat rentals can be arranged at any of the parks, and more adventurous visitors can take guided or

Camping on Cumberland Island

Brickhill Bluff Campground. Way off the beaten path, this primitive campsite is a favorite spot to see manatees and dolphins. For those looking for adventure (and not amenities), Brickhill is worth the long hike from the dock. ✉ *Cumberland Island* ☎ *877/444–6777* 🌐 *www.nps.gov/cuis.*

Hickory Hill Campground. Located in the heart of the island, this primitive camping area is about 1 mile from the beach. Though still in the trees, its canopy is more open than at some of the other sites. ✉ *5½ miles from Sea Camp ferry dock, Cumberland Island* ☎ *877/444–6777* 🌐 *www.nps.gov/cuis.*

Sea Camp Campground. Close to the ferry dock and with plenty of amenities, this is an ideal spot for first-timers, families, and groups. Expect a firepit, food cage, and picnic table at each site. ✉ *½ mile from Sea Camp ferry dock, Cumberland Island* ☎ *877/444–6777* 🌐 *www.nps.gov/cuis.*

Stafford Beach Campground. Located behind the dunes, 3½ miles from the ferry dock, this is the only backcountry site not considered to be in the wilderness. It has more amenities than most of the other, more primitive sites. Expect good tree cover, bathrooms, showers, and a water source. ✉ *3½ miles from Sea Camp ferry dock, Cumberland Island* ☎ *877/444–6777* 🌐 *www.nps.gov/cuis.*

Yankee Paradise Campground. Surrounded by palmettos, this forested and secluded spot is protected from the wind. It's a long hike back to the ferry dock, but the remoteness could be a big draw for some. ✉ *7½ miles from Sea Camp ferry dock, Cumberland Island* ☎ *877/444–6777* 🌐 *www.nps.gov/cuis.*

independent overnight canoe-camping trips into the interior.

GETTING HERE AND AROUND

To get around the Okefenokee swamplands you will need a motorboat, canoe, or kayak, or you'll have to book a tour. Rentals and tours are arranged through individual parks and local outfitters.

Three gateways provide access to the refuge: the eastern (and main) entrance at the Suwannee Canal Recreation Area, near Folkston; a northern entrance at the privately owned Okefenokee Swamp Park near Waycross; and a western entrance at Stephen C. Foster State Park, outside the town of Fargo. There are also two small boat launches (no facilities) at Kingfisher Landing and the Suwannee River Sill on the eastern and western sides, respectively.

The surrounding towns of Folkston, Waycross, and Fargo don't offer much as destinations themselves—they serve as bases from which to visit the swamp.

Suwannee Canal Recreation Area

8 miles southwest of Folkston via GA 121.

Suwannee Canal Recreation Area, the main entrance to the Okefenokee National Wildlife Refuge, is home to the Chesser Island Boardwalk and the historic Chesser Island Homestead. Vendors offer food service, guided boat tours, and canoe and kayak rentals.

Did You Know?

Over 200 species of birds, 40 species of mammals, 60 species of reptiles, and 30 species of amphibians have been identified in Georgia's Okefenokee Swamp.

Sights

Suwannee Canal Recreation Area

NATIONAL/STATE PARK | Extensive open areas at the core of the refuge—like the Chesser, Grand, and Mizell Prairies—branch off the man-made Suwannee Canal, accessed via the main entrance to the Okefenokee National Wildlife Refuge, and contain small natural lakes and gator holes. The prairies are excellent spots for sportfishing and birding, and it's possible to take guided boat tours of the area leaving from the Okefenokee Adventures concession, near the visitor center. The concession also has equipment rentals, and food is available at the Camp Cornelia Cafe. The visitor center has a film, exhibits, and a mechanized mannequin that tells stories about life in the Okefenokee (it sounds hokey, but it's surprisingly informative). A boardwalk takes you over the water to a 50-foot observation tower. Hikers, bicyclists, and private motor vehicles are welcome on Swamp Island Drive; several interpretive walking trails may be taken along the way. Picnicking is permitted. ✉ *Folkston* ✣ *11 miles southwest of Folkston, off GA 121/23* ☎ *912/496–7836* 🌐 *www.fws.gov/okefenokee* 🎫 *$5 per car.*

Restaurants

Okefenokee Restaurant

$ | **SOUTHERN** | Everything's home-cooked at this half-century-old local institution, and it's all good—from the fried shrimp to the black-eyed peas. It opens early for breakfast and has a daily lunch and dinner buffet piled with Southern favorites. **Known for:** breakfast buffet; country-style fare; peach cobbler. 💲 *Average main: $11* ✉ *1507 3rd St., Folkston* ☎ *912/496–3263* ⏲ *Closed Sun.*

Hotels

The Inn at Folkston

$ | **B&B/INN** | This Craftsman-style inn with a huge front veranda, porch swings, and rocking chairs is filled with antiques, and each room is uniquely decorated. **Pros:** inn is beautifully restored; owners make you feel like welcome relatives; spacious, interesting rooms. **Cons:** the many trains that pass by can be noisy; no TVs in rooms; no pets. 💲 *Rooms from: $130* ✉ *3576 W. Main St., Folkston* ☎ *912/496–6256, 888/509–6246* 🌐 *www.innatfolkston.com* 🛏 *4 rooms* 🍽 *Free breakfast.*

Activities

CANOEING AND CAMPING

Okefenokee Adventures

CAMPING—SPORTS-OUTDOORS | Guided overnight canoe trips can be arranged by this rental and guiding business. It also does 90-minute interpretive boat tours ($28) and rents boats, canoes, and kayaks (starting at $40 a day) as well as bicycles ($12 a day) and camping equipment. ✉ *4159 Suwannee Canal Rd., Folkston* ☎ *866/843–7926* 🌐 *www.okefenokeeadventures.com.*

Okefenokee Wildlife Refuge

CAMPING—SPORTS-OUTDOORS | Wilderness camping, by canoe or kayak, in the Okefenokee's interior is allowed by permit only (for which there's a $15 fee per person, per night). Availability is limited and can fill up fast, especially in the cooler seasons. During March and April, the most popular months, trips are limited to two nights. Reservations can be made up to two months in advance. ✉ *2700 Suwannee Canal Rd., Folkston* ☎ *912/496–7836* 🌐 *www.fws.gov/okefenokee* 🎫 *Daily passes $5, good for 7 days.*

Okefenokee Swamp Park

8 miles south of Waycross via U.S. 1.

This park sits at the northern entrance to the Okefenokee National Wildlife Refuge and offers unique opportunities for visitors to interact with the abundant wildlife of the swamp via observation areas, water trails, and boat tours.

Sights

Okefenokee Swamp Park

NATIONAL/STATE PARK | FAMILY | This privately owned and operated park serves as the northern entrance to the Okefenokee National Wildlife Refuge, offering live animal exhibits and orientation programs for the entire family. The park has observation areas, wilderness walkways, an outdoor museum of pioneer life, and boat tours into the swamp that reveal its unique ecology. The 90-foot-tall observation tower is an excellent place to glimpse cruising gators and birds. A 1½-mile train tour (included in the admission price) passes by a Seminole village and stops at Pioneer Island, a re-created pioneer homestead, for a 15-minute walking tour. ✉ *5700 Okefenokee Swamp Park Rd., Waycross* ☎ *912/283–0583* 🌐 *www.okeswamp.com* 🎟 *$20, $30 with 45-minute boat tour.*

Hotels

Holiday Inn Express Hotel and Suites

$ | HOTEL | Among the newer and more updated accommodations in Waycross, the Holiday Inn Express is centrally located in the commercial hub of the city, just down Knight Avenue from the shopping mall. **Pros:** near shopping and dining; clean rooms; pool and fitness center. **Cons:** complaints of noise; service can be inconsistent; breakfast is nothing special. $ *Rooms from: $129* ✉ *1761 Memorial Dr., Waycross* ☎ *912/548–0720* 🌐 *www.ihg.com* *78 rooms* 🍽 *Free breakfast.*

Camping in Stephen C. Foster

Stephen C. Foster State Park. The park has sites for all types of camping as well as basically equipped, two-bedroom cabins that can sleep up to eight. Be aware that the gates of the park are closed between sunset and sunrise—there's no traffic in or out for campers, so you need to stock up on supplies before the sun goes down. You can book sites and cabins up to 13 months in advance. ✉ *17515 GA 177, Fargo* ☎ *800/864–7275* 🌐 *www.gastateparks.org/StephenCFoster.*

Stephen C. Foster State Park

Sights

Stephen C. Foster State Park

NATIONAL/STATE PARK | Named for the songwriter who penned "Swanee River," this 120-acre island park is the southwestern entrance to the Okefenokee National Wildlife Refuge and offers trips to the headwaters of the Suwannee River, Billy's Island—site of an ancient Indian village—and a turn-of-the-20th-century town built to support logging efforts in the swamp. The park is home to hundreds of species of birds and a large cypress-and-black-gum forest, a majestic backdrop for one of the thickest growths of vegetation in the southeastern United States. ✉ *17515 GA 177, Fargo* ☎ *912/637–5274* 🌐 *www.gastateparks.org/StephenCFoster* 🎟 *$5 per vehicle.*

Chapter 13

SOUTHWEST GEORGIA

Updated by
Rachel Roberts Quartarone

Sights ★★★★★ | Restaurants ★★★☆☆ | Hotels ★★☆☆☆ | Shopping ☆☆☆☆☆ | Nightlife ☆☆☆☆☆

WELCOME TO SOUTHWEST GEORGIA

TOP REASONS TO GO

★ **Callaway Resort & Gardens:** 2,500 acres of gardens and parkland make this the raison d'être for visiting Pine Mountain. In spring the rhododendrons and wild azaleas take your breath away.

★ **Thomasville:** It's easy to feel transported to Victorian times in and around the mansions and gracious plantation homes of Thomasville. Several are open to the public and feel like living museums. There's also a thriving foodie scene.

★ **FDR's Little White House:** The cottage where President Franklin Delano Roosevelt stayed while taking in the healing waters of Warm Springs looks much as it did in his day. You can even see the pools where he was treated for polio.

★ **Jimmy Carter's hometown:** President Jimmy Carter and First Lady Rosalynn Carter still live in Plains, Georgia, and still worship at the Maranatha Baptist Church. There are a number of museums and historic sites in Plains dedicated to Carter's legacy.

Scattered along a vast coastal plain that covers much of the southern part of the state, the small towns of southwest Georgia are best explored by car or by the SAM Shortline. The touring train chugs through the countryside between Cordele and Archery.

1 **Warm Springs.** Explore the Little White House and healing pools where FDR found respite.

2 **Pine Mountain.** Enjoy the natural beauty at Callaway Gardens—the gem of Pine Mountain—and at F. D. Roosevelt State Park. To take some local treasures home with you, head to the eclectic antiques shops.

3 **Columbus.** Experience military pride in this town along the Chattahoochee River that is home to Fort Benning as well as plenty of outstanding museums and cultural institutions. For some adventure, raft through the heart of the city on the largest urban white-water course in the world.

4 **Plains.** Learn about Jimmy Carter's heritage at this tiny farming community that was, and still is, home to America's 39th president. The small town fills to the brim on the Sundays when President Carter teaches Sunday school at Maranatha Baptist Church.

5 **Thomasville.** Steep yourself in Southern charm at this once-prominent Victorian Age health resort. Elaborate Victorian mansions reflect Thomasville's tony past, while its revitalized downtown filled with shops and eateries exemplifies its vibrant present.

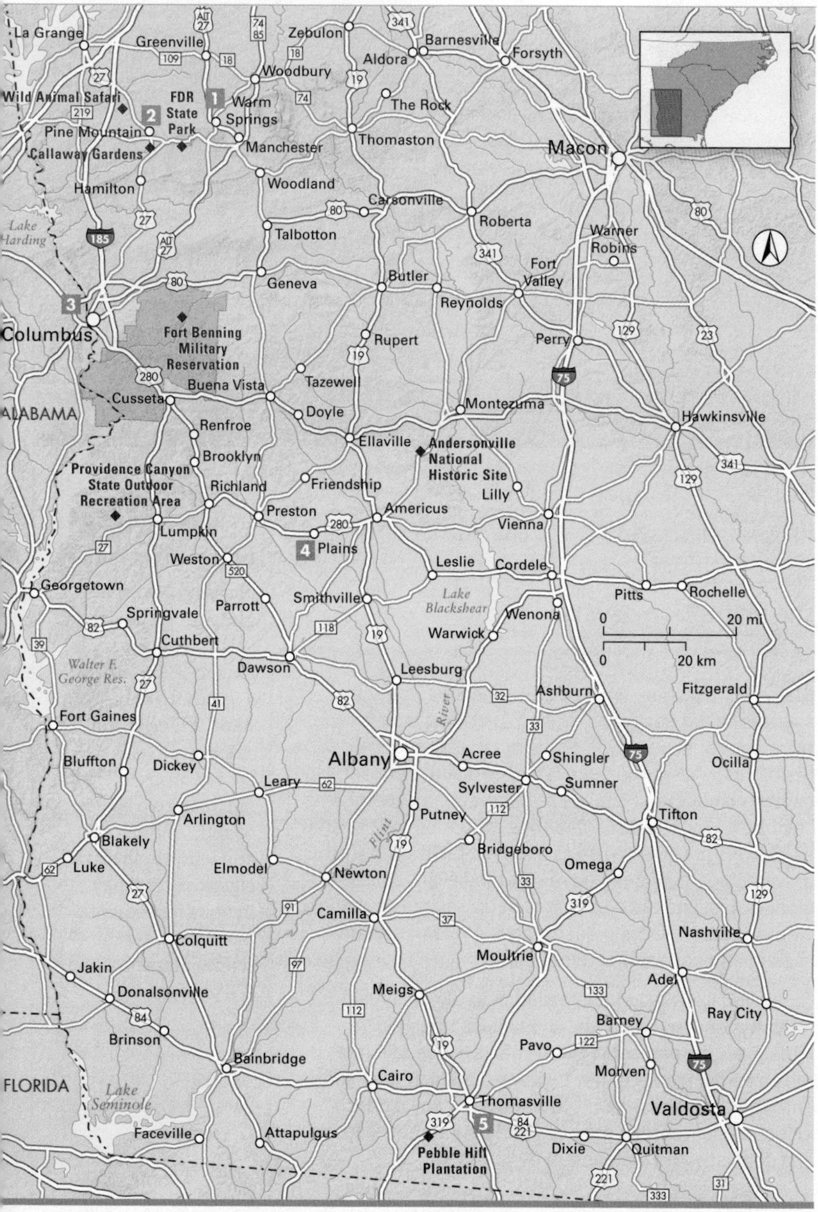

La Grange
Greenville
Zebulon
Barnesville
Aldora
Forsyth
Woodbury
Wild Animal Safari
1 Warm Springs
2 FDR State Park
The Rock
Pine Mountain
Callaway Gardens
Manchester
Thomaston
Macon
Woodland
Hamilton
Carsonville
Roberta
Lake Harding
Talbotton
Warner Robins
Fort Valley
Butler
Geneva
Reynolds
3 Columbus
Fort Benning Military Reservation
Rupert
Perry
Tazewell
Buena Vista
Cusseta
ALABAMA
Doyle
Montezuma
Hawkinsville
Renfroe
Ellaville
Andersonville National Historic Site
Brooklyn
Providence Canyon State Outdoor Recreation Area
Richland
Friendship
Lilly
Preston
Americus
Vienna
Lumpkin
4 Plains
Weston
Leslie
Cordele
Georgetown
Lake Blackshear
Pitts
Rochelle
Springvale
Parrott
Smithville
Wenona
0 20 mi
0 20 km
Warwick
Cuthbert
Walter F. George Res.
Dawson
Leesburg
Ashburn
Fitzgerald
Fort Gaines
River
Bluffton
Dickey
Albany
Acree
Shingler
Ocilla
Leary
Sylvester
Sumner
Arlington
Putney
Tifton
Blakely
Flint
Bridgeboro
Luke
Elmodel
Newton
Omega
Camilla
Nashville
Colquitt
Moultrie
Jakin
Adel
Donalsonville
Meigs
Ray City
Barney
Brinson
Pavo
Bainbridge
Morven
FLORIDA
Lake Seminole
Cairo
Thomasville
Valdosta
5
Faceville
Attapulgus
Pebble Hill Plantation
Dixie
Quitman

SOUTHERN SNACKS

Collard greens with bacon

Collards, grits, mac and cheese—the list of dishes originating from the South is long with a storied history that dates back to the plantation days and the Civil War.

Many of the dishes, which have influences from cuisines as varied as African, Native American, and French, were born of necessity in times of poverty and slavery. Stale bread was turned into bread pudding. Leftover fish became croquettes. Liquid left behind by cooked greens became gravy. The discarded tops of turnips, beets, and dandelions became the stars of a vegetable plate. The unwanted parts of a pig were used to flavor cooked vegetables. Biscuits were used to sop up sauces so nothing went to waste. And a great emphasis was placed on sharing among family and friends.

Today, you likely won't find boiled peanuts on a mainstream menu in the South. And chitlins, the viscera intestines of a pig, aren't often seen outside of Grandma's country kitchen—but things are starting to change. Thanks to the "local food" movement, many old-fashioned regional snacks are now sold at gourmet markets and sophisticated restaurants.

SAY CHEESE

Pimento cheese, the orange mix of cheddar cheese, mayonnaise, pimiento peppers, and salt and pepper, has long been considered a Southern comfort food. It is traditionally served as a spread on crackers or between two pieces of soft, white bread, and variations on the classic recipe may include ingredients like Worcestershire sauce, jalapeños, and dill pickles.

BOILED PEANUTS

Take a country drive and you'll most likely see roadside signs advertising this decidedly Southern snack, which—according to legend—has been on the scene since Union general William T. Sherman marched through Georgia. Raw peanuts are boiled in salted water for four to seven hours, until the shells get soft and the nuts get mushy. They're usually served in a paper bag, which can get soggy, so eat 'em while they're hot.

COLLARD GREENS

Similar to kale, collards have thick, large leaves and a slightly bitter taste. Their origins are traced back to the poor and enslaved, who would cook them with scraps from the kitchen: ham hocks, pork neck bones, fatback, and pigs' feet. Seasonings typically include onions, salt, pepper, and vinegar. Today, it's a Southern tradition to serve collards on New Year's Day, along with black-eyed peas, for wealth in the new year.

HUSH PUPPIES

Legend has it that this snack got its name from an African cook in Atlanta. She was frying catfish and croquettes when her puppy began to howl. To quiet the dog she gave him a plate of the croquettes, saying, "Hush, puppy."

A bowl of grits isn't complete without a pat of butter.

Boiled peanuts are at their best piping hot.

Really, though, a dog's dish is far too lowly a place for these delicious fried cornmeal dumplings. Today you'll find them on simple country menus and in the breadbaskets of fine restaurants throughout the South.

MAC AND CHEESE

In the South, this dish is a vegetable. Though in these creamy, top-browned bowls of pasta and cheese there's not a veggie in sight, many meat-and-three restaurants list mac and cheese as one of the three vegetables you can get on the side. And who are we to argue? Whether we're talking about traditional mac and cheese or a fancier version with homemade shells, truffle oil, and Gouda, it's a rich and delicious snack.

SWEETS

Southerners have a sweet tooth, bless their hearts. And it's satisfied by a number of indigenous desserts. There's chess pie, a simple pie with just eggs, sugar, butter, and flour that supposedly got its name when a Southern cook said she was making "jes' pie." Then there's pecan pie, created by French settlers in New Orleans and a worthy alternative to pumpkin pie at some Southern Thanksgiving tables. And, of course, there is peach cobbler, a favorite in the South, where the climate allows for early harvests and few frosts.

The rolling agricultural landscapes of a slower, older South, where things remain much the same as they were for generations, can be found within a couple hours' drive of Atlanta's high-rise bustle. Here small towns evoke a time when the world was a simpler place, where people lived close to the land and life was measured on a personal scale. In southwest Georgia, peanuts, corn, tobacco, and cotton are the lifeblood of the local economies, and you're as likely to see a tractor on a country road as a car.

People in southwest Georgia's countryside live far from the hassles of Atlanta's modernity—the daily grind of traffic jams and suburban sprawl. Small towns beckon with their quaint town squares, preserved old homes, and charming bed-and-breakfasts. In southwest Georgia the inclination simply to relax is contagious—it can saturate you slowly but completely, like syrup on a stack of pancakes. Yet, the entire region is not to be dismissed as quiet farmland. Columbus is one of Georgia's largest cities and home to several Fortune 500 company headquarters, as well as acclaimed military, academic, and cultural institutions. Outside historic downtown Thomasville, you'll find business headquarters and bustling factories.

Southwest Georgia residents are proud of their communities and those they call their own, including such greats as President Jimmy Carter, writers Erskine Caldwell and Carson McCullers, singers Ma Rainey and Otis Redding, and baseball legend Jackie Robinson. For a time even Franklin Delano Roosevelt was drawn here; he returned again and again for the healing mineral waters of Warm Springs.

MAJOR REGIONS

Western Foothills and Farmland. Take a walk through the past with a visit to Franklin Roosevelt's Little White House retreat or tiptoe through the tulips at the 14,000-acre Callaway Gardens. This area also is home to Georgia's largest state park and massive Fort Benning.

The Southwest Corner. Antiques shopping, peach picking, golf courses, and hunting plantations are abundant in this part of the state, particularly in Thomasville, which is celebrated most for its Victorian homes, plantations, and churches.

Planning

When to Go

Because many of the towns in the region are off the beaten path, crowds are rarely a problem, though spring (which comes early) and fall (which comes late) are the most popular seasons. If you're not fond of the heat, March to May and September to December are the best times to visit. During this time, book well in advance for the more popular hotels and B&Bs in Pine Mountain, Warm Springs, and Thomasville.

Planning Your Time

A traveler could easily get lost on the back roads of southwest Georgia, so perhaps the best way to take in the sites of this region is to park your car and board the SAM Shortline Southwest Georgia Excursion Train in Cordele. The ride will take you to Georgia Veterans State Park, the Rural Telephone Museum, Habitat for Humanity's Global Village, the Rylander Theatre, the Windsor Hotel, and Plains. This way you'll get a sense of what spots deserve more time and which are suited for a drive-by.

Many of southwest Georgia's attractions are ideal day trips from Atlanta. Warm Springs, Callaway Gardens, and Pine Mountain are a 90-minute drive. Thomasville is a little more than four hours from Atlanta, so plan on an overnight stay.

Getting Here and Around

AIR TRAVEL

Delta Airlines has daily flights into Columbus Metro Airport (CSG) from Atlanta.

AIR CONTACTS Columbus Metro Airport. *(CSG) ✉ 3250 W. Britt David Rd., Columbus ☎ 706/324–2449 🌐 www.flycolumbusga.com.*

CAR TRAVEL

A car is the best way to tour this part of Georgia. Interstate 75 runs north–south through the eastern edge of the region and connects to several U.S. and state highways that traverse the area. Interstate 85 runs southwest through LaGrange and Columbus. Do explore back roads—they offer the landscapes and ambience of the real South. Just be sure to travel with a good road map or GPS—cell phone coverage can be spotty in the countryside.

TRAIN TRAVEL

A great means of seeing the countryside, the Historic SAM Shortline Railroad originates in Cordele and runs west through Georgia Veterans State Park, Leslie, Americus, Plains, and Archery. It's important to check the schedule, but as a general rule, trains run on Saturday and some Fridays. On select weekends, you can get on or off at any of the stations, stop over for the night, and take the train again the next morning.

TRAIN CONTACTS Historic SAM Shortline Railroad. *✉ 105 E. 9th Ave., Cordele ☎ 229/276–0755 🌐 www.samshortline.com.*

Restaurants

This region of Georgia does lovely things by slow-cooking pork over green oak. Pit-barbecue joints in the area are homey, hands-on, and relatively inexpensive. There's also a growing food scene in the urban areas of the region as talented chefs have set up shop in the quaint downtown storefronts. *Restaurant reviews have been shortened. For full information, visit Fodors.com*

Hotels

Lodging in the area runs the gamut from elegant, luxurious properties to low-profile but unique B&Bs and reliable and inexpensive chain hotels. RV parks and campgrounds are also available. Many of the state parks in this region have cabin or cottage facilities, which are a great option as well. *Hotel reviews have been shortened. For full information, visit Fodors.com*

What It Costs

$	$$	$$$	$$$$
RESTAURANTS			
under $15	$15–$19	$20–$24	over $24
HOTELS			
under $150	$150–$200	$201–$250	over $250

Warm Springs

97 miles southwest of Atlanta.

Renowned for centuries for the supposed healing properties of its thermal waters, Warm Springs is where the Creek Indians brought their wounded warriors when all other treatments had failed. In the early 1920s news spread that a young Columbus native and polio victim, Louis Joseph, had made a dramatic recovery after extensive therapy in the springs. Word reached Franklin Delano Roosevelt (1882–1945), who had contracted polio, and a 20-year relationship began between him and this remote mountain village, where he built a cottage for his visits that came to be known as the Little White House. Roosevelt's experiences here led to the effort to eradicate polio around the world through the founding of the March of Dimes, and his encounters with his poor rural neighbors fueled ideas for his Depression-era New Deal recovery programs. After Roosevelt's death, the town fell on hard times, but an influx of crafts and antiques shops in the 1980s has revitalized Warm Springs.

GETTING HERE AND AROUND

The best way to visit Warm Springs is to travel from Atlanta on Interstate 85 South to Exit 41. Take a left turn onto U.S. Route 27A/41, then continue for 35 miles to Warm Springs. Columbus is another good point to embark from; Warm Springs is about 40 miles south on Georgia State Route 85 North. Much of Warm Springs is walkable, but a car is necessary if you want to hit all the high points.

VISITOR INFORMATION

CONTACTS Warm Springs Welcome Center. ✉ *1 Broad St.* ☎ *706/655–2558* 🌐 *www.meriwethertourism.com.*

Sights

★ **Little White House Historic Site/FDR Memorial Museum**

MUSEUM | Located on the southern end of town, this fascinating historic site contains the modest three-bedroom cottage in which Roosevelt stayed during his visits. The cottage, built in 1932, remains much as it did the day America's 32nd president died here (while having his portrait painted) and includes the wheelchair Roosevelt designed from a kitchen chair. The unfinished portrait is on display, along with the 48-star American flag that flew over the grounds when Roosevelt died. The FDR Memorial Museum includes an interesting short film narrated by Walter Cronkite (last screening at 4 pm), exhibits detailing Roosevelt's life and New Deal programs, and some of Roosevelt's personal effects, such as his 1938 Ford, complete with the full hand controls he designed. Admission here allows you to also visit the nearby pools where Roosevelt took his therapy. ✉ *401 Little White House Rd.* ☎ *706/655–5870* 🌐 *www.gastateparks.org/LittleWhiteHouse* 🎫 *$12.*

Restaurants

Bulloch House Restaurant

$ | **SOUTHERN** | **FAMILY** | This longtime local favorite is the place to go for down-home Southern cooking in the area. The restaurant serves meals buffet style, with such Southern classics as buttermilk biscuits, golden fried chicken, and baked ham. **Known for:** fried chicken and other Southern staples; generous buffet dining; sides like fried green tomatoes and turnip greens. *Average main: $13* *70 Broad St.* *706/655–9068* *www.bullochhouse.com.*

Coffee and Quick Bites

Lightnin' Bugs Bakery & Café

$ | **AMERICAN** | **FAMILY** | Part shop and part café, this locally owned spot is a great place to grab a coffee, sandwich, or a big ol' slice of homemade red velvet cake or pecan pie. Check out the daily soup and sandwich specials for a variety of options. **Known for:** homemade Southern desserts; soups and sandwiches; gourmet coffee and teas. *Average main: $8* *50 Broad St.* *706/655–2015* *www.lightninbugscafe.com* *Closed Mon.–Thurs.*

Hotels

Hotel Warm Springs Bed and Breakfast Inn

$ | **B&B/INN** | In downtown Warm Springs, this historic hotel has plenty of character—the guest rooms have oak furniture and 12-foot ceilings with crown molding. **Pros:** convenient to Warm Springs' sights; storied history; amazing Southern breakfast. **Cons:** no elevator; some say rooms and public spaces could use some refreshing; child-friendly atmosphere not for everyone. *Rooms from: $110* *47 Broad St.* *706/655–2114, 800/366–7616* *www.hotelwarmspringsbb.org* *14 rooms* *Free breakfast.*

Pine Mountain

14 miles west of Warm Springs via GA 18 and GA 194.

Pine Mountain Ridge is the last foothill of the Appalachian chain, and the town of Pine Mountain rests at the same elevation as Atlanta, making it generally cooler than the surrounding communities. The flora and fauna here reflect the town's Appalachian connections. Most visitors are lured by the surrounding area's large-scale attractions—such as Callaway Resort & Gardens—and are then pleasantly surprised that the small-town burg has a folksy, inviting downtown square. Antiques figure prominently in the area economy, and shops abound in the town center.

GETTING HERE AND AROUND

Pine Mountain can be reached by car from Atlanta via Interstate 85 South and sits 14 miles west of Warm Springs, via Georgia State Routes 18 and 194. A 90-minute drive from Atlanta, it's a popular destination for day-trippers.

VISITOR INFORMATION

CONTACTS Pine Mountain Welcome Center. *101 E. Broad St.* *706/663–4000, 800/441–3502* *www.pinemountain.org.*

Sights

★ **Callaway Resort & Gardens**

GARDEN | **FAMILY** | South of Pine Mountain Village lies the area's main draw: a 2,500-acre golf and tennis resort with a combination of elaborate, cultivated gardens and natural woodlands. This family-friendly destination was developed in the 1940s by textile magnate Cason J. Callaway and his wife, Virginia, as a way to breathe new life into the area's dormant cotton fields. With more than 1,000 varieties, the Day Butterfly Center is one of the largest free-flight conservatories in North America. **Mountain Creek Lake** is well stocked with largemouth bass and bream. **Ida Cason Callaway Memorial Chapel**—a favorite wedding venue—is a lovely stone chapel nestled in the woods alongside a lake and babbling stream. The **Callaway Discovery Center** is a popular choice for families; especially enjoyable is the daily Birds of Prey show. During the holidays, Callaway lights up with the exciting "Fantasy in Lights." *17800 U.S. 27 844/512–3826, www.callaway-gardens.com $25, free for overnight guests.*

F. D. Roosevelt State Park

NATIONAL/STATE PARK | **FAMILY** | At 9,049 acres, F. D. Roosevelt is the largest state park in Georgia. Named for the president who considered this area his second home, it's rich in both history and natural beauty. Several park amenities were built by FDR's Civilian Conservation Corps during the Great Depression, including multiple cottages and the Liberty Bell Swimming Pool fed by local cool springs. The park contains more than 40 miles of trails, including the popular 23-mile Pine Mountain Trail. Dowdell's Knob, an overlook along the trail, was one of the president's favorite spots to picnic; there's even a statue there to commemorate him. Within the park are also two lakes and 115 modern campsites, as well as backcountry and pioneer campgrounds. *2970 GA 190 706/663–4858, 800/864–7275 www.georgiastateparks.org/FDRoosevelt Parking $5.*

Carriage and Horses

$$$$ | **ECLECTIC** | You'll need a reservation at this longtime eatery housed in a quaint Victorian farmhouse, where the emphasis is on high-quality international fare and outstanding service. The menu features classics like escargots, lamb shank, grilled trout (a house specialty), and filet mignon served with garlicky mashed potatoes. **Known for:** traditional fine dining; pastoral setting overlooking horse pastures; gregarious chef and owner. *Average main: $25 607 Butts Mill Rd. 706/663–4777 www.cometodagher.com.*

Callaway Resort & Gardens

$$ | **RESORT** | Accommodations at this sprawling resort range from fairly basic motel-style guest rooms at the **Mountain Creek Inn** to fully furnished two- to four-bedroom luxury cottages and villas, all of them with lovely panoramic vistas and verdant woodland garden settings. **Pros:** access to famous gardens; wide variety of accommodation types; wonderful full-service spa. **Cons:** cottages require two-night minimum; rooms can vary a lot in terms of size and quality; sprawling resort can be difficult to navigate even with a map. *Rooms from: $189 17800 U.S. 27 844/512–3826, 800/225–5292 www.callawaygardens.com 448 rooms No meals.*

Chipley Murrah Bed and Breakfast

$ | **B&B/INN** | One mile from Callaway Gardens and near downtown Pine Mountain, this lavish inn occupies a high-style Queen Anne Victorian dating to 1895. **Pros:** welcoming owner; some cottages are pet-friendly; outdoor pool. **Cons:** breakfast is not included with the cottages; decor is a bit dated; kids younger than 12 allowed only in the cottages. *Rooms from: $130 207 W. Harris St. 706/663–9801 www.chipleymurrah.com 6 rooms Free breakfast.*

Roosevelt Stables

HORSEBACK RIDING | Located within F. D. Roosevelt State Park but operating separately, Roosevelt Stables offers everything from one-hour rides to overnight trips in the expansive state park. There's even a wine and cheese ride offered in the height of the fall leaf season. With over 28 miles of trails, there

Azaleas bloom along the lake at Callaway Resort & Gardens.

are many scenic options. ✉ *1063 Group Camp Rd.* ☎ *706/628–7463* 🌐 *www.rooseveltstablesfdr.com.*

Columbus

35 miles south of Pine Mountain.

During the Civil War, Columbus supplied uniforms, weapons, and other goods to the Confederate army, making the city a prime target for Union troops. But it wasn't until April 16, 1865—a week after the war had ended at Appomattox—that the 13,000 cavalrymen known as "Wilson's Raiders" attacked Columbus and burned all the war industries to the ground. The textile mills soon recovered, however, and grew to a prominence that dwarfed their prewar significance. Textiles still play a major role in the Columbus economy.

Today, Columbus is perhaps best known as the home of Fort Benning, the largest infantry-training center in the world; it's also the site of Columbus College's Schwob School of Music, one of the finest music schools in the South. A project to rejuvenate the downtown area has included the renovation of old manufacturing and ironworks buildings and the creation of the 15-mile **Riverwalk** to highlight the city's river origins; this linear park along the Chattahoochee is ideal for jogging, strolling, biking, and rollerblading.

VISITOR INFORMATION

CONTACTS Columbus Convention and Visitors Bureau. ✉ *900 Front Ave.* ☎ *800/999–1613* 🌐 *www.visitcolumbusga.com.*

Sights

Coca-Cola Space Science Center

OBSERVATORY | FAMILY | Columbus State University's Coca-Cola Space Science Center, part of the Riverwalk, houses a multimedia planetarium with several showtimes offered daily, an observatory, a replica of an Apollo space capsule, a space shuttle, and other NASA-related exhibits, including cool flight simulators.

Visit the 39th president's boyhood farm at the Jimmy Carter National Historic Site.

✉ *701 Front Ave.* ☎ *706/649–1477* 🌐 *www.ccssc.org* 🎫 *$8* 🕓 *Closed Sun.*

Columbus Museum

MUSEUM | The state's largest art and history museum focuses heavily on American art ranging from colonial portraiture to provocative contemporary works. Other permanent exhibits showcase the history and industry of the Chattahoochee Valley. There's always something new and different to see in the temporary exhibit galleries. ✉ *1251 Wynnton Rd.* ☎ *706/748–2562* 🌐 *www.columbusmuseum.com* 🎫 *Free* 🕓 *Closed Mon.*

Historic Westville

MUSEUM VILLAGE | Recently relocated to Columbus near the National Infantry Museum, this living-history museum provides a glimpse of what Georgia was like in the early 19th century. The museum features a collection of 16 original buildings moved from around the region—including a courthouse, two churches, a blacksmith shop, and historic family dwellings—configured to represent a typical small Southern town. Live costumed interpreters provide context, and demonstrations of quilting, cooking, blacksmithing, and other period arts and crafts are offered daily. ✉ *3557 S. Lumpkin Rd.* ☎ *706/940–0057* 🌐 *www.westville.org* 🎫 *$10.*

National Civil War Naval Museum

MILITARY SITE | Those interested in the nation's Civil War past should make it a point to visit this innovative military museum that focuses on the Confederate navy and its influence on the U.S. Navy's subsequent development. Columbus's riverfront location made it a major player in river transport prior to and throughout the Civil War. Interactive exhibits tell the story of shipbuilding and major Civil War ship battles. You can even walk the decks of partially reconstructed Civil War ships and get a glimpse of what combat was like in a full-scale replica of the CSS *Albermarle*. The museum also boasts the largest collection of Civil War naval-related flags on display in the country. ✉ *1002 Victory Dr.* ☎ *706/327–9798* 🌐 *www.portcolumbus.org* 🎫 *$8.*

★ National Infantry Museum and Soldier Center

MILITARY SITE | FAMILY | Located outside the gates of Fort Benning, this museum examines the role of the U.S. infantry for every war in the nation's history through interactive, technology-rich displays. A must for military buffs, the facility holds more than 70,000 artifacts, including weaponry, uniforms, and equipment from the Revolutionary War to the present day, including a re-created World War II Company Street, which includes General Patton's sleeping quarters. On the museum grounds is the moving Global War on Terrorism Memorial, which is rededicated every year to honor service members who have lost their lives. The center also features a Giant Screen theater that shows both documentaries and Hollywood blockbusters. ✉ *1775 Legacy Way* ☎ *706/685–5800* 🌐 *www.nationalinfantrymuseum.com* 🎫 *$5 suggested donation* ⏲ *Closed Mon.*

Springer Opera House

OPERA | Since its opening in 1871, this National Historic Landmark has been known as one of the finest opera houses in the South. In its heyday, its stage boasted legends such as Lillie Langtry and Will Rogers. Today the theater hosts musicals, dramas, and regional talent. It's also the official state theater of Georgia. Call ahead to arrange a tour. ✉ *103 10th St.* ☎ *706/327–3688* 🌐 *www.springeroperahouse.org* 🎫 *Tours $5.*

Restaurants

Buckhead

$$$$ | STEAKHOUSE | At this upscale Southern-style steak house, beef plays a prominent role on the menu with USDA Prime Angus and natural, hormone-free prime rib, New York strip, and rib eye as headliners. Seafood is also done well here, with entrées like cedar-planked Norwegian salmon and lobster tail. **Known for:** wide variety of quality steaks; extensive wine list; family-size sides for sharing. [$] *Average main: $35* ✉ *5010 Armour Rd.* ☎ *706/571–9995* 🌐 *www.buckheadbarandgrill.com* ⏲ *No lunch.*

Country's Barbecue

$ | BARBECUE | In a land where barbecue reigns supreme, Country's cooks with taste and style. You can eat inside the restaurant, a converted bus terminal decorated with '50s flair, or sit at a table in the 1946 bus turned diner. **Known for:** outstanding barbecue cooked over hickory and oak; unique bus station–turned-diner setting; '50s decor. [$] *Average main: $10* ✉ *1329 Broadway* ☎ *706/596–8910* 🌐 *www.countrysbarbecue.com.*

Coffee and Quick Bites

Iron Bank Coffee Co.

$ | AMERICAN | Housed in a historic bank building, this fun little café offers gourmet coffee drinks, pastries, sandwiches, desserts, and other quick bites for breakfast, lunch, and dinner—or anytime in between. Grab a seat in one of the original bank vaults inside or a street-side table outside to enjoy your treat. **Known for:** gourmet coffee drinks; pastries; paninis and salads. [$] *Average main: $7* ✉ *6 W. 11th St.* ☎ *706/992–6609* 🌐 *www.ironbankcoffee.com.*

Hotels

Marriott Columbus

$$ | HOTEL | On the site of a vast 1860s complex of warehouses, factories, mills, and a Confederate arsenal, this hotel is a key component of the Columbus Convention and Trade Center just across the street. **Pros:** excellent riverfront location; modern amenities; historic space. **Cons:** large facility may be a turnoff to some; often booked for events; no free breakfast. [$] *Rooms from: $175* ✉ *800 Front Ave.* ☎ *706/324–1800* 🌐 *www.marriott.com* 🛏 *177 rooms* 🍽 *No meals.*

Rothschild-Pound House Inn

$$ | **B&B/INN** | Listed on the National Register of Historic Places, this B&B includes a main house and separate cottages, and offers a glimpse of old Columbus's elegance—with four-poster mahogany beds, hardwood floors, and period antiques. **Pros:** beautiful architecture; lots of privacy; lovely full breakfast. **Cons:** no pool or spa; upstairs rooms may be difficult to access for some; old-fashioned decor not for everyone. *Rooms from: $160* *201 7th St.* *706/322–4075* *www.thepoundhouseinn.com* *10 rooms* *Free breakfast.*

Activities

Whitewater Express

WHITE-WATER RAFTING | Take a thrilling ride down the longest urban white-water rafting course in the world. The Chattahoochee Whitewater Park flows right through the heart of downtown Columbus. Thanks to the release of two nearby dams, this 2½-mile, man-made course offers Class I–V rapids depending on the time of day you hit the water and the trip you choose. Morning trips are relatively calm while the late-afternoon high-water trips offer pounding Class IV-plus rapids. Whitewater Express offers guided raft trips daily. The outfitter also offers kayaking, fly-fishing, stand-up paddleboarding, ziplining, and bike rentals. *1000 Bay Ave.* *706/321–4720, 800/676–7238* *www.whitewaterexpress.com/chattahoochee.*

Plains

85 miles southeast of Pine Mountain via U.S. 27.

This rural farming town—originally named the Plains of Dura after the biblical story of Shadrach, Meshach, and Abednego—is the birthplace and current home of former president Jimmy Carter and his wife, Rosalynn. Although it's the hub of a thriving farming community, the one-street downtown paralleling the railroad tracks resembles a 1930s movie set.

GETTING HERE AND AROUND

From Interstate 85 or Interstate 75, look for the exit to U.S. Route 280, then exit for Plains.

FESTIVALS

Plains Peanut Festival

FESTIVALS | Each September the town comes alive with the Plains Peanut Festival, which includes a parade, live entertainment, arts and crafts, food vendors, and races. The Carters are usually active participants in the various events and also conduct book signings. *Plains* *www.friendsofjimmycarter.org.*

VISITOR INFORMATION

CONTACTS Plains Welcome Center. *1763 U.S. 280* *229/824–7477.*

Sights

Andersonville National Historic Site

HISTORIC SITE | About 20 miles northeast of Plains, Andersonville National Historic Site is a solemn reminder of the Civil War's tragic toll. Andersonville, also known as Camp Sumter, was the war's deadliest prisoner-of-war camp. Some 13,000 Union prisoners died here, mostly from disease, neglect, and malnutrition. Photographs, artifacts, and high-tech exhibits detail not just the plight of Civil War prisoners but also prison life and conditions affecting all of America's 800,000 POWs since the Revolutionary War. *496 Cemetery Rd., Andersonville* *229/924–0343* *www.nps.gov/ande/index.htm* *Free.*

★ **Jimmy Carter National Historic Site**

HISTORIC SITE | Three different historic sites highlight the life and work of the 39th president of the United States, Jimmy Carter. You can visit the late-1880s **railroad depot** that once housed his 1976 presidential campaign headquarters. Vintage phones play recordings of Carter discussing his

Andersonville National Cemetery is the final resting place of soldiers who died at Andersonville Prison, the Civil War's deadliest prisoner-of-war camp.

grassroots run for the White House. A couple of miles outside town on the Old Plains Highway is the 360-acre **Jimmy Carter Boyhood Farm,** where the Carter family grew cotton, peanuts, and corn; it has been restored to its original appearance before electricity was introduced. Period furniture fills the house, and the battery-powered radio plays Carter's reminiscences of growing up on a Depression-era farm. **Plains High School,** where the Carters attended school, is now a museum and the headquarters of the historic site. Start your visit here with a short orientation film, and pick up a self-guided tour book that explains the sites. ✉ *Plains High School Visitor Center and Museum, 300 N. Bond St.* ☎ *229/824–4104* 🌐 *www.nps.gov/jica* 🎫 *Free.*

Maranatha Baptist Church

RELIGIOUS SITE | The Carters still live in a ranch-style brick house on the edge of town—the only home they have ever owned—and they still worship at the Maranatha Baptist Church. President Carter used to regularly teach Sunday school here at 10 am but it's more of a rarity now. Call ahead or check the website for the schedule. If you are able to catch a date, doors open at 8 and the class fills up fast—in fact, visitors arrive as early as 5:30 to ensure a seat and a security check is required. Selfies with the Carters are possible afterwards: the former president and first lady always make themselves available to take photos with visitors after the 11 am service. ✉ *148 GA 45 N* ☎ *229/824–7896* 🌐 *www.mbcplains.org.*

Providence Canyon State Outdoor Recreation Area

NATURE SITE | Known as "Georgia's Little Grand Canyon," Providence Canyon State Outdoor Recreation Area is actually made up of 16 canyons whose earthen walls display at least 43 different colors of sand. Providence Canyon is a favorite of geologists, photographers, and hikers, who enjoy peering over the canyon's rim and traversing its 10 miles of trails. It's located about 33 miles west of Plains. ✉ *8930 Canyon Rd., Lumpkin* ☎ *229/838–6870* 🌐 *www.gastateparks.org/ProvidenceCanyon* 🎫 *Parking $5.*

Coffee and Quick Bites

Buffalo Cafe at the Old Bank

$ | **AMERICAN** | Housed in an old bank in downtown Plains, this café offers soup, salads, burgers, and sandwiches in a cozy hometown setting. Be sure to try the creamy peanut ice cream. **Known for:** quick and casual meals; chicken salad; down-to-earth and friendly staff. *Average main: $8* *118 E. Main St.* *229/824–4520* *Closed Sun.*

Hotels

Best Western Plus Windsor Hotel

$ | **HOTEL** | Located in nearby Americus, this ornate jewel of a hotel has garnered awards from the National Trust for Historic Preservation. **Pros:** guest rooms with high ceilings; beautiful architectural details; modern amenities. **Cons:** fills up quickly on weekends; no pool; no free breakfast. *Rooms from: $115* *125 W. Lamar St., Americus* *229/924–1555* *www.windsor-americus.com* *53 rooms* *No meals.*

Plains Historic Inn

$ | **B&B/INN** | Each spacious room of this inn, set in a century-old furniture store above an antiques mall, is decorated to reflect the aesthetics of a particular decade between the 1920s and the 1980s. **Pros:** close to tourist attractions; has an elevator; claw-foot tubs in some bathrooms. **Cons:** breakfast is self-serve; not many eateries nearby; can book up quickly, especially on weekends. *Rooms from: $125* *106 Main St.* *229/824–4517* *www.plainsinn.net* *7 rooms* *Free breakfast.*

Thomasville

236 miles south of Atlanta via I–75 and U.S. 319.

This appealing small town in the Tallahassee Red Hills started out as an agrarian community like its neighbors. Cotton and other cash crops lined its plains and rolling hills, while large plantation homes and simple farmhouses graced the countryside. Unlike its neighbors, Thomasville did not see any battles during the Civil War, so much of the town's antebellum architecture was preserved. After the war—thanks to a local doctor's claim that Thomasville's warm winter climate and balsam breezes had curative effects—Thomasville reinvented itself as a health resort, a popular Victorian concept. Wealthy Northerners fleeing the cold wintered here in large luxury hotels. The wealthiest among them built elegant estates in town and hunting plantations in the farmland along the "Plantation Trace."

Although Thomasville's resort era has long since ended, the distinct pine-scented air remains, as does the Victorian elegance of the town's heyday. Known as the City of Roses, it draws thousands of visitors each spring to its annual Rose Festival (the fourth weekend in April). And during the Victorian Christmas, locals turn out in period costumes to enjoy horse-drawn carriage rides, caroling, and street theater.

GETTING HERE AND AROUND

Thomasville, with its rich atmosphere of a bygone era, sits 55 miles south of Tifton and can be reached from Atlanta via Interstate 75 and U.S. Route 319.

King Cotton

Such was Georgia's preeminence in world cotton production at the turn of the 20th century that the international market price was set at the Cotton Exchange in Savannah. And the huge plantations of southwest Georgia were major players in the engine driving the state's economic prosperity. Of course, that prosperity was reliant on the back-breaking labor of an enslaved African American workforce. For more than 100 years, from the first time it was planted in Georgia in 1733 until the beginning of the Civil War, cotton was the most commercially successful crop in the state. But because the seeds had to be separated from the lint by hand, production was laborious and output was limited. In 1793 a young Yale graduate named Eli Whitney (1765–1825) came to Savannah's Mulberry Grove Plantation as a tutor to the children of Revolutionary War hero Nathanael Greene. After watching the difficulty workers were having separating the seeds from the cotton, he invented a simple machine of two cylinders with combs rotating in opposite directions. The "gin," as he called it (short for engine), could do the work of 50 people and revolutionized the cotton industry. So significant was its immediate impact on the U.S. economy that President George Washington personally signed the patent issued to Whitney.

In 1900 the boll weevil insect came to the United States via Mexico and quickly undermined cotton production. The weevil was a major cause of the onset of the economic depression that spread throughout the South. Cotton production was at an all-time low in Georgia by 1978; in 1987 the state began a boll weevil eradication program that has all but wiped out the threat. And the result is that today Georgia is once again one of the top cotton producers in the nation.

TOURS

Taste of Thomasville Food Tour

WALKING TOURS | To explore Thomasville's burgeoning "foodie scene," try a walking food tour that incorporates downtown Thomasville's history with stops and tastings at six celebrated eateries. Tours are offered on Friday and Saturday. There's also an "After Hours" tour focused on food and drink pairings and special holiday-themed tours. They regularly sell out, so it's best to purchase tickets in advance online. ✉ *Thomasville* ☎ *229/227–7585* 🌐 *www.tasteofthomasvillefoodtour.com.*

VISITOR INFORMATION

CONTACTS Thomasville Welcome Center. ✉ *144 E. Jackson St.* ☎ *229/228–7977, 866/577–3600* 🌐 *www.thomasvillega.com.*

Sights

Birdsong Nature Center

NATURE PRESERVE | FAMILY | With 565 acres of lush fields, forests, swamps, and butterfly gardens, this nature center is a wondrous haven for birds and scores of other native wildlife. Miles of walking trails meander through the property, and nature programs are offered year-round. Check the website for the latest hours and program offerings. ✉ *2106 Meridian Rd.* ☎ *229/377–4408* 🌐 *www.birdsongnaturecenter.org* 🎟 *$5.*

The Victorian-style Lapham-Patterson House, built in 1884, is now a National Historic Landmark.

Lapham–Patterson House

HOUSE | When it was built by Chicago shoe manufacturer Charles W. Lapham in 1884, this three-story Victorian house was state of the art, with gas lighting and indoor plumbing with hot and cold running water. But the most curious feature of this unusual house is that Lapham, who had witnessed the Great Chicago Fire of 1871, had 45 exit doors installed because of his fear of being trapped in a burning house. The house is now a National Historic Landmark because of its unique architectural features. The Thomasville History Center staff offers guided tours on weekends. ✉ *626 N. Dawson St.* ☎ *229/226–7664* 🌐 *www.thomasvillehistory.org* 🎫 *$10* 🕓 *Closed Sun.–Thurs.*

★ Pebble Hill Plantation

HOUSE | On the National Register of Historic Places, Pebble Hill is the only plantation in the area open to the public. The sprawling estate was last home to sporting enthusiast and philanthropist Elisabeth "Pansy" Ireland Poe, who specified that the plantation be open to the public upon her death (in 1978). The property dates to 1825, although most of the original house was destroyed in a fire in the 1930s. Highlights of the current two-story main house include a dramatic horseshoe-shape entryway, a wraparound terrace on the upper floor, and an elegant sunroom decorated with a wildlife motif. The second story now serves as an art gallery displaying the Poes' large sporting art collection. Surrounding the house are 34 acres of immaculately maintained grounds that include gardens, a walking path, a log-cabin school, a fire station, a carriage house, kennels, and a hospital for the plantation's more than 100 dogs (prized dogs were buried with full funerals, including a minister). The sprawling dairy-and-horse-stable complex resembles an English village. ✉ *1251 U.S. 319 S* ✣ *5 miles south of Thomasville* ☎ *229/226–2344* 🌐 *www.pebblehill.com* 🎫 *Grounds $5.50, house tour $16* 🕓 *Closed Mon.*

Thomasville History Center

HISTORIC SITE | Located in the historic 1923 Flowers-Roberts House, this museum and history center contains exhibits about the history of Thomas County along with seven historical buildings you can tour. The buildings, carefully preserved and moved to the museum grounds, include an 1870 "dogtrot" log cabin and an 1893 bowling alley believed to be the second-oldest bowling alley still standing in the United States. To see the interiors of the buildings and get the full picture of Thomasville's history, opt for the guided tour. *725 N. Dawson St.* *229/226–7664* *www.thomasvillehistory.org* *Self-guided tour $5, guided tour $8* *Closed Sun.*

Restaurants

Chop House on the Bricks

$$$$ | **STEAKHOUSE** | This upscale steak house is celebrated for its romantic ambience and masterfully prepared meat and seafood dishes. Menu favorites include coffee-rubbed filet mignon, cane syrup–glazed New York strip, and pan-seared gulf snapper with a crawfish cream sauce. **Known for:** high-quality, locally sourced ingredients; outstanding wine list; date-night hot spot. *Average main: $28* *123 N. Broad St.* *229/236–2467* *www.chophouseonthebricks.com* *Closed Sun. and Mon.*

George and Louie's

$ | **SOUTHERN** | The fresh gulf seafood served at this longtime family-owned restaurant is as good as you can find anywhere. Try the broiled shrimp, cooked in olive oil with a smattering of fresh garlic; fresh mullet dinner; or combination platter with homemade deviled crab, shrimp, oysters, scallops, and flounder for one, two, or three people. **Known for:** creatively delicious seafood platters; locally beloved burgers; outdoor dining. *Average main: $14* *217 Remington Ave.* *229/226–1218* *www.georgeandlouies.com* *Closed Sun. and Mon.*

Jonah's Fish & Grits

$$ | **SEAFOOD** | **FAMILY** | Locals line up for a table at this extremely popular locally owned eatery where seafood is the specialty, of course. Jonah's signature rich and creamy white cheddar grits, Parmesan-crusted rainbow trout, and deep-fried catfish with hush puppies are customer favorites. There are plenty of options for landlubbers, and a kids' menu, too. **Known for:** seafood specialties; family-friendly environment; no alcohol. *Average main: $19* *109 E. Jackson St.* *229/226–0508* *www.jonahsfish.com* *Closed Sun.*

Liam's

$$$$ | **ECLECTIC** | With a flair for the unexpected, this bistro turns out a rotating seasonal menu with such updated Southern dishes as pork tenderloin with mashed root vegetable, duck rillette, and prime beef tenderloin, as well as decadent small dishes for sharing. Liam's also serves a full cheese cart of various artisanal cheeses from Europe along with local selections. **Known for:** eclectic and always changing seasonal menu; fun, laid-back atmosphere; outstanding cheese and wine selections. *Average main: $26* *113 E. Jackson St.* *229/226–9944* *www.liamsthomasville.com* *Closed Sun. and Mon.*

Coffee and Quick Bites

★ **Sweet Grass Dairy Cheese Shop**

$ | **AMERICAN** | This award-winning cheese maker makes its home in Thomasville and operates this shop and café, where you can try the farm-fresh cheese, wines, cocktails, and craft beers, as well as peruse the collection of locally crafted jams, honey, and regional food items. You can purchase individual cheeses to go or select an artfully prepared cheese or charcuterie board for a sit-down sampling of the day's offerings. **Known for:** local artisanal cheeses; gourmet desserts and small plates; store selling local food items. *Average main: $14* *123 S. Broad St.* *229/228–6704* *www.sweetgrass-dairy.com* *Closed Sun. and Mon.*

Hotels

Courtyard Thomasville Downtown
$$ | **HOTEL** | New in 2021, this four-story hotel was constructed to blend seamlessly into downtown Thomasville's streetscape and offers stylish, modern rooms in easy walking distance of multiple shops, restaurants, and attractions. **Pros:** new and shiny; walkable downtown location; pool and fitness center. **Cons:** pricey as it's the only hotel downtown; service may be inconsistent as hotel gets established; no free breakfast. *Rooms from: $175* *207 S. Dawson St.* *229/264–4300* *www.marriott.com* *106 rooms* *No meals.*

The Paxton Historic House Hotel
$$$$ | **B&B/INN** | Each room is unique in this immaculate property, a stately 1884 Victorian mansion with a wraparound veranda. **Pros:** luxurious comfort; friendly innkeepers; old-time charm. **Cons:** fills up quickly; no pool; some bathrooms are small. *Rooms from: $275* *445 Remington Ave.* *229/226–5197* *www.1884paxtonhouseinn.com* *9 rooms* *Free breakfast.*

Chapter 14

ATLANTA, GA

Updated by
Chanté LaGon

Sights ★★★★★ | Restaurants ★★★★★ | Hotels ★★★★★ | Shopping ★★★★☆ | Nightlife ★★★★☆

WELCOME TO ATLANTA, GA

TOP REASONS TO GO

★ **The Georgia Aquarium:** The largest aquarium in the United States draws visitors from all over the globe.

★ **A stroll through the park:** April in Paris has nothing on Atlanta, especially when the azaleas and dogwoods are blooming in the Atlanta Botanical Garden and Piedmont Park.

★ **Following in Dr. King's footsteps:** Home of Martin Luther King Jr., Atlanta was a hub of the civil rights movement. Tour the King Center and his childhood home on Auburn Avenue and see his personal documents at the National Center for Civil and Human Rights.

★ **Civil War history:** Artifacts at historic sites throughout the city give you the chance to reflect on those difficult times.

★ **Southern cooking, and then some:** Good Southern food has always been easy to find here, but Atlanta's proliferation of young, talented chefs and its ethnic diversity make it a great place to sample a wide range of cuisines.

1 Downtown. Tourists flock to sites like the Georgia Aquarium.

2 Sweet Auburn, the Old Fourth Ward, and East Atlanta. Sweet Auburn is the epicenter of African American history, while the Old Fourth Ward and East Atlanta have a happening nightlife.

3 Midtown and the Westside. Midtown is home to high-rise condos, while chefs and designers have transformed the industrial Westside.

4 Buckhead. Buckhead has a concentration of ritzy boutiques and stores.

5 Virginia-Highland and the Emory Area. Patio bars, cozy music venues, and great food.

6 Little Five Points and Inman Park. The mansions of Inman Park are a short walk from the bars and shops of Little Five Points.

7 Decatur. Its charming town square is always buzzing.

8 Metro Atlanta. You'll need a car to explore sights like the Chattahoochee River National Recreation Area and Stone Mountain Park.

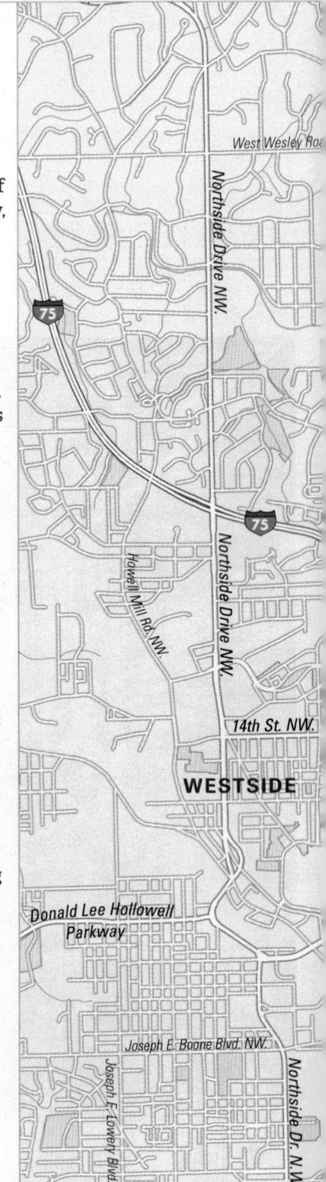

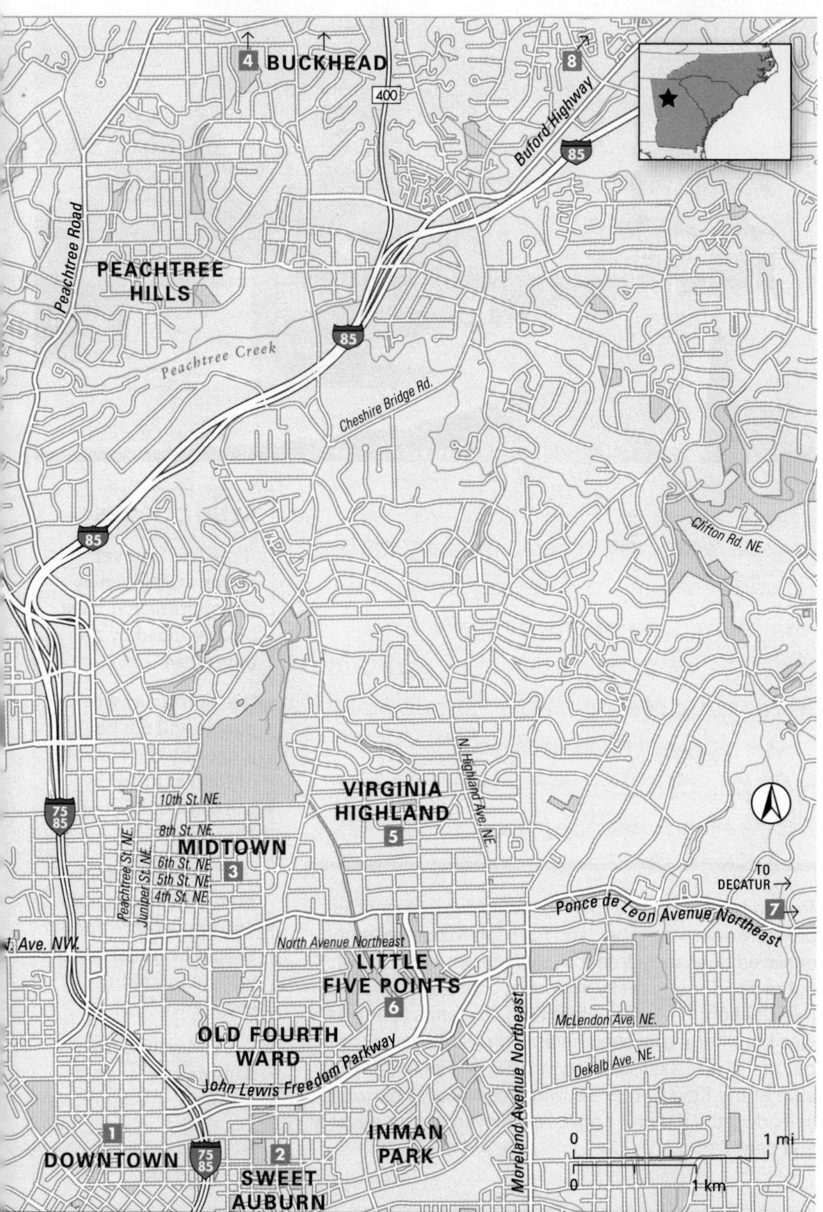
BUCKHEAD
4
8
400
Buford Highway
85
Peachtree Road
PEACHTREE
HILLS
Peachtree Creek
Cheshire Bridge Rd.
Clifton Rd. NE.
N. Highland Ave. NE.
VIRGINIA
HIGHLAND
5
75
85
10th St. NE.
8th St. NE.
MIDTOWN
3
6th St. NE.
5th St. NE.
4th St. NE.
Peachtree St. NE.
Juniper St. NE.
TO
DECATUR
7
Ponce de Leon Avenue Northeast
Ave. NW.
North Avenue Northeast
LITTLE
FIVE POINTS
6
Moreland Avenue Northeast
McLendon Ave. NE.
OLD FOURTH
WARD
John Lewis Freedom Parkway
Dekalb Ave. NE.
1
DOWNTOWN
2
SWEET
AUBURN
INMAN
PARK
0
1 mi
0
1 km

ATLANTA'S CIVIL RIGHTS LEGACY

The tomb of Dr. Martin Luther King Jr. and Coretta Scott King

To some, Atlanta's location in the South may have made it seem an unlikely hotbed for social change, but the city earned an important place in the history of civil rights, particularly through the work and words of Dr. Martin Luther King Jr. Many of the monuments to this rich legacy—including the birth home and church of King—are open to the public.

Tracing back to 1862, when the first African American property owner sold her land for $500 to purchase her enslaved husband's freedom, Atlanta has been a civil rights city. Though many important activists have called this city home, Martin Luther King Jr. stands apart. He was born here, preached here, and raised a family here before he was assassinated in 1968. His legacy is kept alive at the King Center—a living memorial to his work in leading the nation's nonviolent movement for equality and peace.

KING QUOTES

"Freedom is never voluntarily given by the oppressor; it must be demanded by the oppressed."

"I look to a day when people will not be judged by the color of their skin but by the content of their character."

"All labor that uplifts humanity has dignity and importance and should be undertaken with painstaking excellence."

—Dr. Martin Luther King Jr.

CIVIL RIGHTS WALK

A great way to take a tour of Atlanta's civil rights history is to walk through the Sweet Auburn neighborhood. To get here, take the MARTA train to the Five Points station Downtown and switch to either of the two eastbound lines (the Green/Edgewood/Candler Park or the Blue/Indian Creek line). Get off at the King Memorial stop. All tours are self-guided.

Spend time at the Martin Luther King Jr. National Historic Site, also known as **The King Center,** established in 1968 by Coretta Scott King and housing Dr. King's library, a resource center, the Eternal Flame, and the Kings' final resting place. Pause at King's white marble tomb to see its inscription: "Free at last, free at last, thank God almighty I'm free at last."

Stroll along the **International Civil Rights Walk of Fame,** created in 2004 and set up along the National Park Service's Visitor Center to recognize civil rights heroes and cultural icons like Rosa Parks, Stevie Wonder, Hank Aaron, and President Jimmy Carter with 2-foot-square granite markers.

Visit **Ebenezer Baptist Church,** which was founded in 1886 and moved to Auburn Avenue in 1914. King was baptized here and took the pulpit in 1960 as co-pastor with his father. The historic church is open daily for self-guided tours. If you're here on a Sunday, stop by the congregation's current location across the street for a moving service.

Then head to the **Sweet Auburn Curb Market,** which was previously segregated; only white people were permitted to shop inside while black people shopped from stalls lining the curb, giving the market its name.

Ebenezer Baptist Church was founded in 1886.

ATLANTA IN CIVIL RIGHTS HISTORY

1800s: The first African American congressman from Georgia is elected; Booker T. Washington's "Atlanta Compromise" speech is given here.

1900–40: Twenty-five black people die during the Atlanta Race Riots; Martin Luther King Jr. is born in Atlanta.

1950–60: Atlanta's segregated bus system is ruled unconstitutional; members of the Student Nonviolent Coordinating Committee stage a sit-in at segregated lunch counters; public pools and parks integrate.

1954: U.S. Supreme Court declares school segregation unconstitutional in the *Brown v. Board of Education* ruling.

1973: Maynard Holbrook Jackson Jr. is elected as the city's first African American mayor.

1980s: The King Center is named a national historic site.

2000: Shirley Franklin is Atlanta's first female African American mayor.

Originally built as the terminus of the Western & Atlantic Railroad, Atlanta remains a hub for transportation, with the world's busiest airport; industry, with the headquarters for Coca-Cola; art, with treasures on display at the High Museum of Art; and natural wonders, with the nation's largest aquarium.

The city's half million residents enjoy a mix of old-fashioned Southern charm, offbeat artistic funkiness, chic luxury shopping, superb dining, and major attractions. In the past, many of the city's big draws—Stone Mountain Park, for example—were outside the city limits. Today there's plenty in town to keep you occupied. The Georgia Aquarium draws visitors who want to get up close and personal with whale sharks. At the Woodruff Arts Center, you can catch a performance by the Atlanta Symphony Orchestra or listen to jazz while strolling the High Museum of Art. The fizzy World of Coca-Cola is dedicated to the hometown beverage, and the National Center for Civil and Human Rights is a beacon for justice and equality everywhere.

Atlanta continues to experience explosive growth. A good measure of the city's expansion is the ever-changing skyline; condominium developments appear to spring up overnight, while run-down properties seem to disappear in a flash. In Buckhead—once home to a noisy, raucous bar district—most of the taverns have been razed to bring a Rodeo Drive of the South into being. Office and residential towers have risen throughout Midtown, Downtown, and the outer perimeter (fringing Interstate 285, especially to the north). Residents, however, are less likely to measure the city's growth by skyscrapers than by the increase in the already bad traffic, the crowds, higher prices, and the ever-burgeoning subdivisions that continue to push urban sprawl farther and farther into surrounding rural areas.

Known as "the city too busy to hate," Atlanta has become the best example of the New South, a fast-paced modern city proud of its heritage. Transplanted Northerners and those from elsewhere account for more than half the population, and they have undeniably affected the mood of the city, as well as the mix of accents of its people. Irish immigrants played a major role in the city's early history, along with Germans and Austrians. Since the 1980s, Atlanta has seen spirited growth in its Asian American and Latin American communities. The newcomers' restaurants, shops, and institutions have become part of the city's texture.

Planning

When to Go

Atlanta isn't called "Hotlanta" for nothing—in the late spring and summer months the mosquitoes feast, and temperatures can reach a sticky and humid 99°F (thankfully, almost every place in the city is air-conditioned). July 4th weekend can be particularly hectic, due to the influx of runners for the annual 10K Peachtree Road Race. Labor Day weekend also sees major crowds thanks to dozens of popular national festivals, including Dragon Con and the Decatur Book Festival. The best time to visit is in fall and early winter. When many other cities are beginning to get cold and gray, Atlanta typically maintains a steady level of sunshine and cool breezes. Spring is also a beautiful time to visit, with azaleas and dogwoods in bloom. Airfares are fairly reasonable at most times of the year, given that the city is a transportation hub and most Atlanta attractions aren't seasonal.

Planning Your Time

Because it would take too long to explore the city end to end in one fell swoop, consider discovering Atlanta one pocket at a time. In Downtown you can stroll through the Georgia Aquarium, tour the CNN Center, and visit the National Center for Civil and Human Rights, then finish off the day with dinner and a glass of wine at the historic Ellis Hotel's Terrace Bistro restaurant. Another good pocket includes three adjoining, very walkable neighborhoods, all known for their canopies of trees, cute shops, and fun bistros: Virginia-Highland, Little Five Points, and Inman Park. From there you can drive to East Atlanta and check out its casual bars, restaurants, and live music. Your third pocket should be Buckhead, a shopper's mecca. Two constants there are Lenox Square and Phipps Plaza, great shopping spots in their own right. Finally, there's the beer-loving, literary hot spot of Decatur, which is increasingly being recognized for its top-notch restaurants.

Getting Here and Around

AIR TRAVEL

Hartsfield-Jackson Atlanta International (ATL), the busiest passenger airport in the world, is served by more than 15 airlines, including American, Delta, and Southwest. Although an underground train and moving walkways help you reach your gate more quickly, budget a little extra time for negotiating the massive facility. Because of the airport's size, security lines can be long, especially during peak travel periods. Check ATL's website for Trak-a-Line, which will email you updates about wait times and is surprisingly accurate.

The airport is 13 miles south of Downtown. There are large parking facilities, but they tend to fill up quickly. Check their current capacity on ATL's website. Locals know that MARTA, the regional subway system, is the fastest and cheapest way to and from the airport, but taxis and rideshare services like Uber and Lyft are also available. Expect a five-minute walk to the pickup locations on the lower level of both the North and South Terminals. The fare by taxi to Downtown is about $35 for one person. From the airport to Buckhead, the fare starts at $40 for one person. Buckhead Safety Cab and Checker Cab offer 24-hour service.

AIRPORT CONTACTS Hartsfield-Jackson Atlanta International Airport. *(ATL)* ✉ *6000 N. Terminal Pkwy.* ☎ *404/530–7300* 🌐 *www.atl.com.*

BUS TRAVEL

MARTA operates more than 100 routes covering more than 1,000 miles, but the bus system isn't popular among visitors. The fare is $2.50, and a Breeze card ($2 and reusable) is required. Service is limited outside the perimeter of Interstate 285, except for a few areas in Clayton, DeKalb, and north Fulton Counties.

CAR TRAVEL

The city is encircled by Interstate 285. Three interstates also crisscross Atlanta: Interstate 85, running northeast–southwest from Virginia to Alabama; Interstate 75, running north–south from Michigan to Florida; and Interstate 20, running east–west from South Carolina to Texas.

Some refer to Atlanta as the "Los Angeles of the South," because driving is virtually the only way to get around. Atlantans have grown accustomed to frequent delays at rush hour—the morning and late-afternoon commuting periods seem to get longer every year. ■ **TIP→ The South as a whole may be laid-back, but Atlanta drivers are not; they tend to drive faster and more aggressively than drivers in other Southern cities, and they rarely slow down at a yellow light.**

If you plan to venture beyond the neighborhoods served by MARTA, you will want to rent a car or use a rideshare service such as Uber or Lyft. Many national rental agencies have branch offices all over the city, as well as at Hartsfield-Jackson Atlanta International Airport.

STREETCAR TRAVEL

With 12 stops, including Centennial Olympic Park, the Martin Luther King Jr. National Historic Site, and various points in between, residents and visitors alike will appreciate how the line connects neighborhoods, attractions, walk-run-bike paths such as the BeltLine, and MARTA. The one-way fare is $1 and works in tandem with the city rail system's Breeze card.

STREETCAR CONTACT Atlanta Streetcar. ✉ *Downtown* ☎ *404/848–5000* 🌐 *itsmarta.com/streetcar.*

SUBWAY TRAVEL

MARTA has clean and safe subway trains with somewhat limited routes that link Downtown with many major landmarks, like the CNN Center and the Martin Luther King Jr. Memorial. The system's two main lines cross at the Five Points station. MARTA uses a smart-card fare system called Breeze. The cards are available at RideStores and from vending machines at each station by using cash or credit cards. The one-way fare is $2.50, but the cards offer several options, including one-day, seven-day, and 30-day passes.

Trains generally run weekdays 5 am to 1 am and weekends and holidays 6 am to 1 am. Most trains operate every 15 to 20 minutes; during weekday rush hours, trains run every 10 minutes.

■ **TIP→ Locals take MARTA to and from Hartsfield-Jackson International Airport, which has the traffic snarls common with larger airports. The $2.50 fare is a fraction of the amount charged by rideshare services or taxis.** Airport travelers should be careful about catching the right train. One line ends up at North Springs station to the north; the other at Doraville station to the northeast. Daily parking is free at MARTA parking facilities. Long-term parking rates range from $5 to $8 daily. Not all stations have parking lots.

SUBWAY CONTACT MARTA. ☎ *404/848–5000* 🌐 *www.itsmarta.com.*

TAXI TRAVEL

In Atlanta taxi fares begin at $2.50, then add $2 for each additional mile. Additional passengers are $2 each, and there's a $2 gas surcharge added to every trip. You generally need to call for a cab, as Atlanta is not a place where you can hail one on the street. Checker Cab offers 24-hour service. Uber and Lyft drivers are also available throughout the city.

TAXI CONTACTS Checker Cab. ☎ *404/351–1111* 🌐 *www.atlantacheckercab.com.*

TRAIN TRAVEL

Amtrak operates daily service from Atlanta's Peachtree Station to New York; Philadelphia; Washington, D.C.; Charlotte, North Carolina; and New Orleans.

TRAIN CONTACTS Amtrak. ✉ *Peachtree Station, 1688 Peachtree St., Buckhead* ☎ *800/872–7245* 🌐 *www.amtrak.com.*

Discounts and Deals

Visitors can take advantage of the deal offered with **Atlanta CityPass,** "the ticket to a New and Old South vacation." An adult pass—which is valid for a nine-day period—costs $77 and provides access to five attractions: the Georgia Aquarium, World of Coca-Cola, Zoo Atlanta, and a choice between the Fernbank Museum of Natural History, the College Football Hall of Fame, or the National Center for Civil and Human Rights. Visit 🌐 *www.citypass.com/atlanta.*

Performing Arts

For the most complete schedule of cultural events, check the weekly Do Guide section of the *Atlanta Journal-Constitution* (🌐 *www.ajc.com*); the city's free alternative monthly, *Creative Loafing* (🌐 *clatl.com*); or the entertainment monthly, *INsite* (🌐 *www.insiteatlanta.com*). The *Atlanta Daily World* (🌐 *www.atlantadailyworld.com*) and the *Atlanta Voice* (🌐 *www.theatlantavoice.com*), serving the African American community, are also published online weekly.

FESTIVALS

Atlanta Jazz Festival

CONCERTS | The Atlanta Jazz Festival, held throughout the month of May and culminating Memorial Day weekend, gathers the best local, national, and international musicians for free concerts at Atlanta's Piedmont Park and various venues. ✉ *10th St. and Monroe Dr., Midtown* ☎ *404/546–6826* 🌐 *www.atlantafestivals.com.*

Atlanta Pride

FESTIVALS | Since 1971, Atlanta has put on one of the most vibrant and popular gay festivals in the country. Thousands of people gather in Piedmont Park every October for Atlanta Pride, which includes a long lineup of entertainers and a market with vendors and organizations from around the area. The main event is the parade, with festive floats and dancers and folks of all stripes marching through the streets of the city. ✉ *Piedmont Park, 10th St. and Monroe Dr., Midtown* ☎ *404/382–7588* 🌐 *www.atlantapride.org.*

Decatur Book Festival

READINGS/LECTURES | The Decatur Book Festival is the largest independent book festival in the nation. It takes over Decatur's historic square every Labor Day weekend, with readings, signings, and other literary events. Past keynote speakers have included the novelist Jonathan Franzen and former Decatur resident and current Northwestern University professor Natasha Trethewey, the 19th U.S. Poet Laureate. ✉ *E. Ponce de Leon and Clairemont Aves., Decatur* 🌐 *www.decaturbookfestival.com.*

Dragon Con

FESTIVALS | Swarms of sci-fi and fantasy fans from around the world descend on Downtown Atlanta every Labor Day weekend to celebrate everything from zombies to *Star Trek*. The popular Saturday morning parade with hordes of stormtroopers and other movie characters making the route is not to be missed. ✉ *Downtown* ☎ *404/669–0773* 🌐 *www.dragoncon.org.*

National Black Arts Festival

FESTIVALS | Celebrating black literature, dance, visual arts, theater, film, and music, this festival is held in venues throughout the city year-round. Maya

Angelou, Cicely Tyson, Harry Belafonte, Spike Lee, Tito Puente, and Wynton Marsalis have all appeared at past events. ✉ *235 Peachtree St. NE, Downtown* ☎ *404/730–7315* 🌐 *www.nbaf.org.*

Tours

Getting to know the many neighborhoods of Atlanta makes guided tours worthwhile. Although historic locations often offer self-guided materials, there's nothing like a local to share stories of Atlanta's first suburb and the history of Downtown's most beloved attractions. The best options are given by motor vehicle, whether minicoach, e-car, or trolley—all at a slower pace, of course.

ATL-Cruzers
DRIVING TOURS | Small tours by small vehicles—whether electric car or Segway—are this tour's hallmark. Atlanta's neighborhoods are the highlight, from Downtown to Midtown to Sweet Auburn. ✉ *160 Spring St. NW, Downtown* ☎ *404/492–7009* 🌐 *www.atlcruzers.com* 🎟 *From $36.*

Peachtree Trolley
DRIVING TOURS | If you're staying Downtown, this tour will familiarize you with the popular destinations there, including the Georgia Aquarium, World of Coca-Cola, and CNN Center. A trip to surrounding areas, such as Grant Park and its Oakland Cemetery, are also on the route. ✉ *Hilton Garden Inn, 275 Baker St. NW, Downtown* ☎ *404/618-4128* 🌐 *thepeachtreettrolley.com* 🎟 *From $31.*

Restaurants

This is a city known for its food; many a trip to Atlanta is planned around meals in its barbecue shacks, upscale diners, and chic urban eateries. Traditional Southern fare—including Cajun and creole, country-style and plantation cuisine, and coastal and mountain dishes—thrives, as does Asian fusion, traditional Ethiopian, creative vegan, and mouth-scorching Indian food. Catch the flavor of the South at breakfast and lunch in diners and other modest establishments that serve only these meals.

Many restaurants will accept you just as you are; dress codes are extremely rare in this casual city, except in the chicest of spots. Although many restaurants accept reservations, some popular spots operate on a first-come, first-served basis on weekends. Waits at some hot dining locales can exceed an hour, especially if you arrive after 7 pm.

PRICES

Eating in Atlanta is surprisingly affordable, at least when compared with cities like New York and Chicago. Some of the pricier restaurants offer early-bird weeknight specials and prix-fixe menus. Ask when you call to make reservations.

Restaurant reviews have been shortened. For full information, visit Fodors.com.

What It Costs

$	$$	$$$	$$$$
RESTAURANTS			
under $15	$15–$19	$20–$24	over $24

Hotels

One of America's most popular convention destinations, Atlanta offers plenty of variety in terms of lodging. More than 95,000 rooms are in metro Atlanta, with nearly 12,000 Downtown, close to the Georgia World Congress Center and State Farm Arena. Other clusters are in Buckhead, in the north Interstate 285 perimeter, and around Hartsfield-Jackson Atlanta International Airport.

PRICES

Atlanta lodging facilities basically have two seasons: summer and convention (conventions are generally held year-round, though there are fewer in summer).

Hotel reviews have been shortened. For full information, visit Fodors.com.

What It Costs			
$	$$	$$$	$$$$
HOTELS			
under $150	$150–$200	$201–$250	over $250

Visitor Information

The Atlanta Convention and Visitors Bureau, which provides information on Atlanta and the outlying area, has information centers at Hartsfield-Jackson Atlanta International Airport and Centennial Olympic Park.

CONTACTS Atlanta Convention and Visitors Bureau. ✉ *233 Peachtree St., Suite 1400, Downtown* ☎ *404/521–6600* 🌐 *discoveratlanta.com.*

Downtown

Downtown Atlanta clusters around the hub known as Five Points. You'll find the MARTA station that intersects the north–south and east–west transit lines, both of which run underground here. On the surface, Five Points is formed by the intersection of Peachtree Street with Marietta, Broad, and Forsyth Streets. It's a crowded area, particularly when Georgia State University is in session, and traffic can be snarled in the early morning and late afternoon. With the National Center for Civil and Human Rights joining the Georgia Aquarium, World of Coca-Cola, the Children's Museum of Atlanta, and CNN Center, Downtown has taken on greater interest for travelers. Centennial Olympic Park—built for the 1996 Olympic Games—is a great place to let your children play in the Fountain of Rings.

Sights

★ Centennial Olympic Park

CITY PARK | FAMILY | This 21-acre swath of green was the central venue for the 1996 Summer Olympics. The benches at the Fountain of Rings allow you to enjoy the water and music spectacle—four times a day, tunes are timed to coincide with water displays that shoot sprays 15 feet to 30 feet high. The All Children's Playground is designed to be accessible to kids with disabilities. Nearby is the world's largest aquarium and Imagine It! Children's Museum. The park also has a café, restrooms, and a playground, and typically offers ice-skating in winter. **■ TIP→ Don't miss seeing Centennial Olympic Park at night, when eight 65-foot-tall lighting towers set off the beauty of the park. They represent the markers that led ancient Greeks to public events.** ✉ *265 Park Ave. W, Downtown* ✣ *Marietta St. and Centennial Olympic Park Dr.* ☎ *404/223–4412* 🌐 *www.gwcca.org.*

Children's Museum of Atlanta

MUSEUM | FAMILY | In this colorful and joyfully noisy museum for children ages eight and younger, kids can build sandcastles, watch themselves perform on closed-circuit TV, operate a giant ball-moving machine, and get inside an imaginary waterfall (after donning raincoats, of course). Other exhibits rotate every few months. ✉ *275 Centennial Olympic Park Dr. NW, Downtown* ☎ *404/659–5437* 🌐 *www.childrensmuseumatlanta.org* 🎟 *Starts at $16.95.*

CNN Center

FILM STUDIO | The home of Cable News Network occupies all 14 floors of this dramatic structure on the edge of Downtown. The 50-minute CNN studio tour is a behind-the-scenes glimpse of the

The Georgia Aquarium is the world's largest aquarium, with 10 million gallons of water and more than 100,000 animals.

control room, newsrooms, and broadcast studios. Tours depart approximately every 20 minutes. ■ **TIP→ The tour descends eight flights of stairs, making it difficult for some—a limited number of tours have elevator access.** You can make reservations by telephone or online. ✉ *1 CNN Center, Downtown* ☎ *404/827–2300* 🌐 *center.cnn.com* 🎟 *Tour $12–$15.*

★ Georgia Aquarium

ZOO | FAMILY | With more than 10 million gallons of water, this wildly popular attraction is the nation's largest aquarium. The 604,000-square-foot building, an architectural marvel resembling the bow of a ship, has tanks of various sizes filled with more than 100,000 animals, representing 500 species. The aquarium's 6.3-million-gallon *Ocean Voyager Gallery* is the world's largest indoor marine exhibit, with 4,574 square feet of viewing windows. But not everything has gills: there are also penguins, sea lions, sea otters, river otters, sea turtles, and giant octopuses. The 84,000-square-foot *Dolphins in Depth* exhibit includes a 25-minute show (reservations required). Hordes of kids—and many adults—can always be found around the touch tanks. Admission includes entry to all public exhibits, shows, and galleries. Forty-five-minute behind-the-scenes tours start at $15. There are often huge crowds, so arrive early or late for the best chance of getting a close-up view of the exhibits. ■ **TIP→ Try to buy your tickets at least a week ahead. Online ticketing is best, with discounted rates and digital tickets you can print out at home.** ✉ *225 Baker St., Downtown* ☎ *404/581–4000* 🌐 *www.georgiaaquarium.org* 🎟 *$35.95.*

Georgia State Capitol

GOVERNMENT BUILDING | The capitol, a Renaissance-style edifice, was dedicated on July 4, 1889. The gold leaf on its dome was mined in nearby Dahlonega. Inside, the **Georgia Capitol Museum** houses exhibits on its history. On the grounds, state historical markers commemorate the 1864 Battle of Atlanta, which destroyed nearly the entire city. Statues memorialize a 19th-century Georgia governor and his wife (Joseph and Elizabeth Brown), a Confederate general (John B. Gordon), and a former senator (Richard B. Russell). Former governor and president Jimmy Carter is depicted with his sleeves rolled up, a man at work. Visit the website for tour information and group reservations. ✉ *206 Washington St. SW, Downtown* ☎ *404/463–4536* 🌐 *www.libs.uga.edu/capitolmuseum* ⏲ *Closed weekends and state holidays.*

★ National Center for Civil and Human Rights

MUSEUM | This three-level, 43,000-square-foot, hands-on museum offers visitors a multisensory immersion into both the U.S. civil rights movement and global human rights efforts. Each exhibit is a force of its own: the quiet and vicarious look at handwritten journals and personal items from Martin Luther King Jr.; the jolting sensation of sitting in at a lunch counter, hearing the threats and slurs that young protesters would have; or the mirrorlike effect of one-on-one stories told by those who've suffered human rights violations—and the workers whose mission it is to triumph over them. The *Rolls Down Like Water* exhibit is superb, bearing the mark of its curator, award-winning playwright and film director George C. Wolfe. The center hosts one of the biggest celebrations of the Universal Declaration of Human Rights in the world each December. And the building, itself a work of art reminiscent of folding hands, is steps away from parking and a brief walk to World of Coca-Cola and the Georgia Aquarium. ✉ *100 Ivan Allen Jr. Blvd., Downtown* ☎ *678/999–8990* 🌐 *www.civilandhumanrights.org* 🎟 *$16.*

Porsche Experience Center Atlanta

AMUSEMENT PARK/WATER PARK | Select which Porsche you'd like to drive and get one-on-one coaching with a pro, who will show you how to steer, accelerate, and brake your way through the 1.6-mile track. Less expensive options include the simulator lab and tours of the car company's North America headquarters. ✉ *1 Porsche Dr., Downtown* ☎ *888/204–7474* 🌐 *www.porschedriving.com* ⏲ *Closed Sun. and Mon.*

SkyView Atlanta

AMUSEMENT PARK/WATER PARK | Take a seat in one of the Ferris wheel's 42 climate-controlled cars perched 20 stories above Downtown for spectacular views of Centennial Olympic Park and miles beyond. The ride lasts 15 minutes. The wheel comes alive at night with an ever-changing display of colors outlining its rim and spokes powered by the same lighting system as the Eiffel Tower. In true Atlanta fashion, there's a VIP experience that lets you skip long lines and sit privately with your group in a gondola outfitted with Ferrari leather seats and a glass floor for a longer ride. Discount parking is available in nearby lots. ✉ *168 Luckie St., Downtown* ☎ *678/949–9023* 🌐 *www.skyviewatlanta.com* 🎟 *$14.50, VIP $50.*

World of Coca-Cola

MUSEUM | **FAMILY** | This shrine to the brown soda's image, products, and marketing is, at 62,000 square feet, twice the size of its previous building and features more than 1,200 artifacts never before displayed to the public. You can sip samples of 100 different Coca-Cola products from around the world and peruse more than a century's worth of memorabilia from the corporate archives. The gift shop sells everything from refrigerator magnets to handbags. ✉ *121 Baker St. NW, Downtown* ☎ *404/676–5151* 🌐 *www.worldofcoca-cola.com* 🎟 *$18.*

Restaurants

Little Bear

$$ | **FUSION** | Inspired by Jarrett Stieber's pop-up, Eat Me, Speak Me at S.O.S. Tiki Bar in Decatur, the restaurant is named after his dog, a Great Pyrenees. **Known for:** no two meals are exactly alike; chill

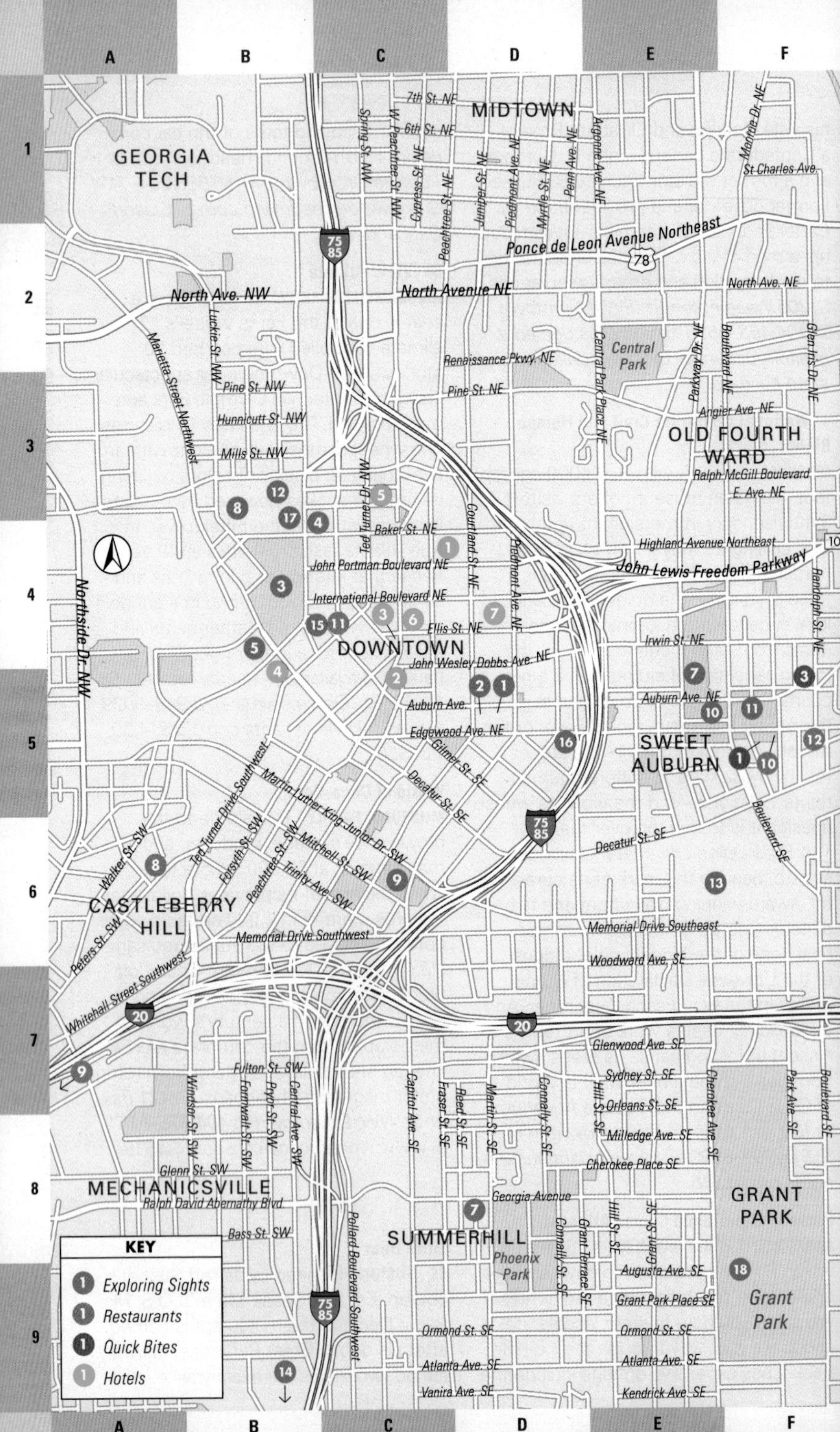

A
B
C
D
E
F
1
2
3
4
5
6
7
8
9
MIDTOWN
GEORGIA TECH
OLD FOURTH WARD
DOWNTOWN
SWEET AUBURN
CASTLEBERRY HILL
MECHANICSVILLE
SUMMERHILL
GRANT PARK
Central Park
Phoenix Park
Grant Park
7th St. NE
6th St. NE
Spring St. NW
W. Peachtree St. NW
Cypress St. NE
Peachtree St. NE
Juniper St. NE
Piedmont Ave. NE
Myrtle St. NE
Penn Ave. NE
Argonne Ave. NE
Monroe Dr. NE
St Charles Ave.
Ponce de Leon Avenue Northeast
North Ave. NW
North Avenue NE
North Ave. NE
Luckie St. NW
Marietta Street Northwest
Renaissance Pkwy. NE
Central Park Place NE
Parkway Dr. NE
Boulevard NE
Glen Iris Dr. NE
Pine St. NW
Pine St. NE
Hunnicutt St. NW
Mills St. NW
Angier Ave. NE
Ralph McGill Boulevard
E. Ave. NE
Ted Turner Dr. NW
Baker St. NE
Courtland St. NE
Highland Avenue Northeast
John Lewis Freedom Parkway
John Portman Boulevard NE
International Boulevard NE
Ellis St. NE
Randolph St. NE
Northside Dr. NW
Irwin St. NE
John Wesley Dobbs Ave. NE
Auburn Ave.
Auburn Ave. NE
Edgewood Ave. NE
Gilmer St. SE
Decatur St. SE
Ted Turner Drive Southwest
Martin Luther King Junior Dr. SW
Walker St. SW
Forsyth St. SW
Peachtree St. SW
Mitchell St. SW
Trinity Ave. SW
Boulevard SE
Peters St. SW
Memorial Drive Southwest
Memorial Drive Southeast
Woodward Ave. SE
Whitehall Street Southwest
Glenwood Ave. SE
Fulton St. SW
Sydney St. SE
Orleans St. SE
Milledge Ave. SE
Cherokee Place SE
Windsor St. SW
Formwalt St. SW
Pryor St. SW
Central Ave. SW
Capitol Ave. SE
Fraser St. SE
Reed St. SE
Martin St. SE
Connally St. SE
Hill St. SE
Cherokee Ave. SE
Park Ave. SE
Glenn St. SW
Ralph David Abernathy Blvd
Georgia Avenue
Grant Terrace SE
Grant St. SE
Bass St. SW
Pollard Boulevard Southwest
Augusta Ave. SE
Grant Park Place SE
Ormond St. SE
Atlanta Ave. SE
Vanira Ave. SE
Kendrick Ave. SE
75
85
78
20
10
KEY
Exploring Sights
Restaurants
Quick Bites
Hotels

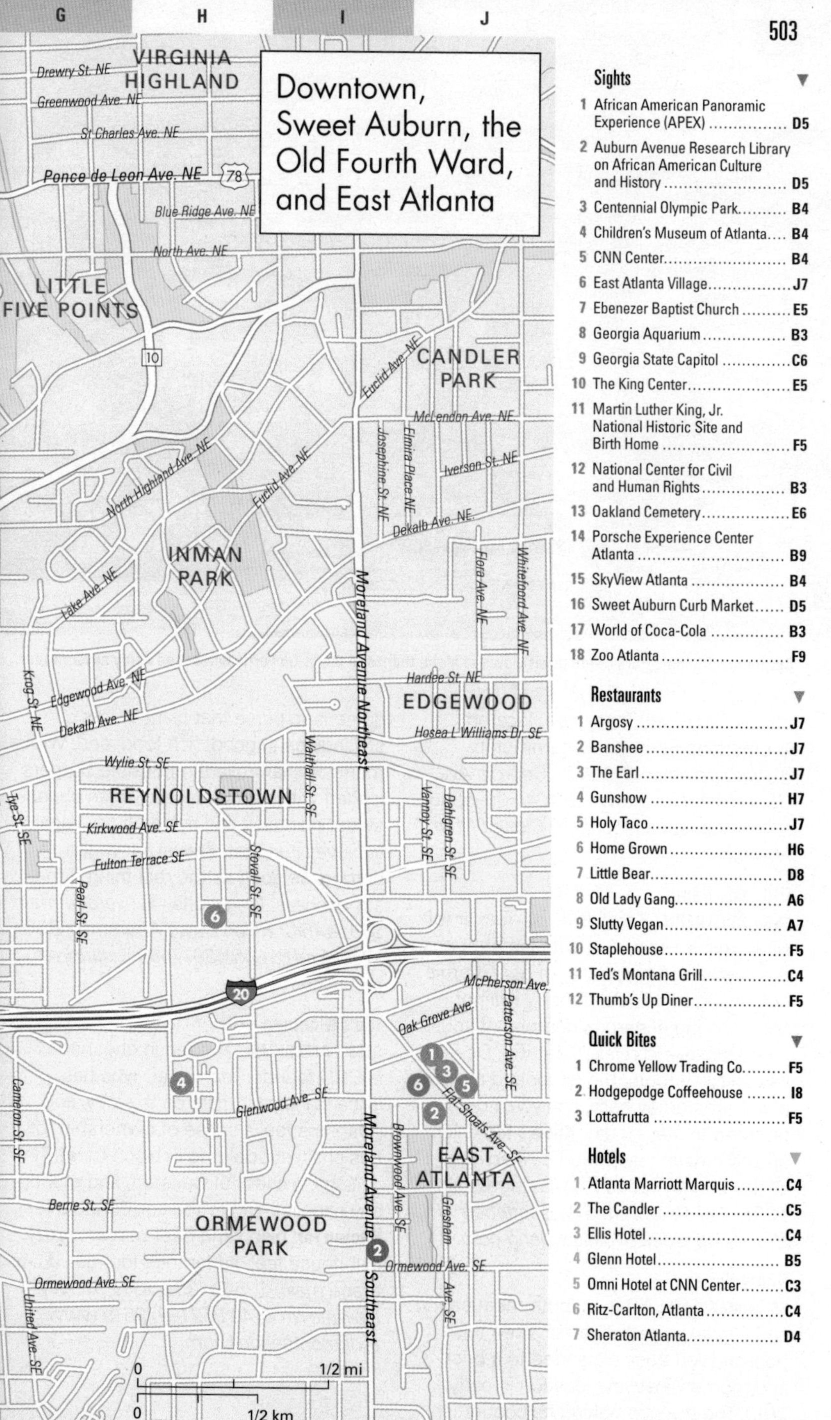

Downtown, Sweet Auburn, the Old Fourth Ward, and East Atlanta

Sights

1. African American Panoramic Experience (APEX) ... D5
2. Auburn Avenue Research Library on African American Culture and History ... D5
3. Centennial Olympic Park ... B4
4. Children's Museum of Atlanta ... B4
5. CNN Center ... B4
6. East Atlanta Village ... J7
7. Ebenezer Baptist Church ... E5
8. Georgia Aquarium ... B3
9. Georgia State Capitol ... C6
10. The King Center ... E5
11. Martin Luther King, Jr. National Historic Site and Birth Home ... F5
12. National Center for Civil and Human Rights ... B3
13. Oakland Cemetery ... E6
14. Porsche Experience Center Atlanta ... B9
15. SkyView Atlanta ... B4
16. Sweet Auburn Curb Market ... D5
17. World of Coca-Cola ... B3
18. Zoo Atlanta ... F9

Restaurants

1. Argosy ... J7
2. Banshee ... J7
3. The Earl ... J7
4. Gunshow ... H7
5. Holy Taco ... J7
6. Home Grown ... H6
7. Little Bear ... D8
8. Old Lady Gang ... A6
9. Slutty Vegan ... A7
10. Staplehouse ... F5
11. Ted's Montana Grill ... C4
12. Thumb's Up Diner ... F5

Quick Bites

1. Chrome Yellow Trading Co. ... F5
2. Hodgepodge Coffeehouse ... I8
3. Lottafrutta ... F5

Hotels

1. Atlanta Marriott Marquis ... C4
2. The Candler ... C5
3. Ellis Hotel ... C4
4. Glenn Hotel ... B5
5. Omni Hotel at CNN Center ... C3
6. Ritz-Carlton, Atlanta ... C4
7. Sheraton Atlanta ... D4

Centennial Olympic Park offers great views at night, thanks to the lit-up Ferris wheel and many skyscrapers.

atmosphere with fancy fare; located in emerging Summerhill community. $ *Average main: $15* ✉ *71 Georgia Ave. SE, Unit A, Downtown* ☎ *404/500–5396* 🌐 *www.littlebearatl.com* ⏲ *Closed Mon. No lunch.*

Old Lady Gang

$$$ | **SOUTHERN** | Kandi Burruss-Tucker (of *Real Housewives of Atlanta* fame) brings the flavors and hospitality of her Georgia upbringing to this Castleberry Hill hot spot, serving generous portions of soul food staples in a relaxed setting. Despite its reality-TV roots, the decor and atmosphere are homey here, and you'll be tempted to stay all day. **Known for:** chicken and French toast; fried deviled eggs; all-day Sunday brunch. $ *Average main: $20* ✉ *177 Peters St. SW, Castleberry Hill* ☎ *404/748–9689* 🌐 *oldladygang.com.*

Slutty Vegan

$$ | **AMERICAN** | ATLiens (both meat eating and vegan) were delighted when this popular food truck expanded to a brick-and-mortar Westview location in early 2019. The mission behind its coquettish name is to prove that plant eaters can still indulge in good, rich food, and, with a menu of charbroiled Impossible Burgers loaded with special sauce, vegan cheese, sweet plantains and more, Slutty Vegan achieves just that. **Known for:** vegan burgers as good as the real thing; fun atmosphere; long waits. $ *Average main: $15* ✉ *1542 Ralph David Abernathy Blvd., West End* ☎ *855/439–7588* 🌐 *sluttyveganatl.com.*

Ted's Montana Grill

$$$$ | **AMERICAN** | The Ted in question is CNN founder Ted Turner, who has left a significant mark on this city, and Atlantans feel a sense of ownership for this chain specializing in bison meat. Tin ceilings, a cheerful waitstaff, and mahogany paneling add to the comfortable feel. **Known for:** bison and beef burgers; cozy, clubhouse feel; its famous founder. $ *Average main: $25* ✉ *133 Luckie St. NW, Downtown* ☎ *404/521–9796* 🌐 *www.tedsmontanagrill.com.*

Hotels

Atlanta Marriott Marquis
$$ | **HOTEL** | Immense and coolly contemporary, the building seems to go on forever as you stand under the lobby's huge fabric sculpture, which hangs from the skylighted roof 47 stories above. **Pros:** great views; convenient to public transportation; lively atmosphere. **Cons:** lobby noise can carry to the lower floors; daily parking starts at $45 a day; unusually crowded during September's Dragon Con festival. *Rooms from: $150 ✉ 265 Peachtree Center Ave., Downtown ☎ 404/521–0000, 888/855–5701 🌐 www.marriott.com 1,663 rooms No meals.*

★ The Candler
$$ | **HOTEL** | History abounds in this Downtown hotel that was once a building owned by Asa Griggs Candler, founder of the Coca-Cola Company. **Pros:** National Register of Historic Places building with modern conveniences; celebrity chef Hugh Acheson as culinary director; Gold Key Awards for Excellence in Hospitality Design nominee. **Cons:** area can be busy when Georgia State University is in session; Woodruff Park homeless; main entrance off side street can be confusing. *Rooms from: $200 ✉ 127 Peachtree St., Downtown ☎ 404/523–1200 🌐 www.hilton.com/en/curio/ 265 rooms No meals.*

★ Ellis Hotel
$$$ | **HOTEL** | A chic lobby, handpicked modern furnishings, and thoughtful in-room touches are the hallmark of this boutique hotel that provides Southern hospitality in a restored 1913 historic landmark. **Pros:** top-of-the line 24-hour fitness center; farm-to-table dining options; close to MARTA stop. **Cons:** some street noise in rooms; no free breakfast; more expensive than other Downtown hotels. *Rooms from: $239 ✉ 176 Peachtree St. NE, Downtown ☎ 404/523–5155 🌐 www.ellishotel.com 127 rooms No meals.*

Glenn Hotel
$$$ | **HOTEL** | This boutique hotel is a mix of New York sophistication and Miami sex appeal. **Pros:** 24-hour business center; walking distance to State Farm Arena and Centennial Olympic Park; rooftop bar with great city views. **Cons:** parking is $40 per night; lighting might be a bit dim for some guests; small rooms. *Rooms from: $240 ✉ 110 Marietta St. NW, Downtown ☎ 404/521–2250, 888/717–8851 🌐 www.glennhotel.com 110 rooms No meals.*

Omni Hotel at CNN Center
$$ | **HOTEL** | An ultramodern marble lobby overlooks Centennial Olympic Park through floor-to-ceiling windows in this sleek two-tower hotel next to CNN's headquarters. **Pros:** convenient location for Downtown tourists; near public transportation; great view of the park from public areas. **Cons:** convention crowds are the norm; heavy traffic during rush hour and State Farm Arena events; $45 per day for parking. *Rooms from: $170 ✉ 100 CNN Center, Downtown ☎ 404/659–0000, 888/444–6664 🌐 www.omnihotels.com 1,067 rooms No meals.*

Ritz-Carlton, Atlanta
$$$ | **HOTEL** | For a luxury experience with useful business amenities, the Ritz can't be beat. **Pros:** top-notch restaurant; ideal for doing business Downtown; impeccable service. **Cons:** the standard rooms can feel small and dated compared to newer options; very expensive; classic decor not for everyone. *Rooms from: $230 ✉ 181 Peachtree St., Downtown ☎ 404/659–0400, 800/542–8680 🌐 www.ritzcarlton.com/en/hotels/georgia/atlanta 444 rooms No meals.*

Sheraton Atlanta
$$ | **HOTEL** | **FAMILY** | In this convention-, family-, and pet-friendly hotel, there's ample meeting and exhibit space, a pool under a retractable roof, and fine dining with delicious takes on Southern fare. **Pros:** convenient location; kid-friendly vibe; large, nicely furnished rooms.

Cons: can be difficult to navigate towers; not everyone enjoys the family-friendly atmosphere; no free breakfast. *Rooms from: $200* *165 Courtland St. NE, Downtown* *404/659–6500* *www.sheratonatlantahotel.com* *763 rooms* *No meals.*

Shopping

ART GALLERIES

Eyedrum

ART GALLERIES | Started more than 20 years ago, this music and gallery space is always on the cutting edge. Its new location continues the mix of avant garde international musical acts, beloved locals, and mind-opening—and sometimes mind-bending—visual art that has kept it indispensable in the Atlanta arts scene. *515 Ralph David Abernathy Blvd., Downtown* *www.eyedrum.org.*

Marcia Wood Gallery

ART GALLERIES | This gallery sells contemporary paintings, sculpture, and photography. *263 Walker St., Castleberry Hill* *404/827–0030* *www.marciawoodgallery.com.*

MINT Gallery

ART GALLERIES | This quaint, nonprofit art space is located in the always evolving Met Atlanta, a 100-year-old gem that's home to creatives and revolving food pop-ups. MINT hosts monthly, ever-changing exhibits, full of local and non-local artists alike who work in mediums from experimental to interactive and more. MINT's goals are for people to truly engage with art and to draw attention to new and emerging talent. As the first W.A.G.E.-certified organization in Georgia, the gallery focuses on regulating the payment of artist fees by nonprofit art institutions. *680 Murphy Ave. SW, No. 2095, Downtown* *www.mintatl.org.*

Activities

BASKETBALL

Atlanta Hawks

BASKETBALL | The Hawks play Downtown in State Farm Arena. *State Farm Arena, 1 State Farm Dr., Downtown* *404/878–3000* *www.nba.com/hawks.*

FOOTBALL

Atlanta Falcons

FOOTBALL | The Atlanta Falcons have played at the huge Mercedes-Benz Stadium since 2017. Their former stadium, the Georgia Dome, was razed to create a parking deck to accommodate the increasing number of fans and tailgaters. In July and August, training camp is held in Flowery Branch, about 40 miles north of Atlanta. There's no charge to watch an open practice session. *1 AMB Dr., Downtown* *470/341–5000* *www.atlantafalcons.com.*

SOCCER

Atlanta United FC

SOCCER | The Atlanta United soccer team was somewhat forgettable when the club started in 2014, but its popularity has skyrocketed in the years since. Its fan base is strong, often filling Mercedes-Benz Stadium with rambunctious energy. The hype grew exponentially when Atlanta United won the Major League Soccer Cup in 2018. Like the Atlanta Falcons football team that plays at the stadium, Atlanta United is owned by Home Depot cofounder Arthur Blank. *1 AMB Dr. NW, Downtown* *470/341–1500* *www.atlutd.com.*

Sweet Auburn, the Old Fourth Ward, and East Atlanta

Between 1890 and 1930, the Sweet Auburn district was Atlanta's most active and prosperous center of black business, entertainment, and political life. Following the Depression, the area went into an economic decline that lasted until the 1980s, when the residential area where civil rights leader Martin Luther King Jr. (1929–68) was born, raised, and later returned to live was declared a National Historic District. Nearby, the Old Fourth Ward and the East Atlanta area have mostly benefited from slow gentrification. Both are nightlife hot spots and home to some beautifully restored houses. Count Grant Park in that number, too, with its lovingly renovated bungalows and Victorians, many of which edge Grant Park itself, one of the city's green-space gems, which houses the Atlanta zoo.

Sights

African American Panoramic Experience (APEX)

MUSEUM | The museum's quarterly exhibits chronicle the history of black people in America. Videos illustrate the story of Sweet Auburn, the name bestowed on Auburn Avenue by businessman John Wesley Dobbs, who fostered business development for African Americans on this street. **■ TIP→ Make a day of visiting APEX and the Auburn Avenue Research Library, with lunch at the Sweet Auburn Market. All three are within a short walking distance.** ✉ *135 Auburn Ave., Sweet Auburn* ☎ *404/523–2739* 🌐 *www.apexmuseum.org* 🎟 *$8* ⏲ *Closed Sun. and Mon.*

Auburn Avenue Research Library on African American Culture and History

LIBRARY | An extension of the Atlanta-Fulton Public Library, this unit houses a noncirculating collection of about 60,000 books of African American interest. The archives contain art and artifacts, transcribed oral histories, and rare books, pamphlets, and periodicals. There are three galleries with rotating exhibits, and frequent special events, all of them free. ✉ *101 Auburn Ave. NE, Sweet Auburn* ☎ *404/613–4001* 🌐 *www.afpls.org/aarl.*

East Atlanta Village

NEIGHBORHOOD | This earthy outpost of edgy-cool shops, restaurants, bars, and concert venues started growing, beginning in 1996, thanks to a group of proprietors with dreams much bigger than their bank accounts. Spurning the high rents of fancier parts of town, they set up businesses in this then-blighted but beautiful ruin of a neighborhood 4 miles southeast of Downtown. Soon artists and others came to soak up the creative atmosphere. East Atlanta, which is centered at Flat Shoals and Glenwood Avenues, just southeast of Moreland Avenue at Interstate 20, has had its ups and downs but has experienced a resurgence. Many of the majestic homes have been renovated, and what remains untouched romanticizes the area's gritty appeal. ✉ *Flat Shoals and Glenwood Aves., East Atlanta.*

★ Ebenezer Baptist Church

RELIGIOUS SITE | A Gothic Revival–style building completed in 1922, the church came to be known as the spiritual center of the civil rights movement. Members of the King family, including the slain civil rights leader, preached at the church for three generations. Sitting in the main sanctuary on a quiet day when light is shining through the stained-glass windows can be a powerful experience. The congregation itself now occupies the building across the street. ✉ *407 Auburn Ave. NE, Sweet Auburn* ☎ *404/331–5190* 🌐 *www.nps.gov/malu* 🎟 *Free.*

Dr. Martin Luther King Jr. was born and raised in this modest Queen Anne–style house.

The King Center

MUSEUM | The Martin Luther King Jr. National Historic District occupies several blocks on Auburn Avenue, east of Peachtree Street in the black business and residential community of Sweet Auburn. Martin Luther King Jr. was born here in 1929; after his assassination in 1968, his widow, Coretta Scott King, established this center, which exhibits such personal items as King's Nobel Peace Prize, Bible, and tape recorder, along with memorabilia and photos chronicling the civil rights movement. In the courtyard in front of Freedom Hall, on a circular brick pad in the middle of the rectangular Meditation Pool, is Dr. King's white-marble tomb; the inscription reads, "Free at last, free at last, thank God almighty I'm free at last." Nearby, an eternal flame burns. A chapel of all faiths sits at one end of the reflecting pool. Mrs. King, who passed away in 2006, is also entombed at the center. ✉ *449 Auburn Ave. NE, Sweet Auburn* ☎ *404/526–8900* 🌐 *www.thekingcenter.org* 🎫 *Free.*

★ Martin Luther King Jr. National Historic Site and Birth Home

HISTORIC SITE | The modest Queen Anne–style residence is where Martin Luther King Jr. was born and raised. Besides items that belonged to the family, the house contains an outstanding multimedia exhibit focused on the civil rights movement. **■ TIP→ A limited number of visitors are allowed to tour the house each day. Advance reservations are not possible, so sign up early in the day.** ✉ *501 Auburn Ave., Sweet Auburn* ☎ *404/331–5190* 🌐 *www.nps.gov/malu* 🎫 *Free.*

Oakland Cemetery

CEMETERY | Established in 1850 in the Victorian style, Atlanta's oldest cemetery was designed to serve as a public park as well as a burial ground. Some of the 70,000 permanent residents include six governors, five Confederate generals, and 6,900 Confederate soldiers. Also here are novelist Margaret Mitchell and golfing great Bobby Jones. You can bring a picnic lunch or take a tour conducted by the Historic Oakland Foundation. The

King Memorial MARTA station on the east–west line also serves the cemetery. ✉ *248 Oakland Ave. SE, Grant Park* ☎ *404/688–2107* 🌐 *www.oaklandcemetery.com* 🎟 *Tours $12.*

Sweet Auburn Curb Market
MARKET | The market, an institution on Edgewood Avenue since 1924, sells flowers, fruits, and vegetables, and a variety of meats—everything from fresh catfish to foot-long oxtails. Vendors also include local favorites Bell Street Burritos and Sweet Auburn BBQ. Individual stalls are run by a diverse set of owners, making this a true public market—especially significant now, considering that Atlanta's black residents were forced to sell their wares on the curb in the market's early days. ✉ *209 Edgewood Ave., Sweet Auburn* ☎ *404/659–1665* 🌐 *www.thecurbmarket.com* ⏲ *Closed Sun.*

Zoo Atlanta
ZOO | **FAMILY** | This zoo has more than 1,500 animals and 200 species from around the world living in naturalistic habitats. The gorillas and tigers are always a hit, as are giant pandas named Yang Yang and Lun Lun. Children can ride the Nabisco Endangered Species Carousel and meet new friends at the petting zoo, and the whole family can take a ride on the Zoo Train. ✉ *800 Cherokee Ave. SE, Grant Park* ☎ *404/624–5600* 🌐 *www.zooatlanta.org* 🎟 *$27–$30.*

Restaurants

Argosy
$ | **AMERICAN** | Dark wood and a welcoming vibe make this cavernous bar with above-average food and a well-curated beer menu feel like a place you can sink into and stay awhile. Ask for their favorite bottled or on-tap brew, or take them up on an offer to sample one that's piqued your interest. **Known for:** massive beer list; wood-oven pizzas; boozy brunch. 💲 *Average main: $12* ✉ *470 Flat Shoals Ave., East Atlanta* ☎ *404/577–0407* 🌐 *www.argosy-east.com.*

Banshee
$$ | **ECLECTIC** | With a food menu inspired by a range of cultures, from Italian to Native American, and a cocktail menu directed by some of Atlanta's best barkeeps, this boutique eatery brings a level of sophistication to an otherwise pub-heavy scene. Rose gold pendant lights and rich blue hues, which tint the heavy velvet drapes separating the bar from the small dining area, give the place a serious bent, but the mini dinosaur figurines tucked away in unexpected spots let you know it's fine to relax and "enjoy yourself"—and a pink neon lighted sign mounted against a hallway wall encourages visitors to do just that. **Known for:** owners who are vets of the Atlanta bar and dining scene; fry bread with pepperoni butter; tight quarters. 💲 *Average main: $15* ✉ *1271 Glenwood Ave., East Atlanta* ☎ *470/428–2034* 🌐 *www.banshee-atl.com* ⏲ *Closed Sun. and Mon.*

The Earl
$ | **AMERICAN** | Scrappy and lots of fun, this bar has a hearty menu of classic pub food. A favorite here is the Greenie Meanie Chicken, a grilled chicken breast topped with roasted poblano peppers and salsa verde. **Known for:** classic bar food; indie-rock atmosphere thanks to live music; smoky atmosphere, especially on weekends. 💲 *Average main: $9* ✉ *488 Flat Shoals Ave., East Atlanta* ☎ *404/522–3950* 🌐 *badearl.com.*

Gunshow
$$ | **ECLECTIC** | Experience a range of tastes at this Southern-style dim sum outpost founded by former *Top Chef* contestant Kevin Gillespie. The menus change frequently, as do the chefs who prepare twists on Southern staples, such as a black-eyed peas fritter. **Known for:** the only experience like it in Atlanta; somewhat awkward moments when refusing a dish; everything à la carte. 💲 *Average main: $18* ✉ *924 Garrett St.,*

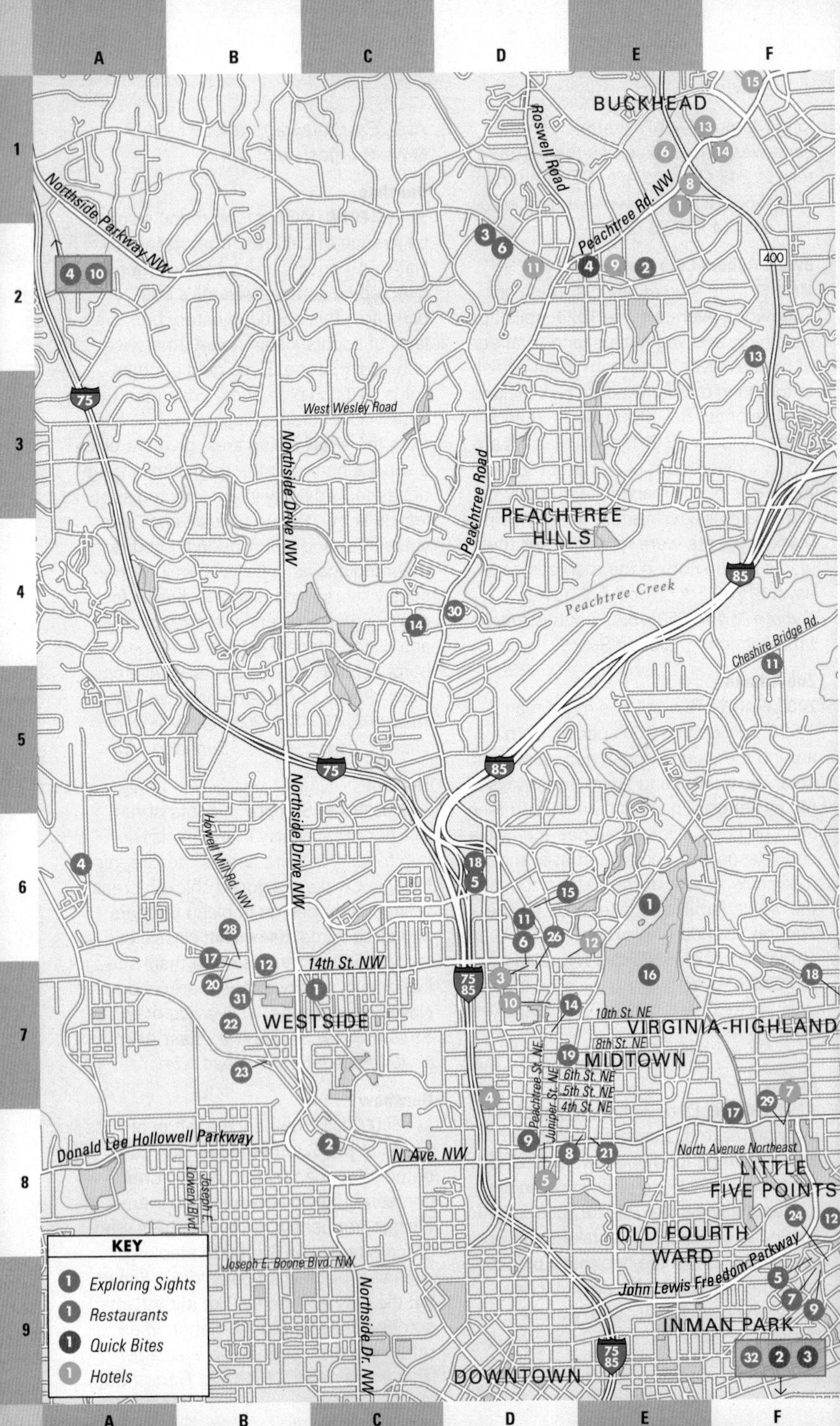
A
B
C
D
E
F
1
2
3
4
5
6
7
8
9
BUCKHEAD
Roswell Road
Peachtree Rd. NW
Northside Parkway NW
400
75
West Wesley Road
Northside Drive NW
Peachtree Road
PEACHTREE HILLS
85
Peachtree Creek
Cheshire Bridge Rd.
Howell Mill Rd. NW
14th St. NW
WESTSIDE
10th St. NE
VIRGINIA-HIGHLAND
8th St. NE
MIDTOWN
6th St. NE
5th St. NE
4th St. NE
Peachtree St. NE
Juniper St. NE
Donald Lee Hollowell Parkway
N. Ave. NW
North Avenue Northeast
LITTLE FIVE POINTS
Joseph E. Lowery Blvd.
OLD FOURTH WARD
John Lewis Freedom Parkway
Joseph E. Boone Blvd. NW
Northside Dr. NW
INMAN PARK
DOWNTOWN
KEY
Exploring Sights
Restaurants
Quick Bites
Hotels

Sights

1 Atlanta Botanical Garden........ E6
2 Atlanta Contemporary........ C8
3 Atlanta History Center........ D2
4 The Battery Atlanta........ A2
5 Center For Puppetry Arts........ D6
6 Cyclorama: The Big Picture........ D2
7 Fernbank Museum of Natural History........ I8
8 Fernbank Science Center........ I7
9 Fox Theatre........ D8
10 Freedom Park Trail........ G8
11 High Museum of Art........ D6
12 Jimmy Carter Presidential Library and Museum........ F8
13 Michael C. Carlos Museum........ I6
14 Museum of Contemporary Art of Georgia (MOCA GA)........ C4
15 Museum of Design Atlanta........ D6
16 Piedmont Park........ E7
17 Ponce City Market........ F8
18 The William Breman Jewish Heritage and Holocaust Museum........ D6

Restaurants

1 Antico Pizza Napoletana........ C7
2 Aria........ E2
3 Babette's Cafe........ G8
4 Bacchanalia........ A6
5 Barcelona........ F9
6 Bar Margot........ D7
7 Bartaco........ F9
8 Bon Ton........ E8
9 Bread and Butterfly........ F9
10 Canoe........ A2
11 Colonnade........ F4
12 Cooks & Soldiers........ B7
13 Eclipse di Luna........ F2
14 Empire State South........ D7
15 Flying Biscuit........ H8
16 Fox Bros. Bar-B-Q........ G9
17 JCT Kitchen and Bar........ B7
18 La Tavola Trattoria........ G7
19 The Lawrence........ D7
20 Marcel........ B7
21 Mary Mac's Tea Room........ E8
22 Miller Union........ B7
23 The Optimist........ B7
24 Sotto Sotto........ F9
25 Soul Vegetarian Restaurant No. 2........ G8
26 South City Kitchen........ D7
27 Sweet Auburn Barbecue........ G8
28 Taqueria del Sol........ B6
29 Tiny Lou's........ F8
30 Varasano's Pizzeria........ D4
31 West Egg Café........ B7
32 Wonderkid........ F9

Quick Bites

1 Dr. Bombay's Underwater Tea Party........ H8
2 Muchacho........ F9
3 Proof Bakeshop........ F9
4 Southern Baked Pie Company........ E2

Hotels

1 Embassy Suites Hotel........ E1
2 Emory Conference Center Hotel........ I5
3 Four Seasons Hotel........ D7
4 Georgia Tech Hotel and Conference Center........ D7
5 Georgian Terrace........ D8
6 Hilton Garden Inn Atlanta - Buckhead........ E1
7 Hotel Clermont........ F8
8 InterContinental Buckhead Atlanta........ E1
9 Kimpton Sylvan Hotel........ E2
10 Loews Atlanta Hotel........ D7
11 The St. Regis Atlanta........ D2
12 W Atlanta - Midtown........ D6
13 Waldorf Astoria Atlanta Buckhead........ E1
14 Westin Buckhead Atlanta........ F1
15 The Whitley........ F1

Suite C, East Atlanta ☎ 404/380–1886 🌐 gunshowatl.com 🕙 Closed Sun.–Wed.

Holy Taco

$$ | MEXICAN | Don't fill up on the tortilla chips at this Tex-Mex joint. They are so tasty that you might miss the rest of the menu, which includes vegan and vegetarian options, as well as standards like fish tacos and fajitas. **Known for:** inventive takes on Tex-Mex; organic margaritas with fresh ingredients; patio dining on sunny days. *$ Average main: $15 ✉ 1314 Glenwood Ave., East Atlanta ☎ 404/230–6177 🌐 www.holy-taco.com.*

Home grown

$ | DINER | Southern comfort food at its finest can be found at this bright, old-school diner. Cheese grits with a good cheddar bite, fluffy biscuits that can be stuffed with anything from sausage and gravy to perfectly fried chicken, and hunks of made-from-scratch cake are just a few of the reasons locals flock to Home grown. **Known for:** huge Southern breakfasts, lunches, and brunches; in-house thrift store; long waits, especially in the morning. *$ Average main: $10 ✉ 968 Memorial Dr. SE, Reynoldstown ☎ 404/222–0455 🌐 www.homegrownga.com 🕙 No dinner.*

Staplehouse

$$ | AMERICAN | Staplehouse was a true staple of Atlanta, with its 2016 James Beard finalist for Best New Restaurant and charitable status widely known. In 2020, the lauded restaurant became a market. **Known for:** high-quality foods that are always made fresh; unique global wine list; relaxing outdoor space. *$ Average main: $15 ✉ 541 Edgewood Ave., Old Fourth Ward ☎ 404/524–5005 🌐 www.staplehouse.com 🕙 Closed Mon.–Thurs.*

Thumb's Up Diner

$ | DINER | You haven't really lived, or at least tested the limits of your heart's health, until you've tried the Heap: a sizzling skillet full of eggs, buttery veggies, and potatoes. Add a fluffy biscuit on the side, and this is one of the city's best breakfasts. **Known for:** fluffy and delicious biscuits; long weekend waits; a diverse mix of locals. *$ Average main: $10 ✉ 573 Edgewood Ave. SE, Old Fourth Ward ☎ 404/223–0690 🌐 www.thumbsupdiner.com 💳 No credit cards ☞ No dinner. Cash only.*

Coffee and Quick Bites

Chrome Yellow Trading Co.

$ | AMERICAN | If you're looking for a pit stop after exploring all Edgewood Avenue, the BeltLine, or Krog Street Market has to offer, Chrome Yellow has you covered. This cool coffee shop hides within a generic black brick building, but once you walk inside, its aesthetic really shines with white paint, industrial metal, and light wood decor. **Known for:** Instagram-worthy design and look; quality coffee and seasonal drinks; walkable location. *$ Average main: $6 ✉ 501 Edgewood Ave. SE, Sweet Auburn ☎ 470/355–1340 🌐 www.chromeyellowtradingco.com.*

Hodgepodge Coffeehouse

$ | AMERICAN | Hodgepodge embodies East Atlanta flair with its murals, free-food fridge, and artsy interior. The baked goods are made from scratch and always local, and the coffee and tea options are numerous. **Known for:** supporting the local community; friendly staff; seasonal drinks with fun names. *$ Average main: $4 ✉ 720 Moreland Ave. SE, East Atlanta ☎ 404/622–8525 🌐 www.hodgepodgecoffee.com.*

Lottafrutta

$ | AMERICAN | Smoothies, fruit cups, and sandwiches—Lottafrutta has a fresh take on them all, and the brilliant colors of the exterior mimic the hues you'll find in those tasty fruit cups. If you prefer a smoothie, options are plentiful. **Known for:** abundance of fruit-related foods; eye-catching outdoor seating and signage; always vibrant vibes. $ *Average main: $6* ✉ *590 Auburn Ave. NE, Sweet Auburn* ☎ *404/588–0857* 🌐 *www.lottafrutta.com.*

Nightlife

529

MUSIC CLUBS | A cavelike bar that opens up into a live music venue with great sound and a patio, 529 hosts local and national emerging indie bands. ✉ *529 Flat Shoals Ave., East Atlanta* ☎ *404/228–6769* 🌐 *www.529atlanta.com.*

Mary's

BARS/PUBS | One of the best gay bars in Atlanta, the divey and fun Mary's is known for its "Mary-oke" karaoke night. ✉ *1287 Glenwood Ave., East Atlanta* ☎ *404/624–4411* 🌐 *www.marysatlanta.com.*

Old Fourth Distillery

BARS/PUBS | Inside a historic building in Atlanta's Old Fourth Ward, Old Fourth Distillery makes vodka, gin, bourbon, and a "Lawn Dart" lemon liqueur. A distillery tour includes tastings of each. The Locker Club, a weekend cocktail lounge inside the distillery's sleek, vintage-inspired tasting room, is a throwback to the pre-Prohibition private drinking clubs once popular in Atlanta. A revolving menu of cocktails exclusively feature O4D spirits, with canned Old Fashioneds, spiked lemonade slushies, and gin served with house-made tonic. ✉ *487 Edgewood Ave. SE, Old Fourth Ward* ☎ *844/653–3687* 🌐 *www.o4d.com.*

Sister Louisa's Church of the Living Room & Ping Pong Emporium

BARS/PUBS | Folk art meets gay pride meets sangria here at "Church" (as this popular dive bar is known), which has nun mannequins in full habit dangling from the ceiling and choir robes for patrons should the spirit move them. There's also an outdoor patio and a spacious second floor with a Ping-Pong table. ✉ *466 Edgewood Ave. SE, Old Fourth Ward* ☎ *404/522–8275* 🌐 *www.sisterlouisaschurch.com.*

Performing Arts

Dad's Garage Theatre Company

THEATER | Founded in 1995, this scrappy playhouse with a sense of humor offers a variety of comedy and improv classes and performances as well as original theatrical works. ✉ *569 Ezzard St., Old Fourth Ward* ☎ *404/523–3141* 🌐 *www.dadsgarage.com.*

Midtown and the Westside

Midtown Atlanta—north of Downtown and south of Buckhead—has a skyline of gleaming office towers that rivals Downtown's. Its renovated mansions and bungalows have made it a city showcase, and so has Piedmont Park and the Atlanta Botanical Garden. It's also the location of the Woodruff Arts Center, one of the largest performing-arts centers in the country, and roughly 20 other arts and cultural venues, including the Museum of Design Atlanta and the Atlanta campus of the Savannah College of Art and Design (SCAD). The neighborhood is the hub for the city's sizable gay community.

The Westside, once considered a part of Midtown, has earned its own identity. Here you'll find some of the city's best and most sophisticated restaurants as well as the Atlanta Contemporary Art Center.

Sights

★ **Atlanta Botanical Garden**

GARDEN | **FAMILY** | Occupying 30 acres inside Piedmont Park, the grounds contain acres of display gardens, including a 2-acre interactive children's garden; the Fuqua Conservatory, which has unusual flora from tropical and desert climates;

and the award-winning Fuqua Orchid Center. Check out the view from the Canopy Walk, a 600-foot suspension bridge 40 feet above Storza Woods. A variety of special exhibits take place throughout the year. ✉ *1345 Piedmont Ave. NE, Midtown* ☎ *404/876–5859* 🌐 *atlantabg.org* 🎫 *$22.95–$24.95* ⏲ *Closed Mon.*

Atlanta Contemporary

MUSEUM | Established by a group of photographers in the '70s as the arts co-op Nexus, Atlanta Contemporary is an arts center that exhibits edgy contemporary art. It has the feel of a sophisticated gallery, but the programming is approachable, and its annual Art Party is not to be missed. ✉ *535 Means St. NW, Downtown* ☎ *404/688–1970* 🌐 *www.atlantacontemporary.org* 🎫 *Free* ⏲ *Closed Mon.*

★ **Center for Puppetry Arts**

ARTS VENUE | **FAMILY** | The largest puppetry organization in the country houses a museum where you can see more than 350 puppets from around the world. The elaborate performances include original works and classics adapted for stage. Kids also love the create-a-puppet workshops. The Jim Henson Museum at the Center for Puppetry Arts houses most of the famed puppeteer's collection and includes rooms that re-create his early days, like his office and workshop. ✉ *1404 Spring St. NW, Midtown* ✣ *At 18th St.* ☎ *404/873–3391* 🌐 *www.puppet.org* 🎫 *$15* ⏲ *Closed Mon.–Wed.*

★ **Fox Theatre**

ARTS VENUE | One of a dwindling number of vintage movie palaces in the nation, the Fox was built in 1929 in a fabulous Moorish-Egyptian style. The interior's crowning glory is its ceiling, complete with moving clouds and twinkling stars above Alhambra-like minarets. Threatened by demolition in the 1970s, the Fox was saved from the wrecking ball by community activists. Today it hosts musicals, rock concerts, dance performances, and film festivals—with an optional rooftop VIP experience at the reservations-only Marquee Club. ■ **TIP→ Tours should be scheduled in advance.** ✉ *660 Peachtree St. NE, Midtown* ☎ *404/881–2100 for box office* 🌐 *www.foxtheatre.org* 🎫 *Tours $18.*

High Museum of Art

MUSEUM | This museum's permanent collection includes 19th- and 20th-century American works, including many by African American artists. It also has some stellar examples of contemporary and outsider art—don't miss the works by the self-taught artist Rev. Howard Finster. The building itself is a work of art; the American Institute of Architects listed the sleek structure, designed by Richard Meier, among the 10 best works of American architecture of the 1980s. An expansion designed by Renzo Piano doubled the museum's size to 312,000 square feet with three new aluminum-paneled buildings. The roof features a system of 1,000 "light scoops" that filter light into the skyway galleries. The High often partners with other major museums, including the Louvre and New York's Museum of Modern Art. ✉ *Woodruff Arts Center, 1280 Peachtree St. NE, Midtown* ☎ *404/733–4400* 🌐 *www.high.org* 🎫 *$15* ⏲ *Closed Mon.*

Museum of Design Atlanta

MUSEUM | The only museum in the Southeast devoted exclusively to design mounts exhibits on fashion, graphics, architecture, furniture, and product design. The eco-friendly building is located just across the street from the High Museum of Art. ✉ *1315 Peachtree St., Midtown* ☎ *404/979–6455* 🌐 *www.museumofdesign.org* 🎫 *$10* ⏲ *Closed Mon.*

★ **Piedmont Park**

CITY PARK | **FAMILY** | A popular destination since the late 19th century, Piedmont Park is the perfect place to escape the chaos of the city. Tennis courts, a swimming pool, a popular dog park, and paths for walking, jogging, and rollerblading are part of the attraction, but many retreat to the park's great lawn for picnics with a smashing view of the Midtown skyline. ✉ *10th St. between Piedmont Ave. and Monroe Dr., Midtown* ☎ *404/875–7275* 🌐 *www.piedmontpark.org.*

★ Ponce City Market

MARKET | The old Sears, Roebuck & Co. building built in 1925 has transformed into Atlanta's hippest place to live, work, shop, and play, especially with the addition of a mini–amusement park on the roof. The historic property is adjacent to the BeltLine, with easy access to several neighborhoods. The 2-million-square-foot development—led by the same group who brought NYC's Chelsea Market to life—is LEED Gold certified. Eco-friendliness aside, the real draw is the food hall. Walk through the crowds and among industrial-style spiral staircases and original concrete columns to devour coveted burgers from Holeman and Finch; Southern-style fried chicken at Hop's; and raw oysters from W. H. Stiles Fish Camp. The Dancing Goats Coffee Bar stays busy, especially when City Winery, a music venue and restaurant in its own right, is hosting events. The rooftop amusement park has all-ages favorites such as skeeball and minigolf. ✉ *675 Ponce de Leon Ave., Old Fourth Ward* ☎ *404/900–7900* 🌐 *www.poncecitymarket.com* 🎟 *Skyline Park $15.*

The William Breman Jewish Heritage and Holocaust Museum

MUSEUM | The history of the Jewish community in Atlanta—particularly those who found their way to the burgeoning city after the Holocaust—is told through a permanent exhibit called *Absence of Humanity: The Holocaust Years, 1933–1945*. The facility is the largest archive of Georgia Jewish history and also contains a research library and an education center. ✉ *1440 Spring St. NW, Midtown* ☎ *678/222–3700* 🌐 *www.thebreman.org* 🎟 *$12* 🕒 *Closed Sat.*

Restaurants

★ Antico Pizza Napoletana

$$$ | **PIZZA** | Antico offers a big slice of cheesy, saucy, chewy, Naples-style heaven. The communal tables, as well as the Italian opera on the stereo, give the place a convivial vibe. **Known for:** authentic Naples-style pizza; communal tables; no substitutions on toppings. 💲 *Average main: $20* ✉ *1093 Hemphill Ave., Midtown* ☎ *404/724–2333* 🌐 *littleitalia.com.*

★ Bacchanalia

$$$$ | **AMERICAN** | Often called the city's best restaurant, Bacchanalia focuses on locally grown organic produce and seasonal ingredients. The current Westside location, a renovated warehouse with 20-foot ceilings, is decorated in deep, inviting tones. **Known for:** splurge-worthy fine dining; farm-to-table ingredients; excellent wine pairings. 💲 *Average main: $85* ✉ *1460 Ellsworth Industrial Blvd. NW, Midtown* ☎ *404/365–0410* 🌐 *www.starprovisions.com* 🕒 *Closed Sun. No lunch.*

Bar Margot

$$$$ | **AMERICAN** | This swanky hotel lounge features a seasonal menu made up of small plates meant to be shared, such as Georgia-sourced cheese and charcuterie, oysters of the moment, and more indulgent offerings like a 16-hour braised short rib. Don't miss the cocktails dreamed up by one of Atlanta's best mixologists, Paul Calvert. **Known for:** luxurious setting; well-crafted cocktails; upscale small plates. 💲 *Average main: $30* ✉ *Four Seasons, 75 14th St., Midtown* ☎ *404/881–5913* 🌐 *www.barmargotatl.com.*

Bon Ton

$ | **FUSION** | When you see the lilac building, you'll know you're in the right place. Inside, say hello to the giant neon sign that reads "Fancy Service," and settle into the eccentric atmosphere. **Known for:** unique fusion foods with an aesthetic to match; intimate space; vibrant vibe.

[$] *Average main: $12* ✉ *674 Myrtle St. NE, Midtown* ☎ *404/996–6177* 🌐 *www.bontonatl.com* ⏲ *No lunch weekdays.*

Cooks & Soldiers

$$$ | **SPANISH** | The goal of Cooks & Soldiers is to serve good yet elevated cuisine, and it succeeds. If you truly get to know someone when you've eaten with them, Cooks & Soldiers makes this possible with tapas, or *pintxos*, meant for sharing, and foods cooked on the *asador*, or wood-fired grill. **Known for:** Spanish tapas; classy interior; wine by the bottle. [$] *Average main: $20* ✉ *691 14th St. NW, Midtown* ☎ *404/996–2623* 🌐 *www.cooksandsoldiers.com.*

Empire State South

$$$$ | **SOUTHERN** | Southern ingredients get the fine-dining treatment without the pretension at the Midtown favorite owned by celebrity chef Hugh Acheson. Empire State South does it all: towering build-your-own breakfast biscuits, beautifully prepared Georgia trout with green beans and pimientos at dinner, and the perfect espresso. **Known for:** diverse wine list; Southern food with flair; extensive coffee bar and coffee menu. [$] *Average main: $30* ✉ *999 Peachtree St., Midtown* ☎ *404/541–1105* 🌐 *empirestatesouth.com* ⏲ *Closed Sun. and Mon.*

JCT Kitchen and Bar

$$$$ | **SOUTHERN** | This comfortable, airy restaurant—with pale wood, white, and silver accents—is part of the now-bustling Westside Provisions District. JCT, a "farmstead bistro" with Southern flair, is a great place for a business-casual lunch or a dinner date. The deviled eggs are to die for, as are the perfectly crisp truffle-Parmesan fries. **Known for:** deviled eggs and truffle Parm fries; fancy yet comfortable vibe; outdoor patio with awesome city views. [$] *Average main: $25* ✉ *1198 Howell Mill Rd., Suite 18, Midtown* ☎ *404/355–2252* 🌐 *www.jctkitchen.com.*

The Lawrence

$$ | **AMERICAN** | The noncorporate upscale pub food at the Lawrence has become a staple in the Midtown neighborhood. Dinner options such as king salmon served with spätzle hash and bacon; oyster po'boys dressed with house tartar sauce; and classic burgers with frites reflect the straightforward menu at this buzzing establishment. **Known for:** creative cocktail menu; one of the best no-fuss burgers in the city; great brunch with patio dining. [$] *Average main: $18* ✉ *905 Juniper St. NE, Midtown* ☎ *404/961–7178* 🌐 *www.thelawrenceatlanta.com* ⏲ *No lunch weekdays.*

★ Marcel

$$$$ | **AMERICAN** | You'd never expect to be treated to such an expansive, fine-dining experience from the corner of Westside Provisions District where Marcel resides. A traditional steak house by way of France—the restaurant's namesake was a French boxer—this place is a knockout in every sense. **Known for:** exceptional steaks; wine list with 500 well-selected options; potatoes four different ways. [$] *Average main: $40* ✉ *1170 Howell Mill Rd., Midtown* ☎ *404/665–4555* 🌐 *marcelatl.com.*

Mary Mac's Tea Room

$$ | **SOUTHERN** | Local celebrities and ordinary folks line up for the country-fried steak and fried chicken here. In the Southern tradition, the servers will call you "honey" and pat your arm to assure you that everything's all right. **Known for:** legendary Southern home cooking; friendly waitstaff; big portions. [$] *Average main: $15* ✉ *224 Ponce de Leon Ave., Midtown* ☎ *404/876–1800* 🌐 *www.marymacs.com.*

Miller Union

$$$$ | **AMERICAN** | The Southern-inflected menu here emphasizes locally sourced food. A highlight is the farm egg baked in celery cream with rustic bread; it's one of the best dishes in town. **Known for:** Southern classics, all with local

ingredients; sustainable, farm-friendly ethos; homemade ice cream sandwiches. *Average main: $26* *999 Brady Ave. NW, Midtown* *678/733–8550* *www.millerunion.com* *No lunch.*

The Optimist

$$$ | **SEAFOOD** | For top-notch seafood, head to this restaurant in a dazzlingly refurbished warehouse space. You can slurp raw oysters on the half shell from the oyster bar or dive into the seafood gumbo, which has dark, complex gravy and is full of meaty hunks of crab. **Known for:** upscale seafood dishes; cool industrial space; noisy crowds. *Average main: $23* *914 Howell Mill Rd., Midtown* *404/477–6260* *www.theoptimistrestaurant.com* *No lunch.*

South City Kitchen

$$$ | **SOUTHERN** | The culinary traditions of South Carolina inspire the dishes served at this cheerful restaurant. This is the place in the city to try out Southern staples like fried green tomatoes, she-crab soup, and buttermilk fried chicken. **Known for:** creatively prepared catfish; fried green tomatoes with goat cheese; hip, artsy crowd. *Average main: $20* *1144 Crescent Ave., Midtown* *404/873–7358* *midtown.southcitykitchen.com.*

Taquería del Sol

$ | **MEXICAN** | Don't let the long lines outside this counter-service eatery discourage you. They move quickly, and once you get in you'll be rewarded with a full bar, a wide selection of tacos and enchiladas, and unusual sides like spicy collard greens and jalapeño coleslaw. **Known for:** long lines and cutthroat table-grabbing; fresh salsa and guacamole; midday "siesta" that can frustrate those who lunch late. *Average main: $10* *1200-B Howell Mill Rd., Midtown* *404/352–5811* *www.taqueriadelsol.com* *Closed Sun. No dinner Mon.*

★ West Egg Café

$ | **AMERICAN** | West Egg is a great place to come for one of the city's best breakfasts, especially if you're staying in Midtown. It serves breakfast all day—locals swear by the blue-plate special and the old-fashioned oatmeal. **Known for:** excellent coffee; huge breakfasts served all day; big crowds. *Average main: $11* *1100 Howell Mill Rd., Midtown* *404/872–3973* *www.westeggcafe.com.*

Hotels

★ Four Seasons Hotel

$$$$ | **HOTEL** | Amenities abound throughout this luxury hotel, one of two five-star properties in Atlanta; these touches include marble bathrooms with extra-large soaking tubs, comfy mattresses, and brass chandeliers. **Pros:** great dining options; top-notch service; indoor saline pool. **Cons:** heavily trafficked area during rush hour; small bathrooms; fee for parking. *Rooms from: $500* *75 14th St. NE, Midtown* *404/881–9898* *www.fourseasons.com* *244 rooms* *No meals.*

Georgia Tech Hotel and Conference Center

$$ | **HOTEL** | In the heart of Midtown, this gleaming building gets kudos for its comfortable, contemporary decor, recently renovated rooms, and a staff that understands the needs of business travelers and meeting organizers. **Pros:** pleasant views of the skyline; walking distance to eateries and attractions; friendly, accommodating staff. **Cons:** short on charm; heavy student traffic when school's in session; lacks luxurious bedding and beds. *Rooms from: $189* *800 Spring St. NW, Midtown* *404/347–9440* *www.gatechhotel.com* *252 rooms* *No meals.*

Georgian Terrace

$$$ | **HOTEL** | Enrico Caruso and other stars of the Metropolitan Opera once stayed in this fine 1911 hotel across the street from the Fox Theatre. **Pros:** the front terrace is a great place for people-watching; proximity to the Fox makes upscale in-house restaurant Livingston a convenient pretheater choice; rooftop pool and penthouse-level fitness room offer incredible city views. **Cons:** rates more in line with legacy of hotel than accommodations; postshow and rush-hour traffic is tough to navigate; hotel is officially no-smoking but guests may smell smoke. *Rooms from: $210* ✉ *659 Peachtree St. NE, Midtown* ☎ *404/897–1991, 800/651–2316* 🌐 *www.thegeorgianterrace.com* *326 rooms* *No meals.*

★ **Loews Atlanta Hotel**

$$$ | **HOTEL** | Georgia's booming film industry brings plenty of celebs to Atlanta, and many of them stay in this sleek glass tower in the heart of bustling Midtown. **Pros:** huge and modern gym and spa; bright, modern rooms; many eateries and bars within walking distance. **Cons:** no pool; large fees for parking; short on complimentary courtesies, like in-room bottled water, expected at finer hotels. *Rooms from: $250* ✉ *1065 Peachtree St. NE, Midtown* ☎ *404/745–5000, 888/304–2514* 🌐 *www.loewshotels.com/atlanta* *414 rooms* *No meals.*

W Atlanta - Midtown

$$ | **HOTEL** | A trip to this trendy hotel in Midtown feels less like Atlanta and more like New York City, with slick details and more black-suited security guards and velvet ropes than seem necessary. **Pros:** exceptionally comfortable beds; gorgeous views; Manhattan-style chic. **Cons:** self-consciously hip theme can be a bit much; customer service can be spotty; daily fee for Wi-Fi. *Rooms from: $200* ✉ *188 14th St., Midtown* ☎ *404/892–6000* 🌐 *www.watlantamidtown.com* *466 rooms* *No meals.*

Nightlife

Blake's on the Park

CABARET | Weekly drag shows, a diverse crowd, and plenty of people-watching all help keep this place near the southwest corner of Piedmont Park popular. ✉ *227 10th St. NE, Midtown* ☎ *404/892–5786* 🌐 *www.blakesontheparkatlanta.com.*

Bulldogs

DANCE CLUBS | A fixture on the gay scene since 1978, Bulldogs is the place to hang out with friends or dance to hip-hop, house, or R&B. ✉ *893 Peachtree St., Midtown* ☎ *404/872–3025.*

Clermont Lounge

DANCE CLUBS | You may have heard of the infamous Clermont Lounge, a strip club unlike any other, but the women who rule the roost at this local landmark are older and sassier. On Saturday nights the dance floor opens up and the DJ plays old-school disco, funk, pop, and R&B. The well drinks are strong, and the clientele is cool—all making for a very entertaining night out in Atlanta. ✉ *789 Ponce de Leon Ave. NE, Midtown* ☎ *404/874–4783* 🌐 *clermontlounge.net.*

District

DANCE CLUBS | Located away from the main strip of Midtown bars, the warehouse-style exterior of this two-level club belies its upscale feel and fashionable crowd. A stellar sound system keeps the international DJs who play here pleased, while the waves of color-changing orbs above the main dance floor give the crowd a reason to smile. ✉ *269 Armour Dr., Midtown* ☎ *404/464–5924* 🌐 *www.districtatlanta.com.*

Laughing Skull Lounge

COMEDY CLUBS | These 73 seats in the back of the Vortex restaurant and bar are Atlanta's most popular destination for local and national touring comedians. ✉ *878 Peachtree St., Midtown* ☎ *404/369–1017* 🌐 *laughingskulllounge.com.*

My Sister's Room

BARS/PUBS | Billing itself as the city's "most diverse ladies' bar," this lesbian club brings the party with hip-hop, DJs, and karaoke. ✉ *84 12th St. NE, Midtown* ☎ *678/705–4585* 🌐 *www.mysistersroom.com.*

Smith's Olde Bar

MUSIC CLUBS | Smith's Olde Bar schedules different kinds of talent, both local and regional, in its acoustically fine performance space. Food is available in the downstairs restaurant. Covers vary depending on the act, but are usually $5 to $15. ✉ *1578 Piedmont Ave., Midtown* ☎ *404/875–1522* 🌐 *www.smithsoldebar.com.*

Swinging Richards

DANCE CLUBS | A gay male strip club, Swinging Richards draws a fun party crowd. Women are welcome, but bachelor and bachelorette parties are not. ✉ *1400 Northside Dr. NW, Midtown* ☎ *404/352–0532* 🌐 *www.swingingrichards.com.*

Terminal West

MUSIC CLUBS | Impeccable sound, balcony views, courteous bartenders, and plentiful parking make this Westside venue a top spot to see indie, soul, and EDM shows. ✉ *King Plow Arts Center, 887 W. Marietta St. NW, Midtown* ☎ *404/876–5566* 🌐 *www.terminalwestatl.com.*

Woofs

BARS/PUBS | Atlanta's first gay sports bar has pool and darts as well as more than 25 TVs. A menu of bar food is also available—perfect for the big game. ✉ *494 Plasters Ave., Midtown* ☎ *404/869–9422* 🌐 *www.woofsatlanta.com.*

Performing Arts

Actor's Express

THEATER | This acclaimed theater group presents an eclectic selection of classic and cutting-edge productions in its 150-seat theater at King Plow Arts Center, a stylish artists' complex hailed by local critics as a showplace of industrial design. ✉ *King Plow Arts Center, 887 W. Marietta St. NW, Suite J-107, Midtown* ☎ *404/607–7469* 🌐 *www.actors-express.com.*

Alliance Theatre

THEATER | Atlanta's Tony Award–winning professional theater presents everything from Shakespeare to the latest Broadway and off-Broadway hits. ✉ *Woodruff Arts Center, 1280 Peachtree St. NE, Midtown* ☎ *404/733–5000* 🌐 *www.alliancetheatre.org.*

Atlanta Ballet

DANCE | The Atlanta Ballet, founded in 1929, is the country's oldest continuously operating ballet company. It has been internationally recognized for its productions of classical and contemporary works. Artistic director Gennadi Nedvigin has aimed to elevate the technical skill of the group since taking the helm in 2016. Most performances, except for the annual *Nutcracker*, are held at the Cobb Energy Performing Arts Centre. ✉ *Michael C. Carlos Dance Centre, 1695 Marietta Blvd. NW, Midtown* ☎ *404/873–5811* 🌐 *www.atlantaballet.com.*

Atlanta Shakespeare Company

THEATER | The Atlanta Shakespeare Company stages plays by the Bard and his peers, as well as by contemporary dramatists. Performances vary in quality but are always fun. The Elizabethan-style playhouse is a real tavern, so alcohol and pub-style food are available. ✉ *Shakespeare Tavern Playhouse, 499 Peachtree St. NE, Midtown* ☎ *404/874–5299* 🌐 *www.shakespearetavern.com.*

Atlanta Symphony Orchestra *(ASO)*

CONCERTS | Under the musical direction of Robert Spano since 2001, the Atlanta Symphony Orchestra (ASO) has 27 Grammy awards to its credit. It performs the fall–spring subscription series in the nearly 1,800-seat Symphony Hall at the Woodruff Arts Center. ✉ *Woodruff Arts Center, Symphony Hall, 1280 Peachtree St., Midtown* ☎ *404/733–5000* 🌐 *www.atlantasymphony.org.*

Ferst Center for the Arts

ARTS CENTERS | The Georgia Institute of Technology's arts center hosts classical, jazz, dance, and theatrical performances. There's ample free parking on weekends. ✉ *Georgia Tech, 349 Ferst Dr., Midtown* ☎ *404/894–9600* 🌐 *arts.gatech.edu.*

gloATL

DANCE | A contemporary dance company helmed by visionary choreographer Lauri Stallings and founded in 2009, gloATL has entranced Atlantans with its site-specific dance performances and collaborations with local artists, which have included Outkast's Big Boi and the Atlanta Ballet. ✉ *The Goat Farm Arts Center, Goodson Yard, 1200 Foster St. NW, No. 17, Midtown* ☎ *470/344–4561* 🌐 *gloatl.org.*

The Goat Farm Arts Center

ARTS CENTERS | A former complex of cotton-factory buildings from the 19th century has been transformed into a 12-acre group of studios and performance and rehearsal spaces for some of Atlanta's most exciting artists and performers. There's a nice on-site coffee shop called the Warhorse, and the Goat Farm also hosts festivals and concerts by local and national touring acts. ✉ *1200 Foster St. NW, Midtown.*

Woodruff Arts Center

ARTS CENTERS | The Alliance Theatre, the Atlanta Symphony Orchestra, the High Museum of Art, and their combined arts education programs are all housed in this complex. ✉ *1280 Peachtree St. NE, Midtown* ☎ *404/733–4200* 🌐 *www.woodruffcenter.org.*

Shopping

Westside

SHOPPING NEIGHBORHOODS | Most of the high-end restaurants and design shops here are located in and around Westside Provisions District, a complex of former meatpacking warehouses transformed into bustling stores. ✉ *Midtown* 🌐 *www.westsideprovisions.com.*

ART GALLERIES

Mason Fine Art

ART GALLERIES | Smaller than its original location, the quality of work is not compromised in the three large, open gallery spaces that exhibit contemporary work from regional, national, and international artists. ✉ *415 Plasters Ave., Midtown* ☎ *404/879–1500* 🌐 *www.masonfineartandevents.com.*

CLOTHING

Sid Mashburn

CLOTHING | This upscale source for classic men's clothing is on the Westside. Next door, Ann Mashburn sells chic ladies' duds. ✉ *1198 Howell Mill Rd. NW, Suite 110, Midtown* ☎ *404/350–7135* 🌐 *www.sidmashburn.com.*

FOOD

Star Provisions

FOOD/CANDY | Fine cookware, gadgets, and tableware, plus top-of-the-line cheeses, meats, and baked goods are what's on offer at this epicurean destination. ✉ *1460 Ellsworth Industrial Blvd., Midtown* ☎ *404/365–0410* 🌐 *www.starprovisions.com.*

MALLS

Atlantic Station

SHOPPING NEIGHBORHOODS | A mixed-use development and outdoor mall, Atlantic Station covers about 10 square blocks, clustered around a green space known as Central Park. Retailers include IKEA, the Dillard's department store, Banana Republic, and H&M. It's easy to reach by car but is also accessible by free shuttle buses from the Arts Center MARTA station. An on-site concierge is happy to help you find your way around or to make dinner reservations for you at the more than a dozen restaurants here. ✉ *1380 Atlantic Dr., Midtown* ☎ *404/410–4010* 🌐 *www.atlanticstation.com.*

Activities

★ Atlanta BeltLine

PARK—SPORTS-OUTDOORS | Hit the BeltLine however you like: run it, walk it, or bike it. This 33-mile loop of parks, trails, and transit is the perfect way to get an eye-line view of the city, and it's the primary way locals take in a bit of the outdoors. There are multiple access points, including the heart of Midtown, the tree-lined West End, and the Freedom Park Trail. There's often art to view as you go, and an official running series to keep things interesting. ⚠ **Be watchful for aggressive cyclists and rollerbladers.** Don't take it personally, just obey the rules of the road: slower traffic should stay to the right. ⊠ *Midtown* ☎ *404/477–3003* 🌐 *www.beltline.org*.

Buckhead

Atlanta's sprawl doesn't lend itself to walking between major neighborhoods, so take a car or MARTA to reach this area, which has some great stores and restaurants. Lenox Square and Phipps Plaza malls are loaded with plenty of upscale shops. Finding a parking spot on the weekends and at night can be a real headache, and long waits are common in the hottest restaurants.

Sights

★ Atlanta History Center

MUSEUM | Life in Atlanta and the rest of the South during and after the Civil War is a major focus of this fascinating museum. Displays are provocative, juxtaposing *Gone With the Wind* romanticism with the grim reality of Ku Klux Klan racism. Located on 33 acres in the heart of Buckhead, this is one of the Southeast's largest history museums, with a research library and archives that annually serve thousands of patrons. Visit the elegant 1928 **Swan House** mansion and the plantation house that is part of **Smith Family Farm.** The Kenan Research Center houses an extensive archival collection. Lunch is served at the Swan Coach House, which also has a gallery and a gift shop. The historic Battle of Atlanta is depicted in *Cyclorama: The Big Picture* and is included in the admission price—just make a reservation to secure your spot. ⊠ *130 W. Paces Ferry Rd. NW, Buckhead* ☎ *404/814–4000* 🌐 *www.atlantahistorycenter.com* 🎫 *$23* 🕒 *Closed Mon.*

★ The Battery Atlanta

SPORTS VENUE | You may be surprised that the Atlanta Braves aren't the only draw for this multiuse complex that houses homegrown restaurants such as Superica and Antico Pizza, specialty stores like DressUp and an Atlanta outpost of Savannah's River Street Sweets, and the 3,600-capacity Coca-Cola Roxy that plays host to pop, rock, and hip-hop acts. With plenty of walkable spaces, outdoor patios, and an on-site Omni Hotel, warm weather brings many patrons to the 1.5-million-square-foot destination whether there's a game or not. ⊠ *800 Battery Ave., Buckhead* 🌐 *batteryatl.com*.

Cyclorama: The Big Picture

MUSEUM | Moved to the Atlanta History Center from a building in Grant Park (named for a New England–born Confederate colonel, not the U.S. president) the 49-foot-tall circular painting depicts the 1864 Battle of Atlanta, during which 90% of the city was destroyed. A team of expert European panorama artists completed the painting in Milwaukee, Wisconsin, in 1887; it was donated to the city of Atlanta in 1898. A brief overview is followed by a 12-minute film, then visitors can get a closer look at the foreground figures on the ground level of the exhibit and learn more about landmarks and how the 10,000-pound scene was created through displays and interactive touchscreens. ⊠ *Atlanta History Center, 130 W. Paces Ferry Rd., Buckhead* ☎ *404/814–4000* 🌐 *www.*

From the creation of the cotton gin to the premiere of *Gone With the Wind,* the Civil War to the civil rights movement, you can learn all about it at Atlanta History Center.

atlantahistorycenter.com *Free with admission to Atlanta History Center, $22.*

Museum of Contemporary Art of Georgia (MOCA GA)

MUSEUM | Although the collection here includes artists from around the world, more than 300 Georgia artists are represented in the space, which is housed in an arts center. More than 1,000 paintings, sculptures, and other works are part of the permanent collection. *75 Bennett St., Suite A2, Buckhead* *404/367–8700* *www.mocaga.org* *$5* *Closed Sun.–Wed.*

Restaurants

Aria

$$$$ | **AMERICAN** | Chef Gerry Klaskala's talent is best captured by his love of rustic and hearty "slow foods"—braises, stews, roasts, and chops cooked over a roll-top French grill. Don't miss renowned pastry chef Kathryn King's mouthwatering dessert menu. **Known for:** perfect desserts from renowned pastry chef; slow-cooked classics; reputation as a go-to spot for special occasions. *Average main: $30* *490 E. Paces Ferry Rd., Buckhead* *404/233–7673* *www.aria-atl.com* *Closed Sun. and Mon. No lunch.*

Canoe

$$$$ | **AMERICAN** | This popular spot on the bank of the Chattahoochee River has built a reputation based on such dishes as slow-roasted rabbit with wild mushroom ravioli and Swiss chard. Sunday brunch—with smoked-salmon eggs Benedict, house-made Georgia pecan sticky buns, and other offerings—is superb. **Known for:** relaxing views of the river; excellent brunch; hard-to-find location. *Average main: $25* *4199 Paces Ferry Rd. SE, Buckhead* *770/432–2663* *www.canoeatl.com* *No lunch Sat.*

Colonnade

$$ | **SOUTHERN** | For traditional Southern food—think fried chicken, ham steak, and turkey with dressing—insiders head to Colonnade, a local institution since 1927 and a magnet for gay men and

the elderly. The interior, with patterned carpeting and burgundy banquettes, is a classic version of a 1950s restaurant. **Known for:** vintage atmosphere; huge helpings of traditional Southern cuisine; homemade yeast rolls. *Average main: $15 1879 Cheshire Bridge Rd., Buckhead 404/874–5642 www.thecolonnadeatlanta.com Closed Mon. and Tues. No lunch Wed.–Sat.*

Eclipse di Luna

$$ | **SPANISH** | Live music and a twist on the standard date night keep this place bustling on weekends. The menu consists of tapas such as *patatas bravas con romesco* (potatoes with olive oil and a spicy sauce) and ceviche. **Known for:** traditional tapas menu; dance-worthy live Latin music; authentic seafood paella. *Average main: $15 764 Miami Circle, Buckhead 404/846–0449 www.eclipsediluna.com No lunch weekdays.*

Varasano's Pizzeria

$$ | **PIZZA** | Software engineer Jeff Varasano was 14 when he set the country's Rubik's Cube record, and he's since changed gears to accomplish the feat of building the perfect pizza. The thin, lightly charred pies are created by closely following Varasano's intense instructions, including the use of an 800°F oven. **Known for:** thin-crust pizzas; quality ingredients ; Italian doughnuts for dessert. *Average main: $16 2171 Peachtree Rd. NE, Buckhead 404/352–8216 www.varasanos.com No lunch weekdays.*

Coffee and Quick Bites

Southern Baked Pie Company

$$$$ | **AMERICAN** | Amanda Wilbanks has come a long way from entering her buttermilk pie in local competitions—she's now the owner of three storefront locations and the author of a cookbook. There's a variety of sweet and savory choices at this chic Buckhead Village location (even a Pie-of-the-Month club). **Known for:** buttery piecrust; chicken potpie; gluten-free options. *Average main: $40 3145 Peachtree Rd., Suite 165, Buckhead 404/263–0656 www.southernbakedpie.com Closed Sun.*

Hotels

Embassy Suites Hotel

$$$ | **HOTEL** | This mostly-suites high-rise is just blocks from the shopping meccas of Lenox Square and Phipps Plaza. **Pros:** convenient to shopping; indoor and outdoor pools; complimentary drinks in the afternoon. **Cons:** Wi-Fi is not free; not all rooms are suites; decor is a bit outdated. *Rooms from: $230 3285 Peachtree Rd. NE, Buckhead 404/261–7733 embassysuites3.hilton.com 316 suites Free breakfast.*

Hilton Garden Inn Atlanta-Buckhead

$$ | **HOTEL** | The excellent location, spacious rooms, and reasonable rates are what make this hotel a worthy consideration. **Pros:** a warm welcome; comfortable beds; next to MARTA. **Cons:** small bar; valet-only parking; no pool. *Rooms from: $180 3342 Peachtree Rd. NE, Buckhead 404/231–1234 hiltongardeninn3.hilton.com 230 rooms No meals.*

InterContinental Buckhead Atlanta

$$$ | **HOTEL** | Marble bathrooms with separate soaking tubs and glass showers, 300-thread-count Egyptian-cotton linens, plush bathrobes and slippers, and twice-daily housekeeping are some of the highlights of the traditionally styled rooms in this hotel, the flagship for the Atlanta-based chain. **Pros:** 24-hour fitness center; convenient to shopping; good on-site restaurant and bar. **Cons:** small spa; complimentary Internet only with rewards program or special room rate; expensive parking. *Rooms from: $230 3315 Peachtree Rd. NE, Buckhead 404/946–9000, 877/834–3613 www.intercontinentalatlanta.com 422 rooms No meals.*

★ Kimpton Sylvan Hotel
$$ | HOTEL | Slow down as you approach this gem of a former 1950s apartment building turned boutique hotel or you may drive by it. **Pros:** near the ritzy Buckhead Village District shops; multiple outdoor spaces to enjoy; yoga mats in every room. **Cons:** easy to miss entrance; no suites; low ceilings. *Rooms from: $185 ✉ 374 E. Paces Ferry Rd., Buckhead ☎ 877/984–6548 🌐 www.thesylvanhotel.com 217 rooms No meals.*

★ The St. Regis Atlanta
$$$$ | HOTEL | By far Atlanta's most prestigious and regal hotel and its second five-star property, the St. Regis is adorned with impressive touches, from the grand "open arms" double staircase in the entry, to the etching on the elevator doors and the crystals dangling from the hotel's many chandeliers. **Pros:** 40,000-square-foot Pool Piazza with Jacuzzi and waterfall; modern touches like in-room tablets to order room service and smart lighting controls; within walking distance of high-end shops and galleries. **Cons:** can sometimes feel overly formal; very expensive; property includes residences. *Rooms from: $500 ✉ 88 W. Paces Ferry Rd., Buckhead ☎ 404/563–7900, 888/627–7231 🌐 www.stregisatlanta.com 151 rooms No meals.*

Waldorf Astoria Atlanta Buckhead
$$$$ | HOTEL | Sophisticated glamour characterizes this upscale 42-story Buckhead hotel. **Pros:** attentive staff; quiet atmosphere; high-end but not stuffy. **Cons:** not much within walking distance besides Buckhead malls and other shopping; lackluster restaurant; Wi-Fi costs extra. *Rooms from: $439 ✉ 3376 Peachtree Rd. NE, Buckhead ☎ 404/995–7500 🌐 waldorfastoria3.hilton.com 127 rooms No meals.*

Westin Buckhead Atlanta
$$ | HOTEL | What draws guests here is the hotel's location and business-traveler focus; from the chic glass-and-white-tile exterior and sweeping two-level lobby to the rooms, the hotel offers a contemporary but comfortable look. **Pros:** in-room service from the Palm, noted for its steaks; plenty of restaurants nearby; large fitness center. **Cons:** expensive for amenities offered; small pool; must pay for Wi-Fi. *Rooms from: $200 ✉ 3391 Peachtree Rd., Buckhead ☎ 404/365–0065 🌐 westin.marriott.com 365 rooms No meals.*

The Whitley
$$$ | HOTEL | An excellent location for high-end shopping, the Whitley boasts clientele that's just as upscale. **Pros:** directly across from both Lenox Mall and Phipps Plaza; sizable fitness room; spa with Himalayan salt room. **Cons:** pricey valet service; crowds when major events are in town; limited seating in lobby. *Rooms from: $240 ✉ 3434 Peachtree Rd. NE, Buckhead ☎ 404/237–2700 🌐 thewhitleyhotel.com 507 rooms No meals.*

SweetWater Brewery
BREWPUBS/BEER GARDENS | A pair of college roommates started this now-popular craft brewery back in 1997, seizing an opportunity to bring West Coast brew knowledge and flavors to the Southeast. Now you can find SweetWater beers (especially the SweetWater 420 Pale Ale) up and down the East Coast. The taproom serves 24 beers and a full kitchen offers pub food like nachos and wings. Tours and tastings are $8, and sign-up is available online in advance. *✉ 195 Ottley Dr., Buckhead ☎ 404/691–2537 🌐 www.sweetwaterbrew.com.*

Ameris Bank Amphitheatre
CONCERTS | The 12,000-capacity Ameris Bank Amphitheatre is situated on 45 acres 22 miles north of Downtown Atlanta. The venue hosts a variety of pop, country, and classical acts, including the Atlanta Symphony Orchestra. *✉ 2200*

Encore Pkwy., Alpharetta ☎ 404/733–5010 🌐 www.amerisbankamp.com.

Atlanta Opera

OPERA | Major roles at the Atlanta Opera are performed by national and international guest artists; many of the chorus and orchestra members come from the local community. ✉ *Cobb Energy Performing Arts Centre, 2800 Cobb Galleria Pkwy.* ☎ *770/916–2800* 🌐 *www.atlantaopera.org.*

Buckhead Theatre

ARTS CENTERS | This restored 1931 Spanish baroque theater has sloped floors that make it ideal for the comedy, rock, soul, and country shows hosted here. ✉ *3110 Roswell Rd., Buckhead* ☎ *404/843–2825* 🌐 *www.thebuckheadtheatre.com.*

Cadence Bank Amphitheatre at Chastain Park

ARTS CENTERS | This theater feels more like an outdoor nightclub than a typical performance venue. Pack a picnic, bring a blanket if you've snagged some seats on the lawn, and prepare to listen to your favorite performers over the clink of dishes and the chatter of dinner conversation. ✉ *4469 Stella Dr. NW, Buckhead* ☎ *404/233–2227* 🌐 *www.livenation.com.*

Shopping

ANTIQUES AND DECORATIVE ARTS

Miami Circle

ANTIQUES/COLLECTIBLES | Upscale antiques and decorative-arts shops are the draw here. ✉ *Miami Circle and Piedmont Rd., Buckhead* 🌐 *miamicircleshops.com.*

ART GALLERIES

Jackson Fine Art

ART GALLERIES | The specialty here is fine-art photography. ✉ *3115 E. Shadowlawn Ave., Buckhead* ☎ *404/233–3739* 🌐 *www.jacksonfineart.com.*

MALLS

Buckhead Village District

SHOPPING NEIGHBORHOODS | With the likes of Dior, Etro, Gucci, and Hermès, this walkable luxury shopping area is frequented as much by daydreaming window-shoppers as no-limit-credit-card holders. ✉ *3035 Peachtree Rd., Buckhead* ☎ *404/939–9270* 🌐 *www.buckheadvillagedistrict.com.*

Lenox Square

SHOPPING CENTERS/MALLS | One of Atlanta's oldest and most popular shopping centers, Lenox Square has branches of Neiman Marcus, Bloomingdale's, and Macy's next to specialty shops such as Cartier and Mori. Valet parking is available at the front of the mall, but free parking is nearby. You'll do better at one of the several good restaurants in the mall—even for a quick meal—than at the food court. ✉ *3393 Peachtree Rd., Buckhead* ☎ *404/233–6767* 🌐 *www.simon.com/mall/lenox-square.*

★ Phipps Plaza

SHOPPING CENTERS/MALLS | Branches of Tiffany & Co., Saks Fifth Avenue, and Gucci are here, as are shops like Lilly Pulitzer and Bally. The mall also is home to Legoland Discovery Center. ✉ *3500 Peachtree Rd. NE, Buckhead* ☎ *404/262–0992* 🌐 *www.simon.com/mall/phipps-plaza.*

Shops Around Lenox

CLOTHING | Quite literally around the corner from Lenox Square mall, this collection of Atlanta favorites, such as fab'rik, and specialty shops, such as Crate & Barrel and lululemon, features modern storefronts and green spaces. ✉ *3400 Around Lenox Rd. NE, Buckhead* ☎ *678/226–5328* 🌐 *www.shopsaroundlenox.com.*

Virginia-Highland and the Emory Area

Restaurants, bars, and boutiques are sprinkled throughout Virginia-Highland, northeast of Midtown. Like Midtown, this residential area was down-at-the-heels in the 1970s. Reclaimed by writers, artists, and a few visionary developers, Virginia-Highland (as well as bordering Morningside) is a great place to explore. To the east, the Emory University area is studded with enviable mansions. Near the Emory campus is Druid Hills, used for film locations for *Driving Miss Daisy* by local playwright Alfred Uhry. The neighborhood was designed by the firm of Frederick Law Olmsted, which also landscaped Asheville's Biltmore Estate and New York's Central Park.

Sights

Fernbank Museum of Natural History

MUSEUM | FAMILY | One of the largest natural-history museums south of the Smithsonian Institution in Washington, D.C., this museum offers more than 12,000 square feet of gallery space and an on-site 3-D theater. The *Giants of the Mesozoic* exhibit includes an exact replica of the world's largest dinosaur. The café, with an exquisite view of the forest, serves great food. **■TIP→ On the second Friday of each month, the museum hosts Fernbank After Dark, which includes live music and food and cocktails for purchase.** ✉ *767 Clifton Rd., Emory* ☎ *404/929–6300* 🌐 *www.fernbankmuseum.org* 🎫 *$20, Fernbank After Dark $22.*

Fernbank Science Center

OBSERVATORY | FAMILY | The museum, a learning and activity center with connections to the county school system, sits in the 65-acre Fernbank Forest and focuses on ecology, geology, and space exploration. In addition to the exhibit hall, there's a planetarium as well as an observatory, which is open Thursday and Friday night 9–10:30, weather permitting. ✉ *156 Heaton Park Dr., Emory* ☎ *678/874–7102* 🌐 *fsc.fernbank.edu* 🎫 *Free, planetarium shows $7* 🕒 *Closed Sun.*

Jimmy Carter Presidential Library and Museum

LIBRARY | This complex occupies the site where Union general William T. Sherman orchestrated the Battle of Atlanta (1864). The museum and archives detail the political career of former president Jimmy Carter. The adjacent Carter Center, which is not open to the public, focuses on conflict resolution and human-rights issues. Outside, the Japanese-style garden is a serene spot to unwind. Both Carter and former first lady Rosalynn Carter maintain offices here. ✉ *441 John Lewis Freedom Pkwy., Virginia-Highland* ☎ *404/865–7100* 🌐 *www.jimmycarterlibrary.gov* 🎫 *$12.*

Michael C. Carlos Museum

MUSEUM | FAMILY | Housing a permanent collection of more than 17,000 objects, this excellent museum, designed by the architect Michael Graves, exhibits artifacts from Egypt, Greece, Rome, the Near East, the Americas, and Africa. European and American prints and drawings cover the Middle Ages through the 20th century. The bookshop sells rare art books, jewelry, and art-focused items for children. ✉ *Emory University, 571 S. Kilgo Circle, Emory* ☎ *404/727–4282* 🌐 *www.carlos.emory.edu* 🎫 *$8* 🕒 *Closed Mon.*

Restaurants

La Tavola Trattoria

$$$$ | ITALIAN | This place serves classic Italian dishes in a beautiful setting that still recalls old-school neighborhood dining. Count on regulars like bruschetta and spaghetti with meatballs to be elevated beyond basic but without being too fancy. **Known for:** authentic trattoria menu; cozy, romantic atmosphere; rotating tours of Italian cuisine. 💲 *Average main: $25* ✉ *992*

Virginia Ave., Virginia-Highland ☎ 404/873–5430 🌐 www.latavolatrattoria.com.

Soul Vegetarian Restaurant No. 2

$$ | **VEGETARIAN** | Vegan comfort food and plant-based barbecue dishes are served up in a no-frills diner setting, with mac and cheese (made with soy cheese), cauliflower and tofu steaks, and kalebone (a wheat-gluten protein) topping the menu. The original location (on Ralph David Abernathy Blvd.) serves similar fare but buffet-style, with more limited daily choices. **Known for:** vegan comfort food; soy mac and cheese; relaxed atmosphere. *$ Average main: $15 ✉ 652 N. Highland Ave. NE, Poncey-Highland ☎ 404/875–0145 🌐 soulvegsouth.com.*

Sweet Auburn Barbecue

$$ | **BARBECUE** | One of several success stories to come from the Sweet Auburn Curb Market, this offshoot of the market makes classic Southern barbecue available in a part of town where it's lacking. The meats are slow-smoked, and the sides are delectable. **Known for:** slow-smoked barbecue; laid-back atmosphere; unique offerings like pimento wontons. *$ Average main: $15 ✉ 656 N. Highland Ave., Virginia-Highland ☎ 678/515–3550 🌐 sweetauburnbbq.com.*

★ Tiny Lou's

$$$$ | **BRASSERIE** | This French-American brasserie at the base of Hotel Clermont doesn't play it small. Decadence is at every turn, from the richly patterned floral wallpaper lining the staircase down to the perfect brioche bread service, cardamom-infused cream desserts, and deftly prepared main courses in between. **Known for:** richly prepared meats such as beef bourguignon; well-curated, French-leaning wine list; impressive date night. *$ Average main: $25 ✉ 789 Ponce de Leon Ave., Poncey-Highland ☎ 470/485–0085 🌐 www.tinylous.com ⏲ Closed Mon. and Tues.*

Hotels

★ Emory Conference Center Hotel

$$ | **HOTEL** | Done in a modified Prairie style, this hotel is surrounded by 26 acres of forest preserve near Emory University and about 6 miles from Downtown Atlanta. **Pros:** indoor pool is fun for kids; rooms on higher levels offer pleasant views of wooded areas; eco-friendly ethos. **Cons:** some small bathrooms; large campus can make walk to hotel from parking area fairly long; far from main Atlanta sights. *$ Rooms from: $190 ✉ 1615 Clifton Rd., Emory ☎ 404/712–6000 🌐 www.emoryconferencecenter.com ⇨ 325 rooms 🍴 No meals.*

★ Hotel Clermont

$$ | **HOTEL** | There's no better stay within walking distance of Ponce City Market and the BeltLine, and for cool factor combined with the conveniences of a modern hotel with vintage touches, there may be no better stay in Atlanta. **Pros:** rooftop bar with great views of the city; plenty of nooks to hang out with friends or take a private call; diverse mix of guests and locals. **Cons:** spotty valet service; late-night bar crowd on weekends; no room service. *$ Rooms from: $200 ✉ 789 Ponce de Leon Ave., Poncey-Highland ☎ 470/485–0485 🌐 www.hotelclermont.com ⇨ 94 rooms 🍴 No meals.*

Nightlife

Blind Willie's

MUSIC CLUBS | New Orleans and Chicago blues groups are the main thing here, although Cajun and zydeco are also on the calendar from time to time. The name honors Blind Willie McTell, a native of Thomson, Georgia; his original compositions include "Statesboro Blues," made popular by the Georgia-based Allman Brothers. *✉ 828 N. Highland Ave., Virginia-Highland ☎ 404/873–2583 🌐 www.blindwilliesblues.com.*

Manuel's Tavern

BARS/PUBS | This local landmark and favorite of left-leaning politicos and media gadflies owes its popularity to its spirit and friendly service. Look for photos of vintage Atlanta sports teams and both local and national politicians, including a younger Bill and Hillary Clinton visiting with the spot's namesake. A crowd gathers around the wide-screen TVs when the Atlanta Braves play. ✉ *602 N. Highland Ave., Virginia-Highland* ☎ *404/525–3447* 🌐 *www.manuelstavern.com.*

Performing Arts

Emory University

CONCERTS | On its idyllic campus surrounded by picturesque houses, Emory University has five major venues where internationally renowned artists perform. ✉ *201 Dowman Dr., Emory* ☎ *404/727–5050* 🌐 *www.emory.edu.*

Shopping

ART GALLERIES

Young Blood Boutique

ART GALLERIES | Young Blood is an edgy hangout with framed artwork, crafts, and gifts created by indie artists. ✉ *632 N. Highland Ave., Virginia-Highland* ☎ *404/358–1286* 🌐 *www.youngblood-boutique.com.*

Little Five Points and Inman Park

About 4 miles east of Downtown, the Inman Park neighborhood was laid out by famous developer Joel Hurt in 1889. Since then it has faded and flourished a number of times, which explains the vast gaps in opulence evident in much of the architecture here. Huge, ornate Victorian mansions sit next to humble bungalows. But no matter the exact address or style of home—be it modest or massive—Inman Park now commands considerable cachet among many different constituents, including young families, empty nesters, and the LGBTQ community. Nearby you'll also find the delightfully countercultural Little Five Points area, with funky boutiques, neighborhood bars, and homegrown eateries.

Sights

Freedom Park Trail

TRAIL | One of the neighborhood's best features is the Freedom Park Trail, a particularly pleasant stretch of the PATH Foundation's more-than-250-mile trail system in the metro area. It gives runners, bikers, and dog walkers a peaceful thoroughfare inside the 210-acre Freedom Park. The PATH is the largest public green space in a major metro area developed in the United States in the last century. ✉ *Moreland Ave. and John Lewis Freedom Pkwy., Little Five Points* ☎ *404/875–7284* 🌐 *www.pathfoundation.org.*

Restaurants

Babette's Cafe

$$$$ | **EUROPEAN** | Sunny yellow walls and back-porch seating add to the homey charm of this renovated bungalow. The restaurant, which describes its cuisine as rustic European, offers such seasonal dishes as New England sole with grilled fennel, and beef tenderloin with Gorgonzola sauce. **Known for:** Sunday brunch popular with locals; dining area full of Southern charm; longtime favorite for authentic French provincial cooking. [$] *Average main: $25* ✉ *573 N. Highland Ave., Inman Park* ☎ *404/523–9121* 🌐 *www.babettescafe.com* ⏲ *Closed Mon. and Tues. No lunch.*

Barcelona

$$ | **TAPAS** | The narrow wraparound patio is the draw at this buzzing Spanish-inspired restaurant and wine bar. The must-try paella and weekly wine specials help to keep patrons happy. **Known for:** crowded but must-try patio; low-key but tasty tapas and other Spanish staples; affordable wine list. *Average main: $18* *240 N. Highland Ave., Inman Park* *404/589–1010* *www.barcelonawine-bar.com/atlanta.htm.*

bartaco

$ | **MEXICAN** | Take an order card, grab a pencil, and decide what you want in your tacos; bartaco offers everything from falafel and fish to cauliflower and chorizo. You'll want at least two, even though it's easy to fill up on the unforgettable guacamole. **Known for:** long taco list with unique fillings; breezy patio; delicious and simple margaritas. *Average main: $10* *299 N. Highland Ave., Inman Park* *470/400–8226* *www.bartaco.com/location/atlanta-inman.*

Bread and Butterfly

$$ | **FRENCH** | Billy Allin helms this bistro that makes you feel like you're hanging on the sidewalks of Paris. The patio is absolutely delightful when the weather is warm, and the pastries, coffee, and wine are just as satisfying. **Known for:** Parisian-style setting; great pastries and full breakfasts; wine-friendly happy hour. *Average main: $15* *290 Elizabeth St., Suite F, Inman Park* *678/515–4536* *www.bread-and-butterfly.com* *Closed Mon. and Tues.*

Flying Biscuit

$ | **SOUTHERN** | There's a long wait on weekends at this spot, which is famous for its biscuits served with cranberry-apple butter. Dinners may include roasted chicken or turkey meat loaf with pudge (mashed potatoes). **Known for:** biscuits with cranberry-apple butter (also available to go); long waits on weekends; surprisingly delicious lunch options. *Average main: $10* *1655 McLendon Ave., Candler Park* *404/687–8888* *www.flyingbiscuit.com.*

Fox Bros. Bar-B-Q

$$ | **BARBECUE** | Here's what pays the bills here: brisket, pulled pork, fried pickles, and an artery-cloggin' take on tater tots, served smothered in Brunswick stew and melted cheese. Try to get a seat on the patio, a great place to soak up sun and sip a cold beer. **Known for:** smoked brisket and pulled pork; buzzing patio; fatty but delectable tater tots. *Average main: $15* *1238 DeKalb Ave., Candler Park* *404/577–4030* *www.foxbrosbbq.com.*

Sotto Sotto

$$$$ | **ITALIAN** | For an adventurous take on Italian cuisine, visit this former commercial space that hops with young, hip patrons dining on seafood risotto, spaghetti with sun-dried mullet roe, and utterly perfect *panna cotta* (custard). **Known for:** inventive Italian dishes; young and hip atmosphere; setting that's perfect for date night. *Average main: $25* *313 N. Highland Ave., Inman Park* *404/523–6678* *www.sottosottoatl.com* *No lunch.*

Wonderkid

$$$ | **AMERICAN** | Jump back in time when disco lights were a delight and wood paneling was all the rage at this diner that somehow feels just the right amount of right-now cool. Who needs Waffle House when there's a spot that serves better coffee—and cocktails by the pouch for sharing—even as you look onto the grill station like you would at the ubiquitous Southern staple. **Known for:** throwback look and feel; location inside newly bustling Atlanta Dairies development; soft-serve ice cream by local favorite King of Pops. *Average main: $20* *777 Memorial Dr., Reynoldstown* *404/331–0909* *www.wonderkidatl.com.*

Coffee and Quick Bites

Dr. Bombay's Underwater Tea Party

$ | **BAKERY** | Dr. Bombay's is full of whimsy. **Known for:** teas sourced from India that go toward a good cause; magical look and feel; private tea parties with delectable pastries. *Average main: $8* *1645 McLendon Ave. NE, Candler Park* *404/474–1402* *www.drbombays.com* *Closed Mon.–Thurs. No dinner.*

Muchacho

$ | **MEXICAN** | The yellow door of the old Atlanta & West Point Railroad station where this coffee shop is housed will undoubtedly draw the eye. Muchacho offers West Coast retro vibes and an assortment of breakfast tacos, matcha lattes, and daily *frescas* in a bright space. **Known for:** eclectic and spacious patio; easy access to the BeltLine; fun merchandise. *Average main: $5* ✉ *904 Memorial Dr. SE, Reynoldstown* ☎ *404/748–9254* 🌐 *www.muchachoatl.com* ⊗ *Closed Mon. and Tues.*

Proof Bakeshop

$ | **BAKERY** | On the outskirts of Inman Park, Proof offers everything from savory breads to decadent desserts, including speciality cake and cookie orders. The shop itself is unassuming, and sits across from the Inman Park/Reynoldstown MARTA station. **Known for:** walkability from MARTA and Inman Park; always fresh pastries; cute interior and aesthetic. *Average main: $6* ✉ *100 Hurt St. NE, Inman Park* ☎ *678/705–3905* 🌐 *www.proofbakeshop.com* ⊗ *Closed Mon. and Tues.*

Porter Beer Bar

BARS/PUBS | Try the salt-and-vinegar popcorn or other bar staples, such as fish-and-chips, fries, and mac and cheese, all with a suggested beer pairing at the Porter Beer Bar. ✉ *1156 Euclid Ave., Little Five Points* ☎ *404/223–0393* 🌐 *www.theporterbeerbar.com.*

★ **Vortex**

BARS/PUBS | Vortex prides itself on being impolite—a look at the "rules" will show you they take no guff—but really it's a friendly bar with great burgers. Ask for the off-menu fried zucchini. Just look for the huge skull, a landmark of Little Five Points, and you've found the door. The bar-restaurant's Midtown location fronts the popular Laughing Skull Comedy Club. ✉ *438 Moreland Ave., Little Five Points* ☎ *404/688–1828* 🌐 *thevortexatl.com.*

Horizon Theatre Company

THEATER | This professional troupe, established in 1983, debuts provocative and entertaining contemporary plays in its 172-seat theater. ✉ *1083 Austin Ave., Little Five Points* ☎ *404/584–7450* 🌐 *www.horizontheatre.com.*

7 Stages Theatre

THEATER | Founded in 1979 and in its current location since 1987, 7 Stages is known for an edgy attitude and exciting works. The adjacent bar and coffee house, Java Lords, serves up delicious brews and affordable drinks before and after shows. ✉ *1105 Euclid Ave. NE, Little Five Points* ☎ *404/523–7647* 🌐 *www.7stages.org.*

Variety Playhouse

CONCERTS | This 1,100-capacity venue was once a movie theater and is now one of the cultural anchors of the hip Little Five Points neighborhood. Music lovers come for rock, bluegrass and country, blues, reggae, folk, jazz, and pop. ✉ *1099 Euclid Ave. NE, Little Five Points* ☎ *404/524–7354* 🌐 *www.variety-playhouse.com.*

ART GALLERIES

Whitespace Gallery

ART GALLERIES | An Inman Park staple, Whitespace exhibits contemporary paintings and installations in its renovated carriage house and a smaller satellite gallery, Whitespec. ✉ *814 Edgewood Ave., Inman Park* ☎ *404/688–1892* 🌐 *whitespace814.com.*

BOOKS

A Cappella Books

BOOKS/STATIONERY | New and out-of-print titles are sold here; the store hosts regular author appearances. ✉ *208 Haralson Ave. NE, Inman Park* ☎ *404/681–5128* 🌐 *www.acappellabooks.com.*

CLOTHING

The Clothing Warehouse

CLOTHING | The Clothing Warehouse is one of the many colorful vintage-clothing stores in Little Five Points. ✉ *420 Moreland Ave. NE, Little Five Points* ☎ *404/524–5070* 🌐 *www.theclothing-warehouse.com.*

Junkman's Daughter

CLOTHING | Kooky wigs, vinyl corsets, and water pipes are all sold at this funky-junky department store. ✉ *464 Moreland Ave. NE, Little Five Points* ☎ *404/577–3188* 🌐 *www.thejunkmansdaughter.com.*

SHOPPING AREAS

Krog Street Market

MARKET | This bustling food hall and market draws both residents who live within walking distance and suburbanites driving in from afar. It houses spots like Ticonderoga Club, a venture of barmen Greg Best and Paul Calvert; Tex-Mex from Superica; and worth-the-wait ice cream from Jeni's. Plus, you can walk around with your beer from Hop City while you shop at the small outposts hawking everything from chocolate to hand-made soaps. ✉ *99 Krog St., Inman Park* 🌐 *www.krogstreetmarket.com.*

Little Five Points

SHOPPING NEIGHBORHOODS | Vintage-clothing emporiums, record stores, and some stores that defy description are what draw thrifters and others here. ✉ *Euclid and Moreland Aves., Little Five Points* 🌐 *www.littlefivepoints.net.*

Decatur

Busy downtown Decatur, 8 miles east of Midtown Atlanta, is one of the metro area's favorite spots for dining, sidewalk strolling, and window-shopping. Its town quad, with a sophisticated, artistic vibe, teems with interesting restaurants, specialty shops, and delectable coffeehouses and cafés.

Restaurants

Leon's Full Service

$$$ | **MODERN AMERICAN** | In a neighborhood flush with craft beer options, Leon's introduced an inventive specialty cocktail menu (as well as its own long list of craft beers). The food menu is full of fun snacks to share while drinking, including fries served with an array of sauces. **Known for:** creative cocktails and craft beers; popular patio with bocce court; standard bar food perfect for sharing. *[$] Average main: $20* ✉ *131 E. Ponce de Leon Ave., Decatur* ☎ *404/687–0500* 🌐 *www.leonsfullservice.com* 🕒 *No lunch Mon. and Tues.*

No. 246

$$$$ | **ITALIAN** | It's fun to come sit at the oversized bar and sample any number of the smaller plates on this happening Italian eatery's menu. The pastas are delicate and delicious, and the pizzas are thin, charred, and chewy. **Known for:** classic margherita pizza; tasty meatballs, served with a plate of fresh red sauce and basil; fresh, locally sourced salads. *[$] Average main: $25* ✉ *129 E. Ponce de Leon Ave., Decatur* ☎ *678/399–8246* 🌐 *www.no246.com.*

Coffee and Quick Bites

Butter & Cream

$ | **BAKERY** | Small-batch ice cream is made on-site at these old-school ice-cream-parlor locations, one in downtown Decatur and the other in the Old Fourth Ward, just off the Atlanta BeltLine Trail. Batches of seasonal and inventive flavors accompany the classics, as well as brownies, cookies, and killer ice-cream sandwiches, like the East Pole Coffee ice cream on a double chocolate cookie. **Known for:** ice-cream sandwiches; second location on the BeltLine; inventive flavors. *[$] Average main: $5* ✉ *416 Church St., Decatur* ☎ *404/378–7272* 🌐 *www.butter-andcream.com.*

Shopping

BOOKS

Charis Books

BOOKS/STATIONERY | This is the South's oldest independent feminist bookstore. ✉ *184 S. Candler St., Decatur* ☎ *404/524–0304* 🌐 *www.charisbooksandmore.com.*

Little Shop of Stories

BOOKS/STATIONERY | **FAMILY** | With story time three times a week, a wide selection of children's books from board to chapter and beyond, and as frequent host to kids' book authors, this may be the best children's bookstore in the Atlanta area. ✉ *133A E. Court Sq., Decatur* ☎ *404/373–6300* 🌐 *www.littleshopofstories.com.*

FOOD

Your DeKalb Farmers Market

OUTDOOR/FLEA/GREEN MARKETS | It may not be a true farmers' market, but this is truly a market experience to remember. In a sprawling warehouse store 9 miles east of Atlanta, some 142,000 square feet are given over to exotic fruits, cheeses, seafood, sausages, breads, and delicacies from around the world. You'll find root vegetables from Africa, greens from Asia, wines from South America, and cheeses from Europe. The store also has one of the largest seafood departments in the country (with some species still swimming) and sizable meat, deli, and wine sections. Just the cafeteria-style buffet alone, with a selection of earthy and delicious hot foods and salads ranging from lasagna to samosas, is worth the trip. **■ TIP→ The market is accessible by MARTA bus from the Avondale rail station.** ✉ *3000 E. Ponce de Leon Ave., Decatur* ☎ *404/377–6400* 🌐 *www.dekalbfarmersmarket.com.*

Metro Atlanta

It's essential to drive to most of these venues, so plan your visits with Atlanta's notorious rush hours in mind.

Sights

Chattahoochee River National Recreation Area

CITY PARK | Crisscrossed by 70 miles of trails, this rec area contains different parcels of land that lie in 15 separate units spread along the banks of the Chattahoochee River. Much of it has been protected from development. ✉ *Visitor Center, 8800 Roberts Dr., Sandy Springs* ☎ *678/538–1200* 🌐 *www.nps.gov/chat.*

Stone Mountain Park

AMUSEMENT PARK/WATER PARK | **FAMILY** | At this 3,200-acre state park you'll find the largest exposed granite outcropping on earth. The Confederate Memorial, on the north face of the 825-foot-high mountain, is the world's largest high-relief sculpture, measuring 90 feet by 190 feet. There are several ways to see the sculpture, including a cable car that lifts you to the mountaintop and a steam locomotive that chugs around the mountain's base. Summer nights are capped with the **Lasershow Spectacular ,** an outdoor light display set to music and projected onto the side of Stone Mountain. There's also 15 miles of nature trails, historical buildings featuring household items from the 18th and 19th centuries, two golf courses, a campground with a pool, an inn, a resort, several restaurants, and a Civil War museum. The SkyHike is a family-friendly ropes course at 12, 24 , or 40 feet high. ✉ *1000 Robert E. Lee Blvd., Stone Mountain* ✣ *U.S. 78 E, Stone Mountain Pkwy., Exit 8* ☎ *770/498–5690* 🌐 *www.stonemountainpark.com* 🎫 *$20 per car, One-Day Attractions Pass $23.*

Hotels

Westin Atlanta Airport

$$ | HOTEL | The 500 guest rooms feature Westin's signature "heavenly bed" along with a flat-screen TV and Starbucks coffee. **Pros:** incredibly convenient to the airport and major highways; affordable room rates; indoor and outdoor pools. **Cons:** not near any restaurants or attractions; typical airport hotel decor; no free breakfast. *Rooms from: $150* *4736 Best Rd.* *404/762–7676* *www.westinatlantaairport.com* *500 rooms* *No meals.*

Nightlife

Punchline

COMEDY CLUBS | The city's oldest comedy club books major national acts. It's ages 21 and up only. *3652 Roswell Rd.* *404/252–5233* *punchline.com.*

Performing Arts

Cellairis Amphitheatre at Lakewood

CONCERTS | Four miles south of Downtown Atlanta, this venue draws national popular music acts all summer. There's seating for nearly 19,000 in reserved areas and on its sloped lawn. *2002 Lakewood Way SW* *404/443–5090* *www.livenation.com/venues/14086/cellairis-amphitheatre-at-lakewood.*

Infinite Energy Center

ARTS CENTERS | A 708-seat theater, a 13,000-seat arena, and a 50,000-square-foot expo center are all here, 30 miles north of Downtown Atlanta. The venue hosts national touring acts and the Atlanta Gladiators hockey team, as well as conventions, sporting events, outlet sales, and jewelry shows. *6400 Sugarloaf Pkwy., Duluth* *770/813–7500* *www.infiniteenergycenter.com.*

Mable House Barnes Amphitheatre

ARTS CENTERS | This 2,500-capacity venue 6 miles west of Downtown Atlanta stages jazz, R&B, and country music. *5239 Floyd Rd., Mableton* *770/819–7765* *www.mablehouse.org.*

Spivey Hall

ARTS CENTERS | Internationally renowned musicians perform everything from chamber music to jazz at this gleaming, modern, acoustically magnificent performance center 15 miles south of Atlanta. The hall is considered one of the country's finest concert venues. *Clayton State University, 2000 Clayton State Blvd., Simpson Dr., Morrow* *678/466–4200* *www.spiveyhall.org.*

Shopping

The interstate highways leading to Atlanta have discount malls similar to those found throughout the country. About 80 miles north of the city on Interstate 85 at Exit 149 is a huge cluster of outlets in the town of Commerce.

ANTIQUES AND DECORATIVE ARTS

Chamblee's Antique Row

ANTIQUES/COLLECTIBLES | You'll find this browser's delight in the suburban town of Chamblee. It's just north of Buckhead and about 10 miles north of Downtown. *Peachtree Industrial Blvd. and Broad St., Chamblee* *770/986–7460* *www.antiquerow.com.*

FOOD

Buford Highway Farmers Market

FOOD/CANDY | Originally started more than 25 years ago as a specialty Asian grocery, the Buford Highway Farmers Market has grown into a full-blown international marketplace; a turn down each aisle is like a trip to a different country. Make sure to stop at the Eastern European deli counter. *5600 Buford Hwy. NE* *770/455–0770* *www.aofwc.com.*

MALLS

Atlantic Station

SHOPPING NEIGHBORHOODS | A mixed-use development and outdoor mall, Atlantic Station covers about 10 square blocks, clustered around a green space known as Central Park. Retailers include IKEA, the Dillard's department store, Banana Republic, and H&M. It's easy to reach by car but is also accessible by free shuttle buses from the Arts Center MARTA station. An on-site concierge is happy to help you find your way around or to make dinner reservations for you at the more than a dozen restaurants here. ✉ *1380 Atlantic Dr., Midtown* ☎ *404/410–4010* 🌐 *www.atlanticstation.com.*

Avalon

SHOPPING NEIGHBORHOODS | Explore Anthropologie, have an authentic Persian meal at Rumi's Kitchen, then indulge in dessert from Cafe Intermezzo at this outdoor mall. This 86-acre community with apartments and a hotel nearby is in the heart of Alpharetta. It features more than 500,000 square feet of retail for hours of shopping, including a 12-screen movie theater—and it's entirely walkable. ✉ *400 Avalon Blvd., Alpharetta* ☎ *770/765–1000* 🌐 *www.experienceavalon.com.*

Perimeter Mall

SHOPPING CENTERS/MALLS | Known for upscale family shopping, Perimeter Mall has Nordstrom, Macy's, Dillard's, Von Maur, and a plentiful food court. Its restaurants include the Cheesecake Factory and Maggiano's Little Italy. ✉ *4400 Ashford-Dunwoody Rd., Dunwoody* ☎ *770/395–5860* 🌐 *www.perimetermall.com.*

Plaza Fiesta

CLOTHING | A 350,000-square-foot Latino shopping mall with more than 280 storefronts, Plaza Fiesta's got everything from cowboy boots to handmade tortillas to *quinceañera* dresses. ✉ *4166 Buford Hwy. NE* ☎ *404/982–9138* 🌐 *www.plazafiesta.net.*

OUTLETS

North Georgia Premium Outlets

OUTLET/DISCOUNT STORES | Here you'll find 140 stores, including Williams-Sonoma, OshKosh B'gosh, and numerous designer outlet shops like Coach, Ann Taylor, Banana Republic, and Polo Ralph Lauren. For the true shopper, it's worth the 45 minutes it takes to get here from Atlanta's northern perimeter. ✉ *800 GA 400 S, Dawsonville* ⊕ *At Dawson Forest Rd.* ☎ *706/216–3609* 🌐 *www.premiumoutlets.com/outlet/north-georgia.*

Outlet Shoppes at Atlanta

OUTLET/DISCOUNT STORES | Head 30 miles northwest of Downtown to get your fill of more than 80 outlet stores, including Coach, Kate Spade, Brooks Brothers, and Nike. ✉ *915 Ridgewalk Pkwy., Woodstock* ☎ *678/540–7040* 🌐 *www.theoutletshoppesatatlanta.com.*

Sugarloaf Mills

OUTLET/DISCOUNT STORES | Twenty-five miles northeast of Downtown Atlanta, this outlet mall has stores that include Saks Fifth Avenue Off 5th, Levi's, and Bass Pro Shops. ✉ *5900 Sugarloaf Pkwy., Lawrenceville* ☎ *678/847–5000* 🌐 *www.simon.com/mall/sugarloaf-mills.*

Activities

Atlanta Gladiators

HOCKEY | The Atlanta Gladiators, a farm team for the NHL's Boston Bruins, play in the ECHL, a nationwide hockey league. Games are played October to April. ✉ *Infinite Energy Center, 6400 Sugarloaf Pkwy., Duluth* ☎ *770/497–5100* 🌐 *www.atlantagladiators.com.*

Chapter 15

CENTRAL AND NORTH GEORGIA

Updated by
Rachel Roberts Quartarone

 Sights	 Restaurants	 Hotels	 Shopping	 Nightlife
★★★★★	★★★★☆	★★★☆☆	★★★☆☆	★★☆☆☆

WELCOME TO CENTRAL AND NORTH GEORGIA

TOP REASONS TO GO

★ **The Antebellum Trail:** Traveling this picturesque trail between Macon and Athens will cast you back in time and introduce you to the elegance of the Old South.

★ **Surround yourself with Civil War history:** The second-bloodiest battle of the Civil War was fought for two days at the site of Chickamauga and Chattanooga National Military Park.

★ **Take a hike:** The starting point of the more-than-2,100-mile Appalachian Trail is at Springer Mountain, a few miles north of Amicalola Falls, the tallest cascading waterfall east of the Mississippi.

★ **Lovely lakes:** Lake Oconee, Lake Allatoona, Lake Hartwell, and Lake Rabun provide numerous recreational opportunities.

★ **Explore the Native American past:** Visit New Echota, the former capital of the Cherokee Nation, which offers tribute to the proud tribe. Nearby is the historic Vann House, a beautiful three-story residence of Cherokee chief James Vann.

1 Rome and the Chieftans Trail. Named after Italy's Eternal City.

2 Chickamauga and Chattanooga National Military Park. It was here in 1863 that Union and Confederate forces fought for control of Chattanooga, the gateway to the Deep South. It's considered one of the bloodiest battles of the Civil War.

3 Dahlonega. Georgia's gold rush town, Dahlonega today boasts a charming town square and has emerged as a hot spot for viticulture in the state.

4 Helen and the Sautee Nacoochee Valley. Beautiful mountain scenery, a thriving art and crafts scene, and a touch of Alpine kitsch.

5 Clayton. The gateway to North Georgia's mountains

6 Hiawassee, Young Harris, and Lake Chatuge. Sparkling blue lakes, gorgeous state parks, winding scenic mountain highways, and Brasstown Bald, the highest point in Georgia.

7 Blue Ridge and Ellijay. Rolling mountain landscapes, abundant outdoor activities, small-town charm, and a scenic railway keep visitors flocking to Blue Ridge and Ellijay.

8 Macon. Known for its colorful cherry trees and historic homes and as the birthplace of many of Georgia's famed musicians, Macon exudes Southern charm.

9 Milledgeville. This quiet college town, home to writer Flannery O'Connor, was the state capital before Atlanta "stole" it away in 1868. The former state capitol, governor's mansion, and many

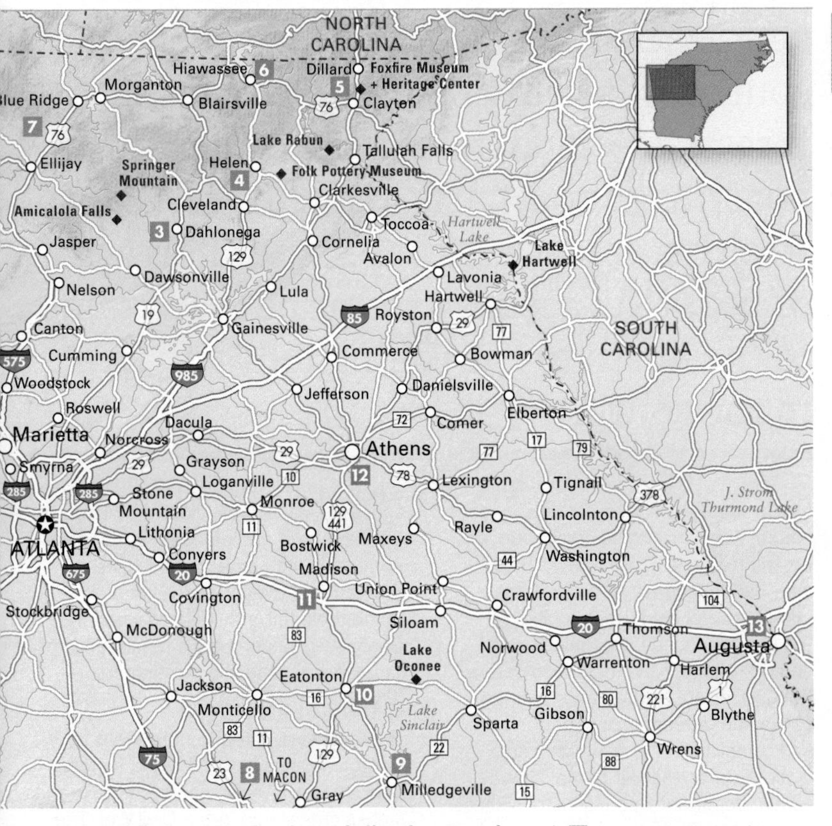

other buildings survived the Civil War and are part of the fabric of Milledgeville.

10 Eatonton. Home to celebrated Georgia authors, this quaint small town sits in the heart of Georgia's lake country.

11 Madison. One of Georgia's oldest and largest national historic districts, Madison boasts beautifully preserved antebellum homes and a quaint town square filled with antiques shops and charming cafés.

12 Athens. Home to the University of Georgia, this vibrant college town offers museums, historic homes, and a dining, bar, and music scene that will keep you busy for days.

13 Augusta. Georgia's second-oldest city, Augusta celebrates its colonial roots. It also has a rich tradition of golfing, with the Masters Tournament focusing the attention of the world on Augusta each spring

It is often said there are two Georgias: Atlanta and the rest of the state. While Atlanta offers bright lights and big-city action, the regions to the north and southeast are filled with farms, lush forests, sleepy hamlets, and larger towns boasting vibrant arts and cultural scenes. In either direction, there is no shortage of beautiful scenery from the mountains to the north to the rolling hills and rivers to the south.

North Georgia is known for its abundant natural wonders and its cool mountain air. The region is home to the 750,000-acre Chattahoochee National Forest, where several bold rivers, including the Chattahoochee, Oconee, Toccoa, and Chattooga, have their headwaters. Rabun, Burton, Nottley, and Chatuge Lakes offer recreational opportunities and camping. To the northwest are quaint river towns like Rome, as well as two important Georgia historic sites: New Echota State Historic Site and the Chickamauga and Chattanooga National Military Park.

Whether planning a day trip from Atlanta or a longer exploration, there is plenty to do and see in Central Georgia. Head down U.S. Route 441—the Antebellum Trail—from Athens to Macon, and you'll quickly see that the elegance of the Old South is new again, with many historic buildings returned to their original splendor. Athens, home of the University of Georgia, pulses with college life, especially when the Bulldogs are playing. For a taste of old Georgia, Macon's historical architecture is unmatched. Farther east, Augusta is the home of the Masters Tournament. Even if you're not drawn to the tees, this city—like so many in Georgia—is undergoing a renaissance of its waterfront and historic districts.

MAJOR REGIONS

The Northwest. A trip to northwest Georgia reveals its fascinating history, from its Native American heritage to the state's critical role in the Civil War. The Cherokee Nation once had its capital in New Echota, before the federal government forced members of the tribe on a long, tragic resettlement march to Oklahoma, marking the infamous Trail of Tears. A few years later, the Civil War's second-bloodiest battle was fought at the site of Chickamauga and Chattanooga National Military Park, which is commemorated by hundreds of monuments and markers in the country's first Civil War battlefield park.

The North Georgia Mountains. North Georgia has become a fascinating meld of the past and the present. Its residents wholeheartedly cherish their Appalachian roots at attractions such as the Foxfire Museum and Heritage Center and the Folk Pottery Museum of Northeast Georgia. They take pride in introducing visitors to their music as well as their natural surroundings: mountains, hiking trails (including the Appalachian Trail), and waterfalls. But residents are embracing the mountains' potential for new ventures, as well. Award-winning wineries are springing up across the region, and a passion for fine dining is a natural accompaniment.

Macon and the Antebellum Trail. The Antebellum Trail begins in Athens and travels 100 miles through seven communities that survived General Sherman's march through Georgia. Stop in Macon for its musical heritage and the National Landmark Hay House, which some say held Confederate gold in a secret room.

Augusta. Though the Masters Golf Tournament put this 200,000-person city on the map, Augusta also charms with its antebellum mansions and tree-lined streets dotted with shops.

Planning

When to Go

Summer in the South can be unpleasant; temperatures of 90°F or higher (plus humidity) cause even the most Southern of Southerners to wilt. The best times to visit Central Georgia are fall and spring, when temperatures are in the 60s and 70s and there are plenty of recreational activities to enjoy. Springtime is particularly lovely in Macon, as the cherry trees are in full bloom.

Spring, summer, and fall are prime times for travel in North Georgia. Weekends are far busier than weekdays, because many visitors drive up from nearby Atlanta for a short getaway. For the mountains, the ideal time is October and early November, when fall color is at its peak. Don't arrive without reservations during spring and early fall festival weekends, when visitors head north to enjoy the spring wildflowers, fall apple and pumpkin harvests, and absolutely blissful weather.

Planning Your Time

As a transportation hub, Atlanta is the jumping-off point for this region. In fact, many of North and Central Georgia's attractions are little more than an hour's drive from the city, making them perfect for a day trip. Panning for gold in Dahlonega, apple picking in Ellijay, and sampling North Georgia wines are worthy excursions. For a more relaxed pace, plan to stay overnight in the beautiful North Georgia mountains.

The bustling college town of Athens is a great place to start if you are interested in exploring the Antebellum Trail winding through Madison, Milledgeville, and Macon. With so much to do and see, consider breaking up the trip with an overnight stay. These cities also stand alone as day-trip destinations or overnight trips, particularly if history and architecture are of interest.

Getting Here and Around

AIR TRAVEL

The gateway airports for North Georgia are Hartsfield-Jackson International Airport (ATL) in Atlanta and Chattanooga Metropolitan Airport (CHA) in Chattanooga, Tennessee.

Direct flights are available from ATL or Charlotte Douglas International Airport (CLT) to Augusta Regional Airport (AGS) with Delta Airlines or American Airlines. The smaller regional airports mostly serve charters and small private planes. The most economical option to reach most destinations in North and Central Georgia is to fly into ATL and rent a car.

AIRPORT CONTACTS Athens Ben Epps Airport. (*AHN*) ✉ *1010 Ben Epps Dr., Athens* ☎ *706/613–3420* 🌐 *www.athensairport.net.* **Augusta Regional Airport (AGS).** (*AGS*) ✉ *1501 Aviation Way, Augusta* ☎ *706/798–3236* 🌐 *www.augustaregionalairport.com.* **Chattanooga Metropolitan Airport.** (*CHA*) ✉ *1001 Airport Rd., Chattanooga* ☎ *423/855–2200* 🌐 *www.chattairport.com.* **Hartsfield-Jackson Atlanta International Airport.** (*ATL*) ✉ *6000 N. Terminal Pkwy., Atlanta* ☎ *404/530–7300, 800/897–1910* 🌐 *www.atl.com.* **Middle Georgia Regional Airport.** (*MCN*) ✉ *1000 Terminal Dr., Macon* ☎ *478/788–3760* 🌐 *www.iflymacon.com.*

CAR TRAVEL

U.S. Route 441, known as the Antebellum Trail, runs north–south, merging with U.S. Route 129 for a stretch and connecting Athens, Madison, Eatonton, and Milledgeville. Macon is on George State Route 49, which splits from U.S. Route 441 at Milledgeville. Washington lies at the intersection of U.S. Route 78, running east from Athens to Thomson, and Georgia State Route 44, running south to Eatonton. Interstate 20 runs east from Atlanta to Augusta, which is about 93 miles east of U.S. Route 441.

Plan on using your car—or renting one—to get around North Georgia. U.S. Route 19 runs north–south, passing through Dahlonega and up into the North Georgia mountains. U.S. Route 129 travels northwest from Athens, eventually merging with U.S. Route 19. Georgia State Route 75 stems off of U.S. Route 129 and goes through Helen and up into the mountains. U.S. Route 23/441 will take you north through Clayton; U.S. Route 76 runs west from Clayton to Dalton, merging for a stretch with Georgia State Route 5/515. Georgia State Route 52 runs along the edge of the Blue Ridge Mountains, passing through Ellijay. Interstate 75 is the major artery in the northwesternmost part of the state and passes near Rome and the Chickamauga and Chattanooga National Military Park.

Restaurants

Central and North Georgia offer an abundance of dining options from hole-in-the-wall barbecue joints to upscale eateries serving sophisticated cuisine. The culinary specialty is Southern food, of course, and a heaping plate of fried chicken washed down with sweet tea is a must. Aside from traditional local fare, plenty of other options are available in larger towns like Athens and Macon. In the North Georgia mountains, you'll find quite a bit of culinary sophistication at many of the charming little bistros on the town squares and near the scenic wineries that dot the Wine Highway. *Restaurant reviews have been shortened. For full information, visit Fodors.com.*

Hotels

The most attractive lodging options here tend to have been around for a long time; the structures often date from the 19th century. At such places—most commonly bed-and-breakfasts but sometimes larger inns—you're likely to find big porches with rocking chairs and bedrooms decorated with antiques. If that's more Southern charm than you're after, you can choose from a smattering of chain hotels or more modern resorts. In the North Georgia mountains and near the recreational areas of Central Georgia there is also a large variety of cabins and home rentals. *Hotel reviews have been shortened. For full information, visit Fodors.com.*

What It Costs

	$	$$	$$$	$$$$
RESTAURANTS				
	under $15	$15–$19	$20–$24	over $24
HOTELS				
	under $150	$150–$200	$201–$250	over $250

Visitor Information

CONTACTS Georgia Welcome Center. ☎ *800/847–4842* 🌐 *www.exploregeorgia.org.*

Rome and the Chieftains Trail

71 miles northwest of Atlanta via I–75 North to U.S. 411/GA 20; 66 miles southwest of Ellijay via GA 53.

Nestled in the countryside of Northwest Georgia is the antebellum town of Rome. Like its Italian namesake, it's built on seven hills with a river running between them. Georgia's Rome sits at the confluence of the Etowah and Oostanaula Rivers and was once a bustling river transportation hub. Cotton was king here, and the city's industry and riverfront location played an important role in the Civil War. With the decline of steamboats and the rise of the automobile, Rome's industry suffered as the interstate highway system reached north to Dalton but did not extend westward to Rome. Nonetheless, Rome reinvented itself as a business and education hub, preserving much of its architecture and green space with scenic river walks and parks. Its central location and historic charm make it a great place to stay and see other points of interest in the northwest Georgia region.

Rome is also an entry point to Georgia's Chieftains Trail. Start at Chieftains Museum, the historic home of Major Ridge, one of the signers of the Treaty of New Echota. The treaty was essentially a forced agreement between the Cherokee and the federal government that launched the tragic Trail of Tears. A significant site on the heritage trail, New Echota returned to farmland after the eviction of the Cherokee but now serves as a state historic site with re-creations and some original buildings depicting the Cherokee capital as it was in the early 19th century. A bit farther north near Chatsworth, you can also visit the Chief Vann House, the 1804 mansion known as the "Showplace of the Cherokee Nation." For a touch of mystery, head east to Fort Mountain State Park to see a massive rock wall that dates back to AD 500. Many theories abound as to who built it—from unknown Indian tribes to the Cherokee legend of "Moon Eyes"—but no one knows for sure.

GETTING HERE AND AROUND

This is a good day trip from Atlanta. Take Interstate 75 to Exit 290. Head west on Georgia State Route 20 until it merges with U.S. Route 411 South to reach Rome.

Sights

★ Chief Vann House

HOUSE | This beautiful home with all the trappings of the wealthy planter lifestyle is fascinating because of the intermingling of cultures that took place here. Known as Diamond Hill, this historic site was home to a 1,000-acre plantation—the largest and most prosperous in Cherokee history. In 1804 James Vann, a Cherokee leader of mixed Scottish and Cherokee parentage, built the plantation's stately redbrick mansion with the help of Moravian missionaries and enslaved workers. When Vann was murdered in 1809, his son Joseph took over the property until he was forcibly evicted in 1835. Diamond Hill and surrounding lands were then given away in a land lottery to white settlers, its Cherokee origins wiped away.

Start your visit in the visitor center where you can view a short film and browse exhibits about the site's history. Rangers lead tours of the home, but outdoor exhibits, such as a re-created Cherokee farmstead and plantation kitchen, are self-guided. The kitchen outbuilding also houses an exhibit focused on the daily lives of the 110 enslaved people who resided at Diamond Hill before Vann's departure in 1835. ✉ *82 GA 225, Chatsworth* ✣ *At GA 52A, 17 miles north of New Echota, 44 miles northeast of Rome* ☎ *706/695–2598* 🌐 *www.gastateparks.org/ChiefVannHouse* 🎟 *$7* ⏲ *Closed Mon.–Wed. Closed Sun. Dec.–Mar.*

Chieftains Museum

HOUSE | This historic home, now a museum, was built by Cherokee leader Major Ridge and is a part of the Trail of Tears National Historic Trail. The 1828 white clapboard plantation home is built around a two-story log cabin. Visitors can peek behind the plaster walls to see the original wooden foundation. Major Ridge and his family lived here and operated a successful trading post and ferry until 1837 when they were forced out to Oklahoma. Although several other families lived in the home and modified it over the years, it came to be known as "Chieftains" in honor of Ridge. The museum features displays detailing the history of the house, the Ridge family, and artifacts from archaeological digs on the property. ✉ *501 Riverside Pkwy., Rome* ☎ *706/291–9494* 🌐 *www.chieftainsmuseum.org* 🎟 *$5* ⏲ *Closed Sun.–Tues.*

Fort Mountain State Park

NATIONAL/STATE PARK | **FAMILY** | This 3,712-acre state park has a 17-acre lake with sandy beach, 14 miles of hiking trails, and 27 miles of mountain-biking trails. The gem of the park is a mysterious wall of rock, 855 feet long, thought to have been built by Native Americans around AD 500. Walk-in tent and premium tent/ RV sites ($18–$36) as well as two- and three-bedroom cottages ($175–$200) are available. The park also offers a unique primitive site for camping with horses. ✉ *181 Fort Mountain Park Rd., Chatsworth* ☎ *706/422–1932* 🌐 *www.gastateparks.org/fortmountain* 🎫 *Free, parking $5.*

New Echota State Historic Site

NATIVE SITE | FAMILY | Made up of a dozen original and reconstructed buildings, this significant historic site allows visitors to explore the capital of the Cherokee nation on the land where the city once stood. It was here that the Treaty of 1835 was signed by a small group of Cherokee leaders, setting into motion the Trail of Tears. The only original building remaining is the Worcester House, a home and Presbyterian mission station. The Cherokee Council House and Supreme Court are reconstructions, as is the print house, where thousands of books translated in Cherokee and the weekly *Cherokee Phoenix* were published. Other buildings, including the 1805 Vann Tavern, were relocated to the site. A museum and film provide more insight on the rich history of the Cherokee in Georgia. ✉ *1211 Chatsworth Hwy., Calhoun* ✣ *GA 225, 1 mile east of I–75* ☎ *706/624–1321* 🌐 *www.georgiastateparks.org/newechota* 🎫 *$7* 🕘 *Closed Mon. Also closed Sun. Dec.–Mar.*

Oak Hill and the Martha Berry Museum

COLLEGE | Dedicated to Martha Berry, founder of Berry College, the museum includes exhibits on the history of the college (located just down the street) and a tour of Berry's 1884 Greek Revival family home, Oak Hill. Berry founded the college in 1902 to help impoverished mountain children gain an education and life skills. Today, it is recognized as one of the top small liberal arts colleges in the country. Oak Hill is preserved as it was when Berry died in 1927. Be sure to stroll the picturesque gardens and outbuildings. If time permits, drive through Berry College for a look at the Gothic-style stone Ford Complex built between 1925 and 1931 and donated by Berry's friend, Henry Ford. ✉ *24 Veterans Memorial Hwy., Rome* ☎ *706/368–6789* 🌐 *www.berry.edu/oakhill* 🎫 *$8* 🕘 *Closed Sun.*

Restaurants

★ Harvest Moon Café

$$ | AMERICAN | With its warm exposed brick walls and folk art decor, this local favorite specializes in Southern-inspired, from-scratch cooking. Everything, from the salad dressings to the bread, is made in-house. **Known for:** comfort food; scratch-made bread and desserts; rooftop bar. 💲 *Average main: $15* ✉ *234 Broad St., Rome* ☎ *706/292–0099* 🌐 *www.myharvestmooncafe.com.*

Coffee and Quick Bites

Swift & Finch Coffee

$ | AMERICAN | The coffee is roasted on-site at this hip coffee shop housed in a former service station in the heart of downtown Rome. The open and airy space offers tons of seating and a wide variety of tasty handcrafted beverages—from basic espresso and fancier coffee drinks, to gourmet teas and smoothies. **Known for:** high-quality beans roasted on-site; spacious, industrial-style interior perfect for hanging out; pastries and snacks. 💲 *Average main: $6* ✉ *600 Broad St., Rome* ☎ *706/237–6750* 🌐 *www.swiftandfinch.com* 🕘 *Closed Sun.*

Barnsley Resort
$$$$ | **RESORT** | This award-winning resort features luxurious and comfortable accommodations, a brand-new 55-room inn, a championship golf course, a boutique spa, elevated on-site cuisine, horseback riding, the Beretta Shooting Grounds, and miles of nature trails. **Pros:** beautiful grounds; tastefully decorated rooms; spa, plus tons of outdoor activity options. **Cons:** pricey; not easy to find at night; may be too remote for some. *Rooms from: $285 597 Barnsley Gardens Rd., Adairsville 770/773–7480, 877/773–2447 www.barnsleyresort.com 150 rooms, 37 cottages No meals.*

Hawthorn Suites by Wyndham Rome
$$ | **HOTEL** | Located in Rome's historic downtown district, the Hawthorn Suites is housed in a beautifully renovated 1890s warehouse with original wood floors, brick walls, and a large skylit atrium. **Pros:** historical charm on the river; tastefully decorated rooms; walking distance of shops, restaurants, and attractions. **Cons:** no pool; can fill up quickly due to events; some rooms can be noisy. *Rooms from: $160 100–110 W. 2nd Ave., Rome 706/378–4837, 800/337–0246 www.hawthorn.com 65 rooms Free breakfast.*

Chickamauga and Chattanooga National Military Park

110 miles northwest of Atlanta via I–75 and GA 2; 42 miles north of New Echota State Historic Site via I–75; 12 miles south of Chattanooga, TN, via U.S. 27.

With nearly a million visitors a year, Chickamauga and Chattanooga National Military Park is one of the most popular battlefields in the country. Here you can gain a fuller sense of one of the Confederacy's greatest military victories by touring the battle lines, standing where the soldiers faced the pain and intensity of war, and imagining the cacophony produced by cannons, gunfire, and battle cries. This site, established in 1890 as the nation's first military park, was the scene of some of the Civil War's bloodiest battles. In Chickamauga alone, 34,624 were killed, missing, and wounded in September 1863. Though the Confederates won the battle at Chickamauga, the Union army retained control of Chattanooga. The normally thick cedar groves and foliage covering Chickamauga were trampled and, according to eyewitness accounts, trees were so shot up that a sweet cedar smell mingled with the blood of fallen soldiers.

Some areas around the park now suffer from suburban sprawl, but the 9,000-acre park itself is made up of serene fields and islands of trees. Monuments, battlements, and weapons adorn the roads that traverse the park, with markers explaining the action.

GETTING HERE AND AROUND

Take Interstate 75 north from Atlanta to the exit for Fort Oglethorpe and follow signs through a small but congested area to the national military park and Cloudland Canyon.

★ Chickamauga and Chattanooga National Military Park
INFO CENTER | A visit to this 9,000-acre military park could easily take all day—or multiple days. The park spans the borders of Georgia and Tennessee, with major sites at Chickamauga, Lookout Mountain, Moccasin Bend, Missionary Ridge, Orchard Knob, and Signal Point. Overall, there are more than 1,400 commemorative features throughout the park

Continued on page 551

A CIVIL WAR TOUR
CHICKAMAUGA BATTLEFIELD

By Rickey Bevington

Chickamauga Battlefield today

With nearly a million visitors a year, Chickamauga & Chattanooga National Military Park is one of the most popular battlefields in the country. Here you can gain a fuller sense of one of the Confederacy's greatest military victories by touring the battle lines, standing where the soldiers faced the pain and intensity of war, and imagining the cacophony produced by cannons, gunfire, and battle cries.

Lithograph of Battle of Chickamauga, 1890

UNDERSTANDING THE BATTLE

Left and center, commanding generals William S. Rosecrans (Union) and Braxton Bragg (Confederacy). Right, General George H. Thomas (Union), also known as the Rock of Chickamauga

Why was the September 19–20, 1863, Battle of Chickamauga so important? To the war-weary people and soldiers of the Confederacy, it was a morale-boosting victory on the heels of losses at Gettysburg and Vicksburg only months before. To the fatigued Union states, it was an important test of their use of Chattanooga, Tennessee, as a supply center from which to launch their advance into the Deep South. Union forces had captured the nearby city less than a month before in a bloodless advance. As they continued their push south into the far northwest corner of Georgia, Atlanta was in their sights. But Confederate soldiers were ready. Over two days of some of the war's fiercest fighting, 16,170 Union and 18,454 Confederate men and boys fell or were injured at the Battle of Chickamauga, named for the nearby creek where hostilities began. On the second day, the Confederates managed to send the Union soldiers into full retreat back to Chattanooga. It would take nine more months of fighting before U.S. General William Tecumseh Sherman was able to reach his original objective, Atlanta.

DECISIVE UNION VICTORIES

On January 1, 1863, President Lincoln issued the Emancipation Proclamation, which declared "that all persons held as slaves" within the seceded states "are, and henceforth shall be free."

Three strategic victories in this year proved crucial to the north's eventual victory over the south. The July 1863 battle of Gettysburg was Confederate

CIVIL WAR TIMELINE

Civil War Union Flag

President Abraham Lincoln

1861

March 4, Abraham Lincoln is inaugurated.

March 11, Confederate Constitution is signed.

April 12, American Civil War begins.

July 21, First Battle of Bull Run.

1862

September 17, Battle of Antietam.

December 13, Battle of Fredricksburg.

1863

January 1, Lincoln issues the Emancipation Proclamation.

July 1–3, Battle of Gettysburg.

1863: A PIVOTAL YEAR IN THE CIVIL WAR

Confederate troops advancing at Chickamauga, drawing by Alfred R. Waud, Civil War correspondant.

General Robert E. Lee's last major offensive; 170,000 men fought over three days with 51,000 casualties, after which Lee retreated to Virginia. The following day, July 4, Vicksburg, MS, surrendered to Union forces laying siege under the command of Union General Ulysses S. Grant. For the north, taking Vicksburg soon meant controlling the Mississippi River south to New Orleans, cutting the Confederacy in half. In early September, Union forces marched into Chattanooga and seized its river, railroads, and a major Confederate supply center. A vital railroad junction, Chattanooga would become the crucial supply center for Union troops advancing south toward Atlanta.

BATTLE OF CHICKAMAUGA

In September 1863 Union forces followed Confederates retreating into Georgia after abandoning Chattanooga. Morale was low among southern forces after the summer's defeats, but a chance skirmish launched what would be the largest battle and final Confederate victory in the war's western theater. The two-day clash ended with Union forces rapidly retreating north to safer ground at Chattanooga. Confederates were ecstatic, but this battle did little but buy the south time. One month later, U.S. General William Tecumseh Sherman took command of the Union force at Chattanooga and set his sights on Atlanta.

July 4, Confederates surrender Vicksburg.

September 19–20, Battle of Chickamauga.

1864

September 2, Sherman captures Atlanta.

November 15, Sherman begins his "March to the Sea."

1865

April 9, Lee surrenders to Grant at Appomattox Courthouse.

April 14, President Lincoln is shot.

December 6, The Thirteenth Amendment abolishes slavery.

Sherman's March to Sea

U.S. General William Tecumseh Sherman

TOURING CHICKAMAUGA BATTLEFIELD

Snodgrass house.

GETTING HERE

From Atlanta, take I–75 north; the 110-mile drive takes about two hours. Take exit 350 (Battlefield Parkway) to Fort Oglethorpe and follow signs to the National Military Park.

PLANNING YOUR TIME

Plan to spend from one hour to an afternoon here. Start with the a visit to the excellent **Chickamauga Battlefield Visitor Center**, which offers a timeline of the battle, a film on the military strategy, a collection of more than 300 antique military rifles, and a well-stocked bookstore. Pack a picnic lunch and go for a hike along one of the park's designated nature trails.

THE AUTO TOUR

Imagine crawling out of a dense wood into an open field only to see a uniform line of thousands of enemy soldiers marching steadily toward you. That's just one of the battle scenes described in the seven-mile auto tour of the battle's most significant events. Pick up a free map and brochure at the visitor center with information on the sights. From Memorial Day to Labor Day rangers lead artillery demonstrations and free two-hour auto caravan tours.

Left, 10th Wisconsin Infantry monument

TOUR HIGHLIGHTS

❶ Starting just outside the visitor center heading south from Stop 1 (where the Florida monument now stands), follow the road that on the second day of battle separated a force of 65,000 Confederates firing from your left toward 62,000 Union troops trying to regain position on your right. The tour follows this battle line nearly the length of the battlefield. Unlike most Civil War engagements, this one did not take place in an open field, and the forested landscape has been preserved much as it was on the day of battle.

❺ Once you veer west at Viniard Field, you are beginning to follow the steps of the retreating Union forces as they succumbed to Confederates pushing them back toward Chattanooga.

❻ The Wilder Brigade Monument is an 85-foot high stone tower honoring Union

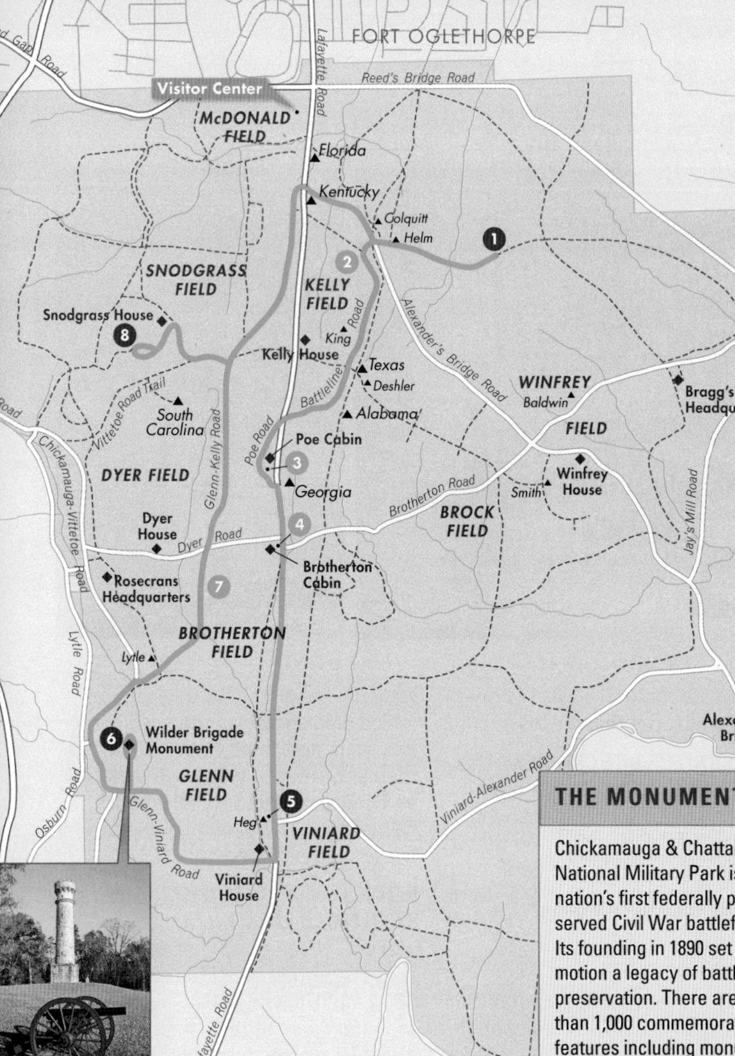

Battlefield and cannon

Colonel John Wilder and his "Lightning Brigade," a group of fast-moving cavalrymen known for their rare but deadly Spencer-7 carbine repeating rifles.

❽ The tour's final stop is Snodgrass Hill. This is the high ground where U.S. General George H. Thomas stayed behind his retreating army to thwart pursuing Confederates, giving Union forces enough time to reach Chattanooga safely. Many of Thomas' men were killed or captured and taken to the notorious Camp Sumter at Andersonville.

THE MONUMENTS

Chickamauga & Chattanooga National Military Park is the nation's first federally preserved Civil War battlefield. Its founding in 1890 set in motion a legacy of battlefield preservation. There are more than 1,000 commemorative features including monuments, markers, and tablets placed by veterans and by states whose citizens saw combat here. Take time to admire the monuments' design and inscription, and look for monuments from your home state. Red tablets describe Confederate action and blue mark Union activity. Large pyramids of naval shells indicate where a brigade commander was mortally wounded in combat.

OTHER GEORGIA CIVIL WAR SITES

Left, Andersonville Prisoner of War Museum. Right, Kennesaw Battlefield.

To experience more Civil War history in Georgia, check out these sites.

RESACA CONFEDERATE CEMETERY. This intimate, shaded cemetery is the final resting place for more than 450 Confederate soldiers. After the Battle of Resaca in May 1864, resident Mary J. Green returned to her farm to find hundreds of Confederates buried haphazardly where they had fallen. She raised the money to re-inter them on 2 1/2 acres in a corner of the family farm. ⊠ *40 miles southeast of Chickamauga, take I-75 to exit 318 for U.S. 41 to Confederate Cemetery Rd.*

ANDERSONVILLE NATIONAL HISTORIC SITE. The infamous Civil War–era Camp Sumter, commonly called Andersonville, was one of the largest prisons built in the Confederacy. Over 14 months, 45,000 Union soldiers were confined within a 26 1/2-acre open-air stockade; 13,000 died from disease and exposure—a rate of more than 30 a day. You can tour the rebuilt stockade walls and historic prison grounds here. The National Prisoner of War Museum, which also serves as the site's visitor center, is dedicated to the American men and women who have suffered as POWs. Andersonville National Cemetery is the final resting place for those who perished here.

KENNESAW MOUNTAIN NATIONAL BATTLEFIELD PARK. More than 160,000 Union and Confederate soldiers battled here from June 19, 1864, until July 2, 1864. This popular mountain park attracts history enthusiasts as well as runners, hikers, cyclists, and families.

ATLANTA HISTORY CENTER. Life in Atlanta and the rest of the South during and after the Civil War are a major focus of this fascinating museum. Displays are provocative, juxtaposing *Gone With The Wind* romanticism with the grim reality of Ku Klux Klan racism. Located on 33 acres in the heart of Buckhead, this is one of the Southeast's largest history museums.

including monuments, markers, and tablets placed by veterans and by states whose citizens saw combat here. Start at Chickamauga Battlefield, the park's headquarters, which makes up the largest part of the park. It was here on September 19–20, 1863, that the Battle of Chickamauga was fought. The excellent visitor center and museum offers a film and exhibits about the battle. There's also a 7-mile self-guided auto tour through the park, and on weekends during the spring and fall, you can join a free two-hour auto caravan, led by a park ranger. During the summer, rangers offer the tours daily at 10 and 2. The rest of the park lies about 30 minutes north of Chickamauga: Lookout Mountain Battlefield and Point Park, a memorial park that overlooks the city of Chattanooga. ✉ *3370 LaFayette Rd., Fort Oglethorpe* ✥ *1 mile south of intersection of GA 2 and U.S. 27* ☎ *706/866–9241* 🌐 *www.nps.gov/chch* 🎫 *Free.*

Cloudland Canyon State Park
CANYON | At this 3,538-acre park you can see firsthand the unusual geology of this remote part of northwestern Georgia. Hike down the canyon, which drops 1,100 feet from the rim, and you're literally walking through millions of years of geologic time. If you make it all the way to the bottom—the trail totals 4 miles—you'll be rewarded with sights of two waterfalls. There are great tent and RV camping sites here, as well as cottages and yurts. ✉ *122 Cloudland Canyon Park Rd., Rising Fawn* ☎ *706/657–4050* 🌐 *www.georgiastateparks.org/cloudland-canyon* 🎫 *Parking $5.*

Dahlonega

65 miles northeast of Atlanta via GA 400 and GA 60.

Hordes of fortune seekers stormed the town of Dahlonega (pronounced dah-LON-eh-gah) in the 1820s after the discovery of gold in the nearby hills. The town's name comes from the Cherokee word for "precious yellow metal." But the boom didn't last long; by 1849 miners were starting to seek riches elsewhere. In fact, the famous call "There's gold in them thar hills!" originated as an enticement to miners in the Georgia mountains to keep their minds away from the lure of the Western gold rush. It worked for a while, but government price-fixing eventually made gold mining unprofitable, and by the early 1920s Dahlonega's mining operations had halted completely.

Many former mining settlements became ghost towns, but not Dahlonega. Today it thrives with an irresistible town square filled with country stores, art galleries, gem shops, old small-town businesses, and several sophisticated restaurants. Gold Rush Days, a festival held the third weekend in October and celebrating the first gold rush in 1828, attracts about 200,000 weekend visitors. The town also shines during December with holiday lights and events.

GETTING HERE AND AROUND

It's easy to spend your entire visit in Dahlonega's quaint town square. But a short drive out of town will allow you to climb down into a gold mine or taste wine at the local vintners.

VISITOR INFORMATION

CONTACTS Dahlonega-Lumpkin Chamber of Commerce and Visitors Center. ✉ *13 Park St. S* ☎ *706/864–3711, 800/231–5543* 🌐 *www.dahlonega.org.*

Sights

Amicalola Falls State Park
BODY OF WATER | This is claimed to be the highest cascading waterfall east of the Mississippi, with waters plunging an eye-popping 729 feet through a cluster of seven cascades. The surrounding 829-acre state park contains a visitor center, lodge, and restaurant and is dotted with scenic campsites and cottages strategically situated near a network of nature

trails, picnic sites, and fishing streams. The southern starting point of the more than 2,100-mile Appalachian Trail begins near Amicalola Falls. ✉ *418 Amicalola Falls Lodge Rd., Dawsonville* ✣ *Off GA 52, 18 miles west of Dahlonega* ☎ *706/265–4703* 🌐 *www.gastateparks.org/AmicalolaFalls* 🎟 *Parking $5.*

Consolidated Gold Mine

MINE | **FAMILY** | Take a guided tour of a real mine, which ceased operations in 1904. With 5 miles of underground tunnels, Consolidated is said to be the largest gold mine east of the Mississippi. Enter the mine (which has been reconstructed for safety), pass through a breathtaking stone passage, and then begin a descent of 120 feet into the mine's geological wonders. Knowledgeable guides expound on historical mining techniques and give demonstrations of tools, such as the "widowmaker," a drill that kicks up mining dust and caused lung disease in many miners. After the tour, guests are invited to pan for gold, prospector style, from a long wooden sluice. Gemstone mining is also available for an additional fee. ✉ *185 Consolidated Gold Mine Rd.* ☎ *706/864–8473* 🌐 *www.consolidated-goldmine.com* 🎟 *$20.*

Crisson Gold Mine

MINE | **FAMILY** | Dahlonega's oldest gold mining establishment open to the public, Crisson offers the opportunity to get serious about gold prospecting. There's indoor and outdoor gold panning and gem grubbing as well as outdoor exhibits that guide guests through the gold mining process. You can also see mining equipment in action, including a 130-year-old stamp mill that's still used to crush gold-bearing quartz. Wagon rides take you by the old tunnels and a functional open pit mine. The gift shop is worth a stop for the gemstone jewelry and unique gold gifts. ✉ *2736 Morrison Moore Pkwy. E* ☎ *706/864–6363* 🌐 *www.crissongold-mine.com* 🎟 *$12.95 per person (ages 4 and up).*

Dahlonega Gold Museum

HISTORIC SITE | Located in the center of the town square, this museum has coins, tools, and several large nuggets on display. Built in 1836, this former courthouse is one of the oldest public buildings in the state. If you look closely at the bricks that form the building's foundation, you'll notice a sprinkling of gold dust in their formation. Along with two floors of exhibits, the museum features a high-definition film titled *America's First Gold Rush*. Arrive an hour before closing to be sure and catch the film. ✉ *1 Public Sq.* ☎ *706/864–2257* 🌐 *www.gastateparks.org/DahlonegaG-oldMuseum* 🎟 *$9.*

VINEYARDS

Grapevines and wineries are popping up all over North Georgia, and burgundy-color signs lead the way to vineyards along the **Georgia Wine Highway.** The Dahlonega area is home to the largest concentration of wineries in Georgia. A listing of current wineries is available at 🌐 *www.georgiawine.com.* **■ TIP→ If time doesn't permit individual visits to the wineries, you can try North Georgia wines in the many tasting rooms on the Dahlonega square.**

Frogtown Cellars

WINERY/DISTILLERY | This 57-acre vineyard and winery offers picturesque mountain views from its deck as well as a dramatic dining room. Since 2010, Frogtown wines have won more than 200 medals. Winemakers Craig and Sydney Kritzer believe it is one of the most awarded wineries in the country not located in California. Wine tastings are offered daily. Lunch is available Thursday to Saturday and dinner is available Friday through Sunday. Sunday brunch is a popular affair, and reservations are recommended for parties of six or more. ✉ *700 Ridge Point Dr.* ✣ *Northeast of Dahlonega* ☎ *706/865–0687* 🌐 *www.frogtown.com.*

Dahlonega's town square is worth a stroll, with country stores, art galleries, and restaurants.

Kaya Vineyard & Winery

WINERY/DISTILLERY | One of Dahlonega's newer wineries, Kaya's wines are produced exclusively from estate-grown grapes, including Chardonnay, Viognier, Touriga, Cabernet Sauvignon, and Merlot. The tasting room offers sweeping panoramic views of Dahlonega's beautiful mountain scenery and regularly features events. Tastings are offered daily along with light lunch items. ✉ *5400 Town Creek Rd.* ☎ *706/219–3514* 🌐 *www.kayavineyards.com* ⏲ *Closed Mon.*

Montaluce Winery

WINERY/DISTILLERY | Reminiscent of a grand Tuscan villa, this 13-acre vineyard features a state-of-the-art, 25,000-square-foot wine-making facility. Montaluce's spacious dining room–restaurant and multilevel terraces provide breathtaking views of mountain scenery. Wine tastings (for a fee) are offered on a first-come, first-served basis at Montaluce's Mediterranean-inspired wine bar and tasting room. You can book deluxe private tastings and a popular wine hike (a 1.8-mile hike plus wine tasting) online in advance. The winery's restaurant is open daily for lunch and dinner, with brunch on Sunday. Reservations are recommended. ✉ *501 Hightower Church Rd.* ☎ *866/991–8466* 🌐 *www.montaluce.com.*

Three Sisters Vineyards

WINERY/DISTILLERY | Dahlonega's first family-farm winery has 20 acres of plantings, including Cabernet Franc, Pinot Blanc, and Chardonnay, along with American varietals such as Cynthiana-Norton. The relaxed winery is named for nearby Three Sisters Mountain, visible from the farm's gazebo. On Saturdays (when weather permits), they feature a food truck and live music. The tasting room is decorated with folk art and pottery from the area, including a poster that proclaims "Thar's Wine in Them Thar Hills." A favorite from the winery is the robust Fat Boy Red. ✉ *439 Vineyard Way* ✣ *Northeast of Dahlonega* ☎ *706/865–9463* 🌐 *www.threesistersvineyards.com* ⏲ *Closed Mon.–Wed.*

Wolf Mountain Vineyards and Winery
WINERY/DISTILLERY | This award-winning winery features a 30-acre vineyard with hillside plantings of Cabernet Sauvignon, Syrah, Mourvèdre, and Touriga Nacional. The Craftsman-style lodge housing the winery and café offers tastings for a fee and serves lunch Thursday through Saturday from noon to 3, and a Sunday brunch with 12:30 and 2:30 seatings. Reservations are required. Wolf Mountain also offers quarterly gourmet dinners and guided tours of the grounds on weekends at noon. Some of the winery's acclaimed labels include Plenitude, a 70% Chardonnay and 30% Viognier blend, and Instinct, a Rhône-style red blend. ✉ *180 Wolf Mountain Trail* ✥ *Off U.S. 19/60, north of Dahlonega* ☎ *706/867–9862* 🌐 *www.wolfmountainvineyards.com* ⏲ *Closed Mon. and Tues. Seasonal hours vary; call ahead.*

Restaurants

Spirits Tavern
$ | **AMERICAN** | This lively pub just off the town square is known for its burgers and craft cocktails. The menu offers appetizers, salads, sandwiches, and a wide variety of certified Angus or grass-fed beef burgers with fun names like the Bearded Goat (topped with goat cheese and green tomato chow-chow) and the Rude Awakening (topped with an egg and hash browns). **Known for:** creative gourmet burgers; craft cocktails and mocktails; lively pub atmosphere. $ *Average main: $12* ✉ *19 E. Main St., Suite D* ☎ *706/482–0580* 🌐 *www.spirits-tavern.com.*

Coffee and Quick Bites

Picnic Cafe and Dessertery
$ | **BAKERY** | With its checkered tablecloths and farmhouse decor, you'll feel as if you've stepped back in time at this adorable café and bakery on Dahlonega's charming town square. The pastry case is filled with cakes, cookies, muffins, and other sweet treats. **Known for:** delicious pastries and desserts; pimento cheese and other Southern-style "salads"; coffee and breakfast all day. $ *Average main: $8* ✉ *30 Public Sq.* ☎ *706/864–1095* 🌐 *thepicniccafe.wixsite.com/picniccafe.*

Hotels

★ **Amicalola Falls Lodge**
$$ | **HOTEL** | One of the most appealing mountain lodges in Georgia is part of the state park system and features panoramic views over the mountains from the massive glass-windowed lobby. **Pros:** Amicalola Falls and numerous outdoor activities are minutes away; stunning views of the mountains; nice variety of room styles, suites, and cabins. **Cons:** no swimming pool; buffet-only restaurant is only on-site dining option; lodge fee charged in addition to daily rate. $ *Rooms from: $159* ✉ *418 Amicalola Falls Lodge Rd., Dawsonville* ✥ *20 miles west of Dahlonega* ☎ *706/265–8888, 800/573–9656* 🌐 *www.amicalolafallslodge.com* *57 rooms, 14 cottages* 🍽 *No meals.*

Dahlonega Square Hotel and Villas
$$ | **HOTEL** | This charming brick-red inn gave new life to the historic McGuire House just off the town square. **Pros:** convenient location, in walking distance of shops and restaurants; modern rooms and conveniences; wine-tasting room on-site. **Cons:** often booked well in advance on weekends; breakfast not included with rate; occasional noise from events and the pub next door. $ *Rooms from: $150* ✉ *135 N. Chestatee St.* ☎ *706/867–1313* 🌐 *www.dahlonegasquarevilla.com* *13 rooms, 5 villas* 🍽 *No meals.*

Mountain Laurel Creek Inn & Spa
$$ | **B&B/INN** | This intimate B&B nestled in the mountains just north of Dahlonega offers an on-site spa and pool. **Pros:** on-site spa, pub, and relaxing amenities; beautiful grounds; gourmet breakfast.

Three Sisters Vineyards has a friendly, down-to-earth tasting room. Be sure to try the Fat Boy Red if it's available.

Cons: some complain that beds aren't comfortable; eclectic decor isn't to everyone's liking; no TVs in rooms. *Rooms from: $164* *202 Talmer Grizzle Rd.* *706/867–8134* *www.mountainlaurelcreek.com* *7 rooms, 1 cottage* *Free breakfast.*

★ The Smith House

$$ | **B&B/INN** | Just a block from the town square, the family-owned Smith House has been serving guests in its inn and family-style restaurant for generations. **Pros:** historic charm with modern amenities; restaurant and country store on-site; great central location, in walking distance of the town square. **Cons:** on-site restaurant does not offer breakfast; historic inn baths are on the smaller side; no fitness room or pool. *Rooms from: $159* *84 S. Chestatee St.* *706/725–8148* *www.smithhouse.com* *39 rooms, 4 villas, 2 houses* *No meals.*

Nightlife

The Crimson Moon

MUSIC CLUBS | Set in the historic Parker-Nix Storehouse, a general store built in the 1850s, this intimate venue features local and nationally known live acoustic music, from blues and bluegrass to Celtic, folk rock, and country, up to five nights a week. It's also a great little café and coffeehouse serving lunch, dinner, and fun signature cocktails like the "Gold Rush" and the "Crimson Mule." *24 N. Park St., Suite A* *706/864–3982* *www.thecrimsonmoon.com.*

Performing Arts

Historic Holly Theater

FILM | **FAMILY** | This restored, classic small-town movie theater, built in 1946, stages live theater, movies, children's performances, concerts, and special events. Check out the schedule online for the latest offerings. *69 W. Main St.* *706/530–5162* *www.hollytheater.com.*

Activities

Appalachian Outfitters

CANOEING/ROWING/SKULLING | Stop here to pick up equipment for self-guided canoeing and kayaking trips on the Chestatee and Etowah Rivers. They also offer 6- to 8-mile guided trips depending on the season. From Memorial Day to Labor Day, Appalachian Outfitters offers tube rentals and shuttle service for tubing trips at an outpost nearby. ✉ *2084 S. Chestatee/ GA 60* ☎ *706/864–7117 for canoe and kayak, 706/864–7116 for tubing* 🌐 *www.canoegeorgia.com.*

Helen and the Sautee Nacoochee Valley

32 miles northeast of Dahlonega; 88 miles northeast of Atlanta.

Helen was founded at the turn of the 20th century as a simple lumber outpost. In the 1960s, when logging declined, business leaders came up with a plan to transform the tiny village of 300 into a theme town, and "Alpine Helen" was born. Today many businesses along Helen's central streets sport a distinctive German facade, giving an initial impression that you've stumbled on a Bavarian vista in the middle of Appalachia. **■ TIP→ Don't expect small-town prices for anything from parking to ATM charges.** This is clearly not Bavaria, but the effect can be briefly contagious, making you feel as if you've stepped into a fairy tale. If it's too touristy, visit nearby areas for delightful crafts, shopping, and dining. Sautee and Nacoochee are the homes of the Habersham Winery, the Folk Pottery Museum of Northeast Georgia, and a number of other speciality and pottery and crafts shops.

GETTING HERE AND AROUND

While the quirky town of Helen may merit a quick stop, other nearby attractions a short drive away are also well worth visiting. Try the Folk Pottery Museum of Northeast Georgia to check out the area's centuries-old pottery tradition and Georgia's famous "face jugs." The Sautee and Nacoochee areas are accessible just south of Helen off GA 75.

VISITOR INFORMATION

CONTACTS Helen Welcome Center. ✉ *726 Bruckenstrasse, Helen* ☎ *706/878–2181, 800/858–8027* 🌐 *www.helenga.org.*

Sights

Anna Ruby Falls

BODY OF WATER | One of the crown jewels of the vast Chattahoochee National Forest, Anna Ruby Falls is actually the junction of Curtis and York Creeks as it forms Smith Creek. With a drop of 153 feet, the stunning twin falls are accessible via a paved 0.4-mile footpath from the visitor center to the base of the falls. For more of a challenge, try the 4.6-mile Smith Creek Trail, which leads from the base of Anna Ruby Falls to Unicoi State Park. ✉ *3455 Anna Ruby Falls Rd., Helen* ☎ *706/878–1448* 🌐 *www.fs.usda.gov* 🎫 *$3.*

★ Folk Pottery Museum of Northeast Georgia

MUSEUM | FAMILY | Located 4 miles southeast of Helen in the Sautee Nacoochee Center, this museum showcases a 200-year unbroken tradition of folk pottery in northeast Georgia (especially in nearby Mossy Creek and the Gillsville-Lula area). Part of the 5,000-square-foot facility outlines how pottery is made and how it was used for essential household purposes. Exhibits showcase a 200-piece collection donated to the museum, including the whimsical face jugs that have become an emblem of Southern folk art. Pottery-making demonstrations are frequently offered. Call ahead for dates and times. ✉ *283 GA 255, Sautee Nacoochee* ☎ *706/878–3300* 🌐 *www.folkpotterymuseum.com* 🎫 *$5.*

Habersham Vineyards & Winery

WINERY/DISTILLERY | One of the oldest wineries in the state, Habersham Vineyards & Winery started producing in 1983. Stop by the winery's tasting room and gift shop to try one of its signature wines, including Chardonnay, Merlot, Cabernet Sauvignon, and popular blends Scarlett, Signet, and Cherokee Rose. ✉ *7025 S. Main St., Helen* ✣ *On GA 75* ☎ *706/878–9463* 🌐 *www.habershamwinery.com.*

Russell-Brasstown Scenic Byway

SCENIC DRIVE | Beginning and ending in Helen, the Russell-Brasstown Scenic Byway is a 41-mile loop through some of the most dramatic mountain scenery in northeastern Georgia. Start the counterclockwise drive from Georgia State Route 17/74 north of Helen, turn left on Georgia State Route 180, left again at Georgia State Route 348, and another left at Georgia State Route 75 Alternate back to Helen. The loop passes the Raven Cliff Wilderness, wildlife management areas, the headwaters of the Chattahoochee River, and a section of the Appalachian Trail, and goes near the state parks of Vogel, Unicoi, Smithgall Woods, and Brasstown Bald Mountain. ✉ *Helen* 🌐 *www.fhwa.dot.gov/byways/byways/13739.*

 Restaurants

Hofer's of Helen

$ | **GERMAN** | Head to Hofer's for authentic, stone-hearth, oven-baked breads and pastries, as well as specialties like Wiener schnitzel and bratwurst. On weekends May through mid-November, grab a table at the outdoor biergarten and enjoy live music along with your meal. **Known for:** fresh bread and pastries; authentic German cuisine; biergarten in the summer and fall. *Average main: $10 8758 N. Main St., Helen 706/878–8200 www.hofers.com No dinner.*

Mully's Nacoochee Grill

$$$ | **ECLECTIC** | Hand-cut steaks, fresh seafood, and seasonal vegetables are the focus at this casual restaurant set in a cheerful old house in Nacoochee Village, just outside town. Shrimp and grits, whole fried trout, and slow-cooked ribs are customer favorites. **Known for:** local trout dishes; hand-cut steaks; local wine and inventive cocktails. *Average main: $20 7277 S. Main St., Helen 706/878–8020 www.mullysnacoocheegrill.com Closed Mon. in winter.*

 Hotels

The Cottages at Smithgall Woods

$$$$ | **RENTAL** | As part of a 5,600-acre park run by the State of Georgia, these six cottages, set in old-growth hardwoods with 5 miles of hiking trails, offer a peaceful retreat. **Pros:** a luxurious and secluded retreat; hiking trails nearby; beautiful mountain stream on property. **Cons:** must bring your own fishing equipment; no food service; two-night minimum (three-night for holidays) required. *Rooms from: $345 61 Tsalaki Trail, Helen 706/878–3087, 800/318–5248 www.gastateparks.org/SmithgallWoods 6 cottages No meals.*

The Lodge at Unicoi

$ | **RESORT** | Choose either the comfortable mountain lodge, with 100 renovated lodge rooms, a one-, two-, or three-bedroom cottage (some with a fireplace), or one of the tent or RV campsites at this state-run accommodation within Unicoi State Park. **Pros:** tons of outdoor recreational activities on-site; less than 3 miles from Helen; pet-friendly accommodations available. **Cons:** breakfast isn't included in the rate; can be crowded in peak season; service can be spotty. *Rooms from: $139 1788 GA 356, Helen 3 miles north of Helen 706/878–2201, 800/573–9659 www.unicoilodge.com 100 rooms, 30 cottages No meals.*

The Gourd Place

CERAMICS/GLASSWARE | **FAMILY** | This unique museum and gourd and pottery store is filled with colorful gourd collections from around the world. Owners Priscilla Wilson and Janice Lymburner sell gourds and supplies to preserve dried gourds (a Southern specialty). They also produce attractive natural-glazed stoneware and porcelain dinnerware, vases, bowls, and luminaries using liquid clay poured into gourd molds. *2319 Duncan Bridge Rd., Sautee 706/865–4048 www.gourdplace.com.*

Hickory Flat Pottery

CERAMICS/GLASSWARE | **FAMILY** | This working pottery studio in a large 120-year-old roadside farmhouse is filled with lots more than "just" beautiful pottery. Vibrant stained glass, a variety of jewelry, and fiber art are featured, along with the vivid, decorative, and functional stoneware of shop owner Cody Trautner, who enjoys sharing his craft by sending little bags of clay home with children. *13664 U.S. 197 N, Clarkesville 4 miles north of Mark of the Potter 706/947–0030 www.hickoryflatpottery.com.*

★ **Mark of the Potter**

CERAMICS/GLASSWARE | FAMILY | In an old gristmill with beautiful views of the Soque River, Mark of the Potter offers an outstanding selection of pottery from more than 30 artisans. The emphasis is on functional pieces, with a great variety of clay and firing techniques and glazes in every imaginable color. Items range from coffee scoops to lamps, mugs to elaborate vases and casserole dishes. The shop is legendary among Georgia-pottery lovers. Children and adults alike will enjoy sitting on the porch and feeding the huge pet trout. A potter works on the wheel at the shop on Saturday and Sunday. ✉ *9982 GA 197 N, Clarkesville* ☎ *706/947–3440* 🌐 *www.markofthepotter.com.*

Old Sautee Store

CONVENIENCE/GENERAL STORES | FAMILY | This unique shop has been operating continuously since 1872. The front part of the store operates more as a museum, with antique farming implements, old-timey tonics and soaps, and even caskets on display. The retail store, influenced by an earlier owner's Scandinavian heritage, continues to sell Swedish farmer's cheese and Norwegian flatbread. Shoppers can also pick up old-time candy and toys. You can even grab lunch at the Old Sautee Market behind the shop. ✉ *2315 GA 17, Sautee* ✥ *5 miles south of Helen* ☎ *706/878–2281* 🌐 *www.oldsauteestore.com.*

Activities

Cool River Tubing

WATER SPORTS | FAMILY | "Tube the Hooch" with Cool River Tubing, which shuttles you on a bus upriver to begin the float back to town. Choose the short (one hour) or long (two hours) float trip. Prices are $10–$14 for a single trip of either length depending on the day of the week. Cool River also operates a waterslide you can add on for $5. For the landlubbers, there's a zipline, climbing wall, and aerial adventure courses at its Headwaters Outpost, plus the new Georgia Mountain Coaster in downtown Helen. Combo tickets are available. ✉ *590 Edelweiss Strasse, Helen* ☎ *706/878–2665, 706/878–9471 zipline and aerial adventures only* 🌐 *www.coolrivertubing.com.*

Clayton

35 miles northeast of Helen via GA 356, GA 197, and U.S. 76.

The town of Clayton, with a downtown filled with shops, is a gateway to North Georgia's mountains. The beautiful lakeshore and the grandeur of Black Rock Mountain State Park and Tallulah Gorge make a day tour of this area a memorable experience.

The culinary scene in Clayton and surrounding Rabun County has blossomed in recent years. Agriculture has a long tradition in these parts, but the marriage of farmers and chefs working together has yielded spectacular results. As a result, the state house of representatives has designated Rabun County as the farm-to-table capital of Georgia. The local tourism authority, Explore Rabun, offers monthly Grow-Cook-Eat Farm and Food Tours with stops at farms, wineries, and restaurants throughout the region.

GETTING HERE AND AROUND

Clayton makes a good base to explore Tallulah Gorge State Park and its falls and Black Rock Mountain State Park. A short drive northwest on U.S. Route 76 will take you to several of the region's most appealing lakes, including Rabun and Chatuge.

VISITOR INFORMATION

CONTACTS Rabun County Chamber of Commerce and Welcome Center. ✉ *10 Seed Tick Rd.* ☎ *706/782–4812* 🌐 *www.explorerabun.com.*

Hike the rim trails at Tallulah Gorge State Park for spectacular views of the canyon below.

Sights

Black Rock Mountain State Park

NATIONAL/STATE PARK | FAMILY | At more than 3,600 feet, Black Rock Mountain is the highest state park in Georgia. Named for the black gneiss rock visible on cliffs in the area, the 1,738-acre park has 10 miles of trails, a 17-acre lake perfect for fishing, 56 campsites, a pioneer group campsite, and 10 cottages. The park offers majestic overlooks and a trail that leads visitors along the Eastern Continental Divide, from which water flows south and east to eventually reach the Atlantic Ocean, and on the other side, north and west to the mighty Mississippi River. ✉ *3085 Black Rock Mountain Pkwy., Mountain City* ✣ *3 miles northwest of Clayton* ☎ *706/746–2141, 800/864–7275 for camping and cottage reservations* 🌐 *www.gastateparks.org/BlackRock-Mountain* 🎟 *Daily-use fee $5* ⏲ *Closed mid-Dec.–mid-Mar.*

Foxfire Museum and Heritage Center

MUSEUM | FAMILY | Set on the slope of Black Rock Mountain, this outdoor museum re-creates life in Appalachia before the days of electricity and running water. The museum features a collection of authentic and reconstructed log cabins, a gristmill, a blacksmith's shop, and an operating weaving workshop, along with tools and displays about life in daily life and mountain culture. The Foxfire organization was born in 1966 when students at the Rabun Gap–Nacoochee School wrote articles for a magazine based on generations-old family stories. Their excitement in chronicling life in the Appalachians has led to more than a dozen Foxfire books, which have sold nearly 9 million copies. ✉ *200 Foxfire La., Mountain City* ✣ *Off U.S. 441 at Black Rock Mountain Pkwy.* ☎ *706/746–5828* 🌐 *www.foxfire.org* 🎟 *$10.*

Lake Burton

FISH HATCHERY | FAMILY | One of the six lakes built by the Georgia Railway and Power Company, this 2,800-acre lake is in the Chattahoochee National Forest. On the lake, at Georgia State Route 197, is the **Lake Burton Fish Hatchery,** alongside **Moccasin Creek State Park ,** which offers a boat ramp, fishing pier, picnic spots, and shady campsites. It also has trout raceways (used to raise trout from fingerlings) and a kids-only trout-fishing area. In extremely hot weather, the hatchery is sometimes closed. ✉ *3655 GA 197 N, Clarkesville* ✣ *Off U.S. 76, west of Clayton* ☎ *706/947–3194* 🌐 *www.gastateparks.org/MoccasinCreek* 🎫 *Park parking $5, hatchery parking free.*

Lake Rabun

BODY OF WATER | Built in 1915, the first of six lakes in the state built by the Georgia Railway and Power Company, Lake Rabun covers only 834 acres. Its small size is misleading, as its narrow fingers dart through mountain valleys. Lightly visited by tourists and populated with weekend homes and old boathouses, it has a low-key charm. The lake offers boating, fishing, and camping. There's a small beach at **Lake Rabun Beach Recreation Area** at the east end of the lake available for day use for a fee. ✉ *5320 Lake Rabun Rd., Lakemont* ✣ *West of U.S. 23/441 via Old Hwy. 441 S and Lake Rabun Rd., 9 miles southwest of Clayton* ☎ *706/754–6221 Chattooga River Ranger District Office.*

★ Tallulah Gorge State Park

NATIONAL/STATE PARK | The 1,000-foot-deep Tallulah Gorge is one of the most impressive in the country. In the late 1800s this area was one of the most visited destinations in the Southeast, with 17 hotels to house tourists who came to see the roaring falls on the Tallulah River. Then, in 1912, to provide electric power, the "Niagara of the South" was dammed, and the falls and tourism dried up. Today the state of Georgia has designated more than 20 miles of the state park as walking and mountain-biking trails. There's also a 16,000-square-foot interpretive center, a suspension bridge with spectacular views, a 63-acre lake with a beach (open seasonally), a picnic shelter, and 50 tent and RV sites. ✉ *338 Jane Hurt Yarn Dr., Tallulah Falls* ✣ *Off U.S. 441* ☎ *706/754–7981* 🌐 *www.gastateparks.org/TallulahGorge* 🎫 *Parking $5.*

Tiger Mountain Vineyards

WINERY/DISTILLERY | Started on a five-generation-old family farm in 1995 by Dr. John and Martha Ezzard, Tiger Mountain Vineyards is known for unusual varietals of French and Portuguese grapes, such as Touriga Nacional and Tannat, as well as the native Norton grape—grown on the slopes of Tiger Mountain. Tastings are available for a small fee. Lunch and dinner are served on the weekends (May–November) in the lovely restored Red Barn Café. The tasting room frequently features live music and events; call ahead for the schedule. ✉ *2592 Old Hwy. 441, Tiger* ✣ *8 mins south of Clayton* ☎ *706/782–4777* 🌐 *www.tigerwine.com.*

Restaurants

The Clayton Market

$ | SOUTHERN | With its retro neon sign, this charming "meat-and-three" café has been a fixture in downtown Clayton since 1931. Now completely renovated and decorated in an industrial-farmhouse style, the restaurant serves a new generation of patrons hearty homemade soups, salads, and sandwiches, and the very best of homestyle Southern cooking. **Known for:** homestyle Southern cooking; fresh veggies and daily specials; market with coffee and baked goods. 💲 *Average main: $10* ✉ *50 N. Main St.* ☎ *706/212–2233 café, 706/960–9245 market* 🌐 *www.claytonmarket.com* ⏲ *Closed Wed.*

Fortify Kitchen & Bar

$$$ | **AMERICAN** | At one of Clayton's designated "farm-to-table" restaurants, chef Jamie Allred's updated Southern cuisine highlights the region's best produce, meats, and spirits in a relaxed, down-to-earth environment. With exposed brick walls and a small wooden bar you'll want to huddle around, Fortify is simply about good food, fun cocktails, and a wine list that includes a few local selections. **Known for:** focus on local, seasonal ingredients; craft cocktails; Georgia pecan-crusted Carolina mountain rainbow trout. *Average main: $24 69 N. Main St. 706/782–0050 www.fortifyclayton.com Closed Mon. and Tues.*

Coffee and Quick Bites

White Birch Provisions

$ | **AMERICAN** | On the square in downtown Clayton, this European-inspired market located next to the White Birch Inn offers a coffee bar, fresh fruit smoothies, house-made baked goods, gourmet cheeses, and a wine cave filled with a wide selection of vino—including a few local choices. **Known for:** espresso drinks; wine, cheese, and gourmet provisions; fresh-baked scones and other goodies. *Average main: $7 60 E. Savannah St. 706/782–2263 www.whitebirchprovisions.com.*

Hotels

★ Beechwood Inn

$$$ | **B&B/INN** | Operating as an inn for more than 100 years, the Beechwood offers sophisticated yet down-to-earth Southern hospitality in a lovely two-story wood lodge overlooking Clayton. **Pros:** beautiful setting in close proximity to Clayton; food and wine focus; historic inn with lots of character. **Cons:** slanted floors in some rooms can be tricky to navigate; most rooms have showers only; highway noise can detract from countryside charm. *Rooms from: $229 220 Beechwood Inn Dr. 706/782–5485 www.beechwoodinn.ws 7 rooms, 2 cabins Free breakfast.*

Dillard House

$ | **HOTEL** | An inviting cluster of cottages, motel-style rooms, and a popular family-style restaurant, this establishment sits on a plateau near the state border. **Pros:** offers a variety of accommodation styles; fishing and horseback riding available; beautiful mountain scenery. **Cons:** on-site restaurant relies too much on its past reputation; breakfast not included in rate; some rooms are dated. *Rooms from: $139 768 Franklin St., Dillard 706/746–5348, 800/541–0671 www.dillardhouse.com 92 rooms, 18 chalets and cottages No meals.*

★ Glen-Ella Springs Inn and Restaurant

$$ | **B&B/INN** | This restored country inn and restaurant, constructed in 1875 and listed on the National Register of Historic Places, has a rustic but polished charm. **Pros:** eager staff; picturesque perennial and herb gardens; saltwater pool. **Cons:** fills up quickly on the weekends; limited number of rooms can accommodate families with children; remote setting may not be for all. *Rooms from: $185 1789 Bear Gap Rd., Clarkesville 706/754–7295, 888/455–8786 www.glenella.com 16 rooms Free breakfast.*

Lake Rabun Hotel

$ | **B&B/INN** | Set in shady hemlocks across the road from Lake Rabun, this romantic hotel, built in 1922, has rough-hewn wood paneling, handmade furniture, and a large working fieldstone fireplace. **Pros:** rustic historic inn rooms and cottages; easy access to Lake Rabun activities; gourmet breakfast included in rate. **Cons:** no room TVs; no elevator; no children under 10 in historic inn rooms. *Rooms from: $149 35 Andrea La., Lakemont 706/782–4946 www.lakerabunhotel.com 15 rooms, 7 cottages Free breakfast.*

Shopping

Goats on the Roof

LOCAL SPECIALTIES | FAMILY | Yes, there really are goats on the roof at this colorful roadside attraction off the main drag near Clayton. While it is kind of a tourist trap, it's a fun one that's down-to-earth and full of charm. The shop features handcrafted items like pottery, goat's milk soaps, Amish furniture, and local jams and jellies, along with toys, T-shirts, and goodies. You can also get fresh-made fudge and "nitro" ice cream in the café across the way. There's even gem mining on-site. Of course, the main attraction is the goats, which you can feed via a pulley system. Kids of all ages love this place! ✉ *3026 U.S. 441 S, Tiger* ☎ *706/782–2784* 🌐 *www.goats-on-the-roof.com.*

Main Street Gallery

ART GALLERIES | One of the state's best sources for folk art, Main Street Gallery carries works by more than 75 regional artists. The store also carries jewelry, pottery, paintings, and sculptures. ✉ *51 N. Main St.* ☎ *706/782–2440* 🌐 *www.mainstreetgallery.net.*

Activities

WHITE-WATER RAFTING

Chattooga River

WHITE-WATER RAFTING | The first river in the Southeast to be designated a Wild and Scenic River by Congress, the Chattooga River forms the border between Georgia and South Carolina. With Class II to Class V rapids, the Chattooga is popular for white-water rafting, especially in spring and summer. Movie buffs should note that this was one of the locations for *Deliverance*. ✉ *Clayton* ✣ *From Clayton drive east 7 miles on U.S. 76 to Hwy. 76 Bridge at Georgia–South Carolina state line.*

Nantahala Outdoor Center

WHITE-WATER RAFTING | The North Carolina–based Nantahala Outdoor Center, the largest rafting company in the region, has an outpost on the Chattooga for Class III and Class IV trips starting at $109 per person. It also offers trips on the Nantahala and Ocoee Rivers. ✉ *NOC Chattooga Outpost, 851A Chattooga Ridge Rd., Mountain Rest* ☎ *828/785–4850* 🌐 *www.noc.com.*

Southeastern Expeditions

WHITE-WATER RAFTING | This locally owned outfitter offers full-day and overnight guided trips on the Chattooga, starting at $90 per person. ✉ *7350 U.S. 76 E* ☎ *800/868–7238* 🌐 *www.southeastern-expeditions.com.*

Wildwater Rafting

WHITE-WATER RAFTING | This is the oldest outfitter in the area, with a campus that also features ziplining and overnight accommodations. Half-day minitrips are offered as well as full-days on Section 3 and 4, and overnight trips on the Chattooga beginning at $80 per person. ✉ *1251 Academy Rd., Long Creek* ✣ *1½ miles north of U.S. 76, 12 miles east of Clayton* ☎ *866/319–8870* 🌐 *www.wildwaterrafting.com.*

Hiawassee, Young Harris, and Lake Chatuge

26 miles northwest of Clayton, via U.S. 76; 21 miles north of Helen via GA 75/17.

The little town of Hiawassee, population 900, and nearby Young Harris, population 1,200, are near the largest lake in North Georgia, Lake Chatuge, and the tallest mountain in the state, Brasstown Bald. The lake has excellent boating and other water-themed recreation. Appealing mountain resorts are nearby as well. A half-hour drive leads to Brasstown Bald, where temperatures even on the hottest

On a clear day, you can see Georgia, North Carolina, South Carolina, and Tennessee from the observation tower at Brasstown Bald.

summer day rarely rise above 80°F. The Georgia Mountain Fairgrounds has a permanent location on the shores of Lake Chatuge. A number of festivals are held at the fairgrounds, including the Fall Festival and State Fiddler's Convention in October and the Georgia Mountain Fair held in the summer.

VISITOR INFORMATION

CONTACTS Lake Chatuge Chamber of Commerce. ✉ *1411 Jack Dayton Circle, Young Harris* ☎ *706/896–4966, 800/984–1543* 🌐 *www.golakechatuge.com.*

Sights

★ Brasstown Bald

MOUNTAIN—SIGHT | **FAMILY** | In the Chattahoochee National Forest, Brasstown Bald reaches 4,784 feet, the highest point in Georgia. Below the bald is Georgia's only cloud forest, an area of lichen-covered trees often kept wet by clouds and fog. From the observation platform at the top of the bald on a clear day you can see Georgia, North Carolina, South Carolina, and Tennessee. A paved but steep foot trail leads from the parking lot (where there are restrooms and a picnic area) to the visitor center, which has exhibits and interpretative programs. You also can ride a bus to the visitor center. ✉ *2941 GA 180 Spur, Hiawassee* ✣ *18 miles southwest of Hiawassee via U.S. 76, GA 75, GA 180, and GA 180 Spur* ☎ *706/896–2556* 🌐 *www.fs.fed.us* 🎟 *$5* ⏲ *Call ahead for winter closings.*

Crane Creek Vineyards

WINERY/DISTILLERY | Nestled in the Appalachian foothills, Crane Creek features scenic ponds and 200-year-old oak trees. The winery produces 15 regional artisanal wines based on the 13 grape varieties it grows. The most popular choices are Vidal Blanc, Seyval, and Norton. Tastings are offered for a fee in the tasting room, located in an old farmhouse. There's also a restaurant on-site for those perfect food and wine pairings. Bottles of wine and take-away food are also available to be enjoyed on decks overlooking the vineyards. On Friday evening, there's live music May through November. ✉ *916 Crane Creek Rd., Young Harris* ✣ *Off GA 515* ☎ *706/379–1236* 🌐 *www.craneecreekvineyards.com* ⏲ *Closed Mon.*

Lake Chatuge Recreation Area
NATIONAL/STATE PARK | This beautiful mountain lake (pronounced "sha-toog") spans 7,200 acres and two states. Some of the best open views can be found near Hiawassee. Here you can access a boat launch and paved walking trail. ✉ *440 Sunnyside Rd., Hiawassee* ✣ *Just off U.S. Hwy. 76* 🌐 *www.fs.usda.gov.*

Hotels

Brasstown Valley Resort and Spa
$$ | **RESORT** | **FAMILY** | For upscale, lodge-style accommodations in a serene mountain setting, this resort is a great option. **Pros:** elegant but rustic rooms; an abundance of activities on-site; cottage rooms and inn rooms available. **Cons:** spa is not located in lodge; dining options are limited in off-season; resort fee can be a surprise. $ *Rooms from: $179* ✉ *6321 U.S. 76, Young Harris* ☎ *706/379–9900, 800/201–3205* 🌐 *www.brasstownvalley.com* *135 rooms* *No meals.*

The Ridges Resort on Lake Chatuge
$$ | **RESORT** | On the shores of Lake Chatuge, this resort offers gorgeous views and is brimming with amenities like a saltwater pool, tennis courts, lawn games, two restaurants, and a marina with boat rentals. **Pros:** restaurant on-site; updated rooms; beautiful lakeside setting with boat rentals available. **Cons:** resort fee charged in addition to room rate; service can be inconsistent; breakfast not included. $ *Rooms from: $159* ✉ *3499 U.S. 76 W, Young Harris* ☎ *706/896–2262* 🌐 *www.theridgesresort.com* *66 rooms* *No meals.*

Blue Ridge and Ellijay

39 miles southwest of Hiawassee via U.S. 76/GA 515; 53 miles northwest of Dahlonega via GA 52 and U.S. 76/GA 515. Ellijay is 15 miles southwest of Blue Ridge via U.S. 76.

Blue Ridge is one of the most pleasant small mountain towns in North Georgia. After you've eaten breakfast or lunch and shopped for antiques, gifts, or crafts at Blue Ridge's many small shops, you can ride the revived Blue Ridge Scenic Railway to McCaysville, a town at the Tennessee line, and then back through the mountains. It's also a paradise for nature lovers. Fannin County (of which Blue Ridge is the county seat) is known as the "Trout Capital of Georgia." The beautiful Toccoa River is a popular destination for fly-fishing, hiking, canoeing, and more.

Just 15 miles southwest is the scenic town of Ellijay. Billed as "Georgia's Apple Capital," Ellijay is also popular among antiques aficionados. The most popular time to visit Ellijay is in fall, when roadside stands brimming with delicious ripe apples dot the landscape. The annual Georgia Apple Festival takes place the second and third weekends of October. Gilmer County is also considered the "Mountain Biking Capital" of Georgia. Numerous bike trails abound in the area, and it's a great place for hiking as well.

VISITOR INFORMATION

CONTACTS Fannin County Chamber of Commerce and Welcome Center. ✉ *152 Orvin Lance Dr., Blue Ridge* ☎ *706/632–5680, 800/899–6867* 🌐 *www.blueridgemountains.com.* **Gilmer County Chamber of Commerce and Welcome Center.** ✉ *696 1st Ave., East Ellijay* ☎ *706/635–7400* 🌐 *www.gilmerchamber.com.*

Blue Ridge Scenic Railway

SCENIC DRIVE | FAMILY | Ride the rails on a four-hour, 26-mile round-trip excursion along the Toccoa River. The trip includes a stop in **McCaysville,** smack on the Georgia–Tennessee state line. Several restaurants, shops, and galleries are open during the two-hour layover. The train, which has open Pullman cars and is pulled by diesel engines, is staffed with friendly volunteer hosts. Premier class is available to those over 18 and includes snacks and a little extra TLC. The ticket office, on the National Register of Historic Places, dates from 1905 and was originally the depot of the L&N Railroad. Children of all ages enjoy the ride. **■ TIP→ In summer you may want to consider the air-conditioned coaches.** ✉ *241 Depot St., Blue Ridge* ☎ *706/632–8724, 877/413–8724* 🌐 *www.brscenic.com* 🎟 *$45–$92, depending on season and ticket type* ⏲ *No train Jan.–mid-Mar.*

Hillcrest Orchards

FARM/RANCH | FAMILY | Buy freshly picked apples (usually early September to late November) at this 80-acre farm. Homemade jellies, jams, breads, and doughnuts are available at the farm's market and bakery. On September and October weekends, the Apple Pickin' Jubilee features live music, wagon rides, apple picking, and other activities. There's also a petting zoo and a picnic area. ✉ *9696 GA 52 E, Ellijay* ☎ *706/273–3838* 🌐 *www.hillcrestorchards.net* 🎟 *$8–$12 for special events, including Apple Pickin' Jubilee* ⏲ *Closed Dec.–Aug.*

Mercier Orchards

FARM/RANCH | This family-owned apple orchard has been producing delicious apples and other fruits for more than 75 years. Apple season is typically from September to November, but even outside the season you can stop in at Mercier's huge farm market and bakery to pick up some of its famous fried apple pies and other homemade goodies. It's open every day of the week. You can also grab lunch in the deli and taste Mercier's own hard-pressed ciders in the farm winery. The orchard is especially buzzing with activity in the fall, when you can take a tractor ride and pick your own apples, and in the summer when blueberry season arrives. Call ahead to find out what fruits are in season and for the latest details on orchard events. ✉ *8660 Blue Ridge Dr., Blue Ridge* ✣ *Off GA 5* ☎ *706/632–3411, 800/361–7731* 🌐 *www.mercier-orchards.com.*

Swan Drive-In Theatre

ARTS VENUE | FAMILY | Originally opened in 1955, this is one of only five drive-in movie theaters operating in Georgia. You can take in a movie under the stars and fill up on corn dogs, onion rings, funnel cakes, and popcorn from the concession stand. ✉ *651 Summit St., Blue Ridge* ☎ *706/632–5235* 🌐 *www.swan-drive-in.com* 🎟 *$10* ⏲ *Closed Mon.–Thurs.; call ahead in winter* ☞ *Cash only.*

Toccoa River Swinging Bridge

BRIDGE/TUNNEL | Located on the Benton MacKaye Trail and the Duncan Ridge National Recreation Trail, this 270-foot-long bridge spanning the Toccoa River is the longest swinging bridge east of the Mississippi River. A shaky stroll across the bridge offers breathtaking views of the river and mountain scenery. Best of all, it can be easily reached thanks to an unpaved Forest Service road. It's a bumpy 3-mile ride, but the road makes accessing the bridge an easy hike. ✉ *Fire Service Rd. 816, off U.S. Hwy. 60, Blue Ridge* ✣ *Look for signs for the Toccoa River Swinging Bridge and follow the gravel road from the parking lot* 🌐 *www.blueridgemountains.com/things-to-do/outdoors/hiking/swinging-bridge.*

Restaurants

Cantaberry Restaurant
$ | **AMERICAN** | "Simple, homemade, good" is the motto at this popular café in downtown Ellijay with exposed brick walls and a cozy covered patio. Open for lunch daily and dinner four nights per week, the café specializes in soups, salads, sandwiches, and homestyle country fare like meat loaf and fried chicken. **Known for:** signature tuna salad and pimento cheese; fresh baked goods; Southern comfort food dinners. *Average main: $12* *5 S. Side Sq., Ellijay* *706/636–4663* *www.cantaberry.com.*

Harvest on Main
$$$ | **MODERN AMERICAN** | Focused on local and seasonal cuisine, this popular Blue Ridge restaurant even harvests its own specialty produce, eggs, and honey. Chef-owner Danny Mellman and his wife, Michelle Moran, have created a sophisticated yet down-to-earth culinary destination housed in an airy cedar "cabin" downtown. **Known for:** true farm-to-table cuisine; upscale comfort food in an inviting, rustic space; excellent bar program. *Average main: $24* *576 E. Main St., Blue Ridge* *706/946–6164* *www.harvestonmain.com* *Closed Tues. and Wed.*

Coffee and Quick Bites

Rum Cake Lady Cuban Cafe
$ | **CUBAN** | This authentic Cuban spot on the edge of downtown Blue Ridge is a lovely surprise. Here you can pick up delicious Cuban sandwiches with fresh-baked bread, empanadas, *croquetas,* and other Cuban specialties. **Known for:** rum cakes in a variety of flavors; authentic Cuban food; Cuban coffee. *Average main: $10* *205 W. First St., Blue Ridge* *706/946–4525* *www.rumcakelady.com* *Closed Sun.*

Hotels

Best Western Mountain View Inn
$ | **HOTEL** | This comfortable but basic two-story motel sits high on a hilltop above East Ellijay, and half of its rooms have mountain views. **Pros:** mountain views; indoor heated pool; close to eating and shopping areas. **Cons:** entrance is hard to find; no elevator; could use some updates. *Rooms from: $109* *43 Coosawattee Dr., East Ellijay* *706/515–1500, 866/515–4515* *www.bwmountainviewinn.com* *52 rooms* *Free breakfast.*

Blue Ridge Inn Bed and Breakfast
$$$ | **B&B/INN** | Housed in an 1890 Victorian just steps from the Blue Ridge Scenic Railway (it was built as the railroad supervisor's home), this lovely B&B blends historic charm with modern creature comforts. **Pros:** in easy walking distance of shops and restaurants; historic charm with modern amenities; delicious home-cooked breakfast. **Cons:** can't accommodate families with children under 13; some bathrooms are small; steep stairs may be a problem for some. *Rooms from: $205* *477 W. 1st St., Blue Ridge* *706/661–7575* *www.blueridgeinnbandb.com* *11 rooms* *Free breakfast.*

Activities

Cohutta Fishing Company
FISHING | Stop at this downtown Blue Ridge shop for fly-fishing equipment and advice, or take a guided trip on the Toccoa or Etowah River with their experienced guides in the "Trout Capital of Georgia." Cohutta Fishing also offers classes, including a Fly Fishing 101 class to help you get the hang of fly tying and casting before you even hit the water. *490 East Main St., Blue Ridge* *706/946-3044* *www.cohuttafishingco.com.*

Macon

85 miles southeast of Atlanta via I–75.

At the state's geographic center, Macon, founded in 1823, has more than 100,000 flowering cherry trees, which it celebrates each March with a knockout festival. With 14 historic districts and 6,000 individual structures listed on the National Register of Historic Places, its antebellum and Victorian homes are among the state's best preserved. Everywhere you turn in the downtown business district there are preservation and rehabilitation projects—new lofts, shops, and restaurants now occupy once-abandoned buildings. Following a $1.2 million restoration, the Capitol Theatre (originally founded as a bank in 1897) is a popular venue for movies and concerts; after a three-year renovation, St. Joseph's Catholic Church is more impressive than ever; and the old Armory, complete with its first-floor dance hall, is finding new life as a special-events space.

Daily news is reported in the *Telegraph*. The *Georgia Informer*, the *11th Hour*, and the upscale *Macon Magazine* are good sources of information on local arts and cultural events.

GETTING HERE AND AROUND

Poet Raymond Farr, in his "Back Roads to Macon," writes of a cozy roadside diner, the sprawling farmland, and a folksy bit of wisdom scrawled on a mailbox in the nearby town of Cordele: "Whatever your destination, thank God you arrive." These kinds of small touches add charm to the back roads to Macon. Or, for a speedier and somewhat less scenic route, jump on U.S. 441.

VISITOR INFORMATION

CONTACTS Macon-Bibb County Convention and Visitors Bureau. ✉ *450 Martin Luther King Jr. Blvd.* ☎ *478/743–1074, 800/768–3401* 🌐 *www.maconga.org.*

Sights

The Allman Brothers Band Museum at the Big House

MUSEUM | Affectionately known as the Big House, this large Tudor-style building was home to members of the Allman Brothers Band and their families during the early 1970s. It was here that they collaborated and wrote some of the band's early songs, which would eventually bring them stardom and launch a new genre of music—Southern rock. In 2010, the home was restored and opened as a museum showcasing the band's guitars, clothing, photographs, posters, gold records, and other memorabilia. It's now home to the largest collection of Allman Brothers Band memorabilia in the world. ✉ *2321 Vineville Ave.* ☎ *478/741–5551* 🌐 *www.thebighousemuseum.com* 🎟 *$15* ⏲ *Closed Mon.–Wed.*

Douglass Theatre

ARTS VENUE | African American entrepreneur Charles H. Douglass built this theater in 1921. A host of great American musicians have performed here, among them Bessie Smith, Ma Rainey, Cab Calloway, Duke Ellington, and locals Little Richard and Otis Redding. It's currently a venue for movies, plays, and other performances. You can take a guided tour of the building weekdays only. Call ahead for an appointment. ✉ *355 Martin Luther King Jr. Blvd.* ☎ *478/742–2000* 🌐 *www.douglasstheatre.org.*

Georgia Sports Hall of Fame

MUSEUM | **FAMILY** | Designed to resemble a turn-of-the-century ballpark, sports enthusiasts will appreciate this shrine to Georgia sports and its Hall of Fame honoring over 400 inductees. Exhibits, though dated, include a variety of artifacts and interactive, touch-screen kiosks and honor sports—including baseball, golf, track and field, and football—at all levels, from prep and college teams to professional. ✉ *301 Cherry St.* ☎ *478/752–1585* 🌐 *www.georgiasport-shalloffame.com* 🎟 *$8.*

★ Hay House

HOUSE | Designed by the New York firm T. Thomas and Son in the mid-1800s, Hay House is a study in fine Italianate architecture prior to the Civil War. The marvelous stained-glass windows and many technological advances, including indoor plumbing, make a tour worthwhile. The home's dining room has recently been restored to its 1870s appearance. Tours depart on the hour. For a small upcharge, you can do the Top of the House tour, which explores the soaring cupola and widow's walk. ✉ *934 Georgia Ave.* ☎ *478/742–8155* 🌐 *www.hayhousemacon.org* 🎟 *$13* ⏲ *Closed Mon. and Tues.* ☞ *Last tour begins at 3 daily.*

Macon Museum of Arts and Sciences

OBSERVATORY | **FAMILY** | Displaying everything from a whale skeleton to fine art, this museum appeals to adults and children alike. *The Discovery House,* an interactive exhibit for children, is modeled after an artist's garret. There's also a mini-zoo and the Mark Smith Planetarium on-site. ✉ *4182 Forsyth Rd.* ☎ *478/477–3232* 🌐 *www.masmacon.org* 🎟 *$10* ⏲ *Closed Sun. and Mon.*

Museum of Aviation

MUSEUM | **FAMILY** | This museum at Robins Air Force Base has an extraordinary collection of 85 vintage aircraft and missiles, including a MiG, an SR-71 (Blackbird), a U-2, and assorted other flying machines from past campaigns. For a small fee, you can also take a ride on a virtual reality simulator as you navigate through outer space. ✉ *Robins AFB, 1942 Heritage Blvd., Warner Robins* ✣ *From Macon take I–75 south to Exit 146 (Centerville/Warner Robins) and turn left onto Watson Blvd., 7 miles to GA 247/U.S. 129,* *then right for 2 miles* ☎ *478/926–6870* 🌐 *www.museumofaviation.org* 🎫 *Free.*

Ocmulgee Mounds National Historical Park
NATIVE SITE | Located 3 miles east of downtown Macon, Ocmulgee is a significant archaeological site as it's been occupied for more than 17,000 years; at its peak, between AD 900 and 1100, it was populated by the Mississippian peoples, who were renowned mound builders. There's a reconstructed earth lodge as well as displays of pottery, effigies, and jewelry of copper and shells discovered in the burial mound. Call or check the park's online schedule for special Lantern Light Tours and other educational opportunities. ✉ *1207 Emery Hwy.* ✥ *Take U.S. 80 E* ☎ *478/752–8257* 🌐 *www.nps.gov/ocmu* 🎫 *Free.*

Tubman Museum
MUSEUM | This museum honors Harriet Tubman, the former slave who led more than 300 people to freedom as one of the conductors of the Underground Railroad. The museum's signature piece is a large mural depicting several centuries of black culture. Permanent galleries are focused on African American inventors, Middle Georgia history, and folk art. Rotating exhibits showcase African American arts and culture. ✉ *310 Cherry St.* ☎ *478/743–8544* 🌐 *www.tubmanmuseum.com* 🎫 *$10* 🕒 *Closed Sun. and Mon.*

Restaurants

Downtown Grill
$$$$ | **AMERICAN** | Tucked away in a city block of renovated warehouses, this old-school English steak house and cigar bar is a Macon institution. Old Georgian brick and dark wood accents give a romantic flair to the decor. **Known for:** classic steak house options like filet mignon; hard-to-find location; cigar bar on-site. 💲 *Average main: $25* ✉ *562 Mulberry Street La.* ☎ *478/742–5999* 🌐 *www.macondowntowngrill.com* 🕒 *Closed Sun.*

The Rookery
$ | **AMERICAN** | There's a definite '70s vibe at this popular downtown eatery, where the burgers are named for Macon's famed musicians and the only president to hail from Georgia. The Big "O," topped with barbecue sauce and an onion ring, is named for Otis Redding; the Allman Burger is smothered with sautéed mushrooms; and the Jimmy Carter comes with peanut butter, of course. **Known for:** creative burgers and sandwiches named for Georgia celebs; milkshakes made with fresh, local milk; fun pub environment with outdoor dining. 💲 *Average main: $12* ✉ *543 Cherry St.* ☎ *478/746–8658* 🌐 *www.rookerymacon.com.*

Coffee and Quick Bites

Taste & See Coffee Shop
$ | **AMERICAN** | Part coffee shop and part gallery, this spacious downtown Macon establishment offers locally roasted coffee and tons of comfy seating. There's also baked goods, sandwiches, and decadent desserts made in-house for a quick snack. **Known for:** handcrafted coffee drinks; yummy baked goods; spacious, artsy interior. 💲 *Average main: $6* ✉ *546 Poplar St.* ☎ *478/238–5191* 🌐 *www.tasteandseecoffee.com* 🕒 *Closed Sun.*

Hotels

1842 Inn
$$ | **B&B/INN** | With its white-pillar front porch and period antiques, it's easy to see why this place is considered one of the region's top inns. **Pros:** a taste of antebellum grandeur; friendly, attentive service; delicious breakfast and evening reception. **Cons:** no suites available; often booked up; no pool. 💲 *Rooms from: $189* ✉ *353 College St.* ☎ *877/452–6599* 🌐 *www.1842inn.com* 🛏 *19 rooms* 🍽 *Free breakfast.*

Hilton Garden Inn Macon/Mercer University
$ | **HOTEL** | There aren't many hotels in downtown Macon, but this trusted chain is just 2 miles from the city center on the campus of Mercer University, making it a safe bet. **Pros:** easy access to downtown and the interstates; suites with sitting areas available; outdoor pool. **Cons:** a bit pricey for the area; can be busy with college groups; breakfast not included in rate. *Ⓢ Rooms from: $140 ✉ 1220 Stadium Dr. ☎ 478/741–5527 ⊕ www.hiltongardeninn.com 101 rooms No meals.*

Milledgeville

32 miles northeast of Macon on GA 49.

Novelist and short-story writer Flannery O'Connor is one of Milledgeville's most famous residents. The author of novels *Wise Blood* and *The Violent Bear It Away* spent the last 13 years of her life at her family farm just north of town.

Locals believe ghosts haunt what remains of the antebellum homes in Milledgeville. Laid out as the state capital of Georgia in 1803 (a title it held until Atlanta assumed the role in 1868), the town was not as fortunate as nearby Madison in escaping Union torches during the Civil War. Sherman's troops stormed through here with a vengeance after the general heard hardship stories from Union soldiers who had escaped from a prisoner-of-war camp in nearby Andersonville. Quite a few antebellum buildings remain, including the Old Governor's Mansion and the old statehouse.

GETTING HERE AND AROUND

Travel by car to Milledgeville, then park and hop aboard the Milledgeville Trolley Tour. This red coach will take you through the city's landmark historic district, with stops at such spots as the Old State Capitol, St. Stephen's Episcopal Church, and the Brown-Stetson-Sanford House. The tour leaves from the Convention and Visitors Bureau and is available weekdays at 10 am and Saturday at 11 am for $15.

VISITOR INFORMATION

CONTACTS Milledgeville Convention and Visitors Bureau. *✉ 200 W. Hancock St. ☎ 478/452–4687, 800/653–1804 ⊕ www.milledgevillecvb.com.*

Sights

Andalusia
HOUSE | A picturesque farm with peacocks, a pond, and a lofty barn, Andalusia inspired much of Flannery O'Connor's work. Now a museum, the 1850s farmhouse has been preserved just as it was (original furnishings and all) in 1964 when O'Connor passed away from complications of lupus at the age of 39. A visit here provides incredible insight into the life of this prolific writer. Guided tours are offered of the home daily on the hour. A small gift shop sells her books and other memorabilia. *✉ 2628 N. Columbia St. ☎ 478/445–8722 ⊕ www.gcsu.edu/andalusia $7 Closed Mon.*

Memory Hill Cemetery
CEMETERY | Flannery O'Connor, who suffered from lupus and died at age 39, is buried at historic Memory Hill Cemetery. Literary scholars from around the world come here to pay their respects. Because Milledgeville was the capital of Georgia from 1807 to 1868, there are many early Georgia governors and legislators buried here as well. *✉ 300 W. Franklin St., Macon.*

Old Governor's Mansion
HOUSE | This grand 1838 Greek revival mansion became Sherman's headquarters during the war. His soldiers are said to have tossed government documents out the windows and fueled their fires with Confederate money. Home to eight Georgian governors, and the founding building of Georgia College and State University, the mansion underwent a painstaking $10 million restoration in the early 2000s. Guided tours of the building

are given daily on the hour. Specialty tours can be arranged in advance for an additional fee. ✉ *120 S. Clark St.* ☎ *478/445–4545* 🌐 *www.gcsu.edu/mansion* 🎫 *$10* 🕑 *Closed Mon.*

Restaurants

The Brick

$ | PIZZA | This eatery has a comfortable, worn-at-the-elbows appeal, the perfect backdrop for munching on massive pizzas with names like the Hogzilla and Hawaii Five-Oh. Vegetarians will appreciate the Environmentally Correct pie with its all-veggie toppings. **Known for:** homemade pizza, pasta, and "pub grub"; good beer selection. 💲 *Average main: $10* ✉ *136 W. Hancock St.* ☎ *478/452–0089* 🌐 *www.thebrick93.com.*

Eatonton

20 miles northwest of Milledgeville on U.S. 129/441.

Right in the middle of the Antebellum Trail, Eatonton is a historic trove of houses that still retains the rare Southern architecture that survived Sherman's torches. But this isn't the only source of pride for this idyllic town. Take a look at the courthouse lawn; it's not your imagination—that really is a giant statue of a rabbit.

The **Eatonton-Putnam Chamber of Commerce** provides printed maps detailing landmarks related to Eatonton native Alice Walker, who won the Pulitzer Prize for her novel *The Color Purple*. It also has information on the many fine examples of antebellum architecture in Eatonton, including descriptions and photographs of the town's prize antebellum mansions, and a walking tour of Victorian homes.

GETTING HERE AND AROUND

As with most cities along the Antebellum Trail, Eatonton is best reached by car. As you travel there via U.S. Route 441, check out the scenic views of pastures, mountain valleys, and rivers.

VISITOR INFORMATION

CONTACTS Eatonton-Putnam Chamber of Commerce. ✉ *108 W. Marion St.* ☎ *706/485–7701* 🌐 *www.eatonton.com.*

Sights

Georgia Writers Museum

MUSEUM | Part of the Southern Literary Trail, this small museum in downtown Eatonton features exhibits on four authors who called Central Georgia home: Joel Chandler Harris, Sidney Lanier, Flannery O'Connor, and Alice Walker. They also display items from the Georgia Writers Hall of Fame in partnership with the University of Georgia's Hargrett Rare Book and Manuscript Library. Check their calendar online for frequent "meet the author" events highlighting current Georgia writers. ✉ *109 S. Jefferson Ave.* ☎ *706/991–5119* 🌐 *www.georgiawritersmuseum.org* 🕑 *Closed Sun.–Tues.*

Uncle Remus Museum

MUSEUM | FAMILY | Eatonton is the birthplace of celebrated novelist Joel Chandler Harris, of Br'er Rabbit and Uncle Remus fame. This museum, built from authentic slave cabins, houses countless carvings, paintings, first-edition books, and other artwork depicting the characters made famous by the imaginative author. It's on the grounds of a park. Note the museum closes for lunch from noon until 1 daily, so plan your visit accordingly. ✉ *214 Oak St.* ☎ *706/485–6856* 🌐 *www.uncleremusmuseum.org* 🎫 *$5.*

Hotels

★ The Ritz-Carlton Reynolds, Lake Oconee

$$$$ | RESORT | FAMILY | This luxurious family-friendly resort on Lake Oconee offers a variety of outdoor activities and is a haven for golfers, with five championship courses to choose from. **Pros:** both rooms and cottages available;

Spend an afternoon wandering around Eatonton's historic district, which is full of antebellum homes.

lakeside luxury with thoughtful amenities; beautiful secluded setting with golf available. **Cons:** daily resort fee added to already expensive rate; amenities can get crowded in peak season; kid-friendly atmosphere may not appeal to all. *Rooms from: $558 ✉ 1 Lake Oconee Trail ✣ 16 miles northeast of Eatonton ☎ 706/467–0600 ⊕ www.ritzcarlton.com 244 rooms, 6 cottages, 1 house No meals.*

Activities

Eatonton sits in the center of Georgia's Lake Country. Lake Oconee and Lake Sinclair, both created and maintained by Georgia Power, are nearby.

Lake Sinclair Recreation Area

PARK—SPORTS-OUTDOORS | Lake Sinclair is a favorite of anglers and is the site of a fishing tournament each year. Georgia Power maintains several parks with boat ramps, fishing piers, and campgrounds. About 11 miles from Eatonton, Lake Sinclair Recreation Area, maintained by the U.S. Forestry Service, has a beach, boat ramp, and campsites. *✉ Twin Bridges Rd. ☎ 706/485–7110 ⊕ www.fs.usda.gov.*

Lawrence Shoals Park

PARK—SPORTS-OUTDOORS | On the shores of Lake Oconee, the second-largest body of water in Georgia, Lawrence Shoals Park offers a boat ramp, beach area, picnic shelter, and camping facilities. *✉ 123 Wallace Dam Rd. ☎ 706/485–5494 ⊕ www.georgiapower.com/lakes.*

Madison

22 miles north of Eatonton on U.S. 129/144.

In 1809 Madison was described as "the most cultured and aristocratic town on the stagecoach route from Charleston to New Orleans," and today that charm still prevails, in large part because General Sherman's Union army deliberately bypassed the town, thus saving it for posterity. From the picturesque town square, with its specialty shops and businesses, you can walk to any number of antebellum and other residences that make up one of the largest designated historic areas in Georgia.

VISITOR INFORMATION

CONTACTS Madison-Morgan County Convention and Visitors Bureau. *115 E. Jefferson St. 706/342–4454 www.visitmadisonga.com.*

Sights

Heritage Hall

HOUSE | Madison is the historic heart of Georgia, and although many of the lovely homes are privately owned, this Greek Revival mansion, circa 1811, is open to the public. Rooms are furnished in the 19th-century style and offer insight into the elegant lifestyle of an average well-to-do family. Combo tickets are available to tour Heritage Hall along with two other historic homes within walking distance. *277 S. Main St. 706/342–9627 www.mchistorical.com $10.*

Madison-Morgan Cultural Center

ARTS VENUE | This 1895 Romanesque revival building was one of the first brick schools in the area. A museum features a restored 1895 classroom and a replica of an antebellum-era parlor. There are also art galleries and other exhibits. Check the online calendar for performances and events. *434 S. Main St. 706/342–4743 www.mmcc-arts.org $5 Closed Sun. and Mon.*

Restaurants

Madison Chop House Grille

$$ | AMERICAN | Popular with locals, this casual eatery in the heart of the downtown shopping district offers bar-and-grill classics like sandwiches, burgers, and steaks and such Southern specialties as fried pork chops and ribs. While the bar is a focal point, it's a family-friendly joint. **Known for:** fresh-from-the-grill steaks and burgers; casual bar setting; family-friendly. *Average main: $15 202 S. Main St. 706/342–9009 www.madisonchophouse.com.*

Town 220

$$$$ | MODERN AMERICAN | Next door to the James Madison Inn, this upscale bistro offers lunch and dinner Tuesday through Saturday. Owner and executive chef Fransisco De La Torre is passionate about fresh, quality ingredients. **Known for:** attentive, knowledgeable service; French cuisine standards; lovely patio. *Average main: $25 220 W. Washington St. 706/752–1445 www.town220.com Closed Sun. and Mon.*

Hotels

The Farmhouse Inn

$$ | B&B/INN | On a sprawling plot, this country inn offers 5 miles of wooded trails to explore, well-stocked ponds to fish, goats and chickens to feed, and a grassy picnic area to enjoy beside the Apalachee River. **Pros:** a great family destination; room options for individuals and groups; picturesque farm setting. **Cons:** fills up often for weddings and events; remote, farm location not for everyone; no on-site restaurant. *Rooms from: $150 1051 Meadow La. 706/342–7933 www.thefarmhouseinn.com 5 rooms, 2 houses Free breakfast.*

The James Madison Inn

$$$ | B&B/INN | Housed in a newer building but still in the heart of the historic district, this boutique hotel across from Town Park has rooms named for Madison's historic homes and landmarks. **Pros:** luxurious touches; spa services available; large well-appointed rooms with fireplaces. **Cons:** expensive for the area; some say breakfast could be improved; no room service. *Rooms from: $204 260 W. Washington St. 706/342–7040 www.jamesmadisoninn.com 19 rooms Free breakfast.*

Southern Cross Guest Ranch
HORSEBACK RIDING | A short drive from Madison you'll see miles upon miles of rolling pastures—an ideal landscape for horses. Located 7 miles outside Madison, Southern Cross Guest Ranch offers horseback-riding excursions with experienced guides. For the horse lovers who can't bear to leave, there are comfy B&B-style accommodations. The ranch specializes in all-inclusive packages, which include lodging, horseback riding, and meals. ✉ *1670 Bethany Church Rd.* ☎ *706/342–8027* 🌐 *www.southcross.com.*

Athens

30 miles northeast of Madison via U.S. 129/441; 70 miles east of Atlanta via I–85 North to GA 316.

Athens, an artistic jewel of the American South, is known as a breeding ground for famed rock groups such as the B-52s and R.E.M. Because of this distinction, creative types from all over the country flock to its trendy streets in hopes of becoming, or catching a glimpse of, the next big act to take the world by storm. At the center of this artistic melee is the University of Georgia (UGA). With close to 40,000 students, UGA is an influential ingredient in the Athens mix, giving the quaint but compact city a distinct flavor that falls somewhere between a misty Southern enclave, a rollicking college town, and a smoky, jazz club–studded alleyway. Of course, this all goes "to the Dawgs" if the home team is playing on home turf, though even then, Athens remains a blend of Mayberry R.F.D. and MTV. The effect is as irresistible as it is authentic.

To find out what's on in Athens, check out the *Athens Banner-Herald* (daily) and the weekly *Flagpole.*

GETTING HERE AND AROUND

Parking can be scarce on the city streets. Leave yourself extra time to find a spot, then take in the city and its shopping, nightlife, campus, and culture on foot. Rideshare services like Uber and Lyft are also an option.

The Historic Athens Welcome Center, housed in the Church-Waddel-Brumby House, offers historic walking tours of downtown, and other special seasonal tours. Call ahead for the schedule and reservations.

VISITOR INFORMATION

CONTACTS Athens Convention and Visitors Bureau. ✉ *300 N. Thomas St.* ☎ *706/357–4430* 🌐 *www.visitathensga.com.*

Church-Waddel-Brumby House
HOUSE | The streets of Athens are lined with many gorgeous old homes, some of which are open to the public. Most prominent among them is the Federal-style Church-Waddel-Brumby House. Built in 1820, it is the town's oldest surviving residence. The museum is home to the Historic Athens Welcome Center, where you can pick up information and arrange for tours. ✉ *280 E. Dougherty St.* ☎ *706/353–1820* 🌐 *www.athenswelcomecenter.com.*

Creature Comforts Brewery
WINERY/DISTILLERY | Founded in Athens in 2014, Creature Comforts has made an imprint in the craft beer community with its award-winning year-round and limited-release beers. Try them all plus creative concoctions like a "Beermosa" at its downtown Athens taproom housed in a former 1950s tire shop. There's often live music and events on the weekends. ✉ *271 W. Hancock Ave.* ☎ *706/410–1043* 🌐 *www.creaturecomfortsbeer.com.*

Georgia Museum of Art

MUSEUM | On the campus of the University of Georgia, the museum serves a dual purpose as an academic institution and the official public art museum of the State of Georgia. The permanent collection contains a wealth of 19th- and 20th-century paintings—some from noted American artists like Georgia O'Keeffe and Winslow Homer. It also houses the Samuel H. Kress Study Collection of Italian Renaissance art. Special exhibitions display cherished works of art from around the world. ✉ *90 Carlton St.* ☎ *706/542–4662* 🌐 *www.georgiamuseum.org* 🎫 *Free* 🕓 *Closed Mon.–Wed.*

Lyndon House Arts Center

MUSEUM | This community visual arts complex centered around the 1856 Ware-Lyndon House features art galleries, artist workshops, and a gallery shop featuring pottery, paintings, jewelry, and more by over 100 Athens-area artists. You can also tour the meticulously restored historic home, Admission is free. Check online for gallery shows and events. ✉ *211 Hoyt St.* ☎ *706/613–3623* 🌐 *www.accgov.com/lyndonhouse.*

★ State Botanical Gardens of Georgia

GARDEN | **FAMILY** | Just outside the Athens city limits, you'll find this tranquil, 313-acre wonderland of aromatic gardens and woodland paths. It has a massive conservatory overlooking the **International Garden** that functions as a welcome foyer and houses an art gallery, gift shop, and café. There's also a 2½-acre children's garden with interactive elements designed to engage children through all their senses. New in 2021 is a porcelain and decorative arts museum featuring eight galleries of nature-inspired artwork. ✉ *2450 S. Milledge Ave.* ✥ *Off U.S. 129/441* ☎ *706/542–1244* 🌐 *www.uga.edu/botgarden* 🎫 *Free.*

Taylor-Grady House

HOUSE | Constructed in 1844, the Taylor-Grady House gives a fine sense of history. It has been restored to its 1860s appearance to accurately represent the time when Henry Grady resided here. Grady, a famed newspaper man and booster of the "New South," lived here while he attended the University of Georgia. ✉ *634 Prince Ave.* ☎ *706/549–8688* 🌐 *www.taylorgradyhouse.com* 🎫 *$3* 🕓 *Closed weekends.*

University of Georgia

BUILDING | Athens has several splendid Greek revival buildings, including two on campus: the **university chapel ,** built in 1832, just off North Herty Drive, and the **university president's house** that was built in the late 1850s. Easiest access to the campus in downtown Athens is off Broad Street onto either Jackson or Thomas Street, both of which run through the heart of the university. Maps are available at the visitor center in the Four Towers Building on College Station Road. ✉ *570 Prince Ave.* ☎ *706/542–0842* 🌐 *www.uga.edu.*

Restaurants

★ Five and Ten

$$$$ | **ECLECTIC** | This cozy yet sophisticated restaurant put the Athens culinary scene on the map almost two decades ago with chef Hugh Acheson's inventive cuisine that blends European technique with down-home Southern cooking. Acheson, an Ottawa native, honed his culinary skills in classical French kitchens in Ontario and San Francisco before settling in Athens. **Known for:** chef-driven menu focused on local, seasonal ingredients; romantic old-house setting; inventive cocktails. 💲 *Average main: $28* ✉ *1073 S. Milledge Ave.* ☎ *706/546–7300* 🌐 *www.fiveandten.com.*

The Grit

$ | **VEGETARIAN** | This vegetarian paradise has been a favorite in Athens for more than two decades, serving freshly made vegetarian food in the casual comfort of a historic building. A popular dish of browned tofu cubes and brown rice may sound bland, but it's far from it—even carnivores say it's delicious. **Known for:** vegetarian fare; tasty breakfasts and weekend brunch. *Average main: $8* *199 Prince Ave.* *706/543–6592* *www.thegrit.com.*

Last Resort Grill

$$ | **AMERICAN** | A favorite of locals and tourists alike, the Last Resort is a popular spot for lunch, dinner, and Sunday brunch. For brunch, entrées like shrimp and grits, stuffed French toast, and breakfast enchiladas please a variety of palates. **Known for:** Sunday brunch; outstanding desserts; inventive Southern cuisine. *Average main: $18* *174–184 W. Clayton St.* *706/549–0810* *www.lastresortgrill.com.*

The National

$$$ | **AMERICAN** | Owned by chefs Peter Dale and Hugh Acheson, this refined but casual eatery evokes the atmosphere of a European café with its Mediterranean-inspired dishes that make creative use of local ingredients. Prosciutto-wrapped grilled figs, hummus with lamb, and slow-roasted beef hanger steak are a few favorites. **Known for:** Mediterranean-inspired fare; creative use of local and seasonal ingredients; laid-back, wine-sipping environment. *Average main: $24* *232 W. Hancock Ave.* *706/549–3450* *www.thenationalrestaurant.com.*

White Tiger Gourmet

$ | **AMERICAN** | Local foodies flock here for chef Ken Manring's delicious smoked meats and burgers at this hip but homey order-at-the-counter restaurant. Housed in an old storefront in the Boulevard Historic District just outside downtown, there aren't many indoor tables, but there's plenty of space to spread out in the picnic area outside. **Known for:** flavorful meats smoked daily; inventive vegetarian dishes; Southern-style Sunday brunch. *Average main: $10* *217 Hiawassee Ave.* *706/353-6847* *www.whitetigergourmet.com* *Closed Mon.*

Coffee and Quick Bites

Jittery Joe's

$ | **AMERICAN** | Athens wouldn't be a legit college town without a quality coffeehouse or two. Jittery Joe's fits the bill with fresh microroasted beans and several locations around town. Check out the downtown location directly across from the University of Georgia to sip coffee amongst the students. **Known for:** microroasted brews from around the world; hip coffeehouse scene; pastries and goodies to go. *Average main: $6* *297 E. Broad St.* *706/613–7449* *www.jitteryjoes.com.*

Hotels

Graduate Athens

$ | **HOTEL** | Centered around a former ironworks facility, this hip boutique hotel offers fresh, modern rooms, a coffee shop, and a restaurant and live music venue—aptly named the Foundry. **Pros:** pool and easy access to amenities; great restaurant and club; comfy rooms with fun, retro decor. **Cons:** live music at the on-site venue can bring a late crowd; room rates are pricey for university event weekends; exterior corridor motel-style layout. *Rooms from: $129* *295 E. Dougherty St.* *706/549–7020* *www.graduateathens.com* *122 rooms* *No meals.*

Hotel Indigo Athens

$$ | **HOTEL** | Sleek and modern, this eco-conscious property is a comfortable and luxurious option for a stay downtown. **Pros:** spacious guest rooms; large bathrooms; pet friendly. **Cons:** fee for parking; pet-friendly aspect may not appeal to all; can be noisy. *Rooms from: $179* *500 College Ave.* *706/309–7263* *www.indigoathens.com* *130 rooms* *No meals.*

Nightlife

40 Watt Club

MUSIC CLUBS | This famed indie-rock club is known for helping to launch the careers of R.E.M., the B-52s, and other local bands that grew out of the college scene. Nirvana, the Flaming Lips, and Sonic Youth all played here back in the day. Today, you'll find a mix of local and national acts gracing the stage—from country to punk and pop. ✉ *285 W. Washington St.* ☎ *706/549–7871* 🌐 *www.40watt.com.*

The Foundry

MUSIC CLUBS | This small but spirited venue at the Graduate Athens hotel hosts both national and local acts, from the Nitty Gritty Dirt Band to Shawn Mullins. At intimate shows in this repurposed historic building, guests can dance the night away in front of the stage and enjoy good service, Southern comfort food, and local craft beers. ✉ *295 E Dougherty St.* ☎ *706/549–7051* 🌐 *www.thefoundryathens.com.*

Georgia Theatre

MUSIC CLUBS | A legendary Athens live music venue, Georgia Theatre continues to host many well-known national and local acts. The historic building once served as a movie theater and Masonic lodge. Catch a show in the theater or head up to the rooftop bar for drinks and snacks. ✉ *215 N. Lumpkin St.* ☎ *706/850–7670* 🌐 *www.georgiatheatre.com.*

Augusta

97 miles southeast of Athens via GA 10 and I–20; 150 miles east of Atlanta via I–20.

Although Augusta escaped the ravages of Union troops during the Civil War, nature itself was not so kind. On a crossing of the Savannah River, the town was flooded many times before modern-day city planning redirected the water into a collection of small lakes and creeks. Now the current is so mild that citizens gather to send bathtub toys downstream every year in the annual Rubber Duck Derby.

The second-oldest city in Georgia, founded by James Oglethorpe, it's also now Georgia's second-largest city. The U.S. Army Cyber Center of Excellence and Fort Gordon bring people from all over the country to settle in Augusta. It's also home to the Medical College of Georgia and Augusta University. While the historic charm remains, its population is ever growing and changing.

Check out the *Augusta Daily Chronicle* and the *Metro Spirit* for up-to-the-minute information about what's going on in town.

GETTING HERE AND AROUND

Explore this part of the classic South via car, then park to wander the streets full of shops and restaurants. You can also canoe on the river or along the 1845 tree-lined Augusta Canal, a natural habitat for herons and other birds.

VISITOR INFORMATION

CONTACTS Augusta Convention and Visitors Bureau. ✉ *1010 Broad St.* ☎ *706/724–4067* 🌐 *www.visitaugusta.com.*

Sights

Augusta Canal Discovery Center

HISTORIC SITE | **FAMILY** | Housed in a converted mill in the Augusta Canal National Heritage Area, this museum traces Augusta's important role in developing Georgia's textile industry. The looms are still powered by the building's original turbines; they also provide the power to juice up the museum's Petersburg canal boats. Tours of the **canal,** usually one hour long, start here and are a fascinating trip through history. Guides are well versed in the passing sights, which include assorted wildlife, a working 19th-century textile mill, and two of Georgia's only remaining 18th-century houses. ✉ *1450 Greene St.* ☎ *706/823–0440* 🌐 *www.augustacanal.com* 🎫 *$6, with boat tour $14* 🕒 *Closed Sun. and Mon. in the summer and winter.*

Augusta Museum of History

MUSEUM | This museum is a great first stop in understanding Augusta's rich history. Begin your visit by taking a 12,000-year journey through the region's past by touring the permanent exhibit, *Augusta's Story*. Other exhibits explore the history of health care in Augusta, the role of the railroads, and of course, the Masters Tournament. Adults and kids alike will enjoy exploring the Transportation Corridor's 1920s trolley car, a 1914 locomotive, and a reconstructed 1930s gas station. Another favorite is an exhibit devoted to native son James Brown. ✉ *560 Reynolds St.* ☎ *706/722–8454* 🌐 *www.augustamuseum.org* 🎟 *$5* ⏲ *Closed Mon.–Wed.*

Augusta Riverwalk

BODY OF WATER | The well-maintained pathways of the Riverwalk (between 5th and 10th Streets) curve along the Savannah River and are the perfect place for a leisurely stroll. The upper brick portion connects downtown attractions like St. Paul's Church and the Morris Museum of Art. There are a few shops and restaurants along the way, but not as many as you might expect. On Saturday mornings between April and November, look out for the Augusta Market at the 8th Street Plaza. The lower paths offer a close-up view of wildlife and a peek at the graceful homes of North Augusta, South Carolina. ✉ *5th to 10th Sts.*

Boyhood Home of President Woodrow Wilson

HISTORIC SITE | The home where President Woodrow Wilson spent the formative years of his childhood still stands in downtown Augusta across the street from First Presbyterian Church, where his father served as minister. The Wilsons lived in Augusta during the Civil War and Reconstruction, from 1860 to 1870, which greatly shaped the future president's point of view. You can take a guided tour of the carefully restored home that depicts life and boyhood in the 1860s. Exhibits provide insight into Wilson's life and time as the 28th president of the United States. ✉ *419 7th St.* ☎ *706/722–9828* 🌐 *www.wilsonboyhoodhome.org* 🎟 *$5* ⏲ *Closed Sun.–Wed.*

Meadow Garden

HOUSE | Augusta's oldest residence, built around 1791, Meadow Garden was the home of George Walton, one of Georgia's three signers of the Declaration of Independence. At age 26, he was its youngest signer. Owned and operated by the Daughters of the American Revolution since 1900, it is one of the oldest house museums in the state of Georgia. ✉ *1320 Independence Dr.* ☎ *706/724–4174* 🌐 *www.historicmeadowgarden.org* 🎟 *$5* ⏲ *Closed Sun. and Mon.* ☞ *Last tour of the day begins at 3:15.*

Morris Museum of Southern Art

MUSEUM | This is a splendid collection of Southern art, from early landscapes, antebellum portraits, and the Civil War period through neo-impressionism and modern contemporary art. The first institution dedicated to Southern art and artists, the museum also holds up to 10 special exhibitions each year bringing important, though sometimes little-known, artists to the forefront. ✉ *Riverfront Center, 1 10th St., 2nd fl.* ☎ *706/724–7501* 🌐 *www.themorris.org* 🎟 *$5* ⏲ *Closed Mon.*

Restaurants

Boll Weevil Cafe and Sweetery

$ | **AMERICAN** | Named for the insect that ruined the cotton industry, this quirky little café on the Riverwalk offers some of the best desserts in Augusta, not to mention soups, sandwiches, and Southern specialties like fried green tomatoes. Step inside the former warehouse and you'll find a pastry case filled with at least 30 decadent desserts, all made on the premises. **Known for:** homemade cakes and decadent desserts; sandwiches on fresh-baked bread; historic building on the riverfront. $ *Average main: $13*

10 James Brown Blvd. 706/722–7772 www.thebollweevil.com.

Frog Hollow Tavern

$$$$ | **AMERICAN** | Reservations are recommended at this stylish downtown restaurant born out of chef-owner Sean Wight's desire to create a sophisticated yet comfortable dining and social club that highlights the freshest local and regional ingredients. Wild-caught shrimp and grits with house-made andouille and local tomatoes and pan-roasted duck breast are just two of the menu items. **Known for:** attentive service; focus on local and regional ingredients. *Average main: $28 1282 Broad St. 706/364–6906 www.froghollowtavern.com Closed Sun.–Tues.*

Augusta Marriott at the Convention Center

$$ | **HOTEL** | Just off the Riverwalk, the Marriott is the city's only full-service downtown hotel. **Pros:** excellent location; pool and fitness center; concierge level available. **Cons:** large and confusing layout; can be busy with convention guests; common areas could use some updates. *Rooms from: $159 2 10th St. 706/722–8900 www.marriott.com 372 rooms No meals.*

The Partridge Inn Augusta, Curio Collection by Hilton

$$ | **HOTEL** | Perched on top of a hill overlooking Augusta, this National Trust Historic Hotel is part of Hilton's Curio Collection. **Pros:** on-site restaurant known for its outstanding Sunday brunch; complimentary valet parking; historic charm with great views. **Cons:** lots of stairs and occasionally uneven floors; some rooms and bathrooms are small by modern standards; corridors can be noisy. *Rooms from: $164 2110 Walton Way 706/737–8888 www.partridgeinn.com 144 rooms No meals.*

GOLF

Forest Hills Golf Club

GOLF | Founded in 1926, Bobby Jones made his "grand slam of golf" here in 1930. The well-kept public course offers tee times seven days a week. *Augusta Magazine* continually names it the best public golf course in the area. Reservations are suggested. *1500 Comfort Rd. 706/733–0001 www.theforesthillsgolfcourse.com $45–$55, 18 holes, 7231 yds, par 72.*

Masters Tournament

GOLF | In early April, Augusta hosts the much-celebrated annual Masters Tournament, one of pro golf's most distinguished events. It's broadcast in 180 countries. Tickets for actual tournament play are extremely limited for the general public, but you can try to get tickets for one of the practice rounds earlier in the week—which, for golf addicts, is still hugely entertaining.

The Augusta National Golf Club, home of the Masters Tournament, is known for its exclusivity. Membership is handed down through families, so unless you know someone, you aren't going to get to play there, much less get a glimpse of the grounds. However, there are plenty of other golf courses in this golfer's town.

Masters Tournament and practice-round tickets are awarded on a lottery basis; apply online at *www.masters.com* by June 1 of the year preceding the tournament. *Augusta 706/667–6700 www.masters.com.*

SWIMMING

J. Strom Thurmond Lake

WATER SPORTS | Located 20 miles northwest of Augusta, 71,000-acre J. Strom Thurmond Lake is where locals head for swimming, boating, camping, and hiking. *510 Clarks Hill Hwy. 800/533–3478 www.sas.usace.army.mil/lakes/thurmond.*

Index

A

B

U

V

W

X

Y

Z

Photo Credits

Front Cover: Mark Waugh / Alamy Stock Photo [Description: The Center for Civil and Human Rights Museum, Atlanta, Georgia, USA]. **Back Cover, from left to right:** Artazum and Iriana Shiyan / Shutterstock, Appalachianviews | Dreamstime.com, SeanPavonePhoto/iStockphoto. **Spine:** Casey Jones/Visit Savannah. **Interior, from left to right:** James Mahan/iStock (1). Sean Pavone/iStock (2). John Seiler/iStockphoto (5). **Chapter 1: Experience Carolinas and Georgia:** WerksMedia/iStock (8-9). WerksMedia/istockphoto (10). Photo courtesy of VisitNC.com (11). Jon Bilous/Dreamstime.com (11). James Duckworth/ACVB & AtlantaPhotos (12). Melissa McAlpine/ACVB Marketing (12). C2 Photography/VisitNC (12). WerksMedia/istockphoto (12). Georgia Aquarium (13). Visit Savannah (13). Photo courtesy of VisitNC.com (14). Photo courtesy of VisitNC.com (14). University of Georgia Public Service and Outreach (14). Photo courtesy of VisitNC.com (14). Chris Council and Emily Chaplin/VisitNC.com (15). Chris M Rogers/Seabrook Island Club (16). Sean Rayford (16). Brent Hofacker/Shutterstock (16). Savannah Canoe and Kayak (16). skiserge1/istockphoto (17). Brett Flashnick (17). Chris M. Rogers Photography, Inc. (18). Sean Pavone/istockphoto (18). RWI FINE ART PHOTOGRAPHY / Alamy Stock Photo (18). David J. Kaminsky/Telfair Museums (18). Visit Myrtle Beach (19). Elena Veselova/Shutterstock (26). Foodio/shutterstock (27). Courtesy_Cape Fear Boil Co (28). Joshua Minso/Shutterstock (29). Credit GoldenIsles.com (30). Credit GoldenIsles.com (30). Levranii/shutterstock (30). Cvandyke/shutterstock (31). Kevin Ruck/shutterstock (31) **Chapter 3: The North Carolina Coast:** MarkVanDykePhotography / Shutterstock (61). digidreamgrafix/iStock (64). Scott Lloyd Photography/Shutterstock (65). Doug Hendricks/Shutterstock (65). karenfoleyphotography/iStock (75). NC Tourism - Bill Russ (79). Robb Helfrick (83). Gianna Stadelmyer/Shutterstock (99). **Chapter 4: Central North Carolina:** SeanPavonePhoto/iStockphoto (113). Swdesertlover | Dreamstime.com (124). NC Division of Tourism - Bill Russ (130). Johnny Stockshooter / age fotostock (152). Nickledford [CC BY 2.0]/Flickr (160). **Chapter 5: Asheville and the North Carolina Mountains:** Appalachianviews | Dreamstime.com (167). Bokdavid | Dreamstime.com (192). Dave Allen Photography/Shutterstock (206-207). Evaulphoto | Dreamstime.com (211). **Chapter 6: Great Smoky Mountains National Park:** jo Crebbin / Shutterstock (213). NC Tourism - Bill Russ (234-235). Bernard B. ILarde [CC BY-SA 3.0]/Wikimedia Commons (236). Pellaea [CC BY 2.0]/Flickr (236). Mary Terriberry/Shutterstock (236). Kelly vanDellen/Shutterstock (236). laessle [public domain]/Wikimedia Commons (236). Steffen Foerster Photography/Shutterstock (237). John Seiler/iStockphoto (237). WiZZiK [CC BY 3.0]/Wikimedia Commons (237). Derek Ramsey [GFDL 1.2]/Wikimedia Commons (237). Jean-Pol GRANDMONT [CC BY-SA 3.0]/WIkimedia Commons (237). Kord.com / age fotostock (238). Jeff Greenberg / age fotostock (239). Thomas Takacs/iStockphoto (239). Pat & Chuck Blackley / Alamy (240). Paul Tessier / Shutterstock (241). Heeb Christian / age fotostock (246). **Chapter 7: Myrtle Beach, SC, and the Grand Strand:** MarynaG/Shutterstock (259). Sean Pavone/iStockphoto (262). StacieStauffSmith Photos / Shutterstock (263). MargaretW/iStockphoto (263). Trisha McQuade/Shutterstock (270). StacieStauffSmith Photos / Shutterstock (287). makasana photo/shutterstock (289). **Chapter 8: Charleston, SC:** digidreamgrafix/Shutterstock (295). Kzlobastov | Dreamstime.com (307). Gabrielle Hovey/Shutterstock (316). Muffet [CC BY 2.0]/Flickr (329). Kevin Ruck/Shutterstock (330). Crlocklear | Dreamstime.com (334). **Chapter 9: Hilton Head, SC, and the Low Country:** SeanPavonePhoto/iStock (339). John McManus Photographer/Shutterstock (342). Sean Pavone/Shutterstock (343). Alison Lloyd, Fodors.com member (343). motion photo/Shutterstock (344). Fanfo/Shutterstock (345). Brent Hofacker/Shutterstock (345). CynthiaAnnF/iStock (364). Courtesy of the Hilton Head Island Visitor & Convention Bureau (366). Adam Colick/shutterstock (377). **Chapter 10: The Midlands and the Upstate, SC:** SuperStock/Agefotostock (379). Sean Pavone/Shutterstock (389). Tashka | Dreamstime.com (394). Robert David Howell/Shutterstock (400). **Chapter 11: Savannah, GA:** Sepavo | Dreamstime.com (405). Rolf_52/Shutterstock (414). trinum/iStockphoto (425). KenosisDre/Shutterstock (435). **Chapter 12: Georgia's Coastal Isles and the Okefenokee:** Vadim 777/Shutterstock (437). Lostsomewhereinfrance | Dreamstime.com (440). Brianwelker | Dreamstime.com (441). Kevin Ruck/Shutterstock (441). Georgia Department of Economic Development (447). Nagel Photography/Shutterstock (450). Dougandme [CC BY 2.0]/Flickr (461). Nolichuckyjake/Shutterstock (466). **Chapter 13: Southwest Georgia:** Tvasas3 | Dreamstime.com (469). Mona Makela/Shutterstock (472). Yuan Tian/iStockphoto (473). Jaimie Duplass/Shutterstock (473). Durden Images / Shutterstock (479). Neal Wellons [CC BY-NC-ND 2.0]/Flickr (480). Ncbateman1 | Dreamstime.com (483). Sundry Photography/Shutterstock (486). **Chapter 14: Atlanta, GA:** Sean Pavone/Dreamstime (489). Ian Dagnall / Alamy Stock Photo (492). Nagel Photography/Shutterstock (493). Yoichi Okamoto [Public domain]/Wikimedia Commons (493). f11photo/Shutterstock (500). Appalachianviews | Dreamstime.com (504). Mondan80 | Dreamstime.com (508). Courtesy of the Atlanta History Center (522). **Chapter 15: Central and North Georgia:** ANCHASA MITCHELL/iStock (535). Library of Congress Prints and Photographs Division (545). BCWH/iStockphoto (545). Historic American Sheet Music, "Bonnie blue flag. 1863", Conf. Music B-1001, Duke University Rare Book, Manuscript, and Special Collections Library (546). Library of Congress Prints and Photographs division (546). Hal Jespersen at en.wikipedia [Public domain]/Wikimedia Commons (546). Hal Jespersen at en.wikipedia [Public domain]/Wikimedia Commons (546). Library of Congress Prints and Photographs Division (546). Mathew Brady [Public domain]/Wikimedia Commons (547). Library of Congress Prints and Photographs Division (547). Library of Congress Prints and Photographs Division (547). Blair Howard/iStockphoto (548). Wayne Hsieh [CC BY-NC-SA 2.0]/Flickr (548). Jeffrey M. Frank/Shutterstock (549). Mikephotos | Dreamstime.com (550). Georgia Department of Economic Development (550). Ian Dagnall / Alamy (553). Three Sisters Vineyards (555). Georgia Department of Economic Development (560). SeanPavonePhoto/iStock (564). Lee Edwin Coursey [CC BY-NC-ND 2.0]/Flickr (573). **About Our Writers:** All photos are courtesy of the writers except for the following: Cameron Roberts, courtesy of Jim Roberts.

**Every effort has been made to trace the copyright holders, and we apologize in advance for any accidental errors. We would be happy to apply the corrections in the following edition of this publication.*

Notes

Fodor's THE CAROLINAS & GEORGIA

Publisher: Stephen Horowitz, *General Manager*

Editorial: Douglas Stallings, *Editorial Director*; Jill Fergus, Amanda Sadlowski, Caroline Trefler, *Senior Editors*; Kayla Becker, Alexis Kelly, *Editors*

Design: Tina Malaney, *Director of Design and Production*; Jessica Gonzalez, *Graphic Designer;* Mariana Tabares, *Design and Production Intern*

Production: Jennifer DePrima, *Editorial Production Manager*; Elyse Rozelle, *Senior Production Editor;* Monica White, *Production Editor*

Maps: Rebecca Baer, *Senior Map Editor*; Mark Stroud (Moon Street Cartography), *Cartographer*

Photography: Viviane Teles, *Senior Photo Editor;* Namrata Aggarwal, Ashok Kumar, *Photo Editors;* Rebecca Rimmer, *Photo Intern*

Business and Operations: Chuck Hoover, *Chief Marketing Officer*; Robert Ames, *Group General Manager*; Devin Duckworth, *Director of Print Publishing*; Amber Zhou, *Business Analyst*

Public Relations and Marketing: Joe Ewaskiw, *Senior Director of Communications and Public Relations*

Fodors.com: Jeremy Tarr, *Editorial Director;* Rachael Levitt, *Managing Editor*

Technology: Jon Atkinson, *Director of Technology;* Rudresh Teotia, *Lead Developer*; Jacob Ashpis, *Content Operations Manager*

Writers: Summer Bozeman, Pamela Brownstein, Chanté LaGon, Stratton Lawrence, Jennifer Leigh Lebos, Rachel Roberts Quartarone, Hanna Raskin, Cameron Roberts

Editors: Jill Fergus (lead editor), Amanda Sadlowski, Douglas Stallings

Production Editor: Elyse Rozelle

24th Edition

ISBN 978-1-64097-412-8

ISSN 1525–5832

Library of Congress Control Number 9780147546975

All details in this book are based on information supplied to us at press time. Always confirm information when it matters, especially if you're making a detour to visit a specific place. Fodor's expressly disclaims any liability, loss, or risk, personal or otherwise, that is incurred as a consequence of the use of any of the contents of this book.

SPECIAL SALES
This book is available at special discounts for bulk purchases for sales promotions or premiums. For more information, e-mail SpecialMarkets@fodors.com.

PRINTED IN THE UNITED STATES OF AMERICA

10 9 8 7 6 5 4 3 2 1

About Our Writers

A Savannah-based freelancer, **Summer Bozeman** is a 2007 graduate of Flagler College in St. Augustine, Florida. Summer was communications manager at Visit Savannah for four years, serving as the organization's primary copy writer and editor, and is also a community advocate and volunteer. She updated the Savannah chapter.

Pamela Brownstein is a freelance writer who lives in Mount Pleasant, South Carolina, with her husband and two young kids. She grew up in New Jersey and moved to the Palmetto State in 2002. She updated the chapters on Hilton Head and the Lowcountry.

Oak Park, Illinois, native **Chanté LaGon** has nearly two decades' experience in all things word-related, from news features to poetry. She moved to Atlanta in the late '90s to join the *Atlanta Journal-Constitution* and later served as managing editor for the weekly *Creative Loafing*. She combined her love of music and words as founding editor of a hip-hop magazine while in North Carolina, where she attended college, and has been an integral part of that scene in Atlanta, along with the electronic music, nightlife, arts and culture scenes there. She updated the Atlanta chapter for this edition.

Stratton Lawrence rambles the globe for much of the year, but his favorite home base is by the sea in Folly Beach, South Carolina, where he surfs and soaks up the sun with his wife and two kids. He's a frequent contributor to Fodor's. He updated our South Carolina content on Charleston, the Midlands and the Upstate, Myrtle Beach, and Hilton Head and the Lowcountry, as well as our chapters on Central North Carolina and the North Carolina Coast. Track his writing at strattonlawrence.com.

Jessica Leigh Lebos, the author of *Savannah Sideways,* has been writing about interesting people, beautiful places, and delicious food for more than 20 years. She writes for Thrillist and *Savannah Magazine* and lives in Savannah's Midtown neighborhood with her family and two rescue dogs. She updated the Savannah chapter. Read her latest at jllnotjill.com.

Rachel Roberts Quartarone is a Georgia native with deep Southern roots. Her family has been firmly planted in North Georgia for more than five generations. She resides in Atlanta with her husband and two sons. She enjoys writing about her passions—history, food, travel, and Southern culture. She updated our content on Central and North Georgia, Southwest Georgia, Georgia's Coastal Isles and the Okefenokee, as well as the Travel Smart chapter.

Hanna Raskin, who lives in Charleston, joined the *Post and Courier* as its food editor and restaurant critic in 2013. She's a frequent contributor to *Garden & Gun* and the Southern Foodways Alliance's publication and podcast. For this edition, she updated the Charleston chapter.

Cameron Roberts writes about travel and entertainment for Fodors.com, Tripsavvy.com, and Fodor's and Michelin guidebooks. She married into a love for the Carolinas and spends most of her time in the mountains outside Asheville. Cameron updated Experience and the chapters on Asheville and the North Carolina Mountains and Great Smoky Mountains National Park.